THE GREAT CONTEMPORARY ISSUES

TERRORISM

THE GREAT CONTEMPORARY ISSUES

OTHER BOOKS IN THE SERIES

DRUGS
   Introduction by J. Anthony Lukas
THE MASS MEDIA AND POLITICS
   Introduction by Walter Cronkite
CHINA
   O. Edmund Clubb, *Advisory Editor*
LABOR AND MANAGEMENT
   Richard B. Morris, *Advisory Editor*
WOMEN: THEIR CHANGING ROLES
   Elizabeth Janeway, *Advisory Editor*
BLACK AFRICA
   Hollis Lynch, *Advisory Editor*
EDUCATION U.S.A.
   James Cass, *Advisory Editor*
VALUES AMERICANS LIVE BY
   Garry Wills, *Advisory Editor*
CRIME AND JUSTICE
   Ramsey Clark, *Advisory Editor*
JAPAN
   Edwin O. Reischauer, *Advisory Editor*
THE PRESIDENCY
   George E. Reedy, *Advisory Editor*
FOOD AND POPULATION
   George S. McGovern, *Advisory Editor*
THE U.S. AND WORLD ECONOMY
   Leonard Silk, *Advisory Editor*
SCIENCE IN THE TWENTIETH CENTURY
   Walter Sullivan, *Advisory Editor*
THE MIDDLE EAST
   John C. Campbell, *Advisory Editor*
THE CITIES
   Richard C. Wade, *Advisory Editor*
MEDICINE AND HEALTH CARE
   Saul Jarcho, *Advisory Editor*
LOYALTY AND SECURITY IN A DEMOCRATIC STATE
   Richard Rovere, *Advisory Editor*
RELIGION IN AMERICA
   Gillian Lindt, *Advisory Editor*
POLITICAL PARTIES
   William E. Leuchtenburg, *Advisory Editor*
ETHNIC GROUPS IN AMERICAN LIFE
   James P. Shenton, *Advisory Editor*
THE ARTS
   Richard McLanathan, *Advisory Editor*
ENERGY AND ENVIRONMENT
   Stuart Bruchey, *Advisory Editor*
BIG BUSINESS
   Leon Stein, *Advisory Editor*
THE FAMILY
   David J. Rothman, Sheila M. Rothman, *Advisory Editors*

THE GREAT CONTEMPORARY ISSUES

TERRORISM

The New York Times

ARNO PRESS
NEW YORK/1979

Theodore Lownik Library
Illinois Benedictine College
Lisle, Illinois 60532

MICHAEL WALLACE
Advisory Editor

GENE BROWN
Editor

Copyright © 1907, 1908, 1909, 1910, 1911, 1912, 1913, 1914, 1915, 1916, 1917, 1918, 1919, 1920, 1921, 1922, 1924, 1926, 1927, 1928, 1929, 1930, 1931, 1933, 1934, 1935, 1937, 1938, 1939, 1940, 1941, 1942, 1943, 1944, 1945, 1946, 1947, 1948, 1949, 1950, 1953, 1954, 1955, 1956, 1957, 1958, 1959, 1960, 1961, 1962, 1963, 1964, 1966, 1967, 1968, 1969, 1970, 1971, 1972, 1973, 1974, 1975, 1976, 1977, 1978, by The New York Times Company.

Copyright © 1979 by The New York Times Company.

Library of Congress Cataloging in Publication Data

Main entry under title:

Terrorism.

    (The Great contemporary issues)
    Bibliography: p.
    Includes index.
    1. Terrorism—Addresses, essays, lectures.
2. Violence—Addresses, essays, lectures. I. Wallace, Michael. II. Brown, Gene. III. Series.
HV6431.T457   301.633   78-20863
ISBN 0-405-11525-3

Manufactured in the United States of America

The editors express special thanks to The Associated Press, United Press International, and Reuters for permission to include in this series of books a number of dispatches originally distributed by those news services.

Book design by Stephanie Rhodes

Contents

Publisher's Note About the Series	vi
Introduction, by Michael Wallace	vii
1. Overthrow of the Old Order	**1**
The Spectre of Anarchy	2
Russia: Terrorism and Reform	8
From Terrorism to Revolution	18
2. The Colonizers and the Colonized	**55**
India	56
Algeria	93
3. Terrorists or Patriots	**127**
The Irgun and the Stern Gang	128
The Palestinians	171
The I.R.A.	212
The F.A.L.N.	261
4. Terrorism and the State Today	**275**
The Western Democracies	276
Perspectives on Terrorism	356
Suggested Reading	**369**
Index	**371**

Publisher's Note About the Series

It would take even an accomplished speed-reader, moving at full throttle, some three and a half solid hours a day to work his way through all the news The New York Times prints. The sad irony, of course, is that even such indefatigable devotion to life's carnival would scarcely assure a decent understanding of what it was really all about. For even the most dutiful reader might easily overlook an occasional long-range trend of importance, or perhaps some of the fragile, elusive relationships between events that sometimes turn out to be more significant than the events themselves.

This is why "The Great Contemporary Issues" was created—to help make sense out of some of the major forces and counterforces at large in today's world. The philosophical conviction behind the series is a simple one: that the past not only can illuminate the present but must. ("Continuity with the past," declared Oliver Wendell Holmes, "is a necessity, not a duty.") Each book in the series, therefore has as its subject some central issue of our time that needs to be viewed in the context of its antecedents if it is to be fully understood. By showing, through a substantial selection of contemporary accounts from The New York Times, the evolution of a subject and its significance, each book in the series offers a perspective that is available in no other way. For while most books on contemporary affairs specialize, for excellent reasons, in predigested facts and neatly drawn conclusions, the books in this series allow the reader to draw his own conclusions on the basis of the facts as they appeared at virtually the moment of their occurrence. This is not to argue that there is no place for events recollected in tranquility; it is simply to say that when fresh, raw truths are allowed to speak for themselves, some quite distinct values often emerge.

For this reason, most of the articles in "The Great Contemporary Issues" are reprinted in their entirety, even in those cases where portions are not central to a given book's theme. Editing has been done only rarely, and in all such cases it is clearly indicated. (Such an excision occasionally occurs, for example, in the case of a Presidential State of the Union Message, where only brief portions are germane to a particular volume, and in the case of some names, where for legal reasons or reasons of taste it is preferable not to republish specific identifications.) Similarly, typographical errors, where they occur, have been allowed to stand as originally printed.

"The Great Contemporary Issues" inevitably encompasses a substantial amount of history. In order to explore their subjects fully, some of the books go back a century or more. Yet their fundamental theme is not the past but the present. In this series the past is of significance insofar as it suggests how we got where we are today. These books, therefore, do not always treat a subject in a purely chronological way. Rather, their material is arranged to point up trends and interrelationships that the editors believe are more illuminating than a chronological listing would be.

"The Great Contemporary Issues" series will ultimately constitute an encyclopedic library of today's major issues. Long before editorial work on the first volume had even begun, some fifty specific titles had already been either scheduled for definite publication or listed as candidates. Since then, events have prompted the inclusion of a number of additional titles, and the editors are, moreover, alert not only for new issues as they emerge but also for issues whose development may call for the publication of sequel volumes. We will, of course, also welcome readers' suggestions for future topics.

Introduction

People kill one another for so many different reasons that searching for patterns to the general slaughter can seem fruitless. It appears simpler to suggest that man is, by nature, a nasty beast. Some analysts propose the existence of a general instinct, which they call aggression, and argue that it is, has always been, and always will be humanity's ruling passion. They issue all-points bulletins to the universe warning that homosapiens, the killer ape, is loose, on the prowl, and should be presumed armed and dangerous.

Blaming violence on "human nature" is a cop-out. Reducing all violent behavior to a single primal urge to kill aborts analysis. History becomes irrelevant, a mere record of the many ways in which the violent impulse manifests itself. Worse still, abandoning inquiry underwrites the status quo: if there is nothing much we can know about violence, there is nothing much we can do about it either. If we conclude that violence, like the poor, will be with us always, we mire ourselves in cynicism or pessimism.

The alternative is to remember that violence grows out of specific historical situations. People come to blows with one another not because they are impelled by mysterious, innate, inevitable forces, but because in the context of their times violence can seem to them an appropriate action to take. People, not instincts, make history, but they do so under conditions they inherit from preceding generations.

As any courtroom observer knows, unravelling the tangle of motivations, opportunities, characters and circumstances involved in a single act of murder is a difficult business. It is more difficult still to lay bare the complex play of social, economic, sexual and political forces that, at any given point in time, form the backdrop for such spectacular events as peasant rebellions or world wars. It is one of the purposes of this collection to demonstrate that while analyzing violence historically may not be easy, it is by no means impossible.

A major reason people have systematically employed violence is to get hold of other people's property. At its most straightforward, this takes the form of plunder. A kills B and takes his property. This may be exceptional behavior, in which case it is called crime. Entire social systems may be organized around the exaction of tribute, in which case crime becomes a legitimate way of life.

Robbery can redistribute wealth, but it cannot create it. Thus the pursuit of other people's property has often involved the construction of a social order in which goods are produced by some people and appropriated by others. In slave societies, masters own laborers and keep whatever they produce, subtracting only what is necessary for the slaves' maintenance. Slaves tend to resent this transfer of wealth and to resist it. Hence slaveowners from ancient Greece to antebellum Alabama, though they developed complex ways of legitimating their rule, at bottom depended on whip and gibbet. In feudal societies also, violence underwrote the transfer of serf-produced wealth to an idle but armed aristocracy.

The rise of capitalism changed the character of accumulative violence. Once fully installed, capitalism diminished the degree of armed coercion at the heart of the productive process. Capitalists got laborers to work for them not by threatening to kill them, but by paying them a wage. The wage, to be sure, was not equal to the value of what the laborers produced, hence the transfer of wealth continued. But lords of the loom differed from lords of the lash, and capitalist societies in Western Europe saw the emergence of freedoms of speech, assembly, movement, and equality under the law.

If capitalist production, once established, relied more on economic than on military sanctions, the initial creation of the capitalist system was often a bloody business. In England, for example, before independent farmers could be induced to work in factories for wages, they had to be dispossessed from their land. Only if prevented from supporting themselves by growing their own food would they be forced to choose between the unpleasant alternatives of working for a boss, or starving. As the farmers knew this, separating them from their lands proved a long and often violent process. Later, when industrial workers organized to demand higher wages—to reclaim, that is, a larger percentage of the value they created and which the capitalists siphoned off as profit—employers responded forcefully. United States history after the Civil War was punctuated with hundreds of large scale battles between striking or unemployed workers, and private or public armies defending vested interests.

Capitalism, moreover, had an international dimension from its inception, and it was on that terrain that it displayed a capacity for ferocity. Hard on Columbus' heels came the conquistadores and slave traders who constructed a new world order. Millions of laborers from Africa were set to work on mines and plantations in America (on land newly wrested, often in savage fashion, from its Indian inhabitants). Africans working for Europeans on American soil sent wealth flowing from New World to Old, wealth that underwrote the further development of Europe.

With the shift from commerce to industry in the eighteenth and nineteenth centuries, looting gave way to a systematic search for needed raw materials—first lumber for ships, cotton for cloth and wheat for urban workers; then copper, zinc, oil, tin and rubber for science-based steel, chemical and auto industries. Rival empires fought colonial wars to secure access to required goods, or to deny them to their competitors; they took up arms at home as well, struggling, for example, to control European stocks of iron ore and coking coal. Colonies also became important markets for the products of western factories, and new wars were waged to remove resistances to foreign trade and to carve out rival spheres of influence.

Finally, as wealth piled up unproductively at home, businessmen seeking profits set up mining, agricultural and industrial enterprises abroad, and the accessory enterprises (banking, trade, railway and port construction) that went with them. More violence followed where necessary, to break down objections to imperial investment and domination of local economies.

The entrepreneurs who energized this expansion did not do so because they were by nature unpleasant people; they were speeded along their course by the imperatives of their productive system. Nor were the most compelling motivations always economic ones: political and military considerations counted heavily in a world of competing imperialist powers. Many Europeans and Americans were also convinced they were bearers of civilization, order, and progress, convictions fueled by assumptions of racial and religious superiority. Brandishing swords, bankbooks and Bibles, they imposed themselves on the planet and fought murderous wars with one another to maintain or extend their various supremacies.

The rest of the world's peoples were not simply passive participants in this process. Some people in colonized countries climbed on the new bandwagon and became local agents of the metropolitan powers. Others took up the gun. Almost from the beginning, imperialism bred its opposite. Indians sporadically sought to drive Europeans into the sea; Africans launched slave insurrections up and down the Americas; Chinese, Turkish, Iranian, Mexican nationalists struggled to free themselves from subordinate status. Cracks in the world order appeared in the nineteenth century, developed into fissures during the early twentieth, and became great gaping gulfs when, after the Second World War had exhausted many of the imperial powers, China, Vietnam, and many African and some Latin American nations made successful bids for political independence. Anti-imperial upheavals, and the resistance to them, have become distinguishing characteristics of our era.

Accumulative violence, the pursuit of other people's property or their labor power, is one of the grand themes of human history, and resistance to such exploitation is another. Together they comprise a long-running and murderous saga. This book examines some scenes from that drama.

The vantage point is that of the various publishers, editors, reporters and contributors to *The New York Times*. It is a perspective that has decided advantages and certain limitations.

Journalism tends to be present minded. Capturing the immediacy of an incident is its special strength. But newspapers often forget that today's event is not fully comprehensible unless it is set in the context of a larger and longer story. A well-warranted attention to the contemporary can have the unfortunate effect of stranding readers in the present, leaving them adrift on the surface of things.

The method adopted here of arranging in chronological order clippings that treat different moments in a single process, overcomes much of the difficulty. As in the old nickelodeons, placing snapshots in temporal sequence creates a moving picture; the sense of a drama developing in time is restored. The actions of violent protagonists become more intelligible as each incident provides a context for the incident that follows.

If the time montage technique finesses some of journalism's limitations, it does not overcome all of them. A newspaper can bring the sanguinary point-counterpoint of Algerian and French forces into sharp focus but still leave the underlying explanation for the conflict—imperialism and the resistance to it—blurry in the background. The press draws our attention to violence—the manifestation of a struggle between people—rather than to the circumstances that generate it. This procedure can, if we are not careful, subtly distort our response.

It is easy, when reading accounts of an assassination and contemplating with horror photographs of the victim's corpse and his sorrowing family, to overlook the drab, but equally horrifying statistics about infant mortality rates. An imperial country murders not only during the initial work of fastening itself on its host's body, but by continually draining its resources and blocking its development. If the connection between imperialism and underdevelopment is overlooked, massive famines, as in Ireland, can seem beyond human agency; regrettable misfortunes but no one's responsibility. Workplace deaths in mines get labelled "accidents" even though the increased expenditures on safety measures which would have prevented them were rejected to preserve profit margins. There is a great deal of difference between kidnapping and murdering a corporate official, and shutting off heat (with fatal results) to an eighty-seven year old arthritic lady who cannot afford to pay her utility bill. Analysis suffers if the one kind of violence is highlighted and the other ignored. Properly intent on covering dramatic bombings and shootings, the press can forget that systems—social, economic, and political arrangements constructed and perpetuated by human beings—can kill too.

It is particularly important to keep the systemic in mind when we move from description to judgment. In many of the following pages, people grapple with the arduous task of assessing the political and ethical legitimacy of acts of violence. For those who do not adhere to a policy of total non-violence, who reject the notion that might makes right, and who deny that exploitation automatically dictates violence as the appropriate response, absolute moral guidelines do not exist. Deciding whether or not an instance of the taking of human life is justified becomes a painful process. The task is made harder by the fact that protagonists debate the legitimacy of their violent deeds as vigorously as they struggle for power in the streets.

These debates take the form of battles over words. Supporters of established systems often characterize violent protesters as thugs or gangsters. Calling them criminals underscores the usually undeniable fact that they have violated existing law, and implies they have done for personal aggrandizement. Others argue that rebels are maladjusted neurotics acting out oedipal fantasies, indulging their own impulses under guise of furthering the public good. Opponents of a regime reject charges of criminality and dismiss the official legal order as an instrument of imperial or class power. They claim for themselves the status of military combatants and argue that in the long run they will be recognized as fighters for freedom. (It is interesting to note how often the victory of the American rebels against the British authority is cited as moral precedent, and how thoroughly the loyalists who bitterly denounced the patriots as criminals have been forgotten).

In the welter of charge and countercharge, how are we to decide if a government's claim to be protecting "national security" or a revolutionary group's claim to be advancing "national liberation" is the more accurate? Horrendous actions have been taken in the name of just sounding causes.

Such questions cannot be answered in the abstract. We must get beyond the labels people choose for themselves (or attempt to fasten to others) and examine historical circumstances in all their complexity and contingency. This book gives the reader some of the contextual evidence needed to make political and ethical evaluations of some violent encounters of the past. It is an unfortunate fact that the training in analysis thus afforded will likely be of value in the future. As long as our world remains marked by relations of domination and resistance, violence will continue to figure prominently in the pages of the *New York Times* for many years to come.

Michael Wallace

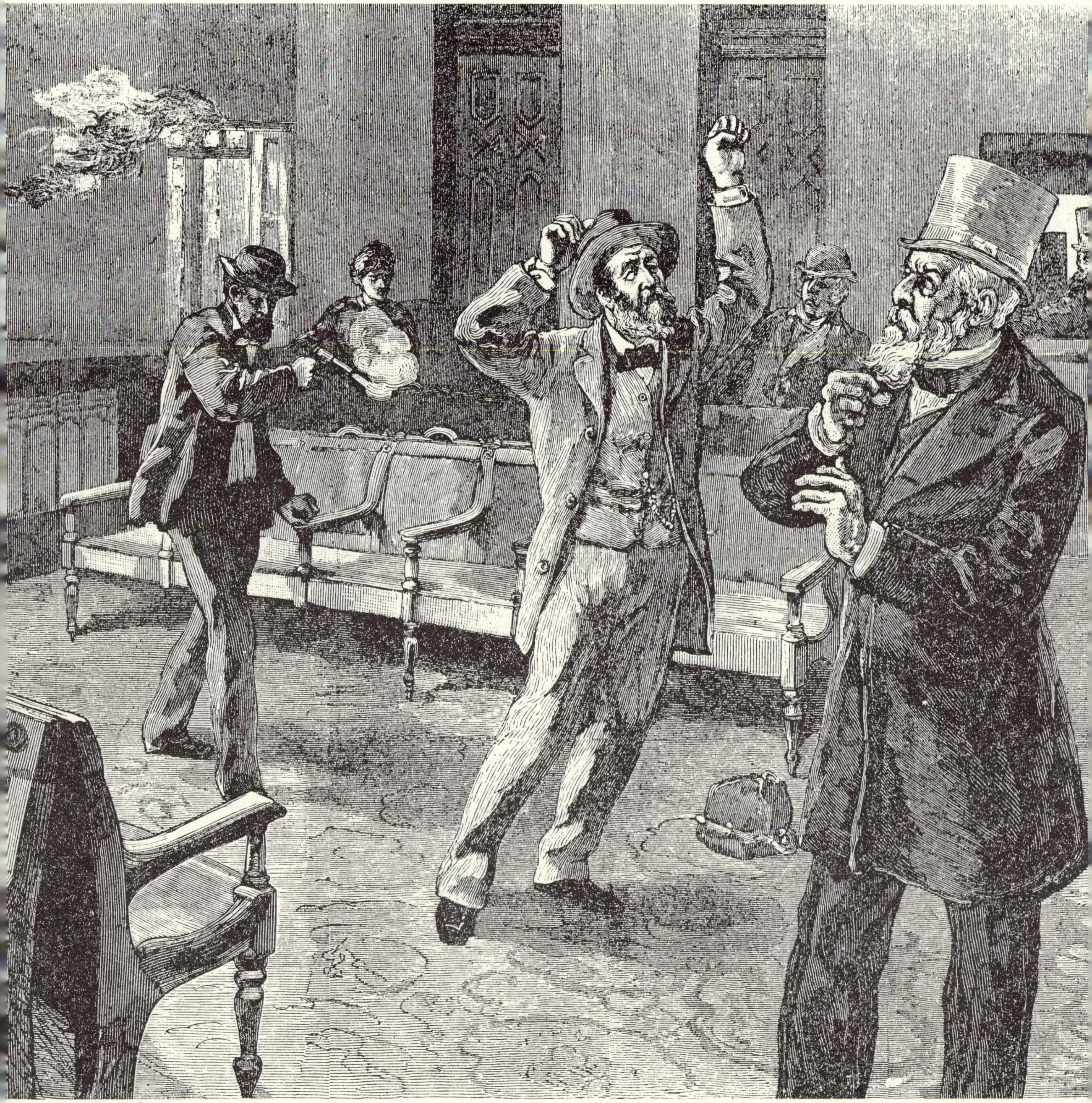

CHAPTER 1

Overthrow of the Old Order

President James Garfield is assassinated
by Charles J. Guiteau in 1881.

THE SPECTRE OF ANARCHY

PROTESTS AGAINST DESPOTISM.

It is not possible for intelligent people in this country to have any sympathy with the theories or methods of the Socialists and Nihilists of European Empires, but we cannot be blind to the fact that they are in some sort, rash and violent though it be, a protest against a despotic system which is equally repugnant to our ideas and feelings. It is not for the citizens of a free Republic, who have won and maintained their liberties through fierce struggles, and whose institutions are based on the fundamental principle that all men have equal rights in shaping and controlling the administration of their own Government, to advocate as a duty apathetic acquiescence in palpable wrongs and quiet submission to whatever tyrannical outrages an autocratic ruler may see fit to impose. The life of the Socialistic movements in Germany and Russia is not derived from the discontent of an ignorant peasantry so much as from the intelligent disapproval of more or less cultivated men of systems which they see to be crushing with cruel severity the energy and the spirit of the people. The Government of neither of these countries will brook any opposition aimed with the slightest show of determination at the policy which it pursues or the theory upon which it acts. They confound all opponents in a common category with those who avow their purposes to be revolutionary and violent, and whose instrumentalities are disorder and assassination. As a whole, the poorest and most ignorant classes both in Germany and Russia are attached to their rulers with a sense of awe and loyal devotion which we can scarcely comprehend. Their lot may be hard and barren, and that fact may be in no small measure due to the system of government under which they live, but they do not realize it, and are not given to rebellious demonstrations.

Socialism and Nihilism are bred in active minds and disseminated by men who think and are disposed to act. Their doctrines are radically unsound, their ends at once unattainable and undesirable, and their methods worthy of condemnation; but they are provoked and driven on by a grinding tyranny, which, in resenting their efforts, makes no discrimination between avowed revolutionists and assassins and those who merely aspire to compel reforms which the enlightened conscience of the world would approve. Men are subject to cruel acts of repression and to penalties which only felony would justify for no offense but an ardent faith in human liberty and the courage to maintain their convictions. In Germany, criticism of the acts of the Administration, disrespect for the Emperor or his Chancellor, discussion of the principles of free government, or any show of the spirit which is the very breath of political life in countries with liberal institutions, are liable to be visited with imprisonment or expatriation. Imperial rule and its harsh exactions must not be resisted or even criticised, though they may be honestly regarded as the source of national misery. In Russia everybody who presumes to question the righteousness of the decrees of autocratic rule, or to condemn or resist the instruments employed to carry them into effect, however they may abuse the powers intrusted to them, is set down as at one with the craziest of Nihilists, and treated with the same severity. Tyrannical restrictions in the universities, sible agents of the Government for private gain or revenge or from the mere caprice of domineering cruelty, abominable abuses in the treatment of prisoners, must be borne in unprotesting meekness, or the iron hand will strike with increased force and in still more unreasoning blindness.

Where this mad conflict will end it is not easy to conjecture. Every new display of violence on one side is met with increased harshness and severity on the other, and this again intensifies the desperation that already smites with little regard for consequences. If tyranny breeds violence, increase of tyranny is not likely to lessen it. With every turn of the relentless screw, more men who feel the pressure are driven to a deadly hostility to the hand that grasps it. It is fortunate for Russia that the great substratum of its society is not as yet much moved with this ferment of opposition to the Government of the Czar. If it were, the almost inevitable result of this policy of repression would be a revolutionary explosion that would shatter the Romanoff autocracy to fragments. As it is, it is preparing for itself an undying conflict and a never-ending danger. Socialism and Nihilism, in a blind and reckless way, are fighting for freedom and liberal principles. Where these prevail they must cease to exist or be devoted to comparatively harmless speculation. Free discussion is the most potent antidote for their pestilent theories, and a representative government affords means for the redress of grievances which leaves no excuse for perilous modes of action.

April 22, 1879

THIRTY YEARS' REGICIDES.
ATTEMPTS TO ASSASSINATE SOVEREIGNS SINCE 1850—A LONG AND BLOODY RECORD.
From the Manchester Examiner, April, 1880.

A paper published at Berne has compiled a list of all the known attempts at assassination that have been made since 1850, under the heading "Recent Regicides," a term which, however expressive, is scarcely accurate, inasmuch as the compilation includes attempts on the lives of magistrates and statesmen, as well as on the lives of Princes and potentates. The first crime recorded in this register is the attempt made in May, 1850, by the Westphalian, Safelage, to shoot the King of Prussia, to the cry of "Liberty for all." On June 28 of the same year, Robert Pate, a retired Lieutenant of hussars, struck the Queen of England with a cane—an assault certainly, but not an assault with intent to kill. In October, 1852, a conspiracy to blow up Louis Napoleon with an infernal machine containing 1,500 projectiles, was frustrated by the activity of the Police. On Feb. 17, 1853, the Emperor of Austria was stabbed in the back by a Hungarian shoe-maker of the name of Libeny. On the 5th of July following a second attempt was made on the life of Louis Napoleon on his way to the Opéra Comique. On March 20, 1854, Ferdinand Charles III., Duke of Parma, was stabbed by an unknown hand. Part of the dagger remained in the wound which it inflicted, and the Duke died after 23 hours of terrible suffering. The murderer escaped. In 1855 the Italian, Pianori, shot twice at the French Emperor in the Tuileries garden. In March, 1856, a Spaniard, of the name of Raimond Fuemes, was arrested just as he was in the act of firing a pistol at his sovereign, and the execution of his murderous design prevented. On Dec. 8, in the same year, Ferdinand II., King of the Two Sicilies, was attacked at a review by one of his own soldiers, who wounded him with his bayonet. In 1857, the Italian conspirators, Tibaldi, Bartoletti, and Grelli, arrived in Paris with the intention of murdering the Emperor, but fell into the hands of the Police before their design could be carried into execution. On Jan. 14 of the following year, Orsini, Gomes, Pieri, and Rudio made their famous attempt to blow up the Emperor and Empress with bombshells on their way to the opera. Their Majesties escaped with some slight contusions, but more than 100 persons of their escort were killed and wounded. In December, 1863, another attempt on the life of Napoleon was made by a band of Italian assassins. The attempt failed, and the would-be murderers were captured. The same year the then Queen of Greece was wounded by a pistol-shot fired by the student, Dosios. On the 14th of April, 1865, President Lincoln was murdered in Ford's Theatre, at Washington, and Secretary Seward dangerously wounded by the actor, Booth. A year later almost to a day, the Emperor of Russia was shot at by a man of good position by the name of Petrouik in the garden of his palace at St. Petersburg. A peasant, who struck up Petrouik's pistol, and so turned the shot aside, and in all probability saved the Emperor's life, was rewarded with a title of nobility and the commission of a Captain in the Army. The month afterward, or, to be precise, in May 1866, Eugene Cohen fired five shots at Bismarck while the latter was walking Unter den Linden, in Berlin, one of which struck and slightly wounded the great Minister. On June 10, 1868, Prince Michel, of Servia, and a lady of his family, were brutally murdered in the park of Topeider. In 1872 Bismarck's life was again attempted, this time by a man of the name of Westerwelle, and in 1874 yet again, this time by Kallmann, at Kissengen. On Aug. 6, 1875, the President of the Republic of Ecuador, Gabriel Garcia Moreno, was murdered in the Government House at Quito, and in April 1877, a similar fate befell the President of the Republic of Paraguay. On May 11, 1878, the German Emperor was shot at by Hoedel, and on June 2, less than a month later, by Nobiling, receiving on the latter occasion wounds by which his life was seriously endangered. Nobiling killed himself in prison, while Hoedel perished on the scaffold. On Oct. 25 of the same year an attempt to assassinate the King of Spain was made by the Socialist, Moncas, who, taken red-handed, paid with his life the penalty of his crime. Less than a month thereafter, Nov. 17, the life of King Humbert, of Italy, was attempted by Passanante, whose sentence of death was commuted, at his Majesty's own instance, to one of perpetual imprisonment. Last year, as will be fresh in the memory of all, the Emperor of Russia had two narrow escapes from death at the hands of his Nihilist subjects, and the closing day of the old year witnessed the latest essay at regicide at present on record—the attempt of Otero to shoot the King and Queen of Spain.

March 14, 1881

ANARCHY'S RED HAND

RIOTING AND BLOODSHED IN THE STREETS OF CHICAGO.

POLICE MOWED DOWN WITH DYNAMITE.

STRIKERS KILLED WITH VOLLEYS FROM REVOLVERS.

THE SLAUGHTER FOLLOWING AN ANARCHIST MEETING—TWELVE POLICEMEN DEAD OR DYING—THE NUMBER OF KILLED OR INJURED CIVILIANS UNKNOWN BUT VERY LARGE — THE BRAVERY OF THE POLICE FORCE.

CHICAGO, May 4.—The villainous teachings of the Anarchists bore bloody fruit in Chicago to-night, and before daylight at least a dozen stalwart men will have laid down their lives as a tribute to the doctrine of Herr Johann Most. There had been skirmishes all day between the police and various sections of the mob, which had no head and no organization. In every instance the police won. In the afternoon a handbill, printed in German and English, called upon "workingmen" to meet at Des Plaines and Randolph streets this evening. "Good speakers," it was promised, "will be present to denounce the latest atrocious act of the police—the shooting of our fellow-workmen yesterday afternoon."

In response to this invitation 1,400 men, including those most active in the Anarchist riots of the past 48 hours, gathered at the point designated. At Des Plaines-street, Randolph-street, which runs east and west, widens out, and is known as the Old Haymarket. The plaza thus formed is about 2,900 feet long and 150 feet wide. It was just off the northeastern corner of this plaza and around the corner into Des Plaines-street, 100 feet north of Randolph, that the crowd gathered. A light rainstorm came up and about 800 people went away. The 600 who remained listened to speeches from the lips of August Spies, the editor of the *Arbiter Zeitung*, and A. B. Parsons, an Anarchist with a negro wife. The speeches were rather mild in tone, but when Sam Fielden, another Anarchist leader, mounted the wagon from which the orators spoke, the crowd pressed nearer, knowing that something different was coming.

They were not disappointed. Fielden spoke for 20 minutes, growing wilder and more violent as he proceeded. Police Inspector Bonfield had heard the early part of the speech, and, walking down the street to the Des Plaines-street police station, not 300 feet south of where Fielden stood, called out a reserve of 60 policemen and started them up the street toward the crowd. The men were formed in two lines stretching from curb to curb. The Inspector hurried on ahead, and, forcing his way through the crowd, reached a point close to the wagon. Fielden had just uttered an incendiary sentence, when Bonfield cried:

"I command you in the name of the law to desist, and you," turning to the crowd, "to disperse."

Just as he began to speak the stars on the broad breasts of the blue coats, as they came marching down the street so quietly that they had not been heard, reflected the rays of light from the neighboring street lamp. From a little group of men standing at the entrance to an alley opening on Des Plaines-street, opposite where Fielden was speaking, something rose up into the air, carrying with it a slender tail of fire, squarely in front of the advancing line of policemen. It struck and sputtered mildly for a moment. Then, as they were so close to it that the nearest man could have stepped upon the thing, it exploded with terrific effect.

The men in the centre of the line went down with shrieks and groans, dying together. Then from the Anarchists on every side, a deadly fire was poured in on the stricken lines of police, and more men fell to the ground. At the discharge of the bomb the bystanders on the sidewalk fled for their lives, and numbers were trampled upon in the mad haste of the crowd to get away. The groans of those hit could be heard above the rattle of the revolvers, as the police answered the fire of the rioters with deadly effect. In two minutes the ground was strewn with wounded men. Then the shots straggled, and soon after all was quiet and the police were masters of the situation.

May 5, 1886

CHAIRMAN FRICK SHOT

DESPERATE CRIME OF A RUSSIAN ANARCHIST.

TWO BULLETS ENTER THE BODY OF MR. FRICK—STABBED TWICE IN THE STRUGGLE TO DISARM HIS ASSAILANT—THE WOUNDS WILL PROBABLY NOT PROVE FATAL.

PITTSBURG, Penn., July 23.—The labor troubles in Allegheny County culminated to-day in a desperate attempt to assassinate H. C. Frick, Chairman of the Carnegie Steel Company.

The would-be assassin is a New-York crank whose name, so far as the police are able to learn, is Simon Bachman. He came to Pittsburg two days ago with the fixed determination to kill Frick, and made several visits to the office for that purpose, but his nerve failed him until to-day, when, having succeeded in obtaining access to the private office of Mr. Frick, he put two bullets in his body, and then stabbed his victim twice in a struggle over his pistol.

To-night Mr. Frick is resting easily and his wounds are pronounced to be of a not necessarily dangerous character.

Bachman is in the Central Police Station. He refuses to talk, further than to declare that he came to Pittsburg to kill Frick, because the latter was an enemy of the working people and deserved death. When informed that Frick would in all likelihood recover, he sighed and said: "I am sad."

Bachman, according to his own statements, is a Russian Jew, who has lived for six years on the crowded east side in New-York. He has learned the trade of cigarmaker and also that of a printer, and has followed both occupations. He refuses to give his address.

To-night Superintendent of Police Roger O'Mara sent Bachman's photograph to Superintendent Byrnes of New-York in the hope that Byrnes could identify the crank. O'Mara himself may go to New-York to-morrow night to consult with Byrnes about the case.

After his arrest, and while sitting for his photograph at the Central Police Station, Bachman made a sensational attempt to commit suicide. His jaws were noticed to move as though he were chewing something. He was ordered to open his mouth, and was hurried into a cell, where it was found that he had been biting a cap composed of fulminate of mercury, which is only used in setting off dynamite. It was with a cap of this description that Louis Lingg, the Chicago Anarchist, blew off his head in prison while under sentence of death for his participation in the Haymarket explosion.

The police do not believe that Bachman has any accomplices. On the contrary, they take him at his word and look on him as a mere crank, a Nihilist, whose head was turned by the reading of the Homestead troubles, and who started forth on a mission of destruction, believing himself to be justified in his course. But, although it is the general opinion that the attempt on Frick's life was not directly connected with the Amalgamated Association, and was not inspired by its officers or by any of the Homestead leaders, the affair has not only aroused intense excitement in the community, but has given a strong additional impetus to the reaction in favor of the Carnegie side of the controversy with their locked-out workmen.

July 24, 1892

ANARCHY AND DYNAMITE.

It may seem strange that the first proposition for an amendment to international law that is plainly in the interest of progress and civilization should emanate from Spain. It is not strange, however, that the country which has been most shocked and most injured by the latest form of crime against progress and civilization should be the first to propose a concert of action against it among civilized nations. Spain is undoubtedly in this plight. The explosion of dynamite at Barcelona may have been aimed at somebody in particular, but it did not reach its aim. Nobody especially obnoxious to the "proletariat" was killed or injured, but some sixty persons, as it now turns out, were killed or injured whose only crime was that they were fairly well-to-do. Manifestly nobody who was not an enemy of civilization and of the human race could defend or extenuate this wanton massacre, but the European organs of Anarchism are prepared to maintain that the persons so cruelly massacred were "expiating" the sins of their class, that is to say, of the industrious, the prudent, and the provident among mankind.

It is quite natural that such a crime, following other crimes not less atrocious in spirit and only by accident less destructive in result, should have filled the Spanish people with horror and indignation and have moved the Spanish Government to appeal for an international union against an organization of miscreants that is also international. The Anarchist is indeed a man of no country, excepting only in Russia, where his provo-

The Spectre of Anarchy

cations are to be considered, and where he may really be actuated by a love of his country and of his kind. Everywhere else he is an enemy of the human race, and the whole human race is interested to suppress and to exterminate him. To call his offense "political" is like calling piracy on the high seas a political offense. His offense is so far from being political that every country has an equal interest in punishing him. We can understand a "despotism tempered by assassination." We can understand that there may be good in a man who, having rightly or wrongly concluded in his own mind that a certain dignitary is the author of his woes and the woes of his class, takes his life in his hand in the attempt to take the life of the oppressor. But it would be gross flattery of the Anarchist to liken him to a political assassin, or to a private assassin who does murder from revenge, or even to a hired assassin who does murder to earn his wages. Unless his plans miscarry he runs no risk at all. His weapon is not a knife or a pistol by which he may destroy his enemy. It is dynamite, by which it is uncertain whether any particular person will be injured, but certain that almost every innocent and promiscuous person within range of the explosion will be destroyed. It is the weapon of cowards and pirates. Those who resort to it should be treated as pirates.

It is a proposition looking to such treatment of them that Spain is reported to have made. Such a proposition ought to be favorably considered by every civilized Government. The "note" of the Anarchist is the employment of explosives, and it is against the unlawful employment of explosives that international action can best be directed. The high explosives invented or introduced within recent years have military uses and industrial uses, and every other use of them is a murderous use. It has proved to be very difficult to detect the authors of explosions after the explosions have occurred. For a score of crimes there has scarcely been, on an average, a single punishment. The unlawful manufacture or possession of high explosives ought to be made a crime. Nobody who has legitimate use for these explosives will have any trouble in explaining his possession of them. It would not be a hardship to require every such person to take out beforehand a license for the manufacture or the possession of them, and to make highly criminal, if not to make absolutely capital, an unlicensed making or possession. If that were the law, then the finding of explosives in the possession of a suspected man would be the foundation of a criminal prosecution, instead of being, as in most countries it is now, at most proof of the breaking of a police regulation. The Anarchists avow themselves enemies of society, and society should avenge itself by making every civilized country too hot to hold them.

November 22, 1893

CARNOT KILLED

The President of France Assassinated at Lyons.

STABBED IN HIS CARRIAGE.

Cesare Santo, an Italian Anarchist, the Murderer.

INSTANTLY SEIZED BY THE POLICE.

PARIS, June 25.—Sadi Carnot, President of the Republic, was stabbed mortally at 9:15 o'clock last evening in Lyons by Cesare Giovanni Santo, an Italian Anarchist, twenty-one years old.

He died this morning at 12:45 o'clock.

President Carnot went to Lyons to visit the Exhibition of Arts, Sciences, and Industries. He left the Chamber of Commerce banquet, given in his honor, a little after 9 o'clock and walked to his carriage, which was waiting in the Place de la Bourse.

He hardly had taken his seat when Santo, a newspaper in his hand, pressed through the crowd and sprang upon the carriage step.

President Carnot started slightly.

Santo snatched a dagger from the newspaper and plunged it into the President's abdomen, near the liver.

The President sank back unconscious. He was taken at once to the Prefecture and the most skillful surgeons in the city were summoned. Meantime, Santo was arrested.

The news spread swiftly to every part of the city. Infuriated crowds filled the streets.

An Italian restaurant had been sacked before 10 o'clock, and the police were obliged to strain every nerve to protect the Italian Consulate.

President Carnot arrived in Lyons Saturday and intended to remain there over Tuesday. He was accompanied by Gen. Borjus, chief of his military household, most of his other household officials, Premier Dupuy, M. Burdeau, and other members of the Cabinet.

He was received enthusiastically at the station by the Mayor and district officials, who, in twenty-seven landaus, drawn by horses draped with the tricolor, escorted him and his party to the Hotel de Ville, about three kilometers distant.

Marie Francois Sadi Carnot.
Late President of France.

Cheering crowds filled the street and gave the President such a welcome as he had seldom received. There was a luncheon at the Hotel de Ville, and in the evening a dinner at the Prefecture.

From the balcony of the Prefecture the President reviewed a large torchlight procession, which was followed by fireworks and an illumination.

The programme of the city officials for Sunday, Monday, and Tuesday was submitted to him in detail, and he expressed his satisfaction with the arrangements. The President and his party yesterday paid a state visit to the exhibition in the Parc de la Tete d'Or, and afterward the President held a reception at the Prefecture.

He planned to go to the Grand Theatre, on the Place de la Comedie, last evening after the banquet at the Chamber of Commerce.

He was in a peculiarly happy mood at the banquet, and was noticeably elated by the cordiality of his reception, not only by the crowd outside the building, but also by the guests within. He was cheered incessantly from the moment he left the Chamber of Commerce until he took the carriage for the theatre.

The demonstrative enthusiasm of the crowd caused the confusion which gave Santo his opportunity, as he was able to push his way forward quite unnoticed until he was at the step of the carriage.

As Santo sprang from the carriage step and tried to escape, he was seized and surrounded. But for the prompt interference of the police, he would have been torn and trampled to death on the spot.

As soon as the police extricated him from the hands of his captors, they hurried him off to the station house.

When Santo was within a few feet of the carriage, he waved a paper as if intending to present a petition, and thus threw off their guard the persons nearest to the President. He was seized just as he was about to jump from the step, and had but half withdrawn the dagger.

The President had repeated hemorrhages after he was removed to the Prefecture. He sank gradually but steadily until 12:45 o'clock this morning, when he died.

June 25, 1894

KING OF ITALY ASSASSINATED

Humbert I. Shot to Death in Monza, Near Milan.

MONZA, Italy, July 30.—King Humbert has been assassinated.

He was shot here last evening about 10 o'clock by a man named Angelo Bressi and almost instantly killed.

The King had been attending a distribution of prizes in connection with a gymnastic competition.

He had just entered his carriage with his aide de camp amid the cheers of the crowd, when he was struck by three revolver bullets fired in quick succession.

One pierced the heart of his Majesty, who fell back and expired in a few minutes.

The assassin was immediately arrested and was, with some difficulty, saved from the fury of the populace.

He gave his name as Angelo Bressi, describing himself as of Prato, in Tuscany.

ROME, July 30.—The news of the terrible event did not arrive here until after midnight last night. Signor Saracco, the Premier, immediately summoned a meeting of the Cabinet, and the Ministers will start at the earliest possible moment for Monza.

The Prince and Princess of Naples are on board the Yela, yachting in the Levant.

July 30, 1900

PRESIDENT SHOT AT BUFFALO FAIR

Wounded in the Breast and Abdomen.

HE IS RESTING EASILY

One Bullet Extracted, Other Cannot Be Found.

Assassin is Leon Czolgosz of Cleveland, Who Says He Is an Anarchist and Follower of Emma Goldman.

BUFFALO, Sept. 6.—President McKinley, while holding a reception in the Temple of Music at the Pan-American Exposition at 4 o'clock this afternoon, was shot and twice wounded by Leon Czolgosz, an Anarchist, who lives in Cleveland.

One bullet entered the President's breast, struck the breast bone, glanced and was later easily extracted. The other bullet entered the abdomen, penetrated the stomach, and has not been found, although the wounds have been closed.

The physicians in attendance upon the President at 10:40 o'clock to-night issued the following bulletin:

"The President is rallying satisfactorily and is resting comfortably. 10:15 P. M., temperature, 100.4 degrees; pulse, 124; respiration, 24.

"P. M. RIXEY,
"M. B. MANN,
"R. E. PARKE,
"H. MYNTER,
"EUGENE WANBIN.

"Signed by George B. Cortelyou, Secretary to the President."

This condition was maintained until 1 o'clock A. M., when the physicians issued the following bulletin:

"The President is free from pain and resting well. Temperature, 100.2; pulse, 120; respiration, 24."

The assassin was immediately overpowered and taken to a police station on the Exposition grounds, but not before a number of the throng had tried to lynch him. Later he was taken to Police Headquarters.

The exact nature of the President's injuries is described in the following bulletin issued by Secretary Cortelyou for the physicians who were called:

"The President was shot about 4 o'clock. One bullet struck him on the upper portion of the breast bone, glancing and not penetrating; the second bullet penetrated the abdomen five inches below the left nipple and one and one-half inches to the left of the median line. The abdomen was opened through the line of the bullet wound. It was found that the bullet had penetrated the stomach.

"The opening in the front wall of the stomach was carefully closed with silk sutures; after which a search was made for a hole in the back wall of the stomach. This was found and also closed in the same way. The further course of the bullet could not be discovered, although careful search was made. The abdominal wound was closed without drainage. No injury to the intestines or other abdominal organs was discovered.

"The patient stood the operation well, pulse of good quality, rate of 130, and his condition at the conclusion of operation was gratifying. The result cannot be foretold. His condition at present justifies hope of recovery."

Leon Czolgosz, the assassin, has signed a confession, covering six pages of foolscap, in which he states that he is an Anarchist and that he became an enthusiastic member of that body through the influence of Emma Goldman, whose writings he had read and whose lectures he had listened to. He denies having any confederate, and says he decided on the act three days ago and bought the revolver with which the act was committed in Buffalo.

He has seven brothers and sisters in Cleveland, and the Cleveland Directory has the names of about that number living in Hosmer Street and Ackland Avenue, which adjoin. Some of them are butchers and others are in other trades.

Czolgosz is now detained at Police Headquarters, pending the result of the President's injuries. He does not appear in the least degree uneasy or penitent for his action. He says he was induced by his attention to Emma Goldman's lectures and writings to decide that the present form of government in this country was all wrong, and he thought the best way to end it was by the killing of the President. He shows no sign of insanity, but is very reticent about much of his career.

While acknowledging himself an Anarchist, he does not state to what branch of the organization he belongs.

September 7, 1901

The Spectre of Anarchy

POPE LEO'S VIEWS ON ANTI-SOCIAL CRIME

Brackets Socialism, Judaism, Freemasonry and Anarchy.

Says Mr. McKinley was a Victim of Unrestricted Liberty—Says Sectaries Aim to Destroy Authority.

LONDON TIMES—NEW YORK TIMES
Special Cablegram.

LONDON, Sept. 21.—The Vienna correspondent of The Times says Die Information, which is in close touch with clerical circles, publishes the following "singular address" from the Pope to the Bishops of South Italy:

"I once more recommend to your best efforts the union of all Catholic resources for the maintenance of harmony among the faithful. We are well pleased with the zeal you have displayed in the study of social questions. It is the duty of all to combat socialism in the form which at present it is developing, which attacks society and threatens it with terrible ruin.

"In the presence of the perils of socialism, Freemasonry, Judaism, and anarchism we must multiply our endeavors."

In expressing his sorrow at the assassination of President McKinley his Holiness said, according to the same dispatch:

"The President of the United States was not the victim of personal enemies. It may be said that he was a victim of unrestricted liberty. King Humbert and President Carnot were similar victims. It is clear that the hatred of the sectaries aims at destroying the principle of authority. It is necessary that Catholics close their ranks and strain every nerve to oppose the enemy."

The Times's correspondent thinks it hardly credible that Pope Leo has taken advantage of the indignation and horror at the assassination of Mr. McKinley to preach an actual crusade against the Freemasons, Jews, and Socialists, which, it is remarked, " would be tantamount to casting the odium of anti-social crime on those whom his Holiness regards as enemies of his Church." The correspondent observes that there is some discrepancy between the Pope's words on this occasion and the co-operation of a certain monastic order in the socialistic disturbances in Milan some years ago.

A large majority of the Anarchists, says the correspondent, come from Catholic countries. Italy heads the list; then come France and Spain. Most Anarchist crimes are committed by Italians and Frenchmen. The United Kingdom and the United States, both Protestant countries, have the smallest number of Anarchists.

The coupling of Freemasonry and Judaism with the social scourge of anarchism is, says the correspondent, unChristian and uncharitable.

September 21, 1901

ANARCHIST LEADER SENTENCED

Malatesta Wrote Articles Applauding the Murder of McKinley—German Anarchists to Meet.

ROME, April 7.—Enrico Malatesta, the Italian Anarchist, was to-day sentenced by a court of justice to five months' imprisonment for contumacy on account of certain articles applauding the murder of President McKinley, which were written for and published in an Anarchist newspaper.

BERLIN, April 7.—A federation of revolutionary laborers, which is working in the name of the German Anarchists, is distributing a mysterious circular calling an Anarchist conference for the third week in May.

The place of the conference is not named, but the circular says it will be designated later by letter, in order to avoid police interference.

April 8, 1902

Scheme for Universal War Against Anarchists

SIR VINCENT HOWARD, who, together with the late Lord Curry and Sir Godfrey Lushington, represented Great Britain at the Anti-Anarchist Conference at Rome convened by the Italian Government after the assassination of Empress Elizabeth of Austria, has issued from Paris the following statement, apropos of the recent fatal bomb outrage in Madrid:

"The outrage in Spain brings prominently into consideration the absolute necessity for European nations and the United States of America to take vigorous and concerted action against anarchic crime. It was soon recognized at the Rome conference that very little could be done in the matter by diplomatic means. I, therefore, took the earliest opportunity in the course of the conference of proposing that the sixteen chief officers of police of different nations who were present or their representatives should be formed into a special committee secretly to consider with closed doors and without minutes or written reports what steps could most advantageously be taken.

In my opinion it is wholly a matter for international police communication. This was the view adopted by all present, and without entering into details as to what was decided upon such an international system was effectually established, and for eighteen months prevented any anarchic outrages of a serious character.

"If these precautions had continued to be observed it is probable that some of those events which the world recently had to deplore would have been averted. But as always happens after a period of freedom from crime or outrage, the police precautions began to be relaxed and the illustrious personages for whose safety they have to be taken themselves got worried by the attentions paid to them by the authorities, and naturally longed for the freedom enjoyed by private individuals. Unfortunately there was the well-known attempt of Sipido at Brussels, followed soon afterward by the assassination of that gallant gentleman King Humbert.

"One of the chief sources of difficulty which is observable at the present time is the power of expulsion from one country to another. This is being exercised excepting by Great Britain. There is no gain for international security by the expulsion of the bad characters of one country to another, often without notice as to the route taken, the intention to expel, or other particulars. I maintain that in the interest of all nations and of public order it is absolutely necessary to establish a permanent international agreement putting an end to the expulsion system. Each country should keep its own bad characters and resort to such measures as it deems desirable for holding them under control.

"At present Italy expels her Anarchists to Switzerland, where the cantonal system renders surveillance extremely difficult. France expels to Belgium, while Germany, Russia, and Belgium all expel to England. It may be that in England Anarchists are quieter than elsewhere because they know that the slightest outrage in that country would lead to such an outbreak of public indignation that they would be deprived of this asylum.

"But we have no right, I maintain, to allow England or our great metropolis to be the refuge of foreign Anarchists or the plotting place of outrages to be executed elsewhere. * * * The American people, who are quite as devoted lovers of liberty as ourselves, have a just conception of their duty in such matters, and refuse access to the United States to Anarchists or persons professing anarchic opinions, furthermore reserving the right to expel them if, having once been admitted, they display their pernicious doctrine within two years."

June 17, 1906

URGES A REIGN OF TERROR.

Emma Goldman's Plan for Readjusting Conditions in America.

AMSTERDAM, Aug. 26.—A small army of detectives of almost every nationality is here to watch the delegates to the Anarchist Congress, now in session. The Dutch authorities are most anxious, and have taken elaborate precautions to guard the Government buildings against outrages.

It is understood that at to-day's session, which was held behind closed doors, Enrico Malatesta and Emma Goldman made violent speeches, the latter advocating a "reign of terror" as a means of readjusting social conditions in the United States.

A. T. Ore of Brussels was chosen president of the Congress.

August 27, 1907

TO DRIVE ANARCHISTS OUT OF THE COUNTRY

Secretary Straus Orders Immigration Men to Co-operate with Police in Locating Criminals.

INDORSED BY ROOSEVELT

Added Precautions to be Taken in Excluding Aliens—Three Assassinations Were Plotted in Chicago.

Special to The New York Times.

WASHINGTON, March 3.—The United States has declared open war on Anarchists. As a result of the great increase in crime and the growing boldness of those who are enlisted under the red flag, Commissioners of Immigration and Immigrant Inspectors have been instructed by Secretary Straus of the Department of Commerce and Labor to ally themselves with the police and detectives of the cities and aid in putting an end to terrorism. The order was issued to-day, and is said to have the hearty indorsement of President Roosevelt.

Secretary Straus orders that the immigration authorities shall take steps necessary to "securing the co-operation of the police and detective forces in an effort to rid the country of alien Anarchists and criminals falling within the law relating to deportation."

Secretary Straus's Order.

The order of Secretary Straus follows:

"To all Commissioners of Immigration and Immigrant Inspectors in charge: It is hereby directed that, with a view to promptly obtaining definite information with regard to alien Anarchists and criminals located in the United States, you shall confer fully with the Chief of Police or the Chief of the Secret Service of the city in which you are located, furnishing such official with detailed information with regard to the meaning of the term 'Anarchist,' as used in the Immigration act of Feb. 20, 1907, and with regard to the inhibition of that statute against aliens of the criminal classes, explaining the powers and limitations imposed by said statute upon the immigration officials with respect to such persons.

"You should call to the attention of the Chief of Police or Chief of the Secret Service the definition of 'Anarchist' contained in Sections 2 and 38 of the act of Feb. 20, 1907, and the provisions of Section 2 placing within the excluded classes 'persons who have been convicted of or admit having committed a felony or other crime or misdemeanor involving moral turpitude,' pointing out that if any such person is found within the United States within three years after landing or entry therein he is amenable to deportation under the provisions of Section 21 of said act.

"The co-operation of said officials should be requested, making it clear that in order that any particular Anarchist or criminal may be deported, evidence must be furnished showing (1) that the person in question is an alien subject to the immigration acts; (2) that he is an Anarchist or criminal as defined in the statute; (3) the date of his arrival in the United States, which must be within three years of the date of his arrest; (4) the name of the vessel or of the transportation line by which he came, if possible, and (5) the name of the country whence he came, the details with respect to the last three items being kept at the various ports of entry in such a manner as to be available if information is furnished with respect to the Anarchist's name, the date of his arrival, and the port of entry.

"It is desired that the above indicated steps shall be taken at once and that no proper effort shall be spared to secure and re'ain the co-operation of the local police and detective forces in an effort to rid the country of alien Anarchists and criminals falling within the provisions of the statute relating to deportation."

Uneasy Over Anarchy's Spread.

The Administration has viewed with increasing uneasiness the spread of Anarchy and Socialistic teachings. The threats made against citizens of wealth and position are becoming more numerous with every month. The attempt to kill the Chief of Police of Chicago, the riot in Philadelphia following the dispersal of an Anarchistic meeting, and the threats made against clergymen have brought the Government to a realization that something must be done to make life and property more secure.

With the activity of the immigration authorities and the police in running down criminals in the United States, there will be taken added precautions against admitting to the country any more of the same class. The examination of the hordes of aliens that come yearly to these shores will be made so severe that it will in the future partake of the nature of an inquisition. The Government is beginning

The Spectre of Anarchy

to realize that it has been employing too lax methods in the past.

A case in point, they say, is the presence in this country of Emma Goldman. This woman is declared to be a firebrand and an Anarchist of the most rabid type. She went abroad some months ago, and at that time it was openly stated that she would not be readmitted to the country. In spite of these declarations Miss Goldman is back again in the United States spreading the propaganda of revolutionary Socialism.

It is cases such as these, in the opinion of officials, that lend encouragement to the vicious element. The laws, in the first place, are held to be too lenient and, secondly, they are not administered with the severity the situation demands. More stringent laws, coupled with emphatic application of them, are said to be the crying need of the time.

As the law now stands, an Anarchist may go about unmolested by the police after he has spent three years in this country, and has not been connected with the perpetration of a crime in that time. He is immune from deportation. It does not matter whether the criminal is a citizen or not, he can legally resist all efforts to return him to the country from whence he came.

It is possible, however, under the existing law to exclude Anarchists. The law declares that, among others, there may be excluded from the country "anarchists, or persons who believe in or advocate the overthrow by force or violence of the Government of the United States or of all government or of all forms of law, or the assassination of public officials."

Section 20 of the Immigration act, which covers the exclusion of aliens, provides: "That any alien who shall enter the United States in violation of the law shall, upon the warrant of the Secretary of Commerce and Labor, be taken into custody and deported to the country whence he came at any time within three years after the date of his entry into the United States."

Section 21 provides "that in case the Secretary of Commerce and Labor shall be satisfied that an alien has been found in the United States in violation of this act, or that an alien is subject to deportation under any law of the United States, he shall cause such alien within the period of three years after landing to be taken into custody and returned to the country whence he came."

This makes it mandatory upon the Secretary to deport any alien Anarchist whom he may discover who has not been in the country three years.

General Enemies of Society.

In addition to these provisions, which ordinarily would cover the case of an Anarchist, a separate section dealing with enemies of society generally was included in the act. Section 38 says:

"That no person who believes in or who is opposed to all organized government, or who is a member of or affiliated with any organization entertaining and teaching such disbelief in or opposition to all organized government, or who advocates or teaches the duty, necessity, or propriety of the unlawful assaulting or killing of any officer or officers, whether of specific individuals or of officers generally, of the Government of the United States or of any other organized government, because of his or their official character, shall be permitted to enter the United States or any territory or place subject to the jurisdiction thereof.

"This section shall be enforced by the Secretary of Commerce and Labor under such rules and regulations as he shall prescribe. That any person who knowingly aids or assists any such person to enter the United States or any territory or place subject to the jurisdiction thereof, or who connives or conspires with any person or persons to allow, procure, or permit any such person to enter therein, except pursuant to such rules and regulations made by the Secretary of Commerce and Labor shall be fined not more than $5,000, or imprisoned for not more than five years, or both."

March 4, 1908

SEE WORLDWIDE ANARCHIST PLOT

Washington Officials Connect I.W.W., Bolsheviki, and Revolutionists in Many Lands.

IRISH AGITATORS ACTIVE

Drastic Action by Federal Authorities Likely if Attempt Is Made to Interfere with War.

WASHINGTON, Dec. 25. — Evidence has been uncovered by Government agents indicating that American Industrial Workers of the World, Russian Bolsheviki, Irish agitators and revolutionists in various countries at war with Germany may be seeking to lay the foundation of an elaborate world-wide plan to overthrow existing social orders.

This was admitted today by officials here in connection with news of the discovery of a quantity of rifles, revolvers, and ammunition in the Russian freighter Shilka, which arrived at a Pacific port on Saturday manned by a mutinous Bolshevist crew. Government agents suspect that the guns and munitions were intended for the Industrial Workers of the World in this country, although it was said a full report on the mysterious cargo has not yet been forwarded by officials at the port of arrival.

The Shilka incident is only one of many cases leading officials to believe the connection between plotters in several of the allied countries may be more tangible than the indefinite link of moral sympathy. Certain Irish agitators and I. W. W. leaders recently have gone from the United States to Russia, after being in close touch with each other here, and reports have been received that Bolshevist organizers would come to America before long to spread their doctrine of direct action for communal organization.

No objection will be raised by the Government to any agitation which does not interfere with the progress of the war, officials declare. Officials do not intend to use the war exigencies as an excuse for suppressing free speech except in so far as it leads to hampering the Government in the fight against the Central Powers. This basis of judgment, however, is recognized as broad and will permit drastic action against foreign agents whose conduct directly or indirectly fosters Germany's war aims.

Action will be particularly swift, officials say, when armed resistance to the law is threatened and when other material forces are employed by the agitators. Customs inspection will serve to prevent importation of arms, and the close supervision of crews of incoming and outgoing vessels is expected to make impossible the traffic of communications on a large scale intended to foster revolutionary activity. There still are means of importing money into the United States, but Government agents can trace remittances and keep a watchful eye on suspicious expenditures. Exports of money are governed so strictly by the Government that officials are certain that the chance of American financing of revolutions in other countries is slight.

Although prosecution of I. W. W. leaders recently has been vigorous, officials have evidence which they claim shows that the menace of this organization, believed to be supported largely by German money, remains strong. Further action against the agitators is forecast. This will be hastened if it is found that the band is working with Russian Bolshevist leaders to bring about a premature peace in Germany's interests or to hamper America at home.

Extreme care is being taken by this Government to avoid antagonizing the Bolshevist movement in Russia, despite the international irritations it has caused. American officials do not care to appear to resist the development of democratic ideals, even if it assumes the form of extreme and chaotic socialism reported in Russia under the new régime. In line with this policy, it is explained, preparations for dealing with the encroachment of Bolshevikism in America is not for political reasons, but only to insure material safety and to promote the moral unity of this nation in the war.

December 26, 1917

RUSSIA: TERRORISM AND REFORM

RUSSIA.

We have now before us the text of the manifesto of the Czar, announcing to his subjects the emancipation of the serfs. His Majesty tells them that on ascending the throne he resolved in all sincerity to acquire the affections of his subjects of every rank and condition—"from the warrior who nobly carries arms for the defence of his country, to the humble artisan engaged in works of industry; from the functionary who pursues the career of the highest employments of the State, to the laborer whose plow furrows the fields." His Majesty proceeds to glance at the patriarchal relations which have hitherto existed between the peasants and their proprietors, and to show that as simplicity of manners has disappeared, the condition of the serfs has been unfavorably affected. He was convinced, therefore, that a great amelioration of their lot was a mission to which he was called by Divine Providence. The steps which have been taken in consulting the nobility, in forming the Committees, and in considering the various propositions, are successively detailed; and the mode of emancipation ultimately agreed to (the substance of which has been given in our columns) is described at length. The cooperation of the nobility is warmly spoken of in the manifesto. "Russia," says His Majesty, "will never forget that the noblesse, moved solely by their respect for the dignity of man and by the love of their neighbor, have spontaneously renounced the rights which the serfdom now abolished had given them, and have laid the foundations of a new future for the peasants." They are then called upon to carry out faithfully and conscientiously the regulations which have been deemed fittest for the great end in view.

The manifesto was read in all the churches of St. Petersburgh and Moscow on Sunday, the 5th ult., and was followed by solemn prayers for the preservation of the health and prolongation of the life of the Emperor. The manifesto and the accompanying regulations are being sent as rapidly as possible to all the chiefs of departments, proprietors of land, and communes of peasants throughout the empire. Myriads of copies are, of course, required, and some weeks, it is said, must elapse before the requisite number can be distributed.

The Emperor of Russia, in an autograph letter to the Duke CONSTANTINE, announces his intention of forming a Special Committee, of which the Duke is to be the President, for establishing the organization of the whole rural classes of the empire after their emancipation in a general and uniform basis.

April 9, 1861

OVERTHROW OF THE OLD ORDER

LATEST VIA QUEENSTOWN.

QUEENSTOWN, Sunday, Nov. 3.
Steamship *Asia*, from New-York, this morning.

LONDON, Sunday, Nov. 3.
Revolutionary movements are taking place among the students throughout Russia. The disturbances at Moscow were quelled by a military force. A petition is being signed largely for a Constitution. Monster meetings of the people were expected on the return of the Emperor at Moscow.

The Bombay Mail reached Marseilles on the 2d.

BERLIN, Saturday, Nov. 2.
The *Prussiche Zeitung* of to-day publishes news from Moscow, without date, announcing that the students in that city had created violent disturbances, which had been quelled by the military force. A petition, requesting the release of the students lately arrested, and that a constitution should be granted to Russia, had been signed by 17,000 persons. The University of Kawan had been closed, because the students had demolished the Rector's house. Students' disturbances had also taken place at Chaisky. It had been proved that a collusion existed between the students of all the Universities. The University of Kien had alone remained quiet.

Count SCHAWALOFF, Chief of the Political Police, had left St. Petersburgh for Moscow to meet the Emperor, to request of him to relieve him of his functions.

The Russian *Zeitung* also states that a Ministerial Secretary had been arrested for having collected signatures to a petition on behalf of the students of St. Petersburgh, which was to be presented to the Emperor on his return to that city. Fears are entertained that stormy scenes, attended by great masses of the people, will take place on the return of the Emperor to St. Petersburgh.

November 15, 1861

The Late Reforms in Russia.

We have spoken already of the great Act of Emancipation, offered by the Russian Government to Poland, as showing both the wisdom and liberal spirit of the Emperor. But the more silent and less revolutionary reforms inaugurated in Russia itself, since the emancipation of the serfs, are a more convincing evidence. On the 1st of January last, according to the Russian Calendar, (the 13th of ours,) a ukase of the Emperor established and perfected a system of municipal reform, begun in 1861, which is among the most wonderful instances recorded in history of governmental and political improvement. A population of nearly fifty millions of people in European Russia—the greater part just emancipated from serfdom—are endowed with the most minute and extended system of municipal reform.

It would be impossible in any narrow compass to describe this remarkable structure of government within government, even as it would be with our own. Briefly we may say that the unit in the Russian Administration, as with us, is the town or *commune*; then above that is the county, and above that the province or State. The county and the State have each their local legislatures, which again choose "executive committees," who carry on the practical detail of their respective fields of labor. The whole local self-government is left in the hands of these authorities; the Government reserving to itself no right to interfere in local legislation, so that at one blow the great political evil of most countries of Continental Europe is struck away—centralization. The field of the local legislatures is distinctly defined, and any passing beyond it exposes the members to trial and punishment, while the neglect of their appropriate duties is equally a legal offence.

There are three distinct classes who have share in the suffrage—the emancipated peasants, (the limitation being by amount of landed property,) the citizens of towns, (here property and trade or professional position determining the right to vote,) and the nobility, with a few of the clergy. On crown lands, the superintendents or officials, placed by Government, have the privilege of voting. It is, in fact, a general suffrage, limited by property, position and intelligence, so far as the vote can fix these.

The Executive Committees, which are very powerful, and are paid by their respective legislatures, are not in all cases allowed to elect their own chairman, that of the Province being *ex officio* the marshal, a member of the nobility; but even these, the Government does not directly control. Nothing could be more complete than the scope of these local bodies. There is hardly a power of our State Legislatures and County boards, referring to local matters, which is not embraced in their powers.

To detail these, or to thoroughly describe the complicated system thus inaugurated, would require a volume. But no American reader needs to be told that it is precisely such a system of local self-government which, first in England and then in America, has educated for centuries the Anglo-Saxon race into their wonderful skill in political affairs, and has prepared them for absolute liberty. It is the want of such an education which has been so fatal to the French and German struggles for self-government. Russia has always had a good deal of self-government in certain parishes. Now she first frees the serfs, then elevates them, under certain conditions, to the suffrage, then offers the whole people a series of municipal institutions, which are seminaries of conservative and national liberty.

If the present Czar originated this most remarkable political system which he has conferred on the nation, he is at once one of the first political philosophers and practical statesmen, as well as one of the greatest benefactors of this age. Nothing could be more adapted to educate the masses for constitutional government, and to elevate the intelligence and character of all classes. It is vastly better than a sudden and wild gift of democratic institutions. It is laying the foundation for Liberty.

A nation of emancipated serfs must ever remember this Emperor as their liberator. But hereafter, other nations and other times will remember him most warmly as the wise builder of free institutions and a constitutional government for hundreds of millions in Europe and Asia.

April 26, 1864

A Revolution in Russia.

Nobody who watches, even superficially, the main currents of European politics, can doubt that the wars of the future will be of a revolutionary rather than a dynastic kind. In every State of the Old World there exist, under one name or other, the elements of popular insurrection. The immediate aims of such movements are varied according to the existing order of things to which they find themselves opposed, but they have the distinction in common of being revolutionary, and of claiming, on that account, a reciprocal fellowship and support. Most things in connection with Russia are more or less mysterious, and as might be expected, its revolutionary impulses are the most occult of anything of a similar nature in Europe. A trial is at present in progress in St. Petersburg which affords some insight into the organization of the political incendiaries of the Empire of the Czar. The alleged conspiracy for which eighty-seven prisoners, consisting of students, priests, merchants and ladies of fashion, are at present arraigned before the High Court of Justice in St. Petersburg, was discovered nearly two years ago. It began with a notable discovery of the Russian Secret Police that the students of the Imperial Academy and other higher schools of the capital were showing symptoms of disaffection. It turned out that the suspicious manifestations in question merely arose from an organized attempt to establish a sort of benefit society for the assistance of the poorer class of students. United action on any question being apparently regarded with suspicion in Russia, the benevolent intentions of the students were summarily interfered with.

Unfortunately, a certain arch conspirator, called SERGIUS NETSCHAJEW, was, in defiance of Police vigilance, ready to take advantage of the disaffection which had been created among the students of St. Petersburg, and which had communicated itself to Moscow and other seats of learning throughout the Empire. This political agitator is a representative man of what is known as the "Russian Section of the Universal Revolutionary Union." The avowed objects of this society are, to break up the monopoly of official patronage enjoyed by the Emperor and a few of his immediate advisers, to vindicate the right of public assembly, to remove the Press beyond Government control, and to render the subject independent of various embarrassing attentions of a paternal Government, such as the spy system, the use of

Russia: Terrorism and Reform

the lash, and the free recourse to the punishment of exile to Siberia. The real programme of the "Section" is, doubtless, a good deal more comprehensive; and, in any case, its objects are held by the public prosecutor to be equivalent to "the overthrow of the established order." The Russian Revolutionary Society is so organized that not more than five members can know each other. Each circle of five holds communication with some acknowledged centre, but they maintain no intercourse one with another, so that as long as one or two leaders are found incorruptible, something like perfect secrecy is obtained. The suspicion of treachery among the members of the Society is almost inevitably followed by the assassination of the party suspected.

This somewhat formidable organization managed to secure the adhesion of considerable numbers of the disaffected students. The repressive measures of 1869 were to be made the incentive to a movement which it was expected might ripen into a popular revolt about the Spring of 1870. The development of the plan was interrupted by a descent made by the Police in November, 1869, upon the house of one of the leaders in Moscow. Very tangible proofs were discovered of the existence of a well-organized conspiracy against the Government. Printed forms, surmounted by the device of an ax, encircled by the words "Committee of the Justice of the People, Feb. 19, 1870," were found in great abundance, and a number of volumes in cypher, and numerous addresses of an incendiary character, showed that the most minute preparations had been made for a popular rising. The eighty-seven culprits now on trial were discovered through the agency of documents captured on this occasion. Drawn as they are chiefly from the upper ranks of society, they give the Russian revolutionary movement the character of an insurrection promoted from above instead of from below. What other features of the political condition of Russia the progress of the trial may reveal remains to be seen.

August 10, 1871

RUSSIAN NIHILISM.

End of the Trial of the First Group of Accused Persons—Severe Penalties.

St. Petersburg (Aug. 4) Correspondence London Standard.

The political trial has ended in the conviction of seven out of the eleven prisoners included in the first group. The accomplices of NECHAIEFF in the murder of IVANOFF are condemned to hard labor in Siberia—one for fifteen, one for twelve, and the third for seven years. Three of the other prisoners are sentenced to close confinement for terms varying from four to sixteen months, and four are acquitted. The real criminal, NECHAIEFF, is said to be enjoying his liberty in London. If he had done nothing but commit a cold-blooded murder there would be a chance of bringing him to justice, but as, besides being an assassin, he is a professor of wholesale slaughter, pillage, and incendiarism, he has a right to the tranquil enjoyment of English hospitality, while his less fortunate dupes have to spend the remainder of their lives in exile. The Russians find it difficult to understand this, and refuse to admit that there is either generosity or wisdom in affording protection to such miscreants as NECHAIEFF. During the preliminary inquiry there was a great deal of vague apprehension as to the extent of the conspiracy, which was thought to have ramifications all over the country; but the result has shown that these fears were perfectly groundless, the leading members of the secret organization being a set of lads, most of whom were learning the mysteries of farming, and the funds at their disposal amounting in all to little more than £40. If the trial had not been a public one, the uneasiness which was manifested last year would doubtless have continued; but as every one who could force his way into the court was permitted to remain, and the counsel were allowed to abuse the Government as much as they liked, everybody was satisfied. One of the advocates, who showed a great deal of skill in defending his client, boldly said that so long as there was any restraint upon liberty, secret societies would continue to be formed; and another defended nihilism, considering that the men of talent who profess this doctrine have done immense service by their writings, and that the reforms of the present reign would not have been half so radical without their agitation. Nihilism seems to be a very favorite subject with this gentleman, who appears to entertain rather advanced opinions in politics. He told the Court that the word "nihilism" was invented by TURGUENIEFF, who introduced it into his admirable novel of *Fathers and Children*, as a term of reproach to the extreme Radicals, but they eagerly adopted it, and have ever since gloried in the name. The trial of the second group has commenced. It consists of thirty-three persons, one of whom is a woman and twenty-seven are students. As the individuals included in this category are even more insignificant than those in the first batch, and as the same ground has to be gone over again, all interest in the trial is at an end.

August 24, 1871

Russian Women Students.

The Russian Government, says the *Pall Mall Gazette*, has just made a remarkable announcement in its official organs relative to the Russian women students in the University of Zurich. During the last two years, says this document, the number of young Russian women who study at Zurich has rapidly increased; there are now more than 100 in the University and Polytechnic school in that town. "Very unfavorable reports have reached the Government," it adds, "relative to the conduct of these young women. At the time when their number began to increase, the leaders of the Russian emigration made Zurich the centre of their revolutionary propaganda, and they spared no efforts to draw the students into it. Under their influence all serious study gave place to a fruitless political agitation; various political parties, representing the most radical opinions, were formed among the Russian youth of both sexes. A 'Slavonic Democratic-Socialist Society,' a 'Slavonic Central Revolutionary Committee,' and a Slavonic and a Russian section of the International Society, have been formed at Zurich, and they number several young Russians of both sexes among their members. In the Russian library, to which certain Russian editors and publishers send their periodicals and newspapers gratis, lectures of a very revolutionary character are delivered. * * * It has become a daily occupation of young Russian girls to attend the meetings of working men; political agitation absorbs these youthful and inexperienced minds, and leads them into wrong courses. * * * The young women who have thus been dragged into politics are entirely under the influence of the leaders of the emigration, and have become their obedient instruments. Some of them go two or three times in the year to Russia and back again, taking with them incendiary letters and proclamations. * * * Others allow themselves to be deluded by the communistic theories of free love, and, under the protection of a fictitious marriage, act in utter forgetfulness of all the fundamental principles of morality and decorum. The misconduct of these Russian women has so provoked the local population that even the lodging-house keepers hesitate to take them into their homes. * * * Such immorality cannot be allowed by the Government to pass unnoticed. It must not be forgotten that these women will, sooner or later, come back to Russia, there to become wives, mothers, and teachers; and it is the duty of the Russian Government to prevent them, as far as possible, from corrupting the youth of the country. To those young women who really wish to obtain a scientific education, ample opportunities are afforded by the higher schools in Russia itself, to which students of both sexes are freely admitted; but there can be no doubt that the Russian young women who go to Zurich are actuated by different motives from that of a love of science. * * * The frivolous articles of some of our newspapers, the false notions as to the position of women in society, the attraction exercised by modern ideas—all these causes have more or less had an influence in bringing a relatively much larger number of young Russian women to Zurich than are to be found there from other European countries to whose universities women are not admitted. The number of women students from Russia is 108; of those from other European States, not 20. * * * In order to put an end to this abnormal state of things, it is hereby announced to all the Russian women who attend the lectures at the University and the Polytechnic School of Zurich, that such of them as shall continue to attend the above lectures after the 1st of January, 1874, will not be admitted on their return to Russia to any examination, educational establishment, or appointment of any kind under the control of the Government."

June 28, 1873

THE NEW RUSSIAN MILITARY LAW.

The terms of the Russian manifesto just issued are as follows:

"We, Alexander II., Imperator and Autocrat of All the Russias, &c., hereby announce as follows to all our loyal subjects: Being ever desirous to promote the welfare of the Empire and improve the institutions of the same, we have directed our attention to the arrangements regulating the service in our army and navy. In accordance with the existing laws, military service is exacted only from the peasants and citizens, a considerable portion of Russian subjects being thus exempt from a duty which ought to be equally imposed upon all. These antiquated arrangements, besides being no longer in harmony with the altered circumstances of our social and political life, are at variance with the military requirements of the present age. Recent events have proved that a State is strong, not by the numbers, but by the moral and intellectual education of its troops. But this education can be secured only by all classes of society alike devoting themselves to the sacred task of defending the country. Recognizing, therefore, the necessity of remodeling the organization of our forces on the experience of modern times, we, in 1870, commanded our Minister of War to draw up a law providing for an improved system of military service on the basis of universal conscription. When we gave this order the well-known patriotic readiness of our subjects to sacrifice everything for the good of the country allowed us to hope that the words we addressed to them at the time would find a ready echo in the Russian heart. In this expectation we were not disappointed. Our valiant nobility, as well as the other classes hitherto exempt from conscription, in many loyal addresses, acquainted us with their anxious desire to share the hardships of military service with the rest of the people. We received the expression of their sentiments with feelings of proud and exalted joy, and we thanked Providence for allowing us to reign over a people who inherit self-denying love of country from their ancestors, and who will leave the same sacred legacy to their children. The principles of the projected reform having been laid down by us, a special commission was appointed, including members of the various departments and other competent persons, to draw up the new military law. The draft submitted to us by the commission, and carefully examined and amended by the Council of the Empire, is entirely in accordance with our own views. Fully acknowledging the principle that the defense of the throne and country is a sacred duty of every Russian, the draft declares every male liable to conscription, and repeals the ancient provisions allowing conscripts to redeem their obligation by payment of a sum of money or the presentation of a substitute. The operation of the new law is, however, not to extend to the Cossacks, whose military service is regulated by special arrangements, nor will the non-Russian inhabitants of the Transcaucasian Provinces and other remote districts enumerated in our Ukase to the Supreme Administrative Senate be liable to the new provisions, it being intended to issue special regulations for these foreign tribes. With these and some other temporary exceptions mentioned in our Ukase to the Senate, the whole male population of the Empire of Russia and the Kingdom of Poland, on attaining the twentieth year of age will be required to draw lots, the result of the drawing settling, once for all, who is to be enlisted for active service and who not. Those drafted into the army will be liable to a fifteen years' service. But after a service of six years, or, if possible, even a shorter period, they will be sent home on furlough, and will be called in only in the event of warlike complications demanding their presence in the ranks. As regards those entering the navy or the corps stationed in remote provinces their time of service will be fixed by special regulations. Young men who have attended any of the schools of the Empire, whether superior or elementary, will in time of peace be allowed a reduction of their term of active service proportionate to the degree and the nature of the instruction received. Other important concessions are likewise accorded to them. While sanctioning the law drawn up in accordance with the above fundamental rules, and calling upon our subjects to acquit themselves zealously of the new duties imposed upon them, we have no intention to abandon the policy we have constantly pursued during our whole reign. We have never aspired, nor do we aspire now, to the splendor of military renown. We have never aimed at privilege to lead Russia to greatness by pacific progress and the gradual development of her domestic resources. This development will not be delayed by the formation of a powerful army and navy; on the contrary, steady progress is insured by securing the Empire from attack and obviating interference with its tranquillity and peace. The important advantages conceded to young men who have received instruction at schools will, it is to be hoped, act as another incentive to encourage the spread of that enlightenment which we regard as the guarantee of the future welfare of our people.

Given at St. Petersburg, Jan. 1.

ALEXANDER.

The details of the new law are still unknown, but enough has transpired to show that the Russian Army and reserve—the latter consisting of those not enlisted for active service—will reach a total of nearly 2,000,000 of men within fifteen years. Adding to this the increased facility of locomotion in the country consequent upon the construction of numerous railways, it is certain that Russia, who has never yet sent more than 150,000 men across her frontiers, will in future dispose of at least 500,000 for a foreign war.

February 5, 1874

END OF A GREAT POLITICAL TRIAL.

The trial which has just been concluded at St. Petersburg is one of great political significance to the Russian Empire. In October last nearly two hundred persons, after having suffered imprisonment for over a year, were placed on trial for alleged complicity in a great Nihilistic conspiracy, and all but twenty of them have been acquitted. They were, technically speaking, accused of having taken part in "a criminal propaganda against the State." The tribunal before which these prisoners were tried consisted of six Senators, two representatives of the nobility, a representative of the commercial class, and a representative of the peasantry. Nearly 500 witnesses were subpoenaed for the Crown, and 150 for the defense. The prisoners were a very miscellaneous body indeed, including, as they did, 60 gentlemen and 22 ladies belonging to the aristocracy, 14 males and 5 females connected with the governing classes, 4 men and 3 women of military origin, 3 sons of priests, 10 merchants, 43 trades-people, 17 peasants, 14 Prussians, a forger, and perhaps a few others.

The actual existence of this propaganda was discovered quite accidentally, though it had long been known that some revolutionary association was at work throughout Russia. In May, 1874, one IVAN PELKONEY, a native of Finland, opened, at Saratoff, a boot and shoe shop, which was soon frequented by such strange people that the Police thought it necessary to visit and search the place, when documents were found which proved beyond doubt that the shoemaker and his friends were members of a secret society, having branches in all parts of the Empire. The society, thus discovered was organized at the Russian capital, and was the offspring of earlier societies of the same kind, notably the Dolgonschin and the Nathanson. One of these adopted "Federalism" as its motto, and the aim of its members was the abolition of all government, and the creation of a new social edifice by means of a free federation of independent and productive consumers. It declared war against property, family, and religion, and thus embraced Nihilism in its most pronounced form. These doctrines seem to have found a sympathetic echo in the revolutionary circles of St. Petersburg, where the Pan-Slavists were already in great force. Naturally, there was considerable affinity between societies which represented, the one revolution at home, the other revolution abroad, and their arguments are repeated in pamphlets, one of which bore the startling title, *Ought We to Occupy Ourselves with the Ideal of the Social Edifice of the Future?* Determined to be consistent in everything, these revolutionists would have no grades, no officers, no giving or receiving of commands. All were equal, and each did what seemed best to himself or herself, both as to the matter and as to the manner of his or her propagandism. In order to gain the confidence of the workmen, numbers of the revolutionists learned trades and opened shops. Toward the end of 1873 the Police discovered that attempts were being made to excite the working population of St. Petersburg; but before any arrests could be made the persons suspected escaped to Moscow, where they lived under false names and started new circles, after the model of those to which they had belonged at the capital. Thus, by dispersing the propagandists, the area of propagandism had been greatly increased.

The method was the same everywhere. In the case of workmen and peasants, stress was laid on the insufficiency of the land allotted to the latter under the Emancipation act, and on the severity of the taxation; and it was pointed out that if the possessors of land among the upper classes were massacred, peasants and workmen might have land in plenty without being taxed at all. To persons higher up in the social scale, the plotters enlarged on the sufferings of the people and represented the economical position as hopeless, adding that there was no escape for them except through a revolution and the destruction of the present political system. These ideas were promulgated, not only among doctors, lawyers, mechanics, and peasants, but among the priests and Army officers. They were whispered not only in the universities, the technological institutes, and the workshops, but in the ecclesiastical seminaries and the military schools of the Empire. In the Army, both Nihilism and Pan-Slavism prevail, although, in truth, the officers are said to bother themselves less about the latter than is generally supposed. The officers of the Russian Army consist of three classes: The upper ranks, which are filled from the territorial gentry; the regimental officers, noble by reason of their parents' service; and those promoted from the ranks. All of these, no matter what their rank, who trouble themselves about politics are either Nihilists or Pan-Slavists. The former, like all Nihilists, believe that whatever is systematic in human affairs must come down, and Nothing is to rule a prostrate universe. They condemn all philosophies, and systems, religions and governments. They say none are perfect, and so dismiss them all. What they hope for is the ultimate triumph of Nothingism. Their motto is that of DANTON, *Destrue!* The chief of the staff of the Czarewitch, writes one correspondent, "is Pan-Slavic to an enthusiastic degree." Another correspondent goes so far as to say that "regimental officers are Nihilists to a man." So extensive have been these ideas that it is believed by many Russians that the war with Turkey alone prevented a revolution at home.

The trial just terminated, notwithstanding that only a very few of those indicted were convicted, may, and undoubtedly will, lead to substantial results. The fate of the convicted ones will, in all probability, be banishment to Siberia. In the meantime, preparations are going on at Odessa and Moscow for the trials of several hundred others charged with like political offenses against their country.

January 24, 1878

Russia: Terrorism and Reform

GENERAL NEWS BY CABLE.

NIHILISM IN THE RUSSIAN EMPIRE.
DISTURBANCES IN MOSCOW, ST. PETERSBURG, AND KIEFF—POPULAR DEMONSTRATION OVER STUDENTS GOING INTO EXILE—THE VERA SASSULITCH ATTACK ON A CHIEF OF POLICE, AND ITS MOTIVE.

LONDON, April 18.—There have been Nihilist riots in the streets of Moscow, the nature and extent of which it is impossible to determine from the official reports. The alleged occasion was the arrival of 15 students from the University of Kieff going into exile, whom crowds surrounded, crying. These men suffer for the truth." An official account says: "Acts of violence ensued. The students were conveyed to prison pending their dispatch to Siberia, and tranquillity was restored."

Private information, however, attributes these disturbances to the excitement growing out of the trial of the woman Vera Sassulitch for her attempted assassination of M. Trepoff, the Chief of Police at St. Petersburg. She admitted shooting M. Trepoff, and said she fired without caring whether she killed, wounded, or missed him, but with the determination to bring his conduct before the public. She, herself, had spent the best years of her life in a dungeon because she was a friend of a relative of a conspirator. There she learned to pity those who suffered in a similar manner. When she read in the newspapers that M. Trepoff had caused a political prisoner to be flogged, she determined to do vengeance on him. This was her whole defense. The speech of the defendant's counsel and the verdict of acquittal, despite the Judge's charge, evoked such expressions of applause from the press and people that it is believed that the Government will modify the present system of trials for political offenses. The outbreaks at St. Petersburg, Moscow, and Kieff, which followed the news of the woman's trial, are said to have been so serious as to give rise to reports in Berlin that a revolution had broken out. The Berlin *Post*, commenting on this news, says: "Russia is threatened with serious dangers. The lesson the trial of Vera Sassulitch affords will be fatal if disregarded."

April 19, 1878

THE DOMINIONS OF THE CZAR.
MARTIAL LAW FOR THE NIHILIST ASSASSINS

LONDON, Aug. 28.—The following is the text of the Russian imperial ukase issued at St. Petersburg temporarily remitting crimes against the State and attacks upon officials to court-martial:

"The frequency of crimes against the State and acts of insubordination and revolt against constituted authority, joined to the repeated attacks upon public functionaries, clearly testify to the existence of a dangerous secret society whose members are imbued with the most destructive ideas, tending to overthrow all governmental order, rejecting the necessities springing from social order, and denying the right of property and the sanctity of family bonds, and even faith in God. These criminals, to attain their culpable ends, shrink from no means however perfidious and hateful. Their abominable crimes disturb the repose of all and menace the public powers charged with the sacred task of protecting society and resisting every bad work. Extraordinary crimes call for extraordinary measures of defense and punishment; wherefore, we have thought it right to confide in future to the military tribunals established for times of war the task of dealing with crimes of this nature."

August 29, 1878

RUSSIA'S NEMESIS.

Were any six ordinary men called upon to define Nihilism, five of the six would probably describe it as an association of Russian Republicans for the purpose of superseding absolutism by popular government. But this definition would be wholly wide of the truth. It would be much more correct to pronounce it a modern revival of that terrible "secret tribunal" of the Middle Ages, known to historians as the Vehmegericht, which punished by assassination the crimes of offenders too powerful to be reached by law. The genuine Nihilist's creed is very much that of the Saxon outlaw HEREWARD, who, when asked by WILLIAM the Conqueror's envoys what he could hope to gain by resisting their master, replied sternly: "I hope to live in these woods till I die, and to kill every Norman I meet." What BURKE said of the French revolution is eminently true of this strange offshoot; it cannot build, but only pull down. Its ablest chiefs, when asked what they would substitute for the Government which they are striving to overthrow, have found no answer. Socialism, indeed, has its programme of an ideal future when the work of destruction shall be done; but Nihilism is the present of Socialism, without its future. Indeed, with all its wonderful ramifications, the Nihilist movement can hardly be considered as an organized system at all; it is rather the fierce natural instinct that makes the lion turn upon the hunter who has wounded him, and the heart of a nation rise in vengeance against the oppression which proverbially "maketh wise men mad."

Two great predisposing causes have fostered revolutionism in Russia—the reign of ALEXANDER I. and the Crimean war. Both ALEXANDER and his Army brought back from their long sojourn abroad many new ideas, which took root and fructified at home with marvelous rapidity. The heart of Russia went out toward the nations which had aided her in her death-grapple with the common enemy and oppressor of all. From 1815 onward Russian society was pervaded by a rage for reading foreign books, studying foreign theories, and copying, or rather parodying, foreign customs, which survived even GRIBOIEDOFF's famous satire of "Gore ot Ouma," ("The Misery of Being Clever,") in 1823. The spirit of progress thus fostered was fatally checked by the accession of NICHOLAS, who, like a second Aaron, cast down his Marshal's baton to change it into a serpent, which swallowed up every other form of national development. But for a time all went well with him. The brilliant triumph over Turkey in 1829 gave a delusive lustre to his gloomy reign. Disaffection was still in embryo, and secret combination obstructed by the want of railways, telegraphs, and posts. The émeute of 1831 was the effervescence of one discontented class, not the spontaneous movement of the whole nation, and the savage cruelty with which it was suppressed struck terror while it inspired hatred.

But the time came at last. As early as 1838, NICHOLAS NEKRASSOFF had begun to denounce popular abuses in words of fire. GOGOL, the greatest of Russian satirists, threw the whole force of his great genius in the same direction. The shock of 1848 thrust forward a man superior to both as a political agitator, who may justly be styled the founder of Nihilism. This was ALEXANDER HERZEN, whose powerful and unsparing journal, the *Kolokol*, (Bell,) published first at Geneva and then in London, exposed the worst vices of NICHOLAS's régime with a minuteness of information on the most strictly-guarded subjects little less than miraculous. Russian Republicanism had found its mouth-piece, and thenceforth its increase was unprecedentedly rapid. The sweeping reforms of ALEXANDER II. deprived HERZEN and his colleague, OGAREFF, of their strongest weapon. They were contemptuously amnestied by the Government a few years later, and their great opponent, M. KATKOFF, the able and contentious editor of the Moscow *Gazette*, representing the "patriotic" or ultra-Russian party, boasted that "the tinkle of the *Bell* was silenced for ever." But the spirit aroused by it was not be silenced so easily. The Crimean war, by the universal discontent which it excited, and the striking proof which it afforded of the internal weakness of Russian absolutism, had given an impetus to revolution such as it had never had before. Successive outbreaks followed each other like waves of the sea. In 1860, the St. Petersburg students made a tumultuous procession through the city, and were dispersed by the Finland Regiment, not without bloodshed. In 1862, the capital was fired in several places, and for months together the streets teemed with revolutionary placards and inscriptions loading the Government with the foulest abuse. In 1866, the Czar himself narrowly escaped the bullet of a Nihilist assassin. Two or three minor émeutes preluded the Netchaieff-Bakounim plot of 1871, and the conspiracy of the five universities of St. Petersburg, Moscow, Kieff, Dorpat, and Kazan, in 1872, both of which, ill-concerted as they were, betrayed an attempt at combined action on an unprecedented scale, which is now being more successfully repeated.

The machinery of Nihilism—the secret printing-presses, the cabalistic marks on walls and houses, the distribution of seditious pamphlets by disguised agents, the presence of well-born and well-nurtured ladies among its adherents, the penalty of death for those who refuse the missions to which they are designated by lot—show that it is terribly in earnest; but its real strength lies in the folly of its opponents. Upon the mass of the people it has no hold whatever. The nobles, ruined by the emancipation—the students, oppressed by the Police—these form the bulk of its recruits. But by scaring the Government into punishing the whole nation for the sins of a few, it has done more to make the latter contemptible as well as hateful, than by any other method. For the "Liberator-Czar" to be found repeating and even surpassing the worst tyranny of his father, is the surest way to make the house of Romanoff odious in the eyes of Russia, and bear out to the full that tremendous sarcasm with which TACITUS branded the worst of the CÆSARS: "To commit every crime with impunity, this is to be an Emperor."

May 4, 1879

POLITICAL MURDER.

THE RUSSIAN REVOLUTIONARY ORGAN JUSTIFIES BLOODSHED IN THE CAUSE OF FREEDOM.

The Russian revolutionary journal, *Zemlya i Volya*, (*Land and Liberty*,) in its issue of April 13 has an article on the "Importance of Political Murder," of which the following is an extract:

"Political murder is, as a rule, an act of revenge. Only when the destruction of political offenders is resented by murder on the part of their surviving colleagues can the revolutionary party exist and assert their independence. Only by avenging the death of their associates can the revolutionary party become a firm, compact and effectual force. Only by shedding blood in a good cause can we rise to that lofty morality from which alone liberty can be born. Only by proving ourselves prompt to kill and to die can we hope to carry the masses with us. No one acquainted with the existing state of things in Russia will deny that, apart from being one of the most effectual means of agitation, murder is the only weapon left in our hands. By spreading terror throughout Government circles we may hope to shake the entire system, and finally overthrow the whole structure. Each bullet fired at our enemies acts like an electric spark, causing trepidation and dismay over a wide area and laming the functions of the official body in extensive provinces. While the champions of liberty were only a handful they concealed their action and formed secret societies. This organized secrecy was their strength. Millions of unorganized divided enemies found it difficult to cope with a small band of closely allied conspirators. As Herzen said in his famous revolutionary journal, *Kolokol*, on Jan. 1, 1861, "our friends met in caverns, in subterranean holes, and there founded those sacred unions of noble desperadoes which could be defeated neither by the horrors of a barbarous persecution, nor by the admonitions of haughty but stupid civilization." But now that the formidable arm of sure and systematic assassination is added to secrecy, conspiracy becomes a power in the State, formidable to its enemies, who never know when and where they will be singled out for retribution. The time has come for murder to take rank among the political agencies of the period. The mysterious subterranean power by which our poniard is wielded has at last determined to arraign before its tribunal all those high and mighty criminals who have so long been reveling in wickedness. And, lo, scarcely have we begun to strike a few blows when the whole lot of them feel the ground shake under their feet, and with fond and quaking see the abyss opened before their quailing eye. Against whom are they to contend? From whom are they to shield themselves? Whom are they to destroy in blind and unscrupulous revenge? A million bayonets, wielded by a million of slaves, are ready to carry out any behests that may be given them. Let the word of command go forth, and they will shoot and stab right and left, no matter how many of their brethren may perish. But against whom are their commanders to direct this terrible force, welded together by the corruption and tyranny of ages? There is no enemy in sight. There is nothing to show whence the avenging blow has come, and whither the hand retired that struck it. It disappeared as suddenly as it came into view, leaving nothing but a corpse and the stillness of death. The habitual repetition of this phenomenon begins to convince our enemies that a time of reckoning has come, and that, however formidable the power that protects them, they will soon have to pass away from the face of the earth. Murder that cannot be averted by whole *corps d'armées*, nor obviated by legions of cunning spies, is the one great resource of the friends of liberty. A few paltry assassinations on our part have forced Government to proclaim a state of siege, double the political Police, place Cossack posts at every corner, and distribute swarms of gendarmes over the country. To all these devices we have driven by a few resolute deeds that autocracy which could not be shaken by years of secret agitation, by centuries of agony, by the despair of the young, the groans of the oppressed, and the curses of thousands murdered in exile, and tortured to death in the wastes and mines of Siberia. Duly taking all this into account, we recognize murder as one of the principal means at our disposal for warring effectually against Russian despotism."

June 4, 1879

NIHILISM AND THE RUSSIAN PEASANTS.

The St. Petersburg correspondent of the *Journal des Débats* gives an account of the manner in which the Nihilists are working upon the Russian peasantry. Finding that it was useless to denounce despotism or declaim against the Czar to them, they have persistently circulated rumors that the Czar himself had authorized a change in the existing tenure of the land, and that the rents payable by the emancipated serfs to their lords would be remitted. These benefits were only prevented from being at once conferred upon them by the wickedness and corruption of the Czar's agents. A more effective mode of action could hardly have been chosen. Ever since the emancipation of the serfs the yearly payment for the land has been looked upon as a serious grievance, and it is felt more and more as times have got harder. The serfs would have been content enough to pay for their liberation, but they do not understand paying for the privilege of cultivating the soil. "I am yours and the land is mine," was the old tale from the serf to his master. Now comes the Nihilist agitator, and whispers that this wrong would have been remedied long ago had their "Little Father" had his own way. All they have to do is to rise against the officers who rob them, and shortly the land will be theirs, and freedom too. Thousands who cannot read *Land and Liberty* have been influenced by this steady propaganda carried on from village to village; and, as nothing is said against the Czar, the people think there can be no harm in following the counsels of men who seem to wish only their good. M. Markoff's circular proclaiming that the Czar had no intention whatever of interfering with the present disposition of property was one result of the success of the Nihilists; the rising of peasants near Kieff was another; and similar troubles may now be expected elsewhere.

August 10, 1879

Russia: Terrorism and Reform

RESTRICTIONS UPON STUDENTS.

RECENTLY-ISSUED REGULATIONS OF THE ST. PETERSBURG UNIVERSITY.

The following is the text of the rules and regulations lately issued to the students of the University of St. Petersburg:

"1. The students, like all other citizens, are forbidden to belong to any secret society or association, even should the society or association have no pernicious aim.

"2. The students, not forming a corporation, are, therefore, strictly prohibited from any collective action, such as the drawing up of addresses and petitions and the sending of deputations.

"3. Any gathering with the intention of making a demonstration or holding a consultation is interdicted.

"4. No amateur concerts, dramatic performances, or readings are allowed.

"5. Where not within the precincts of the university itself the students come under the authority of the Police, but are nevertheless subject to the special supervision of the inspectors of the university.

"6. Every student must be provided with a written authorisation to reside in St. Petersburg for six months, and a student's card authorising him to attend the lectures, which latter he must always carry about him and be able to produce whenever he is called upon to do so, either by an inspector of the university or by a Police officer. Every student is, moreover, to present himself each month with his student's card at the residence of the Vice-Rector, on the day and at the hour which will be determined. Should he fail in this his student's card becomes invalid.

"7. The inspectors of the university are required to visit the students at their homes, especially those who do not live with their parents, and the student should never, under any pretext, offer any opposition to the reception of an inspector.

"8. The students are not allowed to have in their possession any book or engraving prohibited by the Censor in which the Government, any political personage, or public morality is outraged.

"9. The students are required, both within the precincts of the university and in the city, to be continually dressed in decent civil clothes, without any particular sign or distinctive mark by which they can be distinguished from the rest of the civil population. The wearing of the costume of any nationality is also prohibited.

"10. All signs of approbation or disapprobation in the lecture halls are forbidden.

"11. Should any student fail to attend the lecture during three days without having previously given warning of his intention to do so, it devolves upon the inspector to inquire the reason of this absence.

"12. The students are not permitted to lithograph the lectures.

"13. When a student is on leave of absence from the university he is to present himself, with his student's card, before the Police authorities of the town or village where he may be temporarily residing.

"14. Should a student absent himself from the university without permission he will be expelled.

"15. The students are forbidden to receive any private instruction from any one without having previously obtained the authorization of the Vice-Rector of the university. Any infringement of this regulation will be punished by the loss, during the whole of his course of studies at the university, of the student's right to receive private tuition. Should a student infringe this regulation a second time he will be expelled the university.

"16. The infringement of any of these rules and regulations will be punished—first, by a reprimand from the Vice-Rector, with or without inscription on the list of refractory students; second, by arrest, not to extend over more than seven days; third, by a public reprimand; fourth, by rustication for a year, with the right to study in another university; fifth, expulsion from the university forever. The student expelled forever cannot enter another university until after the expiration of three years, and then only with the guarantee of the authorities of the university the student may desire to enter."

October 26, 1879

AFFAIRS IN FOREIGN LANDS

AN ATTEMPT TO KILL THE RUSSIAN IMPERIAL FAMILY.

A MINE EXPLODED UNDER THE DINING HALL OF THE WINTER PALACE—FIVE SOLDIERS KILLED AND THIRTY-FIVE WOUNDED.

LONDON, Feb. 18.—A dispatch to Reuter's Telegram Company from St. Petersburg, says an abortive attempt was made, yesterday, to kill the imperial family by laying a mine in the Winter Palace. Five soldiers were killed and thirty-five wounded.

A later dispatch from St. Petersburg reports that the mine was laid under the guard-room of Winter Palace, which is immediately under the dining hall. Owing to an accidental delay the Imperial family had not entered the latter at the usual time. The explosion occurred at the usual dinner hour, and made a hole in the floor of the dining hall 10 feet long and 6 wide.

February 18, 1880

TWENTY-FIVE YEARS OF EMPIRE.

The opening of the reign which has just completed its twenty-fifth year was the gloomiest period of Russian history; but it was also the most profitable. "We owe gratitude," says the Moscow *Gazette*, "even to England herself, for her blows shattered the pernicious system that was destroying us, opened our eyes to the real state of our internal strength, and cleared the way for all the reforms now in progress." This is no exaggeration. Russia has made more real progress since the accession of ALEXANDER II. than during the whole preceding century. In 1855 she had only 419 miles of railway; she has now upward of 10,000. In 1855 only three cities in the whole Empire—viz., St. Petersburg, Moscow, and Odessa—were even tolerably paved or lighted; whereas, now every leading provincial town is well off in both respects, and the new St. Petersburg Gas Company is one of the most flourishing in the Empire. In 1855 the total number of factories in European Russia was 17,536, representing a yearly value of 350,000,000 rubles, ($262,500,000.) By 1867—the half-way point of the present reign—23,721 factories were at work, with an annual yield of 500,000,000 rubles, and both figures are now considerably higher. The iniquities of the legal system of that day, carried on according to the obsolete forms of mediæval law, were almost too monstrous for belief; whereas, now trial by jury, introduced in 1863, is a national institution. The Russian soldier's terms of service then extended over 25 years, whereas it is now limited to 7. Various cruel and degrading punishments, then in constant use in the Imperial Army, are now almost abolished, only one man having "run the gantlet" in St. Petersburg since 1861. The 23,000,000 peasants who were slaves in 1855 are now freemen, and not a few of them have become land-owners or thriving merchants. Even in actual territory, Russia's gain has been considerable. In Europe she has acquired Southern Bessarabia. In Asia Minor she has annexed part of Northern Armenia. In Central Asia she has won a territory as large as France, while her Siberian frontier has been advanced nearly 1,000 miles at the expense of China, and the important Island of Saghalin, extorted from Japan.

But, apart from all this, Russia has achieved a step which will go far to supply her greatest want. She has formed, not indeed a substantial middle class, but that which will be the germ of such a class, and which is expanding every year. This is the one thing lacking to insure the stability of the Empire. Of the 55,000,000 inhabitants contained by Russia proper in 1861, 29,000,000 were free peasants and 23,000,000 serfs, leaving only 1,000,000 nobles, 4,000,000 burgesses, and 650,000 priests to form the counterbalancing minority. The emancipation of that year, by destroying the power of the nobility, while that of the people was still non-existent, placed Russia in the position of a State with its upper class gone, its lower class not yet come, and no middle class at all. The same sluggish ignorance which makes the Russian "mujik" proof against the whispers of disaffection, renders him absolutely useless to the political life of his country. What is wanting is a reasoning, not a reasonless, obedience. The chosen tools of Nihilism are discontented nobles who have already lost their all, or hot-brained students who have nothing to lose, with heads as empty as their pockets; and Russia's safety lies in the creation of a class of practical and well-to-do men of business, for whom order implies prosperity, and disorder absolute ruin. The existence of such a class in France made the commotion of 1830 short and comparatively bloodless, rendered abortive the attempted outbreak of 1832, and tided over the great political crisis of 1878-9 without any outbreak at all; and the remedy which has succeeded in Paris may be trusted not to fail in St. Petersburg.

March 7, 1880

THE JEWS OF RUSSIA.

A LARGE NUMBER OF THE HEBREW RACE FOUND AMONG THE NIHILISTS.

The Odessa correspondent of the London *Times* writes as follows: "Statements of various kinds now appear in the Russian and foreign newspapers as to the part taken by the Hebrew subjects of the Czar in the plottings of the extreme section of the Nihilists. As in most instances only theories have been propounded hitherto, a few facts are here offered. In the north of Russia, where Jews, as a rule, are not permitted to reside, few in that part have been compromised, but here in the south, which is overrun by them, they have furnished rather a large percentage of those, at any rate, who have been brought to trial. For example, out of 28 Nihilists tried together at Odessa last Summer, eight were Jews, and out of five of the whole number who were hanged, one was a Jew. Out of six Nihilists tried also at Odessa last December, two were Jews, and of the three that were executed on that occasion, one was a Jew. Besides that, the chief of the band, Laiba Deutsch, was also a Jew. He escaped at the time, but afterward blew his brains out at St. Petersburg upon the occasion of the Police discovering the secret printing-office directed by him, in which was printed the *Will of the People* newspaper. Of the 17 Nihilists condemned here a fortnight ago, six were Jews, and in this instance, again, the principal leader, Isaiah Fuchs, was also a Jew, and he, too, managed to escape. Altogether, eight Nihilists have been executed at Kieff, and of these, two were Jews, and of the three hanged at St. Petersburg, one was a Jew. Report makes out Hartmann to be of Jewish origin, and some people believe the same of the Dr. Weimar, whose trial is expected to take place at St. Petersburg shortly. It is only fair, however, to remark that all these Jewish would-be anarchists, except the Doctor, were people of humble origin, without means, and of no position in life to speak of; consequently, they had nothing to lose, and might have gained something in the event of a revolution. You lately presented your readers with some statistics from the *Bereg* in reference to the number and status of Nihilists. The *Novoya Vremya* has supplemented them with the following statement: Twenty-six per cent. of the Nihilists have the rank of gentlemen, 19 per cent. are sons of priests, 13 per cent. are peasants, (among these are included those members of the *noblesse* whose Nihilistic principles have led them to enroll themselves as peasants,) 9 per cent. are petty shopkeepers, 7 per cent. are Jews, (?) 3 per cent. are of the merchant class, and 1 per cent. soldiers; 22 per cent. are unaccounted for, but then, no mention is made of working men, and, besides, these numbers are believed to be only approximative."

May 14, 1880

THE CZAR ASSASSINATED

NIHILIST CONSPIRATORS AT LAST SUCCESSFUL.

THE EMPEROR KILLED WITH A GLASS BOMB.

Alexander II., Czar of all the Russias, met with a violent death in St. Petersburg yesterday afternoon. While returning from a parade about 2 o'clock in the afternoon, in company with his brother, the Grand Duke Michael, a bomb was thrown under his carriage, but its explosion did no further damage than to shatter the back of the vehicle. The Emperor and the Grand Duke immediately alighted, when another bomb was thrown, which exploded at the Emperor's feet, mutilating his legs below the knees in a terrible manner and inflicting other serious injuries. The wounded monarch was conveyed to the Winter Palace, where, in the course of an hour and a half, he expired, surrounded by the members of the imperial family. Great excitement prevails in St. Petersburg, and the sympathy of the people is everywhere expressed.

March 14, 1881

WHAT THE NIHILISTS HAVE DONE.

The Nihilists have slain the Czar, but have they not also slain Nihilism? These savage men and half-crazed women vainly imagined, perhaps, that throne and crown and imperial rule would crumble and be no more when the vital spark had fled from the cruelly mangled body of their victim. They have professed no purpose beyond what has now been achieved. They gloried in a name which stamped them as the apostles of pure destruction; cunning, powerful, remorseless in pulling down, but with no cure beyond that for any human evil, with no plan or wish to reconstitute the State and reorganize a happier society—a hideous and soulless band. Their chief and deadliest aim, often thwarted, but at each succeeding attempt striking nearer the life of the man they so pitilessly pursued, is at length accomplished, and they are brought face to face with the most searching and complete test of any system or policy—a first success. When the shock of horror at their dreadful crime shall have passed away, the world will look to see what next the Nihilists propose to do, and it will see—nothing. Their empty and inhuman creed guides them no further. But they will answer for their bloody work, if not to Russian justice, at least in the loss of the last shred of sympathy with which not a few ill-informed friends of liberty in other countries have regarded their career.

Now, if never before, Nihilism unmasks and stands revealed as the chief foe of the liberty of the Russian people. It has murdered, after a degree of premeditation which surpasses anything in the previous history of attemped or successful royal assassinations, the "Liberator Czar"—the man whom the peasantry loved because he had struck the chains from their hands, and whose only enemies were found in the haughty and illiberal middle class and among the false friends of liberty who called themselves Nihilists. It is Nihilism which has retarded the growth of Russian liberty in its very infancy, and which has now perhaps dealt it a blow from which it will not recover in a generation. It is known that ALEXANDER II. was a man of liberal instincts. There is evidence enough of this, to cite no other proofs, in his emancipation of the serfs and in his warm admiration of, and intimate sympathy with, popular institutions as they exist in the United States. Undoubtedly he meditated the establishment of representative government in Russia as the crowning glory of his reign.

Our late Minister to St. Petersburg, the Hon. E. W. STOUGHTON, wrote upon this matter shortly after his return to this country, as follows: "It is, therefore, but just toward him [*i. e.*, the Czar] and his Government to assume that so soon as the Russian people—the mass of whom were so lately serfs—are capable of exercising that political liberty which a representative Government involves, they will be permitted to enjoy it. Indeed, I have the highest authority for saying that such is the purpose of the Imperial Government, and that for some time past it has been earnestly considering a plan by which, in anticipation of a more general basis of representation, a partial one may be adopted by which the great interests of all portions of the Empire can be represented at St. Petersburg." We cannot suppose that the CZAR intended the creation of a fully organized constitutional government, with means by which the people could express their will and secure their rights, for Governments are not made, they are developed. Moreover, the Russian people are by no means qualified for successful self-government. But ALEXANDER II. was ready to begin the work of their elevation to a higher plane of political and social life, and the Nihilists forbade him. They closed the hand which was ready to sow the seeds of constitutionalism, and the only hand that, under the Russian system, could do that work. He could not invite his subjects to help him govern while these fiends were striving night and day to murder him.

In the mysterious play and counter-play of political forces it has been decreed that in Russia a poisonous weed should spring up upon the ground where a more wholesome growth might have advanced the cause of human rights as much as it has been retarded by these assassins who have served absolutism in the livery of liberty. In France we have seen a strikingly different result from similar conditions. Good men and the might of reason have put aside the Empire and the Red Republic. The ballot, the very force which NAPOLEON III. called into play to legitimize his throne, and as the bulwark of his power, now serves as the impregnable fortress of the Republic. In Germany, though parliamentary government suffers many checks, the same instrument is at work, and it gains in potency from year to year. Even against Bismarckism it is sure of ultimate triumph. Civilization, as it widens, tends everywhere to sweep away autocratic power, whether he who wields it calls himself Emperor or Chancellor, and to install the people as their own sovereign. The current has been staid in Russia by the crime with the news of which the world is ringing to-day. For a time, indeed, all hope of liberalizing reforms in the Empire may be quenched. But an eternal principle is not to be destroyed by the acts of madmen. In the reign of some near successor of him who has been murdered the work he planned will be accomplished.

March 14, 1881

GENERAL NOTES.

That schism in the Nihilist body to which all thinking Russians have long looked as their only hope of peace appears to have begun at last. A new Nihilist journal, the *Black Division*, has arisen in opposition to the *Will of the People*, and anonymous letters supposed to emanate from its managers have assured the Czar and his chief officers that the death sentence passed upon them by the Nihilist committee will not be executed. It would seem, however, that all these comforting assurances have not emboldened the Government to relax its precautions. Two hundred soldiers have reinforced the guard at Peterhof, the Czar's Summer residence, and all the officials employed upon the 16 miles of rail connecting it with St. Petersburg have been photographed in order to facilitate the detection of Nihilist emissaries. Were Gen. LORIS MELIKOFF still in power, such a split in the enemy's camp might be turned to good account, a result, however, which can hardly be hoped for under men like his successors.

June 23, 1881

EVENTS IN RUSSIA.

ST. PETERSBURG, May 19.—It is stated that the Minister of the Household has issued a circular announcing that the coronation of the Czar will take place at Moscow on Sept. 6.

It is reported that riots have broken out among the peasants in the south-west. They demand a redistribution of the land. Two mansions of the nobility have been sacked.

It is reported that the Black Division section of the Nihilists has amalgamated with the "Will of the People" sections, as it is impossible to carry on a peaceful propaganda owing to the vigilance of the Police.

BRODY, May 19.—The misery of the Russian Jews here is indescribable. Ten thousand of them are without shelter. There are fresh arrivals daily. The population of Brody is unable to afford the refugees further relief.

VIENNA, May 19.—The wealthier Jews in Russia are forming secret clubs to facilitate emigration en masse.

May 20, 1882

NECHAYEFF THE NIHILIST

CHAPTERS FROM A BRIEF BUT EVENTFUL LIFE.

REALLY THE FATHER OF TERRORISM IN RUSSIA—POWER HE EXERCISED WHILE IN PRISON AND HIS CONVERTS.

From The London Times.

Secret revolutionary societies have always existed in Russia, but they had no positive programme and were the spontaneous outcome of dissatisfaction rather than the result of a preconceived plan. Even the insurrection of 1825 was completely wanting in organization. It was not till after Karakozoff's attempt upon the life of the Czar, in 1866, that the revolutionary organization which has since exercised so much power was brought into existence. Many contributed to this work, but none were more active than Nechayeff, who imparted a decided direction to the secret circles and societies then in existence. He gave them for definite purpose the overthrow of the Czar. More than this, he was the initiator of Nihilistic terrorism, and was himself the author of the first crime committed in obedience to this new policy. To the outer world the existence of Nihilism as a militant and powerful association was first revealed by the discovery of the body of the student Ivanoff. This unfortunate youth was a friend, it is even said an intimate friend, of Nechayeff, but they ultimately disagreed in political matters, and Ivanoff, deeming his companion was going too far, threatened to resign and quit the secret association. This menace was looked upon as an act of treason, and the conspirators, fearing they might be betrayed to the police, condemned Ivanoff to death, and he was "executed" by his friend Nechayeff.

This was the first notable deed in the career of this remarkable man. Nechayeff was born of humble parents in the village of Khomovtovka, in the Province of Vladimir. His ability procured for him favors at the hands of the clergy. He was sent to St. Petersburg, and became a teacher of religion at the Sergius School. Though but a self-educated man, he was able to lay up a great store of knowledge. He studied deeply German philosophy, political economy, history, and taught himself French by reading Rochefort's *Lanterne*. So great were his powers of organization and persuasion that the Russian Government set a high price upon his head, pursued him even abroad, and finally succeeded in obtaining his extradition from Switzerland. For this purpose the sum of 20,000f. was paid to the Zurich Prefect of Police, Pfenniger, who facilitated the extradition, which, according to all accounts, was more like an act of kidnaping. The Municipal Council, at all events, protested strongly, and passed a resolution to the effect that even common criminals should not be given up to such Governments as those of Russia and Turkey. Tried at St. Petersburg in 1872, Nechayeff merely sought to prove for his defense that the crime was strictly political, but each time he began to speak he was dragged out of court and badly beaten by the gendarmes. Thus silenced and almost stunned, he was sentenced as a common murderer to 20 years' penal servitude in Siberia. The Government, to conceal the dangers by which it was beset, represented Nechayeff as a vulgar criminal, and accused him of killing Ivanoff for purposes of robbery, without allowing any mention to be made in court of his political object.

The condemnation once obtained, the attitude of the Government was very materially altered. As an ordinary criminal, he would undoubtedly have been dispatched to Siberia in accordance with the sentence, but so precious a capture could not thus be sent out of sight. Nechayeff was therefore confined in the most secure and secret part of the fortress of Peter Paul, known as the ravelin of Alexis. Here it was imagined he would be rendered absolutely powerless, his escape put out of all question, while he might, perhaps, if adroitly managed, be made to reveal important secrets. The very reverse was the result. Incredible as it may seem, Nechayeff still continued directing the Nihilist movement, though he never quitted his prison, and while he was able to chastise with his own hands a Government official, his keepers never made him commit the slightest indiscretion affecting the interests of his party. Several high officials visited him from time to time to ask his opinion on the political situation of Russia and to exhort him to make a declaration of repentance. On one of these occasions he was able to communicate with the Czar Alexander II., to whom he boldly declared that absolutism was out of date, even in Russia, and that a Constitution alone would solve the pending difficulties. Among the more distinguished visitors was Gen. Potapoff, the Ataman or Chief of the Cossacks of the Don. This officer had been Governor-General of Lithuania, but was at that time Chief of the Corps of Gendarmery to which the Third Section, or secret police, is attached. It was in this latter capacity that he engaged in a lengthy and animated conversation with the prisoner. He invited Nechayeff to write a paper on the composition, means, and plans of the revolutionary party—a suggestion which was received with contempt. Gen. Potapoff then threatened the prisoner with corporal punishment, and Nechayeff, deeming himself insulted, suddenly administered so violent a slap on the General's face that his nose bled profusely. This unprecedented event caused the utmost sensation, and, to make matters worse, the blow was struck in the presence of Gen. Korsakoff, the Governor of the prison, and several officers, gendarmes, and jailers.

Nechayeff was now put in chains, connected by a metal rod and riveted to the wall. Thus embarrassed, he could neither lie down, stand up, nor sit with anything approaching to ease; but he suffered still more from the shrieks of a madman confined in the next cell. His name was Shevick, formerly an officer. He did not belong to any political organization, but during a review he had left the ranks, accosted the Emperor Alexander II., and reproached him severely for having violated his sister. For this breach of discipline he was imprisoned by order of the Czar, without judicial procedure, and the solitary confinement destroyed his reason. All these incidents favored Nechayeff's deep-laid schemes. He now began to convert the soldiers who were on the watch. He never lost an opportunity of speaking to them, and though they were not allowed to reply, he nevertheless contrived to make them lose patience. By the display of his own suffering, by appealing to their humanity, or else by calling them brutes, pitiless animals, he would at last obtain some word of excuse, the soldiers generally alleging that their oath and discipline made it impossible for them to interfere.

Nechayeff eagerly caught at such replies to explain to the soldiers that their duty toward the country was quite on the other side; that he had not been imprisoned for the committal of any crime, but for seeking to promote the interests of the people of the very class to which the soldiers belonged. He was attempting to free from oppression the men who thought it their duty to watch him so strictly. At the same time he skillfully shadowed forth to these somewhat thick-headed and ignorant soldiers the great fact that he was not standing alone, but belonged to a party exercising influence even at Court, at whose head was the heir apparent himself.

The visits Nechayeff had received from important personages, the respect shown to him by the prison officials even while inflicting measures of rigor, and his courage in daring to box the ears of so lofty a functionary as Gen. Potapoff, all seemed to confirm his assertions. When finally his chains were removed, he naturally pointed to the circumstance as a proof that his party had got the upper hand at Court. He further told each officer in turn that he was the only one to take seriously the orders given him, whereas all the other sentinels were continually speaking to him and executing his commissions. By these artful means he succeeded in entering into relations with two other political prisoners who were confined in the same ravelin—Mirski and Shirayeff. Both had been sentenced to death, the one for attempting to assassinate Gen. Drenteln, and the other for conducting the works of the mine under the Moscow Railway. The soldiers also carried Nechayeff's letters to town, brought him answers, supplied him with papers, and not only enabled him to resume the work of direction and propaganda, but some among them were themselves converted to Nihilism. It was by these letters, written from the depth of his prison, that Nechayeff most contributed to enforce upon the Executive Committee the adoption of the terrorist policy. In the course of time the confidence of the soldiers increased; they commenced to look upon Nechayeff with superstitious reverence. He seemed a sort of saint and martyr, who was always speaking of the good of the people, the regeneration of mankind, and the happy time that was coming. In spite of all orders to the contrary they continued to favor him in every way, and even introduced Jelaboff, the chief promoter of the final plan to assassinate the Czar, into the prison, where he was able to consult Nechayeff on all the plots then in course of preparation.

Some time before this interview Nechayeff had forwarded to the revolutionary party a scheme for capturing the fortress of Peter Paul and taking the Governor and other officials prisoners. Jelaboff did not share these expectations, but he found that the deliverance of Nechayeff and his friends was not only practical but even easy. At the same time a plot had been formed to assassinate Alexander II., and it was felt that both schemes could not be carried out at once—that one must be sacrificed for the other. Jelaboff's chief purpose, therefore, in visiting Nechayeff was to consult him and to let the prisoners themselves decide which plot should have the preference. To this they unanimously replied that they preferred remaining in prison rather than interfere with the prospect of killing the Czar. After this effort to save the prisoners and this new proof of self-abnegation, the Executive Committee no longer hesitated, but pushed the preparations actively forward, and a few weeks later the Czar was assassinated. The arrest, however, of Sophia Perovskaya, who by moving her handkerchief, indicated to Rysakoff and Hryniewiecki the right moment for throwing the bomb, led to the discovery of a letter which had evidently been received from the fortress of Peter Paul. The watch kept over the prisoners became more and more stringent. The relations between Nechayeff and the outside world could no longer be continued, and he was again submitted to many vexations. Deprived of ink, he, however, wrote with his own blood a petition to Alexander III., complaining bitterly of the new Governor of the fortress, Gen. Ganetski, who he represented as a wild beast. He had no light in his cell, a deprivation which was not imposed even by Gen. Potapoff, who, nevertheless, had good reasons for revenge. Nechayeff also mentioned that in 1875 the Government had offered to expose his views, and now he remarked that events had justified the opinions he then expressed, and that the continuation of arbitrary rule and reaction would prove as pernicious in the future as in the past. This petition he was assured would be communicated, if not to the Czar himself, at least to a high official; but as he had a little later another opportunity of communicating with the outer world, he sent a copy of the document to his friends.

In the Summer of 1882 all relations with the prisoner were finally interrupted, the friendly soldiers were ultimately arrested, and the celebrated trial of the 17 ensued. Nothing more was ever ascertained about Nechayeff beyond the fact that he was cruelly beaten in consequence of a dispute with the inspector of the prison, and died shortly afterward, in December, 1882. Some suppose that he committed suicide, others that he was killed by the effects of the blows; but in all cases his untimely end—for he died in the prime of life—was keenly lamented by all the Nihilists. There are not many who go as far or display as much unscrupulousness as Nechayeff; but all recognize his ability, his courage, and utter disregard of self. He was the most ardent promoter of terrorism, and when in Switzerland he was not satisfied even with Bakounine, whom he considered too moderate. He advocated assassination long before it was practiced: and while suffering from the most cruel imprisonment, never relaxed his hold upon the enemy; but, with bulldog tenacity, preferred to see the Czar struck than be himself released. It seems that his policy has survived his death, for we have not only the murder of Gen. Soudaikin, but the promise of several other "removals."

February 19, 1884

THE DECLINE OF NIHILISM.

From a Geneva Letter to the Political Correspondence.

The literature of Nihilism, so abundant a few years ago in pamphlets, tracts, and clandestine newspapers, is now practically reduced to two periodicals of very small importance. The first of these is *La Messager de la Volanté*, a review which appears four times a year, and is edited by Tihorairoff and Lavrov, and the second is the *General Cause*, a monthly review published at Geneva. For want of more exciting materials the latter has lately been publishing extracts from Count Leon Tolstoi's "My Confessions" and "My Religion," works which, though mystical, have nothing of a Nihilist tendency in them. From time to time also the review has published discursive, but very harmless, articles by Plehanhoff and Alissoff, writers who are more busy in contradicting the theories of other Nihilists than in starting any of their own. In its July issue, however, which bears the number 75, the review publishes an article which deserves attention, as containing a most emphatic repudiation of violent methods for the furtherance of the Nihilist cause. This article says: "Truth compels us to own that the fierce struggle between the Russian Government and the spirit of national discontent which gave strength to our party, which was, in fact, its *raison d'être*, has ended in the triumph of absolutism. Sedition has been crushed and the whole Liberal Party have taken flight, abandoning their positions to the enemy. If still some spirit of opposition exists in Russia it is so limp, so terrorized, so wearied that the Government might extinguish it altogether without difficulty. The popular aspirations on which we counted flickered only for a moment and then died out. The people who were at first interested in us have grown afraid; why should we scruple to add that they hate us now worse than they have ever hated their oppressors. A complete darkness has fallen upon Russia, darkness like that of night and fog combined, yet we will not despair. We are struggling for the natural rights of man, and such a struggle must ultimately end in victory, as it has done everywhere else. Meanwhile, let us not defile our cause with violence, murder, or explosions. Let us fight with moral weapons. We have proof enough by this time that the revolutionary violences p[er]petrated in Russia have done nothing for the emancipation of the people, but have, on the contrary, been a benefit to the reactionary party. Violence, criminal and immoral in its essence, is only justifiable for the attainment of certain ends plainly seen and desired by the people. But our Russian people, steeped in ignorance, can see nothing in our violence but the act without the motive. Why, then, work to create only terror among those we wished to serve? What gain has it been to us to see the flower of our youth massacred and execrated at the same time?"

September 13, 1885

RUSSIA'S SCHOOL POLICY

CHANGES ANNOUNCED AS A BLOW TO NIHILISM.

PEASANTS' SONS NOT TO BE ADMITTED TO THE HIGHER INSTITUTIONS—TRADE SCHOOLS FOR THEIR BENEFIT.

ST. PETERSBURG, Sept. 5.—With great political insight and characteristic courage, Count Tolstoï, Minister of the Interior and de facto Premier, has just struck the most mortal blow which has been aimed at Nihilism since its origin some three-and-twenty years ago. A remarkable Ministerial circular was issued a few days since, restricting in a very considerable measure the accessions to the higher schools, gymnasia, and universities. A fair idea of the tenor of the document, which has caused an immense sensation throughout the country, will be gained from the following extract: "The gymnasia, high schools, and universities will henceforth refuse to receive as pupils or students the children of domestic servants, peasants, tradesmen, petty shopkeepers, farmers, and others of like condition, whose progeny should not be raised from the circle to which they belong, and be thereby led, as long experience has shown, to despise their parents, to become discontented with their lot, and irritated against the inevitable inequalities of the existing social positions." In order to carry out these views the directors of gymnasia and schools and the curators of the universities are instructed to closely question the parents and would-be students as to their circumstances, and to obtain information as to the material character of their family life. If the social condition of the parents does not justify the above requirements the children will not be admitted.

Hitherto by modest fees and in other ways all classes in Russia have been encouraged to give their children the benefits of advanced instruction. Among the hasty and premature reforms inaugurated on the accession of the late Czar in 1856, the one which appeared at the time as being most urgent was the necessity of raising the low level of popular instruction. Since then the educational establishments, especially in the provinces, have been crowded with the children of just these classes against which the present Ministerial circular is directed. As there was practically no direct individual expense to be incurred, every peasant, every petty tradesman and artisan was anxious to give his son the advantages of a first-class education with a view to his eventually entering the service of the Government. The latter, they were fully aware, led to the highest offices of the State, and even to this day is the only career available for an educated man in Russia. Of course, the ranks of the Tchinn, as the Government service is called, being already overcrowded by the sons of the wealthier classes, was utterly unequal to meet the multitudinous demands of candidates for employment. There was no means of providing posts for the tremendous and ever increasing influx of highly educated students from the universities and high schools. Russia is as yet so poorly developed a country as regards trade and manufacture, agriculture constituting almost the sole national industry, that on finding the doors of the Government service closed against them they were unable to discover any suitable career open. It would be ridiculous even to speak of the legal and journalistic professions in so despotic a country as Russia, while the clergy is so ignorant, so debased, and so despised by the public that no intelligent man would ever dream of looking for a future in that walk of life. The total absence of any technical education had deprived the students of the possibility of being of any use to the slowly developing manufacturing industries, and they were far too proud of their theoretical and classical acquirements ever to consent to lower themselves to follow their fathers' humble calling. Hence they became the nucleus of a band of malcontents, to whom the celebrated Russian author Ivan Turgeneff first gave the name of Nihilists in his popular novel "Fathers and Sons." Until the year 1883 the ranks of the Russian revolutionists were recruited almost exclusively from this class of ex-students—men without a profession or regular means of livelihood. At least 90 per cent. of the Nihilists brought to trial during the past 20 years have been shown to belong to that class, and in nearly every case they were the sons of some peasant or village priest or petty tradesman. About 8 per cent. of the Nihilists consist of officers of the army, navy, or civil service, who are either exasperated by the fact that the overcrowded ranks have rendered promotions practically at a standstill, or who have been driven to revolt by the harsh conduct of their superior officers, while the remaining 2 per cent. are composed of the fanatics, fools, and knaves who are found in every walk of life, and especially in countries such as Russia, where all men of education are brought up to despise their national religion and its ministers.

In using the term Nihilists I do not include under that denomination the vast body of so-called "malcontents" who have every reason to be dissatisfied with the present despotic form of Government in Russia. The two bodies are entirely distinct, and are far too frequently confounded with one another. The "malcontents" are mostly people of wealth and of social and even official position who have tangible and material interests in the country that are being injuriously affected by the defective administration of the Government. The Nihilists, on the other hand, are mere professional agitators who have nothing but their worthless lives to stake, and who resemble the carpet-bag politician—minus even the carpet bag.

Once before already, during the reign of the late Czar, Count Tolstoï, at that time Minister of Public Instruction, attempted—though in a far more modified form—to restrict the indiscriminate access to the high schools and universities; but the outcry on the part of the public was so great that Alexander II. got alarmed and ordered the withdrawal of the obnoxious measure. Since then the educational establishments above mentioned have steadily gone on swelling the ranks of the Nihilists from year to year until, under the stern rule of the present Czar, Count Tolstoï has been able to carry out his original intention in a much more radical form. In order to more fully demonstrate the necessity of Count Tolstoï's naturally unpopular decree it will be sufficient to cite the case of some peasant's son who, from the age of 8 until that of 17 or 18, is kept at schools where he is taught philosophy, logic, algebra, Latin, Greek, the piano, and other kindred accomplishments, where he eats meat every day, sleeps in a decent bed, and where servants are provided to do all the rough housework. How is it possible to imagine that any young man of intelligence, after having been thus brought up, can be content to go back to his native village, become a mere farm laborer, sleeping in a hovel on straw, eating meat only once a week, if then, and treated to all intents and purposes like a brute beast by a master who is probably his inferior in intelligence and education?

It is needless to add that Count Tolstoï's circular has aroused the most widespread opposition. As has been already stated, the high schools and universities are almost exclusively frequented by the children of the lower classes, those of the more well-to-do being taught either at home by private tutors or at educational establishments abroad. Supported, as the former are, mainly by grants from the communal treasury of the locality, it is contended that it is unjust to debar the lower classes from institutions which they themselves indirectly help to maintain. To this Count Tolstoï answers that by degrees the high schools and universities in the provinces will be abolished, and that a system of technical and trades schools is about to be established, in which almost every trade, from the most elementary forms of manual labor to the higher branches of manufacturing industry, will be taught. This scheme will meet a most pressing want, as at present almost all the skilled labor in Russia has to be imported from abroad. It is unfortunate that the issue of Count Tolstoï's decree could not be postponed until after the establishment of these much-needed trades schools. There was, however, no time to be lost. Nihilism at the present moment is more prevalent than it has been for some time past, although every effort is made by the Government to prevent any news thereof from becoming known either at home or abroad. The movement is especially gaining ground in Russian Poland, and the probable attitude of the population of that portion of the Czar's dominions in the case of a war with Austria furnishes matter for very serious and grave consideration at St. Petersburg.

October 2, 1887

FROM TERRORISM TO REVOLUTION

THE FIRST RUSSIAN STRIKE.

Moscow Letter to the London Telegraph.

The Russian workman, as a rule, is never paid his wages in money, but in groceries, clothing, and fire-wood, all of bad quality, and furnished in shortened quantity—thanks to a widely-spread system of false weights. They are treacherously encouraged to get into their employer's debt to a certain amount, and thus their future services are made sure of. Hours of work are long—in some factories 15 hours a day—and the children work as long as their parents. The English workman's home, with its pleasant aspect, would seem like a dream of fairyland here, where mill-hands sleep in underground cellars, or in cold wooden sheds—men, women, and children all huddled together. The first Russian strike on record has actually occurred. About a month ago, in a cloth manufactory belonging to a Moscow merchant, Nicholas Kaverin, 200 men struck for higher wages. The facts that gained publicity remind us of the abuses that once existed in the West of Europe. Kaverin, like the majority of Russian manufacturers, hired his workmen with the preliminary understanding that they must buy their daily provisions at the store attached to his counting-house. They were furnished with account-books, and bread, meat, tea, tallow, and fire-wood were dealt out to them on credit; on every recurrent pay-day they presented themselves at the counting-house, but went away again with empty pockets. The account-books showed that every kopeck of wages had already been drawn in provisions, though the men looked weak and underfed. There was never coin to send home to their families, they could never buy a new article of clothing.

It must be remembered that not one among them could read or write, and the figures in the account books were to them hieroglyphics. If they begged for a ruble in advance, 10 kopecks out of it were retained as the price of the loan; on New Year's Day Kaverin announced to them that their wages were too high, and that he was forced to lower them. The men stood in the mill-yard, holding council among themselves for an entire day; they argued, scolded, and abused each other, but finally sent their deputies to say they would agree to the lowered rate of wages. One after the other, however, began to talk of the dearness of the store provisions, "much dearer than market prices, dearer even than in other factories." At last, on the 27th of February, the men struck in a body, and asked for higher wages, alleging that it was impossible to live on what they received. The strike had lasted four days when the legal authorities walked in and pronounced sentence in the following manner: Wages to be raised to what they had been before the new year, supplies to be furnished at regular market prices, and the 10 kopeck rate of interest for each ruble lent abolished as illegal. As soon as the authorities had left the premises the workmen went in a body to Mr. Kaverin and thanked him for "his renewed kindness!" They have no guarantee whatever that this fresh engagement on his part will be fulfilled.

April 25, 1880

RUSSIANS SPEAK BOLDLY.

A SHARP ARRAIGNMENT OF THE GOVERNMENT'S RELIEF METHODS.

LONDON, Jan. 30.—The *Daily Graphic* to-day publishes a manifesto which, it says, has been issued by the Russian Zemstovs, (local administrative bodies,) which are composed of country gentlemen and land owners, on the famine in Russia and the inadequacy of the Government measures to afford relief.

The *Globe* and other papers, commenting upon this manifesto, declare that it is the most remarkable expression of public opinion Russia has ever given. The lotteries for the benefit of the famine fund and the way in which public benevolence is systematically thwarted are especially condemned.

The manifesto declares that Tolstoi's efforts to lighten the sufferings of the famine-stricken people are only tolerated because he is a celebrity. It continues:

"The Government, armed with the weapons of a state of siege, is filling Siberia and the jails with suspected persons, fearing a revolutionary propaganda. This Government, which has robbed us of all the reforms inaugurated by Alexander II., and which has deprived society from taking any part in public life, has brought Russia to starvation. Such a Government cannot solve the present problem with its own forces.

"The calamity is only in its initial stage; the Spring will disclose its actual proportions. How will it end if the Government does not change its attitude? Society is in a state of bankruptcy, political enfeeblement, and dismemberment. Russia in a popular rising would be deluged with her people's blood. No one can foresee the end. The advocates of assemblage have elected representatives for a free discussion of the situation."

The Czar Upholds Autocracy.

BERLIN, Jan. 29.—Private dispatches from St. Petersburg say that the Czar was called upon to-day by delegations representing the nobility of the principal cities and many provincial and district assemblies, who congratulated him upon his recent marriage. In replying to their congratulations the Czar said he had learned that in some of the provincial assemblies voices had been raised proposing that the assemblies have a share in state affairs, and expressing other absurd desires. He therefore wished everybody to understand that he devoted all his powers to his dear country, but that he was firmly resolved, as was his dear father, to uphold the autocracy of the Czar.

January 30, 1895

RUSSIAN WARNING TO THE CZAR.

Plain and Forcible Address Against the Dominating Bureaucracy.

LONDON, Feb. 13.—The Daily Chronicle will print to-morrow a column-long manifesto, issued by the People's Rights Party in Russia, and now circulating throughout the empire.

The manifesto is in the form of a letter to the Czar, and is remarkable for plain and forcible language. After censuring him for his recent assertion of his absolutism, the letter says:

"The most advanced zemstvos asked only for the harmony of Czar and people, free speech, and the supremacy of law over the arbitrariness of the executive. You were deceived and frightened by the representations of courtiers and bureaucrats. Society will understand perfectly that it was the bureaucracy, which jealously guards its own omnipotence, that spoke through you. The bureaucracy, beginning with the Council of Ministers and ending with the lowest country constable, hates any development, social or individual, and activity prevents the monarch's free intercourse with the representatives of his people, except as they come in gala dress, presenting congratulations, icons, and offerings.

"Your speech proves that any attempt to speak out before the throne, even in the most loyal form, about the crying needs of the country, meets only a rough and abrupt rebuff. Society expected from you encouragement and help, but heard only a reminder of your omnipotence, giving the impression of utter estrangement of Czar from people. You, yourself, have killed your own popularity and have alienated all that part of society which is peacefully struggling forward. Some individuals are jubilant over your speech, but you will soon discover their impotence. In another section of society your speech caused a feeling of injury and depression which, however, the best social forces soon will overcome, before proceeding to the peaceful but obstinate and deliberate struggle necessary to liberty. In another section your words will stimulate the readiness to struggle against the present hateful state of things with any means. You were the first to begin the struggle. Ere long it will proceed."

February 14, 1895

THE EUROPEAN ISSUES

Labor's Uprising in Russia.

The first bulletins from the census taken on new principles in the Russian Empire last February show just what the political symptoms of the past few years have prepared us for, namely, that the cities and industrial centres have been growing in population at an exceptional rate. Five years ago there were fourteen towns of over 100,000 souls; now there are twenty-one. St. Petersburg now has a population of a million and a quarter, an increase of 25 per cent. in five years. Moscow in a similar period shows an increase of 20 per cent. and Lodz one of nearly 40 per cent. This last place, called the Manchester of Poland, has passed Kharkoff, Kieff, and Riga since 1892, and is now the fifth city in the empire.

I said politics had foreshadowed this, for the distinctive note of political agitation in Russia during the past three years has been its concentration in factory towns. Nihilism has disappeared. In its place we have labor troubles. The Russian Government finds itself confronted now by incessant strikes, with which it has only a very antiquated and inefficient machinery to deal. Trades unions have always been forbidden in Russia, and workmen are slaves to all sorts of stupid and oppressive regulations, but there is nothing which exactly solves the problem of making artisans work when they don't want to. Educated revolutionists have lately been toiling as common mill hands to secure the confidence of the workers, and have been covertly preaching the strike as the only social salvation of their class.

Sixty of these evangels were imprisoned in the Government prison in Moscow the other day, and all are going to Siberia merely for urging a general strike in the district. The Vetroff girl, whose suspicious death in the Petropavlof prison in St. Petersburg created such a sensation in March, was arrested for this same offense of inciting to strike. All the same, strikes are springing up all over industrial Russia, and as they appeal keenly to the Russian's feelings as to the indignity of labor, as well as to his passion for giving the greatest possible amount of trouble short of actual danger to his own skin, they are likely to expand into something like a great labor war, which will mark a new era in Russian history.

May 23, 1897

OVERTHROW OF THE OLD ORDER

MORE RIOTS IN ST. PETERSBURG

Five Students Said to Have Been Killed and Many Injured—Cossacks Guard the Czar.

ST. PETERSBURG, March 19.—Serious riots occurred in St. Petersburg to-day on the occasion of a solemn mass in the Cathedral of Our Lady of Kazan for the repose of the soul of M. Bogoliepoff, the Minister of Public Instruction, who was shot and fatally wounded by Karpovitch. The police fired their revolvers, and it is rumored that five students were killed and eighty others either seriously or slightly injured.

Wholesale arrests followed the rioting. Many women were among those arrested.

Alarm pervades high circles here. The police have notified house owners to have their dvorniks, or house police, report for duty and hold themselves in constant readiness.

A sotnia, or company of Cossacks, passed the Moscow Gate yesterday morning on the way to Tsarskoe-Selo, seventeen miles south of St. Petersburg, where the Czar has just gone. The police said they would escort the Czar back to the Winter Palace, and that he would return by carriage instead of by rail. It appears more probable, however, that the Cossacks were sent to Tsarskoe-Selo as a precaution, since his Majesty is more easily protected there than here.

All the higher schools of the city are closed and all the police headquarters are filled with arrested persons.

A report that three students were killed on Sunday is apparently confirmed. The Cossacks rode into the crowds on the sidewalk, and many faces were cut open by their knotted whips. Students and workingmen threw rubber shoes, canes, and snowballs at the Cossacks. It is reported that one Cossack was killed.

The presence of workingmen among the rioters rendered the demonstration more dangerous than any that had ever before occurred here.

A remarkable feature of the demonstration was the prominent part taken by women of the higher classes of the university.

One of the students read a proclamation by the Students' Committee demanding the abolition of the military service regulations and a jury trial for Karpovitch, who shot and fatally wounded the Minister of Public Instruction, M. Bogoliepoff, last month.

After the reading of the manifesto the students threw crumpled copies of it into the crowd and raised a flag inscribed "For Liberty." The students also shouted, "Help us get our rights," and the mob responded with cheers.

A curious crowd remained in the vicinity of the scene of the disturbance until late in the evening, and persistently spread reports of horrors in Moscow.

It is asserted, though without demonstrable foundation, that the Moscow Chief of Police was killed.

The Official Messenger, which publishes an account of the recent disorders in various Russian cities and of Sunday's outbreak in St. Petersburg, says of the latter:

"When the crowd, which numbered 3,000, became turbulent the Cossacks and police were summoned. The demonstrators retreated to the Cathedral of Our Lady of Kazan, pelting the Cossacks and police with various missiles.

"The students attempted to display red and white flags bearing various inscriptions. On one side of the cathedral the crowd came into violent collision with the Cossacks and police. A portion retired into the cathedral, behaving noisily and smoking cigarettes, although the service was going on, until forcibly expelled.

"Altogether 339 male students, 377 women, mostly students, and 44 other persons were arrested. A Police Commissioner, 20 policemen, 4 Cossacks, and 32 rioters, male and female, were wounded."

March 20, 1901

ATTEMPT TO KILL THE "RUSSIAN TORQUEMADA"

Shots Fired Through a Window at M. Pobiedonostseff.

BEST-HATED MAN IN RUSSIA

He Is Chief Procurator of the Holy Synod, and Caused the Expulsion of the Jews a Decade Ago.

ST. PETERSBURG, March 23.—Privy Councillor Pobiedonostseff, Chief Procurator of the Holy Synod, narrowly escaped assassination early yesterday morning. While he was writing in his study, shortly after midnight, two bullets shattered a window, passed close to him, and buried themselves in the ceiling. Two other shots were fired, but did not enter the room.

The would-be assassin was identified as one Lagowski, a provincial official. The Procurator was unscathed.

An investigation into the causes of the attack is proceeding.

The Students' Organization Committee has issued a call inviting all intelligent members of Russian society to join their ranks in the struggle for freedom.

In the days of the Czar Alexander III. Constantine Petrovitch Pobiedonostseff was termed the most powerful man in Russia, and his influence over the present ruler of all the Russias is declared to be little, if any, less than that which he exercised over Nicholas's father. To say that he is the best hated man in Russia is to repeat a truism. It is declared that not even the cruellest and most autocratic Chief of Police has done a hundredth part as much as has the Procurator of the Holy Synod to earn the detestation of great numbers of the Czar's subjects.

In writing of M. Pobiedonostseff, the late Harold Frederic said:

"This remarkable personage fascinates the imagination. He is as unintelligible to the modern Western mind as Torquemada. Indeed, one must go back to mediaeval times for every parallel which he and his work suggest. The whole situation created by him is like nothing else in history so much as that which Spain presented under Ferdinand and Isabella, where the influence of a man we cannot now at all comprehend persuaded a gentle, wise, and kindly sovereign to stain her reign with the most hideous and stupid of crimes against humanity and to gratuitously work the destruction of her country."

It was Pobiedonostseff who was responsible for the terrible treatment of the Jews in Russia during the last two decades; it was he who caused the persecution of the Lutherans, the Catholics, and the strange sect which has now settled in Canada, and it was he who recently instigated the excommunication of Count Tolstoi.

Pobiedonostseff was appointed Chief Procurator of the Holy Synod in 1880. He was born at Moscow in 1827. He was a successful official in the Legal Department of the Government. He was one of the tutors of Alexander III., who advanced him to one high position after another. When the opportunity came, he eagerly seized on the chance of putting his undoubted abilities to the service of the Church. He had been an earnest Christian—most people say a fanatic—from youth. Even now, at his advanced age, during the great fast of the year he always retires to the Sergieff Monastery, where he mortifies his flesh in the same manner as the anchorites of old, remaining for days on his knees, fasting, and beating his forehead against the stone floor. Add to this fanaticism the capacity for intrigue of a Machiavelli and the grasp of detail of a Loyola, and the result is the man who has been supreme in the religious councils of Russia for twenty years.

The late Czar, if all the accounts of him are to be believed, was a most kindly man by nature, but such was the ascendancy exercised over him by the thin-faced, slender, spectacled man who holds the Procuratorship that he was led to authorize a reign of terror of which the true horror is even yet unrealized in the West. In 1886 the power of Pobiedonostseff had grown so great that his office altogether overshadowed the other branches of the Russian Government. It was in that year and the year following that the Czar signed the edicts which only permitted one Jew in a thousand in many places to be educated, which put terrible burdens on all the Jews in the empire, and which resulted in the expulsion of 6,000,000 Jews from Russia.

"The Grand Inquisitor of Russia" is one of the names by which the Procurator is known. "Russia for the Russians" is his watchword, and when the Russian officials want to praise him they declare that it is to this "modest, unassuming man" that is due the credit of having produced the theory of nationalism which is raising Russia into the ranks of the progressive nations. At the celebration of his fiftieth anniversary as a public official the present Czar wrote to him:

"I cordially wish that it may be given to me to retain you for many years to come as one of my nearest councillors."

March 24, 1901

RUSSIA'S NEEDED REFORMS

The Details of What Tolstoi Proposed to the Czar.

"Modest and Practical" Scheme Which Would Almost Assimilate the Czar to a King or a President.

From The London Times.

We have received from St. Petersburg the following translation of an appeal which, it is stated, has been addressed by Count Tolstoi to the Czar and his Government on the present situation in Russia:

To the Czar and his Advisers:

More assassinations! More street riots! Again there will be executions, while panic and exasperation, giving birth to threats and false accusations, prevail on the one side, and on the other is animated with hatred, the desire for revenge, and the spirit of self-sacrifice. Once more the Russian people are divided into two hostile camps, and preparations are being made to commit the greatest crimes.

It is possible that the present movement, like those which have preceded it, may be suppressed by the employment of military force. But it may happen that the soldiers and policemen, in whom the Government puts so much trust, will realize that to carry out their instructions in this respect would involve the horrible crime of fratricide, and will refuse to obey orders. Even if this agitation is temporarily put down, it cannot be completely stifled. It will continue to spread under the cover of secrecy, and, sooner or later, it will inevitably break out again with redoubled energy, and will lead to more suffering and to crimes greater than those which we now deplore.

Why should this be the case when it can so easily be prevented? We appeal to all who wield power in the Czar's name, to the members of the Council of State, to the Senators and to the Ministers, and even to the uncles and brothers and other relatives of the Emperor, who are able to influence his Majesty's convictions. We appeal to you not as enemies but as brothers. Whether you like it or not, your lot is so closely bound up with ours that all the sufferings which are inflicted upon us, and which, although it is in your power, you make no effort to prevent, affect you more than us.

We beg you to take steps to put a stop to this state of things. Most of you think that it is all the fault of restless and discontented individuals who excite the people and disturb the peaceful course of affairs, that no change of any kind is necessary, and that the only thing to be done is to punish

19

From Terrorism to Revolution

and gag the disaffected. If this were the case, however, the agitation could be brought to an end by imprisoning or executing these individuals. But for more than three years such persons have been arrested, banished, or executed by the thousand. The result has been to increase their numbers. Discontent with the existing order of things not only grows apace, but continues to spread over an ever-increasing area, and has already affected millions of persons among the working classes, who form the great majority of the whole population. It is thus evident that this feeling of dissatisfaction has not been created by the restless and malicious individuals to whom you ascribe the blame, but is due to some other cause.

As a matter of fact, you, the officials of the Government, only need to withdraw your attention for a moment from the sharp contest in which you are now engaged; you only need to cease to think like the short-sighted Minister of the Interior, who has naïvely declared in his circular that everything would come right if the police would only disperse the crowds in time, and if the soldiers would shoot straight when their orders are disobeyed; you only need to cease to believe such nonsense as this in order, clearly, and at once, to recognize the real cause of the discontent existing among the people, and of the agitation which is continually spreading and taking deeper root.

The reason is that, in consequence of the unhappy murder of the Czar Alexander II., the liberator of the serfs—a murder which was committed by a small group of persons, but for which the entire nation was made responsible—the Government of his successor, Alexander III., came to the unwise decision not only to proceed along the path of reform, but even to retrace the steps which had already been taken. They were not even content to let things remain as they were. Instead of discarding more and more the despotic form of administration, which is incompatible with the present conditions of society, they went in for a policy of reaction, being actuated by the belief that salvation was only to be found in this brutal and antiquated form of Government. For nearly twenty years no attempt has been made to bring the political system more into conformity with the general development and greater complications of the conditions of life. This reactionary movement has separated the Government more and more from the people and their wants. It is thus not the malicious and turbulent persons who are to blame, but you administrators yourselves, who care for nothing but your own ease for the time being. It is not a question of defending yourselves from enemies who wish to harm you. No one desires to do anything of the kind. It is merely a question of understanding the causes of the existing discontent, and of taking the measures necessary to remove them. Every one is not fond of discord and enmity. People prefer to live in love and harmony with their fellowmen. If they are now in a state of agitation, and appear to seek your discomfiture, it is simply because, in their eyes, you are the barrier which prevents them from obtaining for themselves, and for their brethren, the greatest blessings of humanity—freedom and enlightenment. It is necessary for you to do so little to put a stop to this agitation and to secure yourselves against attack, and that little is so necessary for yourselves, and so calculated to give you peace and consolation, that it will be astonishing if you do not do it. At present it is only necessary to do very little.

TOLSTOI'S PROGRAMME.

The following measures should be adopted without delay:

In the first place, the peasants should be placed on a footing of legal equality with other citizens; for which purpose it would be necessary—

(1) To abolish the absurd institution of rural administrators, (zemsky natchalniki,) which has no raison d'être.
(2) To repeal the regulations governing the relations of master and man, which would then be subject to the ordinary law of the land.
(3) To liberate the peasantry from all oppressive impositions, such as the necessity of obtaining passports in order to move from one place to another, the duty which falls solely upon the peasants of billeting soldiers and providing country carts for purposes of transport, and the obligations connected with the rural police.
(4) To abolish the unjust system of collective responsibility of peasants for each other's debts, and to remit the land redemption payments, which have long since covered the real value of the land; and, above all,
(5) To do away with corporal punishment, which is useless and degrading, and which is now retained only for the most industrious, the most moral, and the most numerous class of the people.

It is specially important that the peasantry, constituting the vast majority of the population, should have the same rights as other classes. There can be no strength or durability in a social organization when the majority of the citizens are not on a footing of legal equality with their fellow-countrymen, but are kept in the position of slaves bound by special laws. It is only when the laboring majority has been emancipated and invested with the same rights as those which are enjoyed by the other citizens, that a stable social organization becomes possible or conceivable.

In the second place, it is necessary to cease to apply the so-called reinforced measures of public safety, which destroy all existing laws, and place the people at the mercy of stupid, cruel, and, for the most part, immoral officials. The abrogation of these extra measures of public safety is important because they suspend the action of the ordinary law, promote spying and secret denunciation, and cause and encourage the frequent employment of brutal violence against workmen who have disputes with their employers and landlords. Nowhere is there so much cruel persecution as in the districts in which these special regulations are in force. It is owing to them that capital punishment is coming more and more into use and that the authorities are, to an increasing extent, having recourse to that demoralizing punishment which, forbidden by God, is the greatest of human crimes, which is contrary to the Christian spirit of the Russian people, and which was previously unknown in our jurisprudence.

Thirdly, education and teaching should be freed from all obstacles.
(1) No differences should be made between people of different social stations with regard to facilities for education, and books which are allowed to be read by others should not be forbidden to the common people.
(2) Teachers in schools should not be prevented from giving instruction in the language spoken by their pupils, and it is supremely important that
(3) All persons who have not been deprived of their civil rights, and who are desirous of undertaking educational work, should be permitted to conduct schools of all grades.

It is important that the education, training, and teaching of the young should be freed from all the restrictions which now hamper them, because it is by means of these very restrictions that the laboring classes are kept in a state of ignorance, and it is this ignorance which at present serves the Government as an excuse for placing these obstacles in the way of education. The emancipation of the working classes from Government interference in these matters would enable the people to acquire far more quickly the education which they really need, instead of that which is forced upon them. To permit private persons to open and to conduct schools would put a stop to the continual agitation among the young men, who are dissatisfied with the arrangements in the establishments in which they at present pursue their studies. If there were no difficulty in the way of establishing private schools, both for the lower and higher courses of instruction, the Russian students who are dissatisfied with the order of things in the Government educational institutions would leave them for the private establishments which answered their requirements.

Fourthly, all restrictions on religious liberty must be abolished.
(1) All laws should be repealed which provide punishment for any withdrawal from the Established Church.
(2) The establishment and the opening of chapels and churches for the Old Believers and of houses of prayer for Baptists, Molokani, Stundists, and other sectarians should be freely permitted.
(3) Permission should be given for holding religious meetings, and for preaching all forms of belief, except those which teach men to commit unnatural crimes, such as murder and suicide and
(4) Persons of different religious beliefs should be allowed to bring up their children in the form of faith which they believe to be the true one.

The abolition of all restraint on religious freedom is absolutely necessary, because it is universally admitted—and the fact is attested by history and science—that religious persecution does not produce the effect desired by those who practice it. On the contrary, it only strengthens that which the persecutors seek to destroy. Moreover, the interference of the authorities in religious matters produces hypocrisy, which is so strongly condemned by Christ as the worst and most pernicious of vices, and it prevents the attainment of that unity which is the highest good both for the individual and the community at large. This unity can never be attained by using violent means to compel people to observe the outward forms of a religion which has once been adopted and is regarded as infallible; it can only be attained by the unfettered progress of humanity in its search after the truth.

These are the very modest and practical desires of the majority of Russian society. The application of the measures above described would undoubtedly pacify the people and save them from terrible suffering. It would also prevent the crimes, which will inevitably be committed on both sides, if the Government endeavors only to suppress the agitation without seeking to remove the causes that produce it.

We appeal to you all—to the Czar, to the members of the Council of State, to the Ministers, to all persons near to the Czar, to all persons having power to aid in pacifying society and preserving it from suffering and crime. We appeal to you, not as members of the opposite camp, but as colleagues and brothers. It is impossible in a society of people whose interests are bound up together that some should be happy and contented and the great majority be compelled to suffer. People can be happy only when happiness and contentment are enjoyed by the strong, working majority which constitutes the foundation of the whole of society. Help to improve the position of this majority, and, above all, to promote its freedom and enlightenment. Then only will your own position be free from care, and then only will you be truly happy. LEO TOLSTOI.
March 15, (28,) 1901.

June 17, 1901

CZAR TO MAKE INQUIRIES INTO SOCIAL PROBLEMS.

Will Receive 200 Russians in Audience—Takes the Step Against the Advice of His Ministers.

LONDON, July 3.—The St. Petersburg correspondent of The Daily Express asserts that, in defiance of the advice of his Ministers, the Czar has decided to give private audiences to over 200 representative Russians of all ranks, including university professors, publicists, editors, political prisoners, and even convicts, with a view to thoroughly probing social problems and discovering the motives for the assassinations of Ministers and officials.

The visitors will be invited to tell the Czar frankly how the threatened revolution may be averted and by what peaceful means the distress and dissatisfaction of the lower classes may be met.

July 3, 1902

CZAR DECREES REFORMS

Orders Freedom of Religion Throughout Russia.

MEASURES TO AID PEASANTS

Partial Local Self-Government to be Established—The Decree Hailed as Proclaiming a New Era.

ST. PETERSBURG, March 12.—The Czar has issued a decree providing for freedom of religion throughout his dominions, establishing to some degree local self-government, and making other concessions to the Village Committees.

The decree, which was issued to-day in commemoration of the anniversary of the birthday of Alexander III., is considered to be the most significant act of state since the emancipation of the serfs.

The text of the decree is as follows:

"On ascending the throne of our ancestors by the Providence of God we made a solemn vow before the Almighty and our conscience sacredly to guard the centuries-old pillars of Russian power and to dedicate our life to the service of our beloved fatherland in indefatigable solicitude for our subjects. We chose, in order to assure the well-being of our people, the way indicated by the memorable deeds of our predecessors, especially our never-to-be-forgotten father. God pleased to interrupt the deeds of our father by his early death, and thus laid on us the sacred duty of completing the consolidation of order and truth begun by him in conformity with the exigencies of national life.

"The troubles agitating our country, which to our deep regret have partly been sown by designs hostile to the State and partly engendered by doctrines foreign to Russian life, hinder the general work of ameliorating the well-being of our people. These troubles confuse the public mind, remove the people from productive labor, and often ruin families dear to our heart and young energies, among high and low, necessary to the internal development of the country.

"In demanding the fulfillment of this our will, while remaining strongly opposed to any violation of the normal course of national life and having confidence that all will loyally discharge their local duties, we are irrevocably decided to satisfy the needs for which the State has become ripe, and have deemed it expedient to strengthen and decree the undeviating observance of the principles of tolerance laid down by the fundamental laws of the Russian Empire, which, recognizing the Orthodox Church as the ruling one, grant to all our subjects of other religions and to all foreign persuasions freedom of creed and worship in accordance with other rites. And we are further resolved to continue the active carrying out of measures for the improvement of the material position of the Orthodox rural clergy, while enabling them to take a larger share in intellectual and public life.

REVISION OF RURAL LAWS.

"In accordance with impending measures for the consolidation of the national economy, the efforts of the State credit institutions, and especially the nobles' and peasants' banks, should be directed to strengthening and developing the welfare and fundamental pillars of Russian village life and that of the local nobility and peasantry.

"These principles marked out by us for the revision of the laws of the rural population are, when formulated, to be referred to the Provincial Government Councils, so that with the assistance of persons enjoying the public's confidence they may be further developed and adapted to the special conditions of individual localities. In this work the fundamental principle of the inviolability of communal property is to be maintained, while at the same time means are to be found to render it easier for the individual to sever connection with the community to which he belongs, if he so desire.

"Without delay measures must be taken to release the peasants from the present burdensome liability of forced labor.

"Thorough reform is to be effected in the provincial Governments and district administrations by the local representatives, while attention will be devoted to securing closer co-operation between the communal authorities and parochial Trustees of the orthodox churches wherever possible.

"Calling upon all our subjects to co-operate in strengthening the moral foundations of family, school, and public life, under which alone the well-being of the people and the confidence of every one in the stability of his rights can develop, we command our Ministers and chief officials concerned in this matter to submit to us their views regarding the execution of our intentions."

The extension of self-government to the smaller communities, corresponding to the township organizations of the United States, is regarded as a great victory for the Zemstvos, (District and Provincial Assemblies,) while the retention of the communal system with greater freedom of withdrawal therefrom meets the wishes of the peasants and landowners, expressed through the local committees on agricultural depression.

The Czar's desire for the co-operation of the educated public closely follows the action of Alexander II. at the time of the emancipation movement.

JOYFUL EXCITEMENT IN RUSSIA.

The publication of the decree has produced a universal feeling of joyful excitement, and is to-night the chief topic of conversation in every public resort. It is generally attributed to the Emperor's earnest desire to remove the causes which recently produced such deplorable outbreaks among the workmen and students.

Fears, however, are expressed that the powerful party of reaction led by the Minister of the Interior, M. de Plehve, may delay or frustrate the realization of the Czar's aspirations, but great hopes are based on the known fact that Finance Minister de Witte is a strong advocate of whatever reforms he considers the country ripe for. In any case, months must elapse before the projected reforms can be put into execution.

It is understood that the Czar desires to modify the laws by relaxing the penalties against dissenters like the Stundists, but that no attempt will be made to repeal the law compelling children to be brought up in the Orthodox Church unless both parents belong to some other denomination.

One of the most welcome reforms outlined is that enabling the sober and hard-working individual peasant to escape from the responsibility for arrears of taxation incurred by intemperate and lazy fellow-villagers. Many other abuses of the communal system which pressed heavily on the peasantry will be removed.

The paragraph in the decree proposing to refer the reforms to the provincial Government Councils is by many regarded as pointing in the direction of constitutional government.

It is conjectured that the Czar is willing to enlarge the sphere of the Zemstvos by permitting them to deliberate on matters of local administration. In this connection, however, it must be remembered that even last year M. de Plehve strongly resented, and in some cases punished, those invited to Governmental conferences who were bold enough to touch on the need of legislative reforms. It is remarked that the decree does not mention the removal of the restrictions on the press.

For the moment, however, among the general public all these difficulties are forgotten in the spirit of thankfulness at the prospect of the dawn of a new era.

March 13, 1903

RUSSIAN REFORMERS ARE DISAPPOINTED

Czar's Manifesto Regarded as Valueless on Important Topics.

Only Minor Concessions for Education, Local Government, Peasants' Rights, and Finance.

LONDON TIMES—NEW YORK TIMES
Special Cablegram.

LONDON, March 23.—In regard to the four points on which reforms are most required in Russia—education, local government, peasants' rights, and finance—the St. Petersburg correspondent of The Times says the Czar's manifesto is almost valueless. The only useful concessions, he declares, are those abolishing the peasants' collective responsibility for taxation and permitting them to sever themselves from the communes.

In spite of certain hopeful anticipations, says the correspondent, the only journals really satisfied are the reactionary organs, one of which exclaims:

"The Czar has taken our side and placed himself in opposition to our opponents."

The correspondent asserts that the moderate reformers are bitterly disappointed. The revolutionary reformers are pleased rather than otherwise, because the granting of genuine reforms would have struck a severe blow at their agitation.

A leading moderate was interviewed by the correspondent. He thought the passage of the manifesto dealing with religious toleration the only part of the document of much value. He was not sanguine even in that respect, and doubted whether the condition of dissenters like the Doukhobors and Stundists would be improved, while, he said, the manifesto obviously did not apply to the Jews, who enjoyed liberty regarding religious rites, though they were subject to many legal disabilities. He added that he did not believe in reforms drawn up by M. de Plehve, the Minister of the Interior, "in the spirit of Alexander III."

The Times's correspondent concludes that the present agitation will be carried on by the extremists with greater energy than ever, with one of three results—it may be suppressed without producing much effect; it may force the Government to grant important concessions, or it may, as sometimes seems only too probable, lead to a great catastrophe

March 23, 1903

From Terrorism to Revolution

RUSSIA'S BIG STRIKE.

Trouble at Baku the Most Serious Labor Disturbance in Russia's History.

LONDON, July 29.—The Russian correspondent of The Times says in this morning's issue that the strike at Baku seems to have been the most serious labor disturbance that has ever occurred in Russia; that it extended to Tiflis, to Nostoff, and Novo Tcherkask, in the District of the Don Cossacks, and that the Far Eastern railway employes were concerned.

According to the same authority, the disturbances have been renewed at Borisoglehak, on the railway between Voronesh and the Lower Volga.

July 29, 1903

NEW NIHILISM IN RUSSIA

Recent Outrages Due to Socialist Revolutionary Party.

It Caused the Murders of Sipiaguine and Others—De Plehve Believes It Has Sentenced Him to Death.

LONDON TIMES—NEW YORK TIMES
Special Cablegram.

LONDON, Sept. 3.— The Times describes a new revolutionary party formed in Russia, entitled the Russian Socialist Revolutionary Party, which differs from the Russian Social Democratic Party in being less doctrinaire and more violent in tactics. It has revived something of the old terrorism which shook Russian society twenty years ago.

There is a third party, the Russian Revolutionary Party. All three agree as to the necessity of abolishing the existing autocracy.

The Social Revolutionaries publish a number of papers—Revolutionary Russia, of which the motto is "He who would be free must strike for freedom"; The Messenger of the Russian Revolution, The Cause of the People, &c.—of which 260,000 copies were issued last year.

The new party aims at arousing the heart of Russia, reaching the peasants not affected by previous efforts. The peasants now gather frequently and more systematically in order to consult and find means of reducing their burdens. The peasant's belief that the land belongs to him by right now manifests itself in frequent rick burnings and the destruction of harvests.

Minister of the Interior de Plehve, recognizing the strength of the movement, has issued a circular to the Governors instructing them to watch the revolutionary activity and make careful reports.

Since April, 1902, a "fighting organization" has been created as a wing of the Socialist Revolutionary Party in order to meet force with force and terror with terror. The members are bound to strict obedience to the orders from the party; they are only free to choose the means of execution.

To this party are due the murders of Minister of the Interior Sipiaguine, Gen. Obolensky, and Gov. Bogdanovitch. M. de Plehve is said to take special precautions in the belief that he has been sentenced to death by the organization.

September 3, 1903

POLITICS THE CAUSE OF THE KISHINEFF MASSACRE

Report of J. B. Greenhut Made to Secretary of State Hay Says Government Believed Crushing Blow Could Be Administered to Social Democratic Party.

J. B. Greenhut, whose residence is Peoria, Ill., but who has large commercial interests in New York, has recently returned from a trip abroad. He took advantage of the opportunity to visit Russia and especially the region about Odessa and Kishineff. Mr. Greenhut, who is a native of Austria, and was a Captain and Chief of Brigade Staff in the Union Army during the civil war, has embodied the result of his observations in a report which he has transmitted to Secretary of State Hay since his return. The general tenor of the report is absolutely confirmatory of the details of the Kishineff atrocities as described in the newspapers at the time.

Mr. Greenhut speaks particularly of the appreciation on the part of the Russian Jews of the value of the sympathy and moral support of the American Government. He gives native testimony of the satisfactory manner in which relief funds collected in this country were distributed, and calls attention to the circumstances that the majority of the Kishineff Jews were "Social Democrats," declaring that the blow at the Jews was aimed largely at that party, the purpose of which is the eventual subversion of the present autocratic Government of the Czar. Mr. Greenhut writes as follows:

Hon. John Hay, Washington, D. C.:

My Dear Mr. Hay: Last Spring, while in Peoria, I attended a meeting for the relief of the sufferers of the Kishineff massacre, and as I was on the eve of sailing for Europe I was asked and promised to investigate and ascertain, as far as possible, all I could of that terrible affair, as well as the general conditions under which the Jewish population was forced to exist in Russia.

Being aware of the deep interest taken by President Roosevelt and your kind self in the endeavor to moderate as far as possible the sad conditions under which those poor, downtrodden people are suffering, I concluded it would be of interest to you to learn from a source other than regular official channels, but nevertheless fully as authoritative, the true condition of affairs in Russia.

I had the good fortune, during my travels, to come in contact with many Russians, some of whom were eye-witnesses of the late difficulties at Kishineff, and others who were fully conversant with the situation all over Russia, among these latter being Mr. Osiah Chayes, a noted banker of Odessa, who is also President of the Stock Exchange in that city, and bears the title of Commercienrath, and through whose bank most of the relief funds lately sent to Russia were transmitted. Mr. Chayes has been in close touch with all the affairs pertaining to the Jews in Russia, and with Kishineff in particular, which place is only about three hours' distant from Odessa.

Another one of these men, Mr. Moses Kligman, I may mention as having specially impressed me. He is of the wholesale firm of Perlmutter & Kligman of Kishineff. Mr. Kligman is Treasurer of the Relief Committee through which all the relief funds which were lately forwarded to Kishineff were distributed. He, therefore, was in a position to give me a very graphic and accurate account of the two days of terror through which the Jewish residents of that fated city passed last April, of which he also was an eye-witness.

There has been so much publicity given by the newspapers of the horrible details in connection with the murders, brutal treatment, pillage, &c., which were perpetrated on that occasion that I do not think it necessary to recite anything about those atrocities at this time, except to say that the statements of Mr. Kligman and of other men from Kishineff fully confirmed the worst that has been previously reported on the subject, and it would indeed be a hardened individual that could listen to a recital by these earnest men and not feel a touch of sympathy for those poor, downtrodden Jews, who are compelled to eke out such a hopeless existence as theirs in Russia.

I was much interested in learning from these men of how well the funds which were sent to Kishineff had been distributed among those who were in most urgent need of relief. Mr. Kligman stated that in all about 1,000,000 rubles (being about $500,000) had been received by his committee, about one-half of which was raised in Russia, one-quarter was received from other parts of Europe, and one-quarter from America. I was very much pleased with Mr. Kligman, as he did not appear to have any desire to overdraw anything or make any attempt to urge upon me the necessity of more funds being sent for their relief. In fact, he said that he believed the funds already received would enable his committee to care for all the urgent cases in their midst.

However, what impressed and gratified me most was the statement and consensus of opinion of all these men, namely: that while the relief funds, which were so generously forwarded from all parts of the world, were indeed welcome, as it enabled them to give material assistance to those poor creatures whose all had been destroyed and who, if the early assistance had not been received, would have starved to death; but above all, they said, what they prized and welcomed most was the noble and heroic attitude taken by President Roosevelt and Secretary Hay in their behalf. They said, over and over again, that the moral influence exerted through the action taken by our Administration was of more value to them than all other efforts combined which were put forward for their relief, and that notwithstanding that the position of our Administration could not be enforced officially, it nevertheless had immediate effect on the Russian Government and resulted in a change of the Governor and the officials generally in Kishineff, who are said to be less harsh to the Jewish population than their predecessors had been.

They also stated that the public sympathy shown for their race and the abhorrence expressed by the people and the press of the United States against these Russian atrocities had the effect of bringing about the arrest of many of the riotous leaders, who will receive at least some punishment for their evil deeds, and they hope that this action may have some deterrent influence in preventing a similar uprising in the future.

I also made diligent inquiry of these people for the purpose of ascertaining the ulterior or basic cause which instigated the attacks on the Jews of Kischineff. The consensus of their opinion was to the effect that the primary cause of the trouble was on account of the large percentage of the Jews in Kischineff who belonged to the so-called "Social Democratic Party," and they said that undoubtedly the agents of the Russian Government believed that they could give a crushing blow to this party by making a terrible example of the Jews in Kischineff. It seems that this "Social Democratic Party" is organized for the purpose of bringing about a constitutional government in Russia, and therefore is naturally opposed by the present government. I was told that a deputation of Jews had an audience some time ago with the Minister of the Interior to protest against some of the stringent regulations against the Jews. They were told by the Minister that the Jews could not expect better treatment from the Government in view of so many of them having affiliated with the "Social Democratic Party," and when the Minister's attention was called to the fact that the Jews represented but a small percentage of that party the Minister coolly replied that the Christians were natives of Russia, which gave them certain privileges, while the Jews were strangers in Russia, and therefore possessed no such rights.

The absurdity of such a claim was exemplified by the fact, as these men say, that most of the Jews there to-day can trace their ancestry back in Russia for more than a thousand years, which would seem to give them ample right to the claim of being classed as natives, and they say that although classed as aliens, they are nevertheless obliged to pay full tribute in support of the Government not only in paying heavy taxes, but also in being compelled to serve in the army and navy for the protection of the Government.

It is difficult, from the standpoint of an American citizen, to realize that such conditions can exist in a civilized country, but nevertheless such are the facts, and they augur no good for the 5,000,000 of Jews compelled to live in Russia and depend upon the mercy of the Russian Government for protection of their lives and property. I certainly hope that these poor and downtrodden people may always depend upon the Administration, the public, and the press of the United States to raise their protest, as they did lately, against such unjust atrocities as were enacted in Kischineff, for such protest is the only practical protection these people can look forward to and hope to receive from any quarter of the globe.

In conclusion, I wish to add that the detailed information I gathered, from which I summarized the above, will be placed at your command at any time you may desire the same.

Trusting that I have not encroached too much on your valuable time in presenting the above facts to you, I remain yours very respectfully, JOSEPH B. GREENHUT.
New York, Sept. 21, 1903.

September 27, 1903

RUSSIAN PEASANTS' BURDEN.

Arrears Due on Payments for Land Have Greatly Increased in Recent Years.

LONDON TIMES—NEW YORK TIMES
Special Cablegram.

LONDON, Nov. 16.—Particulars of a confidential report on the economic condition of Russia in 1902 which has been presented to the Czar are published in L'Européen and are quoted by the Paris correspondent of The Times.

The report shows a progressive increase in the arrears due from the peasants on their annual payments for the redemption of the land distributed at the time of the emancipation of the serfs. These arrears amounted to 94,000,000 rubles (about $47,000,000) in 1897, and gradually increased to 121,800,000 rubles last year. The conclusion is drawn that radical measures are needed to relieve the peasantry from charges which they cannot bear.

It is declared in the report that the existing economic crisis was caused by the too rapid artificial growth of industry, beyond the capacity of the home market to absorb the products. M. Witte's policy, it is stated, consisted mainly in giving subsidies from the State Bank to manufacturers threatened with ruin and giving them excessively large orders at high figures on behalf of the Government. These advances were made specially to the metal trade, and under conditions which rendered them ultra vires.

November 16, 1903

REFORMERS FILLING PRISONS IN RUSSIA

Increasing Numbers Being Banished or Sent to Siberia.

PEASANTS' RISING FEARED

Prince Ukhtomsky Says Revolt Against Upper Classes May Follow Defeat in Eastern War.

LONDON TIMES—NEW YORK TIMES
Special Cablegram.
Copyright, 1904, THE NEW YORK TIMES.

BERLIN, July 4.—Prince Ukhtomsky, in an interview published here to-day, says the discontent in Russia has become acute. The prisons are being filled with people of intellectual note, while increasing numbers are being banished or deported to Siberia.

At the same time Prince Ukhtomsky is convinced that there will be no revolution, at least none in which the educated classes will participate, since these classes are well aware of the hopelessness of contending against the army and the police.

It is conceivable, however, says the Prince, that in the event of an adverse issue of the present war there might be a general rising of the peasantry, which would be directed not against the existing régime, but against the propertied and educated classes in general.

Prince Ukhtomsky describes the Czar as the chief malcontent, and as being prepared to sacrifice himself if he could relieve the miseries of his people. The Czar, however, although he often gives ear to true accounts of the state of the country, is subject to so many Court influences that he is unable to retain a lasting impression of what he hears or to act under the influence of trustworthy information.

The Prince bases no hopes upon the idea of constitutional government, and, adopting the English phrase, declares that men, not measures, are wanted.

July 5, 1904

From Terrorism to Revolution

MINISTER PLEHVE SLAIN BY A BOMB

Russian Statesman's Assassin Believed to Be a Finn.

MANY PERSONS ARRESTED

ST. PETERSBURG, July 28.—M. de Plehve, the Minister of the Interior, was assassinated at 9:50 o'clock this morning by means of a bomb thrown at his carriage while he was driving to the Baltic Station to take a train for the palace at Peterhof, where he was to make his weekly report to the Emperor.

The assassination is believed to be the outcome of a widespread plot, the existence of which had been suspected for several days. Numerous arrests have already been made, including that of the assassin, a young man who is believed to be a Finn named Leglo, and who is now in a hospital, severely and perhaps mortally injured by the explosion of his own bomb.

An accomplice of Leglo, also apparently a Finn, but whose name is unknown, has been arrested. He had in his possession a bomb, which he tried to throw, but he was overpowered by the police just in time to prevent great loss of life.

The assassin wore a brown overcoat and a railroad official's cap. He stood on the sidewalk just as M. de Plehve's carriage was about to cross the canal bridge near the station. The Minister was escorted by a number of detectives on bicycles, and one of them jostled the assassin, who then rushed into the road and threw the bomb after the carriage, crying "Long live freedom!"

The missile struck the hind wheel and exploded with fearful force, killing or wounding over a score of persons. M. de Plehve and his coachmen were killed outright, and an officer of the guard was mortally injured.

July 29, 1904

CZAR'S COURT TORN BY REFORM REGIME

Prince Mirsky's Liberal Ideas Find Powerful Foes.

TEST WILL COME THIS WEEK

Reactionary Forces Strive to Prevent Provincial Representatives' Meeting—Prince Heads Strong Party.

ST. PETERSBURG, Nov. 18.—This country is facing a great internal crisis, which, in the minds of intelligent Russians, overshadows in importance all questions relating to the war and foreign politics.

A new, broad, and liberal movement seems not only under way, but gaining momentum daily, and the best feature of it is that it is entirely divorced from any radical revolutionary propaganda.

Prince Sviatopolk-Mirsky, the Minister of the Interior, has given impetus to the movement, but has done so against the most powerful influences, and behind the scenes a bitter struggle is waging for imperial support. During the coming week the first test of strength is likely to occur, the result of which may mean much for the history of Russia.

The policy of reaction, which had grown steadily since the accession of Alexander III., seemed suddenly to lose its main bulwark when Minister de Plehve fell. With the advent of Prince Sviatopolk-Mirsky and his frank appeal for a policy of mutual confidence between Government and people a tremendous liberal rebound occurred, raising, perhaps unjustifiably, high hopes and aspirations.

Great Changes Made.

An American, enjoying absolute political freedom, can hardly appreciate the full significance of what the changes that have occurred since Prince Sviatopolk-Mirsky's inauguration mean in a land of absolutism. The Russian policy as regards Finland, if not reversed, has been greatly ameliorated, and the Finnish National Diet will meet next month. Only yesterday prominent Finlanders who were exiled under the de Plehve régime received permission to return to their own country or to go abroad if they desired to do so.

The oppressive activity of the police throughout the Empire has been largely relaxed; banishment by administrative order has been abolished; hundreds of political prisoners exiled to Siberia have been recalled; the Jews have received assurances of the dawning of a brighter day; the doors have been thrown open at two of the biggest trials proceeding in Russia, (the Schaumann treason trial and the Jewish trial at Gomel,) and the method of treating student demonstrations has been radically changed, persuasion being substituted for Cossack charges.

Freedom for Press.

But nowhere are the changes so marked as in the matter of the press. After years of the strictest censorship, Russian papers suddenly found their voices within the last fortnight, and were remarkably plainspoken in the discussion of internal affairs, especially in connection with the forthcoming meeting of zemstvo representatives. Long accounts of the Schaumann and Gomel trials have been printed, and even particulars of student demonstrations, with resolutions offered at the Polytechnic Institute declaring that what was wanted was not confidence, but an end of the war and the immediate convocation of a national assembly.

Such an unprecedented publication made the Russian public rub its eyes in amazement. Prince Oukhtomsky, editor of the Viedomosti, said to-day that never within his memory had Russian newspapers had such liberties; yet the changes had been effected quietly and without public proclamation.

As a rule, said the Prince, no laws had been modified. For instance, the old press law was still hanging above the heads of editors like the sword of Damocles. The machinery of repression existed, but was not in operation.

In the meantime, about the head of Prince Sviatopolk-Mirsky has raged a storm of opposition. All the reactionary elements, including the solid bureaucracy, have used all the weapons at hand to undermine him.

Pobiedonostzeff Warns Czar.

M. Pobiedonostzeff, Chief Procurator of the Holy Synod, has warned the Emperor that if rumors attributed to Court circles are credible the autocracy and orthodoxy will both be in danger if the present movement is not stopped promptly.

A week ago it was actually believed that Prince Sviatopolk-Mirsky had been overthrown but subsequent developments proved the contrary. Nevertheless, his enemies persistently keep reports afloat that the health of the Minister of the Interior is bad, and the nature of the campaign which he is fighting is enough to shatter the health of a strong man.

In the character of the elements which

have rallied to his support, however, lies Prince Sviatopolk-Mirsky's strength. They include neither radicals nor revolutionaries, but the great mass of conservative, liberal-minded, loyal Russians, who believe that the salvation and progress of the empire lie in larger liberties, but who have not a particle of sympathy with violence or revolution.

It is fortunate, indeed, that Prince Sviatopolk-Mirsky has not attracted the support of the radicals, for that would place a powerful weapon in the hands of his adversaries.

Want Conference Postponed.

The enemies of the Minister of the Interior are now moving heaven and earth to postpone the meeting of the Presidents of thirty-eight provincial zemstvos, which is scheduled for next Saturday, and in the present circumstances some of the Minister's own friends are counseling him to allow a postponement until January, fearing that a too radical expression of views in the agitation raised might furnish too much ammunition for the opposition.

M. Shipoff, President of the Moscow zemstvo, who will preside at the meeting, favors this temporizing policy. It is even reported that Prince Sviatopolk-Mirsky is wavering, though his friends declare that this is untrue. The whole question will be decided by the Emperor early in the week.

Some of the Presidents already here are excited over the possibility of postponement, declaring that if the meeting is formally postponed it will be held surreptitiously.

Undoubtedly postponement would be a crushing blow and create an exceedingly bad impression. This is due to the fact that the meeting has been clothed with a sentimental importance hardly justified by its actual powers. It is purely unofficial, without direct authority to act, but it is the first occasion of an authorized assembling of representatives of the zemstvos from all over Russia.

Zemstvo Presidents' Programme.

The meting is not intended to be of a public character. The programme includes the discussion of three points, namely:

First—The conditions which have prevented zemstvo activity, giving wide scope for the consideration of the very questions heretofore prohibited.

Second—The organization of a central administration of agriculture.

Third—The co-operation of local zemstvo hospitals in the case of wounded people.

Although the subjects appear vague and indefinite, all aim at the national co-operation of the zemstvos, which contains a suggestion of a sort of land parliament, where the wishes of the provincial zemstvos could be voiced. The subjects also raise the question of the character of the central zemstvo unit and the collateral question of the elective principle in the matter of representation. However, as the conference will be private, its decisions will be more or less academic.

The best friends of the zemstvos believe that too great haste will be unfortunate, and urge that the Presidents exercise the greatest discretion and avoid giving a final decision, which might be thrown aside and put an end to future possibilities. Instead, they urge that the Presidents work out a clear plan for summoning another conference in the future.

The statement that Prince Sviatopolk-Mirsky has proposed to divide the empire into sixteen districts, from which the zemstvos should select representatives to form a central council, is entirely without foundation. The whole subject remains to be worked out, and if the present movement succeeds eventually, its best friends realize that the plans must crystallize gradually, as any sudden decision which would produce a shock might be fatal to the cause.

November 14, 1904

SUBJECTS OF CZAR DEMAND FREEDOM

Their Leaders Adopt a Protest Against Despotism.

SESSION HELD IN SECRET.

Emperor Finally Withdrew Sanction of Public Meeting—A Rebuff for Prince Mirsky.

ST. PETERSBURG, Nov. 19.—At the last moment the Emperor withdrew his consent to the proposed meeting of Zemstvo Presidents in the City Hall. It is asserted that the spectre of a Constitution for Russia was successfully raised by the reactionaries among the Czar's advisers.

Among these reactionaries those chiefly responsible for the defeat of Prince Sviatopolk-Mirsky's plan are supposed to be the Grand Duke Sergius, M. Pobiedonostzeff, the Chief Procurator of the Holy Synod, and M. Sassonoff, a member of the Council of the empire. MM. Strumer and Suchinsky are also believed to have helped secure the defeat of the project of the new Minister of the Interior. They were M. de Plehve's assistants, and when Prince Sviatopolk-Mirsky took charge of the Ministry of the Interior he dispensed with their services.

The official auspices under which the meeting of the Zemstvo Presidents was to be held having been withdrawn, they assembled at a private house, their place of meeting being kept secret. A hundred earnest men, included among whom were some of the most prominent figures in Russia, discussed a carefully prepared memorandum, practically embodying a recommendation for a national representative body to have a share in the Government, though the use of the word "Constitution" is carefully avoided. This memorandum will be presented to Emperor Nicholas.

Demands on the Czar.

The memorandum comprises ten sections, of which seven were indorsed at to-day's meeting. The remainder, it is expected, will be approved at a meeting to be held to-morrow.

The document, which is bound to hold a conspicuous place in Russian history, is as follows:

"Preamble of proposals on the question of general conditions preventing the normal course and development of our social life, submitted to a private conference of Zemstvo workers Nov. 19 and Nov. 20 in St. Petersburg:

"Section 1. The abnormal system of government prevailing among us, and especially noticeable since the eighties, is due to the complete estrangement of Government and people and the absence of the mutual confidence so necessary to national life.

"Sec. 2. These relations between the Government and the people originate from apprehension of the development of popular initiative and persistent efforts to exclude the people from participation in internal government. With this object, the Government endeavored to extend the centralized administration to all branches of local government and impose a tutelage on every branch of national life, admitting co-operation with the people solely for the purpose of bringing popular institutions into harmony with the views of the Government.

"Sec. 3. The bureaucratic system, causing estrangement between the supreme power and the people, creates a field for a wide scope of administrative arbitrariness and personal caprice. Such a condition deprives the nation of the necessary assurances that the rights of each and all will be protected and undermines confidence in the Government.

"Sec. 4. The normal current of the evolution of State and nation is possible only under the condition of close living and union and the co-operation of the imperial power with the people.

"Sec. 5. In order to exclude the possibility of the display of administrative arbitrariness and to guarantee personal rights, it is necessary to establish and consistently apply a principle by which no one will be subjected to punishment or to the restriction of rights without the decision of independent legal authorities.

Freedom of Speech Required.

"Sec. 6. For the unrestricted expression of public opinion and the free exposition and satisfaction of popular needs, it is essential to guarantee freedom of conscience and speech and of the press, and also freedom of meeting and association.

"Sec. 7. Self-reliance is the chief condition of the proper and successful development of the political and economic life of the country. A considerable majority of the population of Russia belonging to the peasant class, it is necessary, first of all, to place the latter in a position favorable for the development of self-reliance and energy, and this is attainable only by a radical alteration of the present inequitable and humiliating condition of the peasants. For this purpose it is necessary (a) to equalize the civil and political rights of the peasants with those of the other classes; (b) to release rural self-government from administrative tutelage; (c) to safeguard the peasants by proper courts of justice.

"Sec. 8. Zemstvo institutions, in which local and popular life is mostly concentrated, must be placed in a condition in which they may successfully carry out their duties. For this purpose it is necessary that the Zemstvo representation be based on a non-class basis and all the forces of the local population be admitted to share in Zemstvo work; that Zemstvo institutions be brought into closer touch with the people by the creation of a small Zemstvo unit upon a basis guaranteeing absolute independence, and that to Zemstvo institutions there be assured the necessary permanence and independence essential to their proper development and activity and

From Terrorism to Revolution

mutual co-operation of governmental with popular institutions.

"Sect. 9.—But for the creation and maintenance of close and healthy communion and unison of the imperial authority with the people upon the basis above pointed out and in order to assure the correct development of the life of State and nation it is unquestionably necessary for national representation in the form of a specially elective body to participate in legislation.

"Sect. 10.—This conference, considering itself an informal gathering, of which the members express personal views, considers that the settlement of the question of the bases that form the relationship of government and popular representation in the life of the country should be submitted to representatives of the nation, chosen under the conditions above indicated, as essential for freedom in elections."

Prince Mirsky's Position.

There are conflicting reports regarding the attitude of Prince Sviatopolk-Mirsky to the meeting. Some of his friends assert that when he began the negotiations with the Zemstvos, MM. Shipoff and Petrunkavich and Prince Ivoff were sent to explain what the meeting proposed to do.

The Minister found that instead of thirty-four Presidents whom he had invited about one hundred representatives were to be present, and that they proposed to go much further than their powers authorized.

When the Emperor declined to grant permission for the meeting, however, Prince Sviatopolk-Mirsky, it is said, informed the representatives that, although official sanction was declined, they could meet privately, police protection being guaranteed. Moreover, he himself drafted a law for submission to the Council of the empire, authorizing the Zemstvos to elect delegates to sit in a consultative body in connection with the Department of Rural Affairs of his Ministry. This law will immediately be promulgated, in order that the Zemstvos at their approaching meeting in December may choose representatives.

It is said that Prince Sviatopolk-Mirsky's idea that ill-digested, precipitate action might wreck the prospects for the future was supported by a number of the Zemstvo representatives here, but the majority, although moderate in their views, rejected the advice of their colleagues as being simply, as the Russians says, a "sop to a whale," and entered the meeting this afternoon determined to speak plainly.

Another of Prince Sviatopolk-Mirsky's intimates said this afternoon that the Minister's position regarding the meeting was being misrepresented. The Zemstvo Presidents had tried to take advantage of the invitation extended to them, it being understood when the invitation was issued that the conference would be principally for the purpose of the co-operation of the Zemstvos in the Red Cross work, which M. de Plehve refused to sanction.

But, according to this informant, when the Presidents came forward with a programme for the broadest discussion of the general questions of the empire and wanted to commit the Government in advance to their decisions, the Minister took the position that as such matters were entirely beyond their legal competency the meeting could not be held under Government auspices.

As the latest evidence that Prince Sviatopolk-Mirsky has in nowise changed his position toward the Zemstvos was cited the appointment, just announced, of M. Surrousoff to be Governor of Tver to succeed Prince Sheirinsky, one of de Plehve's appointees. The Prince is a notorious reactionary and was selected by de Plehve largely because of his opposition to the Zemstvos.

Radicals Planned Demonstration.

Before the announcement was made that the Presidents' meeting at the City Hall had been forbidden, the Radicals and some student organizations planned sympathetic demonstrations in front of the Hall in favor of ending the war and calling a National Assembly. The secrecy as to the place of meeting prevented these demonstrations.

MOSCOW, Nov. 19.—Popular demonstrations occurred here to-day owing to the refusal of the authorities to authorize an official meeting of the Zemstvos' representatives at St. Petersburg.

Crowds in the streets in front of the palace of the Grand Duke Serglus, Governor General of Moscow, shouted "Down with the Moscow Gazette!" the only newspaper in Russia which is fiercely opposed to the Zemstvos. Later the crowds voluntarily dispersed.

The Zemstvo supporters here telegraphed to M. Shipoff, President of the Moscow Zemstvo, asking him to make a final effort to induce the Government to allow the meeting to be held under official auspices.

ODESSA, Nov. 19.—A majority of the City Councilors have petitioned the Government to restore the freedom of municipal elections and debates as guaranteed under the Law of 1870, and also to suspend the state of siege.

November 20, 1904

CZAR ORDERS REFORM, BUT WARNS SUBJECTS

Pledges Liberty for Peasants and Press and in Religion.

BUT AGITATION MUST END

Manifesto Making Concessions Preceded by Sharp Declaration Against Demonstrations.

ST. PETERSBURG, Dec. 26.—Emperor Nicholas's long-expected reform ukase was issued to-night. The document deals, under eight heads, with practically all the subjects brought to the Emperor's attention by the memorial of the Congress of Zemstvo Presidents held here last month, and, while not specifically pledging the Government to carry out the various reforms in their entirety, as demanded by the memorial, promises that each shall be referred to the Council of Ministers, with orders to report promptly on the fullest measures of relief which can be accorded on the various subjects.

One question not touched by the ukase is that of the Constitutional Assembly. Neither is the Jewish religion specifically mentioned, though freedom for all creeds or sects, whether Christian or otherwise, is among the subjects which will be dealt with.

The various subjects will be referred to committees for early report.

The Imperial decree, which is entitled "A Scheme for the Improvement of the Administration of the State," is addressed to the Senate, and is as follows:

"In accordance with the revered will of our crowned predecessor, and thinking unceasingly of the welfare of the realm intrusted to us by God, we regard it as our duty and the Government's duty, in conjunction with undeviating maintenance of the immutability of the fundamental laws of the Empire, to have untiring care for the country's needs, distinguishing between all that is really in the interests of the Russian people from tendencies not seldom mistaken and influenced by transitory circumstances.

"When the need of this or that change is proved ripe, then we consider it necessary to meet it, even though the transformation to which this leads involves the introduction of essential innovations in legislation. We do not doubt that the realization of such an undertaking will meet with the sympathy of the well-disposed section of our subjects, who see the true prosperity of the fatherland in the support of civil tranquillity and the uninterrupted satisfaction of the daily needs of the people.

The Peasantry His First Care.

"Placing in the forefront of our care thought for the best ordering of the life of the most numerous of our estates, the peasant population, we may remark that this matter is already under examination.

"Simultaneously with a detailed investigation of the initial proposals of the Ministry of the Interior, which are being carried out locally, conferences are now being held by Commissioners specially selected from among the most experienced of the highest administrative officials regarding the most important questions of peasant life, assisted in their investigation of the general needs of the agricultural industry by the knowledge and experience of local committees.

"We command these to labor to bring the laws regarding peasants into unity with the general imperial legislation, thereby facilitating the task of attaining permanent security of this estate, which, by decree of the Czar Liberator is recognized as consisting of free citizens possessing full rights.

"Surveying the wide domain of the people's uttermost needs, we regard as urgent in the interest of the legal strengthening of civic and public life:

"First—The adoption of effective measures for safeguarding the law in its full force as the most important pillar of the throne of the autocratic empire, in order that its inviolable fulfillment for all alike shall be regarded as the first duty by all the authorities and in all places subject to us, that its non-fulfillment shall inevitably bring with it legal responsibility for every arbitrary act, and that persons who have suffered wrong by such acts shall be enabled to secure legal redress.

"Second—That as wide scope as possible should be given to local and municipal institutions in the administration of various matters affecting local welfare, and that they should have conferred upon them the necessary independence, within legal limitations, and that representatives of all sections of the population interested in local matters should be called upon, under equable condiions, to take part in these institutions, with a view to the completest satisfaction possible of their needs. Besides the Governments and zemstvos district institutions hitherto existing there should also be established in close connection with them public institutions for the administration of local affairs in localities of smaller extent.

"Third—That in order to secure equality of persons of all classes before the law, steps should be taken to bring about the necessary unification of judicial procedure throughout the empire, and to assure independence of the courts.

"Fourth—That for the further development of the measures introduced by us for the protection of workmen in factories, workshops, and commercial establishments, attention is to be given to the question of

OVERTHROW OF THE OLD ORDER

the introduction of State Insurance for workmen."

Revision of Exceptional Laws.

"Fifth—That there should be a revision of the exceptional laws decreed at the time of an unparalleled outbreak of criminal activity on the part of enemies of public order, and the application of which was attended with a grave extension of the discretionary power of the administrative authorities; and that at the same time steps should be taken for circumscribing their application within the narrowest possible limits, and for assuring that limitation of the rights of private persons involved in that application shall only be permitted in cases where the actual safety of the State is threatened

"Sixth—That in confirmation of my undeviating heart's desire as expressed in the imperial manifesto of March 8, 1903, for the protection by the fundamental laws of the empire of tolerance in matters of faith, the laws dealing with the rights of communities and persons belonging to heterodox and non-Christian confessions should be submitted to revision; and that independently of this, measures should be taken for the removal of all limitations on the exercise of the religions not directly mentioned in the law.

"Seventh—That there should be such revision of existing ordinances limiting the rights of foreigners and measures in certain territories of the empire that in future there shall remain only such of them as are required by the present interests of the empire and the manifest needs of the Russian people.

"Eighth—That all unnecessary restrictions should be removed from the existing press laws and that printed speech should be placed within clearly defined legal limits: that to the native press, in accordance with the progress of education and the importance thereby accruing to it, should be left the possibility of worthily fulfilling its high calling, namely to be the true interpreters of reasonable strivings for Russia's advantage.

"Acting upon the above principles, with a view to a series of great internal changes impending in the early future, part whereof, in accordance with instructions previously given by us, are already under preliminary examination, we deem it well in view of the diversity and importance of these changes, to fix an order of business for consideration of means and the possibility of their early and complete realization. The closest co-operation is incumbent on the various sections of the administration throughout the whole series of our State institutions.

"With reference to all the above-mentioned subjects the Council of Ministers has to examine the best way of giving effect to our views and to submit to us at the earliest possible date its decisions as to the further shape of the above-mentioned measures in their prescribed order. The committee has also to report to us as to the subsequent progress of the elaboration of the matters mentioned.

Agitation Must Stop.

As a forerunner to the Czar's manifesto the following communication was issued by the Government early this morning:

"In the Autumn of this year there was a meeting in St. Petersburg of several zemstvos of the various Governments, who expressed a series of desires concerning what were, in their opinion, indispensable reforms in the interior government of the empire. These desires were made the subjects of action by members of various other assemblies, which met for the purpose, and also, notwithstanding the provisions of law, were considered at the deliberations of certain town councils and zemstvos.

"Thus by the action of people who endeavored to introduce discord into public and state life, excitement arose in the minds of certain sections of society, chiefly among impressionable youths. In certain towns of the empire there occurred a series of noisy meetings which demanded the presentation to the Government of certain demands which were inadmissible in the face of the sacred foundations of the laws of the empire and the indestructible elements which form the Government.

"These sections of the public made street demonstrations in bands and openly resisted the police and authorities.

"Such movements against the existing order of government, which have fallen adversely upon the bulk of the Russian people, who are loyal to the everlasting foundations of the existing Government, gave to the excitement above referred to an undeserved importance of a general tendency. Th Russian people involved in this movement, forgetful of the grievous year which has fallen to the lot of Russia, blinded by chimerical hopes of profits which they might expect from a radical change in the ancient foundations of the Russian state and life, and not knowing what they were doing, acted to the advantage not of their country but of its enemies.

"Now the duty of the Government is to preserve order in the state and protect the public confidence from all change in the true course of internal life. Therefore, any destruction of order and peace and all meetings of an anti-Government character must and will be stopped by all legal means at the disposition of the authorities, and those concerned in those disorders, especially persons employed in the Government service, will be held responsible.

"Zemstvo and town statutes and every form of institution and company must not go beyond the limits provided for them and must not concern themselves in questions in the consideration of which they have no legal authority. Presidents of public meetings who allow consideration to take place of matters not in their province on questions of general government are liable under the existing laws; and organs of the press, with the knowledge of the responsibility which rests upon them, must for their part introduce the necessary calming effect on public life, which has deviated in recent times from its proper course."

December 27, 1904

CZAR MENACED BY REVOLUTION

Streets of St. Petersburg Full of Troops.

PERIL IN OTHER CITIES

Strike Movement Threatens to Spread—Government Takes Fright and Offers Concessions.

ST. PETERSBURG, Saturday, Jan. 21.—With the Russian capital seemingly on the verge of a revolution, thousands of workmen parading the streets, agitators and fanatics sowing the seeds of disorder, and half the city in darkness and without fire protection owing to walkouts, the situation was hourly growing more tense when the authorities decided last night to adopt energetic measures to preserve order, prevent rioting, and overawe the violent-minded, at the same time seeking to placate the striking workmen by offering satisfaction of their demands in so far as they are just and reasonable, thus acting with combined firmness and moderation.

The Government last night augmented the garrison of the city with 2,500 cavalry and 1,000 infantry from Tsarskoe-Selo, and filled the streets, especially in the disaffected quarter, with heavy patrols of soldiers.

At the meetings yesterday the men drew up a formal petition to the Emperor. A deputation was appointed to take it to the Czar at Tsarskoe-Selo, and it was proposed to ask the Emperor to give a response at the Winter Palace tomorrow, (Sunday.)

It was decided to hold a great mass meeting in the Palace Square at 2 P. M. tomorrow, disregarding any opposition on the part of the authorities, even by armed force.

The strikers agreed to attend the meeting unarmed, saying they were not willing to meet violence with violence. Father Gopon, the leader of the workmen, undertook to head the procession in clerical garb and carrying a cross.

The strikers said they were ready to die in front of the palace, but that they insisted on being heard by the Emperor himself.

Not Allowed to Address Czar.

The men, however, were not allowed to present the petition to the Emperor, and it was made known that the great demonstration planned for to-morrow with its unlimited possibilities of an outbreak would not be permitted.

At the same time, acting in conjunction with a conference of employers, it has been determined to offer concessions in the terms of employment, which the employers declared the great majority of the workmen would be inclined to accept if protection from the more violent faction were guaranteed to them.

A proclamation has been issued this morning forbidding all assemblages, parades, or other demonstrations in the city, and warning well-disposed workmen and other private individuals to avoid gatherings, as the authorities are determined to break up and disperse meetings imperiling public safety.

The proclamation is printed in The Police Messenger, which is the only publication appearing this morning, the police having forced the printers to remain at work until the paper appeared.

Late last night it was reported that Father Gopon had been quietly spirited away from his bodyguard and taken into custody, in furtherance of the plan to disorganize the elements that are threatening the peace of the city.

The situation entered an acute stage yesterday, and the strike assumed an open political phase. The day was one of intense excitement. Mill after mill and factory after factory closed.

Throngs of workmen paraded the streets, and when their colleagues refused to join them broke down gates and forced the men to go out.

No Newspapers Printed.

The whole industrial centre is now idle. All the textile mills and every printing office in St. Petersburg are closed. The newspapers are all forced to suspend publication. By last evening over 100,000 men

From Terrorism to Revolution

were out. One electric light plant and one water plant have shut down.

Throughout the day workmen's meetings were held, many of them being addressed by Father Gapon. Incendiary speeches were made, the wildest threats being uttered as to what would come in the event of the authorities and employers failing to meet the demands.

The nervousness and dread of what the next few days might bring forth were increased by reports that the workmen of Moscow, Kieff, Kharkoff, Kishineff, and other large cities in the interior might join the movement.

The telegraphers and railroad employes threatened to join the walk-out, paralyzing the communications of the country.

Many foreigners are preparing to send their families abroad.

The suddenness of the strike and the far-reaching nature of the workmen's organization were largely a surprise to the Government and employers. Starting with the walk-out of a few thousand employes of the Putiloff Iron Works, due to purely industrial causes, the strike spread as rapidly as a conflagration through the laboring classes of St. Petersburg and became general.

At first only industrial demands were presented, such as shortened hours of labor and increased wages; but poverty and discontent, under the incitement of Socialist-Democratic agitators, led to the formulation of political demands. The workmen's petition was drawn up and largely signed, and this petition attacked the whole capitalistic system of the country, bitterly assailed the present Government as one of bureaucracy, and demanded the reform of both, asserting that death was preferable to existence under such conditions.

The establishments closed yesterday by strikes include the Alexandrovsky Machine Works, 7,000 men; the Steiglitz-Thornton cotton spinning factory, the State distillery, the Keller and Beckman distilleries, the Russo-American rubber factory, the Yukoff soap works, the State playing card factory, the Vargounine paper mills, the Atlas machine works, Wolf & Max's printing works, and the imperial glass works.

The civil employes of the arsenal have gone out. Practically all the small establishments in St. Petersburg are closed.

One of the deputations of strikers visited the office of a recently established news agency and informed the printers that unless they joined the movement the building would be wrecked. The printers promptly quit work, and the agency is now sending out its news in stencilled sheets.

Refuse an Eight-Hour Day.

The employers, after conferences with the Ministry of Finance, which was the first to recognize the gravity of the situation, determined to offer concessions in wages and in conditions of labor, but they declared that it was impossible to grant an eight-hour day without general legislation affecting competition and price regulations for piece work. Compliance with the employes' demands for payment of wages during the strike was held to be out of the question, and the employers declined also to permit of the dictation of terms by other than their own employes. They expressed the belief that most of their employes were desirous of accepting the concessions and returning to work if they could be sure of safety from personal injury.

The priest, George Gopon, is an interesting personality. He is idolized by the workmen, who, since the beginning of the strike, have furnished him with a bodyguard. He has been accompanied everywhere by a score of Izvoschiks, and has not been sleeping at his own home for a week for fear of arrest.

As a peasant swineherd, when a boy, he showed such capacity for learning that he was sent to the Poltava Ecclesiastical Seminary to be educated as a monk. His leaning toward politics led to his exclusion from the seminary, and this prompted a desire to get close to the people and share their lot. He was determined to become a priest instead of a monk, and overcame many obstacles, finally being graduated from the St. Petersburg Ecclesiastical Academy. He then took up work among the laboring classes, whose leader he speedily became. He shows an evident genius for organization.

Father Gopon is believed to be the heart and soul of the whole movement.

Up to an early hour this (Saturday) morning no disturbance has been reported. There are heavy guards at the water works and lighting plants and in the factory district. Patrols of cavalry are constantly in motion throughout the city.

January 21, 1905

STRIKERS' APPEAL TO CZAR.

They Beg for Justice and Say Life Is Not Worth Living.

ST. PETERSBURG, Jan. 20.—Following is the appeal to the Emperor, which the strikers were not allowed to present to him:

"Sire: We, workmen, inhabitants of St. Petersburg, of all classes, our wives, children, and indigent parents, come to you, our sovereign, asking for protection.

"We are poor, persecuted, burdened with labor beyond our strength. We are insulted, treated not as men, but as slaves, who ought to bear their cruel fate in silence. We have suffered, but we are being plunged deeper in the mire and deprived of our rights.

"Uninstructed, stifled by destitution and injustice, we are perishing. We have no strength left.

"Sire, we have arrived at the extreme limits of endurance; we have reached the terrible moment when death is to be preferred to a continuation of our intolerable sufferings. We have left our work, and informed our employers that we will not resume until our demands are conceded. We have not asked much; we have asked but for means of livelihood, without which life is a burden and labor continual torture.

"Our first request is that our masters should investigate our case. They have refused. The right to put forward our claim has been denied to us, it being held that such right is not recognized by law."

After referring to the eight-hour day and other points in their case, the petitioners continue:

"Any one of us who dared raise his voice in the interests of the people of the working classes has been thrown into prison or transported. Kindness and good feeling have been treated as a crime.

"A Shameful War."

"The bureaucracy has brought the country to the verge of ruin by a shameful war. It is luring it to its downfall. We have no voice in the heavy burdens imposed; we do not know for whom or why this money is wrung from an impoverished people, and we do not know how it is expended.

"This state of things, contrary to Divine laws, renders life impossible. It were better that we should all perish, we workers and all Russia. Then, good luck to capitalists and exploiters and poor, corrupt officials, robbers of the Russian people.

"Assembled before thy palace, we plead our salvation. Refuse not thine aid and raise thy people from their tomb. Give them the means of working out their own destiny. Rescue them from intolerable officialdom. Throw down the wall that separates; free thy people; order that they may rule the country with thee. Create for thy people the happiness wrenched from us, leaving us nothing but sorrow and humiliation.

National Representation Demanded.

"We pray your Majesty graciously to receive our demands, which are inspired by a desire for your Majesty's and our welfare and the consciousness of the necessity of escape from an intolerable situation. Russia is too great and her needs are too varied and numerous for officials only to rule. National representation is indispensable, as only the people themselves know the country's real needs.

"Refuse not thy aid, but order a convocation of representatives of all classes, including workmen. Let all be free and equal in the elections, and to this end permit the election of a constituent Assembly and general secret ballot. That is our chief demand, in which all else centres. It is the sole balm for our wounds, which will otherwise speedily bring us death.

"A single measure, however, will not heal all our wounds. Therefore we acquaint you frankly and openly on behalf of the whole of the Russian working classes, as to a father, with our further demands."

Willing to Die for Russia.

After making these demands the petition concludes as follows:

"There, Sire, are our principal needs, satisfaction whereof can free Russia from slavery and misery, make her prosperous, and enable workmen to organize in defense of their interests against the capitalist exploitation and official robbery which are stifling the people. Order and swear they shall be satisfied, and you will make Russia happy and glorious and inscribe your name forever in the hearts of our people and their posterity!, whilst should you repulse and reject our prayer we will die in this square before your palace. We have nowhere else to go.

"Only two paths are open to us; either toward liberty and happiness or to the grave. Should our lives serve as a holocaust for suffering Russia we shall not regret the sacrifice, but shall bear it willingly."

January 21, 1905

DAY OF TERROR IN CZAR'S CAPITAL

Troops Slay Women and Children with Men.

LED BY PRIEST TO DEATH

Workmen Force Guards to Fire to Stop Them.

BARRICADES IN STREETS

A General Killed and Other Officers Attacked—Crowds Shout "Down With the Czar."

ST. PETERSBURG, Jan. 22.—This has been a day of unspeakable horror in St. Petersburg.

Minister of the Interior Sviatopolk-Mirsky presented to his Majesty last night the invitation of the workmen to appear at the Winter Palace this afternoon and receive their petition, but the Emperor's advisers had already taken the decision to show a firm and resolute front, and the Emperor's answer to the 100,000 workmen trying to force their way to the Palace Square to-day was a solid array of troops who met them with rifle, bayonet, and sabre.

The priest Gopon, the leader and idol of the men, in his golden vestments, holding aloft the cross and marching at the head of thousands of workmen through the Narva Gate, miraculously escaped a volley which laid low half a hundred persons.

The figures of the total number killed or wounded at the Narva Gate, the Moscow Gate, at various bridges and islands, and at the Winter Palace vary. The best estimate is 500, although there are exaggerated figures placing the number as high as 5,000.

Many men were accompanied by their wives and children, and in the confusion, which left no time for discrimination, these shared the fate of the men.

One Regiment Mutinied.

The troops, with the exception of the Moscow Regiment, which is reported to have thrown down its arms, remained loyal and obeyed orders.

The military authorities had a firm grip on every artery in the city. At daybreak guard regiments, cavalry, and infantry held every bridge across the frozen Neva, the network of canals which interlace the city, and the gates leading from the industrial section, while in the Palace Square, as the storm centre, were massed Dragoon regiments, infantry, and Cossacks of the Guards.

Barred from the bridges and gates, men, women, and children crossed the frozen river and canals on the ice by twos and threes, hurrying to the Palace Square, where they were sure the Emperor would be present to hear them.

But the street approaches to the square were cleared by volleys and Cossack charges. Men and women, infuriated to frenzy by the loss of loved ones, cursed the soldiers while they retreated.

Strikers Built Barricades.

Men harangued the crowds, telling them that the Emperor had foiled them and that the time had come to act. Strikers began to build barricades in the Nevsky Prospect and at other points, using any material that came to hand, and even chopping down telegraph poles.

Fighting meantime continued at various places, soldiers firing volleys and charging the mob. The whole city was in a state of panic. Women were running through the streets seeking lost members of their families. Several barricades were carried by the troops.

Toward 8 o'clock in the evening the crowds, exhausted, began to disperse, leaving the military in possession. As they retreated up the Nevsky Prospect the workmen put out all the lights.

The little chapel at the Narva gate was wrecked.

On Kaminostov Island all the lights were extinguished.

Every officer wearing the uniform of the Emperor who was found alone was mobbed. A General was killed on the Nicholas Bridge, and a dozen officers were seized, stripped of their epaulets, and deprived of their swords.

January 23, 1905

"HAVE PATIENCE."

"Good day, my children," was the greeting of the Czar yesterday to the deputation of workingmen which he graciously condescended to receive. His consent to receive them was tardily given. They preferred their reasonable request two weeks ago. It was refused. Disorder in the streets followed, the beginnings of a popular uprising, and the Czar's troops had to kill some of his children before the semblance of order could be restored. This seemed hard, but the Czar explained yesterday that his children had been misled by traitors and enemies to the country and to his Government. The lot of the workingmen, he knew, was not easy, but he would take measures to assure all possible betterment of their condition, into which he would inquire "through legal channels." Meanwhile, he told them that they must "have patience."

February 2, 1905

From Terrorism to Revolution

TERRORIST BOMB SLAYS SERGIUS

Czar's Uncle Blown to Pieces in Moscow.

DESCRIBED BY WITNESS

Special Cable to THE NEW YORK TIMES.
[Copyright, 1905. All Rights Reserved.]

MOSCOW, Feb. 17, 8:40 P. M.—The Grand Duke Sergius was assassinated here this afternoon by a bomb. I witnessed the murder from the Kremlin.

Before leaving Moscow I desired to visit the Kremlin, so curious and so picturesque. Leaving the Hotel National, I crossed the Place Rouge and entered by the Holy Gate into the very interior of the Kremlin.

This Holy Gate has its legend, like everything else in this historic place. During the last invasion by the Tartars the defenders of the citadel were exhausting themselves in vain efforts to close the gate, the hinges of which were rusty. Finally, in despair, they prayed for help to a wooden ikon of the Virgin, which stood in a niche over the gate. The Virgin let fall a tear, which moistened the hinges, and thus permitted the closing of the gate. It was by this gate that Napoleon entered.

I was walking along, admiring the vast imperial palace and the panorama of Moscow, which stretched away as far as eye could reach.

The great clock of the Kremlin was striking 3 when I heard a terrific report. An immense sheet of flame at the same time rose 500 meters (550 yards) from me in the middle of the vast avenue which separates the Palace of Justice from the Arsenal. In the midst of the flames I saw several black masses projected into the air and fall in pieces on the ground.

I ran as fast as I could in the direction of the flame.

In an instant I reached the entrance of the Arsenal. A cloud of smoke was lifting, and, scattered on the ground, amid a heap of débris, were pieces of a human body, smoldering beside splinters of wood and broken glass.

A little further on men were stopping two horses, maddened and covered with blood, who were dragging all that remained of a carriage—a spring and two wheels that were twisted and broken.

Sergius's Wife on the Scene.

In a handsome sleigh a young and pretty woman had fainted, and around her a crowd, attracted by the explosion, was pressing. She was immediately recognized as the Grand Duchess Elizabeth Feodorovna, sister of the Empress of Russia and wife of the Grand Duke Sergius.

The terrible truth was at once made clear to me. The smoking human débris scattered around was all that remained of the Grand Duke. His head had been literally blown from his body and lay there, almost unrecognizable. Soldiers who had rushed from the guardhouse, aided by Generals and dvorniks, began to gather up the remains. A cordon of troops was drawn up before the Nicholas Gate.

February 18, 1905

PORTENTS OF REVOLT IN UNION OF RUSSIANS

Workmen All Over Empire Act Under Political Direction.

A PEASANTS' RISING AWAITED

Outbreaks in Cities and Country May Come Together—Situation in the Caucasus No Better.

ST. PETERSBURG, Monday, Feb. 27.—Evidence is increasing that the strikes throughout the Empire, and especially those in St. Petersburg, are not economic in their origin, but inspired by a definite political plan.

The Government and the employers are embarrassed by the tactics of the workmen, whose discontent is being fed and who are increasing their demands with each new concession. This condition is believed to have been fomented by crafty political agitators, who are stirring up the men and at the same time holding them in leash, apparently awaiting some signal for concerted action.

Fear is entertained that this widespread agitation may be connected with a plan to await a possible peasant outbreak in the Spring, with which a general strike will be synchronized, the workmen joining hands with the peasants.

The election of labor representatives on the Imperial Commission, which is to investigate the causes of discontent in St Petersburg, passed off quietly yesterday.

The question of convoking the Zemsky Sobor is apparently not yet settled. Some of the Emperor's advisers are urging the idea that to summon the Land Parliament at this time would be fatal to the autocracy, but that as a preliminary step toward a representative assembly it might be well to invite representatives of the people to sit in the Council of the Empire in a purely consultative capacity and with the existing conservative elements as a balance wheel.

The situation in Riga is again reported to be very serious. The authorities there are apparently unable to cope with the lawless element.

In the Caucasus the situation is extremely bad, practically amounting to civil war.

In Baku the inhabitants, barricaded in their houses, are petitioning the authorities at St. Petersburg for relief from the existing condition of affairs. The Government is sending reinforcements of troops, but while these may be able to stop the reign of terror they will be impotent to start the wheels of industry. Proprietors fear that the oil wells will be utterly ruined if pumping is suspended much longer.

Conditions in other towns in the Caucasus are equally desperate.

Owing to the gravity of the situation in the Caucasus and apprehension based on the depletion of the troops in the district for the war, the Government has appealed to the Armenian Catholicos to exert his personal influence to persuade Armenians to cease their excesses. The Catholicos went to Erivan, where he exhorted the people to remain tranquil.

Dispatches from Batum report that domiciliary searches for arms have been instituted in the quarters of the workingmen.

In Siberia, as well as in other parts of the empire, the Government has granted considerable concessions to railway employes, in some cases according a reduction of the hours of labor to nine a day. This renders the situation of private employers increasingly difficult, as they say it is impossible for them to concede so much.

All the Russian railways, except the Central Asian lines, have been placed under martial law.

Postal telegraph officials at Moscow are threatening to strike unless their demands for the improvement of their condition are granted.

February 27, 1905

CZAR CONCEDES ELECTIVE BODIES

Decrees That People Shall Have Assemblies.

Special Cable to THE NEW YORK TIMES.
[Copyright, 1905.]

ST. PETERSBURG, March 8.—Russia has entered on a vast political experiment, which, if successful, will strengthen the autocracy and crown the hopes and efforts of her best citizens to bring the people and the monarch into closer touch and obtain for the nation a voice in the Government.

It has been a day of bewildering surprises. In the morning the Czar instituted another bureaucratic department instead of the anticipated Zemsky Sobor, and issued a manifesto reaffirming the immutability of the present system of government.

These acts elicited a feeling bordering on despair, since it was generally known that the Emperor was willing to grant representative rights to the people, and had even told a personal friend that he intended to convoke the Zemsky Sobor and let it decide the question of war or peace.

Upon all except the reactionary minority the manifesto acted like a thunderclap from a clear sky. The Bourse became weak and the workmen's delegates, assembled to hear the Government's reply to their demands, took the manifesto to mean a refusal and forthwith resolved to call a general strike.

The authorities thereupon flooded the city with troops, and everything looked like the rehearsal for another tragedy.

It was late in the evening when a supplement to The Official Messenger appeared on the streets, containing a rescript creating a Legislative Assembly.

Amazement, incredulity, and enthusiasm alternated among the crowds, and the wildest rumors were circulated in the city. The people seemed under the delusion that all their wants and cravings were satisfied. Many believed it was the end of the war, the end of all Russia's troubles, internal and external.

To-morrow St. Petersburg celebrates the anniversary of the emancipation of the serfs. The city will also celebrate the birth of a new era.

A civic rights rescript is worth more than many legions in allaying the threatened disorders.

March 4, 1905

JAPANESE CLOSE IN ON TIE PASS

Doubtful If Beaten Army Can Make a Stand.

MUJIKS SLAY AND BURN

Peasant Uprising Spreads Rapidly and Causes Terror Even in Cities—More Terrorist Outrages.

LONDON TIMES—NEW YORK TIMES
Special Cable. Copyright, 1905.

ST. PETERSBURG, March 13.—The full extent of the disaster at Mukden has not yet been established. Gen. Kuropatkin's dispatches indicating the almost total extermination of two regiments are apparently intended to prepare the public for the worst.

Other dispatches, not intended for publication, induce fear in the highest circles that the army now at Tie Pass will be unable to withstand an attack, which is regarded as imminent.

The Japanese, according to Gen. Kuropatkin, are only a gunshot behind the Russian rearguard.

The Thirtieth Infantry Division of the Fourth Army Corps is expected at Tie Pass within a week.

The advocates of peace are distinctly in the minority. General resentment is felt over the peace campaign in the French press.

Russia is overwhelmed by the disaster at Mukden, but is doggedly determined to continue the war, refusing to entertain the possibility of an utter rout in the forthcoming fight at Tie Pass.

The Bourse to-day showed a further decline owing to rumors of an approaching loan.

The revolutionaries are preparing anti-war demonstrations for to-morrow. Officers are being constantly insulted in the streets.

To Mobilize Three More Corps.

A War Council to-day decided forthwith to mobilize the Grenadier Corps and two army corps. The Grenadier Corps consists of three divisions, mostly stationed at Moscow.

The new army will probably be under the command of Gen. Gripenberg. The question of Gen. Kuropatkin's successor has not been definitely decided.

The news from the provinces is daily more alarming. The peasants are murdering landlords and pillaging and burning houses, factories, and sugar refineries. The unrest is fast extending to the whole central belt, so that a feeling bordering on panic prevails in the towns and cities and the alarm has even reached Moscow and Nijni Novgorod.

The threatened cities propose to form town guards, fearing that the police and military will be unable to afford protection.

The revolutionaries are undoubtedly helping to stir up the movement, but the elements of discontent are not of their sowing. It is idle to deny that the movement is assuming the character of an uprising against the landlords and officials. It is a sort of Jacquerie, or what the Russians call a Pugachevshchina, after the eighteenth century rebel Pugichev, who led thousands to revolt under the plea of championing the popular cause of the autocracy against officials, landlords, and all oppressors of the poor.

The same idea appears now to have taken root in the minds of the peasants. The mujik is firmly convinced that the Little Father and he are both victims of the Tchiornik, who have brought an unpopular and unsuccessful war, strikes, cholera, and countless ills upon the country in order to share the plunder with the landlords and manufacturers.

The mujik is strengthened in his fanatical conviction by the Holy Synod's recent denunciation of alien agitators. To the peasant foreigners are all alike, and as the manufacturers are mostly foreigners, his hatred of the capitalist becomes patriotic.

Further Terrorist outrages are reported. Lieut. Kouloff of the Volga Cossacks has been mortally wounded by revolutionists in the courtyard of his house at Kremenchug, it is supposed in revenge for his share in suppressing the disorders in Moscow.

M. Hoffenberg, Chief of Police at Minsk, was attacked by a man armed with a revolver, but escaped unhurt. Many officers concerned in the suppression of disorders have received threatening letters.

Revolutionary proclamations have been discovered at Kronstadt, inciting sailors and dockyard workmen to refuse to fit out warships, or, as an alternative, to damage them so as to prevent them from sailing.

It is rumored that there was an explosion to-night at Moscow close to the walls of the Kremlin.

March 14, 1905

From Terrorism to Revolution

RUSSIAN RULER GRANTS FREEDOM OF RELIGION

Disabilities of Unorthodox Communities to be Abolished.

MUJIKS' DEBTS CROSSED OFF

Czar Remits Arrears of Taxes and Payments on Land—Capital Begins Easter Quietly.

ST. PETERSBURG, Sunday, April 30.— A decree conceding liberty of worship to the Old Believers and abolishing the religious disabilities of the Roman Catholic and other Christian communities and of the Mohammedans will be published to-day.

The decree will provide that secession from the Orthodox Church will not involve any prosecution or the deprivation or curtailment of civil rights. When one of a married couple joins another religious sect the religion of their minor children will remain unchanged, but when a married couple both change their religion their children under fourteen years of age will follow the belief of their parents.

Old Believers and sectarians are to have the right to possess real and personal property and to establish monasteries and build schools, which will be subject to the control of the Minister of Public Worship. The prohibition of the printing and circulating of Old Believers' books on religion will be abolished.

Schismatics will be admitted to cadet and military schools and may be promoted to be officers. The prohibition of the bestowal of the bravery medal on members of the various unorthodox sects will be abolished.

Emperor Nicholas's Easter gifts, in addition to the decree on the subject of religious freedom, consist of a series of rescripts and ukases which will be published in the Official Messenger to-day. One of the Imperial announcements remits the peasants' arrears of taxes and back payments on account of lands given to them at the time of their emancipation, amounting to about $37,500,000.

Although no general amnesty for political offenses will be granted, pardon will be extended to certain classes of prisoners, including those arrested for participation in the disturbances of Jan. 22. Besides this, it is reported that an important official announcement will be made in connection with the rescript of March 3.

Emperor Nicholas will receive Easter felicitations at Tsarskoe-Selo and not at the Winter Palace, as is usually the case.

The recommendations of the Passport Commission in favor of the abolition of interior passports except in the case of Jews when they leave the Pale and the substitution for such passports of life identification cards are now before the Council of the Empire. The recommendations also involve the acquiescence in and universal recognition of foreign passports, thus meeting the American representations on the subject.

This city wore a holiday aspect yesterday. Beautiful weather prevailed and the Nevski Prospect, Grand Moskala, and other boulevards were crowded. There was not the slightest evidence of alarm for last night or to-day. Nevertheless stories of bomb throwing planned in the churches at midnight and of pillage and bloodshed to-day continued to circulate.

The great midnight Easter services passed off without a vestige of disorder. The crowds in the churches were enormous, and there were tens of thousands of persons around the St. Isaac, Kazan, and other cathedrals. The throngs were so dense that the processions of the clergy had to be surrounded by troops and gendarmes in order to force their way through.

April 30, 1905

MUTINEERS TELL TALE OF BLACK SEA REVOLT

Arrest of Men Who Rejected Food Led to Kniaz Potemkine Rising.

A GENERAL MUTINY PLANNED

Mastutchenko, the Leader, Killed Many Officers—Something of the Japanese About Him.

From Le Journal of Paris.

KUSTENJI, Roumania, July 15.—At 11 o'clock, on the evening of July 11, I descended from the Oriental Express, and an hour later I had the good fortune to meet several Russian sailors, who, thanks to an interpreter, related to me the recent stirring events in which they had played a part.

On the following day I saw at the Communal Hospital Able Seamen Ivan Cazlenco, Kovaltof, and Kisselaf; I saw also, at M. Magrin's, Sergt. Major Feodor Pogoirnetz, called Petrof; then I went to Yassy, Braila, Galatz, Calarashi, and Berlad. In these various places I took the testimony of a number of sailors. Thus I succeeded by combining the various accounts, by using what some told me for questions to others, in reconstructing the story of the tragic day of mutiny on board the Kniaz Potemkine. It is as follows:

The Kniaz Potemkine left Sevastopol on June 24 for open sea manoeuvres. The next day it reached the designated place, off Odessa, where they were to experiment with the new guns. Everything seemed peaceful on board. A torpedo boat was dispatched to Odessa for provisions. It returned at midnight.

For breakfast on June 26 " borsch," (Russian broth,) cooked with the meat purchased at Odessa, was served to the sailors. Without a dissenting voice they cried that they would not eat the " borsch," the meat being spoiled and full of worms. Nevertheless, certain sailors did eat the soup, and so their declaration did not become known in the cabin.

SAILORS REFUSE TO EAT.

The day following the soup was remade with the same meat. This time all the sailors refused to eat.

Commandant Gelerowsky, second in command, and a Second Lieutenant came along and demanded to know why nobody ate the soup. Several sailors replied that the meat was tainted. Thereupon the officers returned to the wardroom without saying a word.

Nothing might have happened if the Lieutenant had not seated himself at the table and remained thoughtful without touching his food.

" Why do you not eat? " inquired Commandant Golikoff.

" How can one eat," replied the officer, " when we have on board 800 men who refuse their food? "

An ominous silence followed.

For sometime past the commander of the battleship had heard rumors of a conspiracy against the officers and of the threatened mutiny of the crew. So, after a moment's reflection, he called Sergeant-Major Pogownetz and ordered him to have the crew beat to service quarters on the main deck. When they were assembled, the Commander said:

" Why do you not eat the soup? "

There was no response.

Commander Golikoff repeated his question. Still no voice came from the crew. The Second Commandant said:

" They do not eat because the meat given them is full of worms."

A murmur of approval came from the ranks of the crew.

" Dr. Smirinoff," cried the Commandant, " is it true that this meat is full of worms? "

The Surgeon saluted, and approaching said:

" Commandant, this meat is fresh; it is healthful; it is good. I have never seen better."

Lieut. Gelerowsky turned upon him:

" What, good? I have seen it myself it is alive with vermin! "

The Surgeon, with a dark look, then said: " Possibly you saw it thus when it came from Odessa; since then I have had it salted; it is now good and fit to eat."

LAST SHOW OF DISCIPLINE.

At these words the Commander raised his hand. " Enough for the present," he said. " When the Surgeon says the meat is good, it is good. Those who are content to eat the soup will step to the right; those who do not to the left."

Slowly, one by one, the sailors passed to the right. But they moved with the step of men who act against their will; but—it was discipline.

When there remained only about thirty men who had not yet gone over—although these were preparing to move—the commander stopped them.

" Enough," he said. " Marines, arrest those men! "

Then the marines—even those who had a short time before complained—went after their arms and surrounded their thirty comrades. The commander went aft to his cabin.

One moment later Mastutchenko, a Sergeant Major, with a wild look in his eyes, sprang between decks and presently returned with a rifle. He drew himself up before the officers, crying:

" What would you do with those men? You are going to shoot them. Has not enough blood already been shed in this Russia? After the murders of Liao-Yang and Mukden, of St. Petersburg and Warsaw—after these the murders of the Potemkine? Enough! We might as well, right here, put an end to this reign of barbarity. Long live free Russia! Death to the officers! There are more of us than you. We are the masters. Down with tyranny! "

The Second Lieutenant, almost frantic, interposed: " Hold thy tongue, my poor fellow, or thou'lt be shot instantly! "

" It is thou who wilt be shot," yelled Mastutchenko as he presented his rifle.

The Lieutenant drew his pistol and fired. He missed Mastutchenko, but a sailor named Vakulenchonk fell dead.

There was a moment of stupor, then Mastutchenko cried: " Assassin! Thou hast slain Vakulenchonk! What hath he done to thee. He was innocent! "

With these words he fired on the Lieutenant, and the officer fell with blood dyeing his blonde mustache. Then followed a period of great confusion. The sailors ran about asking each other what should be done.

Pogownetz threw overboard the drum with which he had beaten the men to quarters. Mastutchenko shot two offi-

OVERTHROW OF THE OLD ORDER

cers who rushed upon him to disarm him. The surgeon fled to his cabin and shot himself through the stomach. Mastutchenko marked a fourth officer and instantly killed him.

That was too much. The sailors, wild with fury, ran between decks. Several officers threw themselves into the water and were followed by the petty officers. They swam toward the shore. But Mastutchenko would not have that, for they would betray him. He called eight or ten men to him. They began to shoot at the swimming officers, and soon killed them all.

MURDER OF THE CAPTAIN.

In the meantime the torpedo boat No. 267 noticed that something was wrong on board the Potemkine. Its officers made a shrewd guess, and started for the open sea. Pogownetz ordered a comrade to fire two blank shots at her. After these shots the boat was signaled to approach. When it came alongside the officers were ordered to come on board the battleship, and were then confined. The officer in charge of the dynamo protested.

"If thou wouldst speak to me," said Mastutchenko, "rip off thy shoulder straps and speak as man to man."

"What hast thou done with thy officers?" asked the officer.

"Thou wilt soon see," cried Mastutchenko, as he shot the officer dead.

At that moment the commander appeared from the cabin. He was an old man, with white hair and beard. He trembled convulsively. He cried: "What art thou about? Thou art an assassin!"

"Silence!" yelled Mastutchenko, "or I shall kill thee."

"Wouldst thou slay an old man like me? Thou knowest not what thou doest. Thou art mad!"

Mastutchenko put the rifle to his cheek and said: "Commend thy soul to God. In a second thou shalt be no more!"

Commandant Golikoff shuddered. He crossed himself. He had scarcely done so when he fell to the deck shot through the forehead.

Mastutchenko now gave orders to the sailors: "Arrest the officers that remain!"

The officers were arrested and solemnly stripped of their insignia of rank. Three ripped off their own shoulder straps, saying to the sailors: "We are with you for free Russia."

These three remained on board; one of them, Alexieff, was placed in command. The others were put in a boat and sent to Odessa.

It was half-past eleven when Mastutchenko began the revolt. By a quarter past twelve the sailors were masters of the Kniaz Potemkine. He called the men together and said:

"We are now going to declare war on all Russia which is not for liberty. The revolutionaries will follow us."

"Rabid creature that thou art," interrupted Pogownetz, "hast thou forgotten that on July 5 the crews of the entire fleet were to mutiny. The word has not yet been given to all. Thou beganst too soon. We shall not be followed."

"What is done is done. The mistake has been made. We must go on," replied Mastutchenko, and he began to intone the "International," and was followed by the sailors in unison. Finally the singing ceased. A deep silence prevailed, which was at length broken by groans.

"Who groaned?" demanded Mastutchenko. "Go thou and see Pogownetz."

Pogownetz went to find out. Presently he returned, saying that it was the surgeon lying wounded in his cabin.

"Ah, that pig, who is the cause of all, is sick!" ejaculated Mastutchenko. "What shall we do with him?"

"Death! Death! Let us kill him!" cried the sailors.

Twenty sailors precipitated themselves into the cabin. They grabbed up the surgeon by the feet and arms and threw him into the sea. From the rail Mastutchenko fired at him until the body disappeared beneath the surface.

The sailors became troubled and glanced at the mutineer while they murmured among themselves: "A stupid, unnecessary thing, that!"

They repeated these words under breath, for they were afraid of being heard by Mastutchenko, who with his fierce Tartar eyes watched and dominated them.

Whence came this Mastutchenko? Who knows? He himself says he comes from Siberia, but—there is something of the Japanese about him. He has been in the Russian Navy only three years, and no one knows where he was born or who were his parents.

Pogownetz is a Roumanian, from Bessarabia, which was absorbed by Russia twenty-five years ago. He has been in the navy eight years. He should have has his discharge a year ago, but on account of the war he was not allowed to go. He chafed under the enforced stay, and in him the seeds of mutiny and revolution found rich soil.

July 31, 1905

GRANT OF LIBERTY WRUNG FROM CZAR

Signs Decree, Admitting Peril to Empire.

STRIKERS BACK TO WORK

Railways to Moscow Open ---Factories Resume.

RADICALS NOT PACIFIED

Still Danger of a Clash-- Moderates Rejoice.

London Times—New York Times
Special Cable. Copyright, 1905.

ST. PETERSBURG, Oct. 30.—The people have won the day. The Emperor has surrendered. The autocracy has ceased to exist. A Constitution was signed at Peterhof at 4 o'clock this afternoon.

It is doubtful whether the grant of civic freedom, extended suffrage, a legislative Douma, and Ministerial responsibility, with M. Witte as Premier, and the consequent disappearance of the bureaucracy, which will be promulgated to-morrow, will satisfy the victorious revolutionary leaders, who demanded nothing less than universal suffrage and a constituent assembly.

It is doubtful even whether the reformers will consent to accept the concessions from the hands of the bureaucratic régime.

It is doubtful whether the forced surrender of the Government in the very midst of a revolutionary upheaval can be regarded otherwise than as a signal for further strife. To-morrow's manifesto, autocracy's last manifestation, will, however, bring to an end the acute stage of the Russian crisis and mark the starting point of a new era of political life.

The situation is still replete with possibilities of danger. The very success of the cause of freedom will only stimulate the reactionary elements to greater activity, and so long as the army remains under the present chiefs Russia cannot be safe from the possibility of a pronunciamento. Complete stability is not to be assured until the vast millions of untutored peasants share in the blessings of education.

The news of what was done at Peterhof to-day could not, in the absence of newspapers, be circulated generally among the inhabitants. The city continues to wear a sombre aspect. Troops still patrol the streets and the university remains closed.

The Minister of Finance was hurriedly summoned to the Imperial Bank to-day owing to a threatened strike of the employes. He assured them that if they would only have a little patience they would understand that a strike was unnecessary. Shortly afterward M. Witte telephoned him from Peterhof that the Emperor had signed a Constitution. M. Kokovtsoff immediately conveyed the news to the intending strikers, and they resumed work.

Special Cable to THE NEW YORK TIMES.
[Copyright, 1905.]

LONDON, Tuesday, Oct. 31.—The St. Petersburg correspondent of The Morning Post telegraphs as follows:

Count Witte's appointment was gazetted this evening. It was uncertain until the last moment, it being generally supposed that his traditional tactlessness had evoked a recrudescence of Imperial disfavor and wrecked the chances of the Cabinet project.

Much enthusiasm prevails among the Moderate Liberals, but revolutionary circles maintain an attitude of suspicion. One section demands that popu-

From Terrorism to Revolution

lar pressure be maintained until the real completion of the new régime is displayed. The other is almost hysterical over the victory for representative principles.

The immediately important question is whether Gen. Trepoff, whose energetic measures have baffled the amateurish efforts of the revolutionists, will loyally co-operate with Count Witte. Otherwise the present condition of the capital, which suggests a vast revolutionary picnic, will develop into absolute anarchy. It is too early to see absolutely what measure of support or opposition the new departure will receive from any particular faction.

I got this afternoon a partial list of Count Witte's Cabinet, which, though premature, comes from a well-informed source. It is:

Privy Councilor—M. Romanoff.

Minister of the Interior—Prince Alexis Obolenski.

Minister of Public Instruction—Senator Koni.

Minister of Ways and Communications—M. Zeigler.

Minister of Agriculture—M. Kutler.

STRIKERS RETURN TO WORK.

Lines to Moscow Reopened—Factory Tie-Up Broken.

ST. PETERSBURG, Tuesday, Oct. 31, (3:30 A. M.)—Even before the manifesto of the Czar was known to have been signed yesterday the strike began to break in industrial centres here.

Following the news many railway employes went back to work. The strike has ended on the Moscow and St. Petersburg, the Moscow and Kazan, and the Moscow and Archangel Railroads.

A meeting of the Strike Committee was held last night after the coming promulgation of the Emperor's manifesto was known. The question of calling the strike off was discussed, but a decision postponed until to-day.

A damper was thrown upon the strike enthusiasm by the news that work had been resumed in a large part of the factories of St. Petersburg, including eleven of the twelve departments of the Putiloff works, and that stores had been reopened. The committeemen talked boldly of their ability to call out the men again and to intimidate the store clerks into reclosing, but to-day will probably put a good face on the situation and issue a proclamation calling off the strike until January.

The authorities asserted that only 23,000 factory hands, mostly in the Schlusselberg district along the river, were on strike to-day.

The Strike Committee has brought out the first number of the Workmen's Gazette, the "official gazette" of the strikers' organization, which was devoted to ponderous proclamations in the style of the Government documents and to news of the strike movement in St. Petersburg.

The welcome tidings of the grant of liberty by the Czar reached St. Petersburg shortly before 6 o'clock last evening. Count Witte had spent the day with the Emperor at Peterhof, going over the final draft of the manifesto to which he insisted that certain minor modifications be made. Before taking the train for St. Petersburg he telephoned to a friend that the Emperor had affixed his signature and that the imperial mandate was in his pocket.

An official announcement was issued soon after, saying:

"An imperial manifesto will be issued this evening, appointing Count Witte Prime Minister, with special authority to co-ordinate and unify the powers of the different branches of the administration. Civic liberties are granted to the Russian people and to the National Assembly is given legislative power, while the suffrage is enlarged."

Broad Grant of Freedom.

Count Witte returned to his home in the evening, and the text of the Czar's decree was made known.

A simple perusal of the manifesto shows how complete is the Emperor's abdication of his autocratic power. The very style of the document is clear and direct and devoid of the verbose, vague, and bombastic phraseology which heretofore has characterized his Majesty's decrees.

It not only betrays real authorship, but shows that the Emperor at last has irrevocably bowed to the inevitable. He does not even conceal the fact that the discontent and agitation of his subjects has driven him to take the step and practically yields everything—civil liberty, the inviolability of person, and liberty of conscience, speech, and assembly.

He not only converts the farcical imperial douma, with only consultative power, into a true legislative assembly, without the assent of which no measure shall become law and before which all

---

THE CZAR'S CHARTER OF LIBERTY TO ONE-TENTH OF THE HUMAN RACE

Text of the Historic Document Signed at Peterhof Yesterday by Nicholas II.

"We, Nicholas II., by the grace of God Emperor and Autocrat of All the Russias, Grand Duke of Finland, &c., declare to all our faithful subjects that the troubles and agitation in our capitals and in numerous other places fill our heart with excessive pain and sorrow.

"The happinesss of the Russian sovereign is indissolubly bound up with the happiness of our people and the sorrow of our people is the sorrow of the sovereign.

"From the present disorders may arise great national disruption. They menace the intergrity and unity of our empire.

"The supreme duty imposed upon us by our sovereign office requires us to efface ourself and to use all the force and reason at our command to hasten in securing the unity and co-ordination of the power of the Central Government and to assure the success of measures for pacification in all circles of public life, which are essential to the well-being of our people.

"We, therefore, direct our Government to carry out our inflexible will in the following manner:

"First—To extend to the population the immutable foundations of civic liberty, based on the real inviolability of person, freedom of conscience, speech, union, and association.

"Second—Without suspending the already ordered elections to the State Douma, to invite to participation in the Douma, so far as the limited time before the convocation of the Douma will permit, those classes of the population now completely deprived of electoral rights, leaving the ultimate development of the principle of the electoral right in general to the newly established legislative order of things.

"Third—To establish as an unchangeable rule that no law shall be enforceable without the approval of the State Douma, and that it shall be possible for the elected of the people to exercise real participation in the supervision of the legality of the acts of the authorities appointed by us.

"We appeal to all faithful sons of Russia to remember their duty toward the Fatherland, to aid in terminating these unprecedented troubles, and to apply all their forces, in co-operation with us, to the restoration of calm and peace upon our natal soil.

"Given at Peterhof, October 30th, in the eleventh year of our reign.

"NICHOLAS."

OVERTHROW OF THE OLD ORDER

Governmental authorities must answer, but promises, eventually, universal suffrage. The title, "Autocrat of all the Russians" with which the manifesto begins, now takes its place with title of "King of Jerusalem," borne by the King of Spain and the Emperor of Austria, and with other obsolete titles of European sovereigns.

J. Pierpont Morgan, Jr., and George W. Perkins were with Finance Minister Kokovsoff when the latter received the news. It was a dramatic moment. The Minister was called to the telephone, and when he returned he was greatly agitated, and said:

"Gentlemen, the old order of things has changed. Russia has a Constitution."

October 31, 1905

SEEK A SOCIALIST UTOPIA.

Russian Radicals Want Far More Than the Overthrow of Autocracy.

ST. PETERSBURG, Nov. 11.—Perhaps the most interesting phase of the confused situation in Russia is the attitude of the Social Democrats, who claim all the credit for the overthrow of absolutism and who are determined that they shall not be cheated out of the fruit of victory. Not only a democratic republic, but a universal Socialistic Utopia is their dream.

Their far-reaching programme is announced in two papers, which have just been launched, the Novaia Zhizn (New Life) and Nashalo, (The Beginning.) The staffs of the papers are composed of forty of the most brilliant writers in Russia, including Maxim Gorky and M. Kieff, author of "The Red Laugh."

Political visionaries those men may be, but they have embraced the doctrine of international Socialism with their whole hearts, and are bound to exercise great influence on Russian thought in the present chaotic conditions. They openly scorn the teachings of history, declaring that the world is entering on a new stage of social and political evolution. After the complete overthrow of the present régime in Russia they propose to erect upon the ruins a new politico-social edifice, which will form the nucleus of the future Utopian system of international democracy and the achievement of political equality. The next step will be the leveling of all social ranks. They already speak with contempt of their present allies as the bourgeoisie, for whom the overthrow of absolutism was the final goal. Gorky says:

"For the proletariat the political revolution is only one stage on the road to social revolution. The bourgeoisie are content with half measures and half reforms. We unite with them for the purpose of securing guarantees of political freedom, but later we will demand guarantees from them and we will be entitled to them.

"All the former despotic Governments of Europe were overthrown by the people under the leadership of the bourgeoisie. They resulted, however, only in setting up constitutional monarchies, which are paradises for the bourgeoisie perhaps, but economic hells for the workmen. Russia is the only country owing its evolution to an organized army of workmen who are able to oppose the forces of the Government with a weapon which has paralyzed the nation's heart.

"The greatest credit for the victory thus far achieved belongs to the noble-minded body of students, who years ago began to realize their historic mission. They acted the part of an alarm clock for the working classes, and have been the yeast of the proletariat movement. For years they unsuccessfully tried to arouse the peasantry and wandered through the villages, but they preached to deaf ears and were finally driven to follow the line of least resistance, and turned back to the cities and in the shops and factories found the men who accomplished the October Revolution."

Gorky makes a scathing characterization of the attitude of the bourgeoisie, in which he classes the Zemstvoists and other Constitutionalists, who now, he says, would like to play the rôle of "the progenitors of Mark Twain," adding:

"While the workman's army marched to battle they hung in the rear, but when the army returned after destroying the outer bulwarks of the autocracy they were at the head singing songs of triumph."

Continuing, Gorky draws a contemptuous picture of the self-satisfied tradesmen in the cities, "with their eyes blinded to the great tragedy of life, everlastingly content if they only can live upon the gains stolen from labor, soothing their minds with the delusion that they are cultivating their souls with promises of religion made up of century-old lies."

November 12, 1905

CZAR'S ARTILLERY WIPES OUT REBELS

Moscow Building Wrecked, Burying Hundreds of Insurgents.

MASSACRE BY BLACK HUNDRED

ST. PETERSBURG, Dec. 30.—Gov. Gen. Doubassoff has telegraphed to the Government from Moscow that a meeting of several thousand revolutionists and strikers to-day at the Prokharoff cotton mill outside the city was surrounded by troops of all arms.

The artillery opened a terrific bombardment and made a large rent in the walls, which suddenly crumbled, and the building came down in a heap. Hundreds if not a thousand persons were buried in the ruins.

Admiral Doubassoff regarded the Prokharoff mills as the stronghold of the revolutionists, and he reports that Moscow will be entirely cleared of them in three days.

The Governor General also reports that he prevented several thousand "Loyalists" who assembled in the Sakolniki district, in the outskirts of Moscow, from marching into the city for the purpose of attacking the strikers, revolutionists, and Jews.

No further details have been received of the horrible affair at the Prokharoff mill, except a statement that hundreds perished.

The attempt of the "Black Hundred" to march into the city and wreak vengeance on the revolutionaries and strikers only tends to confirm the fears that the final collapse of the revolt at Moscow will be followed by an awful massacre, and although Admiral Doubassoff succeeded in preventing their entry into the city to-day, and will take stern measures in the future, it will be difficult to restrain the lower classes, who regard the revolutionaries as enemies of the Emperor and the country. Already rowdies are taking advantage of the situation to plunder on a large scale.

Gov. Gen. Doubassoff has not yet given the figures of the losses during the fighting at Moscow, saying that it is impossible at present to do more than make a guess. However, he places the outside limit of the insurgents' losses at 3,000. The troops and police did not suffer nearly so heavily, and it is reported that up to Thursday night there were less than fifty casualties among them everywhere.

The police force of Moscow has been increased by a thousand men and the night watchmen by two thousand men.

In an encounter between workmen and Cossacks yesterday at the Nevski Shipbuilding Yards here, eight Cossacks and twenty-seven workmen were killed and many were injured.

The railroad trains from St. Petersburg to Moscow are not running to that city, but are stopping at a station near Tver.

December 31, 1905

RUSSIAN DEMOCRATS MEET.

First National Political Convention Held in the Country.

ST. PETERSBURG, Jan. 18.—The first national convention organized by a political party in the history of Russia, that of the Constitutional Democrats, opened here to-day. Two hundred and fifty delegates, representing sixty provincial organizations, were present.

Under the Chairmanship of M. Petrunkevitch of Tver, the convention took up the discussion of the first topic on the programme—the party's attitude toward the elections to the National Assembly. Prof. Millukoff, M. Hessen, a well-known editor, and Prince Hakoffsky were the leading speakers. The two first named advocated participation in the Douma, but only so long as it was shown that the majority of the Douma sympathized with the principles of the Constitutional Democratic Party.

Undismayed by the arrests of their successive Executive Committees, a group of Socialistic workmen early this morning elected a new Workmen's Council, whose President issued an address threatening with death all who do not obey the command to abstain from work on Jan. 22, the anniversary of "Red Sunday."

January 19, 1906

35

From Terrorism to Revolution

FUNDAMENTAL LAW DRAFT PROMULGATED IN RUSSIA

Was Thought to Have Perished with Witte Regime.

NEW CABINET IS COMPLETED

Constitutional Democrats Modify Scheme to Supply Landless Peasants with Homes.

ST. PETERSBURG, Tuesday, May 8.—Another of the kaleidoscopic changes in the political situation, to which Russia is becoming accustomed, occurred late last night, when, with utter unexpectedness, the draft of the fundamental law which was supposed to have perished with the Witte régime was officially promulgated and made the permanent basis of the Russian State, unalterable except on the initiative of Emperor Nicholas or his successors.

Published at the present instant, when the people had been led to believe that the unpopular draft had been dropped, and when the dismissal of the old Cabinet was accepted as an indication of the desire on the part of the Government to join hands with the national Parliament, the news will arouse still greater indignation, and threatens to undo all the work of Prof. Milukoff and the other Constitutional Democratic leaders in the cause of moderation.

The new Russian Cabinet has been completed, and will be announced by Imperial ukase to-day as follows:
Premier—M. GOREMYKIN.
Minister of the Interior—M. STOLYPIN.
Minister of Foreign Affairs—Baron ISWOLSKY.
Minister of Finance—M. POKOVSOFF.
Minister of Education—M. KAUFFMAN.
Minister of Agriculture—M. STICHINSKY.
Minister of Commerce—M. RUKHLOFF.
Controller of the Empire—M. von SCHWANEBACH.
Procurator General of the Holy Synod—Prince SHIRINSKY SCHAKMATOFF.
Minister of War—Gen. RUDIGER.
Minister of Marine—Vice Admiral BIRILEFF.
Minister of Justice—M. CHTCHEGLOVITOFF.

The Constitutional Democrats are modifying the original scheme to satisfy the more radical demands of the peasants. As maturing, it is, briefly, a proposition not only to supply land to all landless peasants, but to round out and make adequate the land of those who rent or have insufficient land, the amount of land to be allotted to each to depend upon the region.

The question of financing this gigantic undertaking, involving more than $1,000,000,000 of credit operations, has not yet been approached in detail.

The amount of land which it is proposed shall be distributed can be judged from the present holdings. In forty-nine provinces, comprising 1,054,170,000 acres, the Crown holds 406,080,000 acres, the Imperial family 19,980,000 acres, the church 22,950,000 acres, and the big landowners 250,180,000 acres, while the peasants, numbering about 45,000,000, have 354,890,000 acres, an average of a little more than eight acres per capita.

May 8, 1906

DUMA DISSOLVED; ARMY IN CAPITAL

Martial Law Declared—Dictatorship May Be the Next Step.

NO PARLIAMENT TILL MARCH

ST. PETERSBURG, Sunday, July 22.—Russia's first experiment in parliamentary government came to an ignominious end to-day with the promulgation of two Imperial ukases, the first dissolving the present Parliament and providing for the convocation of its successor on March 5, 1907, and the second proclaiming the capital of Russia and the surrounding province to be in a "state of extraordinary security," which is only infinitesimally different from full martial law. This measure of safety is to provide for the outbursts which undoubtedly will be provoked by the dissolution of the Duma. It is now but a step to a dictatorship.

The texts of the two ukases, both of which are addressed to the Ruling Senate, are as follows:

According to Paragraph 105 of the Fundamental Law we order the Imperial Parliament dissolved, and fix the time for the convocation of the newly elected Parliament as March 5, 1907.

Regarding the time for the new elections to the Imperial Parliament we will later issue special indications.

The Ruling Senate will not fail to take proper measures to place this into effect.
Peterhof, July 21.   NICHOLAS.

In consideration of a report of the Council of Ministers presented to us regarding the necessity in the future for the preservation of order and public safety in the City and Province of St. Petersburg, we consider it necessary to declare in the above city and province, instead of the state of reinforced security which now prevails there, a state of extraordinary security. The Prefect of the City and the Governor of the Province are intrusted with the rights thereto appertaining.

The Ruling Senate will not fail to take proper measures to place this into effect.
Peterhof, July 21.   NICHOLAS.

With these orders, which were promulgated at 3 o'clock this morning, Emperor Nicholas by a stroke of the pen set Russia back to where she stood two years ago—in the full grip of autocracy and irresponsible government—wiping out for six months at least the whole structure of Parliament, erected at such cost.

There is little doubt that the convocation of the new Assembly will be still further postponed unless the new Parliament promises to be more amenable than the present.

The delay in fixing the time for the elections seems to indicate a decision to change the present basis of suffrage to a basis of universal suffrage, by means of which the advisers of the Emperor hope to swamp the educated Liberals, the Socialists, and the workmen with the vast mass of the peasantry.

The only uncertainty is the coming storm—when and where will it break? The advocates of the "mailed fist" believe that by dissolving Parliament and provoking a collision now they will find the revolutionary leaders unprepared for an uprising, whereas further delay would give the Revolutionists the time needed to organize and to continue the corruption of the army.

July 22, 1906

DUMA URGES REVOLT AS IT IS DISPERSED

Moderates Join Radicals When Menaced by Bayonets.

MANIFESTO TO THE NATION

VIBORG, Finland, July 23.—The curtain dropped this afternoon on the final act of the drama of Russia's first Parliament when, under the spur of the threat of Gov. Rechanberg to use military force to end the session, and with troops already converging on the Hotel Belvedere, where the meeting was held, the assembled members of the lower house, 186 in number, hurriedly adopted and signed an address to the people which is thoroughly revolutionary in its nature, elected a perpetual Executive Committee headed by Prince Paul Dolgoroukoff, Vice President of the House, to carry on the work of liberation, and adjourned, amid characteristic Russian embracing and kissing.

A few members, including President Mouromtseff, Ivan Petrunkevitch, and Count Heyden, returned to St. Petersburg by evening trains. The Constitutional Democratic cohorts intend to go to St. Petersburg in a body in the morning, but many of the radical members, fearing arrest on their arrival at the capital, will remain for the present in Finland or return by roundabout routes.

The address, which bears a remarkable similarity to the manifesto framed by the Council of Workmen last November, which landed its authors and the editors of eight St. Petersburg newspapers in cells of the Fortress of St. Peter and St. Paul, strikes the Government in its most vulnerable point, by declaring that the Administration, and not Parliament, is responsible for the delay in the settlement of the agrarian question, and by proclaiming a cessation of payment of taxes and of military service and repudiation of future loans. The address is as follows:

"TO THE PEOPLE FROM THEIR POPULAR REPRESENTATIVES.

"Citizens of All Russia: Parliament has been dissolved by ukase of July 21. You elected us as your representatives and instructed us to fight for our country and freedom. In execution of your instructions and our duty, we drew up laws in order to insure freedom to the people. We demanded the removal of irresponsible Ministers who were infringing the laws with impunity and oppressing freedom. First of all, however, we wanted to bring out a law respecting the distribution of land to working peasants and involving the assignment, to this end, of Crown appanages, monasteries, and lands belonging to the clergy, and compulsory expropriation of private estates.

"The Government held such a law to be inadmissible, and upon Parliament once more urgently putting forward its resolution regarding compulsory expropriation Parliament was dissolved.

"The Government promises to convoke a new Parliament seven months hence. Russia must remain without popular representation for seven whole months, at a time when the people are standing on the brink of ruin and industry and commerce are undermined, when the whole country is seething with unrest, and when the Ministry has definitely shown its incapacity to do justice to popular needs. For seven months the Government will act arbitrarily and will fight against the popular movement, in order to obtain a pliable, subservient Parliament. Should it succeed, however, in completely suppressing the popular movement, the Government will convoke no Parliament at all.

"Citizens, stand up for your trampled-on rights, for popular representation, and for an Imperial Parliament. Russia must not remain a day without popular representation. You possess the means of acquiring it. The Government has, without the assent of the popular representatives, no right to collect taxes from the people nor to summon the people to military service. Therefore you are now the Government. The dissolved Parliament was justified in giving neither money nor soldiers. Should the Government, however, contract loans in order to procure funds, such loans will be invalid. Without the consent of the popular representatives the Russian people will never acknowledge them and will not be called upon to pay them.

"Accordingly, until a popular representative Parliament is summoned do not give a kopeck to the throne or a soldier to the army. Be steadfast in your refusal. No power can resist the united, inflexible will of the people.

"Citizens, in this obligatory and unavoidable struggle your representatives will be with you."

July 24, 1906

STOLYPIN'S NEW POLICY, REPRESSION AND REFORM

Court-Martial for Political Crimes in Russia.

ZEMSTVOS FOR PROVINCES

Black Sea Fleet and Troops at Sevastopol Distrusted—Terrorism for Terrorists.

ST. PETERSBURG, Sept. 5.—An official communication embodying part of the Government programme was published tonight. The programme embraces courts-martial for political crimes and an increase of the penalties for revolutionary propaganda, and expresses a firm determination to preserve order. It also promises a liberal measure of reforms and that useless restrictions on Jews shall be abolished forthwith. Measures are promised in the direction of greater provincial autonomy. Zemstvos will be introduced in Poland and the Baltic provinces. An income tax will be instituted. Reforms in the police and other public services also are promised.

The communication, which was issued after protracted discussion by Premier Stolypin and the Council of Ministers, leaves the situation but little altered. The one thing evident is that the Premier intends to carry out broad reforms on one hand and to pursue a policy of repression on the other. The establishment of courts-martial for political crimes signifies supperial ukase instituting this law is extraordinary insecurity exists.

An imperial ukase instituting this law was issued after the publication of the communication. It empowers Governor Generals, where martial law or extraordinary security exists, to place civilians or military charged with crime upon trial before a military court consisting of five officers, the trial to take not longer than seventy-two hours from the beginning of the process to the execution of the verdict. This is entirely a new law, as heretofore in practice only military or naval mutinies and uprisings, such as that in the Baltic provinces last Fall, were occasions for court-martial, and St. Petersburg, Moscow, Warsaw, and practically the whole of Russia are now under this category.

The programme as announced in the official communication is not the full one of the Government, which probably will be issued at the end of September or early in October.

A general meeting of Octoberists and peaceful regenerationists will be held at the end of September. It is believed that at that time the Octoberist party will be dissolved or merged with the peaceful regenerationists.

The Council of Ministers has sanctioned the plan permitting the Jews to open elementary and secondary schools under the same conditions as people of other creeds.

The long struggle of the Georgian people to regain the autonomy of the Georgian Church, lost after the incorporation of the ancient kingdom with Russia, which has been carried on by interdict and boycott and all the other means at the disposal of the patriotic Church and people, has resulted in a partial victory.

The Emperor, on the recommendation of the Holy Synod, has declared the creation of a Church Council, composed of three Georgian Bishops, of which body a Russian Archbishop will only be the nominal head, and the restoration of the old Georgian language to its place in Church literature. A commission has also been created to translate the Bible into modern Georgian.

It is doubtful, however, if these partial concessions will be effective. It is stated that the Georgians will be satisfied with nothing less than the reinstitution of the ancient Georgian Catholicos as head of the Church instead of the present Archbishop, who is a Russian nominee. The Catholicos was subordinate only to the Emperor or Patriarch, as he was the recognized head of the Greek Church throughout the world. The boycott, which has now been in effect for over a year, will probably be continued until this is attained.

For several months the Georgian Church has virtually been conducting its own affairs, having driven out one Russian Archbishop, and his successor not daring to go to Tiflis until concessions were granted. He arrived at Tiflis to-day, but was not welcomed by anybody except the Russian officials.

Admiral Skrydloff, commander of the Black Sea Fleet, and the military commander at Sevastopol are very apprehensive, both regarding the attitude of the sailors of the fleet and the garrison of the fortress. The annual cruise of the training squadron off the coast of Tendra Island, near the Gulf of Perekop, as well as the regular fleet manoeuvres, have been abandoned. The warships will only make short trips to sea, scarcely venturing beyond the range of the guns of the forts.

The military patrols in the city have been withdrawn inside the walls of the forts, the Governor announcing that the men are needed for their regular military training, but it is said that the step is due to fear that the soldiers will be corrupted if they are allowed to be in contact with the masses.

The merchants of this city have practically been thrown on their own resources in the matter of protection from lawlessness. The Governor, at a recent meeting of merchants, advised them to organize their own guard for the protection of property, as soldiers could no longer be spared for police duty and as the municipality is bankrupt and unable to maintain efficient protection.

In answer to the publication of a notice from the Terrorists that a sentence of death had been imposed on Col. Dumbadze, commander of a rifle regiment here, the officers of that corps in an open letter have announced that in case of an attack being made on the Colonel they will exact vengeance on the leaders of the progressive parties.

The trial of 200 participants in the recent mutinous outbreak, including M. Onipko, one of the peasant leaders in the outlawed Parliament, and 50 other civilians, began at Cronstadt to-day behind closed doors. There are over 1,000 witnesses.

September 6, 1906

From Terrorism to Revolution

RUSSIAN SOCIALISTS AGAINST TERRORISM

Conference in London Likely to Declare for Peaceful Organization.

SPLIT IN DUMA EXPECTED

Both Sides Prepare for It—Constitutional Democrats to Make More Stringent Rules.

LONDON, May 14.—An important statement on the progress and purposes of the Russian Socialist Conference, which is being held here in secret, was made today by Delegate Rothstein.

"The principal points for discussion by this conference are now settled," he said. "Among the most important is the attitude of the Social Democrats toward the Constitutional Democrats. The present trend of feeling is for a definite split between the two parties.

"It is expected that this congress will give authoritative condemnation to the terrorist campaign. A majority of the delegates are of the opinion that the best tactics will be peaceably to organize the working classes. They regard the terrorist as a factor tending to disunite the forces. This view is opposed by the Polish delegates, who are in desperate circumstances and inclined to favor a more militant method.

"The attitude of the party toward trades unionism, which latterly has developed by leaps and bounds, also will be discussed. All the delegates welcome the development of trades unionism as an evidence of the organization of the working classes, which is bound to be valuable when open war is declared. Some go further and desire to see trades unionism developed along distinctly Socialistic lines, while others prefer to leave it unhampered by party politics as in the United States and England.

"It is absurd to say that this congress will decide the fate of the Duma. We do not regard the Duma as a serious legislative machine, but as a useful means for carrying on agitation. If the Constitutional Democrats endeavor to present amendments to the Parliamentary rules designed to strengthen the hands of the President in preserving order, to prevent filibustering by the minority, and increase the working capacity of the House, it will only show that they are becoming more and more reactionary, and it will result in a great increase of recruits to the Social Democratic Party."

The delegates were in session until 11 o'clock last night and met again this morning. The precaution of secrecy is still rigorously maintained. All the delegates travel under assumed names and address each other simply as "comrade."

The Russian Embassy is not taking any action to prevent the conference, which is being held in Whitechapel. An official of the embassy said that any discussion taking place in London could do no harm. He admitted, however, that detectives from Russia were watching the proceedings with the view of preventing the more violent of the agitators returning to Russia.

The little knot of men from Scotland Yard who have been watching the meeting house in Whitechapel were joined today by three members of the Russian secret police.

May 15, 1907

A FAMOUS REBEL IN LONDON.

Lenin Will Be Arrested If He Returns to Russia—Real Name Ulianoff.

ST. PETERSBURG, May 20.—A warrant has been issued for the arrest of Nikolai Lenin, leader of the majority faction now attending the Social Democratic Congress in London, on the charge of high treason. He will be taken into custody if he returns to Russia. The warrant reads "Vladimir Ulianoff, alias Lenin."

It is said that the police have identified Lenin as a noted Radical leader of the early nineties and a brother of the Ulianoff who, with four comrades, all armed with bombs, was arrested in 1887 while lying in wait for the carriage of Emperor Alexander III., and was condemned to death and executed. Vladimir took up the mission of the brother who was executed and was continually hunted for by the St. Petersburg police. He successfully evaded capture until 1897, when he was arrested and sent to Siberia for organizing the first political strike in Russia.

He escaped in 1901 and disappeared. It is stated that he reappeared in St. Petersburg under the name of Lenin after the publication of the amnesty decree of 1905 and immediately assumed his old ascendancy in the Social Democratic Party. He laughed at the endeavors of the police, who believed him to be a new leader, to arrest him, and boldly declared himself a candidate, under his real name, for election from St. Petersburg to the second Parliament. Recently, however, the police determined to arrest him and he removed to Finland.

Lenin is regarded by the police as being the most dangerous and most capable of all the Revolutionary leaders. He is well known as a writer on economic subjects.

May 21, 1907

SOCIALISTS QUIT LIBERALS IN DUMA

Extremists, After Days of Wrangling, Win in the London Congress.

CENTRE PARTY NOT SORRY

Constitutionalists Have Found Co-operation with Socialists Embarrassing—Miliukoff Returns.

LONDON, May 30.—The congress of Russian Social Democrats, which has been in session in this city since May 13, decided to-day by a majority of fifty-three votes definitely to sever all relations with the Constitutional Democrats and other Liberal parties in Russia. Thus the Extremists regain the control of the party, which they lost a year ago.

This decision was reached after days of wrangling and passionate discussion and constant narrow divisions on the clauses of the resolutions.

The Majorities and the Minorities both put forward resolutions, but all attempts to reach a common ground were unavailable. The Majorities, conscious of the strength of their alliance with the Poles and the Letts, refused all compromise. Eventually, the congress decided by a majority of nine to consider a resolution of the Majorities declaring that the Constitutional Democrats had completely turned their backs upon the revolution, that they openly supported the Government in a plan to bring about an anti-Democratic Constitution based on property qualifications, and that their aims did not go beyond the constitution of a monarchy safeguarded by a police régime, the two-chamber system, and a standing army against the attacks of the proletariat.

Social Democracy, the resolution continues, must oppose the extension of these parties of constitutional illusions and must uncompromisingly combat the hegemony of a petty middle class. The resolution further declares that it is necessary to wean the Populist and the Toil parties from the influence of the Liberals, and compel them to choose between the policy of the Constitutional Democrats and the Black Hundreds and that of the Social Democrats.

This resolution was adopted by 159 votes to 108, many of the delegates abstaining from voting.

The Congress is now discussing a motion to call a non-partisan labor congress.

May 31, 1907

OVERTHROW OF THE OLD ORDER

CZAR ENDS DUMA BY COUP D'ETAT

Violates Solemn Pledge by Ordering Election Nov. 14 Under a New Law.

WILL LIMIT FRANCHISE

Troops Fill the Capital and Repressive Measures Are Instituted.

Special Cablegram.
Copyright, 1907, by The New York Times Co.

ST. PETERSBURG, Sunday, June 16.—The Czar dissolved the Duma early this morning after a night session, and while the committee was still considering the indictments against the Social Democrats accused of conspiring against the throne.

All the party leaders were convinced last night that the end of the Duma was in sight.

The general impression is that some of the Socialists probably were engaged in a conspiracy, but that the Government was acting without proper proofs. Count Pototsky, a wealthy Polish Conservative nobleman, a member of the Duma, told me that the long indictment read by the Procurator was only balderdash. It was silly to expect the Duma to convict people instantly on a vague, rambling document like this. The Government's ideas of legal evidence are extraordinary. A month ago, for instance, the Minister of Justice accused a member of the Duma of conspiracy to murder the Czar on the strength of evidence the police would have got had they raided his rooms half an hour earlier. Hence the Poles, though hating terrorism, joined for the sake of justice the majority of the Duma in condemning Premier Stolypin's demand.

ST. PETERSBURG, Sunday, June 16.—Emperor Nicholas affixed his signature this morning to an imperial ukase abolishing the present Duma and ordering that the elections of members to its successor, which is to meet Nov. 14, be held under a new election law which provides against the "submergence of the educated classes by the uneducated masses."

This act constitutes a virtual coup d'etat and overrides the specific provisions of the fundamental laws of the realm, solemnly proclaimed by his Majesty on the eve of the convocation of the first Duma, which declared that the electoral law could never be changed without the consent of Parliament itself.

This breach of the Constitution is justified by the great law of necessity, the advisers of the Emperor holding it impossible, under present conditions, to obtain a Parliament capable of co-operating harmoniously with the Crown to rescue Russia from anarchy and revolution.

The session of the Council of Ministers at which the decision to dissolve Parliament was reached was a long one. It lasted from 9 o'clock last night until nearly 4 o'clock this morning. The Ministers had agreed upon the terms of the ukase before midnight, however, and a draft of the ukase was taken immediately to Peterhof, where the Emperor affixed his signature.

The news of the dissolution was received just before 2 o'clock this morning, but the meeting of the Cabinet was continued until the arrival of the signed document. This document was delivered by Premier Stolypin into the hands of the official printers for publication in the Official Messenger and the Rossia this morning.

Text of the Ukase.

The imperial ukase is addressed to the ruling Senate, and reads as follows:

According to Paragraph 105 of the fundamental laws of 1906 we ordain: Firstly, that the imperial Duma be dissolved; secondly, that new elections of members to another Duma be held, beginning Sept. 14, and thirdly, that the new imperial Duma be convoked Nov. 14 of the present year.

The ruling Senate will not fail to take proper measures to place this in effect.

NICHOLAS.

Peterhof, June 16.

This ukase is countersigned by the President of the Council of Ministers, P. A. Stolypin.

The ukase is accompanied by a manifesto setting forth the motives which led the Emperor to dissolve the Duma. The Czar adverts to the Duma's rejection of temporary laws, its refusal to condemn terrorism, the delay in ratifying the budget, the open revolutionary spirit of a large portion of its members, the abuse of the right of interpellation, and finally the failure of the Duma to comply immediately with the demand for the exclusion of the fifty-five Social Democratic members charged with conspiracy against the present regime.

These various evils are ascribed to defects in the electoral law, consequently the Emperor decided to change the basis of suffrage so that every part of the Russian population should be represented in the lower house of parliament. The representation of the non-Russian nationalities, the manifesto continues, should be decreased in order to prevent these delegates from becoming a decisive factor in purely Russian questions, and elections in the frontier regions, where the standard of civil development is low, should be temporarily suspended.

These necessary changes in the mode of elections cannot be submitted to the Duma, the composition of which is unsatisfactory on account of the defects in the election law itself, but to the authority which was granted the first election law belongs the right to substitute new bases of suffrage.

June 16, 1907

THOUSANDS KILLED IN RUSSIAN TERROR

Forty-four Thousand on the Roll from February, 1905, Until Last June.

ST. PETERSBURG, Sept. 25.—Although the elections to the third Duma are attracting only lukewarm attention, a sensation has been created by the publication in the Novoe Vremya of an article setting forth the number of lives sacrificed in the Russian revolutionary movement from the announcement of the first Duma, in February, 1905, down to the time of the second dissolution last June. Although no name is signed to the article, the statistics in it are said to be furnished from official sources and, for that reason, they should not be regarded as an exaggeration—quite the contrary.

It is stated that during this time 44,020 suffered through the terrorism régime and the reaction against terrorism, of whom 19,144 were killed, 2,381 were executed or lynched, 1,350 committed suicide, 20,704 were wounded, and 441 were the objects of fruitless assaults. The last figure seems surprisingly small, and, in general, these statistics must have a more or less casual character. The total is thus distributed by territories: Russia proper, 20,611; the Caucasus, 7,394; Finland and the Baltic provinces, 4,929; Poland, 4,385; the western provinces, 3,048, and Siberia and Central Asia, 2,268. Collisions with military and police are credited with 12,953 casualties, anti-Semitic riots with 7,969, anti-Armenian riots with 4,540, Black Gang attacks on others than Jews with 2,778, and military and naval risings with 2,193 victims. Agrarian disturbances are credited with only 533 acts of violence against human life, lynch justice claimed 412, and inter-necine warfare among working men 298. In accordance with the usual revolutionary classification, it is found that about a fifth—8,203—of the total were representatives of the Government and of the capitalistic classes.

October 6, 1907

39

From Terrorism to Revolution

SAY CZAR APPROVES JEWISH MASSACRES

German Relief League Hears He Calls Pogrom Leaders Heroes.

PARDONS FOR THEM ALL

None of the Sentences Pronounced Against Them Shall Be Carried Out, He Declares.

Special Cable to THE NEW YORK TIMES.

BERLIN, Feb. 13.—Startling allegations of the Czar's complicity in the pogroms, which in the last two or three years have led to the massacring of hundreds of Jews in various parts of Russia, have reached the German Jewish Relief League from believed to be trustworthy sources.

It is stated that at an audience he granted recently to Count Konownitzyns, leader of the Odessa branch of the "Genuine Russians' Union," the Czar said:

"It is true that the courts, in accordance with the strict letter of the law, have had to convict certain leaders of anti-Jewish mobs; but I give you my imperial word that none of the sentences against these heroes shall be carried out."

The Czar's policy has accorded perfectly with this speech. He has issued pardons by the wholesale, within a short time, to men convicted of leading anti-Semitic outbreaks.

Men recently on trial for organizing pogroms in Orscha shouted to the Judges: "Sentence us to anything you please; the Czar is our protector."

The Czar's sympathy with the Russian pogrom leaders was recently set forth by one of the Russian correspondents of The London Times in a dispatch summing up the anti-Jewish outrages in Southern Russia.

For two years, the correspondent said, the League of the Russian People, called also the Black Hundreds, had been murdering and pillaging in Odessa, encouraged by Gen. Kaulbars, but against the protests of the Prefect of the city, Gen. Grigorieff. Worn out by this state of affairs, Grigorieff proceeded to St. Petersburg to report upon the situation to the Czar. What followed is told by The Times's correspondent, as follows:

"Having arrived at the capital, the General sought an audience with the Emperor. He had made up his mind to tell his imperial master the whole truth, in order that the latter might help him to put a stop to the crimes of the league. The audience was granted, and, laboring under deep emotion, the old General awaited the appearance of his sovereign.

"When the Emperor approached Gen. Grigorieff the latter perceived with dismay that the breast of the Czar was decorated with the badge of the League of the Russian People, the very same that he had seen so often in Odessa on the breasts of the perpetrators of the pogroms. This produced such an effect upon him that, forgetting the speech he had prepared with such care, he stammered out a few commonplaces as a faithful subject of the Czar and retired in confusion.

"Immediately afterward the President of the Council of Ministers informed Major Gen. Grigorieff that his Majesty the Emperor had been graciously pleased to relieve him of the post of Prefect of Odessa and had promoted him to the rank of Lieutenant General. This happened at the end of July, 1907.

"The recall of Gen. Grigorieff, coupled with the subsequent act of the imperial clemency which systematically set free all persons sentenced in the Odessa courts for plundering or murdering the Jews, was sufficiently significant, and had the natural effect of still further encouraging the members of the league. From the month of August to the present time Odessa has in consequence been uninterruptedly under the reign of the Black Terror."

February 14, 1908

"I CANNOT BE SILENT"
By Count Leo Tolstoy

The Frequency of Executions in Russia Provokes a Denunciation of Government That Spares Neither Czar, Church, Nor Duma.

(No Rights Reserved.)

SEVEN death sentences: two in St. Petersburg, one in Moscow, two in Penza, and two in Riga. Four executions: two in Kherson, one in Vilna, one in Odessa."

This, daily repeated in every newspaper and continued, not for weeks, not months, not for one year, but for years! And this in Russia, that same Russia where the people regard every criminal as a man to be pitied, and where till quite recently capital punishment was not recognized by law! I remember how proud I used to be of that, when talking to Western Europeans; but now for a second and even a third year, we have executions, executions, executions, unceasingly!

I take up to-day's paper.

To-day, the 9th of May, it is something awful. The paper contains these few words: "To-day in Kherson on the Strelbitsky Field twenty* peasants were hanged for an attack made with intent to rob, on a landed proprietor's estate in the Elizabetgrad district."

Twelve of those by whose labor we live, the very men whom we have depraved and are still depraving by every means in our power—from the poison of vodka to the terrible falsehood of a creed we do not ourselves believe in, but impose on them with all our sight—twelve of these men, strangled with cords by those whom they feed and clothe and house, and who have depraved and still continue to deprave them. Twelve husbands, fathers, sons, from among those on whose kindness, industry, and simplicity alone rests the whole of Russian life, were seized, imprisoned, and shackled. Then their hands were tied behind their backs, lest they should seize the ropes by which they would be hanged, and they were led to the gallows. Several peasants similar to those who are about to be hanged, but armed, dressed in clean soldiers' uniforms, with good boots on their feet and with guns in their hands, accompany the condemned men. Beside them walks a long-haired man, wearing a stole and vestments of gold or silver cloth, and bearing a cross. The procession stops. The manager of the whole business says something; the secretary reads a paper; and when the paper has been read, the long-haired man, addressing those whom other people are about to strangle with cords, says something about God and Christ. Immediately after these words, the hangman (there are several, for one man could not manage so complicated a business) dissolves some soap, and having soaped the loops in the cords that they may tighten better, seize the shackled men, put shrouds on them, lead them to a scaffold, and place the well-soaped nooses around their necks.

And then, one after another, living men are pushed off the benches which

---

*The papers have since contradicted the statement that twenty peasants were hanged. I can only be glad of the mistake, glad not only that eight men less have been strangled than was stated at first, but glad also that the awful figures moved me to express in these pages a feeling that has long tormented me. Therefore, merely substituting the word twelve for the word twenty, I leave all the rest unchanged, since what I said refers not only to the twelve who were hanged, but to all the thousands who have likely been crushed and killed.

OVERTHROW OF THE OLD ORDER

are drawn from under their feet, and by their own weight suddenly tighten the nooses around their necks, and are painfully strangled. Men, alive a minute before, become corpses dangling from a rope; at first slowly swinging, and then resting motionless.

All this is carefully arranged and planned by learned and enlightened people of the upper class. They arrange to do these things secretly, at daybreak, so that no one should see them done, and they arrange that the responsibility for these iniquities shall be so subdivided among those who commit them that each may think and say it is not he who is responsible for them. They arrange to seek out the most depraved and unfortunate of men, and while obliging them to do this business, planned and approved by us, still keep up an appearance of abhorring those who do it. Even such a subtle device is planned as this: Sentences are pronounced by a military tribunal, yet it is not the military but civilians who have to be present at the execution. And the business is performed by unhappy, deluded, perverted, and despised men who have nothing left them but to soap the cords well that they may grip the necks without fail, then to get well drunk on poison sold them by these same enlightened upper-class people, in order more quickly and fully to forget their souls and their quality as men. A doctor makes his round of the bodies, feels them, and reports to those in authority that the business has been done properly; all twelve are certainly dead. And those in authority depart to their ordinary occupations with the consciousness of a necessary though painful task performed. The bodies, now grown cold, are taken down and buried.

The thing is awful!

And this is not done once, and not to these twelve unhappy, misguided men from among the best class of the Russian people only, but it is done unceasingly for years, to hundreds and thousands of similar misguided men, misguided by the very people who do these awful things to them.

And not this kind of dreadful thing alone is being done, but on the same plea and with the same cold-blooded cruelty all sorts of other tortures and violence are being perpetrated in prisons, fortresses, and convict settlements.

And while this goes on for years all over Russia, the chief culprits of these acts—those by whose order these things are done, those who could put a stop to them—fully convinced that such deeds are useful and even absolutely necessary, either devise methods and make up speeches how to prevent the Finns from living as they want to live, and how to compel them to live as certain Russian personages wish them to live; or else publish orders to the effect that "in Hussar regiments the cuffs and collars of the men's jackets are to be of the color of the latter, while the pelisses of those entitled to wear them are not to have braid around the cuffs over the fur."

This is awful!

II.

WHAT is most dreadful in the whole matter is that all this inhuman violence and killing, besides the direct evil done to the victims and their families, brings a yet more enormous evil on the whole people by spreading depravity—as fire spreads amid dry straw—among every class of Russians. This depravity grows with special rapidity among the simple working folk, because all these iniquities—exceeding as they do a hundredfold all that has been done by thieves, robbers, and by all the revolutionaries put together—are done as though they were something necessary, good, and unavoidable, and are not merely excused but supported by different institutions inseparably connected in the people's minds with justice, and even with sanctity—namely, the Senate, the Synod, the Duma, the Church, and the Czar.

And this depravity spreads with remarkable rapidity.

A short time ago there were not two executioners to be found in all Russia. In the eighties there was only one. I remember how joyfully Vladimir Solovyof told me at that time that no second executioner could be found in all Russia, and so the one was taken from place to place. Not so now!

A small shopkeeper in Moscow whose affairs were in a bad way having offered his services to perform the murders arranged by Government, and receiving a hundred rubles (£10) for each person hanged soon mended his affairs so well that he no longer required this additional business, and is now carrying on his former trade.

In Orel last month, as everywhere else, an executioner was wanted, and at once a man was found who agreed with the organizers of Governmental murders to do the business for 50 rubles per head. But the volunteer hangman, after making this agreement, heard that more was paid in other towns, and at the time of the execution, having put the shroud sack on the victim, instead of leading him to the scaffold, stopped, and approaching the Superintendent, said: "You must add another 25 rubles, your Excellency, or I won't do it!" He got the increase and he did the job.

Taking Men's Lives Subject to Barter and Sale.

The next time five were to be hanged. The day before the execution a stranger came to see the organizer of Governmental murders on a private matter. The organizer went out to him, and the stranger said:

"T'other day So-and-so charged you 75 rubles per man. To-day I hear five are to be done. Let me have the whole job and I'll do it at 15 rubles a head, and you may be sure it shall be done properly."

I do not know whether the offer was accepted or not; but I know it was made.

That is how the crimes committed by the Government act on the worst, the least moral, of the people; and these terrible deeds must also have an influence on the majority of men of average morality. Continually hearing and reading about the most terrible, inhuman brutality committed by the authorities—that is by persons whom the people are accustomed to honor as the best of men—the majority of average people, especially the young, preoccupied with their own affairs, instead of realizing that those who do such horrid deeds are unworthy of honor, involuntarily come to the opposite conclusion, and argue that if men generally honored do things that seem to us horrible, probably these things are not as horrible as we suppose.

Of executions, hangings, murders, and bombs people now write and speak as they used to speak about the weather. Children play at hangings. Lads from the high schools, who are almost children, go out on expropriating expeditions, ready to kill, just as they used to go out hunting. To kill off the large landed proprietors in order to seize their estates appears now to many people to be the very best solution of the land question.

In general, thanks to the activity of the Government, which has allowed killing as a means of obtaining its ends, all crimes—robbery, theft, lies, tortures, and murder—are now considered by miserable people who have been perverted by the Government to be most natural deeds, proper to a man.

Yes: Awful as are the deeds themselves, the moral, spiritual unseen evil they produce is incomparably more terrible.

III.

YOU say you commit all these horrors to restore peace and order.

You restore peace and order.

By what means do you restore them? By the fact that you, representatives of a Christian authority, leaders and teachers approved and encouraged by the servants of the Church, destroy the last vestige of faith and morality in men by committing the greatest crimes—lies, perfidy, torture of all sorts, and the last, most awful of crimes, the one most abhorrent to every human heart not utterly depraved—not just a murder, a single murder, but murders innumerable, which you think to justify by stupid references to such and such statutes written by yourselves, in those stupid and lying books of yours which you blasphemously call The Laws.

Private Property in Land a Cause of Trouble.

You say that this is the only means of pacifying the people and quelling the revolution; but that is evidently false! It is plain that you cannot pacify the people unless you satisfy the demand of most elementary justice advanced by Russia's whole agricultural population, namely, the demand for the abolition of private property in land, and refrain from confirming it and in various ways irritating the peasants, as well as those unbalanced and envenomed people who have begun a violent struggle with you. You cannot pacify people by tormenting them and worrying, exiling, imprisoning, and hanging women and children! However hard you may try to stifle in yourselves the reason and love natural to human beings, you still have them within you, and need only come to your senses and think in order to see that by acting as you do—that is by taking part in such terrible crimes—you not only fail to cure the disease, but, by driving it inward, make it worse.

This is only too evident.

The cause of what is happening does not lie in physical events, but depends entirely on the spiritual mood of the people, which has changed, and which no efforts can bring back to its former condition, just as no efforts can turn a

From Terrorism to Revolution

grown-up man into a child again. Social irritation or tranquillity cannot depend on whether Peter is alive or hanged, or on whether John lives in Tambof or in penal servitude at Nertchinsk. Social irritation or tranquillity must depend not on how Peter or John alone but how the great majority of the nation regard their position, and on the attitude of this majority to the Government, to landed property, to the religion taught them, and on what this majority consider to be good or bad. The power of events by no means lies in the material conditions of life, but in the spiritual condition of the people. Though you were even to kill and torture a whole tenth of the Russian nation, the spiritual condition of the rest would not become such as you desire.

So that all you are now doing with all your searchings, spyings, eviling, prisons, penal settlements, and gallows does not bring the people to the state you desire, but on the contrary increases the irritation and destroys all possibility of pacification.

"But what is to be done?" you say. "What is to be done? How are the iniquities that are now perpetrated to be stopped?"

The answer is very simple: "Cease to do what you are doing."

Even if no one knew what ought to be done to pacify "the people"—the whole people—(many people know very well that what is most wanted for the pacifying of the Russian people is the freeing of the land from private ownership, just as fifty years ago what was wanted was to free the peasants from serfdom)—if no one knew this it would still be evident that to pacify the people one ought not to do what but increases its irritation. Yet that is just what you are doing.

Real Motive for Executions a Purely Selfish One.

What you are doing you do not for the people, but for yourselves, to retain the position you occupy, a position you erroneously consider advantageous, but which is really a most pitiful and abominable one. So do not say that you do it for the people; that is not true! All the abominations you do are done for yourselves, for your own covetous, ambitious, vain, vindictive, personal ends, in order to continue a little longer in the depravity in which you live and which seems to you desirable.

However much you may declare that all you do is done for the good of the people, men are beginning more and more to understand you, and ever more and more to despise you, and to regard your measures of restraint and suppression not as you wish them to be regarded, as the action of some kind of higher collective being, the Government—but as the personal evil deeds of separate evil self-seekers.

IV.

AGAIN, you say: "Not we, but the revolutionaries, began all this; and the terrible crimes of the revolutionaries can only be suppressed by firm measures (so you call your crimes) on the part of the Government."

You say the atrocities committed by the revolutionaries are terrible.

I do not dispute it, but add that besides being terrible they are also stupid, and—like your own actions—hit beside the mark. Yet, however terrible and stupid may be their actions, all those bombs and tunnelings, and those revolting murders and thefts of money—still, all these deeds do not come anywhere near the criminality and stupidity of the deeds you commit.

They are doing just the same as you, and for the same motives. They are in the same (I should say "comical," were its consequences not so awful) delusion, that men having formed for themselves a plan of what in their opinion is the desirable and proper arrangement of society, have the right and possibility of arranging other people's lives according to that plan. The delusion is the same. These methods are violence of all kinds—including taking life. And the excuse is, that an evil deed committed for the benefit of many ceases to be immoral; and that, therefore, without offending against the moral law, one may lie, rob, and kill whenever this leads to the realization of that proposed good condition for the many which we imagine that we know and can foresee, and which we wish to establish.

You, Government men, call the acts of the revolutionaries "atrocities" and "great crimes," but they have done and are doing nothing that you have not done, and done to an incomparably greater extent. They only do what you do. You keep spies, deceive, and spread printed lies, and so do they. You take people's property by all sorts of violent means and use it as you consider best, and they do the same. You execute those whom you think dangerous, and so do they.

So that while employing the same immoral means as they do for the attainment of your aim, you certainly cannot blame the revolutionaries. All you can adduce for your own justification, they can equally adduce for theirs; not to mention that you do much evil they do not commit, such as squandering the wealth of the nation, preparing for war, making war, and subduing and oppressing foreign nationalities, and much else.

You say you have the traditions of the past to guard, and the actions of the great men of the past as examples. They, too, have their traditions also arising from the past, even before the French Revolution; and as to great men, models to copy, martyrs that perished for truth and freedom—they have no fewer of these than you.

So that, if there is any difference between you it is only that you wish everything to remain as it has been and is, while they wish for a change. And in thinking that everything cannot always remain as it used to be, they would be more right than you, had they not adopted from you that curious, destructive delusion, that one set of men can know a form of life suitable for all men in the future, and that this form can be established by force. For the rest, they only do what you do, using the same means. They are altogether your disciples; they have, as the saying is, picked up all your little dodges; they are not only your disciples, they are your products, your children. If you did not exist, neither would they; so that when you try to suppress them by force, you behave like a man who presses with his whole weight against a door that opens toward him.

Revolutionary Not So Vicious as Legal Violence.

If there be any difference between you and them, it is certainly not in your, but in their, favor. The mitigating circumstances on their side are, first, that their crimes are committed under conditions of greater personal danger than you are exposed to; and risks and dangers excuse much in the eyes of impressionable youth. Secondly, that the immense majority of them are quite young people, to whom it is natural to go astray, while you are for the most part men of mature age; old men to whom reasonable calmness and leniency toward the deluded should be natural. Thirdly, a mitigating circumstance in their favor is that however odious their murders may be, they are still not so coldly, systematically cruel as your Schlusselburgs, transportations, gallows, and shootings. The fourth mitigating circumstance for the revolutionaries is, that they all quite categorically repudiate all religious teaching, and consider that the end justifies the means, and therefore they act quite consistently when they kill one or more men for the sake of the imaginary welfare of the many; whereas you, Government men—from the lowest hangmen to the highest of those who command them—you all support religion and Christianity, which is altogether incompatible with the deeds you commit.

And it is you elderly men, leaders of other men, professing Christianity, it is you who say, like children who have been fighting, "We didn't begin; they did"! And that is the best you can say, you who have taken on yourselves the rôle of rulers of the people. And what sort of men are you? Men who acknowledge as God, one who most definitely forbade not only judgment and punishment, but even the condemnation of one's brother; one who in clearest terms repudiated all punishment and affirmed the necessity of continual forgiveness however often a crime may be repeated; one who commanded us to turn the other cheek to the smiter and not to return evil for evil; one who, in the story of the woman sentenced to be stoned, showed so simply and clearly the impossibility of judgment and punishment between man and man. And you, acknowledging that teacher to be God, can find nothing better to say in your defense than that "They began, they kill; so let us kill them"!

V.

AN artist of my acquaintance thought of painting a picture, "The Execution," and he wanted a model for the executioner. He heard that the duty of executioner in Moscow was at that time performed by a watchman. The artist went to the watchman's house. It was Easter-time. The family were sitting in their best clothes at the tea table, but the master of the house was not there. It turned out afterward that on catching sight of a stranger he had hidden himself. His wife also seemed abashed, and said that her husband was not at home; but his little girl betrayed him by saying "Daddy's in the garret." She did not know that her father was aware that he was doing evil, and could not help therefore

OVERTHROW OF THE OLD ORDER

"People Flatter You Because at Heart They Despise and Hate You---And You Know It and Are Afraid of Men"---to the Czar.

being afraid of anybody. The artist explained to the wife that he wanted her husband as a model to paint, because his face suited the picture he had planned, (of course the artist did not say what the picture was for which he wanted the watchman's face.) Having got into conversation with the wife, the artist, to conciliate her, offered to take her little son as a pupil. This offer evidently tempted the woman. She went out and after a time the husband entered, looking askance, morose, restless, and frightened. He long tried to get the artist to say why and for what he required just him. When the artist told him he had met him in the street and his face seemed suitable to the projected picture, the watchman asked, Where he had met him? at what time? in what clothes? And, evidently fearing and suspecting something evil, would not come to terms.

**The Czar and All
Officials Are Participators.**

Yes, this executioner at first hand knows that he is an executioner, and that he does wrong, and is, therefore, hated, and he is afraid of men, and I think this consciousness and this fear before men atone for at least a part of his guilt. But you all, from the Secretary of the Court to the Premier and the Czar—you indirect participators in the iniquities perpetrated every day—do not seem to feel your guilt, nor the shame your participation in these horrors would evoke. It is true that, like the executioner, you fear men, and fear the more the greater your responsibility for the crimes; the Public Prosecutor more than the Secretary; the President of the Court more than the Public Prosecutor; the General Governor more than the President; the President of the Council of Ministers more still, and the Czar most of all. You are all afraid; but, unlike that executioner, you are afraid, not because you know you are doing evil, but because you think other people do evil.

Therefore I think that low as that unfortunate watchman has fallen, he stands morally immeasurably higher than you, participators and part authors of these awful crimes; you who condemn others instead of yourselves, and carry your heads so high.

VI.

I KNOW that men are but human, that we all are weak, that we all err, and that one cannot judge another. I have long struggled against the feeling that was and is aroused in me by those responsible for these awful crimes, and aroused the more the higher they stand on the social ladder. But I neither can nor will struggle against that feeling any longer.

I cannot and will not; first, because, an exposure of these people who do not see the full criminality of their actions is necessary for them as well as for the multitude that, influenced by the external honor and laudation accorded to these persons, approve their terrible deeds and even try to imitate them. Secondly, I cannot and will not struggle any longer, because (I frankly confess it) I hope my exposure of those men will, one way or other, evoke the expulsion I desire from the set in which I am now living, and in which I cannot but feel myself to be a participator in the crimes committed around me.

Everything now being done in Russia is done in the name of the general welfare, in the name of the protection and tranquillity of the inhabitants of Russia. And if this be so, then it is also all done for me, who lives in Russia. For me, therefore, exists the destitution of the people, deprived of the first, most natural right of man—the right to use the land on which he is born; for me the half million men torn away from wholesome peasant life, and dressed in uniforms and taught to kill; for me that false so-called priesthood, whose chief duty it is to pervert and conceal true Christianity; for me all these transportations of men from place to place; for me these hundreds of thousands of hungry workmen wandering about Russia; for me these hundreds of thousands of unfortunates dying of typhus and scurvy in the fortresses and prisons which do not suffice for such a multitude; for me the mothers, wives, and fathers of the exiles, the prisoners, and those who are hung, are suffering; for me are these spies and this bribery; for me the interment of these dozens and hundreds of men who have been shot; for me the horrible work goes on of these hangmen, at first enlisted with difficulty, but now no longer so loathing their work; for me exist these gallows, with well-soaped cords, from which hang women, children, and peasants; for me exists this terrible embitterment of man against his fellow-man.

Strange as is the statement that all this is done for me, and that I am a participator in these terrible deeds, I cannot but feel that there is an indubitable interdependence between my spacious room, my dinner, my clothing, my leisure, and these terrible crimes committed to get rid of those who would like to take from me what I use. And though I know that these homeless, embittered, depraved people—who but for the Government's threats would deprive me of all I am using—are products of that same Government's actions, still I cannot help feeling that at present my peace really is dependent on all the horrors that are now being perpetrated by the Government.

And being conscious of this I can no longer endure it, but must free myself from this intolerable position!

It is impossible to live so! I, at any rate, cannot and will not live so.

That is why I write this, and will circulate it by all means in my power, both in Russia and abroad; that one of two things may happen: either that these inhuman deeds may be stopped or that my connection with them may be snapped and I put in prison, where I may be clearly conscious that these horrors are not committed on my behalf; or, still better, (so good that I dare not even dream of such happiness,) they may put on me, as on those twenty or twelve peasants, a shroud and a cap and may push me also off a bench, so that by my own weight I may tighten the well-soaped noose around my old throat.

To attain one of these two aims, I address myself to all the participators in these terrible deeds, beginning with those who put on their brother men and women and children those caps and nooses—from the prison warders up to you, chief organizers and authorizers of these terrible crimes.

Brother men! Come to your senses! Stop and think! Consider what you are doing! Remember who you are!

Before being hangmen, Generals, Public Prosecutors, Judges, Premier, or Czar—are you not men? To-day allowed a peep into God's world, to-morrow ceasing to be. (You hangmen of all grades in particular, who have evoked and are evoking special hatred, should remember this.) Is it possible that you, who have had this short glimpse of God's world, (for even if you be not murdered death is always close behind us all,) is it possible that in your lucid moments you do not see that your vocation in life cannot be to torment and kill men; yourselves trembling with fear of being killed, lying to yourselves, to others, and to God, assuring yourselves and others that by participating in these things you are doing an important and grand work for the welfare of millions? Is it possible that—when not intoxicated by your surroundings, by flattery, and by the customary sophistries—you do not each one of you know that all this is mere talk, only invented that while doing most evil deeds you may still consider yourself a good man? You cannot but know that you, like each of us, have but one real duty, which includes all others: the duty of living the short space granted us in accord with the Will that sent you into this world, and of leaving it in accord with that Will. And that Will desires only one thing: love from man to man.

But what are you doing? To what are you devoting your spiritual strength? Whom do you love? Who loves you? Your wife? Your child? But that is not love. The love of wife and children is not human love. Animals love in that way even more strongly. Human love is the love of man for man—for every man as a son of God, and therefore a brother.

Whom do you love in that way? No one. Who loves you in that way? No one. You are feared as the hangman or a wild animal is feared. People flatter you because at heart they despise and hate you—and how they do hate you! And you know it, and are afraid of men.

Yes, consider it, all of you from the highest to the lowest accomplices in murder; consider who you are, and cease to do what you are doing. Cease not for your own sakes, not for the sake of your own personality, not for the sake of men, not that you may cease to be blamed, but for your soul's sake and for the God who lives within you.

June 18, 1908.

July 19, 1908

From Terrorism to Revolution

RUSSIAN SPY SHOT STOLYPIN

Bogroff, Police Secret Agent, Admitted to Kieff Theatre to Guard Czar and Premier.

WAS ACTIVE REVOLUTIONIST

Played Azeff's Part and Betrayed Comrades When Named for Previous Attempt.

KIEFF, Russia, Sept. 16.—Dmitry Bogroff, would-be assassin of Premier P. A. Stolypin, who was shot down in the Municipal Theatre here last night in the Czar's presence, and who, it is officially announced, may recover, was a secret police spy brought to Kieff to assist in protecting the Emperor, and was admitted to the theatre especially to aid in guarding the Premier. Such, at least, is the official information given out to-night.

Prompt and searching inquiry, it is said, revealed the fact that Bogroff was a member of the Social-Revolutionary Party known to the "protective police" and employed by them as a "secret agent."

It is declared that the attempt at a revival of terrorism, of which he was the active arm, was planned by the Executive Committee of the Jewish band of Social Revolutionists and Finnish Revolutionists who, according to police information, recently federated. The rapid progress of the inquiry was due, it is asserted, to the eagerness of the municipality to clear itself of a charge of reckless distribution of admission cards to the theatre.

Admission Card No. 406, entitling its holder to a seat in the eighteenth row of the theatre, was found on Bogroff, the would-be assassin. It was issued by the municipality upon a personal request signed by Inspector of Political Police Kuliabko, and by him handed over to the agent of Bogroff. The municipality had taken the precaution to photograph Kuliabko's receipt, and in the face of this overwhelming evidence the protective police headquarters was obliged to admit the facts of Bogroff's past.

Dmitry Bogroff is an orthodox Jew.

He was graduated from Kieff University in 1906. During his course there he joined the Social Revolutionary group, which intrusted to him in 1907 several serious commissions. He was selected for the second attempt on M. Stolypin's life, but did not carry out his orders. Instead, he informed the police and betrayed a large number of his comrades, using the tactics of Eugene Azeff, who in 1909 played the double rôle of leader of the Revolutionary Socialist Party and political spy to gain the confidence of the police chiefs.

Like Azeff, Bogroff in this double rôle was tolerated by the police as their sole means to maintain a permanent spy in the revolutionists' camp through whom they could secure information concerning the consecutive steps of the revolutionists.

As a member of the Central Committee of the Social Revolutionary Party Bogroff visited St. Petersburg last Spring on business of his party, and returned to Kieff Sept. 8 to assist in the protection of the Czar and the members of the imperial family at the manoeuvres.

At the inquiry to-day Bogroff declared that he intended to attempt the life of a higher personage than Mr. Stolypin, but feared this would precipitate an anti-Jewish outbreak. Bogroff's brother Vladimir was arrested here to-day.

September 16, 1911

RUSSIAN STRIKES LIKE REVOLUTION

Unrest Is Growing as the Result of the Government's Reactionary Policy.

160,000 OUT IN CAPITAL

Labor Leaders Plan to Spoil the Reception of the French President —Cossacks Fire on Crowds.

Special Cable to THE NEW YORK TIMES.
LONDON, Wednesday, July 22.—The news reaching the outside world regarding the strike movement in St. Petersburg and other big cities of the Czar's dominions, according to a Russian correspondent of The Daily Chronicle, fails to give an adequate idea either of its dimensions or its true character.

Those who have had an opportunity of following at more or less close quarters the developments of Russia within recent years know that the present huge strikes, attended as they are by street demonstrations under the red flag and by sanguinary conflicts with the police, are but one phase in the recrudescence of the revolutionary movement.

This recrudescence has been noticeable since the assassination of Premier Stolypin, and is daily acquiring new force and new impetus from the thoroughly reactionary policy of the Government. Such moderates as Grutchkoff, the leader of the Octobrists, men of such high political and social standing as Baron Rosen, former Russian Ambassador to Tokio and Peking, and such leaders of the commercial world as Salazkin, Chairman of the Association of Russian Chambers of Commerce, have all in turn within the last year or two loudly warned the Government that persistence in its present policy would lead to a second and still more formidable revolution; but the autocracy, inspired by Rasputin and men of the Purishkevitch type, sees no further than its own nose, with the inevitable result that discontent is growing in all classes of society.

The Lena massacres, the forcible suppression of strikes, the persecution of the labor press, the dissolution of trades unions—all this and much more add to the exasperation of the members of the working class, with whom political strikes have therefore become the order of the day. Every year the number and extent of these strikes increase at an amazing rate, and two-thirds of them are purely political.

In the present instance the movement is a reflex of the general strike at Baku, where fearful conditions of labor, coupled with the tyranny of the police authorities, have brought about a general revolt of labor, which has now lasted for several weeks. Many other industrial cities have proclaimed a general strike, which has a sinister resemblance to those of 1905.

The present movement may run out its course without immediate result; but the general lines of the working-class movement in Russia cannot be obliterated, and these lead straight to a renewal of the national struggle against irresponsible government.

ST. PETERSBURG, July 21.—The strike in St. Petersburg, which was called as a protest against the drastic measures of the authorities at Baku and elsewhere against strikers, is rapidly spreading, and 160,000 men are now out. The streets are swarming with police, gendarmes, and Cossacks, and special precautions have been taken to guard the French President, Raymond Poincaré, in his movements about the city. There is a notable absence of enthusiasm on the part of the people over the visit of M. Poincaré.

Attacks were made upon the street cars today, and the disorders became so serious that the Cossacks fired, wounding several persons.

It appears that the labor leaders, on the eve of President Poincaré's arrival here, held a meeting and decided to do their utmost to interfere with his reception. The authorities heard of this intention and took strong precautions to deal with any disorders. The city was divided into sections, and each was patrolled by troops. Owing to these measures President Poincaré has not been molested.

July 22, 1914

BAD CONDITIONS IN RUSSIA.

Travelers Report Great Lack of Supplies for the Armies.

BERLIN, Sept. 11, (by Wireless to Tuckerton, N. J.)—Travelers who have just returned from a trip to Russia contribute to the Neue Zeitung of Zurich articles concerning their impressions of the conditions under which the Russian armies are fighting. These articles are summarized as follows by the Overseas News Agency:

"Russia has enough soldiers in the field and sufficient food supplies, but has no arms, officers, or ammunition. The army units vary. Some of them are equipped excellently and make a good impression. Others are just to the contrary. The men appear to be unwilling to serve, and enthusiasm is seldom noticeable. The soldiers are interested only in the prospects for peace.

"The lack of officers is particularly noticeable. Frequently large bodies of men may be seen marching without a single officer. In the new formation there is only one gun for ten men. Such guns as are available are mostly of old types, and not repeating rifles.

"The scarcity of ammunition is still more marked. Only three small munitions factories have been operating since the largest Russian plant was destroyed by an explosion.

"Economic conditions are very bad. Large stores of grain are decaying in warehouses while the people go hungry. The lack of communications, inefficiency of organization, and corruption among public officials aggravate these evil conditions. The famine in coal is simply a calamity.

"Recently Belgian workmen were sent to Russia in the hope of increasing the output of the ammunitions plants."

September 12, 1915

OVERTHROW OF THE OLD ORDER

RUSSIAN PEOPLE WIN VICTORY IN FALL OF PREMIER

Public Opinion, for First Time in History, Compels Government to Do Its Bidding.

PETROGRAD, Nov. 24.—Alexander Trepoff, Minister of Ways and Communications, has been appointed Premier to succeed M. Stürmer, who by an Imperial ukase has been appointed Grand Chamberlain of the Imperial Court, retaining his functions as a member of the Council of the Empire.

The Council of the Empire has been adjourned by imperial ukase until Dec. 2.

The resignation of M. Stürmer as Premier and Foreign Minister had long been accepted as an inevitable outcome of the struggle between the present Cabinet and the Duma. It caused no more than mild surprise, and this was due less to the event itself than the rapidity with which the situation matured since the definite break between the Duma and the Government.

It is almost impossible to overestimate not only the political but the national significance of the Duma victory, since for the first time in history Russian public opinion is considered to have triumphed over influences which were regarded as antagonistic to good government.

November 25, 1916

RASPUTIN KILLED BY PROGRESSIVES

British Correspondent Gives Details of the Murder of Notorious Russian Monk.

Special Cable to THE NEW YORK TIMES.
LONDON, Thursday, Feb. 1.—The Daily Mail publishes a dispatch from its special correspondent in Petrograd, dated Jan. 2, explaining recent events in Russia. The dispatch says:

"The British nation must be asking why was Rasputin killed. He was killed because he was the most influential member of a small clique [the Camarilla, it is called here] which wielded an undue influence in the Government of Russia for a long time past. He was influential not by reason of his intellect or character. He was a man of peasant origin, without education, without manners, a libertine, a drunkard, a blackmailer. His influence lay in a certain hypnotic power which he possessed, a power which made him especially dangerous among women.

"He had invented a new kind of religion, one article of which was that men and women should bathe together in order to 'try the flesh.' He pretended to have the miraculous power of healing and it is said he had even induced the Empress to believe that, to him was due the recovery of her son from his former ill health and weakness. Rasputin pretended to 'watch over' the Czar's heir. It seems quite certain that the anxious mother's fears for her son were calmed by the plausible rascal's pretences. In this manner Rasputin kept a substantial footing in the Imperial household and consequently became a very useful tool in the hands of Camarilla. What they wanted they put forward through him, as he had access to court. If his requests were refused or his advice neglected, he could threaten to take himself off and leave the young heir to the throne 'unguarded.'

"Do not suppose the decision to remove Rasputin was taken by the 'revolutionaries.' There is nothing of the old revolutionary spirit in the present progressive movement. It is a movement conducted by men who held the old methods in abhorrence. Those who resolved to kill Rasputin belonged to the very highest families in Russia, some of them to the imperial family. They and others closely related to the Emperor had urged him to be rid of this evil creature, who worked by underground means, trading upon tolerant good nature, pursuing with vindictive malice those who opposed him until he compassed their downfall. Entreaties failed. The Emperor, occupied with the weightiest matters, apparently could not be induced to take Rasputin seriously. It was time to take other measures."

The correspondent then gives particulars of the assassination of Rasputin, who was put to death after the conspirators had learned from him under the influence of drink all they could of the machinations of the Camarilla. According to this account, when Rasputin had a revolver handed to him and was told to choose between suicide and execution he refused to turn the weapon against himself and fired at a Grand Duke, but missed and broke a window. The correspondent continues:

"That any proceedings will be taken against the executioners is unlikely. What every one is asking is will the Camarilla now be intimidated, will it give up its fight against all the best elements in the nation, against the friendship between Russia and England, against the employment of capable, independent Ministers, and against the resolve of the Russian people to continue the war until victory.

"Russia needs men who can and will give her improved railway service, better methods of food distribution, an internal policy aimed at conciliating and consolidating the people. If the Czar consents to call such men to take part in the nation's business and agrees to the measures they propose the army will be satisfied, but not otherwise. That is the situation, and it is better it should be openly described. Germany knows it well and is hoping that the heart of the Czar will be hardened, as was the heart of Pharoah in Egypt. German agents are working hard to that end.

"All the best minds and hearts in Russia are on the side of the Allies. It was because Rasputin stood for what all true Russians hate that he was executed. He represented the forces of darkness and ignorance. His executioners represent those who are seeking to spread the light."

February 1, 1917

REVOLUTION IN RUSSIA; CZAR ABDICATES

ARMY JOINS WITH THE DUMA

Three Days of Conflict Follow Food Riots in Capital.

POPULACE TAKE UP ARMS

PETROGRAD, March 15.—Emperor Nicholas of Russia has abdicated, and Grand Duke Michael Alexandrovitch, his younger brother, has been named as Regent.

The Russian Ministry, charged with corruption and incompetence, has been swept out of office. One Minister, Alexander Protopopoff, the head of the Interior Department, is reported to have been killed, and the other Ministers, as well as the President of the Imperial Council, are under arrest.

A new national Cabinet is announced, with Prince Lvoff as President of the Council and Premier, and the other offices held by the men who are close to the Russian people.

Petrograd has been the scene of one of the most remarkable risings in history, beginning with minor food riots and labor strikes last week Thursday. The people's cry for food reached the hearts of the soldiers, and one by one the regiments rebelled, until finally those troops which had for a time stood loyal to the Government gathered up their arms and marched into the ranks of the revolutionists.

Duma President Leading Figure.

Michael V. Rodzianko, President of the Duma, was the leading figure among the Deputies, who unanimously decided to oppose the imperial order, issued last week, for a dissolution of the House. They continued their sessions, and M. Rodzianko informed the Emperor, then at the front, that the hour had struck when the will of the people must prevail.

Even the Imperial Council realized the gravity of the situation, and added its appeal to that of the Duma that the Emperor should take steps to give the people a policy and government in accordance with their desires and in order that there should be no interference with carrying on the war to a victorious ending.

The Emperor hastened back to the capital, only to find that the revolution had been successful and that a new Government was in control.

The Empress, who, it is alleged, has been influential in the councils opposed to the wishes of the people, is reported to have fled or to be in hiding.

Although considerable fighting took place, it is not believed that the casualties are large. One report says that they do not exceed 300.

A few defenders of the old régime put up a last feeble defense last night from the roofs of the wrecked Astoria Military Hotel and St. Isaac's Cathedral, facing on two sides of the same square.

The city is now quiet and perfect order prevails. So far as is known, no foreigners were injured.

The Imperial Palace at Tsarskoe-Selo is said to have been in a state of siege, but thus far no firing has been reported between the guards defending the palace and the revolutionists and troops.

According to one report the Emperor expected trouble to follow from his decree dissolving the Duma, and so warned the residents of Tsarkoe-Selo to arrange to remain in the suburb for an indefinite period.

Began From Strikes a Week Ago.

The most phenomenal feature of the revolution was the swift and orderly transition whereby the control of the city passed from the régime of the old Government into the hands of its opponents.

The visible signs of revolution began on Thursday, March 8. Strikes were declared in several big munitions factories as a protest against the shortage of bread. Men and women gathered and marched through the streets, most of them in an orderly fashion. A few bread shops were broken into in that section of the city beyond the Neva, and several minor clashes between strikers and police occurred.

Squads of mounted troops appeared, but during Thursday and Friday the utmost friendliness seemed to exist between the troops and the people.

This early period of the uprising bore the character of a mock revolution, staged for an immense audience. Cossacks, charging down the street, did so in a half-hearted fashion, plainly without malice or intent to harm the crowds, which they playfully dispersed. The troops exchanged good-natured raillery with the working men and women, and as they rode were cheered by the populace.

Long lines of soldiers stationed in dramatic attitudes across Nevsky Prospect, with their guns pointed at an imaginary foe, appeared to be taking part in a realistic tableau. Machine guns, firing rounds of blank cartridges, seemed only to add another realistic touch to a tremendous theatric production which was using the whole city as a stage.

On Saturday, however, apparently without provocation, the troops were ordered to fire on people marching in Nevsky Prospect. The troops refused to fire, and the police, replacing them, fired rifles and machine guns.

Then came a clash between troops and police, which continued in desultory fashion throughout Saturday night and Sunday. The Nevsky Prospect was cleared of traffic by the police and notices were posted by the commander of the Petrograd military district warning the people that any attempt to congregate would be met by force.

Until Sunday evening, however, there was no intimation that the affair would grow to the proportions of a revolution. The first serious outbreak came at 3 o'clock, when the men of the Volyn[illegible] Regiment shot their officers and revolted when they received an order to fire upon striking workingmen in one of the factory districts.

Another regiment detailed against the mutineers also joined the revolt. The news spread rapidly to the other barracks and four more regiments went over. Some of the revolting troops marched to the St. Peter and St. Paul Fortress on the left bank of the Neva, and after a brief skirmish with the garrison took possession of it.

Dissension spread among the troops, who did not understand why they should be compelled to take violent measures against fellow-citizens whose chief offense was that they were hungry and were asking the Government to supply bread. Several regiments deserted. A pitched battle began between the troops who stood with the Government and those who, refusing to obey orders, had mutinied, and even slain their officers.

A long night fight took place between the mutinous regiments and the police at the end of St. Catharine Canal, immediately in front of the historic church built over the spot where Alexander II. was killed by a bomb. The police finally fled to the rooftops all over the city and were seen no more in the streets during the entire term of the fighting.

Turning Point in Revolution.

Still, on Monday morning the Government troops appeared to control all the principal squares of the city. Then came a period when it was impossible to distinguish one side from the other. There was no definite line between the factions. The turning point appeared to come about 3 o'clock in the afternoon. For two hours the opposing regiments passively confronted each other along the wide Liteiny Prospect in almost complete silence.

From time to time emissaries from the revolutionary side rode to the opposing ranks and exhorted them to join the side of the people. For a while the [illegible] hung in the balance. The troops appeared irresolute, awaiting the commands of their officers, who themselves were in doubt as to what they should do.

Desultory firing continued along the side streets, between groups of Government troops and revolutionists. But the regiments upon whose decision the outcome rested still confronted each other, with machine guns and rifles in readiness.

Suddenly a few volleys were exchanged: there was another period of silent suspense, and the Government regiments finally marched over to join the revolutionists. A few hours after the first clash, this section of Petrograd, in which were located the Duma building, artillery headquarters, and the chief military barracks, passed into the hands of the revolutionary forces, and the warfare swept like a tornado to other parts of the city, where the scene was duplicated.

At first it seemed a miracle that the revolutionists, without prearranged plan, without leadership or organization, could in such a short time, with comparative ease, achieve a complete victory over the Government. But the explanation lay in the reluctance of the troops to take sides against the people and their prompt desertion to the ranks of those who opposed the Government.

The scenes in the streets were by this time remarkable. The wide streets, where the troops were stationed, were completely deserted by civilians, except for a few daring individuals, who, creeping along walls and ducking into courtyards, sped from one side to the other. But the side streets were choked with people.

Groups of students, easily distinguished by their blue caps and dark uniforms, fell into step with rough units of rebel soldiers, and were joined by other heterogeneous elements, united for the time being by a cause greater than partisan differences.

Unkempt workingmen, with ragged sheepskin coats covering the conventional peasants' costume of dark blouse and top boots, strode side by side with well groomed city clerks and shopkeepers.

This strange army of people, mustered on the street corners, shouldered their newly acquired rifles and marched out to join the ranks of the deserting regiments.

The economic and industrial life of the city came to a complete standstill. Street car service was suspended from the beginning of the disorders and stores were closed. The two leading hotels which housed officers were wrecked. Others restricted their service to regular patrons. In response to an appeal by the revolutionist committees, citizens distributed food to the soldiers.

Duma Declares Government Ended.

On Monday the Duma members, except the Rightists, met in executive session, notwithstanding the order of the Czar dissolving their body. The result was a virtually unanimous vote to place the Duma squarely on the side of the revolution and to authorize the Executive Council of that body to declare the present Government overthrown, and organize a provisional Government.

President Rodzianko, who presided, sent a telegram to the Emperor, informing him of the developments and calling on him to listen to the voice of the people.

"The hour has struck," he said, "when the will of the people must prevail."

It was further stated in the telegram to the Emperor that a special committee, composed of the leaders of the various parties in the Duma, would submit a list of names for the new Cabinet.

Members of the Imperial Council also sent a message to Emperor Nicholas, outlining conditions and recommending a change in the internal policy in accordance with the decision of the Duma, dismissal of the present Cabinet and its reorganization in accordance with the desires of the people and their representatives. The message bore twelve signatures.

Simultaneously it was reported that all the Ministers except M. Protopopoff had resigned.

The following were named as the "staff of the temporary Government": Michael V. Dodzianko, H. V. Nekrasoff, A. I. Konovaloff, L. I. Dmitrukoff, A. F. Kerenski, M. S. Pshkeidze, V. V. Shulgin, S. I. Shidlovsky, Paul N. Milukoff, M. A. Makarauloff, V. N. Lvoff, V. A. Rjevsky, and Colonel Englehard.

Remarkable Scene at the Duma.

The scene at the Duma before the revolution was in full flame was extraordinary. The members stood about the broad corridors talking calmly, the serious priest members in long black gowns, with flowing hair, and members from the provinces in top boots and blouses mingling with well-groomed and frock-coated representatives.

At the front gates the troops began to assemble. They were without arms. They were the revolting regiments. One body in marching order entered the side gate and halted before the entrance. A Duma member spoke from the steps, explaining the attitude of that body and assuring the regiments that the Duma was with them.

Auto trucks packed with men, soldiers, and civilians, with and without arms, rolled up the circular drive and stopped before the door, while some occupant delivered a lurid oration, and then went on cheered by the crowds.

Then came a small army of citizen soldiers, factory workers, clerks, students armed with rifles taken from the captured arsenals, their pale faces and black Winter clothing forming a strange picture against the snow piled high in the Duma garden.

For an hour they stood in more or less military formation before the building, and at dusk marched away toward the centre of the city, followed by the revolting soldiers. The crowd was extremely orderly. A group of a dozen soldiers pushed into the corridor of the building and demanded to be allowed to address the members. A mild-mannered young civilian of the student type took them in hand with a little difficulty and led them into the open. A delegation asked for food. Immediately waiters from the Duma restaurant were sent out with trays of tea and food until the place was cleaned out.

At nightfall on Monday only one small district of the city, containing the War Office, the Admiralty Building, St. Isaac's Cathedral, and the Military Hotel, still resisted the onslaught of the revolutionary forces, and the battle for the possession of Petrograd came to a dramatic conclusion. In the Admiralty Building the Council of Ministers secretly gathered for a conference, and the last regiments loyal to the old Government were drawn up as a guard.

While the Council sat in the last meeting which they were destined to hold, the building was surrounded and the besiegers poured rifle and machine gun fire upon the defenders.

For a few hours the fiercest battle of the day continued: the streets were swept by a steady fusillade and the crowds scattered for the nearest shelter, some of the people being compelled to spend the night in courtyards or corridors of office buildings or wherever they first found refuge.

Toward morning (Tuesday) there was a sudden lull, broken by exultant shouts, which deepened into a roar, and were succeeded by the Russian revolutionary "Marseillaise." The regiments defending the Admiralty had surrendered and gone over to the side of the revolutionists.

The Ministers in the Admiralty Building were then arrested and the Russian national colors were replaced by the red flag of the revolutionists.

During the day revolutionary publications appeared in the streets, with the simple caption "News." These contained a résumé of developments, and they were eagerly read by all classes. Rodzianko's telegrams to the Emperor and others to the commanders of the troops at the front were reproduced. The first message to the Emperor read:

The situation is grave. Anarchy reigns in the capital. The Government is paralyzed. The transport of provisions and fuel is completely disorganized. General dissatisfaction is growing. Irregular rifle firing is occurring in the streets. It is necessary to charge immediately some person trusted by the people to form a new Government. It is impossible to linger, since delay means death. Praying God that the responsibility in this hour will not fall upon a crowned head.

Later President Rodzianko sent the following to the Emperor:

The position is becoming more serious. It is imperative that immediate measures be taken, because tomorrow will be too late. The last hour has come when the fate of the fatherland and the dynasty are being decided.

Similar telegrams were sent to all the commanders at the front with an appeal for their support before the Emperor of the Duma's action. General Alexis Brusiloff, Commander in Chief of the armies of the southwestern front, and General Nicholas Ruzsky, Commander of the northern armies, replied promptly. General Brusiloff sent this message:

"Have fulfilled duty before fatherland and Emperor."

General Ruzsky's reply read:

"Commission accomplished."

Petrograd Resuming Wonted Calm.

Today the city emerged from the week's nightmare of revolution and figuratively smiled under a brilliant flood of sunshine, following a series of gray days, ending with a snowstorm last evening.

Planks were pulled down from windows long closed. Stores, banks, and business establishments of every description reopened their doors for the resumption of ordinary activities as confidence in the new Government gained in force.

With the reopening of bread, sugar, tea, and meat shops queues of women with shopping bags and baskets lined up often to the length of a block to replenish stores exhausted by the long siege.

Truck sledges and little sleighs for hire, the most widely appreciated conveniences of Russian cities, began to appear again in the streets, which for six days had been absolutely void of any means of private transportation.

No newspapers, with the exception of the revolutionary publications, which sprang into life with the success of the revolt, have yet appeared.

The only visible signs of the clash of authority which turned the city into a battleground were the charred ruins of the jail, which are still pouring a cloud of smoke skyward, and here and there the remains of other police institutions

OVERTHROW OF THE OLD ORDER

and the homes of the few individuals who were regarded as offenders against the rights of the people.

In front of other Government institutions, which apparently it was not seen fit to destroy, were piles of charred embers, showing where wreckage and documents had been dumped and consumed.

Spark that Started Conflagration.

It is evident that the strike of workingmen Thursday of last week provided the spark which set aflame the growing unrest and angry discontent with the Government that, pervading the entire population of Russia, had reached the ignition point.

Thus the small manifestations of hungry factory workers, crying for bread, changed in a single day into a revolution which swept the whole city, spread to the Government troops who had been called to hold the crowds in check, and, supported by the Duma, ended in the downfall of the Government.

The revelations in the Duma of Government stupidity and corruption, and the allegations of treason against the chief members of the Cabinet, sent a wave of protest through the country, and all political factions, except a small reactionary group, still cherishing traditional ideas of the old regime which existed before Russia received a constitution, declared themselves firmly against the sinister influences which had been undermining the best efforts of the country successfully to carry on the war.

Even the Imperial Council, which never before in the history of the country had allied itself with the popular will, held special meetings, in which attention was called to the "serious conditions to which the country had been brought by the unscrupulous designs of governmental heads."

People Against Government.

With unanimity unprecedented the entire population presented a solid front against the Government. The belief prevailed everywhere and was expressed that pro-German Court circles and the Government were doing everything in their power to interfere with the proper conduct of the war and to bring about a separate peace.

Stürmer, Rasputin, and Protopopoff formed a picturesque trio, known as "the dark forces" against which the chief animosity of the country was directed, but powerful as they were, these figures were declared to be only symbols of German influence which was "militating against the patriotic desire of the mass of the Russian people for war until victory."

After the assassination of Rasputin and the removal of Stürmer from the Premiership, the same Ministerial influence, wearing a new mask in the form of a changed Cabinet, Duma officials declared, still flourished with undiminished strength. Direct appeals were made to the Emperor by all sorts of representative bodies and influential officials to save the country from the disaster which threatened it and to appoint a new Cabinet which would have the confidence of the people.

But the Government, except for empty concessions and compromises, remained obdurate to all appeals and showed not the slightest inclination to change the direction of its policy or accede to the demands more and more loudly expressed.

It was the opinion of the majority of the Deputies in the Duma that, despite this state of affairs, an open revolution was impossible, as the country realized that a revolution would seriously interrupt the work of the war and would be playing into the hands of those who had this very end in view.

Open letters were printed in the Petrograd newspapers from popular Duma leaders, and proclamations were posted in the streets, urgently begging the population not to create demonstrations or cause disorders which might lead to interruption of the manufacture of munitions or paralyze the industrial activity of the city.

People at Last Convinced.

Manifestations already arranged for March 6, including a general strike and the marching to the Duma of a deputation of workingmen, were in this way averted. But the moment was only postponed. The people, who had been long vaguely disturbed by the political unrest and were convinced that they were being exploited by the hostile Government, received what they regarded as the last proof of the inefficiency and corruption of their own Government when they were apprised that the already insufficient supply of food had become still more meagre and that for some days it would be necessary to go without bread altogether.

Patient and long suffering by nature, this was too much for the population of Petrograd, who knew that the interior of Russia was stored with immense quantities of grain and all kinds of provisions, and, without other motive at first than to voice a demand for bread, the people paraded the streets and the demonstrations began which soon kindled into a revolution.

March 16, 1917

CALLS PEOPLE WAR WEARY.

But Leo Trotsky Says They Do Not Want Separate Peace.

Leo Trotsky, a Russian revolutionist now in America, said last night in the office of the Novy Mir, the Russian Socialist newspaper, that the committee which has taken the place of the deposed Ministry in Russia did not represent the interests or the aims of the revolutionists, that it would probably be short lived, and step down in favor of men who would be more sure to carry forward the democratization of Russia.

Mr. Trotsky said that the cause of the revolution was the unrest of the mass of the people who were tired of war, and that the real object of the revolutionists was to end the war not only in Russia but throughout Europe. He denied that the uprising was in any way a German plot. The revolutionists, even if they had it in their power, would not make a separate peace with Germany. They do not favor Germany, they do not wish to see Germany win," he concluded, " but they are tired of war and the privations of war and they wish to stop fighting."

March 16, 1917

New Russian Government Asks People's Support; States Its Policy as Freedom and Suffrage for All

LONDON, March 16.—The Provisional Government in Russia has issued an appeal to the people, according to a Reuter dispatch from Petrograd. The document begins:

"Citizens.—The Executive Committee of the Duma, with the aid and support of the garrison of the capital and its inhabitants, has succeeded in triumphing over the obnoxious forces of the old régime in such a manner that we are able to proceed to a more stable organization of the executive power, with men whose past political activity assures them the country's confidence."

The names of the members of the new Government are then given and the appeal continues:

"The new Cabinet will base its policy on the following principles:

First.—An immediate general amnesty for all political and religious offenses, including terrorist acts and military and agrarian offenses.

Second.—Liberty of speech and of the press; freedom for alliances, unions, and strikes, with the extension of these liberties to military officials within the limits admitted by military requirements.

Third.—Abolition of all social, religious, and national restrictions.

Fourth.—To proceed forthwith to the preparation and convocation of a constitutional Assembly, based on universal suffrage, which will establish a governmental régime.

Fifth.—The substitution of the police by a national militia, with chiefs to be elected and responsible to the Government.

Sixth.—Communal elections to be based on universal suffrage.

Seventh.—The troops which participated in the revolutionary movement will not be disarmed, but will remain in Petrograd.

Eighth.—While maintaining strict military discipline for troops on active service, it is desirable to abrogate for soldiers all restrictions in the enjoyment of social rights accorded other citizens.

"The Provisional Government desires to add that it has no intention to profit by the circumstances of the war to delay the realization of the measures of reform above mentioned."

March 17, 1917

ANTI-AMERICAN OUTBURST.

Extremists Attempt to Demonstrate at Petrograd Embassy.

PETROGRAD, April 24, (via London, April 24.)—An effort by a small group of ultra-Radicals to make an unfriendly demonstration before the American Embassy today was frustrated by militiamen as the radicals marched down the Nevsky Prospect on their way to the Embassy.

The demonstration was headed by Nikolai Lenine, the radical Socialist leader, who recently arrived here through Germany from Switzerland with a safe-conduct from the German authorities. The demonstration is said to have been due to the alleged killing in America of an anarchist named Mooney, who was under sentence in San Francisco.

A guard was sent by the authorities to protect the embassy.

The Mooney referred to in the above dispatch probably is Thomas J. Mooney, who is under sentence of death for connection with the bomb explosion in San Francisco in July, 1916, in which several persons were killed.

Efforts made at a joint conference to heal the split in the ranks of the Russian Socialists over the question of supporting the provisional Government were unsuccessful, the majority, however, voting to support the Government, according to a cablegram received by the Jewish Daily Forward from Petrograd. The message read in part:

"Attempts to conciliate the two sections of the Russian Socialist have failed. The section headed by Lenin, the extreme Socialist, and the section headed by Plekhanoff, leader of the moderate Socialists, met in conference. The representatives of the Petrograd, Moscow, and provincial organizations were present. Lenin objected to the other section supporting the provisional Government and urged the overthrow of the present régime, formulating his attitude on the following phrase: 'Dictatorship of the working class and democracy of the army.'

"The majority of the delegates present, though, protested against Lenin's suggestion, and have reaffirmed their readiness to co-operate with the provisional Government.

"The first woman in Russia ever to be elected to a public office was elected yesterday Alderman of the municipality of Poltavam, capital of the Province of Poltava.

"The leader of the Black Hundred, Orlov, has been arrested."

April 25, 1917

From Terrorism to Revolution

PEASANTS SEIZE LANDS IN RUSSIA

Soldiers Home from Army Lead Them in Attacks on Estate Owners.

DISREGARD FOOD BOARDS

Grand Committee of Peasants' Alliance Urges Those at Front to Stay There and Fight.

LONDON, April 25.—Dispatches from Petrograd report that the revolutionary spirit is manifesting itself in the rural districts of Russia, bringing the long-standing agrarian troubles to a head. Notwithstanding the organization of food committees, which are doing their best to make the peasants understand that the land question cannot be wisely settled until the Constituent Assembly is elected, the peasants are inclined to take the matter into their own hands.

Soldiers visiting their rural homes, with or without leave, spread the news of the revolution and lead the peasants against the landowners. This is chiefly the case in the Saratov Government, where the people are often inclined to be turbulent. The peasants here, after passing resolutions of confiscation, have proceeded to take possession of the lands and drive the landowners away.

The peasants announced that they would undertake the Spring sowing themselves, but owing to lack of seed this is said to be impossible. In consequence the sowing is likely to be much delayed and a serious shortage of crops is feared. The authorities are taking the matter in hand and hope to prevent such a misfortune.

Peasants' conferences, to which delegates are sent from even the smallest communes, are being organized in every province of Russia to discuss peasant needs. Those already held have insisted on a proper distribution of land. One characteristic resolution demands that all land which private landowners cannot sow must immediately be surrendered temporarily to the peasants, soldiers' wives to receive shares free, and others at moderate rent, to be fixed by the local community.

Considerable ill-feeling is shown in some districts toward landowners. Bessarabian peasants in one instance sacked a country house and estates belonging to a rich family. The peasants of the Tambov Government surrounded the houses of the landowners and compelled them to sign documents surrendering their lands. In many districts the peasants have taken no action, waiting for the authorities to act. In some parts of Bessarabia the country people are highly reactionary and in one district especially the Odessa military authorities have taken strong measures to suppress a counter-revolutionary movement. The Grand Committee of the Alliance of Peasants has addressed the following petition to the peasants at the front:

"Do your duty. Do not fear that the lands will be divided without you. This division cannot be made by isolated villages, for that would provoke internal quarrels by which the enemy might profit. Only the Constituent Assembly, wherein you will be represented, will decide this important question."

At a conference held at the offices of the Minister of Commerce to discuss the question of a Government coal monopoly, it was proposed to place all mineral combustibles at the disposal of the Government and regularize their distribution. No objection was made by coal representatives at the conference, and it is believed that the scheme will be put into effect about the middle of May.

April 26, 1917

Turbulent Record of Russia's Disturber, Lenine

His Acquaintances Here Discredit Theory That He Takes German Money—A Mixture of Extreme Radicalism and Vanity

DISPATCHES from Russia during the last fortnight have been full of a name new to American readers — Lenine. We hear of Lenine traveling through Germany and receiving every sort of courtesy and aid from the German authorities; of Lenine haranguing a crowd from the balcony of the Petrograd home of a famous Russian dancer; of adherents of Lenine driven from one of his lectures by an infuriated mob of Russians as a protest against his peace-at-any-price exhortations; of a parade of Russian soldiers, wounded in battle against the Germans, marching through the streets of Petrograd with banners bearing inscriptions advising "Lenine & Co." to discontinue their pro-German agitation and "get back to William," their boss.

As these dispatches follow each other in quick succession the American reader, accustomed these many years to names of Russian Socialists long on syllables and short on vowels, rubs his eyes and asks, "But who is Lenine?" Yet, new as the name is to most people hereabout, there is nothing new about it in Russia or to the Russians of New York's east side.

If you climb several flights of dark stairs in Seventh Street to the editorial offices of one Russian paper, or descend into a basement that is almost a cellar in St. Mark's Place and interview the editors of another, or talk to the proprietors of dingy bookstores in Grand Street and East Broadway, you will hear plenty about Lenine.

Some will tell you of him as a firebrand and troublemaker, a "scrapper" who advocates peace-at-any-price, one to whom the welfare of Russia is as nothing compared to the progress of international Socialism.

Others, radicals, enemies of all that savors of order, incline rather to emphasizing his achievements as a writer on economic and political subjects, as a standard bearer of Russian radical democracy, who, time and again in hot water with the old Romanoff régime, was forced to save his life by hiding from the police and smuggling himself into exile.

All his life Lenine has been "agin the Government." Not only that—he comes of a family of chronic rebels. Brothers and sisters of his have stood in the ultra-radical ranks of Russia. One brother, while a student at Petrograd in 1887, was hanged for complicity in a plot to assassinate Czar Alexander II.

The man who has now leaped into the limelight as the arch-troublemaker against the new democratic régime in Russia has been prominent among the Socialists of his native land since the early nineties. He is described by Russians here who know him personally as a man about 45 years old, one of the most fiery of all Russian orators, who chooses the simplest of words and phrases in his speeches. He is a personal friend of Gorky and other renowned Russian writers. In the years preceding the war he exerted wide influence among his countrymen.

Lenine is not his real name. It is one of various pen names adopted by him in the course of his journalistic activities. His real name is Vladimir Ilitch Ulianoff, and he hails from the district of Simbirsk in the Volga region of Russia. He first came to the fore as far back as 1895, when he wrote a book on economics strongly impregnated with revolutionary doctrines. That got him "in bad" right then and there with the Czarists. From that year onward Lenine began to spend a good part of his time away from Russia. Now you would find him in Paris, now in Switzerland, now in Austria. Russians here in New York, who knew what the life of a Russian revolutionist was, wink when you ask if his exile was unbroken.

"I know personally that Lenine was in Russia at least on one occasion when he was 'officially' in Switzerland," remarked the editor of a Russian daily here, when questioned on the subject. "And he has been in Russia several times under an assumed name since the revolutionary troubles of 1905," he added.

Lenine's second book appeared in 1899, and is by far the best known of all his works. It is entitled "The Development of Capitalism in Russia," and placed its author in the forefront of the Russian Socialist Party. It was written when there was a bitter struggle on between the two wings of the party—the Social Democrats, with whom Lenine was affiliated, and the Social Revolutionists. The former were imbued with the doctrines of Karl Marx and tended toward internationalism as against the more purely Russian wing, followers of Mikhaelovski, who placed the interests of Russia ahead of internationalistic doctrines.

The fight was furious, and both sides claimed the victory. The split in the party has subsisted ever since.

In 1901 Lenine bobbed up as editor of the Socialistic newspaper Iskra, (the Spark.) It was published in Paris, the desire of the Czar's police to lay hands on Lenine having become so pressing as to render his residence in Russia impossible. This paper had a big circulation in Russia in spite of the fact that any one found with a copy of it in his possession was sent to prison forthwith.

In 1903 Lenine attended the convention of the Social Democrats and wrote the Agrarian program of the party. But there came another split. Lenine became the intellectual leader of the so-called "Bolsheviki," who favored a more radical program than was agreeable to the other side.

In the fateful year 1905 Lenine published another book called "For Twelve Years," consisting of essays and articles on various subjects. After that he became a candidate for the Second Duma, from the District of Petrograd, but he was defeated. He was active in the revolutionary movement of that year, which brought Red Monday and was the most serious with which the Czar's régime had been confronted for a long time. When the rebels had been downed Lenine again found foreign countries more healthful and resided abroad continuously—at least he did "officially"—until the events which have just brought him again into prominence.

At the outbreak of the war he was in Cracow, capital of Austrian Poland, where he was promptly jailed as an alien enemy. But he was soon released by the Austrian authorities, whereupon he returned to his old haunts, Paris and Switzerland. Soon after the beginning of the war he started another paper, the International Socialist, issued in Switzerland.

"Lenine is obstinate, strong-willed, and very hard to get along with," said a Russian here in New York. "His books were forbidden by the censor under the old régime, and all copies of the one on capitalism found by the police were burned."

He shook his head emphatically when asked whether the agitator was in the pay of the Germans.

"I am against him," he said, "and so are most Russians here, but I am convinced that he is doing what he is doing not for the Germans, but for what he thinks are the interests of international Socialism. His actions help the Germans, of course, but he is no German agent. You have the same kind of internationalist here—Hillquit is one—who places internationalism above all else.

"The bulk of the Russian Socialists are opposed to Lenine. They are for the continuation of the war against Germany. Lenine scornfully dubs these men 'social patriots,' and declares that, because they do not want peace for the sake of the development of international Socialism, they are not real Socialists at all.

"They retort by calling him and his crowd 'Porajentsi'—the people who want defeat. And they heap accusations on Lenine of complicity with the Germans and ask him searching questions as to how it happened that he traveled across Germany by special train and was made much of by the authorities there.

"His adherents explain this away by asserting that when he crossed Germany recently there happened to be a special train bearing Russian prisoners of war who had been exchanged for Germans held in Russia, and that Lenine was allowed to ride on the train purely as a matter of courtesy.

"I think it safe to say that if Lenine were actually in the pay of the Germans or really doing German propaganda work he would have been arrested long ago."

May 6, 1917

OVERTHROW OF THE OLD ORDER

SEIZE KRONSTADT, DEFY GOVERNMENT

Workmen's Delegates in Great Russian Fortress Repudiate the Provisional Cabinet.

COMMERCE MINISTER QUITS

PETROGRAD, June 1.—The Workmen's and Soldiers' Delegates reached today the fateful decision to assume control of Kronstadt, the great fortress which defends Petrograd. This decision was carried by a vote of 210 votes against 40, with eight of the delegates abstaining from voting.

It is announced by the Workmen's and Soldiers' Delegates that henceforth the relations of Kronstadt with Petrograd and the remainder of Russia will be only through the intermediary of the Petrograd branch of the delegates. The local Workmen's and Soldiers' Council at Kronstadt announces that it has taken in its hands he effecive power of Kronsadt, that it does not recognize the Provisional Government, and that it has removed all the Government's representatives.

The Minister of Justice has notified his colleagues of this development, and on their instructions has communicated with the Kronstadt Council with a view to inducing it to revoke its orders.

The conflict between Vice Admiral Koltchak, Commander in Chief of the Black Sea Fleet, and the Council of Soldiers' and Workmen's Delegates has been settled, the official news agency announces, the Admiral remaining at his post at Sebastopol.

LONDON, Saturday, June 2.—A dispatch to Reuter's Telegram Company from Petrograd says A. I. Konovaloff, Minister of Commerce and Trade, has resigned, owing to a complete divergence in views with M. Skobeleff, Minister of Labor, concerning the economic and financial measures necessary in the present crisis.

Strikes or other measures to paralyze productoion have been decided upon in more than 120 of the largest factories in Petrograd, most of which are engaged in war work.

After the failure of efforts of the Conciliation Board to reach an agreement on many points, the staffs of the factories resolved to strike or alternatively to paralyze work by carrying out all regulations to the letter. The time and form of strikes are to be decided in each factory separately.

According to the Novaia Zhizn, Maxim Gorky's paper, the demands of the workers include a six-hour day and a minimum wage for women of 150 rubles (about $75) monthly.

It is believed that the latest act of the organized irreconcilable forces of Russia is intended to bring the navy under their dominion, just as the army is already through its delegates.

The Council of Workmen's and Soldiers' Delegates after repudiating, on May 6, the Provisional Government's declaration to the Allies of April 9, announcing its retention of the Allies' policy of freeing small nations and demanding indemnities from the Teutons, has been in constant conflict with the Government's attempt to maintain discipline in the army and navy so seriously menaced by the council's decree early in April to the effect that the soldiers should choose their own officers.

There have been several cases where delinquent soldiers condemned for infraction of the most fundamental discipline have been rehabilitated by the council and their accusers or judges dismissed or ordered to resign, or have voluntarily resigned, as they could not maintain discipline. These things have been going on while speakers of the council, on the invitation of M. Kerensky, were supposed to be at the front appealing to the soldiers to obey their officers.

June 2, 1917

ANTI-CABINET RIOTS START IN PETROGRAD

PETROGRAD, July 16, (Delayed.)—Two demonstrations against the Government resulted in the firing of shots in the Nevsky Prospect at midnight, as a result of which a number of persons were killed or wounded.

The firing apparently was the result of stray shots which brought on a panic, in which the demonstrators turned rifles and machine guns on each other. Quiet was restored after a few minutes.

The demonstrations were organized by the Bolsheviki, the majority faction of the Social-Democratic Party.

LONDON, Wednesday, July 18. Reuter's Petrograd correspondent in a dispatch dated Tuesday, telling of the disorders in the Russian capital, says:

"The Maximalist leaders tried to provoke a mutiny in the Petrograd garrison yesterday in consequence of reports that measures had been taken against some regiments at the front which had been insubordinate. The attempts at the outset met with little success, but gradually some of the soldiers were won over.

"Early in the evening armed groups of demonstrators paraded the streets, and later motor lorries carrying machine guns appeared and moved incessantly to and fro. The people, who at first had for the most part kept to their houses, finding no disorder was taking place, filled the streets as spectators and as auditors at open-air meetings.

July 18, 1917

KERENSKY MADE DICTATOR OF RUSSIA; COUNCILS, FEARING COUNTER REVOLT, APPEAL TO ARMY TO SAVE COUNTRY

PETROGRAD, July 23. — Unlimited powers for the re-establishment of public order, both at the front and at home, were voted to the Government of Premier Kerensky today by the Council of Workmen's and Soldiers' Delegates and the Council of Delegates of the Peasants of All Russia at a joint sitting.

The Cabinet is designated as the Government of National Safety.

Orders have been given to fire on deserters and runaways at the front, and warrants have been issued for the arrest of revolutionary agitators wherever they may be. Rear Admiral Verderviski, commander of the Baltic fleet, has been seized for communicating a secret Government telegram to sailors' committees. Lieutenant Dashkevitch and another executive committeeman of the Workmen's and Soldiers' Council also have been arrested, the former on the charge of inciting the Peterhof troops to remove the Provisional Government.

The decision of the councils to resort to the extreme measure of conferring supreme and unrestricted power on the Government was reached after a session that lasted throughout the night and was embodied in the following resolution, which was passed by 252 to 37:

Recognizing that the country is menaced by a military debacle on the front and by anarchy at home it is resolved:

First—That the country and the revolution are endangered:

Second—That the Provisional Government is proclaimed the Government of National Safety;

Third—That unlimited powers are accorded the Government for re-establishing the organization and discipline of the army for a fight to the finish against the enemies of public order and for the realization of the whole program embodied in the governmental program just announced.

There are indications that the Workmen's and Soldiers' Council, after the events of the past week and all circumstances connected therewith, are apprehensive of a counter-revolution. The Central Committee has issued a manifesto calling local organizations of the revolutionary democracy and army to be ready at any moment to rally round their political centres, namely, the Councils of the Workmen and Soldiers.

The chaotic conditions prevailing on part of the Rusian front were disclosed in a telegram sent to Premier Kerensky, the Provisional Government and the Council of Workmen's and Soldiers' Delegates by the Executive Committee and the Commissioner of the Provisional Government with the Second Army, on the southwestern front. The telegram announced the inauguration of stern measures to combat disaffection.

"We unanimously recognize that the situation demands extreme measures and efforts, for everything must be risked to save the revolution from 'catastrophe,'" the message reads. "The Commander in Chief on the western front and the commander of the Second Army today have given orders to fire on deserters and runaways.

"Let the country know the truth. Let it see it without mercy. Let it find enough courage to strike those who by their cowardice are destroying Russia and the revolution.

"Most military units are in a state of complete disorganization. Their spirit for the offensive has utterly disappeared. They no longer listen to orders of their leaders, and they neglect all exhortations of comrades, even replying by threats and shots. Some elements voluntarily evacuate positions without even waiting for the approach of the enemy.

"Cases are on record in which an order given to proceed with all haste to such and such a spot to assist comrades in distress has been discussed for several hours at meeting, and reinforcements consequently have been delayed several hours.

"These troops abandon their positions at the first shots of the enemy. For a distance of several hundred versts long files of deserters, armed and unarmed, men in good health and robust, who have lost all shame and feel they can act altogether with impunity, are proceeding to the rear. Frequently entire units desert in this manner."

A dispatch to the Bourse Gazette from Nijni Novgorod relates that on July 17 a regiment of troops ordered disbanded for insubordination mutinied, took possession of the town and were still in control July 20. Cadets sent from Moscow to subdue them battled with revolvers, resulting in casualties to both sides and the surrender of the mutineers, who at last accounts were held prisoners. A parley with the Commander of the Moscow garrison after order had been restored resulted in an agreement to surrender control.

As concerns the situation in the capital, the disarming of workmen, including the so-called Red Guards, is proceeding systematically in the Vasilly Island and Viborg quarters. More than 1,200 rifles and revolvers and some machine guns have been recovered. The majority of the revolvers were obtained at the fortress of St. Peter and St. Paul, where cases just arrived from America had been broken open. According to the Russkia Volia, about a third of the arms stolen since the outbreak have been accounted for. Several carts with shells were stopped on the banks of the Neva. The military authorities knew nothing about them. The drivers were arrested and the carts taken to the arsenal.

Three occupants of a motor car dressed as sailors and soldiers shot with revolvers at a group of officers and soldiers on the steps of the People's Palace, two soldiers being wounded. The guard of 150 soldiers rushed from the building and fired on the three men, who attempted to escape, but who were lynched by the crowd. Fifteen civilians were wounded in the firing, some seriously.

M. Pereveizeff, who resigned recently as Minister of Justice, has sent to the press a letter regarding his resignation. He said all his activity against lawbreakers was paralyzed by the general line of conduct of the coalition Government.

July 24, 1917

From Terrorism to Revolution

TROTZKY IS ARRESTED.

Agitator from America Accused of Being Accomplice of Lenine.

PETROGRAD, Aug. 6. By order of the Ministry of Marine Leon Trotzky and M. Lunacharsky were arrested today.

The men are International Socialists and leaders in the Council of Workmen's and Soldiers' Delegates. They are charged with being accomplices of Nikolai Lenine, leader of the Maximalists, during the disorders in July.

Leon Trotzky left the United States for Russia on March 27 with eight other Russian Socialists expecting to take posts in the administration of the new Russian revolutionary Government. British authorities held the party at Halifax and detained them in a camp in Nova Scotia while an examination of Trotzky's record was conducted. He was released in April and allowed to make his way into Russia, where nothing of his activities has been heard until his arrest was reported.

Trotzky was one of the leaders of the Russian revolution of 1905, and finally became President of the Russian Council of Labor Deputies after President Chrustalev Nosar had been arrested in the general strike of October, 1905. During his term the Black Sea mutiny and several revolts in the garrisons of Petrograd were instigated.

Then he was sentenced to two years in Siberia and spent part of this time in the prison at Tobolsk. He had already served a term of two years, beginning in 1900, for his writings against the Russian Government. It was said that he escaped from Siberia before the expiration of his first term and was in Vienna as the guest of Dr. Friedrich Adler, the Socialist who assassinated the Austrian Premier, when news of the "Bloody Sunday" reached him. With the aid of Dr. Adler, it was said, Trotzky disguised himself and returned to Russia, but was discovered and sent to Siberia to serve an additional term.

At the beginning of the war Trotzky was in Berlin editing a Jewish newspaper, and the Foreign Office gave him three hours to pass over the Swiss frontier. It is said he made the journey in two hours. After a few weeks in Zurich he went to Paris and began the publication of a Socialist paper, printed in Russian, called Our Words. His opposition to war was bitter, but his advocacy of peace was unheeded until the arrival of Russian soldiers on the Western front. Then, following the killing of Colonel Krause by intoxicated Russian soldiers who had copies of Our Words in their pockets, Trotzky's paper was suppressed and he was taken to the Spanish frontier by an armed guard.

The commander of the guard telegraphed to the police in Madrid that a dangerous anarchist was to arrive there at a given hour, and Trotzky again received the escort of an armed guard, this time to the Madrid jail, but he was released after three days. A guard at Seville then escorted him to jail and the same guard took him to Cadiz to see that he boarded the Montserrat, bound for the United States. After his arrival here Trotzky continued his writing and talking for peace, Socialism and anarchism.

August 7, 1917

EXTREMISTS WIN PETROGRAD.

Elect 143 Seats Out of 187 in New Municipal Council.

PETROGRAD, Wednesday, Sept. 5.— New municipal elections have been held in Petrograd, resulting in a victory for the radicals. The Social Revolutionaries and Bolsheviki inflicted a severe defeat on the Moderate Socialists and the Constitutional Democrats.

The Social Revolutionaries polled 182,000 votes, the Bolsheviki 174,000, and the Constitutional Democrats 101,000. The Social Revolutionaries elected 73 Municipal Councilors, the Bolsheviki 70, and the Constitutional Democrats 44.

September 7, 1917

Proclamation Issued by Premier Kerensky Ousting Korniloff and Declaring a State of Siege

PETROGRAD, Sept. 10.—Premier Kerensky today issued the following proclamation:

On Sept. 8 a member of the Duma, M. Lvoff, arrived in Petrograd and called upon me, in the name of General Korniloff, to hand over all civil and military powers to the Generalissimo, who would form a new government at his pleasure. The authenticity of this summons was afterward confirmed by General Korniloff himself, who had a conversation with me over the direct telegraphic wire between Petrograd and main headquarters.

Considering this summons, addressed through me to the Provisional Government, as an attempt by certain quarters to profit by the difficult situation of the country and establish a state of things contrary to the conquests of the revolution, the Provisional Government has recognized the necessity of charging me, for the safety of the republican régime, to take the urgent, indispensable measures necessary to cut at the roots all attempts against the supreme power and rights of the citizens won by the revolution.

I, therefore, for the maintenance in the country of liberty and public order, am taking all measures, which I shall announce at the proper moment to the people. At the same time, I order General Korniloff to hand over his functions to General Klembovsky, Commander in Chief of the armies on the northern front, which bar the way to Petrograd, and I order General Klembovsky to assume provisionally the functions of Generalissimo while remaining at Pskov.

Secondly, I declare a state of war in the town and district of Petrograd.

I appeal to all citizens to remain calm, maintain the order necessary for the welfare of the fatherland and the army and navy, and tranquilly and faithfully fulfill their duty in the defense of the fatherland against the foreign enemy.

September 11, 1917

OVERTHROW OF THE OLD ORDER

KERENSKY MENACED BY NEW POLITICAL CRISIS IN RUSSIA

Cabinet Again Split as Bolsheviki Gain Control of Council and Seek Power.

PETROGRAD, Sept. 14.—Friction between the Constitutional Democrats and the Socialists in the Cabinet led to all of the former, save one, withdrawing yesterday, and the crisis continued all day, despite attempts to form a working organization.

The evening newspapers assert that Premier Kerensky is in a very difficult position, and that his resignation is not excluded from the possibilities.

The situation is complicated by the attitude of the Petrograd Council of Deputies, in which at last night's meeting the Bolsheviks for the first time gained an overwhelming majority of 279 against 150 in favor of the extreme radical position, which declares that not only the Social Democrats but all the representatives of property-owning classes must be excluded from power.

This program also demanded an immediate declaration of a democratic republic, the abolition of private property, working class control over production, confiscation of war profits, the "merciless taxation" of capital, an immediate invitation to the warring States to conclude peace, &c.

Korniloff Has Not Surrendered.

The Associated Press is officially informed that General Korniloff has not yet surrendered. Still faithful to him are some of the "striking battalions," and also a considerable number of detachments of Tekke Turcomans.

General Alexieff and M. Virouboff, his civil assistant, according to an announcement by the War Department, were due to arrive at Russian Main Headquarters late today.

Mixed detachments of revolutionary troops, composed of infantry, cavalry, and artillery, concentrated at Orsha, Smolensk, and Vitebsk, have been ordered by Premier Kerensky to march on Mohilev and reinforce the elements of the garrison remaining loyal to the Government and arrest Generals Korniloff and Lokomsky and others concerned in the revolt.

September 15, 1917

DISORDERS GROWING AMONG THE PEASANTS

Russian Masses Discouraged by Results of New Order—Forces of Reaction Busy.

By HAROLD WILLIAMS.
Copyright, 1917, by The New York Times Company.
Special Cable to THE NEW YORK TIMES.

PETROGRAD, Thursday, Oct. 11.—The new Government has published its program and gone to work. The Provisional Council or ante-Parliament is to meet Oct. 19. The Bolsheviks of the Petrograd Soviet have openly declared war on the Government, and are mobilizing their forces and preparing for the struggle. Other Socialist groups are hesitating and debating, troubled and depressed by a sense of disunion and irresolution.

Two months remain until the meeting of the constituent assembly, and this will be the most difficult of all. The Bolsheviks think they are gaining the upper hand among the masses. This is true and untrue. It is true so far as meetings, votes, and resolutions are concerned. It is untrue if it means that the great masses of the people sympathize with the Bolsheviks or are prepared to support them actively. The prevailing feeling is one of apathy, weariness, disillusionment.

In the workmen's committees the Bolsheviks are strong, but most of the workmen have ceased to attend the meetings. In the villages the peasants ignore the elections and express disgust for all committees and have gone back to the old system of having simply an elder and a clerk.

The masses of the people have lost faith in the new order. This does not mean as yet that they desire the restoration of the old régime, but they are baffled, depressed, and disappointed. They see no guiding hand. They have lost faith in extravagant promises. They cannot understand the perpetual strife of parties. They are accustomed to authority and they see no authority. They have been promised a new heaven and a new earth and they see only increasing disorder.

During the last few weeks agrarian disorders have become serious. Whereas earlier the peasants quietly appropriated for their own use the land of neighboring proprietors, they now pillage and plunder, kill valuable livestock, burn corn in the proprietors' barns, and wreck houses and furniture.

The wave of agrarian disorders is spreading from the Central Governments down to the Volga, and the released convicts and undisciplined soldiery are taking a prominent part in the riots. Restraining influences have been removed. The peasants, seeing no evidence of system or order, seeing no authority to guide or restrain, consider that they may as well take advantage of the situation. The wilder spirits among them are breaking loose, and the more sober peasants, who still form a majority, are bereft of force or argument to oppose them.

The disorders are serious. They are symptomatic of a very grave state of affairs, but their possible consequences must not be exaggerated. Russia is a very big country, and the proportion of disorder is still comparatively small. The marvel is, considering the complete absence of real and effective authority, that the country is as quiet as it is.

Tashkent, the capital of Turkestan, has been cut off from the rest of Russia for ten days by a local mutiny. Now that the military force has arrived and the veil is lifted it appears that there has not been any wholesale destruction of life or property.

It would be easy to fill a newspaper with a list of the cruel robberies and brutal murders that take place daily in various parts of Russia. Yet these are far less characteristic of the situation than the gloomy patience and slow working passive instinct for self-preservation that now constitute the only guarantee of security in the country. But for the next two months the Government will have an extremely difficult task in asserting its authority and checking the spread of those forces of disorder which threaten to reduce the patience of the people to despair and foster all the tendencies to reaction.

October 15, 1917

PETROGRAD COUNCIL DEMANDS EARLY PEACE

Accused of Planning Civil War in an Effort to Get the Supreme Power.

The Petrograd Council of Soldiers' and Workmen's Delegates on Monday adopted a resolution proposed by Leon Trotzky, President of its Executive Committee and a leading Maximalist, declaring the salvation of the country lies in the conclusion of peace as quickly as possible.

The resolution accuses Premier Kerensky of a desire to deliver Petrograd into the hands of the Germans and their "imperialist allies," and also of openly favoring the German Emperor. It demands that all power shall pass into the hands of the Councils of Soldiers and Workmen and instructs the Executive Committee to propose an armistice to all the nations. As long as peace is not concluded, continues the resolution, the committee must defend Petrograd and restore the army to the status of a combative force.

In consequence of this resolution the Petrograd Council of Soldiers' and Workmen's Delegates has decided to form a revolutionary general staff for the defense of Petrograd.

In an address to the council, Trotzky explained why the Bolsheviki bolted the first meeting of the Russian Democratic Congress, saying that body had not been representative of the people and was not trusted by the soldiers and workmen.

"With the formation of the Preliminary Parliament," he said, "the independence of the ruling power was confirmed officially. Russia is a republic, but its autocrat is Kerensky."

He urged the Soldiers' and Workmen's Councils to be ready to fight for the handing over of the power to them, saying they would be able to save the country and make peace.

Delegate Lieber, the spokesman of the Minimalists, expressed surprise at Trotzky's attitude, inasmuch as the bolting of the congress had the approval only of a small majority of the Bolsheviki.

M. Avksentieff said that the walkout was only a demonstration which could have no effort on the work of the Congress, since in the eyes of all Russia the body continues to be the same authoritative organization. The Bolsheviki, he said, had lost for themselves the right of further participation in it.

The evening newspapers which publish the program for the meeting of the Central Council of Soldiers' and Workmen's Delegates on Nov. 2 are filled with rumors of a Bolsheviki demonstration and an attempt to seize the Government on that date. The program for the discussions of the council embraces five topics: The revolutionary democracy and its power, the conditions of peace, the constituent assembly, demobilization of the army and the fight against anarchy and pogroms.

The Vechernee Vremya says:

"The Soldiers' and Workmen's Delegates frankly admit that they are planning civil war."

October 25, 1917

From Terrorism to Revolution

REVOLUTIONISTS SEIZE PETROGRAD; KERENSKY FLEES

MINISTERS UNDER ARREST

Winter Palace Is Taken After Fierce Defense by Women Soldiers.

FORT'S GUNS TURNED ON IT

Cruiser and Armored Cars Also Brought Into Battle Waged by Searchlight.

TROTZSKY HEADS REVOLT

Giving Land to the Peasants and Calling of Constituent Assembly Promised.

PETROGRAD, Nov. 8.—With the aid of the capital's garrison complete control of Petrograd has been seized by the Maximalists, or Bolsheviki, headed by Nikolai Lenine, the Radical Socialist leader, and Leon Trotzsky, President of the Central Executive Committee of the Petrograd Council of Workmen's and Soldiers' Delegates. Their action has been indorsed by the All-Russia Congress of Workmen's Councils.

A proclamation has been issued declaring that the Revolutionary Government purposes to negotiate an "immediate democratic peace," to turn the land over to the peasantry, and to convoke the Constituent Assembly.

Premier Kerensky has fled. He is variously said to be headed for Moscow and the northern front of the army, and orders for his arrest have been issued. Last night he was reported to be at Luga, eighty-five miles southwest of Petrograd. Several members of his Cabinet have been taken into custody.

The Preliminary Parliament is declared dissolved.

Little serious fighting has attended the revolt so far. The Provisional Government troops holding the bridges over the Neva and various other points yesterday were quickly overpowered, save at the Winter Palace, the chief guardians of which were the Women's Battalion. Here last night a battle royal took place for four hours, during which the Bolsheviki brought up armored cars and the cruiser Aurora and turned the guns of the Fort of St. Peter and St. Paul upon the palace before its defenders would surrender.

Prior to the attack the Workmen's and Soldiers' leaders sent the Provisional Government an ultimatum demanding their surrender and allowing twenty minutes' grace. The Government replied indirectly, refusing to recognize the Military Committee.

Vice President Kameneff of the Workmen's and Soldiers' Delegates told The Associated Press today that the object of taking possession of the posts and telegraphs was to thwart any effort the Government might make to call troops to the capital. The Russkia Volia and the Bourse Gazette have been commandeered.

The city today presented a normal aspect. Even the noonday band accompanying the guard of relief under the previous administration continued its function. There were the customary lines in front of the provision stores and children played in the parks and gardens. There was even a notable lessening of the patrols, only a few armed soldiers and sailors moving about the streets.

How the Revolt Developed.

The Maximalist movement toward seizing authority, rumors of which had been agitating the public mind ever since the formation of the last Coalition Cabinet, culminated Tuesday night, when, without disorder, Maximalist forces took possession of the Telegraph office and the Petrograd Telegraph Agency.

Orders issued by the Government for the opening of the spans of the bridges across the Neva later were overridden by the Military Committee of the Council of Workmen's and Soldiers' Delegates. Communication was restored after several hours of interruption. Nowhere did the Maximalists meet with serious opposition.

An effort by militiamen to disperse crowds gathered in the Nevski and Letainy Prospekts during the evening provoked a fight in which one man is reported to have been killed. Minor disturbances, some of them accompanied by shooting, occurred in various quarters of the city. A number of persons are reported to have been killed or wounded.

Yesterday morning found patrols of soldiers, sailors, and civilians in the streets maintaining order. Further than a continuation of suppressed excitement, the streets of the city presented no unusual aspects. The shops and banks which had opened for business began closing up about noon.

Shortly after noon a Soviet force occupied the telephone exchange, where a small guard had been stationed for weeks. An effort by Government forces to retake the exchange led to a brief fusillade, by which it is believed a number of casualties was caused. The Maximalists remained in possession of the building.

Toward 5 o'clock in the afternoon the Military Revolutionary Committee issued its proclamation stating that Petrograd was in its hands. It read:

To the Army Committees of the Active Army and to all Councils of Workmen's and Soldiers' Delegates and to the Garrison and Proletariat of Petrograd:

We have deposed the Government of Kerensky, which rose against the revolution and the people. The change which resulted in the deposition of the Provisional Government was accomplished without bloodshed. The Petrograd Council of Workmen's and Soldiers' Delegates solemnly welcomes the accomplished change and proclaims the authority of the Military Revolutionary Committee until the creation of a Government by the Workmen's and Soldiers' Delegates.

Announcing this to the army at the front, the Revolutionary Committee calls upon the revolutionary soldiers to watch closely the conduct of the men in command. Officers who do not join the accomplished revolution immediately and openly must be arrested at once as enemies.

The Petrograd Council of Workmen's and Soldiers' Delegates considers this to be the program of the new authority:

First—The offer of an immediate democratic peace.

Second—The immediate handing over of large proprietarial lands to the peasants.

Third—The transmission of all authority to the Council of Workmen's and Soldiers' Delegates.

Fourth—The honest convocation of a Constitutional Assembly.

The national revolutionary army must not permit uncertain military detachments to leave the front for Petrograd. They should use persuasion, but where this fails they must oppose any such action on the part of these detachments by force without mercy.

The actual order must be read immediately to all military detachments in all arms. The suppression of this order from the rank and file by army organizations is equivalent to a great crime against the revolution and will be punished by all the strength of the revolutionary law.

Soldiers! For peace, for bread, for land, and for the power of the people! (Signed)

THE MILITARY REVOLUTIONARY COMMITTEE.

Delegates from the three Cossack regiments quartered here declared they would not obey the Provisional Government and would not march against the Workmen's and Soldiers' Delegates, but that they were prepared to maintain public order.

Council Welcomes Lenine.

The Petrograd Council of Workmen's and Soldiers' Delegates held a meeting at which M. Trotzky made his declaration that the Government no longer existed; that some of the Ministers had been arrested, and that the preliminary Parliament had been dissolved. He introduced Nikolai Lenine as "an old comrade whom we welcome back."

Lenine, who was received with prolonged cheers, said:

"Now we have a revolution. The peasants and workmen control the Government. This is only a preliminary step toward a similar revolution everywhere."

He outlined the three problems now before the Russian democracy. First, immediate conclusion of the war, for which purpose the new Government must propose an armistice to the belligerents; second, the handing over of the land to the peasant; third, settlement of the economic crisis.

At the close of the sitting a declaration was read from the representatives of the Democratic Minimalist Party of the Workmen's and Soldiers' Delegates, stating that the party disapproved of the coup d'état and withdrew from the Council of Workmen's and Soldiers' Delegates.

Later it was announced that the split in the Council had been healed and that a call had been sent out for a delegate from each 25,000 of the population to express the will of the Russian Army. Following is the text of this document:

To All Army Corps and Divisional Committees:

Today there is a reunion of the Workmen's and Soldiers' Delegates. The army committees are ordered to send delegates for expressing the will of the army. We suggest to you to send delegates immediately from your midst. To refuse to take part in deciding the destiny of the revolution is a sin which history will not pardon. Elect a delegate from each 25,000 and send them to the reunion. (Signed)

THE PETROGRAD WORKMEN'S AND SOLDIERS' DELEGATES.

Congress of Councils Approves.

Subsequently the General Congress of Workmen's and Soldiers' Delegates of all Russia convened with 260 out of 560 delegates in attendance. The Chairman declared that the time was not propitious for political speeches, and the order of business of the congress approved was as follows:

First—Organization of power.
Second—Peace and war.
Third—A constituent Assembly.

The officers elected comprise fourteen Maximalists, including Nikolai Lenine and M. Zinovieff, an associate of Lenine, and Leon Trotzky. In addition seven revolutionary Socialists were appointed.

A delegation was named to initiate peace negotiations with the other revolutionary and democratic organizations "with a view to taking steps to stop bloodshed."

A resolution proposed by the Minimalists that an effort would be made to reach an agreement with the Provisional Government was voted down.

Of the 560 members of the Congress, 250 are Bolsheviki, 150 Socialist revolutionists, sixty Minimalists, fourteen of the Minimalist-Internationalist group, six of the Nationalist-Socialist group, three non-party Socialists, the others being independent.

The official news agency today made public the following statement:

"The Congress of the Councils of Workmen's and Soldiers' Delegates of all Russia, which opened last evening, issued this morning the three following proclamations:

To All Provincial Councils of Workmen's and Soldiers' and Peasants' Delegates.

All power lies in the Workmen's and Soldiers' Delegates. Government commissaries are relieved of their functions. Presidents of the Workmen's and Soldiers' Delegates are to communicate direct with the Revolutionary Government. All members of agricultural committees who have been arrested are to be set at liberty immediately and the commissioners who arrested them are in turn to be arrested.

"The second proclamation reads as follows:

The death penalty re-established at the front by Premier Kerensky is abolished and complete freedom for political propaganda has been established at the front. All revolutionary soldiers and officers who have been arrested for complicity in so-called political crimes are to be set at liberty immediately.

"The third proclamation says:

Former Ministers Konovaloff, Kishkin, Terestchenko, Malyanovitch, Nikitin, and others have been arrested by the revolutionary committee.

Mr. Kerensky has taken flight and all military bodies have been empowered to take all possible measures to arrest Kerensky and bring him back to Petrograd. All complicity with Kerensky will be dealt with as high treason.

Capture of the Winter Palace.

While the All-Russian Congress of Councils had been deliberating the Government forces, including the Women's Battalion, which had been guarding the Winter Palace had been driven inside in the course of a lively machine-gun and rifle battle, during which the cruiser Aurora, that had been moored in the Neva at the Nicolai Bridge, moved up within range, firing shrapnel, and armored cars swung into action. Then the guns of the Fortress of St. Peter and St. Paul, across the river, opened on the structure.

The palace stood out under the glare of the searchlights of the cruiser and offered a good target for the guns. The defenders held out for four hours, replying as best they could with machine guns and rifles, but at 2 o'clock this morning were compelled to surrender.

Meanwhile there had been spasmodic firing in other parts of the city, but the Workmen's and Soldiers' troops took every means to protect citizens, who were ordered to their quarters. The bridges and the Nevsky Prospect, which early in the afternoon were in the hands of the Government forces, were captured and held during the night by the Workmen's and Soldiers' troops.

November 9, 1917

SOVIET PENSIONS NINE REGICIDES

Of Those Who Took Part in the Assassination Of Czar Alexander Only a Few Minor Accomplices Survive

THE Soviet Government commemorated on March 14 a "revolutionary anniversary"—the anniversary of a momentous event. For no one knows what course the Russian history would have taken if Czar Alexander II had not been assassinated in St. Petersburg forty-five years ago, on March 14, 1881. Indeed, would Communists rule in Russia at the present time if the bomb thrown at this most liberal of Russian Emperors had not killed him at the moment he was outlining the reforms that were expected to be the gradual establishment of a constitutional régime in Russia? It is a debatable point.

At all events the Soviet Government has granted to eight women and one man, who took part in the assassination, life pensions of $112 a month. The nine survivors of the deed, whose names are not quoted in the dispatches, participated in it but indirectly, for not one of its real authors is alive. Those pensioned are, so to speak, second rate regicides.

Probably no Russian Emperor less deserved to become the victim of a terroristic act than Czar Alexander, "the Liberator." The abolition of serfdom in 1861, the release of land to the peasants, the introduction of Zemstvos, the radical reform of courts of justice, the introduction of the jury system and more liberal educational measures—these reforms were part of the record of this ruler. On the eve of his death the word "Constitution" was in the air. Together with his Home Minister, Count Loris-Melikoff, he had considered the idea of a sort of a representative chamber.

Eight Plots Against Czar.

Nevertheless, revolutionists pursued him with unrelaxing energy. In the course of one and a half years (August, 1879, to March, 1881) eight plots to assassinate Alexander were organized, one after the other. Revolutionists mined streets and blew up railroad tracks where the Emperor's train was scheduled to pass. On Feb. 24, 1880, they exploded two poods of dynamite in the Winter Palace, wrecking the hall in which the entire imperial family a few minutes later would have been seated at dinner.

The invisible and unapprehended instigator of these attempts was the so-called Party of the People's Will, which had been formed by a handful of young terrorists of both sexes in the Summer of 1879. Their number increased. But up to the last days of its five or six years' existence the whole party could have been easily contained in one good size room. The program adopted by its members was simple. The thing that mattered was to provoke the revolution; the simplest way of provoking it was to arouse the subversive passions of the people by terroristic acts. And what terroristic act could be more startling than the assassination of the Czar?

When, returning from a parade on March 14, the imperial cortège turned from the Inzhenerny Street to Catherine's Canal a terrible explosion wrecked the bottom of Czar Alexander's carriage. But he emerged from it unhurt. He walked to the men of his escort, who were holding the bomb-thrower, N. Rysakov. In a moment a second explosion shook the air.

When the smoke cleared the bewildered courtiers saw the Czar sitting on the ground and leaning with his back against the railing of the canal. His body was torn, his arms and face covered with blood. Near by lay, among other victims, the thrower of the second bomb, I. Grinevitzky, mortally wounded.

Such had been, briefly told, the event which was cheerfully commemorated in Moscow on March 14. And this commemoration challenges a significant historical parallel. Out of thirty-one persons who with unquestionable daring participated, directly and indirectly, in the assassination of Alexander II only five were executed. These were Miss S. Perovskaya, A. Zhelyabov, U. Kibalchich, T. Mikhailov and N. Rysakov. The remainder served their term in prison and were released—among them even men like Trigoni, one of the leaders of the organization.

No ukase against "mass terror" had been issued, as was the case after the assassination of the Communist Uritzky in 1918; no hostages were seized and executed by the hundred. Communists buried their assassinated leaders with much more pomp than attended Alexander's burial.

March 21, 1926

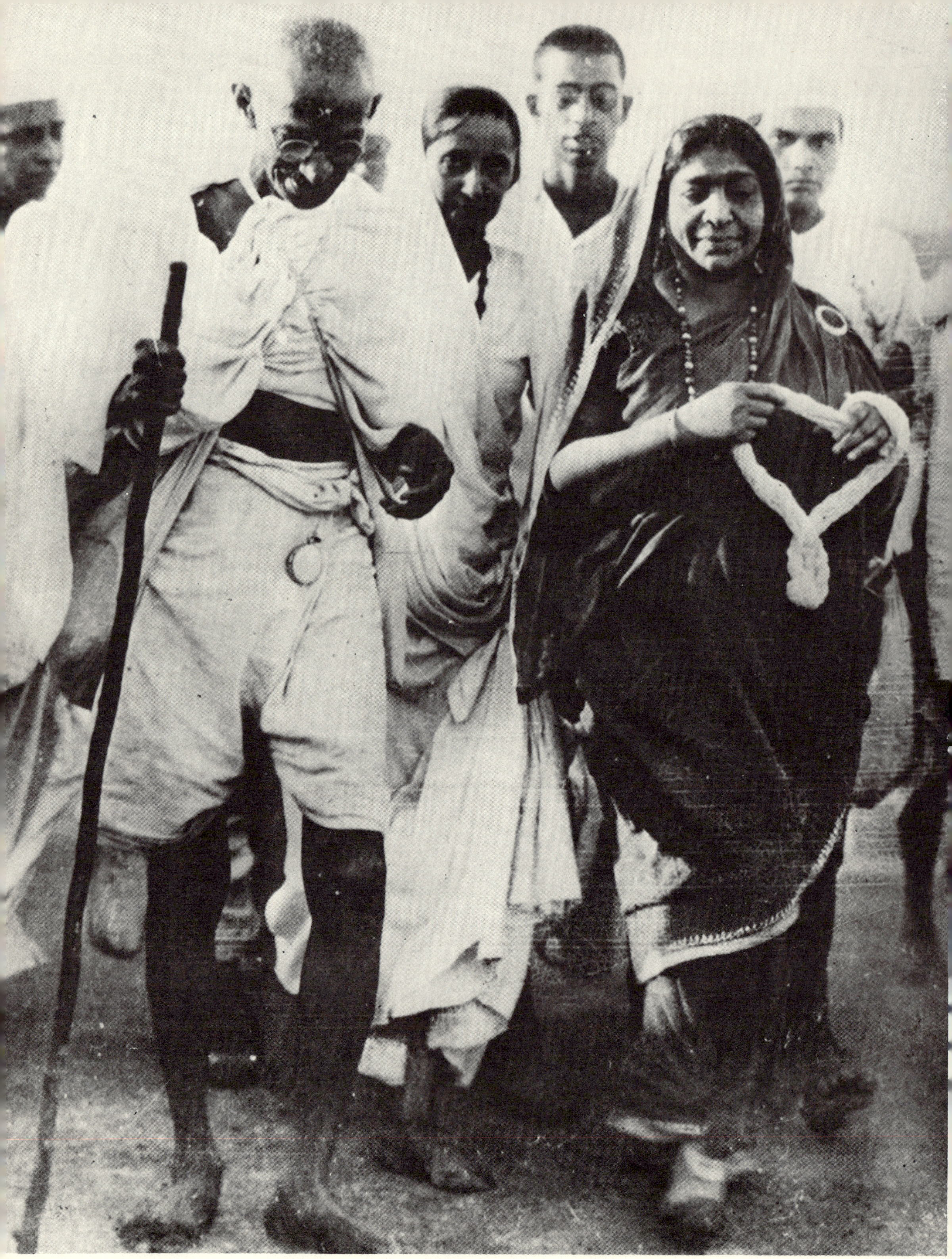

CHAPTER 2

The Colonizers and the Colonized

Mahatma Gandhi, leader of the Indian civil disobedience revolt and proponent of non-violence, leads his followers in a protest against British rule in India.

United Press International Photo

IMPORTANT FROM INDIA.

Revolt and Mutiny Among the Native Troops —Massacre of Europeans at Delhi.

From the London Times, June 27.

It was but the other day we recorded the centenary anniversary of the Battle of Plassy, from which we date the commencement of British power in India. About a month before that full period of one hundred years had elapsed, although on this side of the globe we knew it not, the son of the late Mogul Emperor had been proclaimed King at Delhi by certain regiments of the Bengal Army, which had broken out into open mutiny. This mutiny has assumed a very serious character. We do not write for the purpose of inspiring alarm or suggesting timid counsels. The moment has arrived for action—sharp, stern, and decisive.

An imperial interest is at stake—nothing less than our dominion in British India. It would be easy enough to point out the errors of ommission and commission which have been mainly instrumental in bringing about the present crisis. The course of policy to be adopted for the future is also matter for swift, though serious discussion, but just now it would be idle to waste time either upon recrimination or upon questions of general policy. In the first place the mutiny must be suppressed, and in such a manner as shall impress the minds of the natives with the nature of the power they have defied when its real strength is put forth. If it be true that we are still very much in the dark as to the true feelings and opinions of the natives of India, it is no less true that they know far less of us than we do of them. The disadvantages arising from ignorance may tell upon both sides, but they tell more in our favor than to our prejudice. The crisis is a most serious one. We do not wish to conceal its true nature from the country, but it is not so serious that it should inspire one moment of hesitation. The vigor displayed by the victors of Plassy and Assayo should be the model for our imitation at the present moment—if, indeed, a powerful and resolute people ever need any inspiration from the past. But first let us speak of the facts, as far as they are yet known to us.

The mutinous spirit, which had to a certain extent been checked, if not exinguished, in the more southern portion of Bengal, had spread to Meerut. At this post two regiments of Native Infantry—the 11th and 20th—had united with the 3d Light Cavalry, and had broken out into open revolt. This revolt, as far as it had showed itself at Meerut, had been put down. There had been a collision between the revolted and the European troops, the result of which was, that the mutineers were dispersed, and fled. To the southward, and at no great distance, lies the important city of Delhi, the capital of the old Mogul Empire; and this town appears to have been the centre of the revolt. When the fugitives from Meerut arrived here they were instantly joined by three other regiments of native infantry—the 38th, the 54th, and 74th; and the united forces instantly took possession of the town. Any one who has had experience of the tiger-like ferocity of the Indian in a moment of what appears to him success will be prepared for the result. An indiscriminate massacre of the Europeans was the first act on which the mutineers decided, and this they are said to have carried out in a manner the most remorseless and the most complete. No tenderness was shown to sex, no reverence to age; Delhi was turned into shambles; and so the first act of the tragedy was played out. It might have been expected. The next step, however, may be considered as of a more ominous kind, if it is evidence of any preconceived design. The son of the late Mogul Emperor was proclaimed King, and thus the shadow Sovereign whom we have so long maintained in empty state has been raised into momentary importance—briefly, we trust, to disappear forever from human account. Nor is this all; there has been disquiet on our old Sikh battle-ground. We are informed, under date from Calcutta of the 18th of May, that at Ferozepore also there had been disturbances, but that these disturbances had been suppressed. So far for the blacker side of the picture; and next for what has been done to mitigate or meet the evil. "The Government was taking active measures to suppress the revolt, and was concentrating troops *around* Delhi." The italics are our own, and may, we trust, be justified by the event. It is of the last importance that the rebellion should be extinguished where it has arisen, and that armed fugitives should not be allowed to escape in numbers from the principal seat of the disturbances. When to this intelligence we add that the Rajah of GWALIOE—the Mahratta State abutting on the southwestern limit of Delhi—had placed the troops of which he could dispose at the service of the British Government we have exhausted the brief, but momentous, advices which the electric telegraph brought to us at a late hour last night. The open revolt in the Bengal Presidency of five Regiments of Native Infantry and of one Regiment of Light Cavalry, independently of what may have taken place at Ferozepore, is undoubtedly intelligence as important as any which we have published since the fall of Sebastopol. It must also be remembered that these are not the only Regiments affected with the taint of mutiny; indeed, the very telegraph which brings this news adds that the 34th Regiment of Native Infantry, which had been before suspected, had been disbanded at Barrackpore.

So far from feeling any serious apprehension for the stability of British power in India in consequence of these occurrences, we should be inclined to foretell that they may tend to confirm it, and to give us a fresh lease of empire. We have for a long time been pursuing half measures in India. There can be no doubt that the reign of the mock King at Delhi will be but a brief one, and that a terrible retribution will be inflicted on the mutineers, not merely in that character, but as the bloody and pitiless murderers of the Europeans in Delhi. If it was to come, this revolt could not have occured at a better time. When the Russian war was raging it might have proved a more considerable inconvenience; indeed, a less matter, such as the hostilities with Persia, now happily terminated, might have been a serious obstacle in the way of a satisfactory settlement. What we requires is the presence in British India of the most competent officer who can be found, and an entire revision of our Indian military system. It is not here the time or place to enter upon wider questions of policy, such as the system of double Government, which has gone for so much in producing the present state of affairs. We cannot, however, conclude without urging again upon our rulers, as soon as this revolt is suppressed, the absolute necessity of carrying on the Indian railway system with greater vigor.

The time has arrived when the power of transporting compact and highly trained bodies of European troops from one point of India to another may be all important. In India we are constructing railroads on the expensive English system. Single lines through the jungle and the wilderness, after the cheap American model, could be laid down in a tenth of the time and at less than a tenth of the expense, and these would enable us to hold possession of the country with any army comparatively small in numerical force.

July 8, 1857

THE INDIAN MUTINIES.

THE MASSACRE AT CAWNPORE.

STATEMENT BY THE ONLY SURVIVOR.

The London *Times* publishes the following thrilling letter:

CAWNPORE, Saturday, July 18.

MY OWN DEAREST BROTHER: God Almighty has been graciously pleased to spare my poor life. I am the only individual saved among all the European and Christian community that inhabited this station. My poor dear wife, my darling sweet child Polly, poor dear Rebecca and her children, and poor innocent children Emmelina and Martha, as also old Mrs. Frost and poor Mrs. Osborne, were all most inhumanly butchered by the cruel insurgents on the day before yesterday, and thrown into a well, together with a great number of other ladies and children, reported to be about 150 in number. I am distracted. I am most miserable and wretched. I am like one in a dream. You could not recognize me if you saw me. My life has been spared by a miracle. The will of the Lord be done. He alone can give me comfort, for I am in a terrible state of distress of mind.

I will write you a detailed account of all our sufferings and distresses, such distress as has never before been experienced or heard of on the face of this earth. At present I cannot write, I cannot eat or drink—I am perfectly wretched.

I escaped only yesterday from my miserable prison, where I had been confined with heavy fetters on my legs for twenty-four days by the rebels, who nearly took away my life, but God alone prevented them and spared me. They gave me only parched grain to eat daily and that in very small quantities.

The English troops have come in and restored peace. They have retaken Cawnpore. Their arrival here yesterday was the means of my release, as my term of imprisonment was three years with hard labor. The enemy had from 10,000 to 15,000 troops, and have done great destruction; but the British, with 2,400 Europeans and 700 Sikhs have driven them away, and not a soul of them is to be seen now anywhere.

I know not whether these few lines will reach you, nor do I know if you and your dear children at Agra are still in the land of the living. But I have made this effort to send this letter in the earnest hope that it will reach you. If it do I beg you will send me a reply per bearer, and also write by post, if such is established by that time.

Every officer and soldier, and every merchant, writer, or Christian drummer, &c. that had gone into the entrenchments under Gen. WHEELER on the 4th of June has been killed. The cannonading of the enemy was very, very secure. Twelve guns, taken from our magazine, were brought to play upon us. They had a very large quantity of powder at their disposal, for the magazine was not blown up, and thirty boats of ammunition reached the enemy by the Ganges Canal just in time for them to annoy us. The artillery barracks, where we were intrenched, have been scattered to atoms by the 24-pounder balls that were incessantly fired by the enemy, and many died under the walls. Day and night the guns were kept playing upon us without ceasing for a moment, and the musketry of the enemy poured millions of balls upon us up to the 25th of June—that is for 20 days. The enemy made several attempts to charge upon us; three times they surrounded us on all sides under cover of the compound walls of bungalows in our vicinity, and sounded their bugles to charge but were driven back by our artillery firing canister upon them. We had only six small guns with us, and not a single howitzer.

Had we even had one 24-pounder a great deal could have been done, or had our General taken up his position in the magazine we might all have escaped the very severe calamity that has befallen upon this station, for without guns the enemy could not have done anything. On the 24th of June I was sent out as a spy, on certain conditions, and, as I was dressed like a common Chinaman, I was not killed: for I was taken prisoner almost as soon as I came out of the intrenchment, particulars of which I shall give you in my next, but kept in confinement until the day of my trial, when fetters were put on me, as stated above. After I came out on the 24th it appears the rebel Rajah sent a letter to our General the day after, offering to let him and all his people go to Allahabad, on condition that he would give up all his treasure, ammunition, &c., and vacate Cawnpore within three days. This was accepted by the General, and the usual oaths were taken that no treachery would be used. The Rajah supplied 21 boats and gave carriage to the river side. On the morning of the 27th our people went on board the boats—(Oh! how I felt when in confinement I heard that the English were going in safety. I could not keep my secret; and told the Subadar of the prison guard that I was a Christian and nearly lost my life by this exposure, of which more hereafter;) —but had not time to let the boats go, when the enemy fired canon upon them, and upset some; others they set fire to. Only one boat, I am told, managed to get away, but was afterwards picked up at a short distance and brought back. About 150 women and children, and about 100 European officers and soldiers and men of all classes were taken alive. The former were kept as prisoners up to the 16th of July but the men (among whom was our poor Daniel) had their hands tied behind them, were killed with swords and muskets and thrown into a ditch. The women received parched grain for a few days, but afterwards they got dall and chupaties in small quantities. The rascals have bad motives for sparing them so long.

At the time of their being murdered (on the 16th inst.) I am told that a number jumped alive into the well that was intended to receive their corpses rather than be butchered and insulted so unmercifully as the hard-hearted brutes were using them.

Oh! when I think of it how my heart breaks. I get beside myself, and wish I had not been spared to hear of such dreadful accounts. Oh! my poor dear Polly!! How must they have killed you. So sweet a child never existed. How will I ever forget you! The faces of all I have lost are ever before me. Oh! how dreadful is my state of mind. God Almighty have mercy on me! Oh, God, help Thou me, whom Thou hast spared. Thine affectionate, but miserable.

H.J. SHEPHERD.

October 7, 1857

THE COLONIZERS AND THE COLONIZED

India—The Proclamation of the Queen and of the Governor-General.

The Bombay mails of November 9th, reached London on the 4th of December. They brought the proclamation by which Queen Victoria's direct supremacy over India is finally substituted for the rule of the East India Company. As already announced the document was formally proclaimed throughout India on the 1st of November, and its reading was followed in the principal cities by illuminations, fireworks, and other demonstrations. The following is the text:

"Victoria, by the grace of God, of the United Kingdom of Great Britain and Ireland, and of the Colonies and Dependencies thereof, in Europe, Asia, Africa, America, and Australasia, Queen, Defender of the Faith.

Whereas, for divers weighty reasons, we have resolved, by and with the advice and consent of the Lords spiritual and temporal, and Commons in Parliament assembled, to take upon ourselves the government of the territories in India, heretofore administered in trust for us by the Honorable East India Company:

Now, therefore, we do by these presents notify and declare that, by the advice and consent aforesaid, we have taken upon ourselves the said government, and we hereby call upon all our subjects within the said territories to be faithful and to bear true allegiance to us, our heirs and successors, and to submit themselves to the authority of those whom we may hereafter from time to time see fit to appoint to administer the government of our said territories in our name and on our behalf.

And we, reposing especial trust and confidence in the loyalty, ability, and judgment of our right trusty and well-beloved cousin and councillor, Charles John Viscount Canning, do hereby constitute and appoint him, the said Viscount Canning, to be our first Viceroy and Governor-General in and over said territories, and to administer the government thereof in our name and on our behalf, subject to such orders and regulations as he shall from time to time receive from us through one of our principal Secretaries of State.

And we do hereby confirm in their several offices, civil and military, all persons now employed in the service of the Honorable East India Company, subject to our future pleasure, and to such laws and regulations as may hereafter be enacted.

We hereby announce to the native princes of India that all treaties and engagements made with them by or under the authority of the Honorable East India Company are by us accepted, and will be scrupulously maintained; and we look for the like observance on their part.

We desire no extension of our present territorial possessions; and while we will permit no aggression upon our dominions or our rights to be attempted with impunity, we shall sanction no encroachment on those of others. We shall respect the rights, dignity, and honor of native princes as our own; and we desire that they, as well as our own subjects, should enjoy that prosperity and that social advancement which can only be secured by internal peace and good government.

We hold ourselves bound to the natives of our Indian territories by the same obligations of duty which bind us to all our other subjects; and those obligations, by the blessings of Almighty God, we shall faithfully and conscientiously fulfil.

Firmly relying ourselves on the truth of Christianity, and acknowledging with gratitude the solace of religion, we disclaim alike the right and the desire to impose our convictions on any of our subjects. We declare it to be our royal will and pleasure that none be in anywise favored, none molested or disquieted, by reason of their religious faith or observances, but all shall alike enjoy the equal and impartial protection of the law; and we do strictly charge and enjoin all those who may be in authority under us, that they abstain from all interference with the religious belief or worship of any of our subjects, on pain of our highest displeasure.

And it is our further will that, so far as may be, our subjects, of whatever race or creed, be freely and impartially admitted to offices in our service, the duties of which they may be qualified by their education, ability, and integrity, duly to discharge.

We know and respect the feelings of attachment with which the natives of India regard the lands inherited by them from their ancestors, and we desire to protect them in all rights connected therewith, subject to the equitable demands of the State; and we will that, generally, in framing and administering the law, due regard be paid to the ancient rights, usages, and customs of India.

We deeply lament the evils and misery which have been brought upon India by the acts of ambitious men, who have deceived their countrymen by false reports and led them into open rebellion. Our power has been shown by the suppression of that rebellion in the field; we desire to show our mercy by pardoning the offences of those who have been thus misled, but desire to return to the path of duty.

Already in one province, with a view to stop the further effusion of blood, and to hasten the pacification of our Indian dominions, our Viceroy and Governor-General has held out the expectation of pardon, on certain terms, to the great majority of those who in the late unhappy disturbances have been guilty of offences against our Government, and has declared the punishment which will be inflicted on those whose crimes place them beyond the reach of forgiveness. We approve and confirm the said act of our Viceroy and Governor-General, and do further announce and proclaim as follows:

Our clemency will be extended to all offenders, save and except those who have been or shall be convicted of having directly taken part in the murder of British subjects. With regard to such, the demands of justice forbid the exercise of mercy.

To those who have willingly given asylum to murderers, knowing them to be such, or who may have acted as leaders or instigators in revolt, their lives alone can be guaranteed; but, in apportioning the penalty due to such persons, full consideration will be given to the circumstances under which they have been induced to throw off their allegiance, and large indulgences will be shown to those whose crimes may appear to have originated in a too credulous acceptance of the false reports circulated by designing men.

To all others in arms against the Government we hereby promise unconditional pardon, amnesty, and oblivion of all offences against ourselves, our crown and dignity, on their return to their homes and peaceful pursuits.

It is our royal pleasure that these terms of grace and amnesty should be extended to all those who comply with their conditions before the 1st day of January next.

When, by the blessing of Providence, internal tranquility shall be restored, it is our earnest desire to stimulate the peaceful industry of India, to promote works of public utility and improvement, and to administer its government for the benefit of all our subjects resident therein. In their prosperity will be our strength, in their contentment our security, and in their gratitude our best reward. And may the God of all power grant to us, and to those in authority under us, strength to carry out these wishes for the good of our people."

December 27, 1858

THE EARL OF MAYO.

Assassination of the Governor-General of India.

London, Feb. 12.—A report received here early today of the assassination of the Earl of Mayo, Governor-General of India, has been confirmed by later dispatches. In the House of Lords this evening the Duke of Argyll announced that the Government had received official information of the assassination, and, with several other Lords, pronounced eulogies on the deceased. In the House of Commons Mr. Gladstone stated that on the evening of the 8th inst. the Earl of Mayo was stabbed by a Mohammedan convict, and soon after receiving his wound expired. The Premier proceeded to express the regret the whole country would feel at the sudden death of this distinguished statesmen, and was followed by Mr. Disraeli, who referred to the great public services of the deceased in terms of the highest praise.

It appears that the assassination occurred during an inspection of Fort Blair Prison, in the Andaman Islands, in the Bay of Bengal. A Mussulman convict broke through the surrounding officers and guards, and stabbed the Earl twice in the back. He died immediately. The assassin was instantly secured and placed in irons, and will be tried immediately.

The reception of the news of the assassination here caused the greatest consternation. The news spread rapidly throughout the city, and the expressions of sympathy for the deceased Earl were very general. The influence of the news is already felt on the Stock Exchange. The prices of all securities affected by Indian affairs are lower.

February 13, 1872

ENGLAND'S DANGER IN INDIA.

A NOTE OF WARNING FROM ONE FAMILIAR WITH INDIAN AFFAIRS.

An anglo-Indian writes from Massoorie to the London News in regard to the feeling in India toward the home Government. He says: "I am persuaded that for 40 years past no Government has produced so much distrust in the native mind as the present. The entire machinery of the Administration is deteriorated, and its moral tone lowered to such an extent as to endanger its stability. Corrupt as is the state of your finances in England, ours are ten times worse. A 'license-tax' wrung from a starving population with incomes as low as 3d. per day, and then spent on an unjust war to obtain a scientific frontier belonging to a neighbor; the resources of the country eaten up by a large native army, necessitating the presence of a large European army to keep it in subjection; a semi-military Police, hated most intensely by the entire population, and beyond doubt one of the most terrible instruments of oppression ever brought into existence by any Government among civilized nations; a Public Works Department organized at the cost of millions, and then nearly destroyed by its organizers in a financial panic. I might go on to any extent pointing out the evils of our Administration without exhausting the subject; but enough for the present. My object is to warn England before it be too late. Send us men of common sense to govern us, and not dreamy novelists. The 'mild Hindu' is no longer what he was. We have educated him without the controlling and subduing influence of religion. He is much like a railway engine without brake or brake-van, and we have only to supply him with steam in order to his becoming uncontrollable. I do not think there is a spirit of sedition among the people, but rather one of grief, at the reckless and useless expenditure and the infliction of taxes unsuited to their habits. The present fit of economy inspires no confidence. The chipping begins at the bottom instead of the top. The poor beer-taster is to be cut down or dismissed; but what about the Governor-General, who receives more than the highest-paid functionary in Europe? Engineers of different grades are dismissed or pensioned wholesale; but what about the Bishop of Calcutta, with his more than £10,000 per annum? The promise to introduce natives into the civil service inspires the people with no more confidence than does the promised scheme of economy. A few sycophants may be promoted—men whose only claim to distinction rests on the amount of flattery with which they supply their superiors. Honest men have no chance whatever; and there is no hope of any movement in favor of the really deserving native, whatever his qualifications may be."

October 19, 1879

India

> **BLOODY RIOTS IN MADRAS.**
> THE HINDUS AND MOHAMMEDANS AT WAR—
> HORRIBLE ATROCITIES.
>
> CALCUTTA, Aug. 28.—There has been fearful rioting between Hindus and Mohammedans at Salem, in the Presidency of Madras. One hundred and fifty Hindus and three Mohammedans have been arrested. An eye-witness of the disorders says he saw the disemboweled body of a Mohammedan infant lying on the ground. Its arms were also torn off. Headless corpses of Mohammedan men and women were lying on every side. Houses of Mohammedans were burned and the principal mosque was almost razed to the ground. Dead pigs have been thrown into the wells with the corpses of Mohammedan children. Troops are still patroling the streets. The Mohammedans are a small minority of the population.
>
> August 29, 1882

BRITISH RULE IN INDIA.

Results "serious beyond conception" are predicted in case the bill giving native Judges in India jurisdiction of criminal proceedings against Europeans in certain cases becomes a law. If we may believe the Calcutta correspondents of the London papers, the feeling of hostility to the bill is well-nigh universal among European residents. The volunteers are declaring their intention to resign if the bill is passed, and one officer writes to a Calcutta newspaper to say that the men would be uncontrollable if one of their comrades should be tried and sentenced by a native Judge. The only supporters of the bill are found among the official Europeans and the natives. The former, being secure from criminal prosecution, are influenced in their advocacy of the measure, it is hinted, by a desire to earn the favorable consideration of Lord RIPON, who has gone further than any preceding Viceroy in reforms tending to give the natives the advantages of local self-government and to put them on a more nearly equal footing with the Europeans. The Viceroy and his Council may take as little or as much notice as they please of the public meetings, the memorials of Chambers of Commerce, the excitement and alarm among the unofficial Europeans, and other public demonstrations against the bill; but as India is not a very safe place for radical legislative reforms or for experiments in government, the enactment of the bill may be looked on as extremely improbable.

Mr. Justice STEPHEN has recently given in the London *Times* a sketch of Indian criminal procedure, which makes the provisions of the bill intelligible. The criminal law of India has a double root—the Mohammedan law and the law of England. The native law courts pay the most scrupulous regard to the personal sentiments, prejudices, and social position of those who appear before them, as prisoners or witnesses, so that there is, in effect, one law for Hindus and another for Mohammedans, one for high caste and another for low caste. This is, of course, wholly foreign to English law, but the English in India have taken advantage of the native custom to set up a kind of extra territoriality for themselves. Going a little further in this direction than the European Consular courts of Turkey, Egypt, China, and Japan, they have hitherto confined jurisdiction in proceedings against their own race to the English Judges of the High Courts, the Sessions Courts, and English district magistrates of the first class. This distinction, so exactly contrary to the English principle that all men are equal before the law, is justified by the other equally broad English principle that a man should be tried by his peers. The native Judges are not, and never can be, the peers of the English in India, for they neither understand the language nor the feelings of Englishmen and are naturally liable to the bias of race prejudice. But, as might be expected, this system works a gross injustice to the natives. The courts which have power to try Europeans are in the cities and other centres of European life. For the offenses which Europeans commit in the remote districts the natives have no redress, as it would cost too much to prosecute in Calcutta an Englishman who had beaten or robbed a man in Assam. Justice STEPHEN, who was the legal member of the Council when the Criminal Code was amended in 1872, admits that it was "both a grievance and a scandal that the large and increasing European population established in various parts of the country should practically enjoy impunity for nearly all their crimes."

The bill now before the Council of India was introduced by one of its members, Mr. C. P. ILBERT, to "sweep away an anomaly of the law which allows the appointment of a native Judge in Calcutta and forbids it in the outlying districts." The bill leaves the exclusive jurisdiction of the English courts over all graver offenses untouched, but gives a native Sessions Judge or native magistrate the right to try Europeans for certain offenses of which none but English Judges can now take cognizance. The very dangerous state of feeling which has been aroused by Mr. ILBERT'S bill promises, as we have said, to prevent its passage. But the animated discussion of the proposition has led to some curiously frank avowals of the nature and objects of English policy in India. In the opinion of the London *Times* the bill is odious because it would divest English capitalists, who are India's "best friends," of "the ordinary security of personal liberty." The anomaly of having a native magistrate in Calcutta, where he is surrounded by English Judges and kept from going astray by the "constant and vigilant criticism of an influential Bar," also English, and only an English magistrate at Dargrenling strikes the *Times* as "beneath the notice of any one but a technical purist." That is a forcible and contemptuous way of saying that while the English capitalists are exploiting India, Justice must discreetly turn her back.

The British policy is still more frankly set forth by Mr. Justice STEPHEN, whose Indian experience makes him a competent authority. The assertion that no legal distinction at all is to be recognized in India between natives and Europeans he characterizes as "false and infinitely dangerous." The wrongs which natives suffer when tried before English Judges result from "a defect inseparable from the existence of the British power in India." The British rule is "essentially an absolute Government, founded not on consent but on conquest." It does not represent "the native principles of life or Government," but "represents a belligerent civilization." The Government can be maintained only by keeping the neck of the conquered always under the conqueror's foot. These admissions are interesting. They teach us much of the true character of "British interests" in India. They show, too, that the policy of Lord RIPON is creating a good deal of uneasiness in certain circles in England. There is, as Justice STEPHEN says, much danger in "shifting the foundations on which the British Government of India rests." The mutiny has not yet been forgotten. But there are certain Englishmen who do not look on India merely as a field for the ventures of "English capitalists." They point to the condition of the native population, which grows worse from year to year; to the gradual rise in the price of provisions, accompanied by no corresponding rise in wages; and to the terrible fact that during the past twenty years half a million persons a year have died of starvation in British India. From such persons comes the inquiry, how far the present wholly selfish policy is to be carried. Ireland and British India are about the only countries on the globe where large numbers of people die every year from absolute want.

March 14, 1883

THE COLONIZERS AND THE COLONIZED

REFORMS IN INDIA.

ADDRESSES AT THE OPENING OF THE CONGRESS IN CALCUTTA.

CALCUTTA, Dec. 26.—The National Indian Congress was opened in this city to-day. One thousand delegates were present, and there were 5,000 persons in the audience which listened to the deliberations of the meeting. Among those who attended were Charles Schwann and William Caine, members of the British House of Commons; several Rajahs and Mohammedan nobles, and a number of high-caste native ladies. Advocate Ghose, a leading attorney of the High Court, delivered an address of welcome to the delegates. He described the congress as the inevitable outcome of the generous policy of the British Government.

Mervanji Mehta, a member of the Bombay Legislative Council, in his Presidential address, made declarations as to the loyalty of the movement and its pacific aims. He said the congress desired to assist the Government in the work of social reforms. The time had arrived for consultative councils. Although the diverse nationalities of India were not yet ripe for representative institutions, yet the elective principle ought to be adopted in nominations to the Indian Council, and he appealed to the Viceroy to watch the movement in a spirit of generous sympathy. The speech concluded thus: " Our congress asks but to be allowed to show the pitfalls, and join in the blessing which England will as surely earn as there is an Eternal that maketh righteousness. We appeal to Englishmen not to let the prayer rising from a growing and hopeful nation prove in vain."

December 27, 1890

THE EAST INDIAN CONGRESS.

BOMBAY, Dec. 30.—The Indian National Congress, which is in session at Nagpur, the capital of the central provinces of India, has adopted a resolution declaring it necessary that there shall be established a Legislature in India to which the Indian people shall elect representatives. The resolution says that aside from climatic conditions, the starvation among the masses of the inhabitants of India is largely due to the fact that they have no Parliamentary representation.

The resolution also says it is imperative that reductions be made in the expenditures for the Indian army.

BIARRITZ, Dec. 30.—Among the many congratulatory telegrams received by Mr. Gladstone yesterday was one from the Indian National Congress, which expressed the admiration felt by the natives of India for his character and the hope that he would live to celebrate many more anniversaries of his natal day.

December 31, 1891

THE TROUBLE IN INDIA

Outburst of Anti-English Feeling in the Native Press of Bengal and Bombay.

PLAGUE OFFICIALS BLAMED

Warnings That the Scenes of 1857 Are Imminent—Censorship May Be Revived—Probable Move for an Islam Crusade.

LONDON, July 3.—The outburst of anti-English feeling in the native press, both of Bengal and Bombay, for months past, has had the outcome which might have been expected in the outrages at Poonah and the rioting at Chitpore. Though there is no doubt that the immediate cause of the outbreak is the energy with which the local authorities have been stamping out the bubonic plague, sometimes making necessary interference with the social relations, customs, and traditions of the natives. But the dissaffection would not have become acute except for the activity and malicious accusations of unscrupulous agitators who incited fanatics to vengeance against individuals and to revolt against the Government. One of these newspapers, a fair sample of the others, said:

" The plague authorities are simply butchers, who are torturing and harassing the people of Poonah in the name of sanitary science. If matters are not put right soon, the scenes of 1857 are likely to be rewitnessed there, as neither the Hindus nor the Mohammedans will tolerate the persecution of their wives and children for any length of time. It is the misfortune of the people that the honor, religion, and modesty of women, safe even under Mogul rule, should be violated under the enlightened English Government. We wonder why no notice is taken of the shameful doings of the soldiers in Poonah. They are perhaps secretly instigated by the Government to do these things in retaliation for the tortures once inflicted upon Europeans by the tantia topi, and to punish the capital of the Deccan for taking the lead in all public agitations. Let us hope that the Government will take heed and mend its ways, lest disastrous consequences ensue."

Other newspapers of India openly advocate armed resistance to the search parties. Needless to say, the charges are false. All the search parties who volunteered for that dangerous plague duty have been under the strictest control, and have always been accompanied by officers of tried ability. The death of Commissioner Rand, who was shot by concealed natives while leaving the Governor's reception on Jubilee evening, at the time Lieut. Ayerst of the Commissariat Corps was killed, has added to the bitterness of the feeling in Poonah.

There is reason to believe that the wave of Mohammedan reaction is caused by the successful and unpunished atrocities in Armenia spreading to the Mussulmans of India. There is no reason to fear for the empire, as the white garrison is strong, numbering 75,000 men, but there is reason to fear a succession of municipal outbreaks demanding sanguinary repression. The situation seems to call for vigorous action, and the prompt measure of the Bombay Government in proclaiming Poonah disaffected and occupying the city by a primative police force, the cost of which, amounting to a lac and a half of rupees for a year, will be levied on a certain section of the native community, meets with general approval.

Replying to-day to a question in the House of Commons, Lord George Hamilton, the Secretary of State for India, said the Government was fully alive to the gravity of the case and meant to act promptly. The whole question of the inculcation of sedition through the vernacular press will be considered, and, if necessary, the press censorship law will be revived.

In connection with this serious news from India comes the disturbing information from Afghanistan to the effect that the Ameer has hastily summoned all the influential Mollahs throughout the country to a meeting at Cabul, as he wishes to consult them on important matters concerning Islam. This is believed to be connected with the recent announcement that the Sultan has sent a special envoy to Cabul with instructions to agitate for a general revival of Islamism.

July 4, 1897

THE PROBLEM OF INDIA.

An incident in the history of India which may prove of great and lasting importance has passed almost without notice in the press of the United States.

An address has been presented by the representatives of some 70,000,000 Mohammedans to the British Viceroy, Lord MINTO, and has been answered in the most sympathetic spirit. The basis of the address was the assumption that Great Britain is on the eve of granting some degree of representation to natives in the legislative and executive departments of the Government of India, and if this be done, the Mohammedans urge that they be secured in what they consider to be their especial rights. As they are in a hopeless minority—hardly more than one-fifth of the total population—and are not segregated, but scattered throughout the vast peninsula, representation in the ratio of numbers would leave them practically subject to the majority, whom they regard with jealousy, suspicion, often with contempt, and with an ineradicable animosity that is held in control only by the rule of the British white caste.

Obviously the demand the Mussulmans make of the Viceroy is intrinsically most difficult to satisfy. They suggest that representation, if accorded, be by creeds and not by numbers, and The London Times regards this as neither impracticable nor undesirable, while Lord MINTO significantly declines to reject or even to criticise it. But in application it bristles with difficulties. Even the mere adoption of it, if recommended, would encounter stubborn opposition in England; it would defy every notion of fairness and contradict the whole tendency of English political sentiment for the past three-fourths of a century. It would be particularly hard to secure its acceptance by the party now in power, whose fundamental principles would be stultified by putting one-fifth of the population of India on equality with four-fifths. Mr. MORLEY once distinguished himself in English literature by printing in one of his books the name of GOD without a capital initial and that of MOHAMMED with one, but he could hardly defend that standard of relative importance applied to the Government of India.

It is not, indeed, unfair to suggest that the demand of the Mussulmans in India is treated with a certain expression of respect by the Viceroy and by some of the press in England precisely because it presents an impossible condition to the adoption of serious representative institutions in India. If representation were granted without this condition and the Mohammedans were relegated to what they regard as the oppressive domination of the Hindus,

59

India

there would be grave danger of political disorders throughout the Empire. The Mohammedans as a class are much more energetic, capable, coherent, and aggressive than the remainder of the population. Not that they are of a different race; they are substantially of the same race, or races; but their religion attracts the men of strength and of action, inspires them with fiercer resolution, teaches them to look forward to ultimate conquest as their inevitable destiny, and literally trains them to habitual scorn of all unbelievers. They endure the rule of the British because it is established on that success in war which Allah has permitted.

Even this they endure only as something that in time must end. The rule of those they look upon as inferiors would be a very different thing; it might prove intolerable to them and they might challenge it with the sword. The risk of such a catastrophe is good ground for refusing representation to the natives on the basis of numbers. If no other basis is acceptable the thing falls to the ground.

Unquestionably, however, there is a distinct unrest in India of which the British Government is taking cognizance. Mr. MORLEY, at the head of the Indian Department in the Ministry, in substance admitted the fact in his remarkable speech on the Indian budget. Its origin is much more simple than is the problem of satisfying it. The spread of Western education in India during the past generation has created a class of literates who now seek a share in the government of the country. To some extent their desire has been gratified, especially as to the courts and the minor civil service. But from the army and from the higher offices, involving discretionary authority, they have been excluded. Such recognition as they have received naturally whets their appetite for more, and has tended directly to the creation of a fervent aspiration toward complete self-government. The literate class is not large—probably not more than one in twenty of the population; but it naturally includes the brightest and most eager minds, and it is bound to increase in relative strength and, even more, in influence. What in the long run the British will do with it, or what it will do with British rule—this is an intensely interesting and very puzzling question.

October 26, 1906

THE INDIAN COUNCIL.

In the last debate of the late session of Parliament in which what is called in England " the unrest in India " came up, Mr. MORLEY, the Secretary for India, said that all was now quiet " on the surface." But evidently he did not consider that the unrest would be composed without some distinctly propitiatory measures on the part of the Government. Accordingly he has determined that the Government of India, like that of the Philippines, according to President MCKINLEY, shall be one in which " the natives are admitted to the largest possible participation."

The largest possible participation does not seem to foreigners very great. It consists merely in the appointment to the Indian Council, for the first time since that body was established on the transfer of the Government from the Company to the Crown, half a century ago, of two native members. Of course these two natives could not, if they voted together, exercise any substantial voting power in a body which must by law consist of not less than ten members. Moreover, it is extremely unlikely that they could bring themselves to vote together. One is a Hindu and one a Mohammedan, and Hindus and Mohammedans, even though they were united by common hatred of the English, would yet hate each other much more than they hated the invader. But they are, nevertheless, expert advisers to the body of foreigners, or at the least expert witnesses before it. If they have been well chosen, and it seems to be agreed on all hands that they have been, they can inform the Council authoritatively of the opinions and feelings of the two great bodies which they respectively represent and in comparison with which other denominations of natives of Hindustan are negligible. It would have been a great thing for the English rule in 1857 if there had been somebody to tell the English rulers of the probable effect of ordering native troops to bite cartridges greased with animal fat.

It is to be noted, however, that this concession has pretty plainly been extorted by the conditions, and thus loses the grace of voluntariness. It may be questioned whether, in India any more than in Ireland, it is politic for the Government to let it be known that it will yield to " outrages " what it has refused to appeals in the name of justice. Apparently the " nativistic " movement in India has been ultimately brought about, or at least raised to its threatening dimensions, by the Japanese defeat of Russia. The prestige of the white man throughout Eastern Asia has by that defeat been impaired if not broken. And that probably means that it will take more force to control India hereafter than it has taken heretofore, when the existence of an overwhelming force on the part of the whites has been admitted and did not have to be proved. Meanwhile, the " Swadeshi " in which Indian aspirations have embodied themselves is much to the same effect as the " Sinn Fein " of Irish nativism. It is an economic rather than a political movement, and aims to build up Indian industries at the expense of British. At any rate, the presence of two intelligent and representative native Indians in the Indian Council can hardly produce any result that is not beneficial to all concerned.

September 14, 1907

BLAME FOR INDIA'S TROUBLE.

Major Dunlop Says It Was a Mistake to Educate the Natives.

England's present troubles in India are due to education of the natives, declares Major Arthur Wallace-Dunlop of the Twenty-third Sikh Pioneers, the crack native regiment, who arrived in this city Friday on his way home to London. The Major has seen twenty-one years' service in India. He was with Col. Younghusband in the expedition into Tibet, where he lost two fingers and narrowly escaped with his life.

Discussing conditions in India yesterday in his room at the Hotel Astor, Major Wallace-Dunlop said:

" In Bengal there is real sedition. There the farmers' sons are educated by the Government, and they do not wish to carry on the business of their fathers. They think they should receive a billet from the Government. They are too big for their boots.

" An example of the bad results of educating these people has just been seen in India. Trouble started in the Punjab shortly before I left. The Government had made land allotments to the better class of natives, imposing certain regulations on those to whom the land was given at a small sum. They are obliged, for instance, to raise horses or mules for the army. There was dissatisfaction about the regulations.

" All that is needed is a little firmness. The present Viceroy is capable of dealing with the situation, and so is the Commander in Chief, Lord Kitchener. It will all blow over in time. The people of India possess no arms. They can do nothing unless they win over the native troops, of which there are about 200,000 in India. There are no signs now of any of the troops being won over."

In speaking of the Younghusband expedition into Tibet in 1904, Major Wallace-Dunlop told of the manner in which he lost the first and second fingers of his left hand.

" It was at the first of the campaign," he said, " and we were near Guru. The Tibetans were intrenched and had blocked our way. We were ordered not to fire the first shot in the campaign, and every man in my regiment sincerely hoped that the other side would fire the first shot soon. We fixed bayonets and charged up to the very edge of the intrenchments, and halted only three or four feet away from the enemy. It seems that they had received the same orders—not to fire the first shot.

"There we stood, glaring into each other's eyes. Right in front of me was a peasant soldier with a sabre in his hands. Then some one down the line—I believe it was one of the enemy—fired a shot. That was the signal for the real fighting. The man in front of me made a slash. I fired. The bullet from my rifle entered his body below the arm. It was of such small calibre that it did not stop him. His sabre caught me on the hand just as I killed him with another shot."

The Major said that about half the army in India was now stationed on the northwest frontier, where the trouble is pending. There are about 320,000 troops in India at present, including British and native regiments.

Major Wallace-Dunlop was asked what he thought of Kipling.

"He has unduly vulgarized Tommy Atkins," he replied. "The British soldier of to-day is not the uneducated man that Mr. Kipling makes him out to be in his 'Soldiers Three.' But certainly Mr. Kipling in his writings of army life in India shows a remarkable familiarity with the subject. He is a marvel to the British soldier."

June 23, 1907

FIGHT IN HINDOO CONGRESS.

Home Rulers and Conservatives Beat Each Other Severely.

SURAT, Bombay, Dec. 27.—After two days of futile efforts to elect a President, the Indian National Congress broke up this afternoon in a free fight during which the police had to be called in.

The Congress, which meets annually, was of especial interest this year, owing to the agitation for home rule in India. When the delegates assembled yesterday the Moderates and Extremists at once locked horns on this issue, and the meeting was adjourned amid much disorder. When the delegates reassembled to-day their overheated passions broke loose a second time, and the platform from which moderation and constitutional action had been advised was rushed by the Extremists in a body, loudly demanding the speedy establishment of complete home rule.

Chairs and tables were broken in the scrimmage and table legs and other pieces of shattered furniture were used by the delegates as bludgeons. Many delegates sustained serious injuries before the police finally came in and cleared the hall.

December 28, 1907

BOMB EXPLODED IN CALCUTTA

Intended to Wreck a Street Car, but It Injures Only Natives.

CALCUTTA, May 15.—A bomb which had been placed on the rail of a street car line here was exploded to-day by the wheel of a cart passing over it. Four natives were injured.

It was evidently the intention of the perpetrators of the outrage to wreck a street car containing white persons, as notices in Bengali had been circulated warning natives not to ride in first-class cars. Apparently the bomb was charged with picric acid and not dynamite.

This being the fifth attempt within five months to blow up street cars with bombs, much uneasiness has resulted.

May 16, 1908

ENGLISH IN INDIA ON VOLCANO'S EDGE

Well-Informed Correspondent Says Civilians Go Armed—Women Not Safe Without Escort.

SEDITION IS SPREADING

So Declares a Highly Placed Indian Officer Just Arrived in London—Classes, Not Masses, Affected.

By Marconi Transatlantic Wireless Telegraph to The New York Times.

LONDON, Nov. 21.—Evidences of unrest in India have deepened the apprehensions with which the outlook in that section of the British Empire is regarded in responsible quarters. King Edward's recent proclamation seems to have had the immediate effect of initiating a series of political offenses and demonstrations of disaffection. The alarmists are talking of another mutiny, and one highly placed officer in particular, who has just arrived in London from India, is circulating a statement to the effect that the Indian Government is in the possession of evidence showing that a systematic propaganda has been set on foot with the object of tampering with native troops.

In official circles the idea of another mutiny on any considerable scale is regarded as practically impossible, but, nevertheless, the situation is viewed with considerable anxiety. One authority—that same Indian officer—said:

"We wish that we could ascribe the agitation to the partition of Bengal alone, for then it would die down; but the truth is that sedition and unrest are spreading to all parts of the peninsula."

The Anglo-Indian correspondent of The Daily Mail, who, I am assured, speaks with intimate knowledge, declares:

"The gravity of the situation is not realized in England. In India every European feels that he is on the edge of a volcano that may at any moment become active. When civilians go armed and European women are not safe without an escort, it is evident that race hatred has reached the high-water mark of danger. Yet there are some purblind officials who will not see the danger before their eyes—as in the case of that Governor of a province whose letters announcing an improvement in the situation have been read by friends here simultaneously with the cabled accounts of a second attempt on his own life."

The person referred to is, of course, Sir Andrew Fraser, Lieutenant Governor of Bengal, who was shot at in Calcutta while attending a lecture by Prof. Burton of Chicago.

However, there is still time to avoid a catastrophe, even according to those who paint the dangers in the most lurid colors. One of them suggests the following expedient:

"Certain classes in India have been affected by treason; the millions are practically untouched. But they have forgotten British strength. Lord Kitchener's new concentration of troops has withdrawn the soldiers from the eye of the native. In Lord Roberts's time both native and British troops marched through the country when changing stations. It is twenty-five years since the British troops have so marched, and fifteen years since a native regiment has been seen marching through Bengal."

This suggestion is characteristic of the loose talk which is going on about one of the most complex political problems of the present age. If India could be awed into quiescence by a mere parade of troops, John Morley would not have needed to accept a seat in the House of Lords in order to continue his work at the Indian Office.

November 22, 1908

India

BRITAIN STRIKES IN INDIA.

Leaders of the Movement Against the Government Are Arrested.

CALCUTTA, Dec. 13.—Great excitement prevails here owing to developments in the agitation which has been going on for some time against the Government. The most prominent Bengali leader in Eastern Bengal, Dutta, was arrested at Burrisol on Saturday and conveyed to an unknown destination.

Another prominent Nationalist leader, Mitra, editor of the Sanjibani, has been arrested at Calcutta, while the editor of another native paper has been sentenced to transportation on the charge of sedition.

LONDON, Dec. 13.—The new summary jurisdiction act has been enforced in India with dramatic suddenness by the arrest of Dutta, who personally has been a remarkable force for years past. He has been regarded as the uncrowned King of the district in Bengal of which Burrisol is the chief town.

Dutta is a lawyer of great attainments. He is a born leader of men, and had much influence among all classes of Bengalis. He was at the head of the boycott movement.

December 14, 1908

REFORM IN INDIA BEGINS.

Plan Devised to Lead to Constitution Goes Into Effect.

SIMLA, British India, Nov. 15.—The plan for the reform of the British administration of India, which was outlined by Lord Morley, Secretary of State for India, in the House of Lords last December, and which is designed to give India an embryo constitution admitting the natives to an important share in the legislation of the country, went into effect to-day. Thus begins a new epoch in the history of British rule in India. For more than three years the Imperial Government and the Indian administration have wrestled with the details of the plan recently consummated.

Under the programme adopted all religious and special interests may elect representatives to the Viceroy's council and the provincial councils, but in view of recent Anarchistic outbreaks a safeguard is provided in a qualification which empowers the Imperial and Provincial Governments to declare ineligible those persons whose election is considered contrary to public interests.

The Viceroy's council in the future will have 370 members instead of 126 as formerly, of whom a total of 135 will be elected, as against 39 elected heretofore. The functions of the council will be considerably enlarged, and it will be enabled to take an active part in the making of the budget and all legislations. The new councils will assemble in January.

November 16, 1909

INDIANS URGE MURDER.

Killing of Europeans Not Considered Crime by Hindu Anarchists.

MADRAS, May 7.—The seditious Indians have been circulating surreptitiously an anarchistic broadside, secretly printed at Delhi and professing to be a reissue of the notorious Yugantar. It is probably the most outrageous document inciting natives to murdering Europeans that has yet appeared. It is headed "Killing No Murder," and reads in part as follows:

"We once more appear before you to preach our revolutionary doctrines to all for the redemption of our Mother from the atrocious hands of the Feringhis. Your life is not worth even a dust or a straw if you do not soil your hand with the blood of our oppressor, the Feringhi. You must kill as many of these white sheep as you lay hands on, whether men, women or children. This sort of killing we call no murder, but a sacred duty that devolves on the shoulders of every Indian for the lifting up of our Bharata Mata to the very lofty pedestal filled with glory and splendor. * * * Rise up! Rise up, oh, Sons of India! Rise up! Arm yourselves with bombs and dispatch the white asuras soon to Yama's abode. [Yama is the Indian Pluto.] If you are in need of money, loot down the oppressors' houses. It is the wealth of the poor Indian that fattens the Feringhi."

Then follow directions as to how arms may be procured from arsenals, assurances that British soldiers may be counted upon to offer only a faint-hearted resistance, and the suggestion that domestic servants may assist in the great work of extirpating the British by poisoning their masters, a method described as the "smooth dispatch" in contrast to the use of cocoanut-shell bombs filled with poisoned needles. The article goes on to warn Indians loyal to the Europeans and who shelter them that they "will surely share the fate of the wretched traitor of London," referring probably to the late Dr. Lalcaca, who lost his life in attempting to save Sir W. Curzon Wyllie.

More warnings are followed by an abusive outburst, in which the British are described as "robbers, cowards, dastards, and nobody's sons." And the article concludes with an assurance to patriotic Indians that the killing of Europeans is their "foremost duty" and that "killing is no murder."

June 12, 1910

VICEROY OF INDIA WOUNDED BY BOMB

Attacked on State Entry Into Delhi—Indications of an Extensive Plot.

DURBAR CEREMONIES GO ON

Viceroy's Place Taken by a Member of Council — Lord Hardinge's Wounds Not Dangerous.

By Marconi Transatlantic Wireless Telegraph to The New York Times.

LONDON, Tuesday, Dec. 24.—A great sensation has been caused here by the news that a bomb was thrown by a native at Lord Hardinge, the Viceroy of India, as he was making his state entry yesterday into Delhi, the new capital of India, and that the Viceroy was wounded, though not dangerously. Lady Hardinge, who accompanied him, was not hurt, though she is suffering from shock. Their escape from death was extraordinary. One of their native attendants on the elephant on which they were riding was killed, and another was badly wounded.

A telegram from Delhi to The Times indicates that several men were concerned in the outrage. It says:

"The house from which the bomb was thrown is a large three-storied one, with offices in the lower part and native residential quarters in the other stories. It was densely packed with spectators, men, women, and children, probably 150 in all.

"It is stated that groups of men were seen at a corner of the roof of the house just before the bomb was thrown, and that they disappeared immediately afterward, but not before crying out in Hindustani words expressing satisfaction that the aim had been sure.

"There were great crowds in the street behind the line of troops, and a confused rush took place, as some missiles struck a few spectators. This confusion facilitated the escape of the perpetrators of the outrage, as the police could not surround the house at once.

"It is impossible to say how many occupants got away. A small group was seen entering a winding alley, apparently leading to the neighboring bazaars. They were followed, but the alley proved a cul de sac. A door, however, was found bolted. It was forced and two men with injuries to their faces were arrested, while four others outside who were apparently trying to evade notice were also taken.

"The Viceroy and Lady Hardinge displayed extraordinary coolness and self-possession. The terrible death of their Indian attendant showed that the force of the explosion was very great, but it did not extend to a wide circle, as otherwise the Viceroy's injuries would have been more severe.

"Lady Hardinge's complete escape

THE COLONIZERS AND THE COLONIZED

Lord Hardinge, Viceroy of India, and Lady Hardinge. The Latter Escaped Unhurt.

seems miraculous, as she was on the side of the howdah next to the house whence the bomb was thrown. It must have passed almost over her before striking the attendant.

"The bomb was of native construction and filled with nails, screws, &c., of which a large handkerchief full was collected after the procession had passed. This kind of bomb has been used by Indian Anarchists on previous occasions, such as attacks on trains.

"Sir Louis Dane, Lieutenant Governor of the Punjab, in preliminary remarks at the Durbar, referring to the dastardly attempt made upon the Emperor's representative in the imperial capital of India, said that by the grace of Almighty God the Viceroy's life had been preserved. He was sure the voice of the loyal Punjab of loyal Delhi, of loyal India, of Indians and Europeans, would condemn this atrocious attempt. God grant that it might be the last! It should appeal to all loyalists as amounting to sacrilege on such an occasion.

"Sir Louis said he hoped that every one present would make it clear to his countrymen that such an attempt checked all progress and put back the hands of the clock, it might be for fifty years.

"The deepest feeling has been excited here by the outrage. Delhi contains all the leading Indian members of the Viceroy's Legislative Council, who were invited for the occasion, as well as ruling chiefs. Those present at the Durbar showed the strongest approval of Sir Louis Dane's appeal to loyal feeling and also to Sir Guy Fleetwood Wilson's short speech, in which he said that in the wounded Viceroy's pain and intense disappointment the hearts of all Indians would go out to him, as the hearts of Englishmen would."

The India Office last night issued the folowing report from the Viceroy's surgeon:

"A portion of the projectile struck the back of the right shoulder along the inner border of the shoulder blade, passed upward, and came out through the skin along the upper line of the shoulder, causing a wound four inches long and exposing the muscles and bone. There is no injury to the lungs.

"Another fragment caused a small wound on the right side of the neck, but this is not serious. There are also four small wounds, caused by nails, on the back of the right hip. All these are slight.

"There has been moderate loss of blood, but the shock has been severe and there is some deafness caused by the explosion. His Excellency soon after his injuries lost consciousness, but recovered quickly.

"The wounds have been dressed, and his Excellency is now fairly comfortable."

December 24, 1912

BOMBS IN LETTERS IN INDIA.

Addressed to Editors—Three Postal Employes Mortally Hurt.

CALCUTTA, March 17.—Several bombs intended to kill or maim the editors of leading papers here, sent through the Post Office in the form of letters, exploded this morning while being stamped after they had been sorted. Three of the sorters in the main Post Office were mortally injured. They were taken to a hospital.

The deadly missives were addressed to the editors of four papers—The Englishman, The Statesman, The Capital, and The Empire.

March 18, 1913

Pledges India's Millions to Serve England, Amid Loyal Outbursts at Bombay Congress

BOMBAY, Dec. 27, (via London. Delayed.)—Ten thousand delegates, representing all communities, were present today at the opening of the annual India National Congress, which was notable for the loyal and patriotic utterances of the speakers.

"Millions in India are waiting to serve," was the keynote of the opening speeches. In the Presidential address Sir Satyendra Sinhha said the supreme feeling in India was "admiration for the self-imposed burden England was bearing in the struggle for liberty and freedom, and pride that India had proved herself not a whit behind the rest of the empire in the assistance given the mother country."

Continuing, Sir Satyendra expressed the hope that "the spontaneous outburst of loyalty had dispelled forever all distrust and suspicion between the Indians and their rulers." The speaker admitted that the time had not arrived for self-government in India, but he urged the British Government to approve ungrudgingly the goal to which India aspired, and also to permit the recruiting of a strong national Indian army.

December 29, 1915

WANTED HOME RULE IN INDIA

Protest Meetings Organized After Mrs. Besant Was Curbed.

LONDON, June 23.—Telegrams from Bombay say that the restrictions placed by the Government on Mrs. Annie Besant and her colleagues are the sequel to a violent home rule agitation, which was distinguished by a vilification of everything British and Western. The restrictive measures evoked a storm of adverse comment in the native press, and protest meetings were organised. The local British press welcomes the restrictions silencing the dangerous movement.

Mrs. Besant has been forbidden by the Indian Government to participate in any meetings, deliver lectures, or publish her writings. She and her associates are also prohibited from residing in Madras City, and ordered to remain within certain areas. Their correspondence has also been placed under censorship. Mrs. Besant is head of the Theosophical Society, and was expelled from the Presidency of Bombay last year for preaching revolt in India.

June 24, 1917

HOME RULE SCHEME DRAFTED FOR INDIA

Viceroy and Governor Draw Up Limited Self-Government Plan for Parliament.

CHANGE TO BE GRADUAL

Declarations of British and American Statesmen Credited as Giving Force to the Reform.

LONDON, July 17.—Eventually to set up in India a responsible self-government is the avowed purpose of the plan of limited home rule for that country which has been prepared for submission to the British Parliament by Edwin S. Montagu, Secretary for India, and Baron Chelmsford, Viceroy and Governor General of India.

Before this goal of self-government can be attained, however, the authors of the new plan say the Indian people should have a period of training. They avow that the proposed scheme of government is a temporary expedient intended to provide a method of training in government, and say the ultimate attainment of the desired goal depends upon the Indian people themselves. "It would not be fair to give it to them until they fulfill the necessary conditions," say the Secretary for India and the Viceroy.

The report has been made public by the Government for purposes of discussion and criticism. It has not been definitely adopted in all its details by the War Cabinet.

Leading up to a description of the new plan, the official announcement says that "declarations of both our own and American statesmen concerning the liberalising of the aims of the Allies have given new force and vitality to the growing demand among the progressive section of the (Indian) people for self-government."

The Viceroy and Secretary of India propose that the new Government in India shall be composed of the following:

Provincial Legislatures, to be composed of directly elected representatives.

A Viceregal Legislature for all India, to be composed of two chambers—the Legislative Assembly of India and the Council of State.

The Indian Privy Council, members of which are to be appointed by the King-Emperor.

A Council of Princes.

According to the official announcement of the provisions of the scheme an increasing degree of responsibility is to be given to the provinces. They are to have the largest measure of independence compatible with the authority of the Viceregal Legislature. Certain subjects are to be reserved for action by the Executive Council of these provinces, excluding Burma. These Executive Councils will consist of the Governor and two members, one of them to be an Indian.

"Devolution," says the official announcement, "is to take the form of giving responsibility in certain subjects, to be known as transferred subjects, to the Provincial Legislative Council, which will have a substantial number of elected members to be chosen on as broad a franchise as possible." The subjects over which this provincial electoral body will exercise control are defined as "those offering most opportunity for local knowledge and social service wherein Indians have shown themselves to be keenly interested, those wherein mistakes would not be irremediable, and those which stand in need of development."

"Contributions to the Government of India," the announcement continues, "are to be the first charge of provincial revenues. The remaining provincial revenues are to be administered by the provincial governments."

The Viceregal Legislature of all India will be composed of two chambers—the Legislative Assembly of India and the Council of State. The Assembly is to have a membership of 100. More than half—thirty-six—of the members of the present Legislative Council are nominated by the Governor General, but under the new plan this official majority would disappear and two-thirds of the 100 members of the Assembly would be elective. The remaining one-third would be nominated by the Governor General.

The second chamber, or Council of State, is intended to "develop something of the experience and dignity of a body of elder statesmen. It is to be the final legislative authority in matters which the Government regards as essential. Besides the Governor General, it will consist of fifty members, of whom twenty-nine are to be nominated and twenty-one elected. To obtain legislation necessary for the conduct of the Government, the Governor will have power to certify that enactment of a certain measure is essential to the peace or tranquillity of a province.

The proposed Council of Princes is to consider questions affecting the native States and those of concern either to the empire as a whole or to British India and the native States in common.

Ten years after the proposed new Government is organised a commission is to be appointed to resurvey the whole political situation and judge what further power can be transferred to the native Governments. Similar commissions are to follow at intervals of not less than twelve years. A select Committee on India is to be formed in each session of the British House of Commons.

Throughout the report it is pointed out that the granting of further responsibility to the native Government depends upon active and intelligent voting by the natives.

July 19, 1918

Want Local Autonomy in India.

LONDON, Jan. 8.—At the Nationalist Congress being held at Delhi, India, according to reports from that city, a resolution was adopted by acclamation favoring full provincial autonomy and against special electorates for Europeans. The congress passed formal resolutions of loyalty to the Crown.

January 9, 1919

INDIA RIOTS WIDESPREAD.

British Government Tells of Attacks on Europeans and on Property.

LONDON, April 14.—Widespread disturbances in India were referred to in Parliament tonight as being the outcome of what was described as the "passive resistance" movement against the recent Indian legislation known as the Rowlatt act, intended to combat seditious conspiracy.

The movement originated with the home rule element in Bombay and has taken shape in attacks on officials and Europeans and on property.

The India Office tonight issued a long statement describing the general situation. It was shown that there have been disturbances recently at Lahore and a few casualties at Amritsar, thirty-three miles eastward, where three bank managers were burned to death in the Town Hall, two banks destroyed, the telegraph office wrecked, and three Europeans killed. At Ahmedabad a mob attacked and burned the telegraph office and two Government buildings. Here, also, there were a few casualties.

There have been disorders in which some persons have been wounded at Bombay, but, the statement says, in most of these places military forces are now maintaining order.

April 16, 1919

THE COLONIZERS AND THE COLONIZED

Moslem Leaders of Punjab Take Steps to Check Riots

LONDON, April 22.—Advices from India indicate that the moderate elements are rallying to the support of law and order against the extremists.

From Lahore comes a telegram that the Mohammedan leaders of the Punjab have sent a manifesto, earnestly appealing to their countrymen, especially Moslems, to abandon passive resistance, to obey authority and take effective steps to restore law and order.

SIMLA, India, April 20.—Martial law has been proclaimed in the Gujerat district.

April 23, 1919

PROCLAIMS NEW ACT FOR INDIA SELF-RULE

King George Says That It Points Way to Fully Responsible Government.

URGES RACE FORBEARANCE

Elected Representatives to Share in the Duties of Administration Hereafter.

LONDON, Dec. 23.—King George issued a proclamation today announcing the new measure giving India a larger degree of self-government.

The proclamation characterizes the Government bill as a historic act, giving representation long desired by the natives. It calls for the determination of the people and the officials to work together for the common purpose of making the new plan of government a success.

The proclamation says in part:

"Another epoch is reached today in the annals of India. I give royal assent to the act, which takes its place among the great historic measures passed by the Parliament of this realm for the better government of India and the greater contentment of her people.

"The act, which has now become a law, intrusts elected representatives of the people with a definite share in the Government and points the way to a fully responsible Government hereafter. If, as I confidently hope, the policy which this act inaugurates should achieve its purpose, the results will be momentous in the story of human progress.

"I have watched with understanding and sympathy the growing desire of my Indian people for representative institutions. Their scope has been extended, stage by stage, until there now lies before us a definite step on the road to responsible Government. I shall watch your progress along this road.

"The path will not be easy, and in the march toward the goal there will be the need of perseverance and mutual forbearance between all sections and races of my people in India. I am confident that those high qualities will be forthcoming.

"I rely on the new popular assemblies to interpret wisely the wishes of those they represent and not forget the interests of the masses who cannot yet be admitted to the franchise. I rely on the leaders of the people and the ministers of the future to face responsibility and endure misrepresentation, and to sacrifice much for the common interests of the State, remembering that true patriotism transcends party and communal boundaries.

"A new era is opening. Let it begin with a common determination among my people and my officers to work together for the common purpose."

December 24, 1919

DEFEND AMRITSAR KILLINGS

British Officers Testify to the Violence of Native Crowds Last April.

LONDON, Dec. 29.—The latest newspapers received from India contain details of the investigation of the killing of natives at Amritsar, India, last April, and the testimony given before the commission of inquiry.

General Sir William Beynon, district commander, testifying at Lahore in November, strongly upheld the introduction of martial law. He defended the action of General Dyer, commander of the troops in India at Gallian-Wa.abagh and Amritsar. He said mobile columns had been sent out to impress the natives and make it clear that it was intended to keep order and to counteract false reports spread about that British rule had ended.

Magistrate J. E. Kough testified regarding flogging. He said that only natives of good physique were chosen, twelve being flogged in one day on the same triangle. The punishment was inflicted with the usual cane.

Colonel North, who commanded the fort during the riots, said that the people were offensive, and laughed and jeered at the British quite a month prior to the riots. Early in the morning of April 12 a crowd of 6,000 collected outside the rails of the fort. Many were armed with axes on poles, Colonel North said. They tried to push the rails down and spat at the people inside. They also stoned an officer leaving the fort on a motorcycle. According to Colonel North, many used the expression, "Let us kill the white men."

December 30, 1919

BRITISH CONDEMN SLAUGHTER IN INDIA

Commission Declares General Dyer's Troops Fired Too Long on Amritsar Mob.

DEPLORES ORDER TO CRAWL

Native Members, in a Minority Report, Censure the Punjab Government.

LONDON, May 26.—The findings of the commission appointed by the British Government to investigate the causes of the unrest in India, with the attending disorders, were made public today. The incidents investigated included the Amritsar affair, in April, 1919, in which a slaughter occurred when a crowd of natives in the Jallianwala Bagh inclosure at Amritsar was fired upon by troops commanded by General R. E. H. Dyer, then in command in India.

The commission, under the chairmanship of Lord Hunter, submitted two reports, a majority report by the five English members and a minority report by the three Indian members. An official summary of the two reports given out by the British Government reads in part:

"With the exception of the Jallianwala Bagh and certain minor incidents, both the Indian and English members generally agree in justifying the firing done by the police and the military. They agree in pronouncing unfavorably upon General Dyer's handling of the Jallianwala Bagh meeting and upon certain of the orders passed in the course of the administration of martial law. They further agree in exonerating the Government of India from all blame.

"Regarding Amritsar, the English members hold that the outbreak was anti-Government at every stage, hostility to the Government quickly merging into antipathy for Europeans as such and culminating on April 10 in the brutal murder of five inoffensive persons and savage assaults on others. The Indian members think that the anti-European sentiment developed subsequent to the firing on April 10, but do not dissent from the view that the firing was necessary.

Declare Dyer Made "Grave Error."

"The English members approve the action of the authorities prior to April 13 considering it impossible that de facto martial law could fail to result from the happening of April 10. But while admitting the difficulties of the situation, they consider that General Dyer's conduct at the Jallianwala Bagh is open to criticism in two respects, first, in that he fired without warning, and second, in that he continued firing too long. They do not believe that the mob would have dispersed if warned, and considered that firing would have been necessary in any case. They consider that General Dyer, through a mistaken belief that continued firing would be justified by the effect produced in other places, committed a grave error in firing too long.

"They find no grounds for believing that this action saved the situation and averted a second mutiny. But they do not think that General Dyer can be blamed for not attending to the wounded, as they are not convinced any one was exposed to unnecessary suffering for want of medical attention.

"This opinion is not shared by the Indian members, who, while agreeing in the condemnation of General Dyer's action, take a graver view of the whole incident, stigmatizing his conduct as inhuman and un-British."

The official summary points out that the English and the Indian members differ as to the precise nature of the disorders and as to the justification for the policy pursued by the Punjab government. The English members emphatically state that "open rebellion" was the only suitable description of the disturbances, while the Indian members declare that such a term implies a rising for the purpose of turning out the British government, which was not the intention of the rioters.

The English members assert that the declaration of martial law was justified, while the Indian members censure the Punjab Government "for persuading

India

itself rather easily that martial law was necessary. They declare that martial law was proclaimed when the situation offered no justification for it.

Agree as to Delhi and Bombay.

"Both the Indian and English members," continues the official summary, "are in complete agreement respecting events in Delhi and Bombay, holding that the measures taken by the authorities were reasonable."

The official summary notes that the English members regret that the administration of martial law should have assumed such an intensive form and they condemn certain of the orders issued as injudicious. They object, for instance, to General Dyer's orders that any one desiring to traverse the street where Miss Sherwood, a British subject, was brutally assaulted, should crawl. The orders passed in Lahore against students are condemned as unnecessarily severe.

"On all these matters," adds the official summary, "the Indian members take a more serious view, considering these orders and some others unjustifiable, calculated to humiliate Indians, to punish alike innocent and guilty and to foment racial bitterness."

May 26, 1920

BLAME FOR AMRITSAR

Indians' Commission Says Sir Michael O'Dwyer's Policy Exasperated the People

ALONG with the official British report on the Amritsar disorders a report has just been received here from the commission appointed by the Indian National Congress at its last session in December, at which 8,000 delegates are reported to have been present. Two of the signatories of the report are ex-Presidents of the National Congress, one of them a member of the Viceroy's Legislative Council, M. K. Gandhi, the leader of the Rowlatt agitation; a Justice of the Supreme Court of Baroda, and three other barristers at law.

The Commissioners say they "examined the statements of 1,700 witnesses," and selected for publication 650 of these. Meetings were called at each of the Punjab cities where the disturbances had occurred, and public challenges were invited on the statements made by witnesses. The report says that "no contradictions were made." The majority of the statements made were also presented to the official Hunter Commission, the official investigating body, the report states, but these and the evidence offered by the imprisoned Punjab leaders were rejected. The report also says that "an organized attempt was made to procure false evidence" and the "martial law Commissioners were not bound to record any evidence and their judgments were unappealable."

The report strongly condemns the administration of Sir Michael O'Dwyer in the Punjab, where the events took on a most serious aspect. His methods, the report says, "could only end in exasperating a people who had already been incensed against his rule. We feel tempted to say that he invited violence from the people so that he could crush them. The evidence in the appendix shows that he subjected the people of the Punjab to the gravest provocation, under which they momentarily lost self-control."

Regarding the Rowlatt bills the report says:

"It is this act which raised a storm of opposition unknown before in India. The Government was wholly unjustified in placing on the statute book, on the eve of liberal reform (referring to the Montagu-Chelmsford reform scheme), an extraordinary measure dealing with anarchy, as if anarchy had been endemic instead of being rare in India."

Comment is also made on the Civil Disobedience Movement of Mr. Gandhi, which is characterized as a movement which, "if properly practiced, would render government by force an impossibility, and that an effective enforcement of laws disliked by the people would be difficult." The report voices its opinion that "neither the Satyagraha nor the Hartal (general strike) had anything to do with the mob excesses." What did lead to the mob actions, it says, was the spirit of O'Dwyer, who is declared to have expressed himself before an Indian barrister, with fist raised, in this vein:

"Remember, there is another force greater than Gandhi's soul-force."

The report expresses its disapproval of the mob excesses, declaring:

"We do not, in any shape or form, desire to minimize or defend the murder of Englishmen or incendiarism. We believe that they are indefensible, but no deeds, however dastardly, of an enraged mob can warrant a slaughter of innocent people," which the report characterized as "a calculated piece of inhumanity unparalleled for its ferocity." The report declares that at Amritsar "at least 1,200 persons were killed and 3,600 wounded."

Was there a state of rebellion? ask the Commissioners, and their reply is:

"The theory of rebellion or war completely broke down before the Hunter Commission. There was no proof of organization outside the Punjab, and behind the so-called conspiracy. On the contrary, Colonel O'Brien (one of Sir Michael's lieutenants) had to admit that he had no evidence to support the theory of rebellion; that it was mere guesswork."

The report concludes with the demands for the repeal of the Rowlatt act, the relieving of Sir Michael O'Dwyer and others who participated in enforcing martial law, of any position of responsibility under the Crown, the recall of the Viceroy, and the refund of fines and indemnities imposed upon the people.

May 30, 1920

Gandhi and British India

By CLAIR PRICE

INDIA is one of the wonders of the world, and one of the wonders of India just now is a saint in politics. The fact that he is a saint, however, does not make him popular with the British. For he has made India more uncomfortable for them than it has been since the great mutiny in 1857—and India is the very core of their empire. The structure of the British Empire is such, in fact, that British imperialism would be compelled to evacuate Great Britain itself before it would willingly evacuate India. The Government of India—in its own country the most powerful Government in the world—has met and overcome many an obstacle in one way or another, but today it is up against an obstacle of a sort which is brand new in its experience. It is up against Mohandas Karamchand Gandhi, a dark little wisp of a man, who looks as if he could be picked up in one's arms and carried off like a child. In point of personal following, he is far and away the greatest man living in the world today.

He is a philosophic anarchist, a new Tolstoy without Tolstoy's past. He specializes in reducing his wants. He has fasted so long and so often that he is physically a mere shadow of a man. He is an Idea, living for the moment in a frail and brittle body. At home, he sits cross-legged on a mattress with his disciples. He dresses in a pair of coarse white trousers and a convict's cap of the sort which is known throughout India as "the Gandhi cap." When he is traveling, thousands of his followers throng to the stations through which he is to pass and if he only appears at the door of his third-class carriage, they are content to have seen him. When he leaves the train, they drop to their knees and press forward to kiss the hem of his garment.

Christians, including one or two New York clergymen, have frequently compared him with Christ.

He was born 52 years ago in the Gujarat province of Bombay presidency. He was the son of a low caste Hindu merchant who brought him up for the law. He finished his legal training in London where he donned European dress, read law in the Middle Temple and brought his young Eastern mind into its first contact with our Northern civilization. Here he stopped learning lessons when he read Ruskin's "Unto This Last." He read Tolstoy's "The Kingdom of Heaven Is Within You" and began to shrink from Northern industrialism.

His shrinking developed into a bitter hatred, a hatred which all Eastern minds feel toward a civilization which deifies the Factory Chimney, a hatred in which a larger part of the future history of the world is bound up than is generally believed. Still in European dress, he was sent from London to South Africa 20 years ago to defend an Indian who had been arrested under the new anti-Indian labor legislation. He led an Indian rights campaign and the Transvaal and Natal jails began to fill with his followers. He and his entire family were thrown into jail, an act against which he protested in one of the first of the hunger strikes. He was kept in jail for two years and his health has never completely recovered. In all, he was jailed three times and once he was ambushed by friends for suspected treachery and left for dead. But his long campaign of passive resistance finally compelled General Smuts to negotiate with him and the Smuts-Gandhi legislation is still on the statute books at Cape Town. By this time, he knew that the problem of white men vs. brown men is the biggest problem in any empire which attempts to rule both; he knew that Indians would never receive their full "rights" in any white dominion until they had first won them in India. Still in European dress, he went back to India to fight for Indian home rule.

Now India is a continent in itself. It is as big as all Europe outside of Russia. A third of its area consists of some 700 native States varying in size from Hyderabad, which is as big as Italy, to Lawa, which is as big as a farm. These are controlled by the Government of India through the typically Indian Army device of the political officer, but in theory they are independent, their rulers being entitled to the Seventeen Guns which the Government of India's Salute Sheet accords to independent Asiatic sovereigns. The remaining two-thirds of India is administered by the Government of India direct.

India's population of 330,000,000—one-fifth of the population of the world—is three times as big as the population of the United States and all its dependencies. British India proper numbers 250,000,000, a population more intricate in its complexities of race, religion and stage of civilization than is found in any other country on earth. This population consists of a vast lower stratum of peasantry and a very small educated and propertied class, neither of which is accustomed to playing an official rôle in the Government of India; for the tradition of democracy is the invention of our Northern civilization and is unknown in the East.

Cutting across these strata are many other lines of social cleavage, of which the chief cuts off the Hindus from their former conquerors and traditional enemies, the Mohammedans. The Hindus number about 200,000,000 in all India, and their outlook on life is colored by pantheism and passivism. The Mohammedans, who number only 60,000,000, are of a strong, aggressive sort, who find in warfare the very essence of their religion.

For the last ten years India has been the scene of a rising nationalist movement conducted as a Hindu religious revival, a movement from which the Mohammedans sharply dissociated themselves. Bengal Province greeted it with such vigorous demands that the Hon. E. S. Montagu, Secretary of State for India, went to India from London in 1917 and formulated the Montagu reforms, which were designed to give propertied Indians a very restricted rôle in the government of India. At the same time the Government gave itself added powers to put down "disorder" in Bengal by passing the Rowlatt act, an act whose provisions encountered widespread resentment.

After the signing of the armistice, two terrific influenza epidemics, the unusually high cost of living, the fear of famine due to the failure of the rains and a rapid succession of lightning strokes, which had hitherto never been heard of in India, combined with the Rowlatt act to produce a situation in which anything might happen. Rioting broke out in Calcutta and Delhi and spread throughout the Punjab like wildfire. Five hundred Indians were killed and 2,000 injured in the Amritsar massacre, and still it grew. Finally the Punjab was put under martial law, and in accordance with the provisions of the Rowlatt act thousands of Punjabis were scooped into "preventive detention" and held without trial.

But it was not these things which sent the greatest flame of anger over India. What India smarts under today is the memory of the "crawling orders" which British officers admitted at the subsequent Government investigation into martial law in the Punjab, orders which were designed solely to humiliate. The Punjabis are a proud and fighting race who have furnished famous regiments to the Indian Army, and Bengal province, itself a famous storm centre, is still jeering at the Punjab: "We went down fighting, with a bomb in one hand and a revolver in the other, but you 'martial races' lay down in the streets to be spat upon."

What happened in the Punjab killed the Montagu reforms. When India's first elections were held last year under the Montagu scheme, whole races, classes and religions stayed away from the polls. As the time neared for the Prince of Wales to embark last Winter to open India's first native legislative bodies at Delhi his trip was suddenly canceled and the Duke of Connaught, an older man, was sent out in his place. In opening what there was to open of the Legislative Assembly he said he felt "the bitterness and estrangement of India"; "the shadow of Amritsar" had "lengthened over the land"; he knew "how deep was the concern felt by the King Emperor at the terrible chapter of events in the Punjab"; he appealed to "Indians and Britons alike to bury the past and forgive." In all the history of modern imperialism no member of a European royal family has ever so apologized to an Eastern people, but the royal apology fell on closed ears. The Rowlatt act was still in force and some of the Punjab prisoners were still in jail. The Duke of Connaught had disembarked at Madras into empty streets of closed shops and he embarked at Bombay for England amid a similar silence.

In the meantime the Treaty of Peace with Turkey had cut down the Mohammedan Sultan Caliph to the merest shadow of the power with which Mohammedan law had invested him for thirteen centuries, and the Mohammedans of India were not pleased. On top of the Turkish Treaty came the Esher committee's report to the War Office in London, recommending the continued use of the Indian Army in former territory of the Caliph, and Indian Mohammedans were ready to hurl themselves to Paradise in an immediate holy war against the British Government which had written the Turkish Treaty and which was represented by the Government of India. According to Mohammedan law, any country inhabited by Mohammedans is either Dar ul Islam or Dar ul Harb; i. e., the land of the faithful or the land of the unbeliever, and Mohammedans living in the land of the unbeliever are required either to fight or to emigrate. From the moment the Turkish Peace Treaty was signed Indian Mohammedans began to emigrate, trekking across the frontier into Afghanistan in answer to the same sort of impulse as once moved the Pilgrim Fathers to emigrate to America. Those Mohammedans who remained behind in the hope that the British Government could be made to rewrite the Turkish Treaty put off taking up the Sword of Mohammed and attached themselves to a powerful figure who has arisen outside the ranks of Mohammedanism.

That figure was the new Gandhi, clad in coarse white trousers and a convict's cap, who was crying up and down the political wilderness of India the new gospel of "Back to the Vedas!"

With the passage of the Rowlatt act, he had laid aside his European dress forever. He had become a mahatma, a saint who has transcended the flesh and the world. For him, India had found its soul in the fiery furnace of the Punjab ordeal. By "soul-force," India would purge itself of every vestige of the British and their satanic civilization, and would return to the ancient Vedic wisdom and the peace which antedated the British conquest. And if a purged and purified India should fall in the eyes of the North to progress, that would be its virtue, its proof that it is still sound and healthy at the core.

This was the gospel he was preaching: Let all Indians refuse to serve the British Government. Let those who are now serving give up their positions and their titles. Let all teachers and pupils quit the Government schools and start Indian schools in shaded groves where Indian pupils may gather about Indian teachers, after the manner of the ancient Vedic schools. Let all Indians quit wearing British cotton and return to Indian homespun. Let all Indians quit the use of alcohol and return to Indian food. Let all Indians quit the use of tea and sugar, since Great Britain monopolizes both. Let all Indians quit bearing children into this dark age of British industrialism. Let all Indians refuse to vote at Government elections. To vote is a worse sin than to kill ten holy cows. Let all Indians quit suing in Government courts. Let all Indian lawyers quit practicing in Government courts. "If the lawyers leave off their law and the legal profession is considered as low as that of a public woman, British rule will totter and fall in a single day."

Gandhi's program was arranged in four stages:

1. Refusal to accept Government titles and positions.
2. Refusal to attend Government schools.
3. Refusal to serve in the Government police or the Indian army.
4. Refusal to pay Government taxes.

Thus far he has used only the first two stages. If necessary to rid India of the British, he says he will utilize the third and fourth stages. If all four stages should fail, if "soul-force" fails, 10,000,000 Hindus are to leap to the sword. India is to be purged of the British within three years.

With Gandhi stand the two Mohammedan leaders, Mohammed and Shaukat Ali—huge, bluff men richly clad in green cloaks with tall white astrakhan caps bearing the gold crescent of Mohammedanism. Back of this trio stand the Indian National Congress and the All-India Mohammedan League; back of the congress and the league, Mohammedans are sacrificing goats instead of cows and Hindus are permitted to enter the Great Mosque of the Mogul Emperors at Delhi—both religions joined apparently in such union as India would never have deemed possible.

They are a strange trio, this tiny frugal Hindu vegetarian and pacifist and the two enormous Mohammedan meat eaters and warriors. Were the British not too busily occupied with far more serious matters, they might conceivably permit themselves a smile at the spectacle of these two Mohammedans looming beside Gandhi. For the British have had a long and richly varied experience in Asia and they have met at one time or another nearly all the tricks in Asia's répertoire; the British Army has had many a taste of the Sword of Mohammed and has abundant reason to respect it. But the spectacle of two Mohammedan fighters talking of "soul-force" and engaging in a passive resistance movement is a new one.

Concerning Gandhi, however, not even the British are able to cast the slightest aspersion on the high sincerity of the man. He belongs to the Jain sect of Hinduism, which is distinguished by the sanctity with which it invests all life. Even the Duke of Connaught received a letter from Gandhi immediately after his disembarkation at Madras, assuring him that no attempt would be made on his Highness's life during his stay in India, since India regarded all living things as sacred.

Although Gandhi is the Government of India's greatest foe, the Government is forced to refrain from arresting him; for it is Gandhi, and Gandhi alone, who has directed not only Hindu resentment at the Punjab atrocities but the more explosive wrath of India's Mohammedans over the Turkish Peace Treaty into the silent channels of passive resistance. Take Gandhi away and the Government of India might see at once the dawn of that red day which all white men in the East dread but which they never talk about, the day when the East "breaks loose."

Although he is the most powerful enemy the Government of India has ever encountered, the Government is forced to treat him as a friend. In fact, one of the first official acts of the new Viceroy of India, Lord Reading, was to summon the dark little Hindu in the convict's cap to a long conference at Delhi. All afternoon Gandhi talked to the new Viceroy. He talked more in pity than in anger. There is no anger in him. The anger is rather in the rattling cries of "Mahatma Gandhi ki jai" (to Gandhi the victory), which are resounding throughout India today.

July 10, 1921

FEAR 1,000 KILLED IN INDIA.

Anxiety Felt for English Women and Children as Riots Spread.

LONDON, Aug. 25.—More than one thousand lives, it is feared, have been lost in the rioting in the Malabar district of British India, says an Exchange Telegraph dispatch from Bombay received today. Anxiety is felt for the English women and children in the outlying districts. Several railway stations have been wrecked. Twenty men of the Leinster Regiment at Tirungadi are reported to have been cut off.

It is also reported, adds the message, that the rioting natives are working their way from the interior to Calicut, on the coast.

The centre of the riotous area appears to be in the district of North Ponani, thirty miles southeast of Calicut. Many clashes with military forces have occurred. The outbreak is attributed in British Indian quarters to the work of agitators among the natives in the district.

August 26, 1921

OFFER ISLAM OR DEATH TO HINDUS AT GRAVE

Mohammedan Rebels in India Declare Home Rule and Seize Crops.

CALICUT, India, Oct. 2.—The situation in Melattur is becoming very serious. The rebels are offering Hindus the alternative of death or Islam. If the Indians hesitate to choose, they are ordered to dig their own graves. If they refuse to embrace Islam they then are shot and dropped into their graves.

Complete home rule has been declared. Crops belonging to the Hindus have been confiscated. The Hindus are fleeing.

In the fighting at Nyalla last week, when tribesmen under fanatical leader Abdullah-el-Soghayer attacked the town, 600 of the tribesmen were killed. The British had fifty-one casualties.

LONDON, Oct. 2.—A situation of the utmost gravity is developing in India, says a dispatch to The Daily Herald, the labor organ, in consequence of the declaration of Mahatma Gandhi, the Nationalist leader: "We must repeat the formulae of the Ali brothers and invite imprisonment. We must declare from a thousand platforms that it is sinful for any Mussulman or Hindu to serve the existing Government, whether as a soldier or in any capacity whatsoever."

In response to his, says The Herald, meetings are being held throughout India. Ten thousand persons at a demonstration at Cawnpore repeated, after it had been introduced by Hasrat Mohani, the chairman's wife, a resolution affirming that it was unlawful for Mussulmans to remain in the British Army.

October 3, 1921

India

Troops Again Fire on Bombay Rioters; Disperse Mob That Burned Police Station

BOMBAY, Nov. 20 (Associated Press).—Disturbances occurred Friday at several points in the native quarter of the city. A mob burned a police station and military patrols were called into action. They fired upon and dispersed the rioters, who suffered some casualties.

On Saturday morning the trouble started afresh in a number of places, the patrols again being forced to fire into the crowd.

Both disturbances were confined to the native section, affairs in the European business quarter going on as usual.

In his statement issued yesterday Mohandas Karamchand Gandhi, leader of the "non-co-operationists," deprecating the disturbances which occurred on the occasion of the arrival in India of the Prince of Wales, declared that it was impossible to describe the agony he had suffered during "the last two days, which events stink in my nostrils."

Gandhi emphasized that the Mussulmans ought to be grateful to the Parsee Indians for their liberal contributions to the Caliphate fund. Instead, he declared, the Parsees had been victims of attack.

In his statement Gandhi invited both Hindus and Mussulmans to go home and repent and to implore God for forgiveness. He insisted that reparation should be made to those who had been injured.

Finally, Gandhi blamed himself for having instigated the spirit of revolt and announced that he would refuse to eat or drink anything but water until peace was restored.

Native Hoodlums Started Rioting.
Copyright, 1921, by The New York Times Company.
Special Cable to THE NEW YORK TIMES.
Dispatch to The London Daily Chronicle.

BOMBAY, Nov. 18.—It is now possible to relate in sequence the events of the unfortunate affair that is marring the otherwise successful visit of the Prince of Wales to Bombay. Mohandas Karamchand Gandhi, the leader of the "non-co-operationists, chose the day of the Prince's arrival for a passionate appeal to the malcontents of Bombay and crowned the occasion with the usual bonfire of English cloth and English-made clothes, bought for the purpose second-hand in the bazaar. At the same time he ordered a "hartal" or general strike, of all cabs and public vehicles in Bombay, except taxicabs, a step causing the greatest inconvenience to Englishmen and the better class of his own countrymen, whom he hates at least as much as he hates Englishmen. A warning was also issued on Wednesday that the butchers' shops would be closed on the day of the Prince's arrival, and this was generally done.

The malcontents having been thus stirred up, the inevitable trouble took its course. Even during the Prince's speech in the amphitheatre at the reception by the municipality, the well known Byculla Club was attacked and its custodian, Mr. Rose, severely beaten. The club servants came to his rescue, and the attacking party was driven off.

At first the real significance of this action was not realized, as the attackers were chiefly youthful hoodlums of the district. But, however it began, the disorder was certain to develop along political and religious lines.

A second attack was developed at 1:30 P. M. by a different class of men, but the members of the club had returned, and the assault was easily defeated.

From that time onward the unrest spread in the crowded streets of the city, and reprisals followed till near midnight.

November 21, 1921

TOPICS OF THE TIMES.

A Pacifist Incites to Rioting.

Like many another person of his kind, Mahatma GANDHI has discovered, to what may be his sincere astonishment and horror, that those to whom he has been preaching a peaceful non-co-operation with the British Government in India have acquired his antagonism to that Government, but are not content to limit their expression of it as he advises. Instead, they are resorting to the more militant methods of ordinary revolutionists and of rioters in general, and they are killing and getting themselves killed in a perfectly useless way.

As a remedy for the situation for which he is responsible—a responsibility he has the decency to admit—GANDHI has imposed upon himself a complete fast one day in each week. How that will bring his followers back to the passive resistance in which he believes it is hard to see, but mass psychology is queer, and possibly the thought of their beloved leader going hungry for what he considers their sins may have some effect on the Hindu multitudes—or on such of them as hear of it.

His device of non-co-operation apparently is a little different from the general strike as known in Europe. It belongs to the same family, however, and is a tool that hurts those who use it as much as those against whom it is used. Presumably, that is why it has been abandoned for more vigorous measures, even in India, where pacifists are rather more numerous than in other countries.

November 22, 1921

GANDHI EXTENDS SWAY OVER INDIANS

Nationalists Make Him Sole Executive Authority and Adopt His Non-Violence Policy.

AHMEDABAD, British India, Dec. 29 (Associated Press).—At a full session of the Indian National Congress today the resolution proposed by Mahatma Gandhi, declaring for continuation of the policy of non-violence in the effort to obtain independence from the British Empire, was adopted with only a dozen dissenting votes.

The resolution declares Gandhi the sole executive authority with full powers over the Congress organization.

The resolution was adopted after an amendment offered by extremists proposing the use of "possible and proper means" instead of "legitimate and peaceful means" had been defeated by an overwhelming majority by the special committee of the Congress which had the resolution under consideration. Gandhi warned the delegates that the sympathies of the moderates would be alienated if the non-violence policy were abandoned.

In moving his resolution, Gandhi said it meant that they had grown out of a state of helplessness and dependence and were determined to have their own way. He said the resolution left the door open if the Government or the Moderates sincerely wanted a round-table conference.

Gandhi declared the resolution was a challenge to "a Government enthroned in arrogance, which has disregarded the considered opinion of millions of human beings and wants to crush the freedom of opinion and freedom of forming associations. If non-violence is given up India will never attain her liberty."

The resolution declaring Gandhi the sole executive authority of the movement provides that neither Gandhi nor any of his successors to the leadership be authorized, in case they are arrested, to conclude peace with the Government without previous sanction of the Congress.

Organization throughout the country of public meetings, which are forbidden by law, is urged, and all Indians are exhorted to join the Khalifat Volunteers and to submit quietly to arrest.

December 30, 1921

INDIAN MOB KILLS SEVENTEEN POLICE

Wipes Out Entire Post at Chauri and Strips and Burns Bodies.

RIOTERS SHOT AT BAREILLY

LONDON, Feb. 6 (Associated Press.)—Renewed rioting in several parts of India, involving the killing of at least seventeen police officials and four members of attacking parties, in addition to the wounding of a number of persons and some destruction to property, occurred over the week-end, simultaneously with the issuance of a declaration by the non-co-operationist leader, Gandhi, that civil disobedience would become effective unless the Government granted amnesty.

On Saturday police offices at Chauri, on the Bengal Northwestern Railway, were stormed by Indian Nationalist Volunteers. The mob of 2,000 killed the entire staff and a watchman and eight armed policemen who were rushed to the scene to give aid to the staff. Then the Nationalists burned the offices and stripped the bodies of those killed and burned them.

On the same day rioting took place at Bareilly, in the Middle United Provinces, where several attempts were made by a large crowd of volunteers to seize the Town Hall. Insufficient police forces charged them without success, and then were ordered to fire. The mob eventually was put to rout when after two persons had been killed and five others wounded, among them the District Magistrate and the Superintendent of Police.

Gandhi's declaration was made in a letter to the Viceroy. He said he was prepared to advise postponement of civil disobedience until the whole situation was considered anew if the Viceroy was ready within seven days to declare all political prisoners liberated and the freedom of association and the press restored. He asserted the Government's repressive policy made the adoption of civil disobedience immediately imperative and that the non-co-operators under the existing circumstances were unwilling to attend the proposed conferences.

The Government of Madras has issued its first statement regarding the progress of civil disobedience in Gantur, showing that at the end of January peasants were beginning to pay taxes previously withheld and that even some of the leaders of the agitation were coming forward with their taxes, less their property be confiscated.

Arriving in Bombay on Saturday, Prince Aga Khan, spiritual head of the Mohammedans in India, declared he was working his hardest to secure a favorable settlement of the Khalifat question. He counseled the Indians never to despair, but that it was necessary that co-operators and non-co-operators should work together in the interest of the country.

A serious riot of mill workers in the Pondicherri settlement of French India took place on Thursday, according to a London Times dispatch from Madras. Several thousand men employed in the mill demanded more pay, and many of them went on strike. Then the extreme section barricaded themselves in the mill and assaulted the supervising staff.

Police reserves were summoned and are reported to have fired on the crowd, but inflicted no casualties. The Governor of Pondicherri and the Mayor interviewed the strikers, but could not bring them to terms. There was a further collision with the police, and the mills, owned by a prominent Madras firm, are now closed.

February 7, 1922

BRITAIN THREATENS STERN RULE IN INDIA

Government Warns of New Measures to Put Down Gandhi's Mass Disobedience.

WON'T DISCUSS DEMANDS

Issue Now Is Between Lawlessness and Principles of Civilized Government, Says Statement.

LONDON, Feb. 7 (Associated Press).— The India Office issued an official communication this evening indicating that it was the intention of the Government to adopt stern measures to suppress the campaign of civil disobedience in India.

It adds that no Government could discuss the demands contained in the recent manifesto of Mohandas K. Gandhi, the Indian Nationalist leader.

Civil disobedience as proposed in India must be met with sternness and severity, the communication declares in refuting certain "misstatements" made by Gandhi in his manifesto. In asserting that the demands contained in this manifesto are such that no Government could discuss, "much less accept them," the communication says:

"The alternatives that now confront the people of India are such as sophistry can no longer obscure or disguise. The issue no longer is between this or that program for political advance, but between lawlessness, with all its dangerous consequences on the one hand, and on the other the maintenance of those principles which lie at the root of all civilized government.

"Mass civil disobedience is fraught with such danger to the State that it must be met with sternness and severity. The Government entertains no doubt that in any measures they may have to take for supression they can count on the support and assistance of all law-abiding loyal citizens of his Majesty."

The communication declares that some of the "misstatements" of Gandhi are so important that the Government in India cannot allow them to pass unchallenged. It emphatically repudiates a statement of Gandhi to the effect that the Government has embarked on a policy of lawless repression, and also a suggestion that the present campaign of civil disobedience was forced on the non-co-operation party in order to secure the elementary rights of free association, free speech and a free press.

It adds that the decision to adopt civil disobedience was finally accepted on Nov. 6, before the recent notifications relating to either the Seditious Meetings act or the criminal law amendment to the act to which Gandhi "unquestionably refers" were issued. On the contrary, it asserts that the Government was forced to take these measures because of the acts of professed followers of Gandhi. Nevertheless the operation of the Seditious Meetings act had been strictly limited to a few districts in which there was risk of great disturbances to the peace. The application of the criminal law amendment act of 1908 was confined to associations a majority of the members of which "habitually indulged in intimidation."

The Government, the communication continues, has taken every precaution possible to mitigate, where it is desirable, conditions of imprisonment, and to avoid any action which might have the appearance of vindictive severity. It declares that there "is no shadow of justification for the charge that the Government's policy has been one of indiscriminate lawlessness and repression." "Refutation is made of the charge that the Government's recent measures involved a departure from the policy that the Government should not interfere in the activities of the non-co-operators so long as they remained non-violent in word and deed. The communication adds that the Government will enforce the law relating to offenses against the State, as and when it may think fit, against any persons committing breaches.

With references to the proposed conferences, the communication says that while the Government is asked to make concessions, there is no suggestion that any of the illegal activities of the non-co-operators, other than hartals, picketing and civil disobedience, should cease. Further, it adds, Ghandi has made it apparent that the proposed round-table conference would be called merely to register his decree.

Together with the communication the India Office issued a statement embodying a message dated Feb. 2, reporting additional unrest in the United Provinces. The message says that there was a large procession of volunteers at Ujhani, who were reported to have been planning to seize the municipal offices. The procession was dispersed by the use of truncheons. No firing was required. Brickbats were thrown at the District Magistrate and at the armed guard by the crowds in the street and on the roofs of houses. Two of the ringleaders were jailed. Ujhani is in the District of Badaun, and is situated a short distance from Bareilly, where recently there was rioting, in which two persons were killed and five wounded.

February 8, 1922

"DISOBEDIENCE" ORDER OFF

India Congress Committee Calls For Suspension "Until Wave of Violent Feeling Is Passed."

BARDOLI, British India, Feb. 11 (Associated Press).—A resolution deploring the recent outbreak at Chauri-Chaura and calling for suspension of civil disobedience until the wave of violent feeling has passed was adopted today by the Working Committee of the National Congress.

The resolution declared that "the country's atmosphere is insufficiently non-violent for mass civil disobedience, which will be suspended, and instructs the various local Congress committees immediately to advise the cultivators to pay the land revenues and other taxes.

Suspension of civil disobedience, the resolution declares, should be continued until the feeling has subsided to such an extent that there can not be a repetition of the atrocities at Gorakhpur and the disorders at Bombay in November and at Madras last month.

Another resolution urges that the Congress organizations should be advised to cease activities designed to court arrests and imprisonment, except such normal activities as voluntary hartals, wherever a peaceful atmosphere can be assured; also to cease picketing, except in the case of peaceful warnings to visitors to liquor shops on the evils of drinking.

The resolution advises against holding public processions and mass meetings in defiance of the law. The committee urges enlistment of the 10,000,000 supporters of the National Congress in the National Volunteers, and a more conscientious observance of the Congress' creed.

The resolutions are effective pending a special meeting of the All-India Congress Committee, after which they will be subject to the confirmation of the latter committee.

February 14, 1922

GANDHI SENTENCED TO 6 YEARS IN JAIL; REVOLT TO GO ON

AHMEDABAD, India, March 18 (Associated Press).—Mohandas K. Gandhi, the Indian non-co-operationist leader, who was arrested recently on charges of sedition, was sentenced today to six years' imprisonment without hard labor.

Gandhi's colleague, Shankerlal, banker, Bombay merchant and Nationalist leader, was sentenced today to ordinary imprisonment for one year and fined 1,000 rupees.

That the arrest of Gandhi and the restraint placed upon the country have considerably advanced the Khalifat and Swaraj causes, and that the non-co-operationist leader's arrest will not alter the program outlined at Bardoli recently, which includes individual civil disobedience, is the opinion of the working committee of the All-India Congress committee, expressed in a resolution carried today. A heated discussion, lasting for six hours, preceded its adoption.

The committee calls on all the Congress organizations to devote themselves to carrying out the constructive program agreed upon at Bardoli, and says that it considers universal adoption of the spinning wheel and the use of handspun materials essential to attainment of the country's goal.

March 19, 1922

LEGAL EQUALITY FOR INDIA.

Bill Passed Removing Major Discriminations Against Natives.

DELHI, India, Feb. 22.—After two days' animated discussion, the Legislative Assembly of India has unanimously passed the bill embodying an agreement between the representatives of the European and Indian communities for the removal of the major distinctions regarding the criminal law which resulted in discrimination against the Indians.

Sir Malcolm Hailey, Government leader in the Legislative Assembly, in advocating the measure, declared it represented the better mind of India, which would not let racial animosities impair her political future, as it would be shown that the Europeans and Indians were willing to join in the task of developing that future.

February 23, 1923

India

Gandhi Is Released Unconditionally; Indian Nationalist Is Seriously Ill

BOMBAY, India, Feb. 4 (Associated Press).—"Mahatma" Mohandas Gandhi, the Indian Nationalist leader, has been released from prison unconditionally by order of the Government.

Gandhi on March 18, 1922, was sentenced to six years' imprisonment for sedition in connection with the non-co-operative movement. He gained the title of "Mahatma," or "Wonder Worker," through his power and personal magnetism.

Recently the Nationalist leader has been in a hospital. The action of the Government was taken on recommendation of the attending physicians, who declared that six months at the seaside was necessary for his convalescence.

Mohandas Karamchand Gandhi was arrested at Ahamedabad, 310 miles north of Bombay, on March 10, 1922, on the charge of sedition, and nine days later was convicted by a magistrate's court and sentenced to six years' imprisonment without hard labor. He was first confined in the Yeroda Jail and then in a jail near Poona.

His great power over the Hindus, which at one period united them in a common cause with the Moslems against the British administration of India, consisted of a policy and a creed. The policy was "non-co-operation"; the creed was "the power of the soul." By the first he hoped to make the British administration inoperative by simply considering it nonexistent; by the second he hoped to make the Hindus worthy of self-government and the British to realize that worthiness.

Since his imprisonment began, stories have come from Bombay that he was being cruelly treated — was obliged to clean his cell and do other menial labor. The official word is that the prisoner insisted on performing these labors—the labors of the humblest inmates of the jail. It is added that his keepers have shown him the utmost consideration always.

On the eve of his arrest he called on Police Superintendent Hailey of Ahmedabad and told him he intended to form a non-co-operative demonstration against the visit of the Prince of Wales.

The Superintendent said, "There will be bloodshed."

Gandhi replied, "There will be none."

"There will be," retorted the official. "You cannot control men's passions. Remember, I hold you responsible."

After it was all over—after the mobs and the killing, Gandhi returned to the superintendent, who said:

"I told you what would happen. You are responsible."

Gandhi covered his face with his hands and said: "I know it."

"You know it! Well, can your knowing it bring back to life the men and women whose heads were ground into rust by the heels of your Indian mob?"

"Put me in jail, your Excellency," he moaned.

"Yes, I'll put you in jail, but not just yet. Tomorrow perhaps. Today it would be too much like giving you a crown of thorns."

February 5, 1924

Indian Assembly Flouts Britain.

SIMLA, British India, Sept. 17.—The Legislative Assembly has taken another step in flouting the British Administration by passing the second reading, despite Government opposition, of a native bill repealing a criminal law amendment enacted in 1908 to suppress anarchical crime in Bengal. The vote was 71 to 39. Final reading of the bill has been postponed.

September 18, 1924

EMERGENCY POWERS INVOKED IN INDIA

Viceroy Acts to Suppress Anarchy in Bengal—Twenty-seven Are Arrested.

SIMLA, British India, Oct. 25 (Associated Press).—The Earl of Reading, Viceroy of India, today exercised his emergency powers by the promulgation of an ordinance supplementing the ordinary criminal law in Bengal with a view to suppressing revolutionary crimes on the part of the anarchical movement, which, it was stated, was found to be deep-seated and dangerous.

A statement was issued asserting that the Viceroy was satisfied, as a result of the examination of the evidence placed before him, that it was necessary to arm the Bengal Government with powers to deal with the preparation for crime because he was convinced that preparations and plans for criminal outrages were dangerously developed.

The Calcutta Gazette announces that a man named Bose, who is right-hand man to Chit Ranjan Das, leader of the Home Rule Party; Kumar Mitter of the Bengal Legislature; Ro, Secretary of the National Congress, and twenty-four others have been arrested, mostly under the provisions of the new ordinance, for suspicion of associating themselves with violent criminal methods.

The Commissioner of Police declares that searches are going on throughout the province and that further arrests are expected.

October 26, 1924

---

12 Slain, 100 Wounded and Temples Despoiled In Renewal of Moslem-Hindu Riot in Calcutta

CALCUTTA, India, April 3 (AP).—Rioting between the Hindus and Moslems broke out in Calcutta again this morning. It is estimated that twelve were killed and 100 wounded in today's fighting.

Although widespread disturbances continued throughout the day, the police and military finally obtained control of the situation and normal traffic conditions were restored.

During the rioting many shops were looted and several mosques and temples desecrated.

The rioting today started in College Street, Colootolla Street and the Mechooa Bazaar and spread to the important Howrah Milli district. (The Calcutta University buildings front on College and Colootolla Streets.)

Troops with machine guns were patrolling the streets this morning, endeavoring to check the mobs which were looting and setting fire to shops.

Moslems destroyed a Hindu temple and desecrated the idol, while Hindus set fire to a large mosque.

Calcutta advices yesterday said that twenty persons were reported killed and 150 injured when Moslems barred the way to a procession of Hindus near a mosque in the northern part of the city.

The Hindus and Moslems, the two leading religious sects of India, frequently clash, although the Hindus outnumber the followers of Mohammed in the entire country by about three to one. The Hindus worship several gods and accept the Brahmanical supremacy and the caste system. The Moslems are limited as to their main tenets by the teachings of the Koran.

One of the principal causes of friction is the practice of the Moslems of sacrificing cows, which are held sacred by the Hindus. At Delhi in July, 1924, a riot took place in which several were killed when the Moslems persisted in taking cows for sacrifice through the prohibited area in which the Hindus live. Troops were four hours in restoring order.

April 4, 1926

BRITAIN TO START INQUIRY IN INDIA

Commission to Report Whether Further Measure of Self-Government Is Advisable.

ADVANCES ACTION 2 YEARS

Safeguarding of the Mohammedan Minority a Problem—Sir John Simon Heads Board.

Copyright, 1927, by The New York Times Company.
Special Cable to THE NEW YORK TIMES.

LONDON, Nov. 8.—The British Government, it was announced in Parliament tonight, has decided to appoint a commission, two years earlier than was originally intended, to report whether India is ready for a further measure of self-government.

The date of the appointment has been advanced because of uncertainty regarding the question of how the rights of the Mohammedan minority in India are to be safeguarded under home rule, which has produced a situation where Hindus and Mohammedans are ready to jump at each other's throats.

The commission will be composed of Sir John Simon, prominent Liberal lawyer, as Chairman; Lord Burnham, owner of The Daily Telegraph; Stephen Walsh, Minister of War in the MacDonald Labor Government; Colonel G. R. Lane Fox, Minister of Mines in the present Government; Lord Strathcona, Major the Hon. E. Cadogan, and Major C. R. Attlee, all Conservatives.

It includes no Indians, an omission which is bound to cause feeling in India a self-governing nation could threats of boycott, and is editorially criticized in many newspapers here. The omission is explained on the ground that "the desire, natural and legitimate, of Indian members to see Indian a self-governing nation could hardly fail to color their judgment of her present capacity to sustain that rôle."

Instead, it is proposed that the joint committee of both houses of the British Parliament shall hear Indian views voiced by delegations from the Indian Central Legislature and other Indian bodies.

India has since 1919 enjoyed a limited form of autonomy known as a dyarchy, under which the administration of education, public health, public works, industrial and agricultural development and local self-government is delegated to Indians, while "reserved subjects," including maintenance of law and order, defense and finance are controlled by Britain. It is an admittedly transitory and imperfect stage of political development and it will task the new commission to decide whether the time has come for further evolution.

November 9, 1927

THE COLONIZERS AND THE COLONIZED

INDIA COMMISSION STIRS NATIONALISTS

Exclusion of Natives From Self-Government Inquiry Body Evokes Bitter Protest.

BOMBAY, India, Nov. 9 (*P*).—The Indian Nationalist press is protesting against the exclusion of Indians from the statutory commission which has been named by the British Government to consider the success of the steps taken eight years ago in the direction of self-government for India.

The Nationalist newspapers urge a boycott of the commission, the personnel of which was announced by Premier Baldwin in the House of Commons yesterday.

The Bombay Chronicle declares that Indians have been wounded and their hearts lacerated by the omission of Indians from the commission, which the paper describes as a "Machiavellian device of arrogant imperialists."

The National Herald says with reference to the commission "Let India spurn the unclean thing."

Nationalist party leaders in New Delhi almost unanimously condemn the suggested procedure of the commission as well as its personnel, but they suggest that the question of boycotting the commission should be reserved for a conference thereon.

Sir Muhammed Shafi, President of the Punjab National League, barrister of the Middle Temple, London, and a former member of the Punjab Legislative Council and Imperial Legislative Council, thinks the exclusion of Indians from the commission is a grievous blunder. He attributes the exclusion to intercommunal hatred.

November 10, 1927

RUSSIANS SEND MONEY TO STRIKERS IN INDIA

Wireless to THE NEW YORK TIMES.

BOMBAY, May 13.—Labor troubles which have been causing so much restlessness in India have been accentuated this week by the Russian trade unions sending 7,000 rubles to railway strikers here as well as propaganda to the Workers' and Peasants' Party with Communist posters calling on all workers to unite to smash "imperialism."

Bombay mill owners refused today to accede to the workers' main demands, thus increasing the bitterness which already existed.

Only four of the eighty Bombay cotton mills are now working and more than 150,000 men are idle. The strike began early in April when the owners attempted to reduce production costs by giving highly skilled employes more work but higher pay. There is now an apparent deadlock in this industry and no prospect of a settlement.

The spirit of revolt is even more assertive in the railway union whose members have been inflamed by Communist activities. A preliminary meeting of railway workers last night sent a greeting to workers the world over pledging support in the class war against the "common enemy." Already two railway strikes are in progress, one of ten weeks' duration among the East India Railway employes at Lillooah and the other among the workers in this railway's shops at Howrah. The Howrah strike has been marked by disorders and rioting and the leaders made an open appeal to Moscow. It is possible that their work may cause trouble to spread and it seems likely this week that the Great Indian Peninsular Railway will be drawn in.

May 14, 1928

ASKS A DOMINION STATUS.

All-Parties Committee Proposes a Constitution for India.

SIMLA, Punjab, Aug. 14 (*P*).—A committee appointed by a so-called "All-parties Conference" to determine the principles of a constitution for India, has produced a comprehensive report embodying a constitution on the lines of the governments of the over-seas Dominions of the British Empire.

The committee declares that nothing short of Dominion status will satisfy India and that the real problem consists in the tranference of political power and responsibility from the people of England to the people of India.

Abolition of the post of Secretary of State for India was recommended.

August 15, 1928

LUCKNOW POLICE SHOOT HINDU LEGISLATORS

They Fire on Demonstrators Against the Simon Statutory Commission.

LUCKNOW, India, Nov. 29 (*P*).—The police of this city used firearms today to disperse an unlicensed procession of demonstrators against the Simon Statutory Commission.

Several persons were injured, among them Jawahar Lal, secretary of the National Congress; Pundit Motilal Nehru, member of the Legislative Assembly, and his son, and Govind Ballahgpant, Swarajist leader of the Legislative Council of the United Provinces.

The commission, headed by Sir John Simon, is investigating the possibilities of the extension of responsible government in India.

November 30, 1928

RED BOMBS HURT 5 IN INDIA CHAMBER

Members in Terror Grope Way From the Damaged House of Assembly at Delhi.

TWO NATIVES ARE SEIZED

Sir John Simon, Chairman of the Inquiry Board, Witnesses the Outrage—British Indignant.

Special Cable to THE NEW YORK TIMES.

DELHI, April 8.—Communist terrorism invaded the Indian Legislative Assembly chamber today. While Sir John Simon, chairman of the commission of inquiry, looked on, horrified, from a gallery two bombs were hurled directly at the front government benches.

When the thick smoke fumes had cleared, one English member of the Assembly, Sir George Schuster, who is also financial member of the executive council of the Viceroy, and four Indian members were found to be wounded. Two natives were arrested for the outrage.

President Patel of the Assembly had just arisen to render a ruling on the public safety bill, which would have given the government power to deport non-Indian Communists from the country. A young native in the gallery leaped to his feet and with a shout of "Bande Mataram" [Hail Mother] flung the first bomb straight at the seats where the members of the government were listening to the debate. Another native threw the second bomb. There were two blinding flashes and bits of seats and tables were hurled in all directions, while jagged pieces of metal were projected to the furthest corners of the chamber. A deep hole was blown in the floor.

In the acrid smoke the whole Assembly groped its way to safety, and there was uncontrollable confusion while the police searched the galleries for the perpetrators of the outrage. Meanwhile Communist leaflets fluttered from the balconies to the floor.

Sir George Schuster was struck in the right forearm by a bit of metal. He also suffered severe shock. Sir Bomanji Dalal, non-official member for Bombay, is as seriously wounded in the right thigh. Sir D. Ragvendra, Mr. Rao, budget officer of the Finance Ministry, and Mr. S. N. Roy, one of the nominated members for Bengal, were also injured by flying fragments.

Search of the Strangers' Gallery, whence the bombs were thrown, soon disclosed two natives, one from Punjab and one from Bengal, both carrying revolvers. The first was a student at Lahore University, wearing a dress common to college students in India. The other was sturdily built and dressed in khaki shorts. The police say both confessed they threw the bombs.

Worst Outrage Since 1912.

It was the most serious bomb outrage in India since 1912 when Lord Hardinge, then Viceroy, was wounded while passing through the streets of Delhi in a procession. It marks the culmination of a period of intense and bitter feeling which has been aroused by agitation against the government's trade disputes bill and public safety bill. The former aims at investigation and settlement of industrial disputes and the latter was intended as a government weapon against the Communists.

The political extremists were bitterly hostile to both measures—to the first because it contained penal clauses against the use of trade union organizations for political ends and to the second because it was directed against agitators trying to stir up mass popular movements.

Fuel was added to the flames two weeks ago when the police rounded up labor leaders simultaneously in the leading Indian cities. The presence of Sir John Simon's commission of inquiry has also been as a red rag to the extreme Nationalists and Radicals who organized a boycott of the commission as soon as it arrived.

April 9, 1929

India

150,000 IN CALCUTTA ASSAIL IMPERIALISM

Watch Arrival of Body of Indian Who Died in Prison After 61-Day Hunger Strike.

CALCUTTA, India, Sept. 15 (AP).—A crowd estimated at 150,000 assembled tonight in the streets and on housetops in the vicinity of Howrah Station to witness the arrival of the body of Jatindranath Das. Das, one of sixteen persons arrested in the Lahore conspiracy case, died in Lahore prison yesterday after maintaining a hunger strike for sixty-one days.

Cries of "Down with imperialism!" and "Long live the revolution!" greeted the arrival of the train. The coffin was taken to the Town Hall, where it will lie in state until tomorrow.

Mayor Sen Gupta in an address at the Town Hall extolled the career of Das and ridiculed the position of Indians under the present régime. He said that although he was Mayor he was not permitted to hold public meetings in Calcutta, but that the time had come when persons ought to disobey and court charges of sedition by holding meetings in every park and village in Bengal whether they were prosecuted or not. This, he said, would make the path to home rule.

September 16, 1929

BOMB HURLED IN TRAIN OF INDIAN VICEROY

Special Cable to THE NEW YORK TIMES.

DELHI, Monday, Dec. 23.—An attempt was made today to assassinate Lord Irwin, Viceroy of India, while he was on his way to this city to occupy the new viceregal residence. A bomb was thrown through a window of the dining car of Lord Irwin's train within a mile of New Delhi station.

The car was wrecked, the floor being blown up. No one was in it at the time, but a servant was injured. Lord Irwin had a narrow escape, for his compartment was only three away from the end of the dining car. Crowds at the station heard the explosion but thought it was a fog signal.

Later Lord Irwin arrived safe at the great marble palace which hereafter will house India's viceroys and which Lord Irwin is the first to occupy.

The bomb outrage has heightened the prevailing atmosphere of political tension on the eve of the meeting of the Indian National Congress in Lahore.

The city of Lahore seems half peopled by police. The provincial government has drafted 500 armed police from country districts and ten additional magistrates have been sent there to deal with possible trouble.

Feeling between the Sikhs and Hindus is running high, and at one time the authorities feared the Sikhs would hold a demonstration with a force of 30,000, including 500 cavalry men and eleven elephants, and seize the entire encampment where the congress is planning to meet. The immediate danger is that some slight accidental circumstance may precipitate a bloody outbreak, and responsible leaders in the Sikh and Hindu communities are doing their utmost to prevent any demonstration.

December 23, 1929

INDIA NATIONALISTS VOTE FOR SELF RULE

Only Six Oppose Gandhi Plan to End British Power—Liberty Banner Greets New Year.

BOMB OUTRAGE CONDEMNED

Students in Protest Wave Red Flags —Sikhs Quit Lahore, Leaving Committee to Negotiate.

Special Cable to THE NEW YORK TIMES.

LAHORE, India, Dec. 31.—Mahatma Gandhi's main resolution in favor of complete independence from British rule was carried by the All-India National Congress here today with only six dissentients.

At the exact moment when the clock of the Congress camp pointed to midnight, Pandit Jawaharlal Nehru, president of the Congress, walked from the marquee to the tall flagstaff and hoisted the "liberty" banner. Amid a great outburst of cheering which came from the mists blowing across the river, he was heard shouting "A happy new year and an era of independence!"

Earlier, the Congress, after an acrimonious debate, had passed a resolution, by 897 to 816 votes, congratulating the Viceroy on his escape from the bomb explosion.

Sikhs Quit Lahore.

Mr. Gandhi, clad in the scantiest raiment, as befits a holy man, pleaded softly in Hindu for the resolution, but students waving red flags created a pandemonium. A supporter of Mr. Gandhi shouted "People waving red flags should remember that Communist people do not believe in individual violence but in mass violence. So even the Communist creed does not permit such an outrage."

Over at the fort where the Sikhs were in conference these hardy warriors wrangled all day. The latest news indicates that their leader, Kharah Singh, told of inducements offered by Mr. Gandhi to tempt the Sikhs into the Congress camp. The Sikhs stuck to their decision that they would only cooperate with Mr. Gandhi if the Congress passed a resolution admitting the injustice of the Nehru report and added a stripe of yellow to the green, red and white of the "national" flag. They departed from the city tonight, leaving Kharah Singh and a committee to continue the arguments with Mr. Gandhi.

Congress leaders are perturbed by news from Madras that Sir Tej Bahadur Sapru has persuaded the Liberal party conference to declare for participation in the round-table conference proposed by the Viceroy.

January 1, 1930

GANDHI OPENS DRIVE FOR INDIA SELF-RULE

Leads Volunteers March to Start Civil Disobedience by Breaking Salt Monopoly.

SAYS PEACE MUST BE KEPT

Nationalist Leader Tells People There Will Be No Defeat— Troop Movement Ordered.

AHMADABAD, India (Wednesday), March 12 (AP).—Mahatma Gandhi, Indian leader and mystic, led his pioneer band of volunteers out of his quarters here at 6:30 A. M. today and started his march to the Gulf of Cambay, opening his campaign of civil disobedience to the Indian Government.

Great crowds lined both sides of the route that the little procession was following. As Gandhi, with a firm step despite his 61 years, emerged from his "Ashram," or College of Devotees, at the head of his volunteers a great shiver of excitement ran through the throng.

Almost the entire population of Ahmadabad, nearly 150,000 normally and swollen by visitors that have been flocking here for days to see Gandhi depart was present. The city was virtually deserted all through the night.

Gandhi will address the villagers at Asali, through which he will pass at about 2 P. M.

When the volunteers reach Jalalpur, they will try to manufacture salt in violation of the government's monopoly. In the whole march they will stop at more than a hundred towns and villages, whose inhabitants are expected to furnish supplies.

Completing his preparations last night, Mr. Gandhi, surrounded by enormous crowds of visitors and protected from possible arrest by volunteers, offered up a prayer for the success of his drive, which may prove to be critical for the government.

He told his followers that even if he and his marchers were arrested "the Indian people must preserve peace and carry out the instructions of the National Congress working committee."

In the speech, which constituted what he called his "last message and testament," Mr. Gandhi said there would be no defeat for his people, and he exhorted his hearers to continue marching to Jalalpur, no matter what happened to him, and to uphold the cause of civil disobedience.

Reports from Poona, military headquarters of the British Army in the Deccan, said that the Eleventh Sikh Regiment of the Indian Regular Army had been ordered to proceed on March 17 to Baroda, through which Mr. Gandhi and his volunteers will pass. The Sikhs, noted as fighters and for their faithfulness to the British, will replace a garrison of the Fourth Bombay Grenadiers.

It has been decided that if Mr. Gandhi should be arrested, the band of marchers will be led by Abbis Tyabji, a retired judge of the Baroda high court, or by Chaman Lal Goshi, manager of Ashram, Mr. Gandhi's school.

The police have taken precautions against possible breaches of the peace in connection with the march.

March 12, 1930

THE COLONIZERS AND THE COLONIZED

DIE BEFORE YIELDING IS GANDHI'S APPEAL

He Courts Arrest in Urging His Followers to Resist Seizure of Their Illicit Salt.

Wireless to THE NEW YORK TIMES.
BOMBAY, India, April 8.—Mahatma Gandhi made his latest and most determined attempt to get himself arrested at the village of Atta early this morning by defying not only the salt act but the sedition section of the penal code.

A large crowd had assembled near a dilapidated bridge which spans the creek on the road from Dandi to Jalalpur. Six hundred Congress volunteers had marched over from Bardoli, spending the hour before dawn singing Nationalist songs. Soon after 6 o'clock a car came racing along the track which skirts the mudflats. There was a roar of cheers as Mr. Gandhi stepped out and joined the villagers, who(stripped to their waist, weer collecting salt in a chain of shallow pools along the bed of the creek.

Before entering the water Mr. Gandhi made what was by far his most violent speech since he left Ahmedabad on his 200-mile pilgrimage to the coast.

"Resist With All Your Might."

"The first battle at Aat was a war of love," he said. He exhorted all good passive resisters to lay down their lives before giving up the salt from their hands. He did not explain, however, how this advice could be carried out without offending his creed of non-violence.

"Resist the confiscation of the salt from your grasp with all your might until blood is spilled. All women and children should also resist interference. Let us see whether the police dare to touch our women. If they do, and if the sons and daughters of India are not so emasculated as to take such an insult lying down, the whole country will be ablaze. This is the first non-violent battle for India's freedom. The name of Aat will be written in letters of gold in Indian history. Let every woman of India hold on to her lump of illicit salt as she would hold to her fond child who was being wrenched from her by evildoers."

Apparently disappointed at not being arrested under the penal clauses of the salt act, Mr. Gandhi seemed determined to run his head into the noose of the sedition section of the penal code, which provides penalties up to life imprisonment.

No policeman was on the horizon at Aat this morning and the crowd dispersed, again disappointed at not seeing the much advertised and often postponed martyrdom of "the holy man."

April 9, 1930

30 KILLED IN INDIAN FIGHTS, SPREAD OVER WIDE AREAS; MOB BURNS SOLDIERS IN CAR

TROOPS USE MACHINE GUNS

Mow Down Twenty After Savage Slaying of Three Comrades.

Special Cable to THE NEW YORK TIMES.
LAHORE, April 23.—Two British soldiers were burned alive inside their gasoline-splashed armored car and a city police sergeant was hacked to death with a hatchet in an outbreak of savage rioting at Peshawur, on the Northwest Frontier, this morning.

The infuriated Nationalists became so menacing that British Gurkha troops had to open fire with machine guns and rifles to restore order. The number of casualties among the demonstrators is not definitely known, but the deaths are reported to have numbered at least twenty.

Two armored cars with crews of two soldiers each were patrolling Peshawur when they came upon an unruly crowd. Several Nationalists suddenly poured a bucketful of gasoline over one car, and others threw lighted matches. In an instant the car was a roaring mass of flames. Its two occupants had no chance to escape through its narrow manhole.

Sergeant Hacked to Death.

In another part of the city a police sergeant on a motorcycle found his way blocked by a mob and he was thrown to the pavement. The crowd fell on him with the utmost ferocity and killed him with a hatchet.

A hail of stones and bricks met the British Gurkha troops when they entered Peshawur to end the disturbance. Well aimed missiles from roofs caused several casualties among the troops, including Deputy Commissioner Metcalfe, who was taken to a hospital. The mob was scattered by machine-gun fire, leaving their wounded behind. The city now is quiet, but is patrolled by British troops. All the city gates are guarded to prevent looting by tribesmen.

Aside from its ferocity, today's outbreak at Peshawur is significant as showing that the repercussions of Mahatma Gandhi's campaign have reached the furthest extremities of the vast Indian peninsula. There have been outbreaks so far in Karachi, near the Persian Gulf; in Chittagong, far to the east near Burmah; in Bombay, thousands of miles to the south; and in Calcutta and Madras, 1,500 miles from Peshawur on the east coast of India. Peshawur is inhabited chiefly by tall, swarthy Sikhs and Moslems, who are of an entirely different calibre from the Hindus as fighting men.

H. A. F. Metcalfe, the Deputy Commissioner who was wounded at Peshawur, is an Oxford graduate and was assistant private secretary to the Viceroy from 1914 to 1917. Later he was on the Indian staff of the Prince of Wales during his tour in 1921 and 1922. He was appointed Deputy Commissioner for the Peshawur district in November, 1928.

April 24, 1930

GANDHI SEIZED

CHARGE IS NOT EXPLAINED

The Mahatma Is Arrested and Spirited Away to Jail as Staff Sleeps.

Special Cable to THE NEW YORK TIMES.
BOMBAY, Monday, May 5.—Mahatma Gandhi, leader of the Nationalist civil disobedience campaign, was arrested early this morning at Surat. He was taken by train to Borivli on the Bombay-Baroda Railway and thence by automobile to Poona, where he will be detained.

Within a few minutes of the arrival of the Bombay-Baroda mail train at Surat station, the police called at Mr. Gandhi's bungalow. He was hurried to the station and placed in a reserved compartment and was en route to Poona even before his sleeping staff was aware that he had left the building.

Any demonstration at Poona was avoided by the Mahatma's transference to a closed automobile at Borivli and it swept along roads through deserted villages and into the Poona jail before news of the arrest had spread beyond the dusty streets of Surat.

Strategic points in Bombay were heavily guarded this mornimg and reports from other centres show that the military are prepared for an emergency.

Held Under 1827 Ordinance.

The Indian Government censor has permitted the cryptic statement that Mr. Gandhi was arrested "under Ordinance 25 of the year 1827" and has left it to constitutional lawyers to determine what the charge implies. One interpretation placed upon this ordinance this morning is that the Mahatma can be held indefinitely in Yerroda jail in Poona without trial.

The news that the police had at last taken action reached Bombay when those outside the government's immeliate circles had begun to think that the Viceroy, Lord Irwin, had changed his mind and given Mr. Gandhi a fresh lease on liberty. It was under this impression that the committee of the Bombay European Association decided yesterday to press upon the Governor, Sir Frederick Sykes the urgency of taking a firmer stand.

Cable messages from London had placed it beyond doubt that the Viceroy last week had consulted the MacDonald Government over the question of Mr. Gandhi's arrest and that the British reply was one of full support for the Viceroy in any action he cared to take.

The decision as to whether to arrest the leader of the civil disobedience campaign was left entirely to the Viceroy, as were the time and place of such an arrest if it were considered advisable.

May 5, 1930

India

INDIA CURBS PRESS AFTER NEW TERRORS

Bomb Explosion at Delhi Forces Revival of Repressive Laws to Curb Nationalists.

Special Cable to THE NEW YORK TIMES.

NEW DELHI, India, Dec. 26.—A new flare-up of the revolutionary campaign in India culminated today in a bomb explosion in the central railway station at Delhi and led the Viceroy to reimpose last Spring's repressive ordinances, which expired recently.

The explosion tore off both arms of an elevator boy in the baggage office and resulted in serious injuries to two porters. Dynamite, apparently contained in a cigaret case, fell to the floor from a piece of unclaimed baggage.

The incident was regarded as only one more sign that in the past fortnight there has been a recrudescence of all the most extreme features of the Congress party's campaign against British rule.

The revived ordinances will have the effect of muzzling the press and of threatening the instigators of nonpayment of taxes. Now, as in the turbulent days of last Winter, the Nationalist newspapers have been full of widespread bitter incitement to hate against the police and prison administrations. The campaign has been supported by a mass of wild, unsubstantiated charges. This month several small newspapers, which apparently exist merely to preach violent revolution, have reappeared, especially in the Moslem provinces of Punjab and Bengal.

Blames Newspapers.

Government officials here believe the murder of Colonel Simpson, Inspector General of Prisons in Bengal, the attempted assassination of Sir Geoffrey de Montmorency, Governor of Punjab, and today's explosion are all directly traceable to incitements contained in the new campaign.

Those in touch with affairs realize how anxious the Viceroy, Lord Irwin, and his advisers have been to avoid taking new measures on the lines of the reimposed press ordinance. The Viceroy evidently hoped the round-table conference in London would announce some achievement which would dispel the revolutionary atmosphere created by Mahatma Gandhi's Congress campaign. Above all, the government has been inspired by the greatest anxiety to avert any action which might disturb the round-table conference, but circumstances here have proved too strong.

The new ordinances were announced in a statement from the Viceroy, which spoke of the serious increase in premeditated violence.

"There is no room for doubt," said Lord Irwin, "that inflammatory writings in the press both stimulate recruitment to the revolutionary movement and incite to the commission of violent crimes. It is again the policy of many newspapers consistently to encourage the civil-disobedience movement and thus to foster conditions of disorder, while others, which suspended publication while the ordinance was in force, are again giving direct or indirect incitement to violent revolutionary crime."

In the meanwhile Lord Irwin has been having something of a personal triumph among the European community in Calcutta, which had suspected him of being weak when strength was demanded. His speech before the European Association this week has had the effect of convincing his critics that, although concessions must be made to the spirit of nationalism, there is an unflinching determination on the part of the government to maintain its authority.

Today Lord Irwin rode in a brilliant State procession at the Calcutta races, despite a crippling attack of lumbago and in the face of extraordinary precautions for his safety, taken by the Bengal Government.

December 27, 1930

PLEDGE OF AUTONOMY CLOSES INDIA PARLEY; MOVE TO WIN GANDHI

MacDonald Commits Britain to Work for Early Institution of New Federal Regime.

BESPEAKS EXTREMISTS' AID

Premier Tells Delegates He Is Ready to Urge Amnesty for All Who Support Project.

MINIMUM OF RESERVATIONS

Governor General to Control Army and Foreign Affairs—Powers of Provincial Governors Limited.

By CHARLES A. SELDEN.
Special Cable to THE NEW YORK TIMES.

LONDON, Jan. 19.—The round table Indian conference ended its nine weeks' deliberations today with a statement by Prime Minister MacDonald of the plans and policy of his Majesty's Government for transferring to the Indians themselves the rights and responsibilities of administering their own affairs.

This autonomy is to be given to them in respect both to their central and to their provincial Legislatures and in the independent States under the form of a federal constitution, to which all groups at the conference have agreed. Reservations are stipulated for the early transitional period in this new experiment in nation-building, but these, too, are accepted by most of the Indian delegates as reasonable and inevitable.

The only note of anxiety sounded at the final plenary session came from Dr. Bhimrao Ramji Ambedkar, leader of the "Untouchables," who feared that there was not enough assurance of the safeguarding of the political rights of the depressed classes.

Wins Moslems' Applause.

But the Moslems gave their applause when Mr. MacDonald declared there would be guarantees for the protection of all minorities.

He received one of his greatest ovations when he said that amnesty for India's political prisoners came very close to his own heart and that the British Government would not be backward in responding to this plea if the leaders of the Indian revolt would proclaim civil order.

The Prime Minister was speaking not only for the existing Labor Government of the day, for, whatever party may be in power in Great Britain this year or next, it will find ready for it the foundations of a new Indian Constitution which cannot be abandoned or demolished.

These principles were accepted early in the negotiations by both the Labor and the Liberal delegates. Today even Earl Peel, who has been the doubtful leader of the Conservative delegation, said with reference to the plan of federation: "It would be a great misfortune if this mighty scheme could not soon be started on its great career."

So there was no mockery in this closing hour after Mr. MacDonald finished outlining the new Magna Charta, when English and Indians stood together at their round table while a band in an adjoining room played "God Save the King."

Good-Will Abounds.

Even more significant of the abounding good-will after ten tense weeks of hard tussle were the spontaneous cheers with which these men of many races, creeds and political faiths greeted each other. That was the form in which their relaxation expressed itself in Queen Anne's old drawing room in St. James's Palace, where, under the portraits of four Georges, in whose reigns Britain had strengthened her grip on India, the men of that country heard the farewell message of George V wishing them godspeed in their venture of self-government.

If the recent imperial conference had had such success as this round table has achieved, Great Britain and her dominions would have by this time devised some method of trading with each other to their mutual economic advantage. If the London Naval Conference a year ago had achieved the same proportion of what the general public hoped for as has been gained in the last ten weeks at St. James's Palace, the world would not be worried today about the Franco-Italian Mediterranean dispute, and the United States would not now be contemplating spending hundreds of millions of dollars to build her navy up to the treaty allowance.

Of the many speeches made by Indians at the closing session, that of Sir Tej Bahadur Sapru best indicated the spirit in which he and his eighty colleagues will soon depart for Bombay.

"When we left our own shores," Sir Tej said, "we were told by our friends and our opponents, men of our own and of all other parties, that we were going on a fool's errand, that we were incurring extraordinary risks, that England had made up its mind against us in advance and that we would meet nothing but defeat and humiliation. Those were the warnings given us on our departure from India.

Lauds British Statesmen.

"Well, I don't know whether we came to an England that was hostile. I do know we are leaving an England that is friendly, an England that has sent to this historic conference some of her greatest, some of her wisest, some of her most farseeing statesmen to talk to us on terms of equality, to discuss questions of high import in the spirit of give and take and not to dictate to us from their side. That has been my experience and I venture to think I express the views of many of us at this round table."

Concerning the general results Premier MacDonald said that Britain had gone as far as she could at this moment in the matter of granting self-government.

"Now," he added, "you have to go back to India and we have to go back to our own public opinion. You have spoken here subject to reconsideration and subject to the reaction which your own public will show to your work. We of the British Government and Parliament have spoken in the same way and must also listen to reactions. We must explain, expound, defend. We must also make ourselves the champions of your findings and do our best to bring our people along with us in our pilgrimage of hope to a conclusion."

Indicating something of the work yet to be done, Mr. MacDonald said, "We leave agreed upon certain features of a constitution, but the successful launching of that constitution depends upon a careful study of conditions and structure. I think it was Lord Peel who said we were not so short-sighted and self-centred as to think the only successful constitutional machinery is that under which we work in England. As a matter of fact, I can give you some very bad results of its working here. It certainly is not perfect.

Many Types to be Studied.

"We have got the United States type. We have got the type used in Japan and in some of its aspects it is very interesting to us. There is the type such as was used in Germany before the war and there are the French methods and so on.

"In order that we may have all the world's experience of working legislatures elected in different ways, we shall study these types with you and hope to get from them plans and suggestions by which the new Indian Constitution can be benefited and made workable."

A passage in Mr. MacDonald's final speech which surprised some of his hearers was that paying tribute to the work of the Simon Commission, in view of the fact that the Premier was not willing to have Sir John Simon at the round table either as a delegate or as an adviser. Although the conference had gone far beyond the recommendations made in the Simon report, Mr. MacDonald said this about it:

"The Simon Commission has done remarkable, conspicuous and essential work. You may not agree with it, but without it we could not have gone to the conclusions we have reached at this conference. The Simon Commission opened doors that up to then had been closed. It brought ears into action that up to then had been deaf. India can never be too grateful for the labors of the men who composed the Simon Commission."

The text of that portion of the

THE COLONIZERS AND THE COLONIZED

Premier's address in which he stated his government's policy follows.

Statement of Policy.

At this point I shall read the declaration I am authorized to make by my colleagues in his Majesty's Government.

The view of his Majesty's Government is that responsibility for government in India should be placed upon the Legislatures, central and provincial, with such provisions as may be necessary to guarantee during the period of transition the observance of certain obligations and to meet other special circumstances; and also with such guarantees as are required by the minorities to protect their political liberties and rights.

In such statutory safeguards as may be made for meeting the needs of this transitional period, it will be a primary concern of his Majesty's Government to see that the reserved powers are so framed and exercised as not to prejudice the advance of India through the new constitution to full responsibility for her own government.

His Majesty's Government while making this declaration is aware that some of the conditions essential to the working of such a constitution as is contemplated have not been finally settled, but it believes that as a result of the work done here they have been brought to a point which encourages the hope that further negotiations after this declaration will be successful.

His Majesty's Government has taken note of the fact that the round table conference deliberations have proceeded on the basis accepted by all parties that the central government should be a federation of all India, embracing both the Indian States and British India in a bicameral Legislature.

The precise form and structure of the new federal government must be determined after further discussion with the Indian Princes and representatives of British India.

States to Cede Some Powers.

The range of subjects committed to it will also require further discussion, because the federal government will have authority only in such matters concerning the States as shall be ceded by their rulers in agreements made by them on entering the federation.

The connection of the States with the federation will remain subject to the basic principle that, in regard to all matters not ceded by them to the federation, their relations will be with the Crown acting through the agency of the Viceroy.

With a Legislature constituted on a federal basis, his Majesty's Government will be prepared to recognize the principle of the responsibility of the executive to the Legislature.

Under existing conditions, the subjects of defense and external affairs will be reserved to a Governor General and arrangements will be made to place in his hands the powers necessary for administration of those subjects.

Moreover, as the Governor General must as a last resort be able in emergency to maintain the tranquillity of the State and similarly be responsible for the observance of the constitutional rights of the minorities, he must be granted the necessary power for those purposes.

As regards finances, the transfer of financial responsibility must necessarily be subject to such conditions as will insure the fulfillment of obligations incurred under the authority of the Secretary of State and the maintenance unimpaired of the financial stability and credit of India.

Financial Details Remain.

The report of the Federal Structure Committee indicates some ways of dealing with this subject, including a reserve bank, service of loans and exchange policy, which, in the view of his Majesty's Government, will have to be provided for somehow in the new Constitution.

It is of vital interest to all parties in India to accept these provisions to maintain financial confidence.

Subject to these provisions, the Indian Government would have full financial responsibility for methods of raising revenue and for control of expenditure on non-reserved services. This will mean that, under the existing conditions, the central Legislature and the executive will have some features of dualism which will have to be fitted into the constitutional structure.

The provision of reserved powers is necessary under the circumstances, and some such reservation has indeed been incidental to the development of most free Constitutions.

But every care must be taken to

Chief Points of the British Policy on India Enunciated by Premier MacDonald in London

By The Associated Press.

LONDON, Jan. 19.—The outstanding points of the policy enunciated by Premier MacDonald at the close of the India round-table conference today were as follows:

1. Amnesty for India's 50,000 political prisoners if "civil order" is restored in India.
2. An invitation to the Indian extremists to participate in the negotiations still to come, before the new Indian Government is established.
3. Establishment of full responsible self-government in India, with the Imperial British Government reserving control of finance, foreign affairs and defense.
4. Extension of the voting franchise in India and the lifting of restrictions based on religion and caste.
5. Establishment of a Legislature of two Houses modeled along the lines of the Congress of the United States.
6. Encouragement of Indians to settle their own communal problems.
7. Uninterrupted continuance of negotiations to settle the details of the new government.

prevent conditions arising which will necessitate their use. It is, for instance, undesirable that the Ministers should trust to the special powers of the Governor General as a means of avoiding responsibilities which are properly their own, thus defeating the development of responsible government by bringing into use powers meant to lie in reserve in the background. Let there be no mistake about that.

The Governors of the provinces will be constituted on a basis of full responsibility. Their Ministries will be taken from the Legislature and will be jointly responsible to it. The range of provincial subjects will be so defined as to give them the greatest possible measure of self-government.

Federal Powers Limited.

The authority of the federal government will be limited to the provisions required to secure its administration of federal subjects and to discharge its responsibility for subjects defined in the Constitution as of all-India concern.

There will be reserved to the Governor only that minimum of special powers which is required to secure in exceptional circumstances the preservation of tranquillity and to guarantee the maintenance of rights provided by statute for public services and the minorities.

Finally, his Majesty's Government considers that institution in the provinces of responsible government requires both that the Legislatures should be enlarged and that they should be based on a more liberal franchise.

In framing the Constitution, his Majesty's Government considers that it will be its duty to insert provisions guaranteeing to the various minorities, in addition to political representation, that any differences of religion, race, sect or caste shall not in themselves constitute civic disabilities.

In the opinion of his Majesty's Government, it is the duty of the communities to come to an agreement among themselves on points raised by the minorities subcommittee but not settled there.

During the continuing negotiations such an agreement ought to be reached, and the government will continue to render what good offices it can to secure that end, as it is anxious not only that no delay should take place in putting the new Constitution into operation but that it should start with the good-will and confidence of all communities concerned.

Various subcommittees which have been studying the more important principles of a Constitution which would meet Indian conditions have surveyed a considerable part of the structure in detail, and the still unsettled points have been advanced a good part of the way to agreement.

His Majesty's Government, however, in view of the character of the round table conference and the limited time at its disposal in London, has deemed it advisable to suspend its work at this point so that Indian opinion may be consulted upon the work done and expedients be considered for overcoming the difficulties which have been raised.

His Majesty's Government will consider shortly a plan by which our cooperation may be continued so that the results of our completed work may be seen in the new Indian Constitution.

If, in the meantime, there is a response to the Viceroy's appeal to those now engaged in civil disobedience and if they and others wish to cooperate on the general lines of this declaration, steps will be taken to enlist their services.

I must convey to you all on behalf of the government its hearty appreciation of the services you have rendered, not only to India, but to this country by coming here and engaging in these personal negotiations. Personal contact is the best way of removing those unfortunate differences and misunderstandings which too many people on both sides have been engendering between us in recent years.

Mutual understanding of intentions and difficulties gained under such conditions as prevailed here is by far the best way of discovering the means of settling our differences and satisfying our claims.

His Majesty's Government will strive to secure such an amount of agreement as will enable the new Constitution to be passed through the British Parliament and be put into operation with the active good-will of the people of both countries.

Now, my friends, we go our various ways. Our ten weeks of valuable cooperation, pleasant companionship and friendship are ended.

January 20, 1931

GANDHI TAKES STEPS TO END CIVIL STRIFE

Special Cable to THE NEW YORK TIMES.

NEW DELHI, India, March 4.—What amounts virtually to a British-Indian peace treaty was signed at noon today at the viceregal lodge. Mahatma Gandhi is now understood to be taking measures to call off the civil disobedience campaign.

What is almost as important as this step will follow immediately in negotiations admitting all-India Congress representatives into the next round-table conference, to be summoned to carry on the work begun in London.

The government statement which was expected today, has been delayed until tomorrow to permit its simultaneous publication in London, which may take the form of a statement in the House of Commons by the Secretary of State for India, Wedgwood Benn.

The terms of the truce, as learned from sources close to the government, differ in one respect from those given out by Gandhi's congress party earlier in the day. The government is not to restore property already confiscated for non-payment of taxes, it is said now, but has agreed to consider dropping action against tax-resisters in cases now pending, of which there are a great many.

The debate in the Legislative Assembly Monday left no doubt that the work of the London round-table conference was going ahead, but there still remained an uneasy doubt at the back of the observer's mind that a conference which did not include representatives of the all-India Congress would be like an attempt to settle the Irish question while ignoring the Sinn Fein.

Today's truce assures the participation in the forthcoming sessions of the Congress party, which is the largest and best organized party in India today. It embodies also an agreement that the discussions shall be strictly within the limits laid down by the delegates at London.

Tomorrow's government statement is expected to reveal the terms on which amnesty will be granted to non-violent political prisoners, a result expected as a logical sequel to the calling off of the civil disobedience campaign. Some Indian papers say that there must be an interval of a few days to see how generally Gandhi's new order is obeyed, but that an amnesty may be expected by March 12.

The most vital question remain-

75

ing is how far Gandhi's word will bind the Congress party adherents. As one observer put it today, "Gandhi's spirit is the inspiration of the whole Congress party, and his word is law." In this observer's opinion, since Motilal Nehru's death, there remains no leader strong enough to say him nay.

Lord Irwin's tactics in meeting Gandhi alone have been criticized by his best friends as secret, autocratic and even unconstitutional, but Lord Irwin better than most people understood how the Congress movement is dependent for its very existence on the personality of Gandhi and that therefore, the only method of approach was by the bold stroke of establishing a personal contact. Unless advisers on both sides, as well as the entire Indian press, including the vernacular papers, are wrong, Lord Irwin will probably end his term of office with such a victory in the case of the Indian nation itself as has seldom been vouchsafed to any Viceroy.

The Hindus of India were celebrating today with added significance their annual Holi festival, when they greet the approach of Spring and declare themselves at peace with all the world.

March 5, 1931

SEES WHITE PRESTIGE IN INDIA GONE FOREVER

Lord Irwin Tells Tory M. P.'s Three Things Have Brought About the Change.

Special Cable to THE NEW YORK TIMES.

LONDON, June 23.—Lord Irwin, who was Viceroy of India during the recent critical period of the home rule campaign, told a private meeting of Conservative Members of Parliament last night that the prestige of the white man in India has gone forever.

Addressing some of his foremost critics, including Winston Churchill and Lord Lloyd, the former Viceroy attributed this to three things: first, the defeat of the Russians by the Japanese; secondly, the employment of Indian troops in the World War against white men, and thirdly, the influence of motion pictures on the Indian mind.

There was little chance, Lord Irwin said, of the Moslems and Hindus reaching an agreement in India, but a settlement of the communal question might be found at the renewed conference in London.

While paying tribute to Lord Irwin's courage, many Conservatives called him to task for his government's failure to maintain order, for arresting Mahatma Gandhi's lieutenants before Gandhi and for not trying him when arrested.

Lord Irwin explained that Gandhi had not been arrested first because he had information that Gandhi passionately desired arrest, and the incarceration of his lieutenants forestalled widely planned demonstrations.

June 24, 1931

GANDHI SEES FREEDOM WORTH MILLION LIVES

Special Cable to THE NEW YORK TIME

LONDON, Oct. 12.—Mahatma Gandhi made a startling statement on the future of India at a Labor club meeting here tonight under the presidency of Arthur Henderson, leader of the Labor party.

"I would consider it nothing," Mr. Gandhi said, "if we had to pay a million lives for our liberty, but one thing I hope the Congress has set its heart on is the campaign of non-violence. So, whether it is one life or a million we have to pay, I am praying it will be possible for the future historian to say that India fought and won her liberty without shedding human blood."

Despite Mr. Gandhi's continuous efforts to break down the barriers of caste, representatives of the depressed classes at the round table tonight circulated an outspoken memorandum. Their particular grievance is that Mr. Gandhi, as a condition of accepting the Moslem demands, is reported to have asked them to oppose the claims of the depressed classes and smaller minorities to special representation, and thanks are expressed to the Moslems for refusing. The signatories add:

"We are rather glad, for this attitude of Mr. Gandhi's will go a long way toward exploding the legend that he is the champion of the depressed classes, numbering about sixty millions."

October 13, 1931

INDIAN TERRORISTS BLAMED

Attempt Seen to Prevent Accord With British In Judge's Murder.

Wireless to THE NEW YORK TIMES.

SIMLA, India, July 28.—Coming close on the heels of an attempt to assassinate Sir Ernest Hotson, the murder yesterday of Judge Garlick is regarded here as indication that once again Indian terrorists are doing their best to precipitate a crisis and prevent a settlement with the British.

Naturally, there is talk about the possible effect of these crimes on the present discussions with the All-India Congress, but official parties are going ahead with arrangements for the round table conference.

It is understood that Mahatma Gandhi is still bombarding the Government of India with stories of alleged injustice to Gujarati peasants. News from the congress camp reports the Mahatma incensed, first with his advisers for backing him up so poorly when he came to Simla to lay his case before the Viceroy, and secondly with the government for having given him so little chance. His plans will not be settled until the congress working committee meets in Bombay next week.

July 29, 1931

Viceroy Acts to End Terrorism in Bengal; Courts May Suspend Right to Public Trial

Special Cable to THE NEW YORK TIMES.

CALCUTTA, Nov. 30.—Broad powers for magistrates to deal with terrorism in Bengal are contained in a new ordinance signed today by the Viceroy, Earl Willingdon. Provision is also made for setting up special tribunals with power to pass sentences of death or transportation for life.

Magistrates are empowered to pass any sentence except death or transportation for a term exceeding seven years and may delegate their authority to military or police officers.

The regulation, framed for the conduct of trials, is clearly designed to make impossible such hunger-striking scenes as those that marked the Meerut, Delhi, Lahore and other conspiracy cases. The courts therefore will have the power to hold proceedings in camera and in the absence of the accused.

Limits are placed on the right of appeal from verdicts and on applications for change of venue.

Authority is given to levy collective fines in districts which menace order in the countryside. Provision is made for the compensation out of the funds so collected of persons who have suffered as a result of lawlessness.

The government may demand the services of local officials, municipal officers and school teachers in the task of restoring order after disturbances. Drastic rules are framed for the requisition of buildings and the control of traffic.

Persons behaving in a suspicious manner may be required to furnish immediate proof of their identity and explanation of their movements.

Regarding the sale or storage of arms, the authorities will have power to confiscate arms, to prohibit their sale or to order their removal to such a place as they may think fit. The same regulations apply to tools and machinery which, in the opinion of magistrates, might be employed to manufacture or repair arms.

The terms of the ordinance are bound to let loose a flood of criticism from those who most fear them. The All-India Congress newspapers already profess to see in the appointment of Sir John Anderson as Governor of Bengal, followed by the new ordinance, "the dawn of the blackest day of repression that Bengal has suffered."

For the moment the sections of the ordinance empowering the employment of military aid are applicable only to the Chittagong area, but provision is made for their extension to other parts of the Bengal Presidency.

December 1, 1931

THE COLONIZERS AND THE COLONIZED

M'DONALD DECLARES FOR A FEDERAL INDIA AS CONFERENCE ENDS

By FERDINAND KUHN Jr.
Special Cable to THE NEW YORK TIMES.

LONDON, Dec. 1.—Prime Minister MacDonald today made a declaration of British Government policy which brought the dream of a United States of India a little nearer and left the door open for settling disagreements which still are unsolved.

On the broad issues Mr. MacDonald pledged his overwhelmingly Conservative Government to support the late Labor Government's policy of a Federal India embracing the Princes' States and the British Indian Provinces alike.

"We desire to reaffirm our belief in an all-India federation as offering the only hopeful solution of India's constitutional problems," said the Prime Minister, and he was answered by a burst of applause from the Indian delegates sitting around the great mahogany table in St. James's Palace. "We intend to pursue this plan unswervingly and do our utmost to surmount the difficulties which now stand in the way of its realization."

Work to Be Continued.

To help meet those difficulties, he announced, the round-table conference would be kept in existence in India, and by means of a small working committee would continue the task of building a federal Constitution with the least possible delay.

Within the coming month he promised the government also would establish three special committees to work out the difficult details. The first will draw up a scheme of extending the vote and defining the electoral districts in the new democratic India. The second will investigate the delicate problems of Indian finance and the third will apportion the share of the Indian princes in financing the new federation. When the committees have finished, he said, a round-table conference would be summoned in India to ratify their work.

To the Moslems the Prime Minister promised not only all reasonable protection in the new Constitution but made two important material concessions. First, he announced that the predominantly Moslem northwest frontier province, which now has no self-government, would be made a "Governor's province" immediately like the other Governor's provinces of India. When the new Constitution becomes operative the northwest frontier province like the others would have provincial self-government, subject, of course, to the special defense requirements of the frontier.

Secondly, he announced that Sind, the hot dusty area between Bombay and Baluchistan, would be constituted as a separate province, and here again the Moslems, who are in the majority, would control the provincial government.

Denies Conference Failed.

The Prime Minister insisted the conference had not been a failure. Admitting failure to settle the minorities tangle, he made one more demand that the Indians settle the problem themselves, but warned that if a settlement was not made it would be imposed by the British Government.

Many of the Prime Minister's statements might easily have been made last January when the first phase of the round-table conferences ended. The all-important difference was that this year Mahatma Gandhi sat listening, wrapped in blankets, and next to him sat Indian Nationalist Congress delegates who had taken a full part in the conference debates.

Much more than with Mr. MacDonald it rested with Mr. Gandhi to say whether the conference had been a success or a failure, for upon him rested the decision whether the Nationalist Congress would cooperate with the British Government or declare war on it by a civil disobedience campaign.

Mr. Gandhi still was undecided tonight and some of his closest friends here believe he will choose to resume civil disobedience. One ominous statement by him, however, created more stir today than anything in the Prime Minister's declaration. Moving for a vote of thanks to the Prime Minister for his chairmanship of the conference, Mr. Gandhi quietly delivered a few hints which threw a tense, uncomfortable hush over the conference room.

"It is somewhat likely—I would say only somewhat likely because I would like to study your declaration once or twice or thrice, or as often as may be necessary, scanning every word of it, reading its hidden meaning if there is a hidden meaning in it—and if I then come to the conclusion, as just now seems likely, that as far as I am concerned we have come to the parting of the ways it does not matter to us. Even so, you are entitled to my hearty and sincere vote of thanks.

"The dignity of human nature requires that we must face the storms of life, and sometimes even blood brothers have got to go each on his own way, but if at the end of their quarrel they can say they bore no malice, and that even so they acted as becomes a gentleman and a soldier—if it will be possible at the end of the chapter for me to say that of myself and my countrymen, and if it is possible for me to say that of you, Mr. Prime Minister, and of your countrymen, I will say we parted also well.

"I do not know in what directions my path will lie but it does not matter to me. Even then, although I may have to go in exactly the opposite direction, you still are entitled to a vote of thanks from me from the bottom of my heart."

Premier Answers Challenge.

The Prime Minister did not let such a challenge go unanswered although like the subtle Mr. Gandhi he clothed his phrases in polite friendliness. Replying to the vote of thanks the Prime Minister laid aside the manuscript he had been reading earlier and spoke informally and earnestly to the delegates. He said he would be happy if he could live to see a permanent settlement which would leave India content and would "cement for all time the finest and most spontaneous friendship between India and Britain."

Then, turning dramatically to face Mr. Gandhi, sitting just to his left, the Prime Minister continued:

"I do hope we are going to go away determined to cooperate. It is no good going on any other path, let me assure you. Why has our race been in existence for centuries except to discard old paths and pursue new and better ones? The path of reason, of mutual good-will, is the path of the future, whatever may have been the path of the past.

"My dear Mahatma, let us go on in this way. It is the best way and you may find it will be the only way."

Turning again to wish all the delegates a happy voyage, the Prime Minister made a fervent appeal to them to "stand shoulder to shoulder with us in the exchange of views, and by mutual cooperation, with good luck and good fortune we shall solve the problems that now confront us and see India stand self-governing and self-respecting in the world."

MacDonald Ends Conference.

With a loud bang, Mr. MacDonald brought down the well-worn gavel that had seen service at so many long, weary debates in the last three months. The second round-table conference was over in a sober atmosphere that contrasted strangely with the glaring movie lights and the singing of "God Save the King" that ended the first conference in the same room almost a year ago.

If there was no enthusiasm for the Prime Minister's declaration there also was little open dissatisfaction. It was widely felt the Prime Minister had shown political cleverness in balancing his own pro-Indian convictions with the reaction of his Tory followers, and doing it in such a way that nobody could take much offense.

Even Mr. Gandhi's friend and colleague, Rangaswami Iyengar, editor of the Madras Hindu, said he found the declaration neither disappointing nor satisfactory. Sir Tej Sapru, Hindu constitutional lawyer, was not enthusiastic but was grateful because the government had endorsed the idea of federation and had provided for continuance of the Round-Table Conference.

Mr. Gandhi went back to his office weary and perplexed, unwilling to commit himself immediately. To newspaper men who squatted on the floor with him in front of the fireplace he said he had not read Mr. MacDonald's declaration carefully and would have no opinion until tomorrow on whether it meant "peace or war."

"It is not so much the declaration of what happened at the conference that is worrying me," said Mr. Gandhi, toying with his spinning wheel, "as what is happening in India. You have an English saying, 'Coming events cast their shadows before.' The news from India, especially from Bengal, leaves little hope that something big will come out of the conference."

Condemns Bengal Repression.

Mr. Gandhi complained of the severe repressive ordinance just instituted in Bengal and let his usual instinct for bargaining have full play.

"Apart from the meaning the Prime Minister's declaration of today bears, this ordinance and other things I know to be happening in India fill me with the gravest misgivings," he said, "and may leave the congress no choice in the matter of tendering further cooperation."

The government will have little time for Mr. Gandhi in the next two days, however, for it will be trying to dispose of the equally troublesome Winston Churchill in the House of Commons. The Conservative party's India committee has decided to stand by the government, so only Mr. Churchill and a few diehards will be fighting to amend the Prime Minister's declaration. Tonight Mr. Churchill handed in a motion that the House approve the declaration "provided that nothing in the said policy shall commit the House to the establishment in India of a dominion constitution as defined by the statute of Westminster." Mr. MacDonald is said to be looking forward eagerly to the two-day debate which he now feels will show the country exactly what following Mr. Churchill has in the Commons.

December 2, 1931

PROVINCES OUTLAW INDIAN NATIONALISTS

Wireless to THE NEW YORK TIMES.

NEW DELHI, Jan. 5.—The government of India, having struck the first blow and outlawed the Central Executive body of the All-India Nationalists Congress, the Provincial Governments are now acting independently on their respective fronts.

The government of Bihar and Orissa promptly declared the provincial All-India Congress committee an unlawful assembly and occupied its headquarters at Patna with a small force of police, pulled down the Congress tricolor and hoisted the Union Jack. Similar action is expected elsewhere.

The arrest of Mahatma Gandhi and other leaders was followed by the promulgation of four restrictive ordinances. It had become a commonplace to say Mr. Gandhi's arrest was expected. He was one of the first to predict it, but the strength and rapidity with which the government of India has delivered its succession of attacks have clearly stunned the Congress supporters.

It is recognized a storm may break anywhere at any moment, but there has been nothing like the widespread trouble which marked the similar period following Mr. Gandhi's arrest on May 5, 1930.

In official circles here it is believed the severe sentence given to Jawaharlal Nehru, whose campaign of sedition brought him two years' rigorous imprisonment, and the arrest of Subhas Bose are more likely to lead to violence than the imprisonment of Mr. Gandhi. A bitter fanatic himself, Pandit Nehru has the power to inspire bitter fanaticism in the ranks of his immediate followers while Mr. Bose has long been a popular hero in the eyes of Calcutta Nationalists, from whom terrorist volunteers are largely recruited.

The Delhi bazaars presented a normal appearance this morning. Shops were open and street cars ran despite efforts for a political strike. The Delhi Congress committee was proscribed today.

Dr. M. A. Ansari was appointed president of the All-India Congress today. He is the third president in the twenty-four hours since Mahatma Gandhi's arrest. When Vallabhai Patel, the first president, was arrested he nominated Rojendra Prasad as his successor. After five hours in office Mr. Prasha was arrested and he nominated Dr. Ansari to succeed him.

According to Bombay messages, sixty successive All-India Congress war cabinets have been appointed to last two months if one complete Cabinet is jailed daily.

January 6, 1932

India

Violence by Women Alarms British in India; Independence Drive Also Spreads to Schools

BOMBAY, Feb. 7 (AP).—The attempted shooting of Sir Stanley Jackson, Governor of Bengal, by a 17-year-old girl has drawn the attention of British authorities to the increasing part women are taking in the struggle against the British [Raj] authority.

The girl, Bima Deva, fired five shots at Sir Stanley yesterday as he was addressing a university convocation, but all missed. The girl was arrested. Authorities said Sir Stanley was known to have been long marked for death by terrorist elements.

Thousands of women, it was declared today, had recently taken active parts in the Nationalist movement of Mahatma Gandhi, which aims, by civil disobedience and without force or bloodshed, to achieve India's independence.

In the Bengal district, however, some of the younger women have lately resorted to acts of violence such as yesterday's attack on the Governor and the murder of C. G. B. Stevens, a district magistrate, by two young Indian girls last month. The girls were convicted of murder and sentenced to penal servitude for life.

British authorities today indicated their anxious concern over the situation. Another disturbing factor, they said, was the spread of the independence movement to the schools, where children were said to be showing increased hostility toward the British rule. It was while Governor Jackson was complaining that parents and teachers had lost control over their pupils that the attempt on his life was made.

Feeling among the Nationalist women of the country appears to have been intensified by the severe sentences recently meted out by district magistrates against women pickets and others, many of whom were condemned to serve jail sentences of from six months to two years.

Mr. Gandhi, his supporters declare, has condemned unsparingly all terrorist acts but admitted that his control was weak over the Bengal revolutionists, who have asserted the belief that victory can not be won by the Nationalist leader's formula of non-violence and love.

Another cause of concern to the British is the subterranean character which the Nationalist movement has assumed recently. Although all the important All-India Congress leaders have been imprisoned, the Nationalists are still extremely active, especially in Bombay, where the police have been baffled in their efforts to locate the invisible new chiefs.

February 8, 1932

HINDUS SIGN ACCORD; GANDHI GIVES ASSENT

Special Cable to THE NEW YORK TIMES.
BOMBAY, Sept. 24.—Leaders of the "untouchables" and caste Hindus today signed a historic agreement settling their political differences and foreshadowing a speedy abandonment of Mahatma Gandhi's "fast unto the death."

The "untouchables," who hitherto have demanded separate electorates, now agree to throw their lot in with the caste Hindus. In return, they will receive a guarantee of 148 seats in the Indian provincial Legislatures, twice as many as the British Government's award gave them. The caste Hindus further give assurances they will take practical steps toward lifting the "untouchables" from their degraded social position of thousands of years.

A specific pledge is given that the caste Hindus will try to obtain "a fair share of representation" for the depressed classes in the public services, although for centuries the latter have been shunned as the ditch-diggers and scavengers of India. There is also a promise that "adequate sums" will be set aside for educating the "untouchables" and raising them from the squalor in which they have been compelled to live.

Gandhi Smiles His Assent.
Faint and emaciated after 108 hours without food, Mahatma Gandhi approved the settlement at Yerovda jail in Poona today. He was too weak to say anything, but he indicated his assent by raising his head an inch or two from his cot and smiling wanly. By means of his hunger strike he had won his fight to prevent, as he put it, "the disruption of Hinduism" and "the perpetual segregation" of the depressed classes.

September 25, 1932

Fast Wins Gandhi Unconditional Release; A Week Without Food, He Weighs 90 Pounds

Wireless to THE NEW YORK TIMES.
POONA, India, Aug. 23.—Mahatma Gandhi was released unconditionally from custody this afternoon when doctors at the Poona Civil Hospital warned the government that his fast, in its eighth day, was endangering his life.

He was immediately removed, accompanied by an old friend, the Rev. C. F. Andrews, in an ambulance to Parnakuti House, the palatial home of Lady Vitall Das Thackersey, where he stayed during his three weeks' fast last May. Later he announced he had broken his fast before leaving the hospital.

The effect of the week's abstinence from food had been marked on Mr. Gandhi, who was suffering from minor complications. Mrs. Sarojini Naidu, one of his closest associates in the Nationalist Congress campaign, will arrive at Poona tomorrow to nurse him.

An Indian medical board has been appointed to determine the Mahatma's condition.

There is much speculation as to what Mr. Gandhi will do when he regains his strength. If he resumes his civil disobedience campaign, he will certainly be rearrested.

August 24, 1933

Civil Disobedience Halt Is Ordered by Gandhi

By The Associated Press.
PATNA, India, April 7.—Mahatma Gandhi told his followers today to leave the campaign of civil disobedience and passive resistance to him and to go out themselves and campaign for the forthcoming elections to the Legislative Assembly.

Regarding civil disobedience, the man who seeks the independence of India from British sovereignty said

"Leave it to me alone. It should be resumed by others in my lifetime only under my direction, unless another leader has arisen who claims to know the science better than I do."

Mr. Gandhi will support actively the revived Swaraj, or Independence, party for the elections, which will be held in November.

April 8, 1934

GANDHI QUITS POST IN INDIAN CONGRESS

Wireless to THE NEW YORK TIMES.
BOMBAY, Oct. 28.—While a crowd of 80,000 listened to his words through loudspeakers, Mahatma Gandhi delivered today his farewell as president of the Indian National Congress.

Henceforth he will devote himself to the new All-India Village Industries Association authorized by the Congress at its closing session today. The association will work for the restoration of the ancient industries apart from spinning and for the moral and physical advancement of the villages. Its organization was formally entrusted to J. C. Kumarrapla, an Indian economist with American experience, but he will be under Mr. Gandhi's "advice and guidance."

Mr. Gandhi, who spoke for an hour and a half, confined himself to advocating a change in the congress which would limit its membership to 2,000 and make future meetings less spectacular.

Gandhi Retains Power.
The congress party contains many elements opposed to Mr. Gandhi's policy, but it appeared that he was still the only leader who could carry his wishes with the rank and file. Amendments hostile to resolutions prepared by him have been invariably defeated.

His proposal for altering the party's constitution, although unacceptable to many congress members, has been accepted in principle chiefly because Mr. Gandhi made it and partly because there was no outstanding politician to offer genuine opposition to his leadership.

The amendment proposed last night by Pandit Malaviya on the communal award issue was overwhelmingly defeated. Similarly, Socialist amendments urging a boycott of Legislatures also was defeated, while Mr. Gandhi's policy

THE COLONIZERS AND THE COLONIZED

of "non-violent non-cooperation" was upheld against the Socialist plea for "mass direct action of a peaceful nature as the best possible instrument for attaining complete independence."

Nevertheless, Mr. Gandhi's hold on the political elements of the Congress party has weakened. The loyalty shown to him here derives from loyalty to his personality, not to his politics. The reason is that the Congress is changing. There is a tendency for the party to split into sections which, while stanch on fundamental aims, are divided on methods.

Socialist Strength Increasing.

The growth of the Socialist section is an outstanding development since the Karachi meeting in 1931.

This is composed of youthful elements of the party. Mr. Gandhi has recognized their strength and potentialities and is even prepared to compromise with them on certain issues.

The indications are that, if Pandit Jawaharlal Nehru had been present at this meeting, the Socialists might have consolidated their position sufficiently to embarrass the Congress in the future. Whether they agree with the Communists, who are parading the streets in motor trucks bearing the slogan, "Long Live the Soviet of Hindustan," is not clear. But they are certainly a growing power in the India Congress ranks.

October 29, 1934

INDIA BILL IS LAW AFTER EIGHT YEARS

King's Assent Is Given to the Measure Embodying New Federal Constitution.

TASK WAS MONUMENTAL

Natives Still Denounce 'Sham,' but Congress Party Will Participate in First Poll.

By FERDINAND KUHN Jr.
Special Cable to THE NEW YORK TIMES.

LONDON, Aug. 2.—The ancient formula "Le Roy Le Veult" announced to the House of Lords today that the bill embodying India's new Federal Constitution had received the royal assent.

Thus after eight years of incessant labor one of the greatest legislative tasks ever undertaken by a British Government became the law of the land. Not only was the bill great in its bulk, more than 400 pages, but it probably provided sweeping political changes for more millions of people than had ever been affected by an enactment of a British Parliament.

It remains for the new Constitution to be put into operation and for the Indian political leaders to work it. While the mass of Indian political opinion still denounces the bill as a sham, all news from India indicates that the Congress party will enter candidates in the first elections for provincial legislatures which are expected in 1937.

Deadlocks Sure to Occur.

In the early years of the new scheme there are sure to be crises and deadlocks between the legislatures and the Viceroy, to whom has been given the overriding powers of a dictator in emergencies.

The Constitution as completed falls far short of full self-government or even dominion status for India. The so-called safeguards to protect British interests and satisfy the Conservatives at home have been increased and stiffened until the Indians find them intolerable.

Yet even the Indian leaders agree that the bill gives them the greatest single advance toward self-government since the British conquered India two centuries ago. Looking back on the last eight years, it is remarkable that a Parliament which contains 460 Conservatives should have passed such a measure at all.

That the bill was passed with huge majorities and that it has been whittled down so little in the process is due largely to the courage of Prime Minister Stanley Baldwin, who staked his leadership in defying a rebellious section of his own party, and to the skill of Sir Samuel Hoare, until recently Secretary of State for India, in piloting such a gigantic and complicated measure through the House of Commons.

Simon Commission's Work.

It is almost eight years since the Simon commission was appointed to study the workings of India's system of government. Six years ago the commission returned from a hostile India to prepare its report, which recommended autonomy for the provinces only.

From Sir John Simon and the Viceroy at that time, Lord Irwin, came next the suggestion of a three-cornered conference between the British Government, the Indian princes and a handpicked group of delegates from British India.

When at the opening of the round-table conference the princes dramatically declared their willingness to enter an all-India federation, the broad outlines of the present bill came into sight.

It was based upon three principles—a federation embracing the native States and British India, a wide measure of autonomy for the provinces, and responsibility at the centre. Despite all that has happened since then, these three principles remain the foundation of the bill that has now become law.

Two years ago the present act took shape in a White Paper that sketched the government's proposal in detail. For eighteen months the scheme was examined and revised by a joint select committee of both houses—probably the strongest body ever appointed by Parliament from its own members to deal with a great controversial question of imperial policy.

Course of Bill in Parliament.

The committee's labors gave birth to the India Bill, which followed its recommendations closely. Then came the successive stages of its passage through Parliament, beginning with a three-day debate last December, in which the die-hard group of the Conservative party was routed after its long, bitter campaign against the bill.

On Tuesday the bill emerged from the House of Lords with scores of amendments, but all were minor changes in phraseology, and they were accepted by the Commons in a single day.

The overwhelming mass of British opinion now realizes that the new Constitution is an attempt to stave off a violent upheaval in India by making timely concessions to Indian nationalism. The British Government knows that it had to face now what the Tories call "risks" if the far more serious risk of losing India were not to be faced in the future.

While the provincial governments will be established without serious delay, it may be three years or longer before the federation is launched. Half the princes, on the basis of the population of their States and representation in the upper federal chamber, must sign the instruments of accession before the federation can be brought into existence.

August 3, 1935

INDIA NATIONALISTS TO ACCEPT OFFICE

Party's Working Committee Drops Demand for Pledge From British Governors

GANDHI'S INFLUENCE SEEN

He Had Counseled Moderation—Minority Ministries Ready to Yield to Congress

Wireless to THE NEW YORK TIMES.

WARDHA, India, July 7.—The working committee of the All India Congress [Nationalist] party today voted to accept office after three months of unsuccessful attempt to obtain from the British Government specific assurances that Provincial Governors would not use their "special powers" to nullify the party program.

"Office is to be accepted and utilized," said the committee, "for the purposes of working in accordance with the lines laid down by the Congress election manifesto and to further in every possible way the Congress policy of combating the new act [the Government of India Act of 1935, under which limited provincial autonomy is created] and prosecuting a constructive program."

Terming the present relation between the British Government and the people of India that of "exploiter and exploited," the committee thus left no doubt that the party will continue the fight for complete independence.

Jawaharal Nehru, the party president, said tonight the working committee's decision would be submitted as soon as possible to the full party committee. The resolution, reached at the end of three days of deliberation, said this would have been done beforehand, but that "delay in taking a decision at this time would be injurious to the country's interest and would create confusion in the public mind at a time when prompt, decisive action is necessary."

Minority ministries now will be replaced by Congress leaders in the six provinces the party controls. In five others Moslems and other groups willing to cooperate in launching the new Constitution have been in office since April 1, several carrying on programs of drastic social reform without interference by Governors appointed by the British Government.

Social reforms also are pledged by the Congress party, and the fact that these obviously could not be carried out while the party refused to take on the responsibilities of government is one of the reasons the working committee decided to end the deadlock.

Mohandas K. Gandhi's modification of the Congress demand for a specific pledge that "special powers" would not be used to a demand for assurance that the Governors would not interfere with the day-to-day administration also helped. It gave the Marquess of Zetland and the Viceroy, the Marquess of Linlithgow, an opportunity to pledge that at least there would be no capricious interference with the Congress and that if Congress Ministers and Ministries had any serious disagreements with Governors they would not be removed from office without discussion or explanation designed to iron out their differences.

The working committee, although not satisfied with these assurances, declared they "exhibit a desire to make an approach to the Congress demand" and that anyway "the situation created as a result of circumstances and events that have since occurred warrants the belief that it would not be easy for Governors to use their special powers."

There is no doubt that Mr. Gandhi, who came out of retirement to seek votes for "untouchables" in the provincial elections, is largely responsible for this moderation. The leader of the famous "civil disobedience" campaign did not attend the first of the committee's meetings Monday, but traveled to Wardha yesterday and today by bullock cart from his ashram [retreat] five miles away.

July 8, 1937

India

CONGRESS IN INDIA BACKS UP GANDHI

Moderates Prevail, 218 to 133, in Vote on Party Policy at Opening of Session

LEADER UNABLE TO ATTEND

But His Influence Defeated Party President, Carried In on a Stretcher

By FREDERICK T. BIRCHALL
Wireless to THE NEW YORK TIMES.

ALL INDIA NATIONAL CONGRESS CAMP, TRIPURI, India, March 10.—At a time when national unity in India is menaced by political action as well as religious disputes, when communal disturbances between Hindus and Moslems are taking on a serious recrudescence and when the inevitable struggle between the native States still under princely domination and the provinces rising into representative government has reached a stage of high tension, the All India National Congress party met here today for the most crucial session in its history.

The issue is the old controversy between Right and Left, characteristic of political movements these days. Shall the Congress, which is the only political party of any account in this vast subcontinent of many races, dozens of religions and thirty or forty different tongues which is India, be radical and uncompromising under the leadership of its recently re-elected President, Subhas Chandra Bose, or less extreme and more inclined to moderate methods while still remaining wholly nationalistic in aim under the guidance of a group of other leaders who have grown up under the wise tutelage of Mohandas K. Gandhi?

Party Will Follow Gandhi

For almost a month this has been the issue underlying a strenuous preliminary battle in the ranks of Congress leaders, but tonight, when the first session of the Congress was held, this had already been virtually decided. The Congress party will continue on the path laid out for it by the wise, patient and hitherto continuously successful Mr. Gandhi, who is factually today the real power in the new India that is fast arising from the ashes of the old colonial domain which for several centuries has been a source of some anxiety but of great profit to its British rulers.

Mr. Bose, who engineered his own re-election to the congress presidency against Mr. Gandhi's will and threatened to proceed in his own with the ardent support of Left Wingers, must choose his working committee and consequently direct his own course "in accordance with the wishes of Gandhi."

That is the purport of a resolution adopted this afternoon by the congress working committee, numbering approximately 350 and corresponding roughly to national committees in the United States, although actually counting much more. The vote was 218 to 133 in favor of Mr. Gandhi's policy. This is apparently the ratio of strength in the congress itself of the revolutionaries against the comparative moderates, with the reservation that moderation in politics is always relative.

Means Much to the Empire

This means a great deal in the solution of the Indian problem, which in the larger view may be ultimately the problem of continued cohesion of the British Empire, for ultimately at some future time—perhaps not long in the future—that same ratio may decide whether India shall take on real independence, which is fast coming to her and which no power at present envisionable can avert, within the framework of the British Commonwealth of Nations alongside Canada, Australia and others or outside the Commonwealth, a rich prey to the ambitions of predatory ideologies now arming to refill their bankrupt treasuries with spoils such as this.

But that is in the future. Sufficient today to record the present result achieved after a two-day fight in the committee in which every parliamentary device the subtle Indian mentality could devise has been used to whittle down the significance of the stern admonition delivered.

The battle continued, heedless of food or rest, from morning to late at night in a temperature that New York would classify as torrid. Endless speeches in Hindustani and English alternatively poured from the mouths of fervid orators.

Hundred of reporters and several hundred eager auditors filled every inch of the huge hut of matting and bamboo in which the debate was held. No one ever seemed to tire as endless points of order and a continuous stream of amendments were ruled out or voted down by the same steady majority.

Mr. Bose, the Congress president, under fire himself, presided, despite an illness reputed to be as much mental as physical, which, according to bulletins of his physician, who is also a brother, kept his temperature varying between 99 and 104. He was brought to Tripuri in an ambulance, carried in on a stretcher and presided from a cot flanked by ice tanks, sipping cooling drinks and medicines from time to time while two nieces waved fans above his fevered brow.

Issue Settled in Gandhi's Favor

Mr. Gandhi, his real opponent, although not here, settled in his own favor a larger and wholly different issue regarding the method whereby representatives of the native States in the future Indian Parliament shall be chosen. Soon he will confer with the Viceroy at New Delhi over details of cementing his victory. He has contented himself with occasional telegrams to Mr. Bose, adjuring him to act impartially and invoking divine guidance upon the deliberations. The shrewd old man undoubtedly envisioned the outcome in advance from afar.

With its outstanding issue virtually decided, the Congress organized itself tonight in a great open amphitheatre under the stars preparatory to taking up its normal business tomorrow. It met with Mr. Bose absent and the Left Wingers striving to forget their defeat. Mr. Bose was not even present for the final committee vote. His doctor decided that he had exhausted his endurance, so he was carried out on a stretcher. Mrs. Sarojini Naidu, a poetess, who is the senior ex-president of past congresses, took his place.

Never outside India has there ever been a political convention like unto this. It is held on a roughly level plain beside a river bank near an Indian village. Roads have been built, water piped and electric light, telegraph and telephone lines carried into this plain. The camp comprises a conglomeration of huts constructed of matting stretched over bamboo poles set out in narrow streets. Huge ornamental gateways of papier-mâché dotted intervals at the entrances to the Congress amphitheatre and the committee's equally sizable national hut mark the Congress's national importance.

Delegates bring their own bedding, food and washing appliances. Sanitary arrangements are most primitive.

All Squat on Mats

At meetings all squat on the mat-covered ground before foot-high wooden benches, supposedly for writing purposes. What this means to an unaccustomed American or European during a five-hour session when there is only two square feet in which to wriggle or change one's posture can be imagined. But there are fewer than half a dozen Americans and Europeans in this whole assemblage of several hundred thousands. They include this writer and two British correspondents domiciled in India. Official Britishers are absent: the Congress even has its own police.

Street lights, except on the single main thoroughfare, are lacking, and at night one stumbles through rough dirt streets, seeking his particular hut, guided only by white dhottys and passers-by.

By day, however, the congress is picturesqueness personified, a kaleidoscope of bamboo huts, white robes, multicolored turbans and flashy advertisements.

The proceedings opened this morning with a procession of fifty-two elephants, each bearing a huge portrait of a former president of the congress and all drawing a chariot in which Mr. Bose was to have ridden had he been well enough. Instead, the chariot carried only his portrait, which was an anticlimax, although hundreds of spectators crowded around to rub the dust off the chariot and smear it on their foreheads as a good omen, while other hundreds knelt and kissed the earth as the chariot passed.

There were elephants with howdahs of silver and gold and elephants draped in silken carpets hung on golden chains studded with semi-precious stones, their foreheads painted with fancy pictures. Preceding the chariot came ranks of volunteer congress police in blue shorts, shirts and caps, carrying silver-topped bamboo sticks. Afterward came the girl volunteers, who pass around brass cups of water at the meetings and guide delegates to their seats. They wore orange saris under green bodices, belted in white. The new Indian flag of orange and green white floated over all.

This writer has seen many political conventions in many countries, but none so wonderfully picturesque and none more enthusiastic than this, despite its primitive setting. Its one aim and one slogan is "a free, independent India." All factions demand that, and its slogan is fast becoming a fact.

March 11, 1939

INDIA RENOUNCES TERROR AS WEAPON

Assassination in London Is Followed by Reassurances From All Parties

By JAMES MacDONALD
Wireless to THE NEW YORK TIMES.

LONDON, March 16 — When a wild-eyed Sikh assassinated Sir Michael O'Dwyer, formerly Lieutenant Governor of the Punjab, and wounded the Marquess of Zetland, Lord Lamington and Sir Louis Dane in London this week, the barking of his pistol strangely enough turned out to be a signal that terrorism has become obsolete in the campaign for Indian independence.

This was proved by the remarkable unanimity with which spokesmen representing virtually all classes and all political parties in far-off India, no matter how bitter the differences between themselves or between them and the British Government, hastened to condemn the crime and disavow any connection with it.

All differences momentarily have been submerged in a wave of indignation which, according to reports reaching London, swept through India as soon as the news was received there of the shootings Wednesday afternoon at the conclusion of a public meeting under auspices of the East India Association and the Royal Central Asian Society.

Hindus Deplore Action

There is little doubt in any one's mind that Mohamed Singh Azad, the man who shot down Sir Michael, the witty and forceful former Indian official, was acting on his own and not in connivance with any Indian plotters. Spokesmen for the Hindus, who comprise the powerful Indian majority, which is seeking complete independence from Britain; the Moslems, who, although numbering millions, form a minority that fears Hindu domination, and the Princes of the Native States, who have adopted an attitude of seeming indifference toward the Hindu-Moslem disputes, have all joined in deploring Sir Michael's assassination.

THE COLONIZERS AND THE COLONIZED

Mohandas K. Gandhi, central figure in the All-India National Congress party, which represents principally the Hindus, has denounced the shooting as "an act of insanity." Such crimes, he said, "have been proved injurious to the causes for which they are committed."

Even Subhas Chandra Bose, leftwing leader in Congress, joined in the condemnation, declaring that assassination belongs to a closed chapter in Indian history. Still another Hindu leader, Pandit Jawaharlal Nehru, Congress president, has indicated his aversion for acts of terrorism.

Indian Congress to Meet

These denunciations of terrorism, however, do not preclude the possibility that the Congress may yet resort to civil disobedience in its campaign for independence. The Congress will open its fifty-third session on Tuesday and it is expected that the extremist elements will press Mr. Gandhi to make up his mind on the question of civil disobedience which he hitherto has been reluctant to launch.

The Moslem leaders of India were deeply stirred by this week's act of violence. Like the Hindus, they feel that even though Singh Azad may have acted alone, terrorism hurts rather than helps India's cause. Moslem sentiment will be

INDIAN LEADER

Sahlin
Mohandas K. Gandhi has hesitated to launch "civil disobedience."

crystallized at London this week when the Moslem Association will hold a condemnation meeting. A prayer meeting of all Moslems here will be held tomorrow for the same purpose.

As soon as word was flashed to India Wednesday that Sir Michael had been assassinated and three other distinguished veterans of India affairs wounded, none critically, Maharaja Jam Sahib of Nawanagar, Chancellor of the Chamber of Princes, cabled the sympathies of the entire Princely Order to Sir Michael's family.

Sir Michael was regarded by many Indians as an enemy of Indian nationalism. In a country like India where there is still no unity, where there is no experience in those virtues of compromise which are a necessary part of the democratic processes, and where the vast majority of the people are utterly ignorant of the rudiments of politics, Sir Michael opposed granting parliamentary institutions without preliminary education in their functions over a long span of years.

In the opinion of most observers here it was not the question of India's constitutional problem that prompted Singh Azad to fire two bullets into Sir Michael's heart. More likely the act was an aftermath of the massacre in the sacred Sikh city of Amritsar on April 13, 1919. On that occasion, Amritsar, the wealthiest city in the Punjab State, of which Sir Michael was then Lieutenant Governor, was a scene of wild rioting by a mob of 5,000 Indians. Troops, called out under Brigadier General R. E. H. Dyer to quell the disturbance, fired into the rioters killing 400 and wounding 1,200. General Dyer's order to shoot aroused a great political controversy which eventually resulted in his removal from service in India.

After the general's death in 1928, Sir Michael defended him as follows: "We knew that, unless it was sternly and promptly repressed, what was happening at Amritsar would spread to every station in north India. They were only waiting to hear the news of what happened at Amritsar to play the same game elsewhere."

March 17, 1940

GANDHI REAVOWS POLICY

Scoring Hitlerism, He Writes of 'Bravery' in French Surrender

BOMBAY, India, June 22 (P)—Mohandas K. Gandhi, writing in his weekly newspaper Harijan today, advocated non-violence as the only way to meet Hitlerism, which he called "naked, ruthless force reduced to an exact science and worked out with scientific precision."

"The bravery of the French soldier is well known, but let the world know of the greater bravery of the French statesmen suing for peace."

June 23, 1940

Indian Independence Aim In Abeyance, Gandhi Says

By The Associated Press.

BOMBAY, India, April 26—Mohandas K. Gandhi said tonight that his All India Congress party had dropped temporarily its demand for the independence of India and wanted only "freedom of speech and the pen."

In a reply to a speech before the House of Commons at London Tuesday by L. S. Amery, Secretary of State for India, Mr. Gandhi said:

"Amery has insulted Indian intelligence by reiterating ad nauseam that Indian political parties will have to agree among themselves and Great Britain will register the will of a United India."

He admitted there was "an unbridgeable gulf" between his Congress and the Moslem League, but inquired, "Why don't British statesmen admit it is a domestic quarrel?"

He reiterated that the Nationalists must abide by a policy of non-violence, whatever the odds.

April 27, 1941

INDIA WILL RELEASE NEHRU AND OTHERS

Congress Party Leader Also Among Passive Resistance Prisoners to Be Freed

SOME DELAY IS FORESEEN

Way to New Study of Issues in Path of Dominion Status Discerned in Action

Special Cable to THE NEW YORK TIMES.

NEW DELHI, India, Dec. 3—The Government of India announced today that it had decided to release all passive resistance prisoners, including Maulana Abul Kalam Azad, president of the All-India Congress party, and Pandit Jawaharlal Nehru, former president.

This important step has been expected in India for some time, and it is expected that it will be welcomed by most of the political elements, particularly by those who maintain that the Congress party's policy is now in process of readjustment.

Although release of the prisoners will not in itself end the constitutional deadlock, the general opinion appears to be that it will open up fresh opportunities for re-examining problems hitherto standing in the way of dominion status for India.

Both Mr. Azad and Pandit Nehru have been serving sentences under the Defense of India Regulations. Last Jan. 3 Mr. Azad received a sentence of eighteen months' simple imprisonment. Pandit Nehru was sentenced Nov. 5 last year to four years' rigorous imprisonment.

Text of Announcement

The official announcement reads: "The Government of India, confident in the determination of all responsible opinion in India to support the war effort until victory is secured, has reached the conclusion that those civil disobedience prisoners whose offenses have been formal or symbolic in character can be set free. Effect will be given to this course as soon as possible. There are some provinces in which the numbers and local conditions may mean delay; but before the end of the year the Government of India hopes that throughout India practically all such persons will have been set free. With them there will be released Maulana Abul Kalam Azad and Pandit Jawaharlal Nehru."

Although Mohandas K. Gandhi has said that such a gesture as this will not alter his attitude, it is clear that important members of the Congress party are bound to be affected by it. Commentators both inside and outside the Congress party assert that a new, improved situation will emerge from this decision, which is understood to have been favored by all new members of the Governor General's Executive Council, which was recently enlarged.

Congress party leaders will now be free to examine the position of their party in the circumstances in which it now finds itself. These circumstances disclose a growing feeling of frustration and discontent within the party about a policy regarded as so unrelated to current affairs, both in the domestic and international spheres that there is now an insistent demand that the party should return to parliamentary activities, including that of taking office in the provinces. It is declared that any re-

India

valuation of policy that the party may make will find the import of the organization either enhanced or minimized according to the attitude it adopts toward the prosecution of the war.

Nationalist newspapers have long been urging the adoption of a more realistic policy by the party, although most Congress party commentators imply that the release of the prisoners will have significance only if it represents a preliminary step toward more liberal policies in the constitutional field.

How far the adoption of any new policy by the Congress party will be affected by this view can only be conjectured, but the general belief is that the party's recent policy has had negative results, and it is suggested that any new policy must take cognizance of that fact.

It is held that offers by the Congress party to cooperate in the war effort, if they are qualified by constitutional demands that are considered impossible of fulfillment, will keep the party in a position that most of its members deplore.

December 4, 1941

Nehru to Succeed Gandhi As India Congress Leader

By The United Press.

BOMBAY, India, Jan. 15—Mohandas K. Gandhi announced to the All-India Congress Committee today that Pandit Jawaharlal Nehru would be his successor as leader of the Congress Party.

Maulana Abul Kalam Azad, president of the Congress Party, emphasized that while members disagreed with Mr. Gandhi on the issue of non-violent refusal to cooperate with the British war effort, his guidance, leadership and advice always would be available.

"The British Government has done nothing which could invite us to reconsider our position," Mr. Gandhi told the committee in pleading for continuance of his policy. "There can be no change in the attitude of the Congress toward the war so long as the British Government's attitude is unchanged."

Pandit Jawaharlal Nehru
The New York Times, 1966

January 16, 1942

INDIA IS PULLED THREE WAYS

No Middle Ground Appears in the Dispute Which Is Vital to United Nations

By HERBERT L. MATTHEWS
Wireless to THE NEW YORK TIMES.

NEW DELHI, India, Sept. 12—The first impression of any one arriving fresh in India with an honest desire to find out what it's all about is sheer, overwhelming bewilderment. It is not so much the magnitude of the problems involved as the absence of a middle ground upon which one can take one's stand and calmly survey the countryside.

It is customary for foreigners to come here and discover that India is not a country, that it is a continent and that it has got ever so many races, religions and languages, and that one might as well write about Europe as one nation. Actually that is a superficial difficulty which can be overcome with enough time, patience and energy.

Confusion of Views

The real trouble is the all too human one of different people looking at the same things and drawing opposite conclusions. It is a case of distrust and misunderstanding, of sordid interests being rationalized into pious convictions, of struggles for political power and patronage being disguised as patriotism. Shot through it all is a lot of honesty, sincerity, courage and patience under desperately trying conditions. What is most lacking is the spirit of compromise and good-will.

It would certainly simplify matters if one could take a particular point of view and interpret everything in India along that line. That is what a British official would do, or a follower of the Indian Congress, or a Moslem Leaguer. To them it is all as clear as crystal—granting their premises.

The British say: "We came here at a period when conquest was the natural order of things. We put our genius, our soldiery, our commercial and administrative experience to the service of India and Britain. We brought peace and the benefits of Western civilization to India, and it is we who taught the Indians what democracy and freedom mean. We are willing to go now, and we have promised to do so, but first we have got to win this war, and be assured that our vast interests are protected, and that India herself will not be torn by internal strife."

The Congress View

Congress followers say: "The British are conquerors, usurpers, tyrants. They have exploited India for their own selfish ends and deliberately kept the people in ignorance and poverty. India is a potentially rich country and yet her masses are just about the wretchedest in the world because the British will not let us develop our own industries or intensify our agriculture. The world has gone beyond the age of imperialism, as your Sumner Welles has said, and each nation has the right to independence and self-government. Let the British stay here to win this war. If they give us our own civil government we will help them win the war. But why should we fight for one tyrant against another?"

The Moslem Leaguer is not so sure of that. He too says "We want the British to go, "but he adds that he sees little advantage in exchanging the British Raj for the Hindu Raj. "Your two years and seven months rule in the Prov-

THE COLONIZERS AND THE COLONIZED

"DOORKNOB"—A BRITISH VIEW OF GANDHI'S ROLE

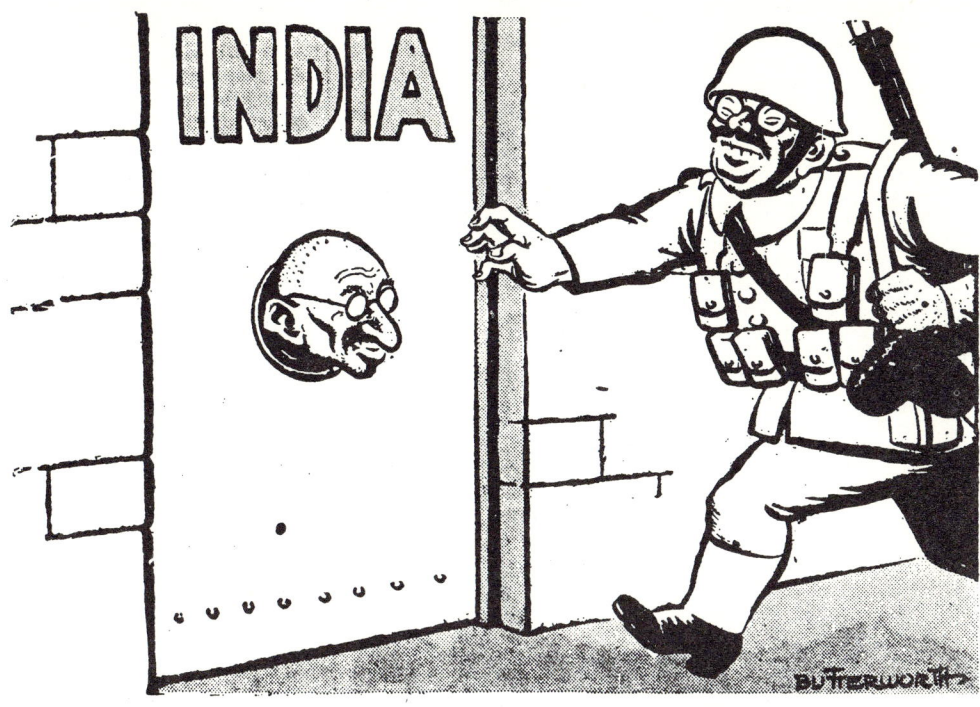

Butterworth in The Manchester Daily Dispatch

inces," he tells the followers of Congress, "has taught us that you intend to keep us in subjection. Therefore, the only solution is for you to give us the same self-determination that you are demanding, and permit us to set up our own nation of Pakistan. Then Hindus and Moslems will live side by side in complete understanding and friendliness, and we will get rid of the British quickly."

It will be noted that the Britisher addresses himself to the world, the Congress follower to the British and the Moslem Leaguer to the Congress follower, and nothing seems so beyond the realm of possibility now than that the three should get together and talk to one another. The Britisher is determined that he will pacify India by force and carry on as he always did. The Congress follower is determined on what Gandhi has called "open rebellion" to drive out the British. The Moslem Leaguer sits on the sidelines and tells his fellow-Indians, "If you want my help, give me Pakistan first."

Those are the main points of view in India and as things are going on now they are irreconcilable. True, complications of the situation lie in such questions as why a handful of British can dominate India, why so many Indians distrust the British, why Hindus and Moslems cannot solve the communal problem. There is much that cannot be settled by logic and reason, much that is emotional, many problems that will work hardship to one side or the other, whatever the solution may be.

The more one studies it the more confused and hopeless the situation seems to get, yet if there is one sure thing about it all it is that, willy-nilly, some solution has got to be found. In the long run there is no question that the British must lose in the sense that they must get out. But they think they can win this particular battle and they are putting everything they have into it.

September 13, 1942

INDIA'S DISTURBERS GO UNDERGROUND

Riots and Demonstrations Are Replaced by Individual Secret Acts of Sabotage

LATTER NOT NUMEROUS

But Security Official Sees a Trend Bothersome to Police —Blames Congress Group

Wireless to THE NEW YORK TIMES.

NEW DELHI, India, Oct. 26—The character of the internal disturbances in India has changed from mass riots and demonstrations to individual acts of sabotage which are harder to deal with and in some ways more dangerous, a government official of India said today. This official deals directly with questions of internal security.

What has happened, according to him, is that the movement has been driven underground to a certain extent, and whereas mass activity can be easily handled by the traditional methods of firing and police charges, individuals working secretly at night are much more difficult to apprehend.

So far there has not been much of this sort of work, but signs are pointing that way, said the official, adding that there have been cases of rails cut by blow torches or acid during the night by small groups. He is convinced that it is organized sabotage and that all that has occurred since Aug. 9 was at least expected, if not organized, by the Congress party.

"We did know exactly what was going to happen," he said, "but Gandhi and Congress party men must have known what was coming. We expected the same old Congress stuff and that is what we got for three days, but then organized sabotage began."

Loyalty of Police Cited

The official stated that a great deal depended on local Indian constables remaining loyal, which they did. He was asked how the Indian Government could count on men whose basic pay is only 18 rupees monthly and who were recruited in home localities and hence were called upon to shoot or arrest their own people.

"Every government has to rely on its servants," the official replied. "The constables remained loyal to their salt. Out of about 230,000 police, less than a thousand are British and of them only 400 are officers. Of course, we had the army behind the police and the army is used more in India for internal security than in other countries.

"Those constables who took a firm line with the mobs were all right, some of those who did not were overwhelmed and killed. I believe India needs a firm government and most Indians agree with me. When they institute their own government it will have to be a firm one."

In reply to a question about the possibility of military developments, the official said that if we attack and things go well in Burma and other parts of the world, then India will calm down. He did not think a wholly Indian Government would mean an increased or more effective war effort.

Another possibility of trouble, he added, was if Mohandas K. Gandhi died. At present, Mr. Gandhi is well and seems to be acting like a spectator of the Indian scene, according to the official. He is allowed to write to his relatives on personal matters, so if he fasted and died they would know quickly.

The official said he was not alarmed by disturbances on the northwest frontier, where Abdul Gaffar Khan has been arousing his "Red Shirts" to acts of civil disobedience. Governor Sir George Cunningham has been taking the line that the Congress party hasn't a big following on the northwest frontier, which is true, said the official, but it might be necessary to take measures against the Red Shirts.

Today's newspapers tell of disturbances in sessions of courts in Peshawar as well as the arrest and subsequent release of 496 Red Shirts at Mardan. Two other arrests took place at the Peshawar cantonment yesterday.

The fact that American correspondents have stopped sending detailed reports of daily disturbances throughout India does not mean they have ended. It is only that they have become commonplace and rarely assume important dimensions in any one place. For instance, yesterday attempts were made to hold processions in several places in Old Delhi and four arrests were made. Other arrests took place in several cities in Bombay Province and at Gauhati in Assam.

October 27, 1942

India

INDIAN CONGRESS REJECTS A REVOLT

Votes Down Disobedience Plan, Choosing to Negotiate With Britain on Independence

BOMBAY, India, Sept. 22 (P)—The All-India Congress party today rejected demands for an uncompromising revolutionary program to win Indian freedom and signified its willingness to negotiate with Britain on the independence problem.

Earlier, the party's Working Committee had denounced Britain's latest proposals as unsatisfactory and designed to maintain "an incompetent and corrupt" rule.

But the General Committee finally adopted a resolution affirming that the Congress party's policy still was to negotiate with the Government when possible and to cease noncooperation when necessary. Five amendments urging an unyielding revolutionary program were turned down.

As the Working Committee lashed at British rule, Pandit Jawaharlal Nehru told the Congress party convention that the same forces welded by the 1942 movement would be used to attain India's liberation. In 1942 the Congress, in a "Britain Must Quit India" resolution, ordered a widespread civil disobedience campaign that erupted into violence. The Working Committee declared the Indian freedom offers by Prime Minister Clement R. Attlee and the Viceroy, Viscount Wavell, were "vague," inadequate and unsatisfactory" and charged that the present Government was "responsible for the widespread corruption that prevails in the country, for the gross mismanagement of the food and cloth problem and the supreme tragedy of the [1943] Bengal famine."

"Yet," its statement continued, "it is declared that, pending the elections and for many months at least, this incompetent and corrupt administration shall continue its misrule."

Declaring the proposals offered little that was new, the Committee stated:

"Neither the end of the war nor a change of Government in Great Britain appear to have resulted in any real change in British policy toward India, which seems to be based on delaying every advance and attempting to create new problems and fresh complications.

"It is significant that there is no mention in these broadcasts of the independence of India, and nothing short of independence can be acceptable to the Congress and the country. The proposals of the British Government become in context still more significant indications of their desire to hold on to power in India as long as they possibly can and with all the means and methods at their disposal."

Mr. Nehru, speaking in support of a resolution charging the British with "wanton suppression" of the 1942 independence movement, said the people briefly liberated several sections of the country despite inadequate organization.

Sadar Vallabhai Patel, former president of the party, asserted the Government had lost its right to govern by permitting the Bengal famine, which he said took 3,000,000 lives. If a third of this number had died in the mass movement, Mr. Patel said, "India would have been free."

The Working Committee approved appointment of a legal committee to defend Indian soldiers charged with fighting under Japanese control.

Mohandas K. Gandhi remained too ill of influenza to attend the Congress party's second session. His fever was reported to have risen to 102 during the night.

September 23, 1945

Unrest in India

Unrest and internal dissension spread across India last week threatening to engulf the subcontinent in large-scale violence. At its root was the three-cornered conflict between the Moslem League, the predominantly Hindu Congress party and the British Government. The Moslems want a separate Moslem nation (Pakistan) composed of the predominantly Moslem provinces of India. The Congress party, India's largest political body, wants a united free country with a democratic government representing all provinces. The British Government has offered eventual dominion status without the right of secession from the empire.

Last week Mohammed Ali Jinnah, head of the Moslem League, served notice that if the British carried out their announced plan of calling a Constitution-making body to grant increased self-government, the Moslems would rise in revolt to obtain their independent state in the six northern provinces of India. This would mean civil war because, for religious and economic reasons, the Hindus would not yield the provinces. These include part of the valley of the Ganges River, sacred to Hindus, much of India's heavy industry and its major agricultural potential, the wheat of the Punjab. Although there are only 94,000,000 Moslems in all of India, the proposed Pakistan territory includes 107,002,000 persons, many of them Hindus and minority groups.

Anti-British Riots

In spite of the uncompromising struggle between the two factions, last week for the first time since 1921 Moslems and Hindus together staged street protests and riots against the British in Calcutta, Bombay and New Delhi. The catalytic agent in this case was the Indian National Army, organized by a Japanese collaborator named Subhas Chandra Bose. A "Bose legend" has been built up by Indians, who claim he was a misguided patriot endeavoring to free India from British rule, and all British attempts to punish members of Bose's army have aroused Moslems and Hindus to fury.

These political differences are sharply aggravated by the food crisis growing daily more acute. By summer the shortage is expected to be more severe than the famine of 1943, in which 1,500,000 Indians perished. Many Indians blame the British for not taking steps to head it off. Last week Pandit Jawaharlal Nehru, one of the Congress party's most popular leaders, warned: "If there is famine in the provinces, I ask the people to revolt against the Government. Let the Government be prepared to face it."

February 17, 1946

Correction

An article in last Sunday's Review of the Week stated that Britain had offered India "eventual dominion status without the right of secession from the Empire." This was an error. Britain's offer of eventual dominion status, made in 1942, said India could "decide in the future its relation to the other Member States of the British Commonwealth."

February 24, 1946

THE COLONIZERS AND THE COLONIZED

BRITISH OFFER INDIA THE RIGHT TO SECEDE WHEN BLOCS AGREE

Full Independence Pledge Made by Attlee Goes Beyond 1942 Bid to Dominion Status

BIPARTY APPROVAL VOICED

Prime Minister Promises Aid if Indians Elect to Break Away From Empire

By HERBERT L. MATTHEWS
By Wireless to The New York Times.

LONDON, March 15—Prime Minister Attlee, speaking on behalf of the British Government, today offered India the right to full independence and not merely dominion status. This was an advance beyond the 1942 offer, carried by Sir Stafford Cripps, of dominion status because it carried the right, under the Westminster statute, of secession from the Commonwealth, and as such it met an insistent demand of the Indian Congress party.

It must be added that independence is not being given to India today or tomorrow nor is it being offered without the constant and fundamental demand that the Indians must themselves agree on their future Constitution. Three Cabinet Ministers are leaving for India Tuesday, and this will be their aim, as it was the primary subject of today's debate in the House of Commons.

Every speaker, whatever his party, agreed that India must receive independence and that Britain sincerely intended to meet India's demand for freedom. There was a clear, earnest desire that the Indians should realize this sincerity and meet the Cabinet mission half way in its arduous task.

Chary of Promises

Though the lack of interest in the issue was reflected by the fact that the benches were at best three-quarters empty during the debate, this also indicated a lack of controversy.

Mr. Attlee took great pains to make it clear that the Cabinet mission, consisting of Lord Pethick-Lawrence, Secretary of State for India; Sir Stafford Cripps, President of the Board of Trade, and A. V. Alexander, First Lord of the Admiralty, was not going to India to give the Indians independence. Other speakers on both sides of the House made that equally plain. This was done partly because the British did not want to be accused of breaking promises about the mission.

"My colleagues are going to India with the intention of using their utmost endeavors to help her to obtain freedom as fully and speedily as possible," Mr. Attlee said. "What form of government is to replace the present regime is for India to decide, but our desire is to help her to set up forthwith the machinery for making that decision. India herself must choose what will be her future Constitution, what will be her position in the world."

Would Cushion Change

The Prime Minister went on to say he hoped India would choose dominion status, "but," he added, "if she does so elect it must be by her own free will, for the British Commonwealth and Empire is not bound together by chains of external compulsion. It is free association of free peoples.

"If, on the other hand, India elects for independence—and in our view she has a right to do so—it will be for us to help to make the transition as smooth and easy as possible."

Again speaking of racial and religious minority difficulties, Mr. Attlee said:

"We cannot dictate how these difficulties can be overcome. Our first duty is to get the machinery of decision set up."

R. A. Butler, who had opened the debate for the Conservative opposition, which did no opposing today, however, likewise stressed that the Indians could have independence as long as they themselves framed the new Constitution.

Another Conservative, Godfrey Nicholson, one of the Parliamentary group that recently visited India, dotted the "i's" and crossed the "t's."

"There is grave danger that it may be thought that the mission is going to India to bring back a solution to the Indian problem," he said. "I believe the main object of the debate today is to impress upon this country and India that we know there is no clear-cut solution or answer to this problem."

Sir John Anderson, former Governor Bengal, participated in the debate. "It has been made clear that what we know as the Cripps offer remains valid in all respects," he said. "It has also been made clear that the British Government and Parliament will accept any Constitution framed by the Indians in India which is acceptable to the main elements in India's national life.

"So long as we are in India there is a responsibility upon us for enforcement of the law and therefore we have a predominant right to a voice as to what the Constitution should be."

March 16, 1946

90 Die, 900 Hurt in Calcutta As Moslems and Hindus Riot

By The Associated Press.

BOMBAY, India, Saturday, Aug. 17—Ninety persons were reported killed and more than 900 injured in Calcutta yesterday in a wild outbreak of violence between Hindus and Moslems during the Moslem League's "Direct Action Day" demonstration against the British plan for Indian independence and the Congress party's interpretation of it.

A curfew was invoked from 9 P. M. to 4 A. M. to clear the streets and troops were sent to the widely scattered battle scenes.

Demonstrators set fire to houses and shops during the height of the demonstration and looting was reported in various localities.

The home of Dr. B. C. Roy, former member of the Congress party's Working Committee and widely known physician who has attended Mohandas K. Gandhi on several occasions, was attacked and fired.

Furniture and property of the Congress party's medical mission to Malaya also were damaged.

Dispatches from Calcutta said the Bengal Provincial Congress party committee office and two Hindu newspaper offices and a Hindu temple were repeatedly attacked and damaged.

Police opened fire several times during the day, which had been declared a public holiday, with all Government offices and business houses closed down.

In Patna, a clash resulted when the Moslem League flag was raised over the Anglo-Sanskrit College, and seven were injured.

The observance of "Direct Action Day" in the rest of India was generally peaceful.

A delayed dispatch from Calcutta said blood spattered the streets in the northern and eastern parts of the city and bodies of the dead and injured littered the pavements.

"Reports of stabbings, assaults, looting and arson poured into police headquarters, which was hard pressed in efforts to keep the situation from getting completely out of hand," the dispatch reported.

"Early tonight (Friday) it became impossible to make contact with police headquarters by telephone."

August 17, 1946

WAVELL CREATES CABINET FOR INDIA HEADED BY NEHRU

By GEORGE E. JONES
Special to The New York Times.

NEW DELHI, India, Aug. 24—The appointment of India's first popular Executive Council was announced today. This is considered a big step forward toward this country's eventual independence.

The fourteen Councilors, only twelve of whose names were disclosed today, will take office on Sept. 2. They will replace the present Council of nine officials who formed the "Caretaker Government" to carry on the administration this summer.

Of the twelve persons named, seven are Congress party members and all of the others are politically acceptable to the Congress party leadership.

The name of Pandit Jawaharlal Nehru, Congress party president and noted internationalist, led the list announced by the Viceroy.

On a communal basis, the Council will include five caste Hindus, one Scheduled Castes (Untouchable) representative, five Moslems, one Parsi, one Sikh and one Indian Christian. Three Moslems were named today, and presumably two will be named later. The three named are opposed to the Moslem League, but all five places will go to the League, if it accepts them, it was stated.

Restraint Is Urged

In an address to the country, the Viceroy, Viscount Wavell, urged "Indians in any authority, in any influence, to show by their good sense and restraint that they are worthy of their country and that their country is worthy of the freedom that it is to receive."

India

Deploring the Calcutta bloodshed, he warned that "a much greater measure of toleration is essential if India is to survive the transition to freedom."

Again he asked the Moslem League to cooperate in the interim and Constitution-making machinery. In the first category he declared that five seats would be allotted to the Moslem League in the Executive Council at any time that it chose to participate. In the long-range evolution he stated that the British Cabinet mission's blueprint would be adhered to, so that the Moslems would obtain proper safeguards.

The Viceroy emphasized that although the Central Government could not interfere in "a very wide sphere of (Provincial) authority, law and order must be maintained in this interim period before the Constitution for an independent India is completed."

Status of Armed Forces

Indicating that the Indian armed forces could not yield to communal differences, he reminded his listeners that the Indian services still owed their allegiance to the King-Emperor.

"The interim Government can be reformed tomorrow if the League decides to come in," said the Viceroy. "Meanwhile, it will administer in the interests of the country as a whole and not of any one party or creed."

The appointment of the new Executive Council culminates a fortnight of discussions between the Viceroy and the Congress party leaders, whom he invited to submit proposals for a suitable panel of names after the Moslem League withdrew from political negotiations.

Although the communal — and political—quotas are the same as those in the Viceroy's offer of June, which was rejected by the Congress party, and first accepted and then rejected by the Moslem League, there is no indication that Mohammed Ali Jinnah, the League president, is prepared to enter this Government.

On the contrary, the League Ministries in Bengal and Sind Province are reported ready to declare the "independence" of their respective Provinces as a protest against the formation of a Congress party-dominated Executive Council.

August 25, 1946

Refugees Tell of Terror in Bengal As Hindu-Moslem Rioting Goes On

Special to THE NEW YORK TIMES.

CALCUTTA, India, Oct. 18 (London Times dispatch)—Unofficial reports reaching Calcutta indicate that acts of violence are continuing on an alarming scale in the districts of Noakhali and Tippera. This is despite the local Government's assurance that the communal situation in eastern Bengal had shown some improvement during the last twenty-four hours.

Hundreds of refugees have reached Calcutta from these districts and they draw a grim picture of the happenings there during the last eight days.

They say that a hundred villages have been burned by hooligans, that hundreds of persons have been butchered or maimed and thousands made homeless and destitute. They report that both districts are infernos of communal fury, and that unless the Government urgently dispatches more troops and police whole minority populations will be wiped out.

[In New Delhi Mohandas K. Gandhi repeated his declaration to Indian women that they should commit suicide rather than submit to dishonor.]

Both Noakhali and Tippera are predominantly Moslem areas. The total population there is just over 5,000,000, and of these only 2,000,000 are Hindus.

The latest reports show that the scenes of the disturbances since yesterday have been moving from Noakhali into Tippera and that they are concentrating in the Chandpur subdivision of that district.

The capital town, Chandpur, is a large railway and river junction toward which refugees are fleeing in an attempt to escape into western Bengal. But most of the roads and the river exits are being guarded by armed rowdies and a large proportion of the cuees has cut into the jungles and swamps to avoid molestation.

Thus far police and military action in the affected areas has been confined to about six firings. The casualties from this source are about twenty killed and an equal number injured.

The total casualties from the riots will perhaps never be known. Official sources [Moslem in Bengal] remain silent over this point but unofficial reports variously estimate the totals between 5,000 and 6,000 killed 1,500 to 2,000 injured. It is reported that a further 50,000 to 60,000 have been forcibly converted to another faith or abducted.

There is grave public anxiety in Calcutta over the inadequacy of the police and military forces dispatched to the stricken areas by the Bengal Government. So far only two companies of troops are known to have been sent to an area covering several hundred square miles. During the August Calcutta riots the authorities had at their disposal about 45,000 troops to protect the city.

Food is another urgent problem. With both railway and river communications seriously dislocated and trade completely at a standstill in most parts of Noakhali and Tippera, thousands face starvation. Local leaders have made urgent representations to the Government to fly food to the starving villages. They have also telegraphed to the Governor of Bengal and the Chief Minister, who at present are at the hill resort of Darjeeling, jointly to visit the affected areas.

The Secretary of the Bengal Hindu Mahasabha party has just received from the Governor's private secretary a message that the Governor proposes to visit Noakhali soon.

Gandhi Advises Suicide

NEW DELHI, India, Oct. 18 (AP)—Mohandas K. Gandhi, "spiritual leader" of the Hindu-led Congress party, again today advised women in eastern Bengal to take their own lives rather than submit to dishonor. In Bombay the provincial Congress party chief called for halting of all business activity as a demonstration of sympathy for riot victims.

Mr. Gandhi said he felt a "call" to go to the trouble areas as soon as the situation in New Delhi permitted. He said that at his request Acharya Kripalani, newly elected president of the Congress party, and Sarat Chandra Bose, recently retired member of the interim Government, had gone to investigate the riot reports.

He was most emphatic in his instructions to women, insisting it was "not an idle idea," and he meant every word he said.

Last night he advised women to suffocate themselves by holding their breath to bring death, but he said tonight that he had been told by physicians that suicide by that means was impossible.

"The only way known to medicine for instant self immolation is strong poisonous doses," he said he was told. He added: "If this is so I would advise every one running the risk of dishonor to take poison before submission to dishonor."

October 19, 1946

MOSLEM LEAGUE JOINS INDIA REGIME

Viceroy, Announcing Accord, Names 5 Members to 14-Man Coalition Government

By The Associated Press.

NEW DELHI, India, Oct. 25—The Moslem League tonight entered the fledgling interim Government to join with the All-India Congress Party in the achieving of Indian independence.

An abatement of the bitter Moslem-Hindu strife that has racked the country may be one of the first tangible results.

The Viceroy, Viscount Wavell, announced the allotment of Ministries in the fourteen-man coalition Government, disclosing that the rival All-India Congress and Moslem League had reached a compromise on an issue that had threatened the Government with dissolution. The Moslems received five portfolios.

Deaths of uncounted thousands, cases of arson, pillage, rape, and forced marriages and religious conversions have occupied leading positions in Indian newspapers for months, overshadowing the political developments.

That the Hindu-Moslem clashes were by no means over, however, were reflected in reports tonight from Calcutta, where eleven persons were reported killed in new outbreaks. For the second night in a row British tanks patrolled trouble spots during curfew hours.

The clashes occurred on the second day of the observance of the Hindu New Year festival. Police clashed with mobs and tram and bus services were stopped in the affected areas.

In Bombay five were killed and fifteen injured in continuing disorders.

The possibility that Congress party Ministers would resign rather than yield any of four important portfolios developed last night, but the compromise found them giving one of the four in question—finance—to the Moslem League.

An authoritative Congress party source said the final agreement included also "satisfactory assurances" from the League that its Ministers would cooperate with the Congress party appointees. The Congress party resisted successfully League demands for one of the top portfolios held by Pandit Jawaharlal Nehru, leading Congress party Minister in the interim Government, or Sardar Vallabhbhai Patel, ranked as No. 2 behind Pandit Nehru.

October 26, 1946

THE COLONIZERS AND THE COLONIZED

Indians Outlaw 'Untouchability' In Formal Action by Assembly

By Reuters.

NEW DELHI, India, April 29—India's Constituent Assembly, discussing the Fundamental Rights Committee's report, today adopted this provision:

"Untouchability in any form is abolished and the imposition of any disability on that account shall be an offense."

This decision by the Constituent Assembly, which does not include the Moslem League, with whom the question of "untouchability" does not arise, sets a constitutional seal on the long campaign against this institution of Hinduism. There are more than 50,000,000 untouchables in India.

[Statutory provisions in British India and in many of the Indian States have long declared against any civil discrimination by reason of caste, but these provisions have not always been enforced when they ran counter to customary religious law and practice.]

"Untouchables"—officially known as Scheduled Castes—may not come into physical contact with caste Hindus. In some parts of the country they may not draw water from public wells, nor may their children enter schools. They gather what learning they can by sitting near the school door.

From these masses India draws her scavengers, sweepers, tanners and many other workers regarded by caste Hindus as "unclean."

Mohandas K. Gandhi, a caste Hindu, has always regarded "untouchability" as the "darkest blot on Hinduism," and first popularized the word "Harijan"—literally "the children of God"—as a synonym for the untouchables. He has campaigned, ceaselessly, for amelioration of their condition on religious grounds.

Fifty-three-year-old Dr. B. R. Ambedkar, leader of the Scheduled Castes Federation, does not see eye to eye with Mr. Gandhi on matters of method, but, since the "Poona Pact" of 1935, which gave the untouchables a chance of representation in the Legislature, for which Dr. Ambedkar worked, both have given their efforts to the abolition of the untouchables' disabilities.

April 30, 1947

GANDHI HAILS BRITAIN FOR DECISION ON INDIA

NEW DELHI, India, May 5 (U.P) —Mohandas K. Gandhi said today that the British decision to leave India was "the noblest act of the British nation." He added that "It would be a good thing if the British were to go today."

The continued presence of British troops, he said, hindered rather than helped India in its progress toward independence because "everybody looks for help to the great military machine they brought into being" instead of being self-reliant.

Mr. Gandhi denied that a partition of India between Moslems and Hindus was needed to solve the communal problem. He pointed out that all his life he had maintained that Indian resistance to British rule should be non-violent. In this connection, he advised Palestine Jews against violence.

"It simply damages your own cause, which otherwise would be a proper cause," Mr. Gandhi said. "You should meet the Arabs and make friends with them and not depend on British or American aid, or any aid save what descends from Jehovah."

May 6, 1947

BRITAIN ACHIEVES SOLUTION IN INDIA; LEADERS ACCEPT IT

Procedure for Partition Is Made Public and Dominion Status Is Offered

SHIFT DUE THIS SUMMER

Parliament to Act Speedily— Churchill Praises Attlee and Mountbatten

By HERBERT L. MATTHEWS
Special to THE NEW YORK TIMES.

LONDON, June 3—The procedure for dividing India, an offer of dominion status and the transfer of British power this summer, and the fact that the Indian leaders had accepted these proposals were all announced today in New Delhi and London.

It was one of the most momentous days in India's long history. But overshadowing all details of the new plan is the astonishing fact that India, and almost certainly Burma—has been kept, at least temporarily, within the framework of the British Commonwealth.

It may well be necessary for the world to reverse its belief that the British Empire is melting away, since India is for all practical purposes, the heart and guts of Britain's Empire. This development seemed impossible only four months ago. Today, there is exultation in London.

Even Winston Churchill, sometimes called the most die-hard of all British believers in the Empire and its historic links to India, got up in the House of Commons and congratulated Prime Minister Attlee and the Viceroy Viscount Mountbatten, on their accomplishment. He conceded that they had succeeded in doing what he had sent Sir Stafford Cripps to India in 1942 to do: to keep India within the British Commonwealth and to get the consent of the major Indian communities to an agreed procedure for the transfer of power.

History Being Made

History was being made fast and furiously today. First, the great news came from New Delhi that the Indian leaders had agreed to work within the new plan. Then came the simultaneous announcements and the reading of the British Government's White Paper containing the details of the plan to both Houses of Parliament.

Meanwhile, the Viceroy, Pandit Jawaharlal Nehru, Mohammed Ali Jinnah and Sardar Baldev Singh were all making broadcasts in India, while here this evening Mr. Attlee also made a brief radio introduction to a rebroadcast of the Viceroy's radio talk. Press conference headlines and stories spread the news like wildfire.

The text of the plan is contained in a brief Government White Paper. It begins by referring to past hopes that the Indians would agree among themselves and by giving credit to the Hindus and Sikhs for setting up a Constituent Assembly in New Delhi and trying to make the Cabinet mission's plan work. It is pointed out that the Moslem League and the Moslems generally refused to participate in the Constituent Assembly.

Won't Frame Constitution

Hence "the task of devising a method by which the wishes of the Indian people can be ascertained has devolved on His Majesty's Government," says the White Paper. It adds that there is no intention to frame an ultimate Constitution for India or to prevent unification in the future.

It goes on to say that present Constituent Assembly will continue, but that its decisions cannot apply to those regions unwilling to accept its jurisdiction.

Hence a plan is offered to ascertain whether the people in those other regions want to form a separate Constituent Assembly.

The procedure is then suggested for getting the Legislative Assemblies of Bengal and the Punjab to decide whether those provinces should be divided, with western Punjab and eastern Bengal going to Pakistan. Rough boundary divi-

India

THE BRITISH PLAN FOR THE PARTITION OF INDIA

June 4, 1947

The shaded regions within the heavy black borders comprise the area from which the Moslem nation of Pakistan is to be evolved; the unshaded territories within these borders are Princely States. Under the British program, the Sylhet district in Assam (1) will hold a referendum to decide whether to join Moslem eastern Bengal if Bengal (2) is partitioned. The Provincial Legislatures of Bengal and the Punjab (3) will meet in Moslem and non-Moslem sections to decide on partition. A referendum in the North-West Frontier Province (4) is provided for, contingent upon the action taken in the Punjab; the Legislature of Sind (5) will make its decision at a special meeting, and Baluchistan (6) will have an opportunity to consider its position. The unshaded areas in the rest of India are states conceded to be Hindu or Princely States.

sions are suggested for voting purposes, but the final boundaries, if there is partition, would be settled by boundary commissions.

The Legislative Assembly of the Province of Sind will make its decision whether to join Pakistan. The North-West Frontier Province, which although overwhelmingly Moslem has a Congress party Government and participates in the Constituent Assembly, will have a popular referendum to choose Pakistan or Hindustan.

Baluchistan will likewise receive an opportunity to make a similar decision but the procedure for this is still being studied.

In Assam the Sylhet District, which is Moslem, will get an opportunity to join eastern Bengal in Pakistan, if Bengal decides upon partition.

The plan then briefly details the voting procedure for Constituent Assemblies so far as Bengal and the Punjab are concerned, supposing that they decide upon partition.

The next section of the White Paper touches on the administrative consequences that will have to be faced in so far as the British Government and the Indian Central and Provincial Governments are concerned.

In one sentence it is stated that the tribes of the northwest will have to deal with the appropriate Indian authority later, and another sentence tells the Princely rulers that this plan has nothing to do with them.

One paragraph is devoted to the "necessity for speed". Then comes the fateful announcement offering dominion status "as the most efficacious and indeed the only practical way of effecting an immediate transfer of power.

"This will be without prejudice to the right of the Indian Constituent Assembly to decide in due course whether or not the part of India in respect of which they have authority will remain within the British Commonwealth", says the White Paper in conclusion.

Quick Action Stressed

Today's tremendous mobilization of energy was calculated, for one of the keynotes of the whole situation is quick action. That is stressed in the plan, it was emphasized by every speaker and driven home to Britons and Indians alike.

Speed is needed here to prepare the legislation for the transfer of power and for Dominion Status. Speed, above all, is needed in India where the communities are almost waging civil war and where one of the most complicated administrative tasks in history faces Indian and British leaders.

The Provinces will have only three, or at most four, weeks to decide whether the Punjab Bengal and Assam will be partitioned and whether the Northwest Frontier Province, Sind and Baluchistan really want to join Pakistan — which they undoubtedly do.

The British Parliament goes into recess at the end of July and therefore it is in the next month that all these developments must get legal sanction. Mr. Churchill promised today that the Conservatives would not make the new India bill a source of controversy, but even so it is a heavy task to complete in so short a time.

Change of Mind Feared

Above all, the British want to rush things through before the Indian leaders have too much time for second thoughts. As always with India, one must inject notes of caution.

Acceptance of general principles has proved much easier in India than the working out of practical details. None of the three great communities—Hindu, Moslem and Sikh—is fully satisfied. Each is hoping to gain advantages; each will be suspicious of the other; all will be importuning Britain.

For today's remarkable achievement two men received the heartfelt thanks of the British people. Tributes to Lord Mountbatten came from Mr. Attlee, Mr. Churchill, Mr. Jinnah, Pandit Nehru and many others. He is credited with having performed a virtual miracle.

But today's triumph goes in an even greater measure to Mr. Attlee and his Labor party advisers whose policies have saved India for Britain.

The House of Commons today was a mutual admiration society. For those who remembered Mr. Churchill's frequent and bitter references to the Labor party's Indian policy his statement today was very impressive.

When he said that the "conditions of the Cripps mission, which were set up under my administration, seem to have been fulfilled" the Labor benches broke into applause.

"The many nations and states of India may find their unity within the mysterious circle of the British Crown," Mr. Churchill continued, "just in the same way as the self-governing Dominions have done for so many years after all other links with the mother country, save those of sentiment, have been dissolved. It may therefore be that through a form of partition the union of all India may none the less be preserved."

Referring to the debate that will have to take place later, Mr. Churchill said:

"It would not be right that such legislation should be deemed contentious or that any long delay should elapse after it has been introduced before it is passed into law."

The leader of the Opposition paid this remarkable tribute to the head of the Labor party:

"If the hopes which are enshrined in this statement should be borne out, great credit will, indeed, be due to the Viceroy and not only to him but to the Prime Minister who advised His Majesty to appoint him."

June 4, 1947

THE COLONIZERS AND THE COLONIZED

INDIA AND PAKISTAN BECOME NATIONS; CLASHES CONTINUE

Ceremonies at New Delhi and Karachi Mark Independence for 400,000,000 Persons

NEHRU ACCLAIMS GANDHI

But He Warns of Trials Ahead—Death Toll in Communal Fighting Reaches 153

By ROBERT TRUMBULL
Special to THE NEW YORK TIMES.

NEW DELHI, Friday, Aug. 15—India achieved her long-sought independence today through the transfer of British power to the two dominions into which that land of 400,000,000 persons has been divided, India and Pakistan.

While the ceremonies marking this major historic event were taking place communal strife continued to cast a grim shadow over the future.

[Communal clashes, fires and looting continued in Lahore, Punjab, with the rising death toll estimated at 153, The Associated Press reported. In London King George conferred an earldom on Viscount Mountbatten for his role in solving the Indian problem and the Government made available to the Indian Government £35,000,000 of India's sterling balance.]

The Dominion of India reached the goal of freedom here at midnight with minimum celebration and a few speeches that stressed the gravity of the tasks ahead of the new nation.

In Karachi, capital of Pakistan, Mohammed Ali Jinnah will take the oath this morning as Governor General of the Moslem dominion which he was the primary figure in creating against the demand for a united India.

Viceroy at Both Ceremonies

This ceremony at the Sind Provincial Government House, which is now Mr. Jinnah's official residence, will be the only event marking the transfer of power from British to Indian hands in that dominion.

The Viceroy, Viscount Mountbatten, addressed the Pakistan Constituent Assembly yesterday—his last official act as Viceroy—and then flew back to New Delhi to attend the formal transfer here.

No special events were scheduled in Karachi, as they were in New Delhi, to mark the actual moment when the rule of the King-Emperor came to an end at midnight except in so far as both dominions continued to owe formal allegiance to the British crown.

Mohandas K. Gandhi, the real hero of the New Delhi ceremony, was absent from the capital of his country in its triumphant hour. At the moment his great dream came true—though not precisely in the form he wished—Mr. Gandhi was in humble surroundings of his own choosing among the Moslems of Calcutta, where he felt he was needed more. But his name was publicly praised by others who remained here to carry on the work to which he has devoted his life.

Climax at Midnight

The Constituent Assembly of the Government of India assumed its sovereign power solemnly in a special session that began at 11 P. M. last night and reached its climax at twelve o'clock. As the hands of the clock in the stately assembly hall of the State Council building met at midnight India's Cabinet Ministers and Members of the Assembly listened in silence to the chimes of the hour.

As the last note died an unidentified member blew a conch shell of the kind used in Hindu temples to summon the gods to witness a great event. Instantly a great cheer arose. India at that moment had become a free member of the British Commonwealth of Nations — free even to leave the commonwealth if she chooses.

The members then stood and repeated after the Assembly President, Dr. Rajendra Prasad, this oath in Hindi and then in English:

"At this solemn moment when the people of India, through suffering and sacrifice, have secured freedom, I, a member of the Constituent Assembly of India, dedicate myself in all humility to the service of India and her people to the end that this ancient land attain her rightful place in the world and make her full and willing contribution to the promotion of world peace and the welfare of mankind."

Then in accordance with a formal motion made by President Prasad and approved by the Assembly, the President and Pandit Jawaharlal Nehru, Prime Minister of the Dominion Government, drove half a mile, to the Viceroy's house—now to be known as Government House—and passed to Viscount Mountbatten two momentous announcements.

Viscount Mountbatten, who ceased to be Viceroy at midnight and thus at that moment ended the long and sometimes illustrious line of British statesmen in India, was told by Dr. Prasad and Pandit Nehru first, that the Constituent Assembly of India had assumed the power of governance of this country and, second, that the same Assembly had endorsed a recommendation that Viscount Mountbatten be Governor General of India from today.

The Chief Justice of India will administer the oath of office to

TWO INDIAN NATIONS EMERGE ON WORLD SCENE

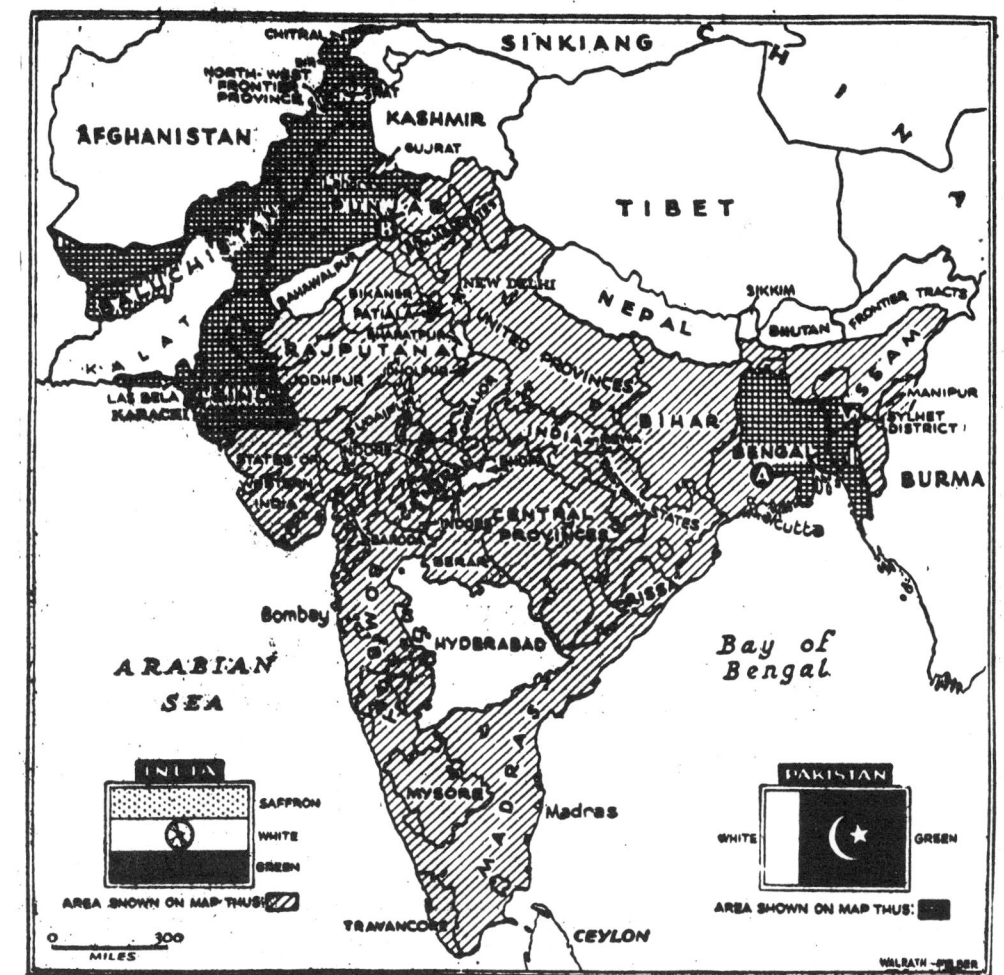

The New York Times   Aug. 15, 1947

Princely states that have not yet adhered to either India or Pakistan are shown without shading. Pakistan has recognized the independence of Kalat, on the Arabian Sea. The boundaries running through Bengal (A) and the Punjab (B) are to be announced by a commission.

India

Viscount Mountbatten at 8:30 o'clock this morning after which the new Governor General will swear in the Indian Cabinet, headed by Pandit Nehru. Later in the morning Viscount Mountbatten will make his inaugural address to the Constituent Assembly.

Thousands at Council Building

Ten thousand Indians crowded about the entrance to the huge round Council of State building as the hour drew near for the Constituent Assembly's historic night meeting. Shopping centers of New Delhi and the adjacent ancient city of Delhi were gay with strings of the new national flag—saffron, white and dark green—the colors of the All-India Congress party—with the symbolic wheel of the great Emperor Asoka.

Unusual crowds were on the streets in both cities. Public buildings and Hindu temples were outlined in electric lights.

A large illuminated flag painted on glass decorated the porch roof of Pandit Nehru's home.

There was, however, little of gaiety that would be associated with such an event as this in the Occident. It is said that exuberance is foreign to the Indian nature though there was no lack of shouting by the crowd at the Council of State building.

Pandit Nehru on entering and leaving received a tremendous ovation and the surging crowd soon broke through the police lines but there was no real disorder, and after the ceremony they soon dispersed.

Stars Held Inauspicious

As a matter of fact the enthusiasm for independence day was dampened by two factors. One was the division of India into Moslem and Hindu nations, leaving large and unhappy minorities in each dominion. The other—a peculiarly Hindu thing that the West might mistakenly underestimate in importance—was the fact that astrologers, on whom millions of Hindus place great dependence in all matters, discovered an inauspicious mating of the stars on Aug. 15. In India this last is a serious consideration that receives no little attention in the press.

Tonight's program in the Assembly was bilingual, most of the speakers, including President Rajendra Prasad and Pandit Nehru, employing Hindi first and then English. The official language of the Assembly is still a matter of debate in which, for sentimental reasons, English is losing out to Urdu and Hindi.

The ceremony opened at 11 P. M. with the singing by a trio of sari-clad women of Vande Mataram composed by the wife of Acharya J. B. Kripalani, President of the All India Congress party.

After President Prasad spoke the entire assembly arose and observed two minutes of silence "in memory of those who died in the struggle for freedom in India and elsewhere."

Dr. Prasad paid tribute to Mr. Gandhi whom he called "our beacon light, our guide and philosopher during the last thirty years or more."

Nehru Sees Trials Ahead

"And now the time has come when we shall redeem our pledge, not wholly or in full measure, but very substantially," Pandit Nehru began, "At the stroke of the midnight hour, when the world sleeps, India will awake to life and freedom." Pandit Nehru dwelt upon the trials that follow the assumption of such great responsibilities as are India's in the days to follow. He called upon his countrymen for an "ending of poverty, ignorance, disease and inequality of opportunity."

Referring to Mr. Gandhi, he said: "The ambition of the greatest man of our generation has been to wipe every tear from every eye. That may be beyond us, but so long as there are tears and suffering, so long our work will not be over."

He reminded India of the indivisibility of "one world" and demanded an end to "petty and destructive criticism * * * ill-will, or the blaming of others"

Pandit Nehru then moved the resolution for the solemn oath which all members took standing at midnight. He was seconded by a Moslem, Chaudry Khaliquzzaman, leader of the Moslem League party in the Constituent Assembly, who promised the fealty of India's Moslems to their state.

Sir S. Radhakrishnan, noted Indian philosopher, paid tribute to the British and asked Indians to look within themselves for faults that in the past had made the Indians "ready victims" for the imperialists.

"From midnight on," he said, "we cannot crowd blame on the British." He called for an end to "nepotism and corruption, which have been a blot on the great name of this country."

August 15, 1947

BANDS ORGANIZE MASSACRES IN INDIA

By ROBERT TRUMBULL
Special to The New York Times.

NEW DELHI, Sept. 13—In India today blood flows oftener than rain falls. No man, woman or child is safe to go where he pleases in this land where primeval savagery has been let loose by religious passion.

In the last two years I have seen every country in Asia and seen a lot of bloody things, but nothing quite like this. For myself I can say that I have never been as shaken by anything, even by the piled-up bodies on Tarawa beachhead, as when a shrieking band of half-dressed Sikhs surrounded my railway train in the Punjab desert, waving spears and battle-axes, their unshorn black hair and beards streaming in the wind.

Since then I have seen dead by the hundreds and, worst of all, hundreds of living Indians without eyes or hands or feet. Thousands of girls are captive in the Punjab—what is happening to them can only be imagined. Among the bodies of the females left behind in the burned villages every nameless mutilation can be seen.

Religious fury has transgressed every civilized bound. Death by shooting is merciful in this war—and uncommon. Men, women and children are more commonly beaten to death with clubs and stones or butchered with knives, spears or axes and left to die slowly with their death agony intensified by heat and flies. The language needs some new words to describe what is happening.

The killing has been well organized. Always it has been by gangs setting upon defenseless individuals or groups. It is not like armies fighting, but rather like organized guerrilla warfare in which sometimes a knowledge of fundamental military tactics is shown. That is not strange, for many marauders are army veterans and some of this wholesale murder has been committed by units of the Indian Army charged with restoring peace. Police have also participated. No one in the troubled areas can feel secure unless his area is guarded by troops or police of his own religious persuasion.

Attacks on Villages

Attacks on villages, usually by night, have been the commonest form of communal onslaught. Men of one village—sometimes women, even children have participated—would set out with whatever weapons they had to assault a near-by village inhabited by people of a different religious persuasion.

While guards were being overwhelmed the defenders would gather womenfolk and children in the central compound surrounded by high mud walls. Soon fire bombs or wads of burning, oil-soaked rags would rain upon the thatched roofs and in a moment the entire village would be engulfed in flames. While men were being shot, speared or battle-axed to death by the invaders in far superior numbers, the women and children trapped in the compound would be dying in the holocaust.

Thus a village is annihilated. Most Indians keep their wealth in coins or jewelry secreted about the home. Whatever homes were not destroyed in the fire would be looted. The inhabitants who might survive would be paupers, afraid to return to their ancestral lands which would now go untilled.

If the attack is made upon a larger settlement there is an orgy of looting and raping. Instances are told of defenders slaying their women rather than letting them fall into the hands of assailants. This is a custom of ancient standing among the Rajputs, dating back to feudal days.

Sadistic Cruelties

In some places in the Punjab, notably Sheikapura, victorious in-

INDIA'S RELIGIONS

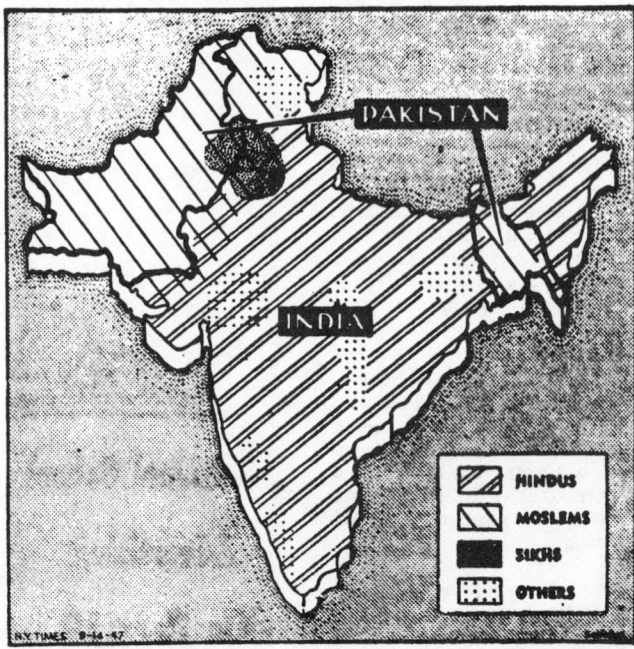

- ▨ HINDUS
- ◹ MOSLEMS
- ■ SIKHS
- ▦ OTHERS

Of India's vast population, 276,000,000 are Hindus, 88,000,000 are Moslems and 5,500,000 are Sikhs.

THE COLONIZERS AND THE COLONIZED

vaders have let their sadistic instincts have full rein, going about from house to house violating and mutilating women, chopping hands and feet from children or jabbing out their eyes.

It is not only the villages whose inhabitants are of one religion that are burned, looted and denuded of all life. Some of the worst trouble is in mixed communities where Hindus and Moslems have lived side by side for centuries. In these places—and they include the great Punjab city of Lahore—communal strife is even more terrible, because one never knows when one will be struck down by a neighbor.

Lahore, capital city of the rich province of the Punjab, was about half Moslem and half non-Moslem. Today, of about half a million Hindus and Sikhs, only a few hundred are left in Lahore. The homes and business establishments of those who are left or were killed are now either looted and burned or occupied by Moslems.

In the cities of Delhi and New Delhi, where serious communal rioting broke out last week, there was a similar balance of population until the Hindu and Sikh refugees flooded in by hundreds of thousands.

The wholesale killing in towns and villages has now passed the peak—at least as far as the Punjab is concerned—because there are few minorities left in the settlements. Now, the refugees who travel the roads of the Punjab by tens of thousands—it is estimated that a million persons on each side of the India-Pakistan border have fled their homes—are bait for marauding bands. Armed groups of one religion or the other roam about the countryside looking for people to kill.

Christians Not Harmed

Eight million Christians in India, half of them Catholics, are generally unmolested in the present disturbances. Christian missionaries are offering such aid as they can to refugees and evacuating Christians to places outside the disturbed zones. Many Indian Christians wear crosses pinned to their shirts indicating that they are neutrals.

As this week draws to a close the rioting has subsided, owing partly to satiety, partly to the Governments' taking hold of the situation. However, there is a dearth of news from Pakistan. Who started this slaughter is beside the point at the moment. Both sides are equally bloodthirsty and ruthless, now that the war is on. Accurate figures will never be available, but authenticated accounts of mass murder and unspeakable atrocities come in equal numbers from Moslem Pakistan and Hindu-Sikh India. There is blood on the flags of both new nations.

Organized slaughter such as I have seen could only have taken form at someone's instigation. In this connection it may be significant that raids have followed the same pattern in widely separated places. It may be important or not that spears and battleaxes in use throughout vast areas are of identical design.

Considerable suspicion has been directed at the Sikh princely states such as Patiala, Faridkot and Kapurthala. It has been pretty definitely established that raiding Sikh bands have their headquarters inside the borders of these principalities ruled by Sikh Maharajahs.

Religious Hatred

There can be no doubt that religious hatred was fed by the Moslem campaign for the separate Moslem nation of Pakistan. That ambition has been achieved.

By fixing of borders between India and Pakistan there was created a promised land for Moslems who felt themselves depressed among the overwhelmingly Hindu population. By the same action there was brought into being a minority people in Pakistan—Hindus—who, though not yet depressed, had reason to believe they might become so. To them especially, when the current massacre of minorities began, the Dominion of India became their sanctuary.

The partition of India left many millions of Hindus in Pakistan, and a comparable number of Moslems in Hindu India. The leaders of both new nations urged these minorities to stay where they were and guaranteed protection. These leaders were simply not in a position to make such guarantees on behalf of the ignorant fanatical masses. Events proved that these assurances were worthless.

Sikhs have been blamed for much of the trouble in the Punjab border area. Their particular complaint has been a division of the main Sikh community of more than three million between Pakistan and India, in almost equal numbers. Even some of the Sikh holy places have gone to Pakistan under the boundary award. On these points the martially minded Sikhs have been the most challenging and bellicose of all groups in India.

Racial Brethren

But after all, Hindus, Sikhs and Moslems are brother Indians by race. There are, of course, differences in ancestral origin, some being descended from the aborigines of this land, others from the conquerors who came from various countries. In past centuries they have, on the whole, been fused to some extent.

But, in addition, the opposed communities have been molded for centuries into different patterns by their varied modes of life, which have been sternly set by the force of religion.

Some of the feeling now being given such tragically free rein may be traceable to economic causes, though these again are bound up with religion. Though we find many instances of the poor rising against the rich, in the Punjab it is the poor Moslem rebelling against the rich Hindu. There is a growing movement toward a better deal for India's terribly depressed masses. But this particular development emerging in Indian life is no important factor in the current bloodshed.

Whatever may be behind the behavior pattern which manifests itself in India's madness may be left to psychologists. How to bring sanity to these two nations is the immediate practical problem. The same leaders who so recently counseled minorities to stay put, now concede reluctantly that a tremendous exchange of populations must take place. It has taken place. It is conservatively estimated that 1,000,000 Hindus have moved to India from Pakistan, and an equal number of Moslems from India to Pakistan. These numbers could, perhaps, be doubled—no one will ever know, for this is a country remarkably sterile in statistics.

Among individual Indians, the one figure with far-reaching influence is Gandhi. By force of his personality he succeeded in pacifying the unruly city of Calcutta, the scene of some of India's maddest bloodshed for three weeks in the most critical period following partition of the country. When violence finally did break out, he resorted to the only means left to him. He fasted until another full day went by with none killed. If in trying to keep peace in India 78-year-old Gandhi fasts again and should die—what we have seen of violence to date will be as nothing.

September 14, 1947

GANDHI IS KILLED BY A HINDU; INDIA SHAKEN, WORLD MOURNS; 15 DIE IN RIOTING IN BOMBAY

By ROBERT TRUMBULL
Special to The New York Times.

NEW DELHI, India, Jan. 30—Mohandas K. Gandhi was killed by an assassin's bullet today. The assassin was a Hindu who fired three shots from a pistol at a range of three feet.

The 78-year-old Gandhi, who was the one person who held discordant elements together and kept some sort of unity in this turbulent land, was shot down at 5:15 P. M. as he was proceeding through the Birla House gardens to the pergola from which he was to deliver his daily prayer meeting message.

The assassin was immediately seized.

He later identified himself as Nathuran Vinayak Godse, 36, a Hindu of the Mahratta tribes in Poona. This has been a center of resistance to Gandhi's ideology.

Mr. Gandhi died twenty-five minutes later. His death left all India stunned and bewildered as to the direction that this newly independent nation would take without its "Mahatma" (Great Teacher).

The loss of Mr. Gandhi brings this country of 300,000,000 abruptly to a crossroads. Mingled with the sadness in this capital tonight was an undercurrent of fear and uncertainty, for now the strongest influence for peace in India that this generation has known is gone.

[Communal riots quickly swept Bombay when news of Mr. Gandhi's death was received. The Associated Press reported that fifteen persons were killed and more than fifty injured before an uneasy peace was established.]

Appeal Made By Nehru

Prime Minister Pandit Jawaharlal Nehru, in a voice choked with emotion, appealed in a radio address tonight for a sane approach to the future. He asked that India's path be turned away from violence in memory of the great peacemaker who had departed.

Mr. Gandhi's body will be cremated in the orthodox Hindu fashion according to his often expressed wishes. His body will be carried from his New Delhi residence on a simple wooden cot covered with a sheet at 11:30 tomorrow morning.

India

MOHANDAS K. GANDHI

The funeral procession will wind through every principal street of the two cities of New and Old Delhi and reach the burning ghats on the bank of the sacred Jumna River at about 4 P. M. There the remains of the greatest Indian since Gautama Buddha will be wrapped in a sheet, laid on a pyre of wood and burned. His ashes will be scattered on the Jumna's waters, eventually to mingle with the Ganges where the two holy rivers meet at the temple city of Allahabad.

These simple ceremonies were announced tonight by Pandit Nehru in respect to Mr. Gandhi's wishes, although many of the leaders desired that his body be embalmed and exhibited in state. India will see the last of Mr. Gandhi as it saw him when he lived—a humble and unassuming Hindu.

News Spreads Quickly

News of the assassination of Mr. Gandhi—only a few days after he had finished a five-day fast to bring about communal friendship—spread quickly through New Delhi. Immediately there was spontaneous movement of thousands to Birla House, home of G. D. Birla, the millionaire industrialist, where Mr. Gandhi and his six secretaries had been guests since he came to New Delhi in the midst of the disturbances in India's capital.

While walking through the gardens to this evening's prayer meeting Mr. Gandhi had just reached the top of a short flight of brick steps, his slender brown arms around the shoulders of his granddaughters, Manu, 17, and Ava, 20.

Someone spoke to him and he turned from his granddaughters and gave the appealing Hindu salute—palms together and the points of the fingers brought to the chin as in a Christian attitude of prayer.

At once a youngish Indian stepped from the crowd—which had opened to form a pathway for Mr. Gandhi's walk to the pergola—and fired the fatal shots from a European-made pistol. One bullet struck Mr. Gandhi in the chest and two in the abdomen on the right side. He seemed to lean forward and then crumpled to the ground. His two granddaughters fell beside him in tears.

Crowd Is Stunned

A crowd of about 500, according to witnesses, was stunned. There was no outcry or excitement for a second or two. Then the onlookers began to push the assassin more as if in bewilderment than in anger.

The assassin was seized by Tom Reiner of Lancaster, Mass., a vice consul attached to the American Embassy and a recent arrival in India. He was attending Mr. Gandhi's prayer meeting out of curiosity, as most visitors to New Delhi do at least once.

Mr. Reiner grasped the assailant by the shoulders and shoved him toward several police guards. Only then did the crowd begin to grasp what had happened and a forest of fists belabored the assassin as he was dragged toward the pergola where Mr. Gandhi was to have prayed. He left a trail of blood.

Mr. Gandhi was picked up by attendants and carried rapidly back to the unpretentious bedroom where he had passed most of his working and sleeping hours. As he was taken through the door Hindu onlookers who could see him began to wail and beat their breasts.

Less than half an hour later a member of Mr. Gandhi's entourage came out of the room and said to those about the door:

"Bapu (father) is finished."

But it was not until Mr. Gandhi's death was announced by All India Radio at 6 P. M. that the word spread widely.

Assassin Taken Away

Meanwhile the assassin was aken to a police station. He identifed himself as coming from Poona.

It was remarked that the first of three attempts on Mr. Gandhi's life was made in Poona on June 25, 1934, when a bomb was thrown at a car believed to be Mr. Gandhi's. Poona is a center of the extremist anti-Gandhi orthodox Hindu Mahasabha (Great Society).

The second possible attempt to assassinate Mr. Gandhi was by means of a crude bomb planted on his garden wall on Jan. 20 of this year.

The only statement known to have been made by the assassin was his remark to a foreign correspondent: "I am not at all sorry."

He is large for a Hindu and was dressed in gray slacks, blue pullover and khaki bush jacket. His pistol, which was snatched from him immediately after the shooting by Royal Indian Air Force Flight Sergeant D. R. Singh, contained four undischarged cartridges.

Lying on a wooden cot in his bedroom, Mr. Gandhi said no word before his death except once to ask for water. Most of the time he was unconscious. When he was pronounced dead by his physician weeping members of his staff covered the lower half of his face with a sheet in the Hindu fashion and the women present sat on the floor and chanted verses from the sacred scriptures of the Hindus. Those who could see these ceremonies through the windows knew then that Mr. Gandhi had expired.

Pandit Nehru arrived at about 6 o'clock. Silently and with burning eyes he inspected the spot where Mr. Gandhi was shot and then went into the house without a word. Later he stood high on the front gate of Birla House and related the tentative funeral arrangements to several thousand persons gathered in the street and blocking all traffic. His voice shook with grief and hundreds in the crowd were weeping uncontrollably.

Several thousand mourners formed orderly and quiet queues at all doors leading into Birla House and for a time they were permitted to file past the body. Later when it became evident that only a small fraction of the gathering would be able to view Mr. Gandhi's remains tonight, the body was taken to a second-floor balcony and placed on a cot tilted under a floodlamp so all in the grounds would see their departed leader.

His head was illuminated by a lamp with five wicks representing the five elements—air, light, water, earth and fire—and also to light his soul to eternity according to Hindu belief.

Pandit Nehru delivered Mr. Gandhi's valedictory in his radio address late this evening. In a quivering voice he said:

"Gandhi has gone out of our lives and there is darkness everywhere. * * * The father of our nation is no more—no longer will we run to him for advice and solace. * * * This is a terrible blow to millions and millions in this country. * * *

"Our light has gone out, but the light that shone in this country was no ordinary light. For a thousand years that light will be seen in this country and the world will see it * * * Oh, that this has happened to us! There was so much more to do."

Referring to the assassin Pandit Nehru said:

"I can only call him a madman."

He pleaded for a renewed spirit of peace, which had been Mr. Gandhi's last project, saying:

"His spirit looks upon us—nothing would displease him more than to see us indulge in violence. All our petty conflicts and difficulties must be ended in the face of this great disaster * * * In his death he has reminded us of the big things in life."

Enmity Incurred

Mr. Gandhi's pleas for tolerance since the far-reaching communal warfare of last August and September had earned him the enmity of extremist elements, notably the Hindu Mahasabha which condemned his fast for inter-religious unity and whose leaders refused to sign his peace pledge. There was also a widespread condemnation of Mr. Gandhi's forgiving attitude among the refugees who had suffered deeply at Moslem hands in the West Punjab.

More serious to India perhaps than loss of Mr. Gandhi's restraining influence on fanatic passions may be the political implications of his death. Though he held no office he was the central figure of India's dominant Congress party and the last of the "old guard" in the long struggle for liberation from foreign rule.

Some Indian observers were predicting tonight that Mr. Gandhi's death would inevitably be followed by a fission in the Congress party and the emergence of a new political pattern after a period of deep confusion.

January 31, 1948

THE COLONIZERS AND THE COLONIZED

ALGERIA

ALGERIA.

A telegram from Algiers, of May 4, says:—The Emperor Napoleon has issued the following proclamation to the inhabitants of Algeria:

THE EMPEROR, TO THE INHABITANTS OF ALGERIA.

"I come among you, to learn in person, your interests, to second your efforts, and to assure you that the protection of the mother-country shall not fail you. You have for a long time past combatted with energy two obstacles—a virgin soil and a warlike people; but better days are at hand. On the one side private companies are about to develop by their industry and their capital, the fertilitity of the land; on the other, the Arabs, restrained, and enlightened with regard to our own benevolent intentions, will no longer be able to disturb the tranquility of the country. Have faith then, in the future. Become attached to the land which you cultivate as to a new Fatherland, and treat the Arabs, in the midst of whom you must dwell, as fellow-countrymen. We must be the masters, because we are the more civilized; we must be generous, because we are the stronger. Let us, then, justify unceasingly, the glorious act of one of my predecessors, who, in planting, thirty-five years ago, on the soil of Africa the banner of France and the cross, unfurled at once the sign of civilization and the symbol of peace and charity."

The Emperor is still making excursions into the environs of the town of Algiers. His Majesty's health continues excellent.

May 22, 1865

THE EMPEROR IN ALGIERS.

THE ADDRESS TO THE ARABS.

The following is the full text of the proclamation addressed by the Emperor NAPOLEON to the Arabs:

ALGIERS, May 5.

When, 35 years ago, France placed her foot on the African soil, she did not come to destroy its nationality, but, on the contrary, to elevate the people from long-continued oppression; she has replaced the Turkish domination by another government, milder, juster, and more enlightened. Nevertheless, during the first years, impatient of foreign supremacy, you combated your liberators.

Far from me be the idea of considering it a crime; on the contrary, I honor the feeling of warlike dignity which led you, before submitting, to invoke by arms the judgment of God. But God has pronounced; acknowledge, therefore, the decrees of Providence, which, in its mysterious designs, often guides us to a good end by disappointing our hopes and deluding our efforts.

Twenty centuries ago, our ancestors, like yourselves, courageously resisted a foreign invasion, but from their defeat dates their generation. The vanquished Gauls became assimilated to the victorious Romans; and from the forced union of the contrasted virtues of two opposing civilizations there arose, in the course of time, that French nationality which in its turn has propagated its ideas throughout the whole world. Who knows if a day will not come when the Arab race, regenerated and blended with the French, shall not regain a powerful individuality similar to that which for ages made it mistress of the southern shores of the Mediterranean?

Accept, then, accomplished facts. Your prophet declares, "GOD gives power to whomsoever He wills."—(Chapter ii, of the Cow, verse 248.) Now the power I hold from Him I wish to exercise in your interest and for your advantage. You know my intentions; I have irrevocably insured to you the property of the lands you occupy; I intend to augment your well-being, and to make you participate more and more in the administration of your country, and in the blessings of civilization; but it is on the condition that you, on your part, will respect those who represent my authority. Tell your erring brethren that an attempt at fresh insurrection would be fatal to them. Two millions of Arabs cannot resist forty millions of Frenchmen—a struggle of one against twenty is madness. You have, besides, sworn allegiance to me, and your conscience, like your sacred book, obliges you religiously to keep your engagements,—(Chapter viii. Of Repentance, verse 4.)

I thank the great majority amongst you whose fidelity has not been shaken by the perfidious counsels of fanaticism and ignorance. You have understood that, being your sovereign, I am your protector; all those who live under our laws have an equal claim to my solicitude. Great reminiscences and powerful interests already unite you to the mother country. For the last ten years you have shared the glory of our arms, and your sons have combated nobly by the side of our own in the Crimea, in Italy, in China and in Mexico. The ties formed on the field of battle are indissoluble, and you have learnt to know our value both as friends and enemies. Have confidence, then, in your destinies, as they are united to those of France, and acknowledge with the Koran, that "He that God leads is well led."—(Chapter 7, El Araf, verse 177.)

NAPOLEON.

May 28, 1865

DE GAULLE, GIRAUD IMPLEMENT ACCORD

Committee Equalizes Pay of French and Native Troops.

By Wireless to THE NEW YORK TIMES.

ALGIERS, Aug. 3—Sealing the agreement of last Saturday, whereby all French fighting forces are united under Gen. Henri Honoré Giraud, while Gen. Charles de Gaulle became permanent chairman of the new Committee of National Defense, the two generals, in letters made public tonight, hailed the settlement in perhaps the most cordial terms they have yet exchanged.

At the same time General de Gaulle and General Giraud, in separate orders of the day to the French forces, expressed, each in his own way, General Giraud's slogan: "Un seul but—la victoire [a single aim—victory]." General de Gaulle called on the former Fighting French Army to accept General Giraud as its chief.

The French Committee of National Liberation met this morning under General de Gaulle's chairmanship. It achieved certain reforms suggesting the democratization of the French colonial set-up that may be regarded by General de Gaulle as the shape of things to come on a larger scale. At Gen. Georges Catroux's initiative, several regulations were promulgated to improve the condition of Moslems in Algeria. The pay of Algerian soldiers was raised to equal that of Europeans.

August 4, 1943

Algeria

Algiers Interns 2 High Arabs

ALGIERS, Sept. 23 (U.P.) — The Algerian Government today announced the internment of two high-ranking Arabic financial figures for provoking civil disobedience, trying to impede the functioning of public institutions and disturbing public order during war. They were Sayah Abdelkader, president of the Arabic section of the financial committee, and Ferhat Abbas.

September 24, 1943

ARABS KILL 50 IN ALGERIA

Europeans Murdered During V-E Day Festivities—Inquiry Begun

ALGIERS, May 12 (AP)—More than fifty Europeans were reported massacred in the Algerian Department of Constantine by Arab agitators during victory celebrations, it was announced today.

The announcement said the Governor General had taken strong action and police and the military had made many arrests. The announcement said victims were mutilated and houses were pillaged during the outbreak.

May 13, 1945

ALGERIAN RESULT CALLED SURPRISE

Arab Nationalists Had Almost No Opportunity to Prepare Election Campaign

By CLIFTON DANIEL
By Wireless to The New York Times.

CAIRO, Egypt, June 4—Recently released from prison, Algerian Moslem nationalists who desire an autonomous Algerian government federated with France won a surprising victory in Sunday's election, a victory that is sure to encourage eastern Arab nationalists campaigning for the independence of French North African territories.

Manifesting considerably more popular strength than the French authorities had generally conceded to them, the nationalists captured eleven of the thirteen seats available to Moslem non-citizens of Algeria, which is now administered as a province of France. Their showing was particularly remarkable because the movement's leaders, imprisoned during the suppression of nationalist manifestations in Algeria in May, 1945, had been released only in March and had publicly reconstituted their prohibited party and produced their list of candidates only fifteen days before the election.

Not having participated in previous elections, they are sending a delegation to the Constituent Assembly for the first time. Their party—the Democratic Union of the Manifesto — campaigning against French "colonial domination," won almost two-thirds of the popular vote in the Departments of Algiers and Oran. The returns from the Department of Constantine are not available here. The "manifesto" is the party's statement of its demands on the French Government, whose presentation preceded the nationalist manifestations last year. Farhart Abbas, a druggist of Sétif, is the party's leader.

Algeria's population is divided into two electoral colleges each with thirteen seats in the Assembly. One, numbering 501,000 registered voters, is composed of citizens of French origin and a Moslem "élite" on whom French citizenship has been conferred. The other, numbering 1,341,000, is composed of Moslem non-citizens. It was in the second college that the Democratic Union won eleven seats, the two others going to the French Socialist party, which advocated a single electoral college.

June 5, 1946

INDO-CHINA REVOLT FATEFUL TO FRANCE

Other Empire Areas Watching Outcome of Dissidence in Troubled East Asia

A TEST FOR BLUM'S REGIME

Communist Influence Is Seen at Work, but Party Has Not Clarified Line in Paris

By C. L. SULZBERGER
Special to The New York Times.

PARIS, Dec. 24 — Unless the weak, temporary and minority Government of Léon Blum can find material ways to implement its leader's pledges to put an end to the Indo-Chinese revolt by positive action during the next month, France faces the possibility not only of losing her prize Far Eastern domain but also of losing eventually a large portion of her overseas empire, especially in North Africa.

Still drained, impoverished and disillusioned by the war and the occupation and torn by internal political rivalries, France is not only hard put to it to find sufficient reinforcements and troops to combat this vigorous Communist-inspired Indo-Chinese insurrection, but is also facing uneasy stirrings in Africa that indicate that other restless former colonies are eagerly eyeing the Viet Nam campaign as a guide to possible future actions on their own part.

With Syria and Lebanon already departed from the French family of nations; with Ho Chi Minh fighting desperately with widely organized support for ultimate independence, and with unquiet hangovers of recent serious troubles in Algeria prevalent, it is evident that the world's second greatest empire is sorely beset by centrifugal forces.

Fewer Cards Up Sleeve

Just as the Socialist Government in Great Britain is gradually being forced to acknowledge the slow dismemberment of former British imperial structures, so Léon Blum's Socialist regime in France is facing a similar and possibly more critical problem. And it has fewer cards up its sleeve.

Individual Communist parties—even though the Communist International remains officially abolished—are playing a strong part in this not unconnected series of maneuvers for native independence. The attitude of the powerful French Communist party appears to be vacillating conveniently as the momentary situations dictate.

Since France's liberation her colonial policy has been evidently confused. The deliberations by the first Constituent Assembly on this subject were unusually vague. After a complex debate the second Constituent Assembly established the general principles of a "French Union," leaving the details to be worked out later with the individual colonies.

Differences of Position

During the last two years the Socialists have consistently talked of autonomous units within an over-all "Union" framework. The Popular Republican Movement and the Right Wing parties have expressed the hope of retaining as much overseas control as possible, but have been vague about it. The Radical Socialists have followed, more or less, the modified line of the Third Republic, while other groups have opposed the idea of giving up any possessions, although admitting that administrative changes must be made.

Until January, 1945, however, there was no detectable interest in the colonial question among the French masses. At that time the vigorous newspaper Combat began a series of articles calling attention to imperial problems. In the following May bloody uprisings in Algeria forced the issue before the public eye. During the last six months almost all the politicians have openly admitted the need for reform.

Amazed by Revolt

Despite this fact, however, many French citizens are still bewildered by the colonial question and are amazed at the Indo-Chinese revolt. The average Frenchman has been brought up in schools that told him that France had no colonial prob-

THE COLONIZERS AND THE COLONIZED

lem; that no native or colored questions existed, since Frenchmen had solved them happily; that French culture was well established and peacefully absorbed in overseas possessions.

Popular rationalization accepted the departure from the French Empire of Syria and Lebanon as a dirty trick fostered by Britain with American support. The schoolbooks used today still teach essentially the pre-war colonial dogma. So the fact that these "happy natives" passionately want freedom comes as a shock.

The powerful French Communist party has played a skillful juggling game, balancing between support of local independence factions and of a new form of imperial structure. This is a role mindful of that pursued by the Italian Communists over the Trieste issue and that of the Greek Communists over Macedonia and Thrace. At first Maurice Thorez, Jacques Duclos and Andre Marty appeared to sponsor full independence for Indo-China, but a wave of popular indignation resulted in a backtracking more attractive to metropolitan French votes.

Alleged Uncertainty

As a result anti-Communist Frenchmen say that the French Communists are uncertain whether "Moscow should control the colonial populations directly or through a Communist regime in Paris." Two facts are certain: First, that communism is active in all the French colonial independence movements except in Morocco, where it has received a rebuff; second, that the French metropolitan Communist attitude and possibly the fate of the colonies depends on what happens in France itself.

At present the Communists officially sponsor a colonial solution, with the federal concepts of an overseas France. But should France ever lean toward the "Western bloc" this attitude would almost certainly change and there would be plenty of agitation by the local Communist parties in the colonies.

With the Levant possessions gone, France is confined to a struggle to maintain a cultural hold in Syria—where she stands little chance at present—and in Lebanon—where the prospects of intellectual, but not political, ties are better.

Indo-China has become a major issue now both actually and symbolically. While the second French Constituent Assembly was meeting a conference was held at Fontainebleau concerning the Indo-Chinese future. Thus, in fact, at that time two separate meetings were simultaneously deciding on colonial policy. The Fontainebleau conference was inconclusive.

The new Constitution approved at the end of this year provides for the establishment of a "French Union," including overseas possessions, and a "Council of the French Union" as one of the organs of the Fourth Republic. The portion of that Council that would be made up of overseas representatives has not yet been fixed.

Under the Minister of Overseas France comes the administration of the Central African possessions, of Oceania and of Madagascar, which are to have new autonomies. If the Indo-Chinese question is ever settled that region would certainly be transferred from the Foreign Affairs Ministry's Section on Protectorates or "Associated States" to the former.

Algeria's Special Status

Tunisia and Morocco are under the direction of the latter section of the Ministry of Foreign Affairs. Although Algeria is still technically part of metropolitan France an opinion exists that this cannot continue and the policy of assimilation there is slowly being abandoned by the reluctant Right Wing. However, at present Algeria, Reunion (near Madagascar) French Guiana, Martinique and Guadeloupe are classified as Departments of France and are so administered by the Ministry of the Interior.

Plans have been rather vaguely set forth granting reforms in all these categories. These include the establishment of legislative assemblies in the regions under the Minister of Overseas France, widened electoral rights and certain local powers such as budgetary review for local allotments and the election of members to the French Upper Chamber.

However, Ho Chi Minh's revolt has in effect scrapped all that machinery for the moment, forcing M. Blum's Socialists into a paradoxical quest to restore order before negotiating. If within the few weeks remaining to M. Blum's Government this insurrection cannot be crushed or held in check even these paper reforms may be invalidated by a coup de force.

Denies He Is Communist

Ho Chi Minh denies that he is a Communist. However, he is a graduate of various Communist institutions in the Soviet Union. Since 1932 he has been recognized by various secret services as the acknowledged leader of the Indo-Chinese Communist party—which he ran from China.

He has spent much time not only in Russia but with Yenan's Chinese Communists. Many of his main supporters are known Communists. Until it became politically embarrassing he was supported by the French Communist party. Therefore, most French politicians regard his Viet-Minh party, Viet Nam's political arm, as a Communist-controlled national front.

The French are worried, not only about him, but also about a pro-Chinese party in Indo-China, whose purged leader is now in Nanking, where he has established a "refugee government." This is believed to be fostered by the Kuomintang, China's Government party. Paris is anxious about what it privately admits is a logical Chinese interest.

Opportunity for Revolt

The assumption here is that Ho Chi Minh felt that his best opportunity for revolt had come when the weak interim Blum Government finally took over in bewildered France.

The French are understood to have only about 75,000 troops in Indo-China, of which two-thirds are European. However, even in this small force—too little to recover the huge area by power alone—there is trouble. Confirmed reports have been received of desertions from one division there of crack foreign legionnaires.

Even to hold her own, France must scrape up new troops and transport. And almost every quarter here admits that in the twentieth century it would be impossible to embark on a full colonial war of military reconquest. This is just about excluded by France's own weakness, in any case.

While this real war is going on in Indo-China, the rest of the stirring French Empire is watching anxiously. There is as yet no indication that North Africa will arise if and when Ho Chi Minh succeeds in an even partial victory. However, the Right Wing parties of France already foresee drastic troubles in North Africa if the Indo-Chinese problem is not definitely settled.

One Serious Outbreak

Since the liberation there has been only one truly serious outbreak in French North Africa. That was so toned down by the French at the time that the world knows little of it. In May, 1945, a virtual revolt broke out in Algeria with particular centers at Guelma and Setif, west of Constantine.

Riots precipitated local massacres. About 200 French were killed and between 7,000 and 18,000 natives (the figure cannot yet be established) were slaughtered in the drastic French reaction, including bombing and mass executions. Bad feeling is still widespread and pamphlets inciting to revolt have not yet been eradicated.

In the summer of 1946 Andre Marty, one of the big three of the French Communist party and certainly its colonial expert, visited Algeria and Tunisia. Details of his activities are meager. However, shortly after his departure the local Communist parties in Algeria and Tunisia sought to set up United National Front parties with local Arab independence groups. This was also attempted a little later on in Morocco, which M. Marty did not visit.

Success in Tunisia

In Tunisia this maneuver succeeded. The Neo-Destour party, headed by Habib Bourguiba, is the principal Arab independence movement there and it has been playing in closely with the Arab League. M. Bourguiba is now a political émigré in the United States, having received his visa from the American consulate in Alexandria.

The Neo-Destour party has in the past been telling its American and British contacts that if it does not receive support from them in its independence efforts it will play with the Communists. There is believed to be some evidence that this is now occurring.

Last September the local Tunisian labor unions reformed themselves into an independent central federation and broke off relations with France's labor federation. The Communists are a minority in these unions, but they occupy most of the key positions.

Curiously enough, from the ideological viewpoint, another trend has been strengthened greatly since M. Marty's visit—the movement to bring back to power the former Bey of Tunis. The Bey was ousted by the French for collaboration with the Axis and is now interned at Pau. This restoration movement is not only popular in Tunisia but, according to reliable evidence, it is also being cautiously if surreptitiously supported by the Communist party.

Following M. Marty's visit the Communists in Algeria attempted a similar national front coalition, without visible success. However, it is understood that a similar labor revolt is now being encouraged by them there.

In Algeria there are two predominant independence movement leaders among the Arabs—Messali Hajj and Ferhat Abbas.

Messali Hajj was interned by the French several years ago and was released only last summer when he returned to the outskirts of Algiers. During the former's internment Ferhat Abbas emerged as a Nationalist leader with a more moderate program—complete autonomy, but within the French Union.

Officially Ferhat Abbas turned down collaboration with the Communists. However, during the second French Constituent Assembly eleven Deputies elected by his movement usually voted with the Communists and held such a key position in tight balloting that some measures were adopted as the result of their coalition. Although there is bad blood between Ferhat Abbas and Messali Hajj personally, with the latter regarding the former as an upstart, there are strong indications of a "deal" between the two; their movements are united among the masses.

Status in Morocco

In French Morocco, so far, the Communists appear to have made no headway. The independence or nationalist movement, called Istiqlal, is secretly supported by the Sultan as well as by Arab notables. It is a Right Wing nationalist movement which has so far rejected all offers of Communist cooperation. But the case of the Bey of Tunis demonstrates that this may not be a permanent condition.

Although the large Independence party in Madagascar is believed to have links with the Communists, the French are confident that for the present there is no fear of any serious trouble there.

At the moment all these independence movements in the French empire seem to be "lying doggo" until they can ascertain the success and the future of Ho Chi Minh's efforts in Indo-China. Possibly they are waiting until the only over-all coordinating force detectable—that of the Communist movements—resolves on a general policy.

Certainly, ideologically, Moscow has always strongly favored the full independence of all Colonial peoples in overseas empires. Russia, of course, has none of these, despite her bid for trusteeship in Tripolitania and the less eager recurrent bid since Czarist days for territory on the Red Sea in or near Eritrea.

How strongly this movement will be organized, whether it will be encouraged if the French Communist party deems it embarrassing, and how it will meet with the aspirations of the hitherto anti-Communist Arab League may well be clarified in 1947. This is especially true if Ho Chi Minh wins his bid for freedom in Indo-China.

December 25, 1946

Algeria

FRANCE APPROVES ALGERIAN REGIME

Votes First Assembly Ever Accorded a Possession, but Retains Final Control

By KENNETH CAMPBELL
Special to The New York Times.

PARIS, Aug. 27—A statute establishing a form of government of Algeria and designed to curb the growing Moslem discontent in North Africa was voted by the National Assembly tonight, 319 to 89.

The statute provides for an Algerian Legislative Assembly, the first such body France ever has accorded to an overseas possession. The Moslem nationalists' hopes for a republic of Algeria within the French Union have gone aglimmering. The country remains as three overseas Départments of France, with a Governor General appointed from Paris.

The Communists, the Assembly's eleven Moslem Deputies and some Rightists abstained from the voting tonight.

Premier Paul Ramadier piloted the statute through the National Assembly in fifteen days of rough and tumble debate, during which he successfully ignored a mandate given him by his Socialist party.

The effect of the statute on Morocco and Tunisia, Moslem countries where France exercises protectorates, is being watched with intense interest. The statute is generally acknowledged to be a compromise.

If it encounters strong Moslem opposition, many persons here usually well informed on Arab affairs fear that Arab League agents may attempt the same tumultuous propaganda now being employed by Egyptian Moslems against the British in connection with the Sudan condominium.

The statute provides for an Algerian Assembly of 120 members, sixty of whom will be elected by the first electoral group made up of Algerians of European descent together with a few Moslem élite, and sixty by the second, all-Moslem electoral group.

The make-up and method of electing this Assembly evoked acrimonious debate, and many believe that the provisions are so complicated that they will be very difficult to apply.

Algerian Moslem spokesmen wanted the Moslems placed on equal footing with the Algerian Europeans. Powerful French Algerians wanted the Arabs shorn of what little political power they now possess. The result was one of those compromises for which Premier Ramadier is becoming famous.

But in spite of the oratory that has rattled the chandeliers of the Assembly chamber night and day for half a month, France retains a firm grip on wriggling Algeria. The Governor General still will be appointed by the Paris Government, and in cases where he does not agree with the Algerian Assembly, the French National Assembly will decide the issue.

Persons reflecting Government opinion feel, however, that while the ultimate power remains with the French, the establishment of an Algerian Assembly is a great step toward conciliating Moslem opinion.

A forerunner of what is expected to be a real concession to Moslem face-saving in Algeria is contained in an amendment casually slipped into the statute last night by unanimous consent by Emmanuel Temple, Independent Republican Deputy from the Department of Aveyron. This amendment establishes the principle of separation of religion and state in the new Algerian Government. The method of applying this is to be left to the Algerian Assembly.

At present, while Roman Catholic Bishops, Jewish rabbis or Protestant pastors are not appointed by the Algerian Government, Moslem religious leaders down to the very mosque janitors must be approved by the French.

August 28, 1947

Paris Confirms Arrests In Tunisia and Algeria

Special to The New York Times.

PARIS, April 21—An official communiqué today confirmed reports of a police action begun a month ago in Tunisia and Algeria against what was described as an underground nationalist movement. Press reports said that some 300 Moslems had been arrested. The communiqué gave no numbers, but officials in Paris said that about fifty arrests had been made in the last three days.

Explosives and arms, including machine guns, were said to have been seized, together with documents that were said to show the existence of a clandestine secret society organized on the lines of French underground movements against the Germans during the war.

This organization was said to have been formed as one expression of the political propaganda of the "Movement for the Triumph of Democratic Liberties," a Moslem nationalist group. Abd el Krim, who led a revolt against the French in Morocco in 1926 and, after a long exile in Madagascar, escaped to Egypt, said recently that a new uprising was seething in French North Africa.

April 22, 1950

Algiers Bars Nationalist Paper

ALGIERS, Algeria, Feb. 6 (Reuters)—An Algiers court suspended for three months today the publication of Free Algeria, official organ of the Algerian Nationalist party. The offices of the weekly paper in Oran and Algiers have been searched in operations by French colonial authorities against the nationalists.

February 7, 1953

TERRORIST BANDS KILL 7 IN ALGERIA; FRENCH SEND AID

Special to The New York Times.

PARIS, Nov. 1—Nationalist terrorism suddenly spilled over into Algeria last night from the adjoining French protectorates of Tunisia and Morocco.

Small unidentified bands made about thirty attacks at widely separated points in the French territory, killing at least seven persons and wounding about thirty others. Most of the attacks took place in the eastern department of Constantine, close to Tunisia, where nationalist bands known as fellaghas have been operating despite French attempts to exterminate them.

Roger Leonard, Governor General of Algeria, which is an integral part of Metropolitan France, immediately called for reinforcements. This afternoon 300 heavily equipped Mobile Guards sent from Marseilles arrived in Bône.

Later, François Mitterand, Minister of the Interior, whose ministry has jurisdiction over Algeria, dispatched 600 Republican security troops by air. This evening it was announced that Premier Pierre Mendès-France had decided to send, in addition, three battalions of parachutists.

M. Mitterand hurried back to Paris today from his week-end retreat in the Nièvre Department in central France.

November 2, 1954

FRENCH INCREASE ALGERIAN FORCES

By MICHAEL CLARK
Special to The New York Times.

PARIS, May 19—The French Cabinet is sending heavy reinforcements to Algeria in an all-out effort to quell the rebellion there.

Alarmed by the recent spread of terrorism in eastern Algeria, the Cabinet approved measures last night that would increase the strength of the French armed forces in the territory to about 100,000 men. The present effectives are estimated at 90,000.

The approved measures were worked out jointly by Interior Minister Maurice Bourges-Maunoury and Gen. Joseph-Pierre Koenig, Minister of Defense and of the Armed Forces.

The efficacy of the Government's anti-terrorist drive is expected to be enhanced by the recent decision to extend the State of Emergency Act to the whole Department of Constantine. The act, passed by the National Assembly on April 1, previously had been applied only in the region around the rebel-infested Aurès Mountains.

May 20, 1955

THE COLONIZERS AND THE COLONIZED

Algeria Core of Paris' Problem With North African Nationalism

Since Area Is Considered Part of France, Programs Implemented in Tunisia and Morocco Are Out of the Question

By ROBERT C. DOTY
Special to The New York Times.

ALGIERS, Algeria, Sept. 15— In Algeria France is at grips with the vital core of the problem of her North African empire.

In Tunisia and Morocco, the flanking protectorates, the effort was to come to terms with native nationalism existing within the framework of vestigial local governments. In both cases the formula was to grant those Governments increased measures of internal autonomy, with provisions safeguarding the links to France.

Here there is no room for such solutions. Here 1,000,000 Europeans and 8,000,000 native Moslems living in a slice of Africa four times as big as France have been incorporated into the mother country itself as French citizens. They dwell in three French departments and the Southern Territories in the Sahara. It is unthinkable to Frenchmen here and in France that there should be any change in the basic juridical position. Therefore the problem, in the view of French authorities, is simply to make the existing organization work.

The material results of 125 years of French control in Algeria are everywhere evident and impressive. Modern cities, rail and highway networks and irrigation systems, and a population, freed from epidemics, burgeoning at a rate that constitutes the root of the economic problem—all these are monuments to French effort.

Social Phase Said to Lag

But in the opinion of many observers, French and foreign, political, social and economic progress has not kept pace with the purely physical aspects of French accomplishment. As a result, since November this extension of Metropolitan France has been the scene of armed revolt and terrorist activity that have cost more lives—native and European—more money and more damage to property than did the Tunisian and Moroccan troubles combined.

Stern repression to be followed by a program of gradual reform is the formula adopted by the French to meet the threat. The reform program, consisting of measures to give the Moslem population more political control at the local level, to improve the economic position of rural and urban Moslem workers and to give greater recognition to Arabic studies in schools, has just been projected by Governor General Jacques Soustelle.

Meanwhile, an estimated total of 200,000 French and colonial troops plus paramilitary and civilian formations are engaged in repressing disorders that are concentrated for the most part in the northern section of the Department of Constantine.

Moslem spokesmen charge that in the week following the savage uprisings in that area Aug. 20 the death toll among Moslems was at least double the 1,275 fatalities officially listed by the French. This assertion was branded as a "lie" by Pierre Dupuch, prefect of Constantine Department. Some responsible French officials, however, acknowledge with regret that scores of innocents perished in the explosion of grief and rage of Europeans over their own innocent dead.

The bitterness generated by this violence has had two principal effects. First, as acknowledged by the military commanders in rebel-infested areas, the relatively small number of activists, probably no more than 1,000, now have the complicity of most of the Moslem population, either through fear or nationalist sentiment.

Second, it has produced threats by Moslem Deputies to both the Algerian and French Assemblies to resign from both bodies. Dr. Mohammed Salah Bendjelloul, Constantine Deputy to the National Assembly, told this correspondent he and other heretofore pro-French Deputies no longer could support, in the face of prevailing Moslem opinion in his department, the idea of integration with France.

Carrying out the threat to resign from the local and national legislatures could not impede either military action or the reform program, but it could serve separatist propaganda aims, in the opinion of observers here.

The French authorities attribute the inspiration for the revolt to propaganda and material aid from Cairo and the Arab League in furtherance of the Pan-Islamic ideal. It has received racial and religious sanction from the councils of Ulemas (Moslem religious leaders) here.

The same officials acknowledge the ground was prepared, however, by failure to deal adequately with the problems of poverty and unemployment in Constantine Department and by a certain "blind optimism" that left depressed regions under-administered and undermanned by security forces.

Whatever were the basic causes, the leadership of the revolt and of its Revolutionary Committee for Unity of Action all are native of northern Constantine.

Europeanized Moslem a Rebel

The over-all commander of the Philippeville region, with at least 150 hard-core activists and an unknown but substantial number of auxiliaries recruited by force or persuasion, is a middle-aged blacksmith named Ziroud Youssef, also known as Si Hamed. He is a former municipal councilor of Condé-Smendou, a town between Philippeville and the city of Constantine.

One of his two "battalion" commanders is Ziguet Smain, 28-year-old commercial representative of Philippeville, a completely Europeanized Moslem who joined the rebels in May.

For the first three weeks after the mass assaults on European centers Aug. 20 these men and the forces they command were able to operate freely in the mountainous areas of the quadrilateral bounded roughly by Philippeville, Collo, Guelma and Constantine.

The French had only enough forces to maintain security in the principal centers and send patrols to known trouble spots between. "They cross the country, but they do not occupy it," a French official said.

Only now, with reinforcements pouring in from France and other areas of Algeria, has the military command been able to plan a network of posts strong enough to maintain security in the countryside and encourage the Moslems who fled to the hills to return to their villages. This is an essential prerequisite for getting the reform program under way.

September 22, 1955

U. N. COMPROMISE ON ALGERIA ENDS FRENCH WALKOUT

By LINDESAY PARROTT
Special to The New York Times.

UNITED NATIONS, N. Y., Nov. 25—The United Nations swung open the door today for France's return to the General Assembly.

Paris immediately announced that France would come back. Although the French delegation here lacked formal instructions late today, its members generally were expected to attend the next plenary Assembly session, probably late next week, and to participate in the work of the various Assembly committees.

The compromise solution was reached when the Assembly adopted unanimously a resolution introduced by V. K. Krishna Menon of India. The international body thus decided "not to consider further the item titled 'The Question of Algeria' and is therefore no longer seized of this item on the agenda of the tenth session."

France walked out of the Assembly Sept. 30 over an Assembly decision to debate French administration in strife-torn Algeria. The resolution for the discussion, introduced by fourteen nations of the Arab, Asian and African group, was characterized by France as interference in her internal affairs. Northern Algeria legally is a part of Metropolitan France.

November 26, 1955

97

ALGERIA FIGHTING MOUNTS SHARPLY

Day's Toll Put at 89 Dead— Nationalists Bid Moslems Quit Government or Die

By The Associated Press.

ALGIERS, Algeria, Dec. 21—Guerrilla warfare mounted sharply in Algeria today.

A climate of fear was increased by nationalist threats to execute any Moslem officials who failed to quit Government jobs. The nationalists oppose France's rule.

Reports, unofficial and incomplete, indicated eighty-nine persons had been killed in the last twenty-four hours.

The French opened a big drive yesterday in the Nemencha Mountains south of Constantine. Planes joined the operation against a handful of rebel bands known to be at large in the area.

French authorities said the drive had cost the rebels thirty-two dead, ten captured and a number of wounded.

In Algiers, nationalists circulated tracts threatening execution for any Moslems who failed to resign Government posts before the French elections Jan. 2.

A number of lesser officials in remote areas are known to have resigned already. Threatening letters have been received by many others.

Resignations by Moslems on a large scale would seriously hamper the already troubled French Administration.

The tracts were signed by the Front for National Liberation, which had previously circulated many threatening handbills directed against the holding of elections in Algeria, also Jan. 2. The balloting was called off by Paris because of the terrorism.

The Algerian elections would have named a number of Deputies to the French National Assembly and to local bodies. The administration of Algeria includes a 120-man local assembly, largely advisory, which is half Moslem and half French.

Nationalists also circulated word through the native quarters of the larger cities to step up terrorist acts over the Christmas season, especially on Christmas Eve and Day.

Increased terrorism has been reflected in road ambushes, bombings, assassinations, burning of farm buildings and schools, and the cutting of telephone lines.

The violence in the last twenty-four hours included a battle near Guelma, where twelve rebels were killed; a clash near Souk Ahras, where four died; a similar fight at Guentis, where ten rebels were killed, and two clashes near the Tunisian frontier, in which a total of fifteen rebels died.

The French Protectorate of Morocco was also troubled by terrorism. Five persons were killed yesterday despite the improved political atmosphere brought about by the restoration of Sultan Mohammed ben Youssef.

FRENCH FIGHT REBELS: Algerian nationalist violence occurred in Guelma and Souk Ahras (1) and in Guentis (2).

December 22, 1955

FRANCE MINIMIZES NEW TROOP MOVES IN ALGERIA CRISIS

By ROBERT C. DOTY
Special to The New York Times.

PARIS, Dec. 23—The French Government sought today to take the political sting out of a decision to send 60,000 soldiers to Algeria soon. It indicated that they were "replacements" rather than "reinforcements."

Opponents of Premier Edgar Faure and his Right-Center Government allies in the electoral campaign have cited the coming dispatch of new military contingents to North Africa as evidence of a deteriorating situation there and of the Government's incapacity to cope with it.

Today, the Ministry of National Defense in Paris and French Governor General Jacques Soustelle in Algiers both issued cautiously worded statements attempting to counter these charges.

The Defense Ministry statement denied press reports that "this was a case of exceptional reinforcements of effectives."

"The ministry once again must state explicitly that these movements are only the normal consequences of the execution of a plan in effect since October in order to compensate for the release of reservists who were recalled to service," the ministry's communiqué declared. "Contrary to the rumors being spread, the situation in North Africa has led to no new measures."

December 24, 1955

ALGERIA FRENCH CLING TO STATUS

Premier's Visit Stirs Riot by Colonials Who Fear Threat to Their Power

By THOMAS F. BRADY
Special to The New York Times.

ALGIERS, Feb. 11—The Algerian French, who this week greeted the Premier of France as a howling mob and hurled tomatoes and clods of earth at him, are a stubborn people. They have been here for 125 years. There are four-generation colonials among them, and they are deeply attached to the land by sentiment as well as by interest. They are farmers in great part and civil servants and shop keepers. More than a quarter of them live in the city of Algiers.

Like people anywhere, the Algerian French cannot see justice in a change that might threaten their way of life and submerge them. They point out that the population of Algeria when the French arrived in 1830 was only a little larger than the local European population is now. Why, they ask, should we be swamped by the consequences of our own sanitation and hygiene? Because the Moslem population is increasing at the rate of nearly 250,000 a year, must we be pushed into the sea?

On a more reasonable level the French argue that Algeria needs France as much as France needs Algeria. The metropolitan country is contributing 98 billion francs (nearly $280,000,000) a year to the Algerian budget, not including military expenditures. This sum permits Algiers to have an unfavorable trade balance of about 80 billion francs a year.

Trade With France

Almost all of this unfavorable trade balance is with France herself, and nationalists insist that Algiers is a captive market for high-priced French manufactures that cannot be sold on the world market.

The average per capita income in France is 240,000 francs (about $700) a year. Here it is 54,000 francs (about $150) a year. The Algerian Europeans have a slightly higher standard of living than their compatriots in France. It may, therefore, be estimated that the Moslem per capita income is about 30,000 francs ($85) a year.

The French say that at the outside there have never been more than 10,000 active rebels in Algeria but their own forces here total between 210,000 and 250,000 men.

In the seven months ended on Jan. 31 published accounts showed 2,939 rebels killed and 3,633 captured. In the same period the French made 9,722 arrests of suspects, most of whom have been sent to concentration camps in the high plateau country to the south.

French military losses in the same period have been 338 killed and 736 wounded.

There have been 850 assassinations by the rebels since last July 1, 312 kidnappings and 1,600 incidents of economic sabotage.

Rebel Attacks Persist

Despite the rebel losses their activities were continuing this week with an average number of military ambushes, attacks on convoys and assassinations. The rebellion has clearly become a

THE COLONIZERS AND THE COLONIZED

sizeable guerilla war. The French believe, apparently with good reason, that it is directed from Cairo. Certainly, Mohamed ben Bella and other exiles who are said to be the chiefs of the "Army of Liberation" are operating from there.

There is no evidence of important Communist participation in the rebellion, but the Communist press has supported it and there is every reason to believe the Communists hope to exploit any breakdown of French authority here if they can get a foot in the door.

If the French cannot find the means to put the rebellion down by force—clearly a monumental task in the mountainous Algerian hinterland—they must deal with its leaders, which would probably mean ultimate independence for Algeria.

February 12, 1956

Algeria Rebel Would Take Arms Of Soviet Bloc or 'Devil Himself'

By OSGOOD CARUTHERS
Special to The New York Times.

CAIRO, Feb. 24—An Algerian guerrilla leader said in Cairo today his forces would accept arms from the Soviet bloc or "even the devil himself" to carry on their fight for liberation from French rule.

The leader is Mohammed ben Bella, 38-year-old much-decorated former major in the French Army, who travels back and forth over the arduous underground routes between Algeria and the sanctuary of Cairo.

At the moment he is in Cairo conferring with political leaders in exile of the Algerian National Liberation Front. Openly supported by the Egyptian Government, the Liberation Front has its headquarters here.

M. ben Bella will return one day soon, he said, to the strife-ridden mountains of Algeria, although the French have put a heavy price on his head as a refugee from a four-year-old sentence of life imprisonment.

The aim of the rebels after liberation from the French, M. ben Bella said, is to set up an Algerian republic along social democratic lines. He added that this did not mean its policies would be socialistic but would aim through agrarian reform and other measures to wipe out social injustices that existed in Algeria.

[Hadj Messali, an Algerian nationalist leader living under surveillance in France, said recognition of Algeria's independence demands was essential to peace.]

"We reject Marxism in any form," said M. ben Bella. "We are nationalists. We have issued stern orders not to permit Algerian Communists into our ranks. Algerian Communists, who are closely linked to French Communists, have opposed our movement. They have declared it is not a true popular uprising because they are not in it."

M. ben Bella is one of the top military leaders of the guerrillas, who call themselves the Army of National Liberation. During the last several months the coordinated operations of this rebel force have cost the lives of hundreds of French soldiers and threatened a crisis in the recently formed Government of Premier Guy Mollet.

"Ours is an army in the real sense of the word," M. ben Bella insists. It has a unified code, officers and insignia of rank, he added.

"We are engaged in all-out war against the French," he said. "We are in dire need of arms to bring up against the modern weapons of the French forces. We will get these arms where we can. And while we are strongly opposed to communism we will accept arms from the Soviet bloc or anyone else who will offer them—even the Devil himself."

Most of Arms Captured

M. ben Bella said there had been "no direct offer" from the Soviet bloc. But his refusal to say whether such arms might be obtained through Egypt seemed heavy with implication.

He said most of the arms the rebels were using had been captured from the French. Others had been smuggled into the country, he added.

France has protested numerous times against alleged Egyptian aid in weapons and training facilities to North Africans under French rule.

The Egyptians also offer other facilities to the men to whom they have granted asylum. One section of the North African headquarters carries on a kind of consular activity, issuing documents and identification certificates to those who flee to exile in Cairo.

"The French say there are 20,000 guerrillas in Algeria," M. ben Bella said, "but as a matter of fact every Algerian is a potential guerrilla if he could get a gun."

The best available information, however, indicates that there has been no such material aid during the last three or four months. Nevertheless the implication was that the Algerian guerrillas would welcome transshipment by Egypt of any of large quantity of the arms she has been buying from Czechoslovakia since last September.

Whether or not the Egyptians would be willing to supply some of those new Communist-produced weapons to the Algerians could not be learned.

The Government of Premier Gamal Abdel Nasser has been forthright in avowing its support of the North Africans of Algeria, Tunisia and Morocco in their struggle for freedom.

The best evidence of this is that exiled leaders from the French protectorates of Tunisia and Morocco and of Algeria, which the French declare is part of Metropolitan France, occupy jointly a suite of offices in the heart of downtown Cairo. They have set up headquarters for the Committee of Liberation of North Africa under subsidy of the nine-nation Arab League.

While M. ben Bella is the military brains of the Algerian revolt, the political chief in the Cairo office is Mohammed Khider. The two men escaped together from an Algerian prison in 1952 after having been sentenced to life terms on charges of plotting the overthrow of French authority. Most of the men in the Cairo office are under similar stiff sentences.

Working with M. Khider in the coordinated campaign against the French are Salah ben Youssef, leader of The Tunisian Neo-Destour party extremist wing, and Allal el Fassi of the Moroccan Istiqlal party.

It is assumed that one of the main courier routes goes across Libya, one of th emembers of the Arab League. According to M. Ben Bella and his Algerian friends, it was while he was in a hotel in Tripoli last December that a members of the French secret service tried to assassinate him.

M. ben Bella implied that he could not be certain the Algerian rebels would continue to reject communism if the Western powers continued to support the stern repressive measures of the French.

He said the Algerians were particularly bitter over the permission granted to France to use the forces committed to the North Atlantic Treaty Organization to fight the rebellion in Algeria.

"Thus we have become disappointed in the United States Government's policies," he said. "The sight of United States-built helicopters being used against our people has made us wonder what has become of anti-colonial tradition in America."

February 25, 1956

100,000 MORE MEN TO GO TO ALGERIA

By ROBERT C. DOTY
Special to The New York Times.

PARIS, April 5—Robert Lacoste, French Minister Residing in Algeria, won approval today for his plan to send 100,000 more French troops to Algeria to quell the rebellion there.

Premier Guy Mollet and others in his left-of-center Cabinet have long been united on the necessity for a major effort to re-establish order in the Algerian departments as a prerequisite to reform. But they have been reluctant to take the politically unpopular action of recalling reservists to meet M. Lacoste's demands.

Premier Mollet, in four days of study of the problem over the Easter week-end, reached the conclusion that it would be impossible to meet Algerian military needs with men already in the armed forces. In a three-hour conference with M. Lacoste, the Premier agreed that 30,000 men in the ready reserve would have to be recalled at once and up to 70,000 others would be mobilized during the coming months.

Most of Troops in Algeria

After having completed eighteen months of active service, French conscripts spend three years as ready reserves who may be recalled by a simple administrative decision. Thereafter, they enter the "first reserve," which may be mobilized only with parliamentary approval.

At last official report there were 330,000 French troops in

North Africa, about two-thirds of them in Algeria. The new reinforcements would put the total for Algeria alone over the 300,000 mark.

[In Algeria itself, eighteen suspected rebels were shot and killed during an attempted escape from a stockade during an extremist attack on a French outpost in the Kabilya Mountains, French authorities announced, according to The United Press. The attack, against Maillot, seventy-five miles southeast of Algiers, appeared aimed at liberating the suspected rebels.]

The necessity for the present Socialist-directed Government to pursue a policy of force in Algeria has brought acute political embarrassment to M. Mollet. The Socialists and their allies of the Republican Front were elected on a program that included prominently a "peace-in-Algeria" plank and condemnation of those whose policies had led to previous recalls of French reservists for service in North Africa.

April 6, 1956

MODERATES JOIN ALGERIAN REBELS

Leader Says All Parties Are One in War on French

By OSGOOD CARUTHERS
Special to The New York Times

CAIRO, April 25 — The leader of the Algerian moderates said today he had joined forces with the National Liberation Front in an all-out war for freedom from French rule.

Ferhat Abbas, who flew to Cairo from France a few days ago, said the Democratic Union of the Algerian Manifesto, of which he was president, "no longer exists."

"There are no more parties in Algeria," he told a news conference. "As of this hour, all forces for the liberation of North Africa are one, united under one command.

"All have become one for the duration of the hostilities against the oppressor. There is but a single force in Algeria, a single indestructible soul. And the National Liberation Front is its voice."

Mr. Abbas at one time was considered one of the most moderate politicians in Algeria.

He told newsmen that the Algerians were willing to negotiate for peace but that France first must "recognize the right of Algerian nationality to every Algerian citizen."

Mr. Abbas spoke in French, and his statement and answers to questions were translated into Arabic. There was considerable divergence between his statement and the English translation that was handed to correspondents.

The English version asserted that France must "disengage her military forces and evacuate them from North Africa, from all North Africa . . . remove every last French soldier and mercenary from our land or we carry the war to France."

Mr. Abbas said that this contained an error in translation and that he had intended to say only that the Algerian guerrilla war would "go on interminably."

He said French Government leaders had declared they could not negotiate peace because there was no responsible Algerian with whom they could speak. The National Liberation Front is a responsible Algerian force, he declared, and the only organization with which France could negotiate.

Mr. Abbas insisted, however, that the French must renounce their claim to Algeria as part of Metropolitan France and recognize the Algerian nation.

Sitting with him at the news conference were Dr. Ahmed Francis, a member of the executive committee of the Democratic Union; Ahmed Tewfik el-Medany, secretary general of the Algerian Association of Ulemas or Islamic scholars, and Sheikh al-Abbas ben Sheikh al-Hussein, a member of the association's high council.

Parleys With Rebel Chiefs

The two members of the Association of Ulemas arrived in Cairo from France two weeks ago. Mr. Abbas pointed to them at the news conference today and said they also had joined forces with the National Liberation Front.

All four men had been in continual conference in the last two days with exiled leaders of the Front—Gen. Mohammed ben Bella, military brains of the Algerian revolt, and Mohammed Kaider, the Front's political leader.

In his statement today, Mr. Abbas said the full liberation of Tunisia and Morocco depended upon the liberation of Algeria.

"Either Algeria is freed," he said, "or the independence of Tunisia and Morocco become illusions."

French Embassy spokesmen declined to comment on Mr. Abbas' remarks.

Mr. Abbas accused the French of having launched a "war of reconquest" and of having "plunged Algeria into a blood bath."

He made a special appeal to French liberals to press the French Government to halt its present efforts to crush the rebellion by force.

"Speaking in the name of the army of liberation," Mr. Abbas said, "I herewith declare that there will be no peace, no respite, no armistice, only intensification of the tempo of the struggle the French have thrust upon us until the colonial forces, including France's mercenaries, are destroyed or evacuated. Algeria will be free."

April 26, 1956

Eastern Section of Algeria Is Put Under Martial Law

By The Associated Press.

ALGIERS, Algeria, May 10—Robert Lacoste, French Minister Residing in Algeria, put the eastern part of the country under a state of martial law today. In the west nationalist forces followed up their farm-burning rampage near Oran last Monday with another attack on twelve farms just a few miles away.

A rebel band burned a vegetable fiber factory and two farms in the area of Bou-Tlelis, seventeen miles southwest of Oran.

The French moved in armored vehicles and fighter planes in an effort to track down and wipe out the bands.

The rebels apparently were unhampered in the raids, despite the fact that thousands of French reinforcements were rushed into the area after the previous attacks. In those attacks forty farms were burned and twenty French farmers were slain.

M. Lacoste acted under near-dictatorial powers granted him by the French Government in March when he put the eastern departments (counties) of Constantine and Bône under the direct control of the military.

The region includes the Aurès Mountains, base of the first rebel attacks against the French on Nov. 1, 1954.

All of Algeria already was under a state of urgency, a step just short of martial law, so no vast policy changes were expected under M. Lacoste's decree. Most of the estimated 300,000 troops in Algeria have been concentrated in the eastern half of the country.

Rebels struck last night at forty-six villages northwest of the city of Constantine. Many houses were set afire, and violent street fighting broke out when French forces arrived.

The heaviest clash reportedly occurred at Rouached, about fifteen miles northwest of Constantine. A witness told newsmen the rebels preceded their invasion of the village with heavy rifle fire. Then they swooped into the town from all sides and tossed flaming bottles of gasoline into the homes.

"Soon long flames shot into the sky," the witness said. "Men, women and children ran from the burning houses, despite bullets whistling by their ears, to seek safety in some villas that escaped attack."

French troops finally ran the rebels out of town after a two-hour fight. They said the rebels left many casualties.

May 11, 1956

ALGERIAN REBELS WARN OF REVENGE

Assert 100 French Civilians Will Die for Every 'Patriot' —To Execute 2 Soldiers

By MICHAEL CLARK
Special to The New York Times.

ALGIERS, Algeria, June 21—The National Liberation Front warned in a handbill today that one hundred French civilians would perish for every Algerian "patriot" executed by French authorities.

The nationalist organization also announced that two French soldiers now in rebel hands would be executed in retaliation for the execution of two convicted terrorists in Algeria Tuesday.

Terrorist attacks in Algiers yesterday cost three Europeans their lives. Fourteen Europeans, including two policemen and a 13-year-old girl, were wounded. One of the wounded died today.

Two terrorists this evening shot and killed the driver of a motor scooter, Marcel Garbagnati, a 20-year-old student. His passenger was wounded.

The police identified those responsible for yesterday's attack as members of a National Liberation Front cell. One terrorist was killed and another was arrested. Two other accomplices were also seized, it was announced today. Other arrests were expected.

The rebel handbill, the authenticity of which was not contested, spoke of the "collective massacre" of Arab inhabitants by the French and of the "summary execution of thousands of peasants." It charged that the French had now resorted to "cowardly acts" against their prisoners.

Executions Were First

This left the "Army of National Liberation" with no choice but to "requite crime with crime and violence with violence," the handbill asserted.

The executions of the two terrorists were the first to be carried out since the start of the nationalist rebellion Nov. 1, 1954. One had been sentenced to death for the slaying of a French forester. The other had been found guilty of having participated in an attack that cost seven French lives on March 7.

The rebel handbill made no mention of these acts but stated that the two French soldiers now in rebel hands would be executed as a preliminary measure of retaliation and that French civilians would be attacked in city and country until each executed Arab had been avenged by the death of one hundred French civilians.

The two French soldiers, Cpl. Louis Aurousseau and Pvt. Raymond Serreau were members of a French patrol lost in the wild Palestro Gorges on May 18. One member of the patrol was freed by French troops on May 23. Corporal Aurcusseau and Private Serreau were the only other survivors.

June 22, 1956

French Seize Five Rebel Chiefs; Draw Algerians' Plane Into Trap

By MICHAEL CLARK
Special to The New York Times.

ALGIERS, Algeria, Oct. 22—A chartered transport plane carrying five top leaders of the Algerian rebellion to Tunis from Rabat was diverted today from its course by order of the French command in Algeria and brought in to an airport near Algiers.

It was announced here tonight that the Algerians, all members of the committee that directs the Algerian rebellion from Cairo, had been placed under arrest after having landed at Maison Blanche Airport. They were Mohammed ben Bella, Mohammed Khider, Mohammed Boudiaf, Hossein Ait Ahmed and Mustafa Lachraf.

The plane, a DC-3, operated by the Air Atlas Company of Morocco, and manned by a French crew, had taken off from Rabat this morning and had put down at Palma, in the Balearic Islands. It scheduled to follow a circuitous route to avoid passing over Algerian territory.

The five rebel leaders had conferred with Sultan Mohammed V of Morocco in Rabat yesterday and were to have taken part in the conference that opens tomorrow in Tunis in connection with the Sultan's state visit there.

[In Paris, Premier Guy Mollet summoned his top ministerial aides to a meeting at 1 A. M. Tuesday to consider the situation arising from the arrests.] Earlier this month the Algerians had gone to Nador in northern Morocco to await the arrival of the 400-ton motor vessel Athos. However the Athos, laded with seventy tons of contraband war material from Egypt, was caured by the French Navy off the cost of western Algeria last Tuesday.

Mr. ben Bella escaped from a French prison in Blida, Algeria, in March, 1952, and made his way to Cairo. There he joined Mr. Khider to organize the guerrilla army that went into action against the French in Algeria Nov. 1, 1954. His capture constitutes one of the most decisive French actions in the drive against the nationalist rebels.

The Air Atlas DC-3 carrying the rebel leaders took off from Palma late this afternoon. Its course was plotted here by directional radio. When the plane reached a point conveniently close to the Algerian coast, the pilot, identified as a Captain Grelier, was invited by radio to land at the Maison Blanche military airport.

He acceded to this request. However, instead of proceeding directly to the point indicated, the pilot circled over the Mediterranean long enough to make his landing at Maison Blanche coincide with his scheduled arrival time at Tunis. He managed in this way to avoid arousing the suspicion of his passengers.

The surprise seems to have been complete. As soon as the plane landed at Maison Blanche, at 9:15 P. M., French police inspectors armed with submachine guns went aboard and clapped handcuffs on the startled rebel leaders.

The plane's hostess was credited with having kept the passengers in conversation during the latter part of the trip so they would not notice the deviation from the scheduled course.

The rebel chiefs offered no resistance when taken, but followed the police in silence. All five were traveling under false names. They were being questioned tonight by officials of the territorial surveillance department of the French police.

October 23, 1956

TERRORIST KILLS ALGERIAN MAYOR

Champion of Rule by France Shot in Busy Algiers Street —Arab Gunman Escapes

By MICHAEL CLARK
Special to The New York Times.

ALGIERS, Algeria, Dec. 28—Amedée Froger, president of the Algerian Federation of Mayors, was assassinated today by an Arab terrorist. The assassin escaped.

The reaction among European inhabitants of the city was one of dismay and exasperation. M. Froger, 74 years old and a man of forceful personality, stood four-square for the maintenance of French sovereignty in Algeria. Europeans looked to him as their spokesman and champion.

Robert Lacoste, French Minister Residing in Algeria, reportedly fearing possible disorders when public burial of the victim is held tomorrow, appealed in a radio address tonight for a "measure of calm and dignity."

M. Lacoste praised M. Froger, Mayor of Boufarik, seventeen miles southwest of Algiers, as a "true Frenchman" and stigmatized today's "odious murder." He described it as a "violent provocation." He said the rebels, defeated in the field despite increasing aid from abroad, were trying now to win a political decision in Paris and at the United Nations.

December 29, 1956

RISKS TO FRANCE IN ALGERIA CITED

Paris Editor Says Military Policy Could Alienate the Whole Arab Population

By HAROLD CALLENDER
Special to The New York Times.

PARIS, March 16—France runs the risk of incurring the hostility, not merely of the rebels in Algeria, but of the whole Arab population, according to an editor who recently completed his military service in that country.

For this risk, the methods of the army were blamed by Jean-Jacques Servan-Schreiber in an article in the latest issue of his weekly, L'Express.

The article, the second of a series on the military operations in Algeria, was in type before the Ministry of Defense announced Thursday that it would prosecute those responsible for a "campaign of disparagement of the army."

The Ministry was referring to an increasing number of newspaper articles, accompanied by two books, charging French soldiers with the indiscriminate shooting of Arabs, both armed and unarmed, the unnecessary destruction of villages, and torture in the questioning of prisoners.

Ministry's Move Questioned

The Ministry said such charges had been investigated and found false or greatly exaggerated. Some commentators here wondered how the Ministry could have investigated every incident. M. Servan-Schreiber, as if anticipating the question, indicated that this was impossible.

"It is lies from top to bottom," he quoted an officer as saying. "The Government misleads the country. The generals and prefects lie to the Minister, the captains and mayors lie to the generals and prefects. If men in my regiment indulge in dirty work, they cover it up as between pals, and if I hear of it, it is by accident."

M. Servan-Schreiber told of French troops surrounding a village to catch rebels who were known to be in a house from which they had fired. He said a general in a helicopter then took over and ordered artillery fire on the village, to the indignation of the infantry officer who previously had been in charge.

Conversations Recounted

M. Servan-Schreiber recounted conservation of officers who he said were appalled by such methods. He contended that the Army must commend itself to the Moslem population, not turn friendly Moslems into rebels by an excess of severity and indiscriminate repression.

"In pillage, assassination and collective torture we yield nothing to the adversary," he quoted one experienced officer as saying.

The French forces in Algeria are engaged in a guerrilla war in which no ground rules restrain the rebels, either against the troops or against civilians believed to be pro-French. According to reports, one atrocity tends to provoke another.

M. Servan-Schreiber was called into the army last July. He went to Algeria strongly opposed to the French policy of "pacification" there. He is an ardent supporter of former Premier Pierre Mendès-France, who likewise opposes the Government's whole Algerian policy.

However, M. Servan-Schreiber is not alone in indicting the methods of the "pacification." This also has been done by other writers, notably in the letters of a soldier who was killed in Algeria that were published in pamphlet form by the Roman Catholic weekly Christian Witness, and in a book entitled "Against Torture," by the novelist, P. H. Simon. This book was praised by the well-known Catholic writer, François Mauriac.

Thus the "campaign," that the Ministry of Defense said would lead to prosecutions, involves some highly responsible writers who contend that a moral issue affecting France's honor is at stake.

March 17, 1957

France Forms Agency to Guard Liberties in Rebellious Algeria

By ROBERT C. DOTY
Special to The New York Times.

PARIS, April 5—The French Government established today a permanent commission to safeguard human rights and liberties in Algeria. This was in answer to charges of excessive brutality in the repression of the rebellion there.

This decision was announced at the end of a four-hour Cabinet meeting called to canvass the situation in Algeria after two and a half years of bitter struggle against Moslem guerrillas and terrorists demanding complete independence from France.

The Cabinet heard another in the long series of optimistic reports on the military situation from Robert Lacoste, Minister Residing in Algeria. While M. Lacoste spoke, many Frenchmen were reading statements by two of France's most respected commentators, Raymond Aron and Maurice Duverger.

The first contended that "the promise of independence" was the only effective policy in Algeria and the second called the methods employed in Algeria "not only immoral" but "stupid."

The Cabinet's communiqué expressed indignation over what it called "a campaign organized by the enemies of France" to depict the French civil administration in Algeria and the 700,000 soldiers who have served in the 400,000-man force there as "so many torturers."

But, at the same time, the Government shared "the sincere emotion of those who hope that any individual lapses from the policy desired by France, attached to the safeguard of the rights of man, should be uncovered and punished." Therefore, Premier Guy Mollet was authorized to select a commission of men of "uncontested moral authority" to work in collaboration with M. Lacoste to uncover violations of human rights and also expose "calumnious or systematically exaggerated" accusations.

The commission was reported to be a compromise between those who had favored an outright committee of inquiry, said to have been proposed by the Premier Wednesday, and those, including M. Lacoste, who opposed any move that could be interpreted as implying distrust of the Algerian administration or of the army.

The Government announced also that one of its most strategically placed critics, Gen. Jacques Paris de Bollardière, had been asked by his military superiors to explain in writing "the act of indiscipline of which he is accused." This was a demand for relief from an Algerian command followed by a published letter in which the general endorsed the activities of a French journalist now under indictment for a series of articles reporting acts of indiscriminate brutality by the French forces.

For more than a year, M. Lacoste has asserted repeatedly that France must hold on, continuing to push the military pacification of Algeria for what he identified some months ago as "the last quarter of an hour."

His optimism today was based on a reduction of the number of terrorist attacks in Algiers from 130 in January to thirty-two in March; on the "return of confidence among the Moslem population" and on an increase of school attendance by Moslem children from seventy Feb. 1, when a Moslem boycott was in effect, to 37,750 last Tuesday.

The views of M. Aron, expressed in his recent book "Hope and Fear of the Century," were given wide circulation today by excerpts published in L'Express, a weekly newspaper published by supporters of former Premier Pierre Mendès-France.

'Policy of Grandeur' Scored

He asserts that France, after the liberation in 1945, adopted a "policy of grandeur" beyond her physical means in Indochina, the Saar and in Africa with an appearance of success for ten years. "In eighteen months [or since the withdrawal from Indochina] the edifice has crumbled," he declares.

In the new book, M. Aron dismisses the theory, maintained with fervor by most Frenchmen, that loss of France's overseas empire would be an economic disaster. France, he writes, exports only 5 per cent of her total goods and services to the French Union and receives from it only 3 per cent.

In the same newspaper, M. Duverger, a left-wing political commentator, came to the defense of such men as General Paris de Bollardière, whose gestures, he said, could save the honor of the country and its army and open the way to a reasonable solution of the Algerian problem.

April 6, 1957

LIBERATION FRONT SPARKS ALGERIAN REBELLION

By THOMAS F. BRADY
Special to The New York Times.

ALGIERS, Algeria, June 8—There is only one significant nationalist group in Algeria, the National Liberation Front.

The Front, which is presumed to have been responsible for the recent massacre of Moslem villagers at Melouza, is a revolutionary organization that has adopted violence as its weapon. It has used that weapon so successfully that an army of half a million soldiers cannot keep the peace in Algeria and cannot assure the safety of its inhabitants.

The Front has succeeded in absorbing every Algerian nationalist group and tendency except a minority party known as the Algerian National Movement, led by a bearded patriarch named Hadj Messali, who is now, as he has been for a large part of his life, in the custody of the French Government.

The Messalists, as the follow-

THE COLONIZERS AND THE COLONIZED

ers of M. Messali are known, have their greatest strength among the Algerians who live in metropolitan France. There are Messalists in Algeria too, but they are relatively rare.

This correspondent has never met an Algerian in North Africa who speaks frankly out of French earshot who does not sympathize with the National Liberation Front. Even in this carefully policed city Moslem merchants, taxi drivers and chance acquaintances have a habit of becoming daringly and convincingly indiscreet when they recognize an American accent.

This does not mean that there are not Moslem victims of Liberation Front violence who hate and fear the organization. But such persons do not speak their minds, except when the French Army is present to protect them, and then it is difficult to distinguish sincerity from opportunism.

Melouza Massacre

The recent massacre of 300 Moslems in the region of Melouza is decided evidence of a division in Algerian ranks, but the impression it has created abroad, because of the dramatic horror attached to the incident, is perhaps exaggerated.

French quarters have emphasized the thesis that this was a killing of Messalists by Front rebels. French army officers on the spot prefer the theory that there was a large element of ethnic antagonism between Kabyle Berbers and their traditional Arab enemies behind the massacre.

The army officers also suggest that the Beni Ileman tribe, from whom the killers chose their victims, was about to "rally" to France by formal declaration and was therefore punished by the nationalist rebels.

The Beni Ileman survivors are somewhat confused. Many of them say they do not know who M. Messali is. Others proclaim their Messalist sympathies in a curious way. One tribesman said this week: "We are for Messali and for France." There are suspicions on the side of the Liberation Front that some French strategists would like to use M. Messali's movement to "divide and reconquer," but M. Messali himself remains an antagonist of French dominion here.

There are, according to French quarters, several hundred Messalist rebels under arms in a roughly triangular section of the country, the blunted apex of the triangle being about seventy-five miles south of Algiers. But the number is small, compared with the more than 15,000 armed combatants who, according to French estimates, constitute the striking force of the Liberation Front.

Clashes between the Messalists and the forces of the Front have been reported from time to time but they have not affected control by the Front of rebel activity in five-sixths of Algeria.

Moreover, all external support of Algerian nationalism from the Arab nations goes to the Front—none of it to M. Messali.

Lesser Evils

There seems little doubt that the French regard the Messalists as the lesser of the evils. They feel the Messali movement is "more democratic" than the Front. It is also weaker and less revolutionary.

The front grew out of a dissident group in M. Messali's party that formed a revolutionary committee for direct action in 1954. The Front itself came into being a few months later when the present guerrilla war began on All Saints Day in 1954. Later Ferhat Abbas, leader of another party, rallied to the Front.

Committee rule still persists. The executive military command is held by a committee of four members who are said to be somewhere in Algeria. A larger committee of about two dozen members, many of them outside the territory, is theoretically in charge of policy, but the military command is the only body that can make quick decisions.

Being an amalgam, the Front is subject to strain among different tendencies in its ranks. There is even dissidence in the military arm in the Aurès-Nementcha Mountains, where the chain of command appears to have been broken.

Tunisian observers say the reason the Front has been so cool to rigorously logical urgings by Premier Habib Bourguiba of Tunisia for negotiations with the French is that front leaders fear splits in their own ranks if external pressure should lessen. "They want the French Army to do their organizing for them," one Tunisian said, "and they think time is on their side, so they do not want to negotiate."

Morale Problem

Members of the Front have suggested themselves that the morale of their guerrilla fighters might slump if negotiations were begun now. And nobody is quite sure what terms would be acceptable to all the elements of the Front, except that they all want independence. It seems clear the leaders prefer to wait and see what the next meeting of the United Nations General Assembly will bring forth on the Algerian question.

June 9, 1957

Carrefour, Paris

AT THE TUNISIAN FRONTIER: "We're poor Algerians in need of rifles, automatic weapons, mortars..."

French Vigilantes Operate in Algiers

By HOMER BIGART
Special to The New York Times.

ALGIERS, Algeria, June 25—Right-wing vigilantism is increasing among the European population of Algiers. One of its manifestations is the newly created Dispositif de Protection Urbaine (Organization for Urban Security).

Liberal French observers say this organization bears a disquieting resemblance to a totalitarian police apparatus. It is, in fact, a corps of civilian informers who operate much like the block-watchers of the Communist world.

The aim of the D. P. U. is to check the terrorist activities of the Algerian nationalists. Its members spy and report on suspicious movements of Moslems. Its table of organization puts two members in each block of apartments inhabited by a mixed population of Europeans and Moslems.

These block-watchers report to their immediate superiors, whose precincts embrace a number of blocks called ilots—little islands. Ilot commanders report to district chiefs, who in turn pass on their information to the headquarters of Gen. Jean Massu, chief of the French security forces in Algiers.

General Massu, who commands a paratroop division, established the D. P. U. a few months ago. He told correspondents today that its strength was 1,500 men, most of them army veterans. He said they were permitted to carry arms and had the power to make arrests when no policemen or soldiers happened to be near.

General Massu is the officer who stemmed urban terrorism last winter by using methods that part of the Paris press denounced as too drastic. He believes these press attacks were inspired partly by the Communists. He said he arrested "twenty European liberals or Communists" during February and March because "I wanted to prove there was only one justice and that we were against the ultras of both sides, whether Moslems or Europeans."

Renewed outbreaks of terror and counter-terror in early June brought General Massu and his paratroopers back to Algiers from the countryside. He was given greater powers and the police were made subordinate to him.

His return was hailed by gangs of European youths who marched through the streets shouting "Massu to power!" after mobs had slain five Moslems in the counter-terrorism of June 11. General Massu attributed those riots to "bums" from the mixed working-class district of Bab el Oued. He expressed surprise over the riots but doubted that they would recur.

"For one thing, we have speeded up the judiciary sys-

Algeria

tem," he said. "The execution of nine terrorists in the past week has done much to calm the Europeans. Second, we have taken more precise methods to control the population. And finally, the European population now knows that the bums of Bab el Oued only hurt the European position."

As for the D. P. U., General Massu conceded an organizational resemblance to the blockwatchers of Fascist and Communist regimes. But he said its members were carefully screened to keep out extremists.

General Massu said he was in complete accord with the program of Robert Lacoste, Minister Residing in Algeria. He said M. Lacoste believed that social, political and economic reforms were necessary if the French were to hold Algeria.

"Militarily, we can win," the general said. "But to assure victory there must be reforms. I would like to see the Europeans treat the Moslems as brothers. I would like to see more Moslems in municipal jobs. M. Lacoste's program of bringing Moslems into the municipal government must be speeded.

"I would like to see a fight against the Bidonvilles [tin shantytowns where Algerians live in incredible squalor]. But rather than build fancy apartments for these slum-dwellers, I would put up simple buildings."

This was implied criticism of Mayor Jacques Chevallier of Algiers, who has erected handsome blocks of apartments adjacent to some of the city's worst Bidonvilles.

June 26, 1957

Events in Algeria

Representation and Protection of Minorities Deemed Essential

The writer of the following letter, a leader of the Gaullist party, is a member of the French National Assembly and a former Governor of Algeria.

TO THE EDITOR OF THE NEW YORK TIMES:

I feel compelled to write to you in order to object to the dispatches of your correspondent in Algiers, Thomas Brady, which appear to me as unfair and misleading.

For instance, it was grossly unfair and inaccurate to describe the veterans and faculty organizations of the University of Algiers as "ultra-colonialist," as Mr. Brady did in his Sept. 17 dispatch. It is misleading to write, on Oct. 5, that "the ultra-colonialists * * * opposed the bill because it would have given Algerians equal voting rights with the Europeans."

First of all I would like to point out that the "Europeans" are "Algerians" as well as the Arabs, exactly as the white or Negro population of the United States is "American," and not only the "Redskin" Indians.

The heart of the matter is that there are in Algeria more than one million citizens of Christian faith and 140,000 Jews. They are not "ultra" or even "colonialist." Their fears are those of men who have everything to lose, including their lives and those of their families, if unwise provisions of the law permit a dictatorial regime to oppress the non-Moslem minority.

That those fears are not groundless is proved by the dreadful record of murders, rapes and tortures committed by the Algerian nationalists against countless men, women and children.

Changes in Text

M. Bourgès-Maunoury's Government felt it necessary to call representatives of all non-Communist parties to a round-table conference which agreed to strike out several dangerous provisions from the proposed text.

Some points still remained to be discussed, mainly concerning the electoral system which many Deputies, including myself, deemed necessary clearly to define in order to establish a proportional representation of the minorities.

I have no doubt that the draft could have been amended had not the Government suddenly cut short all discussion, a move which led 144 non-Communist Deputies to vote against the proposed law.

This is not a matter of "colonialism," "ultra" or not, but a matter of survival for more than one million Algerians. Representation and protection of the minorities seem to me to be one of the requisites of democracy.

It is all very well for Mr. Brady, who is an American and can go back to the United States when he chooses, to look down upon the Algerians. I wonder what he and many American citizens would think if they had seen their friends or relatives butchered by the rebels.

Mr. Brady's description of the Algerian atmosphere after the bill was killed strikes me as most one-sided and biased. He should have seen the hundreds of wires and letters of congratulations I have received from many Algerians, Moslems and non-Moslems alike, for the part I took in defeating the project.

JACQUES SOUSTELLE.

Paris, Oct. 9, 1957.

October 18, 1957

FRANCE CONCEDES ALGERIA EXCESSES

Inquiry's Report Denounces Reprisals as Well as Acts That Provoked Them

By ROBERT C. DOTY
Special to The New York Times.

PARIS, Dec. 13—A report on savagery and brutality by both sides in the Algerian war was made public here today.

The long delayed and hotly disputed report was made by twelve prominent Frenchmen who constituted the official Commission for the Safeguard of Rights and Individual Liberties. It was published in full by the respected Paris newspaper Le Monde before the Government made it public.

After Le Monde's printing, the office of Premier Félix Gaillard made the report available to others.

In approximately 10,000 words the commissioners reported that the Algerian rebels' ferocity had provoked retaliation by individual Frenchmen in violation of express prohibitions. This had taken the form of tortures of Algerian prisoners, abusive use of arbitrary internment and suspect "disappearances" of persons arrested by the French police, gendarmes and army, the report said.

Incidents Detailed

It cited three cases in which groups of rebel suspects were locked up overnight in fume-laden wine cellars. Seventy-eight were suffocated. The officers responsible were subjected to military punishment and indicted for homicide by negligence.

In explanation, if not justification, of the torture of suspects, the report said confessions obtained in this way had saved many lives by permitting authorities to frustrate planned terrorist actions.

The commission made clear, however, that in its opinion neither the provocation of rebel excesses nor the argument of efficacy could justify use of illegal methods in violation of all principles of human rights to which France subscribes.

Against these isolated and sternly punished lapses, the commissioners set rebel terrorism "that knows no quarter" by men who "kill for killing's sake, pillage, burn, slit throats, rape, crush infants' heads against walls, disembowel women, emasculate men."

In its conclusions, the commission paid tribute to the over-all record of the army and civil administration in Algeria but suggested that the Government might take corrective action to end violations of rights and liberties.

Even sterner measures against those guilty of violations of law, some judicial safeguards against abuse of internment procedure and relief of the army from police duties for which it was untrained and had little taste were indicated as desirable steps.

Publication of the report in Le Monde ended a dispute that had raged inside and outside the Government since Sept. 14 when the report was handed in to Maurice Bourgès-Maunoury, then Premier, by the commission's president, Pierre Beteille, a distinguished lawyer.

In general, right-wing forces backing the Government's policies in Algeria fought against publication of the report. They contended that it would serve only to blacken the repute of the Army and Administration and would serve rebel propaganda ends in such forums as the United Nations and the

North Atlantic Treaty Organization.

At the same time, the liberal and left-wing press and opinion that first raised charges of brutality against French forces last spring have pressed insistently for publication of the commission's findings.

Lacoste Criticizes Action

Among those opposing early publication was Robert Lacoste, Socialist Minister for Algeria, although most of his party colleagues have agitated for publication. From Algiers today he issued a statement regretting publication of the report by Le Monde before the Government had completed its comments on the the findings and assembled a new dossier of rebel atrocities to accompany and counterbalance the criticisms of French actions.

Le Monde, however, recalled that access to the text had been promised as early as Sept. 25 and as recently as Dec. 11 by M. Lacoste himself. In these circumstances, the paper observed editorially, it felt "authorized to publish today, after three months of waiting, a document that has been promised unceasingly by the most qualified spokesmen and the revelation of which is demanded by a body of opinion growing larger each day."

Le Monde accompanied the commission report with 4,000 words excerpted from an earlier Government compilation of rebel atrocities. Cited prominently were massacres of hundreds of Moslems in three villages, a total civilian death toll at rebel hands of more than 7,000 men, women and children, European and Moslem, the disappearance of 2,500 others, the killing and mutilation of French soldiers wounded in action.

Continued heavy exactions of support in men and money from the Moslem population under the threat of terror were also reported prominently.

Charges Categorized

From hundreds of complaints received, the commission sorted the apparently serious ones in four categories: charges of torture, of arbitrary imprisonment, of cruelty in the eight Algerian internment camps currently holding about 4,000 persons and, "most troubling," those dealing with "disappearances" from police or army custody.

The report cited no specific examples of tortures but referred to cases discussed in eight preliminary reports submitted since the commission was constituted last May.

The report was critical of the internment in camps by administrative order of fourteen Algerian Moslem magistrates and lawyers against whom no charges ever were substantiated. One young lawyer, assigned by the bar to defend a terrorist, was sent to an internment camp two days after having taken the case.

December 14, 1957

ALGERIA REFORMS ENACTED IN PARIS

Assembly, 296-244, Adopts Bill for Regional Autonomy and Equality in Voting

By HENRY GINIGER
Special to The New York Times.

PARIS, Jan. 31—The Algeria Reform Bill finally became law today amid official concern for the state of military affairs in the embattled North African territory.

The vote on the National Assembly's third reading of the bill was 296 to 244. The three readings were required by differences between the Assembly and the Advisory Council of the Republic.

The bill establishes antonomy on a regional basis, the principle of man-for-man voting equality between Moslems and non-Moslems and maintains full French sovereignty.

Regretting the long delay in passing the measures, on which debate began last September, Robert Lacoste, Minister for Algeria, indicated in the corridors that he was worried by renewed rebel strength and activity. Large supplies of arms have been coming across the frontier from Tunisia.

M. Lacoste said five French parachute regiments had just taken up positions along the frontier in an attempt to halt the arms flow.

The Minister said an electrified barbed wire entanglement erected along a large part of the frontier was not completely effective. He added, however, that the rebels were paying a heavy price in men to get their supplies through.

February 1, 1958

ALGERIANS LOATH TO JOIN NEW RULE

Moslems With Qualifications of Broad Representation Fear Rebel Reprisals

By W. H. LAWRENCE
Special to The New York Times.

CONSTANTINE, Algeria, Feb. 17—Algerian authorities conceded today that they were encountering difficulty in enlisting officials for the new political organs created by the French reform law.

The problem of obtaining men truly representative of the breadth of Moslem opinion is most acute in eastern Algeria, where rebel armed forces are most active.

Politically, there are several reasons for the reluctance among Moslems to assume positions of political leadership now.

Many fear violent reprisals if they cooperate with the French. This group readily believes the talk of a new and bloodier insurgent "spring offensive."

Fear 'Collaborator' Label

Still others fear that cease-fire negotiations or any other kind of political settlement would mark them as "collaborators" deserving of at least political and economic vengeance.

A large section of Moslem opinion still is "in the middle," unwilling to back the rebel National Liberation Front but still unfriendly toward the French. This segment wonders if future developments might not produce concessions more favorable to Moslem rule than those now offered.

The problem is not made any easier by the fact that there is an April 1 deadline for appointing new "special delegations" to replace municipal, town and village governments. These hand-picked delegations will serve until free elections can be held in an atmosphere of calm.

For example, here is Constantine, a city of 160,000 persons, three-quarters of them Moslem. There is no certainty that a new government that would be composed of roughly three Moslems to one person of European descent and that still would be a regime that would command the respect of most Moslems here could be selected in the next six weeks.

This does not mean there is a shortage of Moslem volunteers for official position. But the authorities say that too many of the volunteers represent no one but themselves.

There definitely is a shortage of volunteers among those Moslems who might be considered in the Center or even to the Left of Center but who have so far avoided any direct ties with the rebels. It is to this group that the French are directing new appeals.

The authorities believe that the composition of the first appointed delegation and the respect it can command among the population are of first importance. They believe that any group dominated by Moslem "yes men" would be disastrous.

Unless, as seems unlikely, there is a sudden shift in the political climate, the interim solution for Constantine and other cities like it may be to appoint by April 1 a single official with all the powers of a "special delegation."

"I would much rather have one man appointed than to gamble with the honesty and integrity of the new political reform structure we are attempting to create here," said a Moslem who commands French respect and attention.

February 18, 1958

Algeria

FRANCE TO SET UP A NO MAN'S LAND ON TUNISIAN LINE

By ROBERT C. DOTY
Special to The New York Times.

PARIS, Feb. 19—France decided today to establish a No Man's Land about 200 miles long and averaging fifteen miles in depth on the Algerian side of the Tunisian frontier to check rebel infiltrations.

It was estimated by a high official source that the operation would involve the displacement and resettlement of 70,000 to 80,000 civilians now living in the frontier area. Thereafter French forces behind barbed wire on the Algerian side of the zone and planes flying over it would feel free to fire on any sign of movement in the buffer zone.

In the French view the move would accomplish two ends. It would greatly reduce the ease with which Algerian rebels are believed here to move into Tunisia for rest, training and resupply and back across the border for offensive action in Algeria.

Fewer Incidents Foreseen

At the same time it would reduce the likelihood of frontier incidents with Tunisia of the type that brought about the French aerial bombing Feb. 8 of the Tunisian village of Sakiet-Sidi-Youssef, root of the present crisis in relations between France and her former protectorate.

Practically, the cleared zone would cover the area between the Tunisian frontier and an electrified barbed-wire barricade that runs roughly north-south from Bône to Tebessa. The barricade, known as the Morice Line after former Defense Minister André Morice, who promoted its construction, is meant to help stop the flow of men and supplies.

French civil and military officials acknowledge that it has not been a great success. French estimates of the amount of rebel aid getting through from Tunisia range from 70 to 80 per cent.

February 20, 1958

JUNTA TAKES ALGIERS RULE; FRANCE FEARS CIVIL WAR; PFLIMLIN IS NEW PREMIER

Figures in Algerian Power Struggle

Gen. Raoul Salan

Gen. Jacques Massu
Associated Press

Army Group in Algeria Asks Power for de Gaulle

By Reuters.

ALGIERS, May 13—French troops seized control of Algeria tonight and demanded the return of Gen. Charles de Gaulle as Premier of France. The move was taken by many officials in Paris as a direct challenge to the French Government.

The army's intervention followed rioting by French settlers, who sacked French and United States official buildings during a protest against the confirmation of Pierre Pflimlin as Premier.

"We appeal to General de Gaulle to take the leadership of a government of public safety," said Gen. Jacques Massu, a former comrade of the wartime Free French leader.

Civilians on Committee

General Massu heads a newly-formed "Committee of Public Safety" here. He led a group of paratroopers who took control of the Algiers radio station and ousted the Government director earlier tonight.

Gen. Raoul Salan, the Commander in Chief, declared in a broadcast:

"I have provisionally taken into my hands the destinies of French Algeria.

"I ask you to put your trust in the army and its leaders and to show your calmness and your determination."

General Massu, in a statement read to approximately 30,000 demonstrators massed outside Government House, said General de Gaulle was "alone capable" of heading a French Government that would "ensure the everlastingness of French Algeria, an integral part of France."

The Massu committee, composed of three colonels and seven civilians, said it would "maintain order and avoid bloodshed" in the city.

There were conflicting reports about General Salan's connection with General Massu's committee. Though it had been understood here and in Paris that the generals had sided together, sources close to the Premier's office in Paris said General Salan had acted on instructions from the outgoing Premier, Félix Gaillard.

There were also unconfirmed reports that General Salan was being kept under guard here by some of General Massu's paratroopers, who considered him suspect.

General Massu said Public Safety Committees were being formed in other principal towns of Algeria—Oran, Constantine and Bône.

The term "Committee of Public Safety" is a name once given to a governing institution set up during the French Revolution.

The action came after President René Coty had held an emergency meeting with the army's Chief of Staff, Paul Ely, and the outgoing Government to

The New York Times   May 14, 1958
French paratroops seized radio in Algiers (cross).

seek measures to curb the Algiers disorders.

Shouts of "the army to power" rose from the demonstrators as General Massu and his paratroops arrived at the ransacked Ministry for Algeria. The rioters had been protesting against M. Pflimlin.

A seven-hour general strike called by a European "vigilance committee" led to the formation of the "safety committee."

Demonstrators first attacked the United States cultural center, battering down the front door and hurling books and magazines into the street.

Afterward they paraded to the Ministry for Algeria using trucks to crash through the front gates. They swarmed through the building, smashing furniture and burning files, then toppled from the roof a bust of "Marianne," the symbol of the French Republic.

"Algeria is French—long live de Gaulle," chanted long lines of demonstrators marching twelve abreast through the city streets.

The strike was 100 per cent effective even in the Casbah. At noon steel shutters covered the fronts of stores, cafes, restaurants, offices and theatres.

An announcer in a sound truck preceded the troops and asked the crowds, "Will you abandon French Algeria?" The crowd shouted back, "No."

"Will you defend French Algeria to the end?" the announcer went on. The crowd shouted, "Yes."

A throng of 15,000 persons gathered in front of the main Post Office screaming insults against M. Pflimlin and the Conservative deputy he wanted as his Minister for Algeria, André Mutter.

The Algerian Conservative Federation and the Algiers University Movement for the Maintenance of French Sovereignty in Algeria sent a message to M. Mutter today demanding that he keep out of a Pflimlin Cabinet.

"The French of Algeria are unanimously against the Cabinet of Pflimlin," the message to President Coty said. "They hold you personally responsible for the serious consequences of the investiture."

M. Pflimlin has a reputation among conservatives for liberal views on settling the rebellion, now in its fourth year.

The organizers of the demonstration invited Moslems to take part and large numbers of them did. Moslem troops were loudly cheered as they moved among the Europeans.

A Moslem boy waving a tricolor flag at the foot of the city's War Memorial was applauded, and the cheers increased when a European raised the boy on his shoulders.

A spokesman for the Vigilance Committee read an "Address to the People of France, Algeria and the French Union" which declared that the "proposed government is a government of scuttle." A leaflet said a Pflimlin Government would lose Algeria.

During an earlier news broadcast over the Algiers radio, a voice broke in to abuse the announcer each time he mentioned M. Pflimlin.

The demonstrators also protested last Friday's execution of three French prisoners by Algerian rebels for "torture, rape and murder."

May 14, 1958

FRENCH CRISIS—IN THE WORDS OF KEY MEN

This is a chronology of the French crisis, as illustrated by statements of the key figures who participated in it.

MAY 13

Gen. Jacques Massu, *in asserting the power of the military-civilian junta in Algeria:* "We appeal to General de Gaulle to take the leadership of a government of public safety."

Gen. Raoul Salan, *in defining his role as military commander in Algeria:* "I have provisionally taken into my hands the destinies of French Algeria. I ask you to put your trust in the army and its leaders and to show your calmness and your determination."

MAY 15

Gen. Charles de Gaulle, *in a statement announcing his readiness to take power:* "For twelve years France, at grips with problems too tough for the regime of political parties, has been engaged in a disastrous process. * * * Today, in the face of the troubles that are mounting again in the country, I hold myself ready to take over the powers of the republic."

MAY 17

Premier Pierre Pflimlin, *after receiving emergency powers from the Assembly:* "There was a large majority in favor of giving the Government the powers it needed. We shall use these powers, most certainly, against all those who might attempt to rise up against the law."

MAY 19

General de Gaulle, *in a news conference explaining under what conditions he would assume power:* "If de Gaulle should find himself delegated with exceptional powers for an exceptional task at an exceptional time, that could obviously not be done according to the usual procedure and the rights that are so usual that everyone is tired of them. It would be necessary to adopt a procedure that would also be exceptional. * * * When events speak loudly and there is agreement on substance, procedures can have considerable flexibility. * * * If the need arose I would tell the competent authorities what procedure would in my opinion be the best."

MAY 25

Former President Vincent Auriol, *in a letter to General de Gaulle urging him to clarify his position:* "It is * * * urgent to re-establish compromised unity and that depends now on you. I am persuaded that in the light of events you will do your utmost to bring back to duty those among the generals or superior officers who have disobeyed their supreme chief and to call on all citizens to respect the common law. If you break all solidarity with those who have created a seditious movement, you will regain the confidence of the entire nation."

MAY 28

Premier Pflimlin, *in offering his resignation after winning a vote of confidence in the Assembly:* "The Government obtained the [relative] majority of the votes but an important group separated itself from the Government. Three Ministers belonging to [the right-wing Independents] have left the Government. Thus the Government finds itself weakened at a moment when it must face increasingly heavy tasks."

MAY 29

General de Gaulle, *in a letter replying to Auriol's, released May 29:* "The events of Algeria [were] provoked by the chronic incompetence of the public powers * * *. The launching and developing were carried out without my being in any way involved in them. Things being as they are, I proposed to form by legal means a Government that I think could remake unity, re-establish discipline in the state * * * and promote adoption of a renovated Constitution by the country. But I find myself up against a determined opposition from the side of the national representation [the Assembly]."

President René Coty, *in a message read to the Assembly urging that the leadership go to General de Gaulle:* "With the homeland and the republic in peril, I have turned toward the most illustrious of Frenchmen, toward the one who, during the darkest years of our history, was our leader in the reconquest of our liberty * * *. I am asking General de Gaulle to confer with the Chief of State and to examine with him what, within the framework of republican legality, is immediately necessary to a government of national safety and what can or must be done at a later time for a profound reform of our institutions."

General de Gaulle, *in announcing the terms under which he would accept the call to govern:* "The Government, once invested by the National Assembly, would receive for a fixed time the full powers necessary to act in the present very grave situation. Besides this a mandate would be given to the Government following a procedure provided for by the present Constitution to prepare and to submit to the country through a referendum the changes that must be made in it, notably concerning the separation and the balance of powers as well as the relations of the French Republic with the peoples that are associated with it. I cannot undertake the task of leading the state and the nation unless these indispensable conditions are agreed to with the great and broad confidence that the salvation of France, of the state and of the Republic demands."

June 1, 1958

Algeria

DE GAULLE CURBS ARMY IN ALGERIA; TOP JUNTA YIELDS

By ROBERT C. DOTY
Special to The New York Times.

PARIS, June 6—Gen. Charles de Gaulle brought back from Algeria tonight what most observers here regarded as the key to re-establishment of France's position in Algeria—control of the army there.

The success of the soldier-Premier's three-day mission to liquidate the military-civilian dissidence in Algeria that has defied Paris since May 13 was read in two statements issued within a few hours of his return here tonight.

The first, issued in Oran, his last stop in Algeria, cracked down, politely but firmly, on the dissident Committees of Public Safety set up in the wake of the riots May 13 by the Europeans of Algiers. This movement was set on foot by plotters against the regime who played on the French settlers' fears that the Paris Government was preparing to sell out to the Moslem nationalist rebels.

Power Vested in Salan

The second statement, confirming Gen. Raoul Salan, French over-all commander in Algeria, in possession of all civilian and military power, made it clear that General Salan would henceforth take orders from Paris—in effect, Premier de Gaulle—alone.

[In Algiers, a spokesman for the All-Algeria Committee of Public Safety pledged its help and cooperation to General de Gaulle "without reserve."]

Premier de Gaulle's two declarations were cloaked in language that avoided giving naked offense to the dissidents. Their action, including a threat of civil war, was a major factor in his return to power. In his appearances at the beginning of the week before Parliament and in his dealings in Algeria, General de Gaulle has unveiled hitherto unsuspected talent for political maneuver, compromise and conciliation.

June 7, 1958

Algeria Is Offered Key Role in Union

By W. GRANGER BLAIR
Special to The New York Times.

PARIS, July 13 — Premier Charles de Gaulle opened the door today to the inclusion of Algeria in a new federal system linking France and her overseas territories.

He did so in a radio message to the nation's overseas possessions on the eve of France's national holiday commemorating the storming of the Bastille and the start of the French Revolution on July 14, 1789. It appeared to be the general's clearest expression of his intentions on the future of Algeria since he took office June 1.

The Premier termed his message one of "hope." This was so, he said, because "we are moving away from uncertainty with regard to our future relations."

"We are going toward a vast and free community," he continued. "In 1958 we must build new institutions, establish the links of our union in the federal manner and organize a grand political, economic and cultural entity that will answer to the conditions of modern life and progress.

"I must not fail to say that with Metropolitan France and the overseas departments, with West and Equatorial Africa, with Madagascar, Djibouti, New Caledonia and French Oceania, the place of Algeria, so dear and so torn, is marked out with a choice place."

However, because Algeria itself is legally a department of France and because Premier de Gaulle failed to define specifically what he meant by a "choice place," his message fell short of being an outright call for a federal relationship between France and her rebellious North African holding, according to informed observers.

Significance Stressed

Nevertheless, a Government source did not try to minimize the significance of the general intent of the message or the fact that Algeria was explicitly mentioned in an address that, without question, offered a federal system as a substitute for the present highly centralized French Union.

It also was observed that the Premier's plans for the future relationship between France and her overseas peoples would be embodied in a new Constitution now in process of being drafted. The people of France, Algeria and the territories will vote on the Constitution next autumn.

July 14, 1958

ALGERIANS WAGE TERROR IN FRANCE

Refineries and Shops Fired —7 Dead, 21 Injured

By HENRY TANNER
Special to The New York Times.

PARIS, Aug. 25—Large-scale and coordinated terrorism leaped from Algeria to Metropolitan France today, taking seven lives and leaving at least twenty-one persons injured.

About 2:30 o'clock this morning saboteurs struck simultaneously in Paris and at about twenty places between the English Channel and the Mediterranean. Their targets were gasoline storage facilities, a munitions factory, a railroad signal post and a plant producing military trucks.

Fourth Policeman Slain

The saboteurs killed three policemen and wounded one by machine gun fire when they tried to shoot their way into a police garage on Paris' Left Bank. They threw flaming gasoline torches into the garage in a futile attempt to set it afire.

A fourth policeman was killed a few moments later when the police, alerted by the attack on the garage, foiled an incendiary raid on a munitions factory in the Bois de Vincennes on Paris' east side.

At the same time saboteurs set fire to storage tanks in a big refinery in Mourepiane near Marseilles. Fire-fighting units sought all day to control the blaze, which tonight, sixteen hours after the attack, led to an explosion wounding seventeen firemen, three seriously. Late tonight the blaze still was out of control.

Incendiary raids also were directed against gasoline storage facilities near Le Havre, at Carcasonne and Narbonne in the Pyrenees, in Provence, in several cities west of Marseilles, at Salbris in Central France and in several suburbs of Paris.

All attacks were the work of Algerian nationalists, according to the French Government.

Two Algerians were killed and three wounded in the attack on the Paris police garage. Another was burned to death when he set off a plastic bomb in the Esso refinery at Notre-Dame-de-Gravinchon, near Le Havre, the police reported. The bomb caused no damage.

Scores of Algerians exchanged fire with the police at the scenes of various incidents, official reports say. More than fifty Algerians were arrested during the day.

The violence was said to be the worst of its type in Metropolitan France since the nationalist rebellion began more than four and a half years ago.

The French police had known for a long time that the Algerian National Liberation Front, which controls the Nationalist rebellion in Algeria, has an effective, tightly knit organization also in Metropolitan France.

This organization is understood to consist of two command zones: one for the Paris area and the north of France, the other for the eastern and southern part of country with an extension for Toulouse. The zones are subdivided into smaller regions, sectors, sections and, finally, cells. A cell consists of three or four men.

The strength of the organization is not known. There are said to be about 400,000 Algerians in France. Most of them are believed to have been touched in one way or another by the nationalist organizations and are paying dues—often to save their lives.

Past terrorist activity in Metropolitan France was largely confined to the slayings of Moslems. This was the way extremists extorted dues from their victims, French police officials say. But an important role was being played also by the rivalry between the Nationalist Liberation Front and the older Algerian Nationalist Movement led by Hadj Messali, which has a considerable following among Algerians in France but is weak in Algeria.

Between forty and seventy Algerians in Metropolitan France have been killed by their countrymen every month since the beginning of the year, according to a reliable private estimate. Official figures, which have never ben announced, are believed to be even higher.

Now for the first time the nationalist terrorists have turned from attacks on their countrymen to concerted, well-planned large-scale action against Frenchmen and French institutions.

THE COLONIZERS AND THE COLONIZED

The fact that they were able to strike simultaneously in virtually all parts of the country has caused obvious concern. But French officials, speaking for the record, have an optimistic explanation for the turn of events.

They say the leadership of nationalist rebellion has given an order for all-out terrorism in Metropolitan France as part of its desperate and futile campaign against Premier Charles de Gaulle's referendum Sept. 28 on constitutional reform. These officials say the nationalists are under pressure to demonstrate their military and political power in a dramatic way now, but find it increasingly difficult to do so in Algeria proper.

The Ministry of the Interior, after a day-long session of its top officials, announced that a special police service had been set up to coordinate all countermeasures against nationalist terrorism in Metropolitan France.

August 26, 1958

Algerian Rebels Set Up a Government Free of France

By FOSTER HAILEY
Special to The New York Times.

CAIRO, Sept. 19—The formation of a Provisional Government for a Republic of Algeria free of France was announced here today by leaders of the Algerian nationalist movement. The new regime was immediately recognized by Libya, Iraq and the United Arab Republic as the legal government of Algeria. Recognition by other Arab, African and Asian states is expected. [Tunisia and Morocco also accorded recognition. In Paris the De Gaulle Government termed the rebel regime "artificial" and said it lacked control over the territory.] The Coordination and Executive Committee of the Algerian National Liberation Front, which has been conducting a revolt against French rule of the North African territory since 1954, announced the establishment of the provisional regime.

It named the Cabinet of sixteen Ministers and three Secretaries of state, headed by Ferhat Abbas as Premier. Belkacem Krim, actual leader of the rebel forces, was named a Vice Premier and Minister of the Armed Forces.

A statement of policy also will be made at that time and decisions taken whether to apply for membership in the Arab League and the United Nations, he said.

Mr. Abbas had only five of his Ministers with him when he made the announcement of the Government's formation in the new five-story headquarters building of the Executive Committee in Cairo. Simultaneous announcements were to have been made in Algeria, Morocco and Tunisia.

At 59 years of age, Mr. Abbas and Ahmed Tewfik el-Medani, Minister of Cultural Affairs, are the only graybeards among the Cabinet. Eleven of the seventeen other members are under 40. "General" Krim is only 36.

Until 1954 Mr. Abbas himself was considered a moderate. He had said that if the French would give Algerians citizenship and equal rights with the European settlers, France would have no more loyal subjects.

The formation of a rebel government had been rumored for months, but it could not find a home. The proposal that it be established here had been discouraged until recently by President Gamal Abdel Nasser of the United Arab Republic.

Mr. Abbas, a slightly built man with glasses who looks more like the pharmacist he is by profession than the revolutionary leader he is by trade, read his announcement to a crowded news conference. He spoke in French, the only language in which he is proficient. His words were translated into Arabic and English by Mohammed Yazid, Minister of Information in the new Government.

"In the name of the Algerian people," Mr. Abbas said, "the Coordination and Executive Committee, in accordance with the powers with which it was vested by the National Council of the Algerian Revolution on Aug. 28, 1957, has decided to form a Provisional Government for the Algerian Republic."

He then read the Cabinet list and announced that the Provisional Government "assumes its responsibilities" as of today.

After the brief, informal ceremony the Premier and four of his Ministers posed for photographers with the Algerian Republic's flag—green and white, with a red crescent and star in the center—and that of the Arab Republic as a backdrop.

September 20, 1958

FRANCE GRANTING REBELS CLEMENCY

Algerians' Death Sentences Commuted—Imprisonment of Leaders Modified

By HENRY GINIGER
Special to The New York Times.

PARIS, Jan. 13—France decreed tonight the widest measures of clemency taken for Algerian rebels since they began fighting more than four years ago.

In confirming last week's reports that such measures were forthcoming, France's leaders gave impetus to reports that a new attempt at peace in Algeria was being made.

Today's announcement followed a report from Cairo that the Algerian Provisional Government, political head of the rebellion, had been meeting for the last two days "on important subjects."

The French measures are as follows:

¶Ahmed ben Bella, three other members of the Algerian rebel government, and a fifth rebel leader will be transferred from Santé Prison in Paris to a fortress whose name was not divulged. The men had been in prison since October, 1956, following French interception of a plane carrying them from Rabat to Tunis for a North African conference.

¶Hadj Messali, leader of the Algerian National Movement, which is a rival of the provisional government and more moderate in its tactics, was freed from his forced residence on Belle-Ile, off the coast of Brittany. He will be allowed to live anywhere in continental France. This implied that he could not return to Algeria.

¶The sentences of about 140 rebels who had been condemned to death were commuted by President Charles de Gaulle to life imprisonment. Reports from Algiers put the number at 200.

¶Rebels sentenced to prison will have their terms shortened by a tenth and possibly more.

¶About 7,000 persons interned in camps in Algeria by an administrative decision will be freed. These persons had not been charged with or convicted of crimes but had been considered dangerous.

January 14, 1959

Algeria

PARIS GIVES 3 OPTIONS TO ALGERIA

DE GAULLE SPEAKS

Independence Vote Is Offered Within 4 Years of Peace

By ROBERT C. DOTY
Special to The New York Times.

PARIS, Sept. 16—President Charles de Gaulle promised tonight to let the people of Algeria choose their own future — even independence — within four years after the restoration of peace there.

In a radio and television address to France and Algeria, the President held out to the 9,000,000 Moslems and more than 1,000,000 Europeans of Algeria the right to choose by referendum either independence —what he termed an "incredible and disastrous" independence— integration into the French Republic or a form of federal autonomy retaining close ties with France.

Period of Peace Sought

His plan aims at a period of peace, for a maximum of four years, during which Paris could efface the present bitterness and induce the Algerians to choose to continue in close relationship with France.

The President indicated that generous economic aid and social and administrative reform was planned in the period after fighting ends, to help influence such a decision.

In contrast, it was an unattractive and tightly circumscribed independence that President de Gaulle described. It would involve, he clearly indicated, a partition of Algeria into French and independent areas, with France retaining control of Sahara oil and much other wealth. It would mean "appalling poverty," he said.

The long-awaited declaration represented a major effort by General de Gaulle to bring to an end the Moslem rebellion that has racked Algeria for nearly five years.

Negotiation Ruled Out

Once again he offered the leaders of the rebel National Liberation Front a chance to lay down their arms and to accept an amnesty and full participation in the political debate that will precede the final choice.

[In Tunis the first reaction of quarters close to the rebels' Algerian Provisional Government was markedly negative. In Algiers, large numbers of Europeans and Moslems listened in silence to the President's broadcast and then dispersed quietly, apparently reserving judgment.]

The President again refused to negotiate with the rebel leaders as the representatives of the Moslem population. By conditioning a political settlement on the restoration of peace, he placed responsibility for delaying the exercise of free choice squarely on the rebel leaders.

The offer of independence was a historic occasion. No other French chief of state has ever dared hold out such a possibility, flouting the wishes of the powerful European minority in Algeria.

It was this minority, plus a part of the French Army, that rose up to topple the Fourth Republic in May, 1958, when Premier Pierre Pflimlin was merely suspected of the invention of seeking a negotiated peace.

The French people as a whole would be called upon to ratify by referendum the decision of the Algerians, the President said. He did not specify what the legal position would be if a referendum in Continental France produced a majority opposing the choice of the Algerians.

September 17, 1959

ALGERIAN REBELS OFFER TO DISCUSS PEACE WITH PARIS

Nationalists Accept Major Principle of de Gaulle Bid, but Insist on a Voice

By THOMAS F. BRADY
Special to The New York Times.

TUNIS, Sept. 28—The Algerian Provisional Government accepted today the principle of self-determination for Algeria enunciated Sept. 16 by President Charles de Gaulle.

A communiqué said the Provisional Government "is ready to enter into conversations with the French Government to discuss the political and military conditions of a cease-fire, and the conditions and guarantees of the application of self-determination."

But the nationalists insisted in their statement that the Provisional Government, which General de Gaulle specifically refused to recognize in his declaration, "is the depository and guarantor of the interests of the Algerian people until they have freely pronounced themselves."

Prompt Peace Is Offered

Therefore, the communiqué continued, "there can be a return of peace only with" the agreement of the Provisional Government. Then followed a sentence written in capital letters. "This [peace] can be immediate."

[In Paris, the French Government ignored the rebel organization's declaration. A spokesman said there would be no official reaction because the statement was viewed as unresponsive to General de Gaulle's proposal for peace and self-determination.]

President de Gaulle, in his speech Sept. 16, asked why war should continue in Algeria, after his promise of self-determination, "unless there is at work a group of ambitious agitators, resolved to establish their totalitarian dictatorship by force and terror and believing they can obtain from the [French] Republic one day the privilege of negotiating the destiny of Algeria and thus constituting themselves as the Algerian Government."

President Uncompromising

"There is no chance," he declared, "that France will lend herself to such an arbitrary decision."

Thus the question on which peace in Algeria depends is: What did General de Gaulle mean? The Algerians have proposed "conversations" on the conditions of a cease-fire and guarantees of self-determination. The French President excluded "negotiations" on the "destiny of Algeria."

September 29, 1959

THE COLONIZERS AND THE COLONIZED

ALGERIAN INSURGENTS SURRENDER; LEADER IS FLOWN TO JAIL IN PARIS; DE GAULLE SEEKS DECREE POWERS

TWO ARE IN HIDING

Army Permits Most of the Dissidents to Save Face

By THOMAS F. BRADY
Special to The New York Times.

ALGIERS, Feb. 1—The European uprising collapsed here today and its principal leader was flown to prison in Paris. Another leader was in flight and a third was mysteriously out of sight.

A face-saving formula was provided by the French Army command, which agreed to let the insurgent rank and file keep their arms by remaining "at the disposition of the army in operational units to be attached for the time being to the First Paratroop regiment of the Foreign Legion."

Those who wanted simply to go home were permitted to lay down their arms and walk away.

Home guardsmen, who had been an important element in the week-long hold-out in the middle of Algiers, were ordered to report to their battalion headquarters.

Prosecution Foreseen

The collapse came fifteen hours after insurgent loudspeakers closed down last night, proclaiming that the defenders of the barricades would die rather than surrender.

Pierre Lagaillarde, bearded 28-year-old extremist Deputy of the French National Assembly and an insurgent leader, was taken into army custody. He was not permitted to choose a face-saving course of action because it is expected he will be prosecuted.

He was sent to Paris by plane tonight to be held in Santé Prison, where the French Government first incarcerated Mohammed Ben Bella, Algerian nationalist leader. Mr. Ben Bella's organization, the National Liberation Front, advocates Algerian independence.

The uprising by the Europeans was an attack on President de Gaulle's policy of self-determination for Algeria.

A warrant has been issued for the arrest of Joseph Ortiz, a tavernkeeper and chief of a local Fascist movement. M. Ortiz, another leader of the uprising, slipped out of the barricades last night and went into hiding. He was reported seen this morning in Belcourt, a working-class suburb of Algiers.

Robert Martel, the third leader, was missing. Authorities here said they had no information on him. M. Martel heads the movement of Right-Wing settlers of the Mitidja Plain, south of Algiers.

The men who wanted to "put themselves at the disposition of the Army" were permitted to march out of their stronghold just before noon, after they had torn down the barricades. They were permitted to carry their arms and a French flag, with M. Lagaillarde at their head.

Four hundred and twenty men chose to march out and get into trucks that were to drive them to the rest camp of the First Regiment of legion paratroops at Zeralda, twenty-five miles west of Algiers.

Crowd Cheers Insurgents

M. Lagaillarde was put in a jeep at the end of a line of twenty-three trucks that drove quickly out of town, amid the cheers of admirers. The people of Algiers were strongly sympathetic to the band of men who held out in the barricaded quarter-mile of the main street for eight days until the army finally decided to isolate them.

The surrender took place behind barbed-wire networks and blockades of Army trucks that kept the crowds from seeing much of it. The surrender was negotiated last night by Col. Henri Dufour, commander of the First Regiment of legion paratroopers, which took the surrender.

Early this morning he visited the men in the stronghold and told them they had his word that they would be treated "as soldiers," but that he could give no commitment for M. Lagaillarde. He also declared that Paul Delouvrier, Delegate General and chief of civil government here, had given them no guarantees.

There were 1,200 men behind the barricades yesterday morning, according to army estimates. Those who chose not to attach themselves to the legion slipped out last night and this morning over the barricades of side streets leading into the redoubt.

Many of them were Home Guardsmen, who had been mobilized by the army to force a withdrawal from the barricades. Nevertheless, this morning, more than half the men who got into the trucks wore Home Guard uniforms. The Home Guardsmen could choose the Foreign Legion if they wanted to under the conditions of the surrender.

Some Return to Homes

Not only did more than half the insurgents prefer civilian life to battle against the Algerian Moslem nationalists, but some of those who left in trucks were back home tonight, including the father of M. Lagaillarde, who had embraced his wife and daughter tearfully on the barricades before he rode off.

At Zeralda, where the former insurgents were under no constraint to remain, some 150 automobiles arrived with weeping parents to bring back to Algiers young men who had decided to forego army life.

The status of the men who remain with the legion was not clear. An army press spokesman said tonight that the Foreign Legion would accept enlistment by French citizens, that the enlistment term was five years, and that it provided no shield against prosecution.

But the conditions announced in a communiqué issued by Maj. Gen. Jean Crepin, corps commander for central Algeria, indicated that the former insurgents might form special units, which would remain attached to the legion regiment only temporarily.

The surrender was preceded by bitterness. One defender of the barricades said to a Foreign Legionnaire across the bulwarks: "We're giving up and I don't want to be French any more. I want to be German."

The Legionnaire, himself a German, looked at the man and said: "I don't understand you. Yesterday you were ready to die so that Algeria would be forever French. Today you want to be a German."

The surrender was made somewhat palatable to the men by the fact that the Legion's First Paratroop Regiment was one of those that had fraternized with insurgents during the long inactivity of the Army last week. The refusal of the Army to take any vigorous steps against the uprising until Saturday was what gave it importance.

The insurrection could have been put down within twenty-four hours if the Army acted quickly, observers believe.

The final squeeze came yesterday when troops replaced the paratroops and isolated the insurrectionists from the sympathetic citizens of Algiers.

The uprising began Jan. 24 when demonstrators fired on gendarmes sent to disperse them.

There appeared to be some army anxiety that the surrender "with honor" permitted the insurgents would look like a disloyal compromise in Paris. A truck of the Foreign Legion collected newspaper correspondents here early this afternoon with word that "General Crepin wants to see you."

Gen. Jean Crepin is corps commander for central Algeria and the correspondents hoped for a news conference that would clarify the terms of surrender, so twenty-five climbed into the truck. At General Crepin's headquarters they were met by a major who said:

"The general is desolate that he can't see you. You've been brought here so we can confiscate your films of the surrender."

There were only two photographers in the group and they had already shipped out their pictures of the surrender.

Nevertheless, everyone protested vigorously at the limitation of press freedom. A captain said harshly: "The general has full powers here. Nobody can leave."

After a partial search and exposure of several unexposed rolls of film, correspondents were permitted to walk back to town.

February 2, 1960

Algeria

FRENCH OUTRAGED OVER EXECUTIONS

Slaying of Soldiers Stiffens Opposition to Negotiation With Algeria Rebels

By HENRY GINIGER
Special to The New York Times.

PARIS, Aug. 13—Opposition in France and Algeria to any settlement with the Algerian rebels has stiffened as a result of the execution of two French soldiers by the rebels.

The executions were announced yesterday by the rebel Provisional Government in Tunis and brought an immediate charge of "assassination" from Pierre Messmer, France's Minister of Armed Forces.

The most vehement reaction came from those who have long opposed any settlement that might weaken French sovereignty over Algeria. Conservative political and military circles seized upon the executions as a reason for not undertaking any further negotiation with the rebels.

President de Gaulle made no comment. He is said to be planning another statement on Algeria during a visit to Brittany in September. But his efforts to reach a cease-fire agreement with the rebels, then to obtain their participation in a final political settlement through elections, will be more difficult.

Editor's Reaction Typical

A typical reaction was that of Robert Bony, editor of the conservative paper L'Aurore.

He said the rebel leadership, by taking "the frightful responsibility" to shoot the two soldiers, had placed itself "deliberately outside of any possible negotiation."

There is much criticism of Tunisia for sheltering the rebel officials. A widespread belief that the executions took place in Tunisia led to renewed demands for a tougher attitude toward the Government of Tunisia.

Observers in Algeria reported that many French Army officers were in much the same frame of mind. There had been no enthusiasm for the preliminary talks that began in Melun late in June and broke down a few days later. Today there appeared to be open hostility to resuming talks with the "assassins."

The two soldiers, Michel Castera and Clotaire le Gall, both 22 years old, were condemned and shot for "war crimes," according to an announcement by the rebels. They had been taken prisoners in fighting last May. But most French observers, including those most favorably disposed toward negotiation for a settlement, believed that the executions were reprisals for French executions of Algerian rebels in July.

August 14, 1960

Paris Order Curbs 140 Intellectuals For Algeria Views

By Reuters.

PARIS, Sept. 28—The French Government tonight forbade more than 140 of the country's top intellectuals, including actors, writers and teachers, to appear on the state-run radio and television or in state-run theatres.

The ban was imposed on all who signed a recent manifesto supporting the right to refuse military service in Algeria.

It affects such internationally known figures as Jean-Paul Sartre, the philosopher; Françoise Sagan and Simone de Beauvoir, writers, and Simone Signoret and Daniele Delorme, actresses.

A Cabinet communiqué said the ban was approved at the request of Premier Michel Debré.

The Information Ministry also announced a measure was being prepared to withhold state aid from any film in which signatories of the manifesto appeared.

The ban was included in a decree announced after a Cabinet meeting aimed at strengthening measures against "those favoring refusal of military service or desertion."

Ministers will be able to take immediate disciplinary measures against civil servants—such as teachers, soldiers or magistrates—including suspension from duty and stoppage of up to two-thirds of their salary.

Such action will not prevent legal proceedings being brought under recent measures providing for greater punishment for incitement to evasion of military service or desertion.

More than 140 intellectuals, including writers, actors, teachers, journalists and film stars have signed the manifesto. So far, eighteen have been formally charged by an examining magistrate.

A Cabinet communiqué said the decree was approved after a proposal by Premier Debré to strengthen disciplinary powers over "the few agents who favor refusal of military service or desertion."

September 29, 1960

---

10 SEIZED IN PARIS FOR ALGERIA VIEW

Policemen Raid Offices of 3 Leftist Periodicals—Plot Laid to Intellectuals

By ROBERT C. DOTY
Special to The New York Times.

PARIS, Oct. 1 — Ten persons have been arrested in the last twenty-four hours in the campaign by the French police against Leftist intellectuals suspected of complicity in support for the Algerian rebellion.

Last night and early this morning the police searched the offices of Esprit, Verité et Liberté and Les Temps Modernes, all Leftist periodicals. The last is directed by Jean-Paul Sartre, the philosopher.

The police seized the current issue of M. Sartre's journal and took ten persons to headquarters for questioning.

180 Signers Are Listed

The management of Les Temps Modernes said the seized issue contained a list of about 180 signers of the recent declaration supporting the right of young French conscripts to refuse to serve against the Moslem rebels.

The issue was also said to have included a report on the first congress of a Left-Wing organization, "Young Resistance," witnesses' accounts of "several cases of massacres committed by French soldiers" and a study by Patrick Kessel on "The Civil Power, the Army and Torture in Algeria From 1954 to 1960."

The police action was a manifestation of the increasingly bitter dispute between advocates of a negotiated peace in Algeria and the partisans of an uncompromising war against the rebellion, now nearing its sixth anniversary.

De Gaulle Sets Policy

President de Gaulle is committed to a middle course of seeking to create conditions for a free choice of political status by the Algerian populace without either recognition of the rebel leadership as the valid spokesman for Algeria or resignation to an endless war of repression.

But the most immediate threat to the Government seems to come from a core of intransigents in the army and among the Europeans of Algeria. They have twice combined to menace Paris Governments, successfully in 1958 and unsuccessfully last January, in defense of a "French Algeria."

Therefore, many observers interpreted the Government crackdown on the intellectuals as an effort to appease the army and Right-Wing opinion.

The Government has suspended a number of civil servants who have joined campaigns for insubordination and has banned several artists from future appearances on French radio and television and in state-supported theatres. The banned artists include Simone Signoret, the actress, who signed the manifesto.

Those taken in for questioning were editors and contributors to the three periodicals. According to the newspaper Le Monde, only four of those questioned had signed the manifesto on insubordination. Five were released. The others were held for further questioning.

16 Convicted as Plotters

Shortly before midnight, sixteen persons were convicted in a trial of twenty French men and women, many of them students, teachers and artists, and five Moslem Algerians for active aid to the rebellion. The nine other defendants were acquitted by the military court.

The nine men and seven women who were convicted drew sentences of from eight months to ten years in prison and fines from the equivalent of $100 to $14,000.

Among those convicted were the man accused as the leader of the network, Francis Jeanson, teacher and writer, and another Frenchman and two Frenchwomen who are fugitives from justice.

It was the trial of these defendants over the last month that prompted the signing of the manifesto on insubordination and other actions hostile to the present Government's Algerian policy by the French intellectuals.

October 2, 1960

THE COLONIZERS AND THE COLONIZED

PRELATES ASSAIL ALGERIA EXCESSES

French Catholics Urge Both Sides to End Terrorism

By ROBERT C. DOTY
Special to The New York Times

PARIS, Oct. 17—The Roman Catholic Church in France published a declaration today condemning violent excesses by both sides in the Algerian war.

"From whatever side they come," the prelates said, "acts of terrorism, outrages to the human person, violent methods for drawing confessions, summary executions, measures of reprisal hitting the innocent are condemned by God."

The declaration also said it was inadmissible for French soldiers to refuse to serve against the Algerian nationalists, endorsed the program for self-determination in Algeria and called for continuing efforts to "liberate" the world from an armaments race.

The declaration came out of an assembly of French Cardinals and Archbishops in Paris last week. Pierre Cardinal Gerlier, Archbishop of Lyons and Primate of Gaul, was the senior churchman present. Maurice Cardinal Feltin, Archbishop of Paris, was the host.

Most of the issues under heated debate in French intellectual circles were dealt with in the statement, which came as the Algerian war approached the beginning of its seventh year.

The prelates recognized the anguish of conscience of many young conscripts over the issues of war and approved a soldier's right to disobey an order to commit an "immoral act."

In endorsing self-determination for Algeria, they noted that any plan to enable Algerians to decide for themselves the future of the country must come under conditions safeguarding the interests of all communities in Algeria.

The churchmen also said the United Nations was "indispensable for the establishment of peace." President de Gaulle has repeatedly attacked the present organization of the United Nations.

Indiscriminate terrorism by rebels and the torture of suspects by the French forces have shocked many French consciences and given momentum to the current drive in intellectual circles to agitate for a negotiated peace to end these excesses.

Last month an initial group of 121 French intellectuals published a manifesto asserting the right of French youths to refuse to serve against the Algerian rebels. Jean-Paul Sartre, Leftist fellow-traveling philosopher-playwright set the political tone for the manifesto, which repelled many Frenchmen who were opposed to encouraging insubordination in the army.

On Oct. 5 French educators and their unions published a more moderate appeal for a negotiated peace in Algeria.

The church declaration today quoted the following statement by the late Pope Pius XII to the Congress of International Penal Law in 1953:

"No superior authority is entitled to command an immoral act. There exists no right, no obligation, no permission to accomplish an act in itself immoral, even if it is ordered, even if refusal to act entails the worst personal consequences."

The prelates expressed hope for "a solution of wisdom worthy of France and of the noble example of disinterestedness she has just given to the world with regard to the young African nations."

In less than two years France has brought all of her other African territories except Algeria from colonial status to independence or the threshold of independence.

As the declaration was issued, France's principal student group, the National Union of French Students, proceeded with plans for a mass demonstration and march in Paris next week "for peace in Algeria."

In support of this project the National Union and the Association of Students of the Catholic University of Paris restored relations that were broken in February, at the height of the dispute over state aid to denominational schools.

October 18, 1960

61 DEAD IN ALGIERS RIOTS; TROOPS FIRE ON MOSLEMS; DE GAULLE SHORTENS VISIT

300 ARE WOUNDED

Europeans Retaliate for Algerian Acts of Terrorism

By THOMAS F. BRADY
Special to The New York Times

ALGIERS, Dec. 11—At least sixty-one persons were killed here today as paratroopers, backed by Right-Wing European demonstrators, moved against Moslems who rioted and pillaged in the European quarters yesterday.

Fifty-five of the dead were Moslems, five were European demonstrators and one was a French policeman. In addition, four Moslems were killed on Oran, in western Algeria.

The casualties were reported by Jean Morin, President de Gaulle's Delegate General and chief executive of Algeria's administration.

[President de Gaulle is cutting short his six-day tour of Algeria and will return to Paris Tuesday, a full day earlier than planned, it was disclosed in Algiers Monday, according to The Associated Press.]

Moslems Cheer Him

President de Gaulle remained adamant on his policy. He told a cheering crowd of Moslems: "All of us feel, after so many trials, how necessary it is to make peace here."

Censorship was ordered on press dispatches but not on telephone calls. The censors forbade any indication that the death toll might be greater than the official figure, any reference to the rebel National Liberation Front flags displayed by the Moslems and any reference to the fact that the police and soldiers fired on the Moslems.

Violence spread over three sectors that border on downtown Algiers. These were Bab el-Oued, working-class quarter to the west, where Moslems and Europeans live side by side; the Casbah, the old Moslem quarter on the hillside above central Algiers; and Belcourt, a working-class quarter to the east, where Moslems live on the edge of the European section in a shanty town called Clos Salembier.

[More than 300 persons were wounded, according to The Associated Press.]

Bab el-Oued saw what amounted to a mobbing of Moslems by Europeans. The Casbah was marked by Moslem nationalist demonstrations. The demonstrators there built barricades and fought with French soldiers, who opened fire on them.

In Belcourt, where the Moslems had rioted and pillaged yesterday, there were more Moslem demonstrations today, but there was also severe action to curb the mob by French parachute troops.

Europeans were frightened by the sudden and uncharacteristic surge of violent urban Moslem political agitation—almost all of it in favor of the National Liberation Front, which has been fighting French rule here for more than six years, and also of General de Gaulle's policy of self-determination for the territory.

But the Europeans also seized on the situation to try to discredit General de Gaulle's proposal for an "Algerian Algeria." The Right-Wing Front for French Algeria issued a communiqué that said:

"The true visage of Algerian Algeria reveals itself. F. L. N. [French initials for National Liberation Front] bands armed to the teeth and pushed by the Government now descend into the streets to the cries of 'Vive le F. L. N.' and 'Abbas to power.' French citizens, Europeans and Moslems, all of you come into the streets. The homeland is in danger."

Ferhat Abbas is the president of the rebel Provisional Nationalist Government which has its seat in Tunis. Moslems shouted his name frequently yesterday and today.

The Delegate General said in his statement that "calm is in view" for Algiers. He urged the Europeans, who are on a general strike in protest against President de Gaulle's visit and his policies, to return to work tomorrow.

Archbishop Asks Calm

The Archbishop of Algiers also issued an appeal for calm and order.

Meanwhile, at Bougie, sixty-

113

Algeria

five miles farther east, four companies of guards struggled to push back rival European and Moslem crowds awaiting General de Gaulle's arrival and shouting, respectively, "French Algeria!" and "Abbas to Power!"

Several Moslems were arrested and questioned but were released when leaders of the Moslem crowd agreed to disperse peacefully. They said, "We are for de Gaulle!"

The violence in Algiers was marked by frequent clashes between Europeans and Moslems. One eyewitness saw at least two Moslems killed by a European lynch mob in Bab el-Oued.

In Belcourt the troops fired into the wooded hill for almost an hour as Moslems fled up the slope toward the crest.

One observer, who went into the hills with a detachment of troops, said when he came back: "There must have been a good many dead. It was a good clean-up."

In the Casbah, Moslems continued to demonstrate throughout the day, waving forbidden green-white-and-red flags on the National Liberation Front.

There were exchanges of shots between the Moslems and the French infantry troops in the Casbah.

On a stairway leading up to hills behind Belcourt, a group of several thousand Moslems massed to wave the rebel flag and display a banner reading

ALGERIAN VIOLENCE: Outbreaks in Algiers took place in Bab el-Oued (1), Casbah (2) and Belcourt (3).

"Algeria will live independent." These Moslems were holding their ground at 5 P. M., protected from menacing Europeans by helmeted riot policemen.

The parachutists began to arrive here early this morning. One regiment of the troops in their red berets had been flown in from Batna. The other, wearing green berets of the Foreign Legion, had come from Djelfa.

The commander of one regiment said: "My men were getting ready to go into the mountains against the fellagha when the order came to get to Algiers. They don't understand why they have orders not to fire on the fellagha flag here."

It was this regiment that fired rifles and machine guns for nearly an hour into hills behind Belcourt. The commander said they had been fired on first. Three European women encouraged the marksmen, yelling from a balcony: "Kill them. Kill them."

Four new parachute regiments were said to be arriving in the Algiers region. They were not expected to come into the city unless the situation deteriorated further.

When a regiment of parachutists, which had been relieved at Belcourt late today by the riot police, rumbled past the riot policemen protecting the Moslem demonstrators, the soldiers yelled at the policemen, "Why don't you do something about them?"

A policeman replied, "We have orders."

The parachutists were greeted by Europeans with embraces and cries of "French Algeria!"

The parachutists "cleaned up Algiers" and put a stop to nationalist terrorism in 1957. They fraternized with barricaded European insurgents last January. They are tough troops and have close ties of sympathy with the Europeans in Algiers and little patience with the Moslem nationalists.

The Moslems had had their day yesterday, when about 500 came out of Clos Salembier in the hills above Belcourt and marched into the European quarters, wrecking shops and burning automobiles. In the Ravine of the Savage Women, which leads into Belcourt, twelve burned-out automobiles smouldered. Near one of the cars was the body of a man, not identifiable as either a Moslem or a European.

Clos-Salembier was surrounded by French troops today and the parachutists asked for tanks to go into the quarter because, they said, it was the best way to enter without killing women and children who were "in the front ranks of the demonstrators."

Late this afternoon a column of tanks and armored cars went up the road toward Clos-Salembier, but of eight tanks, three returned almost immediately. There was, as yet, no reliable report of what occurred when the tanks arrived.

Reports from Oran said that a group of young Right-Wing Europeans rushed the new prefecture building there and occupied it. The building was not yet completed, and few offices were being used.

Also at Oran, three French newspaper men were wounded by a grenade, thrown by a policeman at Moslem demonstrators, and caught and thrown back by a Moslem.

December 12, 1960

ALGERIANS KILL 2 IN PARIS HOSPITAL

Terrorists Hunting Member of a Rival Organization Wound 12 in Attack

By HENRY GINIGER
Special to The New York Times.

PARIS, April 6—Three Algerian terrorists invaded a hospital in suburban Montfermeil today and killed two persons and wounded twelve in a hunt for a member of a rival nationalist organization.

The gunmen were believed to be from the National Liberation Front, the organization behind the rebel Provisional Government headed by Premier Ferhat Abbas.

Their intended victim, who was unhurt, is a follower of Hadj Messali, head of the Algerian National Movement, a weak minority group. He was said to have been the witness of a previous gun fight a few days ago in which one person was killed.

The three gunmen shot a police guard to death in the hospital corridor. Seizing the policeman's machine gun, they invaded a ward and wounded nine persons with a spray of machine gun fire. [The victims included a 7-year-old girl and her visiting parents, The Associated Press reported.]

Then the gunmen went to a second room still in search of their Moslem enemy. The intended victim saved himself by diving under a bed, but another Moslem patient in the same room was fatally wounded.

The Algerian terrorists made their escape in a waiting taxi after having wounded three more persons on their way out, including a policeman.

The police later surrounded a North African quarter in near-by Bobigny, but a search for the gunmen produced no result.

The attack, coming after a series of bombings in Paris and other cities in France and Algeria, heightened tension here.

The bombings are attributed to clandestine Rightist organizations that have been sending statements to newspapers and public figures in the last few days claiming responsibility for the attacks and threatening further ones.

After fourteen explosions since the beginning of the year, Parisians are getting manifestly nervous. This morning a package discovered on the floor of a subway car caused the entire station to be cleared and service interrupted for an hour. The package was found by the police to contain some harmless electrical equipment obviously forgotten by a passenger.

An anonymous warning of an explosion in another station caused that one to be cleared too and traffic was stopped for an hour on that line also. Nothing was found.

A hotel and airlines office on the Champs-Elysées received similar warnings, but searches by the police were equally fruitless.

The French Government reaffirmed today its desire to undertake negotiations with the Algerian rebels. But it made no public gesture to meet rebel objections that have delayed tomorrow's scheduled starting date.

Instead, the Government recognized the fact that the talks would not open as planned and placed the responsibility for the postponement on the rebels.

But the Government avoided further cause for strain by saying that Louis Joxe, Minister for Algerian Affairs and chief French negotiator, would not go tomorrow to Evian-les-Bains, French resort on the southern shore of Lake Geneva, and site of the projected talks. There had been speculation that he would go to emphasize who

The laconic communiqué issued after a Cabinet meeting under President de Gaulle this morning said that "the Government is abiding by the spirit and the terms of its communiqué of March 15."

That communiqué confirmed the Government's desire to start official talks on "the conditions of self-determination of the Algerian populations and the problems relating to them."

French Government circles are reported to have no intention of undertaking with Hadj Messali's Algerian National Movement the full-scale negotiation they plan to conduct with the National Liberation Front in Evian. The assurances on this point were not made publicly but may have been conveyed to the Front privately.

President de Gaulle will hold his news conference as scheduled Tuesday and Louis Terrenoire, Minister of Information, said the President intended to make no changes in what he had to say despite the postponement of the negotiations.

April 7, 1961

MUTINY IN ALGERIA ENDS; CHALLE AND SALAN FLEE; LOYALISTS REGAIN CITIES

DE GAULLE VICTOR

Troops Exchange Fire as Revolt Crumbles Under Pressure

By ROBERT C. DOTY
Special to The New York Times.

PARIS, Wednesday, April 26—The French Army mutiny in Algeria collapsed shortly after midnight, with its leaders apparently in flight.

Just four days after Foreign Legion paratroopers commanded by four retired generals seized Algiers, forces loyal to President de Gaulle moved back into the city to end one of the most bizarre episodes in modern French history.

As the loyal forces—gendarmes, Republican Security Guards and infantry regiments—moved in, engaging in sporadic exchanges of shots with the rebels, the four generals moved out in vehicles of the First Foreign Legion Paratroop Regiment. Their destination was not known.

De Gaulle Unyielding

The mutinous generals fled after the military forces supporting them withdrew their allegiance in the face of General de Gaulle's unbending determination to crush the rebellion.

Loyal forces regained control of Oran and Constantine, the second and third largest cities of Algeria, without a struggle yesterday as elements that had supported the rebel generals retired.

The principal figure in the mutiny, Gen. Maurice Challe, once General de Gaulle's Commander in Chief in Algeria, sent an envoy to Paris with a letter offering to place himself "at the disposition of justice," according to the President's office.

But at 1:30 A. M. General Challe and two other leaders of the mutiny, Gen. Edmond Jouhaud of the air force and Gen. Raoul Salan, an army officer who also once served as French commander in Algeria, left the city together, bareheaded but in uniform.

They had failed in a last attempt to rally popular support among the Europeans of Algiers. Their revolt had been called in defense of a "French Algeria" and against General de Gaulle's plan to open peace talks with the Moslem nationalist rebels. The negotiations are likely to lead to Algerian independence.

The fourth leader, Gen. André Zeller, left half an hour earlier dressed in civilian clothes.

In the confused final hours of the rebellion, General Salan was reported to have committed suicide. However, he later emerged from the administration building to drive away with the two other generals.

Left in the Administration building as loyal troops exchanged fire with the retreating rebels was Col. Yves Godard, another top leader of the revolt. The French News Agency quoted him as having said: "I have nothing to do but to put a bullet in my head."

However, he too left a short time later.

All the high-ranking officers deeply implicated in the revolt, have been named in preliminary actions charging them with illegal assumption of command and with leadership of armed insurrection. These charges can be punished by the death penalty.

For the first three days of the revolt, the rebel radio carried reports, never convincingly contradicted by the Government, that almost all Algeria had rallied to their movement.

By Sunday night the situation appeared so critical that Premier Michel Debré warned the nation of an imminent invasion by mutinous paratroopers and called for a mass civilian uprising to help loyal troops repel them.

France spent two anxious nights on the alert, with airfields closed down, runways blocked and thousands of security troops on guard.

But from the first reports yesterday it became apparent that the mutiny had lost momentum. Declarations of loyalty to the Government arrived from generals commanding four-fifths of Algeria.

Pilots Defy Rebels

Twenty-seven air force pilots deserted the rebels and flew their planes to France. Loyal sailors and airmen regained control of some airports, and control of the two other most important cities, Oran and Constantine, passed again to Government forces.

A paratrooper attempt to seize the Mers-el-Kebir naval base for the rebels was repulsed by loyal forces and gunfire from a cruiser off the shore.

By nightfall it was clear that the mutiny was crumbling, but the end came with a rush that surprised even the most optimistic loyalists.

REVOLT FAILS: Gen. Maurice Challe, the leader of the Algerian mutiny.

VICTORY: The Government in France (1) triumphed over the mutiny led by four generals in Algeria (2).

April 26, 1961

Algeria

Algerians Pick Anti-West Leftist As Premier in Place of Abbas

Closer Ties With Reds Seen but Talks With France Are Not Ruled Out

By THOMAS F. BRADY
Special to The New York Times.

TUNIS, Aug. 27—The Algerian rebels have named a Left-wing extremist to replace Ferhat Abbas, a relative moderate, as Premier of their Provisional Government.

The new Premier is Youssef Ben Khedda, 41 years old. He is reported to believe that there is no salvation for Algeria in cooperation with the Western world because the West is fundamentally colonialist and imperialist.

The Algerian Ministry of Information also announced here today a major reorganization of the Provisional Government. The changes were actually voted in Tripoli, Libya, during a month-long secret meeting of the National Council of the Algerian Revolution. The meeting is now ending there.

The reorganization indicates that the tough, revolutionary wing of the Algerian National Liberation Front has prevailed over the moderates in the council session and that the nationalists will now move much closer to the Communist world.

The new Government is expected to intensify the guerrilla warfare in Algeria against the French.

Informed sources here said the nationalists would probably not rule out a resumption of negotiations with France toward settling the long Algerian revolt.

However, they predicted that if peace talks were resumed the nationalists would be even less supple in their bargaining than they were earlier this summer at two rounds of negotiations on the French-Swiss frontier.

One Algerian moderate declared here tonight: "It means that [President] de Gaulle must find a basis with us quickly, very quickly now, if he wants to settle the problem by negotiation."

The Algerian National Council, which chose Mr. Ben Khedda as Premier, is a sort of revolutionary parliament in which representatives of the guerrilla Army of Liberation predominate over the political nationalists.

Their recent decisions indicate that the fighting Algerian militants have "rejected," at least for the time being, the moderate "bourgeois" nationalism of Mr. Abbas.

August 28, 1961

DE GAULLE UNHURT AS BOMB MISFIRES; ASSASSIN IS JAILED

By ROBERT C. DOTY
Special to The New York Times.

PARIS, Sept. 9—President de Gaulle escaped unscathed from an attempt to kill him by an explosive charge last night.

Roger Frey, Minister of the Interior, announced today that the man who planted and tried unsuccessfully to detonate the charge at 9:45 P. M. by remote control had been arrested and had confessed.

The assassin was reported to have divulged the names of three accomplices, but it was not known whether the police had been able to arrest them.

The charge misfired, producing a sheet of flame that touched General de Gaulle's car, but none of the President's party was injured. M. Frey attributed the assassination attempt to the Secret Armed Organization opposed to General de Gaulle's efforts to make Algeria independent.

Score of Rightists Jailed

M. Frey announced at the same time—but without making a direct connection with the assassination attempt—that two French generals were under arrest, suspected of being major leaders of the Rightist organization.

He said that at least a score of other figures in the organization, including its treasurer, had been arrested in four successful police operations in recent weeks.

The officers arrested were Brig. Gens. Paul Vanuxem and Jean Boucher de Crèvecoeur.

M. Frey said a heavy charge of plastic explosive had been concealed in a pile of sand beside Route 19 between Nogent-sur-Seine and Romilly in the Aube Department. Wires buried eight inches deep led to a wood near the road, where a magneto apparently was employed by the assassin to detonate the charge.

September 10, 1961

A City Inured to Terror

Bombings, Shootings and Knifings Are Part of Everyday Life in Algiers

By PAUL HOFMANN
Special to The New York Times.

ALGIERS, Nov. 17 — Plastiqueurs, those who wage the terror with plastic bombs, are keeping ahead of the glass cutters in this convulsed city.

A dozen explosions a night of the putty-like, high-power charges are nothing exceptional, and the least that they do is shatter the windows of a hundred homes and offices. A foreign consul who lives in a frequently bombed neighborhood had the measurements of all the window panes of his villa deposited with one of the overworked glass concerns. After a blast, he telephones: "Rush replacements for windows four and eleven." But even such a client is kept waiting.

The Talk of Algiers

Until a few days ago it was not so bad. Circumspect residents left all their windows open overnight. Now snow is capping the Atlas Mountain peaks near by, and an icy wind blows into one's bedroom. But this is only a minor discomfort in this once-captivating city, which on the eve of its eighth winter of civil war ranks among the most sinister spots on earth.

Strangely, the Mediterranean and Moorish charms of Algiers have not faded completely. A few steps from the barbed wire and the paratroopers in leopard-spotted uniforms, a bistro may still radiate the provincial placidity of the French Midi. Occasionally someone smiles, although most persons have taut faces and hard stares.

THE Casbah is always mysterious and often menacing. The periodic eruptions there are heralded by the "Yooyoo" cries of the women, which often signals anger.

The visitor is warned never to venture into the maze of narrow streets and stairways of the old quarter. But the modern districts, where Moslems and Europeans live side by side, produce most of the lethal statistics.

One may be standing at a bar sipping one's anisette, when suddenly a terrorist enters and tosses a hand grenade. Or one may be driving home from work and be overtaken by another car and sprayed with gunfire. Or, if one is walking, somebody may jump around a corner wielding a gun or a knife.

These things are everyday occurrences. The two local newspapers compile these acts of violence in half a column of small print on an inside page under the standing headline "The Aggressions." They are listed in the terse style of a weather report. The 800,000 inhabitants of greater Algiers have learned, to a degree, to live with the insecurity and violence as if they were meteorological phenomena.

A FEW days ago a Moslem cab driver was shot in the neck and killed in front of the leading waterfront hotel. The gunman, as usual, got away and the body lay for an hour on the sidewalk. Near by, unruffled movie-goers continued queuing up.

Entering the theatre, men automatically held up their arms to be searched and women opened their handbags to show that they had no bombs or guns. The same ritual is observed in the department stores where Europeans and veiled Moslem women shop.

In the children's department, a toy drummer imported from West Germany is politically suspect. When wound up, the

THE COLONIZERS AND THE COLONIZED

drummer makes three quick and two short movements, suggesting the rhythm of "Algérie Française," the slogan of the outlawed movement of European extremists.

Inured to terrorism as the citizens of Algiers are, they feel almost affection for a gang of burglars who, improbably, specialize in haberdashery, repeatedly breaking into the smart men's wear stores on the Rue Michelet, the street where the barricades stood last year when the "ultras" revolted against the Paris Government.

Common thievery provides a touch of normalcy and sanity in a city where 50,000 policemen and soldiers and a midnight-to-5 A. M. curfew have been unable to prevent daily outbreaks of violence.

Pathetically, the Algiers Opera tries to recapture a carefree epoch that seems unbelievable with "The Merry Widow." And a young American conductor, Antonio De Almeida, is rehearsing the local radio orchestra for the première here of Mozart's Symphony No. 29.

"Algiers will appreciate that there are prettier sounds than plastics," the conductor says.

November 18, 1961

Repatriates From Algeria Bitter Over Hostile French Reception

Uncertain of Future and Without Help Given to Others From North Africa, They View 'Homeland' Suspiciously

By W. GRANGER BLAIR
Special to The New York Times.

MARSEILLES, France, Jan. 10—More than 2,500 years ago the Greeks colonized this Mediterranean port, uncertain of what lay ahead of them. Thus was founded Marseilles.

Today a new wave of voyagers is arriving here, also uncertain about their future. These newcomers are the French repatriates from North Africa.

Most of those who have arrived here have come from Tunisia and Morocco since the two former French protectorates gained their independence in 1956. Now it is the turn of the French in Algeria as that land moves toward independence in a climate of mounting strife.

Wherever they come from in North Africa, their attitude as they set foot in metropolitan France, is; in the words of one repatriate, "mistrust and hostility." They are met, more frequently than not, by a matching attitude on the part of the metropolitan French.

The repatriation problem is serious and threatens to become acute. The Government foresees a resettlement of 300,000 to 400,000 French in the four years that follow the independence of Algeria.

Already in France from Tunisia and Morocco, according to official statistics, are 400,000 French. There are no official figures for the number of French who have arrived from Algeria. Estimates of the number of French who have left Algeria since the Moslem rebellion began more than seven years ago range from several thousand to tens of thousands.

Nevertheless, there is growing bitterness here over the lack of Government action to provide for the repatriates from Algeria the same kind of financial help that is available to the French who have left Tunisia and Morocco.

Since 1958, when the Governmental Secretariat for Repatriation was set up, it has disbursed more than $239,000,000 to help resettle the French who have left the former protectorates. Nothing has been done yet officially for the French from Algeria, although a law, voted last month, holds out the prospect for such action in the future.

One Frenchman, who arrived here several months ago from Algeria, said he felt like "an American living in Britain who speaks the same language but knows he's not at home."

Both private and official sources here agree that, while the vast majority of the repatriates are opposed to the Gaullist regime, few of them have so far participated directly in the terrorist activities of the clandestine European Secret Army Organization.

Observers believe that the Rightist convictions of the repatriates has added a new and potentially explosive element to the already turbulent French political scene. One repatriate, a "moderate" who has successfully adjusted himself to life in France and who is spending much of his time trying to help others, said: "I have warned the authorities about their state of mind and what it may lead to if something is not done—and soon."

Metropolitan French Hostile

Almost everyone concerned with the repatriation problem, however, agrees that the repatriates' attitude is largely conditioned by that of the metropolitan French. As one responsible official put it, the French of France seem to be saying to the French from Algeria: "If you're in trouble, it's your own fault."

For most of the repatriates from North Africa the biggest problems are finding a place to live and a job. They prefer the south of France because, as they say, "We are Mediterraneans."

This has produced an "oversaturation" of : patriates in the south. This region, compared to Algeria, has a high cost of living, a serious shortage of housing and an extremely competitive labor market.

When the repatriate comes up against all these problems, beset as he already is by the human tragedy of ripping up deeply planted roots in another and easier land, he is prone to despair. Some of them are preparing to go back to Algeria.

January 11, 1962

BOMB KEY WEAPON IN FRENCH TERROR

By ROBERT ALDEN
Special to The New York Times.

PARIS, Jan. 25—The word that appears most frequently in the headlines of the French press these days is "plastique." Its meaning is sinister—a bomb made out of a clay-like plastic substance.

During the current wave of Right-wing terrorism in France and Algeria, virtually all the explosions have been caused by plastic bombs. The main reasons for the wide use of this explosive are that it is safe to handle, easy to store and readily adaptable for many purposes. There also is a plentiful supply available.

The putty-like substance was developed as an explosive during World War II. Called Composition C-2, it was employed by the United States Army in the latter stages of the campaign in Europe.

Its stability proved an important advantage. Some explosives, such as nitroglycerine, are much more dangerous to use. Any jolt or bump can cause them to explode.

Mixing nitroglycerine with sawdust or any porous material makes the explosive more stable. But the resulting substance, dynamite, is still relatively unstable and extremes of temperature can make dynamite so sensitive that a slight shock can touch off an explosion.

TNT Relatively Safe

Trinitrotoluene, or TNT, is a much safer explosive to handle. In its pure form, it is so safe that a bullet can strike a block of it without causing an explosion. To set off TNT, it is necessary to explode a blasting cap inside a block of the explosive.

The so-called plastic, which more accurately might be called a malleable explosive, is comparable to TNT in stability. If it were not, experts say, President de Gaulle would not be alive today.

This putty-like substance, made by mixing TNT and hexogen, another powerful explosive known also as cyclonite or RDX, can be bent, twisted, stamped upon, hit with a hammer, struck with a bullet, frozen or fried and it will not explode. As with TNT, a powerful blasting cap is necessary to touch it off.

In the attempt on the life of President de Gaulle last Sept. 8, the explosives were placed at the side of a road by which his car was to travel on the way from Paris to his country home at Colombey-les-Deux-Eglises, west of the capital. However, the bars of plastic were not properly placed together and tamped, and the explosion was incomplete. Most of the stable, putty-like material was not detonated.

The explosive power of the plastic or malleable explosive is roughly equivalent to that of TNT, or possibly a little stronger. A half-pound block of TNT or a half-pound bar of plastic can blow a small hole in the ground, make a loud noise and shatter near-by windows. It will kill or severely injure a person standing close by.

Proper tamping of the charges makes it much more destructive. But in their haste, or because of a general lack of technical skill, members of the terrorist Secret Army Organization, which is fighting General de Gaulle's policy of permitting Algerian independence, have generally paid little attention to tamping.

Most of the explosive charges in Paris have been of about the force of half-pound or one-pound charges, with occasional explosions ranging up to two or three pounds in force. Sixty-six pounds, most of which did not explode, were used in the attempt on President de Gaulle's life. Experts estimated that about twenty-two pounds were used by the terrorists who set off an explosion at the French Foreign Ministry that killed one person and wounded thirteen last Monday.

The armed forces of both the United States and France have large quantities of this malleable explosive stockpiled in France and the Secret Army Organization has managed to steal a lot of it from army warehouses and from construction jobs.

Although the explosive comes in the form of bars, its putty-like quality permits it to be flattened or moulded into any shape. It will adhere to surfaces just as putty will.

January 28, 1962

RIGHTISTS BLAST MALRAUX'S HOME

Six Hurt as Secret Army Renews Paris Attacks— Ten Bombs Exploded

By W. GRANGER BLAIR
Special to The New York Times.

PARIS, Feb. 7—Ten bombs generally believed to have been planted by the Secret Army Organization exploded in the Paris region today, including one at the home of André Malraux, novelist and Minister of Cultural Affairs.

The day's blasts, which injured six persons, ended a two-week lull in Right-Wing terrorist activity in the capital.

Among those injured was a 4-year-old girl who was struck in the eye by a splinter of glass as she was playing in a nursery. It was feared she would lose the eye.

[The Secret Army Organization called a strike marked by violence in Constantine, Algeria, in an effort to gain the release of forty of its members seized by the French Army.]

In Paris the homes of a Senator, two law professors, two journalists and two military officers were among the targets.

The Senator was Raymond Guyot, a Communist. The professors were Georges Vedel of the Sorbonne and Roger Pinto of the University of Lille. The journalists were Serge Bromberger of Le Figaro and Vladimir Pozner of L'Humanité, the Communist party newspaper.

Other bombs exploded near a local office of the Communist party and outside the women's prison of Paris. There were no injuries and the damage was not extensive.

Earlier in the day another bomb went off at the home of a Right-wing Deputy, Alain de Lacoste-Lareymondie. It was believed to have been planted by a group opposed to the Secret Army. M. de Lacoste-Larey-mondie is known for his support of the campaign to keep French control of Algeria.

Roger Frey, Minister of the Interior, declared that the bombings, particularly the one that "frightfully mutilated" the little girl, "arouse not only the indignation of all honest people but also a sentiment of revulsion."

"All the police of France, all security forces, must consider themselves permanently mobilized for a fight without mercy or quarter against an ignoble gang of assassins, crooks and racketeers who are trying to dishonor our country," M. Frey said.

The resurgence of terrorism followed by two days President de Gaulle's optimistic forecast of peace in Algeria.

The injured child lives in the ground-floor apartment of the private house in which the Malraux family occupies the first and second floors. The bomb was placed on a window sill of her nursery.

The most injuries and damage were caused by the bomb placed in the building at the Place de la République where Senator Guyot lives. The Senator was away at the time, but his wife and three workers were wounded.

M. Pozner suffered slight cuts from flying glass when the bomb went off at his home.

A copy of a Secretary Army tract dated Jan. 31, was received today by the Paris bureau of The New York Times. It contained orders to eighty Rightist Deputies in the National Assembly to resign. The tract instructed them, among among other things, to demand the arrest of President de Gaulle, and his Cabinet Ministers.

Though the tract was received also in French newspaper offices, not a word about it appeared. The newspapers abided by a Government order prohibiting the reproduction of tracts, communiqués and pirate broadcasts of the Secret Army.

February 8, 1962

AGONY IN ALGERIA GROWS

Right-Wing Violence Seen as an Attempt to Bring Collapse of Organized Society as Truce Nears

By PAUL HOFMANN
Special to The New York Times.

ALGIERS, Feb. 24—On the day when the United States shot John Glenn into orbit, a commando of outlaws in Algiers fired away with a stolen army mortar.

The clandestine artillery emplacement was in Bab El-Oued, the once radical and now racist European suburb whose inhabitants bear mostly Spanish and Italian names and are the loudest partisans of French Algeria.

The mortar shells fell into an adjoining Moslem district and exploded in the vast courtyard of a housing development that is a copy in concrete of the Palais Royal in Paris and is believed to shelter the secret headquarters of the rebel underground network in the Algiers area.

The same day twelve persons, about the daily average, were killed in terrorist incidents throughout the city. Among them were a Moslem teacher mowed down by a machine-gun on the way to school; a young Frenchman who happened to stand with his girl friend gazing at the sea at a moment when a Moslem gunman was looking for a victim, and a Moslem youngster, probably a beginner in bomb-throwing, who was blown up because he held a missile a second too long.

Design of Terror

Algiers' violence has evolved into a new pattern that is apparently designed to cause the ultimate collapse of what has remained of organized society. One day the terrorists fired at stevedores, the next at power workers, the third at aviation personnel and the fourth at postmen. The result was that this city of 800,000 found its harbor paralyzed, its electric current cut, airplanes grounded and post offices closed by strikes.

Towards the week-end, Algiers saw some of the most sanguinary days since the war started. One morning, terrorists struck every twenty minutes, mostly in the heart of the city, and private autos had to be commandeered because there were not enough ambulances.

The terrorism was not only blind, it was also baffling. Nobody knew for sure by whom the postmen were shot down. They could not be classified as "desperados of agonizing colonialism" whom the Moslem rebels claimed to chastise, and the European diehards too disclaimed the murders, blaming them, unconvincingly, on the *barbouzes*.

The slang word, which refers to a spy's proverbial false beard, is the term for the undercover agents sent by the Government to combat European extremism in Algeria with its own conspiratorial methods. Clean shaven Vietnamese *barbouzes* were engaged in bloody bazooka battles this week with German deserters from the Foreign Legion who gutturally shouted they were defending French Algeria.

Leaflets Circulate

At the same time, "intox"—psychological intoxication—reached new degrees. The opposing underground organizations issued their watchwords for the coming emergency in clandestine leaflets, and the cloak-and-dagger outfits circulated fake clandestine leaflets with misleading instructions.

The Government jammed the clandestine broadcasts that rightist technicians poured out of equipment concealed in refrigerators and grand pianos.

Kuekes in The Cleveland Plain-Dealer
"French ornithologist."

The clandestines jammed the Government radio. Inevitably, there was the bogus clandestine broadcast villifying the former generals who were being extolled in the genuine clandestine transmissions.

Fear and discomfort seemed to be the only things Europeans and Moslems had in common this week as they read in their censored newspapers that a cease-fire was imminent and that the road was at last open, after seven years and four months of war, for an independent Algeria "associated" with France.

French leaders believe that what happens, or does not happen, in Algiers and Oran in the first week after the cease-fire will be decisive for the future of this tortured territory. Com-

THE COLONIZERS AND THE COLONIZED

munal clashes might wreck the fragile framework for coexistence hammered out in laborious negotiations since rebel and French representatives first met in June, 1960.

Mobs Feared

Mob passion and mob violence, not continued individual terrorism, are the French Administration's nightmare. The cold reasoning behind the seemingly cynical disregard for the widespread lawlessness is that the multiracial society of the new Algeria will purge itself of crime as soon as its decent and moderate components are strengthened and find they can live and work together.

While the Administration appears to hope for moderation and discipline on the side of Moslem nationalism during the coming period, it tacitly acknowledges that there are almost no moderate elements among the Europeans who dare come into the open now and speak up for the proposed accord.

This is why the army has moved in force into Algiers and Oran this week. Tanks, conscripts from Metropolitan France with tommy guns and tear-gas bombs, marine infantry and, eventually, warships in the harbors of the seething coastal cities are supposed to substitute for civilian common sense—admittedly a precarious and temporary solution, and a gamble at best.

In a snack bar in the center of Algiers an athletic man daintily takes his chopsticks out of his *soupe Chinoise* to point at an armored car that is rumbling by, machine-gunners at the ready fore and aft. "Where do you think they will fire when Moslems start fighting with Europeans?" he asks rhetorically in a continental accent.

Without bothering much to lower his voice, he reports that he is a paratrooper who fought in Indochina, where he learned about revolutionary warfare, and is now a member of the dreaded Secret Army Organization.

He may or may not be what he says. It is difficult to tell in Algiers. Whether the bullies who held a group at gunpoint for hours in the bar of the Aletti Hotel last Saturday night were genuine Secret Army characters or showoffs is a matter of controversy. Since the thirstier part of the foreign press corps was present, the police, in a rare and easy burst of energy, closed the bar, temporarily depriving the city of a landmark where many of the countless plots against Vichy and the Fourth and Fifth Republics were hatched.

AS ALGERIAN CEASE-FIRE NEARS

"Here comes the bride." — Franklin in The Daily Mirror, London

"Algerian sands." — Long in The Minneapolis Tribune / Le Pelley in The Christian Science Monitor

The presumed Indochina veteran goes on: "The *petits blancs* (poor whites) of Bab El-Oued shout about French Algeria in their bistros, but secretly rub their hands because they have heard the French Army will stay on for three years after the cease-fire, and they are already speculating what they can get for themselves out of the deal between de Gaulle and the rebels."

Incidents Planned

The Secret Army will leave the shouting to Bab El-Oued, the man behind the Chinese soup explains, and will not fall into the trap of a big putsch that would end in failure. "We will stage a hundred little putsches, and we will get the Moslems and the petit bourgeois of Bab El-Oued into the streets and at each other, and when the shooting starts, the army will fire in the direction where it sees the green-white rebel flag it has been fighting all these years. There will be chaos, and the Communists in Tunis [the rebel leaders] will find out that all they got from de Gaulle is a worthless piece of paper."

A French Army officer tells a reporter: "Do not quote my name, but you should write that the vast majority in the army thinks de Gaulle may be wrong in many things, yet he is absolutely right about Algeria. Metropolitan France is sick and tired of Algeria. People at home hate the Secret Army and will start hating all the Europeans here."

An influential foreigner who entertains regularly confides: "Whenever I have two or three local businessmen for lunch, they vie in declamations about French Algeria. But when I talk to any one of them alone, he admits an Algerian Algeria is worth a try."

A Moslem intellectual says somberly: "Our people hope to end Ramadan fasting the night of the new moon, March 6, with revelry to celebrate peace. Such is human nature. At the Belgrade conference of nonaligned nations last September, someone said the Algerian nation had paid a fantastic price for independence. I am afraid we will have to pay still more."

February 25, 1962

Algeria

ALGERIAN CEASE-FIRE IS SIGNED

ACCORD AT EVIAN

Truce in 7-Year War Is in Effect Today— Future Tie Defined

By ROBERT C. DOTY
Special to The New York Times.

EVIAN-LES-BAINS, France, March 18 — A cease-fire ending the Algerian war was signed here today by French and Algerian rebel delegations.

The document terminating the rebellion after seven years, four months and eighteen days will go into effect throughout Algeria at noon tomorrow (6 A. M. Eastern standard time). The signing took place at 5:30 P. M.

The accord ended the long fight between the French Republic and the Algerian rebels' National Liberation Front for control of the vast North African territory.

It opened a new phase in the resistance of the Secret Army Organization, made up of extremist Europeans, to a policy certain to lead to an independent, predominantly Moslem Algeria.

Referendum Provided

Only after France and the nationalists have mastered the bloody terror unleashed by the Secret Army will the settlement become really operative.

The accord covers the process by which Algerians will vote on their own political future in four to six months and the cooperation between France and the independent Algeria that will result from a self-determination referendum.

Included also are guarantees for the rights of the 1,000,000 Europeans living among 9,000,-000 Moslems; an interim political regime; provisions for a continued French military presence in Algeria; joint exploitation of oil and other minerals in the Sahara, and a broad amnesty for military and political prisoners on both sides.

The accord was announced here shortly after 6:30 P. M. by Louis Joxe, French Minister for Algerian Affairs. M. Joxe has shepherded it through four open conferences and one secret meeting since June, 1960.

The settlement came at the end of twelve days of hard bargaining here with a rebel delegation headed by Belkacem Krim, Deputy Premier and Interior Minister of the rebels' Provisional Government.

An hour and a half after the announcement here, President de Gaulle went on the state radio and television networks in France and Algeria to proclaim the settlement and to call for massive backing of the Government's Algerian policy in a referendum to be held, probably early next month, in France.

At Aubonne, in Switzerland, the rebel delegation held a news conference to present its version of the accord. It coincided in all essentials with the French announcement.

M. Joxe's statement gave no details of the ninety-three-page document containing the blueprint for Algeria's future. The French radio and television networks and the French News Agency later gave a summary of the main points.

Both were silent on the identity of the twelve men agreed upon by the two delegations to man the Provisional Executive. This will handle Algeria's internal affairs, under continued French sovereignty, between the cease-fire and formation of an Algerian government as a result of free elections.

March 19, 1962

Cost of Algerian Conflict: 250,000 Deaths and Expenditure of $20,000,000,000

PARIS' AUTHORITY ERODED BY STRIFE

Decline of French Prestige and Public Morality Is Among War's Effects

Special to The New York Times.

PARIS—A quarter of a million violent deaths and the loss of about $20,000,000,000—that is the provisional measurable cost of more than seven years of armed conflict in Algeria.

The intangible costs can only be guessed at. They include the erosion of the authority of the French state, the decline of public morality through tolerance of the excesses of the Algerian war and the loss of prestige for France and the West as a whole in the Asian-African world.

Yet there were few Frenchmen or Moslem nationalists who foresaw the long agony ahead on Nov. 1, 1954, when the first rebel bands struck. In seventy attacks, mainly in the rugged Aurès Mountain region of southeastern Algeria, the rebels killed a school teacher, Guy Monnerot, his wife and four French soldiers and wounded a number of other persons.

At first, the Government of Premier Pierre Mendès-France underestimated the significance of the attacks. Interior Minister François Mitterand, later to become one of the strongest advocates of a negotiated peace, asserted that France's only negotiation would be war.

9 Call on 9,000,000

Behind the attacks and the handbills calling on the 9,000,-000 Moslems of Algeria to support the fight for independence were nine Moslem nationalists, banded together in a Revolutionary Committee for Unity and Action.

Of the nine, three later died fighting the French. Five, including Mohammed Ben Bella, a Vice Premier of the Algerian Nationalist Provisional Government, were imprisoned by the French in 1956 and released after the announcement of the truce. Only one, Belkacem Krim, Vice Premier and Interior Minister of the rebel government, was active at the coming of peace.

M. Mendès-France and Edgar Faure, who succeeded him as Premier, sent reinforcements to strengthen garrisons in Algeria. They comprised professional troops, since conscripts were not subject to service outside metropolitan France.

On Aug. 20, 1955, guerrilla bands attacked European civilians in eastern Algeria, killing more than 100 persons. Further French reinforcements were rushed in.

Mollet Adopts New Policy

In January, 1956, the new Premier, Guy Mollet, a Socialist, embarked on a liberal policy, naming a respected anti-colonialist, Gen. Georges Catroux, as Minister-Delegate for Algeria, a new title. M. Mollet spoke of the existence of an "Algerian personality." Later, he proposed a three-fold program of a cease-fire, free elections and the negotiation of a new status for Algeria to end the struggle.

However, the Algerian problem became immensely complicated by increasingly bitter political debate in France and violent resistance to reform by the Europeans in Algeria.

On Feb. 6, 1956, during Premier Mollet's first visit to Algeria, the Europeans demonstrated and he was hooted at and pelted with vegetables. General Catroux, who had aroused the Europeans' wrath, offered his resignation and M. Mollet accepted it.

This was one of the turning points of the war. The Europeans learned that by employing violence they could dominate the policies of weakly based coalition Governments in Paris. This lesson they were to apply successfully many times until the January, 1960, insurrection, which foundered on the determination of President de Gaulle.

Robert Lacoste, a Socialist, was named to replace General Catroux and continued as Minister-Delegate through four successive Governments, until June, 1958. The liberal aspirations he took to Algeria were gradually replaced by acceptance of the European settlers' view that only the integration of Algeria and France was an acceptable solution.

The rebels' Army of National Liberation had been getting more arms, thanks to help from Cairo, and gaining strength as a result of support among the Moslem masses. Military action was still largely limited to raids on French posts, ambushes of French patrols, the sabotage of rail and communication lines, the burning of farms and individual assassinations.

Under Premier Mollet, the French increased their military strength by finally sending conscripts to fight in Algeria.

In August, 1956, the rebel leaders gathered secretly in the Valley of the Soummam and redefined their political and military goals and tactics.

They reaffirmed their demand that the right of Algeria to independence be recognized as a prerequisite for negotiations. They also laid plans to exploit the sympathy of the Arabs and Asians in the United Nations and explore the possibility of

THE COLONIZERS AND THE COLONIZED

Soviet or Chinese Communist assistance.

The reinforcement of the Army of National Liberation, which was to reach a maximum strength of about 120,000 men from 1957 to 1959, was planned at the same conference. Of this strength, 40,000 to 50,000 were hard-core soldiers in organized units. The balance consisted of part-time auxiliaries recruited in villages to reinforce the regular troops for special missions.

In January, 1957, Maj. Gen. Jacques Massu was assigned to purge Algiers of rebel terrorists.

Over the next twelve months, his 8,000 paratroopers smashed the rebel organization in the city, partly by torturing suspects. This tactic was defended by army apologists as necessary to save innocent lives threatened by terrorist attacks. But it produced a crisis of conscience in the army and in France.

The Mollet Government fell in May, 1957. Maurice Bourgès-Maunoury, a Radical, became Premier.

Throughout 1957 and the first half of 1958, M. Bourgès-Maunoury and the two Premiers who succeeded him, Félix Gaillard, another Radical, and Pierre Pflimlin, a Popular Republican, struggled unsuccessfully to achieve enough political freedom from Parliamentary harassment and the pressure of the army and the Europeans in Algeria to reach a political solution of the rebellion. Each fell on proposals tending toward a liberalization of French policy in Algeria.

Peak of Rebel Strength

The rebels achieved a peak of military power in 1957 and 1958, when, for a brief period, they were able to mount battalion-strength attacks with some heavy weapons.

The Algerian problem reached its dramatic high point May 13, 1958, and during the days following. Suspecting that the newly designated Premier, M. Pflimlin, planned to negotiate with the rebels, thousands of the Europeans of Algiers, with the connivance of some army elements, stormed the French Government's headquarters and virtually seized control of the city.

General Massu took active leadership of the Committee of Public Safety set up by the insurgents. His superior, Gen. Raoul Salan, the Commander in Chief in Algeria, exercised his full powers in behalf of the movement.

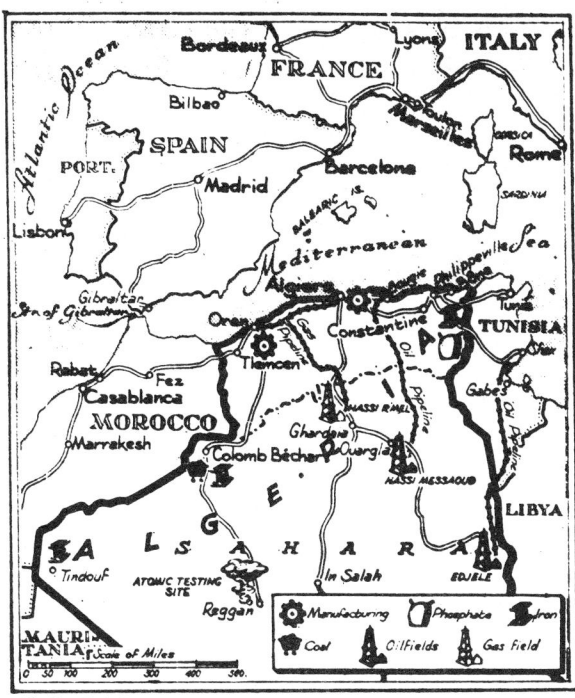

A NEW ERA BEGINS: More than seven years of strife have ended with the agreement on a truce in Algeria.

Waiting just off stage for twelve years, since he gave up the Provisional Presidency of post-war France in 1946, was General de Gaulle. His partisans captured the dissident movement.

De Gaulle Takes Over

The French Government and National Assembly, intimidated by the prospect of civil war, voted full powers to General de Gaulle and he assumed the Premiership June 1, 1958.

As Premier and, after Jan. 8, 1959, as President of the new French Republic set up on a Gaullist pattern, General de Gaulle began the long and delicate task of disengaging himself from his initial supporters and bringing France, her army and the rebels to accept his formula of Algerian independence in friendly association with France.

He sent Paul Delouvrier to Algiers as the Government's civil representative and, after easing General Salan out, appointed Gen. Maurice Challe of the Air Force as Commander in Chief. General Challe began vigorous military operations to break up the major rebel bands.

The political watershed of the rebellion was President de Gaulle's offer on Sept. 16, 1959, of self-determination for Algeria, publicly

The rebel leaders accepted this idea in principle but it took eight months—until June, 1960—to bring them to negotiations, which quickly foundered on the refusal of France to go beyond the question of a cease-fire and discuss political issues.

In January, 1960, Algiers had exploded again, in protest against President de Gaulle's disciplining of General Massu. European extremists killed fourteen policemen, set up barricades and defied the authorities to oust them. Until President de Gaulle gave direct orders to reduce the insurgents, the army stood by in tolerant sympathy. President de Gaulle's firm stand brought about the surrender of the dissidents.

As public statements carried forward President de Gaulle's intention to yield French sovereignty over Algeria, extremist opposition and army discontent grew. In addition, the Left, though sympathetic with the President's goals, reproached him for slowness. But, in January, 1961, more than 70 per cent of the French voters endorsed his Algerian policy in a referendum.

In April General Challe, who had been relieved a year earlier as Commander in Chief in Algeria, returned there and raised the standard of revolt again. With General Salan, a score of other officers and some Foreign Legionnaires and paratroopers, he kept the "generals' mutiny" going for four days. When it became clear that he lacked effective support in the army and among the French people, General Challe surrendered and was sentenced to fifteen years' imprisonment.

Secret Army Set Up

General Salan and most of the other mutineers went into hiding and set up the clandestine Secret Army Organization, enlisting the active or passive support of almost the entire European population of Algeria for last-ditch resistance to the rebels and the Government in Paris. The Secret Army's weapons were assassination and bomb attacks.

Spring and summer brought rebel leaders and Louis Joxe, President de Gaulle's Minister for Algerian Affairs, together twice for negotiating sessions on the French shore of Lake Geneva. These failed, in part at least because the negotiators, in the glare of publicity of a formal conference, were more interested in proclaiming their doctrines than in achieving compromises.

In late fall a new technique was employed. French and rebel delegates held a series of secret meetings in Europe to exchange ideas in private.

A sense of urgency was aroused on both sides by the deterioration of the situation in the big cities of Algeria. There French and Moslem communities, which had lived in relative peace throughout the war, were increasingly at each other's throats.

It was in this atmosphere, with the threat of new revolt in Algeria and an increase in Rightist and Leftist demonstrations on the Algerian issue in France, that the French Government opened a final drive to conclude the secret negotiations.

March 19, 1962

Algeria Secret Army Sets An All-Out Guerrilla War

By HENRY TANNER
Special to The New York Times.

ALGIERS, March 28—The Secret Army Organization proclaimed today "all-out guerrilla warfare" against the French forces and announced that it would not again call out European civilians for mass political demonstrations.

The extremist organization, which aims to prevent by force implementation of the cease-fire in Algeria, made its intention known in leaflets posted and distributed in the center of Algiers. Its decision appeared to represent a basic change of tactics.

[In Paris thirteen bombs were exploded Wednesday night. The targets were homes and offices of individuals and organizations identified with a liberal policy for Algeria.]

All day the Europeans of Algiers stopped in small groups wherever the mimeographed leaflets bearing the Secret Army letterhead were pasted on store windows or tacked to the trees that shade the city's main thoroughfares.

The announcement made it clear that the decision not again to ask the European masses to take to the streets was linked to the shooting in which French soldiers killed about seventy demonstrators last Monday.

The leaflets accused the French Army of having opened fire in cold blood. Therefore,

121

they added, there would be "no peaceful demonstrations in the future—there will be no quarter from now on: it's guerrilla warfare now."

The announcement appeared to confirm the impression gained by neutral observers that Monday's shooting, and also earlier clashes between the army and civilian extremists in the Bab-el-Oued quarter of Algiers, had dealt a severe blow to the Secret Army Organization.

Effect Deeply Sobering

The two events came as a tremendous shock. On the whole, they have had a deeply sobering effect. A large number of Europeans interviewed declared themselves horrified by the realization that things had reached a point where French soldiers and French civilians were killing each other.

Deeply embittered and extreme in their criticism of the French Army, these Europeans said they were more than ever in favor of the Secret Army Organization. At the same time, they gave the impression of being far less eager than in the past to see the masses take an active part in the battles fought by the extremists.

Raoul Salan, former general and commander of the Secret Army Organization, has made popular support a key point in his strategy.

In a captured document described by French Army headquarters as a "directive" sent by Salan to his subordinates, the insurgent leader wrote that Secret Army indoctrination in the cities had reached a point where "armed masses" could be used as a "valuable instrument."

As soon as the situation was ripe, he wrote, the Secret Army Organization would "push masses into the streets."

Observers assume that the organization reached this stage in Salan's plan of action when it appealed to Algiers citizens to stage mass demonstrations last Saturday and Monday.

On the first occasion the turnout was disappointing and the demonstrators appeared unusually subdued. The second demonstration led to the tragic bloodshed.

As a result, observers believe, the Secret Army Organization may have decided to discontinue appeals for popular participation and, instead, to resort earlier than it had intended to direct action by small but highly trained and well-equipped commandos.

Salan in the document ascribed to him by the army listed systematic attacks on army positions, sabotage and such moves as causing spectacular fires by igniting gasoline in all the service stations of the city as methods that should be employed by these commandos.

French officers said today that the army expected attacks of this kind in the near future. One possibility, they said, is that the Secret Army will time attacks to coincide with the arrival tomorrow of the provisional executive of nine Moslems and three Europeans that will administer Algeria during the transition period leading to independence.

The executive is due to arrive tomorrow morning at Rocher Noir, the heavily guarded administrative center thirty miles east of here.

In anticipation of these attacks the French Army now has about 50,000 men massed in and around Algiers, according to authorized sources.

Tanks and armored cars supported the security forces in a demonstration of security arrangements in the center of Algiers yesterday when Christian Fouchet, the new French High Commissioner for Algeria, visited the city.

The army tonight announced completion of the systematic house-to-house search for Secret Army members and their weapons that began in Bab-el-Oued last Friday.

A communiqué said that the curfew, which has kept the 40,000 inhabitants of the European working-class district in their homes for six days, would be lifted at dawn tomorrow.

About 3,500 persons were arrested during the search and about 1,300 weapons were seized, according to authorized sources.

March 29, 1962

ALGERIA RIGHTISTS STRIKE AT RANDOM, KILLING 40 IN DAY

Terrorists Slay 18 Moslems and 5 Europeans Walking in Streets of Algiers

By HENRY TANNER
Special to The New York Times.

ALGIERS, April 6 — Forty persons, most of them Moslems, were killed in Algeria today in a surge of Right-wing terrorism. Many others were wounded.

Terrorists in Algiers, striking at random, shot and killed eighteen Moslems who were walking along the streets of the European quarters. Five Europeans also were killed.

Officials attributed the crimes to the Secret Army Organization, which is seeking to block Algerian independence through terror. The extremists have been trying to provoke the Moslems into attacking the European population in the hope that the French Army will have to be called in to fire on the Moslems and defend the Europeans.

Many Europeans reacted with outspoken revulsion to today's killings. Some of the victims were in the sunlit streets of the business section at a time when housewives, leading their children by the hand, were out in force to do their shopping.

Flags Bedeck Buildings

The bloody scenes on the downtown sidewalks were in contrast to the strangely festive air of apartment and office buildings that have been bedecked with French flags on orders from the Right-wing movement.

The flags were part of an "I am French" campaign timed to coincide with a referendum to be held in mainland France Sunday.

Europeans here are deeply embittered by the fact that France is voting on the Government's Algerian policy and that the French of Algeria, who are French citizens, are not permitted to vote.

The increase in terrorism also appeared to be linked to the referendum. There had been indications for several days that the Secret Army planned major strikes just before and during the voting.

Two Killings on One Street

At midmorning gunmen struck twice within a few moments on the Rue d'Isly, one of the city's two principal shopping streets. Both victims were young Moslem workers. Both were shot in the head at close range.

In midafternoon the killers struck three times within ten minutes a few yards apart on the Rue Michelet, the other principal business street of the European quarter.

Similar attacks took place in other downtown streets as well as in Bab-el-Oued and Hussein Dey, an industrial suburb.

In the working-class district of Belcourt four terrorists cruised in a black car looking for potential victims. The car stopped in front of a neighborhood police station. The four men invaded the station, fatally wounded a Moslem policeman and fled.

The wantonness of the terror was particularly evident when killers shot down a European youth who looked like an Arab. Their next victim, a few yards down the street, was a Moslem. Both men died of bullet wounds in the head.

Until now the great majority of the Europeans in Algiers had found it easy to explain and excuse Secret Army terrorism by saying that the victims must have been leaders of the nationalist rebellion. Today it was unmistakably clear that victims had been picked at random.

Evidence of today's crimes, moreover, remained visible on the sidewalks of fashionable middle-class neighborhoods and was not, as in the past, confined to the quarters of the city that have known violence all along.

For the first time observers gained the impression that a break was developing between extremists of the Secret Army and the mass of citizens who share its objectives, but do not like the idea of being regarded as accomplices to the killings.

Europeans Worried

Several of these Europeans anxiously asked where all the bloodshed would lead.

"No good can come from all this," an elderly man said. "In the end we will have to pay for all this."

The Secret Army suffered a setback today when French troops cordoned off two quarters of the city just before dawn and conducted a house-to-house search.

Thirty-five persons were arrested as suspected members of Secret Army, according to an official announcement. The identities of the arrested men were not disclosed, but several of them were believed to be extremist officers.

Weapons Captured

Military equipment captured during the search included a 57 mm. recoilless cannon, a heavy machine gun, three rocket launchers, nineteen automatic weapons and eighteen rifles, according to the official announcement.

Large quantities of ammunition, grenades and explosives also were found, the announcement said, as well as military uniforms and a number of documents.

The announcement identified the two quarters where the search took place as Redoute, a middle-class suburban area, and Quartier des Facultés, the downtown area where the University of Algiers is situated. Reliable private sources said a large part of the captured equipment was found on the university campus.

The French Army tonight announced that troops pursuing terrorists who raided Army positions near Lamartine, about eighty miles southwest of here a week ago, captured twenty more members of the Secret Army, including eight deserters from the French Army.

April 7, 1962

Size of de Gaulle Victory Shocks French in Algeria

By HENRY TANNER
Special to The New York Times.

ALGIERS, April 9—Frenchmen of Algeria appeared shocked today by the 90 per cent vote in France endorsing President de Gaulle's Algerian policy.

They had expected a majority vote of approval but did not expect near unanimity in yesterday's referendum.

They regard the vote for General de Gaulle as a vote against them and now feel abandoned and betrayed.

"Forty million in France against one million Frenchmen here," an elderly man said bitterly in referring to the populations of the two territories.

[In Paris, President de Gaulle and Premier Michel Debré met to assess the results of the referendum and consider proposals for a general election. In Algiers, according to United Press International, the French announced the appointment of Omar Mokdad, a Moslem village leader, as chief of the 60,000-man Moslem force for policing the cease-fire.]

Gloom Replaces Confidence

Many of the Frenchmen of Algeria now say that they are beginning to realize for the first time that the cease-fire accords with the Algerian nationalists and eventually the independence of Algeria were irreversible.

Two weeks ago many of them still talked about "all-out resistance," boasted that they had "only just started to fight" or coolly asserted that "if the Moslems were able to make war for seven years, we can do the same."

Today this confidence had been replaced by deep gloom, a climate of resignation and anxious questions, such as "Where will it all end?" "What is going to happen to us?"

This new mood also has affected the attitude of the Europeans of Algiers toward the terrorists of the Secret Army Organization, who continued to shoot Moslem victims on the sidewalks of the city.

During the day terrorists killed at least twelve Moslems and wounded eight in Algiers alone. The Secret Army Organization is seeking to prevent Algerian independence by force.

The overwhelming majority of the Europeans of Algeria have long been in favor of the Secret Army Organization and its objectives. Many have given it their active support. But their conversations now show a growing criticism of its methods.

Doubt Is Growing

The insurgent organization still has their sympathy, but the number of those who are critical, or at least doubtful, of its methods appears to grow daily.

There are several reasons. One is that violence has invaded the streets of the fashionable and middle-class quarters of the city for the first time. Previously it was confined mostly to populous quarters.

The impact has been deep. "People just do not like to see blood on their sidewalks," a business man explained.

The Secret Army Organization's call to violence made sense to many Europeans as long as they were convinced that the European insurgents would win and could, in the end, block the cease-fire accords and prevent Algerian independence. It is far more difficult to accept violence for what they are beginning to view as a hopeless cause.

Finally, many of these Europeans seem to be concerned about the consequences that the current terror campaign might have later — after the Algerians take over the government and the French Army is no longer here to protect them.

With increasing frequency Europeans here are beginning to express the fear that in the end they will be the ones who will have to pay for the bloodshed in what some now call "senseless killing."

The Secret Army Organization appears to be aware of this changing mood. Two days ago it distributed a leaflet with an attempt to justify the terrorist campaign.

Violence Is Defended

The leaflet declared that "resistance without violence" was not possible.

Most of today's terrorist attacks in Algiers were individual assassinations of Moslems found walking along streets of various European quarters.

One took place on Rue Michelet, Algiers' Fifth Avenue, which has been the scene of daylight assassinations every day for the last five days.

Algiers and Oran have been the two principal centers of terrorism, but during recent days teams of Rightists have been making forays into smaller surrounding communities.

Terrorism on a smaller scale, individual assassinations and bombings, have been reported also from Bône, Constantine, Philippeville, Mostaganem, Sidi-bel-Abbes and other smaller cities.

April 10, 1962

TERRORISTS SLAY ALGERIAN WOMEN IN WIDER ATTACK

Secret Army Breaks Pattern of Limiting Assaults In Streets to Moslem Men

By HENRY TANNER
Special to The New York Times.

ALGIERS, May 6—European terrorist gunmen have opened fire on Moslem women in the streets of Algiers for the first time.

A veiled Moslem woman was shot dead this morning on her way to work in the Bab-el-Oued quarter of the city. Another woman was killed by a bullet in the head in the same quarter shortly before nightfall. A third woman was wounded.

A Moslem woman was killed and another wounded in similar circumstances in the same neighborhood yesterday.

In all five attacks the gunmen deliberately chose their victims. The attacks are believed to be a result of a decision made by the leaders of the Rightist Secret Army Organization to extend to women their systematic campaign of murder directed against Moslems walking in the streets of the European quarters of the city.

Virtual Segregation Imposed

The Secret Army has imposed virtually complete racial segregation on Algiers by shooting down Moslem men who ventured out of their own quarters. Women and children had been spared by the terrorists.

Observers believe the segregation drive is the first step in a long-range attempt by the Secret Army to impose a de facto partition on Algeria—with the Europeans remaining in control of Algiers and Oran while the interior would be given over to Algerians.

Secret Army insurgents who once hoped to prevent the implementation of the cease-fire agreements signed by France and the Algerian Provisional Government and to keep all of Algeria French are believed by many observers to have scaled down their ambitions. It is believed the Rightists now seek a partition of the country.

Terror Directive Captured

An indication that the terror campaign against Moslems might be extended to women came about a week ago when French authorities captured a Secret Army directive instructing members to exert pressure on European housewives to dismiss their Moslem maids. Traditionally, thousands of Moslem women have been working as maids in European households.

Most of the Moslem women continued to make daily trips from the Casbah, the main Moslem quarter, and other Moslem quarters to the European residential areas long after their husbands and sons had been forced by terrorists to give up their jobs in the European parts of the city.

May 7, 1962

Algeria

MOSLEM GUNMEN KILL 17 EUROPEANS IN ALGIERS RAIDS

44 Wounded by Assassins Firing From Cars as They Drive Through Suburbs

By HENRY TANNER
Special to The New York Times.

ALGIERS, May 14—Gunmen identified as Moslems killed seventeen Europeans and two Moslems in less than two hours tonight in a series of machine-gun attacks. Thirty-five Europeans, five Moslems and four soldiers were wounded.

The attacks were made at seventeen different places in the city's residential suburbs.

They constituted the first instance of mass terrorism committed by Moslems since the cease-fire between France and the Algerian nationalists became effective March 19.

The Europeans of Algiers immediately accused the nationalists of being responsible for the killings. But French officials withheld comment on who they thought had ordered the attacks.

Pedestrians Slain

In all the attacks, the gunmen opened fire from automobiles. In most cases, witnesses said the killers were Moslems.

The fact that cars of the same make were used in several of the attacks led officials to believe that some of the teams of killers struck twice or three times.

Most of the victims were pedestrians or motorists returning from outings.

Today was an important Moslem holiday, Aid el Kebir, which commemorates the Biblical sacrifice of a ram by Abraham in place of his son.

The holiday has been observed here by Europeans as well as Moslems and administration offices and commercial enterprises were closed.

Reprisals Rumored

Rumors had been current in the European community for several days that Moslems planned to avenge the victims of the Secret Army Organization's terrorism on this day. European housewives told of having been warned by their Moslem maids to keep off the streets.

Europeans here have been living in growing fear of Moslem reprisals. Until now, however, the Moslem population had been showing impressive discipline in the face of daily acts of terrorism by the Rightists who are attempting to block independence of Algeria.

Algerian nationalist leaders here and in Tunis recently reaffirmed their policy of no reprisals. One of the main objectives of the Secret Army Organization has been to provoke the Moslems into mass attacks on Europeans. The terrorists hoped that such attacks might force the French Army to open fire on the Moslems and that the peace accords would collapse.

Some observers thought it possible that a dissident group of nationalist extremists had ordered today's action in defiance of responsible authorities.

Observers did not exclude the possibility that the Right-wing terrorist underground had used Moslems to commit the slayings in a desperate maneuver to provoke Europeans to even greater anger against Moslems. The Secret Army Organization is known to have a number of Moslems in its ranks.

The timing of the slayings seemed to exclude the possibility that they could have been a spontaneous outburst.

Europeans in the center of the city learned of the murders when ambulances and private cars, some of them escorted by military vehicles, took the victims to various hospitals and clinics.

Earlier in the day, French authorities announced the murder of a 6-year-old European boy and his 2-year-old brother. The children were killed while their parents were away from their apartment.

The family's Moslem maid was suspected of the crime. She disappeared before the bodies of the children were found.

May 15, 1962

TERRORISTS BOMB ALGIERS CITY HALL AND BIG HOSPITAL

Expanded French Units Fail to Deter Secret Army From Scorched-Earth Drive

CAMPAIGN IN NEW PHASE

By HENRY TANNER
Special to The New York Times.

ALGIERS, June 15—Algiers seemed to edge closer to chaos today as European terrorists made good their threat of a stepped-up campaign of destruction.

Members of the Secret Army Organization destroyed the major part of Algeria's largest and best-equipped hospital, which is in the center of the city. They also damaged a smaller hospital.

They blew up Algiers' massive City Hall, killing at least three French soldiers stationed as guards in the building and wounding forty-three, according to official sources.

They touched off bombs and set numerous fires in almost all the country's urban centers.

The Secret Army was able to renew its scorched-earth campaign in Algiers in spite of the fact that the French Army had moved in heavy reinforcements during the night. Armored cars and soldiers on foot patrolled unceasingly all day. Cars and pedestrians were subjected to searches at many intersections.

Women Join Campaign

Today for the first time since the Secret Army began its efforts to sabotage the French-Algerian accords under which the territory will vote for independence July 1, Algiers saw a different kind of scorched-earth campaign. It was conducted by European residents, including women, instead of trained members of a terrorist organization.

Residents of Bab-el-Oued, the city's principal working-class district, set fire to the covered market place of their quarter, a beloved landmark, in a hysterical scene of tears and laughter.

This is the sort of thing officials have been particularly apprehensive about, not because of the damage, which was relatively minor, but because it is likely to lead more quickly than anything else to general panic and an all-out European exodus.

The city's Moslems showed that their patience was nearing the breaking point and that they were eager to intervene in the European quarters to prevent further destruction and to punish the saboteurs.

Immediately following the explosions at Mustapha Hospital this morning, armed groups of young Moslems left their districts and converged on the hospital to evacuate Moslem patients and cart off medical equipment and supplies.

Similarly, following the bombing of the City Hall at nightfall, Moslem auxiliary policemen stationed near by opened fire with automatic weapons. It was not made known whether there were casualties.

Targets to Be Major

The bombing of Mustapha Hospital and the City Hall was in keeping with an announcement by the Secret Army last night. A spokesman declared in a pirate broadcast that the terrorist campaign would take on "an entirely different character" today and that vital targets instead of secondary objectives would be destroyed.

Terrorists penetrated Mustapha Hospital shortly before 9 A. M. They moved patients, nurses and other personnel out of the way at gunpoint before placing four strong explosive charges. Three of the hospital's six operating units were destroyed, as were its central laboratory and radiology department.

Nine hundred ninety-five patients, more than 700 of them Moslems, were in the hospital, official sources said.

Shortly after the explosion the armed Moslems appeared, followed by a fleet of ambulances, trucks, buses and other vehicles.

The Moslems, apparently obeying strict orders, removed all Moslem patients and then started to carry off supplies and equipment. French troops halted the removal after almost two hours.

The fire in the market place of Bab-el-Oued, which took on the character of a ritual burning and sacrifice, started in midafternoon.

More than a hundred men, women and children of the neighborhood gathered. As the flames went up youngsters danced around them, crying and laughing. An old woman chanted as if in prayer. Several women broke down in tears.

When firemen arrived nearly an hour later, they were greeted with a hail of invective and admonitions not to be quick about putting out the fire.

Meanwhile, the departure of Europeans continued at an increased rate. Observers estimated that nearly 10,000 left during the day, compared with a rate of about 8,000 during the last two weeks.

For the first time since early April the processing of air passengers was in the hands of private airlines. The army took over operations when the Secret Army sought to prevent the departure of Europeans.

Last night, coming full circle, a spokesman for the terrorist organization gave the green light to European men who wanted to leave.

June 16, 1962

SECRET ARMY ORDERS HALT TO TERRORISM IN ALGERIA; MOSLEMS PLEDGE AMNESTY

CONCESSIONS WON

Rightists Gain Degree of Recognition and Role in Police

By HENRY TANNER
Special to The New York Times.

ALGIERS, June 17 — The leaders of the European terrorists in Algeria proclaimed a new truce tonight.

They ordered members of the Right-Wing Secret Army organization to "suspend combat and to halt destruction."

They made their declaration in a broadcast after Dr. Chawki Mostefai, leading nationalist member of the transitional executive council, yielded on three concessions the terrorists had requested in a series of talks earlier.

The exchange of public statements revived hopes that Algeria's transition to independence might henceforth be relatively orderly and that the majority of Europeans would decide to stay here.

Amnesty Is Conditional

Dr. Mostefai, making it plain that he spoke in the name of the Algerian nationalist leadership, promised a general amnesty for crimes committed by European terrorists prior to today. He said the amnesty would be proclaimed after the Algerian Government had obtained sovereignty, and only if Secret Army terrorism did not resume after tonight.

He suggested also that Europeans would be able to serve in newly formed Algerian police forces.

Dr. Mostefai added to the prestige of the Secret Army and gave it a degree of public recognition by pronouncing its name and stating that he had negotiated with its representatives, including Jean-Jacques Susini.

The three points — amnesty, participation in the police forces, and a degree of public recognition were the three principal objectives sought by the representatives of Secret Army in the recent talks with the Moslems.

In its pirate broadcast, the Secret Army command declared that Dr. Mostefai's statement was satisfactory as "a basis for an accord" between "the political forces that confront each other" in Algeria.

If the nationalists keep their promises, it added, the "exodus and the scorched earth will be replaced by a creative brotherly effort."

Observers noted that the spokesman for the Secret Army did not directly advise Europeans to end the exodus and to stay in the country.

The spokesman seemed to imply that there would be additional talks with the nationalists and that the Secret Army expected further concessions.

Observers also saw a possible source of future difficulties in the fact that the spokesman talked in terms of an "accord" between the Secret Army and the nationalist leadership, while the Algerian nationalists regard the developments as two separate statements that are not to be followed by any formal agreement.

The declarations by Dr. Mostefai and by leaders of the European terrorist organization reversed what earlier had appeared to be a trend to even greater violence.

Month-long sporadic talks between nationalist figures and representatives of the Secret Army appeared here to be conday after a "tough" declaration by Premier Benhoussef Ben Khedda of the Algerian Provisional Government. Secret Army members replied by heightening their campaign of destruction on orders from their leaders

June 18, 1962

ALGERIANS PILE UP A MASSIVE MARGIN IN FREEDOM VOTE

70% of Those Eligible Take Part—European Ballots Back Independence

MOSLEMS DANCE FOR JOY

Gunfire in Oran Mars Peace —French and Nationalist Troops Avoid a Clash

By THOMAS F. BRADY
Special to The New York Times.

ALGIERS, Monday, July 2—More than 70 per cent of Algeria's 5,000,000 eligible voters balloted yesterday to pile up a massive majority for independence in cooperation with France. Europeans as well as Moslems generally voted in favor of ending 132 years of French rule.

At 2 A. M. today an unofficial figure for over-all returns in the referendum showed 2,605,203 yes votes and 6,732 no votes. The yes votes amounted to 99.6 per cent of the valid ballots.

In European quarters, those who voted rolled up a strong majority for independence although the participation in some places was not wide. Invalid ballots, a way of rejecting independence, were numerous.

New Strife Threatens

Voting was peaceful for the most part. Moslems in Algiers danced in the streets and embraced Europeans after the polls closed. But in Oran there were moments of shooting and a tense confrontation of French and Algerian troops in the heart of the city.

Behind Algeria's joy over achieving independence, however, there was also the threat of new internal strife that the voters and even the nationalist "militants" tried to ignore.

The men who had led the seven-and-a-half-year struggle for Algerian liberation, standing together against the might of France, had split into two bitterly antagonistic groups now that victory was at hand.

Vice Premier Mohammed Ben Bella of the Algerian Provisional Government in Tripoli and the general staff of the National Liberation Army in Tunisia were openly defying the orders of their own Government, headed by Premier Benyoussef Ben Khedda.

Algiers Awaits Ministers

The majority of the twelve ministers of the Provisional Government, headed by Mr. Ben Khedda, were expected to arrive here later today by plane from Tunis, reinforced in their fight against the dissident Mr. Ben Bella by success of referendum, absence of violence, and European participation in the "yes" vote.

A proclaiming of independence that would end French rule here was also expected during the day to cut short the "vacuum" that might favor dissident nationalist forces.

July 2, 1962

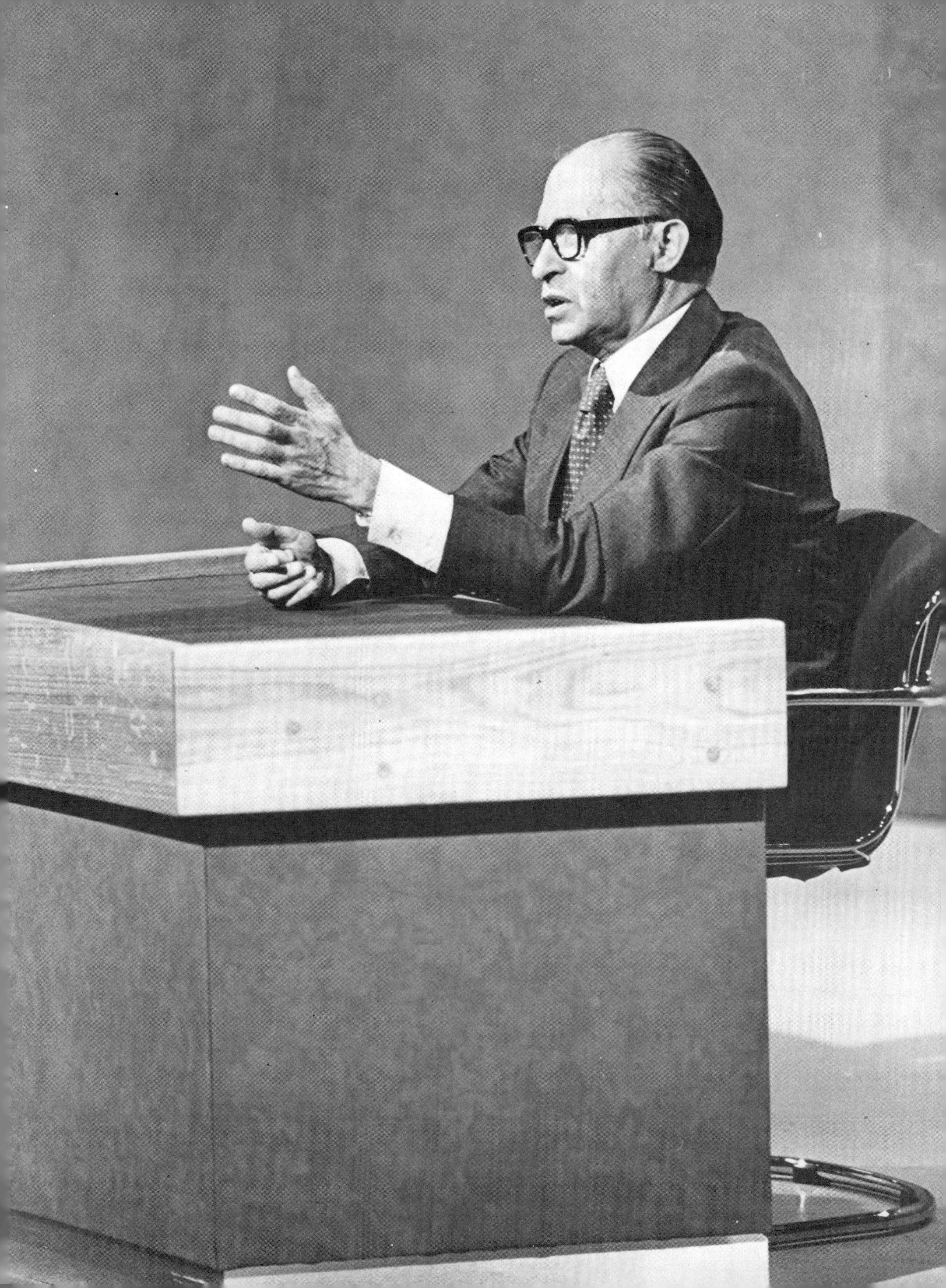

CHAPTER 3

Terrorists or Patriots

Menahem Begin, Prime Minister of Israel, and one-time leader of the outlawed Irgun terrorist group.

NYT Pictures

THE IRGUN AND THE STERN GANG

BACKGROUND OF UNREST IN ANCIENT PALESTINE

Outstanding Events in the History of the Territory Since the War Which Have Led Up to Outbreaks of Violence —Britain's Position as Mandate-Holder

BEHIND the outbreak of strife in Palestine there is a short chapter of international history, going back to the World War and the liberation of the country from the Turks, which helps to explain the present conflict. The outline given below of events leading up to the outbreak has been prepared by the research assistant in Near Eastern affairs of the Foreign Policy Association. Miss MacCallum was born in Turkey and lived there for fourteen years.

By ELIZABETH P. MacCALLUM.

TWELVE years ago Palestine detached from the Ottoman Empire in which it had been included for 400 years. The British and French governments celebrated their victory in the Near East a year later by issuing in November, 1918, a joint declaration of policy:

"The end aimed at by France and Great Britain is the complete and final enfranchisement of the peoples so long oppressed by the Turks, and the establishment of national governments and administrations drawing their authority from the initiative and free choice of the native populations."

This announcement was applicable to Syria and the Lebanon, Mesopotamia, Transjordania and Palestine, all of which are now comprehended within the mandate system of the League of Nations.

Developments in Palestine since the days of the Ottoman régime have been of such an interesting and complex nature as to require a chapter to themselves in the contemporary history of the Near East. During the earlier part of the war Palestine was completely under the control of the Turkish authorities, who advanced from a Palestinian base into Egyptian territory against the British troops. Gradually, however, the Turkish forces were driven back by General Allenby into Palestine and then into Syria, while Arabs from the Arabian peninsula also pushed northward against their former Turkish masters.

Arabs Join the Allies.

The Arabs determined to revolt against the Turks only after their leader, the Sheriff Hussein of Mecca, had won from the British a promise to recognize and support the independence of the Arabs in practically all the territory between Turkey proper, the Indian Ocean and the Red Sea. There were certain exceptions which do not concern us at the moment, since they did not affect Palestine. Great Britain did undertake, however, to guarantee the holy places against all external aggression and to recognize their individuality.

In return, Hussein undertook to seek the advice and guidance of Great Britain alone among foreign powers and to employ no foreign officials or advisers except those of British nationality. On this understanding, and in consideration of certain subsidies for the payment of his men, Hussein threw in his lot with the Allies.

It transpired, however, that during the war Great Britain had also entered into a certain secret agreement with its ally, France, and that this secret agreement (known as the Sykes-Picot agreement) was not altogether compatible with the promises made to Hussein, inasmuch as it involved the creation of a French, as well as a British, sphere of influence within the territory promised to the Arabs. The British and French governments had maps in their possession showing which sections of the liberated territories were to be under direct French control and which under direct British control, which were to form a French sphere of influence and which a British sphere of influence. Palestine, according to these maps, fell within none of these four categories. It was to come under an international administration in which France, as the traditional protector of Christian interests in the Near East, was expected to have a predominant influence.

These secret plans of the French and the British met an unexpected obstacle at the Paris Peace Conference. President Wilson, General Smuts of South Africa and others had come to the conference determined to do what they could to prevent colony-snatching of the traditional sort. Owing to their insistence, and to the support given to their suggestions by public opinion, it was decided before the conference broke up that the territories detached from the Ottoman Empire, along with former German colonies, should be administered under a form of trusteeship by advanced nations on behalf of the entire civilized world. The League of Nations was to supervise the administration of these "mandated" territories and full publicity was to be given to the annual reports of the administrative authorities.

Policy of Peace Conferees.

The Peace Conference decided that the Near Eastern territories had already reached such a high stage of development that their existence as independent nations could be provisionally recognized, subject to the rendering of administrative advice and assistance until they were able to stand alone. In this area the wishes of the inhabitants were to be a principal consideration in the selection of the mandatory powers.

The secret Anglo-French agreement had made no provision, however, for consulting the wishes of the inhabitants before the proposed administrations were set up. And in the end Great Britain and France divided the territory without any reference to the wishes of the people concerned. The Allied Supreme Council met at San Remo in April, 1920, and decided on the disposition of the territories under occupation by allied troops.

France was assigned as mandatory power for Syria and the Lebanon; Great Britain was to take over the mandate not only for Mesopotamia, but also for Palestine, since the international régime originally contemplated for Palestine threatened to be too unwieldy to be feasible. Documents drawn up by the two powers, specifying the principles in accordance with which they proposed to administer the mandated territories, were submitted later to the League Council. The mandate for Palestine was approved by that body on July 24, 1922, although technical difficulties prevented it from going into effect until Sept. 29, 1923.

Guaranty As To Territory.

The mandate for Palestine resembles in a number of ways the mandate for Syria and the Lebanon. It provides, for instance, that the mandatory shall guarantee the territorial integrity of the country; that natives and foreigners shall have their rights protected by an adequate judicial system; that the control of foreign policy shall be in the hands of the mandatory power; that there shall be no economic discrimination against the nationals of any State member of the League of Nations; that archaeological enterprises shall be safeguarded and properly regulated; that inhabitants shall enjoy liberty of conscience and freedom of worship, and that the various communities shall enjoy the right to maintain separate educational institutions of their own.

But the mandate for Palestine contained a number of clauses which had no counterpart in the mandate for Syria and the Lebanon. These special clauses were inserted to provide for the carrying out of one of the most famous social experiments of the post-war period—the establishment in Palestine of a Jewish national home.

In the latter part of the nineteenth century there took shape in Europe a movement having in view the practical realization of this dream of centuries. In 1897 the first Zionist Congress was held in Switzerland, since when a number of Jews the world over have identified themselves with the movement to create for the Jewish people a home in Palestine secured by public law. Companies were formed to acquire land in Palestine in the name of the Jewish people or for individuals and to promote colonization schemes and carry on a banking business. At the outbreak of the World War there were a number of flourishing Jewish enterprises in the country.

The war raised the question in the minds of Zionists as to what would be the position of Jews in Palestine in the future in the event of victory for the allied arms. Remembering that Great Britain had offered in 1902 to set aside land in Uganda for Jewish settlement, the Zionists now approached the British Government on behalf of their Palestine projects and in November, 1917, received the assurance they sought in the famous Balfour declaration, which reads as follows:

"His Majesty's Government view with favor the establishment in Palestine of a national home for the Jewish people, and will use their best endeavors to facilitate the achievement of that object, it being understood that nothing shall be done which may prejudice the civil and religious rights of existing non-Jewish communities in Palestine, or the rights and political status enjoyed by the Jews in any other country."

France and Italy promptly endorsed the British statement, President Wilson expressed his hearty approval of it and the expectations of Zionists rose accordingly. The decision to substitute a British for an international administration in Palestine came at about the same time. It thus ensued, therefore, that it was with British authorities rather than with an international group that Zionists soon began to discuss the special articles relating to the Jewish national home which were to be included in the Palestine mandate.

These articles as finally adopted provided that the mandatory power should be responsible for placing the country under such political, administrative and economic conditions as would secure the establishment of the Jewish national home and the development of self-governing institutions. It was to be responsible, too, for safeguarding the civil and religious rights of all the inhabitants of Palestine, irrespective of race or religion. A Jewish agency (in practice the Zionist organization) was to be recognized as a public body for the purpose of advising and cooperating with the administration in economic, social and other matters affecting the establishment of the Jewish national home and the interests of the Jewish population in Palestine.

This Jewish agency, subject always to the control of the administration, was to assist and take part in the development of the country. The administration was to facilitate Jewish immigration under suitable conditions and to encourage close settlement by Jews on the land, including State lands and waste lands, not required for public purposes. At the same time, the rights and position of other sections of the population were not to be prejudiced. A nationality law was to be so framed as to facilitate the acquisition of Palestinian nationality by Jews settling permanently in Palestine.

Early Disturbances.

When Sir Herbert Samuel arrived in Palestine as the first British High Commissioner, he found that the Arab population suspected the British authorities of intending to expropriate their holdings for the sake of turning them over to the Jews. They anticipated an immediate and overwhelming Jewish immigration. Moslems were afraid that their holy places would be taken from them. There were race riots in 1920 and 1921 in which 104 persons lost their lives and four times as many were wounded. British troops still mobilized in the country quelled the disorders. In time tension eased, all but one unit of the British forces were sent away and from 1924 onward the administration depended on a small battalion of British gendarmes and on the native police to maintain public security.

To make clear the British position for the sake of both Arabs and Jews, Sir Herbert Samuel obtained from the British Government an official interpretation of the Balfour Declaration. This statement explained that the Balfour Declaration did not point to the creation of a wholly Jewish Palestine. It did not contemplate the disappearance or the subordination of the Arab population, language or culture. Palestine as a whole was not to be converted into a Jewish national home; a Jewish national home was merely to be founded in Palestine. In order that the Jewish community should have full opportunity for the free development of its capacities, it was essential that it should know it was in Palestine as of right and not on sufferance. The Palestine community was to become a centre in which Jews as a whole might take, on grounds of race and religion, an interest and a pride.

Petitions to the League.

In spite of this explanation, the Arab inhabitants refused to recognize the Balfour Declaration or to assent to the mandate so long as it contained articles guaranteeing the creation of a Jewish national home in Palestine. Moslem and Christian Arabs sent deputations to wait upon the British authorities and presented petition after petition to the League of Nations.

They asserted that the Balfour Declaration sacrificed the rights of the majority already in the country for the sake of a minority not yet arrived—i. e., the Jewish immigrants who were still to come. To safeguard only the "civil and religious rights" of the Arab majority in Palestine was to treat them as though they themselves were the minority. The Balfour Declaration, they affirmed, was therefore inconsistent with the League Covenant, and Great Britain (in accordance with Article XX of the Covenant itself) should have been forced to repudiate the Balfour Declaration before being permitted to acquire membership in the League.

So bitterly did Moslem and Christian Arabs resent the Balfour Declaration that they refused to cooperate with the authorities when the latter attempted in 1922 to establish a national Legislative Council in Palestine. This body was to have been composed of ten appointed officials and twelve elected members—eight Moslems, two Christians and two Jews.

The Arabs boycotted the elections on the ground that they could not be sure that the rights of the majority would be guaranteed unless the Arab members of the proposed Legislature outnumbered Jewish and official members combined. The boycott being effective, the High Commissioner was forced to give up the plan for a legislative body; since that time government has been carried on by the High Commissioner in consultation with his immediate subordinates and a small advisory council made up entirely of officials. Proposed ordinances are published in the Official Gazette before promulgation, giving interested persons an opportunity to make representations to the authorities before the measures are actually put into force.

Arab Petitions Refused.

During the past year Palestinian Arabs have petitioned both the new High Commissioner, Sir John Chancellor, and the League of Nations for the establishment of "a democratic parliamentary system of government" to take the place of the existing system, described as "absolute colonial rule." But the requests were refused a short time before the recent outbreaks occurred in Palestine.

Disaffection among Arabs in Palestine has been based not only on the Balfour Declaration, however; there has been opposition to the British mandate itself. Arabs have expressed resentment at the artificial division and subdivision of the territories of the Near East to suit the purposes of foreign powers. They have asserted the belief that the erection of customs barriers and political boundaries where none existed before has been detrimental to the economic, social and political interests of the inhabitants. They desire to have these boundaries erased. And one of their main objections to the Balfour Declaration has been that it will tend to perpetuate the isolation of Palestine even should the other territories now under mandate become unified later on.

In the reports submitted to the League of Nations by the British authorities from time to time a number of sources of conflict within the mandated territory have been noted. In sessions of the Mandates Commission of the League such conflicts have been examined and commented upon. Complaints cover economic, social, political and religious matters, many of them dealing with problems which have caused the British authorities considerable anxiety, and toward whose solution considerable effort has been expended.

One of the matters which the Mandates Commission has been called upon frequently to consider is the conflict which has centred in the Wailing Wall of Jerusalem. When the British authorities assumed control in Palestine they realized that they were assuming the trusteeship of a land sacred to the adherents of three faiths—Jews, Christians and Moslems. They assured the world that the shrines of all three would be protected, and that access to these shrines would be guaranteed to those who regarded them as sacred. The mandate for Palestine provided for the appointment of a special commission to study, define and determine rights and claims in connection with the holy places.

Quarrels between Christians of various rites over the trusteeship of Christian shrines, together with conflicts relating to other holy places, all of which developed long before the British régime began, made the work of the proposed commission so delicate that the British authorities decided not to appoint it until there was some prospect of its being able to arrive at a permanent settlement agreeable to all parties. Accordingly, this commission has not yet been created.

Meanwhile, incidents have occurred with increasing frequency to strain relations between Jews (who claim the age-old right to worship unmolested at the Wailing Wall, a relic of Solomon's Temple) and Moslems, who worship at the Mosque of Omar, adjoining the Wailing Wall, where the Prophet Mohammed is said to have sojourned during a miraculous visit to Jerusalem.

Juxtaposition of these two holy places has made them the frequent scene of conflict between Moslem and Jew in the past. And it was here that the spark was struck that started the outbreaks of the past week.

September 1, 1929

BRITAIN'S PALESTINE DISPUTE: THE DOCUMENTS IN THE CASE

Question of Whether the New Policy Contravenes Promises in the Light of the Official Papers and Speeches

IS the new administrative policy for the Palestine mandate announced by the British Government a contravention of the Balfour Declaration of 1917 and of other promises made by Great Britain to the Jews of Palestine and to the Zionist Organization?

This question is answered by implication in the negative by the published report of Sir John Hope Simpson and the British White Paper, and in the affirmative by such leaders in the Zionist movement as Dr. Chaim Weizmann, Felix M. Warburg and Lord Melchett, who have resigned their offices in protest against the action of the British Colonial Office.

Below are presented the important documents and statements bearing on the dispute, including the Balfour Declaration, the pertinent provisions of the Treaty of Sèvres and of the Palestine Mandate, and extracts from the Simpson report, the White Paper and the statements of Dr. Weizmann and Mr. Warburg.

I.
THE BALFOUR DECLARATION.

(Declaration of Sir Arthur (afterward Lord) Balfour, British Foreign Secretary, Nov. 2, 1917.)

"His Majesty's Government view with favor the establishment in Palestine of a national home for the Jewish people and will use their best endeavors to facilitate the achievement of that object, it being understood that nothing shall be done which may prejudice the civil and religious rights of existing non-Jewish communities in Palestine, or the rights and political status enjoyed by the Jews in any other community."

II.
THE TREATY OF SEVRES.

(Article 95 of the Treaty of Sevres, signed by Turkey and the principal allied powers, Aug. 10, 1920.)

"The high contracting parties agree to entrust, by application of the provisions of Article 22, the administration of Palestine, within such boundaries as may be determined by the principal allied powers, to a mandatary to be selected by the said powers. The mandatary will be responsible for putting into effect the declaration originally made on Nov. 2, 1917, by the British Government, and adopted by the other allied powers, in favor of the establishment in Palestine of a national home for the Jewish people, it being clearly understood that nothing shall be done which may prejudice the civil and religious rights of existing non-Jewish communities in Palestine, or the rights and political status enjoyed by Jews in any other country.

"The mandatary undertakes to appoint as soon as possible a special commission to study and regulate all questions and claims relating to the different religious communities. In the composition of this commission the religious interests concerned will be taken into account. The chairman of the commission will be appointed by the Council of the League of Nations."

III.
THE BRITISH MANDATE.

(Extracts from the British mandate for Palestine, approved by the Council of the League of Nations, July 24, 1922; declared in force, Sept. 29, 1923.)

"Article III. The manatary shall be responsible for placing the country under such political, administrative and economic conditions as will secure the establishment of the Jewish national home, as laid down in the preamble, and the development of self-governing institutions, and also for safeguarding the civil and religious rights of all the inhabitants of Palestine, irrespective of race and religion.

"Article IV. An appropriate Jewish agency shall be recognized as a public body for the purpose of advising and cooperating with the administration of Palestine in such economic, social and other matters as may affect the establishment of the Jewish national home and the interests of the Jewish population in Palestine, and, subject always to the control of the administration, to assist and take part in the development of the country.

"The Zionist Organization, so long

The Irgun and the Stern Gang

as its organization and constitution are in the opinion of the mandatory appropriate, shall be recognized as such agency. It shall take steps in consultation with his Britannic Majesty's Government to secure the cooperation of all Jews who are willing to assist in the establishment of the Jewish national home.

"Article VI. The Administration of Palestine, while insuring that the rights and position of other sections of the population are not prejudiced, shall facilitate Jewish immigration under suitable conditions and shall encourage, in cooperation with the Jewish agency referred to in Article 4, close settlement by Jews on the land, including State lands and waste lands not required for public purposes.

"Article XI. * * * The administration may arrange with the Jewish agency mentioned in Article 4 to construct or operate, upon fair and equitable terms, any public works, service and utilities, and to develop any of the natural resources of the country, in so far as these matters are not directly undertaken by the administration.

"Article XV. * * * No discrimination of any kind shall be made between the inhabitants of Palestine on the ground of race, religion or language. No person shall be excluded from Palestine on the sole ground of his religious belief."

V.

THE SIMPSON REPORT.

(Extracts from the report by Sir John Hope Simpson, made public Oct. 2, 1930.)

"It is the duty of the administration under the mandate to insure that the position of the Arabs is not prejudiced by Jewish immigration. It is also its duty under the mandate to encourage the close settlement of the Jews on the land, subject always to the former condition. It is only possible to reconcile these apparently conflicting duties by an active policy of agricultural development, having as its object close settlement on the land and intensive cultivation by both Arabs and Jews. To this end drastic action is necessary. * * *

"If there are Arab workmen unemployed it is not right that Jewish workmen from foreign countries should be imported to fill the existing vacant posts. * * *

"I desire to record my opinion that the observance of the articles of the mandate, and especially Article VI of the mandate, presents extraordinary difficulty. The sole way in which the mandate can be carried out is by intensive development of rural Palestine. * * *

"There exists no easy method of carrying out the provisions of the mandate. Development is the only way. Without development there is no room for a single additional settler if the standard of life of the fellaheen is to remain at its present level. With development that standard could be raised so that it would permit reasonable conditions of livelihood to the backward class of the community and a margin of land could at the same time be provided for additional colonization.

"It is my personal belief, founded on the inquiries which I have made and on my inspections, that with thorough development of the country there will be room not only for all the present agricultural population on a higher standard of life than it at present enjoys, but for not less than 20,000 families of settlers from the outside.

"Any scheme for development presents serious difficulties. Unless such a scheme is accepted by both Jew and Arab it may very well fail. Of both it will require support if it is to have the desired result: namely, the advancement of a neglected but historic country in the path of modern efficiency by the joint endeavor of the two great sections of its population with the assistance of the mandatory power."

VI.

THE BRITISH WHITE PAPER.

(From the statement of Lord Passfield, Secretary for the Colonies, in the British White Paper.)

"The condition of the Arab peasant leaves much to be desired and a policy of land development is needed if the improvement of his condition of life is to be effected. The sole agencies which have pursued a consistent policy have been the Jewish colonization societies, private and public. The Jewish settlers have had every advantage that capital, science and organization could give them. To these and the energy of the settlers themselves their remarkable progress is due.

"On the other hand, the Arab population, while lacking the advantages enjoyed by the Jewish settlers, has by an excess of births over deaths increased rapidly, while the land available for its sustenance has decreased by about 250,000 acres. This area has passed into Jewish hands.

"It can now be definitely stated that at the present time and with the present methods of Arab cultivation there remains no margin of land available for agricultural settlement by new immigrants, with the exception of such undeveloped land as the various Jewish organizations hold in reserve. The provision of a margin available for further settlement depends upon the progress made in increasing the productivity of the land already occupied.

"Clearly, if the immigration of Jews results in the prevention of Arabs obtaining work necessary for their maintenance, or if Jewish unemployment unfavorably affects the general labor position, it is the duty of the mandatory power to reduce or if necessary to suspend such immigration until the unemployed portion obtains work. Under the present circumstances his Majesty's Government considers their suspension of immigration under the labor schedule last May fully justified.

"Any hasty decision in favor of more unrestricted Jewish immigration is to be strongly deprecated, not only from the viewpoint of the interests of the Palestine population as a whole but from the special viewpoint of the Jewish community. So long as widespread suspicion exists as it does among the Arab population that their economic depression is due to excessive Jewish immigration, and so long as some ground exists upon which this suspicion may be plausibly presented as well founded, there can be little hope of any improvement in the mutual relations of the two races. It is upon such improvement that the future peace and prosperity of Palestine must largely depend.

"It is only in a peaceful and prosperous Palestine that the ideals of a Jewish national home can be realized, and it is only by the cooperation of the Jews and Arabs with the government that prosperity can be secured. Palestine has reached a critical moment in its development. In the past the government has left economic and social forces to operate with a minimum of interference and control, but it has become increasingly clear that such a policy cannot continue.

"It is only the closest cooperation between the government and the leaders of the Arab and Jewish communities that can prevent Palestine from drifting into a situation that would imperil on the one hand the devoted work of those who have sought to build up a Jewish national home, and on the other the interests of a majority of the population who at present possess few resources of their own with which to sustain the struggle for existence.

"To the Arabs, his Majesty's Government would appeal for recognition of the facts of the situation and for sustained effort and cooperation in obtaining that prosperity for the country as a whole by which all will benefit.

"From the Jewish leaders his Majesty's Government ask recognition of the necessity for making some concessions on their side in regard to the independent and separative ideals which have been developed in some quarters in connection with the Jewish national home, and for accepting as an active factor in their policy that the development of the country shall be carried out in such a way that both Arabs and Jews receive adequate consideration."

VII.

DR. WEIZMANN'S STATEMENT.

(From the statement by Dr. Chaim Weizmann, in resigning the presidency of the Jewish Agency for Palestine and of the Zionist World Organization, Oct. 20, 1930.)

"It is beyond dispute that neither civil nor religious rights of the non-Jewish community in Palestine have suffered, and the government itself has more than once stated that their economic position has definitely improved, largely as a result, direct and indirect, of the effort of the Jews to build up the Jewish national home.

"The government seems to have laid down the principle that every landless Arab and his family are entitled by right to be settled on the land and that there is an obligation for the government to secure that he be so settled and provide means for settling him. It is clear that so far-reaching and novel a principle is going beyond anything required or implied in the mandate and would seriously hamper the development of the national home.

"The change of outlook is fundamental and points to the deepest misunderstanding of the whole purpose and meaning of the policy of a Jewish national home. The promise of the Balfour Declaration and of the mandate was to the Jewish people in its diaspora and rested the claims of the people upon their historic connection with Palestine. It acknowledged their right to reconstruct a national home in Palestine. The pledge was given to the whole Jewish people, who were to take their place in Palestine 'by right and not on sufferance,' to use the words of the White Paper of 1922. All this by implication disappears from the government's new statement of policy. * * *

"The Council of the League of Nations at its last session warned the mandatory power against a policy 'aimed at crystallizing the development of the Jewish national home at its present stage of development' and the Council's view was accepted without reserve by the accredited representative of the British Government. But the measures now announced by the government will produce precisely the results against which the League of Nations raised its warning voice."

VIII.

MR. WARBURG'S STATEMENT.

(From the statement of Felix M. Warburg on resigning as chairman of the administration committee of the Jewish Agency for Palestine, Oct. 21, 1930.)

"So complete was our confidence and faith in the British Government that millions of pounds were poured into Palestine, as well as unstinted labor and devotion, for the improvement of health and sanitation, for the building of Jewish colonies, the promotion of agriculture and industry and the advancement of education, culminating in the Hebrew University. If today malaria is being stamped out, sanitary and living conditions improved, roads built, agricultural cultivation placed on a scientific plane, waste spaces drained and bleak hillsides reafforested; if industry has been brought into the country with small factories and workshops, electrical power developed and the natural resources of the Dead Sea are tapped—all these civilizing influences have come almost entirely either out of moneys contributed by Jewish enthusiasm, devotion and sacriifces, or from taxes paid largely by Palestinian Jewry. And all of this has inured greatly to the benefit of the Arab population. We have rejoiced that this should be so, for we recognize that no country could prosper if only a part of its population fared well. But it is the simple truth that the whole level of Arab life has been greatly lifted since the upbuilding of the national home was undertaken. * * *

"We now learn that Jewish immigration is to be totally restricted for the present and the purchase of land to be surrounded with difficulties, so that even if funds are furnished to pay, however dearly, for the land, the transactions will still be rendered almost impossible.

"Those of us who tried to support a conservative approach in respect to the future and the upbuilding of Palestine, who assured the Arabs at every session of the agency that we had no ambition to rule over them or to be ruled, but to live and let live, cannot but feel bitterly disappointed this day. * * *

"We rely on the inherent fairness of the British people and enlightened public opinion throughout the world, to enable us to overcome the obstacles which now confront us."

October 26, 1930

TERRORISTS OR PATRIOTS

REVISIONISTS RIOT IN ZIONIST PARLEY

52 Stalk Out, Breaking Up the Basle Session, After Wild Fights and Debates.

WEIZMANN IS CENSURED

By LOUIS STARK,
Staff Correspondent of The New York Times.
Special Cable to THE NEW YORK TIMES.

BASLE, Monday, July 13.—Amid scenes of great disorder, fifty-two delegates of the Revisionist group, led by Vladimir Jabotinsky, bolted the Congress of the World Zionist Organization shortly before 2 o'clock this morning.

This demonstration by the Revisionists occurred after their resolution favoring a Jewish State with a Jewish majority on both sides of the River Jordan, in Palestine and Transjordania, was beaten by 125 votes to sixty-five.

Upon announcement of the defeat, Meyer Grossman, Revisionist leader, jumped to the platform and began making a statement. Taunted by shouts, he declared:

"We have worked in political connection with you for six days, hard as that has been."

An immediate roar of protest arose from the Labor delegates. A fist fight began in the rear of the room between two delegates, while a Laborite tried to shout down Mr. Grossman.

While Labor delegates began singing the Zionist anthem, "Hatikvoh," young Revisionists darted up into the gallery and tore down the Zionist flag.

American Saves Flag.

Colonel Benjamin Evarts, American delegate, seized the emblem and in the melee to gain possession his clothes were almost torn from his back. He managed to wrest the flag away, however, and it was again draped over the balcony amid the cheers of all except the Revisionists.

Meanwhile, Mr. Grossman tried to continue his explanation. Then, irked by interruptions to his associates, Mr. Jabotinsky leaped onto the stand, waving his delegate's credentials in the air.

"This is not a Zionist conference!" he shouted as he dramatically tore up the card and flung the bits of pasteboard into the faces of Labor delegates.

Boos and hisses greeted the declaration.
Above the tumult, Mr. Grossman shouted to the Labor men:

"You are traitors to Zionism."

By this time Elon Motzkin, chairman, had lost control of the meeting and pandemonium continued for ten minutes. Finally Mr. Jabotinsky leaped upon a table, shouting, "All Revisionists out."

Mr. Grossman abandoned his attempt to speak and the Revisionists stamped out of the hall, with Mr. Jabotinsky and Mr. Grossman at their head, to decide their future course. The chairman then adjourned the session until 4 o'clock this afternoon.

Weizmann Is Censured.

Earlier, by a vote of 123 against 106, the delegates "regretted" the views of Dr. Chaim Weizmann, president, who opposed the demand for a Jewish majority on both sides of the River Jordan as "inadequate."

Anti-Weizmannites won several test votes on a report of the political commission, presented after six days of wrangling. The motion was divided into two parts. The first stated the ultimate aims of Zionism as adherence to the long-established Basle program, saying that homeless and landless Jews were striving to re-establish themselves "in our historic homeland, through large and uninterrupted immigration and settlement and by recreating the Israelites' national life with all the essential features of a people's normal existence."

The second part regretted Dr. Weizmann's views as given in an interview to the Jewish Telegraphic Agency. Labor delegates, adhering to Dr. Weizmann, sought to have the first part voted first but their opponents outvoted them by 123 against 106.

Labor then tried to table the second resolution but mustered only 101 against 129. The second resolution was then voted and adopted.

According to veteran Zionists, this morning's scene of disorder was unprecedented in the history of the movement.

The nearest approach to such a demonstration occurred at the Sixth Zionist Congress at Basle in 1903, when the Uganda proposal made by the British Government, offering the Jews British East Africa as a substitute for Palestine, came up for consideration. Menahem Ussishkin, head of the Jewish National Fund and leader of the group which protested against the Uganda proposal, was booed by the Revisionists today for voting against their proposal.

July 13, 1931

PALESTINE COLONISTS PROTEST TERRORISM

At Funeral of Victim of Bomb They Demand More Adequate Protection for Jews.

JERUSALEM, Dec. 28 (Jewish Telegraphic Agency).—Joseph Jakoby, a Jewish colonist of Nahalal, succumbed this morning in a hospital to wounds suffered when a bomb thrown by a person whose identity has not been established exploded in his home on Dec. 22.

Mr. Jakoby is the second fatality in his family. His 9-year-old son died Sunday. The father's hand was amputated and it was believed he was out of danger, when his death suddenly occurred.

The Palestine Government announced today a reward of £500 for apprehension of the bombers.

Funeral services, held this afternoon, were converted into a protest meeting against allegedly inadequate protection accorded to Jews. The consensus was that the bomb was thrown as part of an organized Arab political terrorization plot. Representatives of the Jewish Agency, the Palestine Jewish National Council and other central Jewish bodies attended the services. The funeral cortège included virtually the entire population of Nahalal as well as many persons from neighboring colonies.

The speakers emphasized the need for Jewish self-defense and a larger Jewish immigration. "To replace one Jewish family killed, 1,000 new families must come," one of the speakers declared.

Mr. Jakoby came to Palestine from the United States eleven years ago. He had studied agriculture in California.

December 29, 1932

ZIONIST LABORITES SEEK TO OUST FOES

Begin Drive at Prague Congress to Expel Revisionists as Result of Assassination.

PRAGUE, Aug. 27 (Jewish Telegraphic Agency).—Testimony given in the magistrate's court at Jaffa, Palestine, Friday, alleging that Revisionist extremists had contemplated recourse to murder, overshadowed all other issues here as the eighteenth World Zionist Congress entered its second week of deliberations today.

A determined drive was begun by the Zionist Laborites to have the Revisionists, who form the extreme right wing of the Zionist movement, expelled from the World Zionist Organization.

The testimony was given in the preliminary hearing of three Revisionists, Aba Achimier, Abraham Stavsky and Zvi Rosenblatt, who are accused of the murder in June of Dr. Chaim Arlosoroff, head of the political department of the Jewish Agency for Palestine.

The congress presidium held a secret session with the special commission of inquiry appointed by the Zionist actions committee to investigate Laborite charges against the Revisionists. The latter, who first announced their non-confidence in the commission and their refusal to appear before it, later announced they would do so as individuals but not as representatives of the party and then reversed their stand again and refused to do even this.

The commission, it was learned, wishes to question only the Palestine Revisionists who are now here for the congress.

The Laborites, who with 40 per cent of the total representation are the largest single faction at the congress, are to make a strong demand that the Revisionists be eliminated from all Zionist offices.

August 28, 1933

Fascism No Part Of Revisionism

Its Aim Is Stated to Be a Jewish State In Palestine

To the Editor of The New York Times:

A wireless dispatch from Palestine, entitled "Murder Verdict Stirs Palestine," to THE NEW YORK TIMES contained the following phrase: "the Revisionists or Fascist faction of the Zionist Organization."

Let me say most emphatically that the Revisionists are not Fascists, and nowhere in the program, convention resolutions or official utterances of that organization or its accredited leaders is there anything that hints at fascism.

The Zionists-Revisionists are followers of Dr. Theodor Herzl, the originator of political Zionism. With him they stress that there is an ever-present world-wide Jewish problem, arising from a number of causes, the dominant one being economic. In countries whose economic system no longer readily absorbs the Jews and increasing numbers of them are declassed and become public charges, numerous non-Jewish inhabitants blame the Jews for the general economic ills of the country. Hence troubles, excesses and persecution.

The Zionist-Revisionists maintain that this problem, which is international, is solvable only through mass transplantation of the "surpluses" to one land capable of absorbing them, geographically near the countries of emigration and politically chartered to receive the immigrants. The Land of Israel, they say, is the country, for (1) historically it is Jewish; (2) their historic claim has been recognized by the League of Nations and ratified by the United States in 1922; (3) it is in close proximity to the continent whence the emigration proceeds; (4) its absorptive capacity is between 8,500,000 and 18,500,000 people, depending upon the degree of the industrial and agricultural development of the country, and its present population is only 1,500,000.

Reason Behind Name.

The organization is called "Revisionist" because over a period of years it demanded revision of the attitude of the official Zionist Organization to the mandatory power, which since 1922 has persistently

The Irgun and the Stern Gang

pursued a political course contrary to the letter and spirit of the mandate over Palestine; a course designed to get into the country a maximum amount of Jewish money and a minimum number of Jews; and to spend the minimum amount of Jewish money for Jews. Thus, for instance, the average sum spent by the Palestine Government on a non-Jewish pupil is $25 per annum and on a Jewish pupil about $5, though the Jews constituting between 17 and 20 per cent of the population pay about 50 per cent of the taxes—the government admits 32 per cent.

Fascism has not and cannot have anything to do with revisionism, for fascism advocates a regimented, one-party State where no freedom save the freedom to suppress it prevails; and revisionism merely strives to attain a Jewish State for the Jewish people in Palestine, its social order to be determined, when the State, as a dominion of Great Britain, or in any other form, is established.

Their struggle with the Socialist-Labor party in Palestine arises from the fact that the Revisionists believe that capital and labor disputes in Palestine should, while the process of upbuilding the country is on, be composed by arbitration, and that strikes be reverted to only when the employer fails to abide by the verdict of the Court of Arbitration.   ELIAS GINSBURG.
New York. June 11, 1934.

June 17, 1934

EFFECT OF NAZISM UPSETS PALESTINE

Anti-Jewish Campaign in Germany Has Sent Flood of Immigrants There.

GREAT BRITAIN PERPLEXED

Zionist-Revisionists Are Gaining Recruits and Causing Trouble.

Special Correspondence, THE NEW YORK TIMES.
LONDON, July 27.—A dispatch to The Times from Palestine calls the attention of the British Government and people to the fact that the Jewish national home is turning out to be something very different from what they expected and even from what the first Zionists expected.

"One must come to Palestine," says the dispatch, "to realize how far the anti-Jewish National Socialist Government in Germany has altered not only the whole conception of the Jewish national home in the minds of the Jews but also the problem which it presents to the British Government.

"The sense of persecution has aroused a race-consciousness in thousands of Jews and is directing a spate of Jewish immigrants of all classes and professions toward Palestine. The Palestinian Government limits their numbers to what it considers to be the 'absorptive capacity' of the country; but they find their way in in spite of restrictions.

Much Idle Money.

"The Jewish population, which in 1931 numbered just short of 175,000, must now exceed 250,000. The Jewish town of Tel-Aviv had some 46,000 inhabitants in 1931; it now boasts 80,000. Haifa is half Jewish, Jerusalem more than half. Money has been flowing into the country. A recent estimate of the deposits in the banks was £13,000,000, of which more than half was reputed to be lying idle.

"The development of Jewish race-consciousness has furthered the Zionist-Revisionist movement. The Revisionists, led by the fanatical Vladimir Jabotinsky, have made the symbols and ideology of fascism their own. They constitute the opposition in the ranks of Zionism. They are at daggers drawn with the Jewish Labor Federation (Histadruth), which leads the movement today, because it is inspired by Socialist ideals, which as Fascists they detest, and also because they claim that by accepting the British Government's niggardly conditions for Jewish immigration into Palestine it is betraying the Jewish cause. They believe that if the Zionist Executive only made a stand they could force the British Government to accept their terms, namely, that the mandatary government should turn Palestine and Transjordania into a British colony, sequester all uncultivated land, and settle Jews on it by the hundred thousand.

Move for Illegal Entry.

"Meanwhile they are organizing illegal immigration on a large scale and are bringing into Palestine a class of young Jews full of revolutionary ideas, who give great trouble to the British authorities. Thanks to their activities, Tel-Aviv, which was formerly a model town, has acquired an unsavory reputation with the police and magistrates. Because the Revisionists openly demand unrestricted Jewish immigration into Palestine, while the Zionist Executive has to accommodate its wishes to the conditions laid down by the British Government, they are likely to gain recruits, and Great Britain may yet have to deal with their leaders as the official representatives of Jewry.

"Tel-Aviv, the 100 per cent Jewish city, is always the immigrants' first goal, and there, as often as not, they stay. They first want a roof over their heads. This makes the building trade the busiest industry in Palestine. It employs roughly one in eighty of the whole population of the country, and absorbs perhaps 45 per cent of the Jewish capital invested there. Factories and workshops are arising all around Tel-Aviv. Valuable orange groves are being cut down to make room for them, and the land is being sold at £1,500 to £2,000 an acre.

"In Tel-Aviv itself land has changed hands at ten times the price at which it was sold two years ago. These inflated prices are due to the vast quantity of Jewish capital which is now seeking investment in Palestine. There is evidently a fairly large category of wealthy Jews who for prudential or sentimental reasons are anxious to have a pied-à-terre in the Holy Land and are investing money for this purpose.

"The Jewish Agency justifies its demands for a larger immigration quota by pointing to the shortage of labor in Tel-Aviv and elsewhere and to the work waiting to be done on every hand. The government, in rejecting them, argues that the houses will not provide food for the builders or their inmates, and asks how at least 50,000 immigrants into Palestine are going to live. It believes that much of the investment that is taking place is purely speculative, and that many new Jewish concerns are existing solely on credit. And what if the bubble bursts and Palestine is left with 20,000 unemployed?

"The rate of development of the Arabs is the measure of what the government can do for the Jews. If Great Britain is trustee for the Jews, she is also trustee for the Arabs of Palestine. If the Jews were to flood Palestine the Arabs would be swamped, and this the British Government has no right to permit."

August 5, 1934

PALESTINE UNREST SPREADS TO SOUTH

Arab Wounds Polish Laborer in Grove — Jew Is Shot in Jerusalem on Way to Pray

ARAB IS KILLED AT QUARRY

Special Cable to THE NEW YORK TIMES.
JERUSALEM, March 6.—Several incidents in the past two days show that terrorism, hitherto confined mostly to the north of Palestine, is spreading to the south.

Yesterday afternoon an Arab entered a Jewish orange grove near the colony of Less Tzionah in Southern Palestine and asked for an orange to quench his thirst. When Vladislav Louga, a non-Jewish Polish laborer, bent over to pick up an orange, the Arab shot him in the stomach. Louga was rushed to a hospital at Tel Aviv, where he is in a critical condition.

Today an Arab fired at M. Schneerson, a Jew, as he was walking in the Old City of Jerusalem en route to prayers at the Wailing Wall. He was wounded in the shoulder and was taken to Hadassah Hospital, where his condition is serious.

In the afternoon several Jews passing a quarry were stoned by Arab workers. Two of the Jews were injured. Later two shots were fired near the same quarry and one Arab was killed and one wounded. The wounded Arab and two Arab witnesses said Jews had fired the shots. Several Jews were arrested.

An Arab was wounded today on the Acre-Safed Road in Northern Palestine.

A curfew was declared here tonight for the hours between 9 P. M. and 5 A. M. It is not known how long this will be in effect.

Tension is also high in Jaffa and Tel Aviv, where the police took special precautions all day. Jews are forbidden to travel between Tel Aviv and Jaffa and no Arabs are allowed to travel from Jaffa to Tel Aviv. Armed policemen guard the border between the two cities.

March 7, 1937

PALESTINE DIVIDED INTO THREE PARTS

Version of Royal Commission's Report Traces Frontiers of Jewish and Arab States

THIRD AREA TO BRITAIN

New Mandate Over Jerusalem, Bethlehem, Nazareth and Corridor to Jaffa

By The Palcor News Agency.

LONDON, July 3.—Declaring that only a radical solution can cope with the Palestine situation and that palliatives will not go to the root of the problem, the Royal Commission report, which is to be made public next Thursday, recommends the establishment of two separate States, Jewish and Arab, and the division of the country accordingly, it is learned on reliable authority.

According to the proposals of the commission, there will be in the future three classes of territory in Palestine: Two independent States for the Jews and Arabs, and a part of the country that will remain under a permanent British mandate.

Boundaries of Jewish State

The Jewish State will comprise the whole of Galilee, upper and lower, the whole of the Valley of Esdraelon, the greater part of the Beisan area and the entire coastal plain from Raselnakura in the north to Beer Tuvia in the south.

The northern frontier of the Jewish State will follow the existing frontier of Palestine along the southern boundary of Lebanon from the Mediterranean to Syria. The frontier continues along the present boundary of Syria along the Jordan River and the Sea of Kinnereth to a point north of the town of Beisan. The boundary of the Jewish State turns west along the southern edge of the Valley of Esdraelon to Megiddo, then runs south along the edge of the coastal plain in the foothills with an arc excluding the Arab city of Tulkarem. Thus, it is proposed that all Jewish settlements in Trans-Jordan, namely, the two Deganias, Gesher, Naharaim, and others should be included in the Arab State.

The important harbor city of Haifa will belong to the Jewish State. About 225,000 Arabs, besides the Arab population of the towns of Safed, Acre, Haifa and Tiberias, will be included in the Jewish State enclosed by these boundaries. For some time to come these towns, which are part of the Jewish State will remain under a temporary mandate of Great Britain, and their Arab population will not be obliged to assume Jewish citizenship as long as the mandate remains in force.

The second territorial division of the country will go to Great Britain, which will receive a new permanent mandate over Jerusalem, Bethlehem and Nazareth as well as over a corridor from Jerusalem to Jaffa, covering the area between Jerusalem, the Jaffa Road and Jerusalem and Jaffa Railway. The Arab towns of Ludd and Ramleh will be included under this mandate, but the city of Jaffa will be made part of the Arab State. Under this mandate part of the Negev region bordering on the Gulf of Akaba will be under British administration.

The rest of the country together with Trans-Jordan will form a new Arab State. To bring about the establishment of these two independent States the government will make treaties with the representatives of the Arabs and the World Zionist Organization respectively.

The Arab State will receive a grant of about $10,000,000 and an additional unspecified contribution for the transfer of Arab populations from within the Jewish State into Trans-Jordan.

Treaties with the two States will provide for the transportation of goods from Jewish Haifa to the Arab State and from Akaba and Egypt by railway to the Jewish State. The city of Jaffa will be joined to the Arab State by the Jaffa-Jerusalem corridor under the British mandate. During the period of transition the country will remain under the Central British Government.

The present régime, according to the commission, cannot continue because it must lead to endless troubles. It is the opinion of the body of inquiry which went to Palestine last November under the chairmanship of Earl Peel to investigate the administration of the League of Nations Mandate that the national aspirations of the Jews and Arabs in Palestine are irreconcilable and that the hope once entertained of combining them has not been fulfilled.

Promises Reviewed

Reviewing the promises that were made by the British Government to both Jews and Arabs, the report of the commission says that both the promise to promote the establishment of the Jewish National Home and the pledge to the Arabs to help them establish their political independence were given according to British traditions and in all sincerity. There is the British tradition of friendship to the Arab peoples in all the Middle Eastern countries and there is also the tradition of British sympathy toward the Jews, and it is in the interests of the British to retain the confidence of the Jews.

The report declares that the national aspirations of these two peoples are irreconcilable, because the Arabs want to establish their own empire, while the Jews claim full freedom to recreate Palestine and return to their historic homeland without being subject to limitations. The Jewish Agency insisted before the Royal Commission that the mandate be carried out in full and that Jewish immigration into Palestine be increased.

Neither of these claims can be accepted, the commission finds. The claim of the Arabs, that Palestine is an Arab country, disregards the rights of the Jews in Palestine and the fact that it already has 400,000 Jews. It is inconceivable, the commission report says, that these 400,000 Jews should be handed over to Arab domination, nor can 1,000,000 Arabs be handed over to Jewish domination in the future.

In its recommendation of the creation of two independent States the commission's report says that it had considered the possibility of applying certain palliatives to solve the problem, such as cantonization or drastic restriction of Jewish immigration and land purchase, but it rejected these and others as failing to go to the root of the problem.

Many Proposals Studied

These included such proposals as the fixing of a political maximum of Jewish immigration not to exceed 12,000 yearly for the next five years; the prohibition of land sales to Jews in certain areas and the prevention of Jewish settlement in the hills. In addition, the commission also considered the plan of appointing Jews and Arabs as representatives in the Advisory or Legislative Council, the discontinuance of the principle of allocating a fixed share in public works and services to Jews, and the further restriction of immigration of "capitalists" and dependents; the establishment of an Arab agency with the participation of representatives of Arab Kings to counterbalance the Jewish Agency for Palestine. Finally, the commission weighed the advisability of recommending such modifications in the mandate as would be required to enable the mandatory government to introduce the above-mentioned changes.

All of these plans were rejected by the commission, asserting that a radical solution was necessary and that such a solution could be found only in the establishment of two separate States and the division of the country between Jews and Arabs.

The existing Advisory Council is to be enlarged with the appointment of additional representatives of the Jewish and Arab peoples. If any of them should refuse to serve, a representative of the other will be appointed, nevertheless.

During the interval of adjustment and the establishment of the independent States the acquisition of land by Jews in future Arab territory and by Arabs of land in future Jewish territory will be prohibited. Jewish immigration will be regulated according to the principle of the economic absorptive capacity of the country, taking into account only the area assigned to the Jewish State.

The Royal Commission expressed its appreciation of the Jewish work in Palestine and criticized the Palestine Administration for its ineffective prosecution of Arab terrorists during the disturbances.

July 4, 1937

DIVISION OF PALESTINE

Map shows proposed partition into Jewish and Arab States and new British mandated territory.

Palestine Restricts Jewish Immigration, Basing It on Political Capacity of Country

Wireless to THE NEW YORK TIMES.

JERUSALEM, Oct. 20.—The Palestine Government today promulgated an ordinance restricting Jewish immigration in the sense that it abolishes the principle of immigration based on the economic absorptive capacity of the country. The Government accepts the principle, suggested by the royal commission, of a political maximum for Jewish immigration—that is, the number of immigrants will depend on what the Government considers advisable according to the political conditions of the country.

For the first time in the history of the British mandate Jews are mentioned in an ordinance as "persons of the Jewish faith," thereby, it is declared, violating a condition of the mandate, according to which all religions in Palestine shall stand on an equal basis. The Hebrew press here bitterly attacks the new measure, pointing out that the Council of the League of Nations only recently demanded in a resolution on Palestine that Britain leave in force the principle of economic absorptive capacity.

Early this evening, when a Jewish resident of the Old City of Jerusalem, Eliahu Harush, was returning to his home from work, three shots were fired at him near the entrance to the Christian quarter of the Old City. He escaped untouched, but one bullet hit a passing Arab wounding him slightly in the ear.

This morning when Jewish butchers went to a slaughter house outside Jerusalem they found that eleven oxen belonging to the Jewish Butchers Union had been killed with bullets. Two British policemen were fired on early in the evening just inside the Jaffa gate of Jerusalem.

October 21, 1937

The Irgun and the Stern Gang

BRITAIN TO COMBAT ARAB TERRORISM

Vigorous Measures Will Be Adopted in Palestine by the Colonial Office

Wireless to THE NEW YORK TIMES.
LONDON, Oct. 21.—The British policy to "take the most vigorous measures to combat terrorism" in Palestine before attempting to carry out the partition program was emphasized by William G. A. Ormsby-Gore, Secretary of State for the Colonies, in the opening session of the House of Commons today.

Cheers greeted his statement that Commons would agree with this program.

At the same time the Colonial Secretary described the long and involved procedure necessary to establish three-way partition in the Holy Land as recommended by the royal commission, stating that details would have to be worked out by another special commission that would study and make recommendations regarding social and financial problems on the spot.

As a result of the September outbreaks of terrorism, he told the House, "prompt and effective action" was taken, resulting, among other things, in the arrest and internment of 100 "terrorists."

Now the Government is assigning Sir Charles Augustus Tegart, who made a reputation as the "strongman of Bengal" in dealing with terrorists in India, to Palestine to help uproot the organization that must be eliminated before the political program can be started.

Responding to questions Mr. Ormsby-Gore fully backed the police and military organizations that had carried out reprisals on Arab villagers as the result of the destruction of the civil airport at Lydda.

"Does the Colonial Secretary suggest," asked Aneurin Bevan, Laborite member, "that it is the policy of His Majesty's Government to carry out reprisals upon innocent persons for misdeeds committed by others?"

"Certainly not," Mr. Ormsby-Gore replied, "but when a particular incident was done by local people—it was known where they came from —those who burned and destroyed the building and entire equipment of the civil airport at Lydda, in my view the police and military authorities were quite right to destroy the houses of the people who did act."

The Colonial Secretary said the British Government felt perfectly free to carry out the partition program in the light of the recent approval by the League of Nations, and that accordingly a second commission would be designated to submit a report, which would be submitted to both Parliament and the League.

He declined, however, to accede at the present to a suggestion by Tom Williams, Laborite member, that the second commission's report be submitted to a joint committee of the House of Commons and the House of Lords, saying:

"I should not like to give a final answer to that, but I don't think so. It would necessitate bringing a large number of witnesses from Palestine and cause infinite delay and might lead to a great many complications. We want a settlement to this question."

October 22, 1937

PALESTINE ORDERS DEATH FOR GUNMEN

Military Courts Will Be Set Up Next Thursday to Try Those Who Carry Arms

DECREE TO BE BROADCAST

New Curb Is Put on Jewish Immigration—Terror in Jerusalem Continues

Wireless to THE NEW YORK TIMES.
JERUSALEM, Nov. 10.—As a result of the incessant campaign of murder and terrorism throughout the country the Palestine government has decided to take the most stringent measures. A law, effective Nov. 18, makes the carrying or discharging of firearms an offense punishable by death.

Such offenses will be dealt with by military courts to be established on the same date. The government's communiqué announcing the new measures follows:

"In view of the continuation of an organized murder campaign in Palestine it has been decided in the interest of public security to establish military courts by a defense regulation made under a Palestine Order in Council of 1937.

"The defense regulation will be published Nov. 11 and will come into force on the 18th. In accordance with this decision military courts for the whole of Palestine, consisting of a president, who shall be an officer of field rank, and two other officers, will be set up for the trial of offenses summarized below:

"First, the discharge of firearms at any person, which will be an offense punishable by death; second, carrying arms, bombs, etc., which will be an offense punishable by death; third, causing sabotage or intimidation.

"Full details will appear in the regulations which will be published on the 11th. Sentences pronounced by these military courts will be subject to confirmation by the general officer commanding British troops in Palestine and Trans-Jordan, from whose decision there will be no appeal.

"The officer administering the government wishes it to be understood beyond any doubt that these decisions are prompted entirely by reasons of public security and not because there has been a failure on the part of the civil courts, which will continue to deal with all offenses save those mentioned above. The institution of military courts together with enhanced penalties is designed solely to expedite the operation of the emergency regulations for the suppression of the present campaign of terrorism and sabotage, which it is the determination of the government to exterminate.

"During the period which will elapse between the publication of the new defense regulations and their coming into force on Nov. 18 this communiqué will be published daily in all local daily newspapers and broadcast daily from Jerusalem."

Another communique published today by the Palestine Government makes clear its policy regarding Jewish immigration in Palestine. The communique follows:

"The following announcement is made for the information of the public:

"In official communique No. 1137 of July 7, His Majesty's Government declared that since the period of the current labor schedule expires at the end of July and some provision must be made for the ensuing period, it proposes as an interim measure that a total Jewish immigration in all categories of 8,000 persons be permitted in the eight months' period from August, 1937, to March, 1938, provided the economic absorptive capacity of the country is not exceeded.

"An ordinance is being enacted today with the object of giving effect to the policy of His Majesty's Government expressed in the above paragraph. With the approval of the labor schedule the Jewish quota has been filled. No new application for immigration will be accepted by the Department of Immigration until January, 1938.

"Regarding applications for immigration already accepted by the Department of Immigration but not yet decided on, it will be determined whether any of them may be favorably decided on within the maximum quota or held over for consideration in the light of circumstances surrounding immigration after April 1, 1938."

November 11, 1937

6 KILLED, 14 INJURED IN PALESTINE RIOTS

Terrorist Acts in Jerusalem Threaten to Develop Into Arab-Jewish Warfare

POLICE HAVE DIFFICULTY

By JOSEPH M. LEVY
Wireless to THE NEW YORK TIMES.
JERUSALEM, Nov. 14.—Six persons were killed and fourteen wounded today in terroristic activities in Jerusalem threatening to turn what until recently was a terrorist campaign into a warfare between Jews and Arabs. Of those killed today, five were Arabs and the other was a Jew.

As a result of the rioting A. Jabotinsky, son of the leader of the Jewish Revisionist Party, Vladimir Jabotinsky, was arrested late tonight with twelve other Revisionist youths at Tel Aviv.

In the Jewish colony of Rehovoth ten other Revisionists were arrested. It is expected that about 200 Jews belonging to the Revisionist Party will be apprehended within the next twenty-four hours.

The events of today came in quick succession. At 6:50 A. M. two Arab brothers of the village of Malda were fired on while passing through a Jerusalem Jewish residential quarter. Both were critically wounded and one later died at a hospital.

At about the same time a bomb was thrown at an apartment house on King George Avenue owned by an Arab and tenanted almost entirely by Jews. No damage was done. A passing cyclist saw the Arab who threw the bomb and caught him, turning him over to the police.

Shortly after, in a different part of the city in the Jewish quarter of Beth Israel, seventy Arabs and Jews, all engaged in the construction of a building belonging to an Arab, engaged in a battle. The trouble began with the throwing of stones and ended in the killing of an Arab and a Jew. A Jewish onlooker was arrested. Two Arabs later claimed he was the person who fired the shot killing the Arab.

Arabs Attack a Jew

In the mixed Arab-Jewish quarter of Romemah on the outskirts of Jerusalem Arabs attacked a Jew who was rescued by a policeman. A few minutes later an Arab-owned bus on the Jaffa-Jerusalem Road was attacked and the three bus passengers, all Arabs, killed. Several others were wounded. Two Jewish girls walking along the road were hit by a stray bullet and injured slightly.

The police encountered the greatest difficulty in restoring order. There was talk of a curfew beginning at 2 P. M. but it did not materialize. The curfew now in effect is from 5 P. M. to 5 A. M. Traffic between Jaffa, Tel Aviv and Jerusalem was at a virtual standstill this afternoon.

It appears that the much praised Jewish abstention from retaliation snapped after the killing of five Jewish colonists last week. Retaliation is now the motto of Jewish youths.

Haaretz and Davar, two of the leading Jewish dailies in Palestine, tomorrow will publish strong editorials condemning today's acts and calling on Jews to "take revenge" only through constructive activities.

The sort of propaganda still used by unknown sources to arouse Palestine Arab masses against Britain is best illustrated in the following manifesto distributed today and posted in the streets of Arab villages throughout Palestine. It bears no date name or place.

Addressed to 'Arab Nation'

It is entitled "The First Cry" and is addressed to the "Noble Arab Nation."

The text in part follows:

"The hour has come. Demand death and you will be granted life. We remind you to remember the past, for in doing so it will benefit you as stated in the Holy Book (Koran). At last Britain has uncovered herself and appeared naked. Having experienced your power and bravery she has cast aside sheep's clothing and has appeared as she really is, a preying wolf.

"You noble nation, here is Britain who always pretended to be the friend of Islam now appearing as a poisonous snake in your midst. Every one of you is a Moslem and Arab. Britain is bringing here her various means of destruction in order to exterminate you to bring the rubbish of the earth to establish them in your country.

"For the last seventeen years Britain has been testing your patience by every means but you stood firm. Then she brought against you all her means of destruction, expelled your leaders, put your best men in prison and made others leave the country, then she started her campaign of destruction, killing, robbing and imposing fines on you, taking your cattle and sheep in order to force you to submit.

"But you stood firm again and again. They still are oppressing you, but you are resisting and will never give way."

It was signed "Revolutionary Committee in Palestine."

November 15, 1937

ARAB TERRORISTS GET MONTHLY PAY

Discovery Made After Fight in Palestine—43 Slain by British Forces

Wireless to THE NEW YORK TIMES.

JERUSALEM, Dec. 27.—It is now verified that more than 90 per cent of the Arab terrorist gangs at present operating in Palestine are Syrians, all of whom are equipped with rifles and ammunition and receive monthly salaries from a mysterious source. This was proved in the successful battle of the last four days between British forces and Arab gangs in the hills of Galilee in which forty-three Arabs were killed.

The officer commanding the British forces stationed small detachments of troops in almost every village of the northern district of Palestine and thus prevented the gangs from entering Arab villages to hide or receive food and water. This forced them into open country, where they were surrounded by troops. The military command is acting most energetically and there is little doubt that if the present tactics are continued Palestine will be rid of menacing Arab bands in the very near future.

One of the greatest difficulties that the Palestine government is encountering is murder by sniping in cities, especially on the outskirts. Sir Charles Tegart and his colleague, Sir David Petrie, are now studying carefully the form of the country and are working out plans to combat sniping. Both come from India, where they earned reputations for wiping out terrorism. The government has forbidden the Palestine press to mention their names in any connection or to publish their photographs.

While the government is taking all these stringent measures to restore order and public security here, the Italians continue their anti-British propaganda with increased vigor. It is thought here that the disturbed conditions in Palestine today are no longer the result of an existing Arab-Jewish problem, but rather are due chiefly to an organized campaign by Mussolini against Great Britain.

December 28, 1937

BRITAIN IS COOLER ON PALESTINE SPLIT; LONG DELAY SEEN

Indefinite Stay of Partition Project Suggested in White Paper Recounting Moves

By FERDINAND KUHN Jr.

Wireless to THE NEW YORK TIMES.

LONDON, Jan. 4.—Indefinite and perhaps endless delay in partitioning Palestine was foreshadowed tonight in a new declaration of British Government policy published as a White Paper and signed by Colonial Secretary William G. A. Ormsby-Gore.

The White Paper maintains that partition of the Holy Land into three parts "is the best and most hopeful solution of the problem." At the same time, it shows that Britain is losing whatever enthusiasm it had for the partition scheme recommended by the Peel inquiry commission and accepted in principle by the British Cabinet last July.

In the face of the simultaneous criticism of the scheme by Jews, Arabs, the House of Commons and the League of Nations Council, the new White Paper insists the British Government is not committed in any way to the Peel commission's plan, which envisaged the creation of independent Jewish and Arab States and the retention of a small British mandated area around Jerusalem with a corridor to the sea.

Scope of New Inquiry

A new "technical commission" soon going to Palestine will, according to the White Paper, have "full liberty" to suggest modifications of the Peel commission's proposals, including "variations of the areas commended for retention under British mandate." This would appear to be an attempt to reassure Jews who complained bitterly last Summer that the proposed Jewish State would not include at least part of the city of Jerusalem.

The new commission's inquiries will "undoubtedly take many months," tonight's White Paper admits, and will cover a bewildering complexity of detailed questions. The White Paper explains that only after the new investigators have reported will it be possible for the British Government to judge whether a fair and practicable partition scheme is possible.

The new commission has not yet been appointed, and there is no indication when it can begin its work.

All this indicates that a long period lies ahead, during which Jews and Arabs might attempt voluntarily to settle their differences by some form of peaceful round-table discussion. The White Paper, however, contains not the slightest overture to Jews or Arabs to make the present mandate work as an alternative to accepting partition. The White Paper appears to accept the conclusion of the Peel commission that the mandate is unworkable and that some form of partition is unavoidable.

January 5, 1938

PALESTINE HANGING PROVOKES CLASHES

Many Hurt in Disorders After Jewish Youth Is Executed— Wedding Party Is Bombed

By The Associated Press.

JERUSALEM, June 29.—British airplanes, policemen and troops tonight patrolled a Palestine made tense by the hanging of a Jewish youth today.

Chanting the song of the Revisionist party and dressed in its uniform, 19-year-old Solomon ben Yosef steadily walked to the gallows in the troop-surrounded prison at Acre at 8 A. M. He was the first Jew to be hanged in Palestine since the Turks hanged a Moroccan Jew at Jerusalem's Jaffa Gate in 1916.

The youth had been condemned under Palestine's emergency military regulations after having been convicted of having ambushed an Arab-owned bus last April.

The disorders that the authorities had feared today were not long in coming. They broke out in several places, although most of them were minor and were suppressed by firm police measures.

The police clashed with crowds after two stormy demonstrations in the all-Jewish city of Tel Aviv. Most of the demonstrators were members of the Revisionist party, headed by Vladimir Jabotinsky, which seeks to make Palestine a Jewish homeland.

Seven at Wedding Wounded

The trouble spread to Tiberias, where a bomb was thrown tonight in the midst of a Jewish wedding. Seven persons were wounded. Subsequently, a mob, allegedly Arab, stoned Jews, but the arrival of policemen prevented riots. There were other minor clashes throughout the country.

Ben Yosef was erect as he mounted the dais at Acre Prison and allowed the executioner to place a hood over his head and the noose around his neck. Roads to Acre from Haifa were closed and the police allowed no one to approach until the death notice had been posted on the prison gates.

There had been no casualties in the ambush for which the youth had been convicted and, Jews assert, the bus was not even struck. But mere possession of arms can bring the death penalty by hanging, a dramatic illustration of Palestine's grave problems.

A Royal Commission is here now investigating a proposed plan to partition Palestine into Jewish and Arab States.

Native City Mourns Youth

Wireless to THE NEW YORK TIMES.

LUCK, Poland, June 29.—This native city of Solomon ben Yosef, whose name formerly was Solomon Tabacznik, was greatly shocked today by the news that the death sentence against him in Palestine had been carried out. Relatives and friends had hoped he would be re-

The Irgun and the Stern Gang

prieved at the eleventh hour.

The youth's 60-year-old mother, Rachel Tabacznik, a widow, had prayed all night in the synagogue and early this morning had prayed at the tombs of several famous rabbis reputed to have worked miracles.

Former comrades of ben Yosef in the Zionist Revisionist Youth Organization, Betar, had kept vigil all night in prayer houses.

News of the execution did not reach here until late this afternoon. A black flag was hoisted at the Betar house and an emergency meeting was called.

Ben Yosef's mother, who lives with her daughter and son-in-law and their two children in a one-room log cabin in a suburb, had cabled to the British High Commissioner of Palestine last week a plea that she be allowed to say farewell to her son, but the appeal was futile.

In a letter she received from the youth a few days ago he wrote:

"Try to forget me. You should not be ashamed of your boy. Other Jewish sons have met a more tragic death."

To his friends he wrote:

"Do not be discouraged by my death. It will bring a step nearer the dream of our life—an independent Jewish State."

Ben Yosef went to Palestine ten months ago.

June 30, 1938

JEWISH CIVIL WAR HELD ZIONIST PERIL

Jabotinsky, Revisionist, Asserts Menace Is Rising in Palestine as a Result of Terror

EXTREMIST MOVE GROWS

Moderate Jews Are Becoming Angry as Attacks by Arabs Continue in Holy Land

Wireless to THE NEW YORK TIMES.

WARSAW, Poland, Aug. 16.—A danger of civil war among Jews in Palestine was envisioned here tonight by Vladimir Jabotinsky, leader of Zionist Revisionists, extremist group, in the most sensational declaration made at the "Emergency Conference" of Zionists being held here. Not only in Palestine, he said, "but also abroad there now exists the great menace of civil war between Jews.

"This war," he said, "might arise over the problem of whether Jews should remain passive in Palestine or resort to reprisals. So long as the British Government does not guarantee peace in Palestine and so long as Arab terror continues, reprisals will be inevitable."

Asked a direct question whether he favored or opposed reprisals, Mr. Jabotinsky said it could not be a question whether one favored them or not—it was a question of peace and order. Hitherto, Arabs had killed Jews, and Jews were afraid to appear on the streets, but now Arabs also were afraid to appear on the streets. Everybody must admit, he said, that reprisals did not constitute a method of which one could approve but they were inevitable in the circumstances existing in Palestine today.

Asked how he could reconcile bloodshed methods with the principles of Jewish law, which forbid it, Mr. Jabotinsky replied:

"We, the Revisionists, do not want this bloodshed at all, but it would be sheer cowardice if we tolerated the spilling of Jewish blood alone, which has been going on in Palestine for so long."

He definitely accused the Jewish Agency for Palestine and Leftist parties of organizing what he called a program against Revisionists and using arms that they possessed to shoot Revisionist partisans.

"The Jewish community over all the world," he said, faces a serious problem. It is faced, he asserted, with the possibility in the not distant future that part of the Jewish population in Palestine might be induced to undertake something in the nature of a "Saint Bartholomew's Night" in respect to their political opponents. Naturally, he said, if this were tried in Palestine the war would soon spread to Jews elsewhere.

"I therefore warn everybody that should war start, we, the Revisionists, would be the victors," he said.

He remarked that there were at present not more than 1,500 Arab terrorists, and continued:

"We could mobilize a larger and more effective garrison. We could mobilize the youth, who would stand behind us, and we are certain that if it came to a direct clash with Arab terrorists we would vanquish them."

He added that the question of civil war in Palestine would be an international matter, but he said:

"We can no longer hide the facts of this possibility. Therefore I take the opportunity tonight of warning everybody that this menace exists."

Zionists here were taken aback at this unexpected statement. There undoubtedly exists a sharp difference between Jews in Palestine, as well as elsewhere, on the question whether Jews should remain passive or take reprisals.

August 17, 1938

21 SLAIN BY ARABS IN PALESTINE RAID

10 Children Among Victims as Band Attacks Jews' Homes in Suburb of Tiberias

FIRE AND STABBING USED

Six Killed as Bomb Blows Up House in Jaffa — Tel Aviv Youth Sentenced to Death

By JOSEPH M. LEVY
Special Cable to THE NEW YORK TIMES.

JERUSALEM, Oct. 3.—Twenty-one Jews, including three women and ten children, ranging in age from 1 to 12 years, were killed and three persons wounded last night on the shores of Lake Galilee, in the old Jewish quarter of Tiberias, in a massacre by stabbing, shooting and burning perpetrated by Arabs.

Not since the riots of 1929, when Arabs fell on Jewish men, most of whom were rabbinical students, as well as women and children, in the ancient towns of Hebron and Safed, has there been in Palestine such a slaughter as the attack of last night. The main synagogue of the town was destroyed by fire, and the district offices, the police station and the British police billet were fired on.

The attack apparently was well organized, since the Arab gang, before descending on Tiberias, cut all telephone communications. Coming in two parties from opposite directions at a given signal, which was a whistle blown from the hills surrounding the town, the firing began simultaneously in all quarters.

Beadle Is Killed

At the same time fires broke out in six Jewish-owned houses and in the district offices. The bandits rushed to the central synagogue and, finding there a beadle named Jacob Zaltz, killed him and then set the building afire.

Proceeding from there to the house of Menahem Kabin, an elderly American Jew who came to Palestine only recently, the Arabs knocked at the door. When the occupants heard a reply in Arabic to their question, "Who is there?" they immediately put out all the lights, but the Arabs broke in and stabbed and burned to death Mr. Kabin and his sister. His wife escaped.

From there the bandits went on to the house of Joshua Ben Arieh, where they stabbed and burned to death Joshua, his wife and one son, and then shot dead his infant son. In the same house three children of Shlomo Leimer, aged 8, 10 and 12, were stabbed and burned to death. Proceeding farther, the Arabs broke into the house of Shimon Mizrahi, where they killed his wife and five children, ranging in ages from 1 to 12 years, and then set fire to the house.

Later, rushing through the streets the Arabs encountered Jacob Gross, whom they killed. In the course of the shooting in the town two Jewish constables lost their lives and seven persons were wounded, three seriously.

It is believed that when all debris resulting from Arab plunder is cleared away other bodies may be found.

Six Arabs Slain

The only known casualties among the Arabs were six killed by Jewish supernumeraries who rushed to the assistance of Tiberias from the neighboring settlement of Mizpah. Coming along the main road just above Tiberias, they met an armed gang of Arabs, whom they engaged, killing six. They also seized five rifles, a shotgun and a quantity of ammunition.

When the attack began in Tiberias the police turned out at once, and reinforcements from the Trans-Jordan Frontier Force arrived soon after. The latter were fired on heavily while en route to Tiberias. Shooting in the town continued for two hours, from 9 to 11, when the bandits were finally driven out. Curfew was imposed throughout Tiberias.

The National Council of Palestine Jewry and all rabbinates in Palestine declared the cessation of all Jewish labor and the closing of all Jewish-owned shops from 2 to 4 o'clock this afternoon, as a sign of grief and mourning during the funerals of the victims.

Last night a bomb exploded, reportedly while it was being manufactured by Arabs, in the courtyard of a house in Jaffa. The house was completely destroyed and six Arabs were killed, including a child, and three Arabs were wounded, including a baby.

Early this morning a Jewish engine driver was shot dead by an Arab while driving a freight train across the Acre gate level crossing at Haifa.

Jacob Ben Moshe Kotek, 25, a Jewish youth of Tel Aviv, was sentenced to death today by a military court on the charge of carrying a suitcase containing arms and ammunition.

October 4, 1938

BRITISH ISSUE PLAN TO MAKE PALESTINE INDEPENDENT BY '49

Would Retain Mandate, Curtail Jews' Entry and Have Arabs Outnumber Them by 2 to 1

ZIONISTS TO FIGHT POLICY

25 Are Wounded in Tel Aviv Outbreaks—Country-Wide Demonstrations Called

By ROBERT P. POST
Special Cable to THE NEW YORK TIMES.

LONDON, May 17.—The British Government tonight published the new policy by which it hopes to settle the twenty-year conflict between Jews and Arabs in Palestine. This policy, contained in a White Paper, is aimed at limiting Jewish immigration to 75,000 over the next five years, and at the end of that time the size of the Zionist national home would be frozen at approximately one-third of the total population unless Arabs agreed to further immigration.

At the same time the British laid down the principle that their ultimate objective was an independent State of Palestine, to be created within ten years, wherein Jews and Arabs would live peaceably together. However, Britain will not relinquish her mandate over such a State unless, among other things, she is satisfied that proper provision has been made "for the protection of the different communities in Palestine in accordance with the obligations of His Majesty's Government to both Arabs and Jews and for the special position in Palestine of the Jewish national home."

Aims at Equal Rights

This sentence, it was said, means that the British Government will refuse to contemplate any situation in which Jews, forced to exist forever as a minority in the population, would not have complete equality of political and economic rights.

[About twenty-five Jews were wounded in Tel Aviv, Palestine, yesterday when British troops dispersed crowds demonstrating against the new policy, according to a dispatch from Jerusalem. The crowds previously had invaded a government building. Country-wide demonstrations, including a twenty-four-hour general strike, were called for today, and a long-time policy of non-cooperation and passive resistance was decided upon by Palestine Jews.]

The immediate reaction was what had been expected by the British. The Jewish Agency executive described the policy as "a breach of faith," a "surrender to Arab terrorism" and "a cruel blow." The Zionist body began to lay plans for fighting the policy first in Parliament and then in the League of Nations, as constituting a breach of the mandate. At the same time Jewish circles here predicted that there would be no cooperation with the policy but continuation of illegal immigration. Jewish circles announced that development of colonization in Palestine would be intensified. A loan of £1,000,000 is being floated for that purpose.

The Arab reaction in London was less vocal, though Egyptians announced they disapproved the plan. However, it is a foregone conclusion that Palestine Arabs will reject the proposals, especially since Colonial Minister Malcolm MacDonald announced today that the British would continue to exclude the Grand Mufti from Palestine on the ground he is the active head of terrorists, while neighboring States, though not entirely averse to the policy, are bound to refuse their acceptance.

Cabinet Expects Trouble

But the Cabinet expected these and still worse reactions in the shape of killings and terrorism, but, convinced that the policy is fair to both sides, the government is determined to proceed with it. It will be voted on in the House of Commons a week from Friday.

The White Paper follows most closely the proposals that were rejected by both sides at last Winter's fruitless conference. It also contains much argument to show why the policy is not a breach of the mandate or the Balfour Declaration. Acknowledging that the government "cannot hope to satisfy the partisans of one party in such a controversy as the mandate has aroused," the White Paper nevertheless sets forth proposals in the belief that "in the interest of the peace and well-being of the whole people of Palestine a clear definition of policy and objectives is essential."

On the question of immigration, which roused the greatest Jewish anger, the proposals are for an immigration rate of 10,000 Jews yearly for five years, starting last month and subject to the economic absorptive capacity of the country. Any yearly quotas unfilled would be added to the next year.

In addition to recognizing the contribution that Palestine can make to the present Jewish refugee problem, the British Government proposes to admit 25,000 refugees as soon as an arrangement can be made to take them. It is pointed out that this rate is higher than Palestine's immigration in the past three years, when an average of 12,000 was admitted yearly.

The government also announced a new drive against illegal immigration, adding that any illegal immigration in the future would be deducted from yearly quotas.

"After a period of five years no further Jewish immigration will be permitted unless the Arabs of Palestine are prepared to acquiesce in it," the White Paper says.

The government decided that after five years it "will not be justified in facilitating and will not be under any obligation to facilitate further development of the Jewish national home by immigration, regardless of the wishes of the Arab population."

To meet Jewish arguments that this is a betrayal of the Balfour Declaration and mandate, as well as the principle of immigration up to the ability of Palestine to support and give jobs to all immigrants —a principle laid down by Winston Churchill as Colonial Secretary in 1922—the British White Paper argued that it was fear of unending Jewish immigration that was causing Arab unrest.

Proposal to Be Elastic

"If immigration has an adverse effect on the economic position in the country, it should clearly be restricted," it says. "And equally if it has a seriously damaging effect on the political position in the country, that is a factor that should not be ignored."

If the principle of the economic absorptive capacity, regardless of all other considerations, is followed, "fatal enmity between the two peoples will be perpetuated," it continues.

"His Majesty's Government cannot take the view that either their obligations under the mandate or considerations of common sense and justice require that they should ignore these circumstances in framing an immigration policy," the White Paper states.

It argues that Britain is faced with seeking indefinite expansion of the Jewish national home by force over Arab objections or with freezing the proportion of Jews unless Arabs consent to allow it to be thawed; so under the circumstances, considering the fact that the national home has been raised to 450,000 in twenty years, it was decided to call a halt.

At the same time the White Paper says the Arab demand for an immediate end of immigration is refused because it would damage Palestine's economy, because it would be unjust to Jews and because it would exclude consideration of the plight of Jewish refugees.

On the constitutional question the White Paper proposes a transitional period of five years. During this time Jews and Arabs would gradually be appointed as the heads of the departments of the Palestine Government but their decisions would be subject to veto by the High Commissioner. In addition, they would each have a British adviser, who would have direct access to the High Commissioner.

By gradual stages and subject to review by another conference at the end of the five-year period, it is hoped that a working constitution could be set up and that after a ten-year period the British Government can cut the new State loose. But before doing so, Britain must have assurances that neither party will dominate the other, that holy places will be kept open, that Britain will have protection for her strategic and transport interests, such as the Haifa pipeline, and finally that the interests of other nations will be protected.

The White Paper left the establishment of a Legislature and the final form of the constitution to the future. Whether it will be a unitary State, a Federal State or what, is to depend on what can be worked out.

During the transition period the appointments will be made to departments and the executive council regardless of whether both sides agree. That is to say, if Arabs go along and Jews do not, Arabs will get posts in proportion to their population, while Britons will fill the posts reserved for Jews. The reverse would likewise be followed. The Arab attitude has not been made known yet, but Jews say they will refuse to have anything to do with such a government.

The British emphasize that the transitional government will not necessarily be a model for the new government, and they are ready to give assurances that the proportional system will not be worked out in a permanent arrangement. They emphasize that the transitional government will have Britons over it as a safeguard against the Arab majority dominating the Jewish minority.

On the third great question, land sales, the British set forth that transfers of land from Arabs to Jews must be stopped if Arabs are not to become landless in Palestine. The proposal is to give the High Commissioner power to establish areas where land sales shall be prohibited, where they shall be limited and where they shall be free.

Denies League Jurisdiction

Arguing that the definitions of such phrases as "national home for the Jewish people" are not clear, the British White Paper contends that all this policy falls within the framework of the mandate and, therefore, the League does not have to be consulted, though the British expect the matter to be taken up in next week's League Council meeting.

But Jews make the contention that the mandate is being violated and they plan to take the matter up with the League and possibly with the World Court.

In this connection Sir John Simon, the present Chancellor of the Exchequer, and Viscount Hailsham, Lord Chancellor until a few months ago, wrote a letter to The London Times in November, 1930, denouncing the late Ramsay MacDonald for introducing a temporary limitation of immigration. It was a grave legal question whether this step was not in violation of the mandate, they wrote, recommending that a World Court opinion be obtained before limitation was enforced.

In addition to starting a political fight against the British policy Jews apparently plan passive resistance by refusing to co-operate, by striking and perhaps by active revolt.

Cable messages of protest from individuals and groups in the United States flowed to Prime Minister Neville Chamberlain today. Dr. Chaim Weizmann, head of the World Zionist Organization, had a conference with Joseph P. Kennedy, United States Ambassador here, and Zionists are looking to the United States for much of their opposition.

May 18, 1939

The Irgun and the Stern Gang

JEWS IN PALESTINE WARNED OF FORCE

British General Tells Leaders Violence Will Be Crushed— Passive Resistance Begun

By JOSEPH M. LEVY
Wireless to THE NEW YORK TIMES.

JERUSALEM, May 19.—Lieut. Gen. Robert H. Haining, commander of the British Forces in Palestine, invited the heads of the Jewish Agency for Palestine, the National Council of Palestine Jewry and the Jewish Communal Council to his headquarters here this morning and warned them that he intended to enforce order and would make no exceptions. General Haining added that, while he appreciated the three years of restraint on the part of Jews, he would suppress violence unflinchingly.

The first move in the Jewish non-cooperation movement against the government in protest at the new British policy was a decision of the Landlords Association, composed of rural and urban property owners, to refuse to pay taxes, beginning today, until the White Paper had been repealed.

Despite all stringent measures taken to prevent illegal immigration into Palestine, 300 Jews succeeded in landing clandestinely near Ashkelon, Southern Palestine, but were apprehended by British troops and taken to Tel Aviv for detention.

Jerusalem Quiet But Tense

In contrast with yesterday's turbulence in this Holy City, there was quiet today, although considerable tension still exists. As a result of the violence yesterday, when a mob of Jews attempted to raid the District Commissioner's office, smashed the windows of an English shop and a German restaurant and engaged in fighting in which a British constable was killed and more than 100 Jews were wounded, the military today took far greater precautions to prevent further bloodshed.

All government offices were heavily guarded, various parts of the city were barricaded, and soldiers manned machine guns for action. The only incident today occurred when several Jewish youths penetrated a branch postoffice in the Jewish quarter of Mahne Yehuda here and broke window panes and furniture.

Three British police sergeants and two constables, who yesterday annoyed the Tel Aviv public, it is charged, by wearing helmets marked with the swastika and by shouting "Heil Hitler," were relieved of duty today pending disciplinary proceedings.

May 20, 1939

BOMB BLAST KILLS 18 ARABS AT HAIFA

24 Others Hurt by Explosion in Market—Rigid Curfew on Traffic Is Imposed

WARNING IS GIVEN TO JEWS

Wireless to THE NEW YORK TIMES.

JERUSALEM, June 19.—Palestine's latest wave of terrorism reached a new high level today when eighteen Arabs—nine men, six women and three children— were killed and twenty-four wounded by the explosion of a time bomb in the Arab vegetable market at Haifa near the Central Police Station. Shortly afterward an Arab crowd stoned and seriously injured a Jew who was visiting the mortuary of the government hospital where the bomb victims lay.

Two more bomb explosions in the Jewish quarter of Haifa destroyed a telephone booth and damaged a telephone manhole.

A curfew was declared at Haifa at 9 o'clock this morning but was lifted from 4 o'clock this afternoon until midnight, when it will again be imposed, as usual, until 5 A. M. The curfew includes all traffic in and out of Haifa as far as the Jewish colony of Zichron Yaacob. At that point all vehicles were turned back to Tel Aviv.

Apparently as a retaliation for the explosion at the market, three bombs were thrown this afternoon at Jaffa, one at Jews working near the Jaffa-Tel Aviv border and two at police stations, but there were no casualties. A curfew was also imposed at Jaffa beginning at 2 P. M.

Stern Warning Issued

Palestine authorities seem to believe that Jews were responsible for today's bomb at Haifa and the military commander of the Northern district summoned Jewish leaders there and issued a stern warning.

June 20, 1939

JABOTINSKY DEAD; LED NEW ZIONISTS

Head of Revisionist Group Was Chief of Jewish Legion in Palestine During War

STRICKEN IN HUNTER, N. Y.

Succumbs in Youth Camp at 59 —Tried to Raise Army Here to Fight Italy and Reich

Vladimir Jabotinsky, author, lecturer and world leader of the New Zionist Organization, died on Saturday night in the youth camp of the Zionist group at Hunter, N. Y., of a heart attack, according to word received here yesterday. He was 59 years old.

Mr. Jabotinsky, who had been living at 10 West Seventy-fourth Street since his arrival in this country from London on March 13, headed the Jewish Legion in Palestine during the World War. In recent weeks he had been working on a plan to raise a similar army to fight against Italy and Germany, and also had been conducting a drive for mass emigration of Jews to Palestine from Eastern and Central Europe.

He leaves a widow, Anna, who is in London, and a son, Eri, who is in prison in Palestine because of his nationalistic activities in behalf of the Jewish population of that country.

Spoke to 5,000 Here

Mr. Jabotinsky stirred intense loyalty among his followers and deep bitterness among his opponents in the Zionist movement. His leadership was more pronounced in Eastern Europe and in Palestine— from which he was banned—than in the United States, but on his last visit here last March more than 5,000 persons overcrowded a hall to hear him. They constituted the largest group ever gathered in New York under so-called Revisionist auspices.

Jabotinsky had the multiple appeal of poet, soldier, orator and personal fire and magnetism. His sincerity could hardly be questioned, even by those leaders of other Zionist parties to whom he was anathema. At times he and his followers were denounced as traitors to Jewry, as Jewish Fascists, as trouble breeders, as foes of labor, even as gunmen. But imbued as he was with the ideal of a self-defending Jewish State in Palestine, and with a nature preferring forthrightness to compromise, it was natural that he should be constantly in the center of controversy.

Jabotinsky himself was once sentenced to fifteen years in prison for organizing an anti-Arab defense force, but served only three months. After his exile by the British his son, Eri, continued active, and, with the development of the extra-quota immigration project, openly backed by his father's organization, furthered it to the extent of being jailed himself.

A Linguistic Prodigy

He was born in Odessa, Russia, in 1880 and became something of a literary and linguistic prodigy. He went to high school in his home city, but later studied in Switzerland and Italy. Mr. Jabotinsky did much translating, including the works of Dante and Poe. He translated the "Divine Comedy" into Russian while taking a law degree in Rome.

Five years after his first Zionist poem appeared in a St. Petersburg monthly, Jabotinsky became politically active in the movement. He was a delegate to the Sixth Zionist Congress at Basle in 1903, and his influence rose steadily. But the aspect of his career which brought him international attention and led ultimately to his differences with the other leaders was his organizing and leading of the Jewish Legion, which fought on the British side in the Near East during the World War. He earned an honorary lieutenancy.

Returning to England in 1920 after his release from jail, he became an executive of the World Zionist Organization, but in 1921 resigned because of differences with Dr. Chaim Weizmann, whose policy was to the founder of the Jewish legion one of surrender. Thus the Revisionist movement grew up around him, insisting on more than

VLADIMIR JABOTINSKY

TERRORISTS OR PATRIOTS

a Jewish cultural center or unofficial homeland in Palestine. It had only four delegates at the 1925 world meeting, the figure rising to fifty-eight in 1931. That year the organization had one of its most turbulent sessions, the Revisionists bolting on July 13. Jabotinsky, facing a breach in his own ranks, took a voluntary six months' leave of absence from the leadership.

He had visited America in 1926, arriving with no fanfare, totally ignored by the Zionist Organization of America and by all but a handful of sympathizers. His next visit, in 1935, saw the Revisionists better organized here and able to muster almost 4,000 persons for his first public speech. With the outbreak of another war and the concentration of interest on the refugee problem, his followers in this country increased. The world Revisionist movement became known as the New Zionist Organization, and it was aided here in its refugee work by a new group called the American Friends of a Jewish Palestine. The leadership of the Z. O. A. remained strictly aloof, but the Jabotinsky cause, espoused by a well-known liberal rabbi, Dr. Louis I. Newman, took a firmer grip here. It remained, at the same time, a distinct minority.

Jabotinsky was a small man with a firm chin and a lock of gray hair prone to cut down across his brow. His English was excellent, and he was equally fluent in Russian, French, German, Italian, Hebrew and other tongues—nine in all. His oratory was neither as superbly paced nor as resonant as that of Dr. Stephen S. Wise, nor as direct and keyed to understatement as that of Dr. Weizmann—but it had an uneven brilliance all its own. Jabotinsky clenched his small fist often in the course of a speech, without shaking it. That was a key to the intensity of feeling which characterized him.

A funeral service will be held tomorrow at noon at the establishment of Sigmund Schwartz, 152 Second Avenue.

August 5, 1940

PALESTINE DISSIDENTS WAGE WAR ON POLICE

Abortive Land-Mine Outrages Laid to 'Stern Gang' Survivors

Wireless to THE NEW YORK TIMES.

JERUSALEM, May 3—Three recent abortive land-mine outrages have drawn attention again to the activities of the irreconcilable political terrorist group known here as the "Stern Gang," after their leader, Abraham Stern, who was shot two months ago in a police raid on his hideout on the fringe of the city of Tel Aviv.

These attempts were directed against the Inspector General of the Palestine Police, Alan Saunders, and the assistant inspector general, Michael McConnell, neither of whom was hurt, though Inspector McConnell's Arab servant was killed when he picked up a bomb hidden in a garage. That happened in Jerusalem a fortnight ago.

This week-end a land mine exploded just as the car driven by Assistant Police Superintendent Geoffrey Morton passed a spot near his house outside Tel Aviv. The mine, hidden in a roadside ditch and detonated by a man hiding in a grove, damaged the car badly though it did not injure the occupants, Mr. Morton, his wife and two British constables.

Mr. Morton, as head of the detective force of the Tel Aviv area, was responsible for breaking up the Stern Gang.

The Stern group, of whom there are a number of survivors despite the recent arrests of leading members, is actually a terrorist, if quasi-political, organization that appears to have sworn vengeance against the Palestine police force.

The Palestine government is conducting a vigorous man hunt for the capture of the remaining members of this dangerous group.

May 4, 1942

PALESTINE JEWS DIVIDED ON ARMING

Rightists Say They Must Train to Save Themselves if Arabs Attack Them

PROGRAM ANNOYS BRITISH

Other Jewish Groups Fear the Militants May Cause Trouble in All Arab Countries

By C. L. SULZBERGER

By Wireless to THE NEW YORK TIMES.

CAIRO, Egypt, Aug. 1—In their determination to protect themselves after the war Right Wing Jewish groups in Palestine, which their opponents label as Fascist, have been trying to prepare Jewish youths for trouble with the Arabs.

The Rightists instruct the youths in military science on the grounds that this is the only way the minority can save itself from slaughter if the present seeds of discord sprout into trouble. Their activities embarrass other Jewish groups and irritate the British authorities.

Because Palestine is mandated territory the British never have been in a legal position to recruit there. However the Jewish Agency has been recruiting volunteers among Jewish youths to help win the war and also for political reasons. It wants to demonstrate the extent of active Jewish aid and to prepare Jews for military action if trouble with the Arabs breaks out.

Arabs Have Big Majority

The Jewish population in Palestine is about 550,000. The Moslem Arabs number about 850,000, the Christian Arabs about 120,000 and various others, such as Britons, about 17,000 excluding troops and wartime temporary residents. There are about 22,000 Jewish youths in the British forces, 7,000 auxiliary policemen and 35,000 civil defense workers. There are about 6,000 Arabs in the armed forces, around 4,000 in the police and 10,000 in civil defense.

Last December a decree prohibited the intimidation of alleged Jewish slackers by agents who were anxious to increase the size of the Jewish contingent in the armed forces. There had been several instances of violence or threats.

Voluntary recruiting agencies, after suggesting that young men join the fighting forces, would see to it that they did by getting them dismissed from their jobs or by other forms of boycott. Castor oil was given in the Italian manner.

Bombs were thrown at the homes of some "slackers." One was locked in a coffin and delivered to a Jewish meeting in a cafe as a warning to other youths.

The British have been hard put to it to keep the lid on and avoid friction that tends to come nearer now that the post-war period appears to have arrived in Palestine and the rest of the Middle East. Some Jewish groups fear hotheaded young militants may bring trouble with the British and cause difficulties for Jews in other parts of the Arab world.

British Want Specialists

The British contend that they do not want ordinary soldiers but want specialists, of whom there are many in Palestine, but that the Jews are more anxious to have their men trained in handling arms than in contributing to the technical services.

Some Jews say the British are appeasing the Arabs "in the Chamberlain fashion." They say the Arabs have far greater freedom in their press than the Jews. Officials deny such allegations.

One conclusion that any observer comes to is that a large headache for the United Nations is throbbing in Palestine and that keen study of all aspects of the problems must be made before just decisions can be made.

August 2, 1943

POLITICAL TERRORISM RISES IN PALESTINE

Jewish and Arab Press Urge Suppression of Disorders

By Cable to THE NEW YORK TIMES.

JERUSALEM, Feb. 25—Political terrorist activity has been showing a marked recrudescence lately in various parts of Palestine, probably in the mistaken notion that it would bring about pressure on British authorities to change her present policy drastically in favor of extremist Jewish nationalist demands.

The authors of these outrages—of which the latest was the explosion of two time bombs placed inside British police vehicles at Haifa yesterday—belong to a tiny fanatical group calling itself Irgun Zevai Leumi [nationalist military organization] whose anarchist acts have been condemned by the remainder of the Jewish population as harmful to the Jewish cause. Twenty dissident revolutionaries recently escaped from a detention camp near Jerusalem and are believed to have joined their associates belonging to an even more extremist faction, whose leader, Abraham Stern, was shot dead during a police encounter in February, 1942.

Arab papers have joined the Jewish press in demanding the apprehension and dire punishment of these lawless elements.

February 26, 1944

The Irgun and the Stern Gang

TERRORISTS RENEW PALESTINE ATTACKS

By Wireless to THE NEW YORK TIMES.

JERUSALEM, Sept. 28—Armed uniformed members of the notorious Jewish political extremist group named Irgun Zvai Leumi, which has been directing terrorist assaults against the Palestine police since the beginning of this year, again struck at several police stations last midnight, inflicting casualties on the police and suffering casualties themselves.

A police station on the main highway between Jerusalem and Jaffa was stormed by a large party of armed men, who poured a volley of shots at it and caused about fourteen bomb explosions near by. Later the police found the body of an Arab villager, who probably had run into the firing zone.

At the same time a police station in central Palestine was attacked by twenty men dressed in khaki uniforms with military webbing equipment similar to the British Army's Middle East kit. They threw bombs that caused only slight damage and the police beat off the attack.

The Haifa police station was raided at midnight by twenty-five men, mostly armed with automatic weapons. Explosives with warning notices bearing the Irgun Zvai Leumi [National Military Organization] sign were placed around the station and damaged two passing military vehicles. The police in repulsing the attack inflicted casualties and two arrests were made. In this engagement one Palestinian constable was fatally wounded, a British constable suffered a concussion and a passer-by was wounded.

A fourth attack occurred in southern Palestine, where a number of armed men blasted their way into a police station, stole arms and killed a Palestinian constable and an army corporal traveling on the road near by.

September 29, 1944

PALESTINE BANISHES 251 AS 'TERRORISTS'

By Wireless to THE NEW YORK TIMES.

JERUSALEM, Oct. 19—As a further measure to rid Palestine of the extremist political elements responsible for terrorism in Palestine, the Administration announced tonight that 251 persons who had been detained as terrorists or for complicity had been transferred to military custody and had been moved to a place of detention outside this country.

At the same time the Government announced a plan to use the air raid warning system to signal the outbreak of acts of violence.

When the sirens sound, police and military forces will take prearranged action while all vehicular traffic in streets must stop. The public will then be expected to assist the police by reporting any suspicious movements or persons.

October 20, 1944

PALESTINE JEWS ACT TO HALT TERRORISM

By Wireless to THE NEW YORK TIMES.

JERUSALEM, Oct. 25—Uncompromising opposition to the acts of violence, sabotage and blackmail that small Jewish political extremist groups have been conducting in the Holy Land was voiced in resolutions adopted early today after an all-night meeting of the Inner Zionist General Council, the supreme administrative institution of the World Zionist Movement.

All the speakers at the prolonged discussions gave expression to their profound anxiety over the possible outcome of these activities, which, it was contended, introduce an anarchic element into the Zionist political struggle. At the close of the debate the Zionist councilors adopted recommendations submitted by the Jewish Agency Executive to take drastic preventive measures against terrorism if the perpetrators refuse to heed appeals to desist.

Resolutions of a meeting discussing the same issue, held by the National Council of Palestine Jews—the highest administrative body of the local Jewish "Parliament"—took the same line toward the terrorist groups. Noting that all efforts by authoritative public Jewish institutions to exert moral suasion against the violence had failed, the National Council warned that unless terrorism ceased immediately organized Palestine Jewry would act firmly to end it.

Both meetings also protested against the statement of Oct. 10 by the officer administering the Palestine Government, J. V. W. Shaw, and the Commander in Chief in the Middle East, Gen. Sir Bernard C. Paget, saddling Palestine Jewry and the Jewish people with collective responsibility for the acts of terrorism and ignoring the substantial contribution to the war effort by Palestinian Jews.

October 26, 1944

KILLED BY ASSASSINS

Lord Moyne
Associated Press

BRITISH DIPLOMAT IS SLAIN IN CAIRO

Lord Moyne Shot on Leaving Auto—Two Assassins, Not Egyptians, Mobbed

By The Associated Press.

CAIRO, Egypt, Nov. 6—Two gunmen shot and fatally wounded Lord Moyne, British Resident Minister in the Middle East, and killed his chauffeur today as the diplomat alighted from his automobile at his residence.

Both attackers were captured, one after having been wounded by a constable as he fled. Tonight the Egyptian Government announced that neither was an Egyptian, but their identities and nationality were not disclosed. They apparently had hidden in the entrance to the Minister's residence.

[Gen. Sir Bernard C. Paget, Commander in Chief in the Middle East, in paying tribute to Lord Moyne, referred to "the Jewish assassins," The United Press reported. He may have alluded to Sternists, Jewish extremists in Palestine whom he recently criticized for acts of violence. "In the tragic death of Lord Moyne at the hands of Jewish assassins the British Empire lost a great public servant," General Paget said.]

Lord Moyne was wounded in the stomach and neck when his assailants emptied their revolvers at him. His military driver, apparently killed instantly, slumped over the steering wheel of the car. The diplomat died a few hours later at the army hospital, where he had been taken for an operation to remove the bullets.

The two gunmen attempted to flee across the front grounds of the residence, but one was shot by an Egyptian constable and the other was captured near by. Both were held by Cairo police.

Neither the Governor nor the police have released any explanation of the attack.

Lord Moyne was 64 years of age.

November 7, 1944

TERRORISTS OR PATRIOTS

TWO JEWS ADMIT MURDER OF MOYNE

Terrorists Cite Orders From Sternists—Army Funeral Held for Minister

CAIRO, Egypt, Nov. 8 (P)—The police announced today that two Jewish prisoners had confessed that they had assassinated Lord Moyne, British Minister of State Resident in the Middle East, on orders from the Stern group of extreme Jewish nationalists.

The confessions were obtained, it was announced, after thirty-six hours of questioning by members of the British Palestine police who flew here for the continuing inquiry.

An elaborate military funeral was held for Lord Moyne and his chauffeur, Lance Corp. Arthur Fuller, who were shot dead two days ago as they drove up to the Minister's residence here. The Grand Rabbi of Egypt and the vice president of the Jewish community of Cairo were among the mourners.

British, American, French, Polish, New Zealand and Egyptian troops escorted the flag-draped caskets through the streets on gun carriages drawn by armored cars from Kasr el Nil Barracks to the Saints' English Cathedral. Lord Moyne's heir, Capt. the Hon. Bryan Guinness, flew here from Damascus for the funeral.

Police said that the prisoners, one of whom was wounded by Egyptian police as they fled across the Residence grounds, had declared: "We are members of the Fighters for Freedom of Israel and what we did was on instructions from this organization."

They gave their names as Moshe Cohen and Itzchak Salzman and contended that Lord Moyne's policies were prejudicial to Jewish aspirations for a national home in Palestine.

Zionist leaders, however, have voiced numerous expressions of horror over the assassination and condemned the terrorists' policies in Palestine and elsewhere.

Authorities here said that there were probably "several dozen" other members of the gang at large with missions similar to that of the two who slew Lord Moyne. They recalled the wounding of Sir Harold MacMichael, outgoing British High Commissioner for Palestine, who was shot from ambush near Jerusalem on Aug. 8.

November 9, 1944

CHURCHILL WARNS JEWS TO OUST GANGS

Hints at Withdrawing His Aid to Zionism Unless They Root Out Palestine Terrorism

CITES PLEDGE OF SUPPORT

By CLIFTON DANIEL
By Wireless to THE NEW YORK TIMES.

LONDON, Nov. 17—Prime Minister Churchill demanded today that the Jewish community of Palestine—"every man, woman and child"—destroy the terrorist elements responsible for the recent assassination in Cairo of Lord Moyne, British Resident Minister in the Middle East. He implied that his own support and that of many others might be withdrawn from the Zionist cause if the gangsterism, which he compared with that of nazism, were not eliminated from Palestine.

The Prime Minister told the House of Commons in a statement on Lord Moyne's death that Dr. Chaim Weizmann, president of the Jewish Agency for Palestine, who is now in Palestine, had assured him in a letter that "Palestine Jewry will go to the utmost limit of its powers to cut out this evil from its midst."

The executive body of the Jewish Agency in Palestine, Mr. Churchill added, has called upon the Jewish community "to cast out members of this destructive band"—the Stern gang—two of whose members have been arrested for the Moyne murder.

Plea for Action Applauded

"These are strong words," the Prime Minister said, "but we must wait for these words to be translated into deeds." There was applause for this remark.

The Prime Minister added, "We must wait and see that not only the leaders but every man, woman and child in the Jewish community does his or her best to bring this terrorism to a speedy end."

Describing himself as a "consistent friend of the Jews and a constant architect of their future," Mr. Churchill said, "If our dreams for Zionism are to end in the smoke of the assassin's pistol and our labors for the future are to produce a new set of gangsters worthy of Nazi Germany, then many like myself would have to reconsider the position we have maintained so consistently and so long in the past."

The primary responsibility for the suppression of the Stern gang and the "larger but hardly less dangerous Irgun Zvai Leumi," rests primarily with the Palestine Government, the Prime Minister said, but "full success depends on the wholehearted cooperation of the entire Jewish community."

"This his Majesty's Government is entitled to demand and receive," Mr. Chirchill added.

Two hundred and fifty persons were deported from Palestine on Oct. 19 and numerous arrests have been made since then by Palestine authorities.

After making his statement in the House the Prime Minister attended a memorial service for Lord Moyne in St. Margaret's, Westminster. Other members of the Government also attended.

November 18, 1944

PRESIDENT ORDERS EISENHOWER TO END NEW ABUSE OF JEWS

He Acts on Harrison Report, Which Likens Our Treatment to That of the Nazis

MAKES PLEA TO ATTLEE

Urges Opening of Palestine— Conditions for Displaced in Reich Called Shocking

By BERTRAM D. HULEN
Special to THE NEW YORK TIMES.

WASHINGTON, Sept. 29—President Truman has directed General Eisenhower to clean up alleged shocking conditions in the treatment of displaced Jews in Germany outside the Russian zone and in Austria. He acted on the basis of a report made by Earl G. Harrison, American representative on the Intergovernmental Committee on Refugees, after an inspection.

The report declared that displaced Jews were held behind barbed wire in camps guarded by our men, camps in which frequently conditions were unsanitary and the food poor and insufficient, with our military more concerned with other matters.

Some of the displaced Jews were sick and without adequate medicine, the report stated, and many had to wear prison garb or, to their chagrin, German SS uniforms. All were wondering, it was added, if they had been liberated after all and were despairing of help while worrying about the fate of relatives.

Formal Appeal to Attlee

The President appealed formally to Prime Minister Attlee of Great Britain to open the doors of Palestine to 100,000 displaced Jews of Germany and Austria who want to be evacuated there.

Mr. Harrison, dean of the University of Pennsylvania Law School and former Immigration Commissioner, submitted his report at a personal conference with President Truman in August. The President wrote to General Eisenhower Aug. 31. In the communication he cited the following paragraph from Mr. Harrison's report:

"As matters now stand, we appear to be treating the Jews as the Nazis treated them except that we do not exterminate them. They are in concentration camps in large numbers under our own military guard instead of SS troops. One is led to wonder whether the German people, seeing this, are not supposing that we are following or at least condoning Nazi policy."

The report, while praising "some" of our Army officers in Germany for their handling of the Jews, for the most part severely arraigned the way they were dealing with the problem.

President Truman declared in his letter to General Eisenhower that policies promulgated by Supreme Headquarters, Allied Expeditionary Forces, "are not being carried out by some of your subordinate officers."

Policy Declared Violated

The announced policy of giving the "liberated" prisoners preference in billeting among the German civilian population had not been followed on "a wide scale," he asserted.

"We must intensify our efforts," he wrote, "to get these people out of camps and into decent houses until they can be repatriated or evacuated."

He also asked General Eisenhower to carry out a suggestion of Mr. Harrison for more extensive field visitations by the Army and adequate inspections so that conditions could be promptly and effectively corrected.

"We must make clear to the German people that we thoroughly abhor the Nazi policies of hatred and persecution," he stated. "We have no better opportunity to demonstrate this than by the manner in which we ourselves actually treat the survivors remaining in Germany."

The Irgun and the Stern Gang

General Eisenhower had replied, the White House said, that he was investigating the conditions and would report to the President.

The President had not yet heard from Mr. Attlee on the Palestine question, the White House added, and the President's letter to Mr. Attlee was not given out pending a reply.

Mr. Harrison reported that the conditions affecting the displaced Jews as he observed them were such that unless remedies were applied there was danger of trouble.

They were held in many cases, he said, behind barbed wire camps formerly used by the Germans for their prisoners, including the notorious Berger Belsen camp. Nearly all had lost hope, he stated.

The Germans in rural areas, whom the Jews look out upon from the camps, were better fed, better clothed and better housed than the "liberated" Jews, the report declared.

Unless proper remedial action was taken and promptly, Mr. Harrison warned, "substantial unofficial and unauthorized movements of people must be expected and these will require considerable force to prevent." It could not be overemphasized, he cautioned, that "many of these people are now desperate."

Mr. Harrison urged the opening of Palestine to the displaced Jews, most of whom are Polish, Baltic, Hungarian or Rumanian, in addition to German and Austrian. He declared that the issue of Palestine "must be faced" and voiced hope that we could persuade Britain to make a "reasonable extension or modification" of her White Paper of 1939 which permitted Jewish immigration into Palestine on a limited basis.

There is no acceptable or even decent solution for the future of many European Jews other than Palestine, he contended, adding that his position was "purely humanitarian" and taken with "no reference to ideological or political considerations."

He also urged that the United States admit a "reasonable" number of these Jews under our existing immigration law. Some wanted to come here and others to go to England, the Dominions and South Africa, he added, explaining that the number desiring to enter the United States was not large.

Mr. Harrison urged that "those who have suffered most and longest" receive "first and not last attention" now that the mass repatriation had been so largely completed. Evacuation from Germany, he said, should be "the emphasized theme" and the Jews so wishing should be permitted to return to their own countries without further delay.

Referring to the expiration of immigration certificates for Palestine in August, he stated:

"It is nothing short of calamatous to contemplate that the gates of Palestine should soon be closed."

He quoted Hugh Dalton to show that the British Labor party had stood for a liberal policy on this question.

Those displaced Jews not able to leave the country, Mr. Harrison declared, should be gotten out of the camps and the ill placed in tuberculosis sanitaria or in rest homes. Others should be billeted with the Germans while those who wished to be in camps should be placed in separate ones.

"There seems little justification," he asserted, "for the continuance of barbed-wire fences, armed guards and prohibition against leaving the camp except by passes."

He recommended that as quickly as possible the operations of such camps as remain be turned over to the UNRRA.

Since military authorities must necessarily continue to participate in the program, he urged that there be a review of military personnel selected for camp commandant positions with the aim of obtaining sympathetic officers.

Pending the creation of this setup he suggested that there be more extensive field visitations.

The Combined Displaced Persons Executive, Mr. Harrison said, had generally followed nationality lines, feeling that to treat the Jews separately would make for intolerance and trouble on the part of others. He called this an "unrealistic approach."

Their former barbaric persecution, he pointed out, had made the Jews a seperate group with greater needs.

Because of preoccupation with the mass repatriations and with various difficulties, Mr. Harrison reported, the military authorities had shown considerable resistance to the entrance of voluntary agencies on the scene. In a few places "fearless and uncompromising" military officers had requisitioned whole villages for Jews or required them to be billeted by the Germans, but "at many places" our officers had manifested "the utmost reluctance or indisposition, if not timidity, about inconveniencing the German population."

These officers contend, the report stated, that their job is to get the communities going again while the displaced persons constitute a temporary problem. This has resulted, it was added, in a burgomeister easily persuading a town major to give shabby places with improper facilities to Jews while saving better accommodations for returning German civilians.

"This tendency," Mr. Harrison reported, "reflects itself in other ways, namely, in the employment of German civilians in the offices of Military Government officers when equally qualified personnel could easily be found among the displaced persons whose repatriation is not imminent.

"Actually there have been situations where displaced persons, especially Jews, have found it difficult to obtain audiences with Military Government authorities because, ironically, they have been obliged to go through German employes who have not facilitated matters."

There had been some general improvement in conditions, Mr. Harrison reported, but there had been relatively little done beyond the planning stage.

Many of the Jews, the report said, had no opportunity, except surreptitiously, to communicate with the outside world.

The diet was principally bread and coffee, the report stated, and there are many pathetic malnutrition cases.

Mr. Harrison estimated there would be more than 1,000,000 displaced persons in Germany and Austria this winter, in many instances housed in buildings unfit for cold weather.

September 30, 1945

WARNING OF WAR BARED BY ARABS

Publication of Memorandum to Byrnes Reveals Firm Stand Against Zionists

Special to The New York Times.

WASHINGTON, Oct. 20 — A warning of war in the Middle East if an attempt were made to set up an independent Jewish political state in Palestine was presented to Secretary of State James F. Byrnes in the memorandum that the representatives of four Arab States handed him on Oct. 12. The legations of the four countries—Egypt, Iraq, Lebanon, and Syria—made the memorandum public today.

"Regarding the peace of the Near East in general and of the Arab world in particular," the document said, "one principle is certain: there obviously can be no peace in that region by sacrificing Arab interests for the sake of the Jews. A Zionist political state can be created in Palestine, but only with the help of external force."

The memorandum declared that the "publicity" attending recent Zionist efforts to win political support for their goal of an independent Jewish Palestine nation had resulted in "a great misunderstanding of the real issue in Palestine on the part of American public opinion" and in "a deep feeling of concern throughout the Arab world."

Arabs Offer to Cooperate

"To transform a country that has been non-Jewish for thousands of years and Arab for 1,300 years into a Jewish state," the memorandum said, "is an act that obviously cannot be viewed with equanimity by the Arabs."

The four Arab States offered to cooperate in efforts to solve the Palestine problem but asserted that they wanted no solution at the "expense of the Arabs."

The text of the memorandum as released by the four legations follows:

The renewed general interest on the part of many quarters in the question of Palestine seems to call for a re-statement of this question from the point of view of the Arabs. This re-statement should prove all the more instructive as the Arabs now have formed a League of Arab States which has, since its foundation, expressed the strongest interest in the fate of Palestine.

The bare historical facts are quite simple. Ever since the Balfour Declaration was made known the Arabs of Palestine and the Near East have never failed to express by every means at their disposal their strong disapproval of unrestricted Jewish immigration and the sale of lands to the Jews in Palestine. It is unnecessary to recall the various forms which this expression of disapproval took during the last twenty years.

It is also significant to note that every independent Arab Government has repeatedly made known its view on this matter. All of them have evinced the keenest interest in Palestine and regarded themselves directly involved in any settlement of that issue. The Arab League itself finally gave a more articulate and unified form to this general Arab concern by incorporating it into its constitution.

The essence of the Arab position is that no change in the status of Palestine should take place without the consent of the Arabs. The historical, cultural, religious, political and geographical ties which bind Palestine to the rest of the Arab world have always made this world feel Palestine to be a part and parcel of itself, a part for whose destiny it is directly and unavoidably responsible.

The British White Paper of 1939 recognized this decisive interest of the Arab world in the affairs of Palestine by stipulating that beyond the envisaged quota of Jewish immigration until 1944 any further changes could not be introduced without the consent of the Arabs, and recognizing the right of Palestine to complete eventual independence.

The Zionist leaders throughout the world have been proclaiming lately far and wide that their aim is to transform Palestine into a sovereign Jewish state. This aim seems to have been attended with much publicity. This has resulted, on the one hand, in a great misunderstanding of the real issue in Palestine on the part of American public opinion, and, on the other, in the generation of a deep feeling of concern throughout the Arab world.

In this connection it is right to call attention to the fact that the question of Palestine stirs not only the Arab world, and that regardless of religion, but also the Moslem world at large, and that regardless of nationality. To transform a country that has been non-Jewish for thousands of years and Arab for 1,300 years into a Jewish state is an act that obviously cannot be viewed with equanimity by the Arabs.

The Arab people and states de-

TERRORISTS OR PATRIOTS

sire nothing more sincerely than to be on the best of terms with the people and Government of the United States. The two great peoples have always enjoyed a background of happy relations. It is in the highest interest of peace that these relations be preserved and promoted.

The Arab people have always believed that the United States would not favor the bringing about of any changes in the status and character of Palestine without the consent of the Arabs of that land and at the expense of themselves and the rest of the Arab world.

Fear Change in U. S. Stand

They have lately been perturbed over reports that this policy may have changed. But they cannot believe that the United States, famous as she is in her history and outlook for a very exalted sense of justice, would favor a course of action which would run counter to the freely expressed wishes of the Arabs, especially as assurances have been made by the late and present Presidents that such would not be the case.

The Arabs sincerely deplore the persecutions inflicted upon the Jews in Europe. In this connection it is instructive to note that one of the most brilliant pages of Jewish history was written when the Jews shared with the Arabs the great achievements of their medieval culture.

Feeling a sense of complete solidarity with the civilized world, the Arabs declare their readiness to do their part in helping to solve this world problem. They are sure Palestine will not solve it; and if it does, it will be only at the expense of the Arabs. In helping to shoulder a sacrifice, the Arabs cannot be asked to sacrifice themselves.

Regarding the peace of the Near East in general, and of the Arab world in particular, one principle is certain: There obviously can be no peace in that region by sacrificing Arab interests for the sake of the Jews. A Zionist political state can be created in Palestine, but only with the help of external force.

Such an artificial creation, or even the introduction of further Jewish immigrants into Palestine, is obviously not in the interests of world peace, nor is it conducive to the development of the friendliest relations between the Arabs and the external world.

October 21, 1945

PALESTINE GANGS BLOW UP 2 POSTS ON COAST, WOUND 14

Escape After Firing on Guards—Attacks Follow Seizure of Ship Smuggling In Refugees

CURFEW CLAMPED ON AREA

Mobs Block Troops Searching for Guns—Successful Raid on RAF Arsenal Revealed

By GENE CURRIVAN
By Wireless to THE NEW YORK TIMES.

JERUSALEM, Nov. 25—Armed terrorists, believed to be Zionists, blew up two coast guard stations north of Tel Aviv today and then, with automatic weapons, opened fire on guards, injuring fourteen. The attack was presumably in reprisal against the interception Thursday night of an illegal immigrant ship near the same area.

Guards from these stations patrol the coastal area to prevent illegal immigration, and searchlights from these installations sweep the sea. They are situated on promontories twenty-five miles apart.

The first attack was at Givat Olga, where high explosives were placed in the base of a tower. There were unconfirmed reports that terrorists had warned the occupants of the tower by telephone that the place was to be blown up but that the guards had disregarded the warning. At 1:13 A. M. the tower went sky high. It is believed that no one was in the building at the time.

Immediately after the blast an attacking party opened fire, wounding a British sergeant and three Palestine constables. After an exchange of fire the terrorists fled through the dunes, which they had mined heavily to prevent pursuit.

Second Attack Half Hour Later

Thirty minutes later another explosion under similar circumstances wrecked a second coast guard station on the sandy bluff at Sidna Ali, named for a Moslem shrine near by. The procedure here was exactly the same as in the first instance and may have been carried out by the same mob.

The casualties there were a British police sergeant, four British constables, three Arab constables and two Arab supernumerary constables.

At 2 o'clock this afternoon a clandestine radio station known as "The Voice of Jewish Resistance" ridiculed the British Navy for its "famous victory" over the intercepted schooner, on which twenty illegal immigrants were found, and then made the following announcement:

"Last night after midnight the sound of explosions was heard in the Sharon and Samaria districts. This morning it became known that Jewish volunteers had destroyed police posts at Sidna Ali and Givat Olga. These posts were the basis for a war against Jewish immigrants and were equipped completely for this unholy purpose.

"Precautions" Cited

"Both these bases were active in the hunt on the refugee boat Beri Katznelson on Friday morning. We are informed that all precautions were taken by the volunteers to avoid loss of life among the police, who were advised that explosions were imminent and warned to leave the buildings. The police disregarded the warnings and opened fire instead, compelling our volunteers to defend themselves with their weapons."

The announcer went on to say that the Zionist resistance movement did not recognize the validity of any laws that barred what was termed the right of Jews to "return to the land of Israel."

Another curfew was imposed tonight on two communities adjacent to the coast guard sites, and when troops arrived to search for weapons large crowds gathered to block their way. Reports from these areas did not indicate what progress troops were making in the face of this defiance. In similar incidents in the past the troops withdrew rather than force their way through by fire. [An Exchange Telegraph dispatch from Cairo, cited by The Associated Press, said that riots broke out in Palestine Sunday afternoon. The dispatch quoted information telephoned from Tel Aviv to the effect that clashes had occurred there between police and Zionists. A Zionist who ignored the curfew was shot in the hand when he ignored an order to halt.]

The curfew was placed on a coastal area thirty miles on each side of Tel Aviv and five miles inland. The order was given by Maj. Gen. A. L. Bols, commanding the Sixth Airborne Division.

Coast Scoured for Refugees

It was reported that an extensive manhunt was going on in coastal areas to seek out illegal immigrants who might have escaped the refugee ship before her capture. It was reported at the time of the interception that perhaps two hundred got away before the boarding party arrested twenty on the vessel.

Apart from the interception of the illegal schooner, another incident on Thursday assumed added significance today. At the Petach Tikva Royal Air Force installation two lorries, occupied by seven or eight Zionists, entered with forged passes and carried away a considerable quantity of arms and ammunition. One Zionist was dressed as a British Army corporal. Their papers were checked on the way out and the men drove off without trouble.

Summing up today's explosions, a Government communiqué tonight gave the first indication of casualties among the attackers, saying that they had left blood-stained bandages behind at the Sidna Ali coast guard station and traces of blood at Givat Olga farther up the coast after a prolonged gun duel with the small British and Arab police garrisons.

The communiqué reported that parties of armed Jews attacked both stations early in the morning. At Sidna Ali they opened fire with automatic weapons, rifles and grenades, and the small garrison replied. Three explosions seriously damaged a building. None of the British and Arab casualties was seriously wounded.

Attackers Use Grenades

At Givat Olga, the communiqué said, the station was surrounded by Jews, who opened fire with automatic weapons and grenades. Here, too, the small garrison engaged the assailants. Charges placed against the building wrecked it. Despite this, the police continued to resist vigorously until the attackers withdrew. None of those wounded was in a serious condition.

The communiqué added that a twelve-hour curfew beginning at 5:30 P. M. was imposed in a wide area of the coastal plain excluding municipal areas. Part of this curfew, affecting four administrative districts, also applied a stay-home order.

A tense situation was threatening to develop into ugly proportions at the Zionist collective settlement, Gigath Haim, where thousands of inhabitants, hearing that a village was going to be searched, flocked to it afoot or in buses, horse-drawn carts and bicycles. Food and blankets were sent to them and they were preparing to stay until the troops, who had flung a cordon around the village, were withdrawn. They intended to block any attempts to search the village for illegal immigrants or identification of the attackers of the Coast guard stations.

Similar sitdown demonstrations occurred inside three other Jewish villages farther south, where many hundreds of residents, warned by alarm bells, hurried to the spot and went in to cover up traces of the wanted men. Two British war planes droned over head in the daytime.

November 26, 1945

The Irgun and the Stern Gang

2 ZIONIST GROUPS BOAST OF BOMBINGS

Claim for 'Credit' by Sternists and Irgun Zvai Leumi Gives Hagana Clean Bill

By GENE CURRIVAN
By Cable to THE NEW YORK TIMES.

JERUSALEM, Jan. 3—Posters distributed last night and purporting to be a joint "communiqué" of the Irgun Zvai Leumi and the Stern group, Palestine's two leading underground organizations, claim the credit for last Thursday's bombings of police headquarters here and in Jaffa. They also took a bow for blasting the arms depot near Tel Aviv on the same night.

The attacks killed ten persons and injured a dozen others. The communiqué, written in military phraseology, described in detail most of that night's events and added an interesting angle heretofore unrevealed. It alleged that, while the attacks were going on in Jerusalem, terrorists took up positions in the outskirts opposite two British military barracks and two police stations to prevent reinforcements from reaching the scene of the attack.

This seems logical and in keeping with past performances except that the communiqué added that the attack at these points actually went into action with grenades and mines. If this is true, it is still a military secret here. Grenades were thrown, but only in the vicinity of headquarters during the escape.

"Ambush" Is Charged

The communiqué said that "the attack began under cover of machine-gun and submachine-gun fire and all resistance on the part of the police forces was liquidated and the police and military forces in the Russian compound square were paralyzed. The main gate of police headquarters as well as the building was blown up. While retreating, our soldiers were ambushed by officers and policemen who paid with their lives."

The concluding paragraph of the poster declared: "If the soldiers of Irgun and the Stern group had not tried to spare lives there might have been forty killed instead of only a few."

All this seems to indicate that the two groups have linked for combined operations. Up to now they have been operating separately, with Irgun Zavi Leumi going in for extreme terrorism and the Stern group concerned with assassinations.

Hagana Apparently Cleared

If the communiqué can be accepted as actually emanating from these groups, it leaves Hagana in the clear and corroborates this third underground organization's recent protestations. Hagana, which is concerned mainly with expediting illegal immigration, made denials over its own clandestine radio.

In a recent broadcast it made the following declaration concerning the explosions: "The attacks were made by the Irgun and the Stern group. It is assumed that these attacks were acts of revenge for the brutal behavior of the police toward members of these underground groups and that they were directed particularly against the deportation of members of these groups to Eritrea."

It added: "Yes, this last week of 1945 was crowded with happenings, some joyous, some regrettable. We rejoice in the landing of immigrants; we view it as a symbol of hope and an expression of courage. On the other hand, we regret the loss of life, the suffering that had darkened these last days."

Hagana is probably sincere when it says that it regrets the loss of life. It tries to accomplish its objectives with a minimum of casualties. In a recent case when two Coast Guard stations were blown up because they were instrumental in intercepting illegal landings, the attackers telephoned the police, warning them that the places were about to be blown up. The police disregarded the warning and fourteen were injured—some as a result of the explosions and others by gunfire. At about the same time two police launches were blown up in a harbor, but again no lives were lost.

January 4, 1946

PALESTINE BREEDS TEEN-AGE GUN GIRL

Fanatical Group, Linked to Massacre of 7 Britons, Poses New Palestine Problem

By GENE CURRIVAN
By Wireless to THE NEW YORK TIMES.

JERUSALEM, April 26—Palestine is producing a rare breed of teen-age "gun molls" who are far more vicious and bloodthirsty than anything the United States ever had in real life or on the screen. Some of the guns that took the lives of seven soldiers in Tel Aviv last night were fired by feminine hands.

These girls are fearless and they will fire at the drop of a hat, take a life without blinking an eye or throw a hand grenade with the best of the terrorists. They are fanatical in their ways, believe in what they are doing and are willing to die doing it.

They were among the thirty armed Jews who last night made a well-planned attack on the Sixth Airborne Division car park, where they stole a considerable quantity of arms. When the attack was over and they fled, leaving mined roads in their wake, there were seven dead British soldiers who had had no chance to defend themselves. A communiqué said "they were shot dead in cold blood."

As in past performances, the attack opened with diversionary tactics. To throw everyone off guard a grenade was hurled into the car park from an adjoining house. While attention was drawn in this direction the attackers fired from other quarters and, using this as cover, rushed the guard tent. The soldiers within were mowed down.

At the same time other attackers directed heavy fire against the soldiers who had been caught off guard and then retreated before they could be fired upon.

As they fled the terrorists were fired upon by the police from a station across the way. Bloodstains subsequently were found but all the terrorists apparently escaped.

There is no way of telling which group of terrorists perpetrated this latest mass murder but the tactics indicate the Irgun Zvai Leumi, which calls itself a "military" organization. It is considered significant, however, that several thousand Jewish youths, including teen-age girls, marched through Tel Aviv yesterday mourning the death of Braha Fuld, another teen-age girl who was killed during the terrorist attack on the Sarona police mobile force headquarters a month ago. She was referred to on placards carried by the crowds as a "fighter for immigration."

At her grave these youths took a mass oath "to follow in her path." She died in what these impassioned youngsters believed to be a just cause. They believe in unlimited Jewish immigration and are willing to go to any end to achieve it. Behind them is Hagana, the Jewish underground organization which leaves no stone unturned to expedite illegal immigration.

Many Jews here are ashamed of this latest cold-blooded attack, especially in view of reports that 100,000 Jews may soon be permitted to enter Palestine.

April 27, 1946

PALESTINE TROOPS SMASH JEWS' HOMES

Authorities Hunt Leaders of Group Seeking Vengeance in Death of Seven Comrades

By Wireless to THE NEW YORK TIMES.

JERUSALEM, April 28—Military authorities today were seeking the ringleaders of a party of British soldiers, presumably of the Sixth Airborne Division, who entered last night a number of houses in the Jewish settlement of Beer Tuvia in the Gaza district and smashed furniture in retaliation for the killing of seven soldiers in Tel Aviv on Thursday night.

According to an authoritative statement, the interior of one house was wrecked and two men were severely injured.

A statement described the men concerned as hotheads. Authorities said earlier that the incidents involving British troops, who hitherto had shown admirable patience and restraint in the face of repeated unprovoked attacks culminating in the brutal murder of seven of their comrades, were deeply deplored.

Another incident occurred last night in the seashore township of Nathanya, north of Tel Aviv, where a number of civilians were slightly injured and windows were broken.

The clandestine Voice of Israel radio station of the Jewish resistance movement or an offshoot of the Hagana [Jewish "defense" force] strenuously disassociated itself today from Thursday night's murders and from last Tuesday's raid on the police station in Ramat Gan, outside Tel Aviv, in which arms were stolen.

April 29, 1946

JOINT PALESTINE BODY BARS A JEWISH STATE, BUT URGES ENTRY OF 100,000 REFUGEES

TRUMAN FOR ACTION

Inquiry Upholds His Visa Proposal, Urges End of White Paper

WOULD GUARD ARAB RIGHTS

Report for Change in Holy Land Property Curbs—Demands a Firm Stand on Violence

FELIX BELAIR JR.
Special to THE NEW YORK TIMES.

WASHINGTON, April 30—The Anglo-American Committee of Inquiry on problems of Jews in Europe and Palestine, reporting to the two Governments today on its four-month investigation, urged the admission of 100,000 European Jews into the Holy Land as soon as possible, but flatly rejected the idea of a Jewish state, together with Arab claims for dominance. It asserted Christendom's own interest in the area.

Released simultaneously for publication in Washington and London, the report drew from President Truman an expression of satisfaction that his proposal for the admission of 100,000 Jews into Palestine had been recommended. He added that "the transference of these unfortunate people should now be accomplished with the greatest dispatch."

The President declared it significant that the report aimed at guarantees for Arab civil and religious rights and urged measures to improve Arab cultural, educational and economic position.

Land Changes Asked

"I am also pleased," he said, "that the committee recommends, in effect, the abrogation of the White Paper of 1939."

The report repudiated the 1939 White Paper principles, which made further Jewish immigration dependent on Arab consent and banned Jewish land purchases in a major part of Palestine.

Dependent for its final effect on adoption by both Governments, the report covered a wide range of controversial subjects on which President Truman gave no hint of his attitude except to say that he was taking them under advisement.

However, Mr. Truman seemed to have embraced the major policy statement rejecting "once and for all the exclusive claims of Jews and Arabs to Palestine," which the committee enunciated as follows:

"(I, That Jew shall not dominate Arab and Arab shall not dominate Jew in Palestine. (II) That Palestine shall be neither a Jewish state nor an Arab state. (III) That the form of government ultimately to be established shall, under international guarantees, fully protect and preserve the interests in the Holy Land of Christendom and of the Moslem and Jewish faiths."

Stress on Unique Status

With deliberate emphasis, the Committee of Inquiry declared that "Palestine is a Holy Land, sacred to Christian, to Jew and to Moslem alike; and because it is a holy land, Palestine is not, and can never become, a land which any race or religion can justly claim as its very own."

With equal emphasis, the committee said the same considerations set Palestine apart from other lands, and dedicated it to the precepts and practices of the brotherhood of man rather than to those of narrow nationalism.

The 42,000-word report was signed in Lausanne, Switzerland, by Judge Joseph C. Hutcheson, United States chairman, Sir John E. Singleton, British chairman, Frank Aydelotte, Frank W. Buxton, Bartley C. Crum, James G. McDonald and William Phillips, American members, and W. F. Crick, R. H. S. Crossman, Frederick Leggett, R. E. Manningham-Buller and M. Morrison for Britain.

For the immediate future the committee proposed that Palestine be continued as a British mandate pending execution of a trusteeship under the United Nations. It predicted a long period of trusteeship that would prove burdensome to any single Government, but which could be lightened by the cooperation and understanding of other United Nations.

At the root of the long and bloody struggle of Jew and Arab for dominance of Palestine, the committee discerned a deep-seated and intense fear of each side that the other might attain the ascendancy. The resulting struggle for a numerical majority has bedeviled relations between the groups through the centuries and would be continued unless made purposeless in a self-government constitution, the report aserted.

"We have reached the conclusion," said the report, "that the hostility between Jews and Arabs, and in particular the determination of each to achieve domination, if necessary by violence, make it almost certain that now, and for some time to come, any attempt to establish either an independent Palestinian state or independent Palestine states would result in civil strife such as might threaten the peace of the world."

The committee's insistence on equality of standards between Jews and Arabs in Palestine ran through the entire report but found fullest expression in its Recommendation No. 5.

In this the committee, looking to a form of ultimate self-government consistent with the three major principles, observed that the mandatory or trustee should proclaim the principle that Arab economic, educational and political advancement in Palestine was of equal importance with that of the Jews. It urged preparation immediately of measures "designed to bridge the gap which now exists and raise the Arab standard of living to that of the Jews."

In this way the committee suggested that the two peoples could be brought to "a full appreciation of their common interest and common destiny in the land where both belong." It said that nothing should be done that might lower the high degree of development attained by Jewish social services or halt the constant improvements being made in them.

Government Aid to Arabs

At the same time the Arabs would have to depend to a far greater degree than the Jews on financial aid from the Government since they lacked the financial organization of the Jewish community, the report said. "The Jews of Palestine should accept the necessity that taxation, raised from both Jews and Arabs, will have to be spent very largely on the Arabs in order to bridge the gap which now exists between the standard of living of the two peoples," the committee declared.

Pending establishment of a new trusteeship, the committee proposed that Palestine be administered with due regard to the mandate, which states in regard to immigration that "the administration of Palestine, while insuring that the rights and position of other sections of the population are not prejudiced, shall facilitate Jewish immigration under suitable conditions."

While conceding the right of any Jew to enter Palestine in accordance with its laws. the committee expressly disapproved the position it said had been taken in some Jewish quarters "that Palestine has in some way been ceded or granted as their state to the Jews of the world, that every Jew everywhere is, merely because he is a Jew, a citizen of Palestine and therefore can enter Palestine as of right without regard to conditions imposed by the Government upon entry, and that therefore there can be no illegal immigration of Jews into Palestine."

In recommending repeal of the land-transfer regulations of 1940, the committee said they should be replaced by regulations based on a policy of freedom of sale, lease or use of land irrespective of race, community or creed and providing adequate protection for interests of small owners and tenant cultivators.

Specifically, the report recommended invalidation of leases and conveyances that provided that only members of one race, community or creed might be employed on or about such land.

A further recommendation was that the Government closely supervise holy places such as the Sea of Galilee to protect them from desecration and from uses that offended the consciences of religious peoples.

The committee noted that a number of plans for large-scale agricultural and industrial development of Palestine were under consideration to enlarge its capacity to support an increasing population, as well as improve living standards. It recommended, however, that the Governments of neighboring Arab states affected as well as the Jewish Agency be invited to consult and cooperate in such developments from start to finish.

Leaving aside the question of feasibility of such projects, the committee said they would be certain to fail unless peace were secured in the Holy Land.

To promote a conciliatory spirit between Arabs and Jews and improve the Arab standard of living the committee suggested a complete reform of the educational systems for both Jews and Arabs, including introduction of compulsory education within a reasonable time.

Strict Government control of schools to do away with the "present excited emphasis on racialism and the perversion of education for propaganda purposes," careful supervision of textbooks and curricula, and inspection of schools were urged as means of promoting conciliation.

The committee asserted that improvement of education standards would be possible only by a substantial reduction in expenditures for security.

Finally, the committee strongly recommended to each Government that if its report were adopted it should be made clear to Jews and Arabs that any attempt from either side by threats of violence, terrorism or the organization or use of illegal armies to prevent its execution would be resolutely suppressed.

The Irgun and the Stern Gang

To this end the view expressed that the Jewish Agency should at once resume active cooperation with the Mandatory in the suppression of terrorism and of illegal immigration "and in the maintenance of that law and order throughout Palestine which is essential for the good of all, including the new immigrants."

In recommending the admission of 100,000 Jews to Palestine the committee conceded that this would provide a refuge for only part of the 500,000 who wished or might be impelled to emigrate from Europe. The committee proposed that priority be granted displaced Jews still in camps in the American and British zones in Germany, Austria and Italy.

The report recognized at the outset that Palestine alone could not meet the emigration needs of the Jewish victims of Nazi and Fascist persecution but that countries other than Palestine gave no hope of "substantial assistance" in finding homes for Jews wishing or impelled to leave Europe.

It declared, however, that the whole world shared the responsibility for these victims of persecution and, indeed, for the resettlement of all "displaced persons."

It was recommended, therefore, that the Governments of the United States and Britain in association with other countries, should endeavor immediately to find new homes for all such persons, irrespective of creed or nationality, whose ties with their former communities had been irreparably broken.

May 1, 1946

PALESTINE TERROR MOUNTS AS HARBOR, BRIDGES ARE RIPPED

Haifa Explosions Start Fires After Jewish Bands Blast 8 Highway and Rail Spans

DEATH TOLL GROWS TO 11

By JULIAN LOUIS MELTZER
By Wireless to THE NEW YORK TIMES.

JERUSALEM, June 17—Haifa's harbor was lit up today by a conflagration as a result of explosions at the Palestine Railway's central workshops. The road leading north from Haifa was strewn with mines and booby traps, and police and military reinforcements met difficulty in moving.

Fire engines were summoned from Haifa and neighboring townships to fight the blaze, which was further illuminated by military searchlights.

The fires were brought under control by 11 P. M. after feverish efforts.

The Haifa explosions were the second major act of turbulence in the last twenty-one hours. Eight road and railway bridges in many parts of Palestine were blown up early today and last night. Six Jewish attackers and a British officer were killed. The damage totaled $500,000. The Haifa fire was estimated to have caused further damage of $500,000. Valuable rolling stock was threatened.

[The Haifa sabotage, marked by fifteen explosions, brought the death toll in Palestine's two-night terror wave to eleven, The Associated Press reported.]

Railway Workers Warned

According to one report, workers in the railway's roundhouse, where they were preparing locomotives for tomorrow's services, were advised by an unknown telephone caller to quit the place. Then came the attack under heavy gunfire followed by a series of explosions.

At 10 P. M. a land mine exploded in the area. There were no reports of casualties or damage.

Communications between Palestine and neighboring Arab countries were being restored after explosions set by parties of armed Jews had demolished or damaged four road and four railway bridges in southern, northern and eastern Palestine.

Two of the wreckers were believed to have been killed by a premature dynamite blast, and twelve Jewish settlers were injured, four seriously. Two Jews were in a hospital as a result of manhandling by British troops during a search of Beth Haarava, village on the northern shore of the Dead Sea. Four Arabs were wounded by the attackers.

The British officer was killed while dismantling mines at the Jisr Damiya Bridge.

The raids were carried out by members of Hagana, Jewish resistance movement. The units concerned are called Palmach, an abbreviation of Plugoth Machatz, or striking forces.

Sixty-two men who refused to establish their identity were arrested in the village of Beth Haarava.

Threefold Aim Asserted

The resistance movement's scheduled underground broadcast could not be made today because of a technical hitch, but resistance sources asserted that the purpose of the attacks was threefold:

(1) To prove to British Foreign Secretary Ernest Bevin that if he thought he was unable to transfer another British division to protect the proposed admission of 100,000 Jews to Palestine, a move that he had said last Wednesday would be required, then they would show that he required many more divisions to keep these refugees out.

(2) To demonstrate by force against the alleged intentions of British authorities to liquidate the Palestine Jews' defense organization and cripple its leadership, as outlined in what was described as a secret military document that Hagana captured and broadcast yesterday.

(3) As a protest against an unimpeded arrival of Haj Amin el Husseini, Mufti of Jerusalem, in the Middle East.

June 18, 1946

5 British Officers Abducted, 2 Shot; Palestine Curfew On

By JULIAN LOUIS MELTZER
By Cable to THE NEW YORK TIMES.

JERUSALEM, June 18—Five British military officers were kidnapped in broad daylight today by armed Jewish extremists. From an officers' club on Hayarkon Street in Tel Aviv the officers were taken to an unknown destination. In Jerusalem two Army majors were shot while walking along a street in the center of the city. The shots, which came from a cruising private limousine, inflicted leg wounds on the officers.

Severe military measures faced the Jewish communities of Tel Aviv and Haifa tomorrow. A curfew and orders to stay home until further notice will be imposed, beginning at 5 A. M., to enable large police and military forces to carry out a wide search for the five kidnapped officers, who were reported being held as hostages, and for hidden arms.

[In Cairo the Arab League, in a formal note to the United States Minister, accused "many Americans" of supporting "Zionist terrorists with money and arms." The league advised the United States Government that such action was considered unfriendly.]

The military commander of the Lydda district, in which Tel Aviv is situated, informed the Town Clerk, Judah Nedivi, of the curfew. Similar information was given to the Jewish Community Council in Haifa. A total of 250,000 Jews, almost half of Palestine's Jewish population, is involved.

It was understood that the general headquarters staff, which conferred on the latest outbreak of disturbances, considered a proposal to impose martial law, but the curfew orders represented a compromise.

Tel Aviv was declared off limits to British troops of all ranks. Additional police patrolled the streets in the tense atmosphere.

The Tel Aviv Municipal Council adopted a resolution condemning the kidnapping and urging the perpetrators to free the officers.

The kidnapping and the attack on the officers in Jerusalem, which occurred about the same time, indicated another phase in Palestine's troublesome situation. As individual attacks against the military they recalled recent actions in Cairo and Alexandria.

The Tel Aviv incident was particularly brazen. Several armed Jews entered the club, where a large number of officers on leave were lounging or drinking cocktails before lunch. Most of the officers carried pistols, a compulsory military security precaution, but they were unable to draw quickly enough as the raiders shouted, "Hands up!" Four Army officers and one Royal Air Force officer were selected and escorted outside.

In the Jerusalem shooting the automobile drew up alongside the two officers, who were walking from a club after lunch. A man jumped out, firing a pistol. One officer grappled with him but fell wounded. The men inside the automobile fired automatic weapons, wounding the second major.

The limousine drove off, but a taxi in the Jewish Agency office courtyard, which faces the spot at a principal thoroughfare, sped after the car. The driver managed to take its number. A Jewish passer-by said he believed the attackers were not Jews, but the Government press announcement said they were Jews.

In the Tel Aviv club two officers who resisted the kidnappers were struck with pieces of lead piping. Large police reinforcements were rushed to the scene and found an abandoned taxi a short distance.

146

TERRORISTS OR PATRIOTS

away, indicating that the abductors used another car in planned operations designed to throw off pursuers.

The police theory is that the officers were seized as hostages for two Jewish extremists, Joseph Ashbel and Isaac Simhon, believed to be members of Irgun Zvai Leumi who were sentenced to death Thursday by a Jerusalem military court for having participated in an armed attack while stealing arms from a military camp. These were the first death sentences imposed under the new emergency regulations providing capital punishment for anyone armed or unarmed, found with an armed raiding party.

It was believed that the kidnappers would present an ultimatum that unless their two comrades in death cells were reprieved the lives of the captured officers would be taken.

The death of two more Jews at the Haifa Hospital brought the toll among the attackers of bridges and railway workshops in the last two days to eighteen, according to an unofficial estimate, and to seventeen by official figures. Funerals of Jewish saboteurs in Haifa and Jerusalem were attended by several thousands.

[Press services estimated the total dead at nineteen, including a British officer killed Monday while dismantling a mine at one of the eight attacked bridges.]

Nine Jews were killed last night after they had raided the Palestine Railway's workshops outside Haifa. Two were killed inside the workshop area. As the raiders' truck left the area it encountered a military road block and ambush. The vehicles dashed toward the barrier as if the drivers hoped to crash against it, and the occupants blazed away at the patrol.

They were forced to flee, however, and jumped out, still firing. The troops returned the fire, killing seven Jews and seriously wounding five others, including two women, and slightly wounding six, including a woman.

Fifteen persons, including a woman, were taken in custody from a truck. Pistols and grenades were captured.

The main damage at the railway workshops was in the machine shop, which was hard hit by explosions and fire. One locomotive was wrecked by explosives. Structural damage was caused by blast and fire.

Train service to all neighboring countries except Egypt was still interrupted by the wrecking of bridges Sunday night.

June 19, 1946

BRITAIN LAUNCHES ARMY DRIVE TO END PALESTINE TERROR

At Least 3 Are Slain and 1,000 Held in Nation-Wide Raids to Get Hagana Leaders

JEWISH AGENCY IS SEIZED

4 High Officials Are Placed in Custody on Suspicion of Abetting Resistance

By CLIFTON DANIEL
By Wireless to THE NEW YORK TIMES.

JERUSALEM, June 29—Palestine's Jewish population remained under virtual military siege tonight while thousands of troops and police pursued a country-wide campaign to root out the leadership of Hagana, the Jewish community's underground army, which, so far, has resulted in the arrest of about 1,000 persons for questioning and the deaths of two Jews and one British soldier.

[A London dispatch said that the United States Embassy had been informed of the drive only after it was under way.]

The operations, which began with the first military occupation of the Jewish Agency for Palestine and the arrest of four of its senior officials, are still continuing without any indication of when they will be completed. So far twenty rifles and 30,000 rounds of ammunition have been found in the searches of Jewish settlements.

Passive resistance to the military operations increased as the day wore on, but no major clashes were reported by Palestine Government authorities and there was practically no use of firearms.

There is no indication that Hagana appeared as an organized force.

Meanwhile Dr. Chaim Weizmann, president of the Jewish Agency, was received by the British High Commissioner, Lieut. Gen. Sir Alan G. Cunningham, and discussed the situation.

Drive Opens at Dawn

With full knowledge of the London Government the operations began before dawn and continued through the day with a series of raids, arrests and searches in Jerusalem, Haifa, Tel Aviv and at least eleven Jewish communal settlements. Large portions of the country are in a virtual state of military siege by troops in war kit.

Although official reports accounted for only three dead, late today unofficial accounts mentioned six, including five Jews.

A report circulated in Zionist circles that Hagana leaders had learned of the raids in advance and gone into hiding. Hagana, with a membership sometimes estimated as high as 80,000 active and reserve members, is distinct from the smaller extremist groups of Irgun Zvai Leumi and the so-called Stern gang.

The Jewish Agency's building in Jerusalem was occupied without opposition and throughout the morning big British Army trucks were carting away its files.

Acting chairman of the agency's executive committee, Rabbi J. L. Fishman, leader of the world Mis-Nah Orthodox Jewish movement, and Isaac Gruenberg, a member of the committee, were arrested at their homes in Jerusalem.

Moshe Shertok Detained

Moshe Shertok, a member of the executive committee and director of the political department, was taken from his hotel in Tel Aviv. Doctor Bernard Joseph, legal advisor of the agency, was arrested at his seaside villa at Nathanya, north of Tel Aviv, protesting that his detention was illegal. Nathanya was named for the late Nathan Straus of New York. Dr. Chaim Weizmann "certainly was not arrested."

David Ben Gurion, chairman of the Jewish Agency Executive, is in Europe.

The four agency officials who were arrested were taken to a detention camp at Latrun, where suspected terrorists are interned.

While Palestine Jews and Arabs were awaiting Prime Minister Attlee's statement on his earlier demand for the disarming of underground forces and the British Government's declaration of policy for Palestine, troops and police from among nearly 150,000 in Palestine struck at 4:15 o'clock this morning.

Not Against Whole Community

In a very precisely worded statement, the High Commissioner announced that "especially while discussions are proceeding about the future of the country, His Majesty's Government is determined that law and order are to be maintained in the territory."

"The objective," he said, "is to restore those conditions of order, without which no progress can be made toward a solution of the problem of Palestine.

The operations, he continued, were "not directed against the Jewish community as a whole but solely against those few who are taking an active part in the present campaign of violence and those who are responsible for instigating and directing it."

The Jewish Agency was occupied, he said, "owing to evidence in our hands as to the part it has played in the organization and direction of and in cooperation with the forces which have carried out acts of violence against the Government."

The reaction of members of the Jewish community to this stroke seemed one of anxiety and resentment. Some predicted that it would be the beginning of a Jewish revolt. One remarked wryly: "This must be intended to make things easy for the Mufti [Haj Amin el Husseini] of Jerusalem when he returns to Palestine."

There is no doubt that almost the entire Jewish community is in sympathy with the Hagana underground Jewish militia, which the Jews regard primarily as a defense organization and are alarmed by the attempt to ferret out its secret leadership.

Warns of Consequences

Sir Alan's statement seemed to acknowledge the possible need for private armies in Palestine, but said that "insofar as it may be expedient for such protection to be provided by the communities themselves, it must be brought under proper control of the Government."

Meanwhile he warned of possible unfortunate consequences to any who should be contemplating armed resistance or further violence.

Today's operations are not designed to round up the whole of Hagana but mainly to seize documents that might prove a connection between the Jewish agency and the illegal forces and to round up the high command of "Palmak," the striking force of Hagana.

Hagana since has been growing steadily and arming itself largely by raids on British dumps.

The operation was undertaken on the Jewish sabbath "to save lives," Sir John Shaw, Secretary of Palestine Government, said.

In Jerusalem scores of police and armed and helmeted British troops cordoned off the modernistic headquarters of the Jewish Agency before dawn with armored cars, Bren gun carriers and barbed wire barriers.

Sunrise disclosed a scene like a military encampment.

Machine guns were set up behind the pink stone walls. One was trained on the driveway leading to the agency's front door, where British vans were parked and loaded with big, black wooden boxes of documents and filing cases.

The troops lounging around the area were shaving or eating breakfast. One detail was digging in the back garden of the agency.

Meanwhile about three square miles of the surrounding residential area had been placed under a curfew and barred to unauthorized persons entering or leaving. Within this area agency employees were routed out of bed to open offices and files. Some doors were smashed when the keys could not be found, but the damage was minor, the police stated.

While the operations were proceeding in Jerusalem a light Royal Air Force observation plane constantly buzzed over the rooftops of the Holy City.

Press Dispatches Held Up

Early in the morning a curfew on movement was imposed over all the predominantly Jewish areas of Palestine. News dispatches leaving the country were stopped for six hours and what Sir John Shaw called a "rudimentary censorship" was imposed on foreign correspondents. Sir John expressed the belief that the censorship would be lifted in twenty-four hours, saying that it was intended only to pre-

The Irgun and the Stern Gang

vent misrepresentation for partisan reasons before the facts were complete.

Censorship on the entire contents of local press, except for news from abroad, was also imposed.

At Tel Aviv, which was in the the area of complete curfew, troops and police occupied the premises of the General Federation of Jewish Labor, the newspaper Davar and the Workers Bank and began a thorough search of them, it was reported unofficially.

The British soldier killed at Tel Yosef was struck by the same bullet that one of his comrades fired at a Jew, who also was killed.

At Ain Harod one Jew was killed by a Jewish truck that was attempting to crash a roadblock, the official report said.

Resistance at Ramat Rahel, near Jerusalem, was overcome by a baton charge. Injuries were reported minor.

Tear gas was used at Meshek Yagur, biggest of the Jewish settlements, on Mount Carmel, near Haifa. It was there that the cache of twenty rifles and 30,000 rounds of ammunition was found.

Official reports stated that explosives were used to force entrance to the bank and the Wizo [Women's International Zionist Organization] building. Tel Aviv was quiet, the statements said.

On a hilltop near Jerusalem screaming women and girls attacked British soldiers who were attempting to round up the men of the Ramet Rahel settlement for interrogation. No one was seriously hurt.

Ten other settlements were reported officially to have been entered. Forty persons were detained at Mishmar Hasharon.

Passive resistance was offered at Maabarot in the Vale of Sharon. Jewish youths erected road blocks at Rehoboth and when they were removed they put them up again.

An official statement said that the troops were dealing with curfew breaking there.

The operations are still proceeding according to plan, a statement said, and will continue until their purpose is accomplished.

June 30, 1946

Jewish Faction Threatens to Kill 3 British Hostages in Palestine

By The United Press.

JERUSALEM, June 30 — Irgun Zvai Leumi, a Jewish extremist organization, issued an ultimatum tonight saying it would kill three British hostages if the British executed two Irgun members condemned to death.

Meanwhile, explosions and shootings flared anew in the all-Jewish city of Tel Aviv.

Pamphlet bombs exploded in Tel Aviv, while more conservative Jewish organizations planned hunger strikes and mass campaigns of passive resistance and civil disobedience in protest against the searching of their homes and business establishments by British troops.

Police and troops rushed to Tel Aviv's business district when the bombs exploded and snatched pamphlets from the hands of the jeering populace.

The pamphlets, signed by Irgun, said: "All this, and what will follow, will not change our determination to take the lives of these three if our two die."

The pamphlets referred to three of five British officers kidnapped by terrorists two weeks ago in their Tel Aviv club. Two were released last week after Hagana had warned the terrorists to free all five.

By CLIFTON DANIEL
By Wireless to The New York Times.

JERUSALEM, June 30—Despite the detention of 2,000 persons in the largest mass arrest ever made in Palestine, the secret radio of the Jewish resistance movement announced tonight that its leadership and general staff had not been "silenced" by the campaign that British forces opened against the secret army yesterday morning.

The brief special announcement on the "Voice of Israel" propaganda station of Hagana, the underground Jewish militia, concluded ominously: "Everyone in Yishuv (the Jewish community) must be on the alert and wait for the order that will come as soon as possible, and everyone must then fulfill the duty imposed upon him." This was the first intimation of Hagana reprisals.

As Palestine gradually was returning to normal after two days of searches and seizures, the authorities began to rake through their list of prisoners and their mass of documents for evidence linking the Jewish Agency to the secret forces.

The Palestine Government announced "the first phase of operations which began yesterday morning to restore law and order in Palestine now has been virtually completed." No hint was given of the next phase.

Voice of Israel told its listeners, however, that this was "only the beginning of the assault," and that those places not searched yesterday and today would be visited later.

In announcing that its leadership had not been silenced, the Hagana radio said tonight that the resistance movement would "know how to carry on the battle."

It appealed to American Jewry for help and said the United States Government should associate itself actively either with the Jewish struggle or "with Britain's policy of betrayal."

The first phase of British retributive measures drew to a close with some 2,000 persons having been detained for investigation. Four Jews and one British soldier were killed and thirteen Jews were admitted to hospitals. Dozens of other civilians and soldiers were hurt. The official statement said British forces had shown "great restraint" in the face of "considerable provocation," and only in a few cases had single shots been fired.

During a spontaneous protest demonstration in Haifa today, unofficial reports said, four persons had been wounded, two of them seriously, when a burst of shots was fired from a British vehicle. The area immediately was barred with barbed wire and a curfew imposed tonight on the whole city. The highway curfew was again imposed in all Jewish districts tonight.

Searches in Jewish agricultural settlements continued on a small scale today. So far, authorities have reported finding only two Lewis guns, twenty-seven rifles, forty-eight automatic pistols, 10,000 rounds of small-arms ammunition and some explosives and acid in Meshek Yagur, the largest Jewish settlement near Haifa.

Additional arms caches were discovered today at Mesehek Yagur, a late communiqué said, and the search is continuing.

Six settlements were searched in northern Palestine early this morning. In Gevat, the entire population attempted to obstruct the troops. In Sedot Yam, a barricaded gate had to be broken open by a Bren gun carrier. Arrests were made in several places.

The fatal shooting of a Jewish curfew breaker in Tel Aviv last night was confirmed, making a total of four Jews officially reported killed. The official statement said that search of the Jewish Agency's quarters was continuing.

Apparently, however, the arms of Hagana remain as well hidden as ever. In one recent raid, Hagana obtained more than ten times as much British ammunition as was found in Meshek Yagur.

There was great speculation in Jerusalem today whether the identity of the high command of "Palmak Hagana," the striking force that the British authorities are seeking, would also defy detection.

Many Conceal Identification

Of the 2,000 prisoners taken in the round-up, many of them are believed to have been arrested simply because they refused to identify themselves. Although the vast majority of prisoners are simply held for investigation, it is understood that all senior Zionist officials arrested are suspected of "instigating and directing" the recent campaign of violence.

Rather than rejoicing at the discomfiture of their enemies, the Arabs of Palestine, according to Ahmed Shukairy, head of the Palestine office, said today that British action hadn't gone far enough.

In a written statement, he said: "British authorities have started yawning after a long sleep * * * but we are not confident that this yawning will develop into a full awakening and determination."

The Government's determination to suppress terrorism, he said, was "couched in apologetic terms" and its statement "overestimated the importance of Zionist terrorism."

"A handful of soldiers, coupled with determination, will secure the maintenance of peace and order in the country," the Arab statement said.

"The measures taken will not distract our attention from our struggle for realization of our sovereignty and independence," Mr. Shukairy said. Questioned by correspondents, he asserted the Arabs would fight if they failed by diplomatic means to halt the growth of Zionism in Palestine, taking the "natural course of invoking might when right fails."

July 1, 1946

TWO IN PALESTINE WIN COMMUTATION

By Wireless to The New York Times.

JERUSALEM, Thursday, July 4 —Death sentences on two members of Irgun Zvai Leumi, Jewish underground extremist organization, were commuted to life imprisonment yesterday by Lieut. Gen. Sir Alan G. Cunningham, High Commissioner for Palestine.

This action raised hopes that the three remaining kidnapped British officers would now be released.

Last midnight hopes were high that the release of the three, who had been held nearly sixteen days, might come at any moment. This emerged from a late night broadcast by "Fighting Zion," the underground radio of Irgun Zvai Leumi, that the return of the officers was "imminent." The announcer, speaking in Hebrew, added: "This is because our two men, Joseph Simkhon and Isaac Ashbel, have now been spared from the gallows."

An official communiqué announced Tuesday afternoon that Lieut. Gen. Sir Evelyn Barker, commander of the British troops in Palestine, had confirmed the sentences imposed on the two Irgun men by a military court on June 13. Yesterday the High Commissioner commuted them.

It was the first time that the High Commissioner had been known to have used his power to intervene in such a case.

The two men, Simkhon and Ashbel, were condemned in Jerusalem on charges of discharging firearms, depositing a bomb and removing arms from a military store during a raid on a military camp on March 6 by a band of armed men.

Since their conviction six British officers have been kidnapped.

Three were subsequently released.

Two men—Jews this time—were kidnapped in Haifa early yesterday morning. They were former soldiers in the Czechoslovak Army. They were taken from their quarters by four men in civilian clothes, who wrapped them in blankets after subduing them in a fight. The supposition is that the two men were suspected by their comrades of betraying the presence of arms at the Meshek Yagur settlement near Haifa, where a large store was discovered.

Two additional arms caches were discovered at Meshek Yagur Tuesday, making a total of nineteen, an official statement said. The large haul is still being counted and the search continues.

With the commutation of the death sentences and after the excitement of the week-end raids and arrests, Palestine is settling back into its routine—which is not always a peaceful one—and the threat by the Jewish community of non-cooperation with the British authorities has not yet materialized.

Sir Alan received Isaac Ben Zvi, president of the Jewish National Council, and other council members this afternoon and is understood to have cautioned them about the consequences of a policy of non-cooperation. He also received Chief Rabbi Benzion Uziel.

The agency's building, which is still occupied by British troops, is expected to be returned to its owners before the end of the week.

A delegation of United States Zionists, who called on L. C. Pinkerton, United States Consul General, on Tuesday, presented in writing their views on the British military action against the Jewish community and asked that it be conveyed to President Truman.

The delegation included Charles Rosenbloom of Pittsburgh, national chairman of the United Palestine Appeal; Harold J. Goldenberg of Minneapolis, national vice chairman; Mrs. Rebecca Shulman of New York, vice president of Hadassah, and Meyer W. Weisgal of New York, general secretary of the Jewish Agency office in the United States.

July 4, 1946

KIDNAPPED BRITONS FREED IN PALESTINE

3 Are Dumped in Packing Case in Tel Aviv — Extremists Proclaim 'Independence'

By CLIFTON DANIEL
By Cable to THE NEW YORK TIMES.

JERUSALEM, July 4—True to its promise, Irgun Zvai Leumi today released the three kidnapped British officers whom it was holding as hostages for the lives of its two comrades whose death sentences were commuted yesterday by Lieut. Gen. Sir Alan G. Cunningham, High Commissioner for Palestine.

The three officers reported this afternoon to the central police station of Tel Aviv. They are Capts. K. H. Spencer, G. C. Warburton and A. E. Taylor. They were abducted sixteen days ago from the Officers' Club in Tel Aviv.

Upon the commutation of the death sentences of the two Irgun Zvai Leumi men yesterday the organization's illegal radio immediately announced that the officers would be released.

The officers stated that they were conveyed from their place of detention in a large wooden packing case. After traveling fifteen minutes they were released in Shadal Street in the center of Tel Aviv. They were unharmed and in good health.

While it released the three officers, Irgun Zvai Leumi issued a virtual declaration of war against the British authorities today as a result of the campaign started by the British forces last week-end to rout out the leadership of the Jewish illegal forces.

A handbill containing the Irgun Zvai Leumi program reached this correspondent today dated simply July, 1946. It said:

"There is no other alternative than to fight. In this position it is a sin to hesitate, a crime to delay, a crime to retreat * * * The entire nation in Zion and in despersion must rise as one man to hit back at the savage tyrant by all means and all ways until he departs."

For the first time Irgun Zvai Leumi issued a political program by which it proposed that the Jews might "overthrow the bonds of slavery."

Some of the points in the program were:

The Proclamation of Jewish Independence.

Creation of a Jewish Provisional Government which would collect its own taxes and have its own Parliament.

The formation of a Jewish liberation army which would not lay down its arms until an independent Jewish State was established.

A call to all Jews and all nations of the world to assist the Jews.

Fifty persons detained for interrogation in the recent raids were released from the RAFA detention camp near the Egyptian border today and another fifty are due to be released tomorrow.

The Government announced the formation of a board of survey to assess damage caused to the Jewish Agency building during its occupation by the army preparatory to returning it to the owners.

Chloroformed and Blind folded
By Wireless to THE NEW YORK TIMES.

BEIT DARAS, Palestine, July 4—So many strange things have happened in Tel Aviv lately that when the three British officers crawled out of a packing case just off the main boulevard this afternoon nobody took much notice of them.

That is their story as they told it tonight at headquarters of the Sixth Airborne Division after sixteen days of captivity.

To the three officers the supposedly fearsome figure of the Irgun Zvai Leumi leader, who was chief of their captors, was known as "the type in the sugar bag."

Describing the twenty-four or so young men who stood guard over them in night and day shifts for sixteen days in an outbuilding somewhere in Tel Aviv, Captain G. C. Warburton said:

"They had a very sinister figure with a pink paper mask on—like the KKK—who came in on the first day and told us that we were hostages and that they would not give us any trouble if we did not give them any.

"He came subsequently with an even more flamboyant headdress—a sort of sugar bag affair with holes in it."

Receive Cookies and Money

At one o'clock this afternoon "the type in the sugar bag" informed the officers that they would be released today. He handed some cookies to the captives who had been on a hunger strike for three days and said "you can eat now."

As a parting gift their captors gave the officers a pound note apiece, presumably for expenses.

Just before 6 o'clock, the three officers were blindfolded, put in a large packing case, chloroformed until they were groggy and taken in a truck to the corner of Shadel Street and Rothschild Boulevard in the center of the city and there released.

They staggered out just in time to see their captors fleeing in an ancient truck. Captain Warburton attempted to pursue them in another truck but was outdistanced. He said that at least 400 persons were "sitting on benches playing with their children" and must have seen him giving chase but no one was interested.

The three officers and one other were taken from the Officers' Club in Tel Aviv by a party of armed men who entered the club dining hall at the lunch hour. The fourth man was later released. They were thrown into a taxi and subsequently transferred to a box in which they were carried away by a truck. Eventually they were dumped out into a room about thirteen feet square where there were two pallets on the floor, a stock of food and crude sanitary facilities. The room was "uncomfortably hot," they said, because the window was boarded up. Light came in through a hole in the roof.

The officers had their mouths taped and their wrists bound with cord when first abducted. Afterward they were bound hand and foot with chains cased in rubber tubing. The leg chains were removed when Captain Warburton went on a hunger strike.

Their food at first consisted of brown bread, sausages and water. Later they received eggs and bacon on request. When they asked for reading matter their guards furnished them with Zionist literature, which they found a "bit heavy." When they asked for something lighter they received piles of western stories.

Their guards were all young men, one as young as 16.

"They were very keen on explaining their point of view," said Captain Warburton. They advocated united Jewish immigration to Palestine and for a nation or a Jewish state and they said they "could fight the Arabs, if necessary." The young men very definitely belonged to a military organization, Captain Warburton said, "because they all came to attention when the man with the sugar bag came in."

During all the time they were held the three officers never got more than an intimation that they were being held as hostages for the two Irgun Zvai Leumi men whose death sentences were commuted by the High Commissioner yesterday. When hints leaked out they were denied by the guards. The newspapers they received had bits snipped out of them—presumably dispatches about the officers themselves, and the reason why they had been kidnaped.

After being held for thirteen days in the same room the three men went on a hunger strike because, they said, their pallets were getting "smelly," their clothes "rank" and "ants were crawling about."

July 5, 1946

The Irgun and the Stern Gang

JERUSALEM BOMB KILLS 41 IN ATTACK ON BRITISH OFFICES

52 BURIED IN DEBRIS

Zionist Terror Raiders Accused of Blast in King David Hotel

SHOOT BRITISH OFFICER

Strict Curfew Imposed in Hunt for Killers—Jewish Groups Urge End of Violence

By JULIAN LOUIS MELTZER
By Wireless to The New York Times.

JERUSALEM, July 22—An entire six-story corner and basement at the southwestern wing of the King David Hotel were destroyed and at least forty-one British, Jewish and Arab Government officials were killed and fifty-three were injured soon after midday when terrorists, believed to belong to either Irgun Zvai Leumi or the Stern gang, blew up a large part of the offices of the chief secretary of the Palestine Government.

Prominent Britons, including British Jews, are among the casualties. The dead include eight unidentified bodies, according to the latest semi-official figures, and fifty-two missing persons are buried under a huge pile of debris. They include twelve senior British civil servants and four senior Palestinian civil servants.

I was on the scene, outside the fashionable hotel—a Jerusalem landmark overlooking the Old City—just after the heavy explosions shattered the southwestern corner. Rescue operations had already been begun by British troops and police sweating under the hot July sun. They were bringing out bodies on stretchers, leaving a trail of blood over the rubble.

Postmaster General Killed

People standing outside or just entering or leaving the building were among the casualties. Postmaster General Gerald Donald Kennedy was killed outside the southern wing. The Superintendent of Police, Kenneth Page Hadingham, was badly injured. Richard Mowrer, correspondent of The New York Post, suffered a leg fracture.

The corner was destroyed by a heavy charge of gelignite planted in the basement by four or five armed gunmen. The six floors included a well-known basement cafe called La Regence and consisted of thirty or thirty-five rooms, mostly occupied by the chief secretary's offices. British Army headquarters had the entire top floor of the hotel and only a small section is situated at the southwestern corner. This explains the comparatively small casualties among the British military.

The first detonation occurred at about 12:10 P. M., when a small

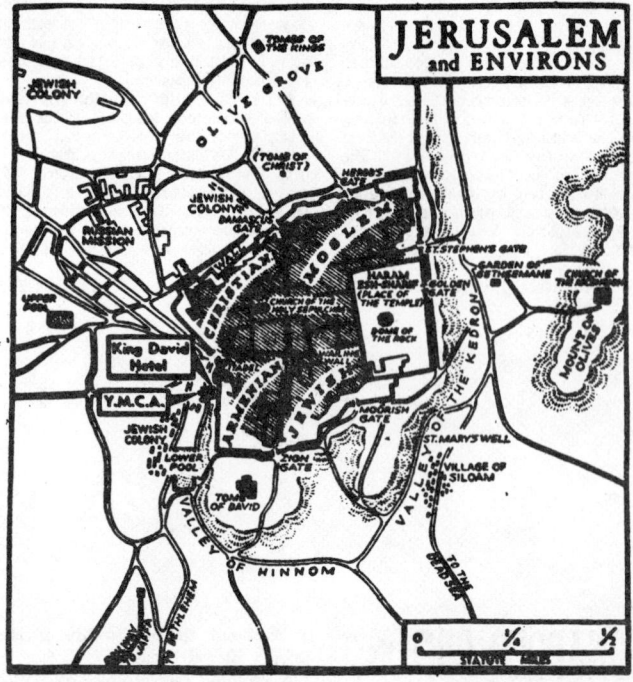

Associated Press, July 23, 1946

The King David Hotel and the near-by Y.M.C.A. building are outside the walls of the Old City of Jerusalem on its west side.

The King David Hotel (right), where explosion occurred, wrecking secretariat of the Palestine Government and part of the British Army headquarters. The bomb was planted in basement of the wing of the hotel nearest to camera. On the left is the Y. M. C. A. Building.

Associated Press

smoke-bomb exploded near a parked automobile on Julian's Way about fifty yards south of the hotel. It was intended to hold up all cars. Then came several shots from automatic guns.

Grenade Is Thrown

The second explosion came almost immediately as a man dressed in Arab clothing alighted from a blue limousine and threw a small grenade along a lane on the northern end of the hotel. A military sentry fired at him and the man threw away a submachine gun and limped to the car, which sped off toward the Jaffa Gate—one of the main gates of the walled Old City. The car was found abandoned later at the foot of the Tower of David, not far from district police headquarters.

Five minutes later came a third, shattering explosion. It was preceded by a mysterious telephone warning to the hotel's switchboard operator by a woman caller who said: "Tell everyone to leave the hotel. It is going to be blown up in a few minutes."

A few minutes before this third detonation a truck drove down the sunken driveway at the northern end of the hotel and four or five men jumped out at the service entrance to the kitchens. They assembled all the hotel staff—cooks, waiters and kitchen boys—below stairs at gunpoint as one man laid several milk cans full of explosives with fuses, wires and detonators. Then the men dashed off and the hotel staff fought to get out at all the exits.

An eyewitness, Maj. Eric Merrill, army public-relations officer who was in the building opposite the hotel, told me: "First there was a great explosion. Then the southwestern corner of the hotel seemed to bulge. It collapsed with a great roar and a huge column of brown-gray smoke billowed up."

A number of Government officials, typists and women clerks who had been standing at their office windows peering out to seek the causes of the first two explosions were trapped and hurtled out as the third went off. E. W. Keys, assistant secretary, was hurled clear across the road into the wall of a Y. M. C. A. gymnasium. He was killed.

Men and women staggered from the hotel, dazed from shock, their faces covered with white dust and many streaked with blood from head wounds. Others unable to walk were being helped. Government employes, British military men, messenger boys and hotel guests came out in a long stream. A passing bus was blown off course and every passenger was injured.

Commissioner Unhurt

The Deputy High Commissioner, Sir John Valentine Shaw, was sitting in his office at the southeastern corner of the hotel when the explosion occurred. He was uninjured. Immediately he assumed charge of the rescue work, directing troops, police officers and plainclothes men. A few minutes later the inspector general of police, Col. W. N. Gray, and other high military officers, joined him.

Executives of the Jewish Agency and the National Council of Palestine Jews issued a statement expressing horror "at the dastardly crime perpetrated by the gang of desperadoes." After expressing sympathy to the victims' families, the statement added: "Jews in Palestine are called upon to rise up against these abominable outrages." This may herald active efforts by responsible Jewish institutions to combat and liquidate reckless terrorist groups.

A detachment of Argyll and Sutherland Highlanders arrived with picks, shovels, acetylene blowtorches, portable cranes and first-aid kits, exactly fifteen minutes after the third explosion. They began clearing the wreckage. At one crevice beneath a twenty-foot pile of wreckage, there was moaning. One man was brought out, followed by two others.

Police Are Active

Police worked unceasingly to seek the culprits. I heard orders crackling and snapping over the short-wave police radio. Commands were issued and patrol trucks and armored cars dashed to the scene. Anti-terrorist sirens wailed and halted all traffic. Police cars with loudspeakers went around announcing complete curfew in the whole municipal area of Jerusalem from 12:45 P. M. until further notice. The curfew was later restricted to the central Jewish area only and this will be removed at 5 A. M. tomorrow.

One report said that an automobile abandoned near the Jaffa Gate had two sticks of gelignite, one revolver and one Arab cloak inside. But the small group of gunmen who held up the hotel staff and planted the explosives in the basement got clear away. A taxi containing a quantity of arms believed used by some of the escaping terrorists was found abandoned at the Jaffa Road.

Army headquarters declared that the men who entered the hotel basement unloaded several milk cans and trundled them along the corridor to the far end, directly below the secretariat and outside the restaurant. A British Signal Corps officer, hearing the noise, came out to investigate and was shot in the stomach twice and severely wounded by a man dressed as an Arab.

The Palestine radio reported that the bodies of five Britons and twenty-three Palestinians had so far been taken from the wreckage of the hotel. Four are still below the wreckage. Hospital reports, however, said that thirty-one bodies had been brought in by 7 P. M.

July 23, 1946

ZIONIST TERRORISTS SAY THEY SET BOMB; DENOUNCE BRITISH

Government Ignored Its Phone Warning, Irgun Zvai Leumi Says in Communique

REGIME DENIES A NOTICE

By CLIFTON DANIEL
By Wireless to THE NEW YORK TIMES.

JERUSALEM, July 23 — Irgun Zvai Leumi, an extremist Zionist organization, announced that it had been responsible for the bombing of the British headquarters here in a communiqué issued tonight in Tel Aviv but blamed the "British tyrants themselves" for the loss of life.

Five more persons were taken from the wreckage of the King David Hotel today, two alive and three dead. The latest official casualty list, issued as three days of further searches appeared probable, showed forty-eight persons killed, forty-one missing and fifty-eight injured. Police seeking the perpetrators of the bombing announced the arrest of twenty-seven Jews and the discovery of one suspect dead and another wounded. The city was under a strict 6 P. M.- 6 A. M. curfew, enforced by roving army patrols.

[Denouncing the bombing, President Truman declared that such terrorism "might well" damage the cause of Zionism. In London, Prime Minister Attlee reported considerable progress toward a permanent solution of the Palestine problem, adding that violence would not sway Britain from her aim of justice.]

Zionists Claim Warnings

Giving a detailed report of the operations of its "soldiers," Irgun Zvai Leumi claimed that telephoned warnings to the King David Hotel's switchboard and a warning bomb placed outside the hotel had given the Government twenty-two minutes — between 12:15 and 12:37 P. M.—to evacuate civilian personnel. "The tragedy which occurred in the civilian offices of the occupying Government was not caused by Jewish soldiers," the communiqué said, "but by the British tyrants themselves, who disregarded that warning and did not evacuate the building at the advice of military experts who undertook to dismantle the explosives." There has been no evidence, however, that there was any consultation of military experts or any attempt to dismantle the explosive charges that were carried into the hotel in milk cans and buckets from a stolen truck, which was found today.

[The Palestine Government vigorously denied that any advance warning had been given to Government and military departments in the King David Hotel before the bomb exploded, according to Reuter. The United Press reported that a mysterious telephone call to police headquarters on Tuesday had warned that the police building would be bombed at any moment and as a result the Jewish section of Palestine was under a guard so heavy that it approximated martial law.]

Of the total casualties, only twenty-two were army personnel —eight killed, five missing and nine injured. The rest were civilian Britons, Arabs, Jews, Greeks and Armenians.

July 24, 1946

The Irgun and the Stern Gang

VIOLENCE IN PALESTINE

It is part of the tragic story in Palestine that violence of the kind that took nearly fifty lives in a single act of terrorism yesterday in Jerusalem is self-defeating. It cannot be expected to modify the position of the Mandatory Power: British opinion in all ranks will stiffen under the impact of such news. It cannot be expected to encourage our own Government to press still more strongly for an increase of immigration into Palestine. Nor can we expect that terrorism of this kind will have any other consequence, within Palestine itself, than to set still more at odds the two groups of people upon whose ability to live in friendly understanding the peace and progress of this little land must ultimately depend. There is no gallantry in a bomb that takes life indiscriminately. Whoever commits such acts, or for whatever purpose, the acts are indefensible.

In the long run, the victims of these tactics of terrorism seem likely to include many of the harassed refugees whose escape from Europe may be postponed still further. We ourselves have strongly favored the immediate admission of 100,000 of these refugees to Palestine. We have hoped that the policies advocated recently by the Joint Anglo-American Committee could be carried out in their entirety, and we have been disappointed at the failure to put them into action. We have urged that the United States use its influence to assist homeless refugees in making a new start in life in friendlier countries than those which so abused them, and we have believed that this country could well open its own doors to more immigrants than those now admitted under the quota system. But to none of these questions and issues will yesterday's violence provide an answer.

July 23, 1946

Patriots, Not Terrorists

TO THE EDITOR OF THE NEW YORK TIMES:

There are points in your editorial of July 23, "Violence in Palestine," which it seems to me are open to question.

If what you term terrorism is self-defeating, as you claim, then the underground patriots in all countries must have failed and those still striving must abandon hope.

Injustice, cloaked as law and order, unfortunately can be met in no other way by oppressed minorities. There is no alternative short of mass suicide.

When resistance groups succeed in their struggle for liberty and right, history transforms the terms terrorist or extremist into hero and patriot. It is 1776 in Palestine. MAY LEWIS.
New York, July 23, 1946.

July 27, 1946

British Halt Palestine Entry, Sidetrack Jews to Cyprus

Statement Holds Immigration Foments Civil War and Sees Effort to Force London's Hand—500 Refugees Leave Haifa

By SYDNEY GRUSON
Special to THE NEW YORK TIMES.

LONDON, Aug. 12—The British Government announced today that no more unscheduled immigration into Palestine would be allowed and that would-be immigrants would in the future be taken to Cyprus "and elsewhere" until their future was decided.

In a long statement announcing the expected decision and the reasons for it, the British declared that such immigration "threatens both civil war and a breakdown of government" in troubled Palestine. Nothing was said about the Jewish refugee immigrants aboard ship in Haifa's harbor, but it was presumed here that they would be transported to Cyprus.

[Two more ships carrying about 1,300 Jewish refugees arrived at Haifa, Palestine, with a British destroyer in escort, as tension rose in Palestine. Transfer of refugees from Haifa's harbor to Cyprus has begun, a National Broadcasting Company correspondent reported Monday night from Cairo. The first ships, bearing Jewish refugees deported from Palestine, "are expected to arrive in the Cyprus port of Famagusta during the night," the British Broadcasting Corporation said.

[The first British deportation ship sailed from Haifa for Cyprus early Tuesday carrying approximately 500 Jewish immigrants who had spent thirty-two hours in sight of their goal, The Associated Press reported.

[Those aboard the first deportation ship were passengers from the dingy little auxiliary schooner Yagur, which arrived at Haifa Sunday after a trip from southern France.]

The British statement charged "a minority of Zionist extremists" with exploiting the suffering of Jews in Europe to obtain a settlement of the Palestine problem that was described as unfair.

With naval strength off Palestine's shores augmented and strong detachments of troops in Haifa to support its decisions, the Government declared that it would "no longer tolerate this attempt to force" its hand in determining a new policy for Palestine.

To this "tough" policy the British added their sympathy for the suffering of Jews, detailed some of the steps taken to prove an assertion that "no country in the world has been a better or more consistent friend of the Jewish people than Britain" and urged the Arabs and Jews to come together with the British to see whether a solution could be reached.

"It is clear that a permanent solution of this complicated question can only be brought about if the Jews and Arabs are prepared to enter upon discussions in a realistic and constructive spirit in order to evolve a practical scheme for harmonizing the claims of these two historic peoples," the statement said. The British hope these discussions will begin this month despite the original objections of Arab and Jewish groups.

Bitter Over Killings

British bitterness over recent events in Palestine was evident in the statement, which recorded Britain's part in helping Jews and in the next paragraph spoke of the wounding, killing and kidnapping of British soldiers and civil servants in Palestine. They were described as "victims of an outrage more worthy of the Nazis than of the Jewish victims of the Nazis."

Hitherto, the statement said, the British allowed immigrants to land out of "sympathy for the suffering of the Jewish people in Europe." The declaration added that "the patience, forbearance and humanity" behind this policy had been interpreted as a sign of weakness and as encouragement for the movement of immigrants.

The point has been reached at which the "illegal traffic is not, as has been maintained, a movement arising spontaneously among the European Jews who see in Palestine their only hope for the future," the statement declared. "Nor are those who encourage and direct it inspired solely by the sympathy which is so widely felt for suffering."

This traffic is widespread and highly organized and supported by large contributions from Zionist sources, the statement asserted. It added that such traffic had been "put into operation by unscrupulous persons in an attempt to force the hand of His Majesty's Government and anticipate their decisions on future policy in Palestine."

Efforts to Plug Exits Told

The British noted the diplomatic representations they had made to European governments to try to halt the traffic at its source and expressed regret over reports of persecution and pogroms against Jews in eastern and southeastern Europe.

Calling on the governments of the countries concerned to end "this shame," the declaration reminded Jews that "in Britain there are no pogroms; Jews enjoy all the rights of civil liberty."

Listed among the reasons for the British decision was "evidence that illegal immigrants were reinforcing the ranks of terrorists" in Palestine and that illegal immigration worked a hardship on Jews who would have been able to enter Palestine legally but could not because the quotas had to be filled from other entrants.

Point was given to British military and diplomatic efforts to back up their immigration decision in an announcement by the Prague radio that the Czechoslovak-Polish frontier had been closed and in word from Valetta that another cruiser, the 8,000-ton Mauritius, had been sent to join the "Palestine patrol."

The British have charged that thousands of Jews have made their way into the United States occupation zone of Germany through the Polish-Czechoslovak corridor. Representations to halt this traffic were made to both Governments. A new British protest to the Greek Government was disclosed following the departure of 433 Jews by sea "from a post on the east coast of the Attica peninsula."

August 13, 1946

TERRORISTS OR PATRIOTS

HAGANAH CENSURES JEWISH EXTREMISTS

Resistance Group Sees Harm to Independence Aim—36 Held in Bank Hold-Ups

JERUSALEM, Sept. 14 (AP) — Haganah, principal Jewish resistance organization, vigorously attacked today Irgun Zvai Leumi and the Stern group, Jewish underground organization, for recent acts of violence, including yesterday's bank hold-ups in Tel Aviv and Jaffa.

Arab-owned businesses in Jerusalem went on a two-hour strike in protest against the Jaffa violence, in which three Arabs were slain by an armed band.

The Voice of Israel, illegal radio of Haganah, said the hold-ups were staged by fanatical groups in efforts to increase dwindling finances.

It added that irresponsible attacks and sabotage endangered the interests of Jews struggling for independence and free immigration in Palestine. The broadcast urged Jewish youth to maintain discipline and follow the leadership of Haganah as "the organized Jewish resistance movement."

The curfew on Tel Aviv and Jaffa was lifted today. No further incidents were reported. Police said they believed Stern band members had staged the bank raids.

September 15, 1946

8 JEWISH LEADERS FREED BY BRITISH

Release Is Unconditional, but Hope Is Voiced for Agency's Role in London Parley

Special to THE NEW YORK TIMES.
JERUSALEM, Nov. 5 — Eight Jewish Agency leaders, detained since the British authorities searched the Jewish Agency offices on June 29, were told at the Latrun detention camp tonight that they were free men.

[According to The Associated Press those released are: Moshe Shertok, head of the Jewish Agency's political department; Dr. Isaac Gruenbaum, Dr. Bernard Joseph, David Remez, chairman of the National Council of Palestine Jews; David Hacohen, head of the Jewish Workers Building Cooperative Society; David Shingarevsky, Josef Shoffman and Mordecai Shatter.]

Simultaneously, curfews maintained on the roads throughout Palestine nightly for many months and in the Jewish areas of Jerusalem since Oct. 19 were abolished.

Speaking for the Government, Richard Stubbs, public information officer, said at a news conference here:

"His Majesty's Government have done the utmost to turn the clock back to June 28 as a gesture in return for the declaration of the Inner Zionist Council and other Jewish institutions that they are seriously determined to end terrorism in this country. His Majesty's Government hope this gesture will lead to the participation of the Jews in the London Palestine conference."

Mr. Stubbs also said that David Ben Gurion, chairman of the Jewish Agency Executive, and another Agency member, Dr. Moshe Sneh, both in the United States, but previously liable to be detained if they returned to Palestine, were now free to come and go as they pleased. Other Jews arrested on June 29 and detained at Rafah, southern Palestine, will be released shortly. [According to The Associated Press this category totals 120.]

The amnesty also included twenty-three Palestinian Arab minor politicians who had been forbidden to return to Palestine since they fled during the 1936-39 disturbances.

The executives of the Jewish Agency will hold a meeting tomorrow. This will be the first full assembly since the leaders were detained.

November 6, 1946

MODERATE ZIONISTS DRIVE ON TERRORISTS

JERUSALEM, Nov. 8 (Reuters) — The Jewish resistance movement's secret radio Voive of Israel announced in a broadcast tonight: "The Haganahs' drive against the Irgun Zvai Leumi and Stern Gang terrorists has already begun."

The broadcast did not disclose what form anti-terrorist action was taking and added: "We shall not be informers."

JERUSALEM, Nov. 8 (U.P.)— British troops in Palestine worked under cover of a security blackout today to set up a guard system for rail lines and it was hoped that trains would be rolling again at nightfall safe from attacks by the Irgun Zvai Leumi.

Traffic was halted last night by a twenty-four-hour suspension of rail travel throughout the Holy Land after a week of heavy attacks that were reported to have inflicted $2,000,000 damage on the lines.

[A section of railway track near Ramleh, forty miles northwest of Jerusalem, was ripped up by the explosion of a time bomb at dawn Friday, other press services reported.]

Irgunists distributed a 2,000-word statement last night giving full details of attacks on rail lines and again assumed responsibility for the bombing of the British Embassy in Rome. The statement included a threat to extend the war against the British to lands outside Palestine. It also attacked the Jewish Agency—calling its members "Vichyites"—and the Haganah "whom we will not allow to stand in our way."

November 9, 1946

PALESTINE WARNED OF DRASTIC CURBS

British Ultimatum, Aimed at Entire Jewish Community, Demands End of Violence

60 SUSPECTS ARE DETAINED

By GENE CURRIVAN
Special to THE NEW YORK TIMES.
JERUSALEM, Jan. 3—A warning that failure to curb terrorism immediately would bring the reimposition of drastic government measures against the entire Jewish population went to the Jewish Agency for Palestine today following the attacks of yesterday and today.

The ultimatum was delivered by Sir Henry Gurney, chief secretary, acting for the High Commissioner, Sir Alan G. Cunningham, to Rabbi Jacob L. Fishman, vice president of the Jewish Agency Executive.

Tonight the Palestine roads were alive with military vehicles. Patrols circulated endlessly, barricades were doubly manned and everyone was on the alert.

The taking of drastic action by the Government would mean a return to the days of last summer when the blowing up of the King David Hotel by terrorists, as part of a series of blows against the Government, resulted in the placing of a ring of iron on Palestine.

Curfews were interminable, road blocks were placed every few miles, searches were carried out ruthlessly and no one was safe on the public highways or urban streets.

There has been an effort to return Palestine toward something resembling a normal level but this latest uprising apparently has destroyed all gains in that direction.

Again the British are fighting mad but they face a powerful underground force that is just as determined to attain its objectives as Britain is to preserve some degree of calm in Palestine while the country's future is being decided elsewhere.

Effect Held Doubtful

This ultimatum may bear fruit, just as a similar one last year resulted in a truce. An appeal such as this is published in the Palestine papers and it is brought to the attention of Haganah, the underground group that has the confidence of the masses.

Haganah is interested primarily in expediting immigration but it does not condone the type of terrorism now being used by Irgun Zvai Leumi. Through Haganah's power and influence the Irgun Zvai Leumi has been restrained in the past but whether it can be done again is another question.

Irgun Zvai Leumi stepped aside and agreed to a truce under pressure when it was pointed out that its aims and objectives were under serious consideration by all concerned. But recently it gave up and decided that American statesmen who had promised deliverence were being swayed by the British.

In pamphlets distributed yesterday by bombs, Irgun Zvai Leumi reiterated its stand and said in substance: "We cannot wait." This group wants Palestine for the Jews, the British evacuated, and all Jews now detained as unauthorized entrants freed. It is willing and ready to go to any extreme to achieve these objectives. Whether it can be deterred at this point, regardless of governmental

The Irgun and the Stern Gang

threats, is a point to be decided by coming events.

Off Duty Troops Armed

Because of the extreme tension caused by recent events, including last night's attacks on government installations and the previous kidnapping and flogging of British personnel, an order went out today to all British soldiers to wear side arms when off duty.

Searches continued in various parts of the country seeking out last night's perpetrators and those who did the flogging. In one quarter of Tel Aviv near Citrus House, military headquarters, 2,500 troops cordoned the area and screened almost 3,000 persons. Sixty were detained. Many whips were found but this is not unusual because many inhabitants of this section keep camels and donkeys for which whips are necessary equipment. Citrus House was the scene of one of last night's attacks.

Another aftermath of last night's attacks, which resulted in the death of one British officer and injuries to more than a score of soldiers, was the blowing up of two more jeeps by land mines. Three British soldiers were hurt today when a jeep hit a mine in the Kfar Sirkin area and five others were injured in a similar accident south of Ranana.

January 4, 1947

BRITAIN SAYS FUNDS OF U. S. ABET TERROR

Advertisements Asking Money for Palestine Causes Again Called to Byrnes' Notice

Special to THE NEW YORK TIMES.
LONDON, Jan. 6—The British Government has again directed the attention of the State Department to advertisements in United States newspapers soliciting funds for the support of "terrorist" organizations in Palestine.

A Foreign Office spokesman said today that Lord Inverchapel, British Ambassador in Washington, had seen Secretary of State Byrnes over the week-end to express British concern over the advertising campaign.

The Foreign Office said that behind Lord Inverchapel's representations was the British Government's belief that money from the United States was financing terrorist activities in the Holy Land.

The spokesman, who said he had not seen the advertisements complained of, was nevertheless emphatic that the appeal for funds was on behalf of "terrorist" organizations and not merely to finance immigration or resettlement work.

The British protested last summer about a similar series of advertisements in United States newspapers, which contained much material critical of British policy in Palestine.

The British seem particularly irritated by the fact that the present advertisements are said to stress exemption of contributions from income tax under clauses relating to "charitable" organizations.

January 7, 1947

PALESTINE HELD BY 100,000 TROOPS

But Lacking People's Support, They Fail To Halt Terror

By JULIAN L. MELTZER
Special to THE NEW YORK TIMES.
JERUSALEM, Jan. 18 — The British armed forces in Palestine are capable of handling a large-scale "frontal" rebellion by either the Jewish or the Arab section of the population. But they are unable to cope as effectively with the sporadic guerrilla warfare that is being carried out by small underground groups who take advantage of the element of surprise in plotting their coups.

The only successful method they found to combat political violence under such conditions is—in the admitted absence so far of the Jewish public's cooperation with the military authorities—to impose stern measures upon everyone in an effort to track down a small number of malefactors.

Much Secrecy Prevails

No real information on the present size of the British and auxiliary forces stationed here can be obtained. Military secrecy is as rigidly maintained as it was during General Eisenhower's surge across Europe two years ago. But it can be assumed that there are now two full divisions and two brigades of the British Army here, with another division reported to be on the way from Egypt. That will give a military strength of more than 80,000 troops, with ancillary services.

The strength of the Palestine police establishment is also being kept secret, with the number of British officers and constables variously estimated at between three and five thousand, the real figure probably being somewhere in between. The Arab constabulary numbers 6,000, the Jewish force another 2,000, perhaps 2,500. There are in addition about 7,000 temporary Arab constables serving on fixed guard duty at army camps or Government buildings and 2,500 Jewish settlement police who have specific duties connected with the security of the outpost Jewish villages in non-Jewish areas. Some 2,000 troopers of King Abdullah's Trans-Jordan Arab Legion are also serving here as airport or Royal Air Force airfield guards or are mounting sentry over Government offices.

That gives a total of more than 100,000 members of the security services, apart from the Royal Navy units that are scouring Palestine waters in search of prohibited ships, and the Royal Air Force, which hitherto has not been used to quell violence but has been employed on reconnaissance errands.

Numbers Not Enough

That figure of 100,000 ought to be adequate to deal with a maximum of 5,000 underground extremists. But judging from the results up to now, numbers do not mean everything.

The present methods of seeking culprits concerned with political violence are entirely punitive—taking place after the outbreak occurs—and only to a small degree preventive. When a terrorist outrage happens, the authorities immediately impose a curfew and clamp down heavily upon the whole public. Rigorous searches are conducted, accompanied by the inevitable hardships for guiltless persons.

Failing Efforts Are Seen

But it 1 all too obvious that such punitive action cannot be avoided where preventive measures fail owing to the passive public cognizance of the tactics of the political extremists—to use no stronger a term than "cognizance."

If stronger measures are taken in the future, they can only mean more tribulation for entire Jewish communities. Indeed, there was a report current some months ago after the King David Hotel blast that General Barker had said at a private gathering, "Give me a fortnight to use my own methods and I'll get every Jewish terrorist in this country."

What the situation boils down to, therefore, is this: the Army and security forces here, totaling at least 100,000 men, are sufficient to crush any major frontal attacks. But they are handicapped by a lack of good intelligence sources in controlling the desultory terrorism that is practiced by compact and daring raiding parties guided by a shrewd underground chief.

The fact must be faced that, to enlist public cooperation in Palestine against the political terror, there must be a prior political settlement.

January 19, 1947

TERRORISTS OR PATRIOTS

JEWS IN PALESTINE REJECT ULTIMATUM ON HELP TO BRITISH

National Council Refuses to Join Campaign to Suppress Holy Land Terrorists

IRGUN REITERATES STAND

By The Associated Press.

JERUSALEM, Feb. 5—The Jewish national council rejected tonight a British ultimatum giving official Jewry until Tuesday to join in stamping out Palestine terrorism. The Irgun Zvai Leumi, an "underground" group, asserted it would "fight to the last breath" against British authority.

In a formal resolution, the national council—Vaad Leumi—told its executive to draft a full answer "in accord with the sentiments" of speeches at tonight's council session, which unanimously expressed opposition to the ultimatum. Members of the Jewish Agency for Palestine and mayors of Jewish towns attended the council's meeting.

The British had warned the agency and national council that they faced the possible imposition of martial law unless they cooperated against underground groups that have resorted to violence against the British. The Irgun's latest expression of defiance, which appealed to "the peoples of the world to come to our help," was contained in a note given to newspaper correspondents by the group.

Evacuation Progresses

It was received as Royal Air Force bombers, each carrying seventeen civilians and one conducting officer, shuttled between Jerusalem and Cairo, evacuating approximately 2,000 British women and children in line with the order issued by the Palestine Government last week. Today about 350 civilians were evacuated by air while 360 others went by train to Egypt, their first stop en route to England.

An unofficial but highly regarded informant said that, if the Jewish Agency refused to assist the British against the Irgun and the Stern gang, the British would withdraw official recognition from the agency. This source said such a withdrawal would probably be announced in a White Paper to be issued on Tuesday.

[The Colonial Office in London declined to say whether it was preparing a White Paper.]

Both the Jewish Agency and its own armed force, Haganah, have refused to cooperate with the British, saying the Jews would not become a "nation of informers." Haganah's spokesman has said it would move against the underground provided it received "a free hand."

New Security Measures

New security measures continued to be imposed by the British today with the announcement of the "segmentation" of Jerusalem into four security areas. Almost 1,000 persons, mostly Jews, were evacuated from their homes to make way for secured areas that will presumably be occupied by Government and possibly military officers.

No appeal has yet been filed on behalf of Dov Bela Gruner, convicted member of the Irgun who is under death sentence. There was no official word of his eventual fate. Jewish leaders fear his execution will signal reprisals from the Irgun and the imposition of martial law in some areas by the British.

February 6, 1947

British Put Palestine Up to U.N.; Admit Failure of Negotiations

By CHARLES E. EGAN
Special to The New York Times.

LONDON, Feb. 14—Formal announcement that Britain had failed in her attempts to find a solution of the Palestine problem and had decided to carry the case to the United Nations was made today by Foreign Secretary Bevin.

Addressing the Arab delegates at the final session of the Palestine Conference, Mr. Bevin said the Cabinet had approved his proposal for appealing to the United Nations.

Mr. Bevin did not disclose what form the reference to the United Nations would take but it was presumed that it would be carried either to the General Assembly when it meets in September or to the Trusteeship Council which is expected to be in operation shortly.

The details of the plan for reference, it was said, would be disclosed by Mr. Bevin in a full statement on the ill-starred Palestine negotiations in the House of Commons early next week.

Reports that Britain would ask for a special session of the United Nations Assembly to consider the problem were denied by officials today.

The following joint British-Arab announcement was issued from 10 Downing Street:

At the final meeting of the Palestine Conference this afternoon Ernest Bevin, Foreign Secretary, reviewed the efforts which His Majesty's Government had made to find a solution to the Palestine problem.

He informed the delegates that since no proposals put forward by His Majesty's Government had proved acceptable as a basis for further discussion, His Majesty's Government had decided to refer the whole problem to the United Nations.

The leaders of each of the Arab delegations re-emphasized that no proposals which involved any form of partition or Jewish immigration would be acceptable as a basis for a solution of the problem.

Mr. Bevin and Arthur Creech Jones, Colonial Secretary, expressed their thanks to the delegates for their courtesy, goodwill and friendliness throughout the course of the discussions.

A full statement will be made in Parliament at an early date.

The Arabs warned Mr. Bevin at their last meeting that any attempt to impose the partition plan would lead to "bloodshed." The heads of the Arab delegation restated their unanimous disapproval of the British Government's proposals. They stood by their counter proposals to give the Jews in Palestine the right of citizenship and guarantees of protection as a minority. As a minority the Jews would be allowed to take their share in the administration of Palestine in the proportion of the existing populations.

Short-Term Policy Door Open

An official of the executive of the Jewish Agency for Palestine said tonight that the agency had rejected any solution short of an independent Jewish state in an adequate area of Palestine and that there was no point in further discussion of the Bevin or Morrison plan.

Although this was apparently the end of the talks on long-term policy, the Agency, he said, had not broken off the talks on the current problems of a short-term nature in Palestine.

Summing up the attitude of the Agency on the British decision to refer the problem to the United Nations, a spokesman said:

"We have not asked for a reference to the United Nations, although the Arabs might have because they are represented, but we do not mind.

"It will take at least nine or ten months if it goes to the United Nations and the position in Palestine will deteriorate unless, of course, the provisions of the mandate are carried out in accordance with international law and the 1939 White Paper, which is in conflict with the mandate, is repealed."

February 15, 1947

16 DIE IN PALESTINE IN MAJOR UPSURGE OF TERRORIST ACTS

By CLIFTON DANIEL
Special to The New York Times.

JERUSALEM, March 1—Answering British Foreign Secretary Bevin's words with bombs and bullets, the Jewish terrorists resumed their activity with a vengeance today.

They caused the death of at least sixteen persons and injury to twenty-two, most of them hit by blast and gunfire when a British officers' club in Jerusalem was blown up.

[Statutory martial law was declared by British authorities for the Jewish quarter of Measherim in Jerusalem, effective at 8 A. M. Sunday, said a United Press dispatch.

[The martial law proclamation, signed by High Commissioner Sir Alan Cunningham, provides for the "withdrawal of normal facilities of civil government," said the dispatch.

[The Cunningham announcement said Government offices and courts would be closed and that "banks may be closed by order of the military, telegraph and postal service may be discontinued and the movement of persons and vehicles may be prohibited," The Associated Press reported.]

Jerusalem Ready for Action

Indications tonight were that some application of martial law would be set tomorrow over Jewish areas of Jerusalem. The stage had been prepared for this by the removal of British women and chil-

The Irgun and the Stern Gang

dren from Palestine.

Today's attacks on British installations were among the most extensive yet made by terrorists.

As reports of bombing, gunfire, mine and mortar attacks poured into Jerusalem from various sections of the country the military authorities imposed a house curfew on the populations of the all-Jewish areas of Tel Aviv, Petah Tikvah and Ramat Gan, in addition to the curfew already instituted in the Jewish quarters of central Jerusalem.

In an afternoon and night of terror thirteen persons died of blast and gunfire when a bomb exploded in the officers' club and fifteen were hurt, two of them dangerously. The dead there included one officer, one enlisted man, four civilian employes, one British policeman and five unidentified persons. The seriously injured were one officer and one enlisted man. Other injured included five officers, one enlisted man and one British policeman. More bodies are believed to be buried in the debris.

Among the civilian dead was a Polish girl telephone operator.

Widespread Attacks

Two British soldiers were killed and two wounded when an army jeep was blown up on Mountain Road, Mount Carmel, Haifa.

One British soldier was injured when a truck struck a mine on a highway north of Haifa near Kiryat Hayim.

British naval vehicles were destroyed in a car park at Haifa, where naval forces had seized 1,398 unauthorized Jewish immigrants yesterday.

A ten-minute attack was made with mortars and small arms on a British military camp near the Jewish resort town of Nathanya on the coast, north of Tel Aviv, killing one soldier and wounding two.

A military truck was damaged by a road mine near the Arab town of Tulkarm on the road from Nathanya.

An attack was made on the police station at Rehoboth, only a short distance from the home of Dr. Chaim Weizmann, Zionist elder statesman and former President of the World Zionist Organization.

A mortar bomb exploded outside a military camp at Hadera, fifty miles south of Haifa.

A mine exploded on the Lydda road at Rehoboth. One of the explosions at Rehoboth shook the town like an earthquake, cut off lights and blasted windows.

Two other blasts occurred, one in front of the police station and another outside the town.

March 2, 1947

MILITARY LAW ENDS IN PALESTINE TODAY; BOMBS GREET NEWS

Terrorists Rip Jewish Agency A Few Hours After British Reveal Lifting of Curbs

OIL PIPELINE IS SERVED

Extremists Caution Zionists Against Soft Policy—Britain Pleased With Jews' Aid

Special to THE NEW YORK TIMES.

JERUSALEM, March 16—The withdrawal of statutory martial law imposed on the Tel Aviv-Petah Tiqva are and a section of Jerusalem on March 2 was announced today.

The withdrawal is effective at noon tomorrow, bringing immediate economic relief to nearly 300,000 Jewish inhabitants, or almost half of Palestine Jewry.

Just a few hours after the announcement on lifting martial law, a Jewish terrorist attack was made on the Jewish Agency for Palestine. An explosion blasted out the interior of the official Zionist organization's press room and tourist information center in the office building in the heart of Jerusalem. Nobody was hurt.

The explosion resounded through the silent and empty streets of the curfew-bound Jewish quarters of the Holy City.

The blast was one of a series occurring soon after the Government's announcement. One explosion ripped open the Iraq Petroleum Company's main pipeline to Haifa, and others—one of which was accidental—killed an Arab and injured five persons.

Intra-Jewish Split Spotlighted

The bomb that damaged the Jewish Agency offices underscored the sharp differences in policy between the official Zionist bodies and the dissident groups conducting the underground campaign against British forces in Palestine. The explosion came while the Jewish Agency Executive was assembled in Jerusalem to consider the internal situation of Palestine and the Zionist appeal to the United Nations.

Some Zionist officials were not ready to believe immediately hat the bombing had been the work of Jews. Comment is awaited tomorrow from the underground press and radio.

Other observers immediately interpreted the blast as a warning to the Executive that a stiff policy would be expected from its deliberations.

It was the second time that the Jewish Agency had been the victim of terrorist acts. The Agency's premises in Tel Aviv were set afire about eighteen months ago.

Tonight's explosion also came at a critical moment in the Palestine Government's campaign to convince the Jewish community and official Zionist bodies that terrorism was as much a menace to them as to the British forces. The lifting of martial law was a gesture of conciliation in return for Jewish assistance to the authorities.

The bombs that wrecked the press room and information office were detonated by electricity, the police report said, although it was not explained how the attackers could have escaped while the whole area was under strict curfew. The bomb must have been placed in the building very shortly before the 6 o'clock curfew deadline, or smuggled in during the curfew when no one is allowed on the streets without a pass.

The British announcement came as no surprise to official Zionist circles or to most of the Jewish population. Since the issuance on March 13 of Communiqué 112, declaring that Jewish cooperation had assisted in the apprehension of seventy-eight terrorists and persons suspected of terrorism, it had been generally expected that some announcement on repeal of the military measures was imminent.

British Now Say "Dissident"

Particular interest, in Zionist circles, centered tonight on two features of the Government communiqué. The first was use of the word "dissident" in referring to the underground groups, instead of the customary "terrorists." The term dissident has been applied by Jewish spokesmen and the Hebrew press to connote the refusal of secret insurrectionary organizations to obey communal discipline. Its adoption in Government phraseology was regarded as a significant move toward political pacification.

The second point is the official tribute to the Jewish community for showing "willingness" to assist in eradicating the "senseless evil which is stultifying any hope of finding a peaceful modus vivendi during the period which will elapse before the Palestine question is considered by the United Nations."

Zionist quarters affirm that the attainment of a pacific modus vivendi of this kind will be made easier if the British Government agrees to increase the monthly immigration quotas during the marking-time period until the United Nations renders its decision.

The declaration that martial law had failed to achieve its avowed security purpose was made tonight by the clandestine Irgun Zvai Leumi broadcasting station, "Voice of Fighting Zion."

The radio announcer said that the military regimen was a punitive device designed to starve out the Jewish community and create "police informers." He declared that not one of the seventy-eight persons arrested as terrorists or suspects belonged to the Irgun Zvai Leumi.

"We haven't had any losses in operations during the past week," the statement said, adding: "If this be the extent of Palestine Jewry's cooperation with the authorities, then we are well satisfied with its paucity."

Other Jewish circles are also inclined to doubt that British security authorities were any more successful in tracking down members of the Irgun Zvai Leumi and the Stern Gang during the period of martial law than they would have been without it.

Government circles, on the other hand, insist they have had an "amazing" amount of cooperation from the public, much more during the fortnight's martial-law period than in the whole of the preceding twelve months. They say they also received a "fantastic" volume of information. For the first time, said those circles, persons had the courage to telephone the police and give information or reveal the whereabouts of suspected terrorists.

New Jewish Attitude Seen

A major Government spokesman told this correspondent tonight that martial law had been valuable in bringing home to the public the Government's determination to isolate terrorism. It is now patently clear, he said, that political violence and the long-term issues, including immigration, must be entirely divorced. The spokesman added that the Jewish population realized there was no possible benefit in permitting truculence to continue and was willing to help the authorities.

The Government felt that the public was beginning to see terrorism in proper perspective: the lawless condition must be stamped out first, and then other matters, such as Jewish immigration, could be taken up.

During the fifteen days of martial law, it is estimated, the Jewish community suffered financial losses running to $7,000,000, or almost $500,000 daily. This loss has resulted from the almost complete halting of trade, commerce and industry, the suspension of traffic and the communications system and the closing of Tel Aviv's port. It includes the halting of citrus exports.

The Arab economy has suffered indirectly from the loss of trade and diminished purchases of farm produce. Numerous commercial connections were maintained between Jewish and Arab merchants in the neighboring towns of Tel Aviv and Jaffa, so that Arab losses were inevitable.

March 17, 1947

TERRORISTS OR PATRIOTS

Gruner and Three Others Hanged; 400,000 Palestine Jews Penned In

By The Associated Press.

JERUSALEM, Wednesday, April 16—An official announced today that Dov Bela Gruner and three other convicted members of the Irgun Zvai Leumi organization were hanged at Acre Prison at dawn.

They were the first Jewish extremists to be executed in Palestine since the hanging of Shlomo Ben Youssef in August, 1938.

Gruner, a 33-year-old veteran of the British Army, was sentenced by a British military court, which convicted him Jan. 1 of having participated in an underground raid on the Ramat Gan police station last April 23. Two policemen were killed in the raid. Gruner was wounded and captured.

The three others executed were Dov Ben-Salman Rosenbaum, Eliezer Ben-Zion Kashani and Mordecai Ben-Abraham Alkachi. All were convicted of having possessed arms and whips when arrested the night four British soldiers were flogged in retaliation for the flogging of a Jew.

They also were members of Irgun Zvai Leumi. Authorities admittedly were apprehensive that the organization would start without delay a "blood for blood" retaliation.

The hangings occurred at the prison at the north end of Haifa Bay.

A short time before the executions British military authorities clamped a rigid security ring on most Jewish quarters in Palestine, putting approximately 400,000 Jews under house arrest.

Armored cars with loudspeakers awoke sleeping Jews in Jerusalem, Tel Aviv, parts of Haifa and a number of other towns and villages to announce the new curfew. Cars attempting to leave Jerusalem and Tel Aviv were turned back.

The security measures were the most rigid ever imposed by the British in Palestine.

Gruner asserted he was a prisoner of war and should be treated as one. He refused to appeal, and pleas by others other courts and to the Privy Council in London, Britain's highest court, were rejected.

Gruner's sister, Mrs. Helen Friedman of Lancaster, Pa., flew here from the United States several weeks ago to aid in the legal fight.

Irgun Zvai Leumi leaders have declared that Gruner would be honored as a martyr. British Colonial Secretary Arthur Creech Jones predicted last February that Gruner's death would be the signal for a new blood bath in Palestine.

April 16, 1947

Irgun Leader Skeptical of Solution For Palestine Through U.N. Inquiry

Beigin Says Only British Withdrawal Can Bring Peace—Willing to Suspend Terror During Study if 'Truce' Is 'Bilateral'

JERUSALEM, May 22 (U.P.) — Menahem Beigin, leader of the Irgun Zvai Leumi, expressed skepticism today that the United Nations would find an acceptable solution for the Palestine problem. He said peace would return only when the British withdrew.

The questions were sent to Beigin two weeks ago. His answers came back today. The questions and his answers follow:

Q. Do you propose to call a truce until the United Nations gives its verdict on the Palestine issue, irrespective of your claims of grievances? A. For an answer on this question please listen in to our broadcast tonight.

The broadcast said: "We have not rejected the appeal of the General Assembly of the United Nations. On the contrary, we made it clear that we were prepared to accede to it provided the enemy [Britain] accedes too. A one-sided truce, even for a short time, is inconceivable."

Attacks Motives

Q. Have you any faith in the inquiry now being conducted into the Palestine issue by the highest world tribunal? A. As submission of the matter to the United Nations was originally intended as a means of gaining time when Britain found her efforts to crush the Jewish resistance unavailing, and as the most superficial observer knows, considerations quite irrelevant to the issue will determine the attitude of the United Nations, our degree of "faith" in such an "inquiry" may be imagined. The question was wrong in describing the United Nations as the "highest world tribunal." It is not a tribunal. It is a political forum with all that that involves.

Q. With which of the two Jewish organizations — the Jewish Agency for Palestine and Peter Bergson's group—would you associate yourself more intimately, and why? A. Our demand is for the withdrawal of British forces and the British regime from our country and the transfer of government to a provisional Hebrew government. We are fighting for the achievement of these objects. Our attitude to all bodies is determined by the degree to which they support and propagate the fight for these objectives.

Q. There have been rumors of the unification of the Irgun and the Stern group. To what extent is this true, and what details would you care to impart? A. The rumors are incorrect.

Upholds "Retribution"

Q. Do you consider that retribution is morally damaging your cause? A. In precisely the same degree as bombing Germany was "morally damaging" to the Allies or the shooting of Heydrich was "morally damaging" to the Czechs. [Reinhardt Heydrich was the assassinated German "protector" of Bohemia-Moravia.]

Q. Do you see a prospect of understanding with Haganah on its submission to the will of the overwhelming majority of the Jewish community? A. We have repeatedly called on Haganah to restore the fighting unity that existed between us in 1945 and 1946 to carry out the "will of the overwhelming majority of the Jewish community" as expressed in elections at the last Zionist congress when some 95 per cent of the electors voted for resistance.

Q.—Do you recognize the moral leadership of the Chief Rabbinate and do you feel bound to obey its precepts? A.—The Jewish religion does not recognize the principle of ex cathedra statements. The Chief Rabbinate is an institution deriving its moral authority from the Jewish religion and Jewish tradition. Its recent pronouncements are demonstrably at variance with these precepts. If compelled to choose between the precepts of Jewish tradition and new precepts determined by secular political pressure, we, like all observing Jews, would choose the former.

Puts Peace Up to British

Q.—Ideology apart, do you realistically see a prospect of peace in Palestine in the coming ten years? A.—We do not like the fixing of terms. There will be peace when the British occupation regime and its armed forces leave the country.

Q.—If peace in Palestine is made a condition precedent to a new effort by the parties concerned to reconsider interim Jewish immigration, would you observe it? A.—The question rests on a false hypothesis. There is no "condition precedent" and also there is no such thing as "interim immigration."

Q. Would you give your blessing to the restoration of Chaim Weismann to the presidency of the Zionist Organization? A. It is not our custom to give blessings or withhold them on this or that political personality. As close followers of Jewish events, we should be surprised to see Weismann restored in view of the clear rejection of his policies by the last Zionist congress, which is the sovereign body of the Zionist Organization. For our part, however, we should be more pleased than otherwise if he should return, as we prefer the open defeatism and Quislingism of Weismann to the cloaked defeatism of the present Jewish Agency executive.

Claims Cut in Arab Attacks

Q. If the present state of insecurity were likely to lead to an Arab-Jewish conflict here, would you lay down your arms to prevent it? A. Our struggle has had the effect of reducing — indeed, eliminating the danger of serious Arab attacks on the Jews. The question is a strange one. Indeed, in the present phase, one factor calculated to encourage Arabs to attack Jews would be the laying down of Jewish arms.

Q. When the Irgun carries out a raid on a bank, is it done because of lack of money or for other motives? A. Money belonging to the enemy is a legitimate target of attack.

Q. If recognized Zionist leaders prove that the insecurity resulting from your operations is detrimental to (a) the chances of the United Nations' inquiry, (b) continued immigration and (c) world public opinion, would you reconsider your present attitutde of using force? A. The most striking of the whole string of false premises in the text of this question is contained in (c). We are understood all over the world. There would have been no inquiry by the United Nations if it had not been for our struggle rendering the British position untenable. The questioner has merely been influenced by British propaganda when he talks of "a state of insecurity" resulting from our operations. With 120,000 foreign British troops in this country, with foreign British naval units stationed in Palestine's waters to prevent Jews from entering Palestine, it is obvious who is causing insecurity in this country.

May 23, 1947

The Irgun and the Stern Gang

3 Slain on Zionist Vessel As Refugees Fight British

By GENE CURRIVAN
Special to The New York Times.

HAIFA, Palestine, July 18—After a prolonged battle at sea with a naval boarding party the largest contingent of unauthorized immigrants ever to reach Palestine shores arrived here today with three of their number dead and scores injured. The boarding party was badly beaten up but only three required hospital treatment.

The immigrants were immediately transshipped to the ferry-ship Ocean Vigour for deportation to Cyprus.

[Meanwhile, one British soldier was killed and seven other soldiers and one Jewish civilian were wounded in a series of bombings and ambushes by Palestine terrorists in a wide upsurge of activity.]

There were 4,550 men, women and children aboard the battered 4,000-ton ship which had its sides stoved in from being rammed by British destroyers when an attempt was made to beach her on the lower Palestine coast.

The battle was bloody and vicious and lasted for three hours early this morning. A broadcast from the ship to Haganah headquarters in Tel Aviv during the height of the fight said that one was dead at that time, five seriously wounded and 100 injured. There was no official confirmation of these figures.

Another death occurred during the voyage from France when a woman died in childbirth and was buried at sea.

When the ship arrived here she was a sorry sight. The passengers looked as though they had been through a major battle.

Among the spectators at port side were Justice Emil Sandstroem, chairman of the United Nations Special Committee of Inquiry on Palestine, and Vladimir Simitch, Yugoslav delegate. Both Haganah and the Jewish Agency for Palestine had made a plea that the committee members see for themselves what the immigrants looked like.

The arrival of this ship, the President Warfield, renamed the Exodus 1947, by Haganah, was the first since the committee came to Palestine.

The ship, a one funneled, three-deck ancient craft, tried to beach herself when she was approached by a destroyer near Rafah above the Egyptian border. The sea was rough and the destroyers had difficulty in drawing alongside. They finally rammed her from both sides and tore away a large portion of the port side, including more than half of the lower deck.

The entire ship was ringed with heavy wire netting to prevent a boarding party from getting aboard.

Boarders Repulsed at First

Of the fifty sailors in the boarding party, none could get on in the first attempt. The passengers lined the decks, throwing missiles, using tear-smoke fireworks, smoke bombs, steam jets and then fuel oil sprayed from high pressure hoses.

After all these failed and the boarding party was climbing aboard, the immigrants released heavy life rafts suspended above the top deck at a forty-five degree angle. These missed the sailors but dropped on the deck of one of the destroyers.

Once on board, after the side of the ship had been smashed in, the sailors ran into hand-to-hand fighting and some of them were temporarily "captured."

As the fight went on, it was necessary for the men on one destroyer to open fire with small arms when one immigrant threatened to decapitate a Navy man with an axe and another was about to fire a rifle. Both desisted when the destroyer fired.

Meanwhile the fight continued for the deckhouse and the immigrants finally surrendered when it looked as if one more ramming operation by the destroyers would sink the ship.

During the fight two sailors and one of the passengers fell overboard. They were picked up by the destroyers.

Radio Describes Battle

According to a series of radio messages from the President Warfield received early today at Haganah, headquarters in Tel Aviv, she first intended to make for Tel Aviv. But after the battle and the rammings the captain decided to head for Haifa because the vessel was taking water and there were several wounded on board.

The radio reported at 2:50 A. M.: "We are being attacked. Shots and tear-gas bombs are being hurled at us without warning."

Nearly two and a half hours later the radio announced:

"We have decided to stop resistance and transfer casualties to a destroyer. The sailors who captured our bridge are now our prisoners. We have disarmed them and thrown their guns into the sea."

A later broadcast claimed that fire was opened on the vessel without warning and that "destroyers rammed our ship and breached a hole in our hull with the full impact of their armor."

Still later the messages began to get desperate:

"Water is pouring into the engine room," one said. "Destroyers are around us and planes are over our heads. The number of British prisoners has reached thirty. We are in danger of drowning. We shall sail full speed for Haifa to save our people."

At 5 A. M., however, the radio reported that the pumps were working and that ship was hastening to Haifa with the wounded, some of whom could not be transferred to the bobbing destroyers.

Captain is Cooperative

It was reported unofficially that the skipper and crew of the President Warfield were Americans. The captain was Bernard Marks, a former merchant marine officer of Cincinnati. The British Navy said he had been very cooperative, once the fight ended, and took the ship into Haifa under her own steam.

Crew members who have been arrested include William Bernstein, first mate, of Los Angeles; Arthur Ritzer, ship's cook, of Brooklyn, and a former Guadalcanal marine, and Cyril Weinstein of New York.

One of the passengers was the Rev. John Stanley Grauel of Worcester, an Episcopal minister representing the American Christian Palestine Committee and a correspondent for The Churchman. His passport and papers were taken up and he will be returned to the United States.

When the immigrant ship arrived at the quay her passengers were singing the Zionist anthem "Hatikvah" although all their fighting spirit seemed to have gone.

There were infants and young mothers and there were aged, bearded men. All looked exhausted.

The ship was so badly battered on the port side that an entire section was missing, revealing tiers of bunks within. There was not even a place to set a gangplank and all the passengers had to be taken from the lower hold exits usually used for discharging freight.

VESSEL FIGURED IN WAR

Acquisition by New York Company Described in London

Special to The New York Times.

LONDON, July 18—Details of the acquisition of the American ship President Warfield by agents in New York for carrying unauthorized immigrants to Palestine were issued here tonight on the basis of official British reports.

The President Warfield carried passengers in Chesapeake Bay before the war. In 1942 she crossed the Atlantic and thereafter ferried troops between Britain and France. After the war the President Warfield was returned to the United States Naval Reserve, was sold to the Potomac Shipwrecking Company for $8,000 and returned to a berth not far from her former waters.

Two days after the sale a man who said he represented the Weston Trading Company of New York bought her for $40,000, intimating that she would be "entering the fruit trade."

When the President Warfield sailed from Baltimore on Feb. 25 this year her "official" destination was China. She had aboard a crew of young Jews, some of whom had been trained for Haganah.

On April 30 she arrived at Spezia, in northwest Italy, and on

June 12 she tied up at Marseille, France.

She began to make preparations early this month for the voyage—ostensibly "to Colombo." At Sète, near Marseille, she took aboard 4,000-odd Jewish passengers.

The Weston Trading Company had a one-room office at 29 Stone Street last March, and spokesmen for the company, when asked at that time about purchase of the President Warfield, were reticent about the destiny of the ship and equally so about the officials of the purchasing company.

The company has since moved and recent inquiries about its purchase of vessels for Mediterranean use have elicited no replies.

The President Warfield ran into difficulties before leaving United States waters. She hit a storm off the Virginia Capes and was towed into Norfolk for repairs.

The same company was reported in June to have bought the former Coast Guard cutter Northland for $50,000.

July 19, 1947

INCENSED BRITONS KILL 5 IN TEL AVIV TO AVENGE HANGING

Troops and Police Run Riot After the Finding of Two Slain Sergeant Hostages

By GENE CURRIVAN
Special to THE NEW YORK TIMES.

NATHANYA, Palestine, July 31

Incensed by the hanging by Jewish terrorists of two British army sergeants, whose bodies were found this morning, British military and police stormed into "off limits" Tel Aviv tonight and killed five Jews and wounded fifteen others.

Indiscriminate shooting was reported all over town.

Three of the dead were riding in a bus that was sprayed with bullets.

[According to the Associated Press the dead were two men, two women and a young boy].

The first fracas occurred in the Beach Cafe where a group of soldiers started to wreck the place. They were disarmed by Jews who outnumbered them ten to one. Shortly afterward the shooting started and windows were shattered right and left.

Witnesses said that the bus in which three persons died was fired on by either three or four armored cars that sped by with their guns blazing.

Residents Flee Streets

The sporadic shooting all over the place suddenly turned Tel Aviv into a deserted town with its streets emptied, its shops and cafes closed, its houses darkened and nothing moving but military cars, apparently looking for prey in this most serious attack on Jews in the Holy Land since the 1936-1939 Arab riots.

Earlier today it was feared that something similar might occur here in Nathanya because of the proximity of army camps and Haganah, Jewish military underground organization, ordered all males to remain in the town rather than be possible isolated targets on the roads outside. Even though the military assured the populace that there would be no reprisals, hundreds of women and children left today for places of sanctuary in settlements.

Late tonight Tel Aviv was cleared of troops except those on duty and everything seemed under control.

In Jerusalem sirens sounded after gunmen fired at a passing armored car in Zion Square but there were no casualties.

The police acknowledged tonight that troops and police had gone berserk in Tel Aviv, killing five persons and wrecking cafes, but added that none of the troops were on duty in the city. All troops on duty were called to barracks and had their guns checked and it was found that no rounds had been fired. Most of the shooting by the invading troops and police occurred in the vicinity of Allenby Road and Ben Yehuda Street and in the Hatikva quarter of Tel Aviv.

Order Pinned to Bodies

The garroted bodies of the two British sergeants who had been held as hostages by the terrorists since July 12 were found hanging this morning from eucalyptus trees a mile and a half southeast of here.

One body was blown to bits by a booby trap as an Army captain cut it down. The victims, who were hanged by order of an Irgun Zvai Leumi "field court" in retaliation for the hanging on Tuesday of three of their members, were Mervyn H. Paice and Clifford J. Martin. It was Martin's body that was booby-trapped.

August 1, 1947

ZIONISTS ANNOUNCE WAR ON TERRORISM

Leaders in Palestine Say They Plan Suppression Despite Internal-Strife Peril

Special to THE NEW YORK TIMES.

JERUSALEM, Aug. 4 — With more determination than they have ever shown before, Zionist leaders are planning a campaign to suppress terrorism that, they hope, will enlist the support of the entire Jewish community.

This campaign is being undertaken with the full realization that it may result very soon in serious strife within the Jewish community. Its general intent is to outlaw terrorists and, by economic and social pressure, to deny them freedom of movement and livelihood.

Among the measures proposed are eviction from industrial jobs and protection for former employers, the refusal of refuge in Jews' houses and active work to prevent the distribution of their propaganda, posters and pamphlets. Jews would also be expected not to lease premises to anyone who might use them for terrorist purposes.

Meanwhile Haganah is continuing its campaign to prevent terrorist actions. Its new program involves more than the use of its forces. Its general policy was decided on last Friday by virtually all leaders of Palestinian politics, religion, industry and labor. They hope their efforts will not be hampered by British Government actions that would destroy the growing anti-terrorist mood of the Palestine population.

Because of Palestinian Jews' feeling toward the British, the Zionist leaders are still not ready to cooperate with the British forces in repressing terrorism. The attitude, rather, is that terrorism has become a serious menace to the Jewish community and to the Zionist cause. On that theory, the Zionist leaders are seeking the cooperation of all organized bodies, particularly the anti-terrorist labor movement, in the coming campaign against the Irgun Zvai Leumi and the Stern gang. Efforts to enlist the man in the street will also be made.

Terrorists raided a branch of Barclay's Bank in Haifa today, killing a staff member and stealing $4,000. The dead man was a member of Haganah. Since the robbery was believed to be the work of the Irgun, the crime may further embitter relations between the two movements.

In Jerusalem the military blew up a house where a large cache of arms was found on Saturday. This indicated that the British were now prepared to blow up any house where a large arms cache was found in order to discourage cooperation with terrorists.

August 5, 1947

The Irgun and the Stern Gang

EXODUS REFUGEES BEGIN FORCED TRIP TO GERMAN CAMPS

British Transports Pull Up Anchor 20 Minutes After Deadline of Ultimatum

ZIONIST PROTESTS MOUNT

Palestine Groups Set Monday for Fasting and Mourning for Jews of the World

Special to THE NEW YORK TIMES.

PARIS, Aug. 22 — Some 4,300 defiant Jewish refugees, whose attempt to reach Palestine aboard the Exodus 1947 was foiled by the British, were on their way to Hamburg, Germany, tonight after having rejected the British ultimatum to debark in France by 6 P. M.

Twenty minutes after the ultimatum's deadline the three British transports Ocean Vigor, Empire Rival and Runnymede Park, lifted anchor and steamed out of Port de Bouc on the French coast toward Gibraltar and eventually Germany. It was estimated that the trip would take about two weeks.

[In Jerusalem the chief rabbinate and the Jewish National Council issued calls to Jews of the world to observe on Monday a day-long fast of mourning and protest against the deportation of the Exodus 1947 refugees to Germany.]

Correspondents who visited the ships this afternoon were told by the refugee passengers that the British would have to use force to get them to land at Hamburg. The refugees said they were determined not to set foot voluntarily in any country but Palestine.

A last-minute renewal of the invitation to debark in France, made by the subprefect of Aix-en-Provence, was rejected this morning, with thanks for French hospitality. [The United Press said that six refugees went ashore.]

Refugees Appeal to Truman

The French news agency said that the refugees aboard the Runnymede Park had appealed to President Truman to intervene to prevent the British from taking them to Germany. The refugees were said to have asked the "President of the most powerful nation in the world to aid them in the eleventh hour of their suffering."

French reports said that sanitary conditions aboard the three ships appeared to be satisfactory considering that the refugees had been living in close quarters for more than a month. Six days' supply of food was aboard. The British had begun loading operations yesterday in the almost certain knowledge that the refugees would reject their ultimatum.

A rumor that the refugees were being taken to the Belsen displaced persons camp in the British zone of Germany was, in effect, denied by the British Embassy here, which issued an announcement today describing two camps in the vicinity of Hamburg in which the refugees are scheduled to be housed.

"The first of the two camps was built in 1945 by the British Army," the embassy said, "to house liberated British prisoners of war. The second was built by the Germans in 1942 to house French and Polish workers. These two camps are the best lodging centers available in Germany at the present time."

The announcement added that as soon as the refugees' identities had been verified the British soldiers guarding the camps would be withdrawn and that in no case would German police be used.

Appeals will be made to Jewish relief agencies and the British Red Cross to supplement food rations and improve living conditions at both places, the embassy said.

August 23, 1947

BRITAIN'S PALESTINE POLICY TIED TO SOVIET AND ARABS

London Believes Troops Guard Against Communism and Middle East Unrest

By CHARLES E. EGAN
Special to THE NEW YORK TIMES.

LONDON, Aug. 9—Why does Britain stay in Palestine, subjecting a huge garrison of her own troops to continual guerrilla warfare from terrorist elements there?

This is a question frequently heard today as indications become clearer daily that the British people, their own Government and the Opposition in the House of Commons would like to rid themselves of an increasingly unpleasant burden.

The answer is not easily found in the variety of responses that come from interested sources. It seems to boil down to the fact that the British Government considers its 100,000 troops in Palestine a bastion against the encroachment of Russian ambition from the east and at the same time wants to be sure that, when it does retire, there will be peace, quiet and a sturdy military force on hand from the United Nations to preserve its interests in that area.

With regard to the reference of the Palestinian problem to the United Nations, it is pointed out that the decision, reached last winter well before the present critical dollar shortage confronted the nation, was even wiser than the statesmen at the time realized. Britain, now in a predicament that has brought her to her knees economically, is no longer able to spend the equivalent of $160,000,000 a year in order to maintain a force of 100,000 men in Palestine.

Officials feel confident that the United Nations will decide to relieve the British of responsibility for the mandate and will have to send an international armed force into the area to enforce its program. Britain can then withdraw her forces, confident that the area is protected against foreign aggression.

Britain's Motives

To say that Britain really has remained in Palestine for altruistic motives stemming from the fact that she has a mandate for the territory would be to blink the facts. Unofficially, the British concede that there are both military and economic reasons for her remaining in Palestine. They will add in an aggrieved voice, however, that the same interests that are compelling her to keep a major military force in so-called occupation are shared by the United States. They speak aggrievedly because they feel that the United States has let them down in contributing criticism but not any comfort nor material aid in carrying out their onerous duties in Palestine.

They complain that while British troops stand between the Arab and Jewish factions in attempting to keep the area tranquil, American extremists have been egging on Jewish terrorists to make trouble and financing unauthorized immigration.

Britons hold that the United States is just as much concerned in preventing a move by Russia into the Middle East as they are.

American Interests

On economic grounds, they insist that the United States has equal interests with the British in the long pipeline that carries petroleum from the rich oil wells of Iraq overland to the Palestinian port of Haifa.

The shifting of British troops on the checkerboard of international politics over the last two years has served to highlight Palestine as the current key point in the Middle East, Britons hold. In Egypt British troops have been withdrawn to the Suez Canal zone and there is the possibility of a complete withdrawal of all British forces even from there.

Under the terms of the Iraq-British treaty Britain maintains only a small garrison in that oil-wealthy country. In Iran Britain now maintains no garrison at all because, under her agreement with the Iran Government, she withdrew her military forces.

This leaves Palestine and the now independent state of Trans-Jordan as the only places in which she has a right to maintain any considerable body of troops.

In seeking for the motivations that add up to the present British stand, it is argued that oil in Iraq and Iran are vital to both British and American interests, so vital that Britain contends that she cannot leave the Palestinian area with an aggressive Russia perched on the fringes of the oil-bearing region.

A recent experience, when a Communist-inspired "Separatist" movement developed in Iran and that nation had a civil war on its hands, is offered as proof of the Soviet hunger for control in that region. The "Separatist" movement was overcome but there were anxious periods for Whitehall during the interval.

The British answer—it is entirely a British response—to the question as to why Britain takes so seriously the Arab threats of retaliation if Britain permits a Jewish nation to be set up in Palestine is that, in the long-term view, Britain would be considerably embarrassed in her world position if the Moslem world united against her.

This is particularly true, it is held, in view of the great upsurge of Arab nationalistic feeling over recent years.

August 10, 1947

BEN-GURION URGES ONE ZIONIST FORCE

Jewish Agency Leader Invites Terrorist to Disband, Join in Defense of Palestine

BY CLIFTON DANIEL
Special to THE NEW YORK TIMES

JERUSALEM, Oct, 16—An invitation from David Ben-Gurion, chairman of the Jewish Agency for Palestine, to the two Jewish terrorist forces to disband and join in defense of the Palestine Jewish community against Arab military threats was published in the Hebrew press today.

Replying to a question at a press conference in Tel Aviv yesterday, Mr. Ben-Gurion said that "no negotiations are in progress with the dissidents, and there will not be any.

"If the dissidents disband their organization and hand over their arms," he said, "they can individually volunteer for defense of the Yishuv [Jewish community] just as any other Jews who are found fit. As long as they fail to do so, resolutions of the inner Zionist Council in regard to them remain in force."

These resolutions called for a campaign to suppress the dissidents.

Despite Mr. Ben Gurion's denial of negotiations, there have been strong rumors of talks between leaders of the Haganah, the official Zionist militia, and Irgun Zvai Leumi, largest of the terrorist forces.

Gossip from the underground says that the Irgun leadership agrees to consolidation on condition that its officers be taken into the high command and that Irgun men be allowed to operate in Haganah as separate units. These conditions reportedly were refused.

Irgun is an offshoot of Haganah; it broke away to pursue a more activist policy and for a larger territory for the Jewish state than that accepted by the majority of Zionist The Fighters for Freedom of Israel [Stern group], smallest of the terrorist forces, was in turn a splinter from Irgun. During the war, the Sternists declined to follow Irgun in cooperation with British forces.

Haganah Sure of Reuniting

Last year, the high command of all three underground forces came into existence for joint operations against the British occupying forces. It was disbanded after the Irgun bombing of the King David Hotel, in which ninety-one persons were killed, and after the British had made damaging raids on Haganah arms and stores.

Haganah officers now are confident that in case of a serious Arab threat, the underground forces could be united again for common defense. A permanent reconciliation is doubtful, however, because of strong opposition by the Irgun and Stern groups to the partition of Palestine, which Haganah's political leaders have accepted. Both the Irgun and Stern groups demand a Jewish state in all of Palestine and Trans-Jordan and repeatedly have declared that they would oppose, although not fight, any Jewish government that accepted less.

Two Irgun members were sentenced to life imprisonment by a Jerusalem military court today after a six-day trial. Yossef Gavriel, 24, and Avraham Katalan, 22, were convicted of carrying arms in a room of the house at Kiryat Shaul where two British policemen were held for nineteen hours last June after being kidnapped from a swimming pool. The kidnapped men were found by an army search party.

October 17, 1947

ASSEMBLY VOTES PALESTINE PARTITION

By THOMAS J. HAMILTON

The United Nations General Assembly approved yesterday a proposal to partition Palestine into two states, one Arab and the other Jewish, that are to become fully independent by Oct. 1. The vote was 33 to 13 with ten abstentions and one delegation, the Siamese, absent.

The decision was primarily a result of the fact that the delegations of the United States and the Soviet Union, which were at loggerheads on every other important issue before the Assembly, stood together on partition. Andrei A. Gromyko and Herschel V. Johnson both urged the Assembly yesterday not to agree to further delay but to vote for partition at once.

The Assembly disregarded last-minute Arab efforts to effect a compromise. Although the votes of a dozen or more delegations seesawed to the last, supporters of partition had two votes more than the required two-thirds majority, or a margin of three.

The roll-call vote was as follows:
For (33)—Australia, Belgium, Bolivia, Brazil, Canada, Costa Rica, Czechoslovakia, Denmark, Dominican Republic, Ecuador, France, Guatemala, Haiti, Iceland, Liberia, Luxembourg, the Netherlands, New Zealand, Nicaragua, Norway, Panama, Paraguay, Peru, Philippines, Poland, Sweden, the Ukraine, South Africa, Uruguay, the Soviet Union, the United States, Venezuela, White Russia.
Against (13)—Afghanistan, Cuba, Egypt, Greece, India, Iran, Iraq, Lebanon, Pakistan, Saudi Arabia, Syria, Turkey, Yemen.
Abstentions (10) — Argentina, Chile, China, Colombia, El Salvador, Ethiopia, Honduras, Mexico, United Kingdom, Yugoslavia.
Absent (1)—Siam.

All other questions before the Assembly were disposed of a week ago, and it ended its second regular session at 6:57 P. M. after farewell speeches by Dr. Oswaldo Aranha, its President, and Trygve Lie, the Secretary General. The Assembly's third regular session is to open in a European capital on Sept. 21.

The vote on partition was taken at 5:35 P. M. Representatives of Iraq, Saudi Arabia, Syria and Yemen, four of the six Arab member states, announced that they would not be bound by the Assembly's decision and walked determinedly out of the Assembly Hall at Flushing Meadow. The Egyptian and Lebanese delegates were silent but walked out, too.

Sir Alexander Cadogan, representative of Britain, which is to terminate the League of Nations mandate over Palestine and withdraw all British troops by Aug. 1, made a brief statement after the vote. He requested the United Nations Palestine Commission to establish contact with the British Government about the date of its arrival in Palestine and the coordination of its plans with the withdrawal of British troops.

The United Nations commission, which will be responsible to the Security Council in the event that the Arabs carry out their threats to fight rather than agree to partition, will be composed of representatives of Bolivia, Czechoslovakia, Denmark, Panama and the Philippines.

This slate, which is understood to have the backing of the United States, was proposed by Dr. Aranha and approved without opposition after the Arab delegates had walked out.

The commission, as proposed by the partition subcommittee of the Assembly's Ad Hoc Committee on Palestine, was to have been composed of Denmark, Guatemala, Iceland, Poland and Uruguay, but the question was left to the Assembly because of United States opposition.

The Assembly, without discussion, also approved an appropriation of $2,000,000 for the expenses of the commission, which will take over authority in Palestine after the British terminate the mandate and will then transfer it to the "shadow governments" of the two states.

The walkout of the Arab delegates was taken as a clear indicationn that the Palestinian Arabs would have nothing to do with the Assembly's decision. The British have emphasized repeatedly that British troops could not be used to impose a settlement not acceptable to both Jews and Arabs, and the partition plan does not provide outside military force to keep order.

Instead, it provides for the establishment of armed militia by the two nascent states to keep internal order and that any threats to peace by the neighboring Arab states are to be referred to the Security Council.

November 30, 1947

PALESTINE FIGHTING GROWS INTO MASS VENDETTA

By SAM POPE BREWER
Special to THE NEW YORK TIMES.

PALESTINE, Jan. 3—Fear and grief are both growing in Palestine as Zionists and Arabs kill each other in a struggle that hardly can be dignified with the name of war because it is more like a great mass vendetta.

Murder, reprisal and counter-reprisal gain momentum daily, while grief for the dead and fear of future horrors put a mark on more and more of the population.

There are Palestinians whose normal life is hardly affected, but by far the greater part of them are having to change their lives to fit the present grim crisis.

Mayor Israel Rokach of Tel Aviv, arriving in New York recently, said the foreign press was exaggerating the situation in Palestine. Its scale is exaggerated if it is called war, but it would be difficult to exaggerate the grimness of the present Palestine atmosphere.

The Irgun and the Stern Gang

There have been no "battles" in the sense of modern armies on a large scale, but there have been fights with as many as 400—almost a battalion—on each side, and automatic weapons, grenades and mortars are used.

Authorities say the main roads are open and they are protecting them—but few persons make the forty-mile ride down Palestine's principal highway from Jerusalem to Jaffa or neighboring Tel Aviv without being fired at unless they are Arabs (and many Arabs also are fired at by Zionists).

Risks Are Scattered

Government services even in Jerusalem itself are rapidly falling apart because Zionist workers are afraid to travel through the city and Arabs say if they are working there alone Zionist terrorists may bomb the building in which they are employed.

It is a situation where the risks of warfare are chopped up and scattered among the population instead of being concentrated in opposing areas.

The percentage of innocent bystanders out of the total population is large and, in accordance with tradition, these bystanders bulk large also among the casualties every day.

It is difficult to know who is doing the shooting. At first, those responsible were small disorganized gangs on the Arab side and small, illegal but organized forces on the Zionist side. The contagion has spread, and now it would be difficult to predict who might or might not join in the shooting.

The Arabs have produced large numbers of "national guards" who bear no insignia except a green armband but assume police powers and fire on those who contest them. These "guards" are tolerated by the police because Zionist bomb attacks prove the need for them.

The Zionists on their side still have Haganah, the members who bear arms. When possible, they avoid meeting the police and having their arms confiscated. The police seize some of the arms of Haganah members but also wink at others bearing them.

The enemy in this fighting is not somebody who wears a special uniform and is known to be in a certain area. He is somebody who may live in the next block or in the next house, who usually does not look much different though he differs somewhat in his habits and dress. The latter is not always true because Jews from the Yemen often are indistinguishable from Arabs.

The question of what lies behind the animosity is apparently simple, but really complex. It looks simple because both the Zionists and the Arabs want Palestine. It is complex because of the opposing factions' inability to reach any compromise, an inability that arises partly from fanatical determination by both parties not to yield, and partly from the Zionists' conviction that the great powers are on their side.

The respective directing forces are the Jewish Agency and the Arab Higher Committee. No outsider can say definitely what share either actually has in the present operations of its people, but each openly acknowledges a certain degree of responsibility.

The Jewish Agency, through its official spokesman, has defended the activities of Haganah, which is to be the official militia when the Jewish state eventually is formed.

Up to the present British authorities refuse to recognize Haganah officially on the ground that they cannot permit any armed force to operate here that is not under the control of British authorities as long as the British hold the responsibility for law and order.

Haganah Reprisals

Another element is that if the British recognized Haganah they would also have to recognize the Arab "National Guard" and the result would be two officially sanctioned armed forces that would undoubtedly fight each other while the British, in the middle, struggled to keep some semblance of order.

The Jewish Agency says the policy of Haganah is to carry out justified reprisals while seeking to avoid hurting innocent parties. Even so, innocent persons still suffer.

The Agency, on the other hand, disapproves the Irgun Zvai Leumi underground's reprisals, which normally take the form of an indiscriminate attack on a crowded cafe or bus station. On New Year's Eve an Agency spokesman formally condemned these attacks and disavowed any Agency or Haganah connection with Irgun.

The Agency also has deplored the Stern group (Fighters for Freedom of Israel), whose operations usually take the form of the assassination of an individual British policeman or soldier in retaliation for the deaths of Jews.

All three forces, however—Haganah, Irgun and Stern—are operating currently and it is sometimes so difficult to fix the responsibility for any special attack, though the groups concerned usually announce their identity through various channels.

On the Arab side there are two elements in the current fights: The "National Guard," which is under more or less responsible direction, and various lawless elements operating on their own.

As explained by Emile Ghory, a member of the Arab Higher Committee who is said to be the mainspring of the whole Arab defense organization inside Palestine, the Arab "National Guards" are under the direction of their local committees, but as yet have no central "general staff."

The Arab Higher Committee has an "emergency committee" dealing with the whole problem of arms and defense. In twenty-five of the principal Arab communities there are "national committees" vaguely responsible to the higher committee, but with broad local authority. Each of them has attached to it an emergency committee to deal directly with "emergency" questions.

Each Arab village has a local committee dependent on the nearest national committee and applying to the corresponding emergency committee for aid in getting the arms and ammunition needed for local defense.

Like members of the Haganah, the Arab "National Guards" are not recognized by the authorities, but are not molested unless they are found using their weapons.

Veteran police officers recently have told this correspondent that already the situation is almost out of hand and that it will get rapidly worse as the British forces move out.

Already British efforts are limited to trying to protect persons not participating in the hostilities, but even that is difficult. Guards on the British "security zones," which have been islands of relative safety, are being reduced already through the shortage of soldiers and soon are expected to be abolished.

All the British hope now is that they can prevent full-scale hostilities between the opposing groups until the United Nations assumes the responsibility for Palestine. After that it is difficult to see how chaos will be prevented. Mr. Ghory says only the cancellation of the partition scheme can avoid it, while Zionist leaders on their side assert they can keep the situation in hand.

January 4, 1948

---

200 ARABS KILLED, STRONGHOLD TAKEN

Irgun and Stern Groups Unite to Win Deir Yasin—Kastel Is Recaptured by Haganah

By DANA ADAMS SCHMIDT
Special to The New York Times.

JERUSALEM, April 9—A combined force of Irgun Zvai Leumi and the Stern group, Jewish extremist underground forces, captured the Arab village of Deir Yasin on the western outskirts of Jerusalem today. In house-to-house fighting the Jews killed more than 200 Arabs, half of them women and children.

At the same time a Haganah counter-attack three miles away drove an Arab force, estimated by the Haganah at 2,500 men, out of the strategic village of Kastel on a hill overlooking the Jerusalem-Tel Aviv convoy road. This village was captured after a six-hour fight during which it repeatedly changed hands. The Jews, who first seized Kastel last Saturday, had been forced out yesterday.

Tonight Fawzi el-Kawukji, commander of the Arab "Liberation Army," was reported, although without confirmation, to be leading large forces of Syrians, Iraqis and Palestinians in an attempt to retake Kastel. The Arabs were equipped with several French 75-mm field guns, many mortars and at least eight armored cars.

On the scene of this, the greatest Arab-Jewish battle to date, the Arabs claimed that 110 Jews had been killed yesterday. On the other hand, Jews said that Arab casualties ran into the hundreds.

In southern Galilee units of the Haganah in the besieged settlement of Mishmar Haemek, a model colony of Jewish Socialists, ended a two-day truce by breaking out and occupying three Arab villages, Abu Shusha, Abu Zureik and Naaieh.

Still other forces of the Haganah were reported to have evacuated Khulda and Deir Muheisan, villages just west of Latrun on the Jerusalem-Jaffa road, yesterday, and to have driven 600 Iraqis out of the near-by Wadi Sarrar camp this morning.

The capture of Deir Yasin, situated on a hill overlooking the birthplace of John the Baptist, marked the first cooperative effort since 1942 between the Irgun and Stern groups, although the Jewish Agency for Palestine does not recognize these terrorist groups. Twenty men of the Agency's Haganah militia reinforced fifty-five Irgunists and forty-five Sternists who seized the village.

This engagement marked the formal entry of the Irgunists and Sternists into the battle against the Arabs. Previously both groups had concentrated against the British.

In addition to killing more than 200 Arabs, they took forty prisoners.

The Jews carried off some seventy women and children who were turned over later to the British Army in Jerusalem.

Victors Describe Battle

The Irgunists and Sternists escorted a party of United States correspondents to a house at Givat Shaul, near Deir Yasin, tonight and offered them tea and cookies and amplified details of the operation.

The spokesman said that the village had become a concentration point for Arabs, including Syrians and Iraqi, planning to attack the western suburbs of Jerusalem. If, as he expected, the Haganah took over occupation of the village, it would help to cover the convoy route from the coast.

TERRORISTS OR PATRIOTS

The spokesman said he regretted the casualties among the women and children at Deir Yasin but asserted that they were inevitable because almost every house had to be reduced by force. Ten houses were blown up. At others the attackers blew open the doors and threw in hand grenades

One hundred men in four groups attacked at 4:30 o'clock in the morning, the spokesman said. The Irgunists wore uniforms of a secret design and they used automatic weapons and rifles.

An Arabic-speaking Jew, the spokesman said, shouted over a loudspeaker from an armored car used in the attack, that Arab women and children should take refuge in the caves. Some of them, he said, did so.

Arab Snipers in Hills

"Within two hours," the spokesman said, "the village was under control.

He conceded that many of the attackers had become casualties— four dead, seven seriously wounded and thirty slightly wounded.

A Jewish plane today dropped six bombs near Enab police station and damaged a wireless mast. Six other bombs fell in open ground. Another Jewish plane yesterday bombed Beersheba in the Gaza district, killing a 12-year-old Arab boy.

Yesterday at Tiberias a three-week-old local truce was broken by a sudden outbreak of sniping. Three Jews and three Arabs were killed, nine Jews and five Arabs wounded.

In a general effort to reduce violence, the British Army ordered a curfew on all nonofficial road traffic from 6:30 P. M. until 5 A. M., to begin Sunday, in a large part of Palestine. The districts affected are Galilee, Haifa, Samaria, Lydda and rural Jerusalem and Bethlehem.

Apart from the fighting at Kastel and Deir Yasin the police today reported twelve Jews and seven Arabs killed, and nineteen Jews and nine Arabs wounded in widespread incidents. One British soldier was killed.

April 10, 1948

HAGANAH, IRGUN UNITE FOR ACTION

By GENE CURRIVAN
Special to THE NEW YORK TIMES.

TEL AVIV, April 27—The Haganah, Zionist militia, announced today that it had put into effect a secret pact with Irgun Zvai Leumi covering all future operations.

There was no mention of the Jaffa campaign in the Haganah announcement but it was understood that the Haganah would continue its hands-off policy unless Tel Aviv were attacked. The Jaffa action, initiated by Irgun Zvai Leumi without the consent of the Haganah, has been deplored by the Jewish Agency for Palestine.

Almost simultaneously the British warned Irgun Zvai Leumi forces now attacking Jaffa to withdraw their forces. The directive was sent to Mayor Israel Rokach of Tel Aviv who forwarded it to Irgun Zvai Leumi.

April 28, 1948

CUNNINGHAM GOES AS MANDATE ENDS

British Commissioner Boards Cruiser Off Haifa — Jews Take Down Union Jack

By The Associated Press.

HAIFA, Palestine, Saturday, May 15—Britain ended her mandate over the Holy Land last midnight. Lieut. Gen. Sir Alan Cunningham, the last British High Commissioner, sailed from Haifa port, finishing British mandate guidance.

Sir Alan's departure from Palestine's richest port caused little excitement among the Jews, who control most of the city.

The British fired a few rockets and searchlights spotlighted the cruiser as it steamed from the harbor.

Wearing the uniform of a British Army general, Sir Alan walked down a few steps of dock into a launch that took him to the cruiser Euryalus.

Upon getting into the launch, he turned and looked soberly up across the docks. There stood an honor guard of the King's Company of Grenadier Guards and Royal Marine commandos

The launch pulled away amid the slap of hands on rifle butts. Puffs of smoke and the small, hollow explosions of a 17-gun salute drifted in to shore from the cruiser outside a breakwater.

Preceding Sir Alan into Haifa was Lieut. Gen. G. H. A. Macmillan, British commander.

As he arrived earlier at Haifa airport, Sir Alan took the salute of a picked fifty-man company of the Palestine police. Then he walked over toward his car, stopping to chat quietly and shake hands with Jewish Mayor Shabatai Levi and Arab Vice-Mayor Haj Ta Er Haraman of Haifa.

His route to the dock was guarded carefully. No crowds were along the way. It lay mainly through Arab quarters, most of whose population had fled a few weeks ago after the Jews had seized control of the majority of Haifa.

The dock area was lined by Comet tanks. Near the dock gates, 200 or 300 curious watched Sir Alan pass. Work stopped inside the harbor and in near-by offices and warehouses so that employes might witness the brief ceremony of his embarkation. About 100 yards away dockers loaded and unloaded ships.

Britain has ruled Palestine since she took it from the Turks in 1917. She has held the mandate, granted by the League of Nations, since 1923.

The first fruits of the Jews' blood struggle—200 Jewish women and children refugees—arrived in Haifa from the Lebanese border about the time the mandate ended. They huddled on the dark sidewalk outside the dock waiting for Jewish Welfare Committee buses to take them to shelter. They came from Chaneta, Mazuoa and Hilom. They were brought overland from those frontier settlements to Nahariya, a German-Jewish settlement on the coast, and then by tug and lighter into Haifa port.

They said the border was quiet now, but they had been under attack previously.

The end of the mandate also halted the British sea patrol against ships carrying unauthorized Jewish immigrants to Palestine. Jewish sources said it was expected immigration ships would begin to arrive soon. The Jewish Agency also is negotiating for the transfer of about 30,000 Jews, held in Cyprus detention camps since they were captured while trying to enter the Holy Land without visas.

Union Jack Is Taken Down

By DANA ADAMS SCHMIDT
Special to THE NEW YORK TIMES.

JERUSALEM, May 14—As Britain's last high commissioner in Palestine left Jerusalem today the Union Jack over Government House was hauled down and a Red Cross hoisted. A solitary bag-piper skirled the Highland lament as Sir Alan walked out of the official residence on Mount Zion for the last time.

Seventy-five minutes earlier the flag of the International Red Cross had replaced the Union Jack over the British Government's offices in King David Hotel, thereby making the building part of "neutral security area for refugees."

Sir Alan left behind "no successor authority" but an independent Jewish state whose army the Haganah had occupied Haifa, Jaffa, Tiberias, Safad, Beisan and countless villages. The Arab parts of Palestine are in chaos. Two hundred thousand Arabs have fled from their homes.

Sir Alan addressed the people of Palestine over the radio last night. "I have never believed that a seed of agreement between Jew and Arab does not exist," he said. "I am convinced that a solution to this problem is not to be reached through bullets or bombs * * * If unhappily conflict must come, there is yet time to insulate the Holy City from it. * * * Let peace for the Holy Land, which certainly must come, have its source in the Holy City to flow therefrom over the whole country."

Both Jews and Arabs agreed that Sir Alan was a man of good intent. But they also agreed that the British had failed in the function to which they devoted their greatest energy for twenty-eight years—that of police power. During the last five and one-half months of Sir Alan's administration about 3,000 Jews, Arabs and Britons have been killed and about 5,000 injured.

May 15, 1948

The Irgun and the Stern Gang

ZIONISTS PROCLAIM NEW STATE OF ISRAEL

THE JEWS REJOICE

Some Weep as Quest for Statehood Ends —White Paper Dies

HELP OF U. N. ASKED

New Regime Holds Out Hand to Arabs—U. S. Gesture Acclaimed

By GENE CURRIVAN
Special to THE NEW YORK TIMES.

TEL AVIV, Palestine, Saturday, May 15—The Jewish state, the world's newest sovereignty, to be known as the State of Israel, came into being in Palestine at midnight upon termination of the British mandate.

Recognition of the state by the United States, which had opposed its establishment at this time, came as a complete surprise to the people, who were tense and ready for the threatened invasion by Arab forces and appealed for help by the United Nations.

In one of the most hopeful periods of their troubled history the Jewish people here gave a sigh of relief and took a new hold on life when they learned that the greatest national power had accepted them into the international fraternity.

The declaration of the new state by David Ben-Gurion, chairman of the National Council and the first Premier of reborn Israel, was delivered during a simple and solemn ceremony at 4 P. M., and new life was instilled into his people, but from without there was the rumbling of guns, a flashback to other declarations of independence that had not been easily achieved.

The first action of the new Government was to revoke the Palestine White Paper of 1939, which restricted Jewish immigration and land purchase.

In the proclamation of the new state the Government appealed to the United Nations "to assist the Jewish people in the building of its state and to admit Israel into the family of nations."

The proclamation added:

"We offer peace and amity to all neighboring states and their peoples, and invite them to cooperate with the independent Jewish nation for the common good of all. The State of Israel is ready to contribute its full share to the peaceful progress and reconstitution of the Middle East."

The statement appealed to Jews throughout the world to assist in the task of immigration and development and in the "struggle for the fulfillment of the dream of generations — the redemption of Israel."

Plans for the ceremony had been laid with great secrecy. None but the hundred or more invited guests and journalists was aware of the meeting until it started, and even the guests learned of the site only ten minutes before. It was held in the Tel Aviv Museum of Art, a white, modern-design two-story building. Above it flew the Star of David, which is the state's flag, and below, on the sidewalk, was a guard of honor of the Haganah, the army of the Jewish Agency for Palestine.

As photographers' bulbs flashed and movie cameras ground out reels of the scene, great crowds gathered and cheered the Ministers and other members of the Government as they entered the building. The security arrangements were perfect. Sten guns were brandished in every direction and even the roofs bristled with them.

The setting for the reading of the proclamation was a dropped gallery whose hall held paintings by prominent Jewish artists. Many of them depicted the sufferings and joys of the people of the Diaspora, the dispersal of the Jews.

The thirteen Ministers of the Government Council sat at a long dais beneath the photograph of Theodor Herzl, who in 1897 envisaged a Jewish state. Vertical pale blue and white flags of the state hung on both sides. To the left of the ministers and below them sat other members of the national administration. There are thirty-seven in all, but some were unable to get here from Jerusalem.

At 4 P. M. sharp the assemblage rose and sang the Hatikvah, the national anthem. The participants seemed to sing with unusual gusto and inspiration. The voices had hardly subsided when the squat, white-haired chairman, Mr. Ben-

THE STATE OF ISRAEL

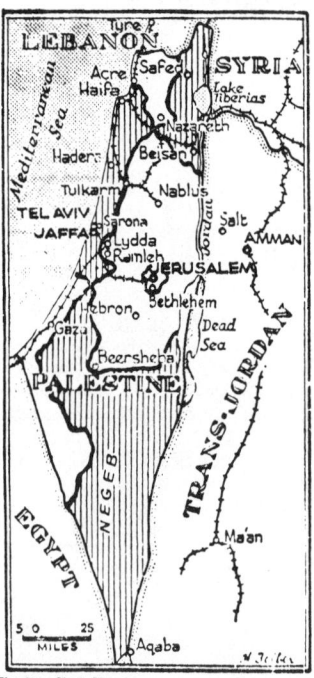

The New York Times   May 15, 1948

Although no boundaries were set by the Zionist leaders in their proclamation of independence, they recently declared that they controlled all the towns and villages in the area assigned to them by the partition resolution of the United Nations General Assembly (shown by shading).

Gurion, started to read the proclamation, which in a few hours was to transform most of those present from persons without a country to proud nationals. When he pronounced the words "We hereby proclaim the establishment of the Jewish state in Palestine, to be called Israel," there was thunderous applause and not a few damp eyes.

After the proclamation had been read and the end of the White Paper and of its land laws pronounced, Mr. Ben-Gurion signed the document and was followed by all the other members of the administration, some by proxy. The last to sign was Moshe Shertok, the new Foreign Minister and the Jewish Agency's delegate to the United Nations. He was roundly applauded and almost mobbed by photographers.

The ceremony ended with everyone standing silently while the orchestral strains of the Hatikvah filled the room. Outside, the fever of nationalism was spreading with fond embraces, warm handshakes and kisses. Street vendors were selling flags, crowds gathered to read posted bulletins, and newspapers were being sold everywhere.

As the sabbath had started, there was not the degree of public rejoicing that there would have been any other day.

The proclamation was to have been read at 11 P. M. but was advanced to 4 because of the sabbath. Mr. Shertok explained that the proclamation had to be made yesterday because the mandate was to end at midnight and the Zionists did not want a split second to intervene between that time and the formal establishment of the state.

In the preamble to the declaration of independence the history of the Jewish people was traced briefly from its birth in the Land of Israel to this day. The preamble touched on the more modern highlights, including Herzl's vision of a state, acknowledgment of the Jewish national homeland by the Balfour Declaration in 1917 and its reaffirmation by the League of Nations mandate and by the United Nations General Assembly resolution of Nov. 29, 1947.

It asserted that this recognition by the United Nations of the right of the Jewish people to establish an independent state could not be revoked and added that it was the "self-evident right of the Jewish people to be a nation, as all other nations, in its own sovereign state."

The proclamation stated that as of midnight the National Council would act as a Provisional State Council and that its executive organ, the National Administration, would constitute a provisional government until elected bodies could be set up before Oct. 1.

Israel, the proclamation went on, will be open to immigration by Jews from all countries "of their dispersion." She will develop the country for the benefit of all its inhabitants, it added, and will be based on precepts of liberty, justice and peace taught by the Hebrew prophets.

The new state, according to the proclamation, will uphold the "social and political equality of all its citizens without distinction of race, creed or sex" and "will guarantee full freedom of conscience, worship, education and culture."

The statement pledged safeguarding of the sanctity and inviolability of shrines and holy places of all religions. It also contained a promise to uphold the principles of the United Nations.

There was great cheering and drinking of toasts in this blacked-out city when word was received that the United States had recognized the provisional Government. The effect on the people, especially those drinking late in Tel Aviv's coffee houses, was electric. They even ran into the blackness of the streets shouting, cheering and toasting the United States.

May 15, 1948

TEL AVIV IS BOMBED, EGYPT ORDERS INVASION

AIR ATTACK OPENS

Planes Cause Fires at Port—Defense Fliers Go Into Action

BORDER IS BREACHED

Cairo Vanguard Takes Colony—Trans-Jordan Reports a Movement

By The Associated Press.

TEL AVIV, Palestine, Saturday, May 15—Air raiders bombed this all-Jewish city at about dawn today.

First reports said there were "some casualties" 'near the power and light station.

[Cairo reported that Egyptian armed forces had been ordered to enter Palestine. Arab armies moved from Trans-Jordan at 12:01 A. M. Saturday to "liberate the Holy Land from Zionism," said a Trans-Jordan communiqué reported by The United Press from Amman.]

Tel Aviv was under complete blackout all night but no sirens were sounded during the raid. Civil guards were alerted and fifteen to twenty ships in the port area moved out to sea.

The planes swooped over Tel Aviv little more than twelve hours after Jewish leaders proclaimed the existence of a new Hebrew state of Israel.

Some bombs fell in the vicinity of the power station along the Yarkum River near Tel Aviv.

Persons at the scene said there was one hit on or near the power station, causing "some casualties."

TEL AVIV, Saturday, May 15 (UP) — Some ten bombs were dropped on Tel Aviv by two aircraft described as bombers and accompanied by two small fighters. One Jew was killed and three were hospitalized. Jewish Army aircraft took to the skies a few minutes after the enemy planes whizzed over rooftops at an estimated altitude of 300 feet.

Several fires could be seen north of Tel Aviv but damage was believed negligible.

Anti-aircraft guns opened up throughout the port area and in Sarona, the Tel Aviv suburb that is the new capital of Israel.

The bombing planes, which disappeared toward the sea after the raid, were believed too small for Egyptian aircraft.

Cairo Orders Invasion Action
Dispatch of The Times, London.

CAIRO, Saturday, May 15—Egyptian armed forces have been ordered to enter Palestine, the Egyptian Government announced in a communiqué issued last midnight.

The communiqué said that their object was the "restoring of security and order in that country and putting an end to the massacres perpetrated by terrorist gangs against the Arabs and against humanity."

[Immediately after the announcement of the communiqué over the official radio, Sheikh Mohamed Mamoun el-Shennawy, rector of Al Azhar University and chief of the Moslem Theological Institute, said, according to The United Press: "The hour for jihad (holy war) has struck."]

Martial law came into force in Egypt at midnight. Premier Mahmoud Fahmy Nokrashy Pasha was named military governor.

Censorship became effective immediately on mail, newspapers, photographs and parcels entering or leaving Egypt as well as on broadcasts, phonograph records and plays.

Captains of merchant ships were warned in a proclamation that their vessels were liable to be searched in Egyptian ports.

[On the fighting front the Haganah reported the capture of Acre, near Haifa.

[At the same time Jewish and Arab forces were locked in battle at Bab el Wad, vital point on the Jerusalem-Tel Aviv highway.]

Lewa [Brigadier] Ahmed Mohamed Aly el-Hawary Bey is Egyptian Commander in Chief on the southern front. According to the pro-government newspaper Al Assas, the order to advance into Palestine was given yesterday at dawn and Egyptian columns have occupied El Auja, which is inside the Palestine border about thirty miles south of Rafah. Brigadier el-Hawary is a 50-year-old staff officer who graduated from the Royal Military College in 1916. His staff consists of four officers.

Al Assas declares that Chief of Staff to King Abdullah of Trans-Jordan is the Egyptian officer Miralai [Colonel] Saad el-din Sabur Bey. His staff also includes Air Force officer Squadron Leader Mohamed Nazih Hashad, who studied flying and reconnaisance in Britain and the United States.

King Abdullah is to be supreme commander of the Arab forces on three fronts. The King will be advised by a war council on which the staffs of all the Arab armies will be represented. This staff will coordinate operations on all fronts.

The Arab Governments have come to an agreement that the Syrian and Lebanese Armies should operate under a unified command on the northern front. Iraqi and Trans-Jordan troops will be responsible for the eastern front, while Egyptian, Saudi Arabian and Yemenite forces will operate on

---

ARAB ARMIES MOVE AGAINST JEWISH STATE

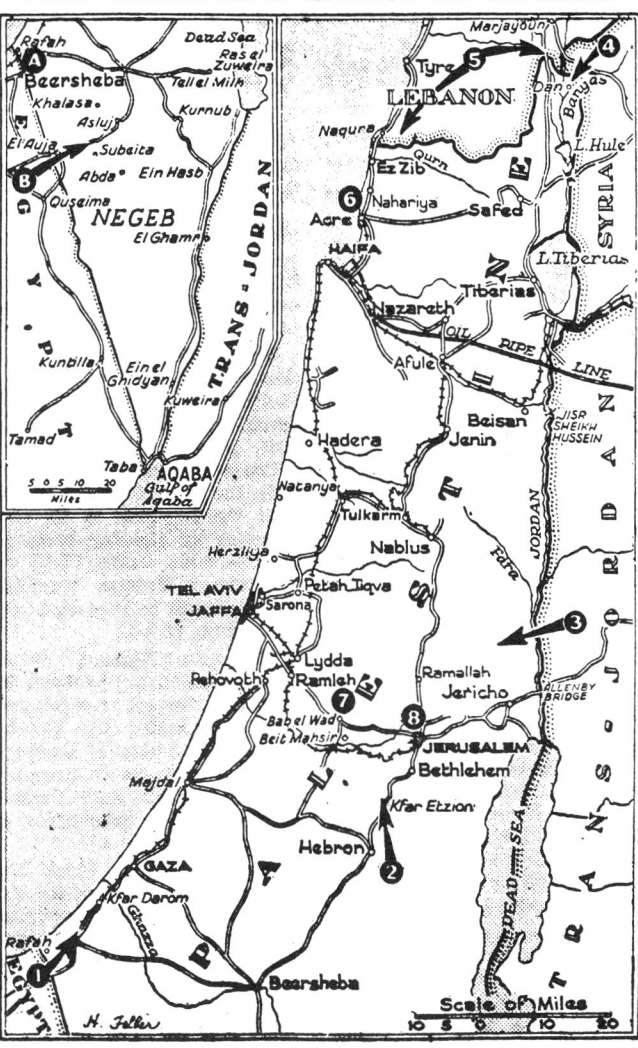

The New York Times — May 15, 1948

Egypt ordered her forces to enter Palestine and columns were reported to have pushed through Rafah (1 and A on inset) and El Auja (B). Trans-Jordan's Arab Legion had captured Kfar Etzion (2); most of the Legion was said to have pushed into the Holy Land (3). Syrians were reported attacking Dan (4) and Lebanese troops were poised along the border from Marjayoun to Naqura (5). Haganah captured Acre (6). Arabs and Jews remained locked in battle for the Jerusalem-Tel Aviv highway at Bab el Wad (7). Haganah seized control of the center of Jerusalem (8).

The Irgun and the Stern Gang

the southern front. Saudi Arabian armored forces are also placed under Egyptian command, but the name of the Commander in Chief was not revealed.

Syrians, Lebanese Poised

CAIRO, Saturday, May 15 (AP)—Syrian and Lebanese troops also are poised on the northern border of the Holy Land apparently awaiting an invasion zero hour expected shortly after midnight, a Damascus dispatch said. A late report said Dan was under attack.

Earlier accounts from Syria said that troops of Iraq and Trans-Jordan were moving up to Palestine's western frontier. However, there was no sign of military preparation in Amman, the capital of Trans-Jordan's King Abdullah, who has announced his leadership of the threatened invasion of the Holy Land.

Irregular volunteers from the various Arab countries already are fighting inside Palestine.

Many units of Egypt's regular army have been reported massed in Sinai, on the southern frontier of Palestine, awaiting orders. Estimates of their number have ranged from 6,000 to 16,000.

A state of emergency has been declared in Syria. The Syrian Parliament is expected to declare martial law later and appoint Premier Jamil Mardam Bey as Military Governor.

Lebanon also declared a state of emergency and the Government said firm measures would be taken to safeguard security. Five hundred additional men were called up for police duty.

An official communiqué announced last night the imposition of martial law throughout Iraq.

Movements of the Egyptian Army were screened by a strict ban on civilian travel into the Sinai Peninsula.

Syrian armor and infantry moved southward from Saida on the Lebanese coast after traversing the outskirts of Beirut, Damascus dispatch said. Lebanese army units were deployed all along the Palestine frontier from Merjayoun to Naqura on the Mediterranean coast.

30,000 Trained Arabs Massed

CAIRO, Saturday, May 15 (UP)—Upwards of 30,000 trained Arab troops had massed on three frontiers of Palestine for an invasion, according to observers here.

It was expected that Egypt, Trans-Jordan and Iraq would provide nearly all the troops for the Palestine invasion. Syria was expected to send a modest force and Lebanon a token one. It was reported that little Yemen, and also Saudi-Arabia, would send some men to show Arab solidarity.

About 3,000 men of the Trans-Jordan Arab Legion had been on duty with the British Army in Palestine as police.

Some of these made what might be called a token withdrawal when British troops evacuated southern areas of Palestine. But they turned back again after crossing the Allenby Bridge over the Jordan. Many of them never even pretended to leave and those who had been in Trans-Jordan all along are reported in Palestine now.

A United Press Aman dispatch said that the bulk of the Legionnaires crossed the Jordan hills and disappeared into the Judean Hills with their artillery, armored cars and a few light tanks. They entered an Arab-earmarked area.

League Declares State of War

DAMASCUS, May 14 (AP)—The Arab League's General Secretariat proclaimed last night that a state of war exists between the Arab countries and Palestine Jewry.

May 15, 1948

Irgun, Sternists End Underground Roles

By The Associated Press.

TEL AVIV, Palestine, May 15—Irgun Zvai Leumi and the Stern Group announced tonight that they would fight to bring all Palestine under the flag of Israel and that they would cease their underground activities within the new state.

Menahem Beigin, Irgun Zvai Leumi's Commander in Chief, said in a speech that his group would continue to fight for all Palestine until "the Jewish flag will fly over David Tower in Jerusalem and Jewish peasants will work in the fields of Galad." Galad is a historic Jewish site in present Trans-Jordan.

Mr. Beigin charged that the Arab states invading Palestine were "British paid agents." He warned the provisional Israelite Government not to be weak and to be "ready for further concessions" or a new underground would emerge.

May 16, 1948

IRGUN SHIP AFIRE IN TEL AVIV BATTLE WITH ISRAELI ARMY

Dissidents Fight Regulars Near U. N. Quarters Over Landing of Arms and Immigrants

HAGANAH GIVES UP BEACH

By GENE CURRIVAN
Special to The New York Times.

TEL AVIV, Israel, June 22—The Israeli Army and Irgun Zvai Leumi, a Zionist dissident band, waged a violent battle today when Irgun attempted to land a cargo of arms and ammunition within a few hundred yards of the headquarters of United Nations truce officials. The struggle ended with Irgun in control of the beach but with its ship ablaze and the cargo exploding sky high.

The area was evacuated when the ship caught fire. Pandemonium gripped the streets during the fight and civilians ran for their lives.

The struggle ended only after Irgun units of the Army had taken control and forced dissidents within the organization who were aboard the ship and on the beachhead to cease firing.

This was Irgun's second attempt in two days to land the cargo in Israel.

When the beached ship went ablaze the struggle was still raging up and down the beach. As it was believed that several tons of ammunition and explosives were aboard, all hotels and other buildings along the waterfront were ordered evacuated. Men, women and children ran into the bullet-raked streets and fled through alleys toward the center of town.

Within a few minutes there was a series of explosions that could be heard a mile away, but there was no major blast, as had been feared.

Where the hundreds who were removed are going to sleep tonight remains to be seen, as the entire beachfront area was taken over by Irgun.

[James G. McDonald, long a champion of a Jewish national home in Palestine, was named by President Truman to be the first United States diplomatic representative in Israel under an agreement for an exchange of missions. The head of the new state's mission in Washington is Eliahu Epstein.]

There was no official report of the casualties in the day's fighting, but this correspondent saw a number of dead and wounded. Some had been hit in front of the hotel where press headquarters had been established temporarily, others on the beach and a few in the landing operation. Some had been shot in the water as they leaped off the ship and others were hit by mortar fragments as they attempted to swim ashore.

Beigin Aboard Ship

The head of the dissidents, Menachim Beigin, was one of the last to leave the ship. He got off only because some of his "suicide" squads had gone back for him. When he was forced off, the other men were leaping into the sea as smoke billowed.

For an hour before, shore batteries had been pouring mortars into the vessel. For hours it was impossible to tell who was shooting at whom. It looked for a time as if everything was out of control.

In addition to the forces fighting on the beach, another unit clashed with one holding one side of a street. The Irgun commanders seemed to have no control over their men, who kept blazing away after having been ordered to cease fire or argued and screamed that they were going to fight to the last.

It took considerable talking and

TERRORISTS OR PATRIOTS

innumerable street-corner conferences, with bullets cutting through the air, before the situation was under control. Calm was restored when the Haganah, Zionist militia, which became the mainstay of the Army, agreed to leave the area and to permit the Irgun "regulars" to deal with their own dissidents.

The Army has given way to Irgun for strategic reasons. Later Army and Irgun men were fraternizing. It now apppears that the situation is completely in hand, with Irgun and the Haganah in agreement.

Although this blow-up may have political repercussions, the arms embargo was not violated.

In a broadcast tonight Mr. Beirin said the ship's cargo included 1,000,000 rounds of ammunition, 1,000 grenades 300 Bren guns, fifty German Spender guns, 4,000 aerial bombs, nine tanks and fifty anti-tank guns. He said that the Israeli Government had known of the ship's arrival and had agreed to a plan to have 20 per cent of the arms to go to Jerusalem and to divide the rest between Irgun men in the Israeli Army and the rest of the Army. He insisted that the Government was not telling the truth about the matter.

Meanwhile Moshe Shertok, Foreign Secretary of Israel, held a press conference in which he accused Irgun of having deliberately tried to break the truce by refusing to surrender its arms to the Government. He said the Government had planned to call on Count Bernadotte, United Nations Mediator, to arrange for the supervision of the cargo, but that Irgun had refused to surrender it. He held that the action taken by the Government was not only in line with its determination not to violate the truce but was primarily an action to defend the sovereignty and authority of the state.

Mr. Shertok acknowledged that the new state was "facing an internal crisis" but said it would see the matter through against "military and political anarchy." He charged that many Irgun members of the Army had deserted.

"The State of Israel was badly in need of arms, but it was better to see it [the cargo] go up in flames than to have it reach the hands of those ready to turn guns against their own state," he said.

To complicate matters, the Stern Group, which recently sent its men into the Army, announced it was going underground again rather than work with a state that fired on its brothers.

The Israeli Army-Irgun clash was one of the world's most fantastic battles. Brother fired on brother and neither side knew half the time who was the enemy. Every time Irgun attempted to bring in its landing craft, loaded with men, arms and ammunition, the battle reached new heights. Irgun men on the beach and on the ship gave covering fire, but the Haganah and the craft zeroed in from a dozen directions. The vessel landed twice but had to give up as the attempt was too costly.

Meanwhile other Irgun units in the Army broke through from the center of Tel Aviv to the beach. They came down near the Armon Hotel, where the Haganah was entrenched, and took up positions in a cafe next door and behind a park wall across the street.

When it looked as if a new battle was about to begin, Irgun and Haganah officers got together and called for a cease-fire. This lasted about five minutes, and then a mortar shell landed in the park across from the Armon, badly wounding an Irgun man. The firing was resumed, but word finally reached the Haganah men on the beach and there was quiet for a while except for certain belligerents who seemed to be carrying out personal feuds.

Irgun started the friction yesterday when it landed on the beach above Nathanya 600 men and 150 women. The Haganah was on hand to meet the vessel and to prevent the landing of arms and ammunition. After a battle on the beach the ship, an American LST (landing ship, tanks), withdrew and came in here just after midnight. She was fired upon heavily as she was beached.

In defiance of Haganah shore batteries, Irgun sent in a small landing craft with men and arms and took up positions on the beach. Haganah held its fire and let the first boat come in but placed a cordon around the beach.

A short time later Irgun sent in another landing craft and the battle was on.

June 23, 1948

BERNADOTTE IS SLAIN

HIS CAR AMBUSHED

Mediator Was Defying Warnings by Tour—French Aide Dies

STERN GROUP IS BLAMED

U. S. Consul Calls Terrorists 'Presumably' Responsible —Palestine Is Tense

By JULIAN LOUIS MELTZER
Special to THE NEW YORK TIMES.

TEL AVIV, Israel, Sept. 17—Count Folke Bernadotte, United Nations Mediator for Palestine, and another United Nations official, detached from the French Air Force, were assassinated this afternoon within the Israeli-held area of Jerusalem.

Count Bernadotte was on his way from the former British High Commissioner's residence in southern Jerusalem and was passing through the Katamon suburb when "Jewish irregulars" held up the Mediator's car.

[John J. MacDonald, United States Consul General in Jerusalem, reported to the State Department that Count Bernadotte and Col. Andre Pierre Serot had been ambushed, "presumably by the Stern Gang."

[Reuters quoted a Stern Group spokesman in Tel Aviv as having said: "I am satisfied that it has happened," but added that the spokesman was unaware whether members of the group were responsible for the killing.

[A Jerusalem dispatch quoted Dr. Bernard Joseph, Military Governor for the Israeli part of Jerusalem, as saying that all possible measures had been taken to apprehend the assassins.]

Truce Staff Announcement

A United Nations truce staff announcement here said:

"Count Bernadotte killed by two Jewish irregulars in hold-up 1700 hours today on way to New City of Jerusalem. In same hold-up United Nations senior observer Col. Andre Serot of French Air Force killed.

"Mediator was on tour of Middle Eastern capitals to bring security and peace to Palestine.

"Arrangements made bring bodies in Red Cross ambulance from Jerusalem to Haifa."

Dr. Paul Mohn, acting chief of staff and legal adviser to the central truce supervision board at Haifa, ordered that all United Nations flags over the buildings that it occupies be lowered to half staff.

The Israeli-controlled "Voice of Jerusalem" radio gave the following account of the assassination of Count Bernadotte:

He was traveling in a car from Government House to Katamon. A jeep with three armed men approached the vehicle and automatic fire opened at the Mediator's car. Count Bernadotte was seriously injured and the French colonel was killed outright. The Count died shortly afterward.

Colonel Lundstroem Unhurt

The radio statement added that Gen. Aage Lundstroem, Count Bernadotte's chief of staff, in the same car, was unhurt. Col. Frank Begley of the United Nations Secretariat was slightly injured.

Numerous wall placards appeared recently in Jerusalem and Tel Aviv over the imprint of Fighters for the Freedom of Israel (Stern Group), declaring that Count Bernadotte should "get out" of Israel as he had failed properly to enforce the truce. One cartoon showed a huge boot kicking the Count.

When he held a news conference recently in the Belgian Consulate General at Jerusalem, two jeeps carrying young men and women of the Stern Group picketed the entrance with large signs. One said: "Stockholm is yours. Jerusalem is ours." The other advised him to clear out. If it is proved that the Fighters for Freedom group had any connection with the slaying, it undoubtedly will provoke rapid action by the Israeli military administration in Jerusalem.

Under the indeterminate position of Jerusalem, pending the solution of its future constitutional status, the Stern Group operates freely in the Israeli areas and, like the Irgun Zvai Leumi, maintains its own private army camps and separate status.

Although the Irgun announced recently an agreement with Dr. Joseph, to accept the authority and discipline of the statutory Israeli authorities, the Stern Group up to now has not reached any such arrangement. Negotiations have been proceeding, however, in a desultory way for some time.

In Tel Aviv both the Irgun and the Stern Group have dissolved their military formations and their members have joined the regular Israeli defense army.

September 18, 1948

The Irgun and the Stern Gang

2 STERNIST CHIEFS REPORTED FLEEING; ISRAEL BARS GANGS

Yellin and Adviser Said to Have Vanished—Emergency Law Is Aimed at Terrorists

BUNCHE REACHES TEL AVIV

Shertok Extends Condolences on Bernadotte's Death, Tells of Search for Assassins

By JULIAN LOUIS MELTZER
Special to The New York Times.

TEL AVIV, Israel, Sept. 19 — The flight of Nathan Friedman Yellin, said to be the leader of the Stern group, and Dr. Israel Scheib, his political adviser, to an "unknown destination" was reported today as the Israeli Government continued its widespread search for the assassins of Count Folke Bernadotte, United Nations Mediator for Palestine, and his French aide, Col. André Pierre Serot.

Dr. Ralph J. Bunche, acting head of the United Nations Mission in Palestine, called on Israeli Foreign Minister Moshe Shertok and Foreign Office aides at the Israeli provisional capital outside Tel Aviv.

The Israeli Government soon will enact a new emergency regulation outlawing all underground or illegally armed organizations.

[Mr. Shertok told Dr. Bunche that the Government already had passed the special regulations, The Associated Press reported. These regulations gave sweeping powers to the Government to "take action against terrorist organizations, their members and accomplices."]

As the Stern group [Fighters for the Freedom of Israel] announced in Jerusalem its dissolution as a separate military organization and the entry of individual members in the Israeli defense army, word reached this correspondent from usually accurate sources that Mr. Yellin left Palestine on Thursday, using forged travel documents and in a disguise.

Mr. Yellin and Dr. Scheib formed recently a shadow faction within the Stern group that was pledged to ultra-extremist action. A number of "elite killers" joined this faction, it is stated. Israeli authorities presumably are planning their eradication.

Dr. Scheib's whereabouts are not known nor can it be ascertained definitely whether he has left the country. When this correspondent tried last Thursday morning to speak to Mr. Yellin about another matter, he was told by an aide, "He left just this morning and will not be back in town for a considerable period."

When this correspondent last saw Mr. Yellin in a Tel Aviv street about three weeks ago, the Sternist had dyed his bristly moustache to an ochre brown color so that even the skin beneath had been stained. Mr. Yellin said: "No one will rule Jerusalem except us."

[The Stern group newspaper Mivrak published Sunday on its front page a denunciation by the group's central committee of what was termed the "base government" of Israel and demanded the liberation of those seized in the Government's round-up, The Associated Press reported.]

An official Israeli announcement stated tonight that more than 100 of the suspects rounded up during Saturday's police and military operations to apprehend the assassins had left Jerusalem this morning under an armed escort for further interrogation elsewhere in Israel. It was rumored that they had been taken to a coastal area camp.

[A combined dispatch from United States correspondents in Jerusalem quoted an Israeli Army spokesman as having said that the Government had transferred nearly 200 arrested members of the Stern group to Jaffa, where it was planned to absorb them into the Israeli Army.]

The curfew in Jerusalem was ended at 5 A. M. today after fifteen hours. Life in the city's Israeli areas has returned to normal. About 300 who broke the curfew were fined small amounts today.

Nevertheless, although the tension has subsided and the three main bases of the Sternists have been seized, Israeli military authorities posted guards outside the consulates of the three nations represented on the Truce Commission —the United States, France and Belgium. The Consuls General of the three nations received notes signed "Hazzit Hamoledeth," Hebrew for "Homeland Front." It was this fragment section of the Stern group, reportedly headed by Mr. Yellin and Dr. Scheib, that is said to have issued a communique yesterday claiming responsibility for the assassination.

Mr. Shertok received a cable today from United Nations Secretary General Trygve Lie acknowledging the former's message that drastic steps had been taken to track down those responsible for the slaying. Mr. Lie said that the Security Council had taken note of Mr. Shertok's statement and had asked to be informed of further developments. He added that the Security Council had asked Gen. Aage Lundstroem, Count Bernadotte's chief of staff, to institute a full inquiry into the circumstances of the shooting.

Dr. Bunche, attended by the new Chief of Staff, Brig. Gen. William Riley of the United States Marine Corps, and Dr. Paul Mohn, his political adviser, received from Mr. Shertok his personal sorrow and that of the Israeli Government at the death of Count Bernadotte. Mr. Shertok outlined the measures to be taken to root out those responsible.

He also described the special legislation being drafted, to be enacted within the next twenty-four hours. He pledged complete cooperation with the United Nations authorities here. Dr. Bunche expressed his satisfaction with the steps taken.

Dr. Mohn handed Count Bernadotte's last two letters to the Israeli Government to Mr. Shertok. One letter gave the ruling of the truce supervision board concerning the southern Palestine villages of Hatta and Haratiyeh, which are under Israeli control and block the Egyptian Army's main lateral supply line inland from the coast. The board said that, contrary to Egyptian assertions, the villages had been occupied by Israeli forces before the beginning of the truce.

The second letter regulated the use of Egyptian and Israeli supply roads in this area. It permitted the Egyptians to travel between 10 A. M. and 4 P. M. daily and the Israelis between 3 A. M. and 9 A. M.

Mr. Shertok took strong issue with Dr. Bunche over the latter's statement yesterday that remarks made by Mr. Shertok at a news conference Thursday were "not calculated to discourage reprehensible acts of this kind."

Mr. Shertok said that all evidence pointed to careful planning of the assassination, for which the preparations had been completed by Thursday. He added that he had passed no stricture whatever on the Mediator's person but, on the contrary, had expressed the conviction that Count Bernadotte and his staff were "striving hard to discharge faithfully their difficult and often dangerous duties."

September 20, 1948

IRGUNISTS DISBAND, JOIN ISRAELI ARMY

Jerusalem Dissidents Submit to Government Ultimatum— 10 More Sternists Seized

By JULIAN LOUIS MELTZER
Special to The New York Times.

TEL AVIV, Israel, Sept. 21— After eleven years of underground activity and four months of public existence Irgun Zvai Leumi disbanded today. Its members began joining the regular army of Israel this afternoon.

Disbandment followed yesterday's ultimatum to Jerusalem's Irgunist commanders by Israeli military authorities demanding immediate, unconditional disbandment on pain of being branded a terrorist organization.

Another ten members of the Stern group—now proclaimed terrorists with their new offshoot the Homeland Front—were arrested today as the hunt for the slayers of Count Folke Bernadotte, United Nations Mediator in Palestine, continued in Jerusalem and Tel Aviv.

At a news conference in Jerusalem this morning an Irgunist spokesman said that the group had accepted the Israeli Government's "abrupt demand" to prevent "civil war" and unnecessary bloodshed. By noon truckloads of arms and ammunition, including mortar shells and hundreds of rifles and machine guns, were removed from an Irgun Zvai Leumi camp in southern Jerusalem to an Israeli army arsenal.

Col. Moshe Dayan, commander of the Sixth Brigade in Jerusalem, told reporters today that "only one army now operates in the Jewish areas of Jerusalem."

The twenty-four-hour ultimatum handed to the Irgunist commanders in Jerusalem consisted of seven brief clauses. It demanded that all eligible members of Irgun Zvai Leumi join the Israeli Army, hand over all arms and take the oath of allegiance. Non-compliance would provoke swift action, it was stated.

The Stern group's afternoon newspaper Mivrak in Tel Aviv was closed down by the authorities. The ten ranking members of the organization's central committee were reported to be still at large, however.

Dr. Ralph J. Bunche, acting head of the United Nations Palestine mission, has written to Moshe Shertok, Israeli Foreign Minister, saying that their week-end meeting was "very satisfying." It related largely to Count Bernadotte's murder. Dr. Bunche took the opportunity to give careful explanation that his reference to Mr. Shertok's statements at a news conference was "not intended to strike any note of recrimination nor to impute any motives to yourself or any other member of your Government which would associate you or them even remotely with the wickedly calculated assassination of Count Bernadotte."

The Executive of the Jewish Agency for Palestine urged the British Government today to free 10,500 Jewish "unauthorized" immigrants detained in camps in Cyprus where the situation was described as "tense and critical."

September 22, 1948

BRITISH RECOGNIZE REGIME IN TEL AVIV

By HERBERT L. MATTHEWS
Special to The New York Times.

LONDON, Jan. 29 — Britain granted de facto recognition to the State of Israel at 11 o'clock this morning. Behind the terse official language of the Foreign Office announcement lay many hopes and fears.

Most Britons concerned with public affairs wanted this to have happened much sooner. Palestine has always aroused mixed feelings in this country. It could not have been any different today when the strange history, with good and bad pages that began with the Balfour Declaration, received its logical conclusion in the acceptance of a state that Britons feel they had made possible. All that remains is to write the epilogue of de jure recognition, but that awaits other formalities.

"His Majesty's Government in the United Kingdom," read the Foreign Office communiqué, "have decided to accord de facto recognition to the Government of Israel. They hope to arrange with that Government for the early exchange of representatives."

January 30, 1949

Menahem Begin, on Extremism and Terrorism

Following are excerpts from a dialogue between Menahem Begin, head of the right-wing Likud Party and the man likely to be Israel's next Prime Minister, and Dr. William Berkowitz, rabbi of Congregation B'nai Jeshurun here. The discussion, last Nov. 15, was part of a program under the synagogue's institute of adult Jewish studies. The transcript was made by B'nai Jeshurun.

Rabbi William Berkowitz: Mr. Begin, you've said that people have called you dogmatic or an extremist. Do you feel you are dogmatic or an extremist? And if not, how do you respond to these charges?

Menahem Begin: I am not impressed with name-calling or these words. Yes, in the course of our struggle in the resistance during the 40's for our just cause there were people who called me an extremist. What do these words mean? We, the Jewish people, have been persecuted, tormented, tortured, and ultimately physically destroyed. What looking behind should we have done during the 40's when we heard from afar the trains running from all over Europe toward one destination: Death to the Jew, whether at Auschwitz, Treblinka, Babi Yar, and all the others where that process of killing a nation continued for five long years.

The world did nothing to try to rescue part of them. At the very same time, Eretz Yisrael, the Land of Israel, the land of our forefathers and of our children, promised by the British as a national home for the Jewish people, was now being subjugated by the British, and its gates were shut to the Jews. When does a human being need a home more than at the time when he is not only being persecuted but even physically destroyed?

And, therefore, we rose in revolt against the British. We did it to make it possible for the Jews to come home in conditions so that never again will

'That is the difference between the Jewish underground and those killers of the so-called P.L.O.'

a bloodthirsty, two-legged beast try to destroy a Jewish child. We had to fight for statehood, for national liberation, to insure the salvation of the Jewish people. Is this dogmatism? Or is this devotion to a just cause and the simple love for a people?

Our fight was for personal liberty and political independence. Otherwise, we would have been handed over to the Arab majority and then the end would have come to the existence of our people. This, then, was more than just a fight for individual liberty. It was the fight to save a nation from complete and utter physical destruction. This is why there hasn't been a fight for liberation as justified as ours in the annals of mankind.

Therefore, there is nothing dogmatic about it, but sometimes people make the mistake of assuming that if a group of men fought for liberation, then they believe in force. It is a complete mistake. Such men never believe in force. They believe in the great moral values of a free human being. Had they believed in force, they could not have started the fight and they surely couldn't have continued in it, because force is always on the other side—the side of the enslaver.

In this struggle, we were again the few against the many, the weak against the strong. We didn't believe in force. We do not. We detested physical force. We believe with Abraham Lincoln that right is might, not vice versa. Only because of this could we have continued fighting. For, at one point a certain equilibrium is created in history between the forces involved. On one side is brutal physical force; on the other side, faith in the justice of a human cause. With that equilibrium, one molecule of self-sacrifice decides the issue, tilting the scales, and the just cause wins. Nothing dogmatic about this.

Rabbi Berkowitz: How would you reply to those who have said that Menahem Begin is an extremist?

Mr. Begin: There is nothing extremist about this point of view. We have never been extremist. What did we want then? What do we want now? Let us take the attitude of the Arab countries vis-à-vis Israel.

The great Arab people, whom we respect, now have 21 sovereign states with an area of 12 million square kilometers. The land of Israel belonging to the Jewish people is a very small little country and yet the Arabs even want this country. Where is the justice in that? They should have 22 states, and the Jewish people should have no country whatsoever?

After 19 centuries of dispersion, persecution and humiliation, we cannot live without Israel. It was true, in previous generations, but it is especially true now, because on Israel depends our national security; and so, if you ask, Is it extreme to believe in the right of one's people to their own country?, I can only reply there is nothing extremist in this. For a Jew to love Zion is moderation because Zion is the faith of our people throughout the centuries that the land of Israel should be the land of the Jews.

The Irgun and the Stern Gang

If this means extremism, then we should ask ourselves, Are we considering the Bible when we use that word? Is the Bible extreme?

When we use that word, are we considering all the teachings, all the history, all the suffering of the Jewish people? Let us make it clear that whoever loves the Jewish people and the land of Israel and stands for that right is no extremist. He's just a patriot.

Rabbi Berkowitz: In presenting the questions to you in which I said that people at one time referred to you and the Irgun as dogmatic and extremist, by the same token some people also have accused you of being a group of terrorists, and my question is this: How do you counteract the accusation of some people, even those who may have believed in the principles you stated, that yours was a terrorist group?

Mr. Begin: Times change, and many people who called us those names then now admit that perhaps they were mistaken. This is why I was invited in 1967 to join the Cabinet—even by the very people who called us those names in 1947. And we worked together for three years in good understanding in a Government of national unity with these same people, with the disciples of Ben Gurion, the members of the Haganah, and Palmach.

Now about that horrible word "terrorism." That word stems from the Latin "terror," meaning fear. Indeed, there were people who used terror. The word in its political use stems from the French Revolution when there was in-fighting between the various groups which overthrew Louis XVI and tried to build a republic. All of them died under the guillotine, and that was called terror. In other words, people were arrested or their heads fell in order to terrorize and instill fear among the French.

A century later there was a group in Czarist Russia which used personal assassination of the Czar or a governor to instill fear in the Czarist Government. The Russian people considered them heroes. They risked their lives. They died on the gallows, and went on fighting because they said it is an oppressive regime. But admittedly they took upon themselves that word.

We never used terror. We never wanted to instill fear into anybody's heart. Ours was a classical fight for liberation. We never used personal assassination. In the Irgun, we carried out *military* operations against an overwhelming force of 100,000 British soldiers equipped with heavy guns, tanks and planes, and supplemented by 30,000 British policemen.

When we started our fight for liberation at the end of 1943, we were 388—less than 400 men. We finished with 10,000 fighting soldiers. Thousands of our members and those who helped us were arrested. Some were executed while others were deported to Africa to concentration camps. Therefore, that term "terrorist," doesn't fit us at all.

Otherwise, all the fights for liberation should be called, and should have been called, terror—including the war of liberation by the American people. They, too, rose in revolt, fighting arms in hand and gaining independence. No one would dare to call that terror.

I would like to add that if anyone should again use that word "terrorist," applying to our struggle for liberation, he takes upon himself the risk of dividing the fighters of the Jewish people, which include the Haganah, the Irgun, the Lechi, the volunteers of 1948 and the members of our victorious army. We never made a distinction between our fighting group and the others.

But if a person should repeat that word in connection with Jewish fighters, he takes upon himself the peril of artificially making a comparison with those who today are referred to as the so-called Palestine Liberation Organization.

We fought to save a people. They shoot in order to destroy a people. Look at the methods we used. We did whatever was humanly possible to avoid civilian casualties, sometimes at the risk of the lives of our own fighting men. We used to warn away any and every civilian, whether Jew, Briton or Arab, from the zone of danger in advance.

What do they—the so-called P.L.O.—do? They make the civilian population the target of their bloody attacks on men, women and children. They never express regret or sorrow when they have "succeeded" to kill an innocent Jewish man or woman or child. On the contrary, they rejoice in it. And that is the difference between fighters and killers. That is the difference between the Jewish underground and those killers of the so-called P.L.O.

Therefore, for the sake of the dignity of the Jewish people, and indeed of all men who fought for liberty, never use that cursed word "terrorist." Always make a distinction between authentic, humanitarian fighters for liberation and the terrorists who want to kill every man, woman and child in Israel. And that difference should always be remembered by every person and by every man who respects the truth.

May 27, 1977

BRITISH AWAIT BEGIN, ONCE A BITTER FOE

Israeli, on 'Most Wanted' Lists in Palestine, Starts Visit Today —Security Will Be Strict

By R. W. APPLE Jr.
Special to The New York Times

LONDON, Dec. 1—Three decades ago Menahem Begin was at the top of the "wanted" lists circulated by the British police in Palestine. He was denounced here as a terrorist and a murderer.

Tomorrow he arrives in London for his first official visit as the Prime Minister of Israel, and the British Government will welcome him with full honors. Prime Minister James Callaghan and other members of the Cabinet will spend about 12 hours with him, hoping to prod him toward a Middle East peace settlement.

Mr. Begin, who was born in Poland, led the Irgun Zvai Leumi, one of the extreme underground groups in Palestine, from 1942 to 1948. Disguised part of the time by a bushy beard, and calling himself "Rabbi Israel Sassover," the future Prime Minister evaded capture, despite a $15,000 price on his head.

He defied both the official Jewish leadership and the British Government, believing that only the use of terrorist tactics would force the "occupying forces" to adopt repressive countermeasures. The resulting cycle of violence, he hoped, would ultimately lead to a loss of British resolve.

British Headquarters Blown Up

A poster from that era, reprinted two weeks ago in The Observer, a London Sunday newspaper, described Mr. Begin in the flat, harsh language of the police blotter: "Thin, sallow complexion, long hooked nose, wears spectacles, flat-footed, bad teeth."

The most spectaular Irgun attack on the British came in July 1946 when a wing of the King David Hotel, then the headquarters of the British Secretariat for Palestine, was blown up. Ninety-one persons were killed and 45 were injured. Mr. Begin insisted that ample warning had been given to enable the building to be cleared and that only British pride kept the warning from being taken seriously.

On another occasion, Mr. Begin ordered that British officers be whipped because, as he later explained, "they were humiliating our boys by whipping them." And he decided to hang two British sergeants "to end the regime of the gallows" after warning that any more hangings of Jewish guerrillas would be avenged.

He got results. The British abandoned whipping and hanging.

The reaction in Britain was extremely bitter, however, with The Daily Express and other popular newspapers whipping up anti-Zionist sentiment, and some of the bitterness has persisted until this day. It is not at all uncommon to hear Britons of the older generation refer to Mr. Begin as "the murderer of British sergeants."

When he visited London in 1972, as

TERRORISTS OR PATRIOTS

leader of the opposition Likud alliance, there were large demonstrations, but no violence.

This time, there have been a few scattered protests, notably from the neo-fascist National Front, but no concerted campaign to stop the visit. Because of the possibility of demonstrations by Britons still outraged by Mr. Begin's tactics of 30 years ago or by members of some of London's dozens of Arab activist organizations, security for the visit is tight.

The name of the hotel to which the Prime Minister will travel after his arrival tomorrow has not been disclosed, and there have been unconfirmed reports that he will be moved several times during his six-day stay here. But the Government is taking great care not to offend the religious sensibilities of Mr. Begin, who is an Orthodox Jew. Any hotel where he stays, a spokesman said, will be no more than a 15-minute walk from a synagogue, and each will be provided with a full kosher menu by a Jewish catering company.

There is no sign of the old bad feeling between Britain and Mr. Begin in the plans for his visit. He will be greeted at Heathrow Airport by Dr. David Owen, the Foreign Secretary, and he will spend Saturday evening and most of Sunday at 10 Downing Street in a series of meetings with Mr. Callaghan and several other ministers.

On Monday, he will meet leaders of the Jewish community in Britain, on Tuesday he will talk with British members of Parliament with special interests in the Middle East and on Wednesday he will hold a news conference.

December 2, 1977

THE PALESTINIANS

PALESTINIANS SET 'LIBERATION' GOAL

Organization Is Formed to Mold Refugee Force

Special to The New York Times

BEIRUT, Lebanon, May 30—Three hundred fifty delegates claiming to represent one and a half million Arab refugees from Palestine vowed this week to "sacrifice our blood for the liberation of Palestine."

They were pledging allegiance to the Palestine Liberation Organization, established at the National Palestine Congress now meeting in Jerusalem's Jordanian sector. They rejected plans to resettle refugees in host Arab countries and declared: "Palestine is ours, ours, ours. We shall accept no substitute homeland."

A large emblem of the organization adorned the assembly hall in Jerusalem's new Intercontinental Hotel, where the congress convened.

The emblem carried a map of Palestine, including the "occupied" area that is now Israel. Inscribed across the map were the words, "We shall return."

Palestine 'Entity' Sought

Ahmed Shukairy, a lawyer from Haifa, is the leader of the new organization. He was chosen last January at a conference of Arab leaders in Cairo to establish what is now referred to as the "Palestine entity."

One plan suggested by him to accomplish this, called the Palestine National Charter, laid down general rights and obligations for Palestinians. It defined Palestine as the area that existed under the British mandate that ended in 1948.

A second plan proposed the liberation organization, which is to have an executive committee and an army of Palestinians.

Mr. Shukairy declared that the organization was based on "faith in the inevitability of the liberation of Palestine and the determination of Palestinians to mobilize all their material, military and spiritual energies toward this end."

The Palestine National Congress and the liberation organization are regarded as the first serious effort since the Palestine war 16 years ago to mold refugees into an effective force.

Although Arab governments agree in principle on the need for a Palestinian "entity," they are divided over the methods through which this should be achieved. Mr. Shukairy's plan falls short of some Arab and Palestinian expectations.

Mr. Shukairy, with the approval of a number of Arab governments, opposed the establishment of a Palestine government in exile at this stage.

May 31, 1964

Arabs Adamant Against Absorption of Refugees

By THOMAS F. BRADY
Special to The New York Times

JERUSALEM (Jordanian Sector), March 30—"The Arab states will not integrate the Palestine refugees because integration would be a slow process of liquidating the Palestine problem," Ahmed Shukairy, chairman of the Palestine Liberation Organization, declared in an interview today.

"Consequently, the refugees don't want to be integrated," he continued. "If there are no Palestinian people, there is no Palestinian cause. We can't conceive of a Babylonian cause today because there are no Babylonians. But we start from the premise that we will achieve the liberation of Palestine soon."

Arab refusal to assimilate the 1.3 million refugees now living in four host countries—Jordan, Syria, Lebanon and the Gaza Strip, controlled by the United Arab Republic—has been the subject of criticism from Israel and from the Western nations that have contributed to supporting the refugees for most of the 18 years since Israel came into existence.

Most of the critics would agree with Mr. Shukairy that the Arabs will not assimilate the refugees because they want to keep the Palestine issue alive. But few of them would be likely to agree that the refugees do not want to be assimilated, and almost none would accept the premise of "liberation of Palestine soon."

A Ready Answer

Indeed, questions about why the refugees persist in their hopes when Israel appears to have consolidated her position bring a different, but fairly standard, Arab retort:

"The Zionists remembered Palestine for 2,000 years. Why should we begin to forget in 18 years?"

When leaders of the Arab nations are asked why they do not assimilate the refugees, they reply that Israel and the West, not the Arabs, were responsible for the refugee exodus in 1948 from the part of British Palestine that became Israel.

These leaders ignore the rebuttal that the Arabs shared largely in the responsibility because their radio stations broadcast propaganda about Israeli atrocities designed to panic the refugees and that the refugees were told to flee.

This debating point matters little to the refugees, who remember chiefly that they were frightened of "the Jews" in 1948. They are not very precise about the sources of the news that frightened them, but one incident is still vivid to many: the massacre at Deir Yasin, a little village near Jerusalem where Arab civilians were killed.

The Arabs declare today that it was Israeli psychological warfare, not their own broadcasts, that produced the exodus.

Refugee attitudes toward integration have two aspects. Conversations and interviews in their camps indicate that virtually all of them want to return to their land. But almost all of them want jobs now, or better jobs than they have. There is every reason to believe they would welcome economic integration to the degree that it would improve their lot.

Peasants Need Land

The basic problem is that integration of the ordinary, uneducated peasant refugee requires land. In Jordan, the only host country that has given refugees the full privileges of citizenship, arable land is not available. The other Arab countries reserve what land they can develop for their own citizens, who want it badly.

Iraq, where there are almost no refugees, has the most favorable land-to-man ratio among the Arab states, but even there any significant assimilation of outsiders would require large-scale development of irrigation.

A Western ambassador in one host country said recently:

"The way to solve the problem is to stimulate Arab economic development to the maximum. If the Arab countries begin to need manpower, refugees will automatically be absorbed."

The psychological and emotional obstacles to integration are great. The refugees and

The Palestinians

their hosts feel strongly that they got a raw deal in 1948, and their self-esteem demands formal reparation, particularly because of the impression that the Israelis are cleverer, abler and more modern than the Arabs.

The Arab armies that moved against Israel in 1948, after the Arabs rejected the United Nations partition of Palestine, were beaten, and the defeat still rankles.

A Refugee's Opinion

One educated refugee said the other day in private conversation that he favored going back to the original partition plan, which would cost Israel 27 per cent of her present territory.

Asked if he agreed with Habib Bourguiba of Tunisia, whom other Arab leaders have denounced for suggesting negotiations with Israel on this basis, the refugee replied:

"Certainly not. Bourguiba wanted to negotiate. The solution must be imposed on Israel by the United Nations to show that Israel has been wrong."

The mystique of the refugees, fed by Arab broadcasts and by nostalgic talk, is based on the conviction that they have been grievously wronged. One commentator, Cecil Hourani, has written:

"In the dim twilight of the camps it is what has been lost that still beckons, not what can be done to take its place."

At a United Nations school in Gaza, a young refugee was learning the trade of an auto mechanic. He was scheduled to go to Sweden for on-the-job training. He spoke a little English.

Asked what he would do if he could get a permanent job in Sweden and if he met a girl he liked, he said: "I would come back. My country needs me."

Hamdi Hirzallah, 40 years old, a representative of the Palestine Liberation Organization, was present at the interview. A native of Beersheba, now part of Israel, he said with great intensity:

"I will tell you something, and I wish you would quote me. If they try to leave, we will stop them, by force if need be."

April 4, 1966

'TOTAL WAR' URGED BY PALESTINE GROUP

CAIRO, Jan. 14—The new leadership of the Palestine Liberation Organization issued a statement tonight that called for "total Arab popular war" against Israeli authorities.

The statement, made public by the Egyptian Government news agency, dashed moderates' hopes that the organization would take a softer line after the ouster Dec. 24 of its fiery chairman, Ahmed Shukairy. The organization says it represents all the Arab refugees from what is now Israel.

The statement said "armed struggle"—terrorism—by Arabs against Israeli occupation authorities on the Jordan River's west bank and elsewhere should be stepped up.

It said direct or indirect negotiations with the Israelis were out of question. The Cairo Government has said that contacts through the United Nations would be acceptable.

The United Nations' special envoy in the Middle East, Gunnar Jarring of Sweden, is expected here tomorrow with specific proposals toward a Middle Eastern settlement. His appointment was authorized by the Security Council resolution of November calling for peaceful settlement of the impasse. That resolution was rejected in tonight's statement by the Palestine Liberation Organization.

January 15, 1968

ARAB GUERRILLAS UNIFY COMMAND

8 Groups Will 'Escalate' Anti-Israeli Activities

By ERIC PACE
Special to The New York Times

CAIRO, Jan. 20—Eight Palestinian organizations announced today that they had formed a joint command to direct guerrilla operations against the Israeli authorities.

Making the announcement at a news conference here, a spokesman for the organizations said guerrilla raids would be "escalated" but would not be directed against Israeli civilians.

The spokesman, a Palestinian heart surgeon, Dr. Isam Sartawi, said the organizations, including the Syrian-backed El Fatah (Conquest), seek the "liquidation of the Zionist state" and would reject any attempts at a peaceful settlement of the Middle East problem.

Closed Meetings Held

For "purposes of military expediency," he asserted, Palestinian commandos would henceforth be divided into three corps, El Asifah (Storm) El Saiqa (Lightning) and Khaled Ibn Walid after a famous Arab commander of medieval times.

Addressing reporters in a shabby Cairo apartment, Dr. Sartawi gave no details as to corps strength, arms or future strategy. But gesturing with a muscular hand he said: "We believe only in our guns, and through our guns we are going to establish an independent Palestine."

The news conference, the first to be held here by Palestinian commando organizations, followed three days of closed meetings by the representatives.

The gatherings were part of the ferment that has been going on among militant Palestinians since last month, when Ahmed Shukairy was forced to resign as head of the best-known Palestinian group, the Palestine Liberation Organization. The group is recognized by Arab governments as representing all the Arabs of Palestine, most of whom have fled their homeland, which is now largely under Israeli control.

The liberation group did not take part in this week's meetings, at which, Dr. Sartawi contended, the majority of militant Palestinians were represented. The meetings were called by El Fatah, which has generally had the reputation of being the toughest of the commando organizations.

The groups taking part in the meetings this week in addition to El Fatah were: The Palestine Liberation Front, the Organization for Support Action, the Palestinian Revolution, the Palestine Revolutionary Youth Movement, the Vanguard for Palestine Liberation, the Palestinian Revolutionaries Front, The Popular Front for the Liberation of Palestine and the Vanguard of the Peoples War of Liberation.

January 21, 1968

FATAH WINS CONTROL OF PALESTINE GROUP

Special to The New York Times

BEIRUT, Lebanon, Feb. 4—Al Fatah, the commando organization headed by Yasir Arafat, has taken control, politically and militarily, of the Palestinian national movement.

This was the effect of the election in Cairo yesterday of a new 11-man executive committee of the Palestine Liberation Organization, which today elected Mr. Arafat as its chairman.

The results of the election, held in secret session, were announced by the Cairo radio.

The new chariman and executive committee, in contrast to the organization's first leadership headed by Ahmed Shukairy, introduce a style of leadership, emphasiizing action.

Speaking briefly after his election, Mr. Arafat promised to intensify the "armed revolution in all parts of our Palestinian territory to make of it a war of liberation." "Armed struggle," he said, "is the only way. We reject all political settlements."

Mr. Arafat, the soft-voiced leader and spokesman of Al Fatah, is generally known by his old pseudonym Abu Amar.

February 5, 1969

TERRORISTS OR PATRIOTS

An Arab Guerrilla Chief Emerges

By DANA ADAMS SCHMIDT
Special to The New York Times

AMMAN, Jordan—Dr. George Habbash, leader of the commando and political organizations behind the recent attack on an El Al jetliner at Zurich and the bombing of a Jerusalem supermarket a few days later, has emerged to explain his groups' preoccupation with spectacular blows against the Israelis.

Denying that such attention-getting exploits were conceived as a shortcut to his political objectives, Dr. Habbash, head of the Arab Nationalist Movement and the Popular Front for the Liberation of Palestine, asserted that he was aware that "even if we repeated this airliner business a thousand times," it would not affect the "liberation" of Palestine.

"We know very well that this can be achieved only by building up our popular army of guerrillas to fight the Israelis on a day-by-day basis," he said. "This will go on for many years to come, until we bring about a shift in the balance of power from the Israeli state to the armed Palestinian people."

Nevertheless, he maintained that there was military justification for the attacks on El Al jets because, he said, the airline's pilots fly combat aircraft and its planes carry troops in time of war, "and we are at war with Israel."

As for the supermarket explosion, he said it was "a direct reprisal for the murder of Abdul Mohsin Hassan, who was killed by an Israeli from the El Al plane after he had laid down his arms" in Zurich on Feb. 18.

Greek Orthodox Background

Dr. Habbash, a 43-year-old Palestinian who is Greek Orthodox—many Christian Arabs are active nationalists—is the leading figure in the Arab Nationalist Movement and the Popular Front. He has lived "underground" during much of the last 20 years because the movement's revolutionary aims make it anathema to all the Arab Governments, including those in Cairo, Damascus and Baghdad.

But as leader of the Popular Front he is tolerated by the Jordanian authorities and has opened a new headquarters a few blocks from that of his fellow "freedom fighter," Yasir Arafat, head of Al Fatah, the other principal guerrilla group.

Colleagues said "the doctor" had not spoken with a foreign journalist for years.

A heavy-set, round-faced man with a mustache, he wore a tweed jacket over a warm sweater against the cold in his office, which still lacked a telephone as well as heat. He greeted his midnight visitors with a smile and then smoked cigarettes incessantly as he discussed his problems in a detached, professorial manner.

He announced that the quarrel between his supporters and a faction headed by Nayef Hawatme, which had cost the life of one man and three wounded recently, had now been settled. Following mediation by the over-all Palestinian political organization, the Palestine Liberation Organization, the factions will observe a three-month truce and the rebellious left wing is assuming a new identity as the Popular Democratic Front for the Liberation of Palestine.

Grain Merchant's Son

Dr. Habbash belittled the conflict, attributing it to "infantile leftism" that would be "all forgotten in a month." But others associated with the movement saw in the dispute an inevitable struggle between the practical-minded old campaigner who puts Palestinian nationalism and results ahead of socialism and theory and the fiery young idealist who is more concerned with Marxism-Leninism and with fomenting social revolution than with the Palestinian cause as such.

Dr. Habbash was born in Lydda, the son of a grain merchant. He was at school in Jerusalem in the last years of the British mandate in Palestine after World War II and could observe the methods of such Jewish groups as Stern and Irgun Zvai Leumi as they fought the British and early Arab nationalist organizations.

In May, 1948, he was studying medicine at the American University of Beirut when the British withdrew from Palestine and the Israelis and the Arabs clashed. Hurrying home, he arrived in time to accompany an exodus of women, children and old men—through searing heat with a minimum of food and water—to the Jordanian lines at Ramallah. Some died on the way.

For George Habbash it was a turning point. He began organizing politically among Arab students. His first group was called Vengeance.

On completion of his studies he moved to Amman and established a clinic whose financial difficulties were matched by its popularity among the poor, to whom it gave free services. But in 1957, when King Hussein was nearly overthrown by supporters of President Gamal Abdel Nasser of the United Arab Republic, Dr. Habbash was suspect and moved to Damascus.

There he established another clinic and married a cousin who bore him two daughters.

Again he got into political trouble when the Baath Socialists took power in 1963, so he fled to Beirut and went underground.

Under Dr. Habbash's direction, the Arab Nationalist Movement was focused on Palestine at first. Socialist ideology and involvement in pan-Arab politics came later as his far-flung university connections opened branches in Damascus, Baghdad, Kuwait and Aden, among others.

Allied With Other Leftists

In most situations the Arab Nationalist Movement has worked in political alliance with other leftist groups, including Nasserites, Baathists, Communists and assorted Socialist.

The movement's commandos merged with two smaller groups to form the Popular Front for the Liberation of Palestine, which had about 2,000 members before the internal struggle. A large proportion of former officers gave its operations a touch of professionalism.

Last May, while Dr. Habbash was convoying a large shipment of arms across Syria, he was arrested by the Syrian Baathist regime, which accused him of planning to use the arms against it. Six months later, while he was being transported from one prison to another, four of his men disguised as military policemen daringly kidnapped him.

In his absence the ardent young extremist Mr. Hawatme, a Jordanian, had taken over. He was one of those who asserted that the Arabs lost in 1967 because of the basic corruptness of their bourgeois societies, even including those of the United Arab Republic, Syria and Iraq, and that a pan-Arab Marxist-Leninist revolution was the essential prerequisite to victory in Palestine.

In his interview Dr. Habbash said that his men were sensitive to references to them in the Western press as terrorists. "Terrorism," he said, "is what made of us refugees—what drove our people to the camps."

Asked what he proposed to do if the United States, Britain, France and the Soviet Union agreed on a political settlement, he observed that he had no doubt that the situation of the Arab Governments required a deal. But he doubted whether the great powers would give Jerusalem and Gaza back to the Palestinian people, and whether they would restore the Golan heights to Syria and control of the Suez Canal to Egypt. He suspected that they might agree to something like the Israeli proposal for a security belt along the Jordan River.

"For us, therefore," he added, "there can be no alternative to continuing to fight."

March 4, 1969

LEBANESE ACCORD SAID TO ENDORSE COMMANDO HAVEN

By DANA ADAMS SCHMIDT
Special to The New York Times

BEIRUT, Lebanon, Nov. 3—Lebanese and Palestinian commando negotiators announced tonight that they had reached "full agreement" on an accord to end fighting and discord between their forces in Lebanon.

Under the agreement, announced in Cairo, Lebanon was reported to have formally endorsed the presence of Palestinian commandos on her territory in return for a pledge by the commandos to "cooperate" with the Lebanese Army.

The terms of the agreement, which was reached by the Lebanese Army's commander in chief, Maj. Gen. Emile Bustani, and the commandos' chief, Yasir Arafat, were not made public. But authoritative sources said that the acknowledgment and pledge constituted the essential provision.

Link to Syria Involved

The main points in the agreement, the authoritative source here said, included the following:

First, from their stronghold in the Arkoub region where their presence now is admitted and permitted, the commandos can openly maintain the line of communications with Syria by road north to the regular border point in Massnaa. This route has been labeled the "new Arafat trail."

Second, from the Arkoub region the commandos can without fear of Lebanese Army interference operate across the Lebanese border to Israel. When, where, how often, and how much are questions that apparently would be covered by the term "cooperation" with the Lebanese Army.

But the commandos would not be allowed to establish

The Palestinians

Maj. Gen. Emile Bustani, right, commander of the Lebanese Army, arriving in Cairo Monday to open talks with Yasir Arafat, left, leader of the Palestine Liberation Organization.

Guerrillas' road link to Syria is to be maintained through Massnaa (cross).

bases outside the Arkoub region, according to the authoritative report on the accord. This is what they especially wanted, and abandoning this objective would be a large concession.

The agreement followed a 13-day military test between Lebanon and Al Fatah commandos, and the reported terms clearly reflect a compromise.

President Charles Helou would surely have preferred to have the commandos withdraw entirely from Lebanese territory. The commandos apparently demanded unlimited freedom of operation.

Each side can be expected to assert that its military success provided the basis for the agreement. The commandos said at the last minute that their forces in the south, in Arkoub, made contact with their forces in the north, near Rasheiya.

Lebanese officers are reported to believe that their army successfully stood up to the commandos' challenge by keeping them out of the south central plain and stopping them at Rasheiya.

Status in All Arab Lands

Political leaders also are said to believe that it was an achievement in that there was never any indication that the country — half Christian and half Moslem—was in danger of falling apart.

The Palestinian commandos represented by Mr. Arafat, who is chairman of the Palestine Liberation Organization, now have agreements and formal standing in all the Arab countries around Israel.

November 4, 1969

Israel Toughens Penalties to Counter Guerrillas

By JAMES FERON
Special to The New York Times

JERUSALEM, Nov. 5 — The Israeli military government is imposing a new level of punishment on Arabs in the west-bank area and the Gaza Strip to compel them to take a stand against the Arab guerrilla movement.

As a result the Arab population of nearly a million in the areas occupied by Israel since the 1967 war is caught between the guerrillas and the officials.

Hints of a tougher Israeli policy have come from leading officials in recent months. Further evidence has become apparent in recent weeks and the Israelis have now confirmed the policy in informal but authoritative discussions.

The main instrument of the new policy is the practice of blowing up houses as a means of administrative punishment in the occupied areas.

Until several weeks ago, occupation officials sought to limit this practice to homeowners or occupants who had either participated in sabotage or who had assisted others engaged in subversion.

Now the Israelis are also blowing up the dwellings of Arabs who they feel are reasonably likely to have known about acts of terrorism committed in their area or who were reported by others to have been involved.

It is seen by the Arabs as a form of collective punishment, and only one of several forms. Another is the seizure of Arab property, which has become frequent recently as group punishment.

In Hebron this week, for example, the security authorities seized 26 Arab shops, 13 on each side of a street where an Arab terrorist had thrown a grenade at a military vehicle earlier in the day. It was the first time this sort of punishment had been applied.

A senior official of the military government said, "You can call it collective punishment; we call it defensive measures."

The local Arabs, meanwhile, are coming under more severe pressure from Palestinian Arab guerrillas, who have murdered 40 to 50 since the war for suspected collaboration with the Israelis.

But collaboration works both ways, and the Israelis see the Arabs of the occupied areas working with infiltrators and subversives more and more. "There has been more collaboration with terrorists recently," the official said.

"At least it is passive acceptance of terrorism, because the local people are afraid," he added.

"We are saying to them, 'if terrorism continues, life will be unbearable and our defensive measures will make life unbearable.'

"If it becomes unbearable, then they will have three choices: either fight the terrorists themselves or denounce them to us or suffer."

Villagers Were Murdered

Two recent incidents demonstrate the tougher Israeli policy. One occurred in Halhul, a village near Hebron, where about two dozen houses were blown up. The other was in Gaza, where eight structures were demolished.

In Halhul, five Arab villagers were murdered by a few months ago by Arab guerrillas for alleged collaboration with Israelis. At least two of them were with victims marked for execution.

A few weeks ago, an Israeli lieutenant was killed in the village while flushing suspected terrorists out of buildings. The terrorist was captured, but the Israelis said he died later of his wounds. Six structures were demolished in the operation, the Israelis said, and the rest were blown up the next day.

An Israeli official, explaining the demolition, said security authorities were disappointed at the lack of cooperation demonstrated by the village leaders in helping them track down the guerrillas.

Collaboration Is Charged

"It was a case of local collaboration with terrorists," the official said.

He denied that it was collective punishment and added that the term did not apply to the Gaza case either.

In Gaza, a Jewish merchant from Bnai Brak, a heavily Orthodox suburb of Tel Aviv, had gone into business in the market area of the Arab town with a local Arab. One day he was murdered by two gunmen.

The next day the Defense Minister, Moshe Dayan, visited the site, as he had Halhul, and after a short discussion it was decided to blow up eight buildings in the lane where the shop stands.

The Israelis did not contend that the owners had participated in the crime, but in the Israeli view they had seen the murderers while they were looking for their victim and had done nothing to assist him or the Israelis in their investigation.

Israeli security authorities say they continue to believe that the demolition of houses remains an effective deterrent.

"We don't know what the state of affairs would have been without it," the official said.

Arab leaders in the occupied areas tell visitors that more than 7,000 houses have been destroyed since the war. The Israelis say the figure is only a fraction, a 15th or 20th, of that. But the Israelis count only homes destroyed as administrative punishment. In other words, the first six houses in Halhul would not be counted.

Postwar Action Excluded

Israeli authorities also mark the end of the 1967 war on June 28, rather than on the 11th, when the fighting ended. This means that bulldozing of Arab villages and town quarters is not counted. Three Arab villages were wiped clean in the Latrun area, for example, to insure Israel's retention of the valley. The destruction of the town of Qalqilya, also on the prewar Jordanian-Israeli border, was halted and the houses pushed over by Israeli bulldozers were later repaired in a postwar change of policy.

Two other towns east of Hebron, Beit Awa and Beit Mirsin, were also rebuilt after being demolished by the Israelis after the war. Hundreds of shacks in abandoned refugee camps far from the fighting also were leveled after the war.

An Israeli Army official said present conditions in the occupied territories had prompted the imposition of the "stricter measures." He recalled previous policies and said, "We retain the option to be more or less strict, as conditions warrant, in applying administrative punishment."

Schools Requisitioned

Another form of Israeli response is the requisition of Arab schools that have become centers of strikes and demonstrations. Last month a high school in Nablus was taken over after several closings. It is being adapted to military use.

The Israelis also deport Arab leaders who are considered by the military governor to have been engaged in organizing subversion and incitement. The Arabs say 90 west-bank leaders have been deported. The number of those whose deportation has been announced comes to several dozen.

Three Bedouin mukhtars, or chiefs, of the Taamara tribe were just deported for alleged involvement in recent sabotage.

The Israelis are putting pressure on the local Arab citizenry, they say, because they find they cannot operate effectively without local support. Arab guerrilla organizations also are worried because they see Arabs under occupation beginning to cooperate with the Israelis.

Arab guerrillas have killed 20 or 30 local Arabs in random violence, such as throwing grenades in market places, and have injured many hundreds that way, the Israelis say.

November 6, 1969

ISRAEL APPEALS FOR WORLD HELP IN PLANE ATTACKS

Cabinet Discusses the Crash Near Zurich—Urges Lines, Pilots and Nations Act

INCOMING FLIGHTS CUT

Several European Carriers Suspend Cargo Service— Swiss See Sabotage

By LAWRENCE FELLOWS
Special to The New York Times

JERUSALEM, Feb. 22—The Israeli Government today called upon governments, civil airlines and pilots' organizations to end the wave of terrorism that is resulting from the Middle East war and, it said, making civil airlines unsafe for travel.

The plea came out of a cabinet meeting that lasted through most of the morning. It reflected the rage and dismay that have swept over Israel since a Swissair jet airliner bound for Tel Aviv exploded and crashed yesterday after having taken off from Zurich.

Fourteen Israelis were among the 47 passengers and crewmen who died.

Arabs Retract Report

A spokesman for a splinter group of Palestinian guerrillas, the Popular Front for the Liberation of Palestine, General Command, said in Beirut, Lebanon, yesterday that his group had been responsible for the explosion. Later in the day, a spokesman for the group in Amman, Jordan, denied that the group had been involved.

Premier Golda Meir was reported to have said in the Israeli Cabinet meeting today that the fact that a terrorist organization would want to take credit for the disaster showed how far such groups had removed themselves from normal behavior.

"These organizations have put themselves outside the laws and morality of human society," Mrs. Meir was quoted as having said. "Only a very strong reaction from countries and civil aviation bodies will put a stop to those criminals and an end to their killings and destructions."

Hijacking to Algiers

Mrs. Meir will make a formal statement tomorrow in the Knesset, the Parliament, Michael Nir, the deputy government spokesman, said after the Cabinet meeting. It can reasonably be assumed that formal approaches are being made to governments, airlines and pilots' organizations, he added, although he declined to discuss details.

Israeli planes and passengers have been the target of terrorist attacks since July 23, 1968, when an El Al plane bound for Israel was hijacked to Algiers just after it had taken off from Rome. The last of the Israeli men aboard was released in August, 1968, as Israel released some Arab prisoners.

On Dec. 26, 1968, an El Al plane was attacked at the airport in Athens and a passenger was killed. The Israelis responded to this attack two days later by raiding the airport in Beirut and destroying 13 planes.

On Feb. 18, 1969, four terrorists attacked an El Al plane at Klöten Airport in Zurich, Switzerland, mortally wounding a trainee pilot. An Israeli security man aboard the airplane shot and killed one of the Arab attackers. The surviving terrorists were later sentenced to 12 years' imprisonment by a Swiss court while the Israeli was freed.

Last Sept. 8, two Arab youths threw grenades into an El Al office in Brussels, injuring an airline employee and a customer.

Grenade Killed Boy

Last Nov. 11, the El Al office in Athens was damaged by a grenade and a 2-year-old Greek boy was killed.

On Feb. 10 this year, three Arab terrorists attacked a group of El Al passengers in the transit lounge at Munich's airport as they were boarding a bus to the plane. One Israeli was killed and eleven persons were injured.

Yesterday, two hours before the Swissair plane exploded and crashed, an Austrian airliner carrying mail for Israel was rocked by an explosion, but landed safely.

The Israeli Cabinet discussed several courses of possible action today, the spokesman said, but for the moment chose to say nothing publicly apart from the approach to governments, airlines and pilots' organizations. The newspapers were demanding at least that much.

"The Arab states must be held primarily responsible for such murderous attacks, since they provide the support which makes them possible," the newspaper Davar said editorially this morning. "The injured countries would do well to draw the correct conclusion and act accordingly."

The newspaper Lamerhav insisted that all nations and international institutions should bring pressure to bear on the Arab governments that support the terrorist groups.

Outside Action Predicted

Al Hamishmar took a tougher line, suggesting that the Israelis would do best to rely on their own hand. "We shall take suitable measures to guard our links with the outside world," the paper said. "Those responsible for the murder will not escape serious punishment."

The Jerusalem Post said that other countries would be forced to act for their own good, because their citizens were being drawn into the Middle East conflict and murdered.

It will no longer be enough, The Post said, for other countries to denounce the terrorists

The Palestinians

as lunatics, and then hope they do not get further involved. The Post continued:

"When the first El Al plane was hijacked to Algiers, there was a stir of unease among the airlines and agreement was very nearly reached that the pilots would refuse to fly to any country that permitted hijacking and harbored the guilty men. On that occasion, the effort was frustrated by the French pilots association, under pressure by Air France, which has major interests in North African airlines. The Swiss air crew of nine that died yesterday might be alive today if the original decision had been carried out."

"The Greeks have done worse," The Post said. "After two attacks on El Al planes at Athens, they have made only meaningless gestures instead of trying the culprits they caught at the time. The Swiss reacted in more orderly fashion and sentenced three terrorists who killed the pilot on an Israel plane at Klöten Airport. Yesterday's act proves that this is not enough."

February 23, 1970

---

11 ISRAELIS KILLED IN ROCKET ATTACK ON A SCHOOL BUS

Most Victims Are Children in Ambush Near Lebanon —Arab Villages Shelled

By LAWRENCE FELLOWS
Special to The New York Times

JERUSALEM, May 22—Eleven persons were killed and 21 wounded, most of them children, when a school bus was ambushed this morning in Israel, about 500 yards from the Lebanese border.

No one escaped unhurt in the crowded bus, which was struck by four bazooka shells fired from a clump of bushes five yards from the road when the bus was about 20 yards away.

[In Beirut, a splinter Arab guerrilla group, the Popular Front for the Liberation of Palestine (General Command), claimed responsibility for the attack. A Lebanese spokesman said that 13 persons were killed and 32 injured when Israeli artillery shelled four Lebanese villages after the ambush.]

Israel Complains to U.N.

Israel lodged a formal complaint with the United Nations Security Council today, only three days after she had been condemned by the Council for an armored attack into Lebanon the week before.

This afternoon, the Deputy Premier, Yigal Allon, attended the funeral service in Safed for the children and warned the attackers and the Government of Lebanon, where they are presumably based, that the deed would not go unpunished.

"The arm of Israel's Army is very long, and its blows are heavy, and those responsible for this crime will pay for it," he said.

From the tracks leading away from the scene, there appeared to have been eight men involved, Israeli officials said.

Thrown Out of Bus

Eight of the dead were children. Two were teachers; one of them a woman. The driver of the bus was killed by the first of the rockets, which hit the front of the bus, just above his head, and glanced off.

One of the injured, a teacher, said that she had watched the driver's limp body sway from side to side as the bus rolled aimlessly along the road for about 60 yards before it came to a stop.

"I was thrown out of the bus," said Hava Yorav, a 23-year-old kindergarten teacher, who was taken to the hospital at Safed. "I saw children lying all over the road. I was afraid to move. I didn't know what would happen next. I didn't know what to do."

Israeli Army patrols searched the area on both sides of the border soon after the ambush, penetrating perhaps half a mile into Lebanon, but none of the assailants was found.

An Israeli officer, walking near the scene of the ambush four hours after it had occurred, stepped on a land mine and his left foot was blown off.

The bus had started from Avivim and was headed for the school at Dovev, picking up children and teachers along the way.

Special to The New York Times

BEIRUT, Lebanon, May 22—Israeli artillery shelled four Lebanese villages, killing 13 persons and wounding 32, half an hour after the fatal attack on an Israeli school bus, it was reported here. The villages that were attacked were Bint Jbail, Yarun, Aitarun and Blida. A Lebanese spokesman said that the dead included seven women and a boy.

Al Fatah, the largest Arab guerrilla group, criticized the attack on the Israeli bus as contrary to its policy of avoiding civilian targets.

May 23, 1970

Cross indicates where the Israeli bus was ambushed. Underlining marks villages in Lebanon that reportedly were shelled in reprisal.

---

4 Jets Hijacked; One, a 747, Is Blown Up

Arab Group Says It Took Planes—El Al Foils Move

Special to The New York Times

LONDON, Monday, Sept. 7—Four jets bound for New York with more than 600 persons aboard were hijacked over Europe yesterday, apparently by members of an Arab guerrilla group. Three of the flights were diverted to the Middle East; the fourth landed at London after a gunfight in which a hijacker was killed.

The United Arab Republic's Middle East News Agency reported early today that one of the four planes, a Pan American World Airways Boeing 747 jumbo jet, had exploded at Cairo International Airport, where it eventually landed. Everyone aboard had already left, the agency said. Spokesmen for the airline said the United States Embassy had confirmed the report.

The four hijackings all took place in the late morning or early afternoon, not long after the planes took off for New York—two from Amsterdam, one from Frankfurt and one from Zurich. The lines involved were El Al Israel Airlines, Trans World Airlines, Pan American and Swissair.

The hijacking attempt that failed took place aboard an El Al jet that landed early in the afternoon at Heathrow Airport in London with one of the two hijackers dead and the other, a woman, wounded. A steward and two other passengers were also wounded. The plane, with a change of crew, took off later for New York.

The three other flights were reported to have landed in the Middle East. The hijackings involved the following planes:

¶El Al's Flight 219 from Tel Aviv, with 148 passengers and 10 crew members aboard, which had been briefly airborne from Amsterdam when a young man and woman armed with hand grenades and a pistol tried to take control. They

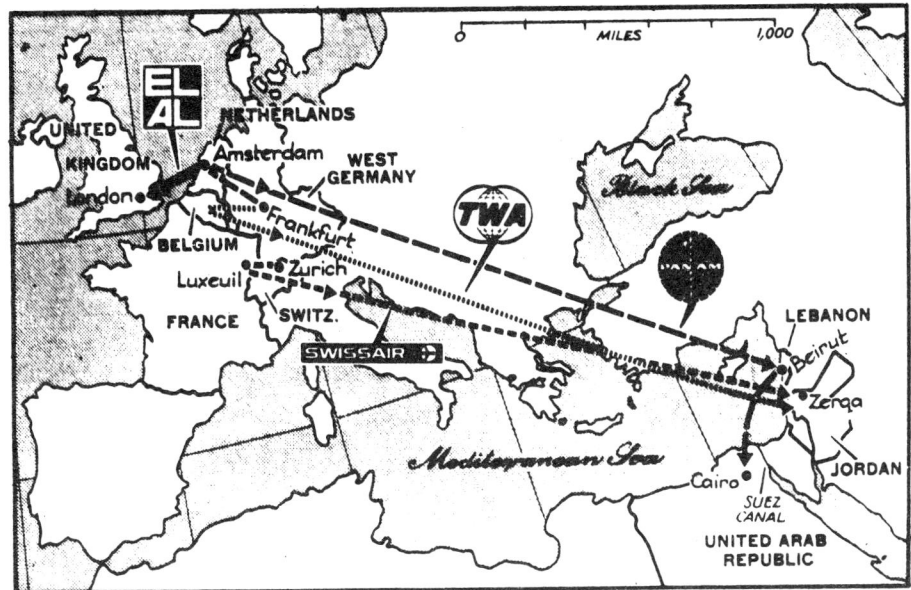

TERRORISTS OR PATRIOTS

Routes taken by the four airliners from points of hijacking toward eventual destinations
The New York Times (by Stephen Hadermayer) — Sept. 7, 1970

were overpowered by the crew and passengers as the pilot threw the plane into a steep dive to throw them off balance.

¶Pan American's Flight 93, with 152 passengers and a crew of 17, which was also hijacked shortly after take-off from Amsterdam's Schipol Airport. The 747 was on the last leg of a flight from Brussels to New York. There were two unidentified hijackers involved, Pan Am said. The plane landed at Beirut, Lebanon, an airline spokesman said, about 11 P.M. **(5 P.M. New York time), and,** after refueling and taking seven more "associates" of the hijackers aboard, took off 2½ hours later for Cairo.

¶T.W.A.'s Flight 741, an around-the-world flight, which was ordered by an unidentified man to reverse course and fly to the Middle East less than 15 minutes after its take-off from Frankfurt with 141 passengers and a crew of 10. The Boeing 707 landed at what an airline spokesman in New York called "a forlorn desert airstrip in Jordan."

¶Swissair's Flight 100, with 143 passengers and 12 crew members aboard, which was diverted less than an hour after its take-off from Zurich. Refused permission to land at Amman, the DC-8 jet was reported to have landed at what was believed to be a military installation at Zerqa, about 15 miles northeast of the Jordanian capital.

Reports of Another Seizure

There were conflicting reports yesterday that a second El Al aircraft had been hijacked during a flight from Nicosia, Cyprus, to Tel Aviv and was on its way to a "secret airport of the revolution." This report was denied by the airline and Israeli officials.

A spokesman for the Popular Front for the Liberation of Palestine, the most militant left-wing Arab commando group, said later yesterday that the organization had conducted the four confirmed hijackings.

The spokesman, in Beirut, said that the American planes had been seized "to give the Americans a lesson after they have supported Israel all these years" and in retaliation for the United States peace initiative in the Middle East.

The Swiss plane was hijacked, the spokesman said, "in order to free our prisoners in Switzerland." This was a reference to the sentencing of three Arab commandos by a Swiss court last December for an attack on an Israeli airliner at the Zurich airport.

As for the El Al plane, the spokesman said: "We are fighting Israel; they are our enemy and we will fight them everywhere."

Account of the Struggle

The only one of the four hijackings for which any first-hand accounts were available was that of the struggle aboard the El Al jet that began 30 minutes after the plane took off from Amsterdam. The schedule for the 707 called for it to arrive at John F. Ken-New York at 2:35 P.M.

"It all started as we were completing the ascent from Amsterdam airport," said Mrs. Florence M. Krasner, a housewife from Cleveland, who said she was sitting just behind the pair of hijackers in the third row of the tourist-class section of the aircraft.

"The pair were aged about 24 to 25. The girl was beautiful, with dark hair that may have been a wig. I could not tell the nationality of either of them."

It was, according to El Al spokesmen, 1:17 P.M. (8.17 A.M. New York time), when in Mrs. Krasner's words, "The two of them stood up as the rest of us still had our safety belts on. The man had a small pistol and the girl was holding two hand grenades."

According to Mrs. Fay Shenk, another passenger in the tourist section, "The man suddenly leapt from his seat with a strange sort of animal bellow. He had a small pistol in his hand and rushed forward toward the first-class section and the flight deck. The girl also jumped up with a grenade in each hand and rushed after him. Next thing I heard some shots that sounded like a cap gun, but I discovered later that they were real bullets."

Although there were conflicting reports of precisely what had happened in the first-class section, all accounts agreed that an unidentified young man, either a security guard or a passenger, had grabbed the woman by the elbows and disarmed her. She was pushed to the floor and her hands and feet bound with string and a man's necktie.

The man with the pistol tried to push open the door to the pilot's cabin but was intercepted by a steward, Shlomo Vider. Shots were fired and Mr. Vider was wounded in the chest. According to another passenger, two more shots were fired by a second security man. The male hijacker was wounded and died before the aircraft reached London.

As the fighting broke out close to the cockpit door, "The plane started banking," said Paul Kaplan, 13 years old, of Philadelphia. "It sort of dived and everyone was screaming. Later we heard that this was to throw the hijackers off balance." The stewardesses, several passengers said, went up and down the aisles, calming the passengers and encouraging them to sing Israeli songs.

Officials at Heathrow Airport said that the pilot had sent a message to the control tower reporting the hijacking attempt and requesting permission to land, which was granted immediately. Police cars, fire trucks and ambulances rushed to surround the plane as it touched down. Security men and Scotland Yard officials were awaiting the Israeli plane as it taxied down the runway at 2:05 P.M. London time.

The passengers were taken off the plane for questioning and the police removed the body of the hijacker and took the young woman into custody. The London police announced soon afterward that both hijackers were Arabs.

An Israeli source in London said that El Al's security personnel believed the two hijackers had been unarmed when they boarded the plane in Amsterdam. "Their personal belongings were thoroughly checked and nothing was found," an Israeli official said. "The question now is, how did they get the weapons?"

Next Stop Uncertain

About 45 minutes after the El Al hijacking attempt, which airline spokesmen said had taken place over the North Sea, T.W.A.'s nonstop Flight 741 left Frankfurt for New York, where it was due to arrive at 3:05 P.M. Less than 15 minutes later, Capt. L. D. Woods, the pilot, said on the radio to Frankfurt: "We are being kidnapped." He was unable to name his new destination, but he later reported to Zagreb, Yugoslavia, that his destination was "the Gaza Strip."

The 707 jet, on the last leg of a round-the-world flight with stops in Los Angeles, Bombay, Tel Aviv and Athens, picked up 39 passengers at Frankfurt, the airline said.

On its flight back across West Germany, the hijacked plane was escorted for a while by United States Air Force fighters stationed in West Germany. The hijacking and the plane's immediate change of course, took place near the West German-Luxembourg border.

A T.W.A. spokesman in Frankfurt said the plane's new route had taken it over Munich, Zagreb and Cyprus before it had headed still further southeast. Contact with the plane was broken over Cyprus, he said. It was later reported to have landed at Amman.

At about the same time that the T.W.A. jet was leaving

177

The Palestinians

Frankfurt, Swissair's Flight 100 was taking off for New York from Kloten Airport in Zurich. It was due to arrive in New York at 3:50 P.M. The aircraft was over Luxeuil, France, near Dijon, an airline spokesman said, when a woman's voice came over the radio to announce, in Arabic and English, that the aircraft was in the control of the Popular Front for the Liberation of Palestine.

The pilot, Capt. Fritz Schreiber, continued to radio frequent reports to Zurich as the plane headed east over the Mediterranean. Late yesterday afternoon in New York, a Swisair spokesman said that the line had learned from Zurich that the plane had landed at Zerqa and that "all passengers are safe."

The Baghdad radio said the passengers on the Swissair plane and the plane itself would be held pending the release of the three commandos sentenced to 12-year terms by a court in Winterthur, near Zurich. They were sentenced in the machine-gunning of an El Al plane in February, 1969, at Zurich's airport, in which a crew member killed one of the attackers. Swissair officials refused to comment on the reported demands.

The Swiss Cabinet, after an emergency meeting in Berne tonight, announced that the passengers and crew were safe and that it would make no decision "until the situation is clearer." The Swiss television network predicted in a special program tonight that the Government would yield to the "blackmail." A commentator said that the Cabinet had no choice when it came to weighing the lives of the 155 persons aboard the plane against those of the three commandos.

Confusion on Landing Site

The commando group said in Amman that the T.W.A. and Swissair planes had both landed at a "revolution airport" in Jordan. Swissair representatives continued to say that their plane had landed at Zerqa, while a T.W.A. spokesman said he did not know the location of the "forlorn desert airstrip" at which the T.W.A. jet had landed.

The T.W.A. spokesman said that "Jordanian aviation officials" had assured the company "that everything possible was being done to expedite the swift and safe return of our passengers and airplane." He said that two T.W.A. executives were en route to Amman from Rome and Paris and that the airline had sent a cable to the Jordanian Government asking for its help.

Pan American's Flight 93, the Boeing 747, was about 90 minutes late in arriving at Amsterdam from Brussels, where it originated, and then in taking off for New York, where it would have arrived about 6 P.M. last night allowing for the delay, a spokesman for the airline said. The jumbo jet, which has a capacity of 362 passengers, was carrying 151 paying passengers and one infant, and a crew of 17.

About 45 minutes out of Amsterdam, at a point that an airline spokesman said would be about "the northern tip of the United Kingdom" on the flight's northwest track, the pilot said on the radio to Amsterdam and London that he was being forced to change course. He asked for navigational bearings for Beirut. The plane was later reported to be heading for Iraq, but did land at Beirut.

Airport officials there said the jet would fly on to Cairo after refueling, but the plane remained at the airport after taking on fuel. The officials said the hijackers were waiting to meet with a leader of the Popular Front for the Liberation of Palestine, who was on his way to the airport.

Instructions for the plane to continue on to Cairo, airport officials said, were relayed by telephone by Abu Maher, who was described as a deputy for Dr. George Habash, the leader of the Marxist group. They said that Abu Maher had telephoned from Amman to the control tower of Beirut's airport, where commandos were already installed.

Dr. Habash, whose group has made a specialty of hijacking and attacking airliners, advocates ridding the Arab world of American business interests.

It was reported that several airports refused to allow the 747 to land because they were not equipped to handle the giant plane. Airport officials at Beirut said that the commandos in the tower had tried to dissuade the hijackers from landing there because of this. A Pan American spokesman in New York, however, said that the 747 was "quite capable of landing at any airfield that can handle a 707," which is smaller. A 707 is 152 feet long, and 747 is 231 feet long.

Landing in Cairo Reported

A spokesman for Pan American in New York said that the 747 took off from Beirut at 7:37 P.M. New York time and that the two hijackers on the plane had been joined by "seven of their associates who boarded the aircraft in Beirut." By 9:30 P.M., Pan American said it had received confirmation of the plane's landing at Cairo, before the reported explosion.

In New York, Najeeb E. Halaby, the president of Pan American issued a statement on the basis of the reports from Cairo, saying: "The most important fact is that our passengers and crew are safe." He said that a Boeing 707 was en route to Cairo "to fly the passengers and crew immediately to New York."

The hijacked 747 was fully insured for $23 million, spokesmen said. The 747, first put into commercial service by Pan Am in January, is the world's largest commercial aircraft. It weighs 355 tons and stands more than six stories high at the tail, with cruising speeds of 584 miles an hour.

September 7, 1970

ARABS BLOW UP 3 JETS IN DESERT AFTER TAKING OFF PASSENGERS

260 ARE RELEASED

Guerrillas Still Detain 'About 5' Women as Israeli Soldiers

By JOHN L. HESS
Special to The New York Times

AMMAN, Jordan, Sept. 12—Palestinian commandos blew up the three hijacked airliners today and announced that they were holding 40 passengers as prisoners of war for the exchange of captives of "imperialist and Zionist powers."

The rest of the 300 persons originally held were released unhurt and some left the country.

A spokesman for the Popular Front for the Liberation of Palestine said that the 40 hostages were nationals of the United States, Britain, West Germany, Switzerland and Israel, including "about five" young women said to be members of the Israeli Army. The rest were men.

Separate Deals Sought

He said the Popular Front was prepared to negotiate separate deals with the countries concerned for their own nationals—the Swiss hostages for the three guerrillas held in Switzerland, the Germans for the three in West Germany, the Britons for the woman hijacker, Leila Khaled, and the Israelis for a list of Palestinian prisoners submitted to the International Committee of the Red Cross but not yet disclosed. The questions of who the United States nationals were and how the United States would negotiate for their release remained unclear.

But the action brought into the open the long rift between the Popular Front, a Marxist group led by Dr. George Habash, and the Central Committee of the commando movement, led by Yasir Arafat, the apolitical guerrilla chief.

The committee suspended the Popular Front tonight for having violated commando discipline and it condemned actions "that could affect the safety and security of the Palestinian resistance."

Although represented in the Central Committee, a military coordinating group, the Popular Front has often flouted the committee's authority.

In recent days, it is believed, the Central Committee has sought to persuade the Popular Front to release the hostages without blowing up the airliners. Along with many Arab governments, it has criticized the hijackings.

The Jordanian Government also denounced the hijackings

178

and their outcome.

Meanwhile, the spokesman, known as Ibrahim, said at a news conference in the Palestine Liberation Organization headquarters here that the organization had blown up the captive airliners 13 hours ahead of the deadline because of "a conspiracy by various imperialist powers to abort this operation."

The reference was to largely broadcast reports of United States naval and air movements in the eastern Mediterranean.

The Popular Front also said in a statement that "Zionism and the United States" had brought pressure on Switzerland and the Red Cross to withdraw earlier offers of a projected exchange. The governments are understood to have insisted firmly on a package covering all the passengers, as well as the planes.

The three aircraft were estimated in value at $25.5-million. They were a Trans World Airline Boeing 707 and a Swissair DC-8, both hijacked last Sunday, and a British Overseas Airways Corporation VC-10, hijacked on Wednesday. A Pan-American World Airways Boeing-747, valued at $24-million, was hijacked Sunday, flown to Cairo and destroyed.

September 13, 1970

Stuff of Arab Legends
Yasir Arafat

He does not look to be the stuff of which legends are made.

Despite his short stature, a rather stocky figure a prominent nose, a receding chin and baldness concealed by his omnipresent kaffiyeh, or headdress, Yasir Arafat is a hero to millions in the Arab world. For multitudes disillusioned by the failures of established Arab leaders in their conflict with Israel, active hope centers on the soft-spoken Mr. Arafat, the 41-year-old leader of Al Fatah, the largest and most active Palestinian guerrilla group, and the head of the Palestinian Liberation Organization, a coordinating body for about 10 commando groups.

Man in the News

Yesterday Mr. Arafat, who has recently taken to issuing his orders under the title Commander in Chief of the Palestinian Revolution, agreed to a cease-fire in Jordan.

These days his leadership among the guerrilla organizations is unchallenged. His decision to stay on in Amman to lead the outnumbered guerrillas in the bitter fighting against King Hussein's army has elevated him to a new level of esteem among militant Arabs.

Amman Muted Criticism

Even the anticommando propaganda pouring from the state-run Amman radio has been devoid of abuse of Mr.

Paris Match—Pictorial Parade
Offers action when others offer rhetoric.

Arafat, who only last month was called "my friend" by the King.

But Mr. Arafat's emergence to pre-eminence confronts him with serious problems. In the past his principal failure was seen in his inability to rein radical elements such as the Marxist Popular Front for the Liberation of Palestine, whose hijacking of commercial airliners is blamed by some guerrilla leaders for their current troubles. Those leaders contend that Hussein would not have ordered an antiguerrilla sweep had it not been for the hijackings.

In addition, and as a result of the recent fighting, Mr. Arafat must rebuild the guerrilla movement, but that is an old and familiar problem, and its solution may be enhanced by the influence and respect he enjoys in Arab capitals.

Mr. Arafat's recorded experience with clandestine and guerrilla warfare extends back more than 20 years; he helped smuggle arms and ammunition to Arabs during a battle for Jerusalem in 1948.

A Native of Jerusalem

Jerusalem is where Mr. Arafat was born—in 1929, a descendant, it is said, of Palestinian nobility.

According to one story repeated throughout the Middle East, legal machinations deprived his family of valuable land it once owned in the heart of Cairo. The story has it that Mr. Arafat's father spent his life in an attempt to reclaim the land through the courts, but without success.

By 1948 the father and an older brother were members of the Holy Struggle Army, fighting against the emergent state of Israel.

When the 1948-49 fighting ended, Mr. Arafat and his parents were refugees in Gaza. He managed to go to Cairo, where he enrolled as an engineering student in what was then King Fuad University, now Cairo University. As chairman of the Palestinian Student Federation, he helped, in his own words, to "lay the basic foundation for our movement."

He also helped to lead and train Palestinian and Egyptian commandos who harassed the British in the Suez Canal area, then served the Egyptian Army as a demolitions expert and battled the British and the French at Port Said and Abu Kabir in 1956.

After working briefly as an engineer in Egypt, Mr. Arafat got a job in Kuwait in 1957, but he returned in 1965 as the Arab world began to hear the name of Al Fatah. In the wake of the 1967 war against Israel, when the Arab armies lay shattered and discredited, people bitter at the failures of the regular leaders began turning to Al Fatah and its chief, who then used the pseudonym Abu Amar.

Unlike other Arab leaders, who often seemed to offer nothing but rhetoric, Mr. Arafat offered action. At a time when the names of the other guerrilla chiefs were shrouded in secrecy, the name of Yasir Arafat, or of Abu Amar, was widely known and his face — the eyes usually hidden day and night behind sunglasses and the cheeks and chin covered with what seemed to be never more or less than a five-day growth of beard— was familiar.

Replying to reporters, he put aside questions of ideology.

"As a refugee," he said, "I have no time to spare arguing over the left and right. What is important is action and its result."

"We have believed that the only way to return to our homes and land is the armed struggle," he said. "We believe in this theory without any complications, and this is our aim and our hope."

September 26, 1970

Newly Militant Palestinian Elite Turns to the Commando Cause

By ERIC PACE
Special to The New York Times

BEIRUT, Lebanon, Nov. 15— Mysterious messengers come and go at a Palestinian doctor's office here. A Palestinian heiress dispenses commando propaganda posters. A Palestinian poet turns his pen to praise of commando feats.

In the 41 months since the 1967 Arab-Israeli war, the sizable Palestinian élite has become more and more caught up in the Palestinian nationalist movement—and in the work of the commandos, or fedayeen.

It is particularly significant for the 2.5 million Palestinians —the Arabs who lived in British-mandated Palestine, and their heirs—because they have a higher percentage of college-educated men and women than most Arab peoples. The Yemeni and South Arabian insurgent movements for instance, suffered from the low level of education of their peoples.

"You don't have to have a college degree to hijack a plane, but it helps," one Palestinian writer contends, and even moderates say that the support of educated Palestinians gives the commando movement much

The Palestinians

of its power.

The Palestinians say they have 40,000 to 60,000 people with college degrees. Thousands of others have become wealthy or powerful without going beyond secondary school.

Many live here in Beirut and in Jordan's capital, Amman, but some are as far away as central Asia, Europe and the Western Hemisphere.

These privileged Palestinians have been given far less publicity than the million refugees who still live in squalor in refugee camps. But thousands of the privileged have been engaged in nationalist activities since the 1967 war, with some Palestinian professional men using their offices here as contact points in commando undercover work.

Individual Palestinians give several reasons in explaining the new militancy of the élite. For one thing, many men had achieved economic security since the 1948 Arab-Israeli war and were in a position to turn to political causes. Many were shamed and angered by the 1967 war, and many have been heartened by the commando movement, which blossomed in its wake.

Most Are Educated

"This is very encouraging; a nation cannot hope to stand on its feet without a brain trust of its own," says Dr. Eugene M. Makhlouf, a Beirut dentist who is active in Palestinian affairs.

The present commando chieftains are mostly educated men. Yasir Arafat, of Al Fatah, was trained as an engineer. George Habash, of the Popular Front for the Liberation of Palestine, has a medical doctor's degree from the American University in Beirut. Dr. Issam Sartawi, of the Action Group for the Liberation of Palestine, studied medicine in the United States.

But the Palestinian élite plays other indirect, though important, roles. Millions of dollars have been poured into the commando movement since 1967 by Palestinians who have become wealthy, largely in the oil industry in the Persian Gulf area.

Also, educated Palestinians have proved to be skilled propagandists, by Arab standards. When King Hussein signed an agreement with Mr. Arafat in Amman recently, commando spokesmen were giving their version of the text and its significance when the ink was scarcely dry.

Multilingual spokesmen for Al Fatah and the Palestine Liberation Organization frequent the lobby of the Hotel Jordan Intercontinental in Amman, ready to dispense their point of view to anyone.

There are, to be sure, numbers of educated Palestinians who do not endorse the commando goals of destroying the state of Israel and replacing it with an independent, Arab-dominated Palestine. King Hussein of Jordan has found no shortage of Palestinians, such as former Premier Ahmed Toukan, to recruit for his short-lived Cabinets. And many middle-class and upper-class Palestinians still seem to reserve all their energies for earning money.

But militant Palestinians contend that educated nationalists play an important role in shaping Palestinian opinion as a whole. They say that villagers who pool their savings to send one of their children to a university respect education, and are therefore impressed when they see prominent intellectuals such as Kemal Nasser and members of old educated families supporting the fedayeen.

On the other hand, there is a noticeable absence of distinguished Palestinians—outside the Jordanian Government—who are willing to speak out in opposition to the commandos' goals.

Critics of the commandos argue, though, that this is because moderates are afraid to speak out for fear of being harassed or even killed by the fedayeen.

The role of the Palestinian élite was somewhat different in past decades. Under the British mandate, a Palestinian aristocrat, Ragheb Nashashibi, was the foremost spokesman of moderation until his voice was drowned out by extremist rhetoric.

Musa Alami, a British-educated scion of an old land-owning family, was one of the Palestinian notables who continued to work for the British authorities as tension rose in the mandate. Other old families, such as the Bitars, favored moderation if for no other reason than to protect their property.

Palestinian nationalists say proudly that both high-born and low-born Palestinians are mainly descended from peoples who lived in the area centuries before Jesus, including the Philistines, Canaanites, Hittites, Amorites and Jebusites.

"They were there when the early Hebrews invaded the land in about 1500 B.C." one Palestinian writer asserts. Palestinian militants contend that their ancestors kept possession of much of what is now Palestine through what they call "The Israelite period," which they consider to have ended in the eighth century B.C.

The Palestinians say their ancestors remained after the dispersal of the Israelites and then became mingled with the Arab conquerors of the seventh century A.D. and, still later, with the Crusaders.

Zionist historians, however, put more stress on the Arab component in the Palestinians' complex ancestry. There are even black Palestinians today—the descendents of blacks who, typically as slaves, arrived in Palestine from Africa.

Many foreign armies have marched across Palestine, notably the forces of the Ottoman empire, which ruled the area—then considered part of Syria—from the 16th century until World War I.

After that war, Palestine became a British mandate and remained so until 1948. The people generally retained the culture that the Arab conquerors had brought centuries before, but the élite was largely Turkish-educated and then, under the mandate, educated in British schools.

This British schooling proved a blessing after the war of 1948, which brought the founding of Israel and what Palestinians now somewhat self-consciously call their diaspora —the scattering of Palestinian refugees through the Arab world to places where they could earn a living.

Helped Set a Pattern

The Arabian-American Oil Company helped to set a pattern by hiring British-educated refugees to work in the Arabian Peninsula, and since then tens of thousands of Palestinians have taken jobs there—40,000 in Kuwait alone.

Tens of thousands of other Palestinians have found good jobs in Beirut. American business influence was greatly increased here after World War II, and Palestinians were in demand here because of their British schooling. The Lebanese were generally French-trained.

Meanwhile, the United Nations relief program was providing schooling for hundreds of thousands of Palestinian children in the refugee camps in the Gaza Strip, Jordan, Syria and Lebanon.

"The quickest way out of those camps was for a boy to get good marks and go away to university," one Palestinian editor recalls. And thousands did. Typically they went to Cairo University, which is free, or to universities in Damascus or Beirut. From these centers many able young people went on to study outside the Middle East.

Dr. Makhlouf, the dentist active in Palestinian affairs, has made a survey of 10,000 Palestinian graduates. He has found that 30 per cent chose medicine or engineering—careers that offer a more-or-less certain livelihood.

Numbers of doctors now help the Palestinian nationalist movement by doing volunteer work with the Palestinian Red Crescent, an equivalent of the Red Cross.

Other Palestinian students went into the liberal arts, mostly as a stepping stone to teaching careers. Nowadays, a traveler in Jordan finds numbers of middle-level commando leaders who formerly taught in schools.

Some Are Bankers

Those Palestinians, educated or not, who have become rich since 1948 have done so generally in oil-industry contracting or in banking. The most famous of them was the late Youssef Beidas, who died after Intrabank, the great Beirut banking house he built up, collapsed in 1966. He was a heavy contributor to various Palestinian nationalist causes.

Another eminently successful Palestinian is Jamal Husseini, a cousin of Haj Amin el-Husseini Mufti — the ranking Moslem religious dignitary — of Jerusalem. Jamal Husseini built a fortune while serving as a close adviser to the late King Saud of Saudi Arabia, and is now retired in Beirut.

A more controversial Palestinian notable is Dr. Ahmed Shukairy, the former head of the Palestine Liberation Organization, which now includes 10 commando groups.

Before heading the organization Dr. Shukairy, a fiery Jerusalem lawyer, represented Syria and, later, Saudi Arabia at the United Nations. His rhetoric got him into trouble, and he lost the Palestinian post after the 1967 war. He now lives quietly in Lebanon.

But it is the young university graduates who are generally the most fiery militants—like the coterie of young intellectuals around Nayef Hawatmeh, the Maoist chief of the Popular Democratic Front for the Liberation of Palestine.

At the American University in Beirut recently, students flocked enthusiastically to hear a speech by Leila Khaled, the young woman who tried to hijack an Israeli airliner over Britain in September. She had been a student there herself.

And during the Jordanian civil war in September Palestinian students here volunteered to drive Palestinian Red Crescent ambulances through Syria to the battleground.

Working-class youths have also grown militant—and commando headwear and placards are prized possessions among the boys of the refugee camps.

But it is in the young intellectuals that Palestinian elders see a special hope for their dream of one day erasing the state of Israel.

"They will be our future," said one Palestinian journalist in Amman recently. "They will be our brains."

November 16, 1970

TERRORISTS OR PATRIOTS

Arab Guerrillas Said to Shift Strategy

By MARVINE HOWE
Special to The New York Times

BEIRUT, Lebanon, Nov. 21— The Palestinian resistance movement is shifting its strategy from regular army operations to urban-guerrilla action inside Israeli-held territory, according to a leading Palestinian theoretician here.

"Guerrillas, it is said, must be as elusive and vicious as fleas but we have been acting like ducks," said the expert, who is a leader of the National Liberation Movement of Palestine, generally known as Al Fatah.

The same source said that if Egypt's President, Anwar el-Sadat, carried out threats to resume hostilities against Israel this would create "a new and more favorable situation for guerrilla action."

"But we are not depending on Egypt to go to war," he said..

The decision to develop an urban-guerrilla movement has not been publicized but is already being carried out, particularly in the Gaza area, informed Al Fatah sources said.

The extremist Popular Front for the Liberation of Palestine has been engaged for several months in urban terrorism in Gaza, Haifa and Tel Aviv, according to Basam Abu Sharif, a spokesman for the organization. He said that the front planned to step up these operations and was cooperating in some cases with Al Fatah.

This reported change in tactics has apparently sprung from a recognition that the Palestine Liberation Army, the regular military arm of the Palestinian movement, succeeded more in antagonizing its Arab host Government—particularly Jordan—than in threatening Israel.

Last-ditch talks are set to open tomorrow in Jidda, Saudi Arabia, for reconciliation between the Jordanian Government and the Palestine Liberation Organization, which links the commando groups.

Whatever the outcome of the talks, Palestinians are likely to move their forces underground for greater efficiency and to avoid further clashes with Arab nations, according to informed Al Fatah sources.

"The basic question is who represents who," said Abu Omar, information chief of Al Fatah here. He said that the Palestinian negotiators would not make concessions on two principles: their freedom of movement and recognition as representatives of the Palestinian people.

King Hussein of Jordan insists that the guerrillas must in no way "infringe on the sovereignty of the Jordanian state" and has made it clear he wants complete control over the commandos stationed in Jordan.

He has reportedly proposed that the number of commandos in Jordan not exceed 1,000 at any time, that they be stationed in two camps selected by the Jordanians, that they carry identity cards issued by the Jordanian Army and that they not be allowed to fire from positions east of the cease-fire line.

"They want to put us in concentration camps," an Al Fatah member said. "To submit to those conditions would be complete capitulation."

There have been strong pressures from many sides for an agreement at Jidda. The talks began in September with mediation by Egypt and Saudi Arabia. If an agreement is reached, Syria has let it be known that she would lift her economic blockade against Jordan, imposed after the Jordanian offensive against the guerrillas in September, 1970. Kuwait and Libya were also expected to resume financial aid to Jordan.

November 22, 1971

FEDAYEEN SEEKING EFFECTIVE UNITY

All Major Arab Units Join New Guerrilla Committee

By IHSAN A. HIJAZI
Special to The New York Times

BEIRUT, Lebanon, July 17— While Jordanian troops battled Palestinian commandos in the hills of northern Jordan this week, the leadership of the guerrilla organizations took major steps toward apparent unity.

All the main commando organizations appear to have rallied around the leadership of Yasir Arafat and they have joined a new executive committee of the Palestine Liberation Organization, the over-all commando group. The 13-member committee is to be the highest authority within the movement, and under it, all 10,000 commandos, or fedayeen, are to have a single military command and a single information unit.

The new executive committee is the successor to the former 27-man central committee.

The apparent unity still falls far short of a merger of the groups, whose political outlooks and methods of operation vary widely, "but it is the highest degree of solidarity achieved to date," an informed guerrilla source said.

Seek Destruction of Israel

The fedayeen are based mainly in Lebanon and Jordan, from where they carry out their missions of harassment against Israel as part of their avowed goal of destroying the Zionist state and replacing it with a Palestinian state.

The steps toward apparent unity were one of the results of the 155-man Palestine National Council, or parliament, which ended a session this week in Cairo. Commando sources reported that the fresh fighting in Jordan, which erupted while the council was in session, had prompted some of the organizations to set aside their reservations about the degree of unity they were willing to establish with other fedayeen.

The Popular Front for the Liberation of Palestine, a Maoist guerrilla group, and the Iraqi-sponsored Arab Liberation Front are represented in the executive committee for the first time. In the past, both groups had refused to join either the executive committee or the Palestine National Council.

The Popular Front, under Dr. George Habash, has insisted on carrying out operations abroad such as the hijacking of international airliners, thus bringing it into conflict with the dominant guerrilla group, Al Fatah, which is headed by Mr. Arafat.

Although the Popular Front does not intend to abandon its operations abroad, informed sources believe that its actions will be more subdued now that it is part of the over-all commando organization.

Ex-Professor Heads Fund

Dr. Youssef Sayigh, a former professor of economics at the American University of Beirut, has been elected head of the Palestine National Fund, or the treasury department of the fedayeen. He is not associated with any particular group.

Dr. Sayigh and Brig. Gen. Abdel Razak al-Yahya, the commander of the Palestine Liberation Army, have been authorized to attend meetings of the executive committee. This in effect brings to 15 the number of committee members. Al Fatah has four members on the committee and As Saiqa, the Syrian-sponsored group, has two.

The Popular Front for the Liberation of Palestine and the Popular Democratic Front for the Liberation of Palestine, another extreme leftist group that had broken away from the Habash organization, each has one member on the committee. The Popular Struggle Front, a smaller group, also has one member.

The representative of Palestinian labor unions in the committee is known to be a close associate of Dr. Habash, which in effect gives his Popular Front two members.

Al Ansar, a guerrilla unit established last year by Communist groups in Lebanon, Syria, Iraq and Jordan, remains outside the over-all commando organization. Its 200 members are believe to be stationed in southern Lebanon, near the Israeli border.

Al Fatah has blocked its entry into the Palestine Liberation Organization because the group has not yet proved itself in action against Israel and because it follows the Moscow policy of advocating a peaceful settlement of the Arab-Israeli conflict.

One group that has not been mentioned in connection with the new executive committee is the Popular Front for the Liberation of Palestine (General Command), led by Ahmed Jebreel. A spokesman for the Palestine Liberation Organization said last week that the tiny Jebreel group was preoccupied with internal conflicts.

Mr. Arafat, who has been re-elected chairman of the executive committee, had worked out details of the Popular Front's entry into the Palestine Liberation Organization with Dr. Habash at a meeting they were reported to have held somewhere in Lebanon earlier this month.

July 18, 1971

The Palestinians

Commandos:

A Quiet End to a Tumultuous Odyssey

AMMAN, Jordan—"The fedayeen are finished, the fedayeen are finished," bystanders murmured as Jordanian Army trucks carried hundreds of captive Arab commandos off to exile in Syria and Iraq last week. There were no cheers from the fedayeen's supporters as the guerrillas passed. Their departure seemed to seal the final crushing of the commandos as an independent force in Jordan. With the army in the saddle, the Palestinians' cheering had to stop.

It was a quiet end to a tumultuous odyssey—the rise and fall of the commando movement in Jordan. Substantial fedayeen forces remain in Lebanon and Syria, to be sure, but Jordan was the heartland of the Arab guerrilla movement. Its capital, Amman, was vaunted as the "Arab Hanoi."

Born before the 1967 Arab-Israeli War, the commando movement flourished after the defeat of the Arab armies. Palestinian militants claim that its strength grew from 700 before the war to 20,000 on the eve of the movement's civil war against the Jordanian army last September.

The commandos flourished because they gave the Arabs hope that they could do real harm to Israel. In 1968, their fight with an invading Israeli force in the Jordanian village of Karameh fed these hopes. Arabs interpreted the engagement as a great success.

The fedayeen preached a doctrine of unrelenting guerrilla warfare aimed at destroying Israel. They proposed to replace it with a nonsectarian state in which, they never tired of telling visitors, Moslems, Christians and Jews would live on an equal basis.

At its peak a year and more ago, the commando movement controlled much of Amman. Guerrillas collected funds in the main hotels—and held guests hostage when they wanted to. Commando trainees posed endlessly for press photographers, and commando leaders spoke with the resonance and hauteur of the Arab princes of old. Funds and volunteers poured into the commandos' offices.

Yet, there was always the nagging fact that the fedayeen were not, in reality, achieving much in the field. For example, they failed to establish a network of guerrillas based inside Israel's lines—even on the Arab west bank of the River Jordan.

Given their military weakness, the commandos were vulnerable to a change in the Arab political climate. The frost came last summer, when the late President Gamal Abdel Nasser of the United Arab Republic endorsed Washington's Middle East peace initiatives.

When fighting along the Suez Canal stopped, Arab truculence waned—and with it Arab support for the fedayeen. There was friction between Cairo and the commandos, which cost them support among the Nasserite masses in many Arab lands.

All this encouraged King Hussein of Jordan to crack down on the fedayeen, who had long since become unwelcome guests in Jordan. With their trucks and their guns, they had insisted on a degree of independence within Jordan's borders that was humiliating to the King's regime.

And then came the multiple airliner hijackings last fall. They were staged by the main left-wing commando group, the Popular Front for the Liberation of Palestine, and the hijacked planes parked in the Jordanian desert were an insult to the King. They also stirred worldwide outrage against the fedayeen.

And so King Hussein moved his army into Amman to clean out the commandos. It was a messy battle, but in the end the army trounced the fedayeen largely because it had vast supplies of American arms and ammunition. It was also better organized than the commando groups, who perennially squabbled among themselves.

In the succeeding months, King Hussein made a series of moves to reduce the commandos' power. The army pushed them out of the key towns of Jarash and Irbid, and army threats got the last substantial commando force out of Amman in April.

This left more than 2,000 fedayeen holed up in the wooded hills between Jarash and Ajlun, north of Amman. Last week, the army attacked them. To assuage outside Arab criticism, it insisted at first that it merely wanted to move the commandos away from villages in the area. Later, however, it claimed to have "rounded up" 2,300.

Other Arab countries made ritual denunciations of King Hussein, but they did not send troops to help the fedayeen, just as they had not done so during the operations in Irbid, Jarash and Amman earlier this year.

This left the King clearly in command throughout his realm. And it left the commandos a broken force in Jordan, although the Government insisted that it would let some of them continue their raids against Israel.

Yet, when the Government announced the release of 2,000 of the captives, it said that almost all of them had left the country or quit the guerrilla movement. Only 30, it claimed, wanted to continue as fedayeen.

—ERIC PACE

July 25, 1971

JORDAN'S PREMIER IS SLAIN IN CAIRO; 3 GUNMEN SEIZED

Tal Was in Egypt for Arab Talks—Suspects Said to Belong to Palestine Unit

By RAYMOND H. ANDERSON
Special to The New York Times

CAIRO, Nov. 28—Premier Wasfi Tal of Jordan was assassinated here today by three gunmen reported to have entered Egypt with Syrian passports.

The 51-year-old Premier fell under a volley of revolver shots as he entered the Sheraton Hotel. He was returning from a meeting of the Arab League's Joint Defense Council discussing strategy against Israel.

The Jordanian Foreign Minister, Abdullah Salah, was reported slightly injured and an Egyptian police officer accompanying the two men was seriously wounded.

Three men ran from the hotel waving revolvers after the shooting. Two were captured near the hotel and the third was found in a nearby apartment.

Linked to Guerrillas

Official sources described the men as members of a Palestinian organization known as Black September, evidently named for the strife that erupted in Jordan in September, 1970, between the Jordanian Army and Palestinian guerrillas. The fighting gravely weakened the guerrilla movement.

A fourth man, identified as a Palestinian with a Syrian passport, was arrested later.

The Egyptian Prosecutor General, Mohammed Maher Hassan, reported after interrogation of the three gunmen that they had arrived in Egypt a few days ago with Syrian passports. Two of the men have confessed the shooting, he said. One was wounded in an exchange of fire with security men, Mr. Hassan declared.

Many Palestinians regarded Mr. Tal, who was closely associated with Jordan's King Hussein, as one of their most deadly opponents in the Jordanian leadership.

November 29, 1971

TERRORISTS OR PATRIOTS

25 DIE AT ISRAELI AIRPORT AS 3 GUNMEN FROM PLANE FIRE ON 250 IN A TERMINAL

72 ARE WOUNDED

Attackers Identified as Japanese—2 Dead, One Captured

By United Press International

TEL AVIV, Wednesday, May 31—Three gunmen armed with automatic rifles and hand grenades attacked a crowd of 250 to 300 people last night at Lod International Airport outside Tel Aviv. Twenty-five persons were killed and 72 were wounded.

The gunmen, identified as Japanese, pulled their weapons from their luggage and began firing shortly after debarking from an Air France jetliner from Paris and Rome. Terror-stricken and screaming, the crowd in the waiting room dropped to the floor or ran for cover.

Among the victims were 11 Puerto Ricans who were members of a delegation of Christian pilgrims beginning a visit to the Holy Land. At Tel Hashomer Hospital, officials said 14 of the 72 wounded were in serious condition. Among the victims was a two-year-old girl.

One Attacker Captured

One of the attackers committed suicide, using a grenade, another was caught by an airport maintenance man, and the third, who was at first thought to have escaped, was killed, apparently by bullets fired by his companions, and was discovered among the dead taken to the hospitals.

The captured attacker told officials he was a member of "the Army of the Red Star," a left-wing Japanese group mobilized by the Arab guerrilla movement. In Beirut, the militant, Marxist-oriented Popular Front for the Liberation of Palestine claimed responsibility for the attack.

Security officials said the dead and captured Japanese were named Nago and Sugizaki but did not give full names or other details.

Premier Golda Meir interrupted a vacation and sped to the airport, then to the hospital. Tired and haggard, she withheld comment on the incident.

Five Grenades Exploded

The attack began shortly after 10:30 P.M. (4:30 P.M. Tuesday, New York time). The gunmen were among the 115 persons who debarked from the Air France plane. They rode buses to the passenger terminal and apparently retrieved their weapons from their luggage.

Suddenly the terminal was filled with screaming persons as the attackers sprayed bullets and grenades throughout the room. "There were bullets flying all over," said Dorit Shriki, a policewoman.

At least five grenades exploded amid long bursts of rifle fire. People in the terminal ran for rest rooms and the first class lounge, seeking cover.

The force of the explosions ripped bodies and luggage alike, leaving blood everywhere. Bullets shattered glass windows and screens throughout the arrival lounge. Holes were splattered in the walls.

"This was a crazy suicide operation," said Police Commissioner Pinhas Kopel.

The Minister of Transport, Shimon Peres, said of the attackers, "We know they are Japanese because of their passports and their looks."

At a later news conference, Mr. Peres declared: "Tonight, there happened one of the most serious things in the history of aviation and in human behavior. I am sorry to say that the bloodbath was extremely terrible. Over 20 dead and scores of wounded, some of them seriously."

"The Government of Israel will take every step to fight this new madness," he pledged. "The human price we paid in blood can never be repaid. This is one of the most terrible things, unprecedented and unknown in the history of aviation."

Action Is 'Quite Strange'

"So far the front has involved only Arabs and Jews," Mr. Peres said. "The introduction of Japanese into the picture is quite strange. It shows what the Arabs think of their ability to fight against us."

An Air France spokesman said in Paris that the gunmen had probably secreted the arms in their luggage but he declined to indicate whether passengers and their baggage had been examined before boarding.

An airport spokesman said that during "calm" periods, passengers and their checked luggage are subject only to spot examinations, but that hand baggage is always inspected.

The Boeing 707 plane left Paris with 122 passengers at 3:30 P.M. (10:30 A.M. New York time) and stopped in Rome. The spokesman said 115 passengers were on board when the plane left Rome. It was not immediately known where the three gunmen had boarded.

Witness Describes Scene

After the gunmen entered the passport-control station, they threw grenades and opened up with bursts from the Soviet-made combat rifle.

"All of a sudden I saw a tall man in a brown shirt pulling a submachine gun and cocking it," said Mrs. Rachel Braunstein, an Israeli who observed the attack while waiting for her son-in-law to arrive.

"Then someone pushed me away," she said. "I heard bursts of fire. It lasted for a few minutes. I don't know where my son and daughter are. Where are they?"

Sammy Shuti, a cab driver, said he had arrived at the airport to pick up a couple and take them to one of Tel Aviv's luxury hotels.

"Then all of a sudden I heard shooting," he said. "I saw people rolling, scattering away. I saw two people limping through the exit doors. I didn't wait around."

Reports from Tel Hashomer Hospital, relayed by the national radio and the police, gave the first indication of the high casualty count.

Dozens of ambulances and troops went to the air terminal, which was a scene of blood and broken glass by the time they arrived.

The shooting followed by three weeks the hijacking of a Sabena airliner with 96 passengers and crewmen to Tel Aviv by four guerrillas. Two of the hijackers were killed, one was wounded and one captured in a raid on the plane by Israeli troops May 9.

Arab Group Claims Credit

BEIRUT, Lebanon, Wednesday, May 31 (UPI)—The Marxist Popular Front for the Liberation of Palestine said today that it was responsible for the attack in Tel Aviv.

"The Popular Front for the Liberation of Palestine announces its complete responsibility for the brave operation launched by one of its special groups tonight in our occupied land," a statement issued by the organization said.

The guerrilla group said the operation had been carried out by three guerrillas, whom it identified as Bassem, Salah and Ahmed. They belong to a group called the "Squad of the Martyr Patrick Urguello," the statement said.

"Those three heroes came thousands of miles to take part with the Palestinian people in their struggle against the forces of Zionism and imperialism," the statement said.

The statement said the raid had been made to coincide with the fifth anniversary of the war of June, 1967, between the Arabs and Israel.

Later, asked about reports that the attackers are Japanese, a spokesman for the front responded, "they may be Japanese; they may be Vietnamese. All that we are saying now is that they belong to the squad of the martyr Patrick Urguello of the P.F.L.P. We may issue a statement later."

Asked who Urguello was, the spokesman identified him as a Nicaraguan who attempted, with Khaled, to hijack an El Al plane over London in September, 1970, but was shot dead by armed guards aboard the aircraft.

The raid also was in reprisal for the killing by Israeli troops of two Arab guerrillas who hijacked a Sabena airliner to Tel Aviv earlier this month, the group's statement said. The Israeli action had been directed by Israeli's Defense Minister, Moshe Dayan.

"The raid launched today was a revolutionary answer to the Israeli massacre performed in cold blood by the butcher Moshe Dayan and his devils against the martyr heroes Ali Taha and Abdel Aziz Elatrash," the statement said.

It added: "This revolutionary answer was a tribute to the blood of two heroes who fell as a result of a cheap trick," the statement said.

May 31, 1972

The Palestinians

9 ISRAELIS ON OLYMPIC TEAM KILLED

A 23-HOUR DRAMA

2 Others Are Slain in Their Quarters in Guerrilla Raid

By DAVID BINDER
Special to The New York Times

MUNICH, West Germany, Wednesday, Sept. 6—Eleven members of Israel's Olympic team and four Arab terrorists were killed yesterday in a 23-hour drama that began with an invasion of the Olympic Village by the Arabs. It ended in a shootout at a military airport some 15 miles away as the Arabs were preparing to fly to Cairo with their Israeli hostages.

The first two Israelis were killed early yesterday morning when Arab commandos, armed with automatic rifles, broke into the quarters of the Israeli team and seized nine others as hostages. The hostages were killed in the airport shootout between the Arabs and German policemen and soldiers.

The bloodshed brought the suspension of the Olympic Games and there was doubt if they would be resumed. Willi Daume, president of the West German Organizing Committee, announced early today that he would ask the International Olympic Committee to meet tomorrow to decide whether they should continue.

Policeman Killed

In addition to the slain Israelis and Arabs, a German policeman was killed and a helicopter pilot was critically wounded. Three Arabs were wounded.

There were some reports that two of the hostages said to have been killed might still be alive. "It is a dim hope," said Dr. Bruno Merk, the Interior Minister of Bavaria, "but I am skeptical on this point."

The bloodbath at the airport that ended at 1 A.M. today, came after long hours of negotiaton between German and Arabs at the Israeli quarters in the Olympic Village where the Arabs demanded the release of 200 Arab commandos imprisoned in Israel.

Finally the West German armed forces supplied three helicopters to transport the Arabs and their Israeli hostages to the airport at Fürstenfeldbruck. From there all were to be flown to Cairo.

A Boeing-707 provided by the Lufthansa German Airlines was waiting.

Two of the terrorists, carrying their automatic rifles, walked about 170 yards from the helicopters to the plane. And then they started back to pick up the other Arabs and the hostages.

Positions Cited

As the Arabs were returning, German sharpshooters reportedly opened fire from the darkness beyond the pools of light at the airport. The Arabs returned fire.

The torment of the entire event was heightened by confusion created in the public mind by contradictory reports from German and Olympic officials after the gunfire erupted at the airport.

Dr. Merk, in a press conference at 3 o'clock this morning said:

"In this situation our task and goal to free the hostages was made more difficult by the lack of agreement from Israel to free prisoners or to get guarantees from the Arabs not to take action against the hostages."

He said the Federal Minister of the Interior, Hans-Dietrich Genscher, had offered to substitute himself and other German officials for the Israeli hostages. This, and money, was rejected by the Arabs.

How the hostages were killed was still in doubt. One theory was that an Arab threw a grenade into a helicopter in which some or all of the hostages were bound hand and foot.

Partial explanation of how the Arabs knew so much about the Israeli compound in the Olympic Village came from Dr. Merk. He said that at least one of the terrorists was an official employe in the village and that there was reason to believe some of his confederates had also obtain accreditation.

The idea of trying to liberate the hostages at the Olympic Village was rejected, Dr. Merk said, because it could have involved athletes from other nations" living nearby.

Hostages Agreed to Flight

He said that though the hostages had acquiesced to the Arab insistence on flying to Cairo "we felt that would have been a certain death sentence for the hostages."

September 6, 1972

A REPRISAL FOR MUNICH

AL FATAH TARGET

Many Reported Killed in Raids on Camps in Syria and Lebanon

By TERENCE SMITH
Special to The New York Times

TEL AVIV, Sept. 8—In a sweeping reprisal for the terrorist shooting of 11 Israelis at Munich, Israeli Air Force planes struck simultaneously today at 10 Arab guerrilla bases and naval installations deep in Syria and Lebanon.

Scores of planes dropped bombs and fired rockets on what Israeli military authorities here described as troop concentrations, training centers, supply depots and headquarters units of Al Fatah, the Arab guerrilla organization. The Black September movement, which claimed responsibility for the killings at the Olympics in Munich, is viewed by Israel as an integral part of Al Fatah.

In scope, number of targets and depth of penetration, today's raids were the most ambitious by the Israeli Air Force since the lightning attack that wiped out the Arab air forces at the outset of the six-day war in 1967.

A military senior officer—whom correspondents admitted to the briefing must agree not to identify—said that initial reports indicated that "scores" of Arab guerrillas had been caught in their camps and killed or wounded. He said later that reports might indicate higher casualties.

All the Israeli planes were reported to have returned safely.

Hopes Fatah 'Gets Message'

The senior Israeli military officer, briefing newsmen on the operation in Tel Aviv tonight, held open the possibility that more air attacks and perhaps ground action might follow in an effort to knock out the terrorists. He stressed that there was "no single way" to eliminate the guerrilla movement and that "a combination of means" would be required.

"I hope the Fatah and the Black September movement get the message," he said. "But if they don't, we will keep our freedom of action. It will be up to the Government of Israel to decide what to do next."

September 9, 1972

TERRORISTS OR PATRIOTS

Arab Guerrillas Are Reported to Get Direct Shipments of Soviet Weapons

By ERIC PACE
Special to The New York Times

GENEVA, Sept. 16—The Soviet Union has recently begun to supply weapons directly to the Arab guerrilla organization Al Fatah, sources close to the Fatah leadership reported this week.

According to Arab informants and Israeli officials interviewed earlier in Lebanon and in Israel, Fatah provides arms as well as money and manpower to the Black September terrorist group.

It was after reporting that Arab terrorists had been gathering in southern Lebanon, an old stamping ground of Fatah, that the Israeli Army crossed the Lebanese border this weekend.

Moscow's first direct shipment of arms to Fatah arrived in the Middle East within the last few weeks, the informants said, but there has been no official confirmation from the commando movement or the Soviet Government. Whether the weapons were delivered before or after the Black September attack on the Israeli Olympic team, in which Soviet arms were used, was not clear.

Word of the weapons delivery caused little stir in informed quarters in Geneva, which has long been a center of Arab intrigue. Fouad Chemali, the Syrian nationalist whom many Arabs credit with planning Fatah and Black September projects in Europe, died of cancer two months ago after having been active here for years, and Western diplomats say that at least one Arab diplomatic mission here has been helping Palestinian guerrillas.

The informants reported that a secret Soviet pledge to send arms directly to Fatah was given when the group's leader, Yasir Arafat, visited Moscow in July at the head of a delegation representing several Arab commando groups. Soviet officials were reported to have told Mr. Arafat then to abandon the use of terror, but now Palestinian militants voice the hope that Moscow will pursue a "two tiered" policy permitting clandestine support for at least some terrorist acts.

As far as is known, the Soviet Union has never before sent arms directly to the Arab guerrillas, or fedayeen, although China began doing so even before the Arab-Israeli war of 1967.

September 18, 1972

Israelis and Arabs Attribute Rise in Guerrilla Terrorism Outside the Middle East to Failure and Frustration

By ERIC PACE
Special to The New York Times

BEIRUT, Lebanon, Sept. 19—The grim succession of terrorist acts against Israeli targets in recent months has set Israelis and Arabs of various political stripes, to addressing themselves to two questions: Why should Arab militants have recourse now, more than 20 years after the birth of Israel, to such spectacular terrorist gestures? And why should they do so largely outside the Middle East? A traveler in the area hears many shades of opinion on the question, but there is a surprising degree of agreement between Israelis and Arabs on one point.

News Analysis

That is that the guerrillas are turning to extremes largely because the Arabs have been unsuccessful in other modes of anti-Israeli action—in diplomacy, in regular warfare and most recently in conventional guerrilla fighting.

The Arab guerrillas, or fedayeen, have been frustrated by security measures behind Israel's borders and by restrictions put on them by Arab governments that fear Israeli reprisals.

But Arab moderates as well as militants also argue that in embracing terrorism the commandos are merely doing what Zionists and Israelis did years before.

And Palestinians are contending in Beirut that, by Arab count, the Israelis have killed more than 200 Arabs in attacks on Syria and Lebanon since the Munich attack—in which, as they repeat tirelessly, fewer than a tenth as many lives were lost. Eleven members of the Israeli Olympic team died as a result of the guerrilla attack.

For their part, some Israeli intellectuals tend to put more stress on other factors, such as the influence on the Palestinians of non-Arab advocates of "revolutionary violence" — notably the late Frantz Fanon, a black who backed the Algerian rebels against France— and on underlying elements in Arab culture.

Death in London

Yet to many Arab observers in Beirut, the reason that envelopes containing explosive devices were sent to the Israeli Embassy in London — one blew up today, killing a diplomat—seems simple enough although no guerrilla group has claimed credit for the attack and none has yet been identified here in connection with the incident.

They say the reason is that someone, presumably the Israelis, killed a prominent Arab guerrilla spokesman and wounded two others with booby traps in Beirut this summer.

The Israelis have not acknowledged responsibility and Jordan might conceivably have done the booby trapping. But in Palestinian nationalist offices in Beirut the conviction is widespread that it was carried out by Israelis in revenge for the guerrilla massacre of May 30 at Tel Aviv airport that led to the deaths of 28 persons.

The spokesman, who was killed by a bomb in his car, was Ghassan Kanafani, a brilliant, tireless and ferociously outspoken ideologist of the Marxist Popular Front for the Liberation of Palestine, which has specialized in airplane hijacking.

His successor as the front's spokesman and another well-known Palestinian intellectual affiliated with the Palestine Liberation Organization, the overall guerrilla group, were both badly wounded by bombs sent through the mails. And Lebanese authorities are said to have intercepted half a dozen other booby-trapped parcels.

"So now it's tit for tat," one Palestinian intellectual said grimly today, and he and other Arabs complained that the West had given little attention to the earlier incidents here.

In addition, the shooting of an Israeli official in Brussels and the assassination in London today are widely considered here as gestures by Arab extremists to show that they will not be deterred by criticism or by the Israeli reprisal raids that followed the Munich attack, for which the guerrilla group Black September claimed responsibility.

Why then did Arab militants attack the Israelis in Munich? If a visitor raises the question at one of the Palestinian offices in Beirut, he is handed what is said to be a careful cataloging of Zionist and Israeli acts of violence, including a number of Israeli Army attacks that left civilian casualties.

The material cites the blowing up of the King David Hotel in Jerusalem in 1946, in which 200 persons, most of them British, are said to have been killed. That action was carried out by the Irgun Zvai Leumi, an underground movement that fought the British before Israel was established in 1948.

Israelis Termed Violent

The catalogue is 21 pages long and has preface by the Palestinian poet Kamal Nasser, who is the liberation organization's chief spokesman. Mr. Nasser has this to say about terrorism:

"It is the Zionist state that has introduced to this area a tradition of violence, collective and terroristic. It has done so in the belief, which characterizes all colonizing supremacist movements and ideologies, that this is the 'language that Arabs understand.' It is obvious that to Israel, violence is a conviction and an institution, while to us it is a defensive and struggling necessity."

Another prominent Palestinian militant, who is sometimes called by the code name Abu Ahmed, said in a recent interview here that he did not care if the outside world was outraged by Arab terrorism. Expressing a view that seems to be widely held by young Arab militants, he said scornfully:

The Palestinians

"They never cared about us. Why should we care about them?"

And, speaking of what he calls the Munich incident, he says: "Call us what you may, but it's good for our morale, and it may help the moderate elements in the movement to take a more militant position. After all our defeats, this comes as an uplift."

"We feel we have to do something," he said. "What does the world expect of young Arabs these days? We have seen too many defeats."

Other views were put forward in Jerusalem recently by Israeli intellectuals, including Dr. Yehoshaphat Harkavi, a professor at the Hebrew University who has long studied the Palestinian resistance movement.

Speaking of the growing use of Arab terrorism outside the Middle East, he said, "The radicals radicalize the nonradicals." And he said that after King Hussein crushed the commando movement in Jordan in 1970, it had to "look for other vistas of action."

Faded Dream

Dr. Harkavi said that the Palestinians had in part been whipped up by what he termed the Palestinian Establishment—older Palestinian intellectuals who have no occupation other than propounding Palestinian irredentism. But he noted that the young Palestinians who actually carried out Arab guerrilla activity behind Israeli lines had been very largely men without university educations.

But he said now the dream of actually creating a Palestinian state through guerrilla warfare had faded, and he added: "When prophecy fails there are two possibilities. You resign yourself to reality—or you become more fanatical."

Israelis contend that the leftist ideologies espoused by many commandos have had a "dehumanizing effect" on their attitudes toward their enemies—and they argue that cruelty and anti-Jewish attitudes have deep roots in Arab culture. They report that many Israeli soldiers whose bodies are returned to Israel by Arab authorities have been found mutilated. Hence they say extreme terrorism is to be expected.

September 20, 1972

Gromyko, in U.N., Assails Terrorism; Cites Palestinians

By ROBERT ALDEN
Special to The New York Times

UNITED NATIONS, N. Y., Sept. 26—Foreign Minister Andrei A. Gromyko of the Soviet Union said today that his Government opposed acts of terrorism and "acts of violence that serve no positive ends and cause loss of human life."

Speaking before the General Assembly, Mr. Gromyko singled out the Palestinian guerrillas for mention.

He said: "It is certainly impossible to condone the acts of terrorism committed by certain elements from among the participants in the Palestinian movement that have led, notably, to the recent tragic events in Munich.

"Their criminal actions deal a blow also at the national interests and aspirations of the Palestinians; these acts are used by the Israeli criminals in order to cover up their policy of banditry against the Arab peoples."

Mr. Gromyko also addressed himself to the question of terrorism in general: "The Soviet Union, from positions of principle, opposes acts of terrorism that disrupt the diplomatic activity of states and their representatives, transport ties between them and the normal course of international contacts and meetings."

September 27, 1972

The Black September Guerrillas: Elusive Trail in Seven Countries

By ERIC PACE
Special to The New York Times

TRIPOLI, Libya, Oct. 7—A hard-living Palestinian intelligence expert whose father was killed by Zionists a quarter century ago . . .

Older Arabs—Al Fatah veterans—who learned about terrorism from the dreaded Moslem Brotherhood. . . .

Poison, Soviet-made hand grenades, British-made submachine guns reportedly passed along by the Libyan regime.

Such are the leaders, and the physical ingredients, of Black September terrorism as reported by informants in six European and Middle Eastern countries and here in Libya, where the revolutionary Government gives zealous backing to what a newspaper it controls calls the "brave lads of Black September."

Black September first attracted attention well before its men attacked the Israeli Olympic team at Munich, West Germany, on Sept. 5. Last November, four of its terrorists assassinated the Jordanian Premier, Wasfi Tal, in Cairo, and one of them is said to have licked his blood.

Arab and Israeli officials and Palestinian militants agree that Black September is an offshoot of Fatah, the largest group of Arab commandos, which has failed to shake Israel with its conventional guerrilla attacks over the years.

In Amman, the Jordanian capital, the authorities say they have had intelligence reports that Black September has made plans to use poison to wreak vengeance on Jordan.

The Jordanian authorities also report that Ali Hassan Salameh, the hard-living Fatah intelligence expert who they say oversees Black September activities, has become a pawn in a rivalry between veteran commando chiefs.

Black September's members themselves have revealed little about their organization, but visits to Beirut, Lebanon, and to Tel Aviv, Jerusalem, Amman, Geneva, and other Middle Eastern and European cities over four weeks have turned up new details about its operations, leaders, internal workings and various allies.

The information, reported largely by security officials and other opponents of Black September, indicates that the Palestinian terrorists have had little success in their latest attacks on Jordanian targets.

It depicts Black September leaders as embittered Palestinian refugees educated mainly in Egypt and hardened by their years with Fatah. And it shows a loose, far-flung organization whose financial support comes principally from Arab oil.

Security officials say there are probably fewer than 200 persons involved more or less full-time with Black September operations, although past estimates have been higher. These operatives are said to have been handpicked and to be fluent in at least one foreign language and willing to die for what the Palestinians term their cause.

Black September hates Jordan because King Hussein's Army crushed the Arab commando movement in that country in a campaign that began in September, 1970—an event that is the origin of the group's name. It hates Israel because it says the Israelis have usurped the Palestinian homeland.

Between the Cairo and Munich killings, Black September claimed responsibility or was blamed for more than a dozen more shootings, explosions and other acts of violence, mostly involving Israeli and Jordanian targets. These were almost all in Europe, where security has been slacker than in the Middle East.

High officials in the Jordanian capital, speaking of indications that Black September planned poisonings on Jordanian soil, said that a plot to poison a Jordanian Cabinet minister was foiled recently when a terrorist agent was caught after having pressed a friend of the minister for details about his eating habits.

The terrorists' violence has included one hijacking and several attempted hijackings of the Jordanian national airline's planes.

Diplomats say that in one instance a hijacker actually pulled the pin on a Soviet-made hand grenade but that a Jordanian sky marshal grabbed the hijacker's hand with the grenade in it. He held on tight, thereby keeping the grenade from going off until the pilot landed in Amman and the authorities managed to dispose of the grenade.

Violence in Europe

In addition the violence has included explosions aboard a Jordanian airliner at the Madrid airport and in a Jordanian office in Geneva—both of which caused no casualties—and the sabotaging of a factory in Hamburg, West Germany, that shipped equipment to Israel.

In another recent incident, Jordanian security officials, acting on a tip, last month intercepted a car loaded with more than 100 pounds of explosives and driven by a man they described as a Fatah commando based in Syria.

TERRORISTS OR PATRIOTS

Black September also showed fallibility last month, the Jordanians say, when it mailed four letter-bombs from Amsterdam to high Jordanian officials in Amman. But some left-wing Arab spokesmen in Damascus, Syria, and elsewhere have suggested that Israel herself sent the letter-bombs as a provocative act.

At any rate, when the letters were intercepted at Amman's main post office, they were found to contain crudely printed Black September cards that seemed intended not for Jordanians but for Israelis.

'We Will Harass You'

The cards, according to an official, said in Arabic and in slightly misspelled English: "Because you have usurped our land, killed out people, and come from all over the world to usurp our rights, we will harass you wherever you are."

The booby traps themselves were homemade. They reportedly yielded no fingerprints or clues about what leader had given the order to mail them along with the dozens of other letter-bombs sent to Israelis, one of which killed an official in the Israeli Embassy in London.

In Beirut, prominent Palestinian militants say that Black September has a loose autonomous "collective leadership" coordinating numbers of more or less isolated "cells," whose members are largely young ultramilitants from Fatah's ranks.

But the view of Western intelligence men and Israeli and Jordanian officials, put forward in increasing detail in recent days, is that Black September is one of Fatah's organizational arms.

Their version is that the terrorists who call themselves members of Black September are actually directed by a small core of men, an operations wing of sorts, in Fatah's intelligence section.

Many experts say it is difficult and misleading to attempt a very precise analysis of Arab commando command structures, which they say are often flexible, changing and fragmented. But they say that regardless of the exact forms involved, it is useful for Fatah to have terrorist operations carried out by men under the separate Black September label.

The arrangment means, the experts say, that Fatah and the over-all commando group, the Palestine Liberation Organization, can disown terrorist acts that would be offensive in moderate quarters. At the same time, they add, the terrorism placates the ultramilitants who crave action against their Israeli and Jordanian enemies.

The Palestine Liberation Organization has disowned Black September, although it has predicted further Arab terrorist blows against Israel.

Most Black September members are said to come from Fatah, but others reportedly come from the Popular Front for the Liberation of Palestine, a smaller Marxist commando group that has carried out several airplane hijackings.

Sources close to the Fatah leadership in Beirut say that a number of the Black September members formerly belonged to élite Fatah units that were trained to operate deep behind Israeli lines. Additional people are said to be recruited temporarily for Black September operations. New faces are useful because they are less likely to be known to policemen and intelligence men.

At least one hijacking expert is reported to have been "borrowed" from the Popular Front.

Black September's guerrillas have reportedly been trained largely in Syria and Lebanon and other Arab countries, with some having received frogman instruction.

The terrorists are said to be split up into small groups scattered through Arab and European countries. There has been at least one report of a handful of them among the thousands of Arab students in the United States, but it has not been confirmed.

Admired in Arab World

The guerrillas in general and Black September in particular command widespread admiration in the Arab world, particularly among Palestinians who have been depressed by Israel's military victories and frustrated by her success in curbing conventional guerrilla activity behind her lines.

The leaders generally move around discreetly, often shuttling between Lebanon and Syria and frequently traveling further afield.

"Sometimes they sleep in two beds in one night," one Arab officer said. "They are afraid the Israelis will kill them."

There is considerable agreement among Black September's various foes on the identities of some of the main figures who are said to oversee its operations.

The foes say that the middle-level commando official directly in charge of carrying out the organization's terrorist plots is Mr. Salameh, a 32-year-old Palestinian refugee from the Jaffa area of Israel. His father, also a Palestinian militant, was killed by the Haganah, the Jewish defense force in Palestine, in 1948.

The following information on Mr. Salameh and other leaders was pieced together largely from reports from Israeli, Jordanian and Western sources and from informants close to the Fatah leadership in Beirut.

Mr. Salameh, a Moslem, is married, has two children and likes to dress well.

His severest critics say he is a compulsive gambler and a part-time narcotics smuggler; others say he smokes and drinks heavily, has a fondness for champagne, speaks confidently and does not like people to talk back to him.

Intelligence Training

While working in Kuwait, he reportedly joined Fatah during its early days, before the 1967 Arab-Israeli war. His first duties were said to have involved dealing with the public, but he reportedly switched to the military branch and was sent to an unspecified non-Arab country in 1968 for training in intelligence techniques.

Later, Mr. Salameh reportedly went to Amman, where he did commando intelligence work for a year or two. After September, 1970, he and some fellow Fatah intelligence experts were said to have moved their operations to Lebanon and Syria.

Last year, Mr. Salameh was reportedly put in charge of terrorist operations under the over-all command of Salah Khalef, one of Fatah's main leaders, who has long been involved with intelligence affairs.

In the past, Mr. Salameh generally worked closely under Mr. Khalef, who is better known under his code name Abu Ayad. But there have been reports of jockeying for power at the top levels of Fatah, and Yasir Arafat, Fatah's leader, is said to have brought Mr. Salameh somewhat under his own wing, thereby placing him a bit of a distance from Mr. Khalef.

"Salameh has become Arafat's man," a Jordanian official said. "Arafat wants to use him to weaken Abu Ayad."

Mr. Khalef is considered more of an extremist than Mr. Arafat, and he is said to give over-all planning guidance to Mr. Salameh and his men.

Strong Hatred of Israel

Mr. Khalef, about 40, has a quiet manner that masks an unbending hatred of Israel. He was educated at Al-Azhar University, an ancient center of Islamic learning in Cairo, and is said to have belonged to the Moslem Brotherhood, an Islamic political organization that has used terrorism.

Mr. Khalef, formerly a schoolteacher in Kuwait, also reportedly joined Fatah before the 1967 war. He is said to be an excellent salesman, skilled at using logic rather than rhetoric to press his points.

Another man who is said to have exercised influence in Black September affairs is Khalil Wazir, a 35-year-old former resident of Gaza who uses the code name Abu Jihad. An intelligent, shrewd man, he too is a devout Moslem, is said to have had ties with the Moslem Brotherhood and was an early Fatah member.

Mr. Wazir was reportedly put in charge of terrorist operations against Jordan after the fighting of September, 1970. His wife is a Palestinian militant, too, and is said to oversee welfare funds paid to widows and children of "martyrs" — commandos who have been killed.

Another reported Black September leader, Fakhri Amri, late last year was in charge of the conspiracy that ended in the assassination of the Jordanian Premier in Cairo. He is said to work on a lower level in the hierarchy and to make his headquarters in Libya, where he is Mr. Khalef's personal representative.

A well-built man, Mr. Amri has a wound scar on his left arm and smokes 80 Rothman cigarettes a day. He was born in Jaffa 39 years ago, is a graduate of Cairo University and has worked as a photographer in Saudi Arabia and a schoolteacher in Jordan. He, too, was reportedly given intelligence training in an unidentified non-Arab country in 1968. Later he was said to have been made responsible for Fatah intelligence affairs in northern Jordan.

Libya is a key country for Fatah and Black September, according to security officials in various countries, because Libyan officials have provided terrorists with passports and other logistical assistance—as well as with Sterling 9-mm. submachine guns used in the assassination of five Jordanians in West Germany last February and in the attempted killing of Zaid al-Rifai, Jordan's Ambassador to London, last December.

Jordanian officials say that the weapons have been traced by their serial numbers to a consignment bought by the Libyan Government last year.

Libya's leader, Col. Muammar el-Qaddafi, is a traditional-minded, fervent Arab nationalist who shares the Arab commando's wish to dissolve the state of Israel. He emphasized his support of Arab terrorism by permitting the burial in Libya of the five Black September members killed in Munich. Several thousand Palestinians are said to be living in Libya.

The Libyan Government recognizes Fatah as the rightful vehicle for "Palestinian liberation" and has expelled a number of Palestinian militants affiliated with other groups. Whether there is an actual Black September office in Tripoli has not been disclosed.

Besides Libyan aid, Black September is said to get help from friendly Arab diplomats, especially Algerians, and sometimes Iraqis and Southern Yemenis. The guerrillas often possess four or five passports, most of them issued by obliging Arab consulates.

Recent Black September pro-

The Palestinians

nouncements issued anonymously in Cairo showed no clear-cut far-left ideological cast, but the sources close to the Fatah leadership say the members are leftist and have friendly ties with radical leftists in West Germany and several more countries who sympathize with the Palestinian cause.

By most accounts, the most important support, in money, training and matériel, comes from Fatah. Estimates by high Jordanian officials of how much money Fatah possesses start at $150-million. But last year, Mr. Arafat went on a fund-raising tour around the Arab world, apparently indicating that Fatah's fortune was not limitless.

Most of the funds have reportedly come from Libya, Saudi Arabia and Kuwait—countries that have grown immensely rich from oil revenues and that are a safe distance from Israel's front lines.

The money has come in direct contributions from governments, from individual leaders, in revenues from special taxes levied by several states and in direct gifts from prosperous Palestinians. Libya is widely thought to make direct contributions to Black September and to be the biggest single contributor to Fatah.

Published Libyan budget figures do not note contributions to any commando organizations. But the Government's oil revenues this year are expected to exceed $2-billion, while the Libyan population is only two million.

In addition, the Libyan regime levies a tax on all personal income for the benefit of the "jihad," or holy war, that it says exists between the Arabs and Israel. This tax ranges between 1 and 3 per cent depending on the amount of income. A 4 per cent "jihad" tax is also levied on the profits of all businesses, with certain exceptions.

Security officials think Libya secretly gives funds to the guerrillas through dummy bank accounts in various countries or, more probably, by having commandos pick up wads of banknotes.

All told, Libyan support for the Palestinian "resistance" movement is thought to run into millions of dollars a year.

October 12, 1972

ARAB GUNMEN KILL 2 U. S. ENVOYS AND SHOOT BELGIAN IN KHARTOUM

2 BELIEVED SPARED

Jordanian and Saudi Arabian Diplomats Reportedly Alive

By HENRY TANNER
Special to The New York Times

KHARTOUM, the Sudan, Saturday, March 3—The Sudanese Government announced early today that Black September commandos had executed two American diplomats who had been held hostage since Thursday night.

The diplomats—Cleo A. Noel Jr., the recently arrived Ambassador, and George C. Moore, the outgoing chargé d'affaires — were among five envoys taken hostage when the commandos invaded and seized the Saudi Arabian Embassy as a farewell reception for Mr. Moore was being held.

A United States Embassy spokesman said that the deaths, by shooting, were confirmed by a Sudanese officer who entered the embassy with permission from the terrorists.

Shots Were Heard

The Sudanese Government also announced that a third hostage—Guy Eid, the Belgian chargé d'affaires — had been killed, but the officer said he was still alive although critically wounded, according to the American Embassy.

The Sudanese officer sought in vain to persuade the terrorists to release the bodies, an American spokesman said. Negotiations for the release of the dead were expected to continue.

The Sudanese Government said that the two other hostages, Sheik Abdullah el-Malhouk, the Saudi Ambassador, and Adliel Nazir, the Jordanian chargé d'affaires, were still alive.

The executions were reportedly carried out at 9:30 last night (2:30 P.M., Friday, New York time) when shots could be heard in the area of the embassy. Sudanese soldiers, sent to surround the building, first reported the executions, and their reports were later confirmed by the Government.

[In Washington, United Press International reported, the State Department said that Mr. Noel had been allowed to make one phone call before his death and that he asked an official at his embassy about "the state of play in the outside world" —meaning world reaction to the guerrillas' act.]

The bursts of fire came as a sand storm hurled clouds of sand around the darkened building, where the hostages were held in a second-floor room behind closed shutters. Visibility was down to about 15 feet.

According to an official Sudanese statement, the killings followed a breakdown of negotiations between leaders of the terrorists and the Sudanese Government.

During the day, the Deputy Premier and Interior Minister of the Sudan, Mohammed Bagir, and other Cabinet ministers had spent several hours negotiating with the terrorists by telephone. The Sudanese had been reported hopeful that the raiders might eventually agree to be flown with their hostages to an Arab capital where both the terrorists and the hostages would be released.

During the morning, the commandos had set 2 P.M. as the deadline by which their demands had to be accepted. At 2, one of them appeared on the balcony outside the room where the hostages were being held, looked at his wrist watch, then disappeared.

In their last exchange by telephone with the Government negotiators, the commandos said at 8:30 P.M. that they had decided to execute the hostages because they had received no acceptable answers from the governments involved.

The Jordanian Government had announced yesterday morning that it would not bow to the guerrillas' demands for the release of Abu Daoud, a leader of Al Fatah, the Palestinian resistance organization, and the release of other Palestinians accused by Amman of having attempted a coup against King Hussein.

"We insist and reconfirm," the commandos had said during the day, "that we will not leave the embassy or release the hostages or even guarantee their lives except if the Palestinian prisoners held in the prisons of the reactionary regime of Jordan are freed."

Many diplomats here expressed the belief that the lives of the Americans had depended primarily on the Jordanian response to the guerrilla demands.

The guerrillas had originally also demanded the release of Sirhan Sirhan, who is serving a life sentence in California for the 1968 assassination of Senator Robert F. Kennedy. [In Washington, President Nixon said at a news conference before it was announced that the envoys had been killed that the United States would "not pay blackmail" for the release of the diplomats.]

In addition, the guerrillas had demanded the release of a number of other people held in Jordan, of all Arab women detained in Israel, and of members of the Baader-Meinhof urban guerrilla group held in West Germany "because they supported the Palestinian cause." The commandos reportedly scaled down their demands during the day yesterday, while continuing to insist on the release of Abu Daoud and his group.

March 3, 1973

The Amuck-Runners

By Gideon Rafael

JERUSALEM—The executioners of Khartoum are of the same mental make as the assassins in the streets of Belfast. They are not alone in the world. They are part of the new international amuck-runners disguised as freedom-fighters, presented by perverted publicity as glamorous guerrillas, idolized by a disoriented community of alienated adolescents.

And what are we doing to ward off this spreading fury? We reel in revulsion, hoping against hope that it won't happen again. But it does, and the happenings become more and more gruesome. Surely submission to violence generates even wider savagery.

If these destructive forces are allowed to rage unchecked they will sap the foundation of society. They threaten to pervert man's mind, and he will be driven to see, as the Bible says, "The shadow of the mountains as if they were men."

The actions of the terrorists compel security forces to maintain a state of vigilance where reaction to threats is a matter of self-preservation. Nothing can be taken for granted.

Take the case of the Libyan airliner forced down by Israeli fighter planes. Was it indeed so far-fetched to suspect that a Libyan aircraft flying over Israeli defense installations might have come with hostile intentions? We have at least as much reason to be watchful as to be careful.

More than one hundred peaceful passengers perished in the Sinai. It was a terrible tragedy. But was it the result of premeditated action? Certainly not. Was it avoidable? This question has been debated by Israelis from all walks of life. Rarely has this country known a similar outbreak of national soul-searching and grief.

People did not seek solace in feasible arguments. Libya regards herself to be in a state of war with Israel; her chief of state, Quaddafi, is one of the most venomous ringleaders of the anti-Israel war coalition. He celebrates the Munich killers as returning heroes and lavishes upon their Fatah organization a reward of $5 million.

We do not abdicate our human compassion. We mourn the victims of the Sinai crash, we compensate their families and we ask ourselves searchingly what can be done to avoid the recurrence of such a tragedy.

This "epidemic insanity," to use a term of Emerson, is spreading.

We must refuse to be deceived by counterfeit ideologies. We must free ourselves of false romanticism. The perpetrators of the crime of Khartoum, of the carnage at Lod Airport, whether they call themselves Red Army Youth or Black September, are not knights in shining armor, but thugs in blood-stained fatigues.

Enlightened governments and public bodies all over the world have repeatedly expressed their abhorrence at terrorist outrages.

There are responsible and concerned governments which have tried to initiate collective action. They have consulted among themselves. They have turned to the United Nations. However, in that world body whose Charter outlaws the resort to force, the use of violence, the fomentation of subversion and proclaims a world order based on the rule of law — in that organization, unfortunately, the Charter-abiding members are in a pitiful minority.

Indeed, upon the initiative of the United States Government the last session of the United Nations was seized with the problem of terrorism, air piracy and assaults against the life diplomats. Proposals for urgent universal action were submitted. But what did the United Nations do? It recommended studying the underlying causes of terrorism, instead of fighting its outrageous effects.

In the fight against terrorism our individual attitudes are important, but what counts are the commissions and omissions of our governments. They must unflinchingly stand up against blackmail. They must not blink when eyeball-to-eyeball with cutthroats.

The governments must deny staging areas to the terrorists from which they have easy and protected access to their targets. Front organizations which serve them as camouflage and cover must be disbanded. The governments should be far more insistent in their refutation of states which assist the outlaws and glorify them when they return from their killing sprees. They should be more persistent in their show of indignation against heads of states who turn a deaf ear to the passionate last-minute appeal of a Prime Minister in the hour of cruel, dire emergency.

Like-minded governments should join in "alliance to combat terrorism," an alignment of states regardless of their political orientation or social organization that are willing to subscribe to a common code of international conduct. Such a charter should define the nature of the subject matter, lay down the guiding principles, prescribe the measure to be adopted, jointly and individually, and specify the mutual obligations, national and international, of the contracting parties.

Since it cannot be worked out within the framework of the United Nations, the governments that care and count should urgently convene a special conference open to all states which are prepared to outlaw and to combat international terrorism. This is the time to act.

Gideon Rafael is the former Director General of Israel's Ministry for Foreign Affairs.

March 16, 1973

Double Standard on Mideast Terror

To the Editor:

It is amazing how different people view one problem. A good example is Gideon Rafael. He views the Black Septemberists as "executioners," "assassins" and "murderers." In the meanwhile he tries, unsuccessfully, to justify the downing of the Libyan airliner by Israeli jets. [Op-Ed March 16.]

His justification is a two-edged sword. On the one hand he condemns the terrorists and on the other he finds in their action a justification for shooting down a civilian plane with more than 100 people on board. The "106" innocent people, according to Mr. Rafael, were the victims of Arab terrorists and not of the Israeli Air Force because terrorist actions "compel security forces to maintain a state of vigilance where reaction to threat is a matter of self-preservation." This, indeed, is the newest and most ingenious in a chain of Israeli interpretations of the incident.

This brings me to the point I am trying to make in regard to terrorism. In discussing terrorism we should not exclude terror inflicted on innocent people by security forces of "civilized" governments. Whenever a "terrorist" hits an Israeli target, Israel hits hundredfold at armless villagers in Syria and Lebanon. Take the case of Munich, where the "terrorists" hit the Israeli athletes. This incident was publicized, and condemned. The same week more than 100 Arabs in Lebanon and 500 Arabs in Syria paid the price for the eleven Israelis. Most of those Arabs, I am sure, do not even know what Munich is, let alone where. This action, committed by the Israeli Air Force, was not widely enough condemned.

Terror should be eliminated whether it is individual or institutionalized.

Institutionalized terror hurts more because it can employ better instruments of death and destruction and because it is done "legitimately." Gibran once said, and I shall try to paraphrase him, that a person who steals a rose from a field is a thief, but the one who steals the whole field is a hero.

Israel is a very strong nation with a very strong army and air force. Israel, now, does not have to resort to terror. She did before when she was not strong. Mr. Rafael should know that, because he belonged to an out-

The Palestinians

lawed organization called the Haganah before the creation of Israel. Now he can afford to condemn terror and the terrorists because his army can terrorize for him.

I am here not to condemn or to defend the Palestinian terrorists or freedom fighters, depending on from where you view them. I am here to condemn hypocrisy. Terror is terror, whether the terrorist is the occupied or the occupier, whether the terrorist is a person or a state.

To condemn the Khartoum incident and not to condemn the Libyan airliner incident is hypocrisy. The intention, if not the magnitude, is the same. A hundred Arabs for an Israeli is not what the Bible says, that same Bible which Mr. Rafael is fond of quoting. HASSAN ABDALLAH
Chicago, March 19, 1973

The writer is director of the Midwest regional office of the Arab Information Center.

April 5, 1973

RAID BY ISRAELIS AT BEIRUT KILLS 2 FATAH LEADERS

OFFICE BLOWN UP

Attackers Enter City After Exchange of Fire With Police

By JUAN de ONIS
Special to The New York Times

BEIRUT, Lebanon, Tuesday, April 10 — Israeli commandos attacked Arab guerrilla bases early today in Beirut and Saida, on the Lebanese coast. The raids, carried out in darkness, followed a Palestinian commando attack yesterday on Israelis in Cyprus.

The Ministry of Defense announced in a preliminary casualty report that two Lebanese security agents and nine civilians had been killed, while an army officer and nine security agents were wounded.

Two prominent leaders of the Palestinian Fatah guerrilla organization were killed in the attack at Beirut.

The raiders blew up the apartment of Mohammed Yussef Najjar, also known as Abu Yussef, a member of the executive committee of Fatah. Mr. Najjar and his wife were both killed. The Israelis reportedly killed several guards and kidnapped a son of the Fatah leader.

Third Death Reported

They also killed Kemal Adwan, another Fatah leader, and blew up the headquarters of the Democratic Popular Front for the Liberation of Palestine, a small but militant commando group led by Nayef Hawatmeh, a Marxist.

There were unconfirmed reports that the Israelis also killed Kemal Nasser, spokesman of the Palestinian Liberation Organization, who lived in an apartment in the same building with Mr. Najjar.

The attacks were carried out in the center of the Lebanese capital in the area of the Palestinian refugee camp called Sabra, which is where most of the commando organizations have their headquarters.

One raiding party came ashore on the Mediterranean beach south of this capital near Khalde where a police post exchanged fire with the Israelis.

The commandos made their way into the center of the capital, reportedly in automobiles that were waiting at the beach, and attacked the fifth-floor apartment of Mr. Najjar, which is only a block away from a police headquarters.

After the attack, the police arrived at the scene and were investigating when a group of armed Fatah commandos arrived and opened fire, apparently believing that the police were responsible for the attack on their leader.

Two Palestinian commandos were hospitalized with wounds after the police returned the fire in the confused incident.

The Lebanese military reported that the Israelis wore civilian clothes and irregular uniforms similar to those used by Palestinian guerrillas. At least two parties landed here by sea.

One group attacked the apartment house were Mr. Najjar and other Fatah leaders lived with a strong guard always at the main entrance controlling visitors.

The other group, coming inland from the coast for nearly a mile through city streets, placed high explosive charges at an apartment house near the Sabra refugee camp holding the officers of the Democratic Popular Front group.

The blast demolished the walls of the building on the first two floors, destroyed two automobiles parked on the sidewalk, and shattered windows in apartment buildings 150 yards away.

Mr. Najjar was one of the best-known Fatah leaders. He was chief of the organization's political department. A soft-spoken man in his 40's, Mr. Najjar often met with Arab chiefs of state on diplomatic missions for Fatah. He was on close personal terms with the Lebanese Premier, Saeb Salam.

April 10, 1973

ARAB GUERRILLAS KILL 31 IN ROME

GRENADES HURLED

Grenade Attack in Rome

By PAUL HOFMANN
Special to The New York Times

ROME, Tuesday, Dec. 18 — Arab guerrillas attacked an American jetliner here yesterday, spraying it with submachine-gun fire, hurling hand grenades into it and setting it on fire.

At least 29 people aboard were killed, and two outside the plane were shot dead.

The guerrillas then hijacked a West German airliner to Athens with a number of hostages aboard and reportedly began shooting them dead, one by one, to back demands for the release of two Palestinian terrorists, who are being held in Greece.

Several Americans and four Moroccan Government officials were among the victims of the attack here on the plane, a Boeing 707 of Pan American World Airways. The attack was witnessed from the airport's transit lounge by Morocco's Premier, Ahmed Osman. He was unhurt.

At least 18 people, including 10 American citizens, were wounded in the shooting and the turmoil that followed, and were taken to various hospitals.

There were 59 passengers and nine crewmen aboard the plane, Flight 110, which was waiting to take off for Beirut, Lebanon, and Teheran, Iran, when it was attacked at 1:10 P.M. (7:10 A.M., Monday, New York time).

All 29 dead were said to have been passengers, and one crew member, a stewardess, was reported missing. The 38 others aboard were able to scramble to safety when the plane burst into flames.

The four Moroccan officials who were among the dead had been on their way to Iran for an official visit. They were identified as Abdelatif Inani, Secretary of State for Planning,

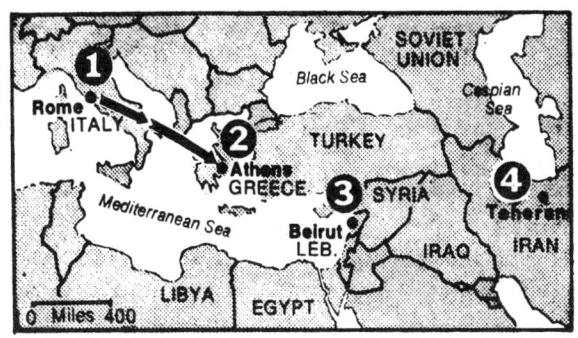

TERRORISTS OR PATRIOTS

Guerrillas attacked Pan American jetliner at Rome (1) and hijacked West German plane to Athens (2). American jet was being prepared for a flight to Beirut (3) and Teheran (4) when the shooting began.

Regional Development and Training; Mounir Doukkali, Under Secretary of State for Youth and Sports; Mohammed Lazrak, secretary general of the Ministry of Commerce, and Mekki Zaylachi, an official of the Cabinet.

The guerrillas were reported by witnesses as numbering from six to eight men. Some of them were described as tall and of olive complexion, with mustaches.

Most or all had reportedly arrived earlier in the day from Madrid on a flight of Iberia, the Spanish national airline. Italian investigators said that the guerrillas might have been met in the transit lounge of Leonardo da Vinci International Airport at Fiumicino, 15 miles west of here, by one or several persons, possibly including a woman, before they started their attack.

The attack at the airport came as preparations were under way for the convening late this week of the Middle East peace conference in Geneva.

In Beirut, the leadership of the Palestinian guerrilla movement condemned the actions in Rome, describing them as against the interests of "our people." The unanimous view in political circles there was that the attack had been carried out by a small extremist group with the objective of upsetting the Geneva conference.

The attack also coincided with the opening of a trial here in Rome of Arabs on terrorist charges. Five persons are accused of having conspired in September to shoot down an El Al airliner with ground-to-air missiles. The trials of three of them opened Friday, but the two others sent telegrams to the court saying they were in hiding for fear of Israeli secret agents.

December 18, 1973

Few Arab Terrorists Are Punished for Hijackings and Killings

By JOHN SIBLEY

Although most Arab terrorists responsible for hijackings, kidnappings and the seizure and execution of hostages over the last few years have been captured or have given themselves up, few have suffered meaningful punishment. Following, in chronological order, is the eventual fate—as best can be determined—of Arab terrorists who preceded those who surrendered Tuesday in Kuwait.

July 23, 1968—Two Palestinians and one Syrian who hijacked an El Al Israeli airliner bound from Rome to Lydda airport in Israel were detained by Algerian authorities but soon released.

Dec. 26, 1968—An Israeli passenger and a stewardess were wounded in a gunfire attack on an El Al plane at the Athens airport. Two Palestinians were sentenced to 17 and 14 years' imprisonment but were freed after the hijacking of a Greek airliner to Beirut, Lebanon, on July 22, 1970.

Feb. 18, 1969—Five Palestinians attacked an El Al airliner at the Zurich airport, killing the co-pilot and wounding the pilot. One attacker was killed; the others were sentenced to varying jail terms but were subsequently released.

Aug. 29, 1969—Two Palestinians hijacked a Trans World Airlines plane from Los Angeles to Damascus but were not brought to trial.

Sept. 8, 1969—Two Arab boys hurled hand grenades into the El Al offices in Brussels. One escaped after taking refuge in the Iraqi Embassy; the other was not prosecuted.

Nov. 27, 1969—A hand grenade attack on the El Al office in Athens killed a Greek child and wounded 13 persons. Two Jordanian terrorists were sentenced to 11-year and 8-year jail terms but were freed after the hijacking of an Olympic Airways plane on July 22, 1970.

Dec. 17, 1969—Two Britons were arrested in an aborted conspiracy to blow up an El Al plane at Heathrow Airport, London. One was sentenced to 12 years in jail; the other went free after turning state's evidence.

Dec. 21, 1969—Three Lebanese were detained after an unsuccessful attempt to hijack a T.W.A. plane in Athens. They were freed after the hijacking of an Olympic Airways plane to Beirut on July 22, 1970.

Feb. 10, 1970—An attack on an El Al plane at Munich killed one passenger and wounded eight more. One Egyptian and two Jordanians were arrested but were set free after the Dec. 6 hijacking of three American airliners.

July 22, 1970 — Six Palestinians hijacked an Olympic Airways plane to Beirut. None were brought to justice.

Sept. 6, 1970—Pan American, T.W.A. and Swissair planes bound for New York were hijacked by Arabs. The Pan American plane landed at Cairo, the others in Jordan, where all were blown up. None of the terrorists were arrested.

Sept. 6, 1970 — A woman terrorist was wounded and her male companion killed in an attempt to hijack an El Al plane bound from London to New York. A steward was wounded. When the plane returned to England the woman was released because the crime had been committed outside British jurisdiction.

July 28, 1971—An attempt to blow up an El Al plane bound from Rome to Lydda with booby-trapped luggage given to a woman by an Arab boyfriend did not succeed.

Sept. 20, 1971—A similar attempt to blow up an El Al plane from London to Lydda with a booby-trapped suitcase given to a woman by an Arab friend also failed.

Nov. 29, 1971—Wasfi Tal, Premier of Jordan, was assassinated by four Palestinian guerrillas while entering his hotel in Cairo. The alleged killers were taken into custody but no prosecutions have been reported.

Feb. 22, 1972—A Lufthansa plane bound from New Delhi to Beirut was hijacked to Aden, where the hijackers were paid $5-million for its release. The hijackers went free.

May 8, 1972—Terrorists hijacked a Belgian Sabena airliner to Lydda. Two men were killed by Israeli security guards and two women were subsequently sentenced to life imprisonment.

Aug. 16, 1972—A booby-trapped tape-recorder exploded in the luggage compartment of an El Al plane in flight from Rome to Lydda, causing slight damage. Two Arabs who gave the recorder to two apparently unaware British women were released by Italian authorities after a short detention.

Sept. 5, 1972—An Arab guerrilla organization called Black September attacked the headquarters of Israeli atheletes in the Olympic Village in Munich. Eleven members of the Israeli Olympic Team were slain. Five of the terrorists were killed in an airport gunbattle with West German police. Three others were later freed under pressure from hijackers.

Oct. 29, 1972—A Lufthansa flight from Beirut to Ankara, Turkey, was hijacked to Zagreb, Yugoslavia, where it was released after Arab terrorists responsible for the attack on Israeli athletes at the Munich Olympic games had been freed by West Germany. The hijackers were never brought to justice.

March 2, 1973—Eight Black September commandoes invaded the Saudi Arabian Embassy in Khartoum and killed three diplomats, including Cleon A. Noel Jr., the United States Ambassador to the Sudan. The terrorists are in custody in Khartoum but have not yet been brought to trial.

April 4, 1973—Two Arabs made an unsuccessful attempt to attack passengers of an El Al plane at the Rome airport. They were arrested but later released and sent to Lebanon.

April 9, 1973—Arab terrorists attempted to attack an Israeli plane at the Nicosia, Cyprus, airport. Eight were arrested and sentenced to seven years' imprisonment. Later, the Cypriote President, Archbishop Makarios, quietly released them, saying he did not want Cyprus to become a battleground for Middle East conflicts.

The Palestinians

April 27, 1973—An Italian employe was killed in the Rome office of El Al by a Palestinian Arab who is now under arrest in the psychiatric ward of an Italian institution. A magistrate's decision to place him under psychiatric observation is widely taken to mean he will never face trial.

July 19, 1973—After an aborted attack on the El Al office in Athens a terrorist took two hostages to an adjoining hotel but released them after negotiations with the police.

July 24, 1973—A Japanese jumbo jet, in flight from Amsterdam to Tokyo, was hijacked and blown up in Tripoli, Libya. Of five terrorists involved, an Arab woman was killed by a grenade she was carrying. One terrorist was Japanese. None were brought to trial.

Aug. 4, 1973—Two Arab terrorists killed five and wounded 55 in a machine gun attack on passengers in the Athens airport lounge. The two were arrested, and Greek authorities have not released them despite a demand by the hijackers in this week's incident.

Sept. 5, 1973—Five Palestinians plotted to shoot down an El Al plane near the Rome airport. The five went on trial —two in absentia—before an Italian court last week. Three defendants are in the dock; the two others have been in hiding, presumably abroad, since they were released in their own recognizance.

December 20, 1973

Arab Guerrillas Kill 18 in Israeli Town, Then Die in Blast at Apartment House

By Reuters

QIRYAT SHEMONA, Israel, April 11 — Eighteen people, mostly women and children, were killed here today by three Arab guerrillas who stormed a four-story residential building.

The guerrillas died in an explosion at the end of a four-hour gun and grenade battle with Israeli troops. The Israeli Acting Chief of Staff, Maj. Gen. Yitzhak Hofi, said the guerrillas had been killed when an explosive-laden knapsack they were carrying was hit by Israeli fire.

Sixteen people were wounded in the incident, the worst since a three-man Japanese "suicide squad" working for the guerrillas killed 27 people and wounded 80 at the Tel Aviv airport in May, 1972.

The guerrillas, said by the Israeli military to belong to an extremist Palestinian group based in southern Lebanon, infiltrated into the northern Israeli town early today after apparently evading a patrol near the Lebanese border, five miles away.

[Premier Golda Meir warned the Government of Lebanon that Israel would hold it responsible for the attack. In Beirut, the Popular Front for the Liberation of Palestine-General Command, a small guerrilla organization, said that the raid had been carried out by a suicide squad composed of a Palestinian, a Syrian and an Iraqi.]

Witnesses of the violence said they had seen children hurled from third-floor windows after the guerrillas stormed into the building and forced their way into apartments, which they sprayed with machine-gun fire as they climbed to the fourth floor. But General Hofi said no children had been thrown from windows.

Tonight, the building at 10 Yehuda Halevy Street, where most of the people died, was a battered, blood-splashed wreck, with huge holes near the fourth-floor room in which the guerrillas made their final stand.

When soldiers moved in they found bodies, many of them children, on the staircases and in the apartments.

A large number of the town's 15,000 inhabitants, many of them recent immigrants, gathered silently outside as the bodies and wounded were taken away.

The military categorically denied reports from Damascus that the guerrillas had attempted to take hostages when they blasted their way into the building. Soldiers here said there were definitely no hostages in the room where they found the bodies of the guerrillas.

The gunmen were carrying explosives as well as Russian rifles and grenades. A television cameraman who was at the scene said he saw Israeli soldiers using recoilless rifles and grenades before they stormed the building.

A grandmother, wounded in a burst of guerrilla fire, dragged herself into a bedroom and pushed two grandchildren under a bed. She died; the children survived.

One child 2½ years old was among the eight who died. Five women and five men were also killed.

The morning of terror for the town began when the three guerrillas infiltrated the outskirts of the town and entered a school, empty because of the Passover holiday.

Witnesses said they began spraying passers-by with automatic fire, but as security forces converged on the area, cordoning it off, the three managed to dash to the nearby residential block, shooting their way in.

The New York Times/April 12, 1974

Arab guerrillas killed 18 people at Qiryat Shemona before being killed in an explosion.

Two hours after the mayhem began, sirens wailed over the town, sending the rest of the inhabitants to shelters.

Soldiers were brought in to reinforce the border police units. Defense Minister Moshe Dayan and General Hofi arrived by helicopter from Jerusalem.

Witnesses said that initially the scene appeared confused with security forces milling around trying to find the best way of getting at the guerrillas, who were firing wildly in all directions from the top floor.

The cameraman said he saw two soldiers appear on the roof to toss grenades into the room occupied by the guerrillas.

April 12, 1974

16 YOUNG ISRAELI HOSTAGES DIE AS TROOPS KILL 3 ARAB CAPTORS

By TERENCE SMITH
Special to The New York Times

MAALOT, Israel, May 15—A day of terror ended in this northern town this evening with a savage, 10-minute burst of gunfire and grenade explosions that killed three Arab terrorists and 16 of the high-school students they were holding hostage.

Early this morning, terrorists took command of the school, where about 90 students out on an excursion were sleeping. The three Arabs demanded the release of 20 prisoners held by Israel in return for the lives of the students.

An Israeli attempt to meet the demand failed and, as the deadline set by the guerrillas approached, soldiers rushed the school.

On 26th Independence Day

In the fighting that ensued, besides those killed 70 students were wounded, at least nine seriously. In the morning, as the day's terror began, a family of three was cut down by the Arab guerrillas as they entered the town. One soldier was also killed.

It was one of the bloodiest terrorist incidents in Israel's troubled history and it came on the 26th anniversary of the nation's independence.

After the decision to rush the

TERRORISTS OR PATRIOTS

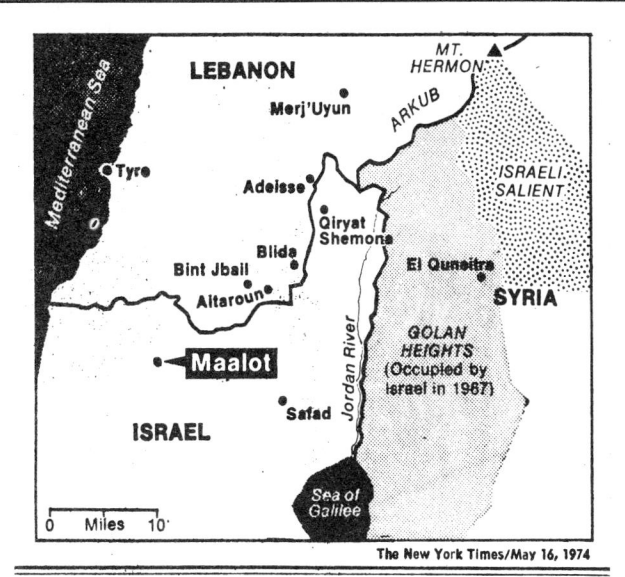

school had been made, soldiers in bullet-proof vests surrounded the three-story building while snipers trained their sights on its shallow horizontal windows.

The firing broke out suddenly, while an officer with an electric megaphone was still pleading with the guerrillas in Arabic to postpone their 6 P.M. deadline.

Two of the three Arabs were hit by the opening burst of fire. One was apparently killed instantly, but the second had the strength to turn his automatic weapon on the students, spraying the second-story classroom indiscriminately.

Sought to Explode School

The third man tossed two grenades out the windows in an attempt to scatter the attacking soldiers. Then, according to one of the officers, the terrorist raced downstairs toward the entrance of the school where explosive charges had been placed. Before he could detonate them, soldiers shot him.

The screams of the terrified teen-agers could be heard a hundred yards away as the shooting erupted. One girl shrieked over and again, "Up here, he's up here," referring to the wounded terrorist who was still firing.

Even before the shooting stopped, the students who could walk fled in panic through a side door. They raced out through smoke from hand grenades toward army ambulances as bullets continued to ricochet off the building.

Only a handful escaped unhurt. The majority were taken from the building on stretchers. All of them seemed to be bleeding. Many were crying as soldiers took them to the ambulances.

Defense Minister Moshe Dayan entered the school to survey the carnage. He emerged grim-faced 10 minutes later, while the last of the stretchers was being brought out.

"Get out of here, get out of here," he shouted to the crowd that had gathered around the entrance. "There's a charge set to go off at 6."

Soldiers, newsmen and townspeople fled down the hill, away from the school.

Several minutes followed, but no explosion occurred. An officer said later that the soldiers feared the guerrillas had left another charge.

The townspeople seemed enraged, either by the way the army handled the incident or simply by the fact that the incident had occurred at all. A crowd tried to attack Mr. Dayan as he emerged from the school. It took a squad of soldiers to push him through and down to the command post that had been established in a house a hundred yards away.

Frustrated, the crowd then returned to the school building, demanding the bodies of the three terrorists.

"Burn them," someone shrieked, "let's make an Auschwitz out of them." This seemed to be an allusion to the crematoria at a Nazi extermination camp.

A double line of police and soldiers held the crowd back and, as darkness fell, people slowly began to disperse.

May 16, 1974

In Lebanon, Just Rubble And Despair

By STEVEN V. ROBERTS
Special to The New York Times

NABATIEH, Lebanon, May 17—An old woman, her head wrapped in a kerchief, trudged through the rubble of this village, talking to herself.

"Everywhere we go," she moaned, "the Israelis are after us."

First her family was driven out of Palestine, she related, and then out of a refugee camp near the town of Saida. Now her village had been pounded by Israeli planes. Standing in its ruins, she voiced the ancient sufferings of war.

"God, this is our destiny!" she kept saying. "This is our destiny!"

Yesterday Israeli aircraft attacked Nabatieh and several other Palestinean refugee camps in southern Lebanon, squalid places that have been breeding anger and violence for 26 years. Government officials said the raids were in retaliation for the Palestinian attack in Maalot yesterday in which 24 Israelis were killed.

A Bullet-Marked Bus

It is estimated that 25 Arabs were killed in Nabatieh yesterday. Today the Palestinian guerrillas took a busload of newsmen from Beirut, about 30 miles north, to view the camp, which is a restricted area that can be entered only with military permission.

The bus, a rickety contraption generously pocked with bullet holes, careened along as if an Israeli patrol was gaining on the driver. Along the coast road an occasional antiaircraft gun poked toward the deep blue sky.

Entering Nabatieh, the first thing to be noticed is bomb craters, some as deep as 20 feet. Lebanese newspapers said today that the raid was the fiercest ever launched against the Palestinians by Israel. The Israelis have insisted that their jets attacked only Palestinian guerrilla concentrations.

The guerrilla command post in the center of town was obliterated. So were dozens of houses.

In one a bed was standing in a room with two walls left. Bulldozers had apparently been through, leveling the debris and covering everything with a thick coat of choking gray dust. But a few odds and ends were still scattered about, signs of the lives that had been lived here—a twisted spoon, a red slipper, a rubber boot that still smoldered with an acrid smell.

The trees had been shorn of their leaves, and bits of clothing hung from the bare branches.

The Nabatieh camp usually holds about 3,500 Palestinian refugees, but most had fled. A few men picked through the rubble, trying to salvage a pan or a blanket. Three hoisted what they could carry onto their backs and headed for the town nearby, hoping to find sleeping space in a mosque.

Guerrilla leaders conducted a news conference in the square, where only a basketball hoop was still standing. Young guerrillas lounged nearby, holding their automatic rifles as casually as a tourist might hold his camera.

The Israeli raids, one said, would only accelerate guerrilla attacks. Said another: "The Kissinger mission and the Israeli attacks are two sides of the same coin. The Kissinger mission is aimed at wiping out the Palestinian cause, while the mission of the Israeli Phantoms is to wipe out the Palestinians themselves."

A third guerrilla, who goes by the name Che Guevara, displayed several toys he said were boobytrapped by the Israelis and dropped on the village. But they were clean and in one piece, and everything else in Nabatieh was dirty and broken, so it was hard to believe him.

As the newsmen departed a villager said several bodies were still buried where they stood. Under the debris a cat cried, another victim of an endless war.

May 18, 1974

The Palestinians

AL FATAH ASSERTS IT SET UP ATTACK ON TOWN IN ISRAEL

By HENRY TANNER
Special to The New York Times

CAIRO, June 25—Al Fatah, the largest and most moderate of the Palestinian resistance organizations, announced today that it was responsible for the guerrilla raid that resulted in seven deaths last night at the Israeli town of Nahariya.

The announcement, made in Baghdad, Iraq, by Fatah's military arm, Al Assefa, came as a surprise. Specialists in Palestinian affairs here said that as far as they could remember Fatah had never before accepted responsibility for such an operation.

The statement was regarded by diplomats here as a sign that moderate Palestinian leaders like Yasir Arafat, who heads both Fatah and the over-all guerrilla group, the Palestine Liberation Organization, had now decided, like their radical counterparts, to maintain pressure on Israel by armed attacks.

Diplomacy and Violence

Mr. Arafat has been pressing for Palestinian participation at the Middle East peace talks in Geneva. He and his moderates are now believed to be committed—as are the militants—to the simultaneous use of diplomacy and violence in an attempt to win Palestinian admission to the Geneva talks.

June 26, 1974

PALESTINIANS GET OFFICE IN SOVIET

By MALCOLM W. BROWNE
Special to The New York Times

MOSCOW, Sunday, Aug. 4— The Soviet Union announced today that it had consented to the opening of an office of the Palestine Liberation Organization in Moscow, in effect recognizing the group as the sole representative of Palestinian Arabs

A joint communiqué by the Soviet Government and a Palestinian delegation that has been visiting Moscow for the last five days reaffirmed Soviet support for the participation of the group in the Geneva peace conference on the Middle East as a full participant.

The communiqué said that Yasir Arafat, head of the Palestine Liberation Organization, had met with Boris N. Ponomarev, a Communist party secretary, First Deputy Foreign Minister Vasily V. Kuznetsov and the deputy head of the international section of the Communist party.

The fact that Mr. Arafat evidently was not received by the highest party leaders or by Foreign Minister Andrei A. Gromyko indicated that Soviet support of the P.L.O. was not so all-embracing as was suggested yesterday by Palestinian spokesmen in Beirut, Lebanon.

August 4, 1974

ARAB GUERRILLAS SHRUG OFF SPLIT

By JUAN de ONIS
Special to The New York Times

BEIRUT, Lebanon, Oct. 5— The breakaway from the Palestine Liberation Organization of an intransigent Marxist faction opposed to any Arab-Israeli political settlement has produced only a surface ruffle in Palestinian ranks.

The withdrawal last week of the Popular Front for the Liberation of Palestine, an extremist group, has been criticized in virtually all Arab quarters, including left-wing publications.

But the withdrawal of the group, which is headed by George Habash, a Marxist radical who advocates unrelenting war against Israel, has been quietly welcomed by Arab governments trying to win international recognition of the Palestine Liberation Organization, the umbrella group for the Palestinian movement, as the rightful representative of the Palestinian people.

These governments, led by Egypt, Syria, Saudi Arabia and Algeria, support Yasir Arafat, the chairman of the Palestine Liberation Organization and the head of Al Fatah, the largest of the Palestinian guerrilla groups, as the leader of the Palestinian movement.

It was these governments that led the successful Arab drive to place the Palestinian question on the agenda of this year's United Nations General Assembly as a separate item. The countries are expected to sponsor the participation in the General Assembly debate on this issue of a Palestinian delegation headed by Mr. Arafat.

Political commentators have said that this effort to obtain broad international acceptance of the Palestine Liberation Organization as a participant in Middle East peace talks would be helped by the withdrawal of Mr. Habash's group, which had denounced the efforts of Secretary of State Kissinger to promote negotiations between the Arabs and Israel. It opposed the Geneva Middle East peace conference as an American-sponsored "plot to bring about the capitulation" of the Arabs.

October 6, 1974

ARAB LEADERS ISSUE CALL FOR A PALESTINIAN STATE; ARAFAT GIVEN MAIN ROLE

By HENRY TANNER
Special to The New York Times

RABAT, Morocco, Oct. 28— Arab heads of state, including King Hussein of Jordan, called unanimously today for the creation of an independent Palestinian state "on any Palestinian land that is liberated" from Israeli occupation.

In a declaration, they recognized the Palestine Liberation Organization, the over-all guerrilla group headed by Yasir Arafat, as the "sole legitimate representative of the Palestinian people." The decision appeared to be a victory for Mr. Arafat.

King Hussein, who had been at odds with the Palestine Liberation Organization over who would administer any areas of the occupied West Bank that Israel might relinquish, accepted the decision "without any reservations," according to Sayed Nofal, deputy secretary general of the Arab League, who read the text of the declaration to reporters tonight.

The Arab declaration raised several questions but left a number of issues in doubt. It was unclear why King Hussein concurred in the declaration

TERRORISTS OR PATRIOTS

and what his role in future Middle East negotiations would be.

Blow to Kissinger Seen

The decision also appeared to leave in doubt the future of Arab-Israeli peace negotiations, since Israel has said she would not deal with the Palestine Liberation Organization.

In addition, the Arab declaration was regarded as a blow to Secretary of State Kissinger, who had hoped to leave the Palestinian issue for a later stage in his step-by-step approach to peace in the Middle East. Instead, it was noted, the Palestine Liberation Organization has now become a major participant in the diplomatic maneuvering.

The declaration, which was approved by the presidents and kings of Arab League countries and by Mr. Arafat, called on Egypt, Jordan, Syria and the Palestine Liberation Organization to hold consultations with the aim of concerting their efforts in the future.

President Anwar el-Sadat of Egypt proposed earlier this year that such four-party consultations be held to decide Arab representation at the Middle East peace conference in Geneva.

Egyptian and other delegates here said tonight that the inclusion of this provision in the declaration, and King Hussein's concurrence in it, were signs that he intended to play a role in the peace talks contrary to his earlier statements. The King had threatened to withdraw from all Arab efforts to bring about a settlement if the Arab leaders recognized the Palestine Liberation Organization—as they did today—as the "sole legitimate representative of the Palestinian people" on the occupied West Bank.

Members of the Jordanian delegation could not be reached for comment tonight on the announcement that the King had concurred despite his earlier statements.

Egyptian and other delegates who had been at the forefront of efforts to reconcile the positions of the Palestine organization and Hussein were jubilant and said that Arab unity had triumphed. But other delegates, said they did not exclude the possibility that King Hussein, once back in his own capital, might yet revert to his earlier position and withdraw from any diplomatic efforts to bring about a settlement in the Middle East.

Assurance Is Hinted

Some conference sources said they thought it possible that King Hussein had gone along with the declaration today after having received informal assurances on the nature of the role he was to play. It was also thought possible that he had received promises of large financial support from King Faisal of Saudi Arabia.

In concurring, King Hussein recognized the Palestine Liberation Organization for the first time as "sole legitimate representative" of the Palestinian people and conceded the Palestinians the right to set up their own national state in "liberated" areas of the West Bank without a plebiscite.

The resolution said that the Arab leaders assembled reaffirmed "the rights of the Palestinian people to set up an independent national authority, under the leadership of the Palestine Liberation Organization as the sole legitimate representative of the Palestinian people, on any Palestinian land that is liberated."

"Arab countries must support this authority when it is established in all fields and at all levels," the declaration added.

The declaration was first adopted this afternoon at a restricted meeting presided over by King Hassan II of Morocco. Those attending were Mr. Arafat, King Hussein, King Faisal and Presidents Sadat of Egypt, Houari Boumediene of Algeria and Hafez al-Assad of Syria.

Immediately after that meeting, it was announced that these leaders had agreed on "the principles giving the Palestine Liberation Organization full national and international responsibilities in the Israeli-occupied areas." These were said to be any areas of the West Bank and the Gaza Strip that Israel might relinquish. The declaration was then adopted by all the heads of state present and by Mr. Arafat.

October 29, 1974

U.N. ASSEMBLY HEARS ARAFAT URGE PALESTINE STATE INCLUDING JEWS; ISRAEL SEES PLAN TO DESTROY HER

DRAMATIC SESSION

P.L.O. Head Says He Bears Olive Branch and Guerrilla Gun

By PAUL HOFMANN
Special to The New York Times

UNITED NATIONS, N.Y., Nov. 13 — The head of the Palestine Liberation Organization, Yasir Arafat, told the United Nations General Assembly today that his organization's goal remained a Palestinian state that would include Moslems, Christians and Jews.

Israel's delegate, Yosef Tekoah, said in rebuttal that this would mean the destruction of Israel and the substitution of an Arab state.

The two speeches at the opening of the debate on "the Question of Palestine" were the highlight of one of the most dramatic and tension-fraught days in the history of the world organization.

Mr. Arafat was applauded by many delegates in the 138-country Assembly when he said he was dreaming of "one democratic state where Christian, Jew and Moslem live in justice, equality and fraternity." In such a state, he said, all Jews "now living in Palestine" could become citizens without discrimination.

Olive Branch and Gun

In what sounded like a threat of intensified guerrilla activity if the Palestine Liberation Organization's proposal for a multifaith Palestinian state was not accepted, Mr. Arafat said toward the end of his speech:

"I have come bearing an olive branch and a freedom fighter's gun. Do not let the olive branch fall from my hands."

Yosef Tekoah, the chief Israeli delegate, branded the Palestinian guerrillas as terroristic and murderous and vowed his Government's determination to fight them implacably.

Mr. Tekoah gravely and forcefully restated "Israel's readiness and desire to reach a peaceful settlement with the Palestinian Arab state of Jordan in which Palestinian national identity would find full expression."

Mr. Arafat, in his 90-minute address, also warned that a fifth Middle East war might end in nuclear destruction, appealed to the American people for friendship and understanding for his movement, described Zionism as "imperialistic" and "racist," and issued a thinly veiled warning to Israel that she might be suspended from United Nations bodies in the same way as South Africa was suspended by the Assembly yesterday.

Later, two senior European delegates commented independently, but in almost the same words, that Mr. Arafat's presentation of the Palestine Liberation Organization's case had been moderate, even statesmanlike, in tone but hard or "maximalist" in substance.

Courtesies of Protocol

Mr. Arafat, who arrived at United Nations headquarters by helicopter from John F. Ken-

The Palestinians

nedy International Airport at 6.50 A.M., appeared in the Assembly hall at 11.40 A.M. The courtesies of protocol extended to him resembled those normally accorded to heads of states.

The Palestinian leader was, uncharacteristically, freshly shaven. He wore the flowing black and white headdress — a kaffiyeh—that is his trademark, a bright windbreaker over a brown shirt without a necktie, and matching trousers.

Cameramen and other people who were near Mr. Arafat noticed that he was wearing a holster under his bulging windbreaker. A spokesmen later denied that Mr. Arafat had carried a gun into the Assembly hall, and asserted that the holster, if there had been one, had been empty.

Most delegates in the hall rose and gave the Palestinian leader a minute-long standing ovation. Mr. Arafat acknowledged the applause, raising both arms and clenching his hands.

Welcome by Bouteflika

The Assembly's President, Foreign Minister Abdelaziz Bouteflika of Algeria, welcomed Mr. Arafat as chairman of the P.L.O. executive committee and "commander in chief of the Palestinian revolution."

Mr. Arafat put his black horn-rimmed glasses on the speaker's lectern and began his long speech in a high-pitched, often staccato, Arabic. He frequently gesticulated with both hands to stress a point. In all, he spoke with ease and displayed consummate rhetorical skills.

Seats for members of the Palestinian delegation who had come to New York with Mr. Arafat had been added to the first row of chairs and desks for representatives of member governments. The Palestinians sat next to the Jordan delegation.

Israeli Seats Empty

The Israeli delegation's seats near the center of the first row remained empty during Mr. Arafat's address, which took up the entire morning meeting of the Assembly. The seats of the South African delegation, which was barred from attendance at the current General Assembly by a vote last night, were also unoccupied. The nameplate, "South Africa" remained.

At this afternoon's meeting, the Palestinians and the delegates of all Arab countries walked out of the hall when Israel's delegate, Mr. Tekoah, started speaking. Mr. Arafat did not appear at the afternoon meeting.

Israel's delegate had originally been scheduled to speak at the morning meeting, which was to have started at 10:30 A.M.

However, the Assembly President unexpectedly ordered a delay until 12 noon, the time at which heads of states normally deliver their addresses to the Assembly. Mr. Bouteflika gave no explanation for his order.

Photographs for The New York Times by EDWARD HAUSNER
Yosef Tekoah delivering Israel's rebuttal to Mr. Arafat

An Israeli spokesman, Yaakov Morris, said in a statement that Mr. Bouteflika's decision reflected "bias" and an attempt to dramatize Mr Arafat's appearance and to make sure that Israel could not present her position at the morning meeting. Actually, the meeting was formally opened by Mr. Bouteflika at 11:37 A.M.

Mr. Arafat was the first person not representing a member government to address the General Assembly since Pope Paul VI visited the United Nations in 1965.

The Palestinian's speech was interrupted nine times by applause. When he finished, a large part of the Assembly gave him a standing ovation that lasted nearly two minutes. The applause before, during and after Mr. Arafat's speech was led by Arab delegates. Black Africans and representatives from other third-world countries joined them. Most West European delegates remained reserved throughout.

Mr. Arafat seemed to enjoy what Arabs here called his "triumph," placing an arm over the backrest of a beige armchair that had been placed to the right side of the rostrum.

Armchair a Symbol

The armchair is a United Nations status symbol usually reserved for heads of states. Mr. Arafat was accorded the symbolic honor on instructions from Mr. Bouteflika, who seemed to be going out of his way to make the Palestinian leader's visit to the world organization solemn and memorable.

In his address, Mr. Arafat named Israel directly only a few times, but referred to her often as "the Zionist entity" or by other disparaging circumlocutions.

Mr. Tekoah used blunt language, calling members of the P.L.O. "murderers," and declaring that "Arafat, today, prefers the Nazi method" of physical annihilation of Jews.

"The murderers of athletes in the Olympic Games in Munich, the butchers of children in Maalot, the assassins of diplomats in Khartoum do not belong in the international community," the Israeli delegate said.

Israelis Adamant

"Israel will not permit the establishment of P.L.O. authority in any part of Palestine," he said. "The P.L.O. will not be forced on the Palestinian Arabs. It will not be tolerated by the Jews of Israel."

The Israeli delegate warned that "no resolution can establish the authority of an organization which has no authority, which does not represent anyone except a few thousands of agents of death it employs, which has no foothold in any part of the territories it seeks to dominate."

There was scattered applause at the end of Mr. Tekoah's speech.

November 14, 1974

Guerrilla Aide Says Raids Will Go on to Force Talks

By JUAN de ONIS
Special to The New York Times

DAMASCUS, Syria, Nov. 19 —A Palestinian guerrilla official vowed here today that Palestinian attacks inside Israel would continue until the Israelis agreed to negotiate with the Palestine Liberation Organization, the main guerrilla grouping.

The assertion was made by the chief of operations of a guerrilla group that announced it was behind an assault early today in the northeastern Israeli town of Beit Shean.

The group, the Popular Democratic Front for the Liberation of Palestine, is a Marxist-oriented organization that supports Yasir Arafat, the P.L.O. chairman. At United Nations headquarters in New York, the chief spokesman there for the P.L.O., Shefiq al-Hout, said at a news conference that "we don't feel any embarrassment" over the Beit Shean raid.

Raid Called 'Military' Action

All guerrilla activities of the Popular Democratic Front, including the attack on Beit Shean today, are "authorized by the P.L.O. Executive Committee," the front's operations chief, who is known by the code name Abou Leila, said in an interview.

He rejected what he described as the "broken record" that Palestinian guerrilla operations in Israel were "terrorist actions." "These are legal military actions," he declared.

Israel however, disputes this and has repeatedly said she will not negotiate with the Palestine Liberation Organization on the ground that it is a terrorist organization.

In the interview, the guerrilla leader contended that the apartment building that was attacked in Beit Shaen today was a "military target" because some of the residents were officers in the Israeli Army. He asserted that several of the officers were engaged in security operations against Palestinian resistance to Israel occupation of the West Bank of the Jordan River.

"I don't know if we got any of them because I have not seen the casualty list," Abou Leila said, "but I can say that no civilians would have been killed if the Israel authorities had complied with our clear and easy demand."

Reports from Beit Shean said that the attack had been carried out by three guerrillas and that all the attackers and four Israelis had been killed.

Abou Leila, however, said that four guerrillas had staged the attack. But only three guerrillas were identified here, and Abou Leila said the name of the fourth was being withheld on the ground that he was from Israel and disclosure of his identity could compromise guerrilla security.

November 20, 1974

ASSEMBLY ADOPTS 2 U.N. RESOLUTIONS AIDING P.L.O. AIMS

Votes 89-8 That Palestinian People Have Right to Be Free and Sovereign

By PAUL HOFMANN
Special to The New York Times

UNITED NATIONS, N. Y., Nov. 22—The General Assembly approved two resolutions tonight declaring that the Palestinian people have the right to independence and sovereignty and giving the Palestine Liberation Organization observer status in United Nations affairs.

The resolution on rights, approved 89 to 8 with 37 abstentions, says that the Palestinian people are entitled to self-determination without external interference and to national independence and sovereignty.

It also affirms "the inalienable right of the Palestinians to return to their homes and property from which they have been displaced and uprooted," and calls for their return.

The resolution also declares that the Palestinian people are "a principal party in the establishment of a just and durable peace in the Middle East."

Widely Supported

The resolution was supported by all Arab states, the Soviet Union and its allies, China, Spain, Portugal and many third-world countries.

The second resolution, which was approved 95 to 17 with 19 abstentions, grants the Palestine Liberation Organization permanent observer status in the General Assembly and gives the movement the right to participate in international conferences under United Nations auspices.

After the voting, Israel's chief delegate, Yosef Tekoah, declared that the United Nation's "has plunged into an abyss from which there is no exit."

By becoming a permanent observer, the P.L.O. attains a position similar to that of some non-member states, such as Switzerland and the North and South Korea.

Most Western European members joined the United States, Canada and Israel in voting against the second resolution. France, Japan and some Latin-American countries abstained.

November 23, 1974

P.L.O. Declares It Will Punish Hijackers

By HENRY TANNER
Special to The New York Times

DAMASCUS, Syria, Jan. 29—The Palestine Liberation Organization announced today that it had decided to treat the hijacking of airplanes, ships or trains as crimes and would impose death penalties on hijackers if their actions led to the loss of life.

If there are no victims, the P.L.O. said, the sentences will be up to 15 years at hard labor.

The Palestinian guerrilla organization took correspondents into the countryside 15 miles southeast of the Syrian capital today to show them a heavily guarded, wall-enclosed former farmhouse in an apricot orchard that was said to be serving as a "corrective camp," or prison, for offenders against regulations of the P.L.O.

Armed Palestinian officials on the scene said there were about 70 prisoners in the camp, ranging from men who had been drinking on duty to others who had sought to "sabotage" the guerrilla movement.

Zaid Abdel-Fattah, a tall young man in a brown velvet jacket who identified himself as head of the Beirut office of WAFA, the official press agency of the Palestine Liberation Organization, read a statement saying that five Palestinians were sentenced last October to terms of 10 to 15 years at hard labor by a P.L.O. court after they had been thwarted in an attempt to hijack a British airliner in Dubai last August.

The Dubai incident had not been reported before and it was not possible to determine whether it had actually happened.

Mr. Abdel-Fattah, in presenting one of the prisoners and reading from what he described as the P.L.O. penal code, made it clear that the purpose was to convince Arab governments and world opinion that the Palestine Liberation Organization was determined to deal firmly with hijackers and that it had the ability to do so.

Asked why the sentencing was announced only today, he said that this was because Israeli propaganda was trying to represent the P.L.O. as an organization that could not and would not prevent terrorism.

The attitude of the Palestine Liberation Organization toward the hijacking of civilian airlines, once equivocal, has been hardening recently out of concern over world public opinion.

Palestinian extremist guerrilla groups outside the Palestine Liberation Organization have publicly rejected its stand on hijacking.

January 30, 1975

Arafat Says Sadat Is Misguided In Pinning Hopes on Kissinger

Yasir Arafat, the Palestinian guerrilla leader, has criticized President Anwar el-Sadat of Egypt as a misguided moderate who is deceiving himself in expecting that Secretary of State Kissinger can achieve for the Arabs a recovery of the lands occupied by Israel in the war of 1967.

Mr. Arafat said he believed that President Sadat was preparing to abandon the Palestinians.

In an interview with Norman Cousins, editor of Saturday Review, Mr. Arafat said he doubted that the Israelis would ever relinquish any of the land unless forced to do so.

Mr. Cousins talked with the Palestinian leader, who kept a machine gun in his lap during the conversation, in Beirut, Lebanon, during a recent tour of the Middle East. A report on the interview is to appear in the March 22 issue of Saturday Review.

Mr. Arafat asserted during the interview that he was convinced that the strategy of Israel was to sit tight and surrender nothing. For 30 years, he said, the Israelis have not made a single conciliatory gesture toward the Palestinians, and for this reason the Palestinians believe they have no choice but to be militant.

'Misconceptions' Cited

In his report on the interview, Mr. Cousins said that it had been arranged by Clovis Maksoud, a Lebanese writer, with

The Palestinians

the purpose of clearing up some "misconceptions" about the objectives of the Palestine Liberation Organization, the grouping of guerrillas headed by Mr. Arafat.

Mr. Arafat sought to justify the tactics of terrorism used by the Palestinian guerrillas, stressing that the Palestine Liberation Organization considered itself in a state of war with Israel.

The guerrilla leader said he doubted that he would have been invited to address the United Nations General Assembly last November if the P.L.O. had not followed a policy of sustained militancy.

Mr. Cousins recounted the discussion of terrorism as follows:

"I said I didn't see how it could help the cause of the Palestinians to shoot up innocent people in airports or planes or crowded theaters.

"He said he agreed with me about the senselessness and brutality of the airport bombings. This is not his policy."

Test of Statesmanship

Mr. Cousins added:

"He said he recognized that violence has to give way at some points to more rational means. He hopes that such a time might be approaching soon. He agreed with me that he would have to meet the test of statesmanship. He is not bound to violence, he said; he can be flexible."

Asked by Mr. Cousins about the feasibility of the proclaimed Palestinian objective of transforming Israel into a "secular state" of Moslems, Jews and Christians, the guerrilla leader implied that he recognized that this was unlikely to be achieved.

"The P.L.O. would not turn down out of hand any serious offer that would give the Palestinians a state of their own," Mr. Cousins wrote in summarizing Mr. Arafat's remarks.

Mr. Arafat said that a "Palestinian ministate" on the West Bank of the Jordan River would not be rejected automatically.

March 12, 1975

Jerusalem, Appropriate Setting for Symposium

Terrorism Is a Subject for Study

By TERENCE SMITH

JERUSALEM — The setting could hardly have been more apt. In a city that has known more than its share of political terrorism, experts were gathered to discuss a worldwide phenomenon: the hijackings, the kidnappings, the bombings and the other acts of terror whose number has increased so dramatically in the past few years.

The city was Jerusalem, the occasion, a recent symposium on "terrorism, pre-emption and surprise," sponsored by the Leonard Davis Institute of International Relations at the Hebrew University. Its participants included professors of international affairs and political science from the United States, Sweden, Norway, West Germany and Israel. The audience included academics and professionals, both students of terrorism and representatives of the army, police and intelligence agencies that attempt to combat it.

The discussions went well beyond local issues. But the Arab-Israeli conflict furnished appropriate background music for the three-day symposium. Palestinian guerrillas fired mortar and bazooka shells across the Lebanese border on the eve of the conference, and during the middle of the sessions a small bomb exploded in the Government Labor Exchange office in Nablus on the occupied West Bank.

The participants read prepared papers on a wide range of subjects, from the psychological implications of the increase in worldwide terrorism to the use of surprise and pre-emption in warfare. Among their conclusions:

• The "technological vulnerability" of modern society has made terrorism more feasible and more profitable at less risk for the terrorists. To cite just one example the growth of international air transportation has created an irresistibly "soft" target. And modern communication techniques mean hostages can be taken at one location and demands made on a government, or a business or political group, thousands of miles away.

• The development of portable, destructive weapons has also opened up terrorists' options. The shoulder-fired antiaircraft missile, for instance, places civilian airliners at the mercy of people who need not even risk boarding them in order to wreak havoc. There has already been one near-miss: In 1973, a group of Palestinians was seized with a Soviet-built Strella antiaircraft missile at the end of a runway at Rome's airport. It turned out that they had hoped to shoot down an Israeli airliner.

More frightening still is the possibility, noted by several speakers, that a terrorist group may soon be able to lay its hands on a nuclear device, and use it to threaten whole countries. Citing the proliferation of so-called tactical nuclear weapons and the laxness of the security conditions under which they are often kept, the speakers concluded that a dedicated group conceivably could steal such a weapon from an army arsenal, or assemble one with plutonium stolen from nuclear plants around the world.

• The trend around the world toward greater tolerance for acts of terrorism and a general laxness in the punishment of terrorists can be partly explained by a "worldwide societal tendency to place more and more value on human life," said George H. Quester. The professor of International Politics at Cornell contended that this is the explanation for widespread abolition of the death penalty and, similarly, for a tendency to give in to the demands of terrorists when the lives of hostages are threatened.

Professor Quester also talked about the unique case of the Palestinian Liberation Movement. Despite its consistent use of terror, it has won political recognition. Palestinian terrorism, he suggested, is tolerated more than other terrorism because "the Palestinians look more like an army, less like a criminal gang."

The Palestinians are "literally getting away with murder," the professor observed, "in part because they are converging on the normal legitimacy of an established political movement, that is, a state and states do not 'commit murder' they 'wage war.'"

The speakers applied a kind of "cost-benefit analysis" to terrorism and counter-terrorism techniques. Improved control over access to weapons and weapons technology; considering terrorism as a factor in the design of socio-technical structures such as airports, mass-transit systems, power plants and energy resource depots, and international cooperation among governments to deny sanctuaries to terrorists: All, they said, would help combat terrorism.

But even as they made these suggestions, most of the experts conceded that it would be unrealistic to expect to eliminate the use of terrorism as a political device. "The best we can aim for," one participant said, "is to make it less inviting and more costly."

Terence Smith is chief of The New York Times Jerusalem bureau.

June 15, 1975

13 Die, Scores Hurt in Jerusalem Blast

By TERENCE SMITH
Special to The New York Times

JERUSALEM, July 4—A huge explosion ripped through Jerusalem's main square at the height of the pre-Sabbath shopping rush hour today, killing 13 Israelis and wounding 72 in the city's bloodiest terrorist incident since the founding of the state.

An explosive charge concealed in an old refrigerator left on the sidewalk detonated at 10 A.M., hurling bodies into the air, scorching the stone building fronts in historic Zion Square and shattering windows for blocks around.

Israeli officials assumed that the blast was an attempt by the Palestinian guerrilla organizations to disrupt the delicate diplomatic negotiations for a new interim agreement between Israel and Egypt.

"We always get something like this when there are serious talks in the offing," one official said, "but usually it isn't this bad."

In Beirut, Lebanon, the General Command of the Palestinian Revolution attributed the attack to a group calling itself the Martyr Farid al Boubaly Brigade, operating in Israel.

Following the explosion, the police rounded up 300 Arabs for questioning and for their own protection against angry Israelis who converged on the scene.

Gangs of Israelis later rampaged through mixed neighborhoods, stoning cars of Arab workers returning to the former Jordanian sector. Reinforced police units broke up several fistfights and arrested a number of Israelis as well as Arabs.

Appeal for Calm

Mayor Teddy Kollek issued an appeal for calm and urged the communities to display "mutual tolerance." He also asked the students from two religious schools in the Jewish quarter of the walled Old City to help patrol the streets in their neighborhood and keep order.

"I can understand the desire for revenge," he said over the Israel radio, "but violence now will only play into the hands of those who want to divide this city again."

The casualties included at least two children and three women. Among the wounded, eight in serious condition, were two American young women tourists. Their names and addresses were not immediately available.

Premier Yitzhak Rabin and several other ministers visited the scene of the blast, conferred with police officials for about 20 minutes, then left without speaking to reporters.

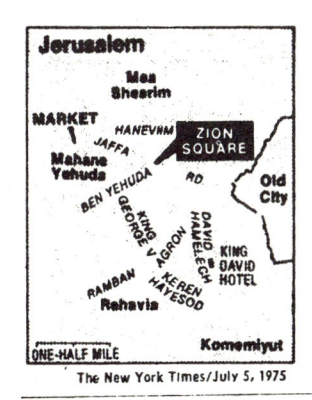

The New York Times/July 5, 1975

As Mr. Rabin's car drove away, an Israeli man shook his fist and shouted angrily in Hebrew: "Do something to stop all this."

A group of several hundred Israelis staged a demonstration in Mahane Yehuda, a crowded market area not far from Zion Square. They pushed through the narrow streets chanting, "Death penalty for terrorists." The market was the scene of a terrorist attack in November, 1968, when 11 persons were killed and 50 injured.

Today's incident was the bloodiest in Jerusalem since the violence that preceded the founding of Israel in May, 1948. Scores of people were killed by explosions in the days of the British mandate government when Arabs and Jews were fighting the British as well as each other.

The explosion this morning could be heard throughout the city.

"I saw a terrific ball of flame and black smoke," said 30-year-old Ephraim Warshavsky, the manager of a nearby tool shop.

About half an hour before the explosion, Mr. Warshavsky said, he and his sister noticed that some men in a truck had deposited an old refrigerator on the sidewalk. He went out twice to inspect it, he said, but found nothing inside. The package of explosives apparently was strapped on the underside.

"I would have called the police right away, but our phone had been out for three days," the shop manager said.

Phone Call to Police

• Mr. Warshavsky and his sister went next door to the Hotel Ron and telephoned the police from there. The police received the call at 9:58 A.M.

A police spokesman said later that a patrol car with bomb experts was 40 yards from the site when the bomb exploded two minutes later.

The blast blew out the fronts of several shops on the square, which is the shopping and business center of the western, or Israeli, half of Jerusalem. The square is lined with banks, stores and five-story stone buildings dating to mandate days. It has often served as the site for the reviewing stand at Independence Day parades.

July 5, 1975

The Palestinians

U.N. VOTES, 72-35, TO TERM ZIONISM FORM OF RACISM

By PAUL HOFMANN
Special to The New York Times

UNITED NATIONS, N.Y., Nov. 10—The General Assembly tonight adopted an Arab-inspired resolution defining Zionism as "a form of racism and racial discrimination."

The vote was 72 to 35 with 32 abstentions. Three delegations were absent.

After the vote, the chief American delegate, Daniel P. Moynihan, said:

"The United States rises to declare before the General Assembly of the United Nations and before the world that it does not acknowledge, it will not abide by, it will never acquiesce in this infamous act."

Waldheim Issues Statement

Secretary General Kurt Waldheim issued a statement saying the vote reflected "a deep and bitter division among the membership at a time when the need for understanding on a wide range of critically important questions is more than ever necessary." He said "the great passions on all sides" aroused by the Zionism issue would not be healed unless urgent progress was made in a search for a solution to the Middle East problems.

Earlier, the Assembly overwhelmingly adopted resolutions calling for the participation of the Palestine Liberation Organization in all efforts for peace in the Middle East and setting up a procedure that would allow the Palestinians to press their demands in the United Nations.

November 11, 1975

TERRORISTS RAID OPEC OIL PARLEY IN VIENNA, KILL 3

Allowed to Leave by Plane With Several Ministers and Other Captives

By CLYDE H. FARNSWORTH
Special to The New York Times

VIENNA, Monday, Dec. 22—Six terrorists, their weapons concealed in sports-equipment bags, burst into a meeting of the Organization of Petroleum Exporting Countries here yesterday, shot three persons to death with submachine guns and held at least 60 people hostage.

Among the hostages were 11 delegates to the conference, including Sheik Ahmed Zaki Yamani, Saudi Arabia's oil minister, Jamshid Amuzegar of Iran and Valentín Hernández Acosta of Venezuela. Early today Chancellor Bruno Kreisky of Austria announced that his Government had agreed to allow the terrorists, who had not clearly identified their organization nor clearly stated their demands, to fly out of the country with some of the oil ministers.

Bus Left for Airport

A bus with curtains drawn over its windows left the OPEC building with the raiders and their prisoners at 7:45 A.M. for Vienna's Schwechat Airport and a waiting plane.

Thirty-three hostages were counted entering the bus. At least 10 hostages were released and were being interrogated by the Austrian police.

The bus arrived at the airport 35 minutes after leaving the OPEC building and the terrorists and their hostages boarded an Austrian Airlines DC-9. The plane took off at 9:15 A.M. (3:15 A.M. New York time).

When the terrorists burst into the OPEC conference room at 11:45 A.M. yesterday (5:45 A.M., New York time), an Austrian policeman and an Iraqi employee of OPEC were killed in an exchange of gunfire. A third body was found in the building after the terrorists had left. One terrorist was wounded, and was taken to a hospital.

Mr. Kreisky said that he had been in touch with Algerian authorities, who had promised landing permission in case the raiders might fly to Algeria. Algeria had sent its ambassadors from Bonn, Geneva and Brussels to participate in the emergency consultations in Vienna, Mr. Kreisky said.

'We Were Pressured'

"We were pressured into this decision by the fear that hostages' lives would be taken," Mr. Kreisky said after an emergency Cabinet meeting.

"We knew we were dealing with very dangerous and determined people," Mr. Kreisky said at an early morning news conference to explain the Government decision. "You cannot rule out terrorism by retaliating, because terror has its own laws."

The raiders, who did not identify themselves other than as "the arm of the Arab revolution," held their prisoners in the eight-story building in the center of Vienna, while the police ringed the area and deployed sharpshooters.

December 22, 1975

For Palestinian Independence and Sovereignty

By Farouk Kaddoumi

The Security Council's debate on the Middle East is predicated upon certain recognized facts: that peace will not prevail in the Middle East until the Palestinian people realize their national rights, including repatriation, self-determination and independence in Palestine; that Palestinian participation in United Nations efforts leading toward peace is absolutely indispensable and that, accordingly, the Palestine Liberation Organization, which is internationally recognized as the legitimate representative of the Palestinian people, was asked and is now participating in the current deliberations of the Council; and that the continuing stalemate in the Middle East, caused by the Zionist insistence on frustrating the internationally recognized national rights of the Palestinian people, will lead to yet another conflict.

There is no question that peace in the Middle East is threatened; that previous agreements, based upon an incomplete and inadequate framework and principles, which brought the fourth Middle East war to a temporary cessation, have demonstrated their limitations; and that what is required now is a comprehensive set of principles and a framework that would constitute the bases leading to the complete withdrawal of Israeli forces from all Arab lands and to the implementation of the national rights of the Palestinians, including independence and sovereignty in Palestine.

There are three and one-half million Palestinians today; they are the descendants of the Palestinian people who have lived on the soil of Palestine since time immemorial. Palestine has been hospitable to all religions and cultures: Jews, Christians and Moslems have lived together in Palestine and contributed to its wealth and to the enrichment of its culture.

Half the Palestinians today live within occupied Palestine; they are governed in accordance with the notorious "defense regulations" that allow the Israeli military authorities to arrest, "administratively detain" and punish any Palestinian suspected of resisting the military occupation.

The other half live in forced exile in the Arab states, which have supported and aided them. More than half of the Palestinians are now "stateless" and all have made it clear that they want to end their territorial and national fragmentation. The P.L.O. embodies this will and commitment.

The Palestinian struggle for independence and sovereignty is not new. Palestinians campaigned for independence during the First World War. It will be recalled that the American King-Crane Commission, which was dispatched to Palestine at the request of the Paris Peace Conference, ascertained that the Palestinians sought national independence and sovereignty. But Britain, which had committed itself through the infamous Balfour Declaration of 1917 to facilitate the colonial Zionist scheme of establishing an exclusive Jewish state in Palestine, crushed the Palestinian drive for independence then.

Throughout the period of British colonial control of Palestine, Palestinians struggled to free Palestine from the dual control of British imperialism and the colonialism of Zionist settlers. The revolutions of 1921, 1929, 1936 and 1948 were waged to obtain independence, a right upheld and eventually applied to all other people.

But the combined weight of British imperialism and Zionism deprived the Palestinians of attaining their legitimate right; instead, Palestine was to be divided into two states according to a United Nations recommendation of 1947, with an international status for Jerusalem; and, in the course of Zionist attacks on the Palestinians in 1948, Zionists succeeded in driving the Palestinians from their homeland to live in forced exile.

With Israel's attack on the Arab states in 1967, Israel succeeded in occupying the rest of Palestine and in expelling more than 500,000 additional Palestinians.

Throughout the period of their exile and under occupation, Palestinians struggled; they did so to realize their rights guaranteed by international law and the United Nations Charter.

Since 1948, the United Nations has

'It would contribute to the establishment of permanent peace.'

passed innumerable resolutions reaffirming the rights of the Palestinians to return to their homes and property. The implementation of these resolutions has been impeded by the unilateral action of the Zionists who intend to increase and consolidate European Jewish settlements on Arab lands.

Initiatives undertaken by various powers, including those of the United States, which were intended to facilitate the repatriation of the Palestinians and the restoration of their national sovereignty in Palestine, met with the same negative Israeli action.

Despairing of arriving at a just settlement that would enable our people to return and to effect their self-determination and independence, the Palestinians resumed their armed struggle in 1965 and offered a constructive program and a new vision that, when translated into reality, would assure all Palestinians — irrespective of faith — a peaceful and dignified life in Palestine.

As a result of our struggle, the international community once more recognized our right to independence; beginning in 1969, the United Nations recognized the colonized status of the Palestinian people and called upon the international community to assist the Palestinians in attaining their national rights.

This steady international recognition of Palestinian national rights culminated in the just resolution of the General Assembly in November 1974 that called for the independence and sovereignty of the Palestinian people in Palestine; this was followed by another resolution in 1975 that called for a specific timetable for independence and specific mechanisms for the attainment of independence and sovereignty.

Thus the General Assembly affirmed the transitional program of the Palestine Liberation Organization, which rejected all other solutions to the Palestinian problem save that of return to and independence in Palestine.

It is ironic that the United States should assume the role of the principal antagonist to the aspirations of the Palestinian people; its representatives were the first to ascertain the aspirations of the Palestinians for independence and sovereignty in 1919; the Government of the United States voted for the establishment of a Palestinian state in 1947 and in 1948 and annually voted for the right of the Palestinian to return to his home and property in Palestine.

Yet for the past few years, the United States has underwritten Israeli expansion and violation of Palestinian national rights. And in the Security Council it threatens to use its veto to pre-empt a resolution consonant with the requirements of a just peace in the region. In doing so, its isolation is complete.

The overwhelming majority of the international community find it natural to support the Palestinian aspiration for independence and sovereignty in Palestine.

An independent sovereign Palestinian state would immediately solve the continuing problem of Palestinian dispersion, would relieve the oppression that the Palestinian suffers under the military occupation of Israel, and thus would enable the Palestinian people to lead an independent, dignified, productive and peaceful life. More than this, it would contribute to the establishment of permanent peace, which has eluded the Middle East for over 28 years.

Farouk Kaddoumi is head of the Palestine Liberation Organization's political department and chairman of its delegation to the United Nations.

January 22, 1976

Arab Terrorism

The Vienna kidnapping of Arab oil ministers by their own Arab compatriots and other pro-Palestinian terrorists will surely rank as one of the great ironies of this era. With dozens of hostages taken, three killed and several wounded so far by the gunmen, the terrible price that can be paid by innocent victims of terrorism has again been made clear to the civilized world. Yet the Arab states for years have refused to cooperate with international action to bring terrorism under any kind of control—as has been done with aerial hijacking.

The collusion in or passive acceptance of the most radical of terrorist activities by the most conservative of Arab states has helped this evil to flourish and proliferate. Hijacking has, in contrast, been brought under control by an international convention agreeing to make it a common-law crime rather than a political act entitling the perpetrators to asylum. Now that trial or extradition faces such criminals, hijacking has virtually disappeared since 1974.

The United States pressed for a similar convention against terrorism at the United Nations in 1972. What finally emerged from the diplomats at the General Assembly in December 1973 was a much-watered-down convention that extends protection not to all hostages and victims of kidnapping and murder, but only to diplomats! Two years later, Tunisia is the only Arab state among the 28 signatories of even this convention.

The Palestinians

The Palestine Liberation Organization yesterday condemned the Vienna terrorist action, which is ironic in itself. Other Arab capitals denounced it as "rash and disgraceful" and the work of "criminals." The more conservative Arab leaders undoubtedly have been shaken by these actions of more radical Arab elements—as well they might. Up to now the predominant tendency in the Arab world, and even elsewhere, has been to see heroism in the acts of terrorists who risk their lives to make a political demonstration. The innocent blood they have spilled has made a lesser impression.

But the virtual disappearance of hijacking has shown that denial of safe havens has a dampening effect on terrorists. Once the Arab states make it clear that these criminals will be prosecuted or extradited, terrorism of this nature will appear considerably less attractive to its perpetrators.

December 23, 1975

ARAB MILITANTS WIN ON WEST BANK

Sweeping Victory in Local Elections Gives Big Role to the Pro-Palestinians

By TERENCE SMITH
Special to The New York Times

JERUSALEM, April 13—A new, militant leadership dominated by Palestinian nationalists and Arab radicals emerged on the occupied West Bank today after the ballots were counted from the municipal elections yesterday.

The final tabulations announced this morning showed that Communists, Syrian Baatists and candidates sympathetic to the Palestine Liberation Organization swept to power in many of the major towns and villages.

The scope of the nationalists' successes surprised Israeli authorities. Some nationalist gains had been expected at the expense of the older, more conservative leadership, but not on the scale that occurred.

Call for a State

Speaking at a news conference in Tel Aviv tonight, Defense Minister Shimon Peres sought to minimize the political impact of the voting. "This is not a day of mourning for Israel," he said. "I see it as a national challenge with which we will now have to grapple."

Mr. Peres also warned the newly elected mayors not to use their municipal offices as forums for Palestinian politics. "That's not what they were elected for," he said.

April 14, 1976

HOSTAGES FREED AS ISRAELIS RAID UGANDA AIRPORT

Commandos in 3 Planes Rescue 105—Casualties Unknown

By TERENCE SMITH
Special to The New York Times

JERUSALEM, Sunday, July 4—Israeli airborne commandos staged a daring night-time raid on Entebbe airport in Uganda last night, freeing the 105 mainly Israeli hostages and Air France crew members held by pro-Palestinian hijackers and flying them back to Israel aboard three Israeli planes.

The hostages and their rescuers were due back in Israel this morning after a brief stopover at Kenya's International Airport at Nairobi, where at least two persons were given medical treatment in a field hospital on the runway. No details of the extent of the casualties were available here pending notification of the families.

Only fragmentary reports of the raid were immediately available here. An unspecified number of commandos apparently flew the 2,300 miles from Israel to Entebbe Airport and surprised the hijackers on the ground.

The hijackers were spending the night with their hostages in the old passenger terminal at Entebbe where they have been confined all week. They had commandeered an Air France airliner last Sunday shortly after it had left Athens on its way to Paris.

News agency reports from Entebbe said that a number of large explosions — perhaps bombs — were set off at a distant point on the airport, apparently to divert the ring of Uganda troops that had surrounded the old terminal all week.

The commandos reportedly broke into the old terminal and fought a gun battle with the heavily armed hijackers. Reports from the scene said that the terrorists had been killed in the skirmish, but military sources here declined to confirm or deny this.

The hostages apparently were then rushed to the waiting Israeli planes and flown away before Uganda forces could intervene.

An Israeli radio report said that the raiders were infantrymen and paratroopers dressed in civilian clothes.

Government sources here said that the decision to stage the military operation was approved unanimously by a special Cabinet meeting in Tel Aviv yesterday. The decision was made, the sources said, when it became clear that the hijackers would not relent in their demands and were holding Israel responsible for the release of the 53 imprisoned

The New York Times/July 4, 1976

Palestinian and pro-Palestinian guerrillas that the hijackers had demanded be freed by Israel and four other countries in exchange for the hostages.

On Thursday, the Israel Cabinet reversed a long-standing policy and agreed to negotiate with the hijackers. The Cabinet decided in principle then to release some Arab prisoners but not all that the hijackers had demanded.

Israel's willingness to negotiate an exchange was communicated to the hijackers through the French and Somali ambassadors on the scene at Entebbe. The hijackers reportedly refused to even discuss the Israeli proposal, insisting that only the mechanics of the exchange could be negotiated. Israel received this reply on Friday.

"It was at that point that a military operation became a real possibility," a senior Government source said. Detailed plans for the operation were worked out Friday night and approved by the Cabinet yesterday at an unusual sabbath session.

Other sources suggested, however, that the original Cabinet decision on Thursday approving an exchange of prisoners for hostages had in fact been designed as a cover to buy time to prepare the military operation. In any event, the operation came as a surprise to the Israeli public, which had accepted the release of Arab prisoners as the only feasible way of freeing the hostages.

July 4, 1976

Arab Goverments Cannot Entirely Turn Away From Arafat

P.L.O. Is Down, but Probably Not Out

By HENRY TANNER

BEIRUT, Lebanon—Yasir Arafat's Palestine Liberation Organization has suffered a crippling military defeat in Lebanon and has seen its political power curtailed. Its influence on events elsewhere in the Middle East has been sharply reduced.

The reverses started in mid-August with the fall of Tell Zaatar, the fortified Palestinian camp in Christian territory outside of Beirut. Last week 1,500 Mr. Arafat's best soldiers were driven out of mountain strongholds north of the Damascus highway and they lost other strategic positions in the hills overlooking Beirut. The Palestinians have also been crucially weakened in southern Lebanon where they have lost control of the area bordering Israel.

The Israelis have organized and armed Christian militias in the border area and have struck a discreet arrangement with the southern command of the Lebanese Arab Army, which was originally fiercely pro-Palestinian. Palestinian guerrillas are no longer in the area. Israeli patrols are.

The question thus may be asked: Is this the end of the Palestinian movement as a powerful factor in Lebanon and the Middle East? The answer is no. Nothing is ever quite ended in this region. Not alliances which, when they break, can always be patched up. Not personal relations between political leaders which may turn to conflict but are never broken off. The Syrian-Palestinian conflict is no exception.

Late last year, when the Syrians originally intervened in Lebanon (acting through As Saiqa, the Syrian-controlled guerrilla organization) they first helped the Moslems and Palestinians who were hard pressed at the time in their civil war against the right-wing Christians.

The Syrians then wanted to control the Palestinian movement, and they still do. They wanted a single front reaching from Aqaba to the Mediterranean and including Jordan as well as the Palestinians, with President Hafez al-Assad in charge. Once this was achieved, Syria could either negotiate for an Arab-Israeli settlement or resume war. In either case, it would act from strength. But in either case, the Syrians would need the Palestinian movement.

It has always been assumed in Lebanon that the Syrians wanted to "tame" the movement, not to liquidate it. Things got out of hand between Damascus and the Palestinian leadership when the Palestinians refused to be "tamed." President Assad in his moments of anger, may have been tempted to try to suppress the Palestinian movement. But he is not free to act as he wants.

Most of the established Arab regimes have been in tacit or public agreement with him as he sought to cut the Palestinians down to size. But there is disagreement among them over how far the operation should go. President Anwar el-Sadat, of Egypt, for one, has come to the Palestinians' rescue, mostly with words, but also with arms deliveries and political support. As long as Arab governments quarrel, the Palestinians will always find an ally among them. It is still good politics for any Arab leader, even President Assad, to be pro-Palestinian and, hence, an Arab nationalist.

There is, of course, no real "Arab unity." The limited Arab solidarity that existed at the time of the October war in 1973 and during the months that followed has largely disappeared. But the quarrels that have taken its place are quarrels "among brothers" even if they involve rockets and heavy artillery. The "Arab cause" that the orators talk about cannot be entirely flouted and the Palestinians, no matter how low their fortunes may sink, represent for most of these leaders the Arab conscience. President Assad thus would not strike at them all-out, even if he were under no other constraints.

This ambiguity in the Syrian policy toward the Palestinians has been obvious. Whenever the Syrians had the Palestinians cornered, they left a back door open for Mr. Arafat to slip through. In June and July the Palestinians and their Lebanese allies were trapped and surrounded in West Beirut, Tripoli and southern Lebanon. They were hemmed in by land and sea with the Israeli Navy and the Lebanese Christians as eager allies. It would have been easy for the Syrians to maintain an effective land and sea blockade and starve the Palestinian-Moslem population centers or at least to cut off the supply lines of the Palestinian fighting forces. Instead, Mr. Assad permitted the blockade to be lifted and supplies to reach West Beirut and Tripoli.

During last week's fighting in the mountains, the Syrians permitted Mr. Arafat to pull out his crack troops intact from the mountain positions. The Syrians went into action with superior armor and artillery but when Mr. Arafat signalled that he had understood the hopelessness of his military situation, they did not block and crush his units.

After the terrorist attack on the Semiramis Hotel in Damascus last weekend, the Assad regime began for the first time openly to call on the Palestinian masses to get rid of Mr. Arafat as well as of his principal aides. This makes it likely that the Syrian-Palestinian conflict will get rougher before it tapers off. But if the Arab-Israeli conflict should break out anew, Syrians and Palestinians would quickly make up. There is also the possibility that the Lebanese right-wing Christians, who have won the upper hand with the help of the Syrians, may overreach themselves and go for a military victory—just as the Palestinian and Lebanese Moslems did last spring—forcing Syria to reverse its alliances.

Henry Tanner is a correspondent for The New York Times who has been reporting on the Lebanese civil war.

October 3, 1976

Palestinians Preparing to Open Office in Washington

By BERNARD GWERTZMAN
Special to The New York Times

WASHINGTON, Nov. 19—The Palestine Liberation Organization has taken steps to open an office in Washington to lobby with American officials and members of Congress and to disseminate information about the Palestinian cause.

The office, which was authorized by Yasir Arafat, the leader of the P.L.O., was registered formally with the Justice Department last night by Sabri Elias Jiryis, a Palestinian-born P.L.O. offficial, described as a moderate, who is presently in Washington. He said in a telephone conversation that he must complete other formalities before he would be able to announce the opening of the office.

The very presence of Mr. Jiryis in Washington and the likelihood of a P.L.O. office here is an extremely sensitive issue for the State Department, which is aware of Israeli suspicions that the United States is looking for ways of modifying its policy of nonrecognition of the P.L.O.

There already is an Arab information center in Washington that circulates a newsletter that strongly supports the Palestinian cause.

No Change in U.S. Policy

State Department officials stressed that there was no change in the policy toward the P.L.O. That policy is that the United States will not deal with that group in a substantive way until it accepts the existence of Israel as a sovereign state and the pertinent Security Council resolutions calling for a negotiated solution for the Middle East conflict.

Mr. Jiryis, who left what is now Israel in 1970, entered this country a month ago with a Sudanese passport. The State Department knew he was coming and knew that he was a leading Palestinian intellectual, who headed the Israel section of the P.L.O. Research Center in Beirut. But officials said they had no indication he would seek to open an office here.

Because he was a member of the Palestine National Council, the top Palestinian organization, Mr. Jiryis was denied any appointments with Administration officials, who flatly refused to see him directly in keeping with the policy of no dealings with P.L.O. officials. He has seen private individuals in Washington, however

Under United States law, there is no prohibition against opening an office on behalf of some foreign government or group. All that is necessary is for the individual to register with the Justice Department as a foreign agent and to supply detailed information about his source of money and his intentions.

In addition, if he plans to deal with members of Congress he must register on Capitol Hill and send a letter to the State Department announcing his intentions.

State and Justice Department officials insisted that the decision of Mr. Jiryis to open a P.L.O. office was taken after he arrived and that there was no law barring him from doing so.

The only question that may arise, officials said, is when his current short-term visa expires and he applies for an extension to run the office. At that point, it is possible that it might be denied.

"We are not a license office," a Justice Department official said. "A person does not come to us and ask permission to open an office. All the law requires is that he inform us of what he is doing and that he label his propaganda as being that of a foreign agent."

Mr. Jiryis, in a phone conversation, also said he had not detected any shift in policy by the United States toward the P.L.O. He confirmed he had not been able to see any officials.

He added that the P.L.O. had an office in Washington in 1965-66 and has had a similar office in New York since 1965, presently at 103 Park Avenue.

In his registration with the Justice Department, Mr. Jiryis said he received $10,000 on Oct. 18 from the P.L.O. headquarters in Beirut to organize an "information office in Washington."

Doubts a Single Palestine State

He said he dealt with Mr. Arafat, chairman of the Executive Committee of the P.L.O.

"Registrant has been and will continue to be engaged in organizing the Washington office of the P.L.O.," he said. "Henceforth he will act as director of that office

Emblem of Palestine Liberation Organization shows the group's banner over a map of Palestine.

and will meet with officials of agencies and departments of the executive branch of the U.S. Government. Members and staff of the legislative branch, members of the press and public, and with representatives of foreign governments, and prepare and distribute and supervise the preparation and distribution of written materials to the above and participate in public meetings and appearances, all with a view to disseminating information concerning the P.L.O., its policies and objectives."

In an interview in 1975 with Americans traveling in the Middle East, published later in an Israeli magazine, Mr. Jiryis said while he "theoretically" supported the P.L.O.'s declared aim of a single, unified state to incorporate what is now Israel, he was in practice "against it."

"I would not like to see a single state now in Palestine," he said in the interview. Rather, he advocated the concept favored by Egypt and other so-called moderate Arabs of giving the Palestinians a state in what is now the West Bank of the Jordan River and the Gaza Strip, both occupied by Israel. Israel, however, continues to oppose any separate Palestinian state and advocates a federated Jordanian-Palestinian state.

November 20, 1976

Palestinians Back Peace Parley Role

Special to The New York Times

CAIRO, March 20—The Palestine National Council adopted a declaration today calling for the establishment of "an independent national state" on "national soil" and authorizing Palestinian attendance at an Arab-Israeli peace conference.

The 15-point declaration, adopted by a vote of 194 to 13 after eight days of at times heated discussion by members of the equivalent of a parliament-in-exile, was considered by Western diplomats to be more moderate than previous Palestinian positions. It made no specific major concessions to Israel.

The declaration called for a continuation of the "armed struggle" against Israel and rejected recognition of Israel or the signing of any complete peace agreement. The Palestinian delegates did not amend the charter of the Palestine Liberation Organization to recognize Israel's right to exist, as Cyrus R. Vance, the United States Secretary of State, had called for during his Middle East tour last month.

However, Western diplomats said that despite the harsh rhetoric included in the declaration, its tone was "considerably more constructive and positive" than the declarations that were issued after the last national council meeting, in 1974.

After the final session of the council late tonight, the P.L.O. chairman, Yasir Arafat, said at a news conference that President Carter "had gone back on" his statement Thursday night calling for a "homeland" for the Palestinian people. He said he was referring to a State Department statement Friday that said Mr. Carter's statement did not represent a change in United States policy.

Mr. Arafat was re-elected chairman of the Executive Committee of the P.L.O. at the end of the National Council session.

The changes in the Palestinian position cited by the Western diplomats included the call for a "national state on national soil." Previously the Palestinians had called for creation of a national authority on any land "liberated" from Israel and had stated that such an authority would be only a stepping stone to further "liberation."

The acceptance by the P.L.O. of the concept of a small Palestinian state, although the idea is still rejected by Israel, is considered to be a vital step in Palestinian movement toward peaceful coexistence with Israel.

The diplomats also saw as a positive change the statement "affirming the rights of the P.L.O. to participate on an independent, equal footing in all international conferences, forums and efforts concerned with the Palestinian question and with the Arab-Israeli conflict."

March 21, 1977

Arab Captives in Gaza Say Israelis Beat Them but Don't Use Torture

The following dispatch, by Bernard Edinger, was submitted to the Israeli military censors, who requested under Israeli law that 166 words be deleted on the ground that they disclosed army interrogation techniques. The rest is as submitted to the censor.

GAZA, July 7 (Reuters)—Palestinian guerrilla prisoners permitted for the first time by Israel to meet freely with journalists have alleged beatings and maltreatment on and immediately after arrest, but none said they had undergone actual torture.

The prisoners, interviewed during a six-hour visit to the Gaza prison, were speaking with the agreement of the Israeli authorities. Though the prison was selected by the Israelis—it is not one where there have been disturbances—I was allowed to choose almost 20 former active members of guerrilla groups at random.

Many of the questions were about their treatment in view of detailed allegations made recently in The Sunday Times of London that Israeli interrogators routinely ill-treated and often tortured Arab prisoners. Israel has strongly denied the allegations and says The Sunday Times declined to have them checked; the newspaper, which has stood by its account, explained that it did not check because the allegations had already been aired and had been denied.

Beatings to Make Them Talk

This is what those interviewed said, followed by the reaction of Israeli officials to whom I relayed the allegations:

Most of the prisoners I spoke with said they were manhandled by the troops who arrested them. Israeli military sources concede that actual arrests can be rough since many suspects are armed and try to shoot their way out of ambush. A good number of those I spoke with said they were beaten to make them talk. Only one said the beatings had had a permanent effect in that his hearing had deteriorated.

Israeli police sources said that beatings were against regulations and that the prisoners had every latitude to complain either to the courts or to the Red Cross.

"I have personally handled many of these complaints," a source at national police headquarters said. "In 95 percent of the cases we found the prisoners were lying. In the other 5 percent of cases we took action against the officers involved. Their punishments are known and have been published in the press."

Some prisoners complained that they had been made to stand against walls with hoods over their heads for long periods while questions put to them were punctuated by blows on the back or buttocks. One said he had been left manacled and naked.

"Again, all these treatments are absolutely banned," the police source said. "Certainly interrogators who sometimes have only a short period to prevent a terror action against civilians, which we know is planned but not for when, are not going to treat men who proudly admit to being killers to V.I.P. treatment."

"But torturing is just not our system, it's theirs," he continued. "We have a case where one of their fellow Arabs, suspected of collaborating with us, was slowly roasted over an open fire to make him talk."

The most serious charges were leveled by Dr. Mohammed Rashad Musmar, who, unlike the other prisoners, who described themselves as soldiers and readily admit their guerrilla roles, does not consider himself an active participant in a war. A Gaza surgeon in his mid-40's, considerably older and better educated than most of the prisoners, he feels his eight-year sentence on charges of possessing weapons and building a bunker under his house, is unjustified.

Dr. Musmar was the only prisoner to complain of maltreatment who agreed to be identified in this article. He also agreed, at my suggestion, to outline his allegations to Israeli officers present, adding: "I am fair. There are no reprisals to be feared here."

Dr. Musmar, arrested in 1971, released and arrested again, challenges the charges brought on the second occasion. He gave the following account in the prison director's office seated facing an Israeli captain who often attends prisoner interrogations:

"On the first occasion I was arrested, in 1971, questioning took a long time, about four months. I was first questioned here in Gaza, then in Sarafand, then in Ashkelon, back here to Gaza and finally in Djalama. It was in Djalama that I was badly maltreated. I was beaten, stripped."

"Did you complain to the Red Cross?" the captain asked. "Yes, I did," Dr. Musmar replied. "And what was their conclusion?" the officer asked. When the doctor said he did not know, the captain told him he doubted the story because the Red Cross would have notified the Israeli authorities.

Earlier Dr. Musmar told me that women members of his family had been slapped to make him talk. When I asked him about tortures such as those outlined in The Sunday Times, he replied: "To me, nothing more happened than what I have described."

Much of the questioning of Dr. Musmar and the other prisoners dealt with techniques, including sexual assaults and electric shocks that, as described by The Sunday Times, would place Israeli practice well into the realm of torture. Despite repeated questions on this, the only mention I heard of sexual assault did not involve the guerrilla prisoners, and none of the guerrilla prisoners said they had been tortured by electricity.

Asked if he knew of any torture, Dr. Musmar replied: "I do not know, but I think that interrogations with maltreatment and severe beatings are almost always present."

Accusations of such treatments were made by Gaza residents at the height of the active guerrilla campaign in the Gaza Strip from 1969 to 1971. Several Israeli officers were discreetly court-martialed then. The strip, a sliver of territory along the Mediterranean at the southwestern corner of Israel, has been generally calm since. The last guerrilla incident was nearly 10 months ago.

July 8, 1977

The Palestinians

P.L.O. Says Sadat Has Forsaken the Palestinians

By MARVINE HOWE
Special to The New York Times

BEIRUT, Lebanon, Dec. 26—The Palestine Liberation Organization charged today that President Anwar el-Sadat of Egypt had forsaken the cause of the Palestinian people in his meeting in Ismailia with Prime Minister Menahem Begin of Israel.

After a two-day emergency meeting of its executive committee, the P.L.O. declared that the talks yesterday in which the Israeli leader had refused to agree to the establishment of a Palestinian state paved the way for Egypt's total surrender on Middle East issues and an overt alliance with "the Zionist enemy."

The organization announced that it was determined to block "the United States-Zionist settlement which is being executed by Sadat's regime at the expense of the Palestinian cause and the national interests of the people of Egypt."

The P.L.O. also warned that any attempts to disrupt the Palestinian national consensus or weaken the unity of the people around the P.L.O. would be condemned and punished.

Arab Official Slain

In line with this stand, an official Palestinian military spokesman said tonight that guerrillas had assassinated a prominent Arab official at Ramallah in the Israeli-occupied West Bank because of his "collaboration" with the occupying authorities and "suspect relations" with the director of Israeli intelligence in the area. The Arab official, Hamdi Kadi, was deputy director of education in Ramallah.

"Out of concern for the security and interests of its masses, the Palestinian revolution has issued orders to liquidate a number of agents inside the occupied homeland, after having warned them to refrain from collaborating with the Israeli intelligence services and from threatening the security of the masses," the military spokesman said in a statement issued by the official Palestinian press agency.

The Palestinians were joined in their hostile reaction to the Ismailia talks by Syria, which leads the opposition to the Sadat peace efforts.

The Syrian Government daily Tishrin called the Sadat-Begin talks a "complete failure" and urged the Sadat Government to resign.

Damascus radio said today that no issues had been resolved as a result of the Ismailia meeting. It stressed that Prime Minister Begin had not met President Sadat's expectations on withdrawal or even pullback from Sinai and predicted Israel would do its utmost to secure further concessions.

Arab political sources here generally dismissed the the Sadat-Begin meeting as a predictable failure because it produced no tangible results. The decision to set up military and political committees was seen as an attempt to cover up this fact.

Some moderate Arab quarters had withheld criticism of Mr. Sadat's moves with the vague hope that he might win concessions from the Israelis on the Palestinian issue. Now, however, a general hardening of Arab positions was expected.

Saudi Arabia, Abu Dhabi and Kuwait made statements yesterday emphasizing their support for Palestinian national rights and for the P.L.O. as the only legitimate representative of the Palestinian people.

Today, the ruler of Qatar, Sheik Khalifa bin Hamad al-Thani, declared in a statement to a P.L.O. delegation, "The Palestinians have the right to an independent state on their national soil."

In its statement tonight, the P.L.O. charged that Mr. Begin and Mr. Sadat were seeking to make a deal that would mean in effect the relinquishing of all Palestine and the Golan Heights for part of Sinai.

December 27, 1977

2 GUNMEN IN CYPRUS KILL TOP CAIRO EDITOR AND TAKE OFF WITH 17

2 P.L.O. AIDES ON ESCAPE PLANE

Victim a Close Friend of Sadat —Some Hostages Released Before Terrorists Depart

By The Associated Press

NICOSIA, Cyprus, Sunday, Feb. 19—Two terrorists believed to be Palestinians killed the editor in chief of Egypt's most important newspaper in the lobby of the Nicosia Hilton Hotel yesterday, then took about 30 hostages to the airport and successfully bargained for an airliner to fly them out of the country.

After several hours they released more than half of the hostages and took off in a Cyprus Airways jet.

The plane flew between several countries early this morning before finally landing in the tiny African country of Djibouti, on the Red Sea, after it reportedly was refused permission to land in Kuwait, Libya, Greece and Southern Yemen.

A spokesmen for the Cypriot Government said that the plane landed without incident but that four hours after it touched down it prepared to take off again, apparently with the gunmen and hostages still on board.

"We just got two cables saying the situation is very grave and desperate," he said. "Now they want to go to Libya or Algeria."

Cypriot officials said the plane, a DC-8, was in the air for 7 hours and 14 minutes and had only enough fuel to remain aloft for 45 minutes when it touched down in Djibouti, the former Territory of the Afars and Issas.

The slayers of the Egyptian editor, Yousef el-Sebai, who was also board chairman and chief executive of Al Ahram, boarded the plane with 11 captives, a crew of four and two representatives of the Palestine Liberation Organization acting as negotiators.

Gunmen Say They Are Palestinians

One freed hostage said the gunmen had identified themselves as Palestinians and said they had acted "for the liberation of Palestine." They were also reported to have called the P.L.O. a puppet.

[In Beirut, Lebanon, a P.L.O. spokesman, Mahmoud Labadi, said his organization had not been involved in the slaying. He noted that four of the hostages were P.L.O. officials. It was not clear whether they included the two negotiators. In Cairo, the Middle East News Agency first said the two gunmen were Eritreans, but later identified them as a Palestinian and an Iraqi.]

The killers of Mr. Sebai boarded the plane at 7:55 P.M. yesterday (12:55 P.M., New York time), nine hours after the shooting. They then freed several hostages before takeoff a half-hour later.

30 Persons Rounded Up at First

For hours, the terrorists held the hostages in a minibus on the airport tarmac. They had threatened to kill a hostage by 2:30 P.M. unless they were guaranteed a safe flight from Cyprus. The deadline passed without incident.

One of the hostages eventually freed, the leader of the Cypriot Socialist Party, Dr. Vassos Lyssarides, carried messages between the terrorists and Cypriot officials in the airport terminal 250 yards away.

The Egyptian editor, Mr. Sebai, was killed after the gunmen, riding up in two cars, had rushed into the hotel lobby about noon yesterday and shot him in the head and chest at point-blank range as he walked through the lobby. He was in Nicosia to lead an African-Asian conference, which was attended by many of the hostages.

At first about 30 persons were rounded up by the gunmen and held for almost two hours in the hotel cafeteria. Twelve of them were then gradually freed. The 18 others, their hands tied behind their backs with their neckties, were herded into the bus in front of the hotel for the 25-mile drive to the airport.

Their captors, gripping grenades and pistols, fired shots into the air to warn off photographers outside the hotel. Police and army escorts led the entourage to the airport.

Witnesses said no words had been spoken before the gunmen opened fire in the lobby.

"It was all so sudden, we thought the noise was plates dropping on the floor or something and then we saw the killers running away from the body," a Cypriot woman said.

"The two gunmen told us they were Palestinians," said Sophia Tsimilli, chairman of a leftist Cypriot women's organization, a hostage freed earlier at the hotel.

"Our people are suffering," she quoted the gunmen as having said. "We are doing this for the liberation of Palestine."

The gunmen told their hostages that they had killed Mr. Sebai because "he published good things about Israel" and was "against the Palestinians." Mr. Sebai, who was 60 years old, was a friend of President Anwar el-Sadat and had accompanied the Egyptian leader on the mission to Israel in November.

Palestinian groups have criticized the peace initiative on the ground that it undermines Arab unity, and some Palestinian militants have threatened to assassinate Mr. Sadat.

Mustapha Amin, a columnist for the Egyptian daily Al Akhbar, said Mr. Sebai had been warned by friends not to attend the Nicosia meeting.

"They told him not to go because of the threats made in Baghdad," Mr. Amin said. He referred to a warning made by a radical Palestinian group in the Iraqi capital that anyone who had accompanied Mr. Sadat to Israel would be shot.

February 19, 1978

UP TO 15 EGYPTIAN COMMANDOS DIE TRYING TO FREE HOSTAGES ON JET WHEN CYPRIOT SOLDIERS OPEN FIRE

CAPTIVES ARE SAVED

Cairo and Nicosia Exchange Charges on Responsibility for Bloodshed at Airport

By The Associated Press

NICOSIA, Cyprus, Feb. 19—Egyptian commandos flew to Cyprus today and attempted to storm a jetliner at Larnaca Airport near here to rescue 15 hostages held by two Arab terrorists, but a battle between the Egyptians and the Cypriot National Guard ensued. The hostages were freed, the terrorists reportedly surrendered, but witnesses said they had seen the bodies of up to 15 slain Egyptians.

The Cyprus radio, however, said 12 of the Egyptians were killed, and 19 Egyptians and seven Cypriot national guardsmen wounded.

It said 38 Egyptians were arrested and would be treated as military prisoners. Cairo reported there were 60 shock troops in the raiding party, 10 more than the Cypriot broadcast accounted for.

Egypt Accused of Needless Bloodshed

The Egyptian raid set off an angry exchange between the Governments of Cyprus and Egypt. Cyprus said that the Egyptians had landed without permission and that the attack had caused needless bloodshed just as the terrorists, who identified themselves as Palestinians, were preparing to free 11 passengers and the four crewmen of the Cyprus Airways DC-8. Egypt said that Cyprus had been notified of the commando action.

[As Egyptian commandos lay on the tarmac in firing positions, a Reuters correspondent said, he saw a Greek Cypriot, apparently an officer, walking upright among them. As bullets whistled around him, he seemed to be angrily ordering the Egyptians off. He forced one Egyptian soldier to his feet, driving him at gunpoint toward the terminal, and fired two shots at the Egyptian, who fell, apparently badly wounded.]

Had Killed Egyptian Editor

The events leading to the battle began yesterday when the two terrorists shot to death the editor in chief of the semiofficial Egyptian newspaper Al Ahram, Yousef el-Sebai, in the lobby of the Hilton Hotel in Nicosia.

The terrorists seized hostages and during negotiations were taken to the four-engined plane that flew them and their captives out of Cyprus. With half a dozen Arab and other countries refusing landing permission, the plane put down in the East African country of Djibouti early today, where it was refueled. It returned here, and three hours later the Egyptian raiders arrived aboard a C-130 transport plane.

The official Greek Cypriot spokesman said, "We told the Egyptian troops not to take any action, but they ran out of the plane and began firing indiscriminately."

Witnesses said Cypriot national guardsmen had fired on the advancing Egyptians and had driven them away from the plane.

The commandos, with at least 10 of their comrades lying dead on the tarmac, turned back and sought shelter as tracer bullets lit the darkness, the witnesses said.

[In the airport tower the Cypriot President, Spyros Kyprianou, ducked bullets and called the United Nations Secretary General, Kurt Waldheim, in New York, asking him to intervene with Egypt, Reuters reported.]

After the hour-long gunfight, Cypriot troops and policemen rounded up the Egyptians, disarmed them and marched them away to an undisclosed destination.

The terrorists were led away by the Cypriot police for interrogation. Both appeared unhurt, witnesses said. Earlier reports said one was wounded.

Two persons, apparently injured during the confused gun battle, were seen being carried off the jetliner. Their identities were not given.

Hours after the firing ceased, a Cypriot official said the last group of Egyptian commandos had surrendered to Cypriot officials. He said that 39 commandos, including the colonel who led the operation, had taken refuge in a Cyprus Airways jet that arrived from Tel Aviv 10 minutes before the battle broke out. Witnesses said Cypriot fire or a demolition charge had rocked the American-built C-130 Hercules.

In Cairo, an official statement said 60 shock troops had staged the raid and the Hercules had been destroyed by an antitank shell fired by the Cypriots. It said both sides had suffered some dead and wounded and blamed the Cypriots for the bloodshed.

During the Egyptian raid, tracer bullets streaked through the night sky as armored personnel carriers began moving onto the tarmac where the Cyprus Airways DC-8 held by the terrorists had been parked since its arrival from Djibouti three hours earlier. There were explosions, apparently from mortars and rockets.

The Palestinians

All the early Egyptian fire appeared to be diversionary and not aimed directly at the plane, witnesses said. One witness said he had seen gun flashes coming from the door of the plane, as the terrorists apparently fired back.

During the fighting, a West German television cameraman, Colin Rosen, was reportedly shot and wounded in the wrist and leg by a Cypriot security guard who had ordered him not to take pictures of the freed hostages.

Miltiades Christodoulou, a Cypriot spokesman, told reporters that the Egyptian military transport carrying the raiders had landed under "false pretenses" at Larnaca Airport on the southeast coast of this Mediterranean island.

"Cairo had informed us it was sending a plane with Egyptian ministers to take part in negotiations," he said. "We told the Egyptian troops not to take any action, but they ran out of the plane and began firing indiscriminately."

Egyptians were shooting at the control tower, the spokesman said, and the Cypriot President, Spyros Kyprianou, "was forced to take cover to avoid being hit; at this point the National Guard opened fire to protect lives."

President Kyprianou was in the tower overseeing negotiations with the two terrorists, who reportedly were seeking safe passage to an unspecified leftist country, when the Egyptian transport landed. The terrorists immediately closed the doors of the jetliner.

The action took place at the airport that Nicosia uses at Larnaca, 23 miles to the southeast. Nicosia's airport, which is astride the so-called "green line" dividing Greek Cypriot and Turkish Cypriot areas, has been abandoned. Ever since the summer of 1974, when Turkish troops invaded Cyprus, more than a third of the island has been under Turkish control.

Yesterday the two terrorists, after seizing the hostages, negotiated with Cypriot officials for a plane to fly them off the island. Most of the hostages were Arab delegates to an African-Asian conference in Nicosia that Mr. Sebai, the Egyptian editor, was to have led.

After a futile journey over much of the Middle East, the plane landed in Djibouti. The terrorists and their captives spent 11 hours on the runway in temperatures that reached 120 degrees before authorities in Djibouti permitted a refueling of the plane on condition that it return to Cyprus.

The Djibouti control tower said airports in Aden, Southern Yemen; Addis Ababa, Ethiopia, and Mogadishu, Somalia, were closed to all traffic until further notice, indicating they would not receive the plane. Libya, Kuwait and Greece said earlier they would not allow the plane to land.

'Shall Deal With You Fairly'

The Cypriot spokesman said the terrorists had decided to return here because "no one else would have them." He said the Government had sent word to the pair that "we shall deal with you fairly."

[In Beirut, Lebanon, Palestinian sources said that the leader of the Palestine Liberation Organization, Yasir Arafat, had sent a 14-man commando unit to Cyprus Saturday to rescue the hostages by force. But, the sources said, Cypriot authorities refused at the last minute to permit the attack, and the jetliner left.]

A Cypriot Government spokesman refused to comment on the report from Beirut.

The executive committee of the P.L.O. denounced Mr. Sebai's killing as "treason against the Palestinian cause" and warned the terrorists not to harm any of the hostages.

A freed hostage, George Batal of Lebanon, said the terrorists had told their captives, "Everybody who went to Israel with Sadat will die, including Sadat."

The terrorists, who were armed with grenades and pistols, released 19 hostages before leaving Cyprus yesterday. One freed hostage quoted the pair as saying they had killed Mr. Sabai because "he published good things about Israel" and was "against the Palestinians."

Cypriot sources said the two men came from Beirut last Tuesday and checked into the Hilton, showing passports in the names of Zayed H. Alali, a 29-year-old Kuwaiti, and Reyad Samir al-Ahad, a 25-year-old Iraqi.

The hostages were identified by the Cypriot Government as four Egyptians, three Palestinians, two Syrians, a Somali and a Moroccan, who had been attending the African-Asian conference.

February 20, 1978

Terrorism: Palestinians Ambivalent About Issue

To some, the very word "Palestinian" is a synonym for terrorist. Yet the number of Palestinians who have engaged in terrorist acts is small and the number of ordinary Palestinians who approve of international terrorism —such as hijacking—is smaller today than it used to be.

At the same time, it is hard to find a Palestinian who will openly condemn a given act of terrorism.

However, the Executive Committee of the Palestine Liberation Organization did condemn the murder of Yousef el-Sebai, the editor in chief of Al Ahram, in Cyprus this weekend as treason to the Palestinian cause.

Most Palestinians make a distinction between the kind of spectacular international terrorism of the 1960's and early 1970's that brought worldwide attention to their cause and the violence that is still occasionally directed against targets inside Israel or the Israeli-held territories.

A Palestinian teacher here, for example, endorsed a recent bus explosion on the West Bank that was said to have killed two Israelis and wounded many others. "That's the way the struggle should be done," she said. "Against the Israelis, inside the occupied territories, and not by hijacking a German plane—how does that serve the cause?"

For many, 1974 was a benchmark in attitudes toward terrorism. In that year, a meeting of Arab heads of state designated the P.L.O. "the sole legitimate representative of the Palestinian people," and Yasir Arafat, the head of the P.L.O., made his milestone address to the General Assembly of the United Nations. International recognition seemed to reduce the need for and usefulness of such headline-grabbing violence as the killing of an editor on Cyprus. Respect declined for the renegades who earlier had been thought of as heroes for indulging in such terrorism.

Today Palestinian professionals wince at their worldwide "terrorist" image and discuss terrorism uncomfortably with foreigners. There is a certain longing for respectability, but attitudes remain complex.

"It didn't register politically on me at all," confessed one well-known Palestinian author, speaking of the "media terrorism" before 1974. "I found the whole thing rather stupid, counterproductive and messily unmoral." Of Leila Khaled, the Palestinians' most celebrated and melodramatic airplane hijacker, the author said, "I don't think anyone took her very seriously beyond the Raquel Welch category."

But opinions are highly fluid, and the advent of Menachem Begin's Government in Israel and the growing belief that the P.L.O. has been left out of the negotiating process have rekindled speculation about a new outbreak of terrorism. It is, Palestinians know, their ultimate, desperate weapon—and it can be used against Arab, American or European targets; or, as in the past, it can be used indiscriminately. Palestinians are, needless to say, the first to recall Mr. Begin's own terrorist past. Many argue today that "the terrorist Begin only understands violence." But, for the most part, they must content themselves with verbal outbursts. Israeli and Arab vigilance on frontiers and the P.L.O.'s organizational incapacities sharply restrict attacks inside Israel or the occupied territories.

February 21, 1978

20 TO 30 DIE IN ISRAEL IN BLAZE AND GUNFIGHT AS INVADERS SEIZE BUS

FATAH ADMITS RAID

Guerrillas Land From Sea, Battle With Policemen and Fire at Cars on Highway

By MOSHE BRILLIANT
Special to The New York Times

TEL AVIV, Sunday, March 12—Between 20 and 30 Israeli civilians were killed yesterday when Palestinian terrorists landed by boat, seized a bus and fought with policemen, the Israeli radio said. About 70 other civilians were wounded in the incident, in which the bus burst into flames during a gunfight between the terrorists and the police on the outskirts of Tel Aviv.

The casualty figures did not include terrorists or Israeli policemen killed or wounded.

[In Beirut, Al Fatah, the largest guerrilla group in the Palestine Liberation Organization, said its forces had carried out the attack.

[The Israeli Defense Minister, Ezer Weizman, said in New York that he had spoken to Prime Minister Menachem Begin several times about the incident. He said 30 people had been killed and 80 injured in the attack, which was carried out by 13 terrorists, including two women.

[Mr. Weizman described the attack as the worst inside Israel in 30 years. Asked about possible military responses by Israel, he said such things "are not always to be discussed."

[Shortly after he spoke, Mr. Weizman cut short his visit to the United States to return to Israel.]

Police Search Area

Most of the casualties occurred when the bus exploded. Others happened when the Palestinians first seized the bus or when the terrorists fired and threw grenades at passing traffic as they drove 25 miles down the coast toward Tel Aviv after reportedly landing south of Haifa.

Witnesses said that they had seen at least two of the terrorists escaping from the bus during the gunfight and that they were then arrested. Another report said that a Palestinian woman had also been taken prisoner.

The police said that there was no evidence any terrorists had escaped but that they were taking no chances and carefully combing the area long after midnight. Army helicopters beamed powerful searchlights at the fields, and roads in the area were closed.

Inhabitants of some Tel Aviv suburbs and the seaside town of Herzlia on the northern outskirts were ordered to remain indoors and to lower their shutters until further notice. After midnight a curfew was imposed as far north as Natanya. This area includes the main resort center for tourists.

The United States Ambassador, Samuel Lewis, was seen at a roadblock and was among those prevented from getting home to Herzlia, a seaside town near the site of the gunfight.

Information about the attack was incomplete and accounts by witnesses differed, but police sources and some witnesses gave the following account of the attack:

The guerrillas landed about 4 P.M. at Maagan Michael, a collective settlement 20 miles south of Haifa, about 30 miles north of Tel Aviv, in two rubber dinghies, which were later found on the beach by the police. A body was also found nearby, and it was suspected the victim had witnessed the landing and had been shot dead.

After coming ashore the gunmen took up positions on the Haifa-Tel Aviv highway at Jisr e Zarka about a mile south of Maagan Michael. They fired through the windshield of a bus that was taking bus drivers and their families home to Haifa after an outing. The passengers left the bus and tried to seek shelter but the gunmen fired after them. They also fired at passing vehicles, inflicting additional casualties.

Meanwhile other Palestinians seized a Mercedes that they filled with arms and explosives. At 4:42 P.M. another bus headed toward Haifa approached Jisr e Zarka, and passengers got off to help the wounded from the attack on the first bus.

The Arabs then sped up to the scene in the Mercedes and at gun point forced back into the bus the passengers and some of the survivors from the first attack. They ordered the driver to turn around and proceed to Tel Aviv.

Police Attempt Interception

The police were alerted at 4:45 P.M. that there had been shooting and made several attempts to intercept the bus. The driver, with a gun pointed at his head, sped past the barriers. Near Hadera the terrorists shot a policeman in a jeep who had fired at their vehicle.

By the time bus reached Natanya, half way to Tel Aviv, helicopters were bringing soldiers to the outskirts of Telaviv.

At 5:25 P.M., the bus reached the Tel Aviv Country Club on the outskirts of the city where the police had set up a huge roadblock. They opened fire from all directions at the tires of the bus and brought it to a halt. The Palestinians threw grenades from the windows and fired automatic rifles. Panic-stricken passengers lay on the floor while others made their way to the exit and escaped.

After 10 or 15 minutes of gunfire, the bus caught fire. One Israeli said he had throw grenades at it, setting it ablaze.

The vehicle was destroyed, but most seen a gunman leave the bus and then

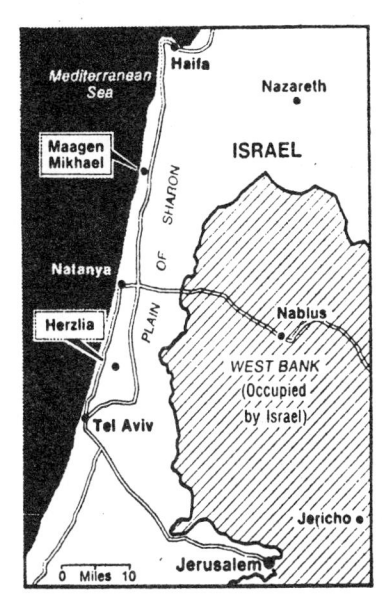

The New York Times/March 12, 1978
Palestinian gunmen came ashore and seized a bus near Maagen Mikhael. Bus exploded in gunfight near Herzlia.

occupants managed to get out before it blew up. Fire lit up the area for a considerable distance.

By the glow of the burning bus, first aid teams began treating survivors lying on the highway. Soldiers and policemen with dogs, flares and searchlights began combing the area.

The police roadblock was arranged in the vicinity of the country club because no residences are in the area and no buildings close to the highway.

The attack was the worst since gunmen seized a schoolhouse at Maalot in 1974. Twenty-eight persons, twenty-two of them children, were killed, and 88 others were wounded.

In 1975 Arab terrorists landed at Tel Aviv and seized a hotel near the seashore. They st off explosives when Israeli troops borke into the building. Eight civilians, three soldiers and seven terrorists died in the raid.

Al Fatah Claims Responsibility
Special to The New York Times

BEIRUT, Lebanon, March 11—The main Palestinian guerrilla organization, Al Fatah, said tonight that the attack on the bus in Israel had been carried out by its guerrillas and that it was Al Fatah's largest operation inside Israel since the 1975 attack on the Savoi Hotel in Tel Aviv.

A spokesman of Al Fatah said that 39 "Israeli soldiers" had been killed in "fierce fighting" on the coastal road between Haifa and Tel Aviv, up to 9 P.M. local time.

The Palestinians

Palestinian political sources here said the attack had been timed to precede Prime Minister Menachem Begin's trip to the United States, which had originally scheduled for tomorrow night but postponed after the raid.

Three units of Al Fatah were said to be taking part in the operation, which the spokesman said began at at 6:40 P.M.

The Palestine Liberation Organization said in a statement tonight that the action was aimed at "the escalation of our armed struggle against the Zionist enemy inside our occupied homeland."

The guerrillas who carried out the attack were described as members of a group named for Deir Yassin, the Arab village near Jerusalem that Palestinians say was the scene of an Israeli massacre in 1948.

Today's operation was named after Kamal Adwan, one of three Al Fatah leaders killed by an Israeli raid in Beirut in April 1973.

March 12, 1978

ISRAELIS SEIZE 4-TO 6-MILE 'SECURITY BELT' IN LEBANON AND SAY TROOPS WILL REMAIN

Israel's Prime Minister, Menachem Begin, left, arriving at the Lebanon border yesterday for a close look at the action. Defense Minister Ezer Weizman is at center, wearing flight jacket and sunglasses.

Associated Press

MAJOR FIGHTING ENDS

By WILLIAM E. FARRELL
Special to The New York Times

JERUSALEM, March 15—Israeli forces routed Palestinian guerrillas today from at least seven strongholds in southern Lebanon, and Prime Minister Menachem Begin said the troops would remain until an agreement was reached to insure that the area could never again be used for raids against Israel.

With land, sea and air operations conducted from the Mediterranean to the foothills of Mount Hermon, Israelis occupied what Lieut. Gen. Mordechai Gur, the Chief of Staff, called a "security belt" along the 60 or so miles of its northern border, with a depth of four and a half to six miles. Late tonight, General Gur said the major fighting was over.

[An Israeli military spokesman reported that 11 Israeli soldiers had been killed in the operation and 57 wounded, according to The Associated Press.]

Air Strikes Near Beirut

Mr. Begin's remarks about how long Israelis would remain in Lebanon were echoed by Defense Minister Ezer Weizman, who told reporters:

"We shall continue to clear the area—prevent the area from being attack positions against us as long as we find it necessary."

The ground offensive, the largest that Israel has ever carried out against Palestinians, was accompanied by air strikes against Palestinian enclaves and camps far north of the Israeli border, including at least two in the vicinity of Beirut.

The Israeli Army spokesman announced that Israeli planes had bombed a Palestinian base near Damur, about 20 miles south of Beirut, which he said had been the staging area for the Arab raiders who infiltrated into Israel on Saturday and seized a bus.

The seizure touched off a wild ride on the Haifa-Tel Aviv highway, with shooting and an explosion that led to the death of 34 Israelis and an American and the injury of more than 70 persons.

The army spokesman said that Israeli planes had struck targets at the Mediterranean port of Tyre and at a site near Beirut that the spokesman described as a Palestine Liberation Organization training and supply base "for terrorist naval units and for their equipment."

In the raid at Damur, the spokesman said the Israeli planes had been fired on by a Syrian unit. The Israeli planes did not fire back at the Syrians, he said, and returned safely to base.

The Syrians have a large military presence in Lebanon under an inter-Arab peacekeeping force installed in the country to enforce a cease-fire in the 1975-76 civil war.

General Gur and Defense Minister Weizman went out of their way at their news conference to say that the Israeli objective in Lebanon was a limited one and that there was no intention to do battle with Syrian forces.

Israelis and diplomats here are apprehensive of a Syrian response because of the possibility it could lead to all-out war.

"I do hope that Syria will understand that this is a limited action in south Lebanon," Mr. Weizman said. "I do hope that the Government of Lebanon understands that this is a preventive action."

"We hope the Syrians will understand," General Gur said.

Asked tonight whether any Syrian ground activity had been detected, General Gur said "no," adding: "Until now, I'm happy to say they were as careful as we were."

Neither General Gur nor Mr. Weizman would say how many Israelis were taking part in the attack. They also did not specify casualties.

High Bombing Toll Expected

General Gur said that at least 100 Palestinian guerrillas were known to have been killed. Mr. Weizman added that when the toll of the bombing missions was learned the total of dead would be much higher.

Foreign press reports placed the combined Israeli force as high as 20,000. Israeli military officials estimated that there were as many as 5,000 Palestinian guerrillas in the enclaves adjacent to the Israeli border. The enclaves have been used over the years to stage terrorist attacks against Israel.

"The operation is a big one," Mr. Weizman said at the news conference. "This is not a reprisal operation in the usual sense. This operation comes—and I believe it will succeed—to destroy and uproot, as far as possible, terrorist concentrations in southern Lebanon."

Mr. Weizman said that the Israelis had taken "a number" of prisoners. "We had a few casualties, they have more," the Defense Minister said.

According to a map provided by the Israeli Army, the main border strongholds attacked by the Israeli forces were Naqura, near the Mediterranean; Yarun, Bint Jbail, Marun al-Ras, Taibe, Khiam and Ibl as-Saqi.

Israeli planes also struck in the Tyre area. There was no confirmation of Palestinian reports from Beirut that Israeli troops had landed in the Tyre area.

General Gur said that during the night attacks "we used mainly infantry forces, with air, naval, armor and enginering corps support."

"Toward morning," he continued, "the operation took on a more mobile aspect, with combined infantry and armored forces, again with artillery and air support and with naval forces operating along the coast."

March 16, 1978

Guerrillas Join Civilian Retreat From Attackers

By MARVINE HOWE
Special to The New York Times

TYRE, Lebanon, March 15 — Many Palestinian and Lebanese families fled in panic today from population centers in southern Lebanon that had been bombarded by Israeli fighter-bombers, gunboats and artillery.

"We're going north, anywhere, to get away from the shelling," said Mohammed Ahmed al-Mohammed, a Lebanese farmer, as he and his family of 12 set out on foot along a road out of Tyre carrying only small bundles of blankets and clothing.

While young Lebanese and Palestinian guerrillas in the towns and villages spoke of their "fierce resistance," it was clear they were retreating in face of the heavy Israeli odds.

"We are not going to let ourselves be annihilated," said a member of the Palestine Liberation Organization's southern military command at Saida. "We cannot destroy the Israeli forces, but we can inflict as many casualties as possible and then make a tactical withdrawal."

The Palestinian military spokesman confirmed reports that the joint Palestinian-Lebanese leftist forces had lost their principal positions in the border area: Khiam, Ibl al-Saqi and Taibe in the east, Bint Jbail and Marun al-Ras in the center and Naqura and Alma al-Chaab in the southwest.

The city of Tyre was a prime target as the main port of entry for arms supplies for the guerrillas. Many of the victims of the attack, however, were said to be civilians.

In the Lebanese government hospital, visitors saw three children brought in after the shelling of the city this morning. A hospital employee said that there were other known civilian casualties but that it was difficult to transport them while the firing continued.

Doctor Talks About Casualties

Next door, in the Palestine Red Crescent clinic, a doctor said that 25 civilians had been brought in with injuries caused by shelling since the Israeli operation was started last night. The wounded came mostly from Tyre and the Palestinian refugee camp of Rashidiye, and nearly half were Lebanese, the doctor said.

As Mirage jets swooped to bomb here early this afternoon, a Lebanese businessman cried to bystanders: "Oh my God, please! My family is in there!"

At the same time, four Israeli gunboats cruising offshore lobbed shells intermittently into residential sections near the port. One of the shells had hit a Toyota, which lay splattered with blood. One of the few residents who had not fled said two children had lost their legs in the shelling.

On the outskirts of Tyre a small group of women and girls waited patiently with their rolls of bedding and a few household utensils. They were Palestinians from the Burj al-Shemali refugee camp and were waiting for the father, who had taken the smaller children to relatives in Saida and was coming back for them.

"The Israelis bombed the camp all night," said 13-year-old Fatima Abdallah, adding that she and the family had spent the night in the camp's bomb shelter. "But we can't take it anymore and so all the people in the camp are leaving."

There were similar scenes in Tyre's two other refugee camps, Al Buss and Rashidiye. Foreign reporters saw huge clouds of smoke rise from Rashidiye while gunboats shelled it this afternoon.

"When the planes came and started bombarding Al Buss, everybody decided to go," said Ahmed Ali, a truckdriver. He was using his brightly painted truck to carry 40 Palestinian women, children and old people with their meager belongings north to Saida.

The main road north was crowded with trucks, taxis and private cars, heaped with household furnishings. Most of the people said they did not know where they were going, that they simply wanted to get as far from the Israeli border as possible.

A tour of the southern interior as far as the market center of Nabatiye showed that even towns and villages that were not attacked were being evacuated. Only three old men and half a dozen Palestinian guerrillas were seen on the streets of Nabatiye, which used to have a population of 40,000.

An 18-year-old old Palestinian student, who identified himself only as Ahmed, warned foreign reporters to leave the area as soon as possible.

"I am sure there is more to come," he said.

March 16, 1978

The Palestinians

Wadi Haddad, Palestinian Hijacking Strategist, Dies

By RAYMOND H. ANDERSON

Dr. Wadi Haddad, the strategist behind the Palestinian guerrilla movement's hijacking of airliners and a shadowy figure linked to international terrorist groups, has died of cancer in a hospital in East Germany, the Popular Front for the Liberation of Palestine announced in Lebanon yesterday.

The Popular Front, which Dr. Haddad founded in 1967 along with Dr. George Habash, said that he "died as a hero" on Tuesday.

The body of the 49-year-old physician was flown yesterday to Baghdad, Iraq, one of the Arab cities where the underground leader had been living out of public view in recent years. Palestinians in Beirut, Lebanon, said he would be brought there for burial at the Palestinians' "Martyr's Cemetery."

Dr. Haddad was at the head of Israel's list of wanted terrorists. He went underground after rockets were fired into his Beirut apartment in July 1970.

Directed First Hijacking

The guerrilla leader directed the first airliner hijacking by Palestinians, involving the seizure of an Israeli plane, an El Al airliner, in July 1968 and its diversion to Algeria.

Last October, already confined by his illness, he was the strategist behind the most recent major hijacking, the takeover of a Lufthansa airliner that was ultimately stormed in Somalia by West German commandos.

One of the most dramatic terrorist actions that Dr. Haddad planned was the hijacking of four airliners in September 1970 and the blowing up of three of them in the desert of Jordan and of the fourth at the Cairo airport.

That gesture of defiance by the Palestinians to Egypt's acceptance of a cease-fire with Israel backfired and led to Jordanian suppression of the guerrilla movement in Jordan.

In 1972 Dr. Haddad split with the Marxist-oriented Popular Front for the Liberation of Palestine in a dispute over airliner hijackings.

In 1976 he and other supporters of hijackings were formally ousted by the Popular Movement, whose leader, Dr. Habash, had come to regard the seizure of airliners as more damaging than beneficial to the Palestinian fight against Israel.

Dr. Haddad was born in Palestine into a Greek Orthodox family. His father was a teacher. A refugee after the creation of Israel in 1948, he studied in Beirut, where one of his closest classmates in the American University Medical School was Dr. Habash.

After graduation, Dr. Haddad did social work in Palestinian refugee camps, and he and Dr. Habash formed a group called the Arab Nationalist Movement, intended for struggle against Israel. This developed into the Popular Front for the Liberation of Palestine.

As a guerrilla leader, Dr. Haddad shunned the spotlight. A guerrilla in Lebanon was quoted yesterday as having said of him: "He was a real revolutionary.

He did what he thought was best for the Palestinian cause, without publicizing himself."

Dr. Haddad had close ties with some of the most notorious international terrorist groups, including the Baader-Meinhof gang in West Germany and the Red Army in Japan. He was also linked to the Venezuelan terrorist known as Carlos.

Dr. Haddad was reported to have been the planner of the Tel Aviv airport attack by the Japanese Red Army in May 1972, in which the attackers pulled submachine guns and grenades from suitcases in the airport terminal and opened fire, killing nearly 30 people and wounding dozens.

He was also said to have been involved in planning the hijacking of an Air France plane to Uganda in July 1976, which ended with an assault by Israeli commandos to free the hostages.

Uncertainty Over Effect

Dr. Haddad's terrorist ventures were said to have been financed by Arab sectors opposed to any peaceful settlement with Israel, among them the Libyans.

There was uncertainty among Palestinians in Beirut yesterday over the effect of Dr. Haddad's death on guerrilla tactics and international terrorism in general.

No certain successor was in sight to command the splinter group headed by Dr. Haddad, called the P.F.L.P—Foreign Operations Branch. But analysts in Beirut said they thought a guerrilla with the code name of Abu Nidal, who operates from Iraq, might take over.

April 2, 1978

THE I.R.A.

TROOPS CRUSH REVOLT IN DUBLIN; TAKE POST OFFICE SEIZED BY RIOTERS

Score of Regulars, Volunteers, and Police Wounded—Losses of Rebels Not Given.

LONDON, Wednesday, April 26.—Almost coincidental with the capture of Sir Roger Casement, leader of the Separatist faction in Ireland, while he was attempting to land arms from Germany on the coast of Ireland, there has occurred in Ireland a revolutionary outbreak of considerable proportions.

So far as has been announced by the British Government only Dublin is affected. Here serious fighting took place Monday between regular troops, volunteers, and policemen against members of the Sinn Fein Society who had captured the Post Office and Stephen's Green and numerous houses in various parts of the city.

Three of the officers of the troops, four or five soldiers, two volunteers, and two policemen were killed, and about a score of others wounded. The losses of the revolutionists have not been made known.

The Government last evening reported that the military authorities had the situation well in hand. The official statement said:

At noon yesterday serious disturbances broke out in Dublin. A large party of men identified with the Sinn Fein Party, mostly armed, occupied Stephens Green, and took possession forcibly of the Post Office, where they cut the telegraphic and telephonic wires. Houses also were occupied in Stephens Green, Sackville Street, Abbey Street, and along the quays.

In the course of the day soldiers arrived from the Curragh and the situation is now well in hand. So far as is known here, three military officers, four or five soldiers, two loyal volunteers and two policemen have been killed and four or five military officers and seven or eight soldiers and six volunteers wounded. No exact information has been received of the casualties on the side of the Sinn Feiners.

Reports received from Cork, Limerick, Ennis, Tralee, and both ridings of Tipperary show that no disturbances of any kind have occurred in these localities.

The first announcement of the trouble was made in the House of Commons yesterday by Augustine Birrell, Chief Secretary for Ireland, who said that the situation was well in hand, but that communication with Dublin was still difficult. There had been several arrests there, but he could not give the names, he said.

While the only details surrounding the situation are the meagre ones contained in the official announcements Government officials expressed the opinion that with Sir Roger Casement and two of his aids in prison in London the troops were in control of the situation.

The arrest of Sir Roger Casement was dealt with by The Pall Mall Gazette yesterday in an editorial which is extremely significant at this moment, but which, for obvious reasons, cannot be dilated upon.

"Before Germany took the trouble to send arms to Ireland," says the newspaper, "she must have been satisfied of the existence of agents in that country who were prepared to receive and use them in her interests. That is to say that there must have been active communication between Irish traitors and their confederates in Berlin despite all existing precautions of censorship and supervision.

"When we find a force devoid of arms undergoing military training in Ireland and a cargo of arms from our enemies seeking a landing place in that country it becomes highly desirable that the connection, if any, between these two striking phenomena should be more fully explained."

April 26, 1916

ORDERS SUPPRESSION OF THE SINN FEIN

British Decree Forbids the Irish Volunteers and Kindred Organizations.

SHAPING HOME RULE BILL

Carson's Silence Considered a Favorable Omen for the New Program.

DUBLIN, Nov. 26.—Widespread suppression of Sinn Fein and other organizations in Ireland has been ordered by the Government.

The Official Gazette today publishes a proclamation prohibiting and suppressing Sinn Fein organizations, Sinn Fein clubs, the Irish Volunteers, the Cunmannamran and the Gaelic League in all counties and boroughs of Ireland.

LONDON, Nov. 26.—A new Home Rule bill setting up two Parliaments in Ireland, with a Council or Senate of forty to be chosen by the two, will probably be introduced in Parliament within the next two weeks.

Daily sessions are being held by the Cabinet committee in charge of the measure, the subject under discussion at present being finance, which is in charge of a sub-committee under the chairmanship of J. Austen Chamberlain, Chancellor of the Exchequer. The control of customs has always been a point of the sharpest difference when other Home Rule schemes have been debated and was one of the rocks upon which the Irish Convention was wrecked. Control of police is another knotty point.

The most hopeful sign of an agreement is the silence which Sir Edward Carson, the Ulster leader, has preserved since the latest Irish kite was flown. Sir Edward has not issued any mandates to the Ulster volunteers " to keep their powder dry," while the presence of two hitherto stanch Unionist leaders, Walter Hume Long and Baron Birkenhead, on the committee, shows that Ulster is tending toward conciliation.

It is the supposition that there has been an understanding on the main points before the committee, and that, in fact, there was a tacit agreement before the committee was named.

The final word, however, does not rest with Parliament, but with the Sinn Fein party. If that organization pursues its policy of refusing recognition of any British law, this British-planned Irish Parliament may come to nothing, since the Sinn Fein polled a majority of the Irish voters at the last election. Moderates believe that the Sinn Fein leaders may not be able to keep the mass of their followers in line against an offer of Home Rule which promises to satisfy most of the ambitions of the old Nationalist party.

The other alternative remains, that the Sinn Fein may capture the new Southern Parliament and promptly declare Ireland an independent republic. It would be possible in such a case to carry on the work of the Parliament without recognizing any imperial overlordship.

November 27, 1919

IRELAND'S PROBLEMS SEEN AT CLOSE RANGE BY AN AMERICAN

Sinn Feiners Control, Yet Dare Not Mention the Names of Their Directing Heads.

OBEY WITHOUT QUESTIONING

"Murders" to Them Are "Killings Under War Conditions"—Disorders Coldly Calculated.

WHOLE COUNTRY PROSPERS

Observer Can Find No Economic Reasons for Discontent—"The Object Is Patriotic."

By CHARLES H. GRASTY.
Special Correspondence of THE NEW YORK TIMES.

LONDON, Aug. 1.—I am just back from Ireland, whither I went to gather impressions of the present conditions there. My mental attitude was impartial and I shall try to report facts and opinions as I encountered them in my visit. If in transcribing my notes, made as I went along, the Sinn Fein viewpoint stands out less than the opposite one, it is because " of low visibility" on that side of the fence.

The Irish Republic is an invisible republic. Its supporters are carrying out a secret program and talking is strictly against the rules. Most of the people I met were Sinn Feiners, and they were all most hospitable and obliging to me as an American. No American who leaves controversial matters severely alone need have any fears in visiting Ireland. In fact, the person of every American is sacred, for America is now the chief cornerstone of Sinn Fein hopes. They shoot pretty freely, but shoot straight and do not often kill by accident. A typical Sinn Fein gunman would put his own brother out of the way, if ordered to do so. He would believe it was necessary for the cause and would not take his personal grief to heart, provided the victim first had absolution.

Murder Domesticated.

In Sinn Fein Ireland murder has become domesticated. Indeed, they do not consider it murder at all. It is "killing." Except in cases where advantage is taken of the general laxity to pay off personal grudges, the whole business is purely mechanical. In the minds of Sinn Feiners connected with this branch of activity there is a state of war, and any patriot would shoot a traitor in the back or any other portion of his anatomy just as freely as a French or English soldier would shoot a German during the war.

In the face of this, general conditions in Ireland are peculiarly unfavorable to the kind of movement which is now at its high tide. Ireland is a relatively prosperous country. The Sinn Feiners do not admit this, and tell you that in Dublin there are 20,000 families each living in a single room. Nevertheless, Ireland, especially in the rural districts, is enjoying conditions which certainly have not existed since the famine of 1846. Land, for which there is a universal lust, has been divided or is in process of division on extraordinarily favorable terms, and whenever these terms do not seem sufficiently generous to the " have-nots " the landowners are compelled to part with their holdings by methods not usually recognized in courts of law.

As will appear later, one of the big impelling forces in the present movement is an insatiable desire among young men for land. It is estimated that the number of young men in Ireland is now about 200,000 above the normal. They did not go to war in large numbers, and were not allowed to emigrate, and now there is a hot scramble among them to get hold of land.

Catholic Ireland, which is three-fourths of the whole population, lives under precisely the same British Government as Northern Ireland, with one-fourth of the population. The larger percentage of the three-fourths is chronically discontented and at times rebellious. About the same percentage of the Belfast district, composed of the two counties of Antrim and Down, and a lesser proportion of four of the other seven counties of Ulster are reasonably prosperous and happy under these same laws and their administration.

Purpose in Ulster's Loyalty.

If Catholic Ireland had the same character and temperament as Protestant Ireland, and had accepted in the same way British rule, Ireland would probably long ago have become one of the most prosperous communities in the world. But British rule does not suit the Irish for reasons of their own. Every concession on the part of British has been made the stepping-stone for new demands. As some one has put it. Southern Ireland's attitude seems to be: " 'Caresses have their charms,' says the mastiff in the fable, 'but the chain is there still.,' "

Ulster accepts the rule that the rest of Ireland despises, works under it, prospers under it, and seems to be as happy as the limitations of that dour Scottish bread permit. Ulster plays for all it is worth her devotion to the Union, but in my visit there I formed the impression that the love of Britain was less potent with them than fear and hate of Catholic Ireland and apprehension of the results that would follow Dublin rule.

It is clear, therefore, that the demand for independence is not due to the causes which usually set off explosive popular movements. There is neither general poverty nor dire oppression. Losses of life in the late war were not suffered to any ruinous extent by the element now rebelling. On the other hand, war profits, mainly drawn from agriculture, were large.

At the time of the open rebellion at Easter, 1916, which was the genesis of the present big movement, none of those conditions seemed to exist which ordinarily arouse passions and invite rebellion. The Home Rule act had been passed and was on the statute books, to be put into effect after the war. Response to the call for voluntary enlistment had been meagre, popular sentiment was largely pro-German, and conscription was impossible. Britain was facing almost insuperable difficulties in the World War. There was the old, undying hatred of her, but it was latent.

New Rebel Calculations Succeeded.

I found in Ireland an almost universal opinion that the organizers of the present movement saw in these conditions the long-awaited opportunity to strike for Irish freedom and went deliberately to work to produce the necessary ferment throughout the country. What was lacking was some fresh action on the part of the British Government that would set aflame the smouldering antagonism.

This was a new method of calculated planning in Irish rebellions. Plans were made carefully and cold-bloodedly and systematically carried out. The object was to draw the Government, never tactful nor wise in handling Ireland, and now sorely perplexed by its war difficulties, into some stupid blundering which, to the Irish, would wear the aspect of British tyranny and thus rouse the people to action.

If, as is believed, this was the purpose for which the rebellion of 1916 was launched, it succeeded almost beyond their expectations. It is undoubtedly true that those who engaged in that rebellion were boys and young men brought in from the country to Dublin, who had not the slightest idea up to the last moment of what they had come for. It seems clear that there was no notion in the minds of the leaders of immediate success of the rebellion as such, but they got what they wanted.

A series of blunders by the deeply preoccupied Government in London supplied the needed issue of fresh tyranny, and from that time on the Republican movement has grown in extent and intensity.

Like methods have been pursued consistently ever since. Power has been concentrated in the hands of a few men, and nobody can be certain who these men are. Invisibility is strictly maintained. Every move bears the stamp of cold calculation and well considered planning. At last Irish politics is controlled by an organization on the general lines of Tammany Hall.

Dare Not Mention Names.

I noticed in Dublin that no one dared to mention names in connection with this omnipotent secret power. Everybody knows and discusses the nominal heads like De Valera, the figurehead " President," and Arthur Griffith, " Vice President and acting President." It is known that there is a Dail Eireann, who the members are of this Irish Parliament, that they have their secret meetings, and that there is an active going Ministry.

Everybody, regardless of religion and politics, lives in a state of mental servitude so far as the program of killing is concerned. Men are dragged from street cars in the centre of Dublin and shot to death. No passenger on the car, nobody in the crowded street, will move a hand to interfere. Not one will go near the victim or inform the police or give testimony in court. All elemental instincts are paralyzed by the certainty of punishment that will be visited upon any act that might compromise the secrecy and efficiency of the program now being put into effect.

Executives of the organization give an order; it reaches those who are to carry it out through channels far removed from the source, and the thing desired is done with mechanical sureness.

Nothing succeeds like success. What is ordinarily called moral sense is in a state of stupefaction and there is little audible protest.

Members of the constabulary and others are marked for destruction in accordance to their value to the Government and with an eye to " getting the nerve" of the whole body of the police and bringing home everywhere a realization that resistance means sure and swift punishment.

How Assassination Is Defended.

The constabulary are nearly all Catholics, but that makes it worse for them because they are regarded as traitors. "We are at war for our country," runs the argument, "and traitors must be disposed of without mercy."

The deadly efficiency with which the program is executed, with hardly a single setback from the British Government, has had the effect reckoned upon by the leaders of the movement. There is a temporary suspension of moral forces which usually check such methods.

Nobody will or can specifically defend shooting in the back, but one hears in highly respectable quarters that while the methods are violent and brutal the object is patriotic. This is war, and war is always hell, they say.

And so the movement has progressed and thrived from week to week. It is stronger now than ever. Neutrals are constantly being drawn into the Sinn Fein ranks and many originally antagonistic are becoming neutral.

The Catholic hierarchy and priests, who were at first aghast at the violence, are less and less outspoken in condemning it, and when they do speak their condemnation is more general and equivocal.

I have roughly outlined the state to which Ireland has been brought, but before a balanced judgment can be formed on the situation there are other matters to be considered. What shall be said of the British Government, which has permitted things to go from bad to worse? If one searches for excuses there are plenty of them. Lloyd George's political difficulties at home are of a kind to enfeeble him in dealing with Irish conditions. If he adopted strong measures, it may be doubtful whether he could hold together the parliamentary coalition upon which he depends for his official existence. There are so many and such conflicting opinions on Irish settlement that any Home Rule bill seems sure to be reduced to impotence by discussion and compromise.

Suppression by force is a policy repugnant to the Prime Minister's instincts, as it is to the instincts of the general British public. And so there has been the policy of drifting. If there had been nothing else to do but handle Ireland, Downing Street would probably have handled it. But probably no Prime Minister in history has ever been confronted at one time with so many dangers and perplexities. It is not alone in Ireland that the British Empire is threatened. It is threatened in the Near East and India. There are signs of conflict and difference of opinion and interest between Britain and its closest ally, France. There is the question involving inevitable differences of how to bring the war to an end and set Europe again on the path of industry and prosperity, and the chief responsibility for this solution lies with the British Prime Minister.

These are but the chief burdens which rest upon the shoulders of the man who has been carrying greater responsibilities for a longer time than any other Government head. For four years there has not been a single moment when a serious mistake by him might not have meant disaster and ruin to his own country and to the world. But the fact remains that the Irish situation has been neglected and mishandled and opportunities for settlement wasted. Lloyd George has recently, in the labor situation presented to him as a part of the Irish question, boldly asserted the character in which he has in so many other things shown in the last four years that he is at home and can be strong. From this starting point he may find his way to the solution of the present problems in Ireland.

August 14, 1920

IRISH HOME RULE PASSES COMMONS ON THIRD READING

Labor Leader's Motion for Rejection Is Defeated by 183 Votes to 52.

PLEAS FOR RECONCILIATION

Premier Says That Ireland's Inheritance Is the Same as England's.

Copyright, 1920, by The New York Times Company.
Special Cable to THE NEW YORK TIMES.

LONDON, Nov. 11.—The Irish Home Rule bill passed its third reading in the House of Commons tonight and was sent up to the House of Lords. A notable change in the atmosphere was evident in the debate, which suggests that while the Government has not changed its intention to push the measure along, there is some hope of slackening of the present tension in the not distant future.

Mr. Asquith was the first to strike a more moderate note. He declined to support the motion for rejection of the bill, made by Adamson, leader of the Labor Party, and after making various criticisms of its provisions he alluded to Armistice Day and asked. "Can we make better use of the emotions such an anniversary arouses than by trying if we can by concerted effort find a basis of real settlement of the greatest and far most difficult of our domestic problems?"

He did not take the view that this was a black and unpromising moment. "Hear, hear," responded the Prime Minister, Mr. Asquith went on to urge that a great majority of the Irish people must repudiate the foul methods of the "wilder spirits," and if a giant effort, generous in its conceptions and possibilities, were made, there might yet be a chance of fruition of the long-delayed hope.

Mr. Lloyd George received Mr. Asquith's advance with frank and becoming cordiality. "We are only too anxious," he said, "to respond in the spirit in which it is made."

Frank reconciliation would be welcome by the people of Britain, and it would be a pleasure to extend the hand of good-fellowship to Ireland in the hope that the two countries should proceed side by side to try to solve the great problems of empire and humanity, he said.

There was no reservation in this full-flowered sentiment of the Prime Minister, and the House indorsed it with a loud cheer. The Premier, however, could not accept a dominion status for Ireland, such as Mr. Asquith recently proposed, and he defended the Government bill as offering Ireland the most generous financial terms ever suggested.

The bill was read as it stood, but the effect of the speeches of the two leaders was to make the members feel that the last word had not ben said and the door had been left open for further negotiations.

Rejection Measure Defeated.

LONDON, Nov. 11.—The Irish Home Rule bill passed the House of Commons on its third reading tonight, after a motion for rejection of the measure proposed by William C. Adamson, the Labor Opposition leader, had been defeated by 183 to 52.

Former Premier Asquith appealed for advantage to be taken of the associations and emotions aroused by the anniversary of Armistice Day, which could not be put to worthier use than an endeavor to find a basis of real settlement for Ireland.

Premier Lloyd George, replying, contended that the present bill was a generous measure, but the Irish people were not in a temper to give it proper understanding and consideration. He declared that documents, to be published at an early date, found in the possession of Sinn Fein leaders in 1918, proving they were involved in a German plot, would show the necessity of England retaining complete control of Irish harbors.

To give Ireland the power to raise a conscript army, he said, would be a dangerous menace to Great Britain, and he warned the Laborites that with an army of that kind in Ireland under full powers of Dominion Home Rule, conscription in England would become inevitable.

The Premier contended that it was equally impossible to allow Ireland her own navy, which was quite needless for her national life and could only be used for the peril of Great Britain and her own destruction.

He argued that it was fruitless to talk of granting fiscal autonomy to people still demanding a republic. Expressing a fervent hope for the removal of misunderstandings which make the future so dark, the Premier closed with a note of emotion:

"It may be that it was an Irish soldier we honored today. Ireland has had a great and brilliant share in the empire. Some of her greatest and most gallant warriors helped to fight for the empire. Some of her greatest statesmen—the shining wisdom of Burke and the stern leadership of Wellington—all contributed to build the empire.

"All we ask is that Ireland should not in a moment of anger cast away an inheritance which is as much hers as ours, but join in the empire it helped to build and adorn."

The fundamental principles laid down by the British Government in the Irish Home Rule bill are:

1. That the people of the six Ulster counties shall not be brought administratively under a separate Parliament in Ireland.

2. That there shall not be any weakening of the reservations which have been made by the Government for the purpose of safeguarding the vital interests of the United Kingdom.

At the time of the introduction of the measure it was stated that the home rule which the Government intended to give Ireland was based primarily on the declaration of Premier Lloyd George in a speech last December that "Great Britain cannot accept separation."

Under the bill two Legislatures with upper and lower houses would be set up, one for the North of Ireland and the other for the South.

If less than half the members of either Legislature are validly elected or fail to swear allegiance to the King, the King may dissolve the Parliament and place the Government in the hands of a committee appointed by the Lord Lieutenant.

A "Council for Ireland," composed of forty members, half of whom would be selected by each Parliament, also is provided for in the bill. The powers of the council would be limited to those granted to it by the two Legislatures.

The framers of the bill, it was said, hoped that the council would form the nucleus around which could be built one Parliament for the whole of Ireland.

November 12, 1920

FROM 1916 REBELLION TO TRUCE IN IRELAND

Chronology of Important Events in Sinn Fein Struggle to Achieve Independence.

The following is a chronology of important events in Ireland from the Easter rebellion of 1916 up to the truce of July 11, 1921, between the Sinn Fein and Crown forces and the negotiations between Premier Lloyd George, Sir James Craig of Ulster and Eamon de Valera, the Irish Republican leader, looking to the establishment of peace:

1916.

April 25.—Revolt in Dublin; 180 civilians killed and 614 wounded; Sinn Fein or Irish Republic flag raised over Dublin Post Office; Ireland proclaimed a republic and Patrick Pearse designated Provisional President.

April 30.—Martial law declared; revolutionaries driven out of St. Stephen's Green; 707 prisoners, including the Countess Markievicz, taken by Crown forces. Property damage estimated at $10,000,000.

May 2.—Seven Dublin leaders, including Provisional President Pearse, executed. Sixteen are sent to prison for life.

May 11.—Seven more Sinn Fein leaders executed; seventy-nine sent to prison and 1,706 deported; 40,000 British troops sent to Ireland.

May 17.—Sir Roger Casement tried for high treason; hanged in Pentonville Prison on Aug. 3.

1917.

Feb. 22.—Sinn Feiners just freed from internments in England are seized by authorities in wholesale raids throughout Ireland.

June 12.—Irish prisoners in internment camp at Lewes, Sussex, mutiny.

Oct. 10.—Lloyd George in House of Commons charges plot for new Irish revolt to be aided by von Bernstorff.

1918.

May 6.—De Valera addresses anti-conscription meeting at Ballaghadereen.

May 22.—John Dillon appeals for American support of Nationalists and condemns Sinn Fein.

June 21.—Irish Republic formally proclaimed by Dail Eireann or Irish Parliament in Dublin.

1919.

March 30.—Twenty Sinun Feiners escape from Mountjoy Prison.

March 29.—Sinn Feiners burn British flag in Dublin street; similar demonstrations in other Irish cities.

Sept. 12.—Suppression of Dail Eireann and all other Sinn Fein organizations ordered by British Government.

Dec. 19.—Viscount French, Lord Lieutenant of Ireland, ambushed while traveling along country road, escapes assassination; one killed, two wounded.

1920.

Jan. 1—Three hundred armed Sinn Feiners raid police barracks at Carrigtohill and later destroy them with dynamite; 14 policemen killed. British Government offers $50,000 reward for capture of raiders.

March 21—Thomas MacCurtain, Lord Mayor of Cork, shot to death and Mrs. MacCurtain wounded by armed men in their home; 15,000 follow body to the grave.

June 6—British troops in Ireland increased to 60,000.

July 25—Seventeen persons killed and wounded in Belfast riots.

TERRORISTS OR PATRIOTS

Aug. 4—Announcement of passage of Irish Coercion bill is followed by resignation of 132 Irish magistrates holding British commissions.

Aug. 15—Lord Mayor MacSwiney of Cork and ten Sinn Fein associates, convicted of sedition, start hunger strike in Brixton Prison.

Aug. 22—Loyalists sack town of Lisburn, Ireland, and burn Sinn Fein houses and shops. Loss $2,500,000.

Aug. 31—Belfast rioting renewed; 52 persons killed; 214 fires in six days.

Sept. 1—Four hundred anti-Sinn Fein Irish police threaten to resign if Lord Mayor MacSwiney is released.

Sept. 21—Balbriggan wrecked and burned by raiders; $1,000,000 loss.

Oct. 25—Lord Mayor MacSwiney dies on seventy-fourth day of his hunger strike.

Oct. 30—Cardinal Logue rebukes "persons engaged in fomenting rebellion in Ireland."

Nov. 17—Committee of One Hundred in Washington starts "to investigate and report on conditions in Ireland."

Nov. 21—Football throng in Croke Park, Dublin, fired upon by police in round-up of Sinn Fein suspects; 26 killed and 70 wounded.

Nov. 26—Arthur Griffith and other Sinn Fein leaders arrested and sent to Mountjoy Prison.

Nov. 28—Eighteen fires and $5,000,000 damage in Liverpool charged to Sinn Fein sympathizers.

Nov. 29—Fifteen auxiliary policemen, or "Cadets," killed in ambush near Kilmichael and many towns burned in reprisal.

Dec. 12—Fires in Cork destroy City Hall, library and eighteen other public buildings, with loss of more than $10,000; 300 other buildings wrecked and looted by masked bands of men.

Dec. 21—House of Commons passes new Home Rule bill providing for Northern and Southern parliaments in Ireland and giving both factions three and one-half years to accept.

1921.

Jan. 18—David Kent, Sinn Fein member of British Parliament, is arrested; seventeen Sinn Fein M. P.'s now in jail.

Jan. 19—Irish Labor Party blames Cork fires on military alone.

Feb. 12—Pope Benedict condemns bloodshed in Ireland; sympathizes with the people.

Feb. 14—De Valera addresses Dail Eireann, telling of British truce negotiations, and later denounces Crown forces in letter to Parliament.

Feb. 21—Six Sinn Feiners executed in Cork jail; Archbishop Walsh protests.

March 3—Lloyd George says he is willing to meet Irish representatives in a peace parley, but bars "guilty Sinn Feiners."

March 7—Michael O'Callaghan, former Mayor of Limerick, shot dead in bed by masked men.

March 14—Six more Irish prisoners executed in Mountjoy Prison.

March 19—Irish Catholics of London protest Cardinal Bourne's pastoral denouncing Irish disorders.

March 25—Dail Eireann orders boycott of certain imports of British manufacture after March 31.

March 31—Committee of One Hundred, in report made public in Washington, blames Great Britain for what it described as the Irish "reign of terror."

April 20—Dail Eireann statement reports 751,359 cases of distress in Ireland and warns all who resort to English courts of justice.

April 28—Four men executed in Cork barracks for attacking Crown forces.

May 4—Review of Irish Republican army's operations for the week shows forty-three attacks on Crown forces.

May 6—Sir James Craig, Ulster leader, confers with de Valera.

May 5—Bishops in reply to Lloyd George declare Government policy toward Ireland is only "inflaming the wound."

May 15—Sinn Feiners raid houses in London; scores of persons slain in Ireland.

May 21—Pope appeals to both Irish and English to abandon violence.

May 25—Dublin Custom House burned; 15 killed and 110 wounded; damage $10,000,000.

May 20—British seize 16,388 rounds of alleged American ammunition in Dublin.

June 7—Three Sinn Feiners executed in Dublin, leave message: "Fight on."

June 15—Cargo of machine guns destined for Ireland seized aboard ship at New York.

June 16—Sir Hamar Greenwood charges 568 killings to "rebels" since July, 1920, results of Irish ambushes or raids on Crown forces which had been of almost daily occurrence.

June 18—Sinn Feiners board steamship and throw supplies for British military authorities overboard.

June 22—Fifteen thousand additional British troops sent to Ireland; King George opens Ulster Parliament and pleads for an end of strife.

June 24—De Valera arrested near Dublin but is quickly released.

June 25—British announce martial law will be extended throughout Ireland on July 12 unless Sinn Feiners agree to settlement.

June 29—Dail Eireann authorities retaliatory measures against reprisal by Crown forces.

June 30—Arthur Griffith, MacNeill and two Sinn Fein members of the British Parliament released from Mountjoy Prison.

July 7—British Government issues orders to limit raids.

July 9—Lloyd George invites de Valera and Sir James Craig to confer with him in London.

July 11—Crown and Sinn Fein forces agree to truce and stop all hostilities at noon pending outcome of parley in London.

December 7, 1921

LLOYD GEORGE REACHES AGREEMENT WITH SINN FEIN

IRISH ACCEPT NEW TERMS

Lloyd George in Long Night Session Gets Assent to Modifications.

MINISTER ANNOUNCES IT

Copyright, 1921, by The New York Times Company
Special Cable to THE NEW YORK TIMES.

LONDON, Tuesday, Dec. 6.—The Irish conference which began at 10 Downing Street at 11:20 o'clock last night ended at 2:15 this morning. As the Sinn Fein delegates were stepping into their automobile to depart Michael Collins was asked for the news.

"Not a word," he said.

"Are you coming back?" he was asked.

"I can't say," he replied.

A few minutes later a Cabinet Minister came out. In answer to inquiries he said:

"The news is not at all bad."

He stepped back into the Premier's residence and conferred with his colleagues. When he then came out again he declared:

"An agreement has in fact been reached. The full terms will be given out for publication in Wednesday morning's papers."

It is stated that as a result of tonight's conference the difficulty over the Sinn Fein oath of allegiance has been eased and that a new formula has been found. No explanation for the delay of the Sinn Fein delegates in reaching Downing Street was forthcoming, but it is rumored that it was caused by the necessity of communicating by telephone the modified offer of the British Government to Sinn Fein leaders in Dublin. Arthur Griffith, Michael Collins, Robert Barton and Erskine Childers were the Sinn Fein delegates at the night conference.

At 10 o'clock yesterday morning Premier Lloyd George had an audience with the King at Buckingham Palace, in which he reported the state of the negotiations with the Sinn Fein delegates and informed the King that one of the crucial difficulties in the way of settlement was the question of allegiance to the Crown.

At 10 o'clock this evening Mr. Lloyd George and his colleagues were to have met the Sinn Fein delegates at 10 Downing Street. The Premier at 9 o'clock was joined by Lord Birkenhead, Winston Churchill and other Ministers and Viscount Fitzalan, Viceroy of Ireland. The Sinn Fein delegates did not arrive until after 11 o'clock, and at 11:20 they went into session.

Had to Come to Decision.

A decision of one kind or other had to be arrived at, for Sir James Craig is waiting in Belfast for new proposals which, as he said in the joint statement he made in the Ulster Parliament on Nov. 29, "must reach the Northern Cabinet by next Tuesday, or the negotiations will be broken off."

A special train was waiting at Euston Station with steam up and a fast torpedo destroyer is ready at Holyhead to convey to Belfast the decision arrived at.

The fact that the protracted conference between the Sinn Fein delegates and the British Ministers was continued to the end without adjournment emphasizes the desire of the Government to keep the pledge given to the Ulster Premier. Sir James Craig is to make a speech at Belfast today, but the question remains whether he will receive the proposals for settlement, agreed upon between the Sinn Fein and the British Government, in time to say definitely whether they are acceptable to his Cabinet or not.

In the day's proceedings Lloyd George, according to the Daily News correspondent, played the leading part "with Herculean force and something like Protean adaptability." The correspondent adds, "one of his admirers in the inner circle at No. 10 described his efforts as being 'almost superhuman.'" Both parties at the protracted meeting of the peace conference in the afternoon took their coats off to the task of threshing out a settlement there and then, in the conviction that no further postponement was possible.

According to The Daily Mail, when the new settlement plan was handed to the Sinn Fein delegates at the afternoon conference it was emphasized that it could be regarded as the Government's final set of proposals.

Last night's 10 o'clock meeting followed a series of conferences which had kept Downing Street as busy as a bee hive all day. At 11 o'clock in the morning there was a gathering of the seven British delegates to the Irish conference. Then at midday there was a full meeting of the British Cabinet. At 3 o'clock in the afternoon by arrangement three Sinn Fein delegates, Michael Collins, Arthur Griffith and Gavan Duffy and Erskine Childers, as Secretary, went to Downing Street and began what proved to be a long session with the British delegates, over which the Prime Minister presided. This con-

215

The I.R.A.

ference lasted about four hours and at the end it became known that certain modifications had been made in the proposals which had been rejected on Saturday by the Sinn Fein Cabinet.

Following this conference the Irish delegates met in their headquarters and had a long discussion before returning to Downing Street at night.

Newspaper reporters who kept watch in Downing Street throughout the day were reminded of Victor Hugo's saying that a crowd is always ready to gather in front of a wall if there is any idea of something happening behind that wall. The crowd of newspapermen knew something was happening within the walls of the Prime Minister's residence, but they could learn nothing.

They saw British Ministers come with anxious faces and go away with even grimmer faces. The Sinn Fein delegates were not one whit more jovial in their aspect.

There were many differences in the circumstances attending today's meetings and those which began the series known as the Irish Conference. At the outset the Sinn Fein delegates came in luxurious automobiles amid the cheers of an assemblage of their compatriots, who sang patriotic songs and recited prayers alternately. Yesterday there was no crowd to shout them a welcome and they came in a single car which seemed to have some difficulty in carrying them all. The small army of photographers which had attended the early gatherings of the conference had departed, as the spectacle of Arthur Griffith's crossing the threshold of No. 10 and of Michael Collins striving in vain to escape the camera had ceased to interest a London public, whose pious prayer, but far from confident hope, was for an Irish peace.

There was much more excitement at Sinn Fein headquarters in Hans Place than in Downing Street. There all was apparently confusion. There was much going and coming, much banging of doors and telephoning galore. None of the Secretariat appeared to know whether they would have to make a hurried departure from London before the day was over.

The Sinn Fein delegates were in earnest consultation for a considerable time this morning and were joined by those of their wives who are in London. This might be taken to signify that preparations were being made for their departure to Ireland.

Hears Dublin Wants Peace.

Dispatches from Dublin published here and written by Irish-born correspondents have indicated, though in guarded language, that the general public in the Southern Ireland capital is more anxious for a settlement than for a hard and fast adherence to the principle of "self-determination," which may lead to a return of the abominable conditions which existed prior to the truce.

The meeting of the Dail Cabinet on Saturday reached the decision to maintain its attitude in regard to the question of allegiance to the British Crown, it is stated in private letters from Dublin, only after prolonged discussion in which there was not complete harmony. The Sinn Feiners themselves, according to these reports, were reluctant to take a decision which might cause a breakdown of the negotiations, but they are said to have closed up their ranks on an imperative injunction from Eamon de Valera. The Sinn Fein President is said to have waved his hand in dramatic fashion and to have told the delegates:

"These are your instructions; they are the instructions of the people of Ireland."

Mr. de Valera gave public expression to his views at Limerick yesterday when he was presented with the freedom of the city. It was by readiness to make sacrifices, he said, that nations were freed. Freedom never yet came to a nation like Ireland, he declared, without sacrifices to purchase it.

If Ireland were ready to become part of England, if Ireland were ready to give allegiance to foreign rulers, she could, he said, at any time within the last 750 years have had peace, but Ireland spurned a peace of that kind. She spurned a certain slavish prosperity, he asserted, because she did not want to become a slave nation, because she thought freedom worth fighting for.

They were not, therefore, he said, going to purchase peace by sacrificing, or by giving up, or consenting to give up that freedom for which Ireland had endured 750 years of sorrow. They would never get a quick decision against physical force, he declared, it was on moral and physical forces that they should depend in order to secure their freedom. They were told that things were offered today that were not offered four or five years ago, which showed the progress that the spiritual forces were making.

It was necessary, he said, to get strong physical backing and he wanted the Irish army to have the full support of the Irish people. The Irish army, he declared, is their strong right hand, and he asked them to give it all the support they could. Let them not be too optimistic nor too pessimistic, he urged, but try to calculate the forces against them, because on their side they had a determination that could not be beaten. There was one thing the enemy could never hope for, and that was success, he said. They might have years of terror, they had it before, but when it was all over the opponents would be as far away from achieving their main purpose as when they started, that of obtaining from the Irish people that sort of allegiance such as Yorkshire gave the rulers of England.

"This, concluded Mr. de Valera, is not Yorkshire; it is a separate nation and they will never, not to the end, get from this nation allegiance to their rulers."

Says Ulster Will Maintain Order.

Colonel Spender, Secretary of the Ulster Cabinet yesterday said:

"Sir James Craig is absolutely determined to maintain law and order within the six counties, and we are not going to recognize or blink at any action on the part of either side which would not be recognized in Great Britain."

Up to the present, Colonel Spender said, the northern Government has received no communication from Premier Lloyd George. The time limit expires tomorrow, but Craig, he declared, will wait until tomorrow night before making any definite statement.

Opinion in Belfast is indicated by the following extracts from press comments. The Belfast News Letter says:

"Ulster will never acknowledge allegiance to a camouflaged republic, and that is what must be understood by the 'Free State of Ireland.' Ulster in the present circumstances will resist to the utmost even the nominal jurisdiction of any Parliament but its own."

The Northern Whig says:

"Though the British Ministers are not yet self-convicted of a betrayal of a readiness to betray which would justify their impeachment for high treason they do already stand self-convicted of the most perilous weakness and ineptitude, of utterly unpardonable levity and of the failure to grasp the elements of the problem which they light-heartedly set out to solve."

The Irish News says:

"A settlement will be reached somehow sooner or later, the sooner the better."

December 6, 1921

DE VALERA FORMS NEW ORGANIZATION

Copyright, 1922, by The New York Times Company.
Special Cable to THE NEW YORK TIMES.

DUBLIN, March 15.—A new move in the fight against the Irish treaty and the Free State was made today by Eamon de Valera. He issued a statement declaring that a union of the National forces could only be secured on the basis of an existing republic, and that the Republican members of the Dail Eireann had decided to launch a republican organization to secure international recognition for the Irish Republic, the unity of the nation and the integrity of its territory, to remove every vestige of foreign authority, to maintain the Dail Eireann undiminished in its sovereign authority, to restore the Irish language and Irish industry, and repudiate the agreement with Great Britain as humiliating to the nation and destructive of its status and rightful claims.

De Valera, speaking at the Volunteer Bazaar in Dublin tonight, appealed to the volunteers not to allow themselves to be disbanded but to remain a strong arm of the Irish Republic. He himself, he said, was back again with them as a volunteer. They had fully justified themselves, he declared. They stood for Irish independence, he asserted, and there would be need for them until that independence was achieved.

March 16, 1922

MICHAEL COLLINS SHOT DEAD IN AMBUSH; CHIEF OF THE IRISH FREE STATE SLAIN WHILE LEADING WAR ON REBELS IN CORK

BELFAST, Aug. 22 (Associated Press).—Michael Collins, head of the Irish Provisional Government and the Irish National Army, was shot and killed from ambush at Bandon, County Cork, tonight, a few hours after he had received an ovation from the people of Cork City, who for the first time saw the Free State hero in the uniform of Commander-in-Chief.

Thus within ten days two of the most prominent figures in the new Irish Government have been removed by death. Just ten days ago President Griffith of the Dail Eireann, considered the brains of the new Administration, died in Dublin. Tonight Michael Collins, the Free State's military genius, was killed at the moment when the dissipation of the irregular forces in the South was considered complete.

CORK, Aug. 22 (Associated Press).—The citizens of Cork saw Michael Collins for the first time today in the uniform of the Commander in Chief and cheered him along the entire route through the city. One rumor, characterized as absurd, represented him as visiting Eamon de Valera in a dugout in a remote part of Cork.

Peace talk of this kind has been industriously circulated by the Irregulars, whose latest terms of peace are said to stipulate that they must be absorbed en masse in the National Army.

News Overwhelms Irish People.

Copyright, 1922, by The Chicago Tribune Co.

DUBLIN, Wednesday, Aug. 23.—The news of Michael Collins's death has overwhelmed the great majority of the Irish, who had seen in him Erin's hope for peace, atfer the long years of fighting.

The General Headquarters of the

TERRORISTS OR PATRIOTS

Irish Free State Army at Porto Bello Barracks is preparing an official statement, which it will make public later.

The Chicago Tribune correspondent learned of the tragedy in a dramatic manner. He was sitting in the Brunswick Street Police Station here when he was startled by the sound of moaning in the corridors. Then Commandant General Beaslie, the chief censor, walking with bowed head and unable to still his grief, came into the room, where he gave the news which he had just received from General Headquarters.

The managing editor of The Freeman's Journal, himself on the verge of tears, hurried across the street on the receipt of the news to order the rules turned for the second time within two weeks.

"It means to Ireland what Abraham Licoln's assassination meant to America." he said.

Some superstititous persons asserted that a curse was on the country. Others asked what would Ireland do now.

Mr. Collins, with Commandant General Lynch, an aid and a driver, left Dublin on Sunday morning in a high powered four-seated motor car of special make which recently had been presented to him by admirers. I saw him on Sunday afternoon at Limerick where General O'Duffy, a members of the Army Council, with Mr. Collins joined the party on an inspection trip through the South-western command.

An armored car led the party which included two motor lorries carrying soldiers and another armored car brought up the rear.

While the route was not announced, it is known that Mr. Collins intended to visit a number of the cities which had been recently occupied by his troops. To reach them it was necessary to pass through many miles of country in which roamed small bands of irregulars.

No details of the tragedy were furnished by general headquarters, but Richard Mulcahy, the Chief of Staff, got out the following order, which was read to all commands:

Stand calmly by your posts. Let no cruel act of reprisal blemish your bright honor.

The dark hours which Michael Collins has met since 1916 seemed to steel his bright strength and to temper his gay bravery.

You are left, each of you, an inheritance of that strength and bravery.

Let each fill his unfinished work. Let there be no darkness and do not let the loss of our comrade daunt you.

Soldiers of Ireland, the army serves—let it be strengthened by its sorrow.

Plot to Kill Him Was Known.

An Associated Press dispatch from London printed yesterday morning said that Americans returning from Dublin had declared that the attempt to kill Michael Collins, head of the Irish Provincial Government, had been forecast and devised in Ireland to remove this outstanding figure of the Irish Free State and as a measure of reprisal for the shooting of Harry J. Boland by the Free State soldiers.

Last week the automobile which he was supposed to be occupying was fired into, but he had transferred to another.

Six weeks ago an attempt was made to wreck a train in which he was thought to be riding.

In Dublin on April 17, while Mr. Collins was on his way home after having addressed a meeting at Naas, County Kildare, he was attacked by a group of men, some with rifles, who rushed his car and opened fire.

The Collins party returned the fire and one of the assailants was captured. Collins was not injured.

Collins Leader in Irish Fight.

Michael Collins, in addition to being Commander in Chief of the National Army, was Finance Minister in the Dail Eireann Cabinet and head of the Provisional Government. He was one of those who succeeded in obtaining a temporary injunction in New York on Monday, restraining Eamon de Valera or his agents from withdrawing funds collected for the Irish Republican cause in banks in New York City.

Collins, always an ardent Sinn Feiner, was among those leaders who, while holding to the fundamentals of tradition for the freedom of Ireland, were still willing to effect a peace with Great Britain. It became necessary, in view of the recent operations of the irregular forces, for Collins to assume active charge of the National Army in the field.

The death of Michael Collins follows very closely that of Arthur Griffith, who was President of the Dail Eireann.

Griffith succeeded de Valera in the Presidency of the Dail, but, unlike de Valera, did not use the term "President of the Irish Republic," as that post was considered abolished by the treaty.

In the long fight of the Irish Volunteers against the British forces following the war, Collins became almost a legendary character, for he was a commander-in-chief who could not be found; no one knew where his quarters were or from what place or places he directed the guerrilla warfare. This mystery completely hid him, and it was not until the truce of last Summer that Collins came out in the open and joined the peace negotiations.

For many months Collins carried on his fight with a large price on his head. The British officials at Dublin Castle wanted him particularly, but in all their raids they never succeeded in catching him.

The life of Michael Collins ends at the age of 31—the life of a young man who, ever since Ireland became one of the storm centres of the world, has played a romantic and thrilling part in the struggles of the Irish people to settle their internal differences and emerge as a peaceful member of the family of nations.

Both in statecraft and in warfare Collins during the months of turmoil lengthening now into years had won for himself a place of respect on the part of disinterested observers and one of unbounded trust and homage from the followers of his own party. And, even in the bitterest recriminations ever hurled at his head by the de Valera faction of bitter-enders, never was it denied that in the fighting Irish sense he was a man.

Leading, apparently, a charmed life amidst the dangers of a country plunged in unbridled revolution, he emerged again and again carrying high the standard of the Free State, turning as occasion demanded from the physical battles of the field to those of politics in the council chamber.

August 23, 1922

ASSASSINS KILL O'HIGGINS, IRELAND'S VICE PRESIDENT, GOING UNGUARDED TO MASS

THREE SLAYERS LIE IN WAIT

Fire Seven Bullets Into Him, Some After He Falls, Then Escape in Car.

Copyright, 1927, by The New York Times Company.
By Wireless to THE NEW YORK TIMES.

DUBLIN, July 10.—Kevin O'Higgins, Vice President of the Irish Free State, Minister for Justice and Minister for External Affairs, was assassinated here this morning by three men as he was walking to mass in the Booterstown Catholic Church, 400 yards from his home.

The assailants drove up in a gray automobile, passing him, and then leaping from the car and pouring a fusillade of pistol shots pointblank into his head and body.

Mr. O'Higgins, wounded, staggered across the road almost to the gate of a friend's house and then fell against the lamp-post and his body slipped to the curb. The assailants crossed the street after him and fired into his prostrate body and then ran to the car, wherein, it is said, two confederates were sitting, one at the wheel, and sped away.

The police had made no arrests at a late hour tonight, but had fair descriptions of the three principals.

The Free State leader died at 4:45 o'clock this afternoon, with his last breath forgiving the men who had slain him.

"I am going to join my father, whom they murdered too," he said, rousing himself from coma in mid-afternoon. "They have murdered me and made no mistake this time."

Soon before the end he said:

"I am dying at peace with my enemies."

The murder has profoundly shocked Dublin, as it will all Ireland. Mr. O'Higgins was regarded as one of the strongest leaders of the Free State. He had just returned from Geneva on Friday, where he attended the League of Nations Conference in his capacity as Minister for Foreign Affairs. O'Higgins left a wife and a baby daughter under a year old.

Few Saw the Shooting.

There were few people near at the time of the shooting, but two women churchgoers saw the crime. The shots were heard by Eamon Fleming, an official of the Ministry of Finance, a neighbor and close friend of the O'Higginses. Fleming and the dead man's brother, Patrick, ran from the house and found the Vice President lying in a pool of blood.

O'Higgins recognized Fleming and asked him to call a priest.

Patrick and Fleming went in search of a doctor and found Dr. James Beckett, a noted Irish athlete, worshipping in the Booterstown Protestant Church. Beckett went quickly to the wounded Minister's side and administered an opiate.

By this time Professor John MacNeill, former Minister of Education of the Free State, had arrived and taken down Mr. O'Higgins's last will, which the Vice President, a barrister by profession, dictated in perfect legal form.

With the arrival of an ambulance, the dying leader was taken home, where a priest administered the last rites.

Crowds in tears stood outside the house all afternoon.

From the beginning there was no hope of his recovery. He was wounded in seven places, one bullet entered the head near the left ear and lodged near the base of the skull, another passed through the neck, a third entered the body under the armpit and passed out through the chest and a fourth pierced the liver and lodged against the lower ribs.

Too Weak for Operation.

Surgeons arriving found Mr. O'Higgins too weak for an operation. Saline infusions were given to maintain his ebbing strength, and later oxygen was administered, but all was useless.

As soon as the news of the attack reached Dublin, President Cosgrave and the other Ministers hastened to his home, where they remained at the bedside until the end.

Friends declared that the assassins must have been biding a chance, watching Mr. O'Higgins's movements closely, since except for today he always had a detective near him, accompanying him even to mass. This morning the Minister sent the detective on an errand just before he left the house, and started to church alone.

KEVIN O'HIGGINS,
Vice President of the Irish Free State, Who Was Assassinated Yesterday.

The I.R.A.

He has been hated by the friends of the Irregulars 1922-23, because as Minister of Justice in those years in quelling the disorders he was responsible for 77 executions of the Guerilla foes of the new Government.

The most dramatic of these executions was that of his close friend, Rory O'Connor, the leader of the insurrection in the four courts. Higgins approved the sentence of his comrade of the pretreaty war against England to death for his part in that ill-fated insurrection and sat up all night awaiting the execution. As the shots of the firing squad rang out O'Connor collapsed.

"I have only done my duty," he said on reviving.

When O'Connor's will was read it was found that he had left all he owned to the O'Higgins family.

Cosgrave Reassures Nation

President Cosgrave tells the story of the O'Higgins murder simply in his message to the nation, issued tonight. "Kevin O'Higgins," he declared, "was shot this morning on his way to mass. The Vice President of the Executive Council, the second minister of the State, has been struck down by the hands of the assassin. In this hour of national loss and national mourning, mindful of the steadfast and heroic figure who has been sacrificed, the Irish people will not falter. Mr. O'Higgins in his dauntless courage and unflinching determination had trodden the path blazed by Arthur Griffith and Michael Collins even unto death. Another great defender of the nation has passed away.

"The Irish people may rest assured that the assassin's bullet will not succeed in terrorizing this country. There are and will be men enheartened by the noble example of the late Vice President and, profiting by his labors, ready to step into his place and maintain his high tradition of devotion to the welfare and safety of the nation."

Republican army headquarters tonight denied any knowledge of the murder, and repudiated any responsibility for it.

"We feel," the statement added, "that when tracked home the responsibility will not involve any of our volunteers. Our organization does not countenance private acts of vengeance against individuals."

July 11, 1927

LONG LIST OF ASSASSINATIONS.

Many Irish Leaders Have Been Done to Death Since 1919.

The assassination of Kevin O'Higgins recalls, according to The Associated Press, a long series of similar crimes having to do with Ireland between 1919 and 1922. Michael Collins, General Sir Henry Wilson, Thomas MacCurtain, Lord Mayor of Cork; the Lord Mayor and former Lord Mayor of Limerick, Miss Barrington, daughter of Sir Charles Barrington; Frank Brooke, member of the Privy Council; Alan Bell, a magistrate; Major Neilson, Brig. Gen. Adamson and many others appointed to enforce the law of the realm are counted among the victims.

Michael Collins was chief of the provisional Free State Government when, on Aug. 22, 1922, he was shot dead from ambush at Bandon, County Cork, on the eve of his marriage. He was 31 years of age. Just ten days before this occurred the death of President Arthur Griffith of the Dail Eireann. Kevin O'Higgins was then Minister of Economic Affairs. William T. Cosgrave took the helm, succeeding Collins.

Field Marshal Sir Henry Wilson, military adviser of the Ulster Government, was shot down and killed in front of his London residence June 22, 1922. Joseph O'Sullivan, a former soldier, and Reginald Dunn, members of the Irish Republican army, were captured red-handed and hanged at Wandsworth Prison Aug. 10.

Brig. Gen. Adamson, commanding the Athlone Brigade of the Irish Republican Army, was murdered by irregulars at Athlone, April 25, 1922.

W. J. Twadell, member of the Ulster Parliament, was shot and killed in Belfast in May, 1922.

Kevin's father, Dr. Thomas O'Higgins, Coroner of Queens County, was shot dead by armed men in Dublin, Feb. 11, 1923. He was Tim Healy's brother-in-law and was 70 years of age.

Thomas MacCurtain, Lord Mayor of Cork, was shot and killed by masked men in March, 1920.

Miss Barrington was killed in ambush in May, 1921.

Frank Brooke, P. C., a unionist and railway director, was killed in Dublin in July, 1920.

Magistrate Bell was dragged from a crowded street car and shot dead in March, 1920.

July 11, 1927

TERRORISM IN THE FREE STATE.

For some two years, and notably in the last nine months, political crimes, intimidation, violence, murder, euphemistically called "execution" by the murderers, have become common in many counties of the Free State. The "gunmen" are at their old work. The Irish Republican Army drills publicly in many places. These forces of disorder and disintegration have nothing in common with Mr. DE VALERA'S party.

They are its worst foes. They tend to discredit the very name "Republican." They injure the constitutional Republicans by their lawlessness. Even when the criminals are caught, terrorism keeps juries from bringing in a verdict of guilty. In 1927, after the murder of KEVIN O'HIGGINS, there was passed a public safety act, never executed and ultimately repealed. Military tribunals were to try political offenders.

In August Minister of Justice KENNEY, declaring that "the recent history of the Free State is blackened by murders as bad as ever blackened the history of any country," said that the Executive Council was preparing a bill to establish military tribunals in certain cases and with the power of capital punishment. This bill, introduced by President of the Council COSGRAVE on Wednesday, is expected to pass the Dail today. It makes membership in the Irish Republican Army and its allied organizations of crime an offense against the State. Mr. COSGRAVE is a man of tranquil courage, not given to exaggeration. He has met many and perilous situations. We may be sure that his picture of the emergency to deal with which the Government asks strong measures is exact. "Killing is common all over the country." It is unpunished because juries are bulldozed by the fear of death. There is a conspiracy to overthrow the Government and the Constitution. Violence and murder are preached as a gospel. The worshipers of the Soviet, whose leaders have learned the holy doctrine at its source, seek to pull down church as well as State.

The Government had its hands full with the economic crisis. It is now compelled to fight for the very existence of the Free State, for orderly and democratic freedom, against the savagery that knows no law but the gun. Mr. DE VALERA'S opposition may be taken as a matter of form. He, too, would be swept under if the extra-parliamentary militants got the upper hand. Mr. COSGRAVE and his Ministers have piloted the Free State with extraordinary sagacity and success through a sea of troubles. Who can doubt that they will be equal to this new call upon their energies?

October 16, 1931

CRAIGAVON VICTOR IN ULSTER ELECTION

Government Gains Two Seats in House—Three Leaders of Opposition Defeated

DE VALERA HELD REBUFFED

Premier Declares Voters Have 'Finally Rejected' Union With Southern Ireland

BELFAST, Northern Ireland, Feb. 10 (Canadian Press).—With all counting in yesterday's general election completed today, with the exception of the four-member constituency of Queens University, Viscount Craigavon's Unionist Government was returned stronger than before. It did not lose a seat while gaining two.

Its 21 victories today, with 14 acclamations on nomination day, gave it 35 seats. In the last House of Commons the Government held 37 seats, including the four Queens University seats. Results in that constituency, where proportional-representation voting was used, will be announced Monday.

Flank attacks by dissentient Unionists failed. The Independent Unionists retained the two seats they had before, but lost their leader, W. M. Wilton. The Progressive Unionists, led by William J. Stewart, failed to elect a candidate.

A third party leader defeated was Harry Midgley of the Labor group, who lost in a three-cornered fight in the Dock Division of Belfast.

From his official residence, Stormont Castle, Lord Craigavon declared the result definitely and finally settled that Northern Ireland would not exchange its unity with the United Kingdom for unity with Eire [Ireland].

"The belief has been current in certain quarters that Ulster blocks the way to a friendly settlement between Southern Ireland and Britain," he commented.

"On the contrary, Ulster will heartily welcome a friendly settlement. * * * I sincerely hope that as a result of the negotiations at Downing Street the present trading difficulties between Southern Ireland and the United Kingdom may be adjusted, that a basis for more friendly relations may be generally established.

"An attempt, however, to make these negotiations the pretext for demanding the surrender of Ulster, her severance from the United Kingdom, is a quite different matter. On this we have now the emphatic judgment of her own people."

Lord Craigavon was elected by acclamation with all except one of his Cabinet Ministers who are members of the House of Commons. The exception, Sir Dawson Bates, Home Secretary since the government was first formed seventeen years ago, was re-elected today in Belfast, Victoria.

DUBLIN, Ireland, Feb. 10 (AP).—Prime Minister Eamon de Valera refused tonight to admit his dream of a united Ireland had been defeated by election results in Northern Ireland.

"Union will be the first item on the agenda in every conference between Eire [Ireland] and Great Britain until that item has been wiped off by the restoration of Ireland's national unity," Mr. de Valera declared.

February 11, 1938

TERRORISTS OR PATRIOTS

BRITISH AND IRISH SIGN 3-YEAR ACCORD ON TRADE, DEFENSE

Broad Agreement Settles the Principal Points of Conflict Between the 2 Countries

By FERDINAND KUHN Jr.
Special Cable to THE NEW YORK TIMES.

LONDON, April 25.—The British and Irish Governments ended their disastrous six-year tariff war today with the help of a £10,000,000 lump sum payment by Ireland and the abandonment by Britain of the last vestige of her control over the soil of the twenty-six counties.

The far-reaching agreement, signed at 10 Downing Street this afternoon, opens the markets of each country to the other and promises to bring more friendly relations than at any time since the 700-year feud of Englishman and Irishman began. From now on the ancient enemies intend to be good neighbors in economic matters and in defense.

Britain now knows she can count on a friendly Ireland at her back, and, incidentally, on a vital source of food supply in case of a European war. Only partition of the North from the South of Ireland remains to cloud Anglo-Irish relations, but even this, it is felt tonight, can be settled some day if the spirit of today's agreement continues.

The agreement, in fact, is regarded as a perfect example of the peacemaking process that Britain would like to see followed elsewhere in distracted Europe. The aptest comment came by accident tonight from the Weather Bureau, which issued the following bulletin after the signing ceremony.

"Further outlook for the British Isles: Fair over Ireland and England."

Easter Rebellion Recalled

Memories of the Easter rebellion and "the troubles" crowded through the Cabinet room as the agreement was signed. Prime Minister Eamon de Valera, who led the Irish signers, just escaped execution at the hands of the British after the Easter fighting in Dublin twenty-two years ago. At the same Cabinet table the Irish Free State had been born, yet the Irish delegates who signed today had fought in a ferocious war against the Free State and its British backers.

Prime Minister Neville Chamberlain must have sensed the history in the scene, for as soon as the agreement was signed he suddenly handed the Irish leader a pair of battered field glasses. Mr. de Valera had not seen them since 1916, when he surrendered them to the British after the Easter uprising. His captor, who lives quietly in an English countryside, sent the glasses to Mr. Chamberlain the other day with the request that they be presented to Mr. de Valera as a symbol of the new relations between the two countries.

April 26, 1938

Irish Hail Birth of Republic With Fanfare and Jubilation

Nation Begins a New Era With Severing of Last Link to the British Crown

By HUGH SMITH
Special to THE NEW YORK TIMES.

DUBLIN, Monday, April 18—Dublin heralded the birth of the Irish Republic at one minute past midnight with a fanfare of trumpets and a salute of twenty-one guns from O'Connell Bridge in the presence of jubilant thousands lining the streets.

As the guns ceased booming a Feu de Joi was fired by a detachment of Irish soldiers. Then reveille was sounded, signifying the commencement of a new era and the midnight ceremonies concluded with the playing of the national anthem.

In Cork the republic also was ushered in at midnight with a fanfare of trumpets sounded at the city hall and reading of the 1916 proclamation of Irish independence. Athlone, Cavan, Dundalk, Galway, Limerick and Kilkenny were among other centers that held celebrations to greet the new republic.

Just after midnight struck the Irish radio announced: "Our listeners will join with us in asking God's blessing on the republic and in praying that it will not be long until the sovereignty of the republic extends over the whole of our national territory."

Late last night thousands of Dubliners and provincials paraded in O'Connell Street, which was bedecked gaily with the Irish tricolor. They watched the workmen putting the final touches to the decoration of the general post office for ceremonies to be held later today.

The focal point of the entire celebration will be the post office in O'Connell Street, where on Easter Monday thirty-three years ago Patrick Pearce and his comrades launched the insurrection of 1916. The building with its Ionic columns has been transformed into an artistic and colorful flood-lit picture. Emphasizing the motif are four large gilt plaques, with the arms of the four provinces of Ireland. A great green map of all Ireland signifies that the new republic is de jure [legal] if not de facto [actual] for the whole of Ireland.

A feeling of regret and disappointment is generally expressed, however, at the decision of former Premier Eamon de Valera's Fianna Fail party not to take part in the national rejoicing.

With the realization that Ireland's status as a republic has been internationally recognized there is an appreciable upsurge in pride in the nation everywhere. "Our flag means something now," one young Dublin man commented as he looked at one of the green, white and orange flags in O'Connell Street.

All through Easter Sunday, while people moved about happily in streets in brilliant sunshine, cables and messages from the heads of states were pouring into Dublin to President Sean T. O'Kelly.

It was with joy that the people heard broadcast last night messages of good-will to the republic from President Truman, King George, Pope Pius, Prime Minister Attlee of Britain, the Prime Ministers of Canada, New Zealand, the Union of South Africa and India. From France, Italy, Norway, Denmark and other continental countries messages were also received.

The greetings from King George, President Truman and the Pope caused particular pleasure in Dublin.

April 18, 1949

Eamon de Valera, 92, Dies; Lifelong Fighter for Irish

By ALBIN KREBS

Eamon de Valera, a chief strategist and fighter in the cause of Irish independence, who became Prime Minister, President, and revered elder statesman of the Republic of Ireland, died early yesterday. He was 92 years old.

Mr. de Valera, a heroic figure to thousands of his countrymen ever since his pivotal role in the 1916 Easter Monday Rebellion, had been suffering a heavy cold for more than a week, and death was attributed to "bronchial pneumonia and cardiac failure."

With Mr. de Valera, who dominated Irish politics for more than a half-century, at his death was a son, Maj. Vivion de Valera, and other relatives, who had been keeping vigil for several days at the Linden nursing home near Dublin. A nursing nun reported that shortly before his death, Mr. de Valera whispered to her: "All my life I have done my best for Ireland; now I am ready to go."

During the last several days, as word spread that "Dev" was not expected to live, many of his old comrades-in-arms had come to Dublin to be near him.

One of them, Sean Tracey, from Tipperary, who is an 87-year-old veteran of the fight for independence, said, "We are thin on the ground now, but we are still able to pay our respects to The Chief."

The passing of "The Chief" was announced on a special national radio broadcast, and throughout the day, normal programs were canceled in favor of somber funeral music and programs relating to Mr. de Valera's life. Irish television also carried special programs.

Mr. de Valera's body will lie in state for two days in Dublin Castle, before a state funeral Tuesday, which will be a national day of mourning. He will be buried in Glas Nevin Cemetery beside his wife with the somber pageantry Ireland reserves for her dead patriots. The ceremony is expected to be in keeping with Mr. de Valera's reputation as a national hero.

Despite his often stubborn and implacable leadership, Ireland had not by 1973—when he re-

219

The I.R.A.

tired after two seven-year terms as President — achieved his most cherished dream, the union of all 32 counties on the island.

To his death, bitter strife has persisted over the separate political existence, under British control, of the six Protestant-dominated counties of Northern Ireland.

A national hero to many of his countrymen, Mr. de Valera at one time supported the militancy of groups such as the Irish Republican Army. But some of his critics maintain that he ferociously suppressed the I.R.A. beginning in the late nineteen-thirties, when the movement again resorted to violence.

Persistently for Independence

He nevertheless waged a persistent battle for complete Irish independence from Britain, which was finally achieved by the Irish Republic of the 26 southern counties in 1949.

His opponents, who probably equaled his supporters, held him largely responsible for the nation's civil war in 1922-23. The bitterness between these political forces plagued Irish politics for decades.

Ever a crusader for independence and the preservation of Gaelic as the official Irish language, Mr. de Valera maintained until his death that "Ireland can never abandon hope of regaining territory hallowed by so many memories and the scene of so many historic incidents in her history; the efforts of her people will inevitably be bent upon undoing partition until all the lands within her four seas are once more united."

Mr. de Valera's granite-like faith in himself seldom wavered, and he was a formidable opponent, one who barely escaped execution by a British firing squad.

In the prime of his career, the tall, darkly brooding Mr. de Valera held many of his countrymen in emotional thrall. There was an element of mystique arising from is appearance, his reserve and a partly Spanish origin that set him apart from contemporaries.

His oratorical style was colorless, however. Many thought his appeal lay rather in an unyielding and single-minded pursuit of goals, a scrupulous habit of self-explanation, idealism and political skill and undeniable rectitude.

Irish-Spanish Descent

The man whom some have called "the father of modern Ireland," was born in New York City, on Oct. 14, 1882, and was of Irish-Spanish descent. His father Vivion, born in Spain, listed himself on the boy's birth certificate as an artist. His mother was the former Catherine Coll, called Kate back in her native Bruree, near Limerick in southwest Ireland.

In later years, some of Mr. de Valera's enemies challenged his Irishness, suggesting that his father was a Portuguese-American Jew. This incensed the fiercely devout Mr. de Valera, who said:

"I was baptized in a Catholic church; I was brought up in a Catholic home. I have lived among the Irish people and loved them and loved every blade of grass that grew in this land. I do not care who says I am not Irish."

When the boy, then named Edward de Valera, was 2 years old, his father died, and he was sent by his mother, who later remarried, to live in Bruree with her youngest brother, Patrick Coll. He lived in Mr. Coll's small cottage and as he grew older helped him till the hardscrabble farm.

Taught by Christian Brothers

Local Christian Brothers teachers saw a certain brightness in the pale, dark-eyed, dark-haired youth. They instilled in him an almost fanatic belief in the Catholic faith and the righteousness of the cause of Irish independence.

The Christian Brothers sent him to Blackrock College near Dublin, and in 1904 Mr. de Valera was graduated with a degree in mathematics from the Roman Catholic National University in Dublin. Mathematics fascinated him, and if he had a special hobby, that was it. After teaching mathematics in several Catholic schools, he became an instructor in St. Patrick's College, a seminary at Maynooth, not far from Dublin.

By then he had become immersed in the nationalistic campaign to increase the use of ancient Gaelic, and at a meeting of the Gaelic League he met 18-year-old Jennifer Flanagan, an actress fluent in Gaelic who changed her name to Sinead Ni Flannagain before their marriage in 1910.

Mr. de Valera, who had changed his name from Edward to Eamon, its Gaelic equivalent, joined the Sinn Fein (We Ourselves) movement, founded in 1912 by the long-time agitator for independence, Arthur Griffith. Tension between the nationalist counties in the south and the unionist ones in the north over the British plan to concede limited independence (home rule) led to the organization of paramilitary forces by both factions.

Joined Secret Group

Mr. de Valera joined the Irish Republican Brotherhood, a secret organization, and the paramilitary Irish Volunteers, forerunners of the Irish Republican Army. He became commandant of the Third Battalion of the Volunteers and adjutant to the Dublin brigade.

Mr. de Valera gained hero status in the Easter Rebellion that began April 24, the Monday after Easter in 1916. While Britain fought the Germans in Flanders, the Irish Volunteers and the Citizens Army staged an armed revolt against the British garrison in Dublin. It was an uprising in which poetry and idealism were intermingled with ambush and wanton murder and incompetence on both sides, but it was a turning point in Irish history.

Commandant de Valera led a force of about 125 men who seized Westland Row railroad station and the huge Boland's mill and bakery, points from which they could cover the British Army installation in Beggars Bush barracks and, if need be, engage enemy reinforcements expected to come by sea into Kingstown.

The rebellion fizzled, but the 33-year-old Commandant de Valera was the last detachment officer to surrender, saying: "Shoot me if you will, but arrange for my men."

16 Leaders Executed

After drumhead courts-martial, the British executed 16 leaders of the revolt, but other executions were delayed so long that public opinion in Britain became so aroused that the death sentences were not carried out.

"My name was next on the list to be shot," Mr. de Valera liked to tell his audiences in years to come, and it may have been so, since he was one of the most prominent and obdurate of the rebel leaders.

The major reason for his salvation was probably public opinion: people in Britain as well as Ireland were becoming sickened by daily news of further executions. Most commentators would agree, however, that his dual citizenship helped spare his life. His wife had gone to the United States Consul in Dublin even before his court-martial to argue his rights as an American citizen, and the Consul got in touch with British officials.

Mr. de Valera was released from an English prison in a general amnesty in June, 1917, and returned to Dublin. Later that year he was elected president of Sinn Fein and of the Volunteers. He was thus formally the leader of both the political and military wings of the struggle against British rule. His prestige with the Irish nationalist population at this time was enormous, both because of his personal magnetism and because he was the senior survivor of the 1916 rebellion. But he played no direct part in the military campaign that was soon to begin.

That campaign was conducted by the I.R.A., and in the main led and organized by members of the small and secretive Irish Republican Brotherhood.

Soon after his release from prison, he won the East Clare by-election to the Westminster Parliament, but in line with Sinn Fein policy refused to take his seat.

Mr. de Valera, who continued to be a thorn in the side of the English, was arrested on May 17, 1918, and packed off without trial to Lincoln Jail in England.

There, while serving mass for the prison chaplain, Mr. de Valera was able to procure candle wax to make an impression of a prison pass key, which was smuggled out of the jail. Then, a key made from the impression was smuggled into the prison in a fruit cake, and on Feb. 3, 1919, Mr. de Valera and several other prisoners escaped and returned to Dublin.

Two months before his escape, the abstentionist policy of Sinn Fein had been triumphantly vindicated when the party swept to victory in the general election of December, 1918. The 76 elected Sinn Fein members formed themselves into a Dail or legislative assembly intent on running the country without reference to Britain. Mr. de Valera became its president.

In June, 1919, he crossed the Irish Sea to Liverpool and stowed away on a ship bound for the United States, where he hoped to drum up support for Ireland's independence struggle.

Collected $6-Million

In the United States, Irish-Americans made Mr. de Valera's presence known and won for him the aid of several influential Tammany Hall figures in New York. His message to Americans was blunt and simple: "The men who established your republic sought the aid of France. I seek the aid of America."

He failed in an effort to have the 1920 Republican and Democratic national conventions adopt resolutions supporting Irish independence, but Mr. de Valera returned to his homeland with $6-million for his cause, most of the money having been raised from the sale of bonds.

Mr. de Valera's critics in later years pointed out that the man who gloried in being a national hero was away from Ireland most of the time from 1919 to 1921, when there was a bitter war of assassination and reprisal between the Irish Republican Army and the British Army, reinforced by the hated auxiliary police groups known as the Black and Tans, named after the colors of their uniforms.

Weary of the violence, both sides finally agreed to negotiate and Mr. de Valera, who was president of the shadow cabinet, sent Arthur Griffith to London for talks with Prime Minister David Lloyd George. Later Mr. de Valera joined in the prolonged, suspicion-laden negotiations. His presence led Mr. Lloyd George to observe that bargaining with the Irishman was like "trying to pick up mercury with a fork."

"Then why doesn't he try a spoon?" was Mr. de Valera's reply.

On another occasion, Mr. Lloyd George complained about Mr. de Valera by saying: "I listened to a long lecture on the wrong done by Britain to Ireland starting with Cromwell. When I tried to bring him back to the present day, he would go back to Cromwell again."

Mr. de Valera: "Aye, he needed a lesson in Irish history."

But despite his ability to match wits with Lloyd George in the early negotiations, Mr. de Valera chose not to go to London for the major conference intended to settle the Irish question, which began in October, 1921. His decision to stay behind aroused controversy, which still continues.

William T. Cosgrave, first president of the Irish Free State and father of the present Prime Minister, said at the time that it was a pity to "leave the best player among the reserves." Far more bitter reproaches were heaped on Mr. de Valera when the tragic consequences of the London negotiations became apparent.

The Irish delegation led by Arthur Griffith and Michael Collins was outmaneuvered by a British team that included Winston Churchill and Lord Birkenhead, as well as Lloyd George. After six weeks of talks, Lloyd George abruptly demanded that the Irish accept the limited form of independence he was offering or face the prospect of "immediate and terrible war."

A Treaty Was Signed

This ultimatum proved effective. A treaty was signed at 2:30 A.M. on Dec. 6, 1921. It was soon repudiated by Mr. de Valera and the more committed republicans, including a large section of the I.R.A.

The treaty gave to the 26 mainly Roman Catholic counties of southern Ireland much of what they wanted, including semi-autonomy. The island had already been partitioned in the previous year, and the predominantly Protestant six counties of Northern Ireland were managing their own affairs through their Parliament at Stormont.

Partition was intolerable to all nationalists, but it was not at the time uppermost in the minds of the anti-treatyites. What offended Mr. de Valera and his followers was the limited, and as they saw it humiliating form of independence conceded by Lloyd George. They had set their hearts on a separate republic.

The British had insisted that Ireland must stay within the Empire and her parliamentarians take a pledge of allegiance to the King. This in particular was anathema to the republicans. They were not impressed by Mr. Collins's arguments that the treaty offered "freedom to win freedom."

Moreover, they accused the London delegation of ignoring strict instructions that any draft treaty should be submitted to the Cabinet in Dublin before signature. Mr. de Valera's strategy in staying behind had been just this: that he could calmly assess any terms negotiated away from the emotion and fatigue of the conference room.

Disagreement over the treaty led to a bloody civil war that lasted from June, 1922, until May, 1923, and, many would say, determined the basic patterns of Irish politics until the present day. Michael Collins was killed in the early months of the war, and the skirmishes, executions and reprisals claimed the lives of many other leaders on both sides. Mr. de Valera was forced into hiding.

By early 1923 it became clear to him that the republican fight was hopeless. Largely through his influence, the I.R.A. command called off the struggle. Mr. de Valera drafted a personal message to the fighting men along with the order to down arms. It said: "Military victory must be allowed to rest for the moment with those who have destroyed the Republic."

Several Years of Confusion

There followed several years of confusion and demoralization for the anti-treatyites. Having abandoned the hope of a military success, they could not bring themselves to participate in constitutional politics, since that meant sitting in the despised Free State Parliament, and taking the oath of allegiance.

But by 1925 Mr. de Valera had decided that the constitutional course, for all its unacceptable features, was the only way forward. Moving with the infinite caution that marked all his political activity, he first proposed to a conference of Sinn Fein that, if the oath of allegiance were removed, participation in the southern Parliament should be judged a matter of policy rather than of principle. This suggestion was narrowly defeated, whereupon Mr. de Valera left Sinn Fein and in a few months formed his own party, Fianna Fail.

This was in time to become the most successful political organization in Ireland, but its beginnings were fraught with anxiety and misgivings. In 1927 it fought its first elections and won more than a quarter of the seats, but there remained the problem of the oath.

In a decision quite as controversial and momentous as his refusal to go to London in 1921, Mr. de Valera suddenly announced that he would regard the oath as no more than "an empty formula."

When he led his supporters into the Dail and was required to sign the oath, he first removed the Bible to another part of the room and then, while he signed, covered the words of the oath with a piece of paper.

This strategy earned him the mockery of his political opponents in the Dail, and the contempt of the irreconcilable republicans who had remained in Sinn Fein, and who were the forerunners of the contemporary I.R.A.

But Irish opinion as a whole welcomed his commitment to ordinary democratic politics, and in 1932, Mr. de Valera came to power for the first time. He was to remain in office for 16 years.

Mr. de Valera earned the undying gratitude of the small farming class, which for the next three decades formed the backbone of his party's support.

During that first 16-year spell in office, Mr. de Valera was both Prime Minister and Foreign Minister. In the latter capacity he became a prominent figure at the League of Nations, being in 1932 President of the Council and in 1938 President of the Assembly of the League.

In 1948 Mr. de Valera and his Fianna Fail had to yield to a coalition that made John Costello Prime Minister. And so he was deprived of the satisfaction of being Ireland's leader when, on April 18, 1949, the last tie with Britain was severed and the fully independent Irish Republic of the 26 southern counties was born.

His public stance was to let it be known grumpily that he felt no particular elation over the establishment of a republic that did not comprise all 32 counties.

In 1951, Mr. de Valera's Fianna Fail returned to power, only to be ousted again in 1954. But three years later, fighting his last parliamentary election at the age of 74, he led his party to a period in power that was to last for 15 years, although he himself retired from active politics in 1959 after having been Ireland's Prime Minister for a total of 21 years.

During the nineteen-thirties, there had been much criticism of his intransigent use of power against the Irish Republican Army, the militant, extremist group that still fights against British rule of Northern Ireland. But Mr. de Valera's supporters say that his actions were the only alternative to anarchy and war.

Constitution in Gaelic

In 1937 Mr. de Valera was largely responsible for the Irish Constitution, which he insisted be written in Gaelic. Not enough of his countrymen were as well-versed in the traditional Irish language as he was, however, and so it had to be set down in English and translated.

The Constitution recognized the "special position" of the

The I.R.A.

Roman Catholic Church as the faith of the great majority of the Irish people, but religious freedom was guaranteed to all. Most of the Protestants in Ulster, where they were and are a majority, remained unconvinced on that point, which was said to be one of the chief causes of continuing strife in Northern Ireland, as well as a deterrent to unification. The special recognition, however, was withdrawn by a referendum in 1972.

During World War II, Mr. de Valera maneuvered shrewdly to keep Ireland neutral—some said "neutral on England's side"—but his position dismayed and angered President Franklin D. Roosevelt, and Winston Churchill tried to entice Mr. de Valera into the war by offering vague but alluring promise of Irish unification. Mr. de Valera ignored the criticism and used Ireland's insistence on neutrality for propaganda purposes.

Economy Stagnates

While becoming a vital, almost legendary figure in his country's political life, Mr. de Valera as he grew older seemed to hang on desperately to his idea of Ireland as a nation of simple, happy — and poor — peasants. The economy continued to stagnate under his leadership, and emigration bled off the best of the nation's youth.

In 1959 leaders of his own party quietly persuaded him to leave active politics and stand for the Presidency, a largely titular office. By that time, his eyesight, which had been bad for many years, had deteriorated so severely that he was almost blind.

He was elected to his first presidential term by a huge margin in 1959, and won re-election seven years later.

Although in failing health, as President he was able to return to the United States 81 years after his birth. He was formally received by President Lyndon B. Johnson, and told a joint session of Congress how grateful the Irish were for American support of Irish independence.

The fighting between the I.R.A. and the British Army and Protestant extremists in Northern Ireland was a source of much concern to Mr. de Valera during the last years of his life.

Deplored Loss of Lives

As President he could express no views publicly on the conditions in Ulster, but close friends reported that in private he deplored the heavy loss of Irish lives on both sides and had become resigned to the prospect that the unity of Ireland would not be achieved in his lifetime.

"Dev," as his suporters called him at the height of his political powers, dominated Irish public life for 30 years. During general election rallies, supporters sang "We'll Crown de Valera King of Ireland." The "anti-Devites" were equally strong, but less fanatical, in their support of such rivals as William T. Cosgrave.

Mr. de Valera spent his declining years being read to and listening to the radio for hours. He and his wife retired to a nursing home in June, 1973. She died in 1974. He enjoyed visiting with his three sons, two daughters and many grandchildren and great grandchildren. Another son, Brian, died in a fall from a horse in 1936.

August 30, 1975

Revolt Within Ulster

A Sidelight of Religious Dispute Pits Militant Cleric Against Government

By DANA ADAMS SCHMIDT
Special to The New York Times

LONDON, July 10—"We call upon Thee, O Lord, to rid us of the archtraitor, the Prime Minister, Capt. Terence O'Neill." With these words booming over a loudspeaker, the Rev. Ian Paisley, moderator of the Free Presbyterian Church, speaking a few nights ago in Lawyer Street in the solidly Protestant section of Sandy Row in Belfast, summed up the present objective of his politics.

News Analysis

Mr. Paisley, whose 6-foot 4-inch and 220-pound physique towered above the denizens of Sandy Row, waved a copy of a summons to appear in Magistrate's Court July 18 to answer charges of holding illegal demonstrations and provoking a riot.

He laughed, apparently relishing the prospect of a showdown fight with the Prime Minister, and the crowd laughed, too. Apparently they also relished the prospect, and they liked Mr. Paisley.

Religious Dispute Obscured

The confrontation between the Protestant Prime Minister and the extremist Protestant minister is curious in that it obscures the basic dispute between the Protestant majority and the Roman Catholic minority in Northern Ireland commonly known as Ulster.

Ulstermen now number about 1.5 million. A third of them are Catholics. The Protestant majority, mostly descendants of 17th-century migrants from England, Scotland and Wales, is composed of Presbyterians (420,000), Church of Ireland Anglicans (350,000), Methodists (72,000) and other denominations.

The Free Presbyterian Church, founded by Mr. Paisley in 1951 after he obtained a religious degree from an American correspondence school, has according to official statistics, 1,000 members, another 3,000 to 5,000 who march in its parades, and perhaps 50,000 potential supporters. Mr. Paisley, however, claims 600,000 supporters.

The truth, as one official of the Government observed, varies from situation to situation. "If the Prime Minister attempted to negotiate union with the Irish [Dublin] Government 600,000 might be about right," he said.

Although the Irish Republic has developed a benign attitude toward Protestants, the Protestants of the North have not.

If North and South were united, the Protestants would be a minority, and that, to them, would be intolerable. In the six counties of Ulster, they are a majority. But for how long? In the primary schools of Belfast the children are already nearly evenly divided between Protestants and Catholics. In another 10 years Catholic children may outnumber the Protestants.

In the political discourse of the dominant Unionist party the evils of "Romanism" and "Papism" are clichés. The Protestant dominance is reinforced by an elaborate system of gerrymandering of election districts, restriction of suffrage and Protestant preference in employment.

Captain O'Neill, a graduate of Eton and Sandhurst, the military academy, has been talking for four years about conciliation between the Catholics and the Protestants.

His most telling gesture was to invite the Prime Minister of the Irish Republic, Sean Lemass, to Belfast last year, and then to return the visit in Dublin.

Captain O'Neill has always made clear his limits of conciliation. He wants to live peacefully with the Irish Republic, do business with her, but maintain forever the partition and the Government of Ulster. However, he or his Government has not shown any inclination to reforms favoring the Catholics.

But in the eyes of Mr. Paisley and his followers, Captain O'Neill has already gone much too far. He is "the archtraitor" who has compromised with "the whore of Babylon, the church of Rome, the enemy of liberty and freedom down through the ages."

The crowd in Lawyer Street is used to that kind of language. It is, after all, merely a rather strong brew of the kind of talk that they have been hearing all their lives from the Unionist party.

Mr. Paisley tells them that it was a Catholic who threw the piece of concrete that hit Queen Elizabeth's car during her visit on July 4, that it was Catholic "gangsters" who a few weeks ago burned down his father's summer cottage and that it was Catholics who pelted his procession and caused a riot.

He sympathises with the Protestants who have been charged with killing Catholics. For all the trouble he blames "the treacherous policies" of Captain O'Neill.

Mr. Paisley dedicated an archway, lovingly erected by the inhabitants of Lawyer Street. It bears the slogan "Remember 1690," the date of the Battle of the Boyne, when King William of Orange, a Protestant, defeated King James II, a Catholic. This battle is to be commemorated by Protestants Tuesday.

Mr. Paisley admires the care with which his followers have painted their houses shades of red, brown and orange, and the curbstones red, white and blue for the occasion. He leads them in singing "God Save the Queen." And it is all marvelously quaint—and anachronistci—and a little frightening.

July 11, 1966

TERRORISTS OR PATRIOTS

Rioting Reopens Old Wounds in Northern Ireland

By JOHN M. LEE
Special to The New York Times

LONDONDERRY, Northern Ireland, Oct. 7 — Old antagonisms between Northern Ireland's Protestants and Roman Catholics have erupted in the worst violence seen since the nineteen-twenties in Londonderry, Northern Ireland's second largest city.

The riots, on Saturday afternoon and Sunday night, are acknowledged by all sides as a setback for the moderate program of Prime Minister Terence M. O'Neill. Mr. O'Neill has sought Protestant-Catholic cooperation to erase the ancient religious scars that still blemish the life of the country.

Prime Minister Wilson invited Mr. O'Neill today to a meeting in London to discuss the situation. No date was set for the meeting. Mr. Wilson asked also for a report on the affair from James Callaghan, the British Home Secretary.

These moves underscored London's concern, but they also demonstrated the relatively weak position of the British government. The 1920 act that divided Protestant Northern Ireland from the Catholic south gave each country its own prime minister and its own parliament with responsibility and authority for local affairs, including law and order.

100 Are Injured

About 100 people, including Gerard Fitt, a Catholic Republican member of the British Parliament, were treated at hospitals for injuries after the Londonderry skirmishes between police and a Catholic civil rights group. Twenty-nine persons were arrested.

In the weekend battles, the Royal Ulster constabulary used batons and water cannon against the demonstrators. The marchers accused the police of brutality.

The demonstrators threw gasoline bombs, stoned police and burned two constabulary huts. They smashed shop windows in the center of Londonderry and looted a few stores.

Late tonight three gasoline fire bombs were thrown at two police Land-Rovers as they crashed through a barricade of oil drums and timber erected by the demonstrators in the center of the old city.

Charge Is Supported

The vehicles, undamaged by the explosions, were stoned by the demonstrators and left the scene. Earlier, policemen had dispersed crowds of young men from the area.

William Craig, Northern Ireland's strong-minded Minister of Home Affairs, said that Communist elements, acting through the Irish Republican Army, had exploited the discontent of Londonderry Catholics to turn a civil rights demonstration into a riot.

R. R. McGimpsey, district inspector of the police in Londonderry, supported this view. He said:

"The civil rights people are quite genuine. But knowingly or unknowingly they are being used. This is our danger. It is left wing, and it is Communism."

The demonstration arose after Mr. Craig had refused permission for the Irish Civil Rights Association to parade through Protestant areas to protest against discrimination in housing and voting. Mr. Craig said that such a route would incite violence. The marchers defied the ban and skirmished with policemen who sought to block off restricted areas.

300 Were Involved

About 300 demonstrators were involved Saturday in an area known as the Waterside Ward across the Foyle River from the city center. Last night, about 800 young men, angered by police tactics on Saturday, assembled in the center of the city in a square known as the Diamond. They fought with the policemen all along the old city walls.

These walls protected Protestant Londonderry from a siege by King James II, a Catholic, in the late seventeenth century. Today, Londonderry is two-thirds Catholic in a country that is two-thirds Protestant. However, the Catholics, through the Nationalist party, hold only eight seats on the City Council compared with 12 for the Protestant Unionist party.

Eddie McAteer, leader of the Catholic opposition and Londonderry representative in the overwhelmingly Protestant Parliament at Belfast, said in an interview that gerrymandering and prejudicial allocation of new houses to Protestants insured Protestant control of Londonderry.

In Ulster local elections, only a homeowner or property taxpayer can vote. Owners of business property are often allocated as much as 18 votes. Unmarried adults living at home have no vote.

October 8, 1968

Ulster a Special Case in British Policy

By JOHN M. LEE
Special to The New York Times

LONDON, Jan. 10—Britain's reluctance to intervene in Northern Ireland is not only dismaying civil rights leaders there but also puzzling outsiders as to the relationship between London and Belfast.

The long-smoldering animosity between Ulster's Protestants and her Roman Catholic minority flared into violence during the last three months.

Civil rights demonstrations protesting Catholic complaints of discrimination in jobs, housing and local voting rights have stirred counteraction by militant Protestants. The sides have battled with the police and with each other, producing hundreds of injuries, smashed windows and burned cars, as in Newry tonight, when four police trucks were damaged.

Some outsiders, recalling Federal intervention to aid Negroes in the American South, have criticized London for sitting by. There has been restrained pressure from London but a more dramatic gesture—even the dispatch of British troops—has been urged by civil rights sympathizers.

Partition in 1922

Some people are confused by recalling that the partition of Ireland created in 1922 an independent, overwhelmingly Catholic state in the south and a predominantly Protestant state in the north, which retained union with Britain and ultimate British authority.

However, the Government of Ireland Act of 1920 first provided for local parliaments at both Belfast in the north and Dublin in the south in an attempt at federalism to avert Irish independence.

The Belfast parliament, know as Stormont because of its location at nearby Stormont Castle, has full local authority, including responsibility for law and order. Neither Scotland nor Wales has such powers.

Voting Regulation Kept

Northern Ireland also elects 12 members to the House of Commons at Westminster, which exercises over-all authority in such fields as defense, foreign affairs and income taxes.

Westminster also subsidizes the Belfast budget by about $240-million a year so that residents of Northern Ireland can enjoy social benefits comparable to those elsewhere in Britain.

Although Northern Ireland's Prime Minister, Capt. Terence O'Neill, has recently reminded his countrymen of their dependence upon Westminster's goodwill, the Belfast parliament pursues an independent course in local matters.

Accordingly, it has continued to impose a property qualification for voting in municipal elections even though Westminster abolished such a role for the United Kingdom in 1947.

Civil rights leaders have demanded abolition of the rule with chants of "one man, one vote," charging that the requirement takes the vote from thousands of ill-housed Catholics.

Members of Parliament at Westminster traditionally refrain from excessive discussion of internal Ulster affairs, although the 12 Ulster members may discuss English affairs.

Eleven of the members represent Ulster's dominant Unionist party, which is identified with Protestantism and the tie with Britain, and sit with the Conservative party. The other member is a Republican-Labor representative and a Catholic, Gerard Fitt. He has said that he intends to lead a deputation to Prime Minister Wilson to demand British intervention.

As Liberal as Possible

Despite some recent warning remarks by Mr. Wilson, most observers believe there is little that he could do. Open interference would be deeply resented in Belfast and, in the view of most observers, would stiffen the resistance to faster change by Captain O'Neill's conservative colleagues.

The deposed Home Affairs Minister in Ulster, William Craig, has already charged British interference, and many Unionists believe that they are being unfairly treated by the Labor Government for political reasons.

Captain O'Neill, while also warning Westminster against interference, has sought support for his own program of moderate reform by disclosing a letter from Edward Heath, the Conservative party leader, which Captain O'Neill said had expressed disapproval of any backward steps.

Captain O'Neill has won

The I.R.A.

strong and wide personal backing for his reforms in housing allocations, reorganization of Londonderry's municipal government and promised appointment of an ombudsman, as well as for his personal efforts to promote better relations between Protestants and Catholics.

It is generally conceded that he is the most liberal Prime Minister possible now and that if he should fall he would be replaced by a more conservative leader.

Accordingly, some observers were surprised last month when Mr. Wilson said that Captain O'Neill should be encouraged to move faster with reforms.

The British Prime Minister is believed to have little desire to embroil himself in an issue that has been one of the shoals of British politics. Mr. Wilson is also in the awkward position of favoring concessions demanded by the Catholics, which militant Protestant say would threaten their religion's supremacy and thereby the link with Britain, and lead to union with the Irish Republic to the south.

Captain O'Neill said last week that many of Northern Ireland's Catholics had relinquished their desire for a united, Catholic Ireland and were content to remain in Ulster. He warned, though, that religious bigotry—and by implication, the political-religious split—would continue for a long time.

January 12, 1969

Irish Girl Casts a Spell in Commons

Bernadette Devlin as she arrived yesterday to address the House of Commons in London
United Press International

By ANTHONY LEWIS
Special to The New York Times

LONDON, April 22—A 21-year-old Irish girl held the House of Commons spellbound today with a maiden speech of quiet eloquence and powerful emotion.

Bernadette Devlin, barely 5 feet tall, wearing a new blue dress, looked like a shy schoolgirl as she stood in the crowded Labor back benches. But there was no shyness as she spoke.

The record books show no other case in which a member made a speech on the day of swearing-in. She also broke tradition by speaking on a controversial subject. Miss Devlin said she felt she had to do those things because of "the situation of my people."

She was there, she said, for "the oppressed people" of Northern Ireland—Roman Catholic and Protestant. She bitterly attacked the Unionist (conservative) politicians who have controlled Ulster for 50 years as men who encouraged religious hatred to preserve their own privileges.

Civil rights demonstrators in Ulster are demanding electoral reforms to establish the principle of one man, one vote for local elections, now subject to property qualifications and districting that insure Protestant control.

In Belfast today, Prime Minister Terence O'Neill demanded that members of the ruling Unionist party support his proposals to carry out the reforms, threatening to resign if they did not.

No single sentence Miss Devlin spoke in the House today is likely to be picked out and preserved among great political utterances. What mattered, in her passion and her courage, was that London was at last hearing a voice not of the Irish Establishment but of the tormented ordinary people of Ulster.

"Electrifying," was the description of one Tory member, Norman St. John-Stevas. He said it was the greatest maiden speech since the celebrated effort of F. E. Smith, later the Earl of Birkenhead, in 1906.

A hardened British Broadcasting Corporation commentator, Conrad Vossbark, called it "a speech for human freedom, illuminated by poetry." The Commons itself, hushed for long moments and then bursting out in delighted laughter at her sallies, seemed to agree.

Miss Devlin, who won a by-election in mid-Ulster last week as an independent, drew a packed house with many curious peers and other visitors in the gallery for her swearing in.

The Speaker whispered with her, held her hand and then broke up the Commons when he said loudly: "It is out of order for the House to be jealous."

The setting was dramatic because the Commons was holding an emergency debate on the crisis in Northern Ireland. It was the more dramatic because one of the first speakers was a representative of the Unionist aristocracy that Miss Devlin opposes, Robert Chichester-Clark.

In an upper-class English accent, he told how he had toured Londonderry after the riot last Saturday night and found "stark misery" of fear among the people. He blamed the Irish Republican Army for the weekend bombings.

Miss Devlin was called next by the Speaker. Beginning "Mr. Speaker, sir," in a small Irish voice, she talked for 22 minutes with only a glance or two at some notes in her hand.

The policy of the Unionists, she said, is to keep Protestant working people agitated against the Roman Catholics so they will not rebel against the general poverty of Ulster.

She agreed with Mr. Chichester-Clark in his phrase "stark human misery" for Londonderry. But, she said, "I saw it not in one night of broken glass but in 50 years of stark human misery.

"There is no place for us, the ordinary peasant, in Northern Ireland. It is a society of the landlords, who by ancient charter of Charles II still hold the rights of ordinary people in Northern Ireland over such things as fishing and paying ridiculous and exorbitant ground rents."

She drew laughter and Labor cheers when she dismissed Mr. Chichester-Clark's I.R.A. charge as "tripe."

She charged Captain O'Neill with failing to carry out promised reforms to give more housing to Catholics, and more civil rights.

Then she spoke again of the rioting last Saturday night in Bogside, the Catholic section of Londonderry, and again scoffed at Mr. Chichester-Clark by inference.

"I was not strutting around with my hands behind my back," she said, "touring the area and examining the damage and tut-tutting every time a policeman had his head slightly scratched.

TERRORISTS OR PATRIOTS

"I was building barricades to keep the police out of Bogside because I knew it was not safe for them to come in.

"I saw that night on the Bogside, with my own eyes, 1,000 policemen come in a military formation to that economically and socially depressed area, six then 12 abreast, like wild Indians screaming their heads off, to terrorize the inhabitants so they could beat them off the streets into their houses."

After the jabs and the ironies, Miss Devlin came to a bitter conclusion, despairing and very Irish. She said this whole debate was coming "much too late for the people of Ireland."

What could the British Government do? she asked. It could have troops take over altogether in Northern Ireland.

"But the one common point among all Ulstermen," she said, "is that they don't like Englishmen telling them what to do."

The same objection applied to the idea of Britain's suspending the Northern Ireland Government and ruling directly. Nor would economic pressure on the ruling Unionists work.

She ended suddenly and sat down to loud shouts of "Hear, hear!"

Afterward, the Home Secretary, James Callaghan, made plain his urgent desire for the Unionist party in Ulster to support Captain O'Neill's proposal to end the gerrymandering that reduces Catholic voting influence.

April 23, 1969

Belfast: Under the Tension, Poverty

By ANTHONY LEWIS
Special to The New York Times

BELFAST, Northern Ireland, April 24—In his first glimpse of Belfast from the surrounding hills, the visitor can see what underlies the communal tension in Northern Ireland: poverty.

The city of 400,000 sits in a dank hollow, with only a few new buildings among the shabby tenements and old mills. A smoky haze lies over it all, pierced by factory chimneys and an occasional church steeple.

It looks like a stereotyped portrait of the industrial north of England in the nineteen-thirties. In the air there hangs the smell of soot and fish.

On Malvern Street, in the Protestant area along Shankill Road, the letters U. V. F. are chalked in blue on some walls. The letters stand for the Ulster Volunteer Force, a group led by the Rev. Ian Paisley, the right-wing Protestant leader, who is in jail now.

Scene of Two Killings

At the corner is the Malvern Arms, a dingy pub. Three years ago, some members of the U. V. F. shot and killed two young Roman Catholic workmen who stopped in late one night for a drink.

The street is lined with two-story row houses, grimy and very small. They have outside toilets. Heat, in this freezing country, comes from one open coal grate downstairs and one upstairs.

At No. 31 live Hugh Warnock, a retired shipyard laborer, and his elderly wife. Their total income, on a Government pension, is $10.80 a week.

Mrs. Warnock was asked what she thought of the proposal yesterday by Capt. Terence O'Neill, Ulster's Prime Minister, for a one-man, one-vote system in local elections. That would meet a long-standing Catholic grievance.

"I don't approve of that," Mrs. Warnock said. "Sure if they get one thing they'll want more. They're not satisfied."

Higher Unemployment

Living standards in Northern Ireland are lower than in the rest of the United Kingdom. The average weekly wage is $45 against $55 in the United Kingdom. The unemployment rate is much higher — 6.7 per cent against 2.2 per cent.

The welfare state still provides better benefits than in the Republic of Ireland to the south. A pensioner there would probably draw only a little more than half of the Warnocks' $10.80. But the country would be more peaceful and much more beautiful.

A few doors down from Mrs. Warnock, two gray-haired women in shawls sat by the coal fire in their tiny front rom.

"It's not safe to go out now, is it, Lily," one who would not give her name said to the other. "It's terrible the way things are going." She went on:

"Bless you, we had the six counties [of Ulster] we were proud of. Now I don't know when it's going to end.

"I wish people were more social, more agreeable. Where is it all leading? To more destruction and that there. Oh let peace come to us.

"Some say it would give the others more than us. But I don't know."

Then, turning from her friend to the visitor, she asked: "What about you in America? How are you getting on? It seems there's trouble everywhere."

Just a few blocks away, with no visible change in the setting, is an all-Catholic area around Falls Road. On many recent nights gangs from Falls and Shankill Roads have fought with bricks and pieces of grating.

On Ardmoulin Avenue, a Catholic street that looks about the same as Malvern Street, Mrs. Teresa Murphy, 50 years old, spoke well of Captain O'Neill.

"He's not a bad man," she said. "We could have worse than Captain O'Neill. But he doesn't seem to have much of a chance."

Her next-door neighbor, 77-year-old Eva Ferguson, thought Captain O'Neill might pull through politically despite the opposition in his Unionist party. "They'll think again when they look at these disturbances and all," she said.

A Report From Detroit

Miss Ferguson also spoke of the United States. "I had a friend over from Detroit a few months ago," she said. "And she said it was terrible—all the fighting."

Then she asked if the visitor had been in the nearby Protestant section. She said, "There's decent people up there, too."

A Catholic taxi driver, Maurice Kennedy, said the people of the two areas "were together for the last time in 1933."

"They marched together for higher wages," he continued. "But a year later they were back at each other's throats. They'd been provoked against each other again by a stone thrown at a chapel or something."

Mr. Kennedy said he was in favor of continuing the union of the six counties with Britain, not trying to join the Irish Republic.

"After all, my people fought for England in the war," he said. "But if I say that to Protestants, they won't believe me."

Another taxi driver, Hugh Baird, is a Protestant. He felt that the trouble with Ulster was that people did not want to work.

"You take these big Catholic families with 12 children," he said. "They get a pound [$2.40] a week for each child after the first, and 8 pounds for the dole—20 pounds [$48] a week for doing nothing."

April 25, 1969

MODERATE NAMED ULSTER'S LEADER

By JOHN M. LEE
Special to The New York Times

BELFAST, Northern Ireland, May 1—Maj. James D. Chichester-Clark, a moderate in the Protestant-dominated Unionist party, was chosen today to become Northern Ireland's fifth Prime Minister. He won, 17 to 16, in a vote by the Unionist members of Northern Ireland's House of Commons.

He acknowledged that his compelling task was to calm the political and religious violence that has brought this corner of Britain to the brink of chaos in the last seven months. The main issue is Protestant resistance to Roman Catholic civil rights demands.

Major Chichester-Clark is a 46-year-old Irish Guards veteran, gentleman farmer and party stalwart, committed to a reform program.

Has No Quick Solution

He said today he had no quick solution for Ulster's troubles, but added, "I'll certainly do my best."

He succeeds his fellow Unionist and distant relative, Capt. Terence O'Neill, 54, who tried to bridge religious animosities and satisfy Catholic grievances with goodwill gestures and mild reforms. Captain O'Neill's program was accelerated only after street demonstrations and Prime Minister Wilson in London applied pressure.

May 2, 1969

The I.R.A.

I.R.A. REPORTS UNITS IN ACTION IN ULSTER

Special to The New York Times

DUBLIN, Aug. 18—Cathal Goulding, who describes himself as the chief of staff of the illegal Irish Republican Army, said in a statement tonight that units of the organization had taken part in the fighting in Northern Ireland.

He called on the Government here to "immediately use the Irish Army to defend the persecuted people of the six counties."

At one time the Irish Republican Army numbered about 2,000 men, but those in a position to know say that its strength has dwindled in recent years to fewer than 1,000 men. Most of the organization's funds come from extremist Irish groups in the United States.

The statement said that northern units of the I.R.A. had been in action in Londonderry and Belfast. The statement did not describe the units.

August 19, 1969

BRITISH TAKE OVER ULSTER'S SECURITY

Also Pledge Discrimination Against Minority Will End —Catholics Jubilant

By ALVIN SHUSTER
Special to The New York Times

LONDON, Aug. 19—The British Government announced tonight that it would assume full authority for security in Northern Ireland and pledged that discrimination against the Roman Catholic minority there would end.

After a six-hour meeting with officials of Northern Ireland, which has been torn by sectarian strife, Prime Minister Wilson said that both sides agreed that all citizens there should be "treated with the same freedom, the same equality before the law and the same freedom from discrimination in all matters."

[In Northern Ireland, Roman Catholic leaders hailed the announcement from London as a victory.]

A joint declaration, issued by Mr Wilson and Prime Minister James Chichester-Clark of Northern Ireland, said that all police officers, including the B Special Constabulary detested by Catholics, would be placed under the commander of British troops there.

The joint declaration also said that the British Government would send two senior civil servants to Belfast to press London's views on the ways to restore order and find long-term solutions to the strife between Protestants and Catholics.

Moreover, the Northern Ireland Government agreed to set up an impartial investigation into the recent Catholic-Protestant fighting, in which eight persons have been shot dead and nearly 800 injured in the last week. It also agreed to urge all members of the public to surrender unauthorized weapons under an amnesty.

Tonight on television, reporting on the meeting, Mr. Wilson made it clear that he and his senior ministers had taken a tough position in the talks with Major Chichester-Clark.

Mr. Wilson raised the possibility of eventually disarming the B Specials—a Protestant volunteer police force—and even suggested that, if progress toward political and social change lagged, his Government would reconsider the question of subsidies. The budget of Northern Ireland, a part of the United Kingdom for 50 years, is now subsidized by about $240-million a year to enable residents to get the same social benefits as elsewhere in Britain.

Must Deal With Causes

He said that London expected the Government of Major Chichester-Clark, in which Protestants are predominant, to proceed with "full momentum in putting into effect civil rights programs dealing with housing, jobs and local voting rights."

"There is no good sending troops if the causes of riots are not dealt with," Mr. Wilson said.

Whether the joint declaration and Mr. Wilson's pledges on civil rights are likely to bring peace to Northern Ireland remains to be seen. While progress was made tonight, Mr. Wilson said. "It is still a very dangerous situation."

August 20, 1969

INQUIRY UPHOLDS ULSTER CATHOLICS ON MANY CHARGES

Panel on Violence Concedes Injustice on Voting, Jobs and Housing Allocation

By ANTHONY LEWIS
Special to The New York Times

LONDON, Sept. 11—An official commission of inquiry into disturbances in Northern Ireland has sustained many Roman Catholic complaints of discrimination and police misconduct.

The commission's report, made public tonight, found that officials of the dominant Unionist party had grossly gerrymandered local voting boundaries to reduce Catholic political influence, favored Protestants in Government jobs and "manipulated" public housing allocations.

While noting the difficulties faced by the Ulster police, the report said that some policemen had used "unnecessary and ill-controlled force" against civil rights demonstrators. It also spoke of "acts of illegal violence" by the police.

Judge Heads Panel

Lord Cameron, a Scottish High Court judge, headed the commission. The other members were Sir John Biggart and James J. Campbell, both on the faculty of Queen's University, Belfast.

The Unionist Government of Northern Ireland itself appointed the commission, last March. Its duty was to investigate the violence that began Northern Ireland's present troubles—in Londonderry in October, 1968, and January, 1969.

Since then the situation in Ulster has sharply deteriorated. Rioting between Catholics and Protestants in Belfast last month led the British Government to send in 6,000 soldiers, who now maintain an uneasy peace.

Document Is Long

The Cameron report lays out the factors — community animosity, fear and tension—that underlie all of Ulster's troubles. The long and careful document, made public here and in Belfast, is likely to become a classic study of the province.

Lord Cameron and his colleagues give weight to Protestant fears of possible domination by the Catholics, who now make up a third of the population in the six counties of the province.

From the time the southern counties of Ireland became a republic in 1922, the report notes, many Catholics in the north refused to accept the border and in effect were opposed to the very existence of an Ulster Government.

The Catholics almost all sent their children to separate schools. And the role of the church in the Irish Republic also exacerbated fears among Northern Protestants.

Today, the report said, most Catholics in the North are willing to work within the constitutional system. Yet Protestant suspicions remain.

Thus, the report said, the recent agitation for civil rights—joined by some liberal Protestants as well as Catholics — has been regarded by many Protestants as "a mere pretext for other and more subversive activities." Lord Cameron said: "We disagree profoundly."

Group's Moderation Hailed

In general, the commission said it was "impressed by the number of well-educated and responsible people who were and are concerned in . . . the civil rights movement." It specifically praised the moderation of the original body of protest, the Northern Ireland Civil Rights Association.

But the report was critical

TERRORISTS OR PATRIOTS

of People's Democracy, a more radical group that was begun at Queen's University after the first Londonderry violence.

The leaders of People's Democracy, the report said, are "dedicated to extreme left-wing political objectives" and are prepared to break the constitutional links between Northern Ireland and Britain. The report found also that they would, if it suits them, "invoke and accept violence."

Bernadette Devlin, the 22-year-old Member of Parliament who recently visited the United States, is a leader of People's Democracy. The commission said she was unquestionably sincere in wanting to correct "social and economic injustices," but "we do think that she would not rule out the use of force to achieve her own purposes if other methods of political persuasion had, in her judgment, failed."

Sectarian Pressure

On the other side, the commission condemned those who "by their appeal to sectarian prejudices and bigotry have assisted to inflame passions and keep alive ancient hatreds." The reference to the Rev. Ian Paisley, the Protestant extremist, was unmistakable.

Leftists, rightists and the police were strongly criticized for events in Londonderry on Jan. 4. A march organized by People's Democracy from Belfast to Londonderry was met by a right-wing mob and the marchers were beaten.

The commission said that the holding of the march was a provocative idea in the first place, opposed by moderates and pushed by radicals with the intention of polarizing the community. It also said that the "vicious" attack bore "the marks of careful preparation" by rightists.

The commission found that some policemen were "guilty of assault and battery and malicious damage to property in the predominantly Catholic Bogside area." Sixteen policemen were charged last week with violation of discipline in this episode.

The earlier Londonderry civil rights march, the previous October, was found by the commission to be peaceful in intent and moderate in leadership. Yet the report found that policemen had used batons and water cannon "indiscriminately," beating, among others, two marchers who were members of the Ulster Parliament.

William Craig, a right-wing Unionist who was then Ulster's Home Minister, banned part of that march on the ground that it was really a treasonable republican demonstration. The report said this judgment was wrong and "did much to heighten tension."

Mr. Craig rejected an invitation to testify before Lord Cameron's group. The commission coldly expressed "serious concern" that a member of Parliament and former minister should refuse to cooperate with an official inquiry.

6 Areas of Domination

On discrimination against Catholics, the report listed six areas of Ulster where Catholics are in the majority but where Unionists control the local governments because of gerrymandering and limitations on the franchise.

"We are satisfied," the commission found, "that all these Unionist-controlled councils have used and use their power to make appointments in a way which benefited Protestants."

It said that the Unionist party, while theoretically open to all, in practice had only Protestant members.

The Government of Northern Ireland, under pressure of the last year's disturbances, has moved to eliminate such discrimination. It is pledged to end gerrymandering, give all adults the vote and assign jobs and housing on an unbiased basis.

The Cameron report praised these reforms. It made one other major proposal, for the creation of an independent board to investigate complaints against the police.

The Northern Ireland Government commended the report "for widespread public study and reflection," seeking only to attach the "condition that it should be taken as a composite whole."

September 12, 1969

Irish Republican Army Warns of Ulster Reprisal

BELFAST, Northern Ireland, April 5 (AP)—The outlawed Irish Republican Army threatened today to shoot a British soldier if a civilian was killed by security forces in Northern Ireland.

"As from now," a spokesman said, "our official policy is to hit back against British troops. If necessary we will kidnap a number of them and if any civilians are shot by the British we will do the same."

The statement was the Irish Republican Army's answer to the new "get tough" policy ordered by Gen. Sir Ian Freeland against rioters and gasoline bombers who have terrorized Belfast since Easter.

April 6, 1970

A Riot Gas Study, Laid to U.S., Heightens British Controversy

By ALVIN SHUSTER
Special to The New York Times

LONDON, April 24 — British controversy over the use of tear gas in Northern Ireland was heightened today by the release of a document reportedly prepared by a United States Army research team detailing the damaging effects of the widely used riot-control agent known as CS.

The 30-page document, entitled "The Effects of Thermally Generated CS Aerosols on Human Skin," told of an experiment on 16 American soldiers conducted three years ago by scientists at Edgewood Arsenal in Maryland.

It said that "second-degree chemical burns occurred in four," of the volunteers and that the gas produced blistering of the skin.

The report was made public by the Irish National Liberation Solidarity Front, which asserted that the document came from a black United States soldier, who was not named.

The Front, formed about a year ago to support Roman Catholic demands for civil rights in Northern Ireland, is a splinter group devoted to the "anti-imperialist struggle and the fight for Socialism."

Despite some pressures in Parliament, the British Government has decided to continue to allow the troops in Ulster to go on using the disabling CS gas to help quell outbreaks of fighting between Catholics and Protestants.

Opponents of its use charged this week that the gas could have caused the death of a two-year-old boy in Belfast two weeks ago after disturbances in which British troops used the gas.

Moreover, Michael Stewart, the Foreign Secretary, recently told Parliament that CS was "not significantly harmful to man in other than wholly exceptional circumstances." He said that international conventions did not bar the use of that type of gas.

April 25, 1970

The I.R.A.

Kindness, Boredom and Terror Mark British Patrols in Ulster

By BERNARD WEINRAUB
Special to The New York Times

BELFAST, Northern Ireland, July 14 — They sit glumly behind sandbags, cradling machine guns and listening to the Supremes over tiny transistor radios. They patrol in jeeps along Falls and Shankill Roads, both littered with barbed wire and smashed bottles. They step nervously along empty Cupar Street.

"Oh boys, oh boys! I have some nice strawberries and milk for you when you're finished duty," said 66-year-old Dora Hunter, opening the door at 24 Cupar Street and waving to two British soldiers, Pvt. Hugh Lanarkshire and Cpl. David Mathieson. "I have a nice cup of tea brewing for you too."

For the 18,000 soldiers and policemen in Northern Ireland — the largest British peace-keeping force ever deployed in the North — the day-and-night duties are a bizarre blend of Protestant-Roman Catholic violence interspersed with kindness, boredom and terror.

"Four months here is just about as long as anyone can take," said a 22-year-old corporal, Michael Durkin, standing near bleak Springfield Road. "I'm tired now. I just want to have the chance to sleep without my boots on."

'Senseless and Archaic'

In a barracks on North Howard Street, on the barbed-wire "peace line" separating Catholics from Protestants, Maj. John Water, commander of Company A of the Gloucestershire Regiment, buttoned on his pistol belt and climbed down the stairs for morning patrol.

"There's an incomprehension for most of us here," the 34-year-old officer said quietly. "This religion thing — it's all so senseless and archaic and irrational."

There are 15 infantry battalions and five armored squadrons of 11,500 soldiers — as well as 7,500 policemen and local Ulster defense troops — in the six counties of Northern Ireland, where the Protestant majority and Catholic minority endure a smoldering peace. Within the last two weeks more than a dozen persons have died in fraternal strife.

For the volunteer soldiers—there are no draftees in the British Army — a mood of weariness, even irritation, has set in following the months of patrols, house-to-house arms searches in the two-story slums and unbroken 18-hour guard tours during weekend alerts.

"The Catholics are on Falls Road, over to the right, and the Protestants are on Shankill Road, to the left, and we're right in the middle," a 27-year-old lance corporal, William Nisbet, said in a sandbagged guard post stacked with copies of Playboy and Auto Mechanics.

'What a Place!'

"The girls used to bring us tea — the Catholics as well as the Protestants — but vigilantes threatened to shave their hair, so they stopped. What a place! What a bloody awful place!"

There are few complaints about the girls of Northern Ireland.

"The girls are absolutely desperate to marry soldiers because this is a release from the way of life here, from this dreadful environment," said Capt. Charles Ritchie, a trim, sandy-haired 28-year-old career soldier of the First Battalion, Royal Scots.

"So many of the young men of Northern Ireland leave and there's this surfeit of girls," he added. "We've had no marriages in the battalion yet but a half-dozen engagements."

Captain Ritchie climbed into his truck and began moving along the rainswept streets. "Most of us came here four or five months ago and we never knew or cared whether a man in the unit was Protestant or Catholic," he said. "But here that's the first thing that people ask you."

"I tell them that I'm Christian," he added with a smile. "They always love the puzzle. They don't seem to know what that means."

July 19, 1970

Gas Bombs Plunge Commons Into an Uproar

By BERNARD WEINRAUB
Special to The New York Times

LONDON, July 23 — Shouting "Belfast! See how you like it!" a demonstrator hurled two gas bombs into the packed House of Commons today, filling the gallery with thick white smoke and leaving members gasping, shouting and crawling beneath benches.

About half a dozen Members of Parliament, coughing and wiping tears from their eyes, were treated in first-aid rooms. Three persons were taken to Westminster Hospital, but there were no reports of serious injuries.

"It was some sort of tear gas or CS gas or something like that," an officer of the Parliament's security force said this evening. "There was utter pandemonium."

The bombs exploded in the oaken Gothic chamber as Anthony Barber, the Minister in charge of Common Market negotiations, was closing his statement on the start of the talks in Brussels on British entry into the market. The two canisters dropped on the mottled green carpet several feet away from him, bursting into smoke and sending fumes through the chamber.

The incident was the most violent in the chamber since 1812 when a Tory Prime Minister, Spencer Percival, was shot and killed by a merchant.

This evening, when the Commons session resumed, the 69-year-old Speaker, Dr. Horace King, announced that one man had been taken into custody "in connection with the recent incident."

"I have directed that he be given into the custody of the civil police," said Dr. King, who had been overcome by fumes hours earlier.

Laborer Faces Charges

Late tonight the police charged James Anthony Roche, a 26-year-old laborer, with possessing a prohibited weapon under the Firearms Act of 1968.

"I saw a man stand up in the public gallery and shout something about 'How do you like it?'" said 63-year-old Bert Crutch, a senior messenger in the House. "He appeared to have two grenades in his hand. He drew out the pins and tossed them."

Other men in the gallery reported that the demonstrator, youthful and fair-haired, shouted: "Belfast! See how you like it!" and "How do you like that, you bastards? Now you know what it's like in Belfast!"

"It seemed to be a particularly strong concentration of CS gas—I have had it before," said the Rev. Ian Paisley, the militant Protestant clergyman in Northern Ireland, who was elected to the House last month. Gas of this type has been used by British troops seeking to quell violence between Roman Catholics and Protestants in Belfast and other Northern Irish cities over the last year.

July 24, 1970

Troops in Ulster Termed Bar to Relief for Catholics

Special to The New York Times

LONDON, Aug. 28 — Two British social scientists who have interviewed political leaders in Northern Ireland have concluded that the intervention of the British peace-keeping force there left the Roman Catholic minority isolated and "put an end to all immediate hopes of reform."

The two, R. S. P. Wiener and John Bayley of the conflict research unit at the London School of Economics, said that Catholic demands for reforms were quelled by British troops who moved into Northern Ireland last August after violent demonstrations in Belfast and Londonderry.

"Ulster Catholics were hoping for rather large measures of reform if the British troops came in, said Dr. Weiner and Mr. Bayley, authors of a book, "Ulster, a Case Study in Conflict Theory," to be published next year. A part of the book appears in the current issue of the British magazine New Society.

Names Are Withheld

The authors say they based their findings on a survey of 63 Catholic and Protestant leaders and representatives of virtually all shades of opinion in Northern Ireland.

In an interview, Dr. Wiener declined to identify the Protestants and Catholics interviewed, saying he and Mr. Bayley had agreed with each not to disclose names.

228

The authors failed to speculate on what might have happened if the British troops had not intervened.

Asserting that "the newly found Catholic weapon of civil rights marches" had previously proved effective, the social scientists added:

"The arrival of the British Army, however, changed the emphasis of the dispute into one of 'law and order.' The very first priority of the British Army in Ulster was to insure law and order, yet this was exactly the first priority for the Catholics' previous attack."

"The presence of the British Army served a number of symbolic functions," said Dr. Wiener, who is the senior officer of the research unit, and Mr. Bayley, who has made previous studies of Northern Ireland. "It seemed to legitimize the Protestant backlash; the Catholics, unable to protest any longer, had to watch the election of Ian Paisley [the anti-Catholic leader] and the establishment of a powerful Protestant bargaining position.

"The Catholics, therefore, found themselves in a worse position than when they had started and a situation had been created where protest was automatically regarded as extremism.

"In reality, the arrival of British troops put an end to all immediate hopes of reform."

The Catholic minority, about 500,000 in a population of 1.5 million, has demanded better jobs, schools and housing from the Protestant-dominated Parliament at Stormont, which governs Northern Ireland. A major emotional stumbling block has been the irregular police force, called B Specials, and the Royal Ulster Constabulary, which are resented by the Catholics as a symbol of Protestant ascendancy.

With the arrival of British troops, the authors write, "the people against whom the Catholic civil rights weapon had been turned, the B Specials and Royal Ulster Constabulary, became invisible, hidden behind the wall of the British Army.

"An attack against the R.U.C. could be presented as an attack on the social policies of the Government; but an attack on the 'neutral' British Army was an act against law and order that could only be committed by the 'lunatic fringe.' The Catholics now feel isolated."

August 30, 1970

IRELAND INVOKES INTERNMENT LAW TO THWART PLOT

Move in 'Armed Conspiracy' Believed Directed at I.R.A. and Splinter Group

By The Associated Press

DUBLIN, Dec. 4 — The Irish Government tonight assumed emergency powers of internment without trial to counter "a secret armed conspiracy" that it accuses of plotting a campaign of kidnapping and lawlessness.

Prime Minister John Lynch acted on the advice of police authorities, who said the conspirators had planned the kidnapping of political leaders and a series of armed bank robberies likely to involve murder.

Mr. Lynch said his Government was invoking the right to bring into operation without further notice Part 2 of the 1940 Offenses Against the State Act. This gives power to intern any citizen without trial.

A statement signed by Prime Minister Lynch and Justice Minister Desmond O'Malley said orders had gone out to prepare detention centers immediately.

Although the statement gave no names of individuals or organizations involved in the alleged plot, it was widely assumed in Dublin that Mr. Lynch's move was directed against the underground Irish Republican Army and an extreme splinter group known as Saor Eire, or Free Ireland. The latter group's gunmen were involved in a series of bank raids earlier this year, until a six-month bank strike thwarted them. The banks reopened last month.

The Irish Republican Army, which is split into two groups, known as "officials" and "provisionals," has re-emerged in the last year after eight years of inactivity.

Seriousness Stressed

The "officials" are dedicated to Marxist revolution, the "provisionals" to the long-standing I.R.A. aim of forcibly abolishing partition of Ireland between the 26 counties of the republic and the six counties of British-ruled Northern Ireland.

Although officially outlawed, both groups have recently paraded openly in uniform in Dublin. Their leaders are known to the police and some even make television appearances in their own names.

By invoking the Offenses Against the State Act, the Government sidestepped some provisions of the European Convention on Human Rights. Mr. Lynch said this was a measure of the seriousness of the situation.

The Government statement declared:

"The police authorities have informed the Government that reliable information has come into their possession to the effect that a secret armed conspiracy exists in the country to kidnap one or more prominent persons. Connected with this conspiracy are plans to carry out armed bank robberies which the police believe may well involve murders or attempted murders.

"The Government view with deep gravity the situation arising from this information which has been carefully checked. They have given the fullest consideration to the problems that this gives rise to and they have decided that, unless they become satisfied that this threat is removed, they will bring into operation, without further notice, Part 2 of the Offenses Against the State Act, 1940, which provides for internment.

"The Government have given instructions that places of detention be prepared immediately and the Secretary General, Council of Europe, is now being informed of the Government's proposals as these proposals will involve derogation from certain provisions of the European Convention on Human Rights.

"This is a serious situation. The Government trust that those who are most directly involved will appreciate just how serious it is and just how determined the Government are to take effective action when they have already gone to the stage of informing the Council of Europe that derogation from an international convention is in prospect notwithstanding the gravity of that step."

December 5, 1970

The I.R.A.

The Red and the Green —The Divided I.R.A.

By ANTHONY CARTHEW

BELFAST.

TWO men in dark raincoats creep along an alley in one of the Catholic ghettos of Belfast. One says: "Joseph, let's pack up now. It's 1 o'clock in the morning, and we have to be at work at 8." The other nods, peering at the cold, damp night: "Ah, well, it's beginning to rain anyhow." They move off quietly, lugging a beer crate containing what remains of their stock of gasoline bombs.

That anecdote is told often these days because it illustrates the attitudes of Belfast's terrorists: they like to finish in time to get a decent night's sleep, and they prefer to work in fine weather. During one recent night's terrorist activity, eight bombs went off, all in the two hours that the rain had stopped. These men may be urban guerrillas, the first in Western Europe—they have been so described by shocked and angry Ulster Unionist Members of Parliament—but they are urban guerrillas of a peculiarly Irish kind.

They are not, of course, a joke, though even in a situation as appalling as that of Northern Ireland it is as difficult as ever to distinguish the fine line which separates Irish reality from stage Irishness, and there is perhaps something of the tragicomedy about the way the natives conduct themselves in their worst times and their best. But certainly there is nothing funny about the latest methods of the Irish Republican Army, methods which have resulted in the deaths of ordinary civilians, of British soldiers, of a child and of their own men.

Probably the most horrible incident in the current troubles was the murder of three young British soldiers, one a boy of 17. The bodies were found in a lonely road on the outskirts of Belfast. All three had been shot through the head. Apparently they had been having an off-duty drink in a pub and struck up a conversation with some men who, by the device of expressing sympathy for the hard job the troops have to do, lured them to a waiting car. The soldiers were driven off and killed by the roadside. This assassination has been generally condemned throughout Ulster, and the British Home Secretary, Reginald Maudling, spoke emotionally of the "wickedness" of the killers, promising that "the battle now joined against the terrorists will be fought with the utmost vigor and determination." As a result of the public outcry, all troops under the age of 18 have been withdrawn from Ulster.

THE I.R.A. is in action again, and for the same age-old motives: to drive the British from their island, to abolish the hated border between the Republic and Ulster and thus unite Ireland and, most important in the short term, to restore their organization to the forefront of the Irish story.

In a way, their greatest achievement so far has been won not in the streets but in the corridors of Ulster power. Their terrorist activities have brought forth such an outcry from the Unionist hardliners that, after weeks of dithering, the liberal-minded Prime Minister, Maj. James Chichester-Clark, was forced to resign March 20. The British Government tried desperately to keep him in office but could not do so without acceding to the Ulster hawks' demands for more troops and a tougher approach to security operations. Shorn of fine words, the hawks' proposal is that terror should be met with terror. The British Government will not countenance this. Major Chichester-Clark's resignation was the only way out of an impossible situation — a situation which many observers now believe must lead to the imposing of direct rule from Westminster. It is probable that be-

ANTHONY CARTHEW is chief foreign correspondent of The Daily Mail, London.

fore summer is out Edward Heath, the British Prime Minister, may have to suspend the Ulster constitution. Small wonder the I.R.A. has taken fresh heart.

Lately, the history of the I.R.A. has been a sorry one. They have been torn by internal dissension which has resulted in beatings and even assassinations. They have lost the political impetus in Ireland, the respect of the people and, worse still, public interest. There was a time when people in Ireland and elsewhere would argue heatedly about whether the I.R.A. members were patriots or fools, heroes or thugs, martyrs or criminals. All these labels have applied at some stage or other in the I.R.A.'s bloody saga, but in the last few years they have seemed to the majority of Irishmen to be merely an irrelevance. In the public mind, the I.R.A. was on the way to becoming an anachronism, an emotive legend to be added to the pile of such legends that litter the island.

It is against this feeling, as much as against the British Army, that the I.R.A. is struggling to re-establish itself as a power. It is possible that a more skillful and intelligent organization would not have got itself into such a position. The I.R.A. has not often been noted for the intellectual caliber of its members, most of whom have appeared to believe that if they blew up enough border posts the border itself would disappear. For years they have fed this simplistic view to the Catholics of the North. The implication has always been that the border was a barrier beyond which lay the Promised Land. But gradually Northern Catho-

The Irish Republican Army, torn between the traditional urban guerrilla warfare and a campaign of social activism, may be having its "last throw"

TERRORISTS OR PATRIOTS

lics have realized that the situation is more complex than the bomb-throwers would have them believe. They have come to understand that the economy of the South is in a far worse state than the economy of the North, and even if they are unemployed, they are at least unemployed within the framework of the British welfare state. So, to the accompaniment of gelignite bombs and machine-gun fire, the I.R.A. makes a new bid to win hearts and minds. Coincidentally, the British Army has entered a new phase of its law-and-order role in Northern Ireland, initiating house-to-house searches for arms. These searches have been rough and unpleasant affairs, perhaps deliberately so in order to provoke reaction and flush out the gunmen. Whatever the intention, the tactic has worked, and the month of February saw sniper battles between the army and the I.R.A.

THE question is: which I.R.A.? There have in fact been two distinctly separate branches for more than a year now. One calls itself the "Regulars," the other the "Provisionals." The people call them the Red and the Green. It has been mainly the Provisionals who have fought the British Army in Belfast.

To understand how the separation came about, it is necessary to go back to the I.R.A.'s border campaign between 1956 and 1962. This was a nasty little war, costly both in lives and property damage, but it was unquestionably a failure. When, on Feb. 26, 1962, the famous I.R.A. announcement was made that "all arms and other materials have been dumped and all full-time active service volunteers have been withdrawn," the time was ripe for the sort of massive recriminations in which the Irish in general and the I.R.A. in particular specialize. Blame was thrown about like gasoline bombs. Moans of accusation and self-pity rent the air. The glories of the past were produced, propped up and marveled over in an effort to forget the present. This pointless activity took up much of the decade. But toward the end of the sixties a kind of common sense set in. Many members forsook arms drill to involve themselves in the social grievances of the ordinary people. They organized demonstrations to protest things like increasing foreign ownership of land and poor housing conditions. It seemed as if the I.R.A. was beginning to grow a modern social conscience.

There was a certain flavor of Marxism in some I.R.A. policy documents. (Though it should be noted that Irish Marxism has no connection with any other brand, even Cuban). A report called "Ireland Today," produced early in 1969, suggested creating a "National Liberation Front," and even endorsed the idea of joining forces with the Eire Communist party. This was too much for the traditionalists, who began to have fevered visions of the I.R.A. sliding into the morass of West European socialism. Besides which, the traditionalists were now rested and ready to return to direct action and physical force. Their chance came at the I.R.A.'s secret convention in January last year. At this, the radicals proposed that the movement's political wing, the Sinn Fein, should abandon its historical abstention from the "Partition Parliaments of British Imperialism" — otherwise known as the Dail in Dublin, Stormont in Belfast and the House of Commons in Westminster—fight elections and take up the seats that could be won.

The radical proposal was carried, but did not gain the necessary two-thirds majority. Most of the 104 men who voted against it immediately broke away and formed the "Provisional Army Council." A number of I.R.A. units and Sinn Feiners throughout the country (no one knows exactly how many) gave the traditionalists their allegiance and pledged to continue the struggle with physical force. The Provisionals were born, and the atmosphere surrounding that birth was a mixture of bitterness and high emotion. It is unwise to read too much into the merely political reasons for the split. While it is true that the traditionalists had become more and more unhappy with the development of a policy of social involvement in the late sixties, their decision to break away was more instinctive than political. It had to do with their obsession with their own history, its heroes and its martyrs. Above all, it meant they could return to violence, and violence was what they knew and understood.

In any case, the return to violence was probably inevitable. Ordinary Catholics in the ghettos of Belfast will tell you they would have felt themselves defenseless without the Provisionals' guns. They may often express their horror at the methods used by the Provisionals, but there is no doubt about their gratitude. This goes back to the troubles of the summer of 1969, when a mob of Protestants swarmed into the Ardoyne, one of the worst ghettos, drove families from their homes at gunpoint and burned down rows of houses. On that night, the frightened Catholics went to the homes of five Regular I.R.A. men. All five had quit the district. One Ardoyne resident said: "The Regulars haven't shown their faces here since, and a good job, too—they'd be lynched." In other words, the Provisionals fill the gap as defenders of a people who feel themselves at the mercy of armed Protestant extremists and hounded by the British Army.

The Provisionals control three of the four main Catholic areas of Belfast: the Ardoyne, the New Lodge Road and Ballymurphy, a newer housing estate of utterly depressing aspect. The Regulars say they still hold the Falls Road district, and certainly it is Regulars who appear when one tries to talk to officials. There is no communication between the two factions. Indeed, there is some evidence, presently being investigated by detectives from Scotland Yard, of assassinations car-

UP THE REPUBLIC—A British recruiting poster in Belfast with an embellishment by an unknown hand. "The presence of the British Army," says one I.R.A. member, "is simply not acceptable to Catholics."

The I.R.A.

ried out by one faction on the other. It is difficult for an outsider to move freely among them, but even after some small contact it becomes obvious that there are considerable character differences between the two branches of the contemporary I.R.A. The Provisionals are mostly in their 30's and are all of working-class background. There is nothing of the student revolutionary about them. Their political knowledge is meager and their interest in political parties is nil.

THEY see their role as a defensive one, to protect Catholics from attack by British troops. They kill without regret because the British Army now has orders to kill. One Provisional said: "We must match gun for gun. This is what people rely on us to do. It is our duty." If they have an aim, apart from day-to-day sniping in the streets, it is to make the peace-keeping role of the British Army in Belfast untenable. This in turn, they think, will sour English public opinion and bring pressure on Westminster for a withdrawal of British troops. There is something in the argument. People on the other side of the Irish Sea, who have no real stake in Ulster, already consider that the problem of Northern Ireland is not worth the loss of a single British life. Now soldiers' lives have been lost and opinion is hardening against the involvement of British troops. Many ordinary Englishmen who neither understand nor care about Ulster have reached the stage of saying, "We should pull out and let them fight it out among themselves." Politically this is impossible, but politicians in Westminster have to take some note of such pressure.

Some Provisionals compare their situation with that of the guerrillas in Cyprus and Aden. They point out that guerrilla activity eventually forced the British to grant independence to those former colonies. Why should not the pattern be repeated here? It is perhaps an appealing theory, but it ignores two important factors: one is that the anticolonial guerrillas were operating with a friendly hinterland behind them, not from ghettos surrounded by hostility, which makes the supply of arms and ammunition immensely difficult. The other is that the Provisionals have to fight within the context of Western Europe, with all its sophistication of communications and transport. There is no precedent for it, and it is hard to see how such a battle could be fought over a long period.

> **The history of the I.R.A. movement is a history of bungling and heroism in equal parts.**

FOR obvious reasons, the Provisionals have a rule about identifying themselves, and they are cautious with newsmen. But one senses that there may be deeper motives than security for their reluctance to talk. The ones I met showed an almost monkish asceticism, pursuing their single purpose with a humorless and fanatic zeal. One Provisional admitted responsibility for the tarring and feathering of some young Catholics suspected of burglary and vandalism during the riots. "We have our own justice," he said, "and we carry it out in our own way. Our intention is to shame people whose behavior betrays the cause." I had the feeling they always talk in capital letters: "ONE IRELAND," "THE COMING OF THE SOCIALIST REPUBLIC," "THE UNITY OF THE 32 COUNTIES."

The Provisionals' conversation seems invariably high-minded and richly seasoned with pride. "We know we are right, and therefore we have no regrets about killing British troops," said one. "Naturally we sympathize with their families, and we have no quarrel with individual soldiers. But they are here to do their duty, and so are we. The presence of the British Army in Belfast is simply not acceptable to Catholics."

The Regulars, or at least those who remain in Belfast, seem to be almost a different race. They tend to be older men, most of them 50 or more. They cling to the old I.R.A. rigidity of command, and their organization is similar to that of the conventional army, with orders passed laboriously down the line. As far as one can judge, they have taken little part in the recent fighting. Indeed, they have gone on record as deploring it, whereas the Provisionals have adopted the modern guerrilla tactic of "claiming credit" for the killings. The Regulars have made such a fuss about dissociating themselves from responsibility that the Provisionals issued a statement in February charging that the official I.R.A. was now in collusion with the British Army to wipe out the Provisional forces. These protestations of innocence by the Regulars are interesting insofar as they show how much the official I.R.A. attitude has changed in a decade. Ten years ago these same men would have been gleeful at the loss of British life and destruction of British property. Today they denounce the use of terrorism to solve Ireland's problems. They speak of the "solidarity and sanctity of the working-class struggle," and in the Regulars' newspaper, The United Irishman, there are articles deploring attempts to divide the working class on religious grounds.

In the pubs on the New Lodge Road you can hear these sentiments expressed nightly as the pints of Guinness go down to the accompaniment of wailing ambulance sirens and rumbling armored cars. The Regulars are proud that they at last have links with the international socialist movement. Toward closing time this pride expands and everyone's conviction grows that it will be through international socialism that Ireland finally becomes united. Guinness is a great inducer of noble dreams. Only later does one realize that one has not been listening to modern international socialism at all, but to the old pub dreams which characterized the British Labor movement of the nineteen-thirties.

In the pubs, with the comforting glasses in their hands, the Regulars are happy to tell you tales of the Easter Rising of 1916 and sing you the songs of the past. Their conversation is nine-tenths nostalgia. To them, nothing has changed. "We reckon the British are still the colonialists they always were," says one. "Ulster is a colony administered by puppets and ruled by the gun. Our task remains the same: to drive the British out and unite Ireland." Ask them what would happen to the Protestants, who make up two-thirds of Ulster's population, and they answer vaguely about the eventual unity of the working class. They are sincere enough in this belief, but to the outsider it all sounds quite unreal.

REALITY is out there on the streets. Reality is the seemingly inevitable pattern of escalation. The British Army arrives for an arms search. The men have no taste for this sort of work, but they have no taste for being shot, either, so they are thorough and, frequently, rough. Furniture is shoved around, drawers turned out. Carpets come up. Floorboards come up. The mess is considerable. Women stream from the houses. They bang dustbin lids and saucepans—the traditional protest of the Irish female. Children, some of them no more than 5 years old, throw stones at the soldiers. Then the gasoline bombs begin to smash onto the cobbles of the narrow streets. The mood changes from protest to fury. The troops reply with rubber bullets, which are a method of riot control found more effective here than tear gas. Rubber bullets were first used experimentally in Belfast to underline the irritant effects of C.S. gas. But now gas has been abandoned in favor of the bullets, large-cartridged, blunt-nosed missiles which produce uncomfortable bruising and on some occasions can cause concussion. Finally, if it is one of the bad nights, the real bullets fly, preceded almost always by nail bombs, which are a kind of homemade version of the Claymore mine. The nails and bullets ricochet murderously off the cobbles and the walls of the mean little houses. It was one of these ricochets that killed a British gunner, the bullets striking up from the street, entering below his jaw and driving upward to make a dent in his steel helmet. Everyone scatters and the sniping battle begins.

The weekends are the worst. On Saturday afternoons the Protestant crowds, returning from football games, march past the entrances to the Catholic ghettos, chanting and jeering. This creates a feeling for violence which is fed through the long evening in

TERRORISTS OR PATRIOTS

the pubs. There is a theory here that the degree of violence is in direct proportion to the amount of beer consumed. It is true enough, for the unemployed men of the Catholic ghettos drink to assuage their despair and end up spiking their courage with alcohol. But it is only part of the story. The role of children is just as vital. On weekdays it has become a routine for the kids to taunt and provoke the troops with catcalls and stones on their way home from school. On weekends this is the children's only pastime.

The truth is that no one in the ghettos has anything else to do. The lives of these people are circumscribed by the walls of the ghetto. You have the feeling that the phrase "mean streets" was invented to describe the slums of Belfast. Files of tumbledown, 19th-century houses lean in terraces against the high blank walls of old mills. This is the worst kind of "company" housing, stressing in lines of red brick the total dependence of the workers on their master. The horizon is blanked off, the view is only of a patch of sky above the mill buildings. The rest of humanity seems a world away.

Accordingly, the children goad the soldiers as in a street game; in an existence of unrelieved drabness, it is exciting to throw stones at authority. These kids establish the atmosphere of a weird sort of carnival. When a city bus is hijacked, set on fire and used as a barricade (a favorite ghetto trick) the children dance and sing round the wreckage. They bring a kind of humor to the situation. They were the ones who, when a Texaco gasoline tanker was hijacked recently, nicknamed it the "Free Ireland Petrol-Bomb Factory." They were the ones, too, who formed a chain to fill milk bottles with gasoline from the tanker. In the last few years, they have learned to live with violence as an ingredient of everyday life, just as their elders have.

I remember standing with a group of British troops late one night when an old man lurched toward us through the flickering darkness. He was very drunk and had two pint bottles of Guinness sticking out of the pockets of his long overcoat. He looked like an extra from the film, "Odd Man Out."

"Sure," he said, prodding a British corporal in the chest, "I know when it's all going to end. I do straight."

"When, tell me when," said the corporal eagerly.

"In about a thousand bloody years," said the old man, and shuffled off, cackling, into the night.

THE British Army estimates that there are about 400 I.R.A. Provisionals in the Catholic ghettos of Belfast. Probably no more than 50 of them are gunmen. The Provisionals do not, of course, reveal any figures; they say only that they are not yet up to the strength required to fight a "proper" guerrilla war against the British. They are inundated with young volunteers, they explain, but they have not got the time or the facilities to train them. They have sufficient weapons but admit to being short of ammunition. They are operating now with small units that act independently of one another; there is no chain of command, no central direction of operations.

The pattern appears to be that the shooting is done by one or two men who are backed up by four or five others. When things go wrong, as they often do, it is the job of the reserves to insure that neither the dead and wounded nor the weapons fall into the hands of the British. Army marksmen are sure they have shot more Provisionals than can be accounted for by the bodies recovered. There are tall tales, for Belfast is a city of tall tales, of bodies being carted away in trucks and of fresh graves dug in the country. The Provisionals deny this, saying that it is their tradition to give their dead comrades funerals with full military honors. The wounded are, however, taken south of the border for treatment because Belfast hospitals are bound to register cases and therefore bound to give the game away.

One technological development in the British Army is giving the Provisionals particular difficulty. This is the "Cyclops" night sight, a vision aid which allows army snipers to see their enemy when the enemy thinks he is invisible in the darkness. The Provisionals' only solution to this problem is to keep constantly on the move.

The army has its difficulties, too, the main one being the sheer numbers of men required to cordon off the ghettos. Belfast is an awkward sprawl of a city, and the ghettos are widely spread out. When a curfew was imposed on one district last year, it took 2,000 troops to hold the area for 24 hours. Gen. Sir Ian Freeland, until lately the military commander of Ulster, calculated that it would take 20,000 men to contain even the main population centers. There are about 7,000 troops in the province, and since the British Army is already fully stretched by its commitments in NATO and elsewhere, even this garrison is considered too large for anything more than temporary deployment.

The soldiers mostly hate the job they have to do. They find the politics of the situation completely incomprehensible. They are almost all Protestants, insofar as they have ever thought about spiritual affiliations, and they cannot understand why people should get so murderously excited about a religious dispute. The work is cold and uncomfortable, the amenities are few and Belfast is socially a disaster area as far as they are concerned.

The senior noncommissioned officers, with experience of peace-keeping in Cyprus and Aden, do not rate their Ulster duty as particularly dangerous. But even they are now worried by the increase in shooting. More than that, they dislike being put in the position of having to fight their own people in their own backyard. A sergeant of the Royal Regiment of Wales said: "It all seems so different when you know these are your own folk taking shots at you. It makes you think a bit before you pull the trigger. I think most of the lads only fire from an instinct of self-preservation." And a Royal Artillery sergeant explained: "You feel almost embarrassed at having to push women around. But you soon learn they're the worst of the lot. The women egg on the men to have a go at you, and that's when the trouble starts."

By mounting a harrying, hit-and-run operation in the middle of a crowded city, the Provisionals are able to tie up and confuse the army. But they cannot survive in such urban conditions, where it is hard to keep any secret, military or otherwise, without popular support. Do they have it? On the whole, I think the answer is that they do. It is true that moderate Catholics are frightened by the street battles and find the violence distasteful. A very large number of moderates have expressed their revulsion at the murder of five civilians whose B.B.C. Land Rover was blown up while they were on their way to a radio transmitter near the border. It is true, too, that the Provisionals have used threats and intimidation, including beatings, to insure the ghetto people's cooperation in demonstrations. But the army's view that law and order can be restored as soon as a handful of hardliners are captured is not entirely accurate. There is in fact some justification for the Provisionals' contention that they are simply responding to spontaneous public reaction to the army's provocation.

Certainly some of the worst battles have begun after the men, women and children of the ghettos have poured into the streets to protest what they considered to be the brutal actions of British troops. These demonstrations appear spontaneous. Spontaneity was not in doubt, for example, at the February funeral of a Provisional killed in action, when more than 3,000 people turned out to cheer the escort of I.R.A. men dressed in the traditional black beret.

There are other reasons for believing that the Provisionals have quite strong popular support. One is the Catholic fear that if the British Army is allowed to pursue its present policy Catholics will soon be completely disarmed and therefore at the mercy of Protestant extremists who have not so far been subjected to arms searches. Catholics point to the unusually high number of "rifle clubs" in Ulster. All these clubs—and there are 108 of them possessing an astonishing total of 72,596 firearms certificates—are Protestant controlled. Their membership has increased significantly since the B-Specials, known as the bully-boy wing of the Royal Ulster Constabulary, were disbanded.

But more than all this, the Provisionals can draw strength from the fear that

The I.R.A.

has been bred in Catholics by the bitter frustrations of their daily lives. The ghettos have some of the worst housing in Western Europe. Even when the slums are demolished the new estates tend to be shoddy, unimaginative and lacking in amenities. Unemployment has sapped the Catholics' will and turned their spirit toward despair. Throughout Ulster the unemployment figure is 9 per cent. But in the ghettos one in four Catholics is out of work, and in some areas—notably Ballymurphy—the figure rises to 47 per cent. The men have nothing to do but draw their dole and hang about the pubs. They thus become natural recruits to violence, though their violence is not so much political as an instinctive reaction, making them strike out at the representatives of a power they believe has victimized them.

IN these ways, the Provisionals can achieve most of the support they need, at least for a while. But it has to be said that such support is entirely negative. The I.R.A. has not been able to effect a cure for the ills of the Catholic minority in Northern Ireland. Indeed, the I.R.A. has failed even to put forward proposals as to how a cure might be managed. The Provisionals have offered merely a physical defense against oppression. The Regulars have wrapped themselves in their dreams and issued statements which have ranged from the irrelevant to the fatuous. When positive pressure for reform was put on the Stormont Government during 1969 and 1970, the I.R.A. simply seemed unable to muster the constructive thinking required. As a result, the I.R.A. lost ground to the civil-rights movement and, in particular, the group known as People's Democracy. There is some small evidence of I.R.A. participation in the great civil rights marches, but mostly the work was left to the Socialists, Republicans and assorted left-wingers of People's Democracy. These marches achieved a great deal. They were the direct cause of much of the reform legislation now on the statute book: one man, one vote; fair housing; the end of discrimination in the hiring of local government employes. The I.R.A. can take credit for none of this, and the people know it.

The people also know, of course, that there is too long a gap between the passing of laws and the putting of reforms into practice. They are impatient, and the I.R.A. is able to play upon that impatience. Hence the I.R.A.'s return to the forefront of the battle. But no one in Ulster is likely to forget that when every voice was needed to cry out for freedom, the I.R.A. was silent. The Irish have longer memories than most and are perhaps less forgiving. The reason for the silence, as we know, was that the I.R.A., as it has been so often throughout its history, was engaged in internal feuding. To be fair to them, many members, chiefly the traditionalists, were keen to join openly and wholeheartedly in the civil-rights struggle. It was an Irish irony that the struggle reached its climax when the I.R.A. was at its most disunited.

IT has often been thus. The history of the movement is a history of bungling and heroism in equal parts. At key moments the men of the I.R.A. have seemed incapable of resisting the temptation to court-martial one another or indulge in some other distraction from the main purpose. If one traces the story from James Stephens's founding of the Irish Republican Brotherhood on St. Patrick's Day, 1858, through Stephens's rebellion in 1867, the formation of the Southern Volunteers in 1913, the Easter Rising of 1916, the creation of the I.R.A. from the Volunteers after the first Dail in 1919, through bombing campaigns in England, a world war, the border campaign in Ireland to the present day, a pattern emerges of skill marred by illogicality, of noble aims obscured by division, of courage ruined by rotten timing.

In other circumstances this could be described as a fatal flaw. Yet the I.R.A. somehow contrives to flounder on. Perhaps this latest split between the Regulars and the Provisionals could turn out to be the most critical the organization has ever had to face. It is possible that we may be seeing the last throw of the I.R.A. If it fails in Ulster in the seventies no more than a rump movement will be left. Obviously its task is a hugely difficult one. The dream of a united Ireland seems as far away as ever, maybe farther. Ulster, its Protestants and its Unionists appear at least as well entrenched as they were at the time of partition in 1921, so much so that the Stormont Government has decided to mark its confidence with a 50th anniversary exhibition this summer. The Irish, who retain their wit even in moments of high tragedy, have already nicknamed the exhibition "Explo 71." ■

March 28, 1971

Ulster Chief Urges Catholics to Back Drive on Terrorism

Special to The New York Times

BELFAST, Northern Ireland, May 26—Prime Minister Brian Faulkner pleaded today with Roman Catholics in Belfast to break the pact of silence that has protected terrorists of the outlawed Irish Republican Army.

Last night an explosion at a police station killed a British Army sergeant and wounded 26 other persons including four women and three children.

The soldier, Sgt. Michael Willets, 27 years old, had hurried a family of four out of the danger zone before placing himself between the smoking 25-pound bomb and two young children. "He could have run for cover like everyone else," said their father. "We owe our lives to him."

But while the sergeant was being carried through the debris there were jeering Catholic teenagers among the weeping women. "I could hardly believe my ears," said an army commander.

Prime Minister Faulkner said: "We need more information, and I believe many people may have vital information which they have so far withheld."

"They should now ask themselves whether they can hold back any longer and risk having on their conscience the deaths and horrible injuries to perhaps their own neighbors and their children."

The soldier, the eighth to die in Ulster this year, was himself the father of two.

On Saturday 26 were injured when a bomb was thrown into a crowded dance hall, and on Monday 19 were hurt in a Protestant pub.

A 2-year-old boy suffered a fractured skull in last night's bombing when he was hurled out of his stroller across the street from the police station.

Inside the building, which is in a Catholic ghetto close to the Falls Road, a police inspector threw himself over two more young children and was injured in the back and legs by flying bricks and glass.

A manhunt is on for the bomber, who left a suitcase containing explosives inside the front door and ran down a side street. One theory is that he was a boy in his early teens, chosen for the job because his presence would go unnoticed.

May 27, 1971

ULSTER INVOKES INTERNMENT LAW; 12 DIE IN RIOTING

300 Suspects Are Arrested as Preventive Detention Act Goes Into Effect

I.R.A. PRINCIPAL TARGET

Buildings Bombed, 12 Buses Hijacked—Many Offices and Factories Closed

By ANTHONY LEWIS
Special to The New York Times

BELFAST, Northern Ireland, Tuesday, Aug. 10 — The Government of Northern Ireland invoked emergency powers of preventive detention yesterday, and the reaction was an explosion of violence that had cost at least a dozen lives by early today.

British army and police patrols seized more than 300 men shortly after 4 A.M. yesterday. The main targets were suspected leaders of the Irish Republican Army, the illegal organization dedicated to destroying the North as a separate, Protestant-dominated state.

Brian Faulkner, the provincial Prime Minister, announced the detention move later in the day. He said he had acted only to protect life and property, and he appealed to the Roman Catholic minority to cooperate.

Reaction Is Bitter

But the Catholic community reacted bitterly. Within an hour of the arrests, bombing and shooting had started. Hundreds of homes burned. Then last night and on into this morning there were prolonged gun battles between security and guerrilla forces.

Late last night, the commander of British army ground forces, Maj. Gen. Robert Ford, said the army and police had killed five men during the day. Two of these were in a group that tried to raid an army post in central Belfast.

One soldier was known to have been killed during the night, and 16 wounded. But the casualty figures were necessarily unreliable in a night of guerrilla warfare that included attacks far out in the country.

Gun Battles Rage

General Ford said the day since the arrest and detention of the suspected terrorists had been "a constant war of attrition against terrorists armed with automatic weapons, gelignite and petrol bombs."

During the night, gun battles raged in several of the Catholic areas of Belfast, and streets were littered with broken glass and the burned out hulks of buses and cars. Twelve buses had been hijacked. Downtown Belfast was a ghostly, deserted city—the pubs and restaurants closed and taxis and all buses off the streets.

While taking the long-debated step on internment, Mr. Faulkner also banned all parades in Northern Ireland for six months. The immediate effect will be to stop the Protestant parade scheduled for Thursday in Londonderry, which the army had feared would produce rioting.

Politically, the two moves were widely seen as a calculated gamble by Mr. Faulkner to save the whole role of the Northern Ireland Government in its present form.

Since he became Prime Minister in March, the bombings and shootings have grown worse. Resentment has mounted in the right wing of the ruling Ulster Union party.

Move to Ease Pressure

Mr. Faulkner's hope was evidently that he could ease the pressure on the right by internment while gratifying Catholic and liberal forces by the ban on parades.

But the first reaction was strong criticism from both right and left.

The most important right-wing Protestant, the Rev. Ian Paisley, denounced internment as a piece of "political expediency" by Mr. Faulkner "to bolster up his tottering premiership."

The leading opposition group, the Social Democratic and Labo party, called for a campaign of civil disobedience against the internment policy and urged the people of Northern Ireland not to pay their rents or taxes.

The Premier of the neighboring Irish Republic, John Lynch, said in Dublin that the internment move showed "the poverty of the policies" long pursued in Belfast.

He said the administration of Northern Ireland, permanently in Protestant hands, was "incapable of just government." Mr. Lynch—a Catholic, like a majority of his countrymen—urged talks to try to create "some alternative method of government" in the North.

In earlier years, the I.R.A. had no broad support among the Catholics, who make up 30 per cent of the Northern Irish population. Now it does—for two reasons.

First, the I.R.A. produced weapons to help defend Catholic areas of Belfast and other towns when they were being invaded by Protestant toughs in 1969. That was before the British army was sent in.

Second, as the British army's tactics in its search for arms aroused increasing resentment in the Catholic ghettos, the I.R.A. has won corresponding sympathy.

Mr. Faulkner, in his statement today, said that the I.R.A. was the principal objective of his policy. But he said Catholics should not resent the use of internment.

"Its benefits," he said, "should be felt not least in those areas where violent men have exercised a certain sway by threat and intimidation over decent and responsible men and women. We are acting not to suppress freedom but to allow the overwhelming mass of our people to enjoy freedom—including freedom from fear and the gunmen, of the nightly explosion, of kangaroo courts and all the apparatus of terrorism."

But long before Mr. Faulkner's voice came over the radio, Catholic fury had burst out in the streets of Belfast, Londonderry, Newry and Fermanagh.

Within minutes of the early morning raids, a form of bush telegraph had spread the word from the ghettos. Young men rushed onto the streets, some carrying gasoline and nail bombs.

By noon, four men were dead—one a factory security guard killed in an explosion, the others apparently shot by army marksmen trying to put down the riots. One soldier, shot last night by a terrorist, also died—the 11th to be killed here since 1969.

Catholic feelings were especially high because of an army error last Saturday—the killing of a Catholic father of six children. He was driving past a Belfast police station when his van backfired. Witnesses said soldiers ran out and shot him dead.

All police leaves were canceled yesterday, and 4,000 part-time army reservists were called into full-time duty. There are already nearly 12,000 British troops in Ulster.

The idea of preventive detention is historically alien to British law. But it is permitted under the Special Powers Act, which applies only to Northern Ireland.

Under the internment order, Mr. Faulkner himself will review the case of every arrested person and decide whether to intern him.

The Prime Minister will rely on police evidence, without any hearing or trial. But he said today that anyone interned would be able to appeal to a special committee that would advise him.

August 10, 1971

Ulster Internment Move Stirs Doubt and Dissent

By BERNARD WEINRAUB
Special to The New York Times

BELFAST, Northern Ireland, Aug. 15 — A week after the Government imposed internment without trial on its militant opponents, the impact of the policy remains uncertain and controversial.

The move by Prime Minister Brian Faulkner on Monday plunged Ulster into a battleground. Dozens died, nearly 5,000 Roman Catholics fled to the Irish Republic and hatred between Catholics and Protestants reached a new peak.

With the bloodshed and burning easing, at least for the moment, Mr. Faulkner's policy of "flushing the gunmen into the open" has come under intensive questioning among moderate Catholics and Protestants as well as British officials.

On the one hand the officials maintain that the internment of 300 suspects — 30 have since been released — has dealt a serious blow to the outlawed Irish Republican Army. With the terrorists in prison, Mr. Faulkner feels that the violence will ebb and that voting and housing reforms in the fall will calm the Catholic minority and blunt the continuing threat of such Protestant extremists as the Rev. Ian Paisley.

Doubt and Criticism

On the other hand the internment policy has met doubt and sharp criticism. Some senior

The I.R.A.

British Army officers remain hesitant, and it is known that Lieut. Gen. Harry C. Tuzo, commander of the 12,500 British soldiers in Ulster, strongly objected to the move before it was announced.

The policy, urged by Mr. Faulkner, was secretly approved two weeks ago by Prime Minister Heath and the Home Secretary, Reginald Maulding.

There are other objections to internment. Catholics feel that it ignores Protestant gunmen active in the ghettos. Moderates maintain that the move may have worsened relations since many Catholics now believe that the rounding up of I.R.A. men has left them defenseless against Protestant extremists.

There are growing doubts among officials whether the 270 internees are the I.R.A. leadership or merely an assortment of political nuisances, radicals and active Catholic opponents of the Ulster Government, which has been controlled by Protestants since it was formed 50 years ago after the partition of Ireland. The 500,000 Catholics believe that their civil rights have been restricted by the million Protestants, who, in turn, fear Catholic attempts to end the partition.

Army Feared Reaction

The army's original objections to internment were that military intelligence could not be certain of seizing the right suspects, that the Catholic minority was bound to turn angry and that internees could be replaced by volunteers from the South, where an internment move in Ulster would probably spur recruitment.

Although the army now says 70 per cent of the men sought were picked up, the I.R.A. ridicules this and says only 30 of its men have been caught. In fact, while Brig. Marston Tickell, chief of staff of the force here, reported at a news conference that the organization had suffered a major defeat, a much-sought leader of its "provisional," or terrorist, wing called his own news conference and denounced the army statements.

"We can still operate effectively in spite of internment being with us," said the leader, Joe Cahill.

Catholics insist that the army's early-morning raid was careless and that its objectives were somewhat confused.

Miss Devlin's Friend Held

One man seized was Michael Farrell, a friend of Bernardette Devlin, the militant Catholic from Ulster in the British Parliament. Mr. Farrell, a youthful New Left leader and university lecturer in Belfast, was widely regarded as a nonviolent but militant opponent of the Protestant regime. The army declines to discuss the arrest, which startled many moderates.

There were other curious arrests. One youth, hearing bursts of gunfire around him, rushed into a doorway and found four soldiers detaining a man. The soldiers promptly seized the youth too.

The 27-year-old printer of a small left-wing weekly newspaper was arrested although he was not responsible for its editorial content and had written only one article last year—in support of lower bus fares.

August 18, 1971

Ulster Women Tar 2 Girls for Dating British Soldiers

Martha Doherty
United Press International

By BERNARD WEINRAUB
Special to The New York Times

BELFAST, Northern Ireland, Nov. 10 — A 19-year-old girl was tied to a lamppost and tarred and feathered in Londonderry last night while a group of 80 women shrieked: "Soldier lover! Soldier lover!"

The incident, in which the girl's head was shaved, underlined the vicious mood among the Roman Catholic minority toward British soldiers—a mood that has radically changed since August, 1969, when the soldiers were welcomed with tea in Catholic ghettos.

[A Catholic girl, believed to be engaged to a British soldier, was tarred by women in Londonderry early Thursday, Reuters reported.]

The British garrison, now numbering 14,000, took over security in Northern Ireland when Catholics, demonstrating for social reform, feared a major pogrom at the hands of the Protestant majority.

Today, Martha Doherty, who was to be married to a soldier on Friday, was seized in the Bogside area and cursed and spat upon before the tar and feathers were poured on her. Later freed, she is in seclusion with friends. The wedding date is in doubt.

'Extreme and Detestable'

"It's an extreme and detestable thing to happen but it's a symptom of Catholic feelings here about the army," said John Hume, a Catholic teacher who has emerged as a powerful leader of the minority. "To Catholics the soldiers are merely acting as agents for the political system whose excesses brought about the army's intervention in the first place."

It was the second incident in three days in which a young Catholic woman was punished for dating soldiers. A 20-year-old factory worker was seized at her home in Londonderry early Monday by six women who blindfolded her and then shaved her head. She was warned that she would be shot or tarred and feathered the next time.

Army officers concede privately that their links to the Catholic community are virtually severed.

Catholic officials, as well as priests, say that the soldiers, who protected Catholics from Protestant gangs in 1969, have since enraged the minority by indiscriminately searching Catholic homes, placing large neighborhoods under curfew and virtual martial law to weed out a few gunmen, allowing "provocative" Protestant marchers in Catholic ghettos and implementing the provincial government's policy of interning suspected terrorists without trial. The Catholics also say the army has seized only Catholics.

At first the soldiers were viewed as a stopgap in the ghettos, where Catholics preferred to assume responsibility for their own defense. Gradually the mood turned against the largely Protestant British force, especially after Easter, 1970, when troops from Scotland were placed in the Catholic ghetto.

In the late spring of 1970 the army and the local constabulary began to cooperate in searches for arms. On July 3 a rock-throwing incident against soldiers exploded into a full-scale riot in which troops hurled tear gas against Catholics and imposed a 42-hour curfew that affected 10,000 ghetto residents.

"In some ways that was the turning point," said the Rev. Padraig Murphy, a ghetto pastor and leader. "We tried to control the situation but the army replied with CS gas and the situation got completely out of hand."

The angry charges grew: there were 4 A.M. searches for arms, with soldiers sometimes breaking cherished knickknacks. When the army allowed Protestants to march in Catholic ghettos there were confrontations between soldiers and Catholics. The army at the urging of the provincial government, forbade Catholics to appear at funerals in black berets or other clothing linked to the outlawed Irish Republican Army.

More recently the army has been used as the instrument of internment, with allegations of brutality against prisoners.

Another Girl Tarred

LONDONDERRY, Northern Ireland, Thursday, Nov. 11, (Reuters)—A Catholic girl believed to be engaged to a British soldier wept and begged for mercy early today as she was manhandled by a hostile crowd, tied to a lampost and covered with tar.

A cardboard placard reading "Soldier doll" was hung from her neck and some 200 spectators watched in silence as a woman used scissors to crop her long dark hair.

A witness said the girl, about 19 years old was stopped in the street by at least seven women, forced into a car and driven to the bogside where she was strapped to the post by her chest and feet.

She was left hanging for about 20 minutes before bystanders took pity and cut her loose.

November 11, 1971

TERRORISTS OR PATRIOTS

An I.R.A. Chief Defends Ulster Terrorism

By BERNARD WEINRAUB
Special to The New York Times

NAVEN, Ireland, Dec. 1—In a secluded house here, a chunky English-born Irishman quietly directs the terrorist tactics of the Irish Republican Army Provisionals in Northern Ireland.

"Killing is inevitable and is going to continue until the British withdraw," said Sean MacStiofain, sitting in his living room beneath a bookshelf that included the Bible and the works of Che Guevara and Mao Tse-tung. "The end is in sight. We're going to win."

As chief of staff of the I.R.A. Provisionals, Mr. MacStiofain is a sternly optimistic guerrilla figure. He is optimistic that the Provisional "freedom fighters" have taken the upper hand over the Marxist Official wing of the I.R.A. He is optimistic that the Provisionals' unrelenting urban warfare will compel the 14,000-man British force, under the pressure of public opinion, to withdraw. And he is optimistic that the 50-year Protestant dominance of Northern Ireland will soon crumble and the six terror-stricken counties will join the Irish Republic.

British Army officers, sharply disagreeing, say that accurate information about terrorist activities is flowing in, that the seizure of weapons and ammunition is growing, that the morale of the Provisionals is sagging and that the Northern Ireland Government's internment of suspected terrorists without trial has seriously shaken the I.R.A. The Provisionals view internment as a crucial turning point.

'That's a Fact of Life'

"Internment opened the way," said Mr. MacStiofain, a tight-lipped 45 year-old Roman Catholic. "We're taking men from 16 upwards and we're getting more than we can handle. We're getting laborers, artisans, self-employed people, a lot of young men."

"We've become the protectors of our people up there," he added. "That's a fact of life. Let me tell you, since internment there's no one up there that the people trust but us."

The Northern Ireland government, with the British Army, began interning suspected terrorists on Aug. 9 in an effort to blunt growing violence. The measure spurred renewed bomb and sniper attacks and enraged the minority which viewed it as an anti-Catholic move. Since then, 65 civilians, 31 soldiers and 9 policemen have been slain.

Discussing the toll, Mr. MacStiofain said he had no feelings of regret when a soldier was killed. He went on: The British Army is responsible for every drop of blood that's shed up there. This is a war against the British Army. The civilians casualties of war.

Making the British Pay

"Since internment, everything is fair game. Before internment our policy was defense and retaliation against the British Army. Our policy was to hit selective targets.

"Now we are determined to make the British pay for their presence here. It's going to be a period of intense activity. It is a war of attrition."

The I.R.A. leader was interviewed in his home on the fringe of a small housing project in Naven, 30 miles northwest of Dublin and about 50 miles south of the border. It is in this house, with curtains drawn and windows shut, that the Provisional strategy is mapped.

A tough, puritanical man—he neither smokes nor drinks—Mr. MacStiofain slips between Dublin and Belfast under the eyes of the British troops although he would be seized immediately in Belfast. He moves freely but elusively in the Irish Republic, remaining free because his arrest would probably cause a political uproar.

Some Provisionals claim a strength of three battalions, or about 1,500 men, in the North, but Mr. MacStiofain declines to be precise. The less militant Officials are believed to have about 500 men.

The young Provisionals, mostly from the North, are often screened for several weeks by intelligence officers before joining. The screening ranges from the pubs that a youth frequents to how much he drinks and who his friends are.

Once admitted to the I.R.A., the recruit is placed on three months' probation and then begins receiving several months' intensive training in small camps in Ireland as well as Ulster. Then he joins a unit in the city where he lives and works.

Visits by journalists to Mr. MacStiofain's home are rare. His Cork-born wife, Mary, greets callers and escorts them into a room where several men are waiting. The phone is constantly ringing, car doors frequently slam, men's voices can be heard.

Mrs. MacStiofain, the mother of two, told an American that she had relatives in Staten Island and Brooklyn. "I'd visit New York but I'm afraid of what goes on there," she said.

Her husband, whose mother was from Belfast, was born with an English name, John Stephenson, in the North London suburb of Epping. He joined the Irish Republican movement in 1950. Three years later he and Cathal Goulding, now head of the Official I.R.A., took part in an arms raid but were caught and sentenced to eight years in prison.

Gaelic and an Irish Name

The prison experience was pivotal. Mr. MacStiofain learned Gaelic, adopted his Irish name and became friendly with Greek Cypriote terrorists who were imprisoned from 1955 to 1959 and from whom he learned tactics. "I learned to speak Greek," Mr. MacStiofain related. "Those Greeks were good boys."

He returned to Dublin with Mr. Goulding, but the two had a bitter and violent break in January, 1970. The newly formed Provisionals walked out of an I.R.A. national conference in Dublin, charging that the leaders were Marxists who were seeking to carry the fight for unification into conventional political arenas.

There were also bitter accusations that the leadership failed to defend the Catholic ghetto in Belfast the previous August when Protestant mobs burned houses there.

The Provisionals—claiming to be a movement of the left but "very anti-Communist"—immediately began a military and political campaign that has developed powerfully in the past year and a half. Mr. MacStiofain works closely with Rory O'Bradaigh, a 38-year-old technical school teacher and Catholic, who is head of the political wing of the Provisionals.

"Our tactics are developing," Mr. MacStiofain said. "We don't have a time limit, but we know things are coming to a head. We are determined in this. The British are going to get out of there."

December 7, 1971

British Army Is Toughening Its Tactics in Ulster

Special to The New York Times

BELFAST, Northern Ireland, Jan. 5 — British soldiers in Northern Ireland have been given new authority to shoot to kill.

Changes in the British Army's regulations, made known today by unofficial sources, coincided with the killing of an 18-year-old soldier by a terrorist sniper. He was the first victim this year of the violence between Protestants and Roman Catholics that has been tearing Northern Ireland apart for more than two years.

The revised instructions permit troops to use machine guns in firing on terrorists. Formerly only pistol and rifle fire was permitted.

Previous instructions, printed on a yellow card carried by all of the 14,000 troops in Northern Ireland, permitted only single, aimed shots. Under the new rules, the commander on the spot can order automatic fire against identified targets. But because automatic fire scatters, it is limited to situations in which there are no unarmed persons in or near the line of fire.

Another change in the code allows a soldier to carry a live round in the breech of his gun when on patrol in dangerous areas, thus enabling him to return fire more quickly.

The new regulations are intended to counter the terrorist policy of using snipers rather than inciting mobs to attack troops, a tactic illustrated by today's fatal shooting. The soldier was shot in the stomach while on foot patrol in the predominantly Catholic Lower Falls area of Belfast. He was the 44th soldier killed since British troops were deployed in Ulster in the autumn of 1969.

While soldiers will welcome more freedom to hit back at the terrorists, observers here fear that the Army's new tactics could result in more accidental shootings. Gunmen of the Irish Republican Army generally operate in narrow slum streets where children often play. In an incident yesterday, mothers showed that they were prepared to push their children into the line of fire to prevent soldiers from shooting.

January 6, 1972

The I.R.A.

BRITISH SOLDIERS KILL 13 AS RIOTING ERUPTS IN ULSTER

Deaths Come as Catholics Defy Ban on Londonderry March

Special to The New York Times

BELFAST, Northern Ireland, Jan. 30—At least 13 persons were shot dead by British troops in Londonderry today when rioting broke out after a civil rights march held in defiance of a Government ban.

It brought to 231 the number of deaths in Ulster since violence first broke out three years ago. Already this year 25 have died.

The army said that the dead were snipers who had fired at troops trying to break up rock-throwing mobs with CS gas, a form of tear gas, and rubber bullets. But local people contended that the soldiers had panicked and fired wildly.

I.R.A. Vows Vengeance

At Altnagelvin Hospital in Londonderry, a spokesman said that the dead men were all in their twenties. Fifteen civilians were also taken to the hospital with gunshot wounds, two of them women. A girl believed to have been hit by an army vehicle is also there.

Three soldiers were reported injured, one with gunshot wounds.

A spokesman for the militant Provisional wing of the Irish Republican Army said that all guns had been cleared from the route of the march and that no shots had been fired until the troops opened fire.

[A spokesman for the official wing of the Irish Republican Army said in Londonderry Monday that British troops would be shot in reprisal, Reuters reported. "Our immediate policy is to shoot to kill as many British soldiers as possible," he said.]

The British Army chief on the spot, Maj. Gen. Robert Ford, maintained that the soldiers fired only at snipers and grenade-throwers.

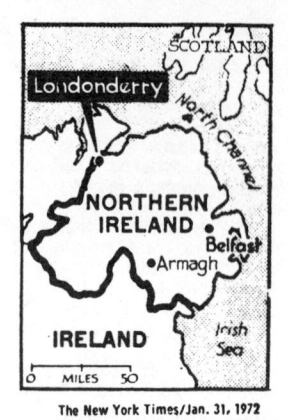

A member of the Northern Ireland Parliament, Ivan Cooper, said that the meeting had just begun and Bernadette Devlin, the fiery civil rights leader, was speaking when the shots rang out.

"The speakers threw themselves to the platform and I shouted for people to keep down," he said. "I could see the army systematically picking off people who had got up to run away."

"There was complete panic and confusion," he went on, "and I thought the best thing I could do was to tend to the injured with a friend. I was carrying a white pillowcase. We were both fired on and my friend was hit on the side of the face. Many of those who died were friends of mine, people I've known all my life.

"I can state absolutely positively that there were no snipers whatsoever. There had been stone-throwing, which had been taken care of. Sniper fire came 10 minutes later from local terrorists.

"The British Army shot down unarmed people and I hope no one has the audacity to stand up and say they were firing at snipers. They murdered innocent men."

Another local member of Parliament, John Hume, said that the soldiers had opened fire indiscriminately in an act that was "nothing short of cold-blooded murder." He said that the city was numb with shock, revulsion and bitterness.

The death toll was the highest for any one day in one city since the disorders in Ulster began. A total of 14 people died in rioting throughout the province on Aug. 10, 1971, the day after the Protestant Government announced that suspected terrorists would be interned without trial.

The march began quietly in a city housing development overlooking the historic city of 50,000 where the Protestant garrison held out successfully against the Catholic army of James II in 1689 and where the civil rights movement was born in 1968.

About 15,000 demonstrators from all parts of Northern Ireland marched on the city center. When their way was blocked by an army barricade about a quarter of a mile from their destination, the organizers diverted the parade toward a meeting point in the Bogside, a Roman Catholic area. But some marchers wanted a confrontation and showered stones and later CS gas cartridges, stolen from the British Army, on the soldiers.

The soldiers replied with volley after volley of gas and rubber bullets and called in water cannon to spray the demonstrators with a purple dye.

The Paratroop Regiment, especially hated by Roman Catholics for their methods, then drove armored cars through the rioters and it was at this stage that rifle fire was heard over the duller thud of rubber bullets.

Civilians were shot down and one report said that a priest giving the last rites to a dying man was arrested and taken away for questioning.

The Roman Catholic Bishop of Londonderry, Dr. Neil Farren, sent a telegram to Prime Minister Heath demanding a public inquiry. William Cardinal Conway, Roman Catholic Archbishop of Armagh and Primate of All Ireland, also called for an independent and impartial public inquiry. "I am deeply shocked at the news of the awful slaughter in Derry this afternoon," he said.

He called on Catholics to maintain their calm and dignity in the face of "this terrible news."

In Belfast, Brian Faulkner,

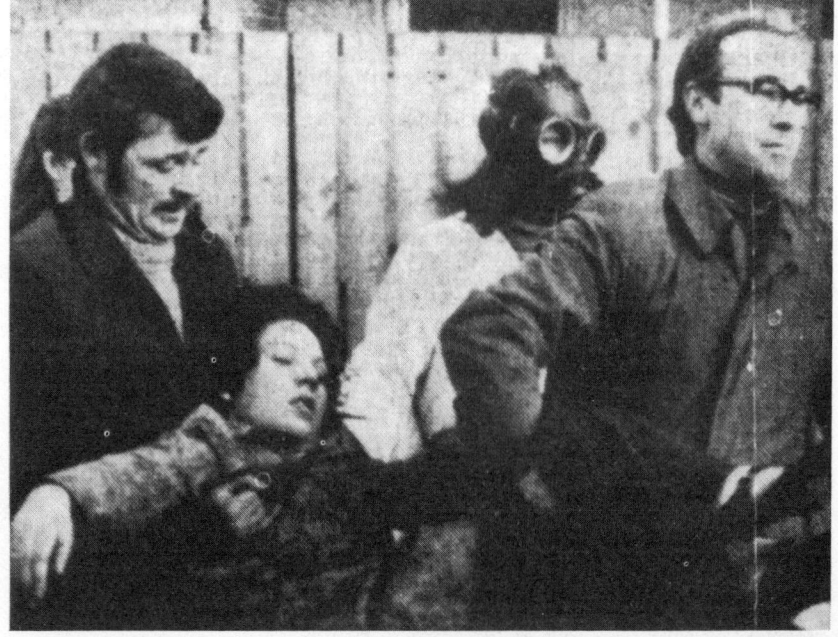

CARRIED TO SAFETY: Girl who fainted being aided. Woman at rear wears a gas mask.

Associated Press

TERRORISTS OR PATRIOTS

the Ulster Prime Minister, issued a statement saying that the day's events "illustrate precisely why it was found necessary, with the full support of the Government at Westminster, to impose a general ban on all processions throughout Northern Ireland." He said that the deaths today arose from "a meaningless and futile terrorist exercise."

The army headquarters, in a statement late tonight from Lisburn, near Belfast, said that the troops had come under nail-bomb attack and a fusillade of from 50 to 80 rounds.

"Fire was returned at seen gunmen and nail bombers," the statement continued. "Subsequently, as the troops deployed to get at the gunmen, the latter continued to fire. In all a total of well over 200 rounds was fired indiscriminately in the general direction of the soldiers."

In Londonderry, Miss Devlin, who is a member of the British Parliament, described the deaths as "mass murder" by the British Army. "This is our Sharpeville," she said, referring to the massacre of 72 black demonstrators in South Africa in 1960. "We will never forget it."

She said the soldiers had shot at a peaceful meeting and declared there was no point in calling for "whitewash" inquiries.

"All we can do is to continue the struggle to rid ourselves forever of this savagery," she said, calling for a general strike until the British Army was withdrawn. Other civil rights leaders have called for a day of mourning in Londonderry tomorrow.

In Belfast the killings are seen as a possible turning point in the Ulster crisis. Already there is speculation in political circles that if the Irish Republican Army retaliates the British may be forced to take over responsibility for security from the Northern Ireland government. In extreme circumstances, the government here might have to be suspended and Ulster ruled directly from London.

Many had predicted a clash like today's and there will be little criticism in Protestant quarters of the army's action.

A clear warning was issued yesterday that the march would be stopped by force if necessary and it was on this assurance that militant Protestant leaders in Londonderry called off a counterdemonstration.

January 31, 1972

Londonderry Clash Study Absolves Troops in Deaths

By ALVIN SHUSTER
Special to The New York Times

LONDON, April 19—An official inquiry absolved the British Army today of gross misconduct in the killing of 13 Roman Catholics in Londonderry, Northern Ireland, on Jan. 30.

The report by Lord Widgery, the Lord Chief Justice of England, questioned some of the tactics of the troops, but concluded that the first shot came from gunmen of the Irish Republican Army. The findings of the inquiry also blamed the organizers of the illegal march for creating a "highly dangerous situation."

Lord Widgery said that the army was not without some blame. He stated that the firing by some troops "bordered on the reckless." And he concluded that if the army had not launched a "large-scale operation to arrest hooligans, the day might have passed off without serious incident."

Major charges from the Londonderry Catholic community were rejected. Lord Widgery insisted that there was no breakdown of discipline among the troops on what has become known as Bloody Sunday and no evidence that the troops acted without provocation.

The report immediately touched off angry charges of "whitewash" from Catholics in Northern Ireland. Spokesmen for civil rights groups said that the Widgery report was an attempt to excuse murder by saying the army was provoked.

"There is no reason to suppose that the soldiers would have opened fire if they had not been fired upon first," Lord Widgery said.

He found no conclusive proof, however, that any of the dead or wounded had been shot while "handling a firearm or bomb." The army has insisted that the troops fired only at gunmen or bombers during the civil rights march.

Government officials here, though worried about renewed bitterness among Ulster Catholics, generally welcomed the report. Lord Carrington, the Defense Secretary, said that the army was "very satisfied" in view of the allegations of "willful murder."

The fatal clash in the Bogside, a Catholic area of Londonderry, Ulster's second largest city, is regarded by some as a turning point in the tragic history of Northern Ireland. It intensified the sectarian conflict and was one of the factors that led to last month's decision by Prime Minister Heath to suspend the Protestant-dominated Government in Ulster and impose direct rule from London.

Mr. Heath ordered the one-man inquiry after Roman Catholics charged that the paratroopers had fired indiscriminately at the demonstrators as part of a deliberate plot. They also alleged that the soldiers who did the shooting were specifically chosen to shoot it out with the underground Irish Republican Army.

Lord Widgery, a former officer in the Royal Artillery, took testimony from 114 witnesses and read statements from more than 200 others. His 25,000-word report was based on more than 750,000 words of testimony and other material.

Even so, his report is not likely to end the controversy over just what happened. He acknowledged that his decisions were reached on testimony that was often contradictory.

On the crucial question of who fired first, for example, Lord Widgery said that he was "entirely satisfied" that the initial firing came from a sniper. He said he came to this conclusion not from the testimony of any one witness, but from listening over many days to evidence and "watching the demeanor of witnesses under cross-examination."

"The soldiers' initial action was to make arrests," he said, "and there was no reason why they should have suddenly desisted and begun to shoot unless they had come under fire themselves. If the soldiers are wrong, they were parties to a lying conspiracy which must have come to light in the rigorous cross-examination to which they were subjected."

Lord Widgery, however, appeared to have some difficulty in finding firm evidence to support army testimony that the troops fired solely at those specifically identified as holding guns or nail bombs — soda or beer cans filled with explosives and nails. During the hearings, Brian Gibbens, the counsel for the Ministry of Defense, said that the troops "replied only when they could identify a gunman or bomber."

Although a number of soldiers told of seeing firearms or bombs in the hands of civilians, Lord Widgery said, "none was recovered by the army" and "none of the many photographs shows a civilian holding an object that can with certainty be identified as a firearm or bomb." He also said no casualties were suffered by the soldiers from firearms or bombs.

While he found no proof that any of the 13 killed was shot while holding a weapon, he said there "is a strong suspicion" that some had been firing weapons or handling bombs during the afternoon. He based that finding on paraffin tests of the hands of those killed.

Of the 13 victims, the report said, 5 bore no traces of having handled weapons. It added, however, that particles found on seven others were inconclusive or suggested that the victims had either handled firearms or been close to someone who did.

Lord Widgery left unresolved a mystery surrounding the 13th victim, 17-year-old Gerald Donaghy. The report said that at least two medical examinations failed to turn up any evidence that he carried weapons. Yet it was later discovered that he had had four nail bombs in his pockets.

The inquiry examined the possibility they were planted on the young man's body, but Lord Widgery said he believed "on a balance of probabilities the bombs were in Donaghy's pockets throughout."

In questioning some of the army's tactics, Lord Widgery said that the move into the Bogside area to arrest the "hooligans" represented a hazard to civilians that might have been underestimated by the brigade commander. He suggested that the tragedy might have been averted if the army had continued its "low-key" approach and merely sought to contain the marchers rather than try to arrest some.

Acted Within Orders, He Finds

Once fired on, he continued, the soldiers acted in accordance with standing orders.

In announcing the findings to the House of Commons, Mr. Heath sought to offset the report's conclusion that some troops were reckless. He said that the soldiers' lives were at risk, "as indeed the world must recognize that they have been and still are during a great part of their time in Northern Ireland."

The Prime Minister also said that such tragedies could be avoided only "by ending the law-breaking and violence which are responsible for the continuing loss of life among the security forces and public" in Ulster.

In announcing itself satisfied with the findings, the Defense Ministry said that no action would be taken against any of the soldiers involved in the shootings. Spokesmen also said that no changes would be made in the standing orders for the troops.

April 20, 1972

The I.R.A.

Londonderry Study Blames Troops

By ALVIN SHUSTER
Special to The New York Times

LONDON, June 7—An independent study today challenged the findings of an official British inquiry that had absolved British troops of gross misconduct in the killing of 13 Roman Catholics last January in Londonderry, Northern Ireland.

The independent study said that the troops fired "recklessly or deliberately" and that military authorities should have known they were "exposing thousands of peaceable citizens to a high risk of death or serious bodily injury." It said the paratroopers used in the operation had a "notorious reputation in Northern Ireland for brutality to civilians."

The report was written by Prof. Samuel Dash, director of the Institute of Criminal Law and Procedure of Georgetown University Law Center in Washington and a former chairman of the American Bar Association's section on criminal law. It was published by the International League for the Rights of Man, a private group with consultative status at the United Nations.

The lawyers who worked with Professor Dash were Prof. Louis Pollak, former dean of the Yale Law School; John Carey, the league's chairman, and Tony Smythe, general secretary of the National Council for Civil Liberties in Britain. It was the council that requested the special study.

Although members of the team visited Northern Ireland, Mr. Smythe said that the report was based primarily on the transcripts of the hearings before Lord Widgery, the Lord Chief Justice of England. Mr. Smythe said that Professor Dash also studied hundreds of statements by civilian witnesses obtained independently.

The Ministry of Defense rejected the Dash report in an unusually sharp statement, saying it could not be described as either independent or impartial. The ministry's statement said that Professor Dash had not observed the demeanor of witnesses under cross-examination, had not seen the photographic evidence and had not heard counsels' speeches.

"It is perfectly clear that he has listened to only one side of the case," the statement declared.

In his report, published in April, Lord Widgery questioned some of the tactics used by the British troops but concluded that the first shot came from gunmen of the Irish Republican Army. He said that the firing of some soldiers "bordered on the reckless" but insisted that there was no breakdown of discipline and no evidence that the troops acted without provocation.

In short, Lord Widgery gave the benefit of the doubt to the British troops. Professor Dash found this unjustified in his report, entitled "Justice Denied."

"The credibility of the testimony of the paratroopers appears to be far less acceptable than Lord Widgery finds it to be," said Professor Dash. "Lord Widgery's finding that the testimony of the paratroopers was, for the most part, truthful constitutes one of a number of internal inconsistencies in his report."

The Dash report specifically challenged Lord Widgery's conclusion on the "first shot," saying that the weight of the civilian testimony was that "the soldiers first fired on the civilians immediately upon leaving their army vehicles." It added, however, that the "record does make it clear that there were some gunmen" who later fired at the paratroopers.

"The presence of some gunmen did not justify the paratroopers in firing aimed or reckless shots at unarmed civilians," Professor Dash said.

The army has insisted that the troops fired only at gunmen or bombers during the civil rights march that led to the violence.

The killings on what the British and Irish press calls "Bloody Sunday" were regarded as a turning point in the current troubles in Northern Ireland. The incident intensified the sectarian conflict and was a key factor in the British Government's decision in March to suspend the Protestant-dominated Government in Ulster and impose direct rule from London.

A major conclusion of Lord Widgery was that there would have been no deaths if "those who organized the illegal march had not thereby created a highly dangerous situation in which the clash between demonstrators and the security forces was almost inevitable."

The Dash report concluded that it was the military command that decided to "accept a high risk of civilian deaths and injuries." It said that the Northern Ireland Civil Rights Association, which organized the march, "wanted to avoid any confrontation with military and police forces."

The British Government has said it is considering compensation for the Londonderry victims. But Mr. Smythe said, "there has not been enough progress" on this issue and he expressed hope that the Dash report would spur the Government to action.

June 8, 1972

BRITISH EMBASSY IN DUBLIN BURNED IN ULSTER PROTEST

Special to The New York Times

DUBLIN, Feb. 2—The British Embassy was destroyed by firebombing tonight as the Irish Republic observed a day of national mourning for the 13 persons killed in Northern Ireland by British soldiers.

A force of 200 Dublin policemen stood by helplessly and the fire brigade could not get past the surging crowd in Merrion Square to save the 18th-century Georgian building.

Before the fire started, stones were thrown, with encouragement from the crowd. Every stone that hit the embassy windows elicited great cheers, but because the panes were bulletproof the stones bounced back. Then gasoline bombs flew, at first sporadically. Each flash was greeted by the crowd with excited shouts of "More! More! More!"

In Londonderry, in the British-controlled province in the north, where British troops killed the 13 persons during a civil-rights demonstration Sunday, thousands of members of the Roman Catholic community, weeping and vowing vengeance, bade them an anguished farewell.

In the Republic of Ireland so high are the passions unleashed against the British that Prime Minister John Lynch may have difficulty controlling them. Last week the Government seemed to be steeling itself, in view of British criticism that it was doing nothing, to deal with the militants seeking a united Ireland. This week the political will seems to have weakened.

The Irish Ambassador in London, Dr. Donal O'Sullivan, has been temporarily withdrawn. There is a general feeling of hopelessness that any understanding on Northern Ireland can be reached by the British and Irish Governments.

February 3, 1972

Britain's Vietnam

By ANTHONY LEWIS

LONDON, Feb. 6—When Senator Edward Kennedy said last October that Northern Ireland was becoming Britain's Vietnam, he outraged a broad spectrum of British opinion. The country's largest-selling paper, The Daily Mirror, spoke for leaders of both parties when it said his call for withdrawal of British troops from Ulster was irresponsible, contemptible, mindless, asinine twaddle.

After Bloody Sunday in Londonderry, things looked different to The Daily Mirror. In a front-page editorial it urged: "Bring back the British troops." Recent events in Northern Ireland, it said, "make it imperative to end this military presence."

That change of mind was no discredit to The Daily Mirror: far from it. The British Army's killing of thirteen civilians in Londonderry, and the reaction, had made the editors see what too many others still cannot—that Britain in Ulster does indeed present some of the terrible symptoms of America in Vietnam.

The reliance on military solutions for political problems will be painfully familiar to Americans. So will the successive assurances by military spokesmen that the tactics are working, the enemy is hurting, the light is appearing at the end of the tunnel.

Then there are the corrupting moral effects of an endless war for ill-defined political objectives. Fury at a clever enemy can rob politicians of their humanity and brutalize the public—in Britain as in the United States.

There was a grisly example of this process when the Home Secretary, Reginald Maudling, spoke in the House of Commons about the Londonderry tragedy. He did not find it in him to say a single word of sympathy about the thirteen deaths.

It should be said that a large part of the British public evidently felt no sympathy for the Londonderry victims. In pub conversations and in letters to the editor, Britons sounded the theme that their soldiers in Ireland had been up against ruthless hooligans who deserved what they got.

One poll showed that only 5 per cent of those asked were inclined to blame the army for the thirteen deaths. Like Americans in the early stages of the Vietnam war, Britons find it extremely hard to believe that their troops can do wrong. British soldiers shouting obscenities at women in the Catholic ghettos of Belfast, beating prisoners, shooting into a crowd—such possibilities are simply not admitted to the imagination.

Britain's motives in Northern Ireland may be entirely honorable. Certainly she has no colonial ambition there; she is staying on in the hope of maintaining the peace. But we learned in Vietnam that men with a sincere belief in peace and freedom may bomb villages and poison forests. Good intentions are not enough.

Again, anyone can see that British forces in Ulster have come under extreme provocation. The best-trained soldier must be oppressed by an atmosphere of hatred and guerrilla terror. But that does not excuse Londonderry even if one suspends disbelief and accepts the army's version that it only responded to massive sniper fire that no civilian observers reported.

It is the duty of those enforcing law and order to avoid loss of life despite the greatest provocation, their burden to bear the provocation without retaliating. The reasons were explained by Winston Churchill when he was Secretary for War, in 1920. He was speaking to the House of Commons about the Amritsar massacre the year before, when 379 Indians were shot to death in a demonstration.

An officer faced with a mob is in a "torturing situation, mental and moral," Churchill said, but there are guides to decision. He must not use more force than necessary, and he should have "a limited and definite objective." Above all he must avoid the "frightfulness" of indiscriminate, exemplary slaughter. "Frightfulness is not a remedy known to the British pharmacopoeia."

When a British Army in British territory uses armored cars against a crowd and kills thirteen civilians, it has failed the test however it was provoked. Churchill said the great danger in harsh military action was "absolute rupture between British administration and the people of the country." He was talking about India, but he said that his thesis applies to Ireland, too. It still does.

London is deeply relieved that the Newry march went off without incident. But officials know that the army will remain in an appallingly difficult posture in Ulster so long as there is no political truce. More violence is likely to change opinion in Britain as it did in America over Vietnam. Pride in the forces will give way to revulsion at what has to be done; the soldiers themselves are likely to lose heart in an impossible role, and their disillusion will reverberate at home.

For all these reasons, the advice that Britain should withdraw her forces from Northern Ireland looks much more compelling now than it did a little while ago. In the end there can be no political solution imposed from outside, any more than in Vietnam. The Irish of the two communities will have to work out their future.

But alas, in some ways it is even harder than Vietnam. Ireland is fifty miles from here, not 9,000. The connection is 800 years old, and the culture is not alien: A million people in Ulster consider themselves British. No British Government will ever find it easy to accept that withdrawal is an honorable way out of the Irish tragedy.

February 7, 1972

BOMBING BY I.R.A. KILLS 7 IN ENGLAND

Officers Mess at Army Base Is Blown Up—5 Women and Priest Among Dead

By ALVIN SHUSTER
Special to The New York Times

ALDERSHOT, England, Feb. 22—Seven persons, including a Roman Catholic army chaplain and five women, were killed today when terrorists of the outlawed Irish Republican Army blew up an officers mess at this sprawling military camp.

A spokesman for the Official wing of the Irish Republican Army in Dublin immediately claimed responsibility for the explosion, which injured at least 17 others. It was one of the worst such incidents in England in the long history of British-Irish troubles.

The spokesman for the I.R.A., which supports the unification of the Catholic Irish Republic with the Protestant-dominated British province of Northern Ireland, said the bombing was in retaliation for the deaths of 13 Catholic civilians killed by British soldiers in Londonderry, Northern Ireland, on Jan. 30.

The wrecked glass-and-concrete building, which is situated off a public road amid woodlands, served as the officers mess of the 16th Parachute Brigade, whose battalions were involved in the Londonderry shooting. The glass in two neighboring mess halls was also shattered when a car parked by the terrorists exploded.

February 23, 1972

HIGH ULSTER AIDE SHOT BY GUNMEN

Special to The New York Times

BELFAST, Northern Ireland, Feb. 25—John Taylor, Minister of State for Home Affairs in the Northern Ireland government, was shot and seriously wounded tonight in Armagh, about 40 miles southwest of Belfast.

Four bullets, fired by two gunmen as he was getting into his car outside the family engineering concern, struck him in the neck, jaw and chest.

Mr. Taylor was found slumped over the wheel, his head covered in blood. He was taken to Armagh City Hospital where after an emergency operation his condition was described as "comparatively good." Later he was transferred to a Belfast hospital for further surgery.

He is the first member of the Northern Ireland government to be the victim of an assassination attempt.

Mr. Taylor, who at 34 is the youngest member of the Cabinet, handled the day-to-day business of maintaining law and order under the Prime Minister, Brian Faulkner, who also holds the office of Minister of Home Affairs.

February 26, 1972

The I.R.A.

British in Ulster Accused of Psychological Torture

By BERNARD WEINRAUB
Special to The New York Times

LONDON, March 12 — Security forces in Northern Ireland were accused today of using psychological torture, brainwashing and interrogation methods that threatened the mental stability of Roman Catholic internees.

The charges were made by Amnesty International, a British-based organization, in a report compiled before the British ban on harsh interrogation methods.

"These techniques constitute a grave assault on the human mind," said the report, which was written by Thomas Hammarberg, a journalist who is chairman of the Swedish section of Amnesty International; Herman van Geuns, a doctor who heads the Dutch section, and Gunnar Lind, a Norwegian lawyer and assistant public prosecutor.

Amnesty, which was set up 11 years ago to help political prisoners, urged an international inquiry last year into the treatment of internees in Northern Ireland after publishing allegations of physical brutality.

"The methods used were deliberately designed to disorientate and break down the resistance of the prisoners, in order to induce them to supply information," said the document. "It is very likely that the combination of sensory deprivation and deprivation of sleep and food caused a pathological state of passive obedience, or of extreme anxiety."

The British Government, reacting to recent charges of brutality, announced on March 2 that security forces would no longer use harsh interrogation techniques on detainees in Northern Ireland. These included the use of black hoods, subjecting prisoners to a continuous noise, deprivation of sleep and a diet of bread and water.

The move by London followed official British inquiries that found evidence of physical ill-treatment of internees. The report by Amnesty, however, charges that psychological, and not physical, mistreatment is most evident in the internment camps.

"The fact that some of the prisoners refused food and water, urinated in inappropriate situations, refused to urinate when appropriate facilities were available and kept the hood on when it could have been removed supports our finding that this treatment had serious mental effects," said the Amnesty report.

"The procedures were designed to disorientate and break down the mind of the suspect by sensory deprivation and the infliction of physical injury was ancillary to this purpose," the report adds.

Internment without trial began in Northern Ireland on Aug. 9 in a Government move to crush the Irish Republican Army. The policy has outraged the Catholic minority, which charges that Protestant gunmen have been ignored and that innocent Catholics are being held in the two internment camps at Long Kesh, south of Belfast, and Magilligan, near Londonderry, as well as on the ship Maidstone in Belfast Harbor. About 820 men are being held.

The Amnesty report deals with the allegations of 30 former detainees. It discusses, in large part, the psychological effect of interrogation techniques allegedly practiced by British soldiers and Ulster security officials.

In one case, of Desmond Smith, who was arrested Aug. 9, the Amnesty report says that he has "suffered convulsive fainting attacks and that his health was disturbed after release."

Mr. Smith maintained that he was beaten and given enforced exercises for about 17 hours, and that he suffered from seizures and epileptic fits in the hours following his arrest.

According to Amnesty, another internee, Patrick Shivers, who said he was subject to continual beating and hooding, "was obviously harmed by the treatment and after release found it difficult to sleep and was unable to work for a considerable time."

In its conclusion, the Amnesty commission found that detainees "had been subjected to brutal treatment by the security forces during arrest and transport.

"Suffering had been inflicted on those arrested to obtain from them confessions or information," it said.

March 13, 1972

6 Killed, 146 Hurt in Blast On Crowded Belfast Street

Special to The New York Times

BELFAST, Northern Ireland, March 20—A large time bomb exploded today in a central Belfast street crowded with shoppers and office workers, killing six and injuring 146.

Many of the victims had gone to the scene, the police said, after misleading telephone calls warned that bombs were set to explode in nearby streets.

Two of the dead were policemen, and one of these was a Roman Catholic. They were helping with the evacuation of the supposedly threatened areas when the bomb exploded on Donegall Street, a narrow thoroughfare a quarter of a mile long, lined with shops and offices.

The explosion was said to be the worst daylight bombing since the crisis began in this Protestant-ruled province two and a half years ago. Earlier this month, an explosion in a restaurant killed two and injured more than 100.

The only previous explosion during the crisis with a higher death toll, it was said, was a nighttime blast in a bar here last December in which 15 were killed.

In Londonderry, meanwhile, a British soldier was shot dead by a gunman firing from a bar on the edge of the Bogside, a Catholic quarter. He was the 55th soldier killed since British troops were deployed in the province in 1969 and, together with those who died in the Donegall Street explosion, raised the death toll in the last two and a half years to 286.

A security force spokesman said the immediate suspects in the explosion were the so-called Provisionals, members of the more militant wing of the outlawed Irish Republican Army. It has reportedly been responsible for most of the bombings in Belfast.

Fear of Rightist Strength

There was some speculation here that, in view of the expected announcement from London soon of reforms designed to end the bloodshed in Northern Ireland, the bomb in Donegall Street might have been intended to stress that the I.R.A. was interested only in removing British troops from the province.

Others saw the explosion as a response to the growing movement by right-wing Protestants concerned that Britain might go too far in meeting Catholic demands for an end to internment of suspected guerrillas without trial and a greater share in government decisions.

William Craig, a former Home Affairs Minister, is the spearhead of the Protestant extremists, whose strength was shown this weekend when more than 50,000 turned out for a rally in Belfast. Mr. Craig told supporters of his Vanguard movement that if the politicians failed, it might be their job "to liquidate the enemy."

Catholic Reaction Promised

Speakers at an anti-internment rally in Belfast yesterday said they were not frightened by threats from right-wing Protestants, and they promised a Catholic backlash to counter any sectarian violence.

In addition to the Donegall Street explosion, there were three other bomb blasts in Belfast in the afternoon. No casualties were reported.

A police spokesman said the explosion in Donegall Street "was a deliberate attempt to kill innocent civilians." He said those responsible "must have known that people were being evacuated into its path."

Among the dead were two garbage men, whose truck was parked behind a car in which the explosive, a 100-pound time bomb, was believed to have been planted. The car was just outside the office of the Protestant newspaper, The Newsletter.

The explosion hurled pieces of the car into the next street 100 yards away. It shattered windows the length of Donegall Street and littered it with debris.

Many of the injured, taken to three Belfast hospitals, were treated for wounds from flying glass. Soldiers joined in the rescue work, handing their weapon to others to dig into the ruins and carry stretchers.

A policeman was one of many who turned away from the scene with tears streaming down his face. An elderly woman, shocked but still clutching her shopping bag, said: "If the swine that did this think they gain anything by it, they have another think coming."

March 21, 1972

BRITAIN SUSPENDS GOVERNMENT IN NORTHERN IRELAND, IMPOSING DIRECT LONDON RULE FOR A YEAR

NEW ULSTER POST

Policy of Internment Will Be Eased and Plebiscites Held

By ALVIN SHUSTER
Special to The New York Times

LONDON, March 24 — The British Government suspended the provincial government and Parliament of Northern Ireland today and imposed direct rule from London.

Prime Minister Heath told a hushed House of Commons that the radical steps, which reverse 50 years of British policy, were necessary to end the strife between Roman Catholics and Protestants in the British-controlled province of Ulster. He expressed hope that the steps would open the way to a lasting solution.

Mr. Heath appointed William Whitelaw, the Leader of the House of Commons, to be Secretary of State for Northern Ireland and to assume all legislative and executive powers now vested in the Ulster Parliament and government. Direct rule, to be authorized for at least a year, is to begin next Thursday after Parliament here approves a Government bill submitted today.

4,000 Troops on Alert

Fearing increased violence, British officials disclosed that 4,000 soldiers were standing by to be sent to Ulster if necessary. They said the soldiers, who would support the nearly 15,000 now there, might have been needed at Easter even without the Heath decision.

Mr. Heath also announced these major decisions:

¶Plebiscites will be held periodically in Northern Ireland on whether Ulster should move toward unification with the neighboring Irish Republic, which is 95 per cent Catholic. Mr. Heath assured the Protestant majority in Ulster that no change would be made in the border without its consent.

¶A start will be made on phasing out the controversial British policy of interning Irish terrorist suspects without trial. Catholics have demanded that the policy end, saying it is aimed only at the minority Catholic community.

¶A commission representing all shades of opinion will be appointed by Mr. Whitelaw to advise him on running Northern Ireland.

Wilson Pledges Support

Mr. Heath said he hoped the measures would "change the climate of political opinion in Northern Ireland" so that representatives of the 500,000 Catholics and million Protestants would sit down together and work out the "future structure" of their government. Officials here made no secret of their view that there would be no return to the old system.

Harold Wilson, leader of the Labor party Opposition, pledged "full support" for the governing Conservatives' measures and said his party would "give every facility" in having the bill passed before "what looks like being a difficult and dangerous Easter period."

Mr. Wilson was Prime Minister in 1969 when British troops were first deployed in Ulster. Recently he has been strongly critical of Mr. Heath's delay in disclosing the long-heralded political initiative.

As Mr. Heath spoke in London, Brian Faulkner, the Prime Minister of Northern Ireland, announced in Belfast that he and the other members of his government would resign next week. Mr. Faulkner's refusal last night to agree to British control over internal security in the province led to Mr. Heath's decision to govern the province from London.

By suspending the provincial government, Mr. Heath went a long way to meeting the demands of Catholics who regarded it as a symbol of sectarianism and a force responsible for years of discrimination. The government in Belfast has been dominated by the Protestant Unionist party since the provincial Parliament was created on the partition of Ireland in 1921.

Direct rule has always been described by London officials as a last resort. A crucial fear has been, and still is, that the Protestant majority would react violently to a take-over.

Militants Express Anger

As expected, militant Protestants in Northern Ireland reacted with anger, charging betrayal and surrender to "terrorist violence." William Craig, leader of a powerful group of Protestants, said, "Ulster is closer to civil war today than it was yesterday."

While acknowledging the obvious risks of further violence in Mr. Heath's plans, officials said it would take several days to determine the depth of Protestant anger. Serious concern remains about the possibility of a severe Protestant "backlash."

There was unhappiness among some Catholic spokesmen that internment was not ended but satisfaction over the downfall of the provincial government. Some Catholics saw the take-over as the beginning of the end for partition, believing that Britain will tire of ruling the province and will eventually agree that it should be united with the Irish Republic.

But that Catholic hope is what Protestants fear. Many Protestants are suspicious of British intentions, despite assurances from London, and would prefer to retain their own parliamentary structure as a symbol of Protestant dominance and as a safeguard against absorption by the South.

This safeguard is underscored by a 1949 act of the British Parliament that says that "in no event" will Northern Ireland or any part of it cease to be a part of the United Kingdom "without the consent of the Parliament of Northern Ireland." But Protestants fear a sellout by a Britain weary of the Irish problem now that Ulster has no parliament.

Lynch Welcomes Move

Prime Minister John Lynch of the Irish Republic said in Dublin that he welcomed the Heath decision as a "step forward in seeking a lasting solution." He urged all Irishmen, North and South, to "consider the proposals maturely and objectively."

The British Government is hoping that Mr. Lynch will crack down on Irish Republic Army guerrillas using the republic as a sanctuary. Sources in Dublin suggested that Mr. Lynch now felt he could move against them without running the risk of being accused of propping up a sectarian regime in Belfast.

In a television speech tonight Mr. Heath appealed to the people of Northern Ireland to remain calm and to seize the opportunity to end the violence.

"Now is your chance," he said. "A chance for fairness, a chance for prosperity, and above all a chance for peace. A chance at last to bring the bombings and killings to an end. Memories of the past are long-lived. In all conscience you have suffered enough."

In a clear allusion to the possibility of Protestant violence, Mr. Heath said the army would stay in Northern Ireland "as long as any faction" sought to terrorize the people. He said there would be no relaxation in the fight against terrorism.

Since the British troops moved into Northern Ireland in the fall of 1969, when sectarian fighting erupted, 287 persons have been killed. Of those 224 have died in the eight months since the Ulster government, with the support of London, announced the internment policy.

Irish Republican Army extremists stepped up their guerrilla attacks and it became clear that Mr. Heath's Government would have to act. For weeks Mr. Heath and his ministers agonized over a formula that they hoped would win the approval of the Catholics without antagonizing the Protestants.

As Mr. Heath explained in the Commons, his Government settled on three key proposals and presented them this week to Mr. Faulkner. They were the plebiscite plan, the beginning of the end of internment, and the transfer of security control from Belfast to London.

However, Mr. Faulkner, who met with Mr. Heath here Wednesday and Thursday, rejected the proposal that he give up jurisdiction over law and order. He said today that to do so would be widely construed as "an acceptance of totally baseless criticism of our stewardship."

Heath Stands Firm

Mr. Heath insisted that Mr. Faulkner agree to all of the plan or resign and accept Brit-

The I.R.A.

ish rule. He told the Commons that he felt the transfer of security to London was "an indispensable condition for progress in finding a political solution."

Mr. Heath said that he had no alternative but to assume full and direct responsibility for Northern Ireland until a "political solution to the problems of the province can be worked out in consultation with all those concerned."

On internment, he said the Government would set free those suspects "whose release is no longer thought likely to involve an unacceptable risk to security." About 100 of 700 persons believed to be held are expected to go free.

"If the measures which we have taken lead to a reduction in terrorist activity, it will be possible to consider further releases," Mr. Heath said, "but this must depend on a clearly established improvement in the security situation."

It was stressed tonight that the internment policy would continue and that new suspects would be handled in the same way.

Heath Denies Surrender

In response to questions, Mr. Heath denied that he had surrendered to the demands of the Irish Republican Army. He said that at least three key demands of the Catholic extremists were not met — amnesty for all prisoners, the withdrawal of all British troops and the abolition rather than suspension of the Ulster government.

Because the government was suspended, not abolished, members of Northern Ireland's Parliament will continue to be paid. Britain hopes that these elected members will join in the search for a solution.

Prime Minister Heath emphasized in his television speech that the next step was up to the people of Northern Ireland.

"You are the ones who have had to endure the years of violence and fear," he said. "We admire the steadiness and courage with which you have done this. Now only you can take the decision to live together in peace."

March 25, 1972

'Free Derry,' I.R.A.-Run Is a State Within a State

By BERNARD WEINRAUB
Special to The New York Times

LONDONDERRY, Northern Ireland, April 22 — Hooded teen-agers gripping submachine guns and carbines patrol the streets of the Bogside. They control traffic, wave on motorists and stop strangers.

"Who are you? Where are you from? Prove it!" This the vigilantes demand as they stand beside the burned-out vehicles and floodlit barricades that seal the entrances to the Bogside and the adjoining Creggan and Brandywell areas.

"Free Derry" — the solidly Roman Catholic quarter where 33,000 of Londonderry's 56,000 people live—is a state within a state now, openly protected by both wings of the outlawed Irish Republican Army. There are no courts and no policemen, rents and taxes are not paid, and gas and electric bills are largely ignored.

"If the army comes in here there'd be a bloodbath," said Thomas McCourt, the 24-year-old leader of the Official wing of the I.R.A. here. "Our job is defense and retaliation. We're not cowboys with guns. We're here to defend our people."

'But We're at War'

On Stanley's Walk in the Bogside, 21-year-old Martin McGuinness, the officer in charge of the Provisional wing, said: "The job, as far as I'm concerned, is fighting the British Army. Ours is an offensive role. No one likes to kill. I don't. But we're at war. These people are invaders."

Since the arrival of the vanguard of 15,000 British troops in Ulster in August, 1969, the Catholics in Free Derry have gradually turned their enclave in this shabby city 70 miles from Belfast into a fortress barricaded with overturned trucks, barbed wire, stones and rubble. The last time soldiers moved in was on Jan. 30, Bloody Sunday, when 13 civil-rights marchers were killed.

Now the area is sealed and, for the first time, young I.R.A. vigilantes openly patrol the broken streets, whose surrounding walls, festooned with the Irish tricolor, bear scrawled slogans: "Irishmen avenge Irish dead" . . . "Beware soldiers' dolls—no Limey lovers."

The mood is at once embattled and eerily normal. Above Creggan Heights, which overlooks the Bogside, is an observation post with an air-raid siren, which wails if the army approaches. Armed patrols work day and night. There is a vigilante for every street (they work one night on and two nights off).

Yet buses, often driven by Protestants, move in and out, taking children to the doctor or dentist and housewives downtown. Two Protestant-owned bakeries deliver bread each morning. Milkmen and butchers' vans and food trucks thread their way through.

"It's a normal society in an abnormal situation," said Michael Havord, organizer of the Derry Civil Rights Association, in the group's tiny headquarters in the Creggan area. "An Establishment in the normal sense doesn't exist here. But there's no anarchy. To most of us there's more anarchy outside—where you can be picked up by soldiers or the Royal Ulster Constabulary — than inside."

Bridget Bond, the mother of four sons and secretary of the civil-rights group, said: "The kids have nothing to do. No one's working here. That's the problem. They can't afford to take out girls. They can't go to a movie or a dance. And they can't and don't go outside." Londonderry has an unemployment rate of 18 per cent; the figure in the Bogside is twice that.

Londonderry has a peculiar place in Ulster's mythology, and its history is embedded in the consciousness of all Irishmen. In the religious wars of the 17th century Londonderry, a Protestant stronghold, was never captured by the Catholics, who were forced to live outside the city gates in the flat, marshy "bogside." The ghetto is nestled beneath the city walls and their cannon, symbols of Protestant domination.

Around the walls now are a handful of heavily barricaded British Army posts, manned by 2,400 soldiers who are under virtually constant threat from snipers and rock-throwing youths.

Committees Maintain Service

The two wings of the I.R.A. control security in the ghetto, but a collection of street committees, citizens' groups and tenants' associations maintain lists of carpenters and electricians, assure the collection of garbage and deal with the sick and elderly.

"These structures give people a sense of order, and there is order here," said Myall Canavan, a moderate who is chairman of the Derry Citizens Central Council. "And people see the I.R.A. as the only force of protection."

Because the community cooperates with the home-grown police force, called the Peace Corps, petty thieves and vandals are quickly tracked down and dealt with, sometimes in a primitive fashion. Several youths who had repeatedly been warned to stop stealing have been tarred and feathered. In more extreme cases offenders have been shot in the leg.

The two wings of the I.R.A. are cooperating, but their senior officers maintain a chilly, sometimes hostile relationship. Among teen-agers the links are closer and joining one wing—as opposed to the other —often depends on one's neighborhood and who controls the block. The Bogside is heavily Provisional, the breakaway wing that relies on bombing and armed attack on the British soldiers. The Creggan area is dominated by the Officials, the more ideological and Marxist group.

Entrance to Bogside area, one of three Roman Catholic areas sealed off by I.R.A.

'We Want the Dedicated'

"We can't take all the lads that want to join," said the bearded Mr. McCourt, leader of the Officials, as he sat in a car near his home. "We want the dedicated. If a fellow says he just wants a gun, we tell him to go to the Provos.

"We're not bloody idiots. We're not here for the showmanship. We want a 32-county socialist republic. We retaliate when we have to, when it's necessary. We killed two British soldiers last week." He explained that the killings were in retaliation for the killing of Joseph McCann, a popular I.R.A. leader in Belfast.

"Sure, sometimes this business gets you down," he continued. "Sometimes you see a few of the lads go across the border to a dance. I'd like to go too. I never go to a picture show. I get low sometimes. But then, well, you think, is any of that important?"

Beneath Creggan, in a house on the fringe of the Bogside, Mr. McGuinness, the Provisionals' leader, sat with several associates, including Sean Keenen, the adjutant, whose brother was recently shot dead in a clash with the army. Asked about Provisional bombing attacks in which civilians are killed or wounded, Mr. McGuinness spoke unemotionally.

"Things are done for a reason," he said. "No one likes to do some things. In Belfast there have been a few bad accidents, not in Derry. But tell me, what sin is there in a

Confusion and Anticipation

man fighting for his country?"

The take-over of Northern Ireland by the Government in London and the toppling of the bitterly resented Protestant-dominated government here have stirred both confusion and anticipation. Even with the report by Lord Widgery, which absolved British soldiers of firing without provocation on Bloody Sunday, there is a glimmer of optimism among moderates, especially priests.

"The Widgery report set things back here, but there's still some hope—a little bit of it," said the Rev. William Rafferty, a frail, gray-haired priest at St. Columba's Church in the Bogside. "We're able to carry on, but life is not normal here. There's a sense of disorder about things."

He stepped outside the church. Two dozen yards away two masked youths with machine guns had set up a checkpoint to investigate strangers.

"What can we do but carry on?" he asked. "What's going to happen? The children are hero-worshipers. This morning an 8-year-old lad said in class that it was all right to throw stones at soldiers because they shouldn't be there. The children think it's great what the I.R.A. is doing."

Referring to William Whitelaw, the new Secretary of State for Northern Ireland, he added: "It's most difficult to be hopeful about any of this, but Whitelaw is trying to ease things up, isn't he? Maybe one of these days he will."

April 27, 1972

A Protestant Militia Takes Hold in Ulster

By BERNARD WEINRAUB
Special to The New York Times

BELFAST, Northern Ireland, July 9—They hover on street corners in Protestant neighborhoods, wearing battle fatigues and masks. They grip wooden clubs.

"We're the army of the Prods," said an 18-year-old, standing at a barbed-wire barricade at Wilton Street off the Shankill Road. "They got their army. We got ours."

Beside him on the street of low red-brick homes, an older man nervously tapped his wooden club against the palm of his hand. He wore a khaki scarf over his mouth and dark glasses. "We're not anti-Catholic, we're anti-terrorist," he said. "We're working-class men and we're sick, tired and bloody sore at the way things have been going."

An Army Comes Into Being

Within the last three months, a militant "army of Prods," or Protestants, called the Ulster Defense Association has mushroomed in Northern Ireland, frightening the Catholic minority and challenging William Whitelaw, the British administrator. Security officials, who worked out the now-cancelled ceasefire with the Provisional wing of the Irish Republican Army are now anxious about the U. D. A. and term the new group — estimated to have 43,000 members — the most disciplined and potentially powerful Protestant militia in years.

What the Protestant group fears is that Britain, in the long run, will become weary of the Northern Ireland problem and, under pressure from the I.R.A., negotiate to unite Northern Ireland with the Irish Republic to the south. Northern Ireland is two-thirds Protestant, while 95 per cent of the Irish Republic is Roman Catholic.

Barricades Are Top Issue

The U.D.A.'s anger, at present, is directed at the British Army's refusal to smash the barricaded Catholic areas of Londonderry's Bogside and Creggan districts. In the last two weeks, the Protestant militiamen have set up concrete and spike barricades in four districts near the Shankill Road and one in the town of Partadown—the first Protestant off-limits areas in Northern Ireland.

The Partadown barricades were cleared by British troops today, seemingly to allow a Protestant parade to pass through the section. The move, denounced by both the Provisional and Official I.R.A., led to shooting which preceded the end of the I.R.A. ceasefire.

Last week, a violent confrontation was barely averted between 8,000 U.D.A. men and British troops when a compromise was worked out to place both the militiamen and British troops in a Protestant area that the U.D.A. had sought to seal off.

The Ulster Defense Association operates in secret— "no names, no descriptions" are the bywords. A visiting journalist, attempting to meet U.D.A. leaders through go-betweens, is awakened by phone at 2 A.M., asked to identify himself, and told to wait for another phone call at 1 P.M. the next day. At 1 P.M. the telephone rings and the visitor is told to go at once to a house in East Belfast. In the pleasant house sits the group's vice commander, a muscled 34-year-old former serviceman who wore a shoulder holster with a 9-mm. pistol. His attractive wife served tea and homemade cake.

"We have a complete range of weapons, an awful lot of them," the vice commander said, "and we are prepared to use them if there is any move to a united Ireland.

'Return of Stormont'

"We don't want a Protestant backlash to come out, but it's here and only to be unleashed. We are big enough, we are strong enough and we'll fight like hell."

Then, referring to the Protestant-dominated provincial parliament suspended by Britain, he said: "What we want is the return of Stormont with the full status quo. We, as the people, will insure that the Catholics get their fair share. In the meantime, we've to be prepared for anything—and we are."

The defense group was built on neighborhood units that sprang up in 1969 when rioting over the religious and civil rights issues began in Ulster. Britain's decision to impose direct rule turned the U.D.A. into a formidable force that reaches deep into working-class neighborhoods.

Although the Protestant group mirrors the style of the I.R.A.—replete with disguise, kangaroo courts and women's auxiliaries—it seeks to blend the training of other guerrilla groups and the British Army. There is a hierarchy of officers, sergeants and men. Often, neighbors who work together on the docks and ride home together on the bus adopt military postures and say "Sir" to each other several hours later. Streets are broken down into platoons of about 50 men, under the command of a "sergeant." Unit or company comanders are "majors."

Training takes place secretly in local halls. "We have physical training, courses in unarmed combat —karate, things like that— we teach them to strip field weapons and we have assault courses outside the city," the vice commander said. "We have no worry about weapons. I can assure you we have plenty of them."

Each member of the U.D.A. pays about 12 cents a week membership dues.

"We wear masks not because of personal fear for our safety," the vice commander said slowly, while his year-old son gurgled at his feet. "Without masks we'd be open to assassination bids and if that took place, there'd be a bloodbath. Our men would run amok.

"Our members are good, working-class lads. For three years we've watched the terrorists pillage and burn the place down. Now they're getting what they want.

"Well, we're going to stop it," he said bitterly. "We're the majority here and we've got the majority of the people on our side. The I.R.A. want a united Ireland against the will of the majority. Well, we won't give an inch, I tell you, not an inch."

July 10, 1972

The I.R.A.

Britain to End Internment Of Ulster I.R.A. Suspects

By BERNARD WEINRAUB
Special to The New York Times

LONDON, Sept. 21—Britain tonight ordered the end of the controversial policy of interning suspected terrorists in Northern Ireland without trial.

William Whitelaw, Ulster's administrator, announced in London that a tribunal would be set up to consider cases with a view to the release of the suspects or their imprisonment for a specific term. Under internment, suspects may be held indefinitely.

Mr. Whitelaw's move, following a Cabinet meeting, was clearly intended to calm the Roman Catholic minority in Northern Ireland and encourage the main opposition group, the Social Democratic and Labor party, to attend a crucial three-day conference next week on the future of the torn province.

The party, representing many Catholics, had announced a boycott of the meeting because of internment. Catholics contended that internment, which was devised to root out terrorists, had been a one-sided policy that exempted Protestant gunmen.

Despite the decision to end internment, there were doubts tonight that the party would attend the conference. Gerry Fitt, the party leader, said that the 241 men still held in the Long Kesh internment camp must be released before the group would attend the talks.

And Paddy Devlin, a party leader from the Falls Road in Belfast, a Catholic stronghold, said: "We are as bitterly opposed to special courts as we are to internment. Such courts would be setting aside the normal processes of justice and could in fact make internment more permanent. There's no question of this persuading us to go to the Whitelaw talks."

Britain's decision to replace internment with a tribunal, or special court, followed weeks of discussion in London among Prime Minister Heath, Mr. Whitelaw and senior legal advisers.

Although the Government was clearly eager to end internment without trial, it faced the problem of how to deal with men believed to be responsible for the Irish Republican Army bombings and other violence in the province.

Officials in London and Belfast said that placing the men on trial was virtually impossible because of the intimidation of witnesses. One witness, a bus driver, was murdered last year the night before he was to appear in court.

Hearings May Be Secret

Mr. Whitelaw said in his statement:

"Certain basic problems of countering terrorism by the normal processes of law still present difficulties. These include the problem of preventing intimidation of witnesses who may be in danger of their lives if they give evidence in court and of bringing to trial many of those who, although responsible for organizing and directing terrorism, take care to avoid, so far as possible, themselves engaging in terrorist operations.

"The system of internment cannot be ended without putting something in its place."

The new tribunal — which will probably consist of three judges—will sit without a jury and may conduct hearings in secret. Cases will be referred to it by Mr. Whitelaw. The judges will pass sentence for a fixed period. So far most trials of terrorist suspects, who are often charged with attempted murder, have resulted in prison sentences of five to seven years.

Mr. Whitelaw's statement indicated that the tribunal was a temporary measure. He said that the Government was setting up "a commission of experienced lawyers and laymen" to advise on legal measures to deal with terrorists and to prepare legislation.

Mr. Whitelaw's move — for which he must seek parliamentary approval when the House of Commons reassembles on Oct. 17—marks the end of a bitter drama that began at dawn on Aug. 9, 1971, when British soldiers swarmed into Catholic districts to seize I.R.A. suspects.

The army action followed a secret decision by the Ulster and British governments to invoke emergency powers to hold suspected terrorists in camps without charges against them, without trial and without fixed sentences.

At the peak of internment more than 900 men were held in camps in Northern Ireland.

British and Northern Ireland officials agree that the internment decision was pivotal in Ulster. Although internment had been used three times before in Northern Ireland—in 1922, 1938 and 1956—the policy last year sparked the most violent Catholic reaction in Ulster's history.

Protestants and Catholic moderates agree that its impact —and the alienation of the one-third Catholic minority—led to the end of the 51-year dominance of the Protestant Unionist party and the start of direct rule by Britain on March 24.

Catholics viewed internment as the traditional instrument used by Protestant governments against them. Allegations of beatings, psychological torture and hardship in internment camps cemented their anger.

The impact of internment— and, to moderates, its "failure" —is underlined by the violence that struck the province after internment began: In the four months before internment, four soldiers and four civilians were killed. In the four months after its introduction, from August to November, 41 soldiers and members of local security forces were killed together with 73 civilians.

Initial Reaction Angry

Perhaps the single turning point linked to internment was the day Catholics call Bloody Sunday — Jan. 30 — when 13 Catholics were killed while taking part in a march in Londonderry to protest the policy. Within two weeks, Prime Minister Heath had begun working out the details of the British Government's takeover of Northern Ireland.

Although the end of internment will be welcomed by many Catholics, the initial reaction to the new tribunal was both muted and angry. Frank McManus, a militant member of the British Parliament from Fermanagh and South Tyrone, said that the proposals were "sophisticated maneuvering" and "an extension of internment under a different guise."

The Government's announcement left unclear how many of the 241 men in Long Kesh would appear before the court, and how many would be freed. One British official said that the first tribunal would sit "in weeks, rather than months," and that it would hear only the the toughest cases."

Security officers say privately that about 80 of the 241 are believed to be "hard-core" terrorists. One of the men held is said to be the key bombmaker of the I.R.A.'s militant Provisional wing.

Late tonight, Mr. Whitelaw said on television that the tribunal was a "much fairer way" of dealing with suspects than an internment order signed by a senior official. He said he did not regard the proposals as a concession to the Catholics.

September 22, 1972

DUBLIN APPROVES I.R.A. CRACKDOWN AS BLASTS KILL 2

Special to The New York Times

DUBLIN, Saturday, Dec. 2— The Irish Parliament approved legislation cracking down on the Irish Republican Army last night, shortly after three explosions in the center of Dublin killed at least two people and injured more than 70.

The explosions, rare for the capital, came as Prime Minister John Lynch was struggling to win parliamentary approval of the tough antiterrorist measures. Before the blasts, the measure had been given little chance of passage.

On hearing the news of the explosions, Parliament recessed its third day of debate and leaders of the parties opposing the bill indicated that they would no longer stand in the way of passage.

When Parliament reconvened later, most of the Opposition members abstained, and the bill cleared the 144-seat chamber by a vote of 70 to 23.

Conviction Is the Goal

The bill, representing the toughest steps taken so far by Mr. Lynch against the illegal activities of the I.R.A., is intended to make it easier to convict members of the organization.

The Opposition parties, led by Fine Gael and Labor, opposed the wide-ranging measures on the ground that they infringed on basic rights. They made it clear that they had no sympathies for the I.R.A. and its campaign of terror aimed at freeing neighboring Northern Ireland from British rule.

Patrick Cooney, speaking for Fine Gael, which led the fight against the bill, said his party "had decided to put nation before party" in withdrawing opposition to the legislation. He said that the decision for most of the party's 50 members to abstain was made after the men responsible for the night's explosions "were revealed as fellow travellers of the I.R.A."

I.R.A. Denies Responsibility

The militant Provisional wing of the I.R.A. denied responsibility for the explosions. There was also a denial from the Ulster Defense Association, the militant Protestant organization of Northern Ireland.

Warnings of the blasts were received here after the fact. The first warning was phoned to the Belfast News Letter, a Protestant paper, two minutes before 8 P.M. The newspaper phoned the Royal Ulster Constabulary's headquarters in Belfast, which in turn relayed the warning to the Dublin police. But it was too late.

The explosions, which came within minutes of each other, created scenes of panic in the downtown area, which was filled with Friday night strollers.

The first bomb exploded just after 8 P.M. outside Liberty Hall, headquarters of the Irish Congress of Trade Unions and about half a mile from Parliament. The Hall, close to O'Connell Street, Dublin's main thoroughfare, was filled at the time with 300 persons playing bingo. Many of its windows were blown out.

The two people killed, a bus conductor and a bus driver, were victims of the second explosion, outside a department store just off O'Connell Street. There was a third, smaller blast in the same general area.

The Liberty Hall explosion, thought to have been caused by a car bomb, shattered windows on both sides of the Liffey River, which bisects Dublin. At least 20 persons were injured and the 14-story building was heavily damaged.

Sinn Fein, the political arm of the official wing of the I.R.A., recently used the hall for its annual conference.

Shortly after the blasts, a spokesman for the I.R.A.'s Provisional, militant wing denied "all responsibility."

A man in the Liffey Bar, just outside the hall, said that all he remembered was "a blinding flash and bodies all over the place."

John McHugh, a police sergeant, said: "I have never seen anything like it in my life. I saw one woman with a gaping hole in her chest."

Injured Are Shuttled

Ambulances and fire engines were hampered at first by hysterical civilians fleeing in every direction as rumors of more explosions spread through the city.

A shuttle service was operated by the ambulances to get the injured to hospitals. Firemen battled fires touched off by the explosions for more than two and a half hours.

Rescue and fire-fighting efforts were complicated by thousands of people drawn downtown by the explosions. The police set up roadblocks in the downtown area.

During the parliamentary recess, Mr. Lynch said over television, that he "deplored and condemned" the explosions and the Republic "would use all its resources to meet this direct threat to democracy."

The bill passed shortly before midnight, ending days of suspense over the measures.

The most controversial provision of the new legislation changes the rules of evidence, making it easier for the Government prosecutor to convict. Under the provision, the sworn testimony of a senior police officer that he believed a defendant to be a member of the I.R.A. can now be admitted as evidence.

Critics argued that this change would shift the burden of proof from the prosecutor to the defendant. Given strict interpretation, they alleged, the basic principle of justice that the accused was innocent until proved guilty would no longer hold.

December 2, 1972

IRISH VOTE TO END FAVORED STATUS FOR THE CHURCH

85% in Referendum Support Measure Designed to Spur Reunion With the North

By ALVIN SHUSTER
Special to The New York Times

DUBLIN, Dec. 8—Irish voters have decided overwhelmingly to abolish the "special position" of the Roman Catholic Church in the Constitution.

The results of a national referendum announced tonight were immediately hailed by Prime Minister John Lynch and other officials as an important symbol of the desire for reconciliation with the Protestant majority in the neighboring British province of Northern Ireland.

The provision on the church, the repeal of which was supported by 85 per cent of the approximately 850,000 people who voted yesterday, has often been cited by Northern Ireland Protestants as one reason why they fear reunification with the independent Irish Republic, which is 95 per cent Catholic.

The provision reads: "The state recognizes the special position of the Holy Catholic Apostolic and the Roman Church as the guardian of the faith professed by the great majority of the citizens."

The immediate practical effect of the voters' decision to end the church's favored status is expected to be small, but it is generally regarded as a significant step toward social change and the evolution of a more secular state.

1.7 Million Were Eligible

Officials are talking privately of moving, perhaps within the next two or three years, toward lifting the prohibition against the import and sale of contraceptives. Legislation is being studied to allow couples in mixed marriages to adopt children. The officials acknowledge, however, that any attempt to remove the constitutional bar to divorce is as much as 15 or 20 years away.

"The decisive vote shows that there is a growing disposition for change among the people in this part of Ireland," said Mr. Lynch. "The results will strengthen the hand of all, in North and South, who are working for peace and reconciliation among all the people of Ireland."

By deciding to put the repeal to the voters, Mr. Lynch was attempting to demonstrate to the Protestants of Ulster that a united Ireland would not simply be an enlarged version of what they have always viewed as a republic dominated by the Catholic Church. Of Ulster's 1.5 million people, about two-thirds are Protestant.

While pleased with the margin of victory, Mr. Lynch and his ministers were disappointed by the low turnout. Only about 50 per cent of the 1.7 million eligible to vote in a population of 3 million went to the polls on the issue of the church and on a constitutional amendment lowering the voting age from 21 to 18. The result on voting age was also about 85 per cent in favor.

The officials, who expressed some concern that the turnout might be interpreted in the North as a lack of enthusiasm for concessions on the church's status, attributed the apathy largely to the absence of controversy surrounding the question. The opposition political parties supported the changes in the 35-year-old Constitution proposed by the Government.

In the view of Government ministers, who had hoped for a turnout of at least 60 per cent, many voters remained away because they saw the outcome as a foregone conclusion. The ministers insisted, however, that the margin of victory accurately reflected the views of the electorate.

"It is clear that had there been a higher poll there would have been a still higher rate in favor," Mr. Lynch commented.

Although the Catholic hierarchy as a unit declined to take a stand, William Cardinal Conway, Primate of both parts of Ireland, said more than three years ago that he would not oppose repeal of the special status.

The provision has been viewed by many as meaningless because it had no bearing on other church-influenced features of the society, such as censorship of books and films, contraception and a prohibition on the adoption of children in cases of mixed marriage.

Underlying the lack of widespread opposition in the church was the confidence that Catholicism is so deeply entrenched in the minds of so many that the provision served little purpose. Members of Parliament are well aware of the voters' convictions.

The vocal opposition was limited to a few archconservatives such as the Most Rev. Cornelius Lucey, Bishop of Cork and Ross, and a small group led by Desmond Broadberry, an accountant with 17 children.

Sitting dejectedly in a building where the votes were being tallied, Mr. Broadberry said: "I am depressed because I think this change represents the thin end of the wedge leading to divorce, contraception and abortion."

The next important vote comes in Northern Ireland early next year, when the people will be asked their views on the abolition or retention of the border. There is no doubt about the outcome, given the opposition of the Protestant majority to unity, but officials here hope it will clear the air for the long-awaited proposals by Britain to improve the situation of the

The I.R.A.

Catholics as part of an Ulster political reform.

Ulster Seems Indifferent

Special to The New York Times

BELFAST, Northern Ireland, Dec. 8—There was little interest in Northern Ireland in the referendum. The Protestants here seemed to regard the vote as a meaningless gesture.

The Protestants are strongly opposed to other articles in the republic's Constitution that are left unchanged, among them the claim to territorial sovereignty over all of Ireland and the ban on divorce. Even if the Constituion was rewritten, it would have no immediate effect on the Protestants' hostility to unity, under which, they fear, they would be submerged.

John Hume, leader of the moderate Social Democratic and Labor party, the major Ulster Opposition party, said the result was clear, decisive and satisfactory, although the vote was not so massive as he had hoped.

The Rev. Ian Paisley, the militant Protestant leader, said it would make no difference to Protestant attitudes. The sparse vote showed that the will of the Irish people to obtain unity was not strong, he added.

December 9, 1972

Catholic Funeral Cortege Raked by Ulster Gunmen

By ALVIN SHUSTER
Special to The New York Times

BELFAST, Northern Ireland, Feb. 7—Northern Ireland erupted in widespread violence today after gunmen fired into a procession of hundreds of Roman Catholics following the coffins of three members of the Provisional wing of the Irish Republican Army who were killed over the weekend by British troops.

Two people were injured in the procession, one an 11-year-old boy.

"They won't even let us bury our dead!" shouted Mrs. Josephine Osborne, a 34-year-old mother. "They're just scum!"

It was one of the ugliest days in months here. Aside from those wounded at the funeral, a British soldier was shot and eight gunmen were reported hit by fire from British troops. One Protestant died later and three unidentified bodies were found tonight. Also tonight, a fireman was shot fatally while fighting a fire in downtown Belfast. He was the first fireman killed on duty since the troubles began in 1969.

The rampant shooting, rioting, looting, arson and intimidation coincided with a one-day strike called by Protestant militant groups.

Just about everything stopped in Belfast except the fighting. There were only a few shops and schools open, and no newspapers, light, heat, buses or trains. Gunfire and explosions were heard throughout the day and into the night.

For security forces, one of the most ominous signs was the increase in activity by militant Protestants. Much of the gunfire and rioting seemed to come from Protestant extremists, angry over the detention of two of their supporters.

The Protestant extremists appear, by their show of strength, to be warning the British Government that they will not tolerate a "sellout" to the Catholic minority in the forthcoming proposals on the future of this troubled province.

Gun battles between Protestant terrorists and the army have been rare here. But today the army reported that fire from the troops had hit four Protestant gunmen after they had shot the soldier. It also said soldiers shot four gunmen in an exchange of fire in a Catholic area.

The army was thus finding itself in the nightmare it has long feared—being shot at by both sides. There are those in London who feel that if this trend continues demands could well arise within Britain to bring the troops home despite the official view that the absence of British soldiers would lead to severe bloodshed.

Protestant youths, who had gathered in protest at a police-army post in east Belfast, moved on to attack the home of a Catholic priest, the Rev. John Courtney, and then wrecked the inside of his church hall near a strongly Protestant area. Religious statues were carried into the street and destroyed.

'Army Saved Our Lives'

"The army saved our lives," said Miss Winnie McCrissican, the housekeeper, who hid in the house with Father Courtney. "We would have been killed if they had not come. I never prayed so hard in my life."

In other incidents, Protestants stoned a convent school for handicapped children, daubed Catholic homes with paint, and burned and looted several Catholic-owned stores near the center of the city.

Much of the day's drama, however, came during the funeral procession as it moved up Divis Street and the Lower Falls Road. At Conway Street, near the "peace line," separating the Protestant Shankhill Road area from the Catholic Falls Road, two bursts of automatic fire cut down the boy and a middle-aged man.

As many fell to the ground, the procession of young Provisional I.R.A. recruits closely following the three hearses remained erect and continued to march. Their faces were obscured by multicolored umbrellas to conceal their identity.

As the wounded lay on the ground, at least two others in the crowd dropped, apparently of heart attacks. The procession reformed and British troops, who had been not far away to keep the factions apart, rushed to the area.

A group of provisional I.R.A. gunmen nearby then opened fire toward the Protestant area. As the Protestants' gunfire faded, the troops and the provisional I.R.A. gunmen then exchanged shots.

The British troops increasingly have become the target for both sides. Militant Protestants, pointing to the recent detention of two members of the right-wing Ulster Defense Association, charge that the soldiers were too soft on the Catholics and that they themselves are being harassed. The Catholics allege that they are the victims of a "one-sided" military policy.

Whatever their views, William Whitelaw, who has administered Ulster since Britain suspended the Protestant-dominated Government here last March, said today that such demonstrations and violence would not influence British policy.

'Will Not Alter Course'

Clearly upset by the day's events, he said: "There have been many victims of widespread intimidation. The sick and the infirm have been seriously endangered. The burning and looting has been of the most disgraceful kind. The law is being applied impartially and we will not alter our course."

The one-day strike was called by William Craig, former Home Affairs Minister who is leader of the Vanguard Movement, a Protestant group, after British troops detained two Protestants under emergency powers for involvement in the tossing of a hand grenade into a busload of Catholic workmen, one of whom was killed. The detention law had previously been applied only to suspected Catholic terrorists.

February 8, 1973

LONDON IS SHAKEN BY TWO BOMBINGS LAID TO THE I.R.A.

By ALVIN SHUSTER
Special to The New York Times

LONDON, March 8—Terrorists struck in London today, setting off two large explosions, near Trafalgar Square and at the Old Bailey, the Central Criminal Court. One man was killed and 243 were injured.

Not since World War II had London seen such chaos. Windows in scores of buildings shattered, ambulances and fire engines screamed through London all afternoon and casualty wards in several hospitals quickly filled with the injured. By tonight, most of the injured had been treated for shock and cuts and released. About 20 remained for further treatment, some for severe injuries.

Both bombs, planted in automobiles, were believed by authorities to be the work of the Provisional wing of the Irish Republican Army. Officials said the blasts had clearly been timed to coincide with the referendum today in Northern Ireland, on whether the province should remain under British control. The I.R.A. opposes the referendum.

Two more car bombs were found and defused. One was found in front of the glass-walled New Scotland Yard building on Broadway, Victoria, and the other on Dean Stanley Street, near the headquarters of the British Forces Broadcasting System.

"They were all aimed at the military, police and the courts," an official said. "Our clear feeling is that it is the I.R.A."

Seven men and three women were detained tonight after police intensified security at

Heathrow, London's airport. All of those detained had been about to board planes for Belfast and Dublin.

The casualties would have been greater if there had not been telephoned warnings. A caller, said to have a slight Irish accent, gave The Times of London the location of three of the automobiles 45 minutes before the first blast.

The initial explosion, which startled tourists and Londoners in Trafalgar Square and Whitehall, came at 2:50 P.M. It was heard throughout the heart of London, and shook 10 Downing Street where Prime Minister Heath was preparing for his Thursday question-and-answer session in Parliament.

The car, containing gelignite explosives, had been parked before the British Army's central London recruiting office on Scotland Yard Street, a narrow lane just south of Trafalgar Square. The blast shattered windows of a nearby pub, of the Ministry of Agriculture and of other Government offices along Whitehall.

The second blast came shortly afterward in front of the Old Bailey, near St. Paul's Cathedral. The police tried to clear the area after the warnings, but they ran out of time.

Hurt on Way to Court

The injured included lawyers, judges and spectators arriving for the afternoon sessions of the historic Central Criminal Court. Many of the more than 180 injured were cut by glass from the windows of a nearby office building used by the Department of Trade and Industry.

A police photographer, who was taking pictures of the suspicious car as the area was cleared, was thrown across the street. A policeman was hurled against a wall and an unidentified man was seriously injured.

The Central Criminal Court was erected in 1902 on the site of the notorious Newgate Prison. Part of the wall of the prison, which dated from the 12th century, is embodied within the court, the setting for many celebrated trials. The central feature of the building is a dome, topped by a bronze gilt figure of Justice, with outstretched arms, holding a sword and scales.

All four bombs, including the two that were defused, had been set to go off an hour before Mr. Heath was scheduled to meet Liam Cosgrave, the new Prime Minister of the Irish Republic and a firm opponent of the Irish Republican Army, which supports unification of the predominantly Catholic Republic with the Province of Northern Ireland, where Protestants are in the majority.

Authorities said the bombings must have been planned well before the announcement of Mr. Cosgrave's visit, disclosed only two days ago. They said that the main purpose appeared to be to cast a shadow over the voting in Northern Ireland where Protestants, who outnumber Catholics by 2 to 1, are expected to give overwhelming support to the province's ties with Britain.

Moreover, the I.R.A. is intent on serving notice to the British Government that despite the blows it has taken from security forces, it still has the power to strike. So far during the recent troubles, it had confined its terrorism to Northern Ireland, with one exception. A car explosion 13 months ago killed seven persons at the sprawling military camp at Aldershot, 35 miles southwest of London. The Official wing, which denied responsibility for today's blasts, took credit for the Aldershot bombing.

5 Were Killed in '39

The shock in London reflects the rarity of such incidents in Britain. The Irish Republican Army, which split into the Official and the militant Provisional factions more than three years ago, has mounted only intermittent campaigns of violence here since it was formed in 1920 from elements of the Irish Volunteers.

The worst previous I.R.A. act here before Aldershot and today's attacks occurred in August, 1939, when five persons were killed in Coventry by a bomb left on a bicycle on a busy shopping street.

British officials have long feared the possibility that the terrorists would turn to Britain. Their concern tonight was whether this was a one-day attack, because of the Ulster voting, or the start of a campaign.

New security measures were imposed immediately in central London. Barricades went up at the entrance to Downing Street, keeping tourists from the traditional walk to the door of the Prime Minister's residence.

The explosions and bomb scares added chaos to a day of disruption caused by a rail strike. Because commuter trains were halted, the heart of London was clogged with automobiles, which complicated the search for bombs.

After the gelignite was found outside Scotland Yard headquarters, the police searched all the cars parked on Horse Guards Parade, between Downing Street and Whitehall. Normally only official cars are allowed to park there, but because of the transit strike the regulations were waived today.

At some of the hospitals treating the injured, nonmedical workers, also on strike, left their picket lines to go back inside and help.

The police said that special security measures, ordered because of the Ulster voting, led to the discovery this morning of the car outside Scotland Yard. Two police officers, members of a special patrol group, found a 150-pound gelignite bomb under the back seat of a stolen Ford Cortina.

John Gerrard, Deputy Assistant Commissioner of Police, pinned the blame on the I.R.A. and ordered the police to intensify their search for other bombs and to increase security at airports and ports. Everyone boarding a plane bound for Ireland was thoroughly checked.

London suffered a spate of bomb scares all day. Sir Alec Douglas-Home, the Foreign Secretary, was among those evacuated for a time from the Foreign Office. The Stock Exchange, Windsor Castle, the Times building and the control tower at Heathrow Airport were evacuated for brief periods.

The Royal Opera House, Covent Garden, was cleared just as the evening performance of the Royal Ballet was about to begin. A member of the staff went on stage and asked the audience to leave. The performance began 70 minutes late, after the police had searched the theater.

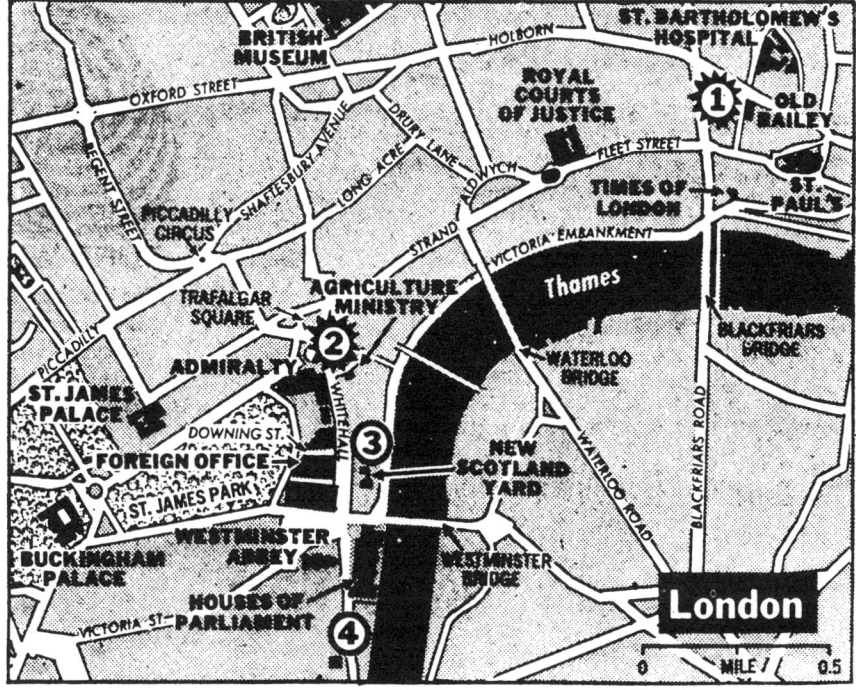

Explosions were set off near Old Bailey, the Central Criminal Court (1), and in the Whitehall area (2). Bombs were found and defused near the New Scotland Yard Building (3) and the headquarters of the British Forces Broadcasting System (4).

March 9, 1973

The I.R.A.

CARDINAL ASSAILS ULSTER ON KILLINGS

Special to The New York Times

BELFAST, Northern Ireland, Nov. 9—William Cardinal Conway, Roman Catholic Primate of All Ireland, said today that not enough was being done by authorities in Northern Ireland to combat what he described as "the campaign of slaughter and intimidation" against Catholics.

The Cardinal, in an official statement issued in Armagh, his ecclesiastical seat, said official measures to end the random assassinations of more than 200 people in two years had been "less than adequate."

The Cardinal's statement came after increased violence by extreme Protestants during the last two weeks. Three Catholics were killed for no seeming reason other than that they were Catholics.

Fifty of the 82 random assassination victims in the province so far this year have been Catholics. The two-year toll stands at 132 Catholics, and 72 Protestants.

"The base deeds of the Irish Republican Army do not justify the campaign of slaughter and intimidation now being waged against the Catholic population as such," Cardinal Conway said.

November 10, 1973

A Retarded Teen-Age Boy Killed in Northern Ireland

Special to The New York Times

BELFAST, Northern Ireland, Nov. 13—A 15-year-old retarded boy died in a hospital here today 15 hours after his abduction from a reform school. He had been shot in the head in a park in northern Belfast with a placard pinned to his clothing saying: "tout," the word used by the Irish Republican Army for "informer."

The boy, Bernard Teggart, and his twin brother, Gerard, Roman Catholics, were abducted at the same time. The reform school, in the predominantly Catholic western Belfast area, did not inform the security forces. An official inquiry has been ordered.

The boys' mother, whose husband was killed in a gun battle in Ballymurphy in August, 1971, said Gerard returned home in a state of shock yesterday. He said his brother had pleaded with the captors to let him—Gerard—go. The boys have been in the reformatory for five years. The slain boy had a mental age of 8, according to his mother. She said he had no connection with terrorism.

November 14, 1973

11-MAN EXECUTIVE TO RULE ULSTER UNDER NEW PACT

Cabinet Make-Up Disclosed—Protestants Are Given 6 Seats and Catholics 4

By RICHARD EDER
Special to The New York Times

LONDON, Nov. 22—The British Government disclosed today the details of the hard-won compromise reached yesterday under which moderate Protestant and Roman Catholic parties agreed to share power in Northern Ireland.

The Secretary of State for Ulster, William Whitelaw, the patient architect of the most important political advance in the shattered province since sectarian strife broke out five years ago, gave the details to the House of Commons.

The executive body to which Britain will entrust the province's affairs, reserving security, justice, foreign relations and some financial matters for herself, will consist of an 11-member inner cabinet plus four members without voting powers.

How Seats Will Be Divided

Six seats on the inner cabinet will go to the Unionist party, which represents about half the Protestant seats in the Assembly. Four will go to the Social Democratic and Labor party, which represents the Catholics, and one will go to the small, nonsectarian Alliance party.

The chief of the executive body will be Brian Faulkner, leader of the Unionists and former Prime Minister of the province. His party will have the finance, education, agriculture, information and public works portfolios. The deputy chief will be the Social Democratic and Labor leader, Gerald Fitt, and his party will get commerce, health and social security and housing.

The Alliance will receive the legal and law-reform portfolio.

Whitelaw Is Praised

Mr. Whitelaw was warmly praised on both sides, yet a few minutes after he started speaking the chamber was more than two-thirds empty. These five years of bloodshed—much of it British — have had the paradoxical effect of making Ulster a distant, almost shunned subject in Britain. Few people here are interested in talking about it any more, and this, despite the heavy national effort being expended there, seems to go for most members of Parliament.

Nevertheless, it was a personal and political victory for Mr. Whitelaw, who has served as minister for Northern Ireland for the last 20 months. As he spoke about the agreement, he was careful to temper his optimism.

"It's a start and a good start," he said, "but I think there's a very long way to go before we can be sure that what is a very new kind of political effort will succeed."

The firm Unionist majority was a considerable, and possibly last-minute, victory for Mr. Faulkner. It had first been thought that a 12-member inner cabinet would be set up, with one seat left vacant so that the Unionist majority could be ended at any moment.

If by accepting the strong Unionist position the Catholics made a considerable concession, both they and the British evidently considered it a necessary one. Mr. Faulkner is the only major Protestant figure willing to accept power-sharing and his decision to do so is weakening him steadily among his own followers. The arrangement announced today should bolster his position.

Mr. Whitelaw was asked at a news conference what concession the Unionists had made.

"Mr. Faulkner has, for the first time, agreed to sink his differences with the minority party and agreed to work together for the future of Northern Ireland," Mr. Whitelaw said. "That is an enormous 'give'."

It was apparent that he was recalling the bitterly held Protestant monopoly during Ulster's 50-year history when he continued:

"The S.D.L.P. has had an enormous success. If anyone had told them 18 months ago that they were to share in government to the degree they now will, they would have been very much surprised."

Mr. Whitelaw's assessment was bolstered by the satisfaction expressed by Social Democratic and Labor leaders and, perhaps more significantly, by the warm approval expressed in the Republic of Ireland both by the Government and the opposition.

The announcement was vague on two subjects on which the Catholic leaders were anxious to win concessions. It said little about changes in the police and, as for detention, said only that it would be ended when security conditions allowed. Mr. Whitelaw said, however, that he hoped to release some detained people by Christmas.

Mr. Whitelaw said that a conference would be held early next month attended by the British and Irish Governments and the leaders of the Northern Irish executive body. It will try to agree on the structure and powers of a Council of Ireland—an all-Irish link that could some day conceivably serve as a transition to a united Ireland. Not until the meeting is held will the new executive body actually take office.

November 23, 1973

TERRORISTS OR PATRIOTS

Dublin Acknowledges the Rule Of Britain in Northern Ireland

Special to The New York Times

DUBLIN, March 13—The Irish Republic's Prime Minister, in a landmark declaration, acknowledged today that neighboring Northern Ireland was a province under British control.

This statement, made to the Irish Parliament by Prime Minister Liam Cosgrave, was aimed at mollifying hard-line members of Northern Ireland's Protestant majority. They oppose the new provincial executive body, in which Protestants share power with Roman Catholics, and they also resist links with the Irish Republic through a new Council of Ireland.

In the recent British elections, such hard-liners won 11 of the 12 seats Northern Ireland is allotted in the British Parliament.

"The factual position of Northern Ireland is that it is within the United Kingdom, and my Government accept this as a fact," Mr. Cosgrave declared. No Irish political figure here has ever made such a statement so boldly before.

The "solemn declaration" made by Mr. Cosgrave on behalf of his Government was regarded by officials here as a clarification of the agreement reached at Sunningdale, near London, last December by the Prime Ministers of Britain and the Irish Republic and members of the Northern Ireland coalition executive.

The agreement, providing for an all-Ireland council with limited executive powers, sought to establish cross-border links between Northern Ireland and the Irish Republic as a means of ending bloodshed in the North. The original Irish Government declaration in the Sunningdale agreement referred to Northern Ireland as a separate entity but did not specifically say it was part of Britain.

Accord Tested in Court

Provisions of the Sunningdale agreement affecting the relationship between Northern Ireland and the Republic were challenged in the courts here recently, and doubts about the sincerity of Mr. Cosgrave and his Government were expressed at the time. The courts found that the agreement was constitutional and that it did not violate the Republic's aspiration for an ultimately united Ireland.

"I solemnly reaffirm," Mr. Cosgrave said today, "that the factual position of Northern Ireland within the United Kingdom cannot be changed except by a decision of the majority of the people of Northern Ireland."

The chief Opposition party, Fianna Fail, accepted Mr. Cosgrave's statement with some reservations. One member of Parliament who did not like it was Vivian de Valera, son of the 92-year-old Eamon de Valera, who recently retired as President of the Republic.

The younger Mr. de Valera said Mr. Cosgrave's statement came dangerously close to recognizing the right of a section of the Irish people to secede from the Irish nation. He said it was unlikely the statement would win new support for Ulster's Chief Minister, Brian Faulkner, and his moderate Unionist grouping, which is committed to sharing power with the Catholic minority in Northern Ireland.

Ratification to Be Sought

Foreign Minister Garret Fitzgerald conceded that the confusion caused by the court action here had hurt Mr. Faulkner politically. He said he would press to have the Sunningdale agreement formally ratified and then registered at the United Nations.

Mr. Cosgrave and his Government have been embarrassed by several recent events, including the assassination of a member of the Irish Senate yesterday.

The prisoner, Kenneth Littlejohn, escaped from Mountjoy Prison in Dublin. A 32-year-old Englishman, Mr. Littlejohn was serving a 30-year sentence for his part in a $160,000 bank robbery. He insisted at his trial last year that he had been acting on instructions from British intelligence witth the intention of discrediting the Irish Republican Army.

The assassination of Senator William Fox occurred near the border with Northern Ireland early yesterday. He was a Protestant, and his killers appear to be associated with the militant Provisional wing of the Irish Republican Army. Earlier confusion attributing the murder to Protestant militants from across the border resulted from what appears to have been a hoax telephone call.

The Provisionals have denied responsibility for the crime, but Irish authorities suspect them. Five young men from Clones, the town where Senator Fox was killed, appeared in a special criminal court today in connection with the crime. They were held without bail.

March 14, 1974

---

23 IN DUBLIN DIE AS BOMBS GO OFF DURING RUSH HOUR

Explosives in 3 Cars Cause Havoc in City Center —5 Killed Elsewhere

IRELAND'S WORST TOLL

By RICHARD EDER
Special to The New York Times

DUBLIN, May 17—At least 23 people were killed and about 80 were critically injured at the height of Dublin's rush hour tonight by bombs planted in three automobiles.

Shortly afterward, five people were killed and more than 20 injured in a bombing in Monaghan, a small town 80 miles to the north.

The bombs, carefully calculated to kill as many people as possible, according to Ireland's Communications Minister, Conor Cruse O'Brien, caused more casualties than any other attack since the fighting over Northern Ireland began five years ago.

For the people of the Irish Republic, almost untouched by the troubles, the scenes of death and mutilation among the rush-hour crowds of this pleasant and peaceful city brought the conflict suddenly and violently close.

Prime Minister's Message

Tonight the Irish Prime Minister, Liam Cosgrave, looking grim but collected, went on television to tell his people:

"This will help to bring home to us here in this part of our island what the people in Northern Ireland have been suffering for five long years. Today's evil deeds will only serve to strengthen the resolve of those north and south who have been working for peace."

Neither Mr. Cosgrave nor any other official has indicated which side is suspected of planting the bombs, but there is a widespread if unproven conviction in Dublin that it was the work of Protestant extremists. This was bolstered by reports that at least two of the cars used were stolen from Protestant areas of Belfast.

A spokesman for the militant Provisional Irish Republican Army said that his organization had had nothing to do with the bombings and denounced them as "vile."

The bombs in Dublin went off just before 5:30 P.M., when crowds coming out of work were thickest on the sidewalks. The explosions were timed so closely that most witnesses thought there had been only one.

May 18, 1974

The I.R.A.

ULSTER COALITION RESIGNS AS STRIKE CHOKES ECONOMY

Chief Minister Says Broad Public Support of Stoppage Forced the Decision

DEFEAT FOR MODERATES

By TERRY ROBARDS
Special to The New York Times

BELFAST, Northern Ireland, May 28—The coalition government of Northern Ireland collapsed today, setting off victory celebrations by extremist Protestant groups whose general strike has crippled the economy and interrupted power supplies throughout the province.

Public support for the strike, now in its 14th day, was so widespread that a majority of the power-sharing Executive, which was made up of Protestants and Roman Catholics, felt it could not continue as a representative governing body, according to Brian Faulkner, who resigned as Chief Minister.

The Executive had been heralded at its formation five months ago as the political organ that would open the way to a new era of cooperation and compromise between the Protestant majority and the Roman Catholic minority, which have been at odds for centuries.

Protestants Want Elections

Its failure today was immediately interpreted by political leaders in Ulster as a substantial setback in the efforts of the moderates on both sides of the sectarian line to end the violence and bloodshed that have devastated the province.

The collapse of the Executive is expected to lead to another period of direct rule by the British Government, pending the formation of a new provincial government—possibly after new elections, which the striking Protestants have demanded.

Merlyn Rees, British Secretary of State for Northern Ireland, flew from Belfast to London tonight and met with Prime Minister Wilson, who cut short a vacation in the Scilly Islands to hold consultations on the Ulster situation.

A spokesman for the Ulster Workers Council, which organized the protest strike, said the shutdown would continue until the strikers were given assurances that new elections would be called. However, the work reduction at the power stations was halted at the present level.

This means that electric power will continue to be made available for only about six hours a day. It also means that such vital services as water supply and sewage disposal will continue to be interrupted and that food shortages will go on.

The occupation of gasoline stations and oil storage depots at strategic points in Northern Ireland by British soldiers will also continue until the strike is called off. Troops took control of fuel distribution at dawn yesterday to assure that certain essential services and goods would remain available to the extent possible.

Military convoys patrolled the streets again today. At checkpoints set up at numerous intersections motorists were halted and their cars thoroughly searched for guns or bombs.

May 29, 1974

LONDON ADAMANT ON ULSTER FORCE

Administrator Says Those Who Ask Pullout Forget Risk of Sectarian War

By ALVIN SHUSTER
Special to The New York Times

LONDON, Nov. 10—Despite rising despair in England over the troubles in Northern Ireland, the British Government has no intention of moving to pull British troops out of the province or yielding to demands for setting a date for withdrawal.

In an interview, Merlyn Rees, the Secretary of State for Northern Ireland, acknowledged that public opinion in England "has had enough" of the sectarian violence in Ulster and the frustrations over finding solutions. But, he added, a withdrawal of the 15,000 troops would lead to a "real civil war" between the Roman Catholic minority and the Protestant majority of the province.

"It is all well to say that, politically, we have to get out and let the people there settle it themselves," Mr. Rees said in his office in the House of Commons. "But when you ask people who call for the pullout about the security situation, they have no answer. The point is that if we withdraw, then there would be serious trouble not confined to Northern Ireland—it could well spread to the Irish Republic and even to cities in England and Scotland."

Mr. Rees rejected proposals that Britain set a date for pulling out in hopes that the extremists of both sides in Ulster would realize that they would have to work together or die together. He said that to announce a withdrawal date would be the same as telling Protestant paramilitary forces that "It's over to you," and they would then take the law "into their own hands."

The 53-year-old Mr. Rees, who has been in charge of British policy in the province since the Labor party returned to power in February, thus sought to stem increasing demands in England for a drastic shift in policy that would bring the troops home. The "Troops Out Movement," including at least six Labor Members of Parliament, has been formed to campaign for a withdrawal in view of the "abysmal failure" of British policy.

The campaign has picked up strength, given the general weariness of the British over the pictures and stories of daily violence in the province and the difficulties in finding a political solution. In Northern Ireland, as well as in the rest of Britain, many have come to the conclusion that Britain has run out of ideas and plans nothing more than indefinite direct rule from London.

4 Soldiers Die in Week

Since 1969, when the fighting began and British troops moved in, 229 soldiers have been killed and nearly 1,400 wounded. In the last week alone, four British soldiers were killed in Ulster.

Meanwhile, the bombing by members of the Provisional wing of the Irish Republican Army has spread to England with an outbreak of explosions in pubs and clubs. In the last 18 months, there have been more than 200 bombings here, and 20 lives have been lost.

Mr. Rees said that the stepped-up I.R.A. campaign in England could well spur pleas to pull out the troops. But, he added, it could also serve to harden attitudes among the British and lead to proposals for tougher action in Northern Ireland and tougher penalties for the terrorists.

He seemed confident, however, that the demands for a troop withdrawal could be kept under control. This depended, he said, in part on what the politicians in Britain said, noting the continuing unity of policy on the issue of Opposition Conservatives and the Labor party.

Rees Sees Slight Letup

Although, from the news reports, the violence never seems to ebb, Mr. Rees said there has been a decline in recent months. "The killings are less, the shootings are less and the bombings less," he said. "I am not suggesting that the security forces are winning the battle but I am saying that it can be held."

Mr. Rees deplored the continuing flow of money from Irish Americans to the gunmen of the I.R.A. He said the contributions from the United States were often misguided because much of the money, ostensibly for humanitarian purposes, feeding and clothing Catholics, has been used to support violence in the province.

In discussing the frustrations in finding a political settlement, the administrator agreed that the latest British plan faced formidable hurdles. Still, he said, there was a "strong chance that it will get somewhere."

November 11, 1974

17 Die as Bombs Destroy 2 British Pubs

Special to The New York Times

LONDON, Nov. 21 — Bombs destroyed two crowded pubs in the heart of Birmingham tonight, killing 17 persons and injuring about 120. Many of them were teen-agers.

It was the worst attack in the series of bombings that have hit Britain over the past two years, an offshoot of the violence in Northern Ireland.

The explosions came at 8:30, bringing death and mutilation to the city's Bull Ring, a glass and steel complex threaded with multilevel roads and ramps that serves as a shopping and business zone by day and an entertainment area at night.

Prime Minister Harold Wilson spoke with Home Secretary Roy Jenkins upon hearing the news. Mr. Jenkins is expected to go to Birmingham tomorrow. Mr. Wilson also sent a telegram to the Lord Mayor of Birmingham saying that he and his colleagues were "profoundly shocked to learn of the outrages which have been committed in Birmingham this evening."

The Government's attention, centered almost totally on the critical economic situation, seems likely now to be wrenched back to the growing threat posed by the intractable Northern Ireland situation.

No immediate statements were issued naming the group responsible for the bombings, but there was little doubt that it was the work of the Provisional wing of the Irish Republican Army. The police rounded up a number of members of Sinn Fein—the guerrilla organization's political arm—in Birmingham, and an "amber" alert went out from Scotland Yard to police forces around the country, signaling them to provide added protection for sites and persons thought to be potential targets of the Irish Republican Army.

Four days ago David O'Connell, a leader of the Irish Republican Army Provisionals, warned in a television interview that violence would be stepped up in Britain. He said that in the case of economic and military targets no warnings would be given. Tonight's warning, phoned by a man with an Irish accent to The Birmingham Post, came only minutes before the first bomb went off.

Brendan Magill, leader of the Provisional Sinn Fein in Britain, called the bombings "disgraceful." He added, however, that it was his policy to neither condemn nor condone such events in Britain. He also said that he did not speak for the Irish Republican Army.

Bomb Thrown at Church

In what appeared to be an isolated militant reaction to the terrorist attacks, a gasoline bomb was thrown at the presbytery of a Roman Catholic church in Aston, an industrial area in the city, Britain's second-largest, with a population of over 1.2 million. The bomb caused little damage and no one was hurt.

The bombings occurred as a British Airways plane waited at Birmingham's Elmdon airport to fly to Belfast the body of James McDade, a guerrilla who blew himself up in a bomb attack in Coventry a week ago. Two other cities in the industrial Midlands were hit at the same time.

The police, backed up by a Government order, had forbidden a planned march to the airport by the Sinn Fein. Tonight's bombings will be interpreted as a response to the ban.

Protestant workers at Belfast's airport had announced their refusal to unload the coffin—a reflection of the savage and endless cut and thrust of the Ulster conflict. Tonight, while ambulances, volunteer taxi drivers and private citizens were taking the shattered victims of the downtown bombings to hospitals, Mr. McDade's body was transferred to an Aer Lingus plane and flown to Dublin.

November 22, 1974

British Enact Laws To Outlaw the I.R.A. And Bolster Police

Special to The New York Times

LONDON, Nov. 29—Legislation outlawing the Irish Republican Army and giving the police unprecedented power to fight terrorism in Britain became law today.

The laws, which authorize the police to search and detain suspected terrorists and to impose curbs on travel between England and Ireland, were approved early this morning without opposition by the House of Commons after a 17-hour session.

Under the new laws, more rigorous controls on travelers from Ireland will be introduced at ports and airports, and Mr. Jenkins will have the power to refuse entry or to order expulsion of suspected terrorists or accomplices.

The measures, proposed only days after 20 persons were killed in two pub bombings in Birmingham, also ban any public display of support for the I.R.A. and the wearing of its traditional parade uniform, black trousers and shirt, beret and sunglasses.

Punishment for anyone belonging to, supporting financially or aiding in any other way an illegal organization under the new laws ranges up to a five-year prison sentence and an unlimited fine.

November 30, 1974

Most Catholics in Ulster Believe That I.R.A.'s Terrorism Is Doing More Harm Than Good

By RICHARD EDER
Special to The New York Times

NEWRY, Northern Ireland— Sunday afternoon it was wet and windy, and 7-year-old Patrick Toner, glued to the television set, almost forgot that it was time to take the cows back up to pasture.

Sunday television is pretty dull, devoted to agricultural programs among other things, and before long a shot of cattle flashed on the screen. Patrick rushed out, taking a friend, Anthony Higgins, with him.

The Toner house, with its nearby cattle shed, is in the tiny hamlet of Forkhill, set in the hilly country just north of the border with the Irish Republic. The I.R.A. Provisionals move freely here, counting on the shelter of the border and the strong republican sympathies of the overwhelmingly Roman Catholic population.

Anthony went ahead to open the gate into the field. Just as Patrick and the six cows cleared the last house in the village, a British Army patrol shouted at him to turn back. They were about 100 yards off, examining a car full of explosives they had towed from beside the police station.

Villagers Were Bitter

Patrick tried to turn the cows. As he stepped off the road an explosion almost underfoot nearly tore his head off.

Next afternoon, as villagers waited to go to the hospital to accompany Patrick's body home for the wake, they were bitter. What particularly outraged them was that the bomb seems to have been set off deliberately; wires led from the crater to a hiding place up the hill.

Patrick Toner's death hit people here harder than most of the 1,100 deaths claimed by five years of violence. Catholics were especially angry. There was already distress in the community because the Provisionals had ignored appeals from all sides and announced the end of their Christmas cease-fire.

But talks were still going on and a tacit semi-cease-fire continued. The killing of the little boy seemed another example of the mindless bungling that has done much in the last three years to estrange the Provisionals from the people they claim to represent.

The considered opinion of the Provisionals among most Catholics—excluding the minority of convinced supporters and a kind of hero worship among the very young—is not that they are wicked or savage, as most Protestants understandably believe; it is that they are disastrously stupid in both tac-

The I.R.A.

tics and strategy.

"We are all Republicans here," a Forkhill woman said. "But we will not forgive them for this. They come from around these parts. And even if they didn't see Patrick, they know that where cows are being driven you always find children."

The goal of a united Ireland is shared by most Catholics, and even those who have few illusions that it can soon be attained sympathize with those who risk their lives to fight for it. There is also a lurking awareness that should civil war ever come, the Provisionals would be a nucleus for a Catholic fighting force.

Most Catholics, including those most critical of the Provisionals, believe that they do not as a rule seek to kill civilians; their object, rather, is to kill soldiers and policemen and judges and to disrupt life by blowing up buildings. Certainly the thousands of bombings would have claimed infinitely more victims if the Provisionals' policy was not to give warnings in advance.

Warnings Badly Given

But warnings are sometimes not given or badly given, and panic, bad judgment and sheer incompetence cause tragedies such as the death of Patrick Toner and the killing of 19 people in Birmingham last fall.

If Catholics often reproach the Provisionals for clumsiness, the deeper objection is not so much to their tactics as to their strategy. Unless the Catholic community is willing to face a civil war, the argument goes, the only possibility is to reach agreement with the Protestants. Provisional spokesmen say they are fighting the British, not the Protestants, but to the Protestants the bombings and shootings seem ultimately aimed at themselves.

The futility of it is put by Frank Lynn, a Catholic storekeeper in the seaside village of Cushendall.

"If the loyalists had tried to shoot or bomb the Catholics out of Northern Ireland, they'd just have got our backs up," he said. "Similarly, there must be sensible men among the I.R.A., but how they propose to bomb the loyalists into a united Ireland I can't see."

The Catholics' republican tradition has more or less been to dismiss the Protestant majority in the North by thinking of them, even though they have been here nearly 400 years, as agents of British colonialism or by arguing that they would be better off in a united Ireland and that their objections to the process can therefore be ignored.

Miriam Daly, a professor of economics at Queens University, Belfast, and something of an intellectual spokesman for the Provisionals' point of view, said in a conversation: "The Protestants can continue to play a colonial role or not. I agree that they have the right not to speak Irish, but they don't have the right to stay in Ireland and not be Irish."

Most Catholics are only too aware, after five years of violent conflict, of the reality of Protestant feelings and of the strength of Protestant arms. That the Protestants are a power in themselves, not simply living off British strength, came sharply into focus last April when they ran a strike—against the British—paralyzed the province and badly frightened the Catholics.

There are signs, in fact, that some I.R.A. Provisional leaders have begun to share this realization and to ask questions about the tactical value of their campaign. Presumably the questions lay behind their decision to call a cease-fire and a rejection of the questions behind its temporary abandonment.

There has been a decided shift of Catholic opinion since the current troubles began. As the minority, and the group more immediately exposed to the consequences of confrontation, the shift—from an emphasis on refighting past battles to a concern with avoiding future battles—may be more apparent here than on the Protestant side.

There is still an ambiguity of loyalties: the inclination to shrug off the complexities of finding a solution and go back to the destructive, let-it-all-rip gaiety that a dreadful history has made into an Irish reflex.

On Side of Compromise

That attitude is brought out by Eamonn McCann in his book, "War and an Irish Town," which quotes a Londonderry Catholic after the Provos bombed the Guildhall. Though the man was a moderate and opposed the Provisionals, he said: "Of course I don't agree with this bombing at all, but I must admit the Guildhall's looking well."

Whatever its views, most of the Catholic community has given its backing to a political leadership that, however divided and prone to self-doubt and ventures into intransigence, is undeniably on the side of compromise.

The Social Democratic and Labor party was the Catholic partner in the effort at constitutional agreement set up by the British two years ago. The brief coalition government, based on power sharing between the communities and a link to the South through the Council of Ireland, collapsed when the Protestants abandoned their moderate leaders last April and struck.

Abandoning Old Positions

The party survived. Furthermore, it is moving away from two positions that seemed to be essential to any group claiming Catholic support but that made agreement with the Protestants nearly impossible. At a well-attended party conference in Belfast, the demand for institutional links to the South was heavily watered down; at the same time there was strong backing for a demand that new thought be given to the party's previously adamant stand against cooperating with the Protestant-dominated Royal Ulster Constabulary.

One evening not long ago a young Catholic urban planner, Tony Kennedy, was reflecting on a wispy recollection that, in its way, says a lot about how Catholic attitudes have changed.

When he went off to Britain to study, a group of friends accompanied him to the ferry. They all had quite a bit to drink, and as he boarded one called after him: "Take off a few of them over there for me, will you."

"That," Mr. Kennedy related, "was the sort of thing you said in those days, before there was any trouble. Nowadays, after all that's happened, nobody would dream of saying something like that."

— February 25, 1975

London Bombings: Now the Richer Targets

By ROBERT B. SEMPLE Jr.
Special to The New York Times

LONDON, Nov. 14—The terrorists of the Irish Republican Army are choosing more fashionable targets these days.

Where once they sought their victims in pubs, department stores and subway stations, they are aiming now at London's prosperous West End, an area that includes some of the people and places with which American tourists tend to identify this city.

Since Aug. 27, when London bombings flared up again after a shadowy eight-month silence, one explosive has been set off in the London Hilton, another in front of a Member of Parliament's house where Caroline Kennedy happened to be staying, still another near a fashionable Italian restaurant in Mayfair.

One bomb was discovered in time in front of the residence of former Prime Minister Edward Heath in a high-priced neighborhood known as Belgravia. Another was found in front of Lockett's, a restaurant near Parliament frequented by politicians. The explosion Wednesday night at Scott's—the bomb was an antipersonnel device packed with ball bearings and it killed one man and injured 15 other persons—fit the pattern. Scott's is one of the most elegant restaurants in town.

In the eyes of Government officials and of the inspectors of Scotland Yard, a bomb is a bomb, whether it goes off among rich or poor. But the terrorists' change of social venue has, in the official view, more than passing significance.

I.R.A. Seen Losing Hold

"We have never had any doubt that the people responsible for the London bombings are members of the Provisional wing of the I.R.A.," an official said, "but the West End bombings represent a new twist in their constant search for publicity and thus an escalation of their pressure on the British Government to remove its forces from Ireland."

In the minds of people close to Roy Jenkins, the Home Secretary, who has responsibility for domestic peacekeeping, the bombings reinforce the view that the I.R.A.'s central command, which is theoretically committed to maintaining a cease-fire here and in Ireland, has lost control over its more militant members. This, in turn, has made officials increasingly pessimistic about the chances for a peaceful political settlement in the British province of Northern Ireland.

The bombings have persuaded Mr. Jenkins and others that the Government must ask the next session of Parliament, beginning next week, for an extension of the Prevention of Terrorism Act, which gives the police unusually broad powers of detention and surveillance.

Finally, the bombings have brought a small but perceptible change in the practices of people who do business in London. "We're carrying on," says Reginald March, director of the

254

company that owns the Mirabelle, a popular and expensive restaurant in Curzon Street. "I think they'll find it hard to bomb people out of the West End."

Wire Mesh and Padlocks

But his resolve has not prevented Mr. March from ordering changes at the Mirabelle. After last month's incident at Lockett's, the Mirabelle installed wire mesh on its windows, put up floodlights out front and installed padlocks on the rear doors. The company took similar precautions at two other West End restaurants that it owns.

Meanwhile, hotels are warning guests to keep their curtains closed for protection against flying glass; the British Museum outinely, if politely, inspects handbags and brief cases at its entrances; restaurants ask guests not to take parcels of any kind to their tables.

The Government had hoped that the cease-fire with the I.R.A. in Northern Ireland, dating to last Feb. 10, would create an atmosphere in which a political solution could finally be achieved between the majority Protestants and the minority Roman Catholics of the province. But while politicians have been meeting and arguing —a report of the Northern Ireland Convention will be presented to Parliament in the next session—the killing has gone on unabated.

214 Ulster Lives in '75

Terrorism has cost 214 lives in Ulster this year, only two fewer than in the whole of 1974.

Strictly speaking, Mr. Jenkins will not seek an extension of the 1974 Terrorism Act but a formal ratification of its powers in a new bill. The Home Secretary's view is that merely to ask for an extension of present legislation would not provide the issue with the prominence it requires; the introduction of a fresh bill, by contrast, will focus attention not only on the legislation but also on the violence it is meant to arrest.

November 15, 1975

Detention Without Trial Ended in Ulster

Special to The New York Times

LONDON, Dec. 5—Britain today announced the end of its controversial policy of detaining terrorist suspects in Northern Ireland without trial.

It released the last 46 people held under the policy, which was adopted in August 1971, from the Maze Prison near Belfast.

"As from today," Merlyn Rees, Secretary of State for Northern Ireland declared, "no one is held under a detention order."

Mr. Rees pledged in July that the detention policy would end by Christmas if the security situation in Northern Ireland improved.

There has been a fragile cease-fire formally in effect since the British Government and the Provisional Irish Republican Army agreed to it a year ago, but bombings and killings have continued throughout the year.

Today, however, a Government official said here that detention without trial—with its bitter harvest in accusations of unfairness and brutality — had "outlived its usefulness." In the four years and four months since detention was introduced, 1,981 men and women have been held without trial.

This year, 1,260 persons have been tried on charges connected with terrorism. "This is the accepted and tested method that we want to use instead of detention," Mr. Rees said in the House of Commons yesterday.

In a statement issued today here and in Belfast, Mr. Rees said that it was now up to the leaders of the Protestant majority and the Roman Catholic minority of Northern Ireland to see that there would be no need to restore the detention policy—a policy that was instituted in the hope of curbing terrorist activity.

The end of the detention policy was welcomed by both the Rev. Ian Paisley, the hardline Protestant leader, and Gerry Fitt, head of the principally Catholic Social Democratic and Labor Party. The two men said the move deprived the I.R.A. Provisionals of a prime emotional issue.

At the same time, the British Conservative Party, which was in power when the detention policy was introduced, condemned its abolition as "dangerous for the people of Northern Ireland."

No immediate comment was available from the Belfast branch of the Provisionals. In Dublin, the political wing of the I.R.A. Provisionals, the Provisional Sinn Fein, issued a statement saying:

"It comes as no surprise that Mr. Rees has now ended the present phase of internment. His timing is geared toward whitewashing the British system of justice at a time when the Dublin regime is pushing the criminal law jurisdiction bill through Parliament."

The Primate of All Ireland. William Cardinal Conway, said it had been "a wise decision" to end detention, which has "cost too much in human lives and human suffering."

The policy of detention without trial was authorized in 1971 by then Prime Minister Edward Heath, a Conservative. It had been urged on him by Brian Faulkner, then the Prime Minister of Northern Ireland, and British army commanders there.

The rationale that the army and police gave at the time, was that suspects could not be put on trial because witnesses were too scared to testify in court. In several cases key witnesses to bombings and shooting were themselves killed.

Within two hours of the detention decree, the security apparatus picked up 377 men. Most of those held under the detention power, were said to have been Catholic republicans, but 107 Protestants have spent some time in prison. The last Protestant was released in March. Thirty-three women, all republicans, have been imprisoned as terrorist suspects.

The reduction in the Maze's population began in June, with the cease-fire agreement between London and the Provisional I. R. A.

Today's decree does not totally close down the Maze. Twenty-five prisoners remain, serving sentences imposed by courts of law.

Mr. Rees, in his statement, said that the rule of law would now be imposed "impartially and firmly through the courts."

"I do not want to go back to detention," he said. "The real responsibility rests with the people of Northern Ireland—above all with the minority community—and not with me. Many people on both sides of the community pressed for it to go. It is their responsibility to see that it does not return."

Mr. Faulkner, now heading a tiny fraction of the split Unionist Party, called the ending of detention "an appalling gamble."

In general there has been a bipartisan approach to the problems of Northern Ireland by the governing Labor Party and the Conservatives.

The Conservative statement deploring the end of the detention policy came from Airey Neave, the party spokesman on Ulster affairs, after he had consulted the party leader, Margaret Thatcher.

Mr. Fitt denounced detention as "the biggest single political disaster during the present troubles," causing "outrage and resentment among the minority community."

Mr. Paisley, said: "Detention without trial threw the entire Roman Catholic population into the hands of the I.R.A. It was the best bonus the I.R.A. ever received."

December 6, 1975

WILSON DENOUNCES U.S. HELP FOR I.R.A.

By BERNARD WEINRAUB
Special to The New York Times

LONDON, Dec. 17—Prime Minister Harold Wilson, in an unusual attack on "misguided Irish-American supporters" of the Irish Republican Army, said tonight that American funds were largely responsible for the terrorism in Northern Ireland.

"The fact is that most of the modern weapons now reaching the terrorists in Northern Ireland are of American origin—possibly as much as 85 per cent of them," Mr. Wilson said. "They are bought in the United States, and they are bought with American-donated money."

Mr. Wilson spoke before the annual dinner of the Association of American Correspondents in London. The speech, devoted solely to American support for the I.R.A., cited the Irish Northern Aid Committee as the principal fund-raising organization in the United States for the outlawed army. The committee, with headquarters in the Bronx, has strongly denied that relief funds for Roman Catholic women and children in Ulster are earmarked for weapons.

'Financing Murder'

The Prime Minister said: "Those who subscribe to the Irish Northern Aid Committee are not financing the welfare of the Irish people, as they might delude themselves. They are financing murder.

"When they contribute their

The I.R.A.

dollars for the old country, they are not helping their much-loved shamrock to flower. They are splashing blood on it. Nor are they helping the minority Catholic population."

It was the strongest denunciation by a British Prime Minister of the American group, and of support among Americans for the I.R.A.

Mr. Wilson said of the conflict in Northern Ireland: "Over 1,000 men, women and children, including babes in arms, have been murdered—blown up in shops or in cars, shot in lonely houses, mown down in the bars and clubs of Belfast, Londonderry and elsewhere.

"In addition about 16,000 soldiers and civilians have been injured or maimed in this campaign, most of them in the bombing, but some of them —by the barbaric practice of shooting away the kneecaps of the victim, perhaps leaving him crippled for life.'

Ammunition Smuggled

Speaking before the 60 correspondents, he continued: "It must be clearly understood in the United States that American money, the million and more dollars that have flowed from there to Ireland since 1971 have directly financed these murders, this maiming, this indiscriminate bombing, as have ammunition smuggled illegally from the United States to Ulster and to the Irish Republic."

"Let me ask this question," he said. "How would the American people react if a British-based organization subscribed a million dollars to, say, finance terrorists in a campaign of murder and bombing within the United States against the people of the United States. Still more if a thousand innocent and politically uninvolved citizens had died as a result?"

The Irish Northern Aid Committee has said that $1.2 million has been raised since 1971 and channeled into relief work for the families of prisoners, mostly I.R.A. members. The money is raised through dinners, dances and bar collections in New York, Boston, Chicago, Philadelphia, Baltimore, San Francisco and other cities. Authorities in Dublin, London and Washington say that the organization's official accounting is too low, and that $2 million to $3 million has been raised.

Mr. Wilson paid tribute to what he termed "the real representatives of the Catholic people in Ireland, North and South," who have condemned the traffic in arms. He cited the Social Democratic and Labor Party, the predominately Catholic party in Ulster, and two of its key figures, Gerry Fitt of Belfast and John Hume of Londonderry.

He also paid tribute to Catholic clergymen as well as Prime Minister Liam Cosgrave of Ireland and his predecessor, John Lynch.

Mr. Wilson asked the American correspondents to "strip away the romantic legends, the myths of 1916 and all that, to which the I.R.A. still so calculatedly cling."

"You can tell the people back home that the killers of today have nothing remotely in common with patriots of 60 years ago," he said. "That the men of the I.R.A. are to the men of the Easter Rising what Al Capone was to Garibaldi. That they are prolonging the agony of Ireland, and so are all of those who support them from afar."

The Easter Rising in 1916 led to the guerrilla war against the British and independence for the 26 counties in the South. The northern six counties of Ulster, predominately Protestant, remained in British hands.

December 18, 1975

Tomorrow's Patriots

To the Editor:

Prime Minister Harold Wilson speaking before the Association of American Correspondents in London (Dec. 17), stated in an effort to curb fund raising by Irish-Americans that the I.R.A. "killers of today have nothing remotely in common with the patriots of sixty years ago." Why then, may I ask, did the English Government of 1916 see fit to execute over a dozen of these "patriots," whom Mr. Wilson now praises? They must have done some evil deed (in English eyes) to provoke such terrible retribution.

That same Government referred to Eamon DeValera as a "murderer . . . with blood on his hands." Yet world leaders paid their final respects to this man, whose recent death ended his dream of a united Ireland fulfilled in his time. It appears that Irish patriots of every generation have been denounced as killers and murderers by successive English governments, as were the Americans in 1776.

The transformation from killer to patriot seems to be a matter of time and accomplishment. Sixty years from now, I picture a British Prime Minister speaking before an Irish-American audience extolling the I.R.A. of the 1970's—who drove the English from Ireland forever and ended the career of the tyrant, Harold Wilson.

There is only one difference between the Irish freedom fighters of today and those of sixty years ago: This time they intend to finish the job.
PETER REICHENBERG
Rego Park, N.Y., Dec. 18, 1975

December 29, 1975

Ulster Group Declares It Murdered 10 In Retaliation for Slaying of Catholics

By ROBERT B. SEMPLE, Jr.
Special to The New York Times

BELFAST, Northern Ireland, Jan. 6 — A group calling itself the South Armagh Republican Action Force claimed responsibility for the machine-gunning to death of 10 Protestants last night, saying it was in retaliation for the murder of five Roman Catholic men in two separate incidents in the same part of Ulster the night before.

The claim was made by a man who said he was a representative of the group in a telephone call to The Belfast Telegraph early this morning. The police would not comment on the claim but said they had picked up four suspects for questioning.

There was little doubt in the minds of Protestant leaders, however, that the Provisional Irish Republican Army — with which the so-called "Action Force" identified itself—was responsible for the massacre. After an emergency meeting this morning between Government officials and leaders of various Northern Ireland political factions, Protestant leaders asserted unanimously that the Government had failed to provide sufficient protection. One of them warned of open retaliation.

Glen Barr, chairman of a committee that coordinates Protestant paramilitary activities, said he was under great pressure to "go on the military offensive" against I.R.A. terrorists.

"We can see no way of avoiding a civil war situation," Mr. Barr declared, unless the Government increases what he described as its "inadequate" security force in southern Armagh, where the killings took place.

Two other Protestant leaders —the Rev. Ian Paisley and Brian Faulkner—made essentially the same points. It was not immediately clear whether today's decision by Prime Minister Harold Wilson of Britain to send an additional 600 soldiers to Northern Ireland would satisfy any Protestant leader.

About the only hopeful sign in an otherwise quickly deteriorating situation was Mr. Paisley's announcement that the Ulster Workers Council had yet to decide whether to take action in the present crisis. The council — Protestant group — used strike tactics to bring down Ulster's last attempt at a coalition government in 1974. The council is expected to meet tomorrow.

Otherwise, the atmosphere was one of fear and gloom. There were those who thought that while a fresh supply of British troops might temporarily passify some Protestant leaders, it might at the same time worsen the situation by giving the I.R.A. an excuse to destroy the last vestiges of a year-long cease-fire that has already become a mockery.

I.R.A.'s Position on Truce

The I.R.A. has long asserted that it agreed to the cease-fire in the first place in exchange for an unwritten Government pledge not to introduce any more troops. Accordingly, there were some here who believed that the introduction of these troops, far from decreasing the possibility of new violence, might in fact increase it.

The Protestant leaders ex-

TERRORISTS OR PATRIOTS

pressed their views after an emergency meeting called by the Secretary of State for Northern Ireland, Merlyn Rees, this morning. Mr. Rees then flew to London to confer with Mr. Wilson and to discuss the Government's decision to send more troops.

Meanwhile in Dublin the Justice Minister, Patrick Cooney, announced today he would confer with Mr. Rees in London on Thursday. He said here that the meeting had been arranged some weeks ago, but obviously the "terrible events" of recent days would have high priority. The two men last met in October 1974 and agreed then on closer cooperation between the police forces in both parts of the island. On Thursday, Mr. Cooney said, they will again discuss common measures to defeat terrorism.

Police Power Limited

But he echoed Mr. Rees's comments after last night's massacre in suggesting there was a limit to what the police could do on their own. He said the communities in the north themselves would have to bring the violence to an end. This would require "full and total cooperation on both sides of the border with the security forces," Mr. Cooney declared.

Hitherto many Catholics in the North who do not support the I.R.A. have refused to help either the police or the British Army.

Mr. Cooney acknowledged that the Government was extremely alarmed by the latest killings. One must wonder if we are all on the brink of a terrible holocaust," he declared. He said he could only hope that the communities, having come face to face with the prospect, would now reject the murderers.

As to the identity of those responsible for the latest massacre, he dismissed the claim issued in the name of the South Armagh Republican Action Force as a piece of subterfuge by the I.R.A. "We get all sorts of euphemisms to cover well-known terrorist organizations," he said. "I think it's a Provisional I.R.A. murder."

January 7, 1976

BRITAIN GIVES UP ON ULSTER TALKS, WILL RETAIN RULE

Convention Elected to Work Out Political Reconciliation Is Ordered Dissolved

NO SOLUTION IS IN SIGHT

Protestant Majority Spurns Any Sharing of Power With the Catholics

By BERNARD WEINRAUB
Special to The New York Times

LONDON, March 5—The British Government, faced with the collapse of efforts to politically reconcile Protestants and Roman Catholics in Northern Ireland, announced plans today to run the province indefinitely.

Britain's Secretary of State for Northern Ireland, Merlyn Rees, told the House of Commons that the 78-seat Northern Ireland Convention — elected last May to work out a political arrangement among Catholics and Protestants—would be dissolved at midnight tonight, and that the British would run Ulster "for some time to come."

Bitter Recriminations

Mr. Rees told the somber Parliament:

"It is clearly not possible to make progress toward a devolved system of government for Northern Ireland. My strongly held view is that there is no instant solution to the problems of Northern Ireland. It would be a grave mistake to pretend that there was one, let alone to rush forward with some new devices."

What led to the failure of the elected Convention—amid bitter recriminations—was the refusal by the Protestant majority to share political power with the Catholic politicians in any future Ulster government. At this point, the British are committed to giving the Catholic minority a say in running the province.

A Lack of Support

"The Convention was born out of a belief that the people of Northern Ireland themselves ought to have the chance to play a constructive part in seeking a solution to their constitutional problems, in the knowledge that final decisions were for Parliament at Westminster," said the British Cabinet official. "The Convention did not, however, agree on the central issue —that is, how, in a divided community, a system of government could be devised which would have sufficient support in both parts of that community to provide stable and effective government."

The expected announcement angered militant Protestants in Ulster who charged that the will of the majority had been rejected by the British. Key Protestant politicians, led by the Rev. Ian Paisley, insist that Protestants control security and government in the province, and reject any decision-making role for the Catholics.

The Irish Republican Army was also furious at the announcement, viewing it as a reaffirmation that Britain intended to remain in Northern Ireland. The I.R.A. has traditionally sought to remove the British from the north, and erase the border between Ulster and the predominantly Catholic Irish Republic in the south.

Moderate Catholic and Protestant politicians in the north, as well as the Irish Government, supported Britain's plans to run Ulster as long as power-sharing seemed out of the question.

Within the six counties of Northern Ireland, Protestants retain a two-thirds majority, and have controlled the political and economic life of the province for more than 50 years. Until 1972 Britain played a secondary, if supportive, role.

In March 1972, following Catholic civil-rights marches, attacks on soldiers and the police and the wholesale internment of Catholics without trial, the British faced a breakdown of law and order in Ulster and assumed responsibility for the province.

Since then Britain has sought, without success, to extricate itself from power in Northern Ireland and to work out a political arrangement that would blunt extremists on both sides and create a Catholic-Protestant coalition. Militant Protestants fear that a compromise with Catholics would lead to a loosening of the border with the Irish Republic.

March 6, 1976

Britain's Envoy in Dublin Killed by Mine

By BERNARD WEINRAUB
Special to The New York Times

DUBLIN, July 21—The British Ambassador to Ireland, Christopher T. E. Ewart-Biggs, was killed today when a land mine was detonated beneath his moving car, about 150 yards from his official residence on the southern outskirts of Dublin.

The blast, which blew a crater 10 feet deep in the road and smashed the car, also killed a 26-year-old secretary, Judith Cooke, who was riding in the front seat of the vehicle.

Two other persons in the car were seriously injured. They are Brian Cubbon, the Permanent Under Secretary of State to the Northern Ireland Office in Belfast, the top British civil servant in Ulster, and Brian O'Driscoll, the ambassador's chauffeur. The police said later that they were out of danger.

"This atrocity fills all decent Irish people with a sense of shame," said Prime Minister Liam Cosgrave, who called an emergency session of the Irish Cabinet after the attack.

[In London, Prime Minister James Callaghan said that those who had assassinated Ambassador Ewart-Biggs were the common enemy of the Irish and British peoples and must be destroyed. In a statement to the House of Commons, Mr. Callaghan said: "These miserable men are the common enemy of both Governments and indeed of all decent people who wish to live in peace and amity in all our islands."]

Later, the Irish Government offered a reward of £20,000 for information leading to the

257

The I.R.A.

arrest of the killers.

According to the police, Ambassador Ewart-Biggs and Mr. Cubbon were on their way to a meeting with the Irish Foreign Minister, Garret FitzGerald, when the blast occurred at 9:32 A.M. The car, a black Jaguar, was hurled high into the air and landed on its roof, trapping the occupants.

It was believed that the land mine, packed with 50 to 100 pounds of explosives, had been set in a culvert beneath the deserted road and detonated by a group of men hiding about 200 yards away, on a hillside covered with high grass and wild scrub.

Security sources said that the police had found a wire leading from the crater to the field. Three men who appeared to be in their mid-20's—two of them carrying rifles — were seen dashing away after the blast by local residents.

By tonight, with flags across Dublin and the rest of Ireland at half staff, Irish plainclothesmen were setting up elaborate security checks at airports, railroad stations and roads in the hunt for the killers.

Although the Irish Republican Army Provisionals remained silent about the blast, the police and Justice Department officials assumed that the killers either were linked to the I.R.A. or were a part of a breakaway group. The assassination itself was clearly well planned and timed with split-second accuracy.

The Irish Government, which has sought in the last two years to blunt the I.R.A. by legal means and thwart the flow of money that pours in from the United States, was stunned by the killings. It sent messages of shock and condolence to Queen Elizabeth II and Prime Minister James Callaghan.

July 22, 1976

DUBLIN PREPARES SWEEPING CURBS AGAINST THE I.R.A.

Would Increase Jail Terms Sharply and Widen Police Powers of Detention

TERRORIST 'CHALLENGE'

By BERNARD WEINRAUB
Special to The New York Times

DUBLIN, Aug. 31—The Irish Government moved today to increase drastically prison sentences for members of the Irish Republican Army and to impose emergency legislation to quell suspected terrorists. The proposed legislation was the most sweeping aimed at the I.R.A. in 50 years.

Prime Minister Liam Cosgrave, in a somber and blunt address to the Irish Parliament, said that the I.R.A. now represented "a direct challenge" to the nation and was an "armed organization dedicated to the overthrow of the institutions of this state."

"The crimes perpetuated by men of violence have brought discredit to the name of Irishmen throughout the world and death and damage to our own people," Mr. Cosgrave said. "Our past has been devalued and our future threatened by their outrages."

Envoy's Killing Cited

Mr. Cosgrave, who termed the I.R.A. "the conspiracy of hate and evil," cited the killings last month of the British Ambassador to Ireland, Christopher Ewart-Biggs, and Judith Cooke, a British civil servant, as a key reason for the proposed legislation.

Mr. Cosgrave said that the deaths of two British officials—who were killed when a bomb was detonated beneath their moving car near Dublin—as well as a series of explosions last month at a special Criminal Court in Dublin, set up to deal with the I.R.A., served to underline the fact that the group was now operating "in a new and menacing fashion."

"The murder of the British Ambassador struck at the conduct of our foreign relations while the explosions struck directly at the administration of justice," Mr. Cosgrave said. "The challenge thus posed called for an unequivocal response."

Warning of Danger

He added: "The challenge is from a body operating within the state but organized on a 32-county basis and with a substantial armed membership in Northern Ireland. In the Government's view, the situation requires that the Government should be able to take emergency powers to whatever extent may be necessary to crush the armed conspiracy against lives and democratic government which faces the nation."

September 1, 1976

30,000 IN ULSTER MARCH FOR PEACE

Women's Rally Is Free of Protest by I.R.A.

LONDONDERRY, Northern Ireland, Sept. 4 (AP)—A crowd of Roman Catholic and Protestant women thought to number about 30,000 met today on a bridge that divides the two sections of Londonderry to call for an end to seven years of sectarian violence in Northern Ireland.

The fourth peace march in as many weeks was the first not disturbed by jeers and stone-throwing by supporters of the Irish Republican Army.

The I.R.A. issued a statement before the rally saying it respected the right of the women to demonstrate for peace, but it cautioned them to "remember the struggle of the past years and do not call for peace at any price—a surrender in fact."

It was a significant change for the Irish Republican Army, which in past weeks had labeled the women "traitors to Ireland." The I.R.A. has been fighting to force the British out of the Protestant-dominated province and to join it to the mostly Catholic Irish Republic.

A 45-Minute Rally

The emotional rally lasted about 45 minutes. Thousands of women poured into Londonderry from all over Northern Ireland and from the Irish Republic in more than 50 buses, two special trains and many cars. The Catholics gathered on the west bank of the Foyle River, which divides the city, and the Protestants on the east bank.

Singing the hymn, "Abide With Me," the groups marched onto the 60-foot-wide bridge toward each other. Some carried white banners saying "Peace, Now" and "Stop the Violence." The atmosphere was tense and emotional. Tears were streaming down the faces of many women.

Betty Williams, who started the peace campaign last month, and Mairead Corrigan, her deputy, threw their arms around two Protestant women. Mrs. Williams, a 32-year-old Catholic housewife from Belfast, began organizing the marches after three children were killed when they were hit by a car driven by an I.R.A. gunman being chased by policemen.

Since the fighting began in 1969 at least 1,614 people have died in Northern Ireland in bombings, assassinations and battles between the Irish Republican Army and British soldiers.

September 5, 1976

I.R.A. Propaganda Move Criticizes Peace Marchers

BELFAST, Northern Ireland, Oct. 9 (AP) —The Irish Republican Army began a propaganda campaign today against the women's peace movement, but thousands of Protestants and Roman Catholics continued peace rallies here, in the Irish Republic and in England.

A spokesman in Dublin for the Provisional Sinn Fein, political arm of the I.R.A., said the poster and leaflet campaign was intended to persuade people that the peace movement is "one-sided and deceptive." Mrs. Betty Williams, founder of the peace movement, said she would not be deterred by the propaganda effort.

The Provisional Sinn Fein spokesman said the propaganda campaign would not include interference with peace marches. The I.R.A. leaflets being distributed in

Catholic slums in the north accuse the women of betraying the Catholic minority, being tools of the British government and duping thousands of well-meaning people.

Demonstrators rallied and marched today in Armagh and Downpatrick and at Leeds in England. More than 5,000 persons turned out for the Leeds rally, the police said.

BELFAST, Northern Ireland, Oct 9 (Reuters)—A woman was killed and four people were injured today when a wave of bombings hit the Northern Irish market town of Ballymena. Ballymena, 25 miles northwest of here, was sealed off after eight bombs exploded in and around the center of the town. A woman died when a firebomb exploded in a boutique.

Local police suggested the injured persons might have been planting the bombs, which were thought to be the work of the Provisional wing of the Irish Republican Army.

October 10, 1976

I.R.A. Aide Slain in Belfast Hospital

BELFAST, Northern Ireland, Oct. 28 (UPI)—Maire Drumm, former vice president of the Provisional Sinn Fein, political wing of the Irish Republican Army Provisionals, was shot to death tonight in her bed at Belfast's Mater Hospital.

The police said three youths, one dressed in a white hospital coat, had walked into the ward where Mrs. Drumm was recuperating from eye surgery and shot her while she lay in her bed. Another woman sitting by her bed was wounded in the leg. Mrs. Drumm, aged 53, had been hospitalized for three weeks.

The Mater Hospital, Belfast's sole Roman Catholic voluntary hospital, is in the Crumlin Road, a predominantly Protestant area, a half-mile from the city center.

The police declined to say whether the woman wounded in the leg was a patient or a visitor.

Mrs. Drumm, her husband, Jimmy, and their two sons and three daughters were all strong supporters of Northern Ireland's Republican movement.

She was detained for three weeks recently under a charge of incitement to hatred following a speech at a rally in Belfast in which she said the city would be destroyed brick by brick. She was released without being brought to trial.

One of Mrs. Drumm's daughters is serving a seven-year sentence in Armagh jail on an arms charge.

A Northern Ireland official once said Mrs. Drumm's presence at Republican rallies seemed inevitably to spark off rioting on the streets.

And Britain's former Northern Ireland Secretary, Merlyn Rees, described her, after she gloated over the killing of British soldiers, as like a woman knitting by the guillotine.

Earlier in the day, gunmen shot two part-time soldiers of the Ulster Defense Regiment in separate incidents, killing one and seriously wounding the other.

Gunmen ambushed and killed the first soldier as he returned to his home from his job as a mailman in the village of Altmore, near Pomeroy, about 40 miles northwest of Belfast. The man's wife said two gunmen held her in their home while others waited outside and killed the mailman at pointblank range.

He was the 60th Ulster Defense Regiment soldier killed since the regiment was founded in 1970, and the ninth killed this year.

The other man was shot and seriously wounded on the doorstep of his home in Londonderry when he answered a ring at the door. The police said two youths armed with automatic pistols had fired six shots at him, hitting him in the chest and stomach.

October 29, 1976

The Awarding Last Week of Nobel Prizes to Two Women Who Lead the Peace Movement Couldn't Hurt

The 'Troubles' In Ulster May, Just May, Be Easing a Bit

By SEAN DUIGNAN

DUBLIN—The award of the Nobel Peace Prize to the Northern Ireland peace movement leaders, Mairead Corrigan and Betty Williams, comes at a time of optimism that the "troubles" may soon end. But peace hopes have been dashed so often since the outbreak of violence in 1969 that there's understandable official reluctance even to speculate about the possibility of a cease-fire by the Provisional wing of the Irish Republican Army, and sources in the group describe the rumors as propaganda. However, the speculation persists, particularly in Belfast, fueled mainly by antiterrorist successes by security forces on both sides of the border between the North and the Republic of Ireland.

The Provisionals' campaign is at its lowest ebb since 1971. The assassinations, explosions and car-bombings which have wracked the North for the last few years have been reduced although there are still sporadic attacks on British Army and Royal Ulster Constabulary personnel. Civilian casualties have recently dwindled to a trickle. The month of September passed without any civilian deaths, a fact proudly proclaimed by Roy Mason, Britain's Secretary for Northern Ireland. The security forces' success is reflected in the growing number of suspects being arraigned before the Northen Irish courts as well as a sharp rise in the number of convictions being obtained. All this has particularly affected the Provisionals but it has also drastically curtailed the activities of Protestant paramilitary organizations such as the Ulster Defence Association and the Ulster Volunteer Force.

An increased flow of information from both sides of the community divide in Northern Ireland is a primary cause of the transformed security situation. In Belfast, many observers say the flow began to be significant soon after the establishment of the peace movement in August of last year, particularly from the Roman Catholic ghettos which are the traditional havens of the Republican Army. At the time, many Catholic members of the peace movement publicly debated the moral question of "turning informer," of providing information to the distrusted Constabulary which could lead to the arrest of boys and girls from their own tightly knit communities. Peace movement leaders advised that such a decision had to be left to individual consciences. Soon afterward there was a substantial increase in the amount of information being received over the confi-

The I.R.A.

dential police telephones.

Police and Special Branch infiltration of paramilitary organizations, especially of Protestant groups, was also a factor and the Provisionals are also believed to be having difficulty in obtaining chemical components for bomb-making. Lack of money is thought to be the Provisionals' most urgent difficulty. The American-Irish, individually and through various organizations in the United States, have been the most important financial supporters of the Republican Army in the past. Soon after "bloody Sunday" in January, 1972, when 13 Catholics were killed by British paratroopers in the Northern Ireland city of Derry, the flow of money from the United States increased spectacularly.

There have been various estimates of this cash-flow at its peak. Republican Army sources hint vaguely at "millions" of dollars being received each year. Recently a United States Justice Department official said donations reported by the Irish Northern Aid Committee alone were as high as $1 million in 1971 but had now shrunk to about $100,000 a year. British Government officials say the donations may now be as low as $30,000 a year. Whatever the correct figure, there's little doubt that there's been a drastic reduction in the contributions. This is due in considerable degree to the concerted efforts of Irish Government emissaries to the United States and American-Irish politicians such as Thomas P. O'Neill Jr., Speaker of the House of Representatives, and Senators Edward Kennedy and Daniel Moynihan, and Governor Carey of New York. Their combined denunciation of the Provisionals and the use of violence in Northern Ireland is thought to have significantly affected American-Irish opinion over the past year.

It is accepted by British and Irish Government sources that the American financial support for the Republican Army can never be completely stopped. However, it is hoped to keep it to a minimum through a continuing program of anti-Provisional publicity in the United States.

Protestant paramilitary funds from outside Northern Ireland are believed to mainly originate in Scotland and Canada. These "Protestant kinfolk" contributions from abroad are not believed to be remotely as significant for illegal Protestant organizations as the American-Irish "donations" have been to the Republican Army.

Despite the reverses, the Provisionals' position remains that there can be no peace without a declaration of intent from the British Government to withdraw from Ireland. There is insistent speculation in Belfast, however, that the Provisionals might be prepared to declare at least a temporary cease-fire to allow for possible political initiatives.

Meanwhile, the political deadlock in Northern Ireland continues. The bipartisan British and Irish Government policies of "no devolved government without power-sharing between the communities" is still rejected by the political representatives of the Protestant community. Prime Minister James Callaghan of Britain is reluctant to mount a British political initiative mainly because of his present precarious majority in the House of Commons. He relies on Liberal Party and Protestant Ulster Unionist votes to stay in office. But Prime Minister Jack Lynch of Ireland is under no such restrictions. His Fianna Fail Party swept to victory in Ireland's June elections and he now enjoys the largest parliamentary majority in the history of the republic. In recent London talks with Mr. Callaghan he re-emphasized his belief in the eventual reunification of Ireland by peaceful consent.

A united Ireland was also the goal of Mr. Lynch's predecessors in office, the coalition Government of Liam Cosgrave. But the new Irish administration came to power with an additional policy, to seek an ordered withdrawal by the British from Northern Ireland. Some of Mr. Lynch's political opponents, notably a former cabinet minister, Conor Cruise O'Brien, have pointed to the similarity between this doctrine and the aims of the Provisionals, and Dr. O'Brien has regularly charged that some elements of the ruling Fianna Fail Party are "soft" on the Republican Army. Mr. Lynch rejects these allegations. He says that the most effective of the republic's tough antiterrorist laws were framed by his party when last in government and that the vital difference between his policies and those of the Republican Army is that he rejects the use of violence.

Mr. Lynch is also concentrating on obtaining international support for his objectives, particularly through Ireland's membership of the European Economic Community and its links with the United States. He places particular emphasis on President Carter's recent offer of financial aid to Northern Ireland if both communities there could agree to a peaceful settlement. "Simply to campaign against violence is too negative an approach to a fundamental problem," said Mr. Lynch last week. "There must be political action as well."

Sean Duignan is a political correspondent for Irish Radio and Television and writes frequently for The New York Times.

October 16, 1977

I.R.A., Far From Broken, Mounts a New Campaign

By ROY REED
Special to The New York Times

BELFAST, Northern Ireland—Britain is grappling with an embarrassing paradox in its Northern Ireland problem. The harder it attacks the anti-British terrorists, the tougher they become.

Near Christmastime, the British quietly began saying that they thought they had defeated the Provisional Irish Republican Army, the chief remaining terrorist group in Northern Ireland. Then the Provisionals found a new source of arms and started a new campaign of shooting, burning and bombing—an efficient, nerve-shattering campaign that demonstrated how far they were from being disorganized and broken.

Four persons were killed in one week recently and although the I.R.A. has taken responsibility for only two of the killings, it is being widely blamed for the other two as well.

The Provisionals have burned and bombed more than $50 million worth of property in the last three months. The British Government, which makes good on terrorist losses, will pick up the bill.

Declining Support

In the face of increased military pressure and in spite of declining support in war-weary Roman Catholic communities, the Irish Republican Army has proved once more that it can strike almost at will.

"Defeat of the I.R.A. is wishful thinking," a middle-aged Catholic priest said the other day. "I don't believe a body of armed citizens can be defeated in these circumstances."

The men of violence once tended to drift away after a few years of "troubles." But now, after nine years of killing and the maturing of an entire generation, the Irish Republican Army seems to have become a permanent terrorist force, a small but deadly fact of life in the Catholic slums of industrial Ulster.

Its enemies in the British Army and the police concede that it is tightly organized with small, secure cells that make the leaders almost impossible to trap.

Keeps Finding New Arms

It has shown repeatedly that it has the imagination and skill to turn up new sources of arms and explosives, no matter how often the old sources are blocked.

Most important for the future, it continues to tap the bottomless pool of anger among Irish nationalists, those who, no matter how their numbers swell or shrink, never forget their bitterness at the British presence on this island. That anger is most inflammable among the young.

Some critics say the I.R.A. has become a children's army. They say that so many

TERRORISTS OR PATRIOTS

of its regulars are in prison that it has to turn to teen-agers to carry its bombs and its newly acquired American-made machine guns. The youngsters, they say, are manipulated by a little band of experienced "godfathers" who make the plans but never risk their own lives.

Friends of the Irish Republican Army deny that. But they acknowledge that as always they are working to draw vigorous young people to their cause.

Interviewed in Dublin

Recently in a room in Dublin, a group of men who are knowledgeable about the Provisional I.R.A. and the republican movement gathered for an interview with The New York Times.

The leader was Ruairi O'Bradaigh, the president of Sinn Fein, the legal political wing of the Provisional movement. Sinn Fein operates in both the Republic of Ireland and the six counties of Northern Ireland. Its chief aim is British withdrawal from the island.

Among the others were Joe Cahill, who has served time in prison for actions against the British, and a young Belfast leader named Ted Howell. Mr. Cahill is now a vice president of Sinn Fein. Mr. Howell is in charge of foreign affairs for the party.

The Provisionals attracted the more militaristic members after a split in the I.R.A. some years ago. The Officials, as the other group is called, tend to be Marxist. They have been only peripherally involved in the violence.

'War Is Going Well'

"The war is going well," Mr. O'Bradaigh, a genial, middle-aged man, said. "People have come through a rough decade. They've suffered a lot. But now they're coming out of their corner again. They've been clobbered by a superior force, but they're not beaten."

They said Sinn Fein was trying to strengthen its political side so it would be ready to pursue its long-term aims when the war ended. Those aims include a federal system of government with Ulster as one of the republic's provinces and reforms such as the breakup of large estates and land redistribution.

There has been speculation that the Provisionals are split by a hawks-doves debate, with older men in the Republic favoring a shift from violence to politics and younger men in Belfast insisting on continuing the fight. Some believe the hawks are in the ascendancy, as evidenced by the renewed campaign here this winter. The men in Dublin simply chuckled at the speculation.

Mr. Howell, a long-bearded man with the look and language of a professor, talked of Britain's efforts to isolate the Provisional movement from the Catholic community. He noted that 1,500 men and women had been imprisoned for terrorist offenses in Britain, Northern Ireland and the Republic.

"The Brits have been unsuccessful because the people identify with the republican movement," he said. "People have been imprisoned, but they continue to work for the movement. The only way they can stop us is to lock us all up."

The British authorities, while not ready to agree with Mr. Howell, are increasingly frustrated as they try to root out the Irish Republican Army.

The British Army and the Royal Ulster Constabulary have recently renewed their efforts to destroy what they see as the group's political infrastructure. The I.R.A. and Sinn Fein operate several "advice centers," offices where people can seek help on problems with housing, health and other matters. They also run newspapers, youth clubs and, like their Protestant counterparts, illegal drinking places called shebeens.

The police have cracked down on shebeens. Community workers among troops and policemen are trying to overturn the republican influence in youth clubs and advice centers. Troops recently raided the republican newspaper and information office here and picked up 17 persons for questioning.

Authorities Seek Support

In addition to raiding offices, chasing gunmen and defusing bombs, the authorities have also started a campaign that is reminiscent of the United States effort in Vietnam to "win the hearts and minds of the people."

Both the soldiers and the police, the latter mostly Ulster Protestants, have put community workers into the tough neighborhoods to try to persuade people to accept the Government's law-and-order forces.

Some of this effort has been successful. Ordinary policemen now patrol many Catholic areas where only soldiers dared go a year ago. But they patrol mainly in armored vehicles, and the soldiers are never far away.

The British Army reports that it is slowly gaining trust in Catholic areas. A few soldiers received presents from Catholic residents at Christmas. More important, army intelligence is getting more tips on the identities and hiding places of young I.R.A. members.

People who see the Catholic slum residents every day say many are tired of the violence and no longer see any point in it. But there is also an old feeling that it might be a mistake to get rid of the Irish Republican Army, for defenders just might be needed again to fight off Protestant rowdies and vigilantes. Protestant terrorists have been relatively inactive since last spring, but no one believes they have been converted to pacifism.

Several public figures recently have condemned the I.R.A. for having lured young people into its ranks and having sent them to do the dirty work. Every week's court calendar lists teen-agers being tried for terrorism.

Police figures indicate that while no greater numbers of young people seem to be joining the terrorists, a larger proportion of the serious acts are being carried out by them. In 1974, for example, 11 terrorist killings and attempted killings were charged to people under 18 years of age. The number last year was 43.

'Godfathers' Criticized

The latest voice raised against the "godfathers" was that of a teacher and politician in southern Armagh County, an I.R.A. stronghold. Seamus Mallon, chairman of the constituency representatives of the predominantly Catholic Social Democratic and Labor Party, said the "godfathers" were cowards who used naive youngsters and then let them take the punishment.

He said in an interview later that his public stand had produced threats against him. He said he had spoken out because five students from his school had been charged with murder and arson. All were under 17 and two were 15.

"One of the most alarming things is that these are not the type who were going into the I.R.A. three or four years ago," he said. "A substantial number now are clever kids, university potential. In the past, they tended to be emotionally committed. Now, some are more ideologically committed."

They will probably be even more committed after a few years in Long Kesh Prison here. Long Kesh has been a kind of institution of higher learning for guerrillas since the turn of the century. The place has been filled for the last several years, and many inmates are completing their sentences. Every month a few more graduates go back into action.

February 13, 1978

THE F.A.L.N.

FOR ALLIANCE WITH ENGLAND.

The Rev. J. F. Carson Also Advocates the Annexation of Cuba, Puerto Rico, and the Philippines.

The Rev. J. F. Carson, pastor of the Central Presbyterian Church, at Jefferson and Marcy Avenues, Brooklyn, preached a sermon on the war last night, in which he advocated the annexation of Cuba, as well as of the Philippines and Puerto Rico. He also advocated an English alliance, and said: "The repulse of to-day is the incentive of to-morrow." His text was Joshua xi., 23— "And Joshua took the whole land, and the land rested from war." The whole church was ablaze with American, British, and Cuban flags.

After rehearsing the causes of the war and defending America's right to intervene in Cuba's behalf, Mr. Carson said:

"Let it not be forgotten that America's intervention is in the interest of peace. By cannon and by sword America will set the oppressed free, and if need be let business stand still. Let the revenue tax be imposed upon every article. Let treasure be poured forth. The high, the supreme business of this Republic, now that this war has been undertaken, is to end Spanish rule in America, and if to do that it is necessary to plant the Stars and Stripes on Cuba, Puerto Rico, the Philippines, or Spain itself, America will do it, and will keep the standard floating there till freedom and peace are secured.

"Through this war America enters upon

The F.A.L.N.

a new epoch in her march of progress. The Republic will emerge from this war with a new and enlarged responsibility. Henceforth she shall be one of the arbiters of the destiny of the world. With the Philippine Islands as an American colony, with Hawaii annexed, with Cuba and Puerto Rico under American control, the Republic will enter upon a new era of National progress and greatness and of international significance and power.

"No longer shall we be a hermit Nation. We have a world-wide mission, a mission which we shall fulfill in alliance and cheerful co-operation with other English-speaking peoples. This war has revealed that almost our only friend in Europe is England. She would not join us in freeing Cuba, but let any nation interfere with us in our duty and in twenty-four hours English ships would be at our side, and the Union Jack and the Stars and Stripes would move forward together."

July 4, 1898

PUERTO RICO AS A PERMANENT POSSESSION.

By AMOS K. FISKE.

There can be no question to perplex any reasonable mind about the wisdom of taking possession of the Island of Puerto Rico and keeping it for all time. There has been the same depressing misrule there as in Cuba, and the only reason why there has not been the same revolt against it is that the case was hopeless. The comparatively small and compact territory and the military weakness of the population have enabled Spain to crush out any attempt with merciless promptitude. At the same time she has taxed the little colony to help put down insurrection in Cuba as well as to enrich the Spanish officials. There can be no doubt that the people of the island, very few of whom are Spanish by birth, would rejoice to be relieved of the oppressive and exhausting rule of Spain, although they have been powerless to resist it, and have hardly dared to give vent to a desire to be rid of it.

There is the same reason for driving the corrupt despotism of Spain out of Puerto Rico as for driving it out of Cuba, save for the melancholy difference between a hopeless submission to wrong and a hopeless struggle against it. The former condition is, indeed, the worse, for the cruelties practiced in trying to suppress chronic revolt excite sympathy and provoke interference from which rescue may come, while the deadening misery of hopeless submission may be allowed to go on forever. It is fortunate for Puerto Rico that Spanish outrages in Cuba have brought about an intervention which will rescue both islands at once. We are under a pledge to leave the fate of Cuba in the keeping of her own people when the Spanish sovereignty over them shall have been destroyed. They have created a claim to this by their own long and costly struggles for independence and by their own part in achieving it, and they have only to justify the claim by proving themselves capable of self-government and worthy of their heritage in order to become a free and prosperous nation. If they find themselves unable to do this, they may yet call upon the United States to take charge of their future destiny, and that may in the long run be better for them.

But we shall free Puerto Rico from Spanish rule practically without any effort on the part of its own people, and at our own proper cost as an incident of the contest to expel it from Cuba. This result is necessary to make that expulsion complete and lasting, for to be rid of the Spanish disturbance to civilization in the Western World, Spain must be thrust from her last foothold on American soil. We are not pledged to give Puerto Rico independence, and she will have done nothing to entitle her to it at our hands. Besides, it would be much better for her to come at once under the beneficent sway of the United States than to engage in doubtful experiments at self-government, and there is reason to believe that her people would prefer it. It would be in accordance with the genius of our institutions to accord them self-government in local affairs as soon and as far as they showed themselves capable of it, and experience would soon teach them how much they had gained by their providential escape from the cruel stepmother country.

The circumstances of the conflict for the enfranchisement of Cuba and Puerto Rico fully entitle us to retain the latter as a permanent possession. Our need of a foothold in the West Indies for naval purposes has long been recognized, and it is now more obvious than ever before. We have made efforts to secure it on the Island of San Domingo which were rendered futile by circumstances that we need not now recall. Once we secured it, so far as negotiation and agreement went, in the Danish Island of St. Thomas, and lost it again by the fatuous conduct of Congress in refusing to ratify the bargain, to the just resentment of Denmark and the humiliation of our Government in the eyes of its own people and of the world. Now we have it within our grasp in a far better form, with Congress and the people in a mood for taking and keeping it, and with every just and proper consideration in favor of our doing so.

As a naval station, the Harbor of San Juan de Puerto Rico is preferable in location to the Bay of Samana, Mole St. Nicholas, or any other place on the Island of San Domingo, and to Charlotte Amalia, the port of St. Thomas. Of the advantage of possessing all the land to which a naval station is appurtenant there can be no doubt. Puerto Rico occupies the central place on the eastern frontier of the great American archipelago, the outpost of the Greater Antilles, and the watch tower between the Bahamas and the Caribbees. The Mona Passage on the west and the Virgin Passage on the east are pathways to the South American coast. It is a commanding position between the two continents of the west, and upon the island rampart between the Atlantic Ocean and the Caribbean Sea. The most deliberate choice of a naval station in the West Indies could not have placed it better than the course of events, which has put the Island of Puerto Rico at our disposal.

And it is an island well worth having—the real gem of the Antilles. A little more than a hundred miles long and a little less than forty miles wide, it has nearly the area of Connecticut. In spite of misrule, exhausting taxation, and a backward state of industry, it is a populous island, having more than 800,000 inhabitants, or about as many as Connecticut. This is because the soil is most prolific and the climate exceptionally salubrious; and twice as many people could live there in ease and comfort. Except for the irregular eastern end, Puerto Rico is almost a parallelogram; and while there are bays and harbors at convenient distances all around its shores, the coast is less broken and less obstructed by reefs than those of any other considerable island in the West Indies. It has no large cities, but many small towns and villages, and the population is well distributed. San Juan, the chief port on the northern shore, has barely 25,000 inhabitants, and Ponce, near the southern coast, the largest and wealthiest city on the island, has less than 40,000.

The chief physical characteristic of Puerto Rico is its variegated and well-watered surface. The Sierra Cayey sweeps from west to east, though nearer the southern than the northern coast, with an average height of 1,500 feet, and, isolated from it in the northeast, the picturesque Triquillo culminates in the peak called El Yunke, "the anvil," some 3,600 feet above the level of the sea. From the long low mountain range many ridges start forth, with wooded slopes, fertile valleys, and broad, rich plains, and there are more than a "thousand hills." Only here and there are the altitudes too great for cultivation, and the variety of level, with rich soil nearly everywhere, affords unusual possibilities of production. There are said to be 1,300 running streams on this island, of which 47 are considerable rivers, and yet one of the needs of the southern slope is irrigation, and one of the drawbacks of the towns is a lack of water supply. Nature's supply is unlimited, but man has not known how to utilize it. The real need is enterprise and industry.

Of the commercial value of Puerto Rico as a possession there is no possibility of doubt. Under a government that discouraged enterprise and prevented improvement, with an almost complete lack of roads and bridges in the interior to make communication and transportation economical, with primitive methods of cultivation and practically no manufactures, and with a stifling system of taxation and official corruption, it has supported a relatively large population and had a foreign trade of $35,000,000 a year. What is it not capable of under an enlightened policy and with a systematic application of enterprise and industry? The mountain forests contain mahogany, ebony, logwood, and other ornamental and useful materials, which may be so dealt with as to become a permanent and inexhaustible source of wealth. The upper ranges of land afford the richest pasturage, and even now the raising of horses, cattle, and sheep is a leading industry. The same levels are capable of producing great crops of fine cereals. Frost never comes, and the raising of tropical fruits can be extended indefinitely. The abundant rains are brought chiefly by the northeast trade winds, and the short southern slope of the mountain range is subject to occasional drought, but the soil is rich and may be easily irrigated. In the lower valleys and the stretches of plain near the seacoast the soil has an almost unexampled fertility.

What have been regarded as the staple crops are sugar, coffee, and tobacco, but they have been raised in a crude fashion and upon a scale that can be enormously extended. As elsewhere, the cane sugar interest has been under a depression on account of the European subsidizing of beet sugar, but by improved methods and economies it can compete against this disadvantage, while the coffee culture could be vastly increased with certainty of profit. It has been the custom to send tobacco to Havana to be manufactured, and there has been little system in its cultivation. The quality is inferior to that of Cuba only because it has not been properly dealt with. A cotton grows in Puerto Rico which has an exceptionally long and strong white fibre, but little has been made of it. Rice is produced without flooding the land, and Indian corn grows luxuriantly. A continuous succession of crops can be raised throughout the year on account of the richness of the soil and the genial and equable climate.

The climate is tropical, but there are no extremes of heat, save here and there and now and then on the lower coast lands. The idea that a tropical climate is of necessity unhealthful or enervating is a delusion. It breeds disease only where there is a neglect of sanitary conditions and disregard of hygienic considerations. In San Juan, as in Havana, there is no system of drainage and little attention to cleanliness, and the penalty of fever is the consequence. The same is true of other towns similarly situated. There is no proper attention to the distribution of wholesome supplies of water in cities and towns, though it would be an easy and inexpensive matter. Suppose American enterprise and capital should go down to this island to put it in order and develop its resources! There is a railroad across from San Juan to Guayama, a short piece from Ponce to Coamo, on the south coast, and another from San German to Aguadilla, on the west coast—about 125 miles in all—but a girdle of railroad could easily be put around the island, with spurs

262

running into the interior. Decent roadways, with bridges across the numerous streams, would give a new impulse to industry by making it easy for its products to get to market. It is admitted that gold, copper, iron, lead, and coal "are found," but it is generally said "not in paying quantities." No adequate examination has been made to ascertain whether they can be obtained in paying quantities or not. American enterprise, once admitted, would speedily find out.

There is nothing in the tropical climate of Puerto Rico to prevent our people from going thither, but the labor force already there has never been half utilized. The real Spanish element is small even in the cities. The white population is mainly like the native element of Cuba—creole descendants of European colonists alienated from the Spanish stock. There are many blacks, possibly a third of all the people, and much mixed blood, but the population is not ignorant or indolent or in any way degraded. It is not turbulent or intractable, and there is every reason to believe that under encouraging conditions it would become industrious, thrifty, and prosperous. It is certain that a great advance could be made upon the present state of things, and the island could be rendered of no small commercial value to us and to its own people.

There is no reason why it should not become a veritable garden of the tropics and an especially charming Winter resort for denizens of the North. Apart from the attractions of climate and scenery, there is a quaint picturesqueness in the old Spanish towns, and many interesting associations with the infancy of America. Columbus, coming up from the Caribbees on his second voyage in November, 1493, came upon the southern coast and was delighted with its beautiful shores. He put in at the Bay of Aguadilla on the west and took water for his ships from the abundant springs which still pour out their limitless supply. He called the island, after his pious manner, San Juan Bautista, and went on his way to Hispaniola (Santo Domingo) to find the settlement he had made at Navidad, as a base for plundering the interior, utterly destroyed by the natives who were to be robbed.

In 1508 Ponce de Leon, who had become Governor of the western province of Santo Domingo, came over and took possession of this fair island of the "noble port," and established its capital where it still bears the name given to the whole territory by the first discoverer. In the casa blanca which still ornaments the variously tinted town of San Juan he planned his expeditions in search of the fountain of perpetual youth, and from here he set forth on the quest which led to the discovery of the Florida coast, whose present name we owe to him—some say on account of the flowery aspect of the land and some on account of its discovery on Easter Day. It matters not, but we owe to Ponce de Leon the close association of our flowery peninsula with the verdant island of Puerto Rico; and perhaps the source of perpetual youth for nations was really found by the disappointed conquistador whom the Indians mortally wounded on our shores.

There are many relics of the aboriginal races of the Antilles in Puerto Rico, including that curious horse collar carved from stone, which is found nowhere else and is supposed to have been associated with the religion or the burial superstitions of the natives. There are neglected opportunities for the study of American ethnology in the island, as well as political, naval, and commercial advantages to be gained, and infinite attractions of tropic scenery and climate to be visited. Whatever may be said or thought of keeping the Philippines or acquiring the Hawaiians, there can be no question of the wisdom of taking and holding Puerto Rico without any reference to a policy of expansion. We need it as a station in the great American archipelago misnamed the West Indies, and Providence has decreed that it shall be ours as a recompense for smiting the last withering clutch of Spain from the domain which Columbus brought to light and the fairest part of which has long been our own heritage.

AMOS K. FISKE.

July 11, 1898

SENOR E. M. HOSTOS TALKS

The Representative of Puerto Rican Juntas in This Country to See President McKinley.

THE FATE OF THE ISLAND

He Believes that If the Spanish Possession Is to be Annexed It Should Be with the Consent of Its Population.

Señor E. M. Hostos, the representative of the Puerto Rican Juntas of Venezuela, San Domingo, and the United States, who came to this country to request an audience with President McKinley relative to the future disposition to be made of Puerto Rico in the event of the invasion and capture of that island by he United States troops, was seen yesterday at the Hotel America, Fifteenth Street and Irving Place.

He explained in detail the object of his mission and the stand which he and a number of his associates are taking with regard to the probable annexation of Puerto Rico by the United States. Señor Hostos comes here from Chile at the request of the Puerto Rican revolutionists living in Venezuela. He holds the position of Director of one of the lyceums in Santiago de Chile, having been called there by the Government in 1888 to help in the reorganization of the system of education in that country.

Referring to his mission to this country, Señor Hostos said:

"It is my intention to ascertain as far as possible the plans of the United States Government relative to the disposition of Puerto Rico when that island becomes by right of capture its possession. It looks now as if my native land is destined to become American territory whether the inhabitants desire it or not, and to this I as well as many of my associates can interpose serious objections. I wish, however, at the beginning to deny any reports to the effect that several Puerto Rican Juntas in foreign countries or in this country have advised their compatriots to offer any resistance to the United States troops in any manner. I fully realize that an expression of that character made on American soil would be treason, and I am quite sure that no sane person would ever utter it.

What He Will Endeavor to Urge.

"Should I succeed in obtaining the desired interview with President McKinley I shall endeavor to impress upon him the fact that if Puerto Rico is to be annexed to the United States it should be with the consent of its population expressed through a regular plebiscite. If the majority of the people desire it we shall all bow to the majority and accept the inevitable.

"But neither I nor any other Puerto Rican patriot and republican would like to see the American people violate their mission as a great democratic nation by forcing our native island to become a dependency of the United States, instead of assisting it to shake off the yoke of its Spanish oppressors and then leave it to build up its own independent government and work out its own destiny.

"We should be only too glad to have the American people act in the capacity of our mentors, our teachers in the art of enjoying and making use of our liberty, which to the masses of the people who have lived for so many years under the ban of Spanish tyranny is a new feeling.

"As soon as I learn something of the readiness of the President and other high functionaries of the United States Government to receive me, I shall proceed to Washington and lay my mission before the President. To prepare the way for my coming and to ascertain the feeling in the White House with regard to my errand, Dr. Henna, the President of the Puerto Rico Junta of this city, has sent Secretary Todd of our organization to Washington. I expect an answer in a few days, and in the meantime a meeting of all our people in this city will be held next Friday, and the situation will be thoroughly gone over.

Suggestions to be Offered.

"If I shall be allowed to offer any suggestions to the President I shall make it my object to point out to him the cause which in my opinion is the only one worthy of the dignity and high aim of the American people. I am certainly entirely in sympathy with the course pursued in sending an expedition to Puerto Rico, as this is absolutely necessary to carry out the joint resolution of Congress, on the merits of which the war was begun.

"Spain must be driven from the Western Hemisphere, and to do this requires men and arms; but there is another provision in this joint resolution which I think should not be left entirely out of sight. I refer to the declaration which says emphatically that this is not a war of conquest, but for the sake of humanity and the independence and liberty of a people entitled to both.

"If Cuba is to be free and its people their own masters, are not Puerto Ricans entitled to the same privileges? Have we not suffered long enough under the yoke of an oppressive government, and should we not have an opportunity to show our capability of governing ourselves?"

Señor Hostos was asked to give his opinion of the strained relations said to exist between the Cubans and the Americans at Santiago. "It grieves me very much to learn of the unfortunate affair, but it should not, in my opinion, create surprise, after the conditions under which the Cubans have been living are looked into. Suffering for many, many years under a tyranny which drove them to extreme despair, is it at all to be wondered at that at the first opportunity that offers itself they should desire in some measure to avenge the wrongs they have endured? It but carries out the idea I have expressed, that all these peoples who have been buried in the thraldom of slavery do not appreciate the responsibilities of liberty, and for that reason must have mentors, teachers, to show them how to act and what to do for their own good. In this role I am sure the Americans, who have demonstrated so well their ability to govern themselves, will be accepted with gratitude and will receive the heartiest co-operation.

He Objects to a Protectorate.

"Let them establish over all their conquered territory not a protectorate, that is too much on the order of a sovereignty, but rather a mentorate, backed by a show of actual interest, and let them reward themselves in whichever manner they may see fit for their trouble, retaining if need be such control of the independent government as will insure their own interests and at the same time guarantee the rights of their protegés."

Señor Hostos is about fifty-five years old, short and slender, and bears a likeness to the portraits of Premier Sagasta. He knows the head of the present Spanish Ministry well, as they were both exiles in Paris in 1867. Señor Hostos is a Puerto Rican by birth, but received his education in Madrid and took part in the September revolution of 1868. After the revolution he came back to America, living for the most part in Venezuela and Chile. He is well known in South America and among Republicans in Spain as the author of several works on political economy, with a decided leaning toward republicanism.

He speaks French excellently, in addition to Spanish, and while he understands English, it is difficult for him to speak the language. Since 1868 he has visited his native land but once, and that was shortly after the treaty of Zanjon, but after becoming convinced that the concessions supposed to have been granted the Puerto Ricans were such in name only, he decided to leave the island and devote himself to the cause of its emancipation, from a distance, where he would be free from persecution.

July 22, 1898

The F.A.L.N.

OUR FLAG RAISED IN PUERTO RICO

Copyright, 1898, by The Associated Press.
GUANICA, Island of Puerto Rico, July 25 —Via St. Thomas, D. W. I., July 26.— The United States military expedition, under the command of Major Gen. Nelson A. Miles, which left Guantanamo Bay during the evening of Thursday last, was landed here successfully to-day, after a skirmish with a detachment of the Spanish troops and a crew of thirty belonging to the launch of the United States auxiliary gunboat Gloucester.

Four of the Spaniards were killed, but no Americans were hurt.

The American troops will be pushed forward promptly, in order to capture the railroad leading to Ponce, which is only about ten miles east of this place. From Ponce there is an excellent military road, running eighty-five miles north to San Juan de Puerto Rico, the capital of the island.

The ships left Guantanamo Bay Thursday evening, with the Massachusetts, commanded by Capt. F. J. Higginson, leading. Capt. Higginson was in charge of the naval expedition, which consisted of the Columbia, Dixie, Gloucester, and Yale. Gen. Miles was on board the last-named vessel. The troops were on board the transports Nueces, Lampasas, Comanche, Rita, Unionist, Stillwater, City of Macon, and Specialist. This was the order in which the transports entered the harbor here. The voyage from Guantanamo Bay to this port was uneventful.

July 27, 1898

READY TO RENOUNCE SPAIN.

Puerto Rican Revolutionary Society Has Made Preparations to Assist the American Army.

WASHINGTON, July 29.—A letter from Gen. Antonio Mattei Lluveras, chief of the Puerto Rican commission which joined Gen. Miles at the port of Guanica, written on board of the auxiliary cruiser St. Louis, was received in Washington to-day. Before the departure of the St. Louis from Newport News Gen. Lluveras received a number of letters from friends of the annexation party in Puerto Rico, describing the situation in the island before the landing of Gen. Miles.

"Gen. Miles will not have a difficult task in subduing the island," he says, "even if Capt. Gen. Macias had determined to make a strong stand against him, which is not the case. He has received orders to shed as little unnecessary blood as possible, and the fact that he has ordered the soldiery from all over the island to the capital, San Juan, indicates that he does not contemplate serious resistance.

"The Puerto Rican annexationists have formed a secret organization similar to the celebrated 'Carboneri,' and in nearly every city and village in the island they have established a branch. Every member of the society has been pledged to use his utmost endeavors to bring one or more friends or acquaintances into the society, which has annexation or independence for its object, and in this way a thorough canvass of the island has been made, resulting in the mustering of a great many volunteers who will fight for the cause of freedom.

"A circular issued by the society, which has adopted for its name 'Justicia,' (Justice,) explains to the ignorant native population of the island the injustice and tyranny of the Spanish Government, and calls attention to the treatment which has been accorded a number of Puerto Ricans who have fallen into the hands of the Spaniards after openly favoring annexation. These prisoners were tried by court-martial and shot without ceremony. At their trials they were tortured to make them reveal the names of their fellow-conspirators, but the organization of 'La Justicia' is so excellent that no one man knows another member by name, but only by signs.

"All of the members of the society are not in favor of annexation to the United States. Their main object is to drive the Spaniards from the island. After that has been accomplished they are willing to take the best they can get from the United States Government, knowing that it will be fair and equitable. What they want is a radical change, which will enable them to forget the present situation.

"Puerto Ricans opposed to Spanish misrule are firmly convinced that the United States, once the island has been rescued from Spanish control, will give them independence to some extent. Even if the island is annexed they believe that the United States will allow them the same home rule which is now accorded every State in the Union, and will not by military or moral force place Americans only at the head of affairs in the island.

"Over 2,000 native Puerto Ricans, from different cities and villages in the interior, have assembled among the mountains on the southern coast to await the landing of the American army of invasion. They will immediately offer themselves, and thousands more will flock to the American standard. These people are a motley crew, armed with pistols, Remingtons, and old-fashioned guns, but they depend upon the American army to supply them with the necessary weapons. They are enthusiastic and will make excellent fighters."

July 30, 1898

PORTO RICANS GIVE LINDBERGH MESSAGE, ASKING FOR FREEDOM

Legislature Inserts Plea to United States in Its Tribute to Flier.

HIS REPLY IGNORES ACTION

By HARWOOD HULL,
Special Correspondent of The New York Times.
Copyright, 1928, by The New York Times Company.
By Wireless to The New York Times.

SAN JUAN, Porto Rico, Feb. 3.— Today will probably best be remembered by the thousands of school children of San Juan as their day with Charles A. Lindbergh. Much of the time and attention during the day were devoted not only for Colonel Lindbergh to see the schools but for the children to see him.

The children got a great "kick" out of it and Colonel Lindbergh stood up or waved to their many greetings.

This afternoon more than 20,000 people gathered on the sloping hillside overlooking El Morro parade ground to watch 2,000 public school children go through mass calisthenics and then pass in troops in front of the elevated stand, where Colonel Lindbergh sat, to salute him. For each troop, the flier stood to receive the salute and when the exercises were finished the whole throng stood while the Sixty-fifth Infantry Band played "The Star-Spangled Banner."

It was a most impressive sight, with flags and school banners flying on the field where the Spanish fought and turned back the Dutch invasion more than three centuries ago, while in the background stood El Morro with its four-centuries-old, graying, weathered walls. Since the shells from Admiral Sampson's fleet in 1898 flew over this field where the children performed, nothing more dangerous than a golf ball has passed.

All Thoroughly Enjoy Show.

The children, all dressed in white, showed every evidence that they knew they were performing before such a distinguished guest, and Colonel Lindbergh appeared equally to enjoy the display. It was the first time such a large demonstration had been undertaken for a visitor to Porto Rico.

At the special session of the Legislature in the forenoon to honor Colonel Lindbergh, a medal was pinned on the flier's coat by Senate President Antonio Barcelo. Then the Speaker of the House, José Tous Soto, read a concurrent resolution, which injected suddenly into the formal proceedings of welcome for Colonel Lindbergh a plea for the freedom of Porto Rico.

The welcoming tribute to the airman who had given this American possession a thrill when he landed here yesterday concluded with a "message from the people of Porto Rico to the people of the United States," which the island legislators entrusted to him.

"To your country and to your people," the resolution said, "you will convey a message of Porto Rico not far different from the cry of Patrick Henry—'Liberty or death!' It is the same in substance with but a difference imposed by the changes of time and conditions.

"The message of Porto Rico to your people is, grant us the freedom that you enjoy, for which you struggled and which you worship; which we deserve and you have promised us."

Flier Is Silent on "Message."

The message was first read in Spanish and then in English. The formal title of the resolution reads: "To confer on the Honorable Charles A. Lindbergh the representation of the people of Porto Rico as the bearer of a message to the people of the United States."

There was no opposition in the Legislature to the adoption of the resolution, which was drafted by Speaker Tous Soto.

Colonel Lindbergh did not refer to it in his address thanking the Legislature for the honor it had done him in conferring the commemorative medal. He spoke instead briefly on the subject of commercial aviation, and said that it would be a simple matter to link Porto Rico and the United States by air lines.

At the close of the session, Colonel Lindbergh shook hands with each member of the Legislature. Asked to whom he would deliver the message, the flier said he could not comment.

The legislative message had not been published in any newspapers here today, and except to some members of the Legislature, its contents were unknown until just before the presentation. While there has been no public comment on it, it was pointed out that the message could have two interpretations, one seeking Statehood for Porto Rico, the other independence. The latter interpretation seemed to have the more general support, with the added suggestion that at least some legislators wanted a place in the sun of local publicity.

Governor Horace M. Towner would not comment on the message, saying that he had made no interpretation of it.

February 4, 1928

264

7 DIE IN PUERTO RICO RIOT, 50 INJURED AS POLICE FIRE ON FIGHTING NATIONALISTS

26 SEIZED IN PONCE

Disorder Grows Out of Overruling of Mayor on Allowing Parade

MARCHERS IGNORE BAN

Police Say a Nationalist Began Clash—They Use Riot Guns and Pistols on Crowd

CLASH IN HEART OF CITY

Demonstration Was Planned in Behalf of Eight Now in Jail on Sedition Charges

Special Cable to THE NEW YORK TIMES.
SAN JUAN, Puerto Rico, March 21.—Nationalist agitation for an independent Puerto Rico led to a serious riot this afternoon at Ponce, second city on the island. Seven or more persons were killed and more than fifty were injured.

The affair grew out of contradictory orders issued by the authorities. A demonstration had been arranged in the course of a campaign of protest against the imprisonment of eight Nationalists who had been convicted of sedition and whose conviction had been upheld by a Federal court in Boston.

Mayor Ormes of Ponce had given a permit for the parade, but when the matter came to the attention of Colonel Enrique de Orbeta, the insular police chief, he forbade it. Thereupon the Nationalist leaders let their followers know that the demonstration would be held anyway.

Police Sent to City

Colonel Orbeta went to Ponce with police reinforcements and took command of the situation. He concentrated his forces along the proposed line of march. A clash came when the paraders reached the Clinica Pila, in the heart of the city.

According to the police version, there was disorder during which some one in the Nationalist crowd fired and some policemen were wounded. The police then returned the fire. They used riot guns, sub-machine guns and pistols.

The known police dead include Patrolmen Loyola and Eusebio Sanchez. Patrolmen Lind and Aponte were injured.

Civilians listed as dead are Ramon Ortiz, Bolivar Marquez, Alfonso Vargas and Juan Rodriguez. One of the dead has not been identified.

Tonight the streets of Ponce were being patrolled by extra police guards and Prosecutor Rafael Perez Marchand started intensive questioning of twenty-six persons arrested in the disturbance.

Recently the Nationalists have been holding parades and rallies partly to increase enthusiasm for their cause and partly to raise funds for the further defense of the eight Nationalists now in jail.

Among the eight is Pedro Albizu Campos, leader of the Nationalist party, who was said to have fostered the formation of a "private army." Following the affirmation of the sedition convictions by the Circuit Court of Appeals in Boston, the Supreme Court granted last week a thirty-day period for the filing of an appeal.

Capital Has No Reports

Special to THE NEW YORK TIMES.
WASHINGTON, March 21.—Officials of the Interior Department as well as the Puerto Rico Reconstruction Administration had received no reports tonight of the Nationalist riots at Ponce.

The riots were believed here to be the outgrowth of a movement led by Pedro Albizu Campos, an American Negro Harvard graduate, and several others, who were convicted of sedition last year after the assassination of Colonel E. Francis Riggs. They are seeking to appeal to the United States Supreme Court.

Colonel Riggs who had been head of the Insular Police since 1933 was shot and killed on Feb. 23, 1936, by two young members of the Nationalist party, Elias Beauchamp and Hiran Rosado. They were shot and killed at San Juan Police Headquarters a few hours later by members of the police force who charged that the youths had tried to seize rifles. The youths said that they had shot Colonel Riggs in retaliation for the "massacre" of four Nationalists at Rio Piedras in October, 1935.

Last April six policemen were indicted for the killing of Beauchamp and Rosado after violent attacks on the administration by the Puerto Rican press. Albizu Campos and six others were charged with sedition in the inquiry that followed the death of Colonel Riggs and their conviction and the subsequent moves to free them have been the principal objectives of the Nationalist party for the last few months.

Violence Has Been Frequent

The Nationalist movement in Puerto Rico, although it has attracted only a small enrollment of active partisans, has become important in the life of the island for two reasons: because the various suggestions for Puerto Rican independence have drawn attention to its aims and because of periodic outbursts of violence involving Nationalists.

Following the assassination of Colonel E. Francis Riggs, retired United States Army officer, who had been head of the insular police, Santiago Iglesias, Resident Commissioner of the island at Washington, was shot in the arm last October during a campaign address at the town of Mayaguez.

The assailant was identified as a Nationalist, and it was reported that the victim had aroused the opposition of the Nationalists by speeches urging closer association between the island and the United States. Mr. Iglesias was not seriously hurt, however, and was returned to office in the November balloting.

Other disorders for which the Nationalists have been blamed included a series of bombings during 1934 and 1935. A Nationalist arrested for setting off a bomb in a branch postoffice in San Juan was sentenced to prison last April.

The head of the Nationalist party, Pedro Albizu Campos, was re-elected to his party post last month, although he is still in jail pending court action on his appeal.

A part of the evidence against Albizu Campos and his co-defendants was that they had promoted the organization of a "private army" to be used in the struggle for liberation. Last May the Puerto Rican police, after student zealots had started disorders in various parts of the island, surrounded the Nationalist club in Ponce and suppressed a drill of the "Cadets of the Republic," described as one of the units of the Nationalist force.

March 22, 1937

HAYS LAYS CLASH IN PONCE TO CURBS

Suppression of Civil Liberties Resulted in Riot, He Says in Report After Inquiry

WINSHIP POLICY BLAMED

Suppression of civil liberties in Puerto Rico resulted in the Palm Sunday riot in Ponce, in which twenty persons were killed and almost 200 were wounded, according to a report yesterday by Arthur Garfield Hays, general counsel for the American Civil Liberties Union.

Mr. Hays returned early this week from Puerto Rico after having conducted hearings for nine days as head of a non-official commission investigating alleged suppression of civil liberties on the island.

Regarding the cause of the riot, the Hays committee found:

"That the insular police on instruction from Governor Blanton Winship refused to permit a group of Nationalist cadets, perhaps eighty in number, to engage in a peaceful parade.

"That the cadets in the face of fifty or seventy policemen, armed with revolvers, shotguns, machine-guns and tear gas bombs, were given the command, 'Forward, march,' and stepped forward one or two paces, when the police opened fire on them and the crowd. * * *

Found Parades Barred

"That civil liberties, for the last nine months, have been denied the people where they wished to hold parades and demonstrations on subjects that interested them, such as Puerto Rican independence, the attitude of Governor Winship and the conviction for a conspiracy of leaders of the Nationalist party.

"That the University of Puerto Rico has passed regulations under which teachers who take part in any of these activities may be penalized or lose their jobs; that such regulations are for the purpose of curbing civil liberty and should be canceled."

The committee urged that Governor Winship be requested "to make a public announcement that hereafter the right of the people to civil liberties shall be recognized and that he will observe their rights as expressed in the Puerto Rico Organic Act. (So far as these rights are concerned, that act is the same as the Bill of Rights and the Constitution of the United States.)"

Mr. Hays arrived in Puerto Rico on May 13 and immediately began to conduct hearings. Other members of the committee included Mariano Acosta Velarde, president of the Puerto Rico Bar Association; Manuel Diaz Garcia, president of the Medical Association, and Lorenzo Pineiro, president of the Teachers Association.

The American Civil Liberties Union has announced that it is planning to establish a branch in Puerto Rico.

May 29, 1937

The F.A.L.N.

FIVE CONGRESSMEN SHOT IN HOUSE BY 3 PUERTO RICAN NATIONALISTS; BULLETS SPRAY FROM GALLERY

CAPITOL IN UPROAR

Woman, Accomplices Quickly Overpowered —High Bonds Set

By CLAYTON KNOWLES
Special to The New York Times.

WASHINGTON, March 1 — Five members of the Congress of The United States were shot down on the floor of the House of Representatives today.

Their assailants, at least three Puerto Rican Nationalists, shouted for freedom of their homeland as they fired murderously although at random from a spectators' gallery just above the House floor. Possibly twenty-five shots were fired.

Bullets rained down from two German Lugers and other pistols of lesser caliber. They crashed through the table of the majority leader and chairs around it, and struck near the table of the Minority Leader beyond. The time was 2:32 P. M.

House members at first thought the sounds were those of firecrackers. But as their colleagues fell or took cover as they heard the slugs hit around them, all realized what was happening.

The wounded House members:

ALVIN M. BENTLEY, 35 years old, multimillionaire Michigan Republican, shot through lung, liver and intestine. Condition critical.

BEN F. JENSEN, 61, Republican of Iowa, shot in back. Condition serious.

CLIFFORD DAVIS, 56, Democrat of Tennessee, shot in the leg. Condition good.

GEORGE H. FALLON, 51, Democrat of Maryland, leg wound. Condition good.

KENNETH A. ROBERTS, 41, Democrat of Alabama, leg wound. Condition good.

Assailants Subdued

Within a matter of minutes, the episode, which threw the Capitol and most of official Washington into an uproar, was at an end. Gallery attendants, aided by spectators, Capitol police and even one House member, quickly overcame and disarmed the three gun wielders.

The three Puerto Ricans, all residents of New York, were booked at police headquarters on charges of assault with intent to kill. They gave their names and addresses as:

LOLITA LEBRON, 34, 315 West Ninety-fourth Street.
RAFAEL C. MIRANDA, 25, 120 South First Street, Brooklyn.
ANDRES CORDERO, or FIGUEROA, 29, of 108 East 103d Street.

A fourth Puerto Rican, also resident in New York, was arrested at a downtown bus station and booked on the same charge.

He was booked as Irving Flores, 27, also of 108 East 103d Street, described by Police Chief Robert Murray as a fourth member of the shooting party who had fled the Capitol successfully. When arrested, Flores still had a .45 caliber pistol.

Later, United States Commissioner Cyril S. Lawrence ordered all four held under $100,000 bonds each. He put off a preliminary hearing until March 10 to give them time to get counsel. Five counts of assault with intent to kill were brought against each of the four, one count for each of the legislators wounded.

Chief Murray reported tonight that all, except Flores, had confessed to the shootings. Edgar E. Scott, deputy chief of detectives, said that Flores, though identified by Mrs. Lebron as one of the party, would not admit being present at the scene.

At police headquarters Mrs. Lebron said none of the four had intended to kill anyone.

She said the shooting date had been picked to coincide with the opening of the Inter-American Conference at Caracas.

Three other Puerto Ricans, all residents of Florida, were picked up as the police threw a dragnet around the whole Capitol area. They were not booked immediately and appeared to have no connection with the shooting.

Mrs. Lebron was identified as an associate of the wife of one of the Puerto Rican Nationalists who made an attempt on the life of President Truman outside Blair House on Nov. 1, 1950.

A note found in her purse by the police read:

"Before God and the world my blood claims for the independence of Puerto Rico. My life I give for the freedom of my country. This is a cry for victory in our struggle for independence. Which for more than a half century has tried to conquer that land that belongs to Puerto Rico.

"I state that the United States of America are betraying the sacred principles of mankind in their continuous subjugation of my country, violating their rights to be a free nation and a free people in their barbarous torture of our apostle of independence, Don Pedro Albizu Campos."

Across the back of the note was scrawled "I take responsible for all."

Strike Without Warning

The two men who stormed Blair House steps seeking to kill President Truman also were followers of Albizu Campos. Today as then, there was no warning as the assailants struck.

The House members—at least 243 of them in the chamber at the time—were set up like sitting ducks for their assailants. The Puerto Ricans literally sprayed the House floor with their fire.

As they shot, they screamed: "Viva Puerto Rico."

Most of the members said later that they thought a string of firecrackers had been set off in the gallery when the guns began to fire. It was only as they saw their colleagues falling about them that they realized what was going on.

"Hit the deck," shouted Representative James E. Van Zandt, Republican of Pennsylvania. He then dashed from the chamber and up one flight to the gallery to help disarm one of the gunmen.

Similar outcries went up from all over the House floor and from the galleries. Piercing the confusion were the screams of the Puerto Rican woman: "Viva Puerto Rico!" She emptied the chambers of a big Luger pistol, holding it in her two hands, and waving it wildly.

Then, she threw down the pistol and whipped out a Puerto Rican flag, which she waved but never did manage to unfurl fully. As she screamed, her companions trained their weapons on the House floor.

Five of the bullets hit Congressmen. Four shots shattered the wood paneling behind the Democrats. Four more pierced or splintered chairs. Two others struck the big mahogany table behind which sat Majority Leader Charles A. Halleck of Indiana and Leslie C. Arends of Illinois, the Republican whip.

A splinter from the desk hit Mr. Arends in the face, piercing the left eyelid. It was only then that he realized that it was "business, not a misguided prank," as he said later.

Beside the majority table, Mr. Bentley keeled over. Representative Jensen, standing near the door, was struck, but kept his feet to stagger to the cloakroom where he collapsed.

Across the aisle, a bullet pierced a chair and lodged in Representative Roberts' leg. Other bullets got Mr. Davis and Mr. Fallon in their legs.

After an exploratory operation at Casualty Hospital about five hours after the shooting, Mr. Bentley tonight was given a "50-50 chance" to live by the surgeon who performed the operation.

Dr. Joseph R. Young, Chief of Staff at Casualty Hospital, said there would be a critical period of "about seventy-two hours," and disclosed that the operation had shown "extensive visceral damage," including damage to the liver.

He reported that the bullet had apparently torn through the liver with "explosive force," so that there was danger of infection. He also described the danger of peritonitis as "very great."

As realization of what was happening spread, members threw themselves to the floor or behind chairs. Others seemed frozen as they looked up to watch the Puerto Ricans shooting.

Representative Pat Hillings, Republican of California, a veteran of fighting in the South Pacific, said:

"I'd been shot at before but never saw who was firing at me."

Speaker Joseph W. Martin Jr. of Massachusetts, presiding at the time, whirled behind a marble pillar for protection. He later said, "I think the shot that got Jensen was meant for me."

Two Dozen Shots Fired

"I think I got hit before I heard the shooting," said Mr. Fallon at the hospital tonight. His reaction was typical. While the force of the shot threw him to the floor, Mr. Fallon did not actually realize he had been shot until he noticed blood on his hip.

Even when some saw the guns smoking, their first reaction was that demonstrators were shooting blank cartridges.

Representative Louis P. Graham, a Pennsylvania Republican, stood watching as did many others on the floor, participating in a vote when the bullets began to rain down.

"Get down, you damn fool! Those are bullets," shouted Representative Benjamin James, a Republican colleague from Pennsylvania.

It was over in a matter of seconds. A full count on the num-

TERRORISTS OR PATRIOTS

ber of shots fired has yet to be announced but the number probably was somewhere between twenty and twenty-five. Two shots, apparently fired by the woman, buried themselves in the House ceiling.

Immediately after the firing ceased, the paralysis that gripped the members and the galleries ended.

There was a rush to the Visitors' Gallery adjacent to the press section, where the Puerto Ricans were fighting their way toward the exit, smoking pistols still in hand.

First out was the woman, still clutching the Puerto Rican flag. She was quickly collared. Then came one of her male companions who was hit from at least four quarters and knocked to the ground.

In the group that struck him down was Boyd Crawford, clerk of the House Foreign Affairs Committee. Mr. Crawford, an excellent pistol shot himself, thrust his finger under the trigger guard of the gun the Puerto Rican carried. It kept him from shooting.

"Then we sat on him until the police arrived," said the 190-pound clerk.

Helping disarm this gunman was Representative Van Zandt, a veteran of both World Wars and former national chairman of the Veterans of Foreign Wars. Also in on the team play was Frank Wise, a suburbanite recuperating from illness and visiting in the gallery to get some of the relaxation his doctor had ordered.

"I didn't know whether to take cover or do my duty," he said. "I closed with him and grabbed his arm."

Another spectator, whose identity was undisclosed, threw a headlock around a second gunman. As they wrestled out the door, the spectator cried: "Look out! He's got a gun."

Doorman Wades In

Closing in to help was another group of willing hands, including those of William Belcher, a doorman, who suffered a heart attack afterward and was hospitalized. The final subduing was administered by a 71-year-old Capitol policeman. Despite his years, Patrolman A. S. (Buck) Rodgers, a former Texas farmer, grabbed the Puerto Rican by the coat collar and brought his own hand down sharply edgewise on the wrist of his victim's gun hand.

A big Luger clattered to the tile floor, close by the other Puerto Rican, head bleeding and still lying on the floor with Mr. Crawford sitting on him.

The actual arrests were made by Capt. Carl Schramp, a city detective heading the city police detail on the House side of the Capitol.

On the floor, meanwhile, hasty first aid was being administered. Representatives A. L. Miller of Nebraska and Walter H. Judd of Minnesota, both medical doctors, gave orders for emergency care of the wounded. Both gave particular attention to Mr. Bentley, who bled profusely.

Dr. Judd, a former medical missionary in China, diagnosed Mr. Bentley's condition as serious.

Representative Percy Priest, sitting beside Mr. Roberts, whipped off his own necktie for use as a tourniquet.

Out in the cloakroom, Mr. Jensen gritted through clenched teeth: "They got me, they got me. Did they hit me in the spine?" Anxious members sought to reassure him.

Many of those in the gallery thought the Puerto Ricans were shouting "Viva Mexico" but some later confessed that they probably made this out of the jumble of Spanish because of the fact that the "wetback bill," governing the flow of Mexican farm labor to the United States, was the business before the House.

At 2:27, shortly before the shooting began, a member had demanded a quorum count. Speaker Martin stated there were 243 members present.

With the quorum established, the resolution before the House for a rule, officially bringing the bill to the floor, was called up for a vote. It appeared to pass on a voice vote but the Democrats demanded a division.

The Speaker asked for all those supporting the rule to rise. He went through his count and just was about to call for the "nays" when the shooting began. He later said he had counted 168 members for the rule.

After the confusion died down somewhat, Mr. Martin returned to the chair, ordered the House floor cleared of nonmembers and proceeded, upon motion, to adjourn the House.

President Eisenhower, informed of the shootings, put through a quick call to Mr. Martin to offer any help he could. Later in the evening, the White House canceled the Congressional reception scheduled for tomorrow night.

Security provisions at the Capitol, White House, Interior and Justice departments were tightened immediately. The Capitol was cleared as both houses quickly quit for the day. Admission to the galleries henceforth will be by card only.

Thousands of persons rushed to the Capitol Plaza within minutes of the shooting. Not since the British burned the Capitol in August, 1814, had there been such an incident there.

Associated Press Wirephotos

Patrolman Jack Brunner of the Capitol police shows correspondents the Puerto Rican flag taken from Mrs. Lolita Lebron, one of the demonstrators. After she had emptied her pistol, Mrs. Lebron cried, "Viva Puerto Rico!" and waved the flag, though she never did manage to unfurl it fully.

Squad cars of the Metropolitan police force sped to join the Capitol police, who guard the building day and night. The entire area was barricaded in fifteen minutes, so quickly that 2,000 persons were caught inside the cordon. Several news photographers were whacked and a few received painful bruises when the police started to swing clubs to disperse the cameramen.

The Plaza, a broad space on the east side of the Capitol, is at the rear of the building. However, most persons enter the national legislative halls there and it has been the scene of inaugurations and historic visits for years.

March 2, 1954

Puerto Rican Terrorists Vow to Press Violence Here

By PETER KIHSS

A communiqué in the name of a terrorist Puerto Rican independence group taking responsibility for the four latest midtown bombings here threatened yesterday to continue "revolutionary violence" against corporations "at the heart of Yanki imperialism."

The same group has said it was responsible for the fatal explosion last January at the Fraunces Tavern annex in the financial district.

Assistant Chief Harold Schryver, in charge of the police investigation, said that "the same organization, maybe, but not necessarily the same individuals" appeared to have brought about the series of explosions.

The group's latest statement, which was typewritten, bore a five-pointed star labeled "F.A.L.N." for Fuerzas Armadas de Liberacion Nacional Puertorriqueña. Like previous statements, it demanded independence for Puerto Rico and the release of five nationalists serving prison sentences—one for the attempted assassination of President Harry S. Truman in 1950 and four for shootings in the House of Representatives in 1954.

Cancer Dispute

In Washington, the Bureau of Prisons denied the state-

The F.A.L.N.

ment's contention that one prisoner, Andres Figueroa Cordero, was dying of cancer. A bureau spokesman said he had been operated on successfully for cancer of the intestine in 1972 and was in good health in the Federal penitentiary in Leavenworth, Kan.

Another prisoner, Lolite Lebron, is serving a 56-year sentence in the women's prison in Alderston, W. Va., for the House shooting. She told the Parole Board in January, 1973 that she would not accept parole unless her group received "unconditional amnesty."

Oscar Collazo, serving a life term in Leavenworth in the Truman case, has waived consideration of parole, for which he became eligible in 1966, the bureau spokesman said.

The others convicted of the House shootings are serving 81-year sentences and are ineligible for parole consideration until July 7, 1981. They are Mr. Figueroa Cordero and Irving Flores, in Leavenworth, and Rafael Cancel Miranda, in the Federal prison in Marion, Ill.

The four latest bombings, according to Fire Department alarm records, took place within 35 minutes—at the New York Life Insurance Company annex, 51 Madison Avenue, at 27th Street, at 11:44 P.M. Wednesday; at the Bankers Trust Company plaza at 46 East 49th Street, at 12:03 A.M. yesterday; at the Metropolitan Life Insurance Company headquarters at 340 Park Avenue South, at 25th Street, at 12:08 A.M., and outside the Blimpie Base restaurant at 5 West 46th Street, at 12:19 A.M.

Given the midnight hour, the buildings and areas were virtually unoccupied. One pedestrian was cut about the head by flying glass in the 46th Street blast; four firemen bloodied their hands clearing glass from Metropolitan Life windows.

Chief Schryver said he doubted that the Blimpie Base had been a target. He conjectured that the bombers were planning to go elsewhere but were frustrated when someone came out of a building, and finally threw their last bomb away because its timing device was about to detonate.

Bomb Lands in Garbage

The bomb burst in the middle of a dozen plastic bags filled with garbage awaiting a carter.

At 12:53 A.M., a man telephoned The Associated Press and said quickly, in a Hispanic accent: "This is the F.A.L.N. We just threw bombs. You will find a communique in a telephone booth at 88th Street and Lexington Avenue."

The news service found the envelope and brought it unopened to the police, who later released the statement.

The bombings of the "Yanki corporations," the statement said, "are the continuation of an offensive aimed at gaining the independence of Puerto Rico and the release of five political prisoners."

Citing special concern for Mr. Figueroa Cordero, the statement said that "his death in prison will result in grave consequences for the Yanki Capitalist class. . . . At no time can we allow an attack by the enemy upon our people to go unanswered. Fascist terror is met with revolutionary violence."

The statement recalled the Jan. 24 bombing, which killed four persons and injured 53 at the Fraunces Tavern Anglers Club annex, and described it as a retaliation against a "ruling class" held responsible for alleged "C.I.A. terror" and a "wave of repression which is being murderously implemented in Puerto Rico."

Chief Schryver recalled that a $50,000 reward was outstanding for information leading to the capture and conviction of the Fraunces Tavern suspects. He urged that information be telephoned to a special number, 349-5844, or mailed to Post Office Box 1000, Church Street Station, New York, N.Y. 10046.

In Washington, a Puerto Rican Commonwealth spokesman said: "The F.A.L.N. as an organization has never been heard of on the island. Neither the Puerto Rican police nor the Federal Bureau of Investigation has ever been able to identify it or ever heard of it in Puerto Rico."

April 4, 1975

F.B.I. ROLE TO GET A HEARING AT U.N.

Puerto Rican Independence Leader Makes Charges

By KATHLEEN TELTSCH
Special to The New York Times

UNITED NATIONS, N. Y., June 7—Juan Mari-Bras, who heads the minority Socialist party in Puerto Rico, is preparing to capitalize here on recent disclosures that the Federal Bureau of Investigation harassed Puerto Rican pro-independence organizations.

Mr. Mari-Bras said he had evidence that the F.B.I. censored his mail, tapped his telephone, checked his bank account regularly and had him followed whenever he left the Island.

He said at a news conference Thursday that he intended to place his evidence before the United Nations Committee on Colonialism, which has agreed to have him testify when it takes up the issue of Puerto Rico, probably in August.

Although the General Assembly decided in 1953 that Puerto Rico had achieved autonomy and had ceased to be a United Nations concern, the colonialism committee will give Mr. Mari-Bras a hearing, mainly at the insistence of Cuba and some Americans.

Unsuccessful Lobby

The United States unsuccessfully lobbied against the move, protesting that the committee was giving a forum to "fringe elements" that polled only 4 per cent in the elections in Puerto Rico.

Until now Mr. Mari-Bras concentrated on charges that the United States had exploited Puerto Rico economically, would like to build a giant petro-chemical complex there that would pollute the island while providing few jobs, and had tried to repress the political freedom of the independence parties.

F.B.I. involvement would be more grist for the campaign to reverse the 1953 Assembly decision and have Puerto Rico put back on the list of "colonies," obliging the United States to submit annual reports.

An F.B.I. program against Puerto Rican independence groups from 1960 to 1971 was recently acknowledged by Attorney General Edward H. Levi.

Mr. Levi said 37 projects were carried out against unidentified militant groups seeking to promote Puerto Rican independence.

Evidence Cited

Mr. Mari-Bras, who is Secretary General of the Socialist party, which he describes as Marxist-Leninist, said he had evidence to give the United Nations committee showing that several United States agencies were conspiring against the independence groups. He displayed a photostat of an affidavit that he said came from a former secretary working for the F.B.I. in San Juan who had quit her job and now was a member of the Puerto Rican Socialist party living in Hartford.

The affidavit was signed by Gloria Teresa Caldas de Blanco in December, 1974, and gave an account of F.B.I. searches of mail, penetration by agents of the independence party organization, surveillance of Mr. Mari-Bras and others when they traveled to the United States and efforts to buy information and recruit party members for the F.B.I.

Mr. Mari-Bras said his goal this year was to "develop the Puerto Rican case" before the United Nations committee. The United States is not a member, having withdrawn in 1971 after protesting that the group's ressolutions were one-sided and its activities dominated by Communist and Third World members.

Mr. Mari-Bras said he had received assurances from Cuba and "friends" on the committee that his position would be received sympathetically.

June 8, 1975

3 Puerto Ricans at U.N. Assail U.S. Rule

By PAUL HOFFMANN
Special to The New York Times

UNITED NATIONS, N. Y., Aug. 14—A leader of the movement for the independence of Puerto Rico charged in a United Nations committee today that the United States had increased repression on the island recently.

The speaker, Juan Mari Bras, said that the Federal Bureau of Investigation, the Central Intelligence Agency, the Secret Service and Puerto Rican police agencies were closely cooperating in the "persecution" of Puerto Ricans who wanted full covereignty for their island.

Mr. Mari Bras, Secretary General of the Puerto Rican Socialist party, was one of three members of the small but militant independence movement who were admitted to be heard by the world organization's 24-country Committee on Decolonization.

The two other Puerto Ricans were Senator Ruben Berrios Martinez of the Puerto Rican Peace Council and Noel Colon Martinez of the Independence party on the island.

The United Nations Special Committee on the Situation with Regard to the Implementation of the Declaration on the Granting of Independence to Colonial Countries and Peoples, commonly referred to as the Decolonization Committee, has held hearings for several years on the relationship between the

United States and Puerto Rico.

A spokesman for the Puerto Rican government said today that Puerto Rican charges against Washington in the Decolonization Committee "have usually been instigated by the Cuban delegation, and supported by a variety of Communist and third world countries."

Cuba's chief delegate to the United Nations, Ricardo Alarcon Quesada, a member of the committee, conferred with the three Puerto Ricans before the hearing.

Mr. Mari Bras, in his statement to the committee, paid tribute to "Comrade Alarcon Quesada," and said Cuba's backing represented "a hope" for the cause of Puerto Rican independence.

The Puerto Rican Government spokesman's rebuttal noted that "less than 5 per cent of the Puerto Rican electorate has supported independence in free democratic elections during the last 20 years."

The Government spokesman added:

"The issue is one of self-determination, and since over 95 per cent of the Puerto Rican people have repeatedly voted in support of political parties standing for permanent union with the United States, Puerto Ricans remain baffled and indignant at suggestions they should become completely independent even if they do not wish to be."

Mr. Mari Bras, in his statement at the committee hearing, accused the United States of "imperialistic exploitation" of the island. He asserted that Rockefeller interests, the First National City Bank of New York and the Morgan Guaranty Trust Company of New York were foremost among American investors reaping immense profits in Puerto Rico.

"The Yankees earn bigger profits in Puerto Rico than in the entire European Common Market," Mr. Mari Bras said.

The Puerto Rican Socialist urged the Decolonization Committee to adopt a resolution acknowledging his island's right to self determination and independence. He also suggested the committee send a fact-finding team to Puerto Rico next year.

The hearings will continue tomorrow. The chairman, Salim A. Salim of Tanzania, said he hoped consideration of the situation in Puerto Rico would be concluded tomorrow night.

In another development, the United Nations announced today that two former Portuguese territories in Africa, Cape Verde and São Tomé, had applied for membership.

August 15, 1975

PUERTO RICAN UNIT SAYS IT SET BOMBS

Police Believe Underground Group's Claim—Blasts in Washington and Chicago

By SELWYN RAAB

A leftist underground group that is demanding independence for Puerto Rico took responsibility yesterday for nine almost sumultaneous early-morning bomb explosions at government buildings, corporate offices and banks in New York, Chicago and Washington.

No one was injured in the blasts, which caused minor structural damage to the buildings, including the offices of the United States Mission to the United Nations here and the State Department building in Washington.

The terrorist band, calling itself the Fuerzas Armadas de Liberación Nacional Puertorriqueña (F.A.L.N.) said the bombings were part of a "coordinated attack against Yanki government and monopoly capitalist institutions." The F.A.L.N., which is now believed responsible for 25 bombings in the United States in little more than one year, reiterated its demands for the release of five imprisoned Puerto Rican nationalists who were convicted of attempting to assassinate the late President Harry S. Truman and the wounding of five Congressmen in the nineteen-fifties.

The Federal Bureau of Investigation and the New York police believe thay may have uncovered their first major clue in the year-long search for the F.A.L.N. with the discovery of an intact bomb that failed to go off in Chicago.

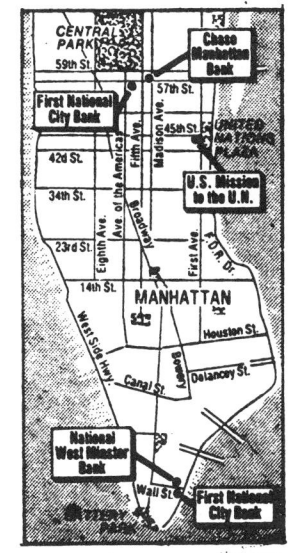

Made of five sticks of dynamite and a detonator, the bomb was found in a flower stand outside the Standard Oil building in Chicago's Loop section. An F.B.I. spokesman said the bomb "is one of the most important leads we have gotten, so far."

In New York, Sgt. Terence G. McTigue of the police bomb section said that in addition to the possibility of finding fingerprints on the device, experts might be able to trace the origin of the dynamite and its other components.

A detective from the city's arson and explosion squad was sent yesterday to Chicago to participate in the investigation there.

1st Anniversary Cited

The F.A.L.N. said yesterday's bombings had been timed for the first anniversary of a similar series of blasts in the city. On Oct. 26, 1974, the terrorist group surfaced publicly with explosions outside five Manhattan banks.

On Dec. 11, the F.A.L.N. claimed responsibility for a booby-trap bomb in East Harlem that cost a rookie policeman his right eye. The F.A.L.N.'s worst attack occurred last Jan. 24, when a noontime explosion in an annex of crowded Fraunces Tavern in the Wall Street area killed four persons and injured 53.

Despite a $50,000 reward for the capture of those responsible for the Fraunces Tavern bombing, the police here privately admitted that they had made little progress in finding the F.A.L.N. members.

The five bombs planted here yesterday exploded during a 29-minute period. According to the police, the sequence was as follows:

At 1:43 A.M., the first explosion occurred at 100 Wall St., outside a branch of the British-owned Westminster Bank. While the Bomb Section officers were heading downtown at 2:01 A.M., the second explosion ripped open the doorway of a branch of the Chase Manhattan Bank at Madison Avenue and East 57th Street. Policemen and firemen were still at the 100 Wall Street explosion near front street when another occurred at 2:04 A.M. nearby at 111 Wall Street, the site of a branch of the First National City Bank.

Amidst the roar of sirens in downtown and midtown Manhattan, the fourth explosion hit the offices of the United States Mission to the United Nations at 45th Street and the United Nations Plaza at 2:11 A.M. This one punched out 55 windows and damaged an entrance door. The last bomb went off a minute later, at 2:12 A.M. It exploded outside another branch of the First National City Bank, at 40 West 57th Street.

Damage Not Extensive

The five bombings here damaged only doors and windows.

Similar explosions were occurring virtually at the same time in Chicago and Washington.

Again, the bombs in Chicago caused minor damage at the Sears Towers, the world's tallest building, the I.B.M. Corporation and the Continental Bank building, all in the Loop, or downtown business section.

In Washington, a bomb placed on a basement window ledge of the State Department blew out 37 windows. There was no damage to the interior of the building.

Secretary of State Kissinger described the act as "completely senseless."

It is unclear what kind of materials were used in the Washington bomb. But Chicago bomb experts believe the devices there contained dynamite.

The city's chief of detectives, Louis C. Cottell, said that the five bombs in New York each contained two to three sticks of dynamite.

"The F.A.L.N. is claiming credit for these explosions and we believe that claim is valid," Chief Cottell said. Despite the "wide investigation" into the F.A.L.N., Chief Cottell warned that there "might be more bombings."

Chief Cottell said a maroon-colored automobile with two men and a woman was seen in the Wall Street area shortly before the explosions. The car, he added, was believed to have Pennsylvania license plates.

Except for the sighting of the car, Chief Cottell said no other suspicious persons were reported in the nearly deserted areas of the bombings.

The police in Chicago said that the bombs there were believed to have been ignited by small propane gas tanks, a method previously used in the metropolitan area by the F.A.L.N.

But none of the bombs used here yesterday contained propane gas tanks, according to the city's bomb section.

Sergeant McTigue, of the bomb section, described the weapons as "well constructed

The F.A.L.N.

and powerful." He said watches had probably been used as timing mechanisms to ignite the explosives.

The bombs that were set off here yesterday, however, were not as powerful as previous ones constructed by the F.A.L.N., Sergeant McTigue said.

"Some of the others, like the Fraunces Tavern one, were designed to kill," he continued. "The ones yesterday were intended to draw attention—to emphasize a message."

Following the explosions, messages were telephoned to The Associated Press and The New York Post that the F.A.L.N. was responsible. Later, reporters for the A.P. and The Post found, as directed, typewritten statements from the F.A.L.N. in a telephone booth at 28th Street and Ninth Avenue.

In a two-page message, headed "Communique No. 6," the F.A.L.N. said the bombings had been intended to mark the 25th anniversary of an uprising by Puerto Rican nationalists on Oct. 30, 1950. With rhetoric similar to other F.A.L.N. statements, the group praised the government of Premier Fidel Castro of Cuba and declared: "Only a protracted, organized armed struggle can force the Yanki invaders out of Puerto Rico."

Besides the bombings here and in the two other mainland cities, the F.A.L.N. warned of simultaneous incidents in Puerto Rico. There were, however, no reports of bombings yesterday in Puerto Rico.

An investigation last January and February by The New York Times discovered that the roots of the terrorist group go back to 1966, when it was organized in Cuba and that it operated under different names here and in Puerto Rico until last year.

Little is known about the F.A.L.N.'s organizational makeup. But, F.B.I. and police intelligence experts believe that the group probably consists of no more than a dozen persons.

The F.B.I., which has been coordinating the hunt for the F.A.L.N., said yesterday that it was cooperating with the local police here and in Chicago, Washington and Puerto Rico.

Because of "security reasons," L. Kost, head of the arson explosion squad, said that police here were aware of the October anniversary significance for the F.A.L.N. Inspector Kost, whose squad is in charge of the local F.A.L.N. investigation, said that private security and guard organizations had been alerted to the possibility of an F.A.L.N. attack.

Because of "security reasons," Inspector Kost declined to indicate whether the police themselves had taken any special steps during the weekend to guard against a possible resumption of the bombings.

October 28, 1975

Puerto Rican Crowds Greet Freed Nationalist

AGUDA, Puerto Rico, Oct. 9 (AP)—Thousands gathered in the rain here today to welcome a Puerto Rican nationalist, Andres Figueroa Cordero, who was jailed 23 years ago for taking part in a shooting attack on the House of Representatives.

President Carter commuted Mr. Figueroa Cordero's 25-to-75 year sentence Thursday as a humanitarian gesture because he has inoperable cancer.

Mr. Figueroa Cordero, 53 years old, appeared to be moved as the crowd of about 6,000 people in his hometown in the north of the island proclaimed him an "idol of the people." He pledged his continuing committment to the struggle for Puerto Rican independence. "It will be kind of long because first we have to free our comrades," he said. The reference was to four other nationalists still serving sentences in Federal prisons.

Mr. Figueroa Cordero and three others were convicted of firing 25 shots from the House gallery on March 1, 1954, and injuring five Congressmen before they were subdued. A fourth nationalist was jailed in 1950 for an attempt on the life of President Harry S. Truman.

Doctors who have accompanied Mr. Figueroa Cordero since his release Thursday from a Federal prison hospital in Springfield, Mo., said they had to administer oxygen to their patient twice today because he was overcome by emotion at the homecoming. He was to return to San Juan tomorrow for medical treatment.

The Committee to Free the Prisoners has announced that Mr. Figueroa Cordero will take part in a demonstration Tuesday to demand the release of the remaining nationalists. Organizers say the protest will be directed at Rosalynn Carter, who is to arrive in Puerto Rico Tuesday to address a meeting of newspaper editors.

October 10, 1977

NATIONALIST'S RETURN SPURS ISLAND DEBATE

Puerto Rico Independence Favored by Prisoner Carter Pardoned for '54 Attack on Congress

By B. DRUMMOND AYRES Jr.
Special to The New York Times

SAN JUAN, P. R. Oct. 10—Andres Figueroa Cordero came home to Puerto Rico to die, but his return has given impetus to the seemingly endless debate about this Caribbean island's relationship with the United States.

Mr. Figueroa Cordero is one of four Puerto Rican nationalists who dramatized a demand for island independence in 1954 by wounding five members of Congress in a shooting spree in the United States House of Representatives.

Each of the gunmen was sentenced to serve from 25 to 75 years in a Federal prison on the mainland. But President Carter freed Mr. Figueroa Cordero last week with a grant of "humanitarian" clemency because the 52-year-old nationalist has terminal lung cancer.

When he returned to the island on Friday, he emerged from the plane in a wheelchair. But there was defiance in his upthrust fist and defiance in his voice.

"If a people asks for a right," he told a cheering airport crowd, "that right has to be claimed with a bullet if the request falls on deaf ears. Every Puerto Rican has the right to think of his nationality and to fight to the end against Yankee imperialism."

Though Mr. Figueroa Cordero, whose goal is believed to be total independence from the United States, has the spotlight here, the issue for most Puerto Ricans is not independence. Rather, the majority of Puerto Ricans seem more concerned about whether the island should become a state or whether it should remain an "associated" commonwealth, its status for the last 25 years.

Hardly a day passes without a loud demonstration, an angry editorial or a strident speech over the status issue. This morning, for example, Gov. Carlos Romero Barcelo spoke out for statehood, comparing commonwealth status to colonialism.

"We are disenfranchised American citizens," he told a group of United Press International editors and publishers who were meeting at the nearby resort town of Dorado.

"Our situation," he continued, "is an affront to the principles of American democracy and is a source of embarrassment in the United Nations as the United States is perennially accused of colonialism. Only by statehood can a sense of political dignity be restored to the Puerto Rican people. Only by statehood will the United States prove that the great principles of democracy are still vibrant."

Governor Romero Barcelo predicted that "in the near future" the Puerto Rican people would ask Congress to approve statehood, a prediction that could be premature. As the most outspoken of the statehood advocates, he narrowly won office last year a race with the most outspoken of the commonwealth advocates, former Governor Rafael Hernandez Colon. Independence candidates ran a very poor third.

The commonwealth status was negotiated in 1952, more than half a century after Puerto Rico was ceded to the United States at the end of the Spanish-American War and some 35 years after American citizenship was granted all Puerto Ricans. The commonwealth agreement freed Puerto Ricans from paying Federal income taxes. But it made them subject to most other Federal laws, while denying them representation in Congress.

However, despite freedom from Federal taxes, Puerto Rico remains one of the most poverty-stricken places under the American flag, an island with an unemployment rate exceeding 20 percent.

Hundreds of thousands of Puerto Ricans have fled to the mainland in hope of finding a better life. Their migration is an uprooting of historic proportion, a tragic commentary on the shabby housing and littered streets that contrast so sharply with the island's golden beaches and verdant mountains.

In an effort to build up its economy, Puerto Rico has offered tax-free status to many industries. A number have accepted, particularly apparel manufacturers. But some have left lately because

TERRORISTS OR PATRIOTS

inflation, fueled by the need to import so many of life's necessities, is boosting the cost of living at an unusually rapid rate. Tourism is a major economic factor, but as elsewhere, Puerto Rican tourism tends to be a low-wage industry.

Statehood advocates contend that full status in the Union would qualify Puerto Rico for more Federal programs and would enable it to revise its local tax structure to make living and working here more attractive. Though Puerto Ricans do not pay Federal income taxes, island income levies are notably high, in part because of the tax breaks given industry.

Commonwealth advocates, while adamantly against statehood, are in favor of renegotiating the commonwealth status.

Former Governor Hernandez Colon says that commonwealth status gives Puerto Rico "the essential bond of common citizenship" with the rest of the United States but also permits the island to "maintain its own personality."

At the moment, Congress is giving no serious consideration to a new status agreement with Puerto Rico. President Carter said recently that any initiatives for change in status would have to come from the island, and he added:

"Whatever Puerto Rico's people want to do is acceptable to me. If the Puerto Rican people want to be a state, I will support it. If the Puerto Rican people want to be a commonwealth, I will support it. If the Puerto Rican people want to be an independent nation, I will support it."

October 11, 1977

There's a place in America where people really believe in the good old hometown virtues.

They believe in voting. They believe in education. They believe in serving their country. They believe in work.

Their hometown: Puerto Rico, U.S.A.

No people under the American flag more strongly endorse the principles that have built this nation than the people of Puerto Rico. In last November's election, over 77% of the voting age population turned out. That's higher than any state in the union. Puerto Ricans have also contributed outstandingly to the defense of the country. In fact, in proportion to population, they have given up more lives in defense of the United States than any of the 50 states. The Puerto Rican worker averages 12.1 years of schooling. Nearly one of every four has been to college.

Puerto Rico's workers are people who get things done. The Puerto Rican worker returns $4.03 in value to his employer for every dollar he himself earns, compared to the U.S. national average of $3.36. Absenteeism and job turnover are significantly lower than on the mainland. They're close to a million strong, with 51% under 35 years old. They're intelligent, industrious, ambitious, with a high ability for learning new skills.

A land whose people believe in themselves—and in the American way of doing business: Puerto Rico, U.S.A.

Skilled, educated, hard working people are only one reason Puerto Rico is the ideal second home for American business. Now consider 17 other good reasons.

No U.S. Restriction On Repatriation Of Profits.
The U.S. Internal Revenue Code Section 936 permits you to bring current profits home to the mainland without U.S. taxes. With only a 7% to 10% Puerto Rico toll gate tax, you keep more of your net profit than is possible anywhere else under the U.S. flag.

Unique Tax Incentives.
In Puerto Rico, you pay no federal corporate income tax. Qualifying industries are eligible for local tax incentives applied to corporate earnings, real estate, personal property, and license fees for as long as 30 years.

Duty Free Entry Into The U.S.
In Puerto Rico, you are on U.S. soil; there are no duties, quotas, or surcharges from Puerto Rico to the mainland.

A Rich Local Market.
Puerto Rico is the world's seventh largest importer of goods from the U.S.A. A tremendous market already exists here for a wide range of industries which set up plants in Puerto Rico.

Familiar Business Climate.
You enjoy the protection and stability of the U.S. and Puerto Rican Constitutions. You operate under the same legal, postal, and telephone systems.

Currency is the U.S. dollar. You can carry on your business in English. And the people are U.S. citizens.

High Profit Potential.
Net profits per sales dollar for manufacturing plants in Puerto Rico exceed those on the U.S. mainland in industry after industry.

Financing Assistance.
Federal EDA and SBA programs are available to assist with your financing. In addition, Puerto Rico offers assistance through the Government Development Bank, its affiliated P.R. Development Fund, the Industrial Revenue Bond Authority, and many international banking facilities.

Dependable Utilities.
The quality and quantity of these vital services are excellent. A $2 billion modern electric system with a total capacity of 4.3 million kilowatts and a reserve margin of 2.3 million kilowatts insure no lack of power.

Excellent Communications.
You can direct dial all major U.S. cities from Puerto Rico. Also world wide telecommunications such as Telex and Data Processing are available.

Efficient Maritime Shipping.
Three major seaports offer extensive dockage and warehousing. The port of San Juan is the fifth largest mover of containers in the world.

Copious Air Freight.
21 airlines compete to speed your shipments to the U.S. mainland, Latin America, and Europe.

Extensive Highway Network.
Approximately 150 trucking companies and over 6,500 miles of good paved roads in an island just 100 miles long and 35 miles wide mean your plant in Puerto Rico is never more than 2 hours by truck from a seaport.

Plant Space Is Plentiful.
Existing industrial buildings are waiting for you to lease or rent for as little as 75¢ per sq. ft. per year.

Abundant Materials And Services.
Industrial materials include a wealth of petrochemicals and intermediate and finished resins and fibers; services include industrial applications such as metal finishing, tool and die making, and textile dyeing, as well as architectural, engineering, accounting, and computer programming firms.

Worker Training.
Puerto Rico provides specially equipped training centers and vocational schools and, if you qualify, shares the cost of training your workers in technical, supervisory, and managerial skills. In many cases, the government will also pay part of the wages for Puerto Rican workers on-the-job training in your company's island subsidiary, on the mainland, or in a foreign country.

Lower Labor Costs.
The Fair Labor Standards Act covers Puerto Rico, but industrial wages are much closer to the statutory minimum than they are on the mainland. As of August 1977, the average per hour wage for industrial workers in Puerto Rico was $3.05, as opposed to the U.S. average of $5.64.

Abundant Labor Supply.
The seventeenth reason is the first reason for doing business in Puerto Rico—the intelligent, industrious, ambitious people who make up your working force.

```
Commonwealth of Puerto Rico
Economic Development Administration
Dept. NY54
1290 Avenue of the Americas,
New York, N.Y. 10019
For specific information on how Puerto Rico can provide a profitable
climate for your business, please call toll free, (800) 223-0772.
In New York State call (212) 245-1200.
Write for your free copy of our brochure, "Gateway to Profits," with all the
facts and figures on worker productivity, tax incentives, and much more.
The products I might be interested in manufacturing in Puerto Rico are:

Name
Firm
Address
City
```

Puerto Rico, U.S.A.
The ideal second home for American Business.

November 17, 1977

Documents Show F.B.I. Harassed Puerto Rican Separatist Parties

By JO THOMAS
Special to The New York Times

WASHINGTON, Nov. 21—Starting in 1960, the Federal Bureau of Investigation conducted an 11-year campaign in New York City and Puerto Rico to disrupt and demoralize political parties advocating Puerto Rican independence, according to documents made public by the bureau today.

Although many pro-independence groups were targets in the campaign, the most consistent recipients of anonymous hate letters and leaflets were the Puerto Rican Independence Movement and its leader, Juan Mari Bras.

Mr. Mari Bras's heart attack in April 1964 was one of the "positive results" the documents cite for the bureau's campaign against him and his party.

The anti-independence campaign began in 1960 with fears that the Communist revolution in Cuba might be exported to Puerto Rico, the documents show. Originally, this F.B.I. program, part of its larger counterintelligence program, was designed to disrupt parties "which seek independence for Puerto Rico through other than lawful peaceful means."

Two Peaceful Groups

The documents show, however, that at least two of the campaign's most consistent targets did not have violence as a goal. The Puerto Rican Independence Movement, founded in 1959, "did not advocate violence but would accept anyone who believed in Puerto Rican independence," one report shows. And the Pro-Independence Federation of Universities was founded at the University of Puerto Rico at Rio Piedras in 1956 to work for independence peacefully and reform the university.

As the F.B.I. campaign began, the documents show, informants were instructed to "report even the slightest bits of information concerning the personal lives" of their subjects in New York City. Trouble with wives, welfare boards or unemployment boards, the documents explained, could be turned to the bureau's advantage "without actual harassment being employed."

In September 1962, a Bronx dentist sympathetic to Puerto Rican independence was the subject of an anonymous F.B.I. letter to New York State officials. The ungrammatical letter accused the man of practicing without a license and asked, "Why don you stop this man from hurt the Spanish people."

In 1964, the bureau sent an anonymous letter to a man accused in a bomb plot informing him that his estranged wife was romantically involved with Mr. Mari Bras. "If you are too much of a fool to resent being a cuckold, I as a friend will not allow it to go on," the letter said.

On another occasion, a letter was sent to a member of the Puerto Rican Socialist League who was "known to be extremely sensitive to criticism and prone to violence." The letter, purportedly written by Mr. Mari Bras's group, was "calculated to infuriate" its recipient.

The purpose of this, according to the documents, was "to promote the current ill feeling" between the two groups and "perhaps provoke further physical violence between members of these groups."

November 22, 1977

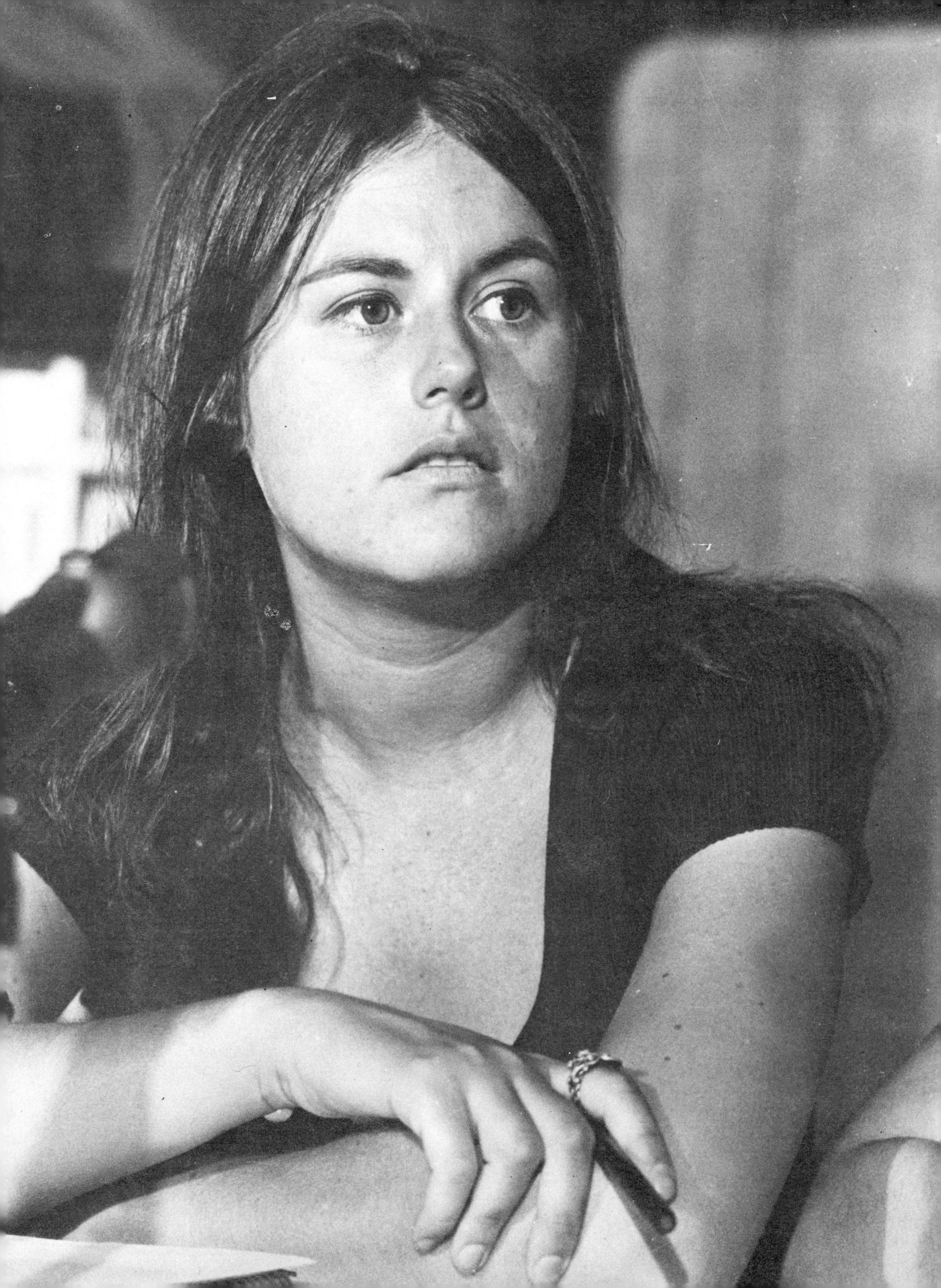

CHAPTER 4

Terrorism and the State Today

Bernadine Dohrn, a leader of the
Weathermen faction of S.D.S.

NYT Pictures

THE WESTERN DEMOCRACIES

'Vandals in the Mother Country'

By JOHN KIFNER

That's what the Weathermen are supposed to be...

"We were talking the other night and we realized that all our heroes are dead," Bill Ayers was saying. "Wow, what a trip!"

"Che, Nguyen Van Troi, the Vietnamese who tried to get McNamara. We're running their pictures in our paper with the line 'Live Like Him!' and they've all been killed. Outtasight, man. We've got a new slogan for the people that are going down to help with the sugar harvest: 'Cuba is for the living!'"

A couple of years and a lifetime ago, Bill Ayers founded Children's Community, a small, gentle, widely acclaimed experimental elementary school in Ann Arbor, Mich. A bespectacled, short-haired young man with a roundish face, he blended with the clutter of students sipping coffee in the cafeteria of the University of Illinois's science - fiction - modern Chicago Circle campus.

"There's a line in that Dylan song: 'The pump don't work 'cause the vandals took the handles,'" he said now. "That's what we're about—being vandals in the mother country."

The Bob Dylan song is "Subterranean Homesick Blues," which also contains the phrase, "You don't need a weatherman to know which way the wind blows," the working title for the program of a small, dedicated, uncompromisingly revolutionary faction of Students for a Democratic Society.

Bill Ayers is an officer and one of the chief theoreticians of the Weathermen. He shares with his fellow Weathermen a background of white, middle-class America, college and families that range from comfortable to wealthy; his own father is the board chairman of Commonwealth Edison, the Chicago utility company.

And, like his fellow Weathermen, he had just participated in "Four Days of Rage," which saw bands of white, middle-class youngsters racing through Chicago's Gold Coast and Loop, smashing windows and attacking policemen in a desperate political psychodrama they hoped would further armed class struggle and the overthrow of the state. It was the first real violence—deliberate, planned attack on persons and property—on the part of the New Left movement and its repercussions are not yet clear. For the Weathermen themselves, it was an experience that was by turns harrowing and exhilarating.

The Weathermen came into being last June at the national convention of Students for a Democratic Society,

---

JOHN KIFNER is a national correspondent of The Times based in Chicago.

---

an ideological orgy of chanted slogans, brandished Red Books, bitter factionalism, walkouts and the eventual purging of the Progressive Labor faction. The Weathermen emerged as the dominant force controlling the S.D.S. national office, now known as the Weather Bureau.

Their political theory is outlined in the Dylan-titled position paper (a slap at the P.L. faction's reliance on close reading of classic Maxist doctrine), which filled five and a half closely printed pages of the tabloid New Left Notes with scholastically reasoned, practically unreadable rhetoric.

The paper begins from the premise that all politics must be formulated in the context of American economic imperialism: "We are within the heartland of a worldwide monster, a country so rich from its worldwide plunder that even the crumbs doled out to the enclaved masses within its borders provide for material existence very much above the conditions of the masses of people of the world."

But, the paper argues, there is a worldwide revolution in progress against American imperialism by the Third World peoples of Asia, Latin America and Africa. Within the "mother country" itself, this revolution is already under way on the part of the oppressed "black colony."

"If necessary," the paper says, "black people could win self-determination, abolishing the whole imperialist system and seizing state power to do it, without the white movement, although the cost among whites and blacks both would be high."

THE Weathermen scenario sees American military might overextended and weakened in losing colonial struggles all over the world and an armed black force rising up and seizing control of the Government. It is imperative, the paper argues, for whites to "get on the right side" of the impending revolution immediately. There is no time left for what Weathermen describe as "leafletting at the factory gate." White revolutionaries must take action that will give material—not merely moral—support to the black and Third World struggles, blows that will "increase the cost of empire," exemplary actions that will show others the way to smash (the favorite Weathermen verb) the state. It is a call for the opening of a new front "behind enemy lines," much as French leftist terrorists increased the cost of the Algerian and Indochinese wars.

But the paper sees white workers as being hopelessly bought off with the small comforts and relatively better positions which have accrued from the exploitation of black and Third World people—what Weathermen term "white-skin privilege" — and thus have been duped into racism. College students, too, are mired in their own middle-class aspirations and are too soft and self-interested to be true revolutionaries.

Rather, the Weathermen seek to organize a new constituency — a Revolutionary Youth Movement — among tough working-class high-school students and dropouts, bikers, greasers, rock freaks and street kids. These white youths, it is argued, are thoroughly alienated, trapped in "jail-like" schools, dropped out into dead-end jobs, scooped up by the draft, propertyless and harassed by the police. They are ready, the paper says, to "burn down their schools."

"Every year," said Bill Ayers, "there's a geometrically greater number of kids watching television and rooting for the Indians. They hate their jobs, hate their schools, hate their parents, hate the authorities. We're trying to show them there's an alternative to hating themselves.

"Cynicism runs real deep with these kids. But cynicism and apathy represent a high level of political consciousness. These kids who dropped out of high school are more perceptive than those of us who went through college," he went on. "They don't relate to peace politics. Struggle is the only healthy response to oppression. There's a band in Ann Arbor called The Up—16-year-old kids. Their pictures show two of them with bayonets on their guitars and the other two with rifles. They play with these bayonets on the ends of their guitars. Fantastic!"

THE Weatherman style evolved over the summer in several Midwestern collectives of about 10 to 30 people —there are now about a dozen across the country. The members of the collectives lived intensely: studying revolutionary doctrine and the works of Mao, writing, organizing and being watched by the police. Much of their time was spent in self-criticism sessions, harsh group therapy in which Weathermen urge one another to "push it out," to exorcise vestiges of bourgeois attitudes. Most of the collectives — largely at the urging of the women—have outlawed monogamy, because mates would stick up for each other in self-criticism sessions and undermine total collective discipline. The Weathermen are very serious about themselves.

"It's hard to be a good communist," says a New York Weatherman. "It's very, very hard, but we have to keep struggling."

The organizing technique that grew out of the collectives was fighting, putting people "up against the wall," creating instant polarization. The tough high-school kids must be shown, the reasoning went, that the radicals were not wimpy intellectuals—soft, privileged hippies — but real fighters, gang members in their own right. (The view imputed to the high-school kids seems to be secretly shared by some of the radicals themselves, and they are desperately trying to rid themselves of it. "We're just middle-class," said one Weatherman, explaining why the Chicago street-fighting was snuffed out so quickly. "We're only learning.")

The tactic called for engaging in a fight with high-school kids to demonstrate the radicals' toughness, or staging an attack on a hated institution such as a school. The youths would then presumably respect the revolutionaries, become curious about the action, and be open to being organized into a citywide revolutionary youth movement.

In Detroit, for instance, Weathermen would take red flags to working-class beaches in order to start fights. The results have not always been successful. A number of Weathermen have been badly beaten while proselytizing in this fashion — including national leader Mark Rudd, of Columbia fame, who was pummeled in a drive-in by youths whose potential revolutionary fervor had been sidetracked to mere surliness by the defeat of their football team — but their enthusiasm remains undimmed.

The Weatherman style really surfaced at an emotional S.D.S. national meeting in Cleveland over Labor Day weekend, where the Midwestern collectives explained their experiences of the summer. "Are you committed to the revolution?" the Weathermen challenged wavering radicals, urging them to become "tools of necessity." The 300 persons present voted to endorse the new tactics and many—including groups from New York and Boston—went home convinced they had found the correct road to revolution.

What Weatherman demands —and where its adherents find much of its appeal— is a total commitment to the revolution. Weatherman says that radicals must abandon their comfortable, hip existence of digging "The Battle of Algiers," the Black Panthers and other people's revolutions, smoking grass and sleeping late, and submit themselves to disciplined lives as revolutionaries. They must purge themselves of all elements of the hated "white-skin privilege." Weathermen know they face long jail terms, beatings and even possible death as a consequence of their actions, and they talk about it frequently among themselves. There is a quality approaching religious fanaticism.

A NUMBER of Weathermen have long been among the most dedicated activists; others were recently radicalized. Many have Establishment credentials saying they are very bright. Brian Flanagan, the 22-year-old Columbia student charged with attempted murder in connection with injuries to the Chicago assistant corporation counsel, Richard Elrod (the grand jury later reduced the charge to battery, for lack of evidence), was a National Merit Scholarship finalist. Some have dropped out of law or graduate schools.

They have come to be Weathermen out of a variety of experiences, with a common thread of frustration at their impotence in the face of what they see as the interlocking, oppressive nature of American institutions. Two of the New York group were teachers last year in the Ocean Hill-Brownsville schools. Several of the members of the Boston collective were leaders in the "moderate" New Left caucus of Harvard S.D.S., which originally opposed the take-over of University Hall led by the P.L.'s Worker-Student Alliance caucus. One of the major influences on this group was the bloody police bust of the building. Their leader, Eric Mann, was the vice president of the Cornell Interfraternity Council in his undergraduate days.

But there has also been a good deal of opposition to the Weathermen within other elements of the left. The former S.D.S. national secretary, Mike Klonsky, split from the Ruddites to form the Revolutionary Youth Movement-II (R.Y.M.-II to Weatherman's R.Y.M.-I), which was to hold its own rival set of demonstrations. R.Y.M.-II adherents, derisively called Running Dogs by the Weathermen, believe in more traditional organizing methods, contending that conditions are ripe for revolution, with blacks in the vanguard, but that white workers are also exploited and can be won over. R.Y.M.-II has formed alliances with the Black Panthers and with new Chicago radical groups like the Puerto Rican Young Lords, but is less cohesive than the tightly knit

❝These high-school kids eat it up when they learn that we're beating up Harvard professors.❞

Weathermen and is somewhat handicapped by a tendency toward even duller rhetoric.

Another group, which includes some of the leaders of the Columbia revolt, disturbed at the tendencies of both factions, split off and is building a new organization in New York known as the Mad Dogs.

An indication of the tensions came in September, when Weathermen barged into a New York meeting of a coalition of radicals planning a demonstration at Fort Dix in support of a group of soldiers charged with rioting in the base stockade—the Fort Dix 38—and announced the march would be held *their* way. Their way, participants in the meeting said later, was to charge the stockade. Any soldier who did not join the ensuing rebellion by turning his weapon on his officers would be "objectively con-

277

The Western Democracies

sidered a pig" and "dealt with." Organizers working with G.I.'s were horrified. The coalition solved the problem by rescheduling the march for Oct. 12, when the Weathermen could be expected to be still tied up in Chicago; more than 5,000 people marched onto the base in defiance of regulations and were eventually driven off with tear gas.

THROUGH the early fall, the Weathermen were staging a series of actions to build "the new Red Army" for their Chicago demonstrations. Seventy-five women from around the country descended on Pittsburgh, tied up five Quakers who had attempted to decline the use of their mimeograph machine, and charged into South Hills High School, brandishing Vietcong flags and shouting: "Jailbreak, jailbreak!" In what was later described as "an uncool getaway," 26 were arrested. In a Detroit suburb, nine women —the Motor City Nine— stormed into an examination at Macomb County Community College and began lecturing on the war, racism and the exploitation of women until two male students got up to leave. "It is reported," wrote New Left Notes, "that the Motor City Nine responded to such an exhibition of male chauvinism and general pig behavior by attacking the men with karate and preventing them from leaving the room." All were arrested.

In Brooklyn, Weathermen struck a high school, tying up and gagging two teachers with adhesive tape and handing out leaflets announcing that they were "part of a big gang" all over the country bent on establishing international communism. Earlier, members of the Brooklyn group had been arrested in a scuffle with a policeman, growing out of a luncheonette owner's refusal to serve them because of their long hair. The youths allegedly took the cop's gun away, then stood about, lecturing the other patrons on the political implications of their act, while police reinforcements came and bagged them all.

The Boston collective has engaged in several fights, taken over a class at Girls' Latin School and staged a raid on the Harvard Center for International Affairs, in which, after ripping out the telephones, they beat an instructor and a librarian.

"These high-school kids eat it up when they learn that we are beating up Harvard professors," explained a Boston Weatherman. "They hate Harvard. They ask us why we did it, and soon we are explaining our whole movement to them."

TENS of thousands of people," said the Weatherman leaflets, were coming to "Tear Apart Pig City," to "Bring the War Home," and the Weathermen fully believed that they would attract at least 5,000 demonstrators to what was billed as a showdown with the Chicago police.

But when the main phalanx marched into Lincoln Park on the night of Wednesday, Oct. 8, white helmets glittering, Vietcong flags sewn to the backs of their stiff, new dungaree jackets, and all the Weathermen in the world gathered on a little knoll near the statue of Giuseppe Garibaldi, the new Red Army numbered only about 300. The first National Action called by S.D.S. since the march on Washington in 1965 had been shunned by everyone but the Weatherman cadres.

"What we have learned from the Chinese people, what we have learned from the Vietnamese people, is that women can fight," a girl shouted in the sing-song rhythm of S.D.S. oratory as the crowd, augmented by about 200 reporters, spectators and plainclothes men, rallied around a bonfire fed by pieces of bright orange park benches on the spot where the tear gas had rolled in the summer of '68. "Right on!" shouted the Weathermen, in the approved Panther manner, shooting clenched fists into the air. "Right on!"

Despite the songs, chants and incantations, and the morale-building rumors that more street fighters were en route, the gathering — called for the second anniversary of the death of Che Guevara— had the desperate rote feeling of a pep rally for a high-school team deep in a losing streak. They were carrying clubs and Vietcong flags on stout poles, but the faces of the Weathermen under the helmets seemed very young and scared. About a third were women, and many of the men, even in their work boots and heavy gloves, seemed slight and small: a dwarf battalion to set against the beefy police legions.

Then a speaker was saying: "We're going down to the Drake Hotel where Pig Judge Hoffman [Julius J. Hoffman, the judge in the Chicago conspiracy trial] lives. On to the Drake!" A pack of helmets were in front, and suddenly everyone was moving through the dark at a run, headed for the southeast corner of the park. It was 10:20, and the first rock of the revolution went through a window of the Chicago Historical Society.

The police were stashed a couple of blocks north, in dozens of cars and small trucks called "squadrols," in their old staging area behind the Fine Arts Building. Two nights before, persons unknown had blown up the statue of a policeman in Haymarket Square (honoring seven officers killed by a bomb when they charged into a labor rally in 1886, setting off the infamous Haymarket riot, in the aftermath of which known radicals were rounded up and eight swiftly convicted of conspiracy to murder). The head of the Police Sergeants Association announced that a "kill or be killed" war had been declared between the radicals and the police. But the police were being held out of sight and under restraint in accordance with the Walker Commission report; like any military force, they were perfectly prepared to fight the last war.

THE Weathermen swarmed out of the park onto Clark Street, in front of the all-glass facade of the North Federal Savings Bank. *Smash*, and an electric shiver ran through the crowd. *Smash, smash*: There were neat, cobwebbed holes in the plate glass. Vietcong banners flying, the crowd was moving south at a quick trot, chanting, "Long live the victory of the people's war!" and creating two, three, many broken windows.

Thunk, crash. Sticks and clubs wiped out the windows of cars guilty of parking in the ruling-class Gold Coast neighborhood. Up ahead, plainclothes men were frantically waving startled drivers out of the road; there were no uniformed police in sight. The Weathermen were scooping up new ammunition—bricks, chunks of concrete, from the debris of a middle-class urban-renewal site.

The first police skirmish line appeared a block south, and the crowd suddenly cut sharply left, east on Goethe, screeching a war whoop— Eeeii-ya-ya-ya-ya-ya-ya! — the cry of the rebel Algerian women, which they had learned from watching "The Battle of Algiers." An old man in doorman's braid, a lifetime of letting out poodles and keeping a close watch on the delivery boys behind him, peered out of his apartment house and a kid, all hair and eyes and elbows, hopped over a shin-high hedge on a dead run with a 3-foot length of 2-by-4 in hand. *Whap, whap, whap.* Three sets of windows were gone, and the old man staggered back, his mouth working and no sound coming out.

A ROLLS-ROYCE was wasted outside the Ambassador East Hotel, and the crowd was running south on State. At the corner of Division, a squadrol, its blue light flashing, was pulled across the intersection and a line of about a dozen cops was waiting, nightsticks held down, horizontal across their thighs in both hands.

"Charge!" yelled a small youth in front, running straight at the police line. A shower of rocks came out of the crowd and everybody kept running and yelling: "Chaaarge!"

The police were astounded. Two cops on the east corner had their arms up against the rocks and were ducking back. The first wave hit the police line and the stunned moment was over. Policemen were bringing down Weathermen with flying tackles and there were quick scuffles all over the street. In the middle of the intersection, a lanky youth with a long pole and a policeman with a nightstick were sparring like medieval yeomen.

The rear of the march turned back and headed north, smashing windows as it went; crowds poured out of restaurants and bars, and a smoke grenade went off in the middle of the street. More police were pouring in to hold the intersection, and Frank Sullivan, the police director of public relations, was shouting: "Where are the cameras now?" The police, as they would at the rest of the public scenes, worked for the most part with a swift, tough efficient professionalism. There were not the wild, cursing, brutal, club-swinging charges of the 1968 convention. This time, the roles were reversed: it was a demonstrator riot.

The Weathermen ran in small bands to the east, north and west, taking a heavy toll of arrests as the action grew tougher in the dark. The police fired pistols and shotguns near Lake Shore Drive; a 22-year-old Seattle youth was shot seriously in the neck, and two other demonstrators were found in a garage on Astor Place with buckshot wounds.

By midnight, workmen were putting up neat tape and plywood patches over the broken windows along Clark Street, 60 Weathermen were being fingerprinted and booked, and the remainder were filtering back to apartments and movement centers.

AT Henrotin Hospital, the emergency room was crowded with police and demonstrators as a short, dark-haired young woman slipped out the door. The police were mostly checking in with bruises ("contusions and abrasions") to secure insurance payments, while the demonstrators were bloody and bandaged. For all the claims by both sides of demonstrator ferocity, most of the injuries to police were minor. A number were bitten.

The Weathermen were told to avoid the hospitals if they were hurt because they would probably be arrested, but the young woman had been brought in by the policemen who subdued her. Last spring, she had dropped out of law school, two months short of her degree, to become a street fighter. Now, her mouth was swollen where the nightstick had landed, and there was a row of big stitches ("They got pig doctors in there, man. He stitched me up without anesthetic and just dug it") across her upper lip.

"How many are in there?" she asked.

"Six of yours, seven cops," somebody answered.

"We won," she grinned through her loosened teeth. "Outtasight."

"THOUSANDS of young women will destroy the Armed Forces Induction Center," announced the schedule on the Weatherman wall poster.

About 70 members of the Women's Militia, wearing helmets, leather jackets, heavy gloves and carrying Vietcong flags, clubs and a couple of lengths of iron pipe, gathered early the next morning at the announced spot in Grant Park. Police lined the park and their tight huddle was completely surrounded by a pack of reporters, cameramen and large plainclothes men as the young women made speeches to one another, chanted, shouted: "Right on!" and sang: "We love our uncle Ho Chi Minh/ Deep, deep/ Down, down/ Deep down in our hearts/ We love our chairman Mao Tse-tung...."

"For the first time in history women are getting themselves together," Bernadine Dohrn, a University of Chicago law-school graduate and leading Weatherwoman, told the huddle. "We're not picketing in front of bra factories now. We're not a woman's organization engaged in self-indulgent — —.... A few buckshot wounds mean we're doing the right thing.... Bullets are not going to stop us. Threats are not going to stop us.... We're living behind enemy lines.... We refuse to be good Germans...."

Then they were in motion, moving off briskly toward the edge of the park. A line of about 20 helmeted policemen blocked them off, and Deputy Chief James Riordan came running up with a bullhorn, shouting, "Hold it, hold it right there." There was a moment's hesitation, a girl shouted, "The sidewalks belong to the people," and the women in front made a little lunge toward the police line.

The scuffle was brief. A dozen women were gritting their teeth, cursing, wiggling and kicking as they struggled in the grip of burly officers. Some were wrestled to the ground by several policemen; others were half-dragged, half-carried to waiting paddy wagons. "The people of the world are going to kill you," screamed one young woman as she was thrown into the van. A plainclothes man scurried about, scooping up an armful of fallen clubs.

The rest of the women fell back a few steps, surrounded by a ring of police. "You are armed and you are carrying weapons," Chief Riordan warned, redundantly, through his bullhorn. "If you set foot on the sidewalk you will be arrested." The women cursed and glared back at the police. Some had their arms around one another's shoulders and several were crying.

"Helmets aren't weapons, you pigs," one spat. "They're protection."

Then, they took off their helmets and dropped their clubs. The police marched them off two and a half blocks to a subway and took their pictures as they passed through the turnstile and left.

At noon, a Weatherman speaker was hooted by municipal workers as he tried to hold a press conference in the Civic Center plaza. Then, in the afternoon, their own actions called off, the Weathermen filtered into the rival demonstration called by R.Y.M.-II outside the Federal Building, where they heard the Illinois Black Panther chairman, Fred Hampton, denounce them as "adventuristic, anarchistic and Custeristic."

Red Squad detectives moved through the crowd, picking out youths they said they recognized from the Wednesday night rampage, grabbing them and hustling them to nearby vans. Lines of uniformed police began to form on the street. The R.Y.M.-II adherents moved off to their scheduled rally at the International Harvester plant, where workers were protesting loss of jobs from the planned moving of the factory. The Weathermen huddled uncertainly, then left too, a number being picked off by detectives.

That afternoon, Gov. Richard B. Ogilvie ordered more than 2,500 Chicago area National Guard men to active duty. The Weathermen regarded the calling out of the Guard as a victory, although, in reality, only two companies —about 300 men—were sent onto the streets and they were soon withdrawn.

Friday began rainy, dreary and quiet. The Weathermen once again called off their planned actions—"jailbreaks" in several high schools and a march on Judge Hoffman's courtroom—to rethink their strategy. Police were in the schools, police were busting Weathermen in the streets, police were everywhere. The R.Y.M.-II people staged a demonstration at the county hospital to protest "butcher shop" medical practices, then held a press conference to dissociate themselves once again from the Weathermen. But, in the wake of the rampages, R.Y.M.-II, the Panthers and the Young Lords were being pegged momentarily as the good-guy, friendly revolutionaries, so they also took the occasion to deny that they were nonviolent.

THE Weathermen were quartered—somewhat uneasily—in seminaries and churches in Chicago and suburban Evanston, an act of charity that enraged many parishioners. Throughout Thursday night and Friday, they spent hour after hour in self-criticism sessions, analyzing their philosophy and their actions. The window-breaking was fine, it was thought, but there was not enough actual fighting of the police. Some objected that Volkswagens as well as ruling-class automobiles were smashed during Wednesday's action. In the middle of all this, a Weatherman recognized a police undercover detective who had arrested him earlier in the week in a group of demonstrators in Evanston's Emmanuel Methodist Church. The radicals fell on the agent, beating him up, until the pastor of the church intervened and asked them to leave.

At 2 A.M. Saturday, a force of about a hundred helmeted Chicago and Evanston police broke open the door to the Covenant United Methodist Church and arrested 43 Weathermen who were staying there. The remaining Weathermen were shaken and tense, but determined to go ahead with their final action —a march into the Loop that afternoon.

The Weathermen began gathering around noon by the stump of the former police statue in Haymarket Square, at first in small groups, apprehensive under the unfriendly looks of the massed policemen. Then larger groups came marching in, raising clenched fists and chanting until the crowd numbered about 200. Some of the groups pulled helmets and dungaree jackets from shopping bags and quickly put them on. A clump of burly men drifted through the crowd, suddenly pulled nightsticks from under their raincoats and began thrashing about. The detectives pulled out five bloodied radicals, including Mark Rudd, and hustled them off, under arrest.

"We are small, but we have stepped into the way of history," John (J.J.) Jacobs, a Weatherman leader wearing a red football helmet and a black leather coat, told the crowd, standing straight by the base of the statue, his arms folded across his chest.

The Western Democracies

"The battle in Vietnam is one battle in the world revolution. It is the Stalingrad of American imperialism. We are part of that Stalingrad. We are guerrillas fighting behind enemy lines.... We have no choice but to fight.... We have to show by example that it can be done.... We do not have to win politically against the pigs—just the fact that we are willing to fight the pigs is a political victory...."

Then a girl in an oversized helmet was speaking: "We went into the streets.... We moved together in the streets and moved into history.... This is the new battleground against American imperialism .... It took us only four days to begin a movement of people who know how to fight .... White America has joined the revolution. We are the first whites to fight back.... We're going to move through the streets and let the Vietnamese, the Latin, the Chinese people know they're not alone ...."

Then the Weathermen were in motion, moving on the agreed-upon march route, lined with policemen, at a quick trot, a black flag with a hammer and sickle flying. "Ho, Ho, Ho Chi Minh, N.L.F. is going to win," they shouted, and the chant and the stomp of their work boots echoed hypnotically as they raced through the underpass of the North Western Railroad.

"That was our real victory, not making this a 'stop-the-shooting' march," said Bill Ayers later. "We thought it was going to be a wipe-out. We were all terrified. We had a joke about how all the people in the front row had to be terrified. But we went ahead anyway. Saturday was the greatest."

At Madison and La Salle, a war whoop suddenly went up, the marchers broke out of line, a huge plate glass window in an abandoned Union Pacific office building went out, and the march was charging into and through the police lines. Glass was crashing, helmeted youths and policemen were running through the crowds of shoppers and there were knots of fighting up and down the street. Elrod, the assistant corporation counsel, was lying motionless in front of the Western Cocktail Lounge. The police said he had been injured as he tried to help prevent a youth from escaping. Clumps of youths were lying, some bleeding, in heaps in the intersections, waiting for the wagons. Others were held against cars, or face down on the pavement, a police brogan firmly in each back. It was all over in a few minutes.

There were 103 arrests in the Loop, making a total of 290 arrests for the four days. Within minutes after the action was over, city sanitation trucks were moving through the streets, sweeping up the broken glass and other debris.

THE immediate reaction to the Weathermen was almost as chaotic as the action itself. Most Chicagoans were outraged; the police found themselves the new heroes of the day and men with beards were assailed on the streets. There would be few liberals coming forward to defend the "Chicago 290."

Within the movement, many regarded the action as a pathetic, lunatic failure which would only provide new excuses for increasing governmental repression, and believed the Weathermen had destroyed themselves and S.D.S. as a mass organization along with them. The radical press was sharply critical, with the weekly National Guardian particularly outraged, calling the action a "penny-dreadful Keystone Kops melodrama."

But many others had admiration for the Weathermen's courage and determination. "For 15 minutes there in the Loop, they were beautiful," said an editor of the underground paper Vortex in Lawrence, Kan.

The Weathermen themselves have built strong defenses to deal with the criticisms of other radicals and their own doubts and fears, and the evaluation they give outsiders is uniform and doctrinaire. "We think it's been a tremendous success, a total success," said one. "For the first time in this country, white people are showing they're willing to fight against imperialism. Even when they raised the level of oppression against us, we raised the level of struggle against them."

But within their own councils, the Weathermen are disturbed by their failure to attract the hoped-for dropout army through their kamikaze techniques and are undergoing what is generally known as an "agonizing reappraisal." One self-criticism skit, for instance, satirizes Weatherman organizing methods. It begins with a Weatherman thrusting a leaflet on a potential convert, then snatching it back, saying: "No, don't read it. Reading's a white-skin privilege," and ends with the Weatherman explaining: "So, there's no other choice; either you're with the pigs of the world or the people of the world. If you side with the pigs, you'll be killed after the revolution. Or you can join the people of the world and come on the streets with us, and be killed anyway."

"Militarily, we lost. We were creamed, beaten and shot at. But it was a beginning, a break with the old New Left," a Weatherman official said a couple of weeks after the action. "And we've got a lot of potential for errors. Maybe the most dangerous is *macho* errors—violence for violence's sake, like in 'The Wild One'"—violence-tripping and death-tripping. But we've got to learn off our errors. And we've got to build a base that's at least sympathetic."

A MONTH after the Weatherman action, some 250,000 Americans took themselves to Washington to march quietly, wave "V" signs and plead with their Government to listen to them. It was, everybody said, a very nice demonstration. The President of the United States was barricaded behind rows of buses and $1-million worth of troops, watching television—the Purdue-Ohio State game.

Late in the afternoon, more than 6,000 young people detached themselves from the main rally and headed on the run for the Justice Department to protest the Chicago conspiracy trial. Bottles and rocks were thrown, breaking 17 windows, and a Vietcong flag was twice run up the building's main flagpole. The police pumped enormous amounts of CS gas into the streets, and, when the youths staggered free and recovered, many went on window-breaking rampages or regrouped and started new demonstrations, only to be gassed again.

Attorney General John N. Mitchell stood briefly on a balcony, smoking his pipe and watching the demonstrations, while his deputy, Richard Kleindienst, muttered angrily nearby, an American flag pinned to his chest. When the Attorney General got home, he told his wife that it "looked like a Russian revolution going on."

A group of Weathermen were in the rear of the plane on the flight back from Washington (half-fare youth cards being a great boon to revolution), draped across the seats, laughing and singing, and Bill Ayers was talking to the stewardess, whose plastic smile never changed.

"You could see the red flags waving over this huge cloud of gas," Bill Ayres was saying. "It looked like the Russian revolution. Outta-sight." ■

January 4, 1970

Bombs, Dynamite and Woman's Body Found in Ruins of 11th St. Townhouse

By DOUGLAS ROBINSON

A large cache of dynamite, homemade bombs and a second body were found yesterday in the water-filled basement of a Greenwich Village townhouse that was destroyed by explosions and a fire last Friday.

The explosives, which included 60 sticks of dynamite, were found 20 feet from a spot where earlier in the day firemen and the police discovered the torso of a young woman in the ruins of the house, at 18 West 11th Street.

After finding the dynamite, the police quickly ordered the evacuation of several houses in the immediate area and asked residents of a large apartment house across the street to move into rear rooms away from windows.

For the first time since the destruction of the townhouse

TERRORISM AND THE STATE TODAY

last Friday, the police officially declared that the initial explosion had been caused by a bomb.

"The people in the house were obviously putting together the component parts of a bomb and they did something wrong," said Assistant Chief Inspector Albert Seedman, who is in charge of the police investigation.

Before the indication of exactly how much dynamite was in the ruins, Inspector Seedman said there was "enough to blow up most of the block."

The first body found in the wreckage of the four-story brick house was that of Theodore Gold, 23 years old, who was identified as a member of the Weathermen, a radical faction of the Students for a Democratic Society.

Two women, who were led from the burning house by rescuers on Friday, have disappeared. One of them has been identified as Catherine Platt Wilkerson, daughter of the owner of the house and also believed to be a member of the Weathermen. She and her companion are still missing.

Last night, however, Miss Wilkerson's stepfather cast some doubt on whether the young woman was still a member of the Weathermen and indicated she had quit the militant group.

The body of the second victim of the blast was not immediately identified and Dr. Elliott Gross, associate medical examiner, said "it will take some time before we have any idea of who she is."

The body was brought from the ruins of the townhouse in the scoop of a large power shovel that has been lifting debris from the basement. The head was badly damaged, both hands were missing and the left leg was severed.

The first hint that the basement of the home has been filled with explosives came when, at 4:20 P.M., the power shovel brought up four 12-inch lead pipes packed with dynamite with wires leading from them.

A few minutes later, workers found three packages of dynamite with about eight sticks of the explosive in each package. The sticks were taped together and each package had a fuse.

Searchers then discovered four cartons of dynamite and 30 blasting caps in the soggy debris of the subbasement. All of the explosives as well as the woman's body were found in a workroom that contained a work bench, a vise and a number of tools.

Two members of the Police Department's bomb squad, Patrolmen Christopher Hayes and Kenneth Dudonis, gingerly examined the dynamite while other policemen began ordering people from nearby homes.

After looking over the dynamite, the bomb squad began to load it into the wire-mesh truck used to transport explosives and dangerous chemicals to the department's disposal area at Fort Tilden in Rockaway.

Last night, a spokesman for the E. I. du Pont de Nemours Company in Wilmington, Del., said that "dynamite is a relatively insensitive explosive that is exploded by a cap, which itself is highly explosive.

"It is not always ignited in a blast or a fire because it is intended to be used in the field as a safe explosive," the spokesman said.

Inspector Seedman, who held an impromptu news conference well away from the ruins of the townhouse, said there was no doubt that those in the house had been making bombs.

Early reports put the cause of the explosions and fire as leaking gas, but, over the weekend, the investigators began to lean toward the dynamite theory because of the magnitude of the blasts.

A neighbor of the Wilkerson family, Mrs. Susan Wager of 50 West 11th Street, the police said, positively identified Miss Wilkerson as one of the two women who ran from the building after the explosion.

Although the police said they had no definite idea of who the second woman was, they said they were looking for 26-year-old Kathy Boudin for questioning.

Miss Boudin, whom the police described as a close friend of the Wilkerson girl, is the daughter of Leonard B. Boudin, a lawyer associated with anti-war cases who was counsel for Dr. Benjamin Spock in a case charging the pediatrician with conspiring to advise young men to avoid the draft.

Mr. Boudin, who was believed to be traveling, could not immediately be reached for comment. His daughter, for whom the police have searched unsuccessfully for several days, has been involved in left-wing militant causes.

March 11, 1970

BOMBINGS ON RISE OVER THE NATION

Police Say Most Are Caused by Left-Wing Militants, Both Black and White

By STEVEN V. ROBERTS
Special to The New York Times

LOS ANGELES, March 12—The mysterious bombings in New York and Maryland this week are only the latest in what appears to be a rising wave of such incidents across the nation.

The bombings have been a problem for at least a year, but they appear to have accelerated in recent weeks, causing sharp concern among citizens and investigative agencies in widely scattered cities throughout the country.

In Seattle, for instance, there were 32 bombings in the last year, with more than two-thirds of them coming in the last four months. The damage in Seattle alone was estimated by investigative agencies at more than $600,000.

In San Francisco, the police report 62 bombings in the last year, with the pace increasing in the last month. On Feb. 16 a bomb exploded inside a police station, killing one officer and wounding five others. Five days earlier a bomb detonated in the parking lot of a police station in Berkeley, injuring two policemen and demolishing three cars.

In Chicago, a large dynamite charge was found last September in a telephone booth in the Civic Center, housing court and local government offices. On Oct. 6, a bomb destroyed a statue erected in the memory of several policemen killed in the Haymarket Square riot of 1866.

There are just a portion of the hundreds of incidents in many cases the bombers have never been caught. According to the police, however, most of the attacks have been planned by youthful left-wing Militants, white and black; a few, the police say, have been the work of right-wingers, including foreign exiles.

The targets have tended to be symbols of the "establishment" and the Vietnam war—corporate offices, police stations, Reserve Officer Training Corps headquarters and other buildings associated with the military.

Law enforcement officials generally agree that the bombings are the work of a very small fraction of the young people who describe themselves as "radical." Moreover the attackers tend to be highly disorganized and fragmented.

'A Crazy Mixed Bag'

"These are the far-out, violent revolutionaries of the ultra-New Left. We've got a crazy mixed bag," said Charles O'Brien, Deputy Attorney General of California. "I wish they would form a conspiracy, they would be much easier to keep track of and deal with."

The rash of bombings burst into prominence last week when two young people were killed in a blast in a Greenwich Village townhouse, apparently while working with explosives. On Tuesday, two associates of H. Rap Brown, the black militant leader, were killed when explosives ignited in a car they were driving in Maryland.

The nest day a bomb exploded in a courthouse in Cambridge, Md., the original site of Mr. Brown's pending trial for inciting to riot. Last night, bombs exploded in three Manhattan headquarters of large corporations.

Bombings are not a new phenomenon in this country. Throughout the 1950's and '60's, Negro civil rights workers were frequent targets. The home of Rev. Dr. Martin Luther King and several black churches were bombed in Montgomery, Ala, in 1956.

On Sept. 15, 1963, a church in Birmingham was bombed, killing five little girls who were attending Sunday school. Attacks were so common in the city that it was called "Bombingham."

Extreme right-wing groups such as the Minutemen have long distributed information to their members on how to make explosives, Mr. O'Brien said. In fact, he added, "It's clear that the ultra-left has benefited from the experience and expertise of the right. Their manuals are obviously cribbed wholesale from right-wing pamphlets."

Right-wingers continue to be active. In Denver, recently, dynamite demolished 23 buses used in the city's school integration program. But most of the activity seems to be coming from the left, as these reports from correspondents of The New York Times indicate:

SAN FRANCISCO—In addition to the police attack, an unexploded bomb was found earlier this month in barracks at the Oakland Army Base housing soldiers bound for Vietnam.

281

The Western Democracies

The same day a second bomb was discovered in a moving freight train headed for a large oil refinery in Martinez.

DENVER—In addition to the school buses, targets in Denver have included the houses of a district judge, a white conservative member of the school board and a Negro who brought a suit demanding school integration.

At the University of Colorado in Boulder, a university police car and a city police car were firebombed earlier this month. The headquarters of the R.O.T.C. was demolished and a Selective Service office in Colorado Springs was also firebombed.

TUCSON, Ariz.—A dynamite charge exploded last month on the sidewalk in front of a building containing four local draft boards. All the windows were broken.

DETROIT—Policemen estimate about 30 incidents in the last year, including dynamite attacks on two police stations. Two draft boards, an Army recruiter, and an Army vehicle were also hit, with little damage. Explosions also occurred at the University of Michigan in Ann Arbor in buildings containing the R.O.T.C., the Institute for Science and Technology and the Central Intelligence Agency.

MADISON, Wis. — Last September, $25,000 of damage was done by a bomb planted in a National Guard armory. In December, several University of Wisconsin buildings were attacked, including a campus landmark — an old red brick gym that houses the R.O.T.C.

Dynamite was found last month outside a plant owned by the Wisconsin Power and Light Company. The incident followed probably the most spectacular attack of all, which occurred when unidentified persons stole a small plane and flew over the sprawling Badger Ammunition plant in Baraboo, 35 miles north of Madison. The plane dropped two small jars filled with gunpowder but the landed in a snow bank and failed to ignite.

SEATTLE — Outside the university, the home of State Senator Fred Dore, who lived on the fringe of a largely black central district, was badly damaged last month. Senator Dore soon moved to another part of town. Stores throughout the black area have been attacked including one owned by a merchant who had shot an armed intruder.

NEW YORK — Ninety three explosions of various sorts were reported in 1969. In addition the police reported 19 unexploded devices and 2,587 threats. For 1968, the police reported 81 explosions, 1,094 threats and 10 unexploded devices.

Among the most serious 1969 incidents were explosions at the headquarters of the United Fruit Company, the Marine Midland Grace Trust Company and the Selective Service Center on Whitehall Street. Four white youths were arrested and charged with a total of eight bombings.

Students Cheer Fire

Twenty-one members of the Black Panthers were also seized on charges of planning the destruction of department stores, a police station, and the New Haven Railroad. Thirteen of the Panthers are now facing trial, and the home of Judge John M. Murtagh, the trial judge, was recently attacked with firebombs.

In other areas, R.O.T.C. buildings were bombed at Texas A.&M., Washington University in St. Louis, and the University of Oregon. Students at Washington cheered as the fire from a Molotov cocktail raged through the building, and booed when firemen brought the blaze under control.

Police and academic experts offer various reasons for the bombings, but many agree with Dr. John Spiegel of the Lemberg Center for the Study of Violence at Brandeis University, who said:

"The young people have had protests and riots and disorders —they've done everything one can do in the way of peaceful and unplanned protest, and not much has changed. To that degree there is an increasing sense of desperation, and a sense of vengefulness."

Among radical youths, talk of "armed struggle" has been common for some time. For most of them it remains just talk, but folowers of the New Left are not terribly surprised that some extreme elements have started bombing.

'Valid Tactic' to Some

"It's the obvious next step in the escalation of violence," said one observer. Another said: "The bombings have to be seen as part of the climate of violence we've had in this country. Violence seems to be a valid tactic across the board."

Several observers also pointed out that bombings had a contagious effect. As Mr. O'Brien put it. "There is no question that one mad act begets another. Zealots tend to be among the more imitative of people. The attention that a successful explosion gets in the press is the source of envy on the part of many psyches who think, by God, that's me way to do it."

March 13, 1970

U.S. to Tighten Surveillance of Radicals

By JAMES M. NAUGHTON
Special to The New York Times

WASHINGTON, April 11—The Nixon Administration, alarmed by what it regards as a rising tide of radical extremism, is planning to step up surveillance of militant left-wing groups and individuals.

The objective, according to White House officials, is to find out who the potential bomb planters and snipers may be before they endanger others.

Preparations for expanding and improving the domestic intelligence apparatus — informers, undercover agents, wiretaps—were disclosed in a series of interviews with key officials, who requested anonymity.

According to these officials, President Nixon is disturbed by the rash of bombings and bomb scares, courtroom disruptions and reports of small but growing numbers of young people who feel alienated from the American system.

On March 12, the same day that bombs exploded in three Manhattan office buildings, Mr. Nixon met over dinner in the White House with Irving Kristol, professor of urban values at New York University.

One aide who attended the dinner said the discussion included attempts to draw parallels between young, middle-class, white Americans who are resorting to violence and the Narodniki—children of the mid-19th century Russian aristocracy who murdered Czar Alexander II, and between militant black nationalists here and Algerian revolutionaries.

Mr. Kristol told the President it was not unrealistic to expect the Latin American resort to political kidnappings to spread soon to Washington. Mr. Kristol confirmed the dinner meeting and commented, "Some of these kids don't know what country this is. They think it's Bolivia.

Some, but not all, of Mr. Nixon's domestic advisers are convinced that the situation is critical. One of the more conservative aides contended, "We are facing the most severe internal security threat this country has seen since the Depression."

The officials have concluded that attempts to bring militants back into society's mainstream are as futile, as one stated it, "as turning off the radio in the middle of a ball game to try to change the score."

The official view is that extreme radicals cannot be won over with welfare, electoral or draft reforms or by White House appeals. It wouldn't make a bit of difference if the war and racism ended overnight," said a highly placed Nixon assistant. "We're dealing with the criminal mind, with people who have snapped for some reason. Accordingly, the Administration sees its prime responsibility as protecting the innocent from "revolutionary terrorism." The President said last month, when he asked Congress for broader Federal jurisdiction and stiffer penalties in bombing cases, that they were the work of "young criminals posturing as romantic revolutionaries."

To keep tabs on individuals referred to by the President as "potential murderers" will require updating an intelligence system geared to monitoring the Communists three decades ago, the aides said.

They said it was easy to keep track of the Communists because they had a highly organized system that undercover agents could penetrate easily. But today's alleged anarchists are disorganized, operating in groups of three or four, and difficult to detect.

"We know there are people training themselves in certain forms of guerrilla warfare and the use of explosives," said one official, "but it's extremely difficult to answer the who, when and how."

A Nixon aide who is aware of the Justice Department's intelligence operations said there was no advance warning of the arson that destroyed a Bank of America branch in Santa Barbara, Calif., last month. He said that "We knew of the New York bomb factory" in a Greenwich Village townhouse, but only just before it exploded on March 6, killing three young people.

White House officials wonder aloud why one of the victims, Diana Oughton, 28 years old, once active in legitimate reform efforts, became a member of a militant faction of the Stu-

TERRORISM AND THE STATE TODAY

dents for a Democratic Society.

"If we had a (phone) tap on Diana Oughton," a Presidential assistant said, "we might have arrested her before the bombs went off and, nobody would have died."

Survivor Is Traced

The official said that Federal agents had traced a survivor of the Greenwich Village blast, Cathlyn Platt Wilkerson, to Canada, but he expressed distress that the intelligence system was not capable of pinpointing her activities before she became a fugitive.

Administration sources would not disclose details of the changes they are preparing in the intelligence mechanism, although they said a good deal of interdepartmental discussion about them was under way.

One suggestion was said to be the possibility of the Justice Department providing grants through the Law Enforcement Assistance Administration to local police departments for training in domestic intelligence gathering.

Only New York City and District of Columbia police men have adequate intelligence systems, one official said, adding: "We need better trained people in metropolitan police departments so they can distinguish between a guy with a beard and a subversive."

The White House is aware of the political sensitivity of domestic intelligence gathering, which one aide described as "hangups in the question of snooping." He contended, however, that the Government was less interested in prosecuting individuals than in gathering information to "prevent the perpetration of an act of violence."

It would help to have "broader public awareness" of the need for improved surveillance techniques, he said. "One of the greatest disservices Senator [Joseph] McCarthy did to this country was to swing the pendulum so far that people no longer want to think about internal security," the official said.

He argued that it would, in fact, increase safeguards of the civil liberties of individuals to have a greater awareness of which members of society posed a threat.

"My concern is that sooner or later this is going to kill innocent people," the official said. "There will be tremendous public outrage and not enough time for restrained, measured response. People will demand that their police start cracking heads.

"The greatest safeguard for rights of individuals is to have good information on what the [radical fringes] are doing. Stop them before the bombings. Bomb legislation [with heavier penalties] is after the fact."

Mr. Nixon, who prefers to decide on Administration policy after receiving a set of clearly defined options, apparently has little choice but to adopt the recommendations of his more conservative staff members for increased surveillance. Liberal advisers have not provided him with alternatives.

Indeed, the liberals do not appear to have any answers to the problem of American radicalism. As one White House liberal put it: "What does Richard Nixon do for these people, short of resigning the Presidency?"

April 12, 1970

Are We in the Middle Of the 'Second American Revolution'?

*The United States is at the beginning of its "Second Revolution,"
spokesmen for the New Left have taken to saying.
Is it true? Is America today in such a state that a revolution—i.e.,
the overthrow of the present system, by force if necessary—
is justified? With what would the revolutionaries replace
the present system? What chances of success do they have?
The New York Times Magazine put these questions
to a group of commentators representing a broad spectrum
of political views. Here are their replies.*

"The most 'revolutionary agent' is the war itself"

By DAVID McREYNOLDS

Field secretary of the War Resisters League; author of a forthcoming collection of essays, "We Have Been Invaded by the 21st Century."

ARE we in the beginning of a Second American Revolution? Yes and no. Paradox: revolutions can occur only after they have occurred. Marx's call for revolution in 1848 was based on the revolutionary changes that had already occurred—the emergence of the proletariat. Revolution as we usually use the word means the violent effort to create new institutions to help share power among new social forces. In England and in the Scandinavian countries, the creation of democratic political parties (a debt we owe the Marxists), trade unions and cooperatives all served to distribute political power to the proletariat without a violent convulsion. In Russia, the revolution occurred less because of the proletariat—a small group in 1917—than because of the inflexibility of Russian institutions combined with the disaster of the war. When the Czar stumbled from power in April, 1917, it was a surprise to everyone, including Lenin. (Which suggests that while we may talk about revolutions, we cannot predict them.)

Revolutions do not occur because of revolutionaries but because of massive social tensions that demand change, combined with a political establishment unwilling or unable to make those changes. That situation exists today in America. Nixon has made the fatal mistake of declaring war on our youth (through his noisome little mouthpiece, Spiro Agnew) and of seeking the allegiance of Southern whites rather than the confidence of American blacks and American youth. In the short run, it is a successful strat-

The Western Democracies

McReynolds.

egy. In the long run, it will prove a disaster.

Blacks, Chicanos, Puerto Ricans, and youth do not constitute a majority, but they are a massive force of social energy and they are unable to feel respect for—or any sense of shared power in—the present white Establishment, made up of the military, the corporations, the conservative A.F.L.-C.I.O. The Chicago trial, the search and destroy missions the police carry out against the Black Panthers, the nomination of Carswell, the absolutely unconstitutional expansion of the war into Cambodia, the failure of the Government to check inflation or to wage a meaningful war on poverty—all of these provoke a loss of confidence in the legitimacy of the Establishment. (The hypocrisy of the "respectable Establishment" is demonstrated by New York Times editorials demanding immediate criminal prosecution of the handful of terror bombers in our nation, while failing to demand similar criminal prosecution of Nixon and all officers of the Government who have conspired in the massive bombing of Vietnam and the waging of a war in which more than a million have died and an entire nation has been ravaged.)

The Pentagon is a greater threat to American institutions than the Weathermen. Spiro Agnew is the real organizer for the violent fringe—every speech he makes drives a few more deeply concerned youths into the tragic tactic of armed resistance. The most "revolutionary agent" of the moment is simply the war itself, which daily persuades more Americans of the criminal nature of the central Government.

WHEN is a revolution justified? Is America in such a bad state that a revolution is justified now? Revolutions are like earthquakes. They are tragic, they cannot be predicted, they do not require justification, they cannot really be organized. Revolutions occur when they occur. They are not caused by conspiracies but, as the Russian theologian Nicholas Berdyaev pointed out, by the indifference and inhumanity and inflexibility of existing institutions. America is in a bad state now and it would be in a bad state after a violent revolution.

What is the aim, beyond destroying the system, of present-day revolutionaries? Revolutions, from our own of 1776 through the Russian, Chinese and Cuban, share a common set of values: freedom, justice, wider distribution of power to previously powerless and oppressed elements of the society. Few revolutions have a blueprint of what they will actually do, and those blueprints are usually scrapped as unusable once the revolution has occurred. For myself, I favor wider distribution of power away from the central Government directly to communities. And I favor the unilateral dismantling of our military machine, so that it cannot oppress us or anyone else. (I would fear a revolutionary military machine as much as I fear the present one.) Such an act would more likely revolutionize the world as a whole, including the Soviet Union, than lead to our facing an invasion. The large corporations need to be broken into smaller units with ownership and control vested in communities and regions. Centralization of economic or political power is dangerous to a free society.

WHAT chances of success do the revolutionaries have? On our own, very little. The central Government still commands the support of the vast majority of citizens, though discussion of revolution helps to remind people that revolution is a very American process. Terror bombings do more to build support for a police state than for revolution, and I suspect that Government agents are involved in some of the bombings. It is possible there will be no revolution but that America, the most advanced power in the world, will prove unable to govern itself in any way and sink into chaos. Youths need to read less Lenin and Mao and more about America. Chants of "Ho, Ho, Ho Chi Minh" are not revolutionary. Ho didn't win power in Vietnam by chanting about Russia or China, but by dealing with Vietnamese problems. The breakfast program of the Panthers is far shrewder than their earlier display of guns. The nonviolence of César Chavez and the nonviolence of the draft-resistance movement suggest that the compassionate tradition of American radicalism, the tradition of Eugene Debs and Martin Luther King, is not yet played out.

Is the revolution here? Something is happening, Mr. Jones, but I'm not sure what it is. The bombings. The campus unrest. Hundreds jailed for resisting the draft, thousands jailed on drug charges, tens of thousands fleeing into Canada, black leaders shot to death in their beds by Chicago cops. Listen to rock music. Observe the culture heroes of the youth.

Popular as Nixon and Agnew may be with a frightened middle America, they lack the charisma needed to sustain the kind of police state the Attorney General is trying so hard to fashion. I won't try to predict the future—just urge those of us who believe in democracy and nonviolence to keep struggling. The editor of Crawdaddy, a leading "rock culture" paper, put the thing perfectly when he said: "Agnew, Nixon and Mitchell have set to sea in a sieve." Sink they will—nothing in today's politics is more certain. The question is whether America will sink with them.

P.S. Just as I prepared to turn this in, I learned troops opened fire on students at Kent State in Ohio, killing four and wounding others. The military junta that rules us is in the open. The chances for a nonviolent and democratic solution—such as Congressional impeachment of Nixon and Agnew—fade hour by hour.

"We must assume that there is hope"

By RICHARD H. ROVERE

Author of the "Letter from Washington" column in the New Yorker.

SO many things are out of joint in this country that if they were all, or nearly all, set right, or nearly right, the changes, by whatever means accomplished, would constitute a revolution of great magnitude.

None of us can know, at this point in our history, how much in the way of change is within the realm of the possible—a realm in which time is now a crucial dimension. If we go by the form sheets—election returns, opinion polls—we have to see ourselves as a conservative people, and getting more so from month to month. Yet the conservative powers-that-be are capable of at least some innovation—e.g., family-assistance programs. And some kinds of change seem to commend themselves on an almost wholly non-ideological basis—e.g., protection of the environment, abortion reform. But this seems to me about to exhaust the categories. Most of the rest involve struggle. Power has to change hands. Wealth has to be redistributed. Institutions have to be junked or reshaped. Most social and political change is brought about through social and political conflict.

Conflict can and usually does take many forms, one of which is violence. For my own part, I see little point in discussing violence as a means toward revolutionary ends in this country in this part of this century. I think I would oppose it under almost any circumstances because I find it abhorrent and corrupting. But even if I felt otherwise and felt also that conditions in this country were so intolerable as to justify an attempt at revolution by violence, I would still oppose it on the ground that the likeliest—indeed, the certain—outcome would be to make conditions even more intolerable. There have been exceptions (fewer than are claimed, though), but this has been the general history of violence, and I should suppose that anyone in possession of his wits and able to give the matter a few moments of thought would find this conclusion inescapable. This country might benefit from revolutionary change, but the overwhelming majority of its people think otherwise. Our society may be deteriorating, but the news hasn't reached deeply into the masses. Of those it has reached, probably a majority blame the deterioration on those who would make the revolution.

In other words a revolution would be quite promptly crushed. Before that happened, a few, perhaps many, edifices would topple, and guerrillas might make life hazardous for a time. But the more bombings there were and the more guerrillas in the streets, the bloodier the retribution and the more repressive the repression. This is not Vietnam. The masses may be deceived and exploited, but political education has not brought them to the point of much awareness on this score. Nor are they apathetic. They are overwhelmingly on the side of authority, legitimate or otherwise, and wish it were used less sparingly than it is. And although certain outbreaks of violence—particularly in the ghettoes—may have had some value as "demonstration effect," the kind of concerted violence that is revolution would bring into the streets not only the police and the military but millions of self-appointed and well-armed vigilantes and counter-revolutionaries.

I said—or tried to say—some of this to some young revolutionaries on a television show recently and was quickly put down as a "cynic" and a "defeatist." My analogies were all from the past—where else can one find any?—and one of them enjoined me to forget history and "study the future." I plead not guilty to cynicism, but guilty of first-degree defeatism when it comes to the proposition of turning this country leftward with guns and bombs. That, at least, is what my study of "the future" leads me to conclude.

BEYOND this, I conclude very little. I have my visions of what I would like this country to be and do in the world, and I think they accord with at least some of those who are in the process of persuading themselves that violence is the only answer. I am not sure they are wrong in believing there is no hope in any of the other approaches. In other words, it could be that our American situation is hopeless. But I see no choice but to proceed on the assumption that there is hope. The argument, in any case, is not closed as of now. The record of democracy, where it has been practiced in some limited fashion, is often far from exhilarating, particularly when it comes to wars and other instruments of foreign policy. It has produced injustices as gross as those produced in many totalitarian societies. But it has had its triumphs, and it is the only system that I know of to be worth trying to bring to something approaching perfection. It cannot be improved or perfected by revolutionary violence. But it can surely be wrecked by counterrevolutionary violence.

"We're in a right-wing counterrevolution now"

By DAVID GELBER

Writer for Liberation Magazine and contributor to The Village Voice.

IN the first place, this symposium is a hustle. We've been asked to respond to four cosmic questions (which insinuate that the principle threat of violent revolution comes from the left) in 1,000 words. Leaving no space for a coherent, substantiated case for views which rarely make their way into the mass media, this format effectively reinforces the smug clichés about "simple-minded leftist fanatics" while giving the reader the illusion that he has "heard both sides."

The Western Democracies

Gelber.

Schlesinger, Rovere, Rand et al may not be very convincing either, but they are very much at home in a business-dominated system which subordinates human development to the production of anesthetizing (and murderous) objects. We're not. They accept the capitalist/warfare state (and the distorted human relationships which inevitably follow) as the loftiest attainable by man. We don't. But if neither side is convincing the status quo wins another round.

The Times, meanwhile, does its bit by focusing on the relatively insignificant violence of the left instead of the massive, legalized violence of Agnew, Mitchell, Nixon and Laird, who are busily hacking away at the Constitution. If The Times called a symposium on the right-wing counter-revolution now under way, it might, God forbid, anger Spiro Agnew. In the hoary tradition of liberal spinelessness, The Times would rather fight the left while caving in to the right.

It is, of course, revolutionary these days to talk about people controlling their own government. Just that. Black and poor white communities have no say as to how or by whom they are policed. Polluting the air is a sacred prerogative of private industry and will remain so as long as profit is the sanctum sanctorum of American values. Voters don't even know what wars their Government is fighting, and, as many Americans have just discovered, it wouldn't make a hell of a lot of difference if they did. So, in the context of violent counterrevolutionaries running things in Washington, you can be a revolutionary if you just take the Constitution seriously.

At the same time, the U.S., which controls 60 per cent of the earth's natural resources for 6 per cent of the world's population, is the chief target of a world revolution. Washington's attempt in Vietnam, and now Laos and Cambodia, to suppress that global revolution has accelerated natural divisions in American society and gives some hope that forces will emerge and unite to make a second American Revolution. In heavy industry, where real wages are declining because of war-induced inflation, young workers are rejecting sweetheart contracts at an unprecedented rate. Blacks, forced to fight a white man's war, have never been so disposed to use militant tactics to achieve dignity in a white-supremacist society. Students are refusing to live out the acquisitive roles slated for them by elders whose enthusiasm for the domination of nonwhites by whites spurred on the U.S. rape of Southeast Asia. In the past decade, millions of blacks, women, soldiers, students, prisoners, homosexuals, young workers and professionals have been sensitized to the intricate patterns of domination and privilege on which the American system rests. Deference to our rulers (or "patriotism," if you will) is a vanishing phenomenon, even among sectors of the population too dulled to put up a fight. All this is enough to justify the assertion that a second American Revolution (inseparable from a world revolution) has at least begun.

In case you haven't noticed, we're not living in a nice, relatively humdrum country like Denmark where the Social Democrats tinker around enough to make life in a class-ridden society tolerable. Those who tenaciously rely on liberalism for gradual solutions to social crises need a strong dose of history.

Liberals have been knocking around for 70 years now without giving us a positive solution to even one major social problem of modern American society. Poverty and unemployment were "solved" not by the New Deal but rather by war and, since World War II, by the production of ecocidal trash. The trusts which engaged the bully-boy progressives in 1900 are more powerful than ever. Eighty per cent of Americans cannot afford the cost of a major illness. The system's answer to the race problem —integration—has integrated 1 per cent of black school children in the South since Brown v. Board of Education. Reform-administered cities are unlivable and will get worse as long as private profit determines how money is spent in America. And two of our last three Presidents, self-avowed messengers of the liberal, humanist tradition, were mass murderers.

Irving Howe intoned in these pages recently that he is "sick and tired" of those who would forsake moderate reformers like Ralph Nader and Sam Brown. In fact, we've had Naderesque muckrakers around since the beginning of time begging Congress to regulate big business, yet consumer products are gaudier and less reliable than ever. As for Sam Brown, less than a month after Howe's article appeared, Brown tucked in his tail and closed down the Moratorium business, having already prevented it from possibly developing into a general-strike movement he and Gene McCarthy could not control. Enough of such timidity. It is a delusion to think that we can create a decent society without first taking power away from the private industrialists, generals and politicians who set the course of this indecent society.

With what would the left replace the present system? The question is misleading. What is positive in the American tradition is not threatened by the left; it is daily being destroyed by the right. Or what do you make of midnight raids on Black Panthers by uniformed murderers? Of laws which make a state of mind illegal? Another misleading implication here is the supposed dividing line between revolution (which The Times reduces to simply a destructive event) and the postrevolutionary system of government. In a revolution worthy of the name (such as the Vietnamese), radically advanced social institutions and human relationships develop in the course of the revolutionary struggle itself.

An example close to home: Last year, the radical community in Berkeley converted a useless piece of land into a people's park. [Governor] Reagan and the university's Board of Regents correctly saw the park struggle as a threat to the principle of private ownership of land. As a result, the Berkeley radicals are up against a coordinated attack spearheaded by Reagan, who declared himself in favor of a juvenicidal bloodbath, the Berkeley City Council, which is about to purchase two surveillance helicopters, and the more liberal University of California, which prefers to destroy the radical community with a housing policy that would convert Berkeley into a well-heeled suburb for professors, obedient scholars and San Francisco executives.

In self-defense, the Berkeley people increasingly are forming supportive community structures: free schools, food cooperatives, democratic living arrangements, rent-strike units and free professional services. This is not the latest utopian flight from the real world. It is a self-conscious effort to strengthen the community for a fight for survival which lies in the imminent future. It is also a partial embodiment of the vision of the revolutionary society which inspires the young left.

The prospects for revolutionary change in America will not be enhanced if the Government is able to murder, exile and jail revolutionary leaders while scaring millions of others into depressive passivity. We may have to face an indefinite period during which the only permissible dissidence will be insipid happenings like Earth Day or privatistic acts such as smoking dope or growing sideburns.

Ten years ago, however, no symposiast in his right mind would have anticipated the emergence of a left potent enough to send one President into retirement and to discredit (in the academic world, at least) liberal imperialists like Arthur Schlesinger, who approve of global interventionism as long as the U.S. can get away with it.

Recent disturbances at state universities and working-class community colleges suggest that the spirit of radical resistance is seeping down the social class ladder. It is not surprising. Lower-middle-class kids who attend college to learn how to feed computers also share in a culture which exalts peace, good sex, gener-

TERRORISM AND THE STATE TODAY

ational solidarity and, in general, better aspirations than flooring a Mustang. The anti-authoritarianism inherent in the young left is politicized by a growing resentment against the socially destructive aims and alienating work of modern industry. This may mean that, within five to ten years, the new generation of workers will be taking over plants and offices insisting (as some French workers did in 1968) on the establishment of workplace democracy and popular control of investment and production decisions. That would not be compatible with the continued hegemony of wealthy shareholders and a managerial élite. For that to happen, the left (the student left, the antiwar left, the women's liberation left, the antipollution left, etc.) will have to come together far more than it has. If these forces manage to join together against a natural target, like polluter-warmaker General Motors (which the U.A.W. will probably strike against next fall), the revolution will seem a lot nearer—and The Times will have to call another symposium.

Schlesinger.

"A 'New Left revolution' is only fantasy"

By ARTHUR SCHLESINGER Jr.

Former White House aide; Albert Schweitzer Professor at the City University of New York.

THE notion of a New Left revolution in the United States—in the sense of a forceful overthrow of the present system—remains a fantasy in spite of the revolutionary stimulus recently provided by President Nixon with his invasion of Cambodia and his encouragement of action against the "bums" on campus. The New Left has revolutionary dreams, not revolutionary plans. It has no program for overthrowing the system and no program for imposing or constructing a new system. For the New Left, revolution is what they term in their patois a "life style"; it is not an overarching conspiracy.

New Leftists, in short, are fantasts of revolution. They see politics as theater and seek to make cautionary and symbolic points against the rigidities and hypocrisies of contemporary life. By being systematically outrageous, they aim to expose and explode the cant that envelops them. When their fantasy maintains touch with reality—as was once the case with Tom Hayden as a reformer and may still be the case with Abbie Hoffman as a satirist—they can be effective. Many criticisms launched by the New Left are uncomfortably close to the mark. By forcing the rest of us to take a fresh look at injustices too complacently accepted or too benignly neglected, the New Leftists have played an undoubted role in stimulating the national conscience.

But saying something like this drives many New Leftists into a fury. Their obsessive anxiety is that society may absorb them as licensed rebels and professional entertainers. Some New Leftists invite such roles, of course, and display obvious relish when offered the chance to bring their act into college lecture halls or television studios. But the more angry among them are propelled by the fear of "co-optation" into drastic attitudes and actions. When this happens, their fantasy loses touch with reality. It has carried some of them into realms of hysteria where their gospel of love becomes an injunction to hate and they seek to verify fantasy by violence.

The more literally they take their revolutionary dreams, the more they jeopardize the revolution of which they dream. If, through their cult of disruption and destruction, the New Leftists should ever succeed in turning American society into a competition of unreason, hysteria and guerrilla warfare, do these playboys of insurrection really believe that Jerry Rubin, Eldridge Cleaver and Herbert Marcuse will bring more armed men into the streets than George Wallace, Ronald Reagan and John Mitchell? Should the New Left bring down the fabric of civility in our society and make force the final court of appeal, they seal their own fate and hand the future to the right. The New Leftists can't make a revolution, but they might conceivably make a counter-revolution.

OBVIOUSLY there are times and places when revolution is justified. The Declaration of Independence offers a lucid explanation of the conditions that make revolution legitimate and necessary. But, however deplorable the present situation of the United States, it can hardly be said that we have exhausted nonrevolutionary remedies. Still the fashion of revolutionary talk — the fact that The Times should stage this symposium—ought to convey a warning to our leaders.

For, though our internal divisions are not revolutionary, they are acute and ominous. President Nixon announced after the election that his purpose was to "bring us together," but his policies have only driven us further apart. Instead of trying to bring the estranged and excluded Americans into the national community, he has evidently decided to accept and exploit the division and side with those he considers the majority. Instead of a politics of reconciliation, he has chosen the politics of polarization and has unleashed the Vice President for this purpose.

One of the few remaining institutions of reconciliation, for example, has been the Supreme Court; to this, almost alone in the panoply of Washington, the alienated groups felt they could look for justice. President Nixon's determination to convert the Supreme Court into one more arm of the established order can only deprive rebels against the system of a last reason to retain faith in the constitutional process. His determination to intensify and widen the Vietnam war in spite of Congressional and popular opposition can only increase disenchantment with the democratic process.

Should the Administration thus continue to make our institutions more rigid and regressive, our internal divisions will certainly deepen. As John F. Kennedy once said, "Those who make peaceful revolution impossible will make violent revolution inevitable." But also, in the words of Adam Smith, there is a lot of ruin in a country. The further hardening of the Nixon policies will, I trust, lead to an overthrow of the Government, but through elections, not explosions.

"The New Left represents an intellectual vacuum"

By AYN RAND

Author ("The Fountainhead," "Atlas Shrugged," etc.) and editor (The Objectivist).

THE New Left does not portend a revolution, as its press agents claim, but a *Putsch*. A revolution is the climax of a long philosophical development and expresses a nation's profound discontent; a *Putsch* is a minority's seizure of power. The goal of a revolution is to overthrow tyranny; the goal of a *Putsch* is to establish it.

Tyranny is any political system (whether absolute monarchy or fascism or communism) that does not recognize individual rights (which necessarily include property rights). The overthrow of a political system by force is justified only when it is directed against tyranny: it is an act of self-defense against those who rule by force. For example, the American Revolution. The resort to force, not in defense, but in violation, of individual rights, can have no moral justification; it is not a revolution, but gang warfare.

No revolution was ever spearheaded by wriggling, chanting drug addicts who are boastfully antirational, who have no program to offer, yet propose to take over a nation of 200 million, and who spend their time manufacturing grievances, since they cannot tap any authentic source of popular discontent.

287

The Western Democracies

PHYSICALLY, America is not in a desperate state, but intellectually and culturally she is. The New Left is the product of cultural disintegration; it is bred not in the slums, but in the universities; it is not the vanguard of the future, but the terminal stage of the past.

Intellectually, the activists of the New Left are the most docile conformists. They have accepted as dogma all the philosophical beliefs of their elders for generations: the notions that faith and feeling are superior to reason, that material concerns are evil, that love is the solution to all problems, that the merging of one's self with a tribe or a community is the noblest way to live. There is not a single basic principle of today's Establishment which they do not share. Far from being rebels, they embody the philosophic trend of the past 200 years (or longer): the mysticism - altruism - collectivism axis, which has dominated Western philosophy from Kant to Hegel to James and on down.

But this philosophic tradition is bankrupt. It crumbled in the aftermath of World War II. Disillusioned in their collectivist ideals, America's intellectuals gave up the intellect. Their legacy is our present political system, which is not capitalism, but a mixed economy, a precarious mixture of freedom and controls. Injustice, insecurity, confusion, the pressure-group warfare of all against all, the amorality and futility of random, pragmatist, range-of-the-moment policies are the joint products of a mixed economy and of a philosophical vacuum.

There is a profound discontent, but the New Left is not its voice; there is a sense of bitterness, bewilderment and frustrated indignation, a profound anxiety about the intellectual-moral state of this country, a desperate need of philosophical guidance, which the church - and - tradition-bound conservatives were never able to provide and the liberals have given up.

Without opposition, the hoodlums of the New Left are crawling from under the intellectual wreckage. Theirs is the Anti-Industrial Revolution, the revolt of the primordial brute—no, not against capitalism, but against capitalism's roots—against reason, progress, technology, achievement, reality.

WHAT are the activists after? Nothing. They are not pulled by a goal, but pushed by the panic of mindless terror. Hostility, hatred, destruction for the sake of destruction are their momentary forms of escape. They are a desperate herd looking for a Führer.

They are not seeking any specific political system, since they cannot look beyond the "now." But the sundry little Führers who manipulate them as cannonfodder do have a mongrel system in mind: a statist dictatorship with communist slogans and fascist policies. It is their last, frantic attempt to cash in on the intellectual vacuum.

Do they have a chance to succeed? No. But they might plunge the country into a blind, hopeless civil war, with nothing but some other product of antirationality, such as George C. Wallace, to oppose them.

Can this be averted? Yes. The most destructive influence on the nation's morale is not the young thugs, but the cynicism of respectable publications that hail them as "idealists." Irrationality is not idealistic; drug addiction is not idealistic; the bombing of public places is not idealistic.

What this country needs is a *philosophical* revolution— a rebellion against the Kantian tradition—in the name of the first of our Founding Fathers: Aristotle. This means a reassertion of the supremacy of reason, with its consequences: individualism, freedom, progress, civilization. What political system would it lead to? An untried one: full, laissez-faire capitalism. But this will take more than a beard and a guitar.

"Dissolution before decay!"
By PAUL COWAN

Former Peace Corps member; author of "The Making of an Un-American."

I'M writing this a few hours after the Ohio National Guard murdered four students at Kent State; a few days after President Nixon incited such violence by calling students "bums," announced the invasion of Cambodia, resumed the bombings of North Vietnam. New declarations of war on two fronts, a redeclaration of war on one. Who knows what will have happened by the time this is printed?

We got rich too quickly in this country, defined our freedom as the right to exploit others, replaced our cultural and moral roots with a crazed desire to chase the big buck. We prided ourselves on an undefeated, untied, unscored-upon war record, lost all personal feeling for what it's like to be devastated. We decided that our affluence was willed by God and immunized ourselves to the complexity and tragedy of life, the suffering of others.

I have serious doubts about presenting a fuller, reasoned argument here. Are there words that will persuade you that The New York Times, Time and Newsweek should print articles exploring the psyches of the clean-cut generals who order the wanton destruction of thousands of Asians, not of radicals who respond to such provocations by fighting? That the white-collar fascists in power now hope to gain total control of this country by insulting, imprisoning and even murdering young people, black people and poor people? Can you be convinced that Richard Nixon and his advisers are war criminals who should be tried accordingly? That there are no conventional means at all by which the problems of this country can be solved?

HERE are seven proposals. Some readers may have mind sets that make it hard for them to take such suggestions seriously. To me, and many people I've talked to, such ideas—not necessarily these specific ones—represent the minimum necessary for survival.

(1) Force the United States to admit and accept defeat in Southeast Asia.

(2) That means that the end of the war in Indochina—and of the war against dissenters at home—must become the absolute first priority of every American institution. Strikes can be organized like those on the campuses. Social workers can force their agencies to join clients in combating the war and its disastrous effect on poor people. Teachers and students; poverty lawyers and their clients; doctors, nurses and their patients can enter into similar sorts of alliances. People in agencies like the Peace Corps and AID can organize to shut down those operations. Liberal Justice Department lawyers, if there still are any, can disrupt the functioning of that thoroughly corrupt agency. Federal employes in agencies like Health, Education and Welfare and the O.E.O. can stage massive demonstrations at the Pentagon for a reversal of national priorities. Workers throughout the country can organize antiwar strikes in their unions. Such actions could inspire a nationwide general strike.

(3) Also, petition the United Nations General Assembly (where the U.S. has no veto) to brand this country the aggressor in Southeast Asia and recruit an international army to fight it in a sort of reverse Korea.

(4) Impeach Nixon — then the rest of the ghostly parade of successors who have complied with the United States' criminal policies: Agnew, John McCormack, Richard Russell, etc.

(5) Force the Government, private institutions and large corporations to recognize that America's affluence is largely based on the exploitation of domestic colonies. Negotiate reparations treaties with blacks, Indians, Puerto Ricans, Mexican-Americans. Free political prisoners like Huey Newton, Bobby Seale and Martin Sostre, some of the bravest, most far-sighted members of their communities.

(6) Establish new communities, "liberated zones," in cities or sections of states.

There we can build the kind of humane institutions we believe in—schools, hospitals, child-care centers, old peoples' homes, mental institutions that are dedicated to serving people. Our loyalties will not be to the piggish United States, but to people throughout the world. In such communities, we will have to learn to transcend the racism, erotism and product addition that we have developed during our lives in this culture of greed—to undergo personal revolutions that parallel the political revolution we are trying to bring about.

If we can create such communities and defend them, people throughout the country will relate to them enthusiastically, see them and the politics and life style they represent as vibrant alternatives to the horrors of Nixonia.

(7) Work toward the eventual dissolution of the United States into a number of smaller autonomous regions. Only indispensible technological systems like communications and transportation should be continental—and those should include Canada and Mexico as equal partners with the rest of the separate North American states.

In some regions, of course, people will form alliances with Europeans, Asians, Africans or Latins that are closer than their alliances with other parts of the present United States.

This nation is too big for any group to govern it humanely. Few people really identify with it except in a commercial sense: they get tears in their eyes when they go overseas and hear some patriotic or popular song that reminds them of the hamburgers or huge hunks of steak they miss. Living in smaller, self-governing regions, Americans might recover some of the roots they lost when they came to this country, recover some of the modesty. We might become decent citizens of the world.

But maybe that is impossible. Maybe our history has injected a poison into our blood stream that forces us to be violent. Then, I would rather see Kansans fight Oklahomans than be part of a country where Kansans and Oklahomans are drafted into an army which forces them to drop bombs on Cambodians, Laotians, Vietnamese, their houses, schools and hospitals.

My slogan is: Dissolution before decay!

OF course, much of America's ruling class will suffer if any such ideas are adopted. The Nixon Administration knows that. It is terrified by all threats to its greedy plans to turn the United States into a giant factory town and use its mechanized people to control this planet and space.

It will try to stifle even small threats with repression at first, as it is doing now. Perhaps, when that doesn't work, there will be a military dictatorship. If that happens, the bloodshed will be ghastly. Could anything humane survive the wreckage that would be in store for this country?

I often think that the name of the thing we are headed for is not fascism, not revolution, but national suicide. ∎

May 17, 1970

Political Terrorism: Hysteria On the Left

By IRVING HOWE

THE life of the political terrorist is overwhelmed by loneliness, not merely because he can no longer trust completely friend or comrade, but because he cuts himself off from all movements and communities in which choices can be weighed. Staking everything on the act, he blocks off all that comes before it and all that comes after. Deciding whom to smite, he replaces God. Choosing whom to punish, he replaces the justice (be it good or bad) of society. And since the conflicts of social classes must be bent to his will, he replaces history, too. The terrorist carries a moral burden only saints or fanatics would undertake—worst of all, fanatics mistaking themselves for saints.

IRVING HOWE, author of "The Decline of the New," a collection of literary essays, is on the faculty of the City University of New York.

Greater still is his political loneliness. The terrorist surrenders the possibility of sharing the experiences of a mass political movement, be that movement democratic or authoritarian. He discards responsibility to his people, his class, his generation. For you cannot hold an open discussion on where to throw the next bomb, and, while you may keep mumbling "power to the people," you deny in effect whatever power the people may have over your behavior. In a hallucinatory transaction you "become" the people.

We have had plenty of terrorism in the United States, mostly by far-right lunatics and racists; lynching is an American contribution to the repertoire of death. But the far right, shrewder than its symbiotic opposite on the far left, has never articulated an ideology of the rope and the bomb: it has done its dirty business and kept its mouth shut.

A few years ago it would have seemed—it would have *been*—a gross slander for anyone to ask whether terrorism might become a weapon of the dissident young, so hopeful did many of them seem in their idealism and fraternity. Today, that question must be asked about a fringe of the New Left. Serge Nechayev,* heroic and ruthless terrorist of 19th-century Russia, would until recently have seemed a creature alien to our national experience; now it is possible that his spirit has migrated to our shores.

I say this not because I accept the scatter-shot malevolence that men in authority direct against students, but because I have witnessed the conduct and read the journals of the New Left grouplets. The great majority of the young, dissident or not, still seem to believe in democratic norms and nonviolent methods, though they are sadly unable to reach coherent articulation. But fragments of the New Left, by now fractured to the point of jungle warfare, are inflamed with

---

*Serge Nechayev (1847-1882), a Russian revolutionary fanatic who, scorning the Marxist idea of "going to the masses," advocated the use of terror, arson, robbery and spying on comrades. His "Catechism of the Revolutionist," a classical exposition of political amorality, begins with the sentence: "The revolutionist is a doomed man." In 1869, while forming underground groups, Nechayev arranged for the murder of Ivanov, a comrade who had begun to doubt Nechayev's grandiose claims to being the leader of a vast movement. Three years later, Nechayev was captured by the police and sentenced to solitary confinement, where he spent the remainder of his life.

The Western Democracies

Language of violence: a cartoon from New Left Notes, a weekly publication of Students for a Democratic Society.

the rhetoric of violence. Some flirt with sabotage and terror; others inflict minor physical brutalities on intra-left opponents. Perhaps there have also been a few ventures in actual bombings. We don't yet know.

About the recent incidents I have no revelations. All I propose to do here is to look into the rationales developed by the far-out wings of the New Left, the responses these get from half-sympathetic students and the likely repercussions of terrorism. I confess at the outset that I have no comprehensive theory to account for everything.

THERE is a standard liberal explanation for the growth of terrorist moods in or near the New Left, and like all standard liberal explanations it is neither entirely right nor wrong. The young rebels, we are told, tried every method of peaceful persuasion; they protested and picketed; they marched and electioneered. But the country, choosing Nixon and Agnew, turned its back on their outcry. As a result, they have become desperate and see no solution but guerrilla warfare. At this point, usually over a drink or in a faculty lunchroom, the more chuckleheaded kind of liberal will add, "Of course I don't approve of such methods, but still . . ."

Though it contains a good portion of the truth, perhaps even a decisive portion, this analysis strikes me as too simple, and the "but still" as a proviso that could lead us to disaster.

There is plenty of reason for dismay and disgust at the state of American society. Every sensible person knows the list of our troubles. The thought of three, or seven, or more years of an Administration that regards Judge G. Harrold Carswell as a fit candidate for the Supreme Court and the barbaric regime in Athens as an appropriate ally fills many of us with bitterness. But—and I want to underscore this point—there is no necessary political, logical or moral connection between this response to our present condition and the methods the *kamikaze* segments of the New Left are turning to.

It does not follow that if you feel the country to be in a desperate condition you should necessarily start throwing bombs. First, you ought to do some thinking. You must take into account the sentiments of millions of middle- and working-class Americans; you must reckon the power of the state; you must ask whether the consequences of terrorism, whether "successful" or not, would be worse than the problems we already have. All this is on the prudential level; I will come to the moral issues later. If you do consider such matters, the only rational conclusion is, I believe, to continue political activity—the creation of movements and alliances—so that, through elections, public programs and militant protest we can turn this country onto the path of social reconstruction.

To say that all means of peaceful action have been exhausted is nonsense: they have barely begun to be

TERRORISM AND THE STATE TODAY

"The terrorist bears a moral burden only saints or fanatics would assume—worst of all, fanatics thinking themselves saints"

employed. To say that nothing has been achieved by opponents of the war is a masochistic delusion: the results of protest have been notable. True, some of the New Left young have by now devoted as much as five or six years to politics and appear shocked that the centuries-long struggle for social justice did not come to instant triumph in 1969. It is not callous, it is merely humane, to suggest that this struggle seems likely to continue a while longer, and that among the requirements for it are the maturity needed for speaking with patience and decency to the unconverted. No one has ever been convinced by a bomb.

I am impatient with the maudlin claim that the young "have tried everything." For those who wish to change society there is no shortage of tasks: help Sam Brown organize the Moratorium against the war; join Cesar Chavez in unionizing grape pickers and Leon Davis in unionizing hospital workers; campaign for Allard K. Lowenstein's re-election to Congress; work with Ralph Nader for consumer rights and Philip Stern for tax reforms; and a thousand and one other things crying to be done and far more useful, *far more radical*, than the posture of bomb-throwing. What's more, if you don't like my list, make up your own.

Now, I do not mean to say that the despair felt by thousands of young Americans has nothing to do with the turn a few of them seem to have taken toward terrorism. Obviously, there is a strong connection, but mainly as an encompassing condition rather than as a direct and immediate cause. For since the despair is widespread and the terrorism very limited, there must also be other sentiments and convictions behind the throwing of bombs.

THE despair felt by the extremist segments of the New Left is given an explosive or, if you prefer, hysterical quality by their having yielded to ideologies such as Maoism and Castroism, which has cut them off from both American realities and democratic norms. And the severe internal disintegration of the New Left seems also to have driven some of its adherents to the thought of desperado tactics.

The two main wings of Students for a Democratic Society—the Maoists chained to a totalitarian ideology and the anarcho-authoritarians running wild in search of another ideology—analyze precisely the dilemmas of one another. The Maoist cadres, hair cut and contemptuous of drugs, make devastating criticisms of the dilettantism and political "Custerism" (last-ditch bravado) of their factional opponents, especially the Weathermen. But it is precisely the unreality of Maoist dogma, with its faith in a proletarian revolution in the United States, that leads many young radicals to the scatter of opposing groups. In turn, the increasingly suicidal and pathological character of groups like the Weathermen, to say nothing of their political incoherence, creates a strong revulsion among the more rational young leftists. All are trapped. To be profoundly caught up in the fevers of ideology, to be unable to settle upon one that has a touch of realism, to drive oneself through rituals of "discussion" and then to exhaust one's body and imperil one's skin in hopeless street battles—all this must lead to desperation.

Though its sympathizers may have increased in number, the New Left meanwhile is incapable of reaching organizational or political stability. Its inner life is befouled by dreary factionalism and, sometimes, plain hoodlumism. It remains a sect, even if a large one, that cannot gain acceptance from any major segment of the population beyond the campus. To have grown and then to fracture, to know wild hopes and yet to be unable to suppress intimations of futility—this, too, must lead to despair.

Such, I wish to suggest, is the immediate or triggering factor in the outbreak of desperado moods. There are others. American radicalism, alas, has almost always looked abroad for its models. Today, none of the traditional wings of the European left, neither Social Democracy nor Bolshevism, command much authority among the young, since, for all their differences, they are both too rational and disciplined to satisfy the moods of youth. Brezhnev—who but a bureaucrat could identify with him? Mao—a warlord of the left. The style that captures romantic imaginations is that of Guevara: personally heroic, dashing, free-lance, though a mediocre thinker and a scandalously inept revolutionist (he did not even know the language of the Bolivian peasants he meant to "liberate," any more than his local admirers know the language of the American workers). Guevara signifies to the radical young a vision of instant revolution, personal risk, guerrilla exposure: the old Hemingway notion of discovering one's manhood through physical risk, but now in the context of political exaltation.

LET us also remember that a large percentage of the New Left young are the children of the middle class and the rich. (It is curious that a movement calling itself Marxist does not perform a class analysis on itself. Why does New Leftism appeal mostly to upper-class youth and not to young proletarians?) The affluent young leftists have little experience in doing significant work, either work that is socially useful or that could give them a sense of personal independence. They are riddled with guilt, they have no clear awareness of their place in the world, they have been raised to expect instant gratification. And, therefore, they often debase the admirable impulse to social involvement and sympathy with which they begin.

In the past I have avoided the view that the desperado wings of the New Left show symptoms of being the "spoiled children" of affluence, but it becomes hard to resist precisely that impression. A significant proportion of the young desperadoes we have no statistics—comes from the upper *bourgeoisie*. Untrained at persisting in behalf of personal or public ends, unwilling to dig in at the job of persuading the American people to accept their ideas — and perhaps afraid that even making that effort would create the risk of being influenced by the very "masses" they have yet to meet—at least a few of these children of the rich, at once idealistic, disturbed and very bright, abandon themselves to the delirium of terrorist fantasy.

In utterly American style, it is a delirium with a large portion of innocence. They talk about and may even take a crack at violence, but deep down they seem still to expect that the society will treat them with the indulgence they have come to expect from at least some of their liberal teachers. They are innocent of history and innocent of social reality. A Columbia student is quoted in justification of terrorism: "If we don't take an active part in the revolution, the workers won't listen to us." Poor deluded boy. Does he have any idea what the

The Western Democracies

PHASE I? — *Serge Nechayev, 19th-century Russian revolutionary fanatic, who advocated terror, arson, robbery and spying on allies. "It is possible," says the author, "that his spirit has migrated to our shores."*

American workers think of him, his politics and his methods?

Tragedy in comedy, comedy in tragedy. Identities shuffled, costumes tried on, the revolution as theater. Nobody knows who he is, everyone plays parts. Abbie Hoffman, accredited clown of the moment, chants praise to the bombs— "Boom!"—and his educated admirers chant back, "Boom, boom!" Jewish boys and girls, children of the generation that saw Auschwitz, hate democratic Israel and celebrate as "revolutionary" the Egyptian dictatorship. Some of them pretend to be indifferent to the anti-Jewish insinuations of the Black Panthers; a few go so far as to collect money for Al Fatah, which pledges to take Tel Aviv. About this I cannot say more; it is simply too painful.

MEANWHILE, the ideology of the New Left itself creates strong inducements to political desperation. That ideology runs along these lines: There is a worldwide class war between imperialism, led by the United States, and the third world of revolutionary nations. In this international class war it is "our" job to weaken, disrupt and help destroy the main enemy, which is the American Government. In this view, which might be called the politics of Dean Rusk stood on its head, there is a tiny plausibility and a mountain of errors.

The third world does not exist as any sort of unified, let alone revolutionary, force; the underdeveloped countries have enormous differences in political character, social progress and economic need. Some, like India and Venezuela, are democratic and to propose "revolution" in these countries is to favor imposing élitist dictatorships. Others require modest beginnings in both industrialization and democracy. The "revolutionists" celebrated by our New Left are often tiny bands of deracinated intellectuals and students who have no contact with the people of their countries. And, finally, the relation between the United States and the third-world nations, while requiring radical correction, is far more complicated than the New Left picture allows. Yet, even if one does accept the Guevarist analysis, Weathermen tactics don't necessarily follow—unless, perhaps, a "final conflict" is expected within the next year or two.

TO all of which I would add two factors, not as direct causes but as aggravating conditions: the mass media and the intellectuals.

That the mass media, especially TV, have been irresponsible in their coverage of "youth rebellion" and black upsurge seems to me beyond question. (Living in California last year, I sometimes felt the S.D.S. was a creation of TV, providing it with an unfailing flow of usable items; on reflection, I concluded it was a phantom dreamed up by Ronald Reagan to insure his re-election.) The irresponsibility of the mass media takes

PHASE II?—*Some modern revolutionaries, all members of Students for a Democratic Society. From left: Jeff Melish; Dionne Donghi; Ted Gold, recently killed in a blast in a so-called "bomb factory" on West 11th Street; Bernadine Dohrn, a Weatherman leader who has expressed some admiration for the murderers in the Sharon Tate case in California; Kathy Boudin, missing in connection with the explosion on 11th Street, and Eleanor Raskin.*

TERRORISM AND THE STATE TODAY

the form of a raging thirst for sensation, and this, I am inclined to think, is built into the very nature of modern communications. If the medium is the message, then the message is bad news: gross simplification and exploitation. There is no time for qualifying nuances, no appetite for complex reflection; the idiot box processes the life of man into polarities of mindlessness. If a Roy Wilkins spends a lifetime fighting Jim Crow and a Bayard Rustin comes up with a program for training ghetto kids for jobs, that hardly constitutes news by the standards that allow fly-by-night loudmouths to scream "Burn, baby, burn!" at audiences of wide-eyed or dull-eyed suburbanites. Television seems inherently melodramatic and thereby made to order for farceurs like Abbie Hoffman; it encourages New Leftists, born to the corruptions of publicity, to act out an endless serial: *Which building will be liberated today?*

More serious is the role of the intellectuals, too many of whom have proved susceptible to the delights of being 90-day campus heroes. I think of the distinguished movie critic, yesterday an absolute pacifist, who helped raise money for S.D.S. after the Columbia events; the brilliant novelist who told his admirers they must prove their courage by feats of bravado and speculated on the moral propriety of beating up 50-year-old candy-store keepers; the erudite Hegelian philosopher who taught the young that tolerance is bourgeois deception and liberal values are a mask for repression; the fierce sociologist who kept reminding us that "violence is as American as apple pie," without troubling to ask whether that pie might give one a bad case of food poisoning; the bright young journalist who announced that "morality comes out of the barrel of a gun"; the stylish literary paper that ran a diagram on its cover, perhaps as part of an adult-education program, describing how to make a Molotov cocktail.

Of course, none of these people favor terrorism; their only violence is of the phrase. But at some point sorcerers must take a bit of responsibility for their strayed apprentices. For it's not as if everything leading up to the present debacle on the New Left—the élitism, the authoritarianism, the contempt for democracy, the worship of charismatic dictators, the mystique of violence—hadn't already been visible two or three years ago, when such intellecutals began offering the New Left an aura of intellectual responsibility. What the young radicals needed from the intellectuals was sober criticism; what they got too often was a surrender of critical faculties. And it did no one any good.

As for the sympathetic young, unhappy with the idea of terrorism yet inclined to murmur *"but still . . . "* let me print a little dialogue, all too true to life, between one of them, whom I'll call *He*, and an interlocutor, whom I'll call *I*. No illusions need be entertained that *I* persuades *He*:

He: "If this country can drop endless numbers of bombs on defenseless Vietnamese, why get so outraged when these fellows, whoever they are, drop some here?"

I: "If I thought that dropping them here could speed up the end of dropping them there, I'd still be against doing it, but at least I'd admit there's something to argue about. But you know as well as I do that dropping bombs here isn't going to help end the Vietnam war; if anything, quite the contrary. Besides, why can't we be indignant toward both?"

He: "Well, I don't like terrorism any more than you, but nothing else has worked."

I: "Does that mean that if bombing emptied buildings doesn't 'work,' they'll take the next step?"

He: "And bomb buildings with people in them? I don't know. So far they've only bombed buildings, but not hurt people."

I: "Sorry, that won't do—for three reasons:

"First, I don't trust their aim.

"Second, I don't share your faith in the efficiency of the police. Suppose the cops hadn't proved fast enough in responding to one of those phone calls that give them 20 minutes to empty out a building. Or suppose they'd been distracted from a 'revolutionary' phone call about a real bomb by a nut's phone call about an imaginary bomb.

"Third, they already have, it seems, killed some people: themselves."

About the political consequences of continued terrorism there can be no doubt. The first and mildest consequence would be Reaganism. ("The one indispensable element in Reagan's political survival," says Jesse Unruh, who ought to know, "is campus unrest.") The Reagan backlash suave in manner and graced with a Hollywood smile, depends more on police than street mobs, and it rests upon the assurance of winning elections. Ultimately, Reaganism might be the least of it, for this country can produce far worse. It has.

For most New Leftists, the argument concerning backlash in particular and consequences in general has little persuasive power. They affect to see little or no difference between Reagan and a liberal Democrat, and some even prefer a victory for Reagan out of the suicidal expectation that after apocalypse their turn will come. A good portion of the S.D.S. campus guerrillas can retreat, if necessary, to their parents' town and country houses, or quickly find the money to flee the country. But no such luxury of choice is open to the residents of Watts, the patients in California's hospitals, the teachers and students in its colleges; they must suffer the consequences of Reagan's policies.

Now, in a country with an atomized population, weak military forces, widespread illiteracy, feeble structure of government and no tradition of national unity, terrorist methods might prove effective. But it is really a sign of political dementia to suppose that a few hundred people could terrorize a country with unprecedented wealth and power, enormously vigorous agencies of government and a population with a large conservative segment. All terrorism might do in the United States is to frighten or enrage authority that now acts with a measure of restraint but could brutally smash its opponents.

Some New Leftists, however, are enchanted by their "clever" tactics: they don't have a centralized organization that can be infiltrated on top, so they reason, they are not as vulnerable as were past radical groups. Another delusion! For while it's true that "confrontationist" tactics have been shrewd and at first have caught authorities unprepared, radicals ought to recognize that there are intelligent and determined people on the other side too. Each time "confrontation" has brought into play student ingenuity, it has resulted in an escalation of retaliatory measures. Nevertheless, it speaks rather well for the people of this country that, despite what they consider to be provocations and outrages, they have thus far refrained from letting themselves be stampeded into hysterical and repressive moods.

Terrorism by small groups is admittedly hard to detect, but one consequence of this could be that if limited responses don't cope with bank-burners and bomb-throwers, men in authority will be driven to employ total measures, e.g., large-scale "preventive detention." Those of us who believe in civil liberties would fight as hard as we could against such proposals, just as Norman Thomas fought for the rights of Communists who had steadily abused him. But who is prepared to say that in the kind of social atmosphere created by terrorism we would have much chance of success? Every state, whether good or bad, must react against terrorism; otherwise, it ceases to exist.

What for the Government might be an intermittent nuisance could, for American radicals, be a complete disaster. It is hard enough for the American left to gain a hearing, hard enough to convince our fellow citizens that we wish an extension of democracy into all areas of social and political life and share their loathing for all varieties of dictatorship.

But now, if that amorphous entity called "the left" is in the slightest to be identified with terrorist methods, we will be thrown back 100 years —literally 100 years—to the point where, in both Europe and America, the left movements had to spend decades disassociating themselves from a handful of anarchist bomb-throwers. How one despairs of the indifference to history shown by the radical young! If only they would read, say, the second volume of G. D. H. Cole's authoritative "History of Socialist Thought," in which he shows with crushing detail the way the terrorists hurt the Socialist movements of Europe

293

The Western Democracies

Brown.  **Chavez.**  **Davis.**

Lowenstein.  **Nader.**  **Stern.**

MODELS?—"I am impatient," says Howe, "with the maudlin claim that the young 'have tried everything.' For those who wish to change society there is no shortage of tasks: help Sam Brown organize the Moratorium against the war; join Cesar Chavez in unionizing grape pickers and Leon Davis in unionizing hospital workers; campaign for Allard K. Lowenstein's re-election to Congress; work with Ralph Nader for consumer rights and Philip Stern for tax reforms."

and America, exposing them to provocation and smear. Cole goes still further by remarking of the bomb-throwers: "In the 20th century they would have become Fascists or Nazis; and some of them got as near to this as they could by joining the special anti-Anarchist police after a spell of Anarchist activity."

FOR civil-libertarians, the consequences of terrorism will be equally disastrous. In the past, people of the liberal-left community could usually assume that charges of "plotting to overthrow the Government," when brought by prosecuting attorneys against radicals, were politically motivated and false in substance. When Communist leaders were so charged in the nineteen-fifties, those of us on the left who had long been anti-Stalinist could nevertheless react immediately in opposition to such prosecution. We knew that people like Eugene Dennis and Gus Hall weren't manufacturing dynamite or planning a coup. They were trying to strengthen their position in the unions and other institutions. But whatever else, they were not fools.

In the future, however, how will we know? By its reckless talk and mindless acts, the far-out fringe of the New Left lays itself open—but also lays open all other sections of the left, old or New—to endless legal harassment and, to be blunt, to a maze of provocations and frameups. Yet, such provocations and frameups will be greatly helped if there is at least a smidgin of reality behind them, if there are in fact sticks of dynamite as well as the rhetoric of dynamite. Given that possibility, civil-libertarians will be hard pressed to distinguish between victims of persecution and candidates for prosecution.

Lest anyone think I am exaggerating, here is a statement put out by a committee in defense of three persons charged in New York City with bombings:

"Either the accused did strike a magnificent blow against those who make profit through the destruction of our lives and our world and they are our most courageous and beloved comrades; or they are being framed by a government bent on destroying our movement. . . . In both cases, they deserve our total support."

In short, hurrah if they threw bombs and hurrah if they did not. But what about those people who choose to be more discriminating with their hurrahs?

IT would be a grave error to argue against terrorism mainly on grounds of expediency. To throw bombs is wrong. It is wrong because it is inhumane, because it creates an atmosphere in which brute force settles all disputes, because even if the bomb-throwers could win power through such methods they would no longer be (if they ever had been) the kind of people who could build a good society. Above all, it is wrong because minorities in a democratic society, as long as their right to dissent and protest is largely protected, do not have the right to impose their will upon the majority through violence or terror. This has always been a central argument of democratic socialism, an argument classical liberalism also accepts.

I would extend this argument to property. In a democratic society minorities have no right to inflict damage on property simply because they oppose the arrangements of capitalism. The aim of Socialists is to socialize the control of property, not to vandalize or destroy it. Toward this end we must first achieve a certain little detail: persuading millions of our countrymen that our goal is a desirable one. Until and unless we do that, we must abide, no matter with what pain, by the judgments of the majority, so long as our rights of criticism and dissent are protected. There is a still more essential matter: that, as the history of our century shows, any effort to establish "socialism" through terror ends and must end as a ghastly caricature of our hope.

THERE remains one issue concerning the consequences of terror, and I wish to stress it more strongly than all the others. *What kind of people are you going to become if*

TERRORISM AND THE STATE TODAY

you turn to such methods? "Those who set out to kill monsters should take care not to turn into monsters themselves." These words were spoken by Nietzsche before the experience of totalitarianism, and all the blood and pain of our century confirms their wisdom. Ironically, some seven or eight years ago, when the then-young radicals were turning away from Leninism, it was precisely such perceptions that struck them as central.

The moral consequences for the lives of the young terrorists are already clear. Bernadine Dohrn, a Weatherman leader, is quoted by a New Left paper, The Guardian, as saying that the Weathermen "dig" Charlie Manson, accused leader of the gang that allegedly murdered several people in Beverly Hills. "Dig it, first they killed the pigs, then they ate dinner in the same room with them, then they even shoved a fork into a victim's stomach! Wild!" is how The Guardian quotes Miss Dohrn. Other New Leftists have expressed their admiration for Sirhan Sirhan, killer of Robert Kennedy. Some have even toyed with the notion that fascism is a necessary prelude to the introduction of utopia: first arsenic and then strawberries and cream. Are these the kind of people who are going to create a bright new world and to whom we are to entrust the future of our children?

But a youthful voice answers me: "Our moral integrity will be protected by our revolutionary commitment, by our fight against injustice, by our sacrifice and ideology."

Alas, too slender a reed! Do you suppose that some of the G.P.U. men who tortured innocent victims in Stalin's prisons had not once told themselves the same thing? Do you suppose that some of them might not have imagined that their maiming and murdering was in behalf of "the revolution," and that in the end "history" would vindicate them? No, what matters is the quality and discipline of the life one leads at a given moment, and what one sees at the outer edges of the New Left—I do not speak of it as a whole—is at least as discouraging as what one sees in American society at large.

THE bomb-thrower and the jailer are brothers under the skin. Is it not possible to revitalize in America the politics of democratic norm and radical change? Our traditions, our best impulses, our most humane energies, our needs all speak for it. Do that, and terror will die. ■

April 12, 1970

Letters

TERRORISM, LEFT AND RIGHT

To THE EDITOR:

As a friend and great admirer of Irving Howe, holding a similar political point of view — if anything a more nonviolent one — I am saddened by his analysis of the present terrorism by the left ("Political Terrorism: Hysteria on the Left," April 12).

Mr. Howe ignores a crucial point, a crucial experience that the young people have had in this country: the political terrorism and torture by the right.

Nobody knows how many young people have been radicalized by their military experience, either through service or resistance, but I have met literally hundreds of them, and many, perhaps a majority, do not come from the well-heeled homes of which Mr. Howe writes.

The blacks have had a very special experience with democracy in this country, an experience of repression and violence. Now the young white generation has been faced with an analogous situation when they don't go along with prevailing policies. They know they are not "free." Some know firsthand of the tortures and killings that go on in prison camps here and abroad under the traditional names of stockades and brigs. They know that it is not, as Mr. Howe puts it, with seeming innocence that we simply ally ourselves with the barbaric regime in Athens, but that we made that regime possible.

There is a group of young radicals who are nonviolent. With great difficulty and perseverance they started a coffeehouse in Wrightstown, N.J. They never threw a bomb, nor did they believe in such tactics. They were continually harrassed by the right. The man who rented them their little building was threatened, and his child was threatened. The coffeehouse was broken into continually; finally, it was bombed beyond repair. But this has not ended the terror of the right. These young people are so threatened that they have to guard their home night and day.

This type of violence is kept very quiet. This is an experience that blacks, whites, rich and poor young radicals know well. This is where the generations gap.

JOAN SIMON.
New York.

Mr. Howe replies: "Of course, as I wrote in my article, 'We have had plenty of terrorism in the United States, mostly by far-right lunatics and racists; lynching is an American contribution to the repertoire of death.' And, of course, authority — especially military authority — is often oppressive. But none of these urgent truisms controverts, even touches upon, what I wrote about recent tendencies toward terrorism along a fringe of the New Left. It's too simple to say that outcroppings of adventurism and authoritarianism in 'far left' circles are the result of despair following upon defeats in trying to change this country. There is just too much evidence that, while despair is a major cause (I said that, too), left authoritarianism has acquired a momentum and glamour of its own.

"The main question is this: Granting shades of difference in analysis, what conclusion would Mrs. Simon draw that is in any way different from my own? Surely, she too recognizes that hooliganism and terrorism on the left is politically suicidal and morally repugnant.

"American liberals and radicals must make up their minds: Do we choose, with whatever difficulties, to remain committed to democratic methods, norms and institutions, or do we succumb to corrupt fantasies about 'revolutionary' bank-burning and bomb-throwing?

"It's like seeing a distraught man on a high ledge preparing to commit suicide. Whatever our notions about the ultimate causes driving him to such a step, our first obligation is to cry, 'Don't jump!' In time, it may even become clear that this cry constitutes an act of moral solidarity."

May 10, 1970

Berkeley (Calif.) street corner

The Western Democracies

MAN DIES AS BOMB RIPS MATH CENTER

Special to The New York Times

MADISON, Wis., Aug. 24—An explosion that the police said was caused by a bomb ripped through the Army Mathematics Research Center on the University of Wisconsin campus early today, killing a graduate student and injuring four other persons.

The math center, a frequent target of antiwar demonstrations, was severely damaged.

Two minutes before the explosion, a dispatcher at the Madison police station received an anonymous call. "Hey, pig," the caller said, "there's a bomb in the math research center."

The explosion occurred at 3.45 A.M. The dead man was Robert Fassnacht, 33 years old, a research assistant in physics who was working late in a section of the center shared with the university's physics department. He was in a basement laboratory doing research on low-temperature phenomena.

The bomb, described as a high-quality explosive device enclosed in plastic, was said to have been inside a truck that was parked in an alley alongside the center. According to Capt. Stanley Davenport, chief of detectives of the Madison Police Department, the truck—a Ford Falcon van—was stolen from a university parking lot last Thursday.

The force of the blast tore apart the six-story, reinforced-concrete building and destroyed most of its contents, including a $1.5-million computer on the third floor. A police spokesman estimated damage to the area at between $6-million and $8-million.

August 25, 1970

Rejection of Terrorism

To the Editor:

The time has come for those of us on the left to speak out against the senseless, irresponsible bombings which are being carried out on university campuses and elsewhere, ostensibly in support of radical political goals and principles.

I am angry that vicious acts of murder and destruction are committed in the name of humanitarian socialism. I refuse to be associated with the wild fantasies of those deranged young men and women whose frustration and rage have driven them to useless, malicious adventures.

They claim, in their defense, that all the destruction of their deeds cannot compare with the horror inflicted upon the Vietnamese people by a single B-52 raid; and they are right. But the unspeakable evil of America's acts in Vietnam does not relieve radicals of responsibility for their acts here in the United States.

It is said that the terrorists are originally decent youths who have been driven literally mad by the wickedness of America's policies and the unresponsiveness of our supposedly democratic political system. I believe that to be substantially true. But although it explains their behavior, it does not excuse it. No man has the right to indulge in evil merely because his enemies indulge in greater evil.

If there were a factual basis for supposing that the murder of tens of thousands of Vietnamese could be stopped by the bombings of college buildings and corporate offices, then there might be some justification for the bombings. But there is absolutely no evidence whatsoever that terrorist attacks accomplish the slightest alteration in our Government's policies.

If there is to be any hope for the advancement of radical socialist policies in this country, responsible men and women of the left must firmly dissociate themselves from these terrorist escapades.

ROBERT PAUL WOLFF
Professor of Philosophy
Columbia University
New York, Sept. 2, 1970

September 13, 1970

Morality of Bombings

To the Editor:

In a letter published Sept. 12, Robert Paul Wolf, professor of philosophy at Columbia, lectures his fellow leftists against bombings on campus or off. Unfortunately, his confusion must perforce diminish his persuasiveness.

He first asserts that another's evil does not justify one's own—that violence committed by the United States in Vietnam does not give the opponents of the war the right to commit violence at home. However, he then concedes that if there were some basis for thinking that bombings here would halt U.S. action in Vietnam, "then there might be some justification for the bombings."

But "there is absolutely no evidence whatsoever" that the Government's policies will be altered by the bombings, Professor Wolff goes on to observe, thus leaving the implication that the bombings would be justifiable if there were such evidence, and thereby repudiating his earlier condemnation of bombing on moral grounds.

MICHAEL HAKEEN
Professor of Sociology
University of Wisconsin
Madison, Sept. 20, 1970

October 5, 1970

Terrorism 'for Peace'

To the Editor:

Over the past decade I must have signed dozens of antiwar statements and appeals, many of which have been published as full-page ads in The Times. I would like to suggest that it is time for another "Stop the Bombing!" ad, but this time addressed by opponents of the Vietnam war and the American "warfare state" to those who share those objectives but have chosen to turn to more extreme strategies of action to win them.

My personal opposition to the bombings, snipings, and other forms of terrorist activity "for peace" has several levels. My immediate concern is with the fact that these things can only prove to be counterproductive, bringing the whole peace movement into disrepute and "turning off" great numbers of people we should be winning over to our cause.

Fear of Repression

I am concerned, too, with the almost certain repression these acts are going to unleash against the essentially fine and deeply committed young people who are involved and who will have to pay a cruel price for permitting their perfectly understandable impatience and frustration to provoke them to such excesses.

Finally, I am concerned over the injustice suffered by the victims—not only the innocent bystanders but, more specifically, the policemen and officials against whom the acts are directed. I see no justification for the indiscriminate killing of a man just because he is a member of some category, whether national, racial or occupational.

All such things are murders and should be condemned as such, regardless of whether the victim is wearing black pajamas in some Vietnamese rice paddy, the jacket of some militant group in one of our urban ghettos, or a policeman's uniform in Chicago or Philadelphia.

To protest these actions publicly is not to abandon the agreement on substantive issues which binds all segments of the antiwar movement. A new "Stop the Bombing!" appeal could, and should, include a forthright condemnation of the continued slaughter of the innocent in Vietnam (and now in Cambodia as well). It would have to be explicit in rejecting our presently disordered national priorities which permit human needs to go unmet while precious resources are squandered in foreign wars and diplomatic deals that support oppressive, even dictatorial, regimes all over the world.

These are all betrayals of the moral conscience of our people, and this must be made clear. Nevertheless, they do not justify any program of action which finds some of our most dedicated opponents of the war joining people like General LeMay and others who believe, each in his own way, that the only way to get the peace we want is by more and more violence and bigger and better bombs.

GORDON C. ZAHN
Professor of Sociology
University of Massachusetts
Boston, Sept. 3, 1970

September 14, 1970

Role of Terror and Bombing

To the Editor:

Prof. Gordon C. Zahn [letter Sept. 14] has presented an accurate analysis of the role of bombing and terrorism in the current phase of American history, with one significant exception. When he states that he finds "some of our most dedicated opponents of the war joining people like General LeMay . . . who believe that the only way to get the peace we want is by more and more violence and bigger and better bombs," his analysis is unsound.

It is a socially dynamic contradiction to associate bombing with the peace movement. Those who are dedicated to the principle that societies can resolve their socioeconomic problems and learn through various systems to live effectively with one another, could not in any way, in their most anguished and frustrated endeavors, resort to violence and bombing as a logical sequential development in their struggle for enduring peace.

The association that Dr. Zahn made gives tremendous ammunition to the minority that is against the peace movement and alienates the healthy segment of people on the fringe of the peace movement. Whenever there is bombing and terrorism, allegedly on behalf of the peace movement, only those who are against the peace movement profit from such actions.

Bombing in the name of peace takes on the aura of the Reichstag fire syndrome; those who can gain the most from the reaction of people to such violence may be the very ones to condone or foster such actions, thereby discrediting the people in the peace movement.

The campus bombings have done much to undermine the genuine antiwar movement and alienate a large segment of supporters of peace. They have given ammunition to the high officials of this and the past Administration to permit the continuation of the war without criticism.

Bombing and terrorism should be stopped. They should never be viewed as symptomatic of the anguish of the failing struggle of the peace movement.

ALBERT M. BIELE, M.D.
Assoc. Professor Clinical Psychiatry
Thomas Jefferson University
Philadelphia, Sept. 18, 1970

September 29, 1970

Bombings Cost Militants Potential Gains in Support

Incidents Are Alienating Many Radicals and Youths Who Might Join Cause —Student Ambivalence Is Found

By DOUGLAS E. KNEELAND
Special to The New York Times

SAN FRANCISCO, Dec. 13— "We told them to bomb it, to blow it up. And then they blew it up. And we said, 'My God, they blew it up!'"

The slender, dark-haired girl, pretty in blue jeans and a loose pullover top, paused, her brown eyes hurt, confused. Most of the eight or nine other young radicals casually surrounding two pitchers of beer and the greasy remains of hamburgers and french fries in the back room of the Plaza, a bowling alley, bar and restaurant a few windswept blocks from the State Capitol in Madison, Wis., nodded understandingly.

Nearly all were members of the staff of Kaleidoscope, an underground weekly that, like innumerable others around the country, had printed instructions for making bombs and had repeatedly exhorted militants to action.

They had been discussing the bombing last Aug. 24 of the Army Mathematics Research Center at the University of Wisconsin that killed a graduate student, injured four other persons and caused $6-million damage. And they were still shaken.

A team of correspondents, in several weeks of reporting across much of the nation, has determined that the continued bombing by such groups as the Weathermen is alienating large numbers of radicals and many college youths who would be potential supporters of the movement—that if the bombers are trying to rally adherents to their cause, they are failing.

They also seem not to be bringing about the harsh repression that some militants say they are willing to face to lure others to their side in a struggle against the Government.

On the campuses and among many radicals, there is a feeling of real ambivalence — a sense that the bombers are wrong and are hurting the chance for any meaningful political change, accompanied by a deeply entrenched empathy with their disillusionment.

Many youths, even while they disagree with the tactic, understand the bombers' rationalizations that their acts are necessary to call attention to "repressive" institutions and that the destruction of property is not violence — that violence can be perpetrated only against people, as in the killing in Vietnam.

Among faculty members and much of the general public, there seems to be a similar ambivalence for somewhat different reasons. The radical left has almost always warned the occupants of a building that was to be bombed and they have usually timed explosives to go off when there was a minimum chance of hurting anyone. While many people are distressed by the bombings, few seem frightened or angered to the point of supporting repressive measures.

Some views were encountered frequently around the country:

"Bombings are suicidal and are not bringing any change except an increase in repression," said Harvey Ovshinsky, long active in radical movements in Detroit. "Blowing up the C.I.A. building will not bring home the troops."

Most radicals are not following the Weathermen, Mr. Ovshinsky added, but once a bomber is caught and charged with conspiracy, radicals and other youths will support him.

Support For Victims

"They identify," he explained. "You show support for victims of oppression. They become heroes because they fought the law. Many would harbor Bernardine Dohrn or Angela Davis."

Miss Dohrn is a Weatherman leader who is on the Federal Bureau of Investigation's "most wanted" list. Miss Davis is a black militant who is wanted in California to face charges in connection with an abortive attempt to free prisoners last August in which a trial judge and three other persons were killed.

"The Weathermen personify the frustrations of the radical movement now," said Michael Charney, a 20-year-old history major who is a spokesman for the Oberlin Radical Coalition. "They show a contempt for the people of the United States.

"What they're really saying is that you can't organize a mass movement in the United States for a revolution so they're resorting to terrorism. It's dangerous for the whole radical movement, because the reaction of the average American is that all radicals are bombers."

Case For Indifference

Sitting at the counter in Johnny's Restaurant near Wayne State University in Detroit, Bruce Hern, 18, a freshman, said:

"I just don't like what both sides are doing—the Weathermen or the Government. I guess being indifferent is the best way. I myself can't suggest any ideas on how to solve things. Everyone should mind his own business. That would be the best way if it was possible."

And Herman Bates, a Westchester conservative who worked in Barry Goldwater's Presidential campaign in 1964, on a plane ride between Chicago and New York declared of the bombings:

"People don't like them, but they're not outraged. They're just annoyed."

Most people who have studied radical groups agree that political bombings are the desperate acts of a weakened movement that has not attracted a mass following.

Nonviolent Tradition

One reason for the bombers' failure to win many followers is that most radicals, college students and other segments of the youth culture are steeped in the nonviolent traditions of the civil rights and peace movements.

They sincerely deplore the possibility of killing or maiming innocent people. And while many sympathize with the frustrations and the goals of the extremists and would willingly shelter them from the police, they consider their tactics "adventuristic" and "counterproductive," inviting unwanted repression and scaring away potential supporters.

Moreover, the bombings have brought no heavy repression that would sharply polarize the country.

The Federal Government and some states have tightened up their laws on the sale, use and transportation of explosives. The F.B.I. has stepped up its efforts to find suspected bombers. The police departments of many cities have increased the size of their bomb squads, partly because of the soaring number of threats that must be checked out. But there have been no mass arrests and the public has shown no appetite for witch-hunts.

Law-and-Order Drive

For example, the Nixon Administration's law-and-order campaign against the "radical-liberals" and "anarchy," which was in crescendo in October at the same time the far left was taking credit for bombings in the Weathermen's "fall offensive," was considered by most observers to have been largely unsuccessful.

Even in Wisconsin, where the bombing death of the graduate student caused widespread revulsion, Republican attempts to make violence an issue failed.

Lieut. Gov. Jack B. Olson, the Republican candidate for Governor, used television spots picturing him standing in front of the devastated math center, while a sound track indicated that liberal professors were partly responsible for the bombing. Mr. Olson lost to a Democrat, Patrick J. Lucey, by the unexpectedly large margin of 125,000 votes, and the Democrats upset the Republicans to win control of the State Assembly by 67 to 33, their largest edge in history.

Finds Sympathy

"I think the bombing really provided some sympathetic reaction," Robert Taylor, a vice president of the University of Wisconsin, said. "People thinking twice know you can't prevent a bombing or that we don't support it. It's not the same as having radicals bring in people to disrupt conservative speakers. That, they blame the university for. They think we could run a tighter ship."

Still, the bombings go on with what most experts agree is a rapidly increasing frequency and intensity in the last few years. A lack of national records, except for recent months, makes comparisons almost impossible with earlier periods when violence swept the country and bombings were in vogue.

However, the bomb section of the New York Police Department has kept thorough records for a number of years. These present a startling picture of the rise in incidence. In 1961, the section handled 722 cases; in 1965, it had 1,011 cases; in 1969, cases rose to 3,192, and as of the second week of November this year, they totaled 8,745.

From Threats to Defusing

In bomb squad parlance, every duty that members are called upon to perform is a "case." This ranges from checking out anonymous false telephones threats to defusing bombs and incendiary devices to searching out a building that a dignitary is to visit.

There has been no complete breakdown of cases in New York for 1970 as yet, but in 1969 the total included 2,587 anonymous and unfounded threats of bombs, 93 exploded bombs, 19 unexploded bombs that had to be defused, and 443 other cases that actually involved such things as explosives or incendiary devices. The 50 other cases listed in this total were not explained.

Such national figures as are available are conflicting, but they give some idea of the extent of the bombings.

Last summer the Alcohol, Tobacco and Firearms Division of the Internal Revenue Service presented to the Senate's Permanent Subcommittee on Investigations bombing statistics it had collected for the period of Jan. 1, 1969, to April 15, 1970, from local and state law enforcement agencies.

The statistics showed that during that period there were 975 explosive bombings in the nation, 3,355 incendiary bombings and 35,129 bomb threats. The Department of Justice, in a study of its own, recorded 350 explosive bombings between last Jan. 1 and Oct. 25.

Almost anyone, in government or out, who speaks of bombings these days is talking or thinking about the Weathermen or other radical leftists.

In fact, the experts say bombers are a diverse group, embracing the radical left, the radical right, black militants, racketeers, persons involved in labor disputes, immigrants, such as Cubans, who have a grievance against the present government in their homeland, and the mentally ill who have a real or fancied grudge against society.

Still, there is little doubt that disenchanted young leftists have contributed significantly to the bombing totals.

"The radicals are driving the racketeers out of the bombing business," said Detective William Schmitt, a stocky, 20-year veteran of the New York police bomb section. He added almost wistfully:

"In the old days, when we caught a bomber such as George Metesky, the threat was over. Now, if you catch one, you haven't stopped the organization. There are others to take his place."

This is a problem that troubles the Department of Justice and the F.B.I. A Justice Department official in Washington, admittedly guessing, put the number of Weathermen at fewer than 500. These, he noted with some chagrin, are scattered around the nation in groups of three or four, making infiltration by informers or the F.B.I. almost impossible.

Speaking of the Black Panthers, the Communist party, the Klan and the right-wing Minutemen, a Justice Department spokesman said, "We know pretty well what they're doing — they're pretty structured."

The young radicals are anything but structured and most law enforcement officials do not see their bombings as a national conspiracy in any but the loosest sense—small groups with similar aims spread across the country.

Who are the bombers?

A taped message, purportedly from Miss Dohrn, was released by the Yippies on Oct. 8, the third anniversary of the death of Che Guevara, the Cuban revolutionary, in Bolivia. Calling for the "fall offensive of youth resistance," it declared in part:

"Now we are everywhere and next week families and tribes will attack the enemy around the country. It is our job to blast away the myths of the total superiority of The Man."

Within days, Federal buildings, R.O.T.C. buildings and armories were bombed in various parts of the country. Many of the actions were quickly claimed by groups such as the Quarter Moon Tribe in Seattle and the Perfect Park Homegrown Garden Society in Santa Barbara, Calif.

Are they Weathermen? Or freelance radicals? Or youngsters out for excitement? What is a Weatherman? Anyone who says he is? There are no cards to carry, dues to pay. Any person or group can choose a romantic name from the youth culture and expound some revolutionary ideals.

Instructions for making bombs and carrying on guerrilla warfare are easily available from the underground press, libraries or from any number of radical groups that insist they do not take part in such actions themselves.

A young woman social worker in Columbus, Ohio, who was active in demonstrations last spring at Ohio State University, explained the attraction for at least some of the bombers.

"There's a crisis in the movement," she said. "Things have split apart and many people are tired. There's a lot of attraction when a few people can blow up a building and do millions of dollars in damage and the news media carries it all over the country. Then the people can slip underground, look at each other and say, 'Ha, ha.'

"There is a romantic thing about it. You can be the revolutionary for a day but not really get involved. Like you and your girl going around blowing up bridges. It gives you a feeling that you're doing something."

The following New York Times staff members assisted Mr. Kneeland in the reporting for this article: Agis Salpukas, Douglas Robinson, John Kifner, Martin Waldron and Michael T. Kaufman.

December 14, 1970

Weatherman Dormant After Fiery Start

By LES LEDBETTER

Weatherman went underground in 1970, and most of the members of the militant left-wing organization have been hiding ever since to avoid prosecution on charges that include violation of Federal antiriot laws and destruction of property.

Law enforcement officials generally consider the organization dead or dormant — an opinion generally shared by members of the left who have had contact with or knowledge of members of the group.

These people, who declined to be identified and who spoke guardedly yesterday, said the key members of the Weather Underground, as the group is now known, were more concerned with protecting their identity and residences than with meeting or planning further action as an organized group.

These theoreticians, organizers and original members of the radical left advocated violence as a proper political tool in 1969. Now they are reported to be deeply worried about police infiltration and surveillance and are said to shun all

TERRORISM AND THE STATE TODAY

direct contact with former associates in the anti war movement. They dress in nondescript clothing, carry well-forged false identification and live away from areas associated with radicalism.

For example, Howard Norton Machtinger, listed by the Federal Bureau of Investigation as a member of the Weather Underground, was arrested a week ago on the Upper West Side, reportedly carrying a fake draft card and other false identification. He had been sought on a Federal fugitive warrant for more than three years.

Similarly, Bernadine Dohrn, a Weatherman member also sought by the F.B.I., was said to have been seen in Boston last spring wearing a dress and looking more like a secretary than a fugitive radical.

Law-enforcement officials say that the three years of hiding have made the highly secretive Weather Underground cells, or chapters even more cautious, to the extent that many cells, which rarely number more than seven members, are not in contact with each other and make no attempt to coordinate activities.

Nevertheless, some meetings apparently do occur, as attested to by an "Open Letter from Underground" written in May, 1973, by another fugitive, Jane Alpert, who pleaded guilty to a bombing-conspiracy charge in 1970 and then jumped bail.

Discussing her conversion from radical-left activity to radical feminism, the woman denounced Weatherman as sexist.

She recalled meeting the Weather Underground leader Mark Rudd at a public lecture and thinking him "either an agent or a dangerous fool" and denouncing the fact that Mr. Rudd and two other men controlled the five-member central committee of the Underground that is known as the Weather Bureau.

Although she was never an official member of the Weather Underground, Miss Alpert in her letter indicates that the group is more structured and more active than most law-enforcement officials believe.

Leftists here, in the Boston area and on the West Coast said yesterday that since Miss Alpert's letter was published there had been increased efforts by the Federal Bureau Investigation to find the 30 young radicals who have successfully evaded capture for the last three years.

These radicals report repeated visits by Federal officers to their residences and to the residences of their parents. In San Francisco, a Federal grand jury is said to have issued contempt citations to a number of subpoenaed witnesses who have refused to discus whether they have harbored any of the wanted radicals.

Weatherman was born in 1969 when a segment of the Students for a Democratic Society advanced the thesis that violence was a necessary means of increasing "the cost of empire." The Weatherman name was taken from a song by Bob Dylan, "Subterranean Homesick Blues," which says: "You don't need a weatherman to know which way the wind blows." The new group called for direct physical action to replace peaceful demonstrations.

During four "Days of Rage" in October, 1969, scores of youths from radical "collectives" rampaged through downtown Chicago, and an alleged bombing campaign was begun that included the June, 1970, explosion at Police Headquarters at 240 Centre Street here. After the "Days of Rage," leaders of Weatherman were indicted by a number of local and Federal grand juries and then went underground.

September 29, 1973

Miss Hearst Says She Joins Terrorists

In a Broadcast Message, Kidnapping Victim Vows to Fight for 'Oppressed'

By EARL CALDWELL
Special to The New York Times

SAN FRANCISCO, April 3—Patricia Hearst said in a tape-recorded message received today that she had chosen to join the forces of the Symbionese Liberation Army and fight for "the freedom of oppressed people."

She said that she had been offered the choice of being released or the chance to join the underground terrorist group.

"I have chosen to stay and fight," she said.

The message, delivered to Berkeley radio station KPFA, came one day after the group that calls itself the Symbionese Liberation Army had announced that it was planning to release the 20-year-old daughter of the newspaper executive, Randolph A. Hearst. The police say she was abducted from her apartment at gunpoint last Feb. 4.

In a brief meeting with reporters several hours after the message from his daughter was broadcast, Mr. Hearst said he did not believe that his daughter had joined the terrorist group.

"We've had her 20 years," he said. "They've had her 60 days, and I don't believe she is going to change her philosophy that quickly and that permanently, and I'll never believe it until she comes to me, or her mother, or her sisters, or one of her cousins and is free to talk without any interference whatsoever. At that time if her choice is to become a member of an organization like this, we'll still love her and she's free to do whatever she wants."

However, earlier, Mrs. Hearst said, after listening to the tape, that the voice was her daughter's.

In the tape, which was delivered to the radio station early this afternoon, Patricia was deeply critical of her parents. She told her fiancé, Steven Weed, that much had changed since her disappearance.

"I have changed — grown," she said.

In addition to the message from Miss Hearst, the Symbionese spokesman who calls himself General Field Marshal Cinque spoke at length.

He identified three people whom he described as "enemies of the people" and maintained that they would be shot on sight. They were identified as Robin Steiner, Chris Thompson and Colston Westbrook. He asserted that all three were informants for the Federal Bureau of Investigation. Miss Steiner is white and the men are black.

The S.L.A. spokesman asserted that Miss Steiner was 20 and a "past resident of Berkeley now living in Florida, an informer to the F.B.I."

He contended that Mr. Thompson was a Berkeley resident, was "a Government agent, paid informant for the F.B.I."

Cinque said that Mr. Westbrook was 35, a "Berkeley language instructor, resident of Oakland, a Government agent, worked for C.I.A. in Vietnam ... now working for military intelligence while giving cross-assistance to the F.B.I."

At the outset of the message, Miss Hearst made a point of saying that her words reflected her own feelings.

"I have never been forced to say anything on any tape," she began. "Nor have I been brainwashed, drugged, tortured, hypnotized or in any way confused." She then quoted George Jackson, a black convict and author who was shot and killed at San Quentin Prison.

"It's me," she said, "the way I want it, the way I see it."

Unlike previous communiqués from the Symbionese, today's message did not have any date. There were reports that the package contained half of Miss Hearst's driver's license, but that could not be confirmed.

In his message Cinque said that "the prisoner [Patricia Hearst] had been freed" but added that "she refused to go home."

Of Miss Hearst, he said: "There is no further need to discuss the release of the prisoner, since she is now a comrade and has been accepted into the ranks of the people's army as a comrade and fighter." And, he continued, "there is no further basis for negotiations since the subject may leave whenever she feels that she wishes to do so and she is armed and perfectly willing and able to defend herself."

After saying she had chosen to stay with the Symbionese, Miss Hearst said:

"One thing which I learned is that the corporate ruling class will do anything in their power in order to maintain their position of control over the masses, even if this means the sacrifice of one of their own.

"It should be obvious that people who don't even care about their own children couldn't possibly care about anyone else's children. The things which are precious to these people are their money and power—and they will never willingly surrender either."

She added that "people should not have to humiliate themselves by standing in lines in order to be fed, nor should they have to live in fear of their lives and the lives of their children."

Miss Hearst addressed her parents first. She said:

"Mom, Dad, I would like to comment on your efforts to supposedly secure my safety. The P.I.N.[People in Need] giveaway was a sham. You attempted to deceive the people, the S.L.A. and me with statements about your concern for myself and the people. You were playing games—stalling for time—time which the F.B.I. was using in their efforts to assassinate me and the S.L.A. elements which guarded me.

299

"You continue to report," the girl went on, "that you did everything in your power to pave the way for negotiations for my release—I hate to believe that you could have been so unimaginative as to not even have considered getting Little and Remiro released on bail."

Miss Hearst referred to Joseph Remiro and Russell Little, two acknowledged members of the Symbionese who were arrested and indicted in the murder of Dr. Marcus A. Foster, the black superintendent of the Oakland, Calif., public schools, last November.

"While it was repeatedly stated that my conditions would at all times correspond with those of the captured soldiers, when your own lawyer went to inspect the 'hole' at San Quentin, he approved the deplorable conditions there—another move which potentially jeopardized my safety.

"My mother's acceptance of the appointment of a second term as a University of California Regent, as you well knew, would have caused my immediate execution had the S.L.A. been less than 'together' about their political goals. Your actions have taught me a great lesson, and in a strange kind of way, I'm grateful to you."

She then spoke to her fiancé, who was with her Feb. 4. To him, she said:

"Steven, I know that you are beginning to realize that there is no such thing as neutrality in time of war. There can be no compromise as your experiences with the F.B.I. must have shown you. You have been harassed by the F.B.I. because of your supposed connections with so-called radicals, and some people have even gone so far as to suggest that I arranged my own arrest.

"We both know what really came down that Monday night —but you don't know what's happened since then. I have changed — grown. I've become conscious and can never go back to the life we led before. What I am saying may seem cold to you and to my old friends, but love doesn't mean the same thing to me anymore.

"My love has expanded as a result of my experiences to embrace all people. It's grown into an unselfish love for my comrades here, in prison and on the streets. A love that comes from the knowledge that 'no one is free until we are all free.' While I wished that you could be a comrade, I don't expect it — all I expect is that you try to understand the changes I've gone through."

The tape recording was delivered by a messenger. Along with the tape there was a color photograph of Miss Hearst standing in front of the Symbionese flag that bears the imprint of a seven-headed cobra. She was photographed carrying a submachine gun.

In the message some of her strongest comments were directed at her father. She said:

"Dad, you said that you were concerned with the life and interests of all oppressed people in this country, but you are a liar in both areas, and as a member of the ruling class, I know for sure that yours and Mom's interests are never the interests of the people.

"You, a corporate liar, of course will say that you don't know what I'm talking about, but I ask you then to prove it, tell the poor and oppressed people of this nation what the corporate state is about to do, warn black and poor people that they are about to be murdered down to the last man, woman and child."

April 4, 1974

5 Terrorist Suspects Die In Coast Gunfight and Fire

Reported Members of Group Linked to Hearst Kidnapping Killed in Siege— Blaze Destroys Slum Hideout

By JON NORDHEIMER
Special to The New York Times

LOS ANGELES, May 17— Five persons believed to be members of the Symbionese Liberation Army were killed here tonight in a savage gun battle and fire as hundreds of heavily armed policemen laid siege to a house where the fugitives had taken refuge.

Hours after the walls of the blazing house collapsed, the police and spokesmen for the Federal Bureau of Investigation said the five bodies found in the ruins had been burned too severely to permit immediate identification.

Earlier unconfirmed reports —attributed to, but subsequently denied by, the F.B.I.—had identified two of the dead as Donald D. DeFreeze, the 30-year-old escaped convict who called himself General Field Marshal Cinque, and Camilla Hall, 29, a member of the radical group.

An F.B.I spokesman said late tonight that the bodies would probably not be identified until late tomorrow morning The same spokesman said there was no indication that Patricia Hearst, who was abducted by the same group on Feb. 4, was among those in the house.

Tear gas, shotguns and automatic weapons were used in the gun battle. During the fight, the house caught fire and ultimately became a raging inferno.

A middle-aged black woman, with a pink hair-roller in her hair, stumbled from the house after the blaze started and was quickly taken into custody.

Officials said she told investigators that two men and two women had been in the house with her when 130 policemen surrounded and laid siege to the house in a black slum near the Watts section in south-central Los Angeles.

The confrontation, which was carried live by Los Angeles television stations and watched by hundreds of neighborhood residents at close range, erupted when automatic

Donald D. DeFreeze

weapons fire from the house greeted the first police overtures for the occupants to surrender.

The gunfire, which started about 6 P.M. Pacific daylight time, continued unabated for an hour before the unidentified woman stumbled from the burning house. A police marksman in a flak jacket reported that he saw two bodies at the door near the rear of the house. Both were wearing ammunition belts, and both were apparently dead.

Flames engulfed the doorway before the police could move in. An hour after the shooting stopped, the firemen were still hosing down the rubble.

The gun battle and fire occurred as the authorities here made their second raid of the day on the suspected hideout of the self-styled Symbionese Liberation Army. The first raid occurred a few miles away, when the police and F.B.I. agents, acting on a tip, surrounded and stormed a similar structure. They found a few scattered boxes of ammunition, some wigs and other clothing, but the unfurnished premises had been abandoned.

It was the first confrontation between the authorities and members of the radical group since Miss Hearst, the 20-year-old daughter of Randolph A. Hearst, the San Francisco newspaper executive, was kidnapped early in February by the group

Although there were initial and unconfirmed reports that Miss Hearst was in the building that burned here tonight, police units in the state of Washington were alerted earlier today to be on the lookout for Miss Hearst and several members of the radical group. They were reported to be driving from Portland, Ore., to Spokane, Wash.

A 'People's Struggle'

The enigma of Miss Hearst's captivity has not been resolved. Initially, after her abduction, she pleaded with her father to meet her abductors' ransom demands so that she could be released. But in subsequent messages, Miss Hearst portrayed herself as a convert to the terrorist group and said she was now committed to a "people's struggle" against persons like her father.

Last month, she participated in a San Francisco bank robbery with three other members of the group, adding to the mystery around her strange conversion.

Today's events developed quickly after three members of the group, believed to be Emily Harris and her husband, William, and a second unidentified woman, were involved in a shootout yesterday in nearby Inglewood.

The police said that a man and woman, stopped for shoplifting by a sporting-goods store employe after they had purchased about $30 of heavy outdoor clothing, escaped after another woman seated in a parked van scattered the employes with a burst of machine-gun fire.

After abandoning the van and stealing several cars, their trail was lost near Hollywood Hills.

Speculation Over Clothing

There was immediate speculation that the purchase of heavy garments at this time of the year in Los Angeles was an indication that Mr. and Mrs. Harris and the unidentified woman—and possibly others—had planned to live in a cooler climate, either in the rugged mountains of California or elsewhere.

The F.B.I. found the hideout last night or early today, presumably on a tip from an informer, after television reports about the bizarre shoot-out. The incident occurred in the predominantly black Inglewood section of Los Angeles. The Harrises and the unidentified woman are white.

Before dawn, an attack force of F.B.I. agents and special units of the Los Angeles police surrounded a small, unfurnished house in a black slum near Watts. They rushed it about 9 A.M. Pacific standard time, but found the house empty except for shotgun ammunition, wigs and clothing.

"There is no doubt that this was their hideout," an F.B.I. spokesman said. "We now have to assume that these three are on the run in the L.A. area, are armed, desperate and dangerous."

William Sullivan, head of the F.B.I.'s Los Angeles office, announced that there was "no doubt" that the fugitives were part of the same group that kidnapped Miss Hearst.

Black neighbors told F.B.I. agents they had thought it unusual to see three whites move into the house last Friday, but no one called the police.

Apparently, the three never returned to the hideout. After the store shoot-out they abandoned the van, which had been stolen, and then stole a series of cars at gunpoint.

The last vehicle, a Ford van, belonged to an 18-year-old Lynwood youth, Thomas Matthews, who had a "For Sale" sign on it and had parked it outside of his home. He told the police a woman inquired at his door last evening about the van and asked for a demonstration ride.

A Meandering Trip

After they drove one block, the man and the second woman scrambled into the van with guns, forced the youth into the rear of the vehicle, and began a meandering, hours-long trip around Los Angeles. They even took the youth to a drive-in, where they bought him food and a drink.

The police believe that the three were able to purchase a hacksaw during the evening and cut the handcuffs from the man's wrist.

The youth, blindfolded but unhurt, was left in the parked van that the three deserted in the city's Hollywood Hills district about 3 A.M. He said they had two "long rifles" and two hand guns, and at one point apparently were trying to reach accomplices by telephone. Several times during the drive-in movie. "Thomasine and Bushrod" (described in the trade papers as a black "Bonnie and Clyde"), one of the women left the van to make telephone calls, reporting back each time: "She is not at home. They're not there."

May 18, 1974

BARGAIN WITH TERRORISTS?

Is America's no-negotiating policy a deterrent or an invitation to murder?

By Judith Miller

WASHINGTON. Rockets rip through the United States Embassy in Beirut. . . . An American military adviser is gunned down on a street in Teheran. . . . In Khartoum, two American diplomats held hostage by Palestinian terrorists are riddled with machine gun bullets after demands for political concessions are not met. . . . Caskets containing the bodies of an American Ambassador and his economic counselor are received in Washington by President Ford to a 19-gun salute. . . .

Although the biggest headlines in the rising incidence of international terrorism have gone to Arab actions against Israeli nationals, such as the slaying of Israeli athletes at the 1972 Olympics in Munich and the abduction and dramatic rescue of the passengers of an Air France jet two weeks ago, American Government missions abroad have also been a primary target. In the 77 episodes from 1968 to 1975 in which hostages were held for ransom, the victims included about 30 American officials, six of whom were killed. And for nearly six years now, Washington has adhered to a policy of "no concessions" to the terrorists. It will not accede to demands put forward as a condition for the hostages' release, it will not negotiate such terms, and it will not put pressure on other Govern-

Judith Miller is the Washington correspondent of The Progressive.

ments to yield. In the interests of deterring future terrorism, America hangs tough.

But now this rigid policy has come under fire. Critics within the State Department and elsewhere are calling for a more flexible approach—one that would permit negotiations with terrorists and, under certain circumstances, acquiescence to demands for money and political concessions to save American lives. This debate over the deterrent value of the hard-line policy has until recently been shielded from public view, but now the critics have begun to express their views more vociferously and publicly.

The Israeli rescue of 103 hijacking hostages and crew members from Entebbe Airport in Uganda has called attention to the agonizing decisions that confront American policy makers when American hostages are involved. Fortunately, terrorism is still an insignificant form of violence in terms of numbers. Between 1968 and mid-1975, only 250 people were killed in terrorist episodes—less than the annual homicide rate of any major American city. But terrorism cannot be measured by statistics. It is violence in its most pernicious form; its victims are the innocent; it is unpredictable. And its impact is all the greater because it makes one's own Government seem either helpless or heartless —unable to protect its citizens or callous in the remedies its employs.

The United States has chosen the hard-line approach well aware of its limitations and liabilities.

State Department proponents of this policy know, for instance, that it is likely to make Washington seem indifferent to the safety of Foreign Service officials and American citizens abroad. The Ford Administration, nonetheless, is deeply committed to the hard line, and the American response to terrorism is not likely to change so long as Henry Kissinger remains Secretary of State. But unrest within the State Department over the current stance is growing; there is little ground for hope that acts of terrorism involving Americans will subside in the near future, and the whole dilemma is likely to come up for reassessment by the next Administration.

☐

In the early 60's, terrorist incidents were rare. In 1968, however, diplomatic kidnappings and attempted assassinations increased markedly in number. Among the victims that year were four American officials kidnapped and killed in Latin America and two wounded. Washington dealt with each incident as it occurred; there was no consistent policy. In some cases, the Government ignored the terrorists' demands; in others, while refusing to pay ransom, Washington pressed the Governments of the countries where the abductions took place to meet the terrorists' conditions. For example, when Ambassador Charles Burke Elbrick was kidnapped in Brazil in 1969, the United States put pressure on Brazil to free 15 "political prisoners," as demanded by the captors. *(Continued)*

301

Brazil reluctantly complied, and the Ambassador was released, unharmed.

In July 1970, Dan Mitrione, an American public-safety adviser stationed in Uruguay, was abducted by the Tupamaros, the "urban guerrillas" then on the rampage in that country. In the developing drama (which has been fictionalized in the Costa-Gavras movie "State of Siege") the Uruguayan Government rejected the Tupamaros' offer to release Mitrione in exchange for a group of political prisoners. At this juncture, Washington's policy hardened. As one State Department official said, "We decided not to pressure the Uruguayans to meet the terrorists' demands. We were beginning to realize that such actions would only encourage others to use the same tactic." Efforts to rescue Mitrione were unsuccessful. His dead body was found in an abandoned car.

The number of terrorist incidents rose sharply in 1971, but it was not until the slaughter at the 1972 Olympics that the United States began to take concerted counteraction. President Nixon established a Cabinet Committee to Combat Terrorism, composed of the Secretaries of State, Defense, Treasury and Transportation, the Attorney General, the Ambassador to the United Nations, the directors of the C.I.A. and the F.B.I., and the President's top national-security and domestic-policy aides. The committee appointed a Working Group of officials of these and other Government agencies. This group, meeting twice a week, began to lay down plans for coordinated action. What it boiled down to was "no concessions."

On the evening of March 1, 1973, that policy was put to its first major test.

In Khartoum, capital of the Sudan, eight Palestinians of the Black September terrorist faction stormed and seized the Saudi Arabian Embassy during a farewell party for the deputy chief of the American mission, George Curtis Moore. They soon released all their prisoners except two Arab diplomats, the Belgian chargé d'affaires, American Ambassador Cleo A. Noel Jr., and Moore. In exchange for the lives of these five, the Palestinians demanded the release of hundreds of "political prisoners" held in the Mideast and the West—including Sirhan Sirhan, the slayer of Robert Kennedy.

The Working Group in Washington assembled an emergency task force, which set up camp in the State Department's Operations Center, a communications room down the hall from the office of the Secretary of State. Telex messages from the embassy in Khartoum were speeded to various members of the Government by phone, pneumatic tube and a facsimile transmitter equipped with a scrambler to insure secrecy. President Nixon sent a Deputy Under Secretary of State, William Macomber Jr., to Khartoum to advise the Sudanese in their negotiations with Black September.

It seemed to many on the task force that there was a chance of saving the hostages' lives. A cable from the embassy in Khartoum said Black September had dropped all its demands except for what seemed to be its bedrock condition—release of 17 Palestinian guerrillas imprisoned by the Jordanian Government after the suppression of the Palestinian commando forces on Jordanian soil. Macomber and his entourage landed in Cairo. The publicity surrounding their mission appeared to have pleased the Palestinians. There were indications that they were prepared to fly to Cairo with their hostages, to continue the negotiations there.

Quite suddenly, things seemed to fall apart. Black September refused to move the talks to the Egyptian capital. Macomber, setting off for Khartoum, was diverted by a sandstorm. The guerrillas issued a "final deadline" for the release of their comrades in Jordan. The Jordanian Government refused to comply. At a White House press conference, reporters asked President Nixon about the Sirhan Sirhan demand. He replied that the United States would not give in to blackmail. "We cannot do so and we will not do so," he said. "Now, as to what can be done to get these people released, Mr. Macomber is on his way there for discussions; the Sudanese Government is working on the problem . . . but we will not pay blackmail."

The cables to the task force became increasingly ominous. The Palestinians, who, from all indications, were growing anxious and irritated, heard of Nixon's widely reported statement. Soon afterward, they permitted Ambassador Noel to speak by telephone to his embassy. Noel was told Macomber was on his way to Khartoum from Asmara and would arrive later that evening. "That will be too late," the Ambassador said. The next morning, the Palestinians gave themselves up. The bodies of the two Americans and the Belgian were found in the basement.

The new American policy was given more official expression by the President a few days later at a State Department ceremony honoring Noel and Moore. "All of us would have liked to have saved the lives of these two brave men," Nixon said. "But they knew and we knew that in the event we had paid international blackmail, it would have saved their lives, but it would have endangered the lives of hundreds of others all over the world, because once the terrorist has a demand that is made, that is satisfied, he then is encouraged to try it again; that that is why the position of your Government has to be one, in the interest of preserving life, of not submitting to international blackmail or extortion any place in the world. That is our policy, and that is the policy we are going to

TERRORISM AND THE STATE TODAY

continue to have."

The death of the two popular diplomats stunned the Foreign Service. For many in the State Department, the shock was followed by anger. Some felt the handling of the incident had been bungled. Several Foreign Service officers demanded a full-scale study of the Khartoum episode instead of the routine post-mortem conducted by the Working Group. Seven months later, the Rand Corporation, the California-based "think tank," was hired to review the whole question of negotiating for the release of kidnapped diplomats and to make recommendations. Khartoum was one of some 30 cases to be examined. The project was headed by Brian Jenkins, a senior Rand analyst who had long been warning the State Department of the growing threat of terrorism.

Last May, a draft of the report was issued in the form of working notes and was circulated for limited distribution within the State Department. Those familiar with the work describe it as an analysis and indictment of the hard-line policy.

One of the fundamental errors made in the Khartoum incident, according to the draft report, was Nixon's "no blackmail" statement at his White House press conference at the time Macomber was on his way to Khartoum. "The guidance given to him [Nixon], if asked about the affair, was to remain noncommittal," Jenkins wrote. "[The] President's statement . . . suggested that there was not much to negotiate, even when Macomber arrived. . . . [Macomber's] long flight was working as a stall, which the President's statement may have effectively torpedoed." Moreover, Jenkins added, Macomber was sent half-way around the globe from Washington, with the result that no American in a position of authority arrived in Khartoum in time; sending someone closer might have made more sense. And when Macomber was dispatched, no one in Washington had a clear idea of what he was supposed to do or why he was being sent.

Among Jenkins's recommendations were that high-level Government officials remain silent during such episodes, that all official statements be checked with the task force set up to handle the crisis, and that all information to the press be screened. Even a biographical sketch listing a kidnapped diplomat's previous assignments can have a detrimental impact on his chance of survival, Jenkins argued, since he may have been accredited to a Government regarded by the terrorists as their enemy. The Working Group has accepted these recommendations and revised its guidelines accordingly. It has also agreed with his finding that greater expertise and professionalism are required, and it is expanding its membership to include psychiatrists, police specialists and others experienced in "coercive bargaining" with terrorists. The most controversial section of the study, however, deals with the efficacy of the "no-concessions" policy.

The current hard-line position, Jenkins points out, is based on the assumptions that, first, refusing to negotiate, pay ransom or make political concessions deters terrorists from kidnapping American officials; and, second, that any deviation from such a policy would lead to a proliferation of such incidents. Both in his still-classified study and in his public writings, Jenkins contends that the evidence to support these assumptions is "squishy" at best. Terrorism, he reasons, has many objectives; the wringing of concessions is only one of them, and often not the most important; the terrorists may, for example, be hoping to gain publicity for their cause and project themselves as a force that merits recognition. One objective the terrorists do *not* have, he argues, is mass murder. "Terrorists want a lot of people watching and a lot of people listening, not a lot of people dead," he told the House International Relations Committee during hearings last summer. Their target, therefore, is not so much the hostage as the larger audience. In this sense, terrorism is theater. A hard-line policy, while it can add to the theatrical effect, can do little to deter.

Jenkins has considerable support for his views among other experts on the subject. Prof. Richard Falk, of Princeton University, told the same committee, "We don't have real evidence that deterrence works." While agreeing with Jenkins that massacring large numbers of hostages does not fall within the political terrorist's plans, Falk held that in some cases the deaths of some hostages "actually serves the interest of the terrorist group better than would the receipt of ransom demanded (release of prisoners, money, etc.)." Hence, he said, the hard-line policy can often play into the terrorists' hands.

What really deters, according to Jenkins, is not a hard line during the crisis but determined action afterward to capture and convict the terrorists. In this country, he says, there have been only 647 kidnappings for ransom in the past 30 years—and the reason is not far to seek. "If one looks at the record of ransom payment, the ransom has almost always been paid by the family. . . . [But] of the 647 cases, all but three have been solved. The F.B.I. has a better than 90 percent capture record. The conviction rate is extremely high, and the sentences are harsh." Hence the relative unpopularity of kidnapping for ransom within the United States.

This argument is supported by the American Foreign Service Association, the Foreign Service officers' "trade union." The association has established a Committee on Extraordinary Dangers to negotiate with the State Depart-

The Western Democracies

ment management on problems of terrorism, and there have been frequent meetings with Kissinger and his top aides. The committee has several objectives.

One is better protection for the 31,000 American officials stationed overseas—and, in that regard, much has been done already. Congress has appropriated $20 million for closed-television monitoring systems, electronic alarms, armored cars, extra Marine guards at American Embassies and other security measures; and American officials—and businessmen living abroad—are briefed on the rudimentary precautions they should take for their own safety. Another demand is for broader medical coverage for former hostages and their families. But the committee's main complaint is against what its members see as the State Department's unwillingness to impose strong sanctions against governments that harbor terrorists or allow them to go free.

The Department's records on that score substantiate the complaint. A terrorist involved in a kidnapping has about an 80 percent chance of escaping death or capture. For those who are caught and tried, the average sentence has been only 18 months. Of the 267 international terrorists apprehended since 1970, less than half were still in jail as of September 1975. In the Khartoum case, the Black September guerrillas were convicted of murder and sentenced by the Sudanese to life imprisonment. Soon after, however, all were flown to Egypt, where they are now living under "house arrest." For a brief period, the United States Ambassador to the Sudan was withdrawn and aid was suspended. When the flap died down, normal relations were restored.

"What good is a 'hang tough' posture during a kidnapping," said a Foreign Service committee representative, "if the Department is unwilling to be firm on pressure for punishment? They're perfectly willing to sacrifice us in the name of deterrence, but unwilling to rock the diplomatic boat afterward."

As to the hang-tough policy itself, the Foreign Service has not taken a formal position. Some of its members support it. Others are critical of it, and added their voices to the calls for a more flexible policy that were heard during a two-day conference on international terrorism sponsored by the State Department three months ago.

□

Despite the growing criticism within and outside the Government, the State Department clung to the hard-line approach in word and deed.

In May 1973, just a few months after the Khartoum incident, Terrance Leonhardy, United States Consul General in Guadalajara, was kidnapped by left-wing militants, who demanded that the Mexican authorities release 30 prisoners and read the kidnappers' communiqué over the air. According to a State Department official familiar with the episode, the United States counseled against acquiescence. But the Mexican Government complied with the demands and Leonhardy was released, unharmed.

In March 1974, the United States refused to comply with demands for money made by the kidnappers of Vice Consul John Patterson, stationed in Hermosillo, Mexico. Despite the efforts of his family to meet the demands, Patterson's body was found near Hermosillo in July.

During the crisis, Lewis Hoffacker, then head of the Cabinet Committee to Combat Terrorism, reaffirmed the "no-concessions" policy in Congressional hearings. "Tactics vary in each crisis situation," he said, "but one consistent factor should be understood by all parties concerned: The United States Government will not pay ransom to kidnappers, nor will it release prisoners to satisfy blackmail demands. We advise other Governments, individuals and companies to adopt similar positions because we believe to do otherwise will multiply terrorist attacks."

In the summer of 1975, three American students were kidnapped in Tanzania. The ransom was raised by their families, and the students were released. But the American Ambassador, W. Beverly Carter Jr., was sternly reprimanded by Kissinger for his involvement in the negotiations. "It is our policy, in order to save lives and in order to avoid undue pressure on Ambassadors all over the world," Kissinger told reporters, "that American Ambassadors and officials not participate in negotiations on the release of victims of terrorists, and that terrorists know that the United States will not participate in the payment of ransom and in the negotiations for it. In any individual case, this requires heartbreaking decisions ... but there are important issues of principle involved here."

State Department officials who support that policy insist that it does deter terrorism. They point out that other governments that have had a more flexible policy—West Germany, the Netherlands and Britain—have recently toughened their positions on negotiations and ransom payment. They argue that kidnappings of diplomats would have increased at an even steeper rate had the United States not held firm to its position. In the absence of international agreement on a code of sanctions and punishment—one man's "terrorist" is, in many instances, another man's "freedom fighter"—it should be, they contend, the obligation of each government to demonstrate to the terrorists that their tactics will be unproductive.

The hard-line approach, these officials claim, can sometimes even enhance the victim's own bargaining power. By way of example they point to the 1974 kidnapping of Barbara Hutchison, of the United States Information Agency, by terrorists in the Dominican Republic who sought the release of imprisoned comrades. She persuaded her captors to free her by convincing them that the United States would never pressure the Dominican Government to accede to their demands and that killing her would be pointless.

Actually, the Jenkins recommendations would retain some of the benefits, real or imagined, of the present posture. A flat "no-concessions" policy, he says, limits the range of possible responses and stifles innovative action aimed at saving a hostage's life. Those managing these crisis situations, he contends, should not be forced to rule out any option in advance. Nothing should be prohibited—either negotiating formally, or bargaining informally or secretly, or even paying ransom, if it can be arranged through third parties without publicity.

TERRORISM AND THE STATE TODAY

In other words, the United States could continue to espouse a hard line publicly, while becoming more flexible privately.

Jenkins dismisses the objection that such a two-tier policy would readily become apparent in the era of Watergate journalism. Because each incident is unique and complex, there is already a degree of ambivalence and confusion surrounding such episodes. When Col. Edward Morgan was held hostage in Beirut last year, the United States publicly refused to consider ransom. But ransom was paid—ostensibly by a group of unidentified Lebanese businessmen—and the colonel was released. While Washington officials insist that the United States did not deviate from its "no-concessions" line, they concede that speculation about the source of the funds persists. The American Government, Jenkins suggests, ought to be able to capitalize on ambivalence of this kind. "To assume that private flexibility would immediately become apparent is to assume gross stupidity and incompetence in the management of such crises."

There is another consideration that is often cited by Jenkins's supporters within the State Department—the difficulty for any government to implement a "no-concessions" policy consistently and evenhandedly. The United States would not negotiate for the lives of Noel and Moore in Khartoum, but would it refuse to negotiate or consider ransom if the hostage were Henry Kissinger or Susan Ford?

Even Israel, regarded as an exemplar of the toughest policy possible, has negotiated with terrorists in several particularly difficult hostage episodes. After an El Al jet was hijacked to Algiers in 1968, Israel agreed to release Arab prisoners as a gesture of "goodwill" to save the plane's crew and passengers. A year later, Israel exchanged two captured Syrian Air Force pilots for two Israeli hostages of a hijacking. The Israelis were also willing to negotiate with the Palestinians for captured Israeli schoolchildren in the town of Ma'alot in 1974. In that instance, deciding the negotiations would not prove fruitful, the Israelis stormed the school and one of the terrorists sprayed the children with bullets, resulting in the death of 24.

The raid on Entebbe Airport has renewed debate within the Administration. Some see the Israeli action as vindicating the hard-line approach. Acording to this view, the Israeli "negotiations" were merely a shield behind which the Government planned its bold and risky mission. Others come to the opposite conclusion. They believe the Israeli officials who insist that the negotiations were serious, and they thus see the talks as a departure from Israel's usual hard-line policy. Whatever the case —and officials here have no hard evidence to contradict the Israeli assertions of good faith—policy makers believe the Israeli response to the hijacking is not relevant to American planning and decision-making. "The option the Israelis chose," said one high-level official, "would never be possible for us." The feeling is that Israel, already a pariah to many in the United Nations, stood to lose little through such an assault, whereas the United States, as a world power, could not engage in such unorthodox action without suffering a tremendous loss of prestige.

The United States role as superpower, Administration officials argue, also limits the retributive action that Washington can seek against nations harboring terrorists or allowing them to go free. While the United States may like to "punish" such nations, the officials say, broader foreign-policy interests often make the withholding of economic and military aid, or the withdrawal of an ambassador, counterproductive. In addition, given the year-long Congressional investigation of the C.I.A. and other intelligence agencies, formation of special squads to hunt down and capture or kill international terrorists has been ruled out as an option. Finally, the United States has publicly supported solutions to international terrorism through the United Nations, and extreme unilateral responses such as the Entebbe mission would not be consistent with the stated American goal of achieving an international consensus.

Therein lies the full painfulness of the dilemma. "Be more flexible, do everything possible to save our people's lives during the crisis — and come down hard afterward on the terrorists and those who support or tolerate their actions," say the critics of the present policy. "But we're already as flexible as we can be," reply the policy makers. "We communicate with the kidnappers through third parties in every way short of negotiation or bargaining. We take advantage of every option we have. The inescapable fact is that some options during and after the crisis are simply not open to us." It is also inescapable that the terrorists are becoming increasingly sophisticated, daring and innovative, and the pressure on the United States Government to match them in these attributes can only increase. ■

July 18, 1976

U.S. IS TRAINING UNITS TO FIGHT TERRORISTS

By BERNARD WEINRAUB
Special to The New York Times

WASHINGTON, Oct. 19—At least two Ranger battalions of the United States Army have been trained as antiterrorist units and are capable of dealing with terrorist incidents involving Americans abroad, according to Pentagon sources.

The two Ranger, or "black beret," battalions are based in Fort Stewart, Ga., and Fort Lewis, Wash. They were formed in 1973 by Gen. Creighton Abrams, the late Chief of Staff, who sought "an elite, light and most proficient infantry battalion" capable of doing things "with its hands and weapons better than anyone else."

As international terrorism continues— such as the hijacking last week of the Luftshansa airliner from Palma to Frankfurt—the somewhat secretive Ranger battalions have stepped up their antiterrorism training.

Mock Raids to Free U.S. Hostages

Recent exercises, held amid some restraints on information, included an assault on a mock oil refinery to "free" 30 American workers held hostage and a raid on a desert camp in Texas to "liberate" American diplomats held by terrorists behind barbed wire.

Each Ranger company, with about 170 men, is highly mobile and is armed with nine M-60 machine guns, two 60-millime ter mortars and three 90-millimeter antitank weapons. Each soldier carries an M-16 semiautomatic as well as grenades and knives.

According to Pentagon sources, the carefully chosen volunteers undergo elaborate training in weapons and hand-to-hand combat. About once a month, each Ranger parachutes into swamps, woods or jungles.

As many as 85 percent of the men in the battalion are "on call" at all times.

Details Given in Army Magazine

Information about the two units—each battalion has about 580 men—remains veiled, but some details about it were printed in the May issue of Army, a magazine published by the Association of the United States Army.

The F.B.I. is known to have an antiterrorism unit, but the two Army battalions are believed to be the key units to be deployed in the event of a hijacking rescue.

Pentagon officials said yesterday that the United States had a specially trained unit, including troops and equipment from all the services, to deal with terrorism. But the sources said that the special commando unit was an Army unit—the Rangers—and that the Navy and Air Force would be involved primarily in transporting the force to whatever part of the world it was needed.

October 20, 1977

Pentagon Game Simulates a Nuclear Blackmail Case

By RICHARD BURT
Special to The New York Times

WASHINGTON, Nov. 14—In a sign of how seriously the United States Government has come to view the problem of international terrorism, the Pentagon recently simulated a hypothetical situation dealing with the theft of an American nuclear weapon by terrorists.

The exercise, conducted by the Defense Department's Studies, Analysis and Gaming Agency, was based on so-called game theory, which employs mathematical rules to determine possible choices of strategies in a real situation. The game was said to have given its participants—some 35 decision-makers in the national security community—a realistic picture of the problems that could emerge if a group were to seize a nuclear weapon and threaten to use it to blackmail the United States.

As a result, the week-long exercise is seen by officials as aiding the Carter Administration in its efforts to improve preparations against terrorism.

International terrorism has emerged as a key area of concern, with officials particularly worried over the possibility that criminal or political extermists might acquire advanced conventional weapons, nuclear bombs or toxic chemicals to further their claims. In August, a special working group was established within the State Department to coordinate government activities to combat terrorism, but officials acknowledge that they are a long way from fashioning an integrated approach to the problem.

Officials have been especially concerned with the security of nuclear weapons deployed in Western Europe and South Korea. Their storage sites are identifiable, and some Congressional committees have suggested that these sites constitute an attractive target for terrorists. Consequently, the Defense Department has begun to strengthen the protection of nuclear installations.

Participants Divided Into Teams

The Pentagon exercise was secret and officials refused to discuss its outcome or the identity of the participants. They were drawn by Gen. George Brown, chairman of the Joint Chiefs of Staffs, and from several agencies, including the State Department, the National Security Council and the Central Intelligence Agency.

On arriving at the game, the participants were divided into three groups, two teams and a control group. Both teams represented the United States, while the control group provided them with information concerning a hypothetical crisis in which terrorists seized a nuclear weapon that ultimately ended up in the hands of an unpredictable third-world leader.

Officials close to the game said the situation appeared plausible and was based on extensive research. As the game progressed, the two teams were confronted by the control group with a variety of contingencies that might occur in such a situation, including faulty communications between the terrorists and the United States Government, the interference of outside powers and the necessity of dealing with the press.

Since it was established in 1952, the Pentagon's gaming agency has conducted 58 such games simulating possible conflict situations, usually hypothetical crises between the United States and the Soviet Union. In most cases, lower-level officials take part, but once a year senior officials participate in a game that is selected for its topical relevance.

The game nearly coincided with the release last weekend of a report by the Arms Control and Disarmament Agency's chief scientist, Robert H. Kupperman, warning that "there is no doubt that mass annihilation is feasible and resourceful, technically-oriented thugs are capable of doing it."

Noting that the potential leverage of nuclear terrorists over governments would be "disproportionately high," Mr. Kupperman urged the creation of a government-wide crisis-management team and said simulated exercises were an excellent means of preparing officials for the real thing.

November 15, 1977

Washington & Business
A Seminar on Threat of Terrorism

By JUDITH MILLER

WASHINGTON — Statistically, an American businessman's chances of being killed in a terrorist attack are less than death by dog bite. But terrorism is what experts term a "high leverage" form of violence—a few episodes can spread panic within a community or a country.

The business sector has increasingly become the target of terrorist attacks, and as a result, fear has spread in corporate quarters in many parts of the world. So much so that about two weeks ago, some 35 corporations spent $150 each to send executives to a daylong conference on "Terrorism in U.S. Business," a meeting sponsored by the Georgetown University Center for Strategic and International Studies.

In a somberly lit conference room at Washington's International Club, the businessmen heard panel after panel of intelligence officials, psychiatrists, statisticians, academics, and consultants describe the terrorist threat, and what companies could do to minimize the risk to their executives, especially those overseas.

The seminar was just one of many such sessions being offered to allay the anxiety generated by terrorist incidents, or "episodes," as they are known in the trade.

Combating terrorism appears to be a growth industry. Increased security is estimated to run to hundreds of millions of dollars in the business sector alone. Academic institutions, such as the Georgetown Center or the Rand Corporation, a pioneer in the study of "transnational" terrorism, provide private and public counseling. In November, the first issue of a journal devoted exclusively to terrorism was published.

Even the Federal Government has recently stepped up its counter-terrorism initiatives. Brooks McClure, a former Foreign Service officer in the United States Information Agency, is currently a member of a working group on terrorism formed six months ago within the Commerce Department that is handling most of the increasing inquiries from businessmen. The working group, according to Mr. McClure, is preparing pamphlets on terrorist threats in individual countries. So far, the group has completed eight country papers, with 36 planned.

"There have been a lot of requests

lately for information to combat terrorism," said Mr. McClure.

• • •

Dr. Charles A. Russell, chief of the Air Force's Acquisitions and Analysis Division in the Directorate of Counter-Intelligence, outlined the extent of the threat. According to a data base that he and some Air Force colleagues have assembled (which Dr. Russell asserts varies a percentage point or two from the classified Air Force base for which he is also responsible), businessmen are increasingly the focus of terrorist assault.

Excluding terrorist episodes in Israel, Northern Ireland and the United States, there have been some 1,800 terrorist episodes — kidnapping, hijackings, bombings and attacks on facilities between Jan. 1, 1970, and Nov. 1, 1977.

During that period, 512 persons were killed, 551 wounded and 363 kidnapped. Of the kidnap incidents, 80 percent of which were successful, 43 percent of the victims were businessmen; one-fifth were Americans. The kidnapping trend, according to Dr. Russell, is growing, with 78 percent of the incidents in the last three years.

Statistics for assassinations show a similar upward trend. During the same period, there were 390 victims in 257 incidents—38 percent in Latin America and 46 percent in Western Europe. About one-fifth of those killed were police; another fifth were rival terrorists. But 17.2 percent were businessmen, topping diplomats at 15.7 percent. Once again, 49 percent of the assassinations took place in the last two years; 69 percent in the last three years.

• • •

Corporations, and especially American corporations, were the focus of terrorist bombs in half of the 924 incidents recorded in the domestic and foreign press and terrorism chronologies, from which Dr. Russell compiled his data base. The trend in bombings is down, but Dr. Russell is not cheered by this.

"Bombing is really a very unsophisticated form of terrorism," he observed. Since inexperienced terrorist groups begin with bombing and work up to more sophisticated forms, such as assassinations and kidnappings, Dr. Russell said he feared that "the trends may mean that many of these groups are becoming more sophisticated, and hence, more dangerous."

To demonstrate the point, the corporate executives were shown a slide show regarding what Dr. Russell termed a truly "sophisticated" operation: the kidnapping and subsequent murder of Hanns-Martin Schleyer, the spokesman for West German industry, by German terrorists.

The episode demonstrated enormously good intelligence and surveillance capabilities, possession of automatic weapons, the preparation of safe houses and other means of logistical support, according to Dr. Russell.

"This is excellent fire discipline," said Dr. Russell, pointing to 50 closely clustered bullet holes through the back windshield of the police vehicle that followed Mr. Schleyer's bulletproof car to insure the industrialist's safety.

Dr. Russell also pointed out that the terrorist groups were increasingly well-financed. According to the best records available, more than $146 million in known ransoms have been paid since 1970. "A ransom of $1.9 million, which was the fee for one executive's release recently, can really eat into your profit margin," Dr. Russell said.

Businessmen at home and abroad are increasingly spending money on improving internal security, of course, and the panelists had some more general managerial advice for combating and preventing terrorism. Robert Rabe, assistant chief of the Washington Police Department's Office of Inspection Service, said he "got a doctorate in terrorism on the streets" during the Hanafi kidnappings in the Capital last spring.

Chief Rabe advised corporate officials to know local law enforcement officials wherever the company is situated, check for vulnerable spots in the company's operations, know where employees are supposed to be when traveling and work out jurisdictional guidelines within a company in the event of a terrorist attack.

After a day of ominous statistics and accounts of gruesome incidents and terrorist upsurge, the panel had a final word to assuage their corporate paying guests. "Don't panic," said one analyst. "Don't overreact."

January 5, 1978

A SLAYING UNITES GERMAN STUDENTS

Mass Protest Binds Them in Front Demanding Reform

By DAVID BINDER
Special to The New York Times

BERLIN, June 9 — The killing of a West Berlin student by a police bullet in a violent political demonstration has led to an extraordinary mass protest by university youths throughout West Germany.

The occasion was the funeral yesterday of Benno Ohnesorg, 26 years old, in his native Hanover. More than 7,000 students from universities and colleges all over West Germany and West Berlin gathered in Hanover to stage a silent protest march.

Thousands more held memorial services on their own campuses. The ceremonies bound the students into a kind of political front demanding social and academic reforms.

Germans are comparing the event to the so-called Wartburgfest of 150 years ago, when rebellious university students gathered in the Thuringian town of Wartburg to protest against absolutist rule in Germany.

The focal point of the current unrest is West Berlin, where students have coalesced into a mass movement as a result of the shooting of Mr. Ohnesorg last Friday.

Since then the students of the Free University and other higher schools in West Berlin have been carrying on continuous meetings demanding the resignations of Mayor Heinrich Albertz, Police Chief Erich Duensing and Wolfgang Busch, Senator for the Interior in the city administration.

Today authoritative sources reported that Mr. Duensing had been dismissed.

The clash last Friday was the latest and bloodiest of a series of West Berlin student demonstrations on a variety of political issues.

It was aimed against the Shah of Iran, Mohammed Riza Pahlevi, who was here on a state visit. To the West Berlin students he is a symbol of dictatorship and oppression of academic freedom.

What began as a more or less peaceful demonstration quickly turned violent when about 50 agents of the Shah dismounted from buses and attacked the demonstrators.

The agents' appearance was ordered by the Shah and authorized by the West German Government. The West Berlin Senate has made representations to Bonn because of it.

Mr. Ohnesorg was shot in the back of the head after police riot squads wielding clubs had waded into the chanting students outside the Berlin Opera House while the Shah was inside. At least a dozen other students were severely injured by clubbing and kicks.

Victim Accompanied by Wife

Unlike the militant leftist students who spearheaded the demonstration, Mr. Ohnesorg attended more out of curiosity than commitment, according to friends. He was unarmed and accompanied by his pregnant wife.

The man who shot him is Detective Karl-Heinz Kurras, 40, who was in plain-clothes. He alleges that he acted in self-defense, although there is contradictory evidence from witnesses. Tonight the police disclosed that Mr. Kurras possessed a large personal collection of arms.

Speaking yesterday before the West Berlin City Assembly, Mayor Albertz ascribed the outbreak of violence to "an extremist minority" of students who stirred "a chain of irresponsible provocations" aimed at "liquidating the basic democratic order." But he also promised an investigation of police excesses.

The police chief, Mr. Duensing, lost the confidence of the West Berliners and his superiors last Tuesday when he used unpalatable military phraseology to describe his actions during the violence.

A former army officer, he spoke of his "battle assignment" and his "battle station."

He described the student crowd as "a liverwurst with a stinking left end. . . You press it in the middle to squeeze it out at the end."

West Berlin professors blame the city administration under former Mayor Willy Brandt, now West German Foreign Minister, for having ignored the problems of the university too long.

The chain of incidents to which Mayor Albertz alluded began two years ago when leftist political activists organized the first of many public demonstrations.

Their targets included the United States Information Agency's Amerika Haus and Vice President Humphrey when he arrived on a visit. They are against United States policy in Vietnam, against the archaic German university system and against what they believe to be authoritarian aspects of West German society.

The hard core, numbering fewer than 400 out of a West Berlin student population of 29,000, belong to a variety of loose groupings. The names include the Socialist German Student League, Liberal Students of Germany, Humanist Union, Horror Commune and Polycommune.

These students' sympathies range from Mao Tse-tung, Communist China's leader, on the far left, with proposals to burn down West Berlin's department stores, to moderate Socialism

The Western Democracies

in the middle left.

Where they had formerly been political splinters on the edge of the student body, this self-styled "new left" now commands the student movement and runs the major student organizations at the Free University.

Yet the student movement as a whole remains almost totally isolated from the rest of West German society, and particularly from the West Berlin populace.

This became evident yesterday. While Mayor Albertz was speaking at City Hall, 5,000 students were attending a memorial service at the Free University in the Dahlem district for Mr. Ohnesorg. At the service Bernhard Wilhelmer, deputy student body leader, complained, 'We still stand alone."

The isolation of the student movement has also been evident in unsuccessful attempts of student militants to rally the support of West Berlin workers by trying to debate with them in the streets. When they entered workers' districts such as Kreuzberg and Wedding, they were punched and harshly insulted by the residents.

This is not untypical for Germany, where workers and intellectuals have never found common ground. In fact, the majority of the West Berliners seem to despise the students and are despised by them in return.

A more hopeful aspect has arisen in the form of debates organized by the students on West Berlin's main street, the Kurfürstendamm.

These have been going on every night since last Sunday, lasting as late as 3 A.M. Up to 300 students gather in small groups and try to engage passers-by in a dialogue about their problems and the problems of the universe. So far there has been no violence.

City government representatives and long-time observers of the Berlin scene believe these Kurfürstendamm debates may open prospects for bridging the wide gap between the students and the rest of the populace.

Prof. Richard Löwenthal of the Free University, who was partly responsible for inspiring these debates, thinks there is a possible benefit for West Berlin.

"It could be that the students will have the effect of a catalyst on the populace, which has been slowly petrifying," he said in an interview.

He and some members of the Government are trying to engage the students more and more in the public life of the city.

The outcome could be the transformation of West Berlin into a kind of national market place for the exchange of ideas about the future of the German people. The alternative, said a high Government official, is mounting tension and "the closing of the Free University."

June 10, 1967

VIOLENCE MOUNTS IN WEST GERMANY

U.S. Offices, Napalm Maker and Paper Are Targets

Special to The New York Times

BERLIN, Feb. 3—A wave of violence apparently politically motivated swept West Germany and West Berlin today.

In Frankfurt a time bomb attached to the outside of a window exploded in the offices of Dow Chemical, a American company that manufactures napalm, used against the enemy in Vietnam. The window was broken, but damage was negligible.

Also in Frankfurt, three windows were smashed at the United States Consulate-General and four at the American library and cultural center.

The Frankfurt police force said the attacks were regarded as a demonstration against American policy in Vietnam.

In West Berlin, several hundred students and left-wing demonstrators clashed with the police on the Kurfürstendamm, the city's fashionable thoroughfare, following a sit-down demonstration by 1,500 staged outside the building of the Greek mission here in protest against the military regime in Athens.

Earlier in the day two men smashed the windows of a branch office of the "Berliner Morgenpost", a newspaper owned by Axel Springer, West Germany's biggest publisher. The attack followed similar incidents the night before at seven other branch offices of the publishing house in Berlin.

In Munich earlier this week a member of the right-wing National Democratic party died of a heart attack as a result of fisti cuffs at an indoor anti-Nazi rally in the Bavarian capital.

All week long high-school and university students and other left-wing groups clashed with the police in such cities as Kiel, Bochum, Freiburg and Hanover over a variety of issues.

West German officials voiced concern over the apparent radicalization of a considerable proportion of the young generation.

In a number of cases the left-wing groups were viewed as having used political protests as a pretext to stage clashes with the police.

Students Change Tactics

In Berlin, following the peaceful sit-in at the Greek mission, a student shouted: "Let's change this demonstration and unmask police brutality!," whereupon several hundred boys and girls rose to dash to the Kurfürstendamm, a block and a half away.

Police units were under orders to show restraint, but for about two hours they used high-pressure water cannon to disperse youths who were blocking traffic by sitting down in the middle of busy intersections. Twenty-four persons were arrested. One policeman and three others persons sustained injuries.

Acting Mayor Kurt Neubauer accused the demonstrators of seeking to disturb law and order in the city.

"The peaceful demonstration at the Greek mission was misused by elements who are not interested in restoring democratic conditions in Greece, but in creating disorder and lawlessness in Berlin," he declared.

In Kiel and Bochum youths rioted this week against a raise in streetcar fares, following similar incidents the week before in Bremen.

The Clash in Munich

In Munich, pro and anti-Nazis battled during a rally called in commemoration of Hitler's takeover as Chancellor 35 years ago. Carl Hofmann, a 56-year-old National Democrat, collapsed and died of heart failure after ushers had ordered him to leave the hall.

The anti-American aspect of the demonstrations, largely youthful opposition to the United States involvement in Vietnam, was held to have figured heavily in the rash of civil disobedience.

Mr. Springer's publishing house, which controls about 70 per cent of the West German national press, has become a favorite target of left-wing attacks.

Last Thursday about 800 Berlin students announced that they would stage a tribunal in April to prove the publisher was manipulating public opinion. Another group siad it planned to hold a hearing against Mr. Springer next weekend.

February 4, 1968

West Berlin Gunman Wounds Leader of Left-Wing Students

Special to The New York Times

BERLIN, April 11—A gunman fired three shots at Rudi Dutschke on Kurfürstendamm, Berlin's main shopping street, today, critically injuring the 27-year-old left-wing student leader.

It was the first attempt at political assassination in Germany in the postwar period. Mr. Dutschke was rushed to a hospital with two shots in his head and a breast wound.

An hour later, the West Berlin police captured the assailant after a gun battle in a nearby basement where the man had barricaded himself. He was hit by two police bullets and was seriously injured, officials said. The man carried no papers and his identity was not known.

Kurt Neubauer, Deputy Mayor of West Berlin, said he was "shocked at the crime," and called on Berliners to remain calm and come to the aid of the police in the investigation. Mr. Neubauer and other officials made it clear they feared the murder attempt could intensify unrest among radical students and other left-wing groups.

Late tonight, as doctors fought to save Mr. Dutschke's life in a four-hour operation, clashes broke out in various parts of the city.

The police used water cannon in an attempt to disperse some 2,000 students who marched to the newspaper publishing house of Axel Springer to protest the shooting. Police officials said demonstrators hurled rocks and flaming torches at the multistory office building in downtown Berlin, breaking windows in the lower floors. They set fire to several automobiles parked near the building.

The Springer concern has long been the target of radical student protest because of what the students consider the right-wing trend in the newspapers' political reporting.

Mr. Dutschke is a leading member of the radical Socialist League of German Students, which has advocated the overthrow of the present parliamentary system in Germany. But the student leader has frequently asserted his opposition to the use of force in Western industrial countries. "We must convince people that a change is necessary through the force of our argument," he contended.

The student leader is married to an American girl, the former Gretchen Klotz of Chicago, who was a student of theology until their marriage last year. They have a 3-month-old son, Hosea Che, who is named after the Old Testament prophet and after Ernesto Che Guevara, the Latin American guerrilla fighter who was killed in Bolivia.

Mr. Dutschke's life had been threatened before and he moved his living quarters repeatedly to avoid being molested. He had no police protection.

April 12, 1968

STUDENT RAMPAGE IN WEST GERMANY FOLLOWS SHOOTING

Youth Says He Shot Leftist After Reading of Killing of Martin Luther King

By PHILIP SHABECOFF
Special to The New York Times

BERLIN, April 12 — The young West German who shot Rudi Dutschke, the radical student leader, said today that his murder attempt had been prompted by the assassination of Dr. Martin Luther King Jr.

The student rampage set off in West Berlin by the shooting yesterday reached a new pitch of violence today as clashes between the students and the police broke out in downtown West Berlin and in many parts of West Germany.

"I read about Martin Luther King and I said to myself, 'You must do this too,'" 23-year-old Josef Bachmann told investigating officials who questioned him as soon as he was able to speak after an operation for gunshot wounds. He was captured after having been shot by the police shortly after the attack on Mr. Dutschke yesterday.

Terms Victim a Red

Bachmann said he decided to "bump off" Rudi Dutschke because the Berlin student was a "Communist."

A police official reported that Bachmann kept a painting of Hitler in his room and, like Hitler, was a house painter and an amateur artist.

Mr. Dutschke, a 28-year-old graduate student and professional revolutionary, was reported improved after an operation for wounds in the head, neck and shoulders, and was said to have a "real chance to live." Mr. Dutschke regained consciousness this morning and managed a cheerful "Hello, sister" to his nurse.

The police used water cannon, horses and rubber clubs in an unsuccessful attempt to keep some 2,000 students from marching on the West Berlin city hall at John-F.-Kennedy-Platz.

Police Formation Broken

The students, carrying red banners and chanting "Ho Chi Minh!" and "Ru-di Dutsch-ke! Ru-di Dutsch-ke!" forced their way through a massed formation of club-swinging policemen to reach their destination.

At the city hall, the students stood their ground for more than 30 minutes against attacking water cannon and repeated advances by massed policemen. A number of people, both students and policemen, were carried away in ambulances. Some had blood pouring down their faces.

The students taunted officials in the building with chants of "Murderers!" "Nazis!" and "Fascists!" They repeatedly called to Mayor Klaus Schütz to come to the microphone and enter a discussion. Mayor Schütz who was in the City Hall after flying back to Berlin last night from a vacation, stayed out of sight.

The only reply to the student chanting was a fresh attack by water cannon. A group of about 200 students refused to give way before the powerful jets of water, but crouched on the ground huddled together as the armored water trucks hovered almost directly above them.

These students were said to be members of the League of Socialist German Students, the leftist group that forms the core of the student rebellion sweeping West Germany. One student danced and capered in indifference to three jets of water turned directly on him.

The square was cleared only after seven of the water cannon, followed by hundreds of policemen in ranks three deep, advanced on the students from three sides and forced them slowly backward.

U.S. Radio Station Attacked

After leaving the square, the students moved to the headquarters of RIAS, the American radio station in Berlin, where they smashed windows with rocks.

RIAS is one of the targets of the "action program" announced today by the "extra-parliamentary opposition," the name used by the student revolutionaries to describe their movement. The students are demanding that the United States give up control of the Berlin station.

Among the other demands by the students are the resignation of the Berlin Senate and Mayor Schütz, the creation of a city council of workers, government officials and students, an hour-a-day free television time for the students to present their case to the people and the break-up of the newspaper and magazine empire of West Germany's press lord, Axel Springer.

The Springer publishing plant, near Checkpoint Charley at the Berlin Wall, looked like a battlefield today following student attacks on the building late last night. An area of more than ten square blocks around the plant is sealed off with barbed wire and protected by hundreds of policemen, some carrying submachine guns. With at least half its windows smashed by stones, the building looks as if it had been bombed. Burnt-out Springer trucks litter nearby parking lots.

Tonight students fought half a dozen battles with policemen as they sought to prevent the delivery of tomorrow's Springer newspapers by blocking routes leading from the publishing plant. The students barricaded the streets with cars, steel beams, concrete tubes from nearby construction sites and rubbish. They also lit fires in the middle of the streets and surrounding fields of weeds.

The students said it was the first time in their "revolution" that they had thrown barricades up in Berlin.

Both policemen and students were in an ugly mood. The students, some of whom armed themselves with wooden staves and hurled stones at police cars, tried to stand their ground at the barricades. But they were driven back time and time again by the high-pressure water cannon and often scattered in panic as the grim-faced policemen moved slowly forward.

Springer delivery trucks started to go through about an hour and a half behind schedule as police cleared one street at a time.

Mr. Springer, a conservative who controls a large share of West Germany's newspaper circulation, is one of the students' most hated enemies. Springer newspapers, for their part, have been vitriolic critics of the West German student radicals.

Today a student spokesman accused Mr. Springer of "murdering" Rudi Dutschke by inflaming public opinion against him.

A six-man student delegation went to the city hall tonight at Mayor Schütz's invitation, to discuss a truce with the city administration. The talks fell through, however, when the Mayor refused a demand by the students that the conversation be tape recorded.

April 13, 1968

The Western Democracies

The Followers of Red Rudi Shake Up Germany

By PHILIP SHABECOFF

BERLIN.

IT was a sunny day some weeks ago in West Berlin, but a cold wind was blowing in from the sand heaths of the Mark Brandenburg. Sunday strollers were warming themselves inside the cafes lining the Kurfürstendamm, drinking coffee with whipped cream and lazily watching the passers-by. Small lines had formed at the movie-house box offices. Old ladies, their thick bodies encased in ankle-length coats, moved heavily along the sidewalk in groups of two or three, pausing now and then to stare at the miniskirts and chic leather boots displayed in the glittering shop windows.

It seemed to be an ordinary, unhurried Sunday along the "Kudamm." Except for one discordant element. There were too many policemen—hundreds of them in blue-gray uniforms standing along the curbs, gathered in small knots and talking quietly, occasionally glancing toward the Kaiser Wilhelm Memorial Church at the end of the broad avenue.

An amorphous mass of humanity had been gathering in the square surrounding the church. Suddenly, the mass congealed and began moving up the Kurfürstendamm. There was a sound of scraping feet and then chanting — faint at first, growing steadily louder: "Ho, Ho, Ho Chi Minh! HO, HO, HO CHI MINH!"

The knots of blue-gray uniforms broke up as the policemen hurried to their posts. The people in the cafes left their seats and pressed against the windows. The old ladies looked at one another, their bitter mouths made more bitter by grimaces of disgust. One of them said loudly: "It's the students again."

Her companion made a spitting noise and ejaculated a single word "Dutschke."

And, yes, there was Rudi Dutschke, the famous student revolutionary, leading a long column of young people up the avenue. The spectators recognized him immediately. After all, his picture had appeared in every newspaper and on the cover of almost every major magazine in West Germany during the previous year and his face was at least as familiar to Berliners as that of Chancellor Kiesinger. "Yes, there he is," said voices in the crowd. "There is Red Rudi. There is Dutschke."

Rudi Dutschke lived up to the onlookers' expectations. He was unshaven and his lank black hair was falling over his forehead. He was wearing a black leather jacket and his arms were linked through those of two young men who towered over his short, husky frame. He bent forward, straining, seemingly trying to drag the procession with him.

Dutschke was leading still another protest demonstration, just the sort of thing he was always associated with in newspaper stories. The target was familiar, too: American aggression in Vietnam.

Behind him marched thousands of young people, grouped into phalanxes of 100 or so. They chanted about Ho, sometimes switching to "Hey, hey, L.B.J.! How many kids have you killed today?" They carried placards saying "Peace in Vietnam," "End American Aggression" and "Hang L.B.J." They displayed large photographs of Ho Chi Minh, Ché Guevara and Mao Tse-tung. They also carried pictures of Rosa Luxemburg and Karl Liebknecht, the German Socialist heroes of the early 20th century, because many of the students fancied themselves Marxists and identified with those of an earlier era. Above the marching ranks, hundreds of the red, blue and yellow flags of Vietnam's National Liberation Front whipped about in the wind.

The procession wound into and filled the big square in front of Berlin's opera house. The next day the left-wing newspapers would say that 20,000 people took part in the demonstration and the right-wing papers would say 5,000. The correct figure was probably 10,000; in any case, the demonstration was said to be the largest anti-Vietnam assembly ever held in Berlin.

When Dutschke spoke, the crowd was completely his. He told them that the United States was committing crimes against humanity in Vietnam. He vilified American imperialism. He declared that the revolution being fought in Vietnam must also be fought here and now in Germany. He promised action against those who hold and abuse power. He spoke on and on in a high-pitched but rather hoarse voice, exploding his sentences in almost hypnotic cadence.

The words poured from him with the speed and impact of machine-gun bullets: "revolution," "counter-revolution," "obstruction," "manipulation," "manifestation," "integration," "transformation." The crowd of students, many of them only half grasping what he was driving at, stood silent and spellbound.

"Tell the Americans," he yelled, "that the day and the hour will come when we will drive you out unless you yourselves drive out imperialism," and the 10,000 roared their approval.

WHILE others were talking, Dutschke sat back on the rostrum, relaxed and smiling, chatting with the young men and women who came up to shake his hand. He was obviously exhilarated and enjoying himself. But then there was an incident. Two men wearing construction workers' helmets appeared and began tearing down the Vietcong flags that some students had tied to a half-completed building. The men set fire to the flags and waved them tauntingly at the crowd. There was an ugly muttering and several hundred students surged toward the men.

Dutschke jumped up and pulled the microphone away from the speaker. "Do not let yourselves be provoked," he shouted. "That is what the police want. Leave those poor simpletons alone." The muttering stopped and the angry students turned their backs on the two men holding the burning flags.

When the last speech was over, Dutschke took the microphone again. "We have changed our plans and will not march on the American military settlement," he said. "Leave here quietly and spread out in small groups across the city to distribute your pamphlets."

The 10,000 students began filing quietly out of the square. They picked

---

PHILIP SHABECOFF has been a correspondent for The Times in Germany since 1964.

TERRORISM AND THE STATE TODAY

Dutschke, who terms himself a "professional revolutionary," hopes to build a better world. Right, a Swiss cartoon criticizes his Maoist beliefs.

Horst in Nebelspalter, Rorschach, Switzerland

up their pamphlets, broke into small groups and began spreading out across the city. Nobody went near the American settlement, which had been sealed off by hundreds of policemen.

Throughout the rally, a middle-aged man with a crooked nose had been sitting on the roof of a low building heckling the speakers. He was drunk or a provocateur from the right-wing National Democratic Party or perhaps both. As the meeting broke up he stood and shouted: "Dutschke, you bastard, why don't you go back to your Communist friends in East Germany?"

IN Rudi Dutschke, a 28-year-old graduate student in sociology at Berlin's Free University and a self-described professional revolutionary,

West Germans seem to have found both their first authentic folk hero and their first public villain since World War II. During the last 20 years or so, they have tended to steer clear of both heroes and antiheroes. Presumably one important lesson of the Nazi era was that idols and villains sometimes turn out to be something other than expected. The late Chancellor Konrad Adenauer was probably the most popular man in postwar Germany, but he was a father figure, not a hero.

The intensity of the Germans' feelings about Dutschke has been demonstrated in the reaction to a pro-Nazi assassin's attack on him April 11. As Dutschke began his long recovery in a hospital, dangerously wounded by bullets in the head, neck and chest, students by

the thousands poured into the streets—first in West Berlin, then in city after city throughout the country—to show their sympathy and anger. They battled the police for five days, chanting "Nazi swine!" "Gestapo!" and "Dutschke murderers!"

Long before the shooting, it had been virtually impossible to engage in an extended conversation in this country without eventually discussing Dutschke. He is talked about at diplomatic cocktail parties in Bonn as often as in neighborhood bars in Berlin. Many West Germans, especially those over 40, bristle with outrage when talking about the student leader. They have called him "the Goebbels of

311

The Western Democracies

the left," "an antiauthoritarian anarchist," "a Red Fascist," "an Antichrist," "an agent of East Germany," "a Führer," "an enemy of democracy," "a psychopath" and "a bum."

For German students, however, the name Dutschke is a rallying cry. He is the first postwar German to fully capture the imagination of young people, to pull them out of their political lethargy and to bring them to the barricades to battle for social and political causes. The police in Frankfurt recently picked him up as soon as he arrived at that city's airport. The chief of police, in justifying the action, said, "Dutschke brings unrest with him." Although it may have been a flimsy excuse for the police action, Dutschke did bring unrest with him. His appearance in a university town often presaged Vietnam demonstrations, attacks against Amerika Houses, demands for school reform, protest marches and, occasionally, acts of violence. Dutschke may not have planned or directed this unrest, but he did inspire it.

Even when Dutschke does not appear, his name is used as a kind of talisman by West German students. During a meeting of the ultra-right-wing National Democratic party in Hanover last fall, for example, students tried to organize a demonstration to prevent the nationalists from assembling. At the appointed time, only a handful of students showed up; they stood in a cold rain watching futilely as the National Democrats filed into their hall. But the demonstrators did not give up hope. "Did you hear?" they murmured to one another. "Dutschke is coming with a thousand students from Berlin." Dutschke did not come.

"THERE are many Dutschkes," a young sociologist told an interviewer recently, explaining that the student rebellion did not depend on Dutschke. He has become the symbol, if not the apotheosis, of the student rebellion for most West Germans, but there are many other influential student leaders. As a journalist commented some months ago: "The student revolution began long before Dutschke appeared on the scene and would be taking place now even if he did not exist."

Most observers agree that the "Movement," as students call it, germinated at Berlin's Free University in the early nineteen-sixties. I first visited the campus in 1965 to investigate reports that some students were defying the school administration to demand academic reform. The news was hardly to be believed. Even at the politically oriented Berlin school, German students simply did not challenge the authority of Herr Professor, the autocratic deity of Germany's hoary academic structure.

It was true, though. A group of liberal students, borrowing such methods as sit-ins and hunger strikes from the Free Speech Movement at the University of California, were demanding that the university grant more academic freedom and democratize the entire educational process.

The Berlin movement was limited, however; only a couple of hundred students were directly involved. The preoccupation of the majority of students with their own personal affairs seemed to remain absolute. One liberal student leader explained the apathy by saying: "The ideal German university is designed to produce a series of Fausts who know everything but who live above the mundane problems of society."

Three years later, thousands of Berlin students are taking to the streets to protest injustice in Southeast Asia or the attack on their hero. And the new engagement is not limited to Berlin. In Bonn, Frankfurt, Cologne, Munich, Hamburg, Bremen, Kiel, Freiburg and dozens of other cities and towns, students are demonstrating, protesting, demanding, striking, attacking and, in the process, driving school and Government officials up the walls.

More than any other single issue, it was the Vietnam war that brought West Germany's students to a state of political engagement. Vietnam is a cause that commands total commitment from many young Germans. In the name of justice in Southeast Asia, they have bombed an office of the Dow Chemical Company, the American concern that makes napalm; have smashed windows at American consulates and have tried to block ships carrying war goods. At a recent rally in Berlin, a young girl with the delicate features of a Fra Angelico Virgin publicly declared her intention to pick up American soldiers and sleep with them as a means of persuading them to desert.

But Vietnam and the Dutschke shooting are not the only issues spurring the students to action. In Bremen, for example, thousands of schoolboys rioted for a week to protest a 2½-cent increase in the city's streetcar fares. Of course, there was a deeper reason. "Young people feel alienated from the Government," one of the student leaders said at the end of the riots. "We feel that the political power is not interested in what we think or what we want." Students have demonstrated against the power of the conservative West German press lord, Axel Springer; against the National Democratic party; against Bonn's grand coalition, and for sexual freedom and the pill for everyone.

Springer is enemy No. 1 to the radicals, who have accused him of "manipulating public opinion" and who have been waging a permanent campaign to "dispossess Springer." Recently, the students have blamed the Springer press for "inflaming hatred" and thus causing the shooting of Rudi Dutschke. During the night after the attack, chants of "Springer the murderer!" echoed through the dark streets of German cities.

EVEN at this stage, the true activists are still probably in a minority among West German students. But their number is growing, and more and more of them are listening to the siren song of ideology as sung by the radical students who form the hard core of the Movement. The radicals are a mixed bag of Marxists, Trotskyists, Maoists, anarchists, syndicalists, pacifists, humanists and utopians. Many of them belong to the *Sozialistischer Deutscher Studentenbund*, the League of Socialist German Students. They are a grimly earnest group of young men and women intent on overthrowing the established order in West Germany —in all of the West, for that matter—so that they can build a better and more equitable world.

Marx remains the chief deity of the student radicals, but they pay homage to a new prophet. He is Herbert Marcuse, the Berlin-born Marxist philosopher now teaching at the University of California at San Diego who preaches the failure of the Western capitalist society and the need for a healing rebirth of democracy. Marcuse, who has called Dutschke "a sweet demagogue," describes his democratic structure as a "liberated society," which, he says, means that it is "free from every kind of forced integration of people into a structured social order." This free society would be a kind of association of citizens who would participate in the social order of their own free will.

The students, following the gospel of Marcuse, look to the Third World, to Fidel Castro and Ho Chi Minh, for salvation. They are militant activists. Their idols are Ché Guevara and Stokely Carmichael, not Gandhi or Dr. Martin Luther King.

LAST year, two events moved the radicals from the outer fringe to the very heart of the student movement. One was the formation of the grand coalition of Christian Democrats and Social Democrats in Bonn. To many young liberals, the Socialists' decision to join their arch-enemies in the Government was a betrayal that ended all effective political opposition and protest in the country. There was only one other place for liberals to turn—the radical movement.

The second event, strangely enough, was a state visit to West Germany by the Shah of Iran. When the Shah arrived in Berlin, students staged a demonstration against Iranian "despotism" that led to a clash with the police. Tempers flared and a shot was fired; a 27-year-old student named Benno Ohnesorg fell to the ground. Ohnesorg, whose name means "without care" and who had just been married, died in the hospital the next day.

In Ohnesorg, the Movement had found its martyr. Though not a member of the radical groups, he had nonetheless been killed by the Establishment. Students throughout the nation began to wonder if the radicals were not right when they charged that the West German power structure was corrupt. The shock of Ohnesorg's death jolted thousands of university students into a new sense of political engagement. The League of Socialist German Students, previously a small, isolated, lightly regarded group of extremists, suddenly found itself in the van of a mass movement. And the head of the league in Berlin was an eloquent young revolutionary named Rudi Dutschke.

Dutschke is often referred to as "the chief ideologist of the student rebellion." In fact, he does not speak for all the students. Even the national leadership of the league has come close to disavowing him, and in Berlin itself many of the radical students speak bitterly of the "cult of personality" that has built up around Dutschke. There are some ideological differences between Dutschke and the league's national leaders, who were moved to a public expression of annoyance when Dutschke denounced several league branches for accepting money from East German Communists. Nevertheless, Dutschke is undoubtedly the most charismatic leader among the student radicals, if not among all West German politicians. His theoretical concepts of the revolution are the most powerful ideological fuel available to the Movement.

Several weeks before he was shot, Dutschke agreed to talk to me about the Movement—what it is and what it seeks. At the time he was living at the League of Socialist Students headquarters on the Kurfürstendamm. Appropriately, the building itself, a former Nazi headquarters, looks thoroughly out of place on the sleek, fashionable boulevard. Its stone walls are crumbling, most of its windows are broken and a stone imperial eagle over the entrance has long since been decapitated. On the ground floor of the building is a funeral parlor.

The league headquarters is a warren of rooms several floors up. A door marked "Secretary" was opened by a young man wearing nothing but a pair of brief underpants. A girl, holding a baby, was in the room behind him. The young man, seeing my wife next to me, grinned broadly and held a newspaper in front of him. He beckoned to the girl. "She'll find Dutschke for you," he said.

The girl led us to a large kitchen crowded with about 10 young people — mostly bearded, slightly seedy boys—sitting at a table drinking coffee. There were a few girls, too—sweet-faced, with clean, long hair and neat miniskirts or leather jerkins. An argument was in progress about whether Ché Guevara really had been killed in Bolivia or reports of his death had been falsified by frightened capitalist dictators trying to end the myth of the revolutionary hero.

Dutschke arrived about 20 minutes later, carrying a bag of groceries. He was unshaven, as usual, and wore a thick green and black striped sweater. He smiled and apologized for being late. Lateness for appointments has become a part of the Dutschke legend.

He led the way to his room, which was spotlessly clean and contained little furniture except for a couple of mattresses covered with bright cloths and several well-stocked bookshelves. On the wall was a picture of Jomo Kenyatta and a sign saying, "AMIS RAUS!" ("Americans, out!") A guitar stood next to a desk upon which were several open books on early Christianity. Dutschke leaned forward, folded his hands between his knees and began to talk, speaking slowly and in short sentences so that the American visitors could understand his German. His tone was nothing like his ranting public style but was soft, almost apologetic.

The student uprisings, he began, are a consequence of an internal crisis in the capitalist middle class in West Germany. They are an indication that the German social, economic and political systems are growing ripe for a change.

"There is a real structural crisis here. Anxiety and fear are growing all over West Germany. The old economic and labor structure is unworkable. Coal, agriculture and industry are in deep trouble. The Government gives subsidies but does not try to solve the basic problems. We are in for a long period of stagnation. We have had our so-called Economic Miracle, and now it is over; but nobody will say it is over. The existing power structure just asks for new sacrifices, new victims.

"The political structure is even worse. The established parties no longer enjoy the trust of a wide segment of the population. There is no dialogue between the parties and the people. Those with power simply use power to manipulate the masses."

For a brief moment, Dutschke's dark eyes took on the almost fanatic glitter that newspaper photographers try to capture when he is speaking.

"West German democracy is a sham," he said. "The people vote but they have no faith in those they vote for. They know nothing will be done for them. The Federal Republic under Kiesinger is not really much better off than Germany before World War II."

The only answer for Germany is a complete change in the power structure, he insisted. That is the goal of the radical movement. "We will only have reached our goal when we take over power."

Who are "we"? I asked.

"The extraparliamentary opposition. Extraparliamentary, because no opposition is possible within the old system, which maintains a monopoly on political power. There are 10,000 to 12,000 people in this opposition in West Berlin. Most are students, but there are other small groups who have indicated solidarity with us. The Movement is spreading throughout Germany faster than we had hoped. We are a minority, but an engaged, convinced minority with definite goals."

JUST then the door opened and Dutschke's wife, Gretchen, entered the room. Mrs. Dutschke, slim, dark-haired, with shy, deep-brown eyes, is the 25-year-old daughter of an Illinois druggist. She came

TERRORISM AND THE STATE TODAY

66 For the students, the name Rudi Dutschke is a rallying cry. He is the first postwar German to pull the young out of their lethargy and bring them to the barricades to fight for social and political causes. 99

to the Free University to study theology and met Dutschke in a restaurant. She recently gave birth to a son named Hosea Ché Dutschke, after the Old Testament prophet and the Argentine guerrilla leader. The standing joke in Berlin is that in 25 years the chant, "Ho, Ho, Ho Chi Minh!" will be replaced by "Ho, Ho, Ho Ché Du!" Mrs. Dutschke sat down and listened without saying a word herself.

Dutschke smiled at his wife and continued to talk about the opposition. Its role, he said, is to prepare the groundwork for the revolution. Unlike most revolutions, which are short, sharp encounters, this one will be a long process, lasting 10 years or more, he explained. Germany, he said, is in an intermediate stage: those in power want to rule but cannot, while those on the bottom are not strong enough to take over. But in time, the extraparliamentary minority will become a majority.

The basic goal of the revolution is to create a direct democracy to replace the present system of representative democracy — "yes, a plebeian democracy if you like. We envisage something on the order of the Paris Commune. Every citizen must be answerable to himself. He must be convinced that his vote is necessary and good—not useless, the way it is today. The revolution will end the manipulation of the masses by those with power; it will end the domination of man over man.

"But first we must produce changed men. The future has no place for an élite establishment. People do not want to be led, but to be answerable for their own actions and ideals."

This utopian strain is characteristic of Dutschke, and indeed of most of the student

The Western Democracies

radicals. Even the Soviet Communists rarely talk about "the new Socialist man" these days. But in a speech last year, Dutschke could say: "The Biblical Garden of Eden is the fantasy fulfillment of mankind's oldest dream. But never in history has its realization been as possible as it is today." Dutschke's critics have pounced upon this utopianism to dismiss him as a dreamer out of touch with reality. They have pointed out—accurately, but perhaps not pertinently—that he and the other students have no strategy for taking power and no program for utilizing power if they win it. Dutschke himself, however, claims to have few illusions.

"We are in no position to use violence," he said. "First of all it is not human to use terror against other people. Secondly, we do not have power to match that held by the Establishment. But the social confrontation inevitably will lead to the use of force by the other side. Then we will have to defend ourselves. The police already use weapons against us. The death of Benno Ohnesorg brought the terrorist methods of the Establishment into the open. It showed people that the power for evil is not just potential, but actual. So there already are signs of civil war. The Establishment has no other answer to our arguments.

"The revolution cannot take place in just one country—it must be international. The Third World—Vietnam, Cambodia, Laos, Cuba, Africa—will play an ever greater role. There is a steady polarization between the Third World and the monopolistic power structures in the big capitalist and Communist countries. The need for revolt against this power monopoly is growing. Perhaps there will be, as Guevara said, two, three or more Vietnams."

DUTSCHKE, who left East Germany shortly before the Berlin Wall went up, finds that country's Stalinism even more oppressive than the West German Establishment:

"Over there they have it even harder than we do. There the alienation between the power structure—that is, the party—and the masses is greatest. Here we can at least seek a dialogue on Vietnam and other issues. But there is no dialogue at all in the D.D.R., which is becoming increasingly Stalinistic."

Dutschke considers himself a Marxist. He explained that he was strongly influenced by Marxist friends when he was young and leans toward the Marxist view of history. He is also drawn to Mao Tse-tung's and Trotsky's concepts of the permanent revolution.

"My values spring from Marx, Mao and Marcuse—yes. But also from many other sources, including the Bible. There are many factors that I myself still do not understand about the way I think. Marxism is a creative science —one that is right and necessary—but it is not a finished system. Historically, Marx founded the world revolution. Now, however, we must again fight for new truths. Before and after Marx there were those who supplied these truths, men like Bakunin, Sorel and Lenin. In Communist countries today there is a monopolistic Marxism, but all material science is not Marx."

RUDI DUTSCHKE was born on March 7, 1940, in Schönefeld, which is now in East Germany. As a schoolboy he was active in both Communist and Protestant youth organizations. His Christian background, in addition to influencing his political ideology, has left a permanent strain of Puritanism in him; he eschews alcohol and tobacco. His church experience also seems to have left him a passion for preaching his political sermons from pulpits. This predilection earned Dutschke a bloody head on Christmas Eve when, with a group of friends, he entered Kaiser Wilhelm Memorial Church and attempted to speak from the pulpit against the bloodshed in Vietnam. Irate members of the congregation, no doubt regarding Dutschke's antiwar tirade as impious, threw him out of the church. One middle-aged man used his walking stick to lay open Dutschke's scalp. This defense of the faith by the middle-aged Berliner, a self-described anti-Semite and admirer of the Nazis, was widely applauded.

An outstanding track and field athlete as a youth, Dutschke intended to become a sportswriter. However, when, as a churchgoer "influenced by Christian socialism," he declined service in East Germany's army, he was denied the opportunity to become a writer and trained instead as an industrial salesman. Soon after he moved to West Berlin and later entered the Free University and joined the League of Socialist German Students.

Before the shooting, Dutschke spent most of his time traveling, making speeches, participating in forums and organizing "the extraparliamentary opposition." He was one of the most sought-after speakers in Germany, appeared on television, conducted a cadre school and worked on his doctoral thesis. Considered an outstanding student, he was writing his thesis on antiauthoritarian movements within Marxism.

Recently, he had begun to travel abroad. He appeared in London during an attack on the American Embassy; in the Hague, where Dutch officials treated him as a public enemy, and in late March he visited Prague for an "All-Christian Conference" of East European nations. In foreign capitals, Dutschke, the envoy of revolution, was usually made as welcome as the bubonic plague.

The Dutschkes lived modestly on about $200 a month, according to his estimate. The money came from fees for speeches, payments for magazine articles and a $100-a-month allowance sent by his wife's father. Recently he has started asking money for interviews, prompting some acid comments about "Dutschke the capitalist." But as a friend said—and it seems fair enough—"the Dutschkes have to live, don't they?"

In our conversation a few weeks ago, Dutschke was not at all certain about his future except that he would go on trying to change the world. He hoped to go to America to study political science and perhaps to meet Professor Marcuse, but beyond that was not sure what he wanted to do. "I can't see myself as a college professor," he said. A newspaperwoman in Bonn who knows Dutschke well summed him up this way: "We were driving around Bonn one evening in December and he was talking about how much he loved the Christmas holiday. It suddenly occurred to me then that, despite all his brilliance and fire, he is basically an innocent young man who really thinks he can make the world a perfect place."

AT the moment, however, it seems unlikely that Dutschke and his students will bring any major change to West Germany, much less remake the world. The Movement has attracted no mass support; West Germany's self-satisfied workers have expressed little but scorn for the intellectual élite in the universities. Dutschke and Professor Marcuse would say that the opinion of the masses has been manipulated into this attitude, but the attitude remains. It is conceivable that repeated antiauthoritarian provocation by the left-wing students could push conservatives into the camp of the ultra-rightist National Democratic party and create the kind of political polarization in Germany that paved the way for the Nazis' rise to power. But most observers here are convinced that this polarization could not take place without an economic and political catastrophe, and no such catastrophe is in sight.

Some West Germans have dismissed the student movement as nothing more than a group of young intellectuals trying to impress their teachers with how well they have learned their lessons. This is surely a serious underestimate, a fact that has become increasingly clear since the attack on Dutschke.

If nothing else, the student revolt has exposed some deep flaws in the West German social fabric. West German education is badly in need of reform. The West German press is tending toward a monopoly situation. There is a problem of communication between West Germans and the politicians who govern them. Many West Germans are indifferent to the suffering in Vietnam and other places outside their own country or, indeed, their own families.

Some members of the West German power structure — only a few up to now—even admit a positive aspect in the student revolt. They believe that the movement is basically a good thing for the nation, that it will inject new life into the sluggish West

TERRORISM AND THE STATE TODAY

German democracy. Dutschke and his fellow students are demonstrating that authority can be questioned, that discipline is not the only virtue, order not the only goal. They are proving that citizens can make their voices heard all the way to the Olympian peak of German bureaucracy if they will yell loud enough.

"These young men and women are better than we were," one leading educator wrote not long ago. "We never challenged authority. We did what we were told, deferred to our superiors and stayed out of trouble. And, of course, we got what we deserved: Hitler." ■

April 28, 1968

BONN HOUSE VOTES EMERGENCY LAWS

Bundestag in Final Reading —Students Protest to Last

By PHILIP SHABECOFF
Special to The New York Times

BONN, May 30—The Bundestag, or lower house of the West German Parliament, approved today the third and final reading of the controversial and long-pending emergency laws. They must now be approved by the Bundesrat, the uper house, before they become law. The vote is scheduled for June 14 and approval is considered virtually certain.

The laws, which would give n emergency government powers to limit certain civil rights in time of national danger, have been the most bitterly opposed legislation in West Germany.

Even as the legislation was being adopted by the surprisingly wide margin of 384 votes to 100 with one abstention, students and some workers in all parts of the country continued to hold strikes and other protest demonstrations in a last-ditch effort to defeat it.

Today about 100 policemen forced their way into the University of Frankfurt and evicted left-wing students who had occupied the building since last Friday. The students had voted to change the name of the school to Karl Marx University and had smeared the name in red paint across the facade of the building.

School Ordered Closed

The rector of the University of Giessen, 30 miles north of Frankfurt, ordered the school closed because he could no longer control it in the face of student protest demonstrations.

At the University of Cologne students barricaded the buildings with lumber and other building materials. In Bochum about 60 students stormed into the Krupp steel works and tried to persuade workers to join them in a protest strike before they were evicted by the police.

A two-thirds majority of the Bundestag was required to pass the far-reaching constitutional changes adopted today.

Although the deputies voted on name cards, the individual votes by name were not announced immediately.

Willy Brandt, Vice Chancellor and Foreign Minister and head of the Social Democrats, pledged in today's debate that his party would see that the laws were never abused. He added that they would not be applicable if West Germany had a crisis similar to France's present one.

May 31, 1968

FRENCH WORKERS JOIN HUGE PROTEST

Student Ranks Swelled to Hundreds of Thousands in Marches in Many Cities

By JOHN L. HESS
Special to The New York Times

PARIS, May 13—Hundreds of thousands of French students and workers joined today in an extraordinary protest against "police repression" and the de Gaulle regime.

It was the most massive outpouring in the recent international wave of student-led demonstrations. Students here, latecomers to the movement, chanted "Berlin, Warsaw, Rome—Paris!"

A majority of organized labor held a one-day strike in sympathy with the students, who had battled the police for 10 nights in the Latin Quarter.

In cities across the country, students occupied universities, and unions joined demonstrations as large as scores of thousands.

Size of Crowd Disputed

In Paris, the actual size of the demonstration was disputed. The police estimated the crowd at 200,000 people, while leaders of the protest put it at 500,000 to a million. The French state television network said the figure was "somewhere between."

In any case for four hours, marchers, 40 abreast, chanting "De Gaulle assassin!" filled a three-mile route from the Place de la République on the Right Bank, across the Seine and up the Boulevard St.-Michel to Place Denfert-Rochereau.

The police were invisible, and order was maintained by thousands of volunteers. Elsewhere, heavy police forces barred the Seine bridges to keep activists from approaching the area of President de Gaulle's residence, the Elysée Palace, and the United States Embassy nearby. But there was no serious trouble.

Meanwhile, university student and teacher organizations announced that their strike would continue until basic reforms were won. The students say that they are overcrowded because of inadequate construction since the war, that the universities' teaching practices are archaic, that they have an inadequate voice in the running of the schools and that, in general, the "capitalist establishment" must be changed or overthrown. They also seek amnesty for their recent demonstrations.

Day With Festive Air

The day, fine and sunny, began with a festive air. Power had been cut and transport services were drastically reduced, but Parisians are used to stoppages. Subway operations were soon restored, but they were free. The ticket-punchers were on strike. Power came on again in the afternoon.

Students from the middle-class suburbs to the west and workmen from the "Red Belt" of suburbs, where the Communist party is strong, converged on the Place de la République by car and bus or afoot in organized groups.

The students, in tens of thousands, some wearing school caps and many bearing homemade placards, assembled half a mile away at the Gare de l'Est.

The great square and its side streets were filled with workers of the Communist-led and Roman Catholic-led union federations. There were also a number of banners of the smaller, strongly anti-Communist Force Ouvrière — Workers Force — whose national leaders had endorsed the strike but opposed the demonstration.

'Make Way for Students!'

Thousands of teachers assembled at the Bourse du Travail (Labor Exchange) next to the Place de la République. But there was no question who was leading the show. As the march got under way, marshals with bullhorns cleared a path through the packed square by shouting, "Make way for the students!"

Ahead was a benner reading, "Students, Teachers, Workers Together."

In the first line were the top teacher and labor officials, in neat city suits, arm in arm and singing "The Internationale" with half a dozen tieless, unshaved, weary but happy-looking student militants. Conspicuous among them was the red-haired Daniel Cohn-Bendit, called "Danny the Red," leader of the extremist students of Nanterre who began the agitation two months ago.

Immediately behind were three red banners and one black one representing the Trotskyite, anarchist and other revolutionary youth groups.

Hundreds of placards recalled that on May 13, 1958, settlers in Algiers began the uprising that brought General de Gaulle to power. "Happy Anniversary, General," the placards said. Marchers chanted, "Ten years, that's enough!"

Thousands of volunteers, holding hands along the line of march, maintained order. Not a policeman was to be seen. In the Latin Quarter, where scores of thousands of sympathizers were waiting, a triple row of workmen blocked the Place de la Sorbonne, where a company of riot policemen had stood for 10 days.

The stone bust of Auguste Comte in front of the Sorbonne wore a red bandanna. The buildings were empty.

Demands Outpace Him

Premier Georges Pompidou had opened the Sorbonne, conceding to one of three demands posed by the students last week. He also met others by removing the police and by releasing on appeal today the last four students jailed in the rioting. But demands had outpaced him.

Fifty-three teachers at the university branch in suburban Nanterre called a "constituent assembly" there tomorrow to

315

replace the "bankrupt existing structures" of the institution.

Student marchers from Nanterre raised a variety of complaints and demands. They said they wanted the right to discuss politics freely in class, more night classes for students with daytime jobs, and smaller classes. The typical class, they said, now has 50 students.

A girl in corduroy slacks said scholarship stipends, worth $60 a month, were too small. A room at Nanterre costs $24 a month, and a meal 30 cents, she said.

Premier Pompidou received a delegation of students and teachers this afternoon, called on General de Gaulle and then met with Alain Peyrefitte, the Education Minister.

Several hundred ultrarightists gathered at the Arc de Triomphe this afternoon and marched down the Champs-Elysées in a counterdemonstration. Turned aside by the police, some of them stoned the Chinese Communist Embassy before being driven off.

On the Left Bank, there were several minor clashes between bands of youths and police patrols near Montparnasse. But roving detachments of volunteer guards restrained the activists, and there was no serious trouble.

May 14, 1968

POMPIDOU ASSERTS MOUNTING UNREST IMPERILS FRANCE

Tells Nation the Government 'Must Defend Republic'— Gendarme Units Called

MORE PLANTS OCCUPIED

Three Renault Factories Are Taken Over by Strikers— Students to Join Them

By HENRY TANNER
Special to The New York Times

PARIS, May 16 — Premier Georges Pompidou, faced with growing unrest among students and workers in many parts of the country, said today that a handful of troublemakers were out to "destroy the nation and the very foundations of our free society."

"The Government must defend the Republic—it will defend it," Mr. Pompidou said.

The upheaval spread during the day. At least six factories were occupied by striking workers, including three nationalized Renault plants. About 1,000 students marched from the Latin Quarter of Paris to one of the struck plants, seeking to sit in with the workers. Insurgents were also still holding the state-controlled Théâtre de France at the Odéon. Performances have been suspended.

'Listen to Reason'

Mr. Pompidou said: "I address myself to you with calm but also with gravity. Students, do not follow the provocateurs. Listen to the voice of reason."

A few minutes after his nationwide broadcast, the Government announced the call-up of certain reserve units of the gendarmes, the paramilitary state policemen, the equivalent of the United States National Guard.

The grim-faced Premier, who is acting chief of state while President de Gaulle is in Rumania, spoke at the end of an eventful day during which the two-week old student revolt spread to more factories.

20,000 Workers Move

Some 20,000 striking workers took a leaf from the students' book and occupied the three Renault automobile plants — in the auto racing town of Le Mans; in Flins, 25 miles northwest of Paris; and at Sandouville, near Le Havre.

Strike movements were touched off in many other parts of the country and in several different industries. As far as could be ascertained, these other strikes had not yet led to the occupation of plants, except for a small factory at Elbeuf in Normandy.

In Paris, directors and producers of newscasts on the state-owned radio and television network walked off their jobs just before Télé-Nuit, the day's last news program, at 11:30 P.M.

The striking newscasters accused the Government of having exerted censorship and otherwise interfered with their work. They called for an "assembly" of personnel tomorrow.

Paris newspapers ran off the presses but a part deliverers' strike hampered distribution. The deliverers, employed by a single agency, staged a sit-in on the agency's premises at La Villette, in the north of Paris.

Students Walk 7 Miles

During the evening, students marched seven miles down the Seine from the Latin Quarter— the name derives from the days teaching was done in Latin— to the industrial suburb of Boulogne-Billancourt to link up with striking workers.

At the entrance of the factory they were stopped by a detachment of workers who told them they could not enter. Their presence might bring the intervention of the police, the workers said.

The student occupation of universities and high schools continued for the third day in defiance of the Government.

Mr. Pompidou resolved to make his appeal a short time after extremist student leaders announced their intention to stage a mass march on the headquarters of the state radio and television network.

Citizens Also Concerned

Mr. Pompidou's statement disclosed that the Gaullist Administration, like many private citizens, is convinced that a truly revolutionary situation exists and that the democratic institutions of France are threatened.

The principal threat lies in the spontaneous, popular and utterly uncontrolled nature of the movement, which was started by a handful of New Leftists but then was joined by hundreds of thousands of students and more recently by thousands of workers.

The movement unleashed forces that neither the Government nor the traditional Opposition parties seem equipped to handle.

The Communist party is making a strong effort to capture the revolt.

'Ripe' for Removal

A statement issued by the party tonight declared that conditions were "rapidly getting ripe" for the removal of the Gaullist regime and that the unity of workers and students had been achieved. But in an echo of Mr. Pompidou's appeal it added: "The Politburo of the party warns the workers and the students against taking instructions from adventurers who are likely to impede the movement."

The Communist party statement was issued after one of the student leaders, Daniel Cohn-Bendit, called the Communists "Stalinist creeps." Mr. Cohn-Bendit, called Danny the Red, appears to hold views close to anarchism.

The Communist-dominated General Labor Federation issued a similar warning against taking instructions from "adventurers" and told its members to stay away from tomorrow's march on the radio and television headquarters, which it said would "play into the hands" of the Gaullist Government.

Resignation Asked

The non-Communist Federation of the Left, a major Opposition party, called for the resignation of the Government and new general elections. It said that the Government had proved its inability to cope with the problem raised by students, teachers, workers and farmers.

Mr. Pompidou's speech represented a sharp reversal of Government policy.

Mr. Pompidou, in an address Saturday, announced a policy of mildness and forbearance toward the students. He withdrew the police from the Sorbonne and the Latin Quarter and announced an amnesty for those who had been arrested during bloody clashes in which more than 1,500 civilians and policemen were wounded.

The Premier hoped to restore calm to the universities. Instead the student revolt spread to the workers.

Mr. Pompidou has returned to a policy of toughness. Before he spoke, the police had re-entered the Latin Quarter. Scores of black buses were parked in back streets and on strategic squares or were cruising along the boulevards.

The unpredictable character of the protest became evident last night when more than a thousand young people occupied the Odéon, three blocks from the Sorbonne, after the curtain fell.

The move, it turned out, was led by a group of young actors and hangers-on. The "student assemblies," in their third all-night session in the 19th-century building at the Sorbonne were not consulted.

Through the day there were rumors that student groups would move to other public buildings, including the Opéra, in the heart of the city.

The Renault workers on strike at the four major plants around the country demand that their working hours be cut to 40 hours a week without loss of pay and call for a guaranteed minimum salary of 1,000 francs ($200) a month. They now work 44 or 45 hours, depending on the factory.

An estimated total of 9,500 Renault workers at Flins, 25

miles northwest of Paris, occupied their plant and hoisted a red flag over the main building. The plant has 10,000 workers.

The strike at Flins is for an unlimited duration. The same is true for the Renault plant at Le Mans. In France, such strikes are very rare; usually strikes are called for 24 or 48 hours.

Renault workers at a plant near Rouen called part strikes.

There were strikes also in the mineral water plant at Contrexéville in central France; at Unelec, a manufacturer of electrical equipment in Orléans; at a rubber-boot factory near Bordeaux, at the potassium mines in Alsace, and at a glass works in Lorraine.

The wave of worker protests and plant occupations started Tuesday night in Nantes, where 2,000 striking workers at the aircraft plant of Sud-Aviation welded the factory gate closed and told the plant manager he and his aides could not leave the plant until the workers' demands for a small salary increase were met.

May 17, 1968

A Bas—Everything!

By SANCHE de GRAMONT

PARIS.

"It is impossible to see how France today could be paralyzed by crises as she has been in the past. . . . In the midst of so many countries shaken by such confusion, ours will continue to give an example of order. . . . Frenchmen, Frenchwomen, I salute the year 1968 with serenity."
—PRESIDENT DE GAULLE, New Year message to the French people.

IN the beginning there was *hubris*, a pride so inordinate that it summoned the wrath of the gods. In some of his recent speeches, President de Gaulle called himself the "guide." And it seemed, after 10 years of power, that he was a guide who seldom looked over his shoulder to see whether he was still being followed. The structure of France was pyramidal. Everything came from the top. Twice a year the general told his people how well off they were. His vision of France as a nation of satisfied and obedient subjects had little relation to what history had taught of a people quick to revolt.

The style of the regime was a blend of arrogance and smugness. The general was so sure of his own people that he could gloat about the difficulties of other countries whose houses were not in such immaculate order. The regime asked to be judged on the merits of its foreign policy alone. To build up international prestige, de Gaulle initiated such policies as the independent nuclear force and the stockpiling of gold reserves, which slowed the country's economic growth. Prestige was bought at the expense of domestic welfare. The peasants' and workers' demands could wait. The *force de frappe* could not.

Technocrats, like laboratory technicians experimenting with guinea pigs, drafted a five-year plan that postulated an unemployment figure of half a million as one of the conditions for the desired annual increase of 5 per cent in gross national product. The objectives of the plan could be met only by not giving in to labor demands. A man like Finance Minister Michel Debré preferred the abstract, ideal world of statistics to human problems.

The Government controlled public opinion through the technique of referendums and through the shrewdly censored radio and television network. But despite de Gaulle's self-congratulatory pronouncements that he was revolutionizing French society, his habit of governing without counsel and his rigid centralization actually strengthened the conservative French establishment. The *notables* have managed to survive far less hospitable regimes. Here was a regime based on the principle of authoritarian paternalism that they themselves advocated to run their businesses and industries. The temptation was strong for men in important positions to imitate the example that came from on high. Thus, university rectors named by the Government acted as if they ruled by divine right. Directors of the great nationalized plants, such as the Renault works, behaved like five-star generals and told the workers it was unpatriotic to ask for a raise.

It was not a matter of misery or oppression. There was nothing critical about the domestic French scene. It was more a question of taking a people for granted despite the lessons of history. "De Gaulle," one French commentator wrote, "offered the French people the destiny of force-fed geese."

After the students and the workers had rebelled, one of the recurring themes in the National Assembly debate on the motion of censure was incredulity. "How could we have reached this point with a Government that was able to do exactly what it wanted?" wondered the Socialist leader Guy Mollet. René Billères of the Federation of the Left reminded Premier Georges Pompidou that he had once called education the Government's most successful program.

There was a note of incredulity, too, in Premier Pompidou's speech when he recalled, as if evoking some distant past, the France of only a few weeks before, with orderly students preparing for their exams, a rise in employment and a bright economic outlook.

The Deputies groped for explanations. Some expressed a feeling of shame that French domestic events were once again on the front pages of the world press. It was a shock, like discovering that your maiden aunt is a secret tippler. Valéry Giscard d'Estaing, head of the Independent Republican party, paraphrased Shaw's "Pygmalion:" "'Why are you so hostile after all I've done for you?' asks Professor Higgins: 'Because I want some consideration,' replies Eliza."

* * *

"Something is happening here, but you don't know what it is."
—BOB DYLAN.

THE student rebellion did not come from the Sorbonne, with its patina of tradition and archaism, but from the Gaullist-designed, oppressively new Nanterre University, which has problems of its own but no traditions. It was another irony of these strange weeks to hear Robert Poujade, secretary general of the Gaullist party, the Union for the New Republic, in a confessional frame of mind at the National Assembly, de-

SANCHE de GRAMONT *reports regularly on French affairs.*

317

The Western Democracies

scribing Nanterre as "a Kafkaesque universe where concrete is king, where trees are rare, and which symbolizes the dismay of the students."

Planned to relieve university overcrowding in Paris, Nanterre was built on the site of a deactivated army camp a few miles northwest of the capital, in the middle of one of the worst suburban slum areas. It is still a construction site, but 12,000 students already attend it. They come to class on trains that leave from the Gare Saint-Lazare and they get off at the station they call *La Folie*—Complexe Universitaire.

It was in Nanterre, removed from Paris and the habits of the Sorbonne, that a small group of students formed a study group in 1967. Just as Nanterre was outside the Paris university system, the leader of the group, too, was an outsider. He was a 23-year-old carrot-topped sociology student named Daniel Cohn-Bendit, a German Jew.

Later, when events had made him notorious, "Danny the Red" was stigmatized in the left-wing press as a German anarchist and in the right-wing press as a Jewish anarchist. He drew chauvinist and racist prejudices like a magnet.

These were not the children of Marx but of Mao and Marcuse. The film director Jean-Luc Godard was the first to draw attention to the peculiar nature of the Nanterre group in his 1967 film "La Chinoise." But he drew the mistaken conclusion that these young men and women of bourgeois background would never achieve any real mass action.

The appeal of Fidel Castro, Mao Tse-tung and other Third World leaders was that they were leaders of active minorities who successfully took power, whereas in the French experience active minorities have been doomed, as the Commune of 1871 was doomed. Thanks to the example of Third World revolutionary leaders and student movements in Germany and the United States, the Nanterre group became convinced that in certain situations the active minority can succeed.

The philosopher Herbert Marcuse taught them that in a modern technological society any conventional opposition group inevitably assumes the values of the system it opposes and is eventually absorbed by it. The Nanterre students refused to adopt a program or form a conventional organization. As Cohn-Bendit was later to explain: "If we had founded a party, Pompidou would have been reassured and he would have said, 'Well, now these boys are playing it our way and we can handle them.' The strength of our movement was precisely that it was uncontrollable. There are two ways to do things—the first is to get five politically minded students together to draw up a program and say, 'Here is our position; do what you want with it.' The other is to get a large number of students to understand the situation they are in. To do that you must avoid creating a program which inevitably paralyzes your action. The movement's only chance lies in maintaining a state of disorder."

From Marcuse, too, came the idea that reform is a trap which again makes you part of the system and that the only valid goal is an overthrow of the social order itself, whose prosperity and cohesion he believes is founded on exploitation, brutal competition and hypocrisy.

Cohn-Bendit and his fellow radicals fanned what they called the "objective situation" of discontent at Nanterre. The 400 resident students demonstrated because they were not allowed to have members of the opposite sex in their dormitories. There were protests against a number of other university practices: mandatory seminars, which the 15 per cent of job-holding students could not attend; alleged blacklists of student agitators whom teachers were instructed to flunk; plainclothes policemen who infiltrated the university and attended classes; a sociology professor who refused to show a film on Cuba in the classroom.

There were also the normal protests about French higher education, which were not specific to Nanterre: the icy remoteness of the professors, the huge classrooms, the lectures that had to be taken down verbatim, the exam as a disciplinary proof of attendance rather than an evaluation of judgment. In short, the results of a long tradition of contempt for the student.

Agitation mounted until the first serious clash with the police on March 22, which gave the movement its name. There were 42 founding members. Students who occupied one of the big classrooms for a political meeting were routed by the police, who used the steel rods propping up notice boards as spears.

Nanterre was closed for the first time just before Easter vacation. After Easter, the number of militant students had grown to several hundred and political meetings were held daily. Members of the German S.D.S. movement came to Nanterre to give Cohn-Bendit the benefit of their experience. Student sources say they were arrested, beaten and flown out on the first plane to Germany. Perhaps that is what Premier Pompidou meant when he told the National Assembly he had proof that the student riots were set off by foreign agitators (he reassured the Communist group that he did not mean the Soviet Union).

IN May, Nanterre was closed once again, which made the militant students decide to go to the Sorbonne for support. Cohn-Bendit and other leaders were to be judged by a faculty court on charges of agitation. On Friday, May 3, a Nanterre group met a Sorbonne group in the Sorbonne courtyard to plan a protest meeting for the following Monday. None of those present had the remotest notion of occupying the Sorbonne. Cohn-Bendit himself said later that "the movement took on an extension we had not foreseen."

This was the Sorbonne's first real contact with the radical Nanterre group. Alarmed, Rector Jean Roche called Education Minister Alain Peyrefitte and said, "Mr. Minister, I think we should close the Sorbonne. Several students are committing depredations, and the deans insist I take this action."

"Are things really that bad?" Peyrefitte wanted to know.

"Yes, I'm certain of it. Do you give me your permission to act?"

"Yes, but do it within existing regulations."

Peyrefitte's advisers had told him that the *enragés*—the mad dogs—were only a handful, and that firm police action would bring them into line. The others, so close to exam time, wouldn't follow, they said. It was the Government blunder of calling in the police that provided Cohn-Bendit with the "objective situation" he needed. The Government violated a venerated Sorbonne tradition. "One day when I was a student," a lawyer explained, "we were lis-

TERRORISM AND THE STATE TODAY

tening to old Lévy-Bruhl giving the same Roman law course he'd been giving word for word for 20 years, mumbling into his beard. We shouted, we sang songs, we threw folded newspapers at him. There was such a racket that the police came into the auditorium. Old Lévy-Bruhl rose to his full height of 5 feet 2 inches and said with great authority: 'Leave at once, gentlemen. We in the Sorbonne are accustomed to settling our own differences. We do not require interference from the police.' He became a student hero."

THE quality of the teaching has not changed since then, but the attitude toward student disorder has. The more authoritarian a regime is, the less it can tolerate disorder. Centralization is a two-edged weapon. It permits the Government to control education. But it also makes any attack on the educational system an attack on the Government. Rioting students at Columbia University do not threaten President Johnson, but the students in the Sorbonne courtyard were threatening a part of the pervasive state apparatus, and, indirectly the Elysée.

The man in the Elysée was closeted in his study, writing out in longhand the speeches with which he was going to impress the people of Rumania. Premier Pompidou was in Iran on a state visit. The remaining Ministers responded in a conventional way to an unconventional situation: Force of habit was too ingrained for them to consider anything except police repression.

Later, when Interior Minister Christian Fouchet explained the police attack on the Sorbonne to the National Assembly, he said: "You must understand that we had to react. The situation was inadmissible — the university courtyard was full of students!"

There was a week of rioting in the Latin Quarter—bloody faces, arrests, streets clouded with tear gas. But instead of dying out, the movement grew. For the first time since the Commune of 1871, with the exception of the 1944 liberation, there were barricades in the streets of Paris. Baron Haussmann, who rebuilt Paris to make it barricade-proof, must have been whirling in his grave.

The Government attitude was that the students were unruly children who had to be taught a lesson. This attitude was reflected in the behavior of the police. I am not talking about police brutality, which is one of the predictable elements of any street riot. But the students had to be humiliated as well. An 18-year-old American girl who is an anthropology major at Nanterre, and who was arrested at the Rue Gay-Lussac barricade and locked up with 70 other girl students in one cell of the Beaujon detention house near the Etoile, said:

"We were detained without charges for 36 hours. We were given no food. We could have all the water we wanted, but were not allowed to go to the toilet, which was a constant source of glee to the police, who said, 'You girls must learn to hold yourselves back.'

"When things got dull, one of them would come into the cell with a truncheon and say, 'Well, who is going to shout "Police assassin!" now?' and then take a crack at one of the girls. After that, they turned gallant: 'What are you doing tonight, chérie?'"

The American girl was re-

DEMONSTRATORS—Striking students climb an allegorical statue on a monument to "*la gloire française*" in the Place de la Republique, Paris.

leased after a lecture: "So you're one of these foreign agitators like that German Jew Cohn-Bendit. Go back where you came from. Make trouble in your own country."

* * *

A spark can set fire to the entire plain.
—MAO TSE-TUNG.

THE student disorder had grown from 42 enragés to 40,000 who occupied the Latin Quarter. The movement channeled the smoldering discontent of the nation. It spread to the provinces, to all the groups and classes that had felt frustrated during the Gaullist decade because they were never consulted except to say "Yes" or "No" in a referendum every three or four years. But as the movement spread to nonstudent groups, it lost its revolutionary content to become reformist.

This becomes clear when one compares the occupation of the Sorbonne with the occupation of Nanterre, where the "22d of March" group kept control thanks to the isolation of the campus. At Nanterre there was no program—no motions proposed, no votes. Action was taken by small cells or study groups and then presented to the rank and file and passed by proclamation. The Nanterre people maintained their determination to remain outside the system. When Alain Touraine, a sociology professor, proposed a reform program, he was booted. "I've resigned from the university," he said to prove his good faith. They made him write on a blackboard, "I, Alain Touraine, have resigned from Nanterre University."

The Sorbonne students fell into the old ways of administration, bureaucracy and parliamentary procedure. The Sorbonne was crowded with committees — an Occupation Committee, an Investigation of Repression Committee, an Action Committee for the Secondary Degree, an Action Committee for Students in Countries Under French Rule and 20 others. A woman brought her paints and brushes to the Sorbonne and said she wanted to paint over the muddy 19th-century frescoes. The Culture Committee named an action subcommittee, which told her it was all right. The next day she started painting but was stopped by members of the *Service d'Ordre*, who told her: "Listen, comrade, you must not paint on the walls." At Nanterre, the classrooms looked as if a dozen Jackson Pollocks had been let loose. No one had been consulted— it just happened.

The Nanterre leaders did not take any position on exams, or student government, or the inadequacy of their teachers. As one of them said: "Our theory is that we cannot commit the movement to any program. We must always be ahead of every program. We are ready for direct action whenever the situation requires it. In the present case, we acted as the detonator, and now the reformists have taken over."

At the Sorbonne, the mood was one of exultation that the students had successfully occupied the premises. "Do you realize," one student asked, "that two weeks ago there were signs in this courtyard saying, 'Politics is forbidden here'? Now the signs read, 'Patriotism Is Collective Egotism,' 'Anarchy Is the Mother of Order' and 'There are just and generous insurrections, those where the people repulse force with force—Robespierre.'"

The most urgent activity was talk. It was as if the French had been muzzled for 10 years and were making it up with an orgy of discussion, a permanent banquet of words, a Niagara of debate. The Sorbonne became the forum, and the Odéon Theater, also occupied, became Hyde Park. "Is the nesting of the egg necessary to the revolutionary development of the hen?" one long-haired young man was solemnly asking another one evening at the Odéon. "Ionesco says that the future lies in the egg," the other replied.

I REALIZED the extent to which the student movement had spread to other groups when I wandered one afternoon into the Sorbonne Committee for Revolutionary Cultural Agitation and was met by a bright-eyed, smiling young man who offered to brief me. "What do you study?" I asked. "Oh, I'm not really a student," he said. "I'm a circus artist, a tightrope walker. Myself and seven others, we are the Astarlis troupe. We have an international reputation. We are some of the 1,800 circus artists who have gone on strike. The owners said they would bring in foreign artists. You don't know how we are exploited, comrade. We drive the trucks, we pitch the tents, we distribute the posters, we feed the animals and then we have our own rehearsals, and all we get is a lousy $80 a day split eight ways."

The rebellion revealed some of the areas of French life that are still organized along restricted, antiquated lines. In hospitals, for instance, the Balzacian institution of the *Grand Patron*, or dictatorial head doctor, still prevails. The *patron* has total responsibility and thus total authority, with all the abuses and inadequacies the system entails. At the Broussais Hospital, the *patron* of the cardiology department was unceremoniously evacuated from his office and the department was placed under the authority of an elected committee. The same thing happened in other hospitals, and the Sainte-Anne insane asylum was invested by several hundred students, who formed a Committee of Psychiatric Action.

Architects are burdened by a highly restricted professional order to which they must belong in order to practice — a kind of feudal guild designed to limit the number of architects.

The architects met at the Ecole des Beaux-Arts and voted to dissolve the order. Several burned their membership cards. But here, as in other instances, the French love of debating fine points made their gesture lose much of its meaning. The architects had decided to invest the order's headquarters when news came that the order had accepted its own dissolution. So they had a debate on whether self-dissolution was acceptable, because one who dissolves himself can reconstitute himself. And then they passed a motion not to burn their cards because if they did they would not be able to get into the building in order to destroy it.

Journalists working for the Government radio and television network pledged to supply honest, complete and objective news, an admission that up until now the broadcasts have been dishonest, incomplete and subjective. It is common knowledge that a Government body called the *Service des Liaisons Interministériels* meets each morning with the network department heads to give them directives on what to censor and what to stress. The network bows daily to multiple Government pressures. The journalists announced that they would no longer accept Government directives and would provide news instead of propaganda. This deserving stand was not immediately evident, for the street fighting in Paris received far less network time than have similar disturbances in Chicago and Detroit.

* * *

Since these mysteries are beyond us, let us at least feign to have organized them.
—JEAN COCTEAU.

ONE of the groups that did not take advantage of the student agitation to press its own demands was the Communist party. Its newspaper, L'Humanité, attacked the students as "pseudorevolutionaries led by the German anarchist Cohn-Bendit." The novelist Louis Aragon, French Communism's Grand Old Man, toured the student barricades and was greeted with insults. Incidents were avoided, thanks to Cohn-Bendit, who said, "Here everyone has the right to speak, even the Stalinist scoundrels."

But when they realized the breadth of the student movement the Communists made a 180-degree turn, and by May 9 L'Humanité was talking about "the just cause of the students." The Communist-controlled labor union, the C.G.T., or General Federation of Labor, grudgingly threw its support to the students, not because of any genuine sympathy but because it could not afford to be left out of a major protest movement. This was the stand that led to the huge demonstration of May 13, when the great mass of students and workers marched without incident from one end of Paris to the other. From the start it was clear that the unions intended to keep their distance from the students. They insisted on marching in separate groups, and it took a three-hour discussion before they agreed to let Cohn-Bendit join them in the front line of the march.

TERRORISM AND THE STATE TODAY

THE students had given the example, not to the Communist party or the unions but to the young workers, who proceeded to occupy factories just as the students had occupied the Sorbonne. As Jean-Paul Sartre explained at a Sorbonne meeting: "Cohn-Bendit opened a breach in the system with the student revolt. The young workers said, 'Why not us?' They were way ahead of their unions. The C.G.T. had to follow if it wanted to keep control of its rank and file. It was an example of direct democracy upsetting institutions, and the C.G.T. is an institution. It was also an example of bourgeois students, who have a nonclass reaction, of the nonoppressed wanting to form an alliance with the oppressed."

THE first factory occupations, at Sud-Aviation in Nantes and at the Renault works in Cléon, were decided by the workers in defiance of union directives.

The C.G.T. was forced to give its imprimatur to the movement, and within days most of the economic activity in France came to a halt. One of the few unions not to strike was the National Union of Penitentiary Workers, "because of the particular nature of our responsibilities."

Life unreeled like a film in slow motion, and it appeared that France in 1968 was again divided into three orders, like the France of the *ancien régime*: the students, the strikers and the hoarders. The hoarders had the atavistic French reaction to any national crisis, from a strike to an occupation: stockpile. Housewives sagging under the weight of canned foods and a six-month supply of salad oil and sugar, men filling their bathtubs with gasoline, bourgeois who withdrew their savings to buy gold napoleons, these were the backbone of conservative France whom General de Gaulle could count on to vote "Yes" in any referendum. They even hoarded Mother's Day: the Association of Merchants asked that it be put off until June 16, when dutiful sons would presumably be in a better frame of mind to honor their *mamans*.

The student is someone who by definition will become something other than a student. There is no student class, except insofar as in France more than 90 per cent of university students are recruited from the middle and upper classes. The student is someone who is being trained to take a role in the élite of the society against which he is demonstrating. At the same time, his oppressor is not an employer but society itself. This is why the students could so easily escalate their protest from a reform of the educational system to a complete overthrow of society.

The worker, who is involved in a class struggle, does not view his protest in such grandiose, overwhelming terms. His goals are narrower and more precise. André Gouin, a 27-year-old postman who makes $125 a month plus a $20-a-month Paris living allowance, went to work as usual on May 20. Although he does not belong to a union, he and his 80 co-workers decided to occupy the post office and they got the keys from the postmaster.

By midmorning, a union official called to approve their action. The strikers set up a round-the-clock guard at the post office and drafted their demands: a 20 per cent salary increase, a fifth week of annual paid vacation and a five-day week.

"I went to the Sorbonne to talk to the students," Gouin recalled. "One of them said it was natural for the man who designed the Eiffel Tower to be paid more than the worker who put in the bolts. I said, 'What about the miner, with his working conditions?' But I lost my footing talking to those fellows. There is too much difference in our backgrounds."

ON the big iron doors of the Citroën plant on the Quai de Javel, which employs 20,000 workers, there were signs reading "This Plant Occupied." The plant director, a man named Berçot, was hanged in effigy from the branch of a chestnut tree outside. Young workers leaned over the plant walls, laughing and whistling at passing girls. Inside, workers showed their wives and children the rows of gleaming black chassis and the machines they worked on. This must have been the way it was in 1936 during the Popular Front lock-ins, when the unions won the right to collective bargaining.

At the Citroën plant today, however, fewer than 10 per cent of the workers are union members. This is partly because half the workers are immigrant labor and hard to organize. It is also because the Citroën management, acknowledged to be the most reactionary in the French automobile industry, sabotages union efforts. Daniel Doiselet, the 37-year-old C.G.T. secretary general for the plant, explained:

"When they find out you want to join the union, they give you a dirty job, or they move you to a suburban plant, or if your wife works in the plant they threaten to separate you, or if you want to buy a car and get the 7 per cent price reduction they tell you they won't give it to you.

"It's only four years ago that we obtained the right to distribute union literature at the plant gates. Before that, the management called the cops and they'd pull us in. Since we can't organize, collective bargaining is a dead letter. Instead, we try petitions. We got 10,500 signatures for a $50 bonus when the 1968 models came out, but they told us, 'No, it's not the moment. Our sales are down.'

"We took the plant over at 7:30 A.M. on Monday, May 20. We had the shop stewards take a vote on it. The management deigned to receive a union delegation and they told us, 'Look, this isn't the moment to strike. This is a peak period for sales. If you strike now, foreign cars will move ahead of French cars on the export market!'"

The Citroën workers were asking for a minimum wage of $200 a month (skilled workers now make $170), a fifth week of paid vacation for workers under 21, a retirement age of 60 for men and 55 for women (now 65 for both), recognition of the union's right to organize, and job security for migrant laborers, who can now be fired at the end of a six-month temporary contract.

As I talked to Doiselet, other workers filled the room, and one young bearded man said, referring to the students' role, "You'll have to admit we jumped aboard the train after it started moving."

"Who asked you?" snapped Doiselet. "Are you a C.G.T. delegate?"

"I thought this was a democracy," the bearded man said.

"Is that what you call democracy," Doiselet said, "where they all grab the microphone from each oother?

"The students called us yesterday," Doiselet went on, "and wanted to come to the plant to express their solidarity. We told them we didn't want them around and would not let them in. That's all we need, *provocuteurs* to start trouble and give the police a chance to move in. After all, we're responsible for the plant. We can't let anything happen here."

The great brotherhood between students and workers turned out to be eclipsed by suspicion. The students complain that the workers aren't even aware of their condition, that they have become a part of the consumer society. Bearing this out, one young worker questioned after the student barricades said: "Sure I sympathize with them, but what about those cars they burned? What if one of those cars belonged to a worker who took two years to pay it off? Who's going to get him another one?"

To the students, the C.G.T. is part of the establishment, a conservative organization that doesn't want to rock the boat, while the Moscow-directed French Communist party is mainly concerned with making sure de Gaulle stays in power.

The workers scorn the students as *fils à papa* — rich men's sons—with nothing to lose, and say they ought to try raising a family in Paris on $170 a month. Before the students start giving us lessons on revolution, they say, they ought to spend some time on an assembly line.

The events in France seemed to confirm Marcuse's theory. The young, marginal members of the society, the radical students and the young workers, revolted against the establishment, which includes not only the Government but the labor unions and the political parties as well. The establishment appropriated the rebellion and brought it back into the traditional framework of labor demands.

GENERAL de Gaulle, upon his return from Rumania, was faced with the task of putting

The Western Democracies

the genie back into the bottle. By allowing the process of Fifth Republic institutions to play itself out normally, he averted a collapse of the regime. He showed that the days when uprooted paving stones and assaults on public buildings were enough to overthrow a Government were yet another facet of France's archaic past. Instead, there was a motion of censure, an Assembly debate, a Presidential television address and the announcement of another referendum.

A conference with labor leaders and management was hurriedly summoned. It had the immediate result of putting a stop to workers' demonstrations and isolating the students. As the last remaining demonstrators, the students risked alienating a growing sector of the population if they kept up their strategy of street violence. Student leaders, realizing that further agitation would contribute to the growth of "the party of fear" who will vote for de Gaulle, called for new tactics: a national student campaign against the Gaullist referendum.

This referendum is a political gamble disguised as a proposal for social and economic reform. De Gaulle has chosen to place his own survival in the balance. By promising to resign if he does not obtain a massive endorsement, he has asked the French voter for a vote of confidence on his personal leadership.

Thus, an end to Gaullism has been made possible, not by street violence and strikes, but because of the General's own decision to seek proof that a majority of the French people still want him in power.

The referendum will be held in a climate of disaffection with the regime, at a time when the spectrum of opposition has been mobilized as never before. It would be an unconditional Gaullist indeed who could comfortably predict victory for the general, particularly since his seven-minute televised address disappointed even his sympathizers. There was no indication from his speech that he has any understanding of the deep psychological motives for the rebellion, or that the discontent went beyond specific demands to question the very nature of the regime.

THE May events were a personal tragedy for a great statesman convinced that history would remember him in part for having made France an orderly nation while he governed. To those who asked what would follow him, he was fond of saying, "The delights of anarchy." Anarchy came instead during his reign, and perhaps that in itself was enough to end the Gaullist era.

Even if de Gaulle wins the referendum and remains in power, it will not be the same power he once had. He can never again govern on the principle that he is the incarnation of France. His policies, based on a mystical belief in French grandeur, do not correspond to the aspirations of French youth.

The orientation of French students is cosmopolitan, not nationalistic. They are a part of the student international, which has common problems, methods and aims. De Gaulle cannot grasp this, as his decision to ban Cohn-Bendit shows. When several thousand students marched on the National Assembly to protest the decision, shouting in chorus, "We are all German Jews," they were doing much more than taking the defense of a student leader. They were repudiating the Gaullist philosophy of the nation.

The students, who can continue to back their demands with street action, are determined to change the old university more profoundly than it has ever been since it was founded in the 13th century by Robert de Sorbon, who liked to say that a final exam should be more severe than the Last Judgment.

Despite his achievements, de Gaulle was unable to change the French historical pattern. It is in the nature of French society to advance through crisis. The last time French labor made any major progress was with the Matignon agreements that followed the lock-ins of 1936. For 32 years after that, there were no top-level negotiations among management, labor and the Government, which operates one-fourth of French industry. One reason the settlement will hurt the French economy is that there is such an accumulation of unmet demands to consider. The other groups who grafted themselves onto student and worker agitation, from circus artists to professional soccer players, had in common the modest aspiration of being associated with the decisions that determine their destiny. But that, although expressed in its simplest form, has been the idea behind every French revolution. ■

June 2, 1968

Shooting of a Striker by Police Is the First During Paris Strife

By LLOYD GARRISON
(Special to The New York Times)

PARIS, June 11—The killing of a demonstrating worker by a policeman at Sochaux today probably came as no great surprise to Frenchmen, but the fact that the man had been killed by police gunfire stunned them.

Until now most people have evidenced surprise that only three persons have been killed during more than a month of clashes between policemen and demonstrators, student and worker.

The Sochaux incident was a tragic exception to the rules that have governed the handling of street violence in France—unlike the United States, where shooting deaths in street rioting have been a frequent occurrence in recent years.

Although club-swinging and rock-throwing and hand-to-hand combat with the police have become the pattern in the demonstrations here, the shooting of 23-year-old Jean Beylot at Sochaux, in eastern France, raised fears that future confrontations could take a far more violent turn.

Until now, the police have used truncheons, tear gas and even concussion grenades. While many policemen are armed with rifles, only the butts had been employed.

Firemen Considered Neutral

Students could tear up the streets, build barricades out of overturned cars, even throw homemade gasoline bombs, but shooting and sniping were out. Firemen, who have often come under attack in the United States, are considered neutral here. In the same category are student stretcher-bearers, usually young medical students, and internes who treat the wounded on both sides.

French policeman have had good excuses to open fire, not only to prevent property damage, but as a measure of self-defense, but until today they had not fired a shot, even in warning.

Thousands on both sides have been injured, some seriously, but there had been only three deaths attributable to the violence. One person was stabbed to death on the edge of a riot zone and the other deaths were more or less accidents.

Despite restraint in using firearms, the mobile French riot police force has an evil reputation, and students have likened it to the Nazi Elite Guard.

The bad reputation of the riot police is partly due to traditional suspicion of "les flics," the cops on the beat. But much of it springs from widespread and well-documented examples of brutality that dates to the force's suppression of demonstrations during the Algerian war and of Communist-led strikes in the wake of World War II.

Merciless Beatings

Young students, workers and passers-by have been beaten mercilessly before being dumped unconscious into the arms of stretcher-bearers. Women are often targets. Beatings often continue once the detained are out of sight.

Tactics have changed on both sides since the first barricades went up after the police forced left-wing student demonstrators from the Sorbonne early in May.

Policemen are quicker to charge under a protective screen of tear gas fired in grenades at long range. Students and workers defend their positions until the last moment, then retreat to yet another barricade.

"In urban guerrilla warfare," one student leader explained, "we never try to take and hold ground. It is hit and run."

He was dressed in a typical street fighter's uniform—levis, motorcycle helmet and heavy gloves—and was armed with an iron pipe and a bag full of construction bolts, and had a garbage-can lid for a shield.

His back pockets were stuffed with wads of cotton soaked in lemon juice to treat his eyes for tear gas burns and a surgical mask hung around his neck.

June 12, 1968

Marcuse Defines His New Left Line

In terms of day-to-day effect, Herbert Marcuse may be the most important philosopher alive. For countless young people, discontented, demonstrating or fulminating, on campus or in the streets, here and abroad, this 70-year-old scholar is the angel of the apocalypse. "Away with the world's mess," his message seems to say. "Let us have a clean, revolutionary, new start." Born in Berlin, a Social Democrat in his youth, Marcuse came to the United States in 1934 and has been a citizen since 1940. His writings, particularly "One-Dimensional Man" (1964), have made him a hero of the New Left. Since 1965, he has been teaching at the University of California in San Diego, where there are constant clamors for his ouster (and where a death threat last summer brought him a spate of publicity). Recently, three staff members of the French magazine L'Express, Jean-Louis Ferrier, Jacques Boetsch and Françoise Giroud, found him on holiday on the Riviera. This translation by Helen Weaver of their conversation sets forth the man and his ideas.

SIX months ago, sir, your name was almost unknown in France. It came to prominence in connection with the student revolt in Berlin, then in connection with student demonstrations in America. Next it was linked with the May demonstrations here. And now, all of a sudden, your last book has become a best-seller. How do you see your own position in relation to the student uprisings all over the world?

MARCUSE: The answer is very simple. I am deeply committed to the movement of "angry students," but I am certainly not their spokesman. It is the press and publicity that have given me this title and have turned me into a rather salable piece of merchandise. I particularly object to the juxtaposition of my name and photograph with those of Che Guevara, Debray, Rudi Dutschke, etc., because these men have truly risked and are still risking their lives in the battle for a more human society, whereas I participate in this battle only through my words and my ideas. It is a fundamental difference.

Still, your words preceded the student action.

MARCUSE: Oh, there are very few students who have really read me, I think. . . .

No doubt, especially in France; but there are also very few students who have chosen a doctrine for their revolt. Can we say that for these students you are the theorist?

MARCUSE: If that is true, I am very happy to hear it. But it's more a case of encounter than of direct influence. . . . In my books, I have tried to make a critique of society—and not only of capitalist society—in terms that avoid all ideology. Even the Socialist ideology, even the Marxist ideology. I have tried to show that contemporary society is a repressive society in all its aspects, that even the comfort, the prosperity, the alleged political and moral freedom are utilized for oppressive ends.

I have tried to show that any change would require a total rejection or, to speak the language of the students, a perpetual confrontation of this society. And that it is not merely a question of changing the institutions but rather, and this is more important, of totally changing human beings in their attitudes, their instincts, their goals, and their values.

This, I think, is the point of contact between my books and the worldwide student movement.

But you feel that they did not need you to arrive at these ideas, is that right?

MARCUSE: One of the essential characteristics of the student movement is that the students apply to reality what has been taught them in the abstract through the work of the masters who have developed the great values of Western civilization. For example, the primacy of natural law over established law, the inalienable right to resist tyranny and all illegitimate authority. . . . They simply cannot comprehend why these great principles should remain on the level of ideas instead of being put into practice. And that is exactly what they are doing.

Do you mean that fundamentally this is a humanist movement?

MARCUSE: They object to that term because according to them, humanism is a bourgeois, personal value. It is a philosophy which is inseparable from a destructive reality. But in their minds there is no point in worrying about the philosophy of a few persons; the point is to bring about a radical change in the society as a whole. So they want no part of the term "humanist."

You know, of course, that here in France we are very far from that "affluent society" whose destruction you propose and which for the moment exists, for better or worse, only in the United States.

MARCUSE: I have been accused of concentrating my critique on American society, and this is quite true. I have said so myself. But this is not only because I know this country better than any other; it is because I believe or I am afraid that American society may become the model for the other capitalist countries, and maybe even for the Socialist countries. I also believe that this route can be avoided, but again, this would presuppose a fundamental change, a total break with the content of the needs and aspirations of people as they are conditioned today.

A break ... that is, a revolution.

MARCUSE: Precisely.

Do you believe in the existence of a revolutionary impulse in the industrial societies?

MARCUSE: You know quite well that the student movement contains a very strong element of anarchy. Very strong. And this is really new.

Anarchy—new?

MARCUSE: In the revolutionary movement of the 20th century, I believe it is new. At least on this scale, it is new. This means that the students have perceived the rigidity of the traditional political organizations, their petrification, the fact that they have stifled any revolutionary impulse. So it is outside of these organizations that the revolt spontaneously occurs.

But spontaneity is not enough. It is also necessary to have an organization. But a new, very flexible kind of organization, one that does not impose rigorous principles, one that allows for movement and initiative. An organization without the "bosses" of the old parties or political groups. This point is very important. The leaders of today are the products of publicity. In the actual movement there are no leaders as there were in the Bolshevik Revolution, for example.

In other words, it is anti-Leninist?

MARCUSE: Yes. In fact, Daniel Cohn-Bendit has severely criticized Leninism-Marxism on this ground.

Does this mean that you rely on anarchism to bring about the revolution you desire?

MARCUSE: No. But I do believe that the anarchist element is a very powerful and very progressive force, and that it is necessary to preserve this element as one of the factors in a larger and more structured process.

And yet you yourself are the opposite of an anarchist.

MARCUSE: That may be true, but I wish you'd tell me why.

Isn't it because your work is dialectical? Your work is very carefully constructed. Do you think of yourself as an anarchist?

MARCUSE: No. I am not an anarchist because I cannot imagine how one can combat a society which is mobilized and organized in its totality against any revolutionary movement, against any effective opposition; I do not see how one can combat such a society, such a concentrated force—military force, police force, etc.—without any organization. It won't work.

No, *it won't work. The Communists will quote you Lenin's analysis of "leftism" which, according to him, was the manifestation of "petits bourgeois overcome with rage before the horrors of capitalism ... a revolutionary attitude which is unstable, unproductive, and susceptible of rapidly changing into submission or apathy or going mad over some bourgeois fad or other."*

MARCUSE: I do not agree. Today's left is far from the reaction of a *petite bourgeoisie* to a revolutionary party, as in Lenin's day. It is the reaction of a revolutionary minority to the established party which the Communist party has become, which is no longer the party of Lenin, but a social democratic party.

If anarchy doesn't work and if the Communist parties are no longer revolutionary, what do you hope for from the student unrest but a superficial disorder which only serves to stiffen the repression?

MARCUSE: All militant opposition takes the risk of increasing repression. This has never been a reason to stop the opposition. Otherwise, all progress would be impossible.

No doubt. But don't you think the notion of the "progress" that might result from a revolution deserves to be better defined? You denounce the subtle restraints that weigh upon the citizens of modern societies. Wouldn't a revolution result in exchanging one series of restraints for another?

MARCUSE: Of course. But there are progressive restraints and reactionary restraints. For example, restraints imposed upon the elemental aggressiveness of man, upon the instinct of destruction, the death instinct, the transformation of this elemental aggressiveness into an energy that could be used for the improvement and protection of life—such restraints would be necessary in the freest society. For example, industries would not be permitted to pollute the air, nor would the "White Citizens Council" be permitted to disseminate racism or to possess firearms, as they are in the United States today. . . . Of course there would be restraints; but they would be progressive ones.

The ones you mention are commonplace enough. The possession of firearms is forbidden in France, and in America it is a survival, not a creation of the affluent society. Let us consider freedom of expression, which means a great deal to us. In the free society which you advocate this freedom disappears, does it not?

MARCUSE: I have written that I believe it is necessary not to extend freedom of the press to movements which are obviously aggressive and destructive, like the Nazi movement. But with the exception of this special case, I am not against freedom of expression....

Even when this means the propagation of racist, nationalist or colonialist ideas?

MARCUSE: Here my answer is no. I am not in favor of granting free expression to racist, anti-Semitic, neo-Nazi movements. Certainly not; because the interval between the word and the act is too brief today. At least in American society, the one with which I am familiar. You know the famous statement of Justice Holmes, that civil rights can be withdrawn in a single case: the case of immediate danger. Today this immediate danger exists everywhere.

Can't this formula be turned against you in connection with students, revolutionaries, or Communists?

MARCUSE: It always is. And my answer is always the same. I do not believe that the Communism conceived by the great Marxist theorists is, by its very nature, aggressive and destructive; quite the contrary.

But has it not become so under certain historical circumstances? Isn't there something aggressive and destructive about the Soviet policy toward Hungary in 1956, or toward Czechoslovakia today?

MARCUSE: Yes. But that isn't Communism, it is Stalinism. I would certainly use all possible restraints to oppose Stalinism, but that is not Communism.

WHY *do you criticize America more severely for its deviations from the democratic ideal than you do Communism for its deviations from the Communist ideal?*

MARCUSE: I am just as critical of these deviations in Communist countries. However, I believe that the institutions and the whole culture of the capitalism of monopolies militate against the development of a democratic socialism.

And you believe that one day we shall see an ideal Communist society?

MARCUSE: Well, at least there is the theory. There is the whole Marxist theory. That exists. And there is also Cuba. There is China. There is the Communist policy during the heroic period of the Bolshevik Revolution.

Do you mean that Communist societies do these reprehensible things in spite of themselves? That the Soviet Union invaded Czechoslovakia in spite of herself?

MARCUSE: In spite of the idea of Communism, not in spite of the Soviet Union. The invasion of Czechoslovakia is one of the most reprehensible acts in the history of Socialism. It is a brutal expression of the policy of power that has long been practiced by the Soviet Union in political and economic competition with capitalism. I believe that many of the reprehensible things that happen in the Communist countries are the result of competitive coexistence with capitalism, while poverty continues to reign in the Communist countries.

HERE *you are touching upon an important point. It does not seem possible to reduce poverty without an extremely coercive organization. So once again we find that restraint is necessary.*

MARCUSE: Certainly. But here, too, there can be progressive restraint. Take a country in which poverty coexists with luxury, waste, and comfort for the privileged.... It is necessary to curb this waste to eliminate poverty, misery, and inequality. These are necessary restraints.

Unfortunately, there is no economic correlation. It is not the curbing of waste that eliminates poverty, it is production.

MARCUSE: That's true. But my point is that the restraints that certainly exist in, say, Cuba, are not the same as those that are felt in capitalist economies.

Cuba is perhaps not a very good exmple of a successful Socialist economy, since the country is totally dependent on daily deliveries of Soviet petroleum. If the Soviet Union were to stop those deliveries for two weeks ...

MARCUSE: I don't know what would happen. But even under these conditions of dependence on the Soviet Union, Cuba has made tremendous progress.

In comparison with what she was that's certainly true. Have you been there?

MARCUSE: No. I can't get authorization from the Americans.

Why do you despair of all progress within the framework of the American democracy?

MARCUSE: Do you really think that democracy is making progress in the United States?

Compared with the period of "The Grapes of Wrath," yes.

MARCUSE: I disagree. Look at the elections, the candidates for the Presidency of the United States, fabricated by the huge political machines. And who can find the differences between these candidates? If that's democracy, it's a farce. The people have said nothing and they have been asked nothing.

True. But at the same time thousands of young Americans have shown in recent months that they were against the war in Vietnam, that they were willing to work to eliminate the ghettos, to act in the political sphere.

MARCUSE: This movement is encountering a more and more effective repression.

Do you feel, then, that we are witnessing a definite obstruction of American society?

MARCUSE: The answer is a little more complicated than that. There is a possibility of progress toward democracy in the United States, but only through movements that are increasingly militant and radical. Not at all within the limits of the established process. This process is a game and the American students have lost interest in playing this game, they have lost confidence in this allegedly democratic process.

DO *you believe in the possibility of revolution in the United States?*

MARCUSE: Absolutely not. Not at all.

Why not?

MARCUSE: Because there is no collaboration between the students and the workers, not even on the level on which it occurred in France in May and June.

In that case, what role do you attribute to the students?

MARCUSE: They are militant minorities who can articulate the needs and aspirations of the silent masses. But by themselves they are not revolutionaries, and nobody says they are. The students know that very well.

The Western Democracies

So their only role is to reveal?

MARCUSE: Yes. And this is very interesting. Here as well as in the United States, the students can truly be called spokesmen.

And who will make the revolution in America, in Germany, in France, if the students do not make contact with the working class?

MARCUSE: I cannot imagine. In spite of everything that has been said, I still cannot imagine a revolution without the working class.

The drawback—at least from the viewpoint of revolution—is that the working class is more interested in belonging to the affluent society than in destroying it, although it also hopes to modify certain aspects of it. At least this is the case in France. Is it different in other countries?

MARCUSE: You say that in France the working class is not yet integrated but that it would like to be. . . . In the United States it is integrated and it wants to be. This means that revolution postulates first of all the emergence of a new type of man with needs and aspirations that are qualitatively different from the aggressive and repressive needs and aspirations of established societies. It is true that the working class today shares in large measure the needs and aspirations of the dominant classes, and that without a break with the present content of needs, revolution is inconceivable.

So it will not happen tomorrow, it seems. It is easier to seize power than to change the needs of men. But what do you mean by aggressive needs?

MARCUSE: For example, the need to continue the competitive struggle for existence—the need to buy a new car every two years, the need to buy a new television set, the need to watch television five or six hours a day. This is already a vital need for a very large share of the population, and it is an aggressive and repressive need.

Aggressive to watch television? But it would seem on the face of it to be a passive activity.

MARCUSE: Are you familiar with the programs on American television? Nothing but shooting. And they always stimulate the consumption that subjects people to the capitalist mode of production.

There can be a different use of television.

MARCUSE: Of course. All this is not the fault of television, the fault of the automobile, the fault of technology in general. It is the fault of the miserable use that is made of technological progress. Television could just as well be used to reeducate the population.

In what sense? To persuade people that they do not need cars or television sets or refrigerators or washing machines?

MARCUSE: Yes, if this merchandise prevents the liberation of the serfs from their "voluntary servitude."

Wouldn't this create some problems for the people who work in the factories where they make cars, refrigerators, etc?

MARCUSE: They will shut down for a week or two. Everyone will go to the country. And then the real work will begin, the work of abolishing poverty, the work of abolishing inequality, instead of the work of waste which is performed in the society of consumption. In the United States, for example, General Motors and Ford, instead of producing private cars, will produce cars for public transportation, so that public transportation can become human.

IT will take a lot of television programs to persuade the working class to make a revolution that will reduce their wages, do away with their cars, and reduce their consumption. And in the meantime there is reason to fear that things may take a different turn, that all the people affected by the economic difficulties may potentially furnish a fascist mass. Doesn't fascism always come out of an economic crisis?

MARCUSE: That's true. The revolutionary process always begins with and in an economic crisis. But this crisis would offer two possibilities: the so-called neo-fascist possibility, in which the masses turn toward a regime that is much more authoritarian and repressive, and the opposite possibility, that the masses may see an opportunity to construct a free society in which such crises would be avoidable. There are always two possibilities. One cannot, for fear of seeing the first materialize, stop hoping and working for the second through the education of the masses. And not only by words, but by actions.

For the present, aren't you afraid that these actions, especially when they are violent, will produce the opposite effect, and that the society will become even more repressive in order to defend itself?

MARCUSE: Unfortunately, that is a very real possibility. But that is not sufficient reason to give up. On the contrary, we must increase the opposition, reinforce it. There will always be privileged classes which will oppose any fundamental change.

It is not the privileged classes which have manifested their opposition in France. It is the middle class and part of the working class. The privileged classes have been content to exploit the dissatisfaction.

MARCUSE: Next you'll tell me that the revolutionary militants are responsible for the reaction. In Germany they are already saying that neo-Nazism is the result of student action.

In France, the result of the elections is incontestably the response of the majority of the country to the May movement, which frightened them.

MARCUSE: Well, we must fight that fear!

Do *you think that one can fight fear with violence?*

MARCUSE: Violence, I confess, is very dangerous for those who are the weakest. But first we should examine our terminology. People are always talking about violence, but they forget that there are different kinds of violence, with different functions. There is a violence of aggression and a violence of defense. There is a violence of police forces or armed forces or of the Ku Klux Klan, and there is a violence in the opposition to these aggressive manifestations of violence.

The students have said that they are opposing the violence of society, legal violence, institutionalized violence. Their violence is that of defense. They have said this, and I believe it is true.

Thanks to a kind of political linguistics, we never use the word violence to describe the actions of the police, we never use the word violence to describe the actions of the Special Forces in Vietnam. But the word is readily applied to the actions of students who defend themselves from the police, burn cars or chop down trees. This is a typical example of political linguistics, utilized as a weapon by the established society.

There has been a lot of fuss in France over the burned automobiles. But nobody gets at all excited about the enormous number of automobiles destroyed every day on the highways, not only in France but all over the world. The number of deaths in highway accidents in America is 50,000 per year.

And between 13,000 and 14,000 in France.

MARCUSE: But that doesn't count. Whereas one burned automobile is terrible, it is the supreme crime against property. But the other crime doesn't count!

How do you explain this phenomenon?

MARCUSE: Because the other crime has a function in production. It is profitable to society.

But people don't kill themselves to make a profit. How can you separate the society from the people who compose it? Society is not some special tribunal of people who meet in secret and say to each other: we are going to see to it that people kill themselves on the highways so that we can sell a lot of cars! Society is everyone, and everyone consents. You have a car yourself and you drive it . . . .

MARCUSE: But there is a very good reason for all this. It is that this society, at the stage it is at, must mobilize our aggressive instincts to an exorbitant degree to counteract the frustrations imposed by the daily struggle for existence. The little man who works eight hours a day in the factory, who does an inhuman and stupefying work, on the weekend sits behind a huge machine much more powerful than himself, and there he can utilize all his antisocial aggressiveness. And this is absolutely necessary. If this aggressiveness were not sublimated in the speed and power of the automobile, it might be directed against the dominant powers.

This seems to be what is happening in spite of the weekend traffic!

MARCUSE: No. It is only the students who are revolting and crying, "We are all German Jews!" that is, We are all oppressed.

And why do you think this diffuse oppression is more precisely experienced and formulated by the students? Why is it that the torch of revolution which seemed to be wavering, to say the least,

326

in the industrial countries, has passed into their hands?

MARCUSE: It is because they are not integrated. This is a very interesting point. In the United States, for example, there is a vast difference in behavior between the students and teachers in the social sciences and the humanities on the one hand and the natural sciences on the other. The majority comes from the first group. In France, I believe it is not the same....

No, it isn't.

MARCUSE: And in the study of these sciences they have learned a great deal. The nature of power, the existence of the forces behind the facts. They have also become very much aware of what goes on in societies. And this awareness is absolutely impossible for the vast majority of the population, which is, in some sense, inside the social machine. If you will, the students are playing the role of the professional members of the intelligentsia before the French Revolution.

You know that Tocqueville denounced the role of writers in the revolution of 1789, precisely because they were on the fringe of political life, lacking experience in public life, constructing arbitrary schemata.

MARCUSE: Magnificent! And here is my answer to Tocqueville. I say that it is precisely *because* the students and intellectuals have no experience in what is today called politics that they are in the avant-garde. Because the political experience today is the experience of a game that is both faked and bloody.

POLITICS *has always been a bloody game which kings and heads of state played among themselves. Do you mean that today it is faked because the people have the illusion of participating in this game?*

MARCUSE: Yes. Who really participates in politics? Who takes part in it? Any important decision is always made by a very small minority. Take the war in Vietnam. Who really participated in that decision? A dozen people, I would say. Afterwards the Government solicits and receives the support of the population. But in the case of Vietnam, even Congress did not get a chance to learn the facts. No, the people do not participate in decisions. We do not participate. Only in secondary decisions.

But if the American Government stops the war tomorrow—they certainly will some day—won't it be as a result of public opinion? Of the revolt in public opinion?

MARCUSE: Precisely. And who is responsible for this change in public opinion?

American television.

MARCUSE: No, no! First there were the students. Opposition to the war began in the universities.

THE BEATLES ON 'REVOLUTION'

In their new hit song of that name, the innovative rock group takes to the political stump—with words (see below) by John Lennon, right, and music by Paul McCartney.

*You say you want a revolution,
Well you know,
We all want to change the world.
You tell me that it's evolution,
Well you know,
We all want to change the world.
But when you talk about destruction,
Don't you know that you can count me out.
Don't you know it's gonna be alright, alright, alright.
Alright, alright, alright, alright, alright, alright, alright, alright.*

*You say you got a real solution,
Well you know,
We'd all love to see the plan.
You—ask me for a contribution,
Well you know,
We're doing what we can.
But when you want money for people with minds that hate,
All I can tell you is brother you have to wait.
Don't you know its gonna be alright, alright, alright.
Alright, alright, alright, alright, alright, alright, alright alright.*

*You say you'll change the constitution,
Well you know,
We all want to change your head.
You tell me it's the institution,
Well you know,
You better free your mind instead.
But if you go carrying pictures of Chairman Mao,
You ain't going to make it with anyone anyhow.
Don't you know it's gonna be alright, alright, alright.
Alright, alright, alright, alright, alright, alright, alright, alright.*

Copyright © 1968 Northern Songs, Ltd. Used by permission All Rights Reserved

There is a slight contradiction in what you say, since you have written that this opposition is tolerated insofar as it has no power.

MARCUSE: It may have the power to alter American policy, but not the system itself. The framework of society will remain the same.

And to try to destroy this society which is guilty of violence, you feel that violence is both legitimate and desirable. Does this mean that you think it impossible to evolve peacefully and within the democratic framework toward a nonrepressive, freer society?

MARCUSE: The students have said it: a revolution is always just as violent as the violence it combats. I believe they are right.

But you still think it is possible, in spite of the judgment of Freud, to whom you refer frequently in "Eros and Civilization," to create a free society. Doesn't this betray a remarkable optimism?

MARCUSE: I am optimistic, because I believe that never in the history of humanity

The Western Democracies

have the resources necessary to create a free society existed to such a degree. I am pessimistic because I believe that the established societies—capitalist society in particular—are totally organized and mobilized against this possibility.

Perhaps because people are afraid of freedom?

MARCUSE: Many people are afraid of freedom, certainly. They are conditioned to be afraid of it. They say to themselves: if people only had to work, say, five hours a week, what would they do with this freedom?

This is a condition which is not related to capitalism. The whole Judeo-Christian civilization is founded on work and is the product of work.

MARCUSE: Yes and no. Look at feudal society. That was truly a Christian society and yet work was not a value in it; on the contrary.

Because there were slaves, villagers. It was very convenient for the feudal lords.

MARCUSE: There were slaves, but the system of values was altogether different. And it was within this system that the culture was created. There is no such thing as bourgeois culture. Every genuine bourgeois culture is against the bourgeoisie.

In other words, we should return to the feudal system, but with machines taking the place of the slaves?

MARCUSE: We must have machines in place of slaves, but without returning to the feudal system. It would be the end of work, and at the same time the end of the capitalist system. Marx saw this in that famous passage where he says that with technological progress and automation, man is separated from the instruments of production, is dissociated from material production, and acts simply as a free subject, experimenting with the material possibilities of the machines, etc. But this would also mean the end of an economy founded on exchange value. Because the product would no longer be worth anything as merchandise. And this is the specter that haunts the established society.

Do you regard work, effort, as a repressive value?

MARCUSE: It all depends on its purpose. Effort is not repressive by itself. Effort in art, in every creative act, in love. . . .

Would you work if you were not obliged to do so?

MARCUSE: Certainly. I work if I am not obliged to do so.

Do you consider yourself a free man?

MARCUSE: Me? I believe that nobody is free in this society. Nobody.

Have you been psychoanalyzed?

MARCUSE: Never. Do you think I need to be?

It's quite possible, but that's beside the point. What seems curious is that you have made such a thorough study of the work of Freud and his views on the inevitably repressive quality of all civilization without asking yourself about your own obstacles to the exercise of your personal freedom.

MARCUSE: I have discussed Freud only on the level of theory, not on the level of therapy.

DON'T *you give European civilization any credit for being able to create its own values in reaction to American civilization while at the same time appropriating the positive element in that civilization, that is, the technical progress which you yourself have said is absolutely fundamental to the liberation of man?*

MARCUSE: It is almost impossible to speak of a European civilization today. Perhaps it is even impossible to speak of a Western civilization. I believe that Eastern civilization and Western civilization are assimilating each other at an ever increasing rate. And the European civilization of today has already absorbed much of American civilization. So it seems impossible to imagine a European civilization separated from the influence of America. Except, perhaps, in a few very isolated sectors of intellectual culture. Poetry, for example.

So you think the battle is lost. That we are Americans?

MARCUSE: We mustn't say it is lost. It is possible to change, to utilize the possibilities of American civilization for the good of humanity. We must utilize everything that enables us to facilitate daily life, to make it more tolerable. . . . We could already, today, end air pollution, for example. The means exist.

What role do you envision for art in the free society of which you dream, since art is by definition denial, challenge?

MARCUSE: I am not a prophet. In the affluent society, art is an interesting phenomenon. On the one hand, it rejects and accuses the established society; on the other hand, it is offered and sold on the market. There is not a single artistic style, however avant-garde, that does not sell. This means that the function of art is problematic, to say the least. There has been talk of the end of art, and there really is among the artists a feeling that art today has no function. There are museums, concerts, paintings in the homes of the rich, but art no longer has a function. So it wants to become an essential part of reality, to change reality.

Look at the graffiti, for example. For me, this is perhaps the most interesting aspect of the events of May, the coming together of Marx and André Breton. Imagination in power: that is truly revolutionary. It is new and revolutionary to try to translate into reality the most advanced ideas and values of the imagination. This proves that people have learned an important lesson: that truth is not only in rationality, but just as much and perhaps more in the imaginary.

The imaginary is above all the only realm where man's freedom has always been complete, where nothing has succeeded in curbing it. Dreams bear witness to this.

MARCUSE: Yes. And this is why I believe that the student rebellion, whatever its immediate results, is a real turning point in the development of contemporary society.

Because the students are reintegrating the imaginary with reality?

MARCUSE: Yes. There is a graffito which I like very much which goes, "Be realists, demand the impossible." That is magnificent. And another: "Watch out, ears have walls." That is realistic!

You have no desire to go back to Germany?

MARCUSE: I don't think so. Only to give lectures. But I like the German students very much, they are terrific!

Have they succeeded any better than the others in making contact with the working class?

MARCUSE: No. Their collaboration has been even more precarious.

Is it true that in the United States you received threats from the Ku Klux Klan?

MARCUSE: They were signed Ku Klux Klan, but I don't think it was they who sent them.

Is it true that you moved out of your house following these threats?

MARCUSE: Yes. Not in a panic, but I did leave. Frankly, I wasn't afraid. My students came and surrounded the house with their cars to protect me. . . . In one sense, they were right in thinking that there was a risk.

And do you feel that your life in the United States can continue, now that your notoriety has put you in the public eye?

MARCUSE: I'm not sure, not at all sure. At the university there's no problem. But universities are always oases.

Do *you think that the American university as it is set up now can be a model for the French university, for example?*

MARCUSE: One must distinguish among American universities. The large universities are always sanctuaries for free thought and a rather solid education. Take mine, for example, the University of California in San Diego. This is probably the most reactionary area in the United States—a large military base, a center of so-called defense industry, retired colonels and admirals. I have no difficulty with the university, the administration, or my colleagues. But I have a great deal of difficulty at the hands of the community, the good middle-class townspeople. No problems with the students. Relations between professors and students are, I think, much more informal than here and in Germany.

In this respect, you know, there really is an egalitarian tradition in the United States. The sanctity of the professor does not exist. It is the American materialism that prevents it. The professor is a salaried man who has studied, who has learned certain things, and who teaches them; he is not at all a mythical personage identified with the Father, not at all. His political position depends upon his position in the university hierarchy. If you reach a permanent position it is practically im-

"I tried to make a critique of society in terms that avoid all ideology"

possible to fire you. My own situation is precarious, and I am very curious to find out whether I will be able to retain my position at the university.

What you say is very serious. If freedom of expression no longer exists in the United States, it will no longer exist anywhere... or perhaps in England?

MARCUSE: Yes. England may turn out to be one of the last liberal countries. The democracy of the masses is not favorable to nonconformist intellectuals....

This is the crux of the matter. You have often been criticized for wanting to establish a Platonic dictatorship of the elite. Is this correct?

MARCUSE: There is a very interesting passage in John Stuart Mill, who was not exactly an advocate of dictatorship. He says that in a civilized society educated people must have political prerogatives to oppose the emotions, attitudes and ideas of the uneducated masses.

I have never said that it was necessary to establish a Platonic dictatorship because there is no philosopher who is capable of doing this. But to be perfectly frank, I don't know which is worse: a dictatorship of politicians, managers and generals, or a dictatorship of intellectuals.

Personally, if this is the choice, I would prefer the dictatorship of the intellectuals, if there is no possibility of a genuine free democracy. Unfortunately this alternative does not exist at present.

THE dictatorship of the intellectuals must first be established to educate and reform the masses, after which, in a remote future, when people have changed, democracy and freedom will reign. Is that it?

MARCUSE: Not a true dictatorship, but a more important role for intellectuals, yes. I think that the resentment of the worker movement against the intellectuals is one of the reasons why this movement has stopped today.

The dictatorship of the intellectuals is rather disturbing, to the extent that intellectuals often become cruel because they are afraid of action.

MARCUSE: Is that really so? There is only one example in history of a cruel intellectual: Robespierre.

And Saint-Just.

MARCUSE: We must compare the cruelty of Robespierre and Saint-Just with the cruelty and the bureaucratized violence of an Eichmann. Or even with the institutionalized violence of modern societies. Nazi cruelty is cruelty as a technique of administration. The Nazis were not intellectuals. With intellectuals, cruelty and violence are always much more immediate, shorter, less cruel. Robespierre did not use torture. Torture is not an essential aspect of the French Revolution.

You know intellectuals: they are not, or are only slightly, in touch with reality. Can you imagine a society functioning under their direct government? What effect would this have on trains running on time, for example? Or on organizing production?

MARCUSE: If you identify reality with established reality you are right. But intellectuals do not or should not identify reality with established reality. Given the imagination and rationality of true intellectuals, we can expect great things. In any case, the famous dictatorship of the intellectuals has never existed.

Perhaps because an intellectual is by his very nature an individualist. Lenin said this, too. What form of dictatorship do you prefer? One that operates directly as is the case in the Soviet Union, for example, or one that adopts the mask of democracy?

MARCUSE: It is absolutely necessary not to isolate a given situation from its tendencies for development. There is a social and political repression which can foster human progress, which can lead toward a true democracy and a true freedom. And there is a repression which does the opposite. I have always said that I utterly reject Stalinian repression and the repressive policy of Communism, although I recognize that the Socialist base of these countries contains the possibility of development toward liberalization and ultimately toward a free society.

It is a question of not being too skeptical about the end....

MARCUSE: I am very skeptical about the end, in both cases.

Do you think that man can be free and at the same time believe in the existence of God?

MARCUSE: The liberation of man depends neither on God nor on the nonexistence of God. It is not the idea of God which has been an obstacle to human liberation, but the use that has been made of the idea of God.

But why has this use been made of it?

MARCUSE: From the beginning, religion has been allied with the ruling strata of society. In the case of Christianity, not from the very beginning, but still, rather early on.

In short, one must belong to the ruling strata of society! That is the sad conclusion that one could cynically draw from what you say. All the rest is adventure, more or less doomed to failure. Of course, one can prefer adventure, need adventure, and dream of being Guevara, in Paris or Berlin.

MARCUSE: Guevara was not adventure; it was the alliance between adventure and revolutionary politics. If revolution does not contain an element of adventurism, it is worthless. All the rest is organization, labor unions, social democracy, the establishment. Adventure is always beyond....

What you call adventurism, others call romanticism....

MARCUSE: Call it what you will. Adventure is transcendence of the given reality. Those who no longer wish to contain the revolution within the framework of the given reality. Call it what you will—adventurism, romanticism, imagination—it is an element necessary to all revolution.

No doubt. But it would seem that a concrete analysis of the situation in the countries in which one wants to make a revolution is also not an entirely negligible element. Provided, of course, that one wants to bring it off, and not merely to dream. One more question. You denounce as a painful form of oppression and one from which we suffer the deprivation of solitude and silence inflicted on us by modern society. Isn't this a plague that is just as characteristic of collectivist societies?

MARCUSE: First of all, we must eliminate the concept of collectivist societies. There are many modes of collectivization. There is a collectivism that is based on true human solidarity. There is a collectivism that is based on an authoritarian regime that is imposed on people. The destruction of autonomy, silence and solitude occurs in the so-called free societies as well as in the so-called collectivist societies. The decisive problem is to determine whether the limitations imposed on the individual are imposed in order to further the domination and indoctrination of the masses, or, on the contrary, in the interest of human progress.

It would be interesting to learn which noises are the progressive ones, if only so as to bear them with a smile. Sorry... we were being facetious.

MARCUSE: So was I. There is no free society without silence, without the internal and external space of solitude in which individual freedom can develop. If there is neither private life, nor autonomy, nor silence, nor solitude in a Socialist society—well, it is very simple: it is not a Socialist society! Not yet.

October 27, 1968

The Western Democracies

Sartre Accuses the Intellectuals of Bad Faith

PARIS.

JEAN-PAUL SARTRE has a knack for making news. Long considered France's greatest intellectual, a man who has influenced two generations of writers all over the world, Sartre has also contributed to the developing social consciousness of the post-World War II era through his determined, if at times erratic, political commitment. Until the 1956 Russian invasion of Hungary, his political activity was closely allied to that of the French Communist party; he participated in most of the period's antiwar and anti-American demonstrations, and was a regular contributor to the Communist-sponsored peace congresses.

After 1956, when he openly denounced the Soviet invasion, Sartre's position was no less vehement but much more independent. He played an important role in the French anti-Vietnam-war movement, and was so active during the Algerian war that French right-wing extremists tried to kill him various times. Sartre also wrote, spoke, and demonstrated against the regime of Charles de Gaulle, and led numerous protests against the U.S. Vietnam war. In 1966 and 1967, he was president of the International War Crimes Tribunal, which condemned the U.S. for genocide in Vietnam.

For all his political acumen, however, Sartre was caught by surprise by the events of May, 1968, when French students launched a disorganized rebellion against de Gaulle which almost led to his overthrow. Sartre reacted by justifying youth's rejection of traditional values, and became what the French call a *gauchiste*, meaning a militant semispontaneous leftist. In effect, Sartre took the position that anything on the far left goes, hence gave his support to any group that found itself too far afield of French traditional left-wing politics to benefit from the country's civil-liberties policies.

He became "responsible editor" of various newspapers which the police tried to suppress, chaired "people's courts" wherever the left attempted to focus attention on what it considered official injustice, and lent his name to any new organization whose avowed purpose was to stimulate revolution without the participation of the French Communist party. In June, he was finally arrested and indicted for libeling the police. The trial is expected to open soon.

Living very modestly in a one-room apartment off Montparnasse, Sartre collects no possessions save books, and gives away most of his sizable income to needy left-wing writers or to the struggling *gauchiste* press. He insists that the committed intellectual must never use his status for special privileges and he claims that the only relevant writing possible today is the political tract.

Yet he himself has just finished a 2,000-page work on Flaubert, and though he used that great 19th-century novelist as a tool to dissect France's *bourgeoisie*, the two-volume opus is certainly in contradiction to his stated position. Sartre also made news recently for his open break with Fidel Castro over the case of the Cuban poet Heberto Padilla, who had been jailed temporarily for his "counterrevolutionary attitudes." Though valiantly insisting that all genuine revolutions must honor, indeed defend, creative freedom, Sartre's position on Padilla actually reaffirmed what he had tried to deny—namely, that intellectuals have a privileged status.—JOHN GERASSI

Mr. Gerassi is an American journalist now living in Europe. His books include, as editor, "The Coming of the New International"; he is currently at work on a biography of Sartre.

GERASSI: *In a few days, part one of your massive work on Flaubert will be published. Yet you have often told me in recent times that the only viable activity for the intellectual today is the political tract. Is that not a contradiction? And would you explain what you mean by viable activity?*

SARTRE: My book on Flaubert may, indeed, be a form of petty-bourgeois escapism vis-à-vis the exigencies of the times, though it is a very political work. What I mean is simply that the status of the intellectual has changed. He must now write with the masses, and through them, therefore, put his technical knowledge at their disposal. In other words, his privileged status is over. Today it is sheer bad faith, hence counterrevolutionary, for the intellectual to dwell on his own problems, instead of realizing that he is an intellectual because of the masses and through them; therefore, that he owes his knowledge to them and must be with them and in them: he must be dedicated to work for their problems, not his own.

In my case, as you know, I have put myself on the line in various actions. For example, I worked for the people's tribunal of Lens [where rebellious workers were charged with various crimes], put my skill at the service of the people's prosecution, explained in tracts why it was the bosses and directors of the Renin-Lietard firm who were the true criminals, wrote out the judgment, etc.

I wrote this material but I was only the mouthpiece of the miners. Also, I write articles for revolutionary newspapers, such as J'Accuse, even though I may not be in total accord with the paper's ideology. I've lent my name to any revolutionary paper that requested it. Why? Well, of course, at the beginning it's part of the star system, letting my name be used to help launch such papers. Simone de Beauvoir, as you know, has done the same, but the objective is to collectivize these papers, to eliminate names altogether, and eventually to create newspapers written by masses who fight, the role of the editorial collective being only to help, technically, to put these papers together and publish them. Each time there is a seizure of a plant by workers, for example, our job is to make sure that it is the workers themselves who explain why they did it, what they felt and learned from it. Our job is to help them, etc., but never interpreting them, never telling them what they should say. Self-determination is not a ballot-box principle; it's a political act which must lead to power of the people.

In what way does this differ fundamentally from the task of the Communist party which has always had intellectuals but is based on workers?

The Communist party has always separated the intellectual from the masses. Its principal mode of operation is the cell, of which there are two kinds—the enterprise cell and the neighborhood cell. In both cases, the intellectuals, either because they do not work in the enterprise, the factory, or because they do not live in working-class neighborhoods, are separated from the masses. In the past, during the revolutions of 1848 and 71, for example, there were intellectuals who integrated themselves with the masses and, indeed, earned the right to speak in their name. But the Communist party has always been opposed to such liaison, which would have de-bourgeoisied the intellectual, and so has kept them separate. And, you know, I am convinced now that, for all the obvious difficulty (the difference in language, to name the most obvious), such integration is very possible.

There's the difference in life style too, isn't there?

Yes, but, you know, the masses never

(Continued)

TERRORISM AND THE STATE TODAY

really hold that against you. I've noticed that in my own case many times. It's that I am with workers in actions that counts, not the fact that I may live differently and better in Paris. No, language is a much more serious problem. Intellectuals take for granted all sorts of propositions which workers do not.

You know it's much easier for a philosopher to explain a new concept to another philosopher than to a child. Why? Because the child, with all its naiveté, asks the real questions. So do workers. To reach them, we have to use a different language, not talk down to them—that always fails—but use a language that is honest, by which I mean we have to use words which are not loaded with a past. We have to demystify our words. If you look at Rouge [the newspaper of the Fourth International in Paris], for example, you will understand what I mean: it's unreadable, full of Marxist concepts, each with a past, half words whose meaning is clear only to the initiated. What we want to create is a language that explains the necessary political realities in a way that everyone can understand.

But are such newspapers, no matter how simply written, read by the masses? It doesn't seem to me to be the case for J'Accuse, and I know it's not the case with leftist newspapers in England or the U.S.

The only solution to that is militant distribution. A committed newspaper must show its commitment not only in its content but in its distribution as well. It is not enough to plunk a pile of papers at the vendor, or wage a subscription campaign. The paper must be distributed in the factories, in the working-class neighborhoods, in the ghettos—by militants going up to individual workers. In France, this is being done by La Cause du Peuple and J'Accuse. What's more, the militant distributors must not just sell or give away the paper but talk about it, ask the worker what he thinks about it, and why it is the reader who must ultimately make the paper. Say the paper talks about the seizure of a plant in Grenoble, in articles written by workers who participated in the seizure, well then, the militant distributor asks the worker in front of the Renault plant at Billancourt to read it, comment on the article, write about it or talk into a tape recorder, which then becomes an article for the next issue. The militant distributor, who is inevitably an intellectual at first, thus operates merely as a sort of mediator between the workers of Grenoble and Billancourt.

That may be possible in France where the workers are politicized, have a class conscience, but in the U.S., where this is not the case, where, in fact, many unionized workers are against you, would the tactic be appropriate?

I would say the tactic should be the same, though the risks are different. In the U.S. your distributors may be beaten up more often. But that happens here in France, too. Our people are often roughed up, sometimes very, very seriously, by the goon squads of the C.G.T. [General Confederation of Workers—which is run by the Communist party]. That's why it is my job to do things like that, as there is more of a chance for me to get to talk to workers than a student.

You would say that big-name intellectuals in America should do the same?

Absolutely. It is very easy to denounce the war in Vietnam by signing petitions or marching in a parade with 20,000 comrades. But it doesn't accomplish one-millionth what could be accomplished if all your big name intellectuals went into the ghettos, into the Oakland port, to the war factories, and risked being manhandled by the roughs of the maritime union. In my view, the intellectual who does all his fighting from an office is counterrevolutionary today, no matter what he writes.

Are you ready to risk your own skin in this tactic?

Yes, and I have—at Renault, in Lens, in Paris streets. Of course, I am fully aware that it is easier for me as my name, my prestige, protects me somewhat, always. But would this not be the case of your big-name intellectuals too? Usually, wherever you go, wherever I appear, there is a group of people for you, a group against, and a majority, who are just curious, usually neutral, perhaps amused. It's to them you must talk. Depending on the relationship of these forces, the risk is minimal or great. But let's face it, had they beaten me up, there would have been certain political advantages from that, no?

But a big-name intellectual such as you can have access to the straight press which is read by the masses. Why not then take advantage of that?

Careful. The masses do not read the straight press to be informed but to be entertained. That's why they read L'Aurore here and—what?—The Daily News in New York.

Should they read a leftist newspaper, they may not agree with it, they may in fact be totally against, but they know the object is to inform, not entertain. The concept of freedom of the press is a bourgeois concept. The masses don't worry about such things, and you will never see workers protesting press censorship, here in France at least, and I would conjecture that neither in the U.S. would masses wage a campaign against the censorship of reports from Vietnam. The masses know instinctively that the press belongs to the *bourgeoisie*, not to the masses. Freedom of the press is capitalist freedom of the press, which means that, perhaps unconsciously, the masses view the press as the enemy. Hence they don't expect from it anything that is really meaningful in terms of their own lives. This was not true, of course, in Czechoslovakia, where the workers and students were united in demanding a press that would inform them as their own, that is, as a socialist press.

But in a capitalist country the straight press doesn't really count, so why write for it? As for the independent left-wing weeklies or monthlies, they are not read by the masses, only by the leftist *bourgeoisie*. In general, I will write, here in France at least, only for newspapers that are militant, even if I don't always agree with their ideological position—that is, newspapers whose staff understands that their role is to break the vicious circle by going to the masses militantly, and that doesn't mean hawking the newspapers in front of the cafes.

And you think these papers will be read by the masses and not intellectuals?

Yes. But the papers have to be better organized. Also, there are too many of them, one for each little group.

Isn't that a question of the sectarianism of the left?

Well, yes, but the left is always sectarian at first. However, here in France, I think we can detect some significant progress. I don't think that the Trotskyists of the Fourth International and the Maoist groups will ever be able to work together consistently, yet in Secours Rouge [Red Aid, a *gauchiste* organization], which was begun by 20 so-called personalities, important changes are taking place. The personalities are on the way out—for example, I have resigned from the directorate—and are being replaced by militants from the base. Some of the independent Trotskyists and the Maoists are working well together. Regional chapters are

331

bringing workers and intellectuals together efficiently. True, whenever students join in, fights break out. But, by and large, Secours Rouge is developing into a united front of militant leftists. For the May 1 Paris march, they brought together some 30,000 people, while the Communist party mustered only 70,000, a significant shift in the relationship of forces.

Considering the many defeats the movement and you personally have suffered over the last three decades, how do you manage to stay optimistic?

I do what I believe an intellectual should do today, but that doesn't mean I'm optimistic. I'm in the system and I'm forced to stay in it, but I also feel the revolution must triumph. This is a choice. It is not necessarily evident. And if it does triumph, then what? Will the human condition be cleansed of exploitation, alienation, and all that we find disgusting in this society? I'm not so sure. All I hope is that if we are successful in bringing about a revolution without terror, then we'll be able to face things squarely, that is, look at our oppressive past, all the ideas imposed on us by machines but which today we consider—falsely—our own, and deal with them together.

A revolution without terror, yes, but is it conceivable? Can we really expect a successful revolution without revanche? Can we expect the winners to forget the brutality, the viciousness, the tortures of those in power today? Can a George Jackson be expected to forgive his sadistic guards?

No, but that might not be so bad. It is better that revolutionaries wipe out the guilty than one another. Unfortunately, in the past, the winners have always thought about stopping. Historians claim revolutionaries never know where or when to stop. But it is the contrary. They always do stop, so that the next generation of revolutionaries has felt obliged to go after the previous generation. It happened four times during the French Revolution of 1789-94. Perhaps it would be better if for once a revolutionary movement was ready and willing to go all the way.

This, of course, means totally junking all the bourgeois values we have been taught in schools, in the press, at home. My feeling is that of all the groups within the left today, the undogmatic Maoists, which here we call "*les Maos*," are most prepared to do that—that is, they have most understood that to be genuinely successful a revolution must be what bourgeois historians claim is impossible, namely a revolution that is total yet without terror.

Is that why you will not work with the Communist party any more? There was a time when you did. And it is still, in France anyway, a mass party.

During the occupation I did indeed work with the Communists, as did all resistants who were genuinely anti-Fascist. After the liberation, the opportunistic maneuvers of the party made our adherence impossible, and I was often attacked as an enemy in their newspapers. But at the beginning of the nineteen-fifties, specifically during the massive U.S. encroachment, NATO, etc., and after the French Communist leader Jacques Duclos, a deputy, was arrested (totally illegally, since he had parliamentary immunity and in fact was far away from the "Ridgeway go home" demonstrations of which he was accused of being the organizer), I decided to side with them.

The Communists were also leading the opposition to the war in Vietnam —ours, then—and I helped publicize the case of Henri Martin, a French Communist sailor who refused to participate in the war and was being tried for treason. So I helped as much as I could. I even went to Vienna for the Peace Congress. Then the U.S.S.R. invaded Hungary. To me this was monstrous. Up to then, yes, the Soviet Government had perpetrated horrible crimes, what we call Stalinism, but never before had its troops invaded an independent nation to put down a popular internal insurrection.

To me this was imperialism, pure and simple, as was its invasion of Prague in 1968. The French Communist party supported the invasion of Hungary so I broke with it. Then, during the Algerian war, the C.P. showed itself very lukewarm in its support of the F.L.N., primarily because the F.L.N. was not Communist, and so, though at times the whole left united to stage joint anti-French-colonialist demonstrations, it became clear that it was time to create a movement to the left of the C.P. That left emerged seriously with the Vietnam war—yours—and I was part of it. But I was still a typical intellectual. That is, I did my work at my desk, and occasionally joined a parade in the streets or spoke at some meeting.

Then May, 1968, happened, and I understood that what the young were putting into question was not just capitalism, imperialism, the system, etc., but those of us who pretended to be against all that, as well. We can say that from 1940 to 1968 I was a left-wing intellectual [*un intellectuel de gauche*] and from 1968 on I became an leftist intellectual [*un intellectuel gauchiste*]. The difference is one of action. A leftist intellectual is one who realizes that being an intellectual exempts him from nothing. He forsakes his privileges, or tries to, in actions. It is similar, I think, to what in the U.S. you would call white-skin privileges. A white leftist intellectual, in America, I presume, understands that because he is white he has certain privileges which he must smash through direct action. Not to do so is to be guilty of murder of the blacks—just as much as if he actually pulled the triggers that killed, for example, Bobby Hutton, Fred Hampton, Mark Clark, and all the other Black Panthers murdered by the police, by the system.

Are you saying then that the responsibility of the intellectual is not intellectual?

Yes, it is in action. It is to put his status at the service of the oppressed directly. Just as the German intellectual who fled Hitler and talked about his anti-Nazism while he earned money writing scripts for Hollywood was as responsible for Hitler as the German who closed his eyes, just as the American intellectual who only denounces the Vietnam war and the fate of your political prisoners but continues to teach in a university that carries out war research and insists on law and order (which is a euphemism for letting the courts and police repress active dissenters) is as responsible for the murders and repression as is the Government and its institutions, so too, here in France, the intellectual who does not put his body as well as his mind on the line against the system is fundamentally supporting the system— and should be judged accordingly.

But concretely, what can committed intellectuals do?

In America, it is not for me to say. Surely, your intellectuals know that themselves. They must know that if Ericka Huggins and Bobby Seale are jailed or killed, it is not the police, the courts, the F.B.I. or the Government alone that jails or kills them. They will have let that happen and hence are similarly accountable. Every intellectual who cries nonviolence to those who try to free political prisoners—and I understand you have thousands and thousands in America—he is responsible for their not being free. Concretely, I can talk only of France where I am more familiar with the facts. Here, when we have political trials, our job is to immediately stage people's trials, to be in the streets and accuse the real culprits. Here, when the youth confront the police, our job is not only to show that it is the police who are

TERRORISM AND THE STATE TODAY

INTELLECTUEL GAUCHISTE—Sartre (with Simone de Beauvoir in the background) demonstrates his commitment to action by hawking copies of a Maoist paper.

the violent ones, but to join the youth in counterviolence. Here, when political prisoners go on a hunger strike, all of us who can physically do so must also go on a hunger strike.

What it comes down to is this—and George Jackson expressed this beautifully in his prison letters—that the intellectual, more than anyone else, precisely because of his privileged status, must understand, and act accordingly, that there are only two types of people: the innocent and the guilty, or as your Black Panthers have also said: "If we're not part of the solution, we're part of the problem."

Do you then openly support the use of revolutionary counterviolence to the violence of the system?

Absolutely. But obviously, as a man of 66, I cannot participate in it just like that. But whenever there is an important action which is not clandestine I must join it, and in my writing support the clandestine acts as well.

Do you think that these leftist groups here in France, which relatively, are minuscule...?

Yes, minuscule....

Who use counterviolence, can bring about a revolution?

I think that they themselves are the product of a revolutionary situation, not in the sense that there will be a revolution soon, but in the sense that there is a real division today between official France—the state, the Government, the institutions—and truth. There is a violent refusal of official power. Be it by small shopkeepers, truckdrivers, peasants, students, or workers who seize plants, we have the embryo of a total rejection of power. Of course this is still mostly unconscious, as these very same people, come election time, vote for official France. But they know, by their actions when their self-interest is at stake, that real change can come about only through violence. I feel that only these minuscule groups understand this, that is why they are the vanguard. As long as they keep plugging away, consciousness can only grow and the split in the society will become more apparent. Once the two sides become clear, revolution becomes inevitable.

So you would approve of the Weatherman tactics in the U.S.?

Except that the Maos here are less violent and they are not trying to lay the foundation of a revolutionary party but to create conditions which will mobilize the masses from which, and *only* from which, such a party will surge. But, you see, the conditions are not the same. Here we often win. The hunger strike was successful. After our people's trial at Lens, the accused miners were freed by their courts. After forcing them to arrest big-name intellectuals, including me, they stopped trying to prohibit La Cause du Peuple. In the U.S. repressions are vicious. They kill. Of course, I think you could win too if big-name intellectuals and personalities became more active. Would they have opened fire at Kent State if every antiwar professor teaching there had been in the front lines? Would the police have been so brutal if every one of those so-called liberal antiwar Congressmen and Senators *inside* the Democratic convention had been outside with the people? One of those Senators referred to the police as Gestapo. What effect did that have? But ask yourself: What effect would it have had had he been beaten with the people and had made his denunciation with blood pouring from his head? It seems to me that much more could be done on the question of Vietnam, capitalizing on the contradiction of the Government, which claims to want to end the war—yet, in fact, widens it.

But from a revolutionary point of view, that does not necessarily bring about a movement willing to bring down the system. After all, Algeria didn't create such a left in France, did it?

No, and God knows we tried. I think the error is that such a policy is, after all, fundamentally moral. There's nothing wrong with that; on the contrary. To refuse to fight in Vietnam, or Algeria, or Chad, etc. is fine and should be encouraged, but a revolutionary policy aims locally: exploitation at home, racialism at home, injustice at home. In a capitalist country, exploitation, racialism, injustice lead necessarily to wars, but it's secondary as far as establishing a mass-based revolutionary movement is concerned. And that's the real test, today, of those intellectuals who pretend to be committed. It's easy for us to denounce the war—and do nothing. It's harder for us to pretend to want a just and

The Western Democracies

humanitarian society and confront the injustices and inhumanities in our own bailiwicks, in the very places we live—and which give us our life of ease. But that's where the action is. That's where the fight really is. I imagine that every intellectual who claims to be committed and lives in New Haven must have been first of all committed to the freeing of Bobby Seale....

No, Yale's intellectuals seemed to find too many things to criticize about the Panthers to have been active supporters of Ericka and Bobby.

Ah, well, I fear that's as if I had said that, the main resistance against Germany being led by the Communists and my being anti-Communist, I cannot join the resistance. There's only one word for such a position: collaborationist. We have a lot of such collaborationists here in France, too. They never understood May, 1968. They refused to understand that the protected status of the intellectuals is over, that there are no sanctuaries. The university, the laboratory, the research center, these are all state institutions and hence just as much part of the system as the C.R.S. [France's antiriot tactical police force]. The task of the intellectual is not to decide where are the battles but to join them wherever and whenever the people wage them.

And, I take it, to serve as the media through which the people express themselves, hence to be the fighting people's mouthpiece?

But he can be the mouthpiece only if he fights at the same time. Commitment is an act, not a word. ■

October 17, 1971

Notes on Violence

By WILLIAM V. SHANNON

WASHINGTON, Oct. 20—"The intellectual who does all his fighting from an office is counterrevolutionary today, no matter what he writes," Jean-Paul Sartre told John Gerassi, a radical American intellectual, in an interview printed in The New York Times Magazine of Oct. 17.

"Are you saying then that the responsibility of the intellectual is not intellectual?" Gerassi asked.

"Yes, it is in action," Sartre replied. "The intellectual who does not put his body as well as his mind on the line against the system is fundamentally supporting the system—and should be judged accordingly."

The French, being a worldly-wise people, may take Sartre a shade less seriously than Americans do. They have had, after all, a good deal more experience with barricades rhetoric and revolutionary gestures. Yet Sartre is influential in the United States among intellectuals and the college-educated young. He is a philosopher and literary critic of considerable distinction. "Being and Nothingness" and "What Is Literature?" are important books. He has therefore to be taken seriously. Like the turgid works of Herbert Marcuse, Sartre's writings may be more talked about than carefully read but his ideas have consequences.

But what are we to make of Sartre's message as expounded to Gerassi? Of his idealization of the wise, honest "masses," his call to intellectuals to rush into bloody combat with police and hardhats, his praise for revolutionary terrorism, his vague indictment of "the system" and his sweeping assessments of guilt?

Sartre demonstrates once again that a man can be an eminent philosopher and a perceptive literary critic and still have no political sense. The essence of politics is specificity, limits, timing, the critical interplay between particular personalities and particular ideas and particular events.

But Sartre does not discuss any problem or even an ideology. He seems to have abandoned any notion of causality. The social framework within which the intellectuals and the "masses" are supposed to act is never made clear. Instead, violence has taken the place of program, ideology or political strategy.

Brave men and fools have been risking their lives since the beginning of time. The shedding of blood in and of itself proves nothing. The questions always have to be asked—what was this violence meant to accomplish? Was there no other way to reach the same objective?

To be washed in the blood of the lamb is a very old religious concept, but to borrow that idea from religion, where it is valid, and transpose it to politics is wholly irresponsible. The injustices of an old society cannot be washed away in a baptism of blood and a new society, clean and fresh, then be born.

Human societies are too stubborn for that to happen. The Soviet Union more than fifty years after its revolution, for example, has achieved many positive changes but it still has an awful lot of Czarist Russia in it, including secret police, Siberian camps, persecuted Jews, half-strangled intellectuals screaming for freedom and millions of mute peasants.

Sartre cannot escape the inherent limits of political action by romanticizing working people. It is obscurantist to write that the intellectual "must now write with the masses and through them, realizing ... that he owes his knowledge to them and must be with them and in them."

The "masses" is as repulsive a phrase as "the little man." There are no masses or little men. There are only persons like you and me who work, fall in love, are happy and are afraid, suffer when they are hurt, grow old and die.

To preach violence, whether revolutionary or counterrevolutionary, is to deny one's common humanity. Violence is not an abstraction. Violence means that an eighteen-year-old British soldier, shot in the head in Belfast, will never see his girl again, that a Vietnamese woman holds her dead husband in her arms. There is not a single word in the Sartre interview about love, about binding up anyone's wounds. There is only sterile hate and loose talk about "the system" and "the guilty."

Violence has always had a nervous fascination for many intellectuals. There is in the Sartre-Gerassi exchange the same twittery talk about the presumed necessity for political violence ("A revolution without terror, yes, but is it conceivable?") as runs through Regis Debray's recent interview with President Allende of Chile.

The masculine fantasies so evident in the writings of Hemingway and Mailer are clearly not an exclusively American daydream. Pale, bespectacled French intellectuals who lead outwardly passive lives also have dreams of testing their courage, of striding through the streets like heroes. Ordinary human beings would be safer if intellectuals left these crude, vulgar fantasies to Hollywood instead of projecting them on the world as political theories.

October 21, 1971

Kidnappers Release Renault Official As French Maoists Ponder Isolation

By HENRY GINIGER
Special to The New York Times

PARIS, March 10—An official of the Renault automobile plant who was kidnapped two days ago by a group of Maoist guerrillas was released unharmed early this morning from what his captors called "the people's prison."

Robert Nogrette, a 63-year-old assistant personnel director at the plant, in suburban Boulogne-Billancourt, was set free in the Rue Desnouettes on the Left Bank despite rejection by the Government of demands for the release of seven Maoists now under arrest and for the rehiring of 14 Maoist workers that had been discharged after disorders two weeks ago in which René-Pierre Overney, a 23-year-old Maoist, was shot to death.

Mr. Nogrette said that his captors, numbering three or four, including a girl with a submachine gun, conceded they had committed a blunder in kidnapping him. This was an opinion shared by some of their ideological comrades, who in interviews deplored the loss of the sympathy that they had gained by the Overney killing.

Guerrillas Isolated

The extreme leftist guerrilla group, calling itself the New Popular Resistance, found itself isolated on several fronts.

The police were engaged in an intensive hunt that included searches of hundreds of apartment buildings and the setting up of checkpoints in the streets of the capital throughout the night.

Every party and labor union condemned the act, and the Maoists themselves, while upholding the need for violence at times, could see little point in this particular example.

The kidnapping case has been turned over to a Court for the Security of the State and the kidnappers could get as much as 20 years in prison if convicted.

The severity with which the Government was acting and speaking against the Maoists was contrasted by some French commentators with the lack of any similar condemnation of the Overney killing, for which a Renault plant security official is being held.

Mr. Nogrette's captors said in a statement that one of their motives was to underline "the incredible injustice" that consisted of assassinating a worker, then of arresting or discharging others who had expressed their anger at the killing.

France, which has been trying to develop as friendly relations as possible with the China of Mao Tse-tung, has treated his disciples here as Pariahs.

They were little noticed until 1968, when they came to the fore as one of the major driving forces of a revolutionary movement that almost toppled President de Gaulle.

The 1968 effort failed partly because then, as now, the revolutionaries were unable to develop any centralized and coordinated direction.

"This is our greatest difficulty and our greatest weakness," Gilbert Mury, a 52-year-old former philosophy teacher and a leading theoretician of the Maoist movement, acknowledged.

Mr. Mury, who was discharged as a university professor two years ago, referred constantly to the movement as truly Marxist-Leninist, in that its doctrine calls for keeping the revolutionary movement closely tied to the masses and responsive to its needs and desires.

Mr. Mury and other Maoists denounce as "revisionists" the leaders of the Soviet Union and its satellites and, in France, the Communist party, of which Mr. Mury was once a member, and its labor movement, the General Confederation of Labor.

"They are integrated into the bourgeois state," Mr. Mury said of the Communists. "They want to gain power by using peaceful electoral means and by collaborating with Social Democrats."

The Maoist aim is the end of the capitalist state. "At a given moment we must have recourse to armed struggle," Mr. Mury said. "We cannot do this now. We must first raise the level of political awareness of the working masses so that they realize that the end of their oppressed state will require armed struggle."

Photographs of Chairman Mao sitting with President Nixon may have been unsettling to some Maoists, but none will admit it. Mr. Nixon's visit is explained as a Chinese victory and a defeat for American imperialism since it was Mr. Nixon who sought to go to China and thus acknowledged the Communist regime. No compromise with Maoist principles of armed struggle and national liberation from capitalist oppression is seen and none is desired by Maoists here.

Maoists acknowledge that there are all kinds of obstacles to their campaign, some of them self-created. There is virtually no Maoist group that is national in scope. The three to four thousand people that consider themselves Maoists are scattered into hundreds of tiny groups. Those who have attempted to organize nationally have often split into quarreling sections.

Mr. Mury complained: "The groups don't know and have no contact with each other."

Another handicap is the constant surveillance and repression of the Government.

In the Renault uproar, the Communists have rivaled the Government in condemning the extreme leftists. They have even charged a "plot" by the Government to use the ultra-leftists to discredit the whole left with the voters.

Then, too, the Maoists have a rival in the ultra left camp, the Trotskyites, themselves divided into three or four groups.

A dramatic event such as the Overney killing can produce a mass movement, as evidenced by the huge crowd that followed the youth's coffin to the cemetery last Saturday.

Then the Maoists find some temporary unity among themselves, with the Trotskyites and other leftists and with a mass of mainly young people with latent sympathies but no real urge toward day-to-day militancy.

The ambivalence of French youth was borne out in a poll published in Le Figaro today of opinions of those from 15 to 20 years of age.

Of the group, 53 per cent said they felt drawn toward those who contest present-day society, 69 per cent predicted profound upheavals in France and 58 per cent said there could be no improvement in the lot of the French people without a "profound transformation of French society."

But when the young people were asked in what countries they would like to live, only 7 per cent named China, 6 per cent Cuba and 9 per cent the Soviet Union. The favorite countries were France, 61 per cent; the United States, 48 per cent; England, 39 per cent, and Sweden, 31 per cent. Even Israel, with 8 per cent drew more interest than any Communist country except the Soviet Union.

March 11, 1972

Tiny West German Group Vows to Overthrow State

Special to The New York Times

BERLIN, June 16—A small group of West German leftist political extremists has served notice that it plans to set up a guerrilla organization to overthrow the parliamentary system in the state and in West Berlin.

The group of three or four, headed by Ulrike Meinhof, a 36-year-old woman journalist, is believed to be in Beirut, Lebanon. They were said to have fled there June 8 after having freed a convict from prison while using guns.

The freed prisoner, Andreas Baader, sentenced to three years for setting fire to a Frankfurt department store, is believed to be with the group.

Miss Meinhof left a taped manifesto that proclaimed her plans, excerpts of which were printed this week in the Hamburg news magazine Der Spiegel. She said: "We must learn from the revolutionary movements of the world—the Vietcong, the Palestine Liberation Front, the Tupamaros, the Black Panthers."

June 17, 1970

The Western Democracies

Anarchist Leaders Seized in Frankfurt

By DAVID BINDER
Special to The New York Times

BONN, June 1—The state and federal police captured two ringleaders of a West German anarchist band in Frankfurt early today who are believed to have been responsible for a wave of bombings that killed four American soldiers and injured 30 persons last month.

The two were identified by the authorities as Andreas Baader, 29 years old, and Holger Meins, 30. Two other suspects were seized but not immediately identified and one was later released. The group is popularly known as the Baader-Meinhof gang.

Baader and Meins had been sought in a countrywide dragnet along with 17 other alleged gang members, including a former journalist, Miss Ulrike Meinhof, 37, in connection with a series of terrorist actions dating from 1963.

The Baader-Meinhof group had declared its participation in these bombings and other terrorist acts as members of an assemblage of leftist-anarchists the Red Army Faction. This group preaches terror against "imperialism" as a means of achieving "revolution."

Group Clashed with Police

They are believed in police circles here to have international connections to like-minded groups in Italy, Japan and France. Baader and Miss Meinhof and others reportedly received weapons training in the Middle East from Palestinan guerrillas during the summer of 1970 after Baader was freed from jail in Berlin by masked gunmen. He had been sentenced for setting fire to a Frankfurt department store in 1968.

Last year the group turned for a time to bank robbery, operating with fast cars and armed with automatic rifles, and amassing hundreds of thousands of marks. Then came a series of clashes with the police that left at least three gang members and three patrolmen dead.

The well-appointed three-story apartment house in north Frankfurt where today's action took place had evidently been under police observation for some time.

Shortly after 5 A.M. a special squad of Frankfurt, Hessian state and federal police cordoned off the corner building and called on the suspects to leave their hideout, a garage on the property. "Come out, your means are limited but ours are unlimited," called an officer through a bullhorn, as recorded by West German television.

When there was no response, tear-gas grenades were fired into the building from an armored car in the courtyard.

The suspects began firing with pistols and automatic rifles. Some of the bullets were later found to have been filed down to dumdums. The police fired a few rounds in return. When the armored car started to ram the closed garage door the man identified as Holger Meins came out. He was stripped to his undershorts and led away.

Then out came Andreas Baader, shooting wildly with a .45-caliber pistol.

Baader was hit in the right hip by a police bullet and he cried out twice.

From a stretcher he called the police "pigs, pigs." With huge sideburns and bleached hair, he was scarcely identifiable from the police photo that showed him with short dark hair.

The two were later identified by fingerprints. Like other members of the gang under arrest, they refused to answer interrogators.

A red Porsche Targa outside the apartment was found to contain hand grenades and a large homemade bomb, police officials reported later

West German authorities who are overseeing the dragnet disclosed the license numbers of five other cars being sought and warned that they might contain bombs.

A bomb went off in a West Berlin apartment this afternoon and was also attributed to the terrorists.

A bomb threat in Frankfurt this evening, reportedly by a cell of the Red Army Faction, caused the police to strengthen patrols, close theaters and warn people to avoid the downtown area.

June 2, 1972

TERRORIST LEADER SEIZED IN GERMANY

Special to The New York Times

BONN, June 16—The state police in Hanover today announced the capture of Ulrike Meinhof, a founding member of a leftist terrorist group known popularly as the Baader-Meinhof gang.

Miss Meinhof, 37 years old, had been considered the leading ideologist of an anarchist group calling itself the Red Army Faction, which took responsibility for bombings last month in which 4 American servicemen were killed and 30 others injured.

The gang's other top leader, Andreas Baader, and two accomplices were arrested in Frankfurt June 1 after a gunfight.

Miss Meinhof was captured by surprise last night in a second-floor dwelling in Langenhagen, a Hanover suburb, and gave up without resisting, according to police.

June 17, 1972

West Germany's Leftist Guerrillas Reawaken Sensitive Political Issues

By PAUL KEMEZIS
Special to The New York Times

BONN, March 3—West Germany's left-wing guerrilla movement was considered by many to be close to collapse after the arrest in 1972 of many of its key figures.

But in the last year the movement has reappeared seeming more effective and daring than ever, to plague a country where political extremism and police security are highly sensitive issues.

The daylight kidnapping in West Berlin last week of Peter Lorenz, the city's Christian Democratic party leader, and the subsequent demand for the release of six terrorists held in West German prisons were preceded by bombings, shootings and prison protests, which have become more important political issues than the uncompromising Marxist ideology that the terrorists are trying to spread.

The terrorists themselves are mostly former students in their mid-twenties who are veterans of the political struggles that swept German universities in the late nineteen-sixties.

The group that has taken responsibility for the West Berlin kidnapping takes its name, the June 2 Movement, from the killing of a student by the West Berlin police at a demonstration in 1967. The incident was considered the spark that set off the radical student movement in West Germany and West Berlin.

Many of the terrorists have been on the West German wanted posters for years, although few are well known. They have shown skill at existing underground despite intensive police investigations.

West German opinion has tended to give the guerrillas a single label, the Baader-Meinhof gang, named for two radicals who were arrested in 1972 and are still in prison. But recent events seem to indicate that there are at least two separate—and perhaps rival—bands with similar political goals.

The Red Army faction was active up to 1972, but then splintered with the arrest of many of its leaders—Andreas Baader and Ulrike Meinhof among them

The June 2 Movement, which was already active in 1971, is believed to have attracted many of the radicals who drifted away from the Red Army faction after 1972. The June 2 group has recently been considered by the West Berlin police to be the most active and dangerous in the city.

Much like the Symbionese Liberation Army in the United States, the group seems entirely devoted to revolution through violence, with little of the intellectual reflection used by the early Baader-Meinhof faction to justify its acts.

Lately the Red Army faction has been mainly involved in protests over alleged harsh treatment of its many members in prison. Included was a hunger strike last fall during which one member, Holger Meins, died despite intravenous feeding. Few people seemed convinced by the protests that the group was being unfairly treated.

Two days after Mr. Meins's death Judge Günter von Drenkmann, president of West Berlin's highest court, was assassinated presumably by leftist terrorists. During November, as public outrage over the shooting remained high, the West German police conducted a number of raids that netted dozens of radicals and sympathizers.

The activity of the June 2 Movement goes back at least to 1970, when, with the Baader-Meinhof faction, it carried out a series of spectacular bank raids. In February, 1972, a bomb blast at a British boat club in West Berlin that killed one person was laid to the group.

Last June the band killed one of its own members, Ulrich Schmücker, who had become a police informer.

By mid-1974 several of the group that had been captured and officials began to fear that they would take a prominent hostage in an attempt to win freedom for the prisoners. The shooting of Judge von Drenkmann is thought to have followed an unsuccessful attempt at kidnapping.

The police believe a key leader of the June 2 Movement is Ralf Reinders, 26 years old, whom they had connected by evidence to the killing of Judge von Drenkmann. He is also believed to have taken part in a bank robbery in December, 1974.

Angela Luther, 34, a former teacher who was identified by Mr. Lorenz's chauffeur as one of his kidnappers, has been sought since 1971. Last June an apartment she had rented in West Berlin under a false name caught fire, revealing a bomb factory.

The six radicals whose freedom the kidnappers had demanded in exchange for Mr. Lorenz — who was a candidate for Mayor of West Berlin in elections this weekend — were all unknown except for 39-year-old lawyer, Horst Mahler.

Though the West German police estimate the hard core of left-wing radicals at fewer than a hundred, they have noted that violent incidents traced to political groups have risen steadily in 18 months.

The recent acts, which also included an unsuccessful shooting attack on the home of a prominent Christian Democratic Deputy, Walter Kiep, are particularly chilling since political figures have become targets. Although a number of German diplomats have been kidnapped by terrorists groups abroad, especially in South America, no major public figure had been kidnapped in West Germany in the postwar period.

March 4, 1975

West German Prosecutor Is Slain; Led Fight Against Urban Guerrillas

By The Associated Press

KARLSRUHE, West Germany, April 7—Assassins riding a motorcycle pulled alongside a limousine carrying West Germany's chief prosecutor today and sprayed it with submachine-gun fire, killing him and his driver and critically wounding another official.

The prosecutor, Siegfried Buback, 57 years old, had been leading proceedings against leaders of the Baader-Meinhof gang, an anarchist group, on trial in Stuttgart since May 1975 in two bombings that killed four American servicemen in 1972.

Mr. Buback drew up the charges in connection with the bombings against five members of the gang—Andreas Baader, Ulrike Meinhof, Gudrun Ensslin, Holger Meins and Jan-Carl Raspe. Mr. Meins died in a hunger strike before the trial began. Miss Meinhof was found hanged in her cell last May. Her death was ruled a suicide.

The news agency D.P.A. said it had received calls from a man saying that the shootings were the work of the Ulrike Meinhof Action Committee. He warned that more violence would follow.

Cyclists Waited Half an Hour

The Government announced an $85,000 reward for the arrest of the assassins. One person was taken into custody about five hours after the shooting, but officials said it was not known whether the prisoner was a "genuine suspect."

Mr. Buback had said that investigators expected a new round of terrorist attacks. He was considered to be in danger and was entitled to a bodyguard and protection of his house, officials said. But he used the bodyguard only on special occasions and was without protection today.

April 8, 1977

German Ruling Disturbs U.S. Lawyers

By CRAIG R. WHITNEY
Special to The New York Times

BONN, April 14—West Germany's highest court has approved Government limitations on defense lawyers for an important trial of leftist anarchists—a move that some American jurists say is a blow to principles of free speech and legal protection.

The measures spring from a deep West German fear that a few hundred leftist radicals pose a threat to the stable values of postwar West German society, and from a West German wish to use the law to combat that threat.

West German criminal law, substantially formulated under the Prussian Empire late in the 19th century makes possible some measures that Americans find shocking or unjustifiable. In this case, four Americans, including former Attorney General Ramsey Clark, have sought to protest in a West German court.

These four lawyers—all from New York—argue that the constitutional protection of freedom knows no political boundaries, and they want to intervene on behalf of the West German defense lawyers.

In its ruling today, the Constitutional Court in Karlsruhe declared that the Government could limit the number of lawyers a defendant may use. It also approved the exclusion of a left-wing attorney, Klaus Croissant of Stuttgart, as a court-appointed lawyer in the trial of Andreas Baader, Ulrike Meinhof, and others accused of being "urban guerrillas." That trial is set to begin in Stuttgart, May 21. But it left open the question whether Mr. Croissant could be excluded if he was the defendants' explicit choice.

The American lawyers who are protesting the exclusion are, in addition to Mr. Clark, William M. Kunstler, William H. Schaap and Peter Weiss. Another of the Baader-Meinhof lawyers, Kurt Groenewold, whom prosecutors want to exclude, says that he will file the American lawyers' legal brief with the Stuttgart court during argument on the case Wednesday.

Both Mr. Groenewold and Mr. Croissant were technically court-appointed because the defendants have no money, Mr. Groenewold said today. Some of the Baader-Meinhof defendants have been in jail, under investigation and awaiting trial since 1972.

What the West Germans see at issue in the case is the possible participation by these and other lawyers in illegal activities of the "Baader-Meinhof gang" defendants—smuggling letters and plans to other leftist terrorists still at large, directing a hunger strike by some of them last fall, and the like. The Constitutional decision today said that limiting the number of defense lawyers guarded against the possibility that the court proceedings might be "misused" by the terrorists, some of whom were represented by more than a score.

The other question for the West Germans is whether lawyers can be excluded altogether from the defense for "improper activities," and how to define thsse; the court ruling today was a partial answer.

The Americans' brief points out that none of the attorneys whose exclusion is at issue has been convicted of any crime or indicted, and adds: "Resort to such extralegal means for keeping defense attorneys 'in line' cannot, it seems to us, be justified by the special quality of German political life. If attorneys Croissant and Groenewold are guilty of crimes, let them be charged with crimes. If they are not, let them represent the defendants who have chosen to be represented by them."

April 15, 1975

The Western Democracies

3 Die as Guerrillas Seize and Blow Up West German Embassy in Stockholm

By The Associated Press

STOCKHOLM, Friday, April 25 — Three persons were killed as terrorists shot their way into the West German Embassy here yesterday, took up to a dozen hostages and then blew up part of the building after their demands for the release of 26 anarchists jailed in West Germany had been refused.

The guerrillas first mortally wounded the embassy's military attaché and then killed one of the hostages after a deadline for the release of their jailed comrades had passed. The third person killed was a guerrilla who died in a hospital after having attempted suicide as he was about to be captured, authorities said.

The police said that the series of explosions that rocked the embassy and set it afire shortly before midnight was designed to cover the terrorists' escape but that all seven terrorists known to have been in the building had been captured.

Several of the hostages were injured in the explosions, as were a number of policemen and firemen.

"The building was mined heavily on the third floor," policemen said. "The terrorists and the hostages were all on the ground floor at the time of the explosion, and that's why no one was seriously hurt."

Six of the terrorists were captured after a brief gun battle following the explosions, the police said, and the seventh was taken later after being pinned down by police fire in the burning four-story embassy. One terrorist was reported in grave condition in a hospital with gunshot wounds.

Shortly before the explosions ripped the building the terrorists released three women hostages unharmed.

The terrorists, including at least one woman, killed Lieut. Col. Andreas Baron von Mirbach, the military attaché, while blasting their way into the building at midday.

The terrorists had threatened to blow up the building with nearly 35 pounds of TNT if police tried to storm the building. No such attempt was made by the police. They also had threatened to kill the ambassador and the other hostages unless 26 members of the so-called Baader-Meinhof gang of anarchists were freed from German jails, given $520,000 and flown from the Frankfurt airport to an undisclosed country.

Named for Dead Anarchist

The terrorists identified themselves as the "Holger Meins Commando," named for a member of the Baader-Meinhof gang who died after a hunger strike in a West German jail last November.

The Baader-Meinhof gang has claimed responsibility for terrorist bombings in West Germany in 1972 that killed four American servicemen and wounded more than 50 other persons. They also allegedly killed several German policemen. The group's leaders, Ulrike Meinhof, 40 years old, and Andreas Baader, 30, are scheduled to stand trial in Stuttgart, Germany, on May 21.

The embassy take-over began at noon when one of the terrorists entered the building and inquired about a passport. When he was told to go to the consular section, four other terrorists burst in with submachine guns and pistols.

The military attaché was brought out three hours later. The police said that he had been shot four times in the head and legs and had died in a Stockholm hospital. He is survived by his wife and 12-year-old twins, a son and a daughter.

The terrorists blamed the Swedish police for the killing because, they said, the police had not left the embassy building "despite repeated requests."

They said if their demands for the release of the prisoners in Germany were not met, they would start executing their hostages one by one.

About 150 policemen with rifles and bullet-proof vests surrounded the embassy and evacuated the nearby embassies of the United States, Britain, Japan and Norway.

Shortly after the mortally wounded attaché was taken out of the building, the police carried sandbags into the ground floor of the embassy. But officials said they had no intention of storming the upper floors, where the terrorists and hostages were.

They said that they were in telephone contact with the terrorists but were not allowed to speak to the hostages, including Ambassador Stoecker, who is 60.

President Walter Scheel of West Germany cut short a visit to France and headed back to Bonn because of the embassy siege.

Premier Olaf Palme of Sweden called his cabinet into emergency session, and he was in direct contact with West German officials in Bonn.

Shortly before 10 P.M. Premier Palme said that he had been told by the Bonn Government that it would not meet the terrorists' demands.

Mr. Palme's spokesman, Thage Petersson, said that the Bonn refusal was "supported by all regional governments in West Germany as well as by the Federal Government in Bonn, with the Opposition united behind the Government on all levels."

The escape attempt began later with a tremendous flash and explosion on the top floor of the building.

The Swedish Minister of Justice was in a lower wing of the embassy building when the first major explosion occurred but he escaped unhurt.

Ladders were raised to the building to help the hostages escape.

A dozen fire engines were used to fight the fire at the embassy and the surrounding grounds, set ablaze by flaming objects thrown by the explosions.

April 25, 1975

Ulrike Meinhof, an Anarchist Leader In Germany, Is Found Hanged in Cell

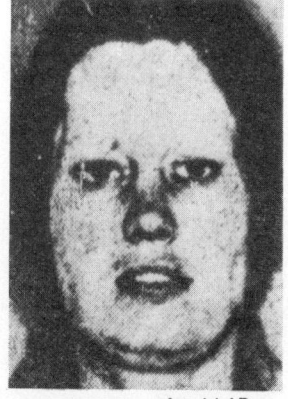

Ulrike Meinhof (Associated Press)

STUTTGART, West Germany, May 9 (AP)—Ulrike Meinhof, on trial for nearly a year with three other members of the Baader-Meinhof anarchist group, was found hanged today in her maximum security cell, the Stuttgart prosecutor's office reported.

A spokesman said the 41-year-old former journalist was last seen alive last night by a guard and that she was heard typewriting in her cell until 10:30 P.M.

When another guard opened her cell this morning, he found Miss Meinhof hanging at the window rails from a piece of her prison toweling.

The spokesman said the papers she left behind gave no indication of any intent to commit suicide. He said further details would be released after an inquiry.

West German authorities put security forces on alert in fear of retaliation by sympathizers of the leftist radical group.

Until 1968, Miss Meinhof was a successful journalist who wrote her own column in a Hamburg-based satirical leftist magazine owned by her husband, Klaus Rainer Röhl, father of her two children. But she parted with her family that year and left her job.

She appeared in West Berlin where authorities said she helped free Andreas Baader, who was serving a sentence for an arson attack on a Frankfurt department store. A guard was shot and seriously wounded when Mr. Baader was liberated from the prison library on May 14, 1970.

Miss Meinhof and Mr. Baader went into hiding and organized the Red Army Faction, which the police say was responsible for acts that terrorized most of West Germany in the next few years. The faction became commonly known as the Baader-Meinhof group.

Following the rearrest of Mr. Baader, the arrests of Jan-Carl Raspe and Gudrun Ensslin, Miss Meinhof was apprehended in Hanover-Langenhagen on June

7, 1972. A West Berlin court sentenced her to eight years in prison for the prison attack that freed Mr. Baader.

After her trial in Berlin in 1974, at which she said an "armed battle" to achieve a change in society was legal, Miss Meinhof and the three other members of the group were brought to Stammheim, which was specially constructed outside of Stuttgart for the Baader-Meinhof trial, which began under maximum security precautions on May 21, 1975.

The four were charged with masterminding a wave of anti-state bombings and shootings that killed four United States servicemen and a policeman, wounded several others and endangered at least 54 persons.

The trial, halted by numerous protest motions and outbursts by the defendants, is expected to last at least two years. Most of the time, the defendants have been kept out of the court proceedings or have chosen to remain in their cells.

Miss Ensslin surprised the court last Tuesday by accepting responsibility for all the accused for the three bombings that in 1972 killed the four Americans and injured at least 40 persons.

May 10, 1976

SECURITY INCREASED FOR GERMAN LEADERS

Concern Voiced for the Prominent as New Targets of Anarchists After Slaying of Banker

By PAUL HOFMANN
Special to The New York Times

BONN, Aug. 1—Protection for West Germans prominent in politics, the judiciary and business was quietly reinforced today following the killing Saturday of Jürgen Ponto, an influential banker, by two women and a man in Mr. Ponto's home near Frankfurt.

However, Armin Grünewald, a senior Government spokesman, warned in Bonn that the police forces were not nearly sufficient to protect all hose whom terrorists have singled out.

"We must be prepared for the worst," the chief of the antiterrorism division of the Federal Criminal Police Department, Gerhard Boeden, said today.

West Germany's formidable economic leaders, who so far had been spared politically motivated violence, are now thought to be new targets of anarchist plotters. The previous victims were for the most part judges, prosecutors, police officials and diplomats.

Some financiers and industrial managers will apparently not wait for the police to take additional safety measures. The market in privae bodyguards — wiry Yugoslavs seem to be preferred — and electronic security equipment are brisk, according to consultants of commercial protection services in Frankfurt, Hamburg and other business centers.

The consultants said they regarded every assignment as confidential and would not offer even approximate descriptions of their new clients.

While some West Germans are hiring "gorillas" and having new surveillance systems installed, an old debate has arisen once more, about the thought processes, the ideological and social backgrounds, the active membership and tacit supporters of clandestine terrorist networks.

The Women in Anarchist Ranks

One of the questions frequently asked by here is why there are so many armed female militants in the anarchist factions that have assumed responsibility for much of the violence. Yesterday the police named four young women wanted in the inquiry into the murder of Mr. Ponto, the chairman of the board of the Dresdner Bank, who was 53 years old.

The principal suspect, the police say, is Susanne Albrecht, the 26-year-old daughter of a well-to-do Hamburg lawyer. According to the police, the young woman has been active in far-left causes for years.

Today, public interest and the police search centered on Miss Albrecht. She was personally known by the slain banker and thus could easily have gained admittance to his tightly guarded villa for herself and her alleged co-conspirators— Silke Maier-Witt, 27, Sigrid Sterneback, 28, and Angela Speitel, 25.

The name of the man has not been divulged, and the police have not said specifically what roles the various suspects played in the killing. Today the West German Chief Prosecutor, Kurt Rebmann, requested an arrest warrant against Miss Albrecht. The federal court in Karlsruhe said a decision could not be expected before tomorrow.

Protest for Poor or Boredom of Rich?

Miss Albrecht's social background evoked reiterations by newspaper editorialists today of the old contention that terrorism in West Germany was not a protest by the exploited and oppressed but a pastime of the bored children of the affluent, who had gone underground in quest of new thrills.

Miss Albrecht was depicted as typical of frustrated young West Germans who choose to quit comfortable lives and become plotters. Until recently, she is said to expressed a desire to become a teacher. Eventually she moved out of her parents' home, in a prosperous Hamburg neighborhood, to join a commune in a two-room walkup in the St. Pauli waterfront district.

Meanwhile, the police announced today that they had found two cars in which the killers of Mr. Ponto escaped Saturday, and that a bloodstained jacket believed left by one of the terrorists was in one of the cars.

A Kidnapping Theory Reaffirmed

The cars were not the Volkswagens that the police had originally identified as the getaway cars. The Volkswagens were found yesterday in Hamburg, and there was no hint that they had recently been driven outside the city.

The autos found today were a Ford Granada stolen near Frankfurt last week, and a blue Volkswagen bus, also stolen. The police said that the plotters had been using false license plates and had abandoned the bus near Mr. Ponto's home and the Ford on the outskirts of Frankfurt.

Investigators reaffirmed a theory, first advanced yesterday, that the two women and the men planned to kidnap the banker to extort a ransom to finance underground activities and back up demands for the freeing of imprisoned anarchists.

Mr. Ponto, the police theory went, apparently resisted and died after he was shot.

Politicians, officials and press commentators are voicing particular concern over what they term insufficient help by the population in the police search for terrorists. There are misgivings about hidden, if only passive, support and sympathies that the anarchist conspirators may enjoy.

August 2, 1977

GERMAN KIDNAPPED; 4 GUARDS ARE SLAIN

By Reuters

COLOGNE, West Germany, Sept. 5—Gunmen kidnapped one of West Germany's leading industrialists and killed four of his bodyguards today in an attack on his automobile during the evening rush hour.

Chancellor Helmut Schmidt, in a television broadcast, confirmed that Dr. Hanns-Martin Schleyer, 62 years old, the president of the West German Confederation of Employers Associations and president of the Federation of West German Industries, had been abducted. He appealed for anyone able to provide the police with information "about these murders and the kidnapping of Hanns-Martin Schleyer" to come forward.

Five gunmen in a small yellow bus attacked Dr. Schleyer's motorcade at a crossroads in the evening rush hour and sprayed it with machine-gun fire, the police reported. Two police escorts, a security agent and a driver died instantly, they said.

Caller Threatens Killing

The police speculated that the killers might have been left-wing urban guerrillas, but there was no immediate indication of who they were.

The Western Democracies

[An anonymous caller telephoned the Munich office of the mass-circulation newspaper Bild Zeitung later and said Dr. Schleyer would be killed at 5:15 P.M. Tuesday unless Andreas Baader and other convicted terrorists were released from prison, The Associated Press reported. Two West German news agencies reported receiving similar calls from a group called the Red Army Faction.]

Dr. Schleyer was an adviser to the Government on labor and economic problems. He was also a member of the board of the Daimler-Benz automobile company.

The Confederation of Employer Associations, which he heads, represents 12 regional employer organizations and 45 trade associations. The Federation of West German Industries, which he also heads, is an umbrella group that represents the associations of various industries such as the automobile and petroleum industries.

A grim-faced Mr. Schmidt said in Bonn that the attack made the Government more than ever determined to pursue its fight against terrorism.

The Chancellor described the attack as "a bloody provocation which is a challenge to us all" and appealed for anyone able to provide information to come forward.

Cologne was quickly surrounded by a tight security cordon.

A meeting of key ministers was called, and Dr. Burkhard Hirsch, Interior Minister of the state of North Rhine-Westphalia, in which Cologne is situated, described the attack as "brutal murder."

The increase in urban guerrilla activity in West Germany followed the passing of life sentences in April on three leaders of the Baader-Meinhof group.

The three—Andreas Baader, Jan-Carl Raspe and Gudru Ensslin—are in the top-security Stammheim Prison in Stuttgart where they ended a 26-day hunger strike on Friday after winning an assurance that prison conditions would be improved.

Immediately after the murder of the head of the Dresdner Bank, Jürgen Ponto, on July 30, a previously unknown left-wing organization telephoned news agencies to threaten more killings of representatives of West Germany's "exploiting class."

Dr. Schleyer, a lawyer and father of four, is one of West Germany's most influential industrialists and an obvious target for guerrillas.

West German television showed film of the ambush scene, a body lying sprawled in the gutter beside a car amid glass fragments from shattered windows. The police later gave the registration number of the bus as K-C 3849 and appealed for witnesses.

Three of the dead escorts had apparently been traveling in a car that was immediately behind Dr. Schleyer's limousine.

September 6, 1977

West German Terrorism Is 'Heroic' Step to Genet, Who Finds All Life Violent

By JONATHAN KANDELL
Special to The New York Times

PARIS, Sept. 6—Most of the European intellectual left has, in recent years, condemned urban terrorism of the sort that has erupted in West Germany.

A notable exception has been the novelist and playwright Jean Genet, who has defended political violence in Western parliamentary systems as a "heroic" effort by revolutionaries to unmask the "brutality" that Genet feels lies behind the bland democratic facade of European governments.

Only a few days before leftist terrorists kidnapped Hanns-Martin Schleyer, the president of the West German Employers' Association, and killed four bodyguards, the writer reiterated his views in a front-page article published in the French newspaper Le Monde.

Mr. Genet begins by stating philosophically that "violence and life are almost synonymous," citing even childbirth as an example in support of his case.

He sees violence throughout modern society—not simply in acts of war, police shoot-outs and, social and economic inequalities, but also in everyday, run-of-the-mill events such as "the priority given in traffic to speed over the slowness of pedestrians, the authority of machines over the men they serve, the enactment of laws governing customs, the use of secrecy to prevent knowledge that is in the public interest."

According to Genet, society owes a lebt to the West German terrorists "for making us understand, not only by their words, but by their acts, outside prison and within prison, that only violence can put an end to the brutality that the playwright sees all around him."

He ends his essay by arguing that attempts to stamp out the terrorists will only boomerang by giving West Germany "a terrifying, monstrous image" that the urban guerrillas sought to expose in the first place.

September 7, 1977

West Germany's Orderly Society Proves Vulnerable to Terrorists

By PAUL HOFMANN
Special to The New York Times

BONN, Sept. 18—Within hours after urban guerrillas kidnapped Hanns-Martin Schleyer, West Germany's leading industrialist, in Cologne on Sept. 5, police officers in Bavaria set up roadblocks to catch any terrorists who might try to flee abroad.

But at the same time public-service broadcasts kept cautioning motorists to avoid traffic jams caused by the police controls, and recommended alternate routes without roadblocks.

Mr. Schleyer's abductors may never have tried to leave West Germany or even the Cologne metropolitan area. Yet the incident is one of many examples of how things may go wrong in a well-organized, even over-organized, country, and how red tape and long-established routines in effect invite subversion and sabotage.

These days there is much talk here about how vulnerable an advanced industrial and technological society like West Germany's is whenever a tiny band of fanatics, who may be highly intelligent and imaginative, chooses to attack.

More and more West Germans are also asking uneasily why their police are unable to find the murderers and kidnappers. The criminals are by no means anonymous.

Five Women Have Vanished

The wanted posters show the pictures of five young women who are being sought as suspects in the murder of Jürgen Ponto, a leading banker, in July. All five have vanished.

The Federal Criminal Bureau also has a fairly clear idea of who participated in the Cologne ambush in which Mr. Schleyer was abducted and his driver and three police bodyguards killed. Data on hundreds of terrorists and persons believed to be capable of terrorist violence are stored in computers; investigators are said to have narrowed the field of suspects to about 50. Many of these also seem to have disappeared.

The 62-year-old president of the West German Confederation of Employers' Associations and of the industry federation was the latest prominent target of terrorist actions.

In April, gunmen riding heavy Japanese motorcycles shot and killed Siegfried Buback, West Germany's chief prosecutor, in Karlsruhe.

Then Mr. Ponto, chairman of the board of Dresdner Bank, was murdered in his well-guarded villa near Frankfurt by three visitors who were led by the daughter of a school friend, Susanne Albrecht. The young woman was carrying a bunch of red roses when she called at the Ponto mansion.

In the Cologne ambush, a baby carriage, pushed across a one-way street, served as a decoy to stop the motorcade that was to take Mr. Schleyer to his home. The baby carriage was loaded with submachine guns that were immediately picked up and fired by the terrorists. The police escorts also had submachine guns, but they were in the luggage compartment of their car.

The nature of the targets, even more than the cunning techniques of West Germany's ultraleft terrorists, explain why their operations have such a paralyzing effect.

They aim high. A directive by a group of jailed left-wing extremists, issued from a Stuttgart penitentiary two years ago, ordered their associates who remained at large to "hit the imperialist apparatus, its military, political, economic and cultural institutions, its functionaries."

A dead chief prosecutor, a dead top banker and a kidnapped head of the industrial establishment show that the terrorists have been quite succesful so far. Now many people here ask apprehensively who is next on the terrorists' list.

On the Adenauerallee in Bonn, double barbed-wire coils, one above the other, and a mobile security wall of armored cars and heavily armed police patrols with watchdogs protect the offices and residences of West Germany's head of state and head of Government.

Sandbagged gun emplacements and miles of barbed wire are all over the West German capital. The effect is that of an unstable country awaiting the next coup d'etat.

Terrorism in West Germany, unlike political violence in, for example, Northern Ireland or the Middle East, is by no means indiscriminate now. It is accurately aimed at the country's top figures and at the ganglia of the country's power system.

This is a nation where pedestrians will patiently wait for a green light at an intersection even if there is no oncoming traffic for half a mile. Germans generally like rules and expect to be told what to do. The terrorist offensive, with its unforeseen shocks, unsettles them more than similar events would in a less highly organized society.

Whenever one asks here about the failure of the police to capture the terrorists, one is told about the incompability of the Siemens computers that some law-enforcement agencies are using with the I.B.M. systems on which others rely.

But there are certainly other, less technical reasons for the failure to stop the terrorists.

Unable to Infiltrate

The police here have never managed to infiltrate the small radical groups. Granted, the extremist cells are small, secretive and suspicious of any outsider. But in France, Britain and other countries, police informers have penetrated clandestine organizations.

Officials here say that to win the trust of the terrorist conspirators, an informer would have to establish credentials by participating in some crime, and that a nation based on the rule of law cannot condone such practices.

Neither can the West German authorities resort to widespread, indiscriminate wiretapping and other intrusions on individual rights without laying themselves open to the charge of erecting a police state.

All major parties in West Germany today stress their determination to maintain a liberal system that, although it is denounced as "fascist" by the radicals is far removed from both the Nazi dictatorship and the police states of the Soviet bloc.

September 19, 1977

GERMAN TROOPS FREE HOSTAGES ON HIJACKED PLANE IN SOMALIA; AT LEAST 3 TERRORISTS KILLED

PASSENGERS UNHURT

Soldiers Attack 90 Minutes Before New Deadline and After Pilot Is Slain

By HENRY TANNER
Special to The New York Times

BONN, Tuesday, Oct. 18 — Ninety minutes before a threatened massacre deadline, a West German commando unit stormed a hijacked Lufthansa airliner on an airport runway in Mogadishu, Somalia, today and ended a five-day, 6,000-mile hijacking episode by shooting the four terrorists and freeing all 86 hostages unharmed, the Interior Ministry announced early today.

The attack ended the ordeal for the passengers and crew of Lufthansa Flight 181, which was taken over by the four terrorists less than an hour after it had left the Mediterranean island of Majorca Thursday on a routine flight to Frankfurt.

The West German Government announced that all four hijackers had been killed. [Somalia's official press agency reported that three of the hijackers had been killed, but that a fourth, a woman, had been captured, Reuters reported from Mogadishu.]

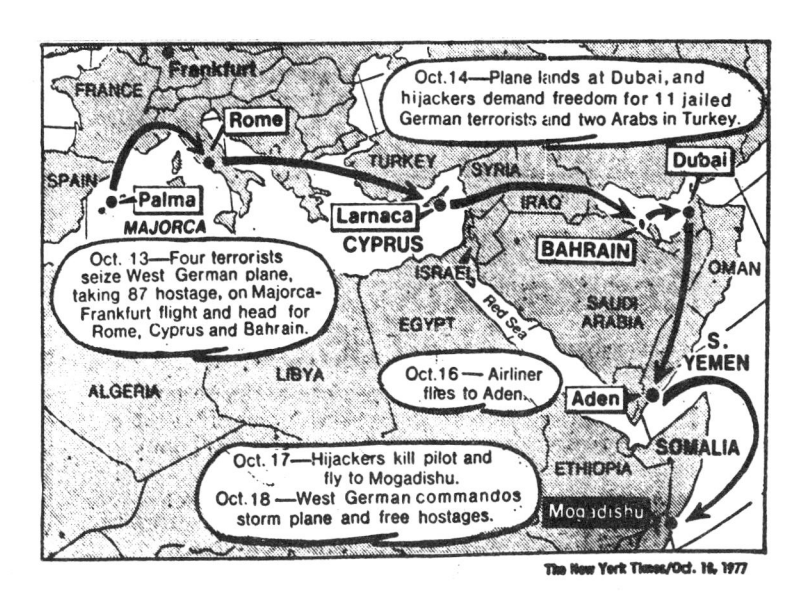

The terrorists had taken the Boeing 737 on a 6,000-mile odyssey to Rome, Cyprus, Bahrain, Dubai, Aden and finally Mogadishu, killing the pilot en route and setting several deadlines to blow up the jet and the hostages unless the West German and Turkish Governments met their demands to free 11 members of the terrorist organization known as the Baader-Meinhof gang and two Palestinians imprisoned in Turkey. They also demanded a ransom of $15 million.

The Western Democracies

The storming of the plane came after a day in which pressure on the West German Government mounted and international concern over the fate of the plane's 82 passengers and four crew members grew. In Rome, Pope Paul VI said that, "If it were useful we would offer even our person for the liberation of those hostages."

Triumph for Helmut Schmidt

The successful rescue operation was regarded here as a triumph for the Government of Chancellor Helmut Schmidt, which had refused to accept the demands of the hijackers. It was carried out by a specially trained force of West German border police organized after the Munich massacre in 1972. The entire operation lasted only five minutes, according to first reports reaching here.

The West German commandos blasted the doors of the airliner open and then rushed inside, the reports said. Two of the soldiers were wounded in the attack. A ham radio operator in Israel interviewed on West German radio said he had heard radio conversations from Mogadishu saying that one of the West German flight attendants aboard had been slightly injured but that all the passengers were unharmed.

The West German's raid recalled the July 1976 Israeli action at Entebbe in Uganda, in which commandos freed 102 hostages held aboard an Air France jet.

Sixty of the commandos involved in the attack on the plane were flown to Mogadishu earlier today from Crete, according to West German official reports. Others may have come from other destinations. A group of commandos is known to have been flown to Teheran, Iran, while the hijacked plane was on the ground in Dubai on the Persian Gulf from Friday morning until Sunday afternoon.

A plane full of special troops of the border police was dispatched to Cyprus during the first hours of the hijacking but reached there, after the hijacked plane had already moved on. The plane was then sent to Ankara and the commandos were kept in readiness there.

When the hijackers learned of the commandos' presence in Ankara they demanded they be withdrawn to Germany. The West Germans agreed and the Germans news media reported they had returned to Bonn. What was not known at that time was that other contingents of the commandos were still in the eastern Mediterranean and in Iran, within a few hours' flight of the hijacked plane.

Statement Praises Somalis

In an early morning press conference here, the Government spokesman, Klaus Bolling, said that one of the passengers had been treated for exhaustion at a hospital in Mogadishu. The other passengers had received medical attention at the airport, he added.

The spokesman read a statement issued jointly by the Government and the leaders of all the parties in Parliament that praised the Somali Government of President Mohammed Siad Barre and said that without full agreement and help from the Somali authorities the military action against the plane could not have been carried out and the passengers could not have been saved. Chancellor Schmidt sent President Barre a telegram saying "We will never forget," Mr. Bolling said.

Mr. Bolling made it clear that the Government had never seriously contemplated meeting the hijackers' demand for the release of 11 terrorists. "The Government had no real choice," he said. "Releasing these 11 terrorists would have led only to new crimes. We weighed the risks as thoroughly as we could."

He appealed to the kidnappers of Hanns-Martin Schleyer, the head of the West German Employer Association, to release their prisoner and warned them that the road of terrorism was the road to self-destruction.

The kidnappers, who abducted Mr. Schleyer six weeks ago, have demanded in several messages the release of the same 11 prisoners that were named by the hijackers and had threatened to kill Mr. Schleyer unless the hijackers' demands were met. West German authorities are convinced that the hijacking was a "follow-up" action intended to obtain what the Schleyer kidnapping had not achieved.

Even at its moment of jubilation over the outcome of the raid on the hijacked airliner in Mogadishu, the Schmidt Government could not forget about the fate of Mr. Schleyer.

Nothing has been heard from his kidnappers since their last ultimatum on Friday. In that message they said that Mr. Schleyer would be killed Sunday afternoon unless the 11 members of the Baader-Meinhof organinzation had been freed by then. There is a lingering fear that Mr. Schleyer may still be discovered murdered.

"If our action [in Mogadishu] had not succeeded," Mr. Bolling said, "we would have had to face many questions. We accepted the risk." He added that the Government had felt that it had to put the safety of everyone over the safety of any one individual.

October 18, 1977

3 JAILED GERMAN TERRORISTS REPORTED SUICIDES AS HOSTAGES FROM HIJACKED PLANE FLY HOME

DEATHS CAUSE FUROR

Officials Unable to Explain the Presence of Pistols in Top-Security Cells

By PAUL HOFMANN
Special to The New York Times

BONN, Oct. 18—Three West German terrorist leaders committed suicide early today in a maximum-security prison in Stuttgart hours after German commandos stormed a hijacked Lufthansa plane in Somalia and blocked an attempt to free them, Justice Ministry officials announced.

The officials said that 34-year-old Andreas Baader, founder and leader of the Baader-Meinhof terrorist organization, and Jan-Carl Raspe, 33, had shot themselves and that Gudrun Ensslin, 37, had hanged herself. A fourth prisoner, 30-year-old Irmgard Möller, tried to stab herself with a bread knife, the officials reported.

The four were among the 11 imprisoned West German terrorists whose release had been demanded by four hijackers in exchange for the lives of 82 passengers and five crew members aboard the Lufthansa plane. The hijackers killed the pilot of the plane, but West German commandos, hurling special flash grenades, struck at 2 A.M. today, Somalia time (7 P.M. Monday, New York time), and in seven minutes killed three of the four hijackers and freed the remaining 86 hostages.

Joyful Welcome in Frankfurt

This afternoon, 80 of the hostages, still shaken by their ordeal, arrived in Frankfurt. Six others remained temporarily in Mogadishu, Somalia.

West German officials, politicans of all major parties and many private citizens throughout the country voiced joy and relief over the spectacular rescue of the hostages. But this mood was soon overshadowed by shock at the announcement by officials that three members of the Baader-Meinhof gang had been able to kill themselves in their cells at the maximum security Stammheim prison in Stuttgart.

Officials said they could not explain how the two men had managed to obtain pistols or how the woman terrorist had obtained the bread knife. Officials and others here and elsewhere in West Germany called for a thorough investigation. The Government expressed concern, and Franz Josef Strauss, the leader of the opposition Bavarian Christian Social Union, said the events at the prison "will have political consequences."

The release of the hostages today ended part of a drama that began Sept. 5 with the abduction of Hanns-Martin Schleyer, president of the West German employers and industry federations, by urban guerrillas who demanded the release of the same 11 jailed terrorists that the hijackers had tried to free. His whereabouts today still were unknown.

After the commando raid at Mogadishu, reports circulated that Dr. Schleyer had been killed, but these were disputed by the West German Government.

With the West German Government maintaining secrecy on the case, there was no official word here on the identity of the hijackers, three men and a woman, who seized the plane shortly after takeoff last Thursday from Palma, Majorca, for Frankfurt and then forced it to fly to Rome, Larnaca in Cyprus; Bahrain, Dubai, the United Arab Emirates, and Aden, Southern Yemen, before landing yesterday in the Somali capital of Mogadishu.

Woman Wounded and Captured

Two of the men were killed immediately during the attack by 60 West German commandos, and the third, who called himself "Mahmoud," died in a hospital of wounds. The woman was also wounded and captured, and she reportedly flashed a "V" sign and displayed a picture of Che Guevara to her captors.

Some reports said that at least the hijacker known as Mahmoud spoke Arabic, and some hostages recalled having heard commands in German.

Chancellor Helmut Schmidt said in Bonn during the day that the West German commando raid at Mogadishu had "set a standard for the fight against international terrorism."

The Chancellor, looking tired though self-assured, made his remark in an address to the Somali Ambassador, Yusuf Adan Bokah, when the diplomat and his African country were honored during a formal Cabinet meeting here. Somalia and its President, Mohammed Siad Barre, were praised for consenting to the West German commando raid on Somali territory.

In Stuttgart, Justice Minister Traugott Bender of the West German state Baden-Wurttemberg, told reporters at a hastily summoned briefing that he had "no explanation" how the prisoners had obtained their weapons. He said prison warders had been "under orders to search the prisoners' cells daily." Nor could he explain how the prisoners had heard the news that the hijackers' attempt to free them had failed.

In reply to questions, the Justice Minister said he could not exclude the possibility that there had been "outside help" in smuggling weapons into the cells. He said Mr. Baader had used a 7.65-millimeter Heckler & Koch pistol, and that Mr. Raspe had used a 9-millimeter weapon of the same make.

Otto Schily, a defense attorney for Miss Ensslin, said he could not exclude the possibility of "foul play." He said that in his view it was impossible for a prisoner to hide a weapon in the prison cell.

Evidently shocked at the prison suicides, Mr. Bender said non-West German medical authorities will be asked to conduct autopsies of the dead terrorists. Representatives of the International Red Cross and of Amnesty International, the London-based organization that just won the 1977 Nobel Peace Prize for its work for political prisoners, also are due to be admitted, it was learned.

Stammheim Prison was the scene of a terrorist suicide last year, when Ulrike Meinhof, another of the original guerrilla leaders, hanged herself.

Mr. Bender said that Mr. Baader and Mr. Raspe had last been seen alive at 11 P.M. yesterday when they received prescribed medication from a prison warder. The two women were last seen at 6 P.M. when they were locked up in their cells.

He said the terrorist prisoners had not been allowed contact with their lawyers, family members or other visitors since the kidnapping of Mr. Schleyer six weeks ago. It was then that the Bonn Government ordered a temporary ban on all outside contacts for convicted terrorists in an attempt to prevent new crimes. Mr. Baader had long been thought to direct terrorist activities throughout West Germany from inside his cell.

The Justice Minister said prison personnel had not heard the shots or any other untoward activities. "At night there is only one man on duty at the seventh floor maximum security section," he stated.

The terrorists at Stammheim were each held in a separate cell and had been barred from seeing one another or other prisoners since conditions were tightened in early September. "It is possible they were able to call to each other from their windows," the minister noted. "Whether Baader gave out the orders for the others to take their own lives, I do not know."

Mr. Baader, Miss Ensslin and Mr. Raspe along with Miss Meinhof belong to the original group of West German terrorists who formed a secret band in the late 1960's, later known as "Baader-Meinhof gang" to commit violent crimes against what they termed imperialism and West Germany's capitalist parliamentary system.

They were captured in 1972, and after a long trial at the fortress-like Stammheim Prison, especially built for the purpose, received life terms this April for killing five persons, among them four American servicemen, and for the attempted murder of scores of others.

Some experts on West German terrorism speculated that the deaths of three leaders of the Baader-Meinhof gang, which calls itself the Red Army Faction, might not mean the destruction of the extreme left-wing underground movement. They said that while the three had been revered as heroes and symbols by clandestine groups, a younger generation of radicals had assumed actual leadership.

These experts also said they were concerned that the urban guerrillas still at large might attempt to recoup from the latest setback to their cause by staging new spectacularly violent incidents.

Early today the Schmidt Government and all major parties, stressing that Dr. Schleyer's life must be saved, appealed to the kidnappers to release the industrial leader and warned that the "way of terrorism" was a road to self-destruction.

A number of members of Parliament expressed the view that the Government's handling of the Mogadishu raid had enhanced the prestige of Chancellor Schmidt. Many congratulatory messages over the mission were received from various heads of state and chiefs of government, among them one from President Carter.

October 19, 1977

Abducted German Industrialist Found Slain in France

Caller Says Schleyer, Kidnapped on Sept. 5, Was Killed in Retaliation for Somalia Raid

By PAUL HOFMANN
Special to The New York Times

BONN, Oct. 19—The body of Hanns-Martin Schleyer, the West German industrial leader who was kidnapped Sept. 5, was found today in the trunk of an abandoned car in the eastern French city of Mulhouse.

French policemen were directed to the scene by an anonymous telephone call saying that Dr. Schleyer had been slain out of "pain and anger" over the West German commando raid yesterday that ended a plane hijacking in Somalia and killed three of the four hijackers.

The caller also cited the officially announced suicides yesterday of three imprisoned West German terrorist leaders, whose release had been demanded by both the hijackers and the kidnappers of Dr. Schleyer.

French officials said Dr. Schleyer's throat had been cut. The news of his death, though not unexpected, caused deep shock in West Germany, already agitated by the series of interconnected violent events.

Government officials, seeking to explain how terrorist leaders could obtain the weapons to kill themselves in maximum-security cells in Stuttgart, rejected suggestions that the three had been slain by others.

The Western Democracies

"We have found no evidence that speaks against the deaths being suicides," the Stuttgart prosecutor's office said in a preliminary report issued tonight following autopsies performed on the bodies by a team of five specialists, three of them non-German.

Meanwhile, extremists hurled firebombs at West German property in cities across Italy and France today to avenge the prison deaths of the terrorist leaders.

There was nationwide elation over the success of the commando mission in Mogadishu, Somalia, in freeing 86 hostages from the plane that had been hijacked last Thursday after taking off from Majorca, Spain, for a flight to Frankfurt. That elation was then tempered by dismay over the deaths of Andreas Baader and two other terrorist leaders at Stuttgart, and today the mood turned even more somber when the news of Mr. Schleyer's death came.

Television stations canceled programs and substituted funeral music. Chancellor Helmut Schmidt called an emergency meeting of his crisis team, including leaders of all parties in Parliament.

The Chancellor is scheduled to report to Parliament tomorrow on the latest development.

The Government's chief spokesman, Klaus Bölling, declared in a televised press conference that the authorities would pursue the killers of Mr. Schleyer "with all means at our disposal."

"We will not have any rest," he said. "We will not give the murderers any chance."

Car Parked Outside Tenement

The body of Mr. Schleyer, the 62-year-old president of the West German Employers and Industry Federations, was found in a green Audi car that had been parked since yesterday outside a dilapidated tenement in Mulhouse, in the French border region of Alsace.

The local police were alerted after French and West German organizations received identical messages purporting to come from the kidnappers announcing that they had ended the industrialist's "miserable and corrupt" life.

The messages asserted that Mr. Schleyer had been killed 43 days after he was seized, which could mean yesterday morning. The text also said his death was "insignificant" as measured against the pain and fury caused by the "massacre" in Somalia and in the Stuttgart prison.

The message concluded by warning that Chancellor Schmidt and the "imperialists backing him" would never be allowed to forget the blood that has been shed. "The fight has only begun," it said.

After the message was received, French and West German officials quickly established liaison, and soon police officials of both countries converged on Mulhouse.

Fear of Booby Trap

Investigators hesitated to open the trunk of the green car before bomb experts had been called to the spot because of fear that it was a booby trap.

Government sources here said tonight that the kidnappers had apparently decided to kill the industrialist when they lost hope after the Somalia commando raid that the authorities would grant their demands.

October 20, 1977

Schleyer, Key Figure in Industry, Once a Top SS Official in Prague

Special to The New York Times

BONN, Oct. 19—When Hanns-Martin Schleyer, the bull-necked, chain-smoking automobile executive who was abducted by terrorists in Cologne on Sept. 5 and was found dead today at age 62, became president of the West German employers and industry federations last year, a newsman called him "the top boss in the country."

Mr. Schleyer had been president of the West German employers federation—the leading spokesman for management in negotiations with organized labor—since 1973.

By combining the two influential posts, he became one of the most powerful men in West Germany. He surely knew that he was high on a secret list of potential targets for assassination or kidnapping that radical plotters were known to have drawn up.

After terrorists killed a top banker, Jürgen Ponto, in a bungled attempt at abduction from his villa near Frankfurt late in July, Mr. Schleyer at last agreed to protection around the clock by a detail of three police volunteers. All three bodyguards, and Mr. Schleyer's driver, were killed in a hail of submachine-gun fire in the Cologne ambush.

Knew He Was in Danger

Mr. Schleyer apparently had no illusions as to how much danger he was in. He is reported to have written a memorandum months ago, stating that if he was captured by terrorists he would refuse to be traded for jailed extremists. That was the deal the urban guerrilla group that captured him had in mind when it offered to spare Mr. Schleyer's life in exchange for the release of 11 imprisoned ultraleftists.

In a letter to the federal criminal bureau, the Cologne guerrillas labeled Mr. Schleyer a "fat magnate" of the hated capitalist system, and enclosed a black-and-white photo showing him hunched in a chair in a gray undershirt, with a sign over his vast chest reading "Prisoner of the Red Army Faction."

Earlier, when Mr. Schleyer became known to the public through pictures in the newspapers and television appearances, the bulky industrial executive with the dueling scars on his face looked to some West Germans almost like a caricature of the "ugly capitalist."

However, labor officials who had to deal with him grudgingly conceded that his gruff, even abrasive ways were combined with fairness in negotiation and an agile mind. Lately he had stubbornly opposed labor proposals for giving workers a larger role—"codetermination"—in industrial management.

Hanns-Martin Schleyer
Sven Simon/Katherine Young

In his big-money, high-powered jobs and at home with his family, Mr. Schleyer was "always very calm," a friend said.

After he was kidnapped, Prague broadcasts reported at length about the attack and betrayed some sympathy for the captors of "the despoiler of the Czech economy." Thus many West Germans learned for the first time of Mr. Schleyer's role during World War II, a period in his life that had been glossed over by his official biographies.

Joined Nazi Party and SS

As a law student in Heidelberg and Innsbruck he had joined the Nazi Party and the SS, and in 1943, at the age of 28, he became the administrative chief at the headquarters of the industrial federation in Nazi-occupied Prague. In that capacity he had to channel Czech economic resources into the Nazi war effort.

After the collapse of the Nazi regime, Mr. Schleyer became an economic administrator, headed the foreign trade department of the Chamber of Commerce and Industry of Baden-Baden, and in 1951 joined the Daimler-Benz concern, manufacturer of the Mercedes auto.

In only eight years he worked his way up to a seat on the Daimler-Benz board in charge of personnel and labor questions. With Mercedes as his managerial base, he became influential in the metal industry. In 1963 he was instrumental in a lockout of 300,000 metal workers in a bitter labor dispute.

Mr. Schleyer, who was married and had four sons, had a home in Stuttgart and was on his way to an apartment on the outskirts of Cologne, headquarters of the employers association, when he was ambushed. The attackers opened fire, ripping holes in Mr. Schleyer's Mercedes. The Daimler-Benz director's vehicle had no bulletproof glass or any other special safety features.

October 20, 1977

The German Terrorists Have a Bond; It's Hatred

By HENRY BRANDON

BONN—Despite their links to terrorist groups abroad and the sympathy, however limited, they evoke among other German radicals, the violent young men and women responsible for the recent kidnappings, murders and bombings in West Germany belong to a different tradition. Terror in Northern Ireland or among Palestinians has an obvious objective—to further the cause of Irish or Palestinian nationalism. But among the adherents of Andreas Baader and Ulrike Meinhof no apparent aim or ideology can be found except the hatred of political stability, of economic affluence and of middle-class aspirations.

Their "politics of hatred" has much in common with the ragged and unruly Nihilists of the 1860's in Russia; like the Nihilists they scorn all social bonds and family authority and are more intent on destroying the existing order than on trying to build a new one. If they have a political outlook, it is the one expressed by Herbert Marcuse, the philosopher of anarchy. In the late 1960's in California, when the Weathermen were causing much concern in the United States, he was asked what he expected to happen in the wake of the revolutions as he preached and foresaw them and what new ideology he expected to rise from the scrapheap of the shattered structures of society. He only shrugged his shoulders and said he did not know.

The German terrorists from all that they have said do not know either. They come mostly from upper-middle and upper-class homes, the children of the affluent managers of West Germany's postwar economic miracle. There is nothing, from fast Porsches to expensive drugs, they could not afford. The woman guerrilla, Susanne Albrecht, the daughter of a wealthy Hamburg lawyer and who is accused of engineering the killing of her godfather, Juergen Ponto in July, summed up her ideology in one line to a family friend. "I'm tired of all that caviar-gobbling," she said.

Although hundreds of supporters attended the funeral last week of Mr. Baader, Gudrun Ensslin and Jan Carl Raspe last week in Stuttgart, the group's total support is limited, even among students. German students today are not in the kind of rebellious mood they used to be in the sixties. The atmosphere is not dissimilar from that on American university campuses, except for two or three universities where the radical left is exceptionally strong, as for instance, at the University of Marburg. The trade unions, who might be expected to be sympathetic to attempts to weaken the industrial leadership, in fact oppose radicalism. The unions are one of the more stable elements in German society.

An example of this limited support was provided recently when only a few hundred students assembled in the largest auditorium at the University of Frankfurt to discuss terrorism. Despite the subject of the conference it took quite a while before anyone would broach the central question that occupied many German minds: whether the three Baader-Meinhof gang leaders had been murdered or had committed suicide in prison. Even the one-time leader of the rebellious students at the Berlin and Paris universities, Daniel Cohn-Bendit, admitted that he did not know against or for whom to demonstrate. Quite a few of those present, however, dared to openly challenge the aims of the Baader-Meinhof group, or at least their terrorist methods, for, as one girl argued, "humanity cannot be achieved with inhuman means."

By coincidence, the Trilateral Commission, the discussion "tank" that Zbigniew Brzezinski and David Rockefeller created to stress the need for close cooperation among the highly industrialized nations of North America, Western Europe and Japan, held its annual meeting in Bonn in the midst of the terrorist atmosphere. To the terrorists, trilateralism has its own meaning even though the United States is no fertile ground for it now. By all the evidence, they hate everything these three pillars of the industrialized societies represent and it is a hatred that seems to have some support under the surface in some of the western European countries as has been shown by the violence in Italy and elsewhere that followed the deaths of Mr. Baader and his associates in Stuttgart.

With some premonition the Polish Marxist philosopher, Leszek Kolakowski, who now lives in London, in an address at the recent Frankfurt Book Fair analyzed the "politics of hate" as a danger to Western society. He argued that the indiscriminate use of terror robs one of one's critical faculties toward oneself and toward those one hates, for to be able to be critical one must be able to distinguish between good and evil. At the same time he said "to give up hate and fanaticism does not mean giving up the battle.... However to deploy it in the name of justice leads to self-destruction. It is the secret weapon of totalitarianism."

The Germans are very much aware of the consequences of the hatred the Nazis stirred up. And this is of course the reason why Germans are profoundly disturbed by the terrorists and the challenge they represent to the balance of the German mind. A nation that lost pride in its history, that does not identify with the state, as for instance, the French identify with France, but only with its government, depends for a stable outlook on wise political leadership. The enthusiasm for a united Western Europe, the young say, has evaporated, the political party system offers no alternative between the bourgeois Social Democrats and the Communists, economic and political stability have engendered boredom. The issues of the environment and nuclear proliferation offer only a partial outlet. "Freedom from conflict," as Mr. Kolawski put it, "is seemingly a virtue, but one that is reminiscent of the chastity of the castrated."

Why is it then that the responsible authorities expect terrorism to continue? No one has a plausible explanation, except the irrationality of the guerrillas and something that links them that is more than hatred: the fact that they have become outlaws There are also enough non-German terrorists with their own specific causes willing to help them keep going.

But the support in Germany seems likely to dwindle. Although extreme radical students call for a "war" against the current social order, they don't get the support even among their own. As one of the conferees at the University of Frankfurt said: "I'm not ready to go to war, because the masses are not ready to join us."

Henry Brandon is chief North American correspondent for The Sunday Times of London.

October 30, 1977

The Western Democracies

Of Terrorism, Marcuse and an 'Effort to Smear'

To the Editor:

Publication of Henry Brandon's demagogic attempt to link the name of Herbert Marcuse with the followers of Baader-Meinhof (Week in Review Oct. 30) calls fundamentally into question The New York Times's devotion to responsible journalism.

In one paragraph Brandon tries to associate 19th-century Russian nihilists, Baader-Meinhof, the U.S. Weatherpeople and Marcuse, who is dubbed "the philosopher of anarchy" and portrayed as preacher of hatred against "society." Nihilists and Baader-Meinhof are held to "scorn all social bonds and family authority." Presumably, this holds true for Marcuse.

That just the opposite is true should be evident to anyone who has bothered to read what Marcuse has written. Rather, he, together with his late colleagues of the Institute for Social Research, Max Horkheimer and Theodor W. Adorno, has been intent on preserving the integrity of private existence, including family relationships, against the one-dimensional assault on nonadministered forms of life in late capitalist society. As for "social bonds," Marcuse has emphasized the need to sustain and *re-create* them, in opposition to the tendency of that society to undermine all bases for human solidarity.

At no time has Herbert Marcuse advocated destruction for its own sake, not to speak of skyjacking or kidnapping. This effort to smear the name of the 79-year-old socialist philosopher itself smells of terrorism, of the kind that so long ago drove him into exile from his native Germany. Surely, The Times owes an apology both to Marcuse and its readers for Brandon's appalling attack on this distinguished thinker.

THEODORE MILLS NORTON
Vassar College
ROBERT PAUL WOLFF
WILLIAM E. CONNOLLY
University of Massachusetts
Amherst, Mass., Oct. 31, 1977
This letter was also signed by 11 other faculty members at four colleges and universities.

November 15, 1977

Herbert Marcuse
Camera Press/Pix

Of Marcuse, Terrorists And a Shared Hatred

To the Editor:

Professors Norton, Connolly and Wolff are correct in asserting that Herbert Marcuse has never advocated skyjacking, kidnapping or "destruction for its own sake" (letter Nov. 15). It should, however, be also noted, in all fairness to the terrorists of our times, that they did not advocate "destruction for its own sake" either. They advocate destruction and engage in acts of terrorism in order to weaken and discredit Western democratic societies.

What they share with Marcuse is the implacable (and in my opinion irrational) hatred of Western democracies. To this hatred, and to the misperception of Western societies, Marcuse has made a far from insignificant contribution by making it more difficult for many people to appreciate the political freedoms at their disposal (in Western societies) and in particular by trying to obscure the difference between truly repressive societies and "repressively tolerant" ones (in the West).

The relationship between ideas and actions is complex and often difficult to fathom. Belief in free expression is not compatible with faulting people for the misuse of their ideas. Yet it must be recognized that Marcuse's ideas have not been inconsequential in regard to the emergence of an ethos (in the late 1960's) which spawned the recent acts of political terror. This, I hope it will be recognized, is a proposition somewhat different from holding Marcuse responsible for political violence.
PAUL HOLLANDER
Professor of Sociology
University of Massachusetts
Amherst, Mass., Nov. 15, 1977

November 24, 1977

Of Herbert Marcuse and Anarchy

To the Editor:

The tone and the claims contained in the Nov. 15 letter by Professors Norton, Wolff and others in defense of Herbert Marcuse may not have surprised the informed, but to most others they could be highly misleading.

When I wrote in my Week in Review report on Oct. 30 that if the German "Baader-Meinhof gang" had a political outlook it was one expressed by Herbert Marcuse's philosophy of anarchy, I based it on a conversation I had with Marcuse in October 1966 at the University of California in San Diego. He then acknowledged that the extreme Weatherman student movement got some of its inspiration from his writings. He also stated that, while he did not advocate anarchy but revolution, there was nothing wrong with the former because even out of anarchy would emerge something new and better. In an interview published in The New York Times Magazine on Oct. 27, 1968, when asked whether he relied on anarchy to bring about the revolution he desired, he replied: "No. But I believe that the anarchist element is a very powerful and very progressive force and that it is necessary to preserve this element as one of the factors in a larger and more structured process."

Martin Greiffenshagen, professor of political science in Stuttgart, writing about the "Baader-Meinhof gang" in Der Spiegel of Oct. 31, calls Herbert Marcuse the "crown witness" of the politics that are "directed against civilization, technology, rationality, parliamentarianism, pluralism, and thereby against the rational political comprehension of the Western model."
HENRY BRANDON
Chief North American Correspondent
The London Sunday Times
Washington, Nov. 16, 1977

November 28, 1977

Marcuse and Weathermen

To the Editor:

The Nov. 28 letter by Henry Brandon concerning the baleful influence of Herbert Marcuse on the "Baader-Meinhof gang" contained one error of fact so vital that it tends to put his thinking itself into question. Referring to that influence, Brandon writes, ". . . I based it on a conversation I had with Marcuse in October 1966 at the University of California in San Diego. He then acknowledged that the extreme Weatherman student movement got some of its inspiration from his writings." This would have been a remarkable admission since there was no Weatherman faction in 1966, nor in 1967, nor in 1968.
EMILE DE ANTONIO
New York, Dec. 5, 1977

December 12, 1977

TERRORISM AND THE STATE TODAY

Baader-Meinhof—How Come? What's Next?

By Ralf Dahrendorf

LONDON — The hijackers have failed; except for the Lufthansa pilot, their hostages have survived; Ulrike Meinhof hanged herself last year, and now Andreas Baader and the hard core of their gang are dead (and the German Chancellor, Helmut Schmidt, has earned just praise for his nerve and sense of responsibility from many parts of the world). But two questions remain. One is, what next? It is a practical question and I for one am pleased that it is, in West Germany and elsewhere, in the hands of known defenders of freedom and the rule of law. The other question is, how could terrorism reach such proportions in West Germany in the first place? We are all groping, but unless we understand, we shall be unable to cope.

This is one attempt to understand, and perhaps it is all in the following story:

The girl, Susanne Albrecht, was no stranger to the Pontos. The daughter of a distinguished Hamburg lawyer, she had had many a fierce though apparently amicable discussion with her parents' friend, the brilliant head of the Dresdner Bank, Jürgen Ponto. He tried to talk the girl out of her extremist views, as so many of us have done with young people since the late 1960's. This time, on July 30, Susanne not only brought him his favorite flowers, a bunch of red roses, but came with two friends. The chauffeur-butler let them in, of course, and asked them to wait in the living room while the master of the house finished a phone call. Jürgen Ponto came in; they raised a submachine gun and told him to come with them as their hostage; he refused, and as he turned around they shot him in the back; he died two hours later. The murderers have not yet been found.

Jürgen Ponto and I were students together at the University of Hamburg after 1945, along with Helmut Schmidt and some others who have taken public responsibility. Both, Ponto and Schmidt, had come out of the war with the vow that neither totalitarianism nor war must ever happen again. They may have parted company politically, but their basic philosophies remained the same, and they were practical: What they had rebuilt with their own hands (and we literally did that with the University of Hamburg) they were not going to lose, nor were they going to abandon the air of liberty and role of law that we were breathing at last.

I ought to add that to me and my friends—10 years younger than the ex-army officers and less directly affected by the war—the position of our older friends often seemed a little tough, even authoritarian in defense of anti-authoritarianism. But in essence we shared their views.

So did Germany, or at least that half of it that was allowed to determine its own future. There are not many examples in history of a society changing so fundamentally in so short a time as that of the western part of Germany. (Nor are there many examples of one society changing so quickly into two almost diametrically opposed directions as the two Germanys—one of the less studied and more explosive developments of postwar history.)

Where there was a history of state domination of economic affairs, one of the most successful market economies of the world evolved. Where there was a society pervaded by authoritarian structures, participation and individual rights became a guiding principle. Where there was a political system persistently looking for certainty and the one leader who embodied it, parliamentary democracy gained a more than temporary foothold. This is the real German miracle—that the society has become liberal, and not only on its political surface.

I have thought for some time that 1969 played an important part in this process: the *Machtwechsel* ("change of administration") that made the Social Democratic opposition under Willy Brandt, and a rejuvenated Liberal Party under Walter Scheel, the parties of Government.

Contrary to Japan, Germany has proved its democratic potential by changing course without rocking the boat. Willy Brandt and Helmut Schmidt—but also the victims Jürgen Ponto and Hanns-Martin Schleyer, the kidnapped industrialist, no less symbolize the profoundly liberal potential of a new German society.

Leaders may disagree on levels of taxation and methods of co-determination, and other matters, but they do not disagree on the institutions and rules by which they want to live. And

Seymour Chwast

The Western Democracies

the overwhelming majority of the people support them.

But there are clearly some who do not. This is not in itself surprising. There is no society in the world that commands the support of all its members. What makes the German case special is two things: that it is, above all, the children of the successful who object, and that they find supporters, even if they rob banks and take hostages and kill unconcerned bystanders. There are "sympathizers" among a few hundred intellectuals and others—"knee-jerk" liberals (as they are called in America).

There is no simple explanation of this phenomenon, and in any case general statements do not take one very far. Hitler's children? There is something in this, especially if one considers how the killers use Marx's notion of "character mask" to dehumanize human beings. Affluence crime? This is a term (Wohlstandskriminalität) used by the German Chancellor, and clearly we are concerned with a version of white-collar crime. Yet the roots of the problem may well be deeper.

Yes, Germany has become democratic. Yes, German society has become liberal. Yes, the market economy has served people well. But what is it all about? This may not be a very sensible question; one may wonder whether societies are about anything; yet the question is asked quite often and answered rarely.

Helmut Schmidt and Jürgen Ponto knew what their efforts were about. My own generation knew and knows, too, on the whole. But after that, there is a vacuum. Germany is neither a Switzerland that is content with the safe prosperity of its citizens, nor a United States that is responsible for the security and prospects of many others—but what is it? What is the raison d'état of the Federal Republic of Germany?

There is an international aspect to this question that may have little to do with the murder of Ponto and the abduction of Schleyer, but which has surely contributed to the new doubts in the world community on the future of Germany. What is it that the Federal Republic wants?

How about, for example, the relationship between German unification and European union? What is the purpose and object of German foreign policy? Such questions must not be misunderstood.

Germany's Foreign Minister Hans-Dietrich Genscher has just made a credible case in the United Nations for Germany's commitment to peace, to economic development everywhere, and to the Western alliance. But there remain the bigger questions of German unity, ideas about Central Europe and the burden of an unfinished history.

I am not suggesting that there is any direct link between terrorism and these questions—but the inability to answer them contributes to the insecurity, the sense of self-doubt, that pervades the country. As a country — dare I say "nation"?—Germany has so far found neither purpose nor identity.

In an important sense, this is true for the internal processes of the Federal Republic, too. Despite the "guest workers," German society is essentially homogeneous; great issues like busing and the Bakke case are absent. There is no question of a people's front taking over. There is no economic predicament à la Britain, no historical compromise à la Italy to debate, not even the Scandinavian questions that arise from decades of Social-Democratic government.

The great slogans of Willy Brandt's Government (in which I, as one of its members, believed at least as much as most Germans) — "internal reforms," "daring more democracy" — remained slogans, paper promises, and never became serious social objectives. There is not only no major position to agree with; there is not even one to disagree with—unless one wants to disagree with everything, with "the system," which is of course exactly the sentiment that the terrorists are trying to exploit.

Perhaps what becomes evident here is one of the deepest deficiencies of German society: In the absence of an entrenched tradition of social cohesion, of values that are accepted without dispute, the country is wavering between total indiscipline and total discipline, between the destructive desire to violate all rules and the dangerous desire to create rules for every contingency. There was, perhaps, not enough time for changes to gain a real hold on successive generations of insecure young people.

But here I must stop an analysis that is already in danger of extenuating the inexcusable by dissolving it into the dust of theory.

The plain fact is that one of the democratic and liberal societies of the day, in which the rule of law is under no doubt at all, is threatened by both a middle-class children's protest against it and a general reaction to such protest that evokes unfortunate memories.

Those who govern Germany today are beyond doubt guarantors of liberty and the rule of law. But they need support, and they deserve it—from all those in the world who want to prove that change is possible and that the Federal Republic of Germany has done its part to support the cause of freedom in the last quarter of a century.

Ralf Dahrendorf, a former Parliamentary State Secretary in the West German Foreign Ministry, is now director of the London School of Economics.

October 20, 1977

Compensating for a Childhood in Germany

By Frederick Weibgen

Dear Mary,

It was when German terrorism had again made the headlines that you asked—after a powerful industrialist had been abducted and eventually killed; a chief federal prosecutor had been assassinated; a plane had been hijacked, grounded on some desolate airstrip in Somalia, the hijackers eventually shot to death by German commandos; Ulrike Meinhof, at one time leader of the terrorist Red Army Faction, had been found hanged in her cell in Stuttgart-Stammheim, West Germany's most secure prison, and Andreas Baader, co-leader of the Red Army Faction, along with two other terrorists in the same prison, had died violent deaths—it was then that you asked me what it all meant. I was German, you said, could I help you understand. And so, let me try.

For indeed, I am as German as the members of the Baader-Meinhof gang. I belong to their age group, somewhere between 25 and 35 years old. I have shared their past.

When Ulrike Meinhof and Andreas Baader and I grew up, we were ashamed of our country. We were told what had happened there—the marching and the boots, the *Sieg Heils* and the beatings, the loud, brutal and vulgar crowds, the people we loved being driven out — like Albert Einstein, Thomas Mann, Bertolt Brecht—their books, paintings and music scores burned. Other people we had never heard of, those nameless millions who so silently went to the camps, where their voices were gassed, forever silent.

This was no country to be proud of. That it was poor then was of little import. On the contrary, it was when Mercedes cars cruised the streets again, when neon lights went up everywhere, when furs and good meat and new houses again appeared that these symbols of affluence struck us as obscene rewards for obscene practices and added to the shame we felt. And so, the country was a stranger to us. We were expatriates living in Germany.

Then, on a personal level (should

I not say "even more personal," if one's country is to be more than a geographical locale?), we were also exiles, pained, lonesome kids amid adults who could not, must not, ever be trusted.

How could I trust my parents who, balancing me on their knees, sang "Deutschland, Deutschland, Uber Alles" with me? Who would make me call after a man in the street, a man I didn't even know, "Jew! Jew!" Who, with my father once a high-ranking SS officer, would tell me they'd never, never, heard of any camps. And who, when I asked them about the six million Jews that had been put to death (I got the figure, as pretty much all of the solid, reliable information, from some book—some *samizdat*, since family and school would not talk) insisted it was "4.5 million," the figure I quoted having been made up by the notoriously deceitful Jewish media— 4.5 million, while my heart was counting one and one and one and one and is still counting to reach that simple, neat, short figure.

Trust my teachers who taught me nine years of Latin, six years of Greek, two years of English (oh, yes, a gesture to the new *Zeitgeist*), philosophy, sciences and fine arts, and yet were so clumsy at the fine art of teaching history? Two hours were spent on some of the more questionable aspects of the Nazis' reign (including camps), some days on the German Army's heroic exploits, and some weeks on more lasting aspects of the Third Reich like the Führer's doing away with unemployment, building highways and curbing inflation.

We were young then. Not dumb. Not without insight. We could tell right from wrong, scoundrels from decent men. We knew the difference between inflicting pain and suffering pain, between the mighty and the defenseless. We could tell lies. But, being young, we had to disguise our knowledge. Store it. Never forget it. Preserve it. Defend it until the day would come when, old enough, we could speak. The day when we could respond. Reveal our pain, the pain of kids without country and family, the answer born out of shame and in anger.

Thus we grew up. There were many different answers, depending on individual temperament. But all bore the sign of a curious determination, the determination of people who not only have to build their lives, but build it from scratch, like settlers: invent an ersatz country, an ersatz family, a new life, untainted. . .

And so, one of my sisters adopted a Korean, then a Vietnamese child. Here is to you, my parents, who so much believed in, and contributed to, the Aryan ideal of tall and blond and blue-eyed offspring — Homo sapiens' finest achievement.

And another of my sisters became not just any, but a fervent Pentecostal Christian. Here is to you, my father, who spent all those years away from your children, waging some war or other, then returned, still with all the hatred, still without love.

And yet another of my sisters, turning to any and all left-wing causes. Here is to you again, my father, who so neatly exchanged the black of the SS uniform for the business executive's suit.

Then myself. Not so unselfish as to adopt children. Not a believer, somebody who would espouse religion, traditional or left. (How could I after a childhood in a country run into the ground by believers?) But searching all the same for this new family, this new country.

So I joined the United Nations: a family of nations, a no-man's-land beyond the folly of any single one country, and who is to say that simplistic answers, in and by themselves, are always wrong ones?

At about the same time, emerging from similar backgrounds, carrying similar wounds, Ulrike and Andreas and the other German terrorists formulated their answer. It was to be terrorism

Terrorism as a philosophy transcended and rendered obsolete the need for country and family (far from being accidental — the *international makeup* of Baader-Meinhof terrorism must have attracted gang members). As a philosophy it also laid claim to the Truth: Away with the lies of the past.

As the self-professed war against fascism and capitalism, (the unholy alliance of which Baader-Meinhof had seen so intimately), it was Evil itself they were fighting against and you don't fight fire other than with fire; so they fired.

As action, terrorism proved (to which parents?) that these kids had listened enough, shut up too much and been waiting so long to prove (to which jury?) that they were different, that they would not stand by when wrong was done.

As a statement, finally, it said: "I am me now. I am grown up. I hate you, parents. I hate you, country. I will do away with you." And that's what they set out to do.

I am not sure, Mary, whether I helped you understand. I am sure I understand (not condone, mind you— *understand* some of the underlying pathology). I am sure Ulrike and Andreas are dead because they understood.

Frederick Weibgen works for the United Nations Food and Agriculture Organization. The "Mary" to whom the letter is addressed is his wife.

January 17, 1978

Suspicion Festers in Prison Deaths of German Terrorists

By JOHN VINOCUR
Special to The New York Times

STUTTGART, West Germany, Jan. 17— Three months after the deaths in Stammheim Prison here of three West German terrorist leaders, doubts remain about what the Government has said were suicides rigged by the victims to look like murders.

If Andreas Baader, Jan-Carl Raspe and Gudrun Ensslin sought to discredit the West German Government and create an aura of martyrdom for themselves, as the Government believes they did, they failed in the view of the vast majority of West Germans.

Among many young people, and especially young leftists, there is a continuing suspicion that the terrorists were murdered on Oct. 18 after other terrorists failed to win their freedom by hijacking a West German plane. This suspicion is commonplace elsewhere in Western Europe, notably in France, Spain, Italy and Scandinavia, according to reports from New York Times correspondents, and in spite of an autopsy finding that the deaths were suicides.

Misgivings Scrawled on Walls

"Gudrun, Andreas and Jan—tortured and murdered" is the message occasionally scrawled on walls in West Germany.

"I think just about every university student, and most intellectuals in the country have very serious misgivings about what actually happened," said Haug von Kuenheim, managing editor of the liberal weekly Die Zeit. "It's become a bit of an obsession."

In France, the leftist newspaper Liberation published a special magazine, which had on its cover a drawing of Mr. Baader gently stroking Miss Ensslin's cheek. The concluding article said: "If the conviction of a massacre has hardened, it's simply because it has become plausible. It's this potential of the German state, at least marginally, to commit such an act that is frightening."

An investigation now being conducted by the Baden-Württemberg state government has failed to clear the air. Most importantly, a basic contradiction in testimony has confronted an explanation by a federal official that was seemingly meant to provide a final convincing account of how three convicted terrorists, two armed with pistols, could commit suicide simultaneously in a supposedly inviolable maximum-security prison.

The main ingredient of disbelief was the failure in the initial accounting, issued a week after the deaths, to explain how pistols were obtained by Mr. Baader and Mr. Raspe. Last week, the chief federal prosecutor, Kurt Rebmann, seemed to furnish the conclusive missing element when he said to the commission that information from a terrorist cooperating with the investigation had made clear that the weapons had been smuggled into Stammheim in hollowed-out court documents by Arndt Müller, a radical lawyer. The explanation remained credible for five days until three police offices disavowed Mr. Rebmann's testimony before the commission.

Police Testimony Impugned

The prosecutor incorrectly stated, they said, that lawyers were excused from sur- of a packet of documents containing a every case, they added, the documents were tested by metal detectors, "examined, shaken and leafed through." Besides, an officer said, the unusual weight of a packet of doccuments containing a pistol would have given it away.

A high official of the state Justice Ministry dismissed the value of this police testimony, saying privately: "The police look very bad in this affair. They obviously have to protect themselves and must say they did their job properly."

But on the same day as the police officers' testimony, Irmgard Möller, a fourth convicted terrorist who was found in her cell with superficial knife wounds in her chest at the time of the three deaths, told the commission that her comrades had considered suicide to be out of the question because "we had decided to continue the struggle." On the contrary, she said, the Stammheim group feared being killed by their guards.

"The last thing I remember," she said, "was finding myself, freezing and trembling on a stretcher in a corridor. I heard a man's voice say: 'Baader and Ensslin are cold already.'"

The woman suggested that she had been drugged and insisted that she had not stabbed herself.

Although a group of physicians specializing in forensic medicine, three from outside West Germany, reported in the autopsy that all signs pointed to suicide, lawyers and supporters of the terrorists have been attacking their conclusions.

In the case of Mr. Baader, the critics of the suicide theory point to signs of a struggle in his cell—bullets fired into the wall and mattress—and to the manner of his death, a bullet fired into the back of the head. Mr. Baader's lawyers say that he was left-handed and find it incomprehensible that powder burns and flecks of blood were discovered, according to the autopsy report, on the thumb and forefinger of his right hand.

Other friends of Mr. Baader, noting that traces of what appears to have been sand were found on his shoes, have even suggested that he might have been transported to Somalia for negotiations with the hijackers of the Lufthansa jetliner, then returned to Germany and killed.

In the case of Miss Ensslin, who was found hanged with wires from a radio she owned, critics have pointed to unexplained scratches on her chest and bruises on her knees as suggesting that she had been involved in a struggle.

In each instance, there is a strong official answer to the charges. The bullets fired into the wall and mattress and the wound in the back of the head were obviously meant to suggest murder, the initial report said. Mr. Baader's gun, according to a source close to the investigation, was possibly held with two hands, one grasping the barrel, making it possible for either to bear traces.

The "sand" found on the shoes appears to come from the prisoner's gardening work earlier in the year, the investigators said. They said it would be physically impossible for a prisoner to be transported to Africa and returned here between the time of the last check on Mr. Baader by a guard and the time that his body was discovered

As for the scratches and bruises on Miss Ensslin's body, they are explained as likely to have come from involuntary and unconscious movement seconds before death.

Other public statements by officials have led to even more confusion over the deaths.

A Baden-Württemberg state official has conceded, for example, that the state government took no concrete action to search the terrorists' cells more thoroughly after the discovery in September of an unauthorized miniature camera in one of them. Then, in testimony before the commission, officials of the state's Justice and Interior Ministries attacked each other, insisting that the other bore responsibility for security at Stammheim.

A police union official criticized the federal prosecutor for suggesting that his men had been negligent, and a member of the investigation commission acknowledged to a reporter that because the terrorists had contacts inside the prison with prisoners serving time on other charges, it was possible that they could have obtained weapons or communications equipment from them.

The commission's report to the state parliament is expected about the middle of next month. "There won't be any surprises in it," said Helmut Engler, a state Justice Ministry official. "And I don't doubt that the people who want to believe there were murders will continue to do so regardless of how strong and complete the evidence is to the contrary."

January 22, 1978

Blast in Milan Kills 13, Hurts 85; 3 More Bombs Injure 16 in Rome

Special to The New York Times

ROME, Dec. 12 — A terrorist bomb in Milan killed at least 13 persons today and injured about 85. Three more blasts, in Rome, injured 16 persons.

The explosion in Milan this afternoon devastated the lobby and public room of the National Bank of Agriculture in Piazza Fontana.

In Milan's Italian Commercial Bank in the Piazza della Scala, near La Scala opera, policemen found a newly bought satchel that contained a box of high explosives weighing about 20 pounds.

The target of one of the three bombs in Rome was also a bank. Fourteen persons were injured, none seriously, when a bomb exploded shortly after 5 P.M. in the cellar of the National Bank of Labor just off the Via Veneto and a short distance from the United States Embassy. The blast shattered windows in the bank and in neighboring buildings.

At least two other persons were injured when two bombs exploded at about 5:20 P.M. at the white marble monument dedicated to King Vittorio Emmanuele II in the Piazza Venezia — the "center" of Rome. One bomb showered marble fragments on passers-by while the other blasted in the doors of a small museum and shattered the windows of the Ara Coeli Church behind the monument.

The bombings, termed "ghastly" and "brutal" crimes by President Giuseppe Saragat, produced a new upsurge of public outrage, fear and insecurity in a nation already shaken by political instability and violent confrontation of extremist forces — the "Maoist" left and the neo-Fascist right.

Late tonight, Milan policemen said that 70 people had been detained for questioning. They were described as "extremists of all directions."

Extremists have exploited an autumn of widespread strikes by provoking clashes with security forces during peaceful demonstrations by orthodox labor union members. The bombings were the latest in a wave of violence this year that began in April when 20 persons were injured when a bomb exploded in the Fiat automobile company's pavilion at the In-

TERRORISM AND THE STATE TODAY

ternational Milan Trade Fair.

In August, 11 persons were injured when 8 bombs exploded on 7 trains.

The latest bombings had immediate repercussions in the Parliament. Deputies from almost all political parties called upon the Government to tell the nation what measures it was planning to take the meet the violence.

Premier Mariano Rumor, in a television broadcast, vigorously condemned the "vile criminals" and promised that the Government would take all steps to capture them. Calling for respect for the law, he warned the nation that a community could "lose itself" if it did not uphold the laws.

President Saragat, in his message to the nation, said the bombings were a "ring in a chain of terrorist attacks that must be broken at all costs."

Policemen said the bank bombing in Milan took place about 4:20 P.M. The bomb had been placed under a large table in the center of the public room where about 300 people had gathered.

The explosion was said to have sent bodies flying through the air and shattered windows up to a hundred yards away. It tore a hole three feet across in the floor of the bank.

The agricultural bank is not normally crowded. However, on Friday afternoons it becomes a type of "market place" where farmers and farm agents gather to buy and sell agricultural products and land.

In a message to President Saragat, Pope Paul VI expressed his "intimate participation of pain and prayer." Such acts are "wholly contrary to the civilization and Christian tradition of the Italians," the Pope said.

December 13, 1969

Machine of State Stalled, Italians Feel

By PAUL HOFMANN
Special to The New York Times

ROME, March 28—These are days of bombings and plots, spectacular robberies and urban guerrillas, an election campaign full of cabals and alarming rumors, and on top of it all the death of a famous publisher, a friend of Fidel Castro, in a mysterious explosion at the foot of a power pylon.

An internationally known writer, asked for an article on "Italy's future" for a United States publication, guffaws and says, "Italy has no future!"

The Easter tourists who are crowding into Rome see little reason for such gloom. One may have trouble getting luggage at the ramshackle Fiumicino Airport because the ground personnel are striking intermittently, and one may have to subsist on sandwiches because restaurant workers walk out, but everything seems cheerful and prosperous enough.

All over Italy new cars fill the highways and smartly dressed people throng the streets. "Surely this is one country where life is still pleasant," a visitor from Paris observed. "I get a lot of smiles here. What a relief after those French scowls."

Yet many Italians are bewildered, troubled, even anguished as they are confronted daily by a barrage of baffling and ominous news.

Sociologists say that the protests and the tensions are the results of economic growth that has been too quick and too uneven. The affluence created by the efficient industries in northern Italy remained spotty and left large patches of poverty. The central bureaucracy in Rome is as lethargic as ever. The deep South is still one of Europe's backward areas.

Six million poor Southerners have migrated to northern Italy since World War II seeking jobs —two million more have gone abroad—and many of them feel exploited and discriminated against. Discontented Southerners are often in the vanguard of the worker and student protests. While post-Fascist Italy has managed to build one of the most efficient road networks in Wested Europe, it has failed to modernize its outdated social structures. Disorganized schools, hospitals and law courts, poor public transit, inadequate housing and other grievances have led to increasingly frequent outbreaks of rage.

"Italy is shaken by turbid ferment; it runs the risk of becoming a country on the outskirts of civilization and reason," said a leading newspaper, La Stampa of Turin.

Every foreigner who has lived here for some time is being asked by friends: "If you were an Italian, for which party would you vote?" It seems that there are many more people who can give convincing reasons why not to support any of the eight or nine major parties in the general elections on May 7 and 8 than people professing firm political loyalties.

The statement that Italy had no future was not just a witticism; the man who made it explained:

"The neo-Fascists are going to pick up a lot of votes in the coming elections because the people yearn for order, and if the Christian Democrats make a government with them, the workers will rise and we'll have a civil war.

"If instead the Christian Democrats form a government with the Communists, the chances are we'll have a civil war too. Since the Christian Democrats aren't strong enough to run the country alone, the best that can happen is another indefinite, messy period of just muddling through."

Advice From Foreigners

Government ministers who ought to know what is going on ask foreign callers what they think will happen—and actually seem to listen. Many newspapers have taken to reprinting foreign press comment day after day.

Italians, questioned about the uncertain mood will say that they feel let down by the politicians, manipulated by state television and disappointed by a democratic system and administrative machinery that threaten to fall to pieces. "Italy has been drifting for years," a lawyer remarked.

The country has indeed lacked far-sighted political leadership since the late Alcide De Gasperi, was eased out in 1953 after serving as Premier for seven crucial years.

His party, the Christian Democrats, remained the biggest vote-getting group but quickly degenerated into a loose confederation of warring and scheming factions. The Communist party remained the biggest Marxist force in the West but turned into a bureaucratic machine with a marked appetite for power.

3 Years of Turmoil

Something new has happened since 1968. The wave of protest that started on American campuses and almost overthrew President de Gaulle in France spilled into this country — and has not abated.

For three years schools have been in turmoil, industries are shaken by wildcat strikes and small extremist groups have been battling with each other and the police.

On Dec. 12, 1969, an explosion in a Milan bank killed 16 persons. An inquiry exposed police inefficiency and the chaotic procedures of an archaic judicial system.

An anarchist, Pietro Valpreda, has been in jail for 27 months on charges of having planted the bomb. A few days ago a neo-Fascist, Giuseppe Rauti, was imprisoned on suspicion of having engineered the bombing. That the public is disconcerted is no surprise.

The chief prosecutor in Milan told newsmen that the anarchist and the neo-Fascist, despite their ideological differences, might have acted jointly — or again they might not. The same official confided that he did not allow his assistant prosecutors to give him important information by phone "because in our dear Italy, one never knows."

The case of Giangiacomo Feltrinelli, the millionaire by inheritance who became a successful publisher and a backer of ultraleftist movements, deepened the general feeling of conspiracy and confusion.

Leftists Charge Frame-up

Mr. Feltrinelli had gone underground. The circumstances in which his body was found seemed to suggest that he had been killed accidentally while trying to dynamite a power line in a protest against "the system."

Leftists charged that the publisher had been murdered by neo-Fascists or Italian secret-service men or by the United States Central Intelligence Agency. Mr. Feltrinelli was no Che Guevara (whom he had admired), the leftists said, but his murder was designed to frighten people into voting for right-wing law-and-order tickets.

The judicial investigation has nibbled away at that theory. Luigi Barzini, the journalist and author, who was once married to Mr. Feltrinelli's mother, says that while a conspiracy cannot be entirely ruled out, it is hard to imagine a secret agent with the talents "of a great novelist or a great play director, capable of staging a death so in keeping with the personality, style and character" of the 45-year-old publisher.

The trend of recent events has built the impression that the leftist and neo-Fascists extremists are encouraging each other's militancy and that in effect they complement each other.

The chief representative of the central Government in Milan, Libero Mazza, estimated some time ago that about 20,000 extremists of all brands were enrolled in paramilitary organizations in that city, a center of urban guerrilla activity. Throughout the nation the clandestine left-wing and right-wing fringes may number 50,000 people, according to the most reliable guesses. In a traditionally nonviolent nation of 55 million people, informed observers comment, it should not be too hard to bring the extremists under control.

The Italian Communist party

has condemned ultraleftist "adventurism" in the same stern terms as the French Communists use. At the same time the parliamentary branch of neo-Fascism, the Italian Social Movement, is trying hard to look respectable and moderate. The leaders are urging organizers of campaign rallies to display no black shirts and no Mussolini portraits, and to hang lots of Italian tricolors.

The neo-Fascist leader, Giorgio Almirante, a onetime actor and a Government aide under Mussolini, is a formidable campaigner, all suavity and reasonableness. The new Communist party chief, Enrico Berlinguer, a sad-looking Sardinian aristocrat, sounds more like a Social Democrat than a revolutionary.

The electoral strategy of the Communists and neo-Fascists clearly betrays their worry that the violence and plots may favor the middle-of-the-road parties.

No Single Leader Seen

These are the Christian Democrats, whose many factions—united only in their professions of loyalty to the Roman Catholic Church—range from conservatives to near-Marxists; the Socialists and Social Democrats, both Marxist; the Republicans, left of center but anti-Marxists, and the right-of-center Liberals.

No one of the many Christian Democratic notables is able to speak for the entire party. However, the smart money is on former Premier Amintore Fanfani as the most likely to patch together another coalition after the elections. It may be a shade more to the right than the center-left alliance whose collapse brought about the disbanding of Parliament in February, more than a year ahead of schedule.

March 29, 1972

Troubled Italy

By Rosario Romeo and George Urban

The following interview, which originated with Radio Free Europe, is excerpted from The Washington Review of Strategic and International Studies, a quarterly published by Georgetown University's Center for Strategic and International Studies. Rosario Romeo is professor of history at the University of Rome and author of several works on Italian history. George Urban, a scholar and journalist, is editor of the book, Détente, published in Britain.

George Urban: Wouldn't you say that Italy is, by virtue of the temperament of the people and the conservatism of her institutions, in a state of permanent not, far from malign, much less bloodthirsty, civil war?

Rosario Romeo: I would hesitate to describe our situation as civil war even in the benign sense in which you have tried to depict it, but it is certainly true that we are always on the brink of precipitating a serious crisis. Why this is so is something very hard to understand if you are an American or even a Briton.

In Italy the difference between having [Enrico] Berlinguer [head of the Communist Party] and a Christian Democrat at the head of the Government is a matter heavy with consequences for the entire future of the state and the nation.

I know Americans who think the Italians exaggerate, that the [Communist Party] is really a Social Democratic party, that there would be nothing very terrible in having Berlinguer as Prime Minister, and so on. But this is misreading our situation. Since the 1968 upheavals in France and Italy, our country has never returned to normality. We are suffering from what could be described, with some exaggeration, as a permanent general strike.

There is continuous agitation at the schools, universities, railways, airports, post offices, in the press, and in the factories. And the strikes are more and more often clinched by violence and the threat of violence. Our economic life, civic security and international position have all been deeply affected.

You have to live in Italy to get the full measure of this: It has become practically impossible to manage public institutions or private enterprise, because the legitimacy of all authority has been challenged and defeated. We have examples of this every day. At the moment we are suffering from the suspension of the law in favor of terrorists. There are two principal leftwing terrorist groups in Italy: the Red Brigades in the north and the Proletarian Armed Guards in the south. Some members of these gangs have been arrested and put on trial in Turin and Naples. But when the arrested men's colleagues began attacking the police and the judges, the trials were halted and no more arrests followed.

The terror is being successful—both the judiciary and the police are frightened of being shot in the streets, as some have been. The most recent [May 1977] example of the defeat of the law has been the abandonment of the trial of a group of Red Guard terrorists in Turin. The intimidating effect of threats and recent murders has been so thorough that no jury could be found to sit at the trial.

Or take another kind of disorder. You have no doubt read in the Italian papers that so-called "young proletarian committees" have set up house in the University of Milan. They occupied the university, stopped all teaching and research, and went on a rampage, destroying books, documents, scientific instruments, as well as wrecking the premises. The rector did not call in the police, and when asked why, he said he was anxious to avoid more serious incidents which might have included loss of life.

And you could see what he meant: When you call in the police to expel young people armed with iron bars, knives and Molotov cocktails, the possibility of someone getting hurt or killed can never be ruled out—it has happened in the past—and if a student gets killed, the rector is held responsible, for wasn't he the one who had called for police protection?

At that point, up goes the cry in every radio and television program and in every newspaper in the land that the university teachers do not understand the young—and look what has happened: They've caused the death of a student! There then follows an emotion-packed funeral which thousands attend, and the sight of which on the television screen further magnifies the demand for the rector's head. The rector is, by now, completely alone. The political ruling class have disowned him. In fact, they reinforce the charge that he alone was responsible. Can you blame the rector for refusing to assert his authority?

The irony is that in our latest round of troubles the extreme left has started armed attacks on members of the Communist Party, and the Communist press is calling for police protection. And while this is going on, Berlinguer continues to demand power for his party on the grounds that "without the Communist Party it is impossible to govern Italy."

So when Americans tell me that the Italian Communists are Social Democrats or social reformers, we tend not to be in complete agreement. I have long given up trying to explain Italian politics to Americans.

Urban: I am strongly, and perhaps wrongly, under Luigi Barzini's influence in thinking that the basic good nature and opportunism of Italians would somehow take the heat out of, or at any rate corrupt, the extremism of any Italian political party.

Romeo: I have heard this argument before and I'm far from certain that it is true. Where is this great humanity of the Italians? Italy is, and has always been, a country of violence. Some of the most famous assassins in world literature are Italians, usually imported for their skills. There are cities and entire regions in Italy today where murder is an everyday occurrence.

Only yesterday I was talking to a former student of mine who is now a member of the regional government of Calabria. "There are two million people in Calabria," he said, "of whom only 80,000 have gone to school, and even these have no work commensurate with their qualifications. One of the results is that anyone with a little

TERRORISM AND THE STATE TODAY

100˙000˙000 di TAGLIA
RICERCATO

AVV. GIANNI AGNELLI

INCENDIARIO & GOLPISTA

LA VERITA' E' RIVOLUZIONARIA

LOTTA CONTINUA

An Italian political poster

money in the bank is exposed to blackmail: If you are a shopkeeper or a lawyer or a doctor or anyone suspected of having savings, you are made to pay protection money if you want to stay in business. If you are known to be rich, your chances of being kidnapped and released only against large sums of money are high. The situation is completely out of hand.

"Recently we and the Communists [the man is a Socialist] organized a mass demonstration, with Red flags and a great deal of worker participation, against the spread of this evil. A few days later the police tried to arrest some of the criminals involved—there was an exchange of fire and one of the wanted men was killed. A funeral was arranged and the Mafia let it be known that it expected the entire population of the small town where the man was to be buried to be present. Well, all shops were dutifully shut, all offices were closed for the day, and the entire population appeared in the funeral procession—not because they had any sympathy with the dead extortioner but because they were frightened of the consequences of not doing what the Mafia had ordered them to do."

Where, I ask you, is the exceptional wisdom and humanity of the Italians? In Lombardy and Piedmont, for some years after the war, criminality was rampant. In Emilia there was a "triangle of death," composed of the cities of Regio, Parma and Bologna, where the assassination of landowners and capitalists for reasons no other than their "class" was a common feature of life. These were all Communist strongholds. Even now, if you go to Turin or Milan or some of the other large industrial centers, the atmosphere is so thick with political hatred that you can almost touch it with your hands. And you say the Italians are kindly folk?

Naturally, there is good and bad in every nation. There is a bit of the brute in all of us as well as some faint glimmer of the gentle Jesus. But to say that the Italians have a special knack for sinking their differences and letting reason prevail does not make sense to me. It is an old truth that it takes two to make peace but one is enough to make war.

Of course in Italy, as elsewhere, the man in the street is a good-natured fellow. He is happiest when he is left alone, for his concerns are a secure job, a roof over his head, a satisfactory sexual life, and the odd weekend at the seaside. But it isn't this sluggish majority that makes things tick in history. The Fascists weren't the majority of the Italian people, but they took power, and it was not very easy to say to them: "But what has become of your good nature?" They had simple answers to complicated questions and the power to tolerate no others.

Today, again, we have a determined minority waiting in the wings to exploit the first turbulence in our political, economic or social equilibrium. And if this were to happen I would not vouch that civil strife could be avoided.

January 2, 1978

MORO SLAIN, BODY FOUND IN ROME

HE IS SHOT 10 TIMES

Ex-Premier Is Discovered in Car on Downtown Street 54 Days After Abduction

By HENRY TANNER
Special to The New York Times

ROME, May 9—The bullet-riddled body of former Prime Minister Aldo Moro was abandoned by his kidnappers today in a parked car in the historic center of Rome, a short distance from the headquarters of both the Communist and Christian Democratic parties, whose alliance the terrorist Red Brigades are fighting to destroy.

The discovery of the body behind the back seat of a burgundy red French Renault R-4 came 54 days after Mr. Moro, who was expected to be the next president of Italy, was abducted in a hail of gunfire in a street near his suburban home by urban guerrillas belonging to the Red Brigades.

Policemen raced to Via Caetani shortly after 1 P.M. today after intercepting an anonymous phone call to one of Mr. Moro's secretaries. The caller said, "In Via Caetani there is a red car with the body of Moro," and hung up, officials at Rome police headquarters said.

The kidnapping of Mr. Moro led to a nationwide manhunt by thousands of policemen and soldiers. Roadblocks were set up throughout the Rome area and a number of suspected terrorists were arrested in extensive house-to-house searches.

Mr. Moro was killed sometime early yesterday, according to first estimates by the police. He had at least 10 bullet holes in his chest. The cuffs of his trousers were full of sand as if he had been walking on a beach or been dragged across rough soil shortly before his death, the police said.

He was dressed in the clothes he had worn on the day of his abduction: a navy blue suit, a heavy overcoat, striped shirt and dark tie. He was found lying in the luggage compartment of the small car, his head leaning against the back of the rear seat. His face had been covered by a blanket. Next to his body was a plastic bag containing his watch, razor and other personal effects.

Mr. Moro was killed before being placed in the car, according to police sources, who said that there were no bullet holes in his overcoat. He was lying in a pool of blood.

The news of the discovery of Mr. Moro's body spread rapidly through Rome after radio stations broke into their programs with bulletins at about 1:30.

There were no crowds in front of the Communist headquarters, but in front of the offices of the Christian Democrats, throngs of grieving men and women shouted their anger. "Moro is alive!" some cried. Others shouted, "Death to the Red Brigades!" or just "Murderers!"

When a car with Christian Democratic officials left the building it was booed by some of the bystanders. A man shouted "Berlinguer murderer!" presumably because he blamed the Communist Party, whose leader is Enrico Berlinguer, for the tough stand the Government had taken.

All over Italy flags on government buildings and the offices of political parties were lowered, and special prayers were offered in most churches. Trade unions called a half-day general strike for tomorrow afternoon as a sign of mourning for Mr. Moro and of protest against terrorism.

Special editions of the morning newspapers, some with several pages of text and pictures of Mr. Moro, were out by midafternoon. The extra edition of the Rome afternoon daily Vita Sera announcing Mr. Moro's death was being sold on the streets by the time the body was removed from the car. Demonstrators in front of the Christian Democratic headquarters waved it over their heads as they shouted their anger at the terrorists.

In killing Mr. Moro, his abductors lived up to the threats they had made in public statements over the last several weeks. They announced on April 15 that they had sentenced him to death during a "people's trial" held at the place where they kept him hidden. On April 24, they offered to spare his life if the Government agreed to free 13 prisoners, including six members of the Red Brigades, from Italian jails. When the Government rejected their demand, they renewed their death threats.

Throughout the 54-day drama, the Red Brigades controlled the situation. The police and armed forces conducted a countrywide search but found no solid clues to the whereabouts of the "people's prison" where Mr. Moro was hidden. It now seems that he was kept in or near the capital all the time.

Last Taunt by Terrorists

The terrorists last taunting gesture was in leaving his body within 300 yards of

TERRORISM AND THE STATE TODAY

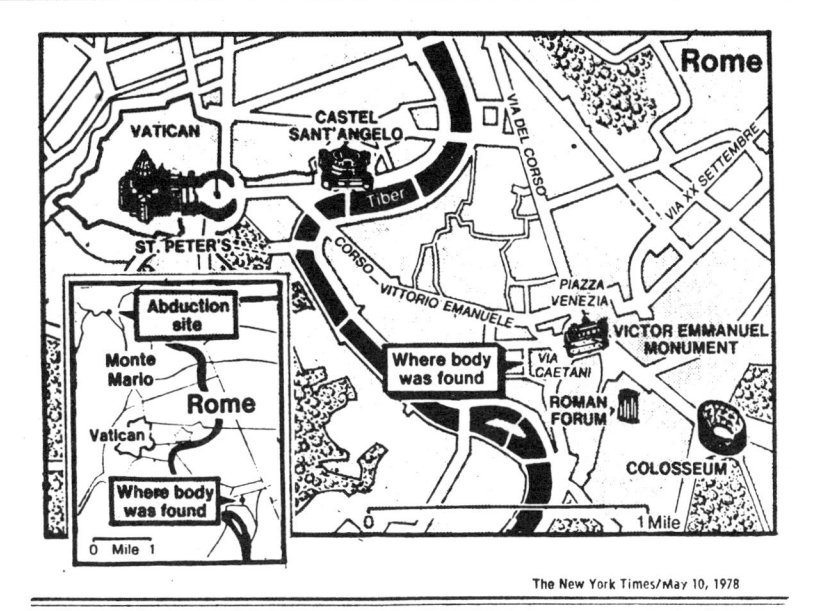

the headquarters of the Christian Democratic Party and perhaps 200 yards from the heavily guarded headquarters of the Communist Party.

The Communist Party and the Christian Democrats together make up the political establishment that the terrorists, who consider themselves the "real" Communists, want to bring down through a civil war that they hope their acts of terrorism will help unleash.

The two parties together determine Italian politics. The Cabinet of Prime Minister Giulio Andreotti is made up exclusively of Christian Democratic ministers, but the Communists are formally committed to supporting it in Parliament and thus keep it in power.

The leaders of the Communist Party were even more strongly opposed than the Christian Democratic leadership to any kind of deal with the Red Briagdes to free Mr. Moro. It was in large part because they knew that their working alliance with the Communists would break down that the Christian Democratic leaders, most of them lifelong friends and associates of Mr. Moro, turned down his family's appeals for negotiations with the kidnappers and his own emotional pleas for a prisoner exchange.

The body had barely been removed from the car when Mr. Moro's wife and children publicly reminded the Christian Democratic leaders that one of his last wishes had been that none of them should be present at his funeral. Mr. Moro had expressed the wish in at least two letters written from captivity.

The family made its statement in a public announcement to the press.

Murder Surprises Many

The news of Mr. Moro's death came as a surprise to many Italians. After the Red Brigades let pass a deadline they had set for his "execution," the impression gained ground that the terrorists were reluctant to kill their victim and were seeking a way to spare him. There were rumors of last-minute contacts between the terrorists and various politicians and of a compromise under which Mr. Moro would be exchanged for a single prisoner.

Mr. Moro's body lay undiscovered for about five hours in the small car parked on a narrow cobblestoned street near a church. The car—a compact with an open space for luggage behind the back seat—had been parked between 7:30 and 8:15 in the morning.

The secretary of the Center for American Studies, on the other side of Via Caetani, had seen the car when she came to work shortly after 8 A.M., the police said. The center, a private organization, has a library of American books and arranges English and Italian courses and lectures.

The Carabinieri, Italy's elite police corps, closed off the street, which is only one block long, with their blue-and-white Alfa Romeo patrol cars. Word had spread that the car was booby-trapped. Explosive experts of the Rome fire brigade opened the hood and gingerly cut the electric wiring. Then they opened the trunk, equally carefully.

A priest from a nearby Jesuit church blessed Mr. Moro's body and sprinkled it with holy water before it was transferred to a red ambulance of the fire department. At 3:20, more than an hour after the body had been discovered, the ambulance moved off at breakneck speed preceded and followed by Carabinieri.

The body was taken to the Institute of Legal Medicine of Rome University.

On Via Botteghe Oscure, two short blocks away, the red flags of the Communist Party had been lowered to half-mast, and party guards in civilian clothes at the entrance had been doubled or tripled. On Piazza del Gesù, a short block further, the flags of the Christian Democratic Party also had been lowered and black ribbons had been attached to them.

Supporters of Mr. Moro in the Christian Democratic Party as well as his friends and family are expected to accuse the leaders of the party as well as the Communists of having made his death inevitable by refusing to negotiate with the terrorists. The leaders of the two parties are expecting such a campaign and want to counteract its potentially divisive effect.

Red Lavish in His Praise

Mr. Berlinguer, the Communist leader, today praised Mr. Moro in terms never before used by a Communist politician about a leader of the Christian Democratic Party.

"A great democratic leader has fallen, murdered by an organization of criminal terrorists," he said. "The republic loses one of its major statesmen, one of the personalities who have had the greatest impact on the recent history of our country."

Mr. Berlinguer noted that Mr. Moro, as president of the Christian Democratic Party, had promoted collaboration with the Communists. He will be remembered "not only by democratic Catholics but by the entire Italian people," he said.

Benigno Zaccagnini, the secretary general of the Christian Democratic Party and one of the men most deeply affected, personally, by Mr. Moro's death, told reporters outside the party offices: "I don't think I am able to say adequate words in this momemt. There aren't any, I don't find them. I can't find them.

"I think of his family, his loved ones, of their unspeakable sorrow. I think of what Aldo Moro has meant to all of us, to Italian democracy."

Mr. Zaccagnini was a lifelong friend of Mr. Moro's and one of his closest collaborators. Yet, with great grief and visibly aging during the 54-day ordeal, he refused to negotiate with the terrorists. He broke openly with Mr. Moro's family over the issue, arguing that a "deal" with the Red Brigades would destroy the authority of the Government and perhaps bring the destruction of the republic.

May 10, 1978

Extremist Red Brigades Seek to Destroy the Italian State and Society

Special to The New York Times

ROME, March 16—At the forefront of the political violence that has been sweeping Italy are several hundred mostly well-educated, middle-class men and women whom the police have called "political mystics." They call themselves Red Brigades, and to Italians in general they are the nation's most feared terrorist group.

Their aim is to destroy the present Italian state and society, and today they proclaimed that they had struck at the "heart of the state" with the kidnapping of Aldo Moro, the leader of the governing Christian Democratic Party, and the murder of his five bodyguards.

This, they feel, is the way to bring revolution to Italy, for in their eyes the Italian Communist Party has sold out to the bourgeoisie by cooperating with the Christian Democrats. The Communists, in turn, have condemned the Red Brigades.

While this terrorist group is estimated to number several hundred, 150 of them, including their leader, Renato Curcio, are

The Western Democracies

in prison.

Many other smaller terrorist organizations, most of them extreme leftists but some also from the extreme right, are operating around the country, and the police put the total membership of all guerrilla groups, including the Red Brigades, at about 2,000. The Communist Party, however and other sources say it may be as high as 5,000.

But in addition, it is said, the terrorists have the support of several thousand sympathizers.

The Red Brigades have adopted a five-pointed red star with a submachine gun superimposed upon it as their symbol for their drive to bring about what they regard as a real Marxist upheaval led by a "revolutionary proletariat." The drive, they say, has been pursued so far with more than 40 assassinations, 30 kidnappings, numerous robberies and sabotage attacks.

Some of the brigade members, like Mr Curcio, now on trial in Turin with 14 of his aides, were left-wing students in the northern city of Trento. Others came from among trade union delegates also in the industrial northern area. Some were students in technical schools in the traditionally Communist area of Reggio Emilia in central Italy, and still others came from the Communist youth movement.

The nucleus of the group, which was born of disillusionment with the traditional left, was formed in the late 1960's at the School of Sociology in Trento. The Christian Democrats had established the school, hoping to raise a new crop of political leaders, but many of the students turned further and further left, led by Mr. Curcio, a young man of Roman Catholic background.

Mr. Curcio and his followers moved from Trento to Milan where they hoped to persuade the workers to join in an armed revolution.

By the spring of 1970, a clandestine newspaper called Proletarian Left began to appear. Its writers preached armed struggle. At the same time, leaflets carrying attacks on the unions and and exhorting workers to armed revolution began to appear in factories.

Families of leaders and factory managers began receiving threatening phone calls, and their automobiles were smashed.

In January 1970, three trucks belonging to the Pirelli rubber factory in Milan were burned. The Red Brigades claimed responsibility, first with a phone call and later with a note carrying the red star.

In March 1972, the radicals kidnapped a right-wing trade-union leader in Milan from SIT-Siemens, a mutlinational compay that produces household appliances. The red-starred note said: "No one among the functionaries of the counterrvolution will ever sleep soundly again."

In the spring of 1974, the group kidnapped Judge Mario Sossi in Genoa and held him for 34 days. In exchange for the judge, they won an agreement that eight of their members would be released from prison, but the order to release them was countermanded by Francesco Coco, th general prosecutor of eGnoa. He was later killed.

The first deaths attributed to the extremists, however, came in Padua in June 1974. The Red Brigades were raiding the headquarters of a neo-fascist group when the neo-fascists opened fire. Two of the rightists were killed and the Red Brigades termed the deaths "an accident in the line of work."

Policemen captured some of the leaders of the Red Brigades in September 1974 with the help of a priest who had infiltrated the group. Other leaders were killed in shootouts. The police began to discover the extremists' hideouts.

There were more kidnappings, bombings and threats. By 1977 the group had begun to shoot journalists, factory managers, middle-level political leaders and others in the legs, causing severe disabilities.

Since April of last year, five persons connected with the trial in Turin of Mr. Curcio and his aides have been killed.

With the abduction of Mr. Moro, the Red Brigades attacked their most prominent victim.

March 17, 1978

PERSPECTIVES ON TERRORISM

Robert Kennedy Says Sabotage Is a Major Peril to Free Nations

By FELIX BELAIR Jr.
Special to The New York Times

WASHINGTON, Feb. 28—Attorney General Robert F. Kennedy said today that sabotage, banditry and terrorism had replaced the small war as a mean of toppling governments and seizing control of free societies.

He told the first graduating class of the International Police Academy here that this was "the age of hit-run terrorist activities coordinated on a global scale."

In this situation, he said, civil police forces are "a very real first line of defense, and the fate of governments and nations hangs in the balance."

Mr. Kennedy never referred to international Communism as the instigator of tactics short of war for taking control of free nations. His meaning, however, was clear to the 31 high-ranking police officials from 16 nations of Latin America, Asia and Africa who had just completed a 13-week course in modern police administration that included "insurgency in Communist Theory."

The new academy is operated by the Office of Public Safety of the Agency for International Development, which directs the foreign aid program. Its first class was for senior police officials only. This year an estimated total of 450 senior and intermediate officials will go through the academy.

Only English is spoken in the classes, lectures and seminars of the academy, the first of its kind in the world. It occupies the top two floors of a remodeled car barn in the Georgetown section of the capital.

In a companion academy in Panama, also operated by AID, only Spanish is spoken. It is attended by police officials of junior and intermediate rank and will train 500 more of these in the year ahead.

Underlying both academies is the concept that economic and social progress require internal political security as well as freedom from external aggression.

February 29, 1964

Frantz Fanon

A Critical Study.
By Irene L. Gendzier.
300 pp. New York: Pantheon Books. $10.

By PHILIP GREEN

In 1956, while stationed at an outpost of the Free World, I read in the Stars and Stripes one morning that a young Negro woman named Autherine Lucy had been admitted to the University of Alabama, at the point of a court order and bayonets. That news item was also read by two other residents of our barracks, a couple of rather elemental white Southerners whom I shall call Julius and Flem. Julius threw the paper aside with an expression of mixed disgust and anger and said, "By God, Flem, an reckon it's about time to go home an' git the ol' shotgun off the wall an' shoot us up some of that nigger meat."

I don't know what has happened to Flem and Julius since 1956, but I can say two things with a fair degree of certainty: Wherever they are—and their ilk exists everywhere some men dominate the lives of others—the chance of achieving a reasonable degree of civilization is a little less because of their existence; and yet the current orthodoxy among democrats is to "understand" their virulent racism, while bending every effort to secure their votes. This is called toleration; it is part and parcel of an American liberalism that is, for example, able to find its canonized philosopher in Albert Camus, whose last political act was to side with oppression by lending his tacit support to the French colonialists against the Algerian revolutionaries. Flem and Julius, in a more sophisticated and murderous guise, were on the same side as liberalism's lay saint.

To "understand" the violence of racism but to condemn the violence of resistance to it: that has been typical of our unserious liberalism, and nothing is more symptomatic of that attitude than the reception accorded in this country to the work of the most significant homegrown philosopher of national liberation, the late Frantz Fanon, a major figure to the rebellious left, but by others either ignored or seen as a philosophical pariah, a dangerous apostle of violence. Ours is a strange culture to be able to cultivate such intellectual schizophrenia; it is too bad that Fanon was never among us to analyze Julius and Flem (though he analyzed them elsewhere) and our liberal commentators, or to describe the symptomology of our illness.

For what one finally sees clearly from Irene L. Gendzier's excellent biography (though the latter part of Fanon's "The Wretched of the Earth," the work with which Americans are most familiar, might have led to this view years ago) is that Fanon was preeminently a psychological analyst, a psychiatric theorist, one of the first of the radical therapists whose perspective has now become commonplace. In the best tradition of genuine professionalism he moved slowly but necessarily from a stance in which psychiatry functions as therapy for "personal" tragedy (and thus as an unwitting handmaiden of the social order) to a stance in which that order itself is revealed as the destroyer of personality, and must itself be opposed and, finally, overthrown.

Gendzier's work shows biographically the development that Fanon's essays in "Black Skin, White Masks" and "A Dying Colonialism" demonstrate intellectually. From Fanon's failure to achieve satisfactory clinical results with Moslem (and French) patients; from his inability, as Chief of Services at the Blida-Joinville Psychiatric Hospital, to reorganize patient care along the lines that a patient-oriented therapy seemed to demand; and from the growing intrusion of the Algerian civil war and its effects into his work, Fanon reached not merely a moralistic condemnation of oppression but a profound philosophical understanding of colonialism as a system, an understanding of the deformation of both rulers and ruled by that system's operation, and an understanding of revolution (national liberation) as the only "therapy" capable of creating (though by no means certain to create) conditions in which personal adjustment to the new social order would be life-giving rather than death-dealing.

In fact, for those of us who still adhere to the restrictive and deficient notion of "values" as separate from "facts," as mere attitudes that we choose like a favorite flavor of ice cream, Gendzier's work may, one hopes, be a revelation. (She is associate professor of history at Boston University and a fellow of the Radcliffe Institute.) Her concentration on Fanon's professional career is but one aspect of a more general and generally successful effort to situate her subject as none of his previous biographers or critics have sufficiently done. Fanon was not only a psychiatrist, but a West Indian, educated at French schools, who came to work for the liberation of an Arab nation; to understand him we must understand his developing consciousness of his profession and of colonialism and revolution in three different cultural milieux. All of this Grandzier provides admirably in her discussions of the philosophy of *négritude*, of the Algerian liberation movement, of French colonial politics, and of the response of French intellectuals—of whom one, Jean-Paul Sartre, quite properly stands at the center of this book: a towering figure whose like our own culture could dearly use. Thus an attentive reader will be able to understand Fanon's philosophy of revolution from its exemplary ambivalence about black cultural nationalism to its final appeal to violence, not as the irrelevant or even offensive viewpoint of one man who was marginal everywhere he moved, but as a deeply reasoned and appropriate response—though one not without its ambiguities, of course—to a history in which we all have been immersed.

Indeed the only serious fault one should find with this book is that when dealing with Fanon's climactic work, "The Wretched of the Earth," the author tends to retreat from her earlier approach and treat aspects of the book as abstract sociological or philosophical statements. This is true in particular of her discussions of Fanon's rediscovery of the *lumpenproletariat* and his paean to the cathartic effects of violence. One can sympathize with these omissions: To rescue Fanon's notion of the new, revolutionary *lumpenproletariat* — a notion which after all also grew out of his own Algerian experience—both from dogmatic Marxists of the old school who dismiss it out of hand and from New Leftists who, like the Black Panthers in America, have un-

Perspectives on Terrorism

derstood its relevance but misapplied it in their particular circumstances, would require a major and perhaps separate essay.

As for the question of cathartic violence, Gendzier strongly criticizes Fanon on this point but stops short of relating his claims—as they so obviously should be related—to the very same professional experience that she has elsewhere integrated so well with his thought. To be sure, when psychological categories are used for purposes of intellectual criticism rather than explanation, it is too often done by intellectual hacks looking for a cheap weapon with which to denigrate the ideas of individuals or movements they dislike; but Gendzier's mind is obviously so much more subtle than theirs that one would like to have seen her make the effort to accomplish her critical task, in this instance, more completely.

That criticism aside, this remains an important and serious study. Any white person who teaches at one of our more-or-less integrated colleges, and pays any kind of sympathetic attention to black students, has sooner or later been told, in just these words, "Listen Professor so-and-so, I'm not here to help you learn how to deal with black people." Precisely: in just the same way Fanon was not here to add a footnote to the previous history of Western philosophy, but to help make a necessary revolution, one that is not yet completed. If Irene Gendzier's biography leads American readers to take a more intelligent interest in the way he came to define that task, it will have served its best possible purpose. ■

Philip Green is a member of the Department of Government at Smith College.

February 25, 1973

'Terrorism' or Liberation Struggle? Violence Begets Many New Nations

By PAUL HOFMANN
Special to The New York Times

UNITED NATIONS, N.Y., Oct. 30—A few age-old nations, like China, seem to have existed since the dawn of history; others were born in the collapse of once-mighty empires and through civil war or revolution; and yet others have emerged through a painful process of violence by relatively small groups.

Semantics are highly controversial in the making of new states. Today's plotters may become tomorrow's Presidents or Premiers.

The United Nations, the world's registrar for new members of the international community, has in the last few years legitimized the statehood of a number of new entities after conflicts that were described both as terrorism and as struggles for liberation, depending on the point of view.

"The birth of a new nation, like the birth of a new human being, is a messy business," a West African diplomat observed.

'Heinous Crimes' Noted

A Latin-American delegate remarked: "Of course, many revolutions leading to new statehood are promoted by minorities. But fighting for freedom is one thing; another thing is committing heinous crimes with innocent persons, maybe unwitting bystanders, as targets."

The Latin American added: "If you justify criminal acts on the ground that they serve a noble purpose, you suspend Christian ethics."

The President of the current General Assembly here is an Algerian, Foreign Minister Abdelaziz Bouteflika, who comes from a movement, the National Liberation Front, that only 15 years ago was widely regarded as terrorist by the French.

The new Algerian Republic, born amid bombings and killings, is today a leader of African and nonaligned countries.

Several African territories achieved independence, or are about to attain that goal, after long 'guerrilla warfare started by relatively few militants. Guinea-Bissau, Mozambique and Angola, all emerging from long periods of Portuguese rule, are recent examples.

Now, the Palestine Liberation Organization, the political superstructure of guerrilla groups that have ben fighting Israel for years, seems well on its way toward international legitimacy.

Israel has vehemently opposed such recognition for the Palestinian organization, citing the many hijackings, killings and other terrorist actions in the last few years that have been attributed to various Palestinian groups.

Speaking at the General Assembly on Oct. 14, the Israeli delegate, Yosef Tekoah, characterized the Palestine Liberation Organization as "the approximately 10,000 murderers trained and paid for the slaughter of innocent human beings."

Arab spokesmen, while attributing some of the recent terrorism to fringe groups unconnected with the Palestine Liberation Organization, have contended that Israel too was born amid terrorism.

The Arab group in the United Nations recently issued a document titled "criminal acts and acts of sabotage committed by the Zionist gangs" since 1939. This was an obvious response to an earlier list issued by the Israeli delegation, "the principal crimes perpetrated by the Palestine Liberation Organization in pursuance of its nefarious goals."

To the accompaniment of such charges and countercharges, the United Nations General Assembly thus overwhelmingly voted to invite the Palestine organization to participate in its forthcoming debate on the "Question of Palestine."

A Palestinian delegation is expected at United Nations Headquarters next week when the debate is scheduled to start.

It is much less likely that the General Assembly will get around to discussing during this session another item on its long agenda—the question of terrorism in the world and how to curb it.

The official heading of the item, No. 91, gives an indication of the complexity of the problem. It reads: "Measures to prevent international terrorism which endangers or takes innocent human lives or jeopardizes fundamental freedoms, and study of the underlying causes of those forms of terrorism and acts of violence which lie in misery, frustration, grievance and despair and which cause some people to sacrifice human lives, including their own, in an attempt to effect radical changes."

The question of international terrorism was also on the agenda of last year's Assembly, but it was never debated, ostensibly because of a lack of time.

The world organization has for several years been unsuccessfully grappling with the surge of terrorist activities. Western countries have in vain advocated an international convention that would reaffirm the old principle, "aut dedere aut judiciare"—"either surrender or judge" terrorists.

This principle would oblige governments either to extradite persons held responsible for terrorist acts or bring them to trial before their own courts.

However, a majority of member states, led by Arab and African countries, want to explore principally the causes that supposedly lead to acts of terrorism rather than draw up new international laws that would deter such acts.

Even definition of the term "terrorism" has run into difficulties at the United Nations. Representatives of developing nations contend that violent acts committed by oppressed peoples should not be described as terrorist and should not be condemned.

The world organization did manage last year to approve a convention that defined diplomats as "internationally protected persons" and called for prosecution and extradition of assailants against them.

Apart from this international agreement, so far signed by 21 countries including the United States, the United Nations has been dealing gingerly and in woolly language with terrorists.

A Dutch law expert says gloomily: "It sometimes looks as if there were an international premium on terrorism—instead of being punished, it is rewarded. I know that Soviet and other Communist delegates are privately outraged by the spreading of terrorist methods, which they call 'adventurism,' but in public they all too often seem to condone them.

"So I'm afraid we have to get used to a new international level of disorder and crime."

October 31, 1974

The Violence Plague

Like a dread plague in medieval times that moved relentlessly and invisibly from one walled town to another and that walls were powerless to keep out, terrorist violence breaks out today in one great city after another and sophisticated security systems are powerless to prevent it. Within days a bomb goes off in the State Department in Washington, there is a murderous explosion at Fraunces Tavern in New York, planes are shot up and hostages seized in an airport in Paris. No city—Stockholm or Rome, Birmingham or Buenos Aires—is immune, and in the least favored, such as Belfast, violence has become endemic.

These acts of terrorism breed so much anxiety because they are so random. Nothing is more terrifying than a menace that is totally unpredictable. Since human beings cannot stop going to lunch or taking airplanes or walking crowded streets or working in public buildings, they develop a protective sense of gallows humor about the unknown adversaries who at any moment may be setting off a bomb in their midst. But humor and stoicism notwithstanding, this random terrorism preys on the nerves of all but the most hardy fatalists.

* * *

When a political motive is ascribed to a particular bombing, it still seems senseless. Repeated acts of terrorism by the Irish Republican Army and the various Palestinian organizations have brought renewed public attention to long-festering issues in Northern Ireland and the Middle East. But the absolutist aims of these fanatics are as difficult of attainment today as they were five years ago or twenty years ago.

The bombings of Fraunces Tavern, ostensibly by Puerto Rican nationalists, and of the State Department, ostensibly by a branch of the Weathermen, are even more futile. Since Puerto Rico is not a colony, bombing cannot liberate it. The Puerto Rican people through their free political processes remain masters of their own destiny no matter what happens in New York.

Since the United States Government is not a totalitarian tyranny, bombing cannot overthrow it. The American people through their free political processes remain masters of their own destiny no matter how many government buildings are evacuated or blown up.

The political senselessness and moral nihilism of these terroristic acts may be clues to their essential nature. The fanatics are rebels against—not only a particular grievance or injustice—but against the modern world itself. The modern world was created by sciences and technologies that are cabalistic mysteries to millions of people. This world is organized and directed by huge, impersonal, hierarchical bureaucracies which have many managers and few heroes. This world produces profits and better living standards but erases eccentricity, muffles discontent, curbs the wayward and the restless.

* * *

Not every man and not every community is willing to accommodate to the rational, economic-oriented values of the world created by the Industrial Revolution. Such men and such communities of people take refuge in extreme nationalist or revolutionary ideals. Pure ethnicity and perfect socialism are alike ideals that can generate heroes and fantasies, nourish old hatreds, legitimize wayward lives and violent impulses.

The slums of Derry and Belfast and the refugee camps of the Middle East exist outside the mainstreams of modern economic life. So do many segments of the now-disrupted, traditionalist, rural societies of Asia, Africa and Latin America. In the advanced wealthy countries of North America and Western Europe, discontented, disoriented individuals choose to identify with wrongs remote from themselves or wholly imagined because they, too, can then posture on the stage of history.

Like scourges of the past before the age of modern medicine, this plague of violence has no swift, sure remedy. It has to be lived through and survived. Rational men and women can only combat it indirectly as they struggle to find humane ways to transform the affluent modern world into that more just and generous society of which men have dreamed in every age.

February 2, 1975

Flight With 92 Aboard Is Diverted To Montreal; Officer Dies in Blast

By ROBERT E. TOMASSON

Six persons hijacked a Trans World Airlines jetliner carrying 92 people on a New York-to-Chicago flight last night and forced it to fly to Montreal.

And when the Boeing 727 landed at Montreal's Mirabel Airport, the hijackers forced the pilot to transmit a radio message that sent New York City police to a locker near Grand Central Station where a bomb was found along with two letters from a group called "Fighters for Free Croatia."

The bomb, contained in a sealed pressure cooker, exploded as the bomb squad sought to deactivate it at the bomb range in the Bronx, killing one officer and seriously injuring three others.

List of Demands

There were two letters. The text of the first, containing demands that the hijackers said must be met immediately, read as follows:

"Both of these texts must appear in their entirety in tomorrow morning's editions of the following newspapers: New York Times (all three editions), Los Angeles Times, Chicago Tribune, International Herald Tribune, and Washington Post.

"At least one-third of each text must be printed on the first page of the first section, the remainder in the first section.

"Through a prearranged code word, we shall hear if these demands have been met by tomorrow's deadline. If they have not been met, a second timed explosive device, which is likewise in a highly busy location, shall be activated. In the event that these texts are printed as per instructions, this device will be deactivated.

"The fate of many people hangs in the balance if any attempts whatsoever are made to circumvent our instructions."

The letter was signed, "Fighters for Free Croatia."

September 11, 1976

Perspectives on Terrorism

Text of 'Croation Fighters'

The text of an "appeal to the American People" from a group called "Fighters for a Free Croatia" follows:

"The American people, in 1776, proclaimed in the Declaration of Independence that every nation has a right to national self-determination and freedom, and this declaration, which inspired later the protagonists of the French Revolution in their formulation of the "Declaration of the Rights of Man," has served as a model to many other nations throughout the years, which have strived to free themselves from colonialistic or imperialistic forces.

"One can truly say that world decolonization began when the original 13 Colonies proclaimed independence from Great Britain. Later, Woodrow Wilson perpetuated this guiding principle in American policy, stating his support of national self-determination of nations at the Versailles Peace Conference in 1919, a position that America, in 1941, in the Atlantic Charter, continued to support and honor.

"According to various persons in influential government positions, this philosophy continues, theoretically, to be adhered to in questions of American policy. The Secretary of State, Henry Kissinger, stated recently, as quoted in The New York Times, April 28, 1976, that 'there can be no doubt that the United States remains committed to the principles of its Declaration of Independence. We support self-determination.

"These are the reigning principles included in the United Nations Charter, and provide the basis upon which the politics of the United Nations should rest.

"At the 25th anniversary convention of the United Nations, this declaration, which succinctly detailed and formulated the inalienable right of national self-determination, was unanimously accepted. In principle, the inviolable right of nations who are legitimately entitled to, but denied, self-determination, is upheld, even to the extent that an armed resistence is necessary.

"Unfortunately, memorandums sent all over the world reporting of the unbearable economic, cultural and political exploitation in Croatia were, for the most part, ignored. Recently, however, the State Department replied to one of these. The reply read that the United States would in the future support and respect the "integrity and unity of the state of Yugoslavia." We have also been informed that Secretary of State Kissinger sent a letter, with the same contents, to Yugoslavia.

"This letter was read aloud before the Yugoslav Presidium, providing this artificial government with additional support in the continuation of its oppressive policies, which are the epitome of "Great Serbianism", totalitarianism, Stalinism. and Nazi terror.

"Thus, the United States supports the colonialistic enslavement of the non-Serbian nations within Yugoslavia. An ugly paradox arises when one realizes that the theoretical and practical applications of American support for self-determination are in direct opposition to one another.

"Democratic and Communist countries alike, or more accurately, their governments, often justify the use of force upon smaller nations with the same terminology, even utilizing the identical terminologies of Hitler, Mussolini, and other Nazi ideologues and theoreticians.

"It is difficult to criticize many American politicians, and especially the American people, for the fact that official U.S. politics shows no awareness of or sympathy for the desires of small, occupied nations. This is quite clear and comprehensible to those who have an understanding of American history, since America, in her entire 200-year history, has never once experienced any form of national problems, problems which Europe and other parts of the world have known and continue to encounter.

"As one illustration, which all who are familiar with the exact situation in Yugoslavia can comprehend, let us make an interesting and instructive analogy.

"Yugoslavia, or translated, South Slavia, is a product of the forced consolidation, created by the Big Powers, of the southern Slav nation: Croatians, Serbians, Solvenians, Macedonians, and Montenegrins, and, thus, is the quintessence of terror, a continuing ideological and expansionist hoax.

"If the formation of South Slavia has solved the problems between the southern Slav nations, and created an "historical ideal" through this forced consoliation, why should not the big powers follow this glowing example, forming, the Middle East, as in South Slavia, a purportedly voluntary union of Syrians, Palestinians, Jews, Jordanians, Libyans, and Egyptians?

"Through the creation of a unified state, the Middle East section of the State Department would, then, to avoid further headaches in this area, merely appoint one of these nations as the ruling force, (as the Serbs are in South Slavia), with supreme authority over all the other nations, and supply this chosen nation with all the weapons necessary to defend the new state from any opposition, or to impose its will on the others.

"This ludicrous idea would find no support from any faction or government whatsoever, but, nevertheless, total support for South Slavia is often all too apparent. If South Slavia is not a criminal and political absurdity, then the Middle East State would be even less!

"We decided to undertake this particular action for many reasons. First, our goal was to present an accurate picture of the brutal oppression taking place in Yugoslavia. When the eventual uprising against Serbian imperialism begins, the American people will not, then, allow themselves to be further manipulated regarding the justifications of such an occurrence.

"Next, we decided on this method in order to illustrate the idea that there indeed exists nobler values than the preservatior of a bloody, totalitaristic and imperialistic creation. Is freedom for Croations less important or necessary than the freedom of other nations?

"Croatians have optimistically attempted, many times, to effect legal changes in the oppressive political climate of Yugoslavia. Stjepan Radich, founder of the Croatian Peasant Party and a confirmed pacifist, was assassinated in the Belgrade Parliament in 1928. In the spring of 1971, the Croatian Communist Central Committee, headed by Miko Tripalo and Dr. Savka Dapcevic-Kucar, were, with the full support of Washington and Moscow, purged militarily from power by the Belgrade Government.

"Thousands and thousands of Croatians were imprisoned, without even attempting to calculate the number who emigrated as a result.

"We hold no illusions that Serbian imperialism will allow (as imperialism by its very nature prohibits this) the Croatian national self-determination: we hold no illusions that it shall understand in the future, as it has failed in the past, any methods of resistance excluding those it itself employed in the occupation of Croatia and in the maintenance of this occupation.

"The final question which comes to mind is then: why was an American aircraft taken? The United States has systemically provided the Belgrade regime with billions of dollars of economic and military aid, as outright gifts, regardless of the fact that Yugoslavia is a multinational state, and the weapons intended to prevent outside invasion would not, in the event of internal unrest, be used against a foreign aggressor.

"The non-Serbian nations would, under no circumstances, defend Yugoslavia against any invader, from the East or the West, but, rather, would use the first opportunity to obtain national independence.

"The United States, as recently stated in The New York Times, prohibits the selling of arms to states who do not support basic human rights. This is yet another striking example of the discrepancy between the theoretical and practical application of U.S. policy.

"This, then, was the only possible method to employ in appealing to the American people to protest the sending of any form of aid to the imperialistic Belgrade regime. The 3 million Americans of Croatian descent, who have fulfilled their obligations as U.S. citizens, militarily, economically and especially politically, have a moral right to demand a radical change in the American policies regarding occupied Croatia.

"We expect all 'peace-loving' forces in the world to describe us as terrorists, criminals and murderers. From the time of Caesar, through Hitler, Stalin, Franco and Salazar, as well as with numerous other colonial and neo-colonial governments, those fighting for national liberation have always been described in such terms.

"The point to be made here, obviously, is not to conclusively define 'terrorism,' an impossible and unnecessary task, but, rather, to explain the ultimate necessity for our extreme decision and to ask others to judge this decision objectively and unemotionally.

"Recently, a U.N. diplomat expressed this idea, stating that today, only a small number of diplomats had never been imprisoned or convicted of terrorism or criminal acts. One man's terrorist is another man's patriot, depending solely on one's national and political objectives and suitability.

"We must remember that today's 'terrorists' are often tomorrow's policymakers, having participated in the formation of a new, independent state. Such was the position of the supporters of the Declaration of Independence, after the American Colonies were freed from British subjugation. Thus, the unsuccessful continue to be 'terrorists,' but, upon success, are courted by all governments. With this reality reappearing dependently from one day to the next, all ethical and moral revulsion felt for so-called 'terrorist' acts is necessarily irrational.

"Illegal actions against a government take place in every country, regardless of the governmental system. However, where a possibility for constructive change through legal channels exists, a forum for discussion and an opportunity to publicize one's dissatisfaction, violence and terror is rarely condoned, and groups practicing violence under such conditions rarely enjoy any popular base of support. Thus, fringe groups such as the S.L.A., [the Symbionese Liberation Army] the New World Liberation Front, or the Red Guerrilla Family may succeed in getting publicity but fail even to recruit enough members or sympathy to realize their aims.

"In countries where no opportunity for democratic change, peaceful lobbying or publication where one's views exist, another method must necesarily be utilized. Sean McBride, winner of the Nobel Peace Prize, expressed this idea well: "If oppression amounts to genocide . . . people are entitled to fight back. The framers of the Universal Declaration of Human Rights recognize that; in the Declaration, they point out that unless human rights are protected under the rule of law people will be driven to violence.

"Aware of the fact that violence, even when justified, still temporarily invokes fear and revolution in some of the populus, we shall use as little, violence as possible to achieve our demands. As these demands are quite easily fulfilled and involve nothing more than disseminating accurate information, all should run smoothly and come to a satisfactory conclusion. If our goal is accomplished, we gladly accept all punishment and consider these ideas worthy of suffering for.

"The failure of our demands to be met would result in actions which would rightly lie not on our consciences, but on those of the people in a position to meet such trivial demands.

"We have undertaken this action in the upmost seriousness, conscious of all its possible consequences and far-reaching effects on world peace.

"Send all critiques or support to this address: Croatia Press, POB 1767, Grand Central, New York, N.Y. 10017."

September 11, 1976

I Am God! Do You Hear—God! (For a Minute.)

By Manès Sperber

PARIS—In 356 B.C., a man named Herostratos set fire to the most famous temple of the goddess Diana—merely, as he confessed, to make himself famous. Even though the mention of his name was declared a capital offense, this criminal is still famous today. When the attention of contemporaries is drawn to a man totally unremarkable except for some unusually destructive act he has committed or threatened to commit, we speak of herostratism.

Today it is much easier to become famous than in his time, for the news of a great deed or even greater misdeed, say a repugnant extortion, travels to every inhabitant of the earth in just a few minutes. Because of such instant sensationalism, even intelligent people have the mistaken notion that acts of terrorism demand unusual boldness and masterful planning. And yet terrorists, like any common criminal, succeed because of an assumption that we renew every day: The mutual trust by which people live together.

It is thus not a sign of stupidity if we let terrorists take us by surprise, and it is no proof of the terrorist's superiority that he misuses this universal, mutual, permanent trust by attacking "—like a bolt from the blue," to employ a pet phrase of Hitler's.

Terrorists, who unscrupulously endanger the lives and freedom of other human beings, may feel like demigods and despise their victims for their defenselessness. And the press, which often spreads stupidity, and public opinion, which spreads it further and more often, tend to admire the wrongdoer all the more, the more the press and opinion use fear to justify their hasty unconditional surrender. That's one reason for the growth of terrorist groups who cite a so-called ideology, a more-or-less persuasive idea of national liberation or total social revolution.

Whether the terrorist acts alone or joins up with like-minded men into a secret group demanding blind obedience—no matter. In both cases, as amazing as it may sound, he is trying to solve a personal problem. In the usually unclear interplay of the conscious and the unconscious, we can discover the internal contradiction of the criminal, his strange mixture of reasons and motives, which delude him and make him seem different from what he really is.

Thus we can certainly assume that a terrorist *thinks* he is acting on behalf of an entire class, say the proletariat, or a national emancipation—even though an analysis of the actual results of terrorist actions generally proves that none of the goals can be achieved by means of terror. The terrorist is thereby using ideology and politics as a *pseudo-motivation*, such as we often encounter in daily life, especially in neurotics. The true, actual motive remains *unidentifiable* and as good as fully covered up in the terrorist's consciousness by ideological extremism.

A man turns to terrorism usually under the influence of political illusions or, vice versa, after embittering losses of illusion, from which he refuses to learn anything. But the very fact that he remains on this path, despite all indications of its leading into the void, can be explained by the unrestrainable need for a position in which the terrorist will feel personally, politically, morally superior to all who are not of his kind. This feeling of superiority strengthens his defiant dogmatism; he resists all arguments even though the facts may daily invalidate his ideological, tactical and other rationales.

For a time, terrorists could win herostratic victories that gave them a temporary illusion of being master of fate—the same feeling that a kidnapper has when he uses the threat of killing a child at any moment to hold a family or the people of a town on tenterhooks. Insofar as politics is a struggle for power, terrorists may believe at such moments that they, these *wanderers into the void*, are storming ahead on the shortest path to power.

A man chooses revolt or even revolution for any number of reasons, under the influence of the most varied personal and social experiences and under the effect of great events. Any such decision involves a personal

Perspectives on Terrorism

motivation, visibly or unconsciously, for the character of the individual is always in play. That is why we must distinguish all the more sharply between two kinds of people here: those seeking a political possibility to take part in common efforts, and those others hoping to find dramatic adventure in politics and turning to individual or group terror as a vehicle and instrument of their personal rebellion and as a refuge for their disappointments in themselves. The men who disguise this neurotic rebellion as a revolutionary stance transform the great cause they are fighting for into a matter of personal vendetta, so to speak, an unhappy love affair in which rape is meant to camouflage an inability to love.

The principle of the ends justifying the means is not merely an atrocious general amnesty for all crimes, but also a miserable, misleading inducement to purposeful action. Ever since World War I we have seen not only a political practice that functions on that principle, never shying away from any means, and justifying the worst crimes with the sublimity of the ends to be achieved. But we have also witnessed something far more absurd and ultimately far more dangerous: People have been making those means operate independently, turning them into reasons, meanings, and justifications for themselves—that is, for all actions. *The means have replaced the end; terror has become an end in itself.*

These terrorists dash around in a vicious circle. The actions are alienated from the ends; their violence isolates them from the world that they wish to arouse or conquer. They have made fools of themselves, *dangerous* poor devils.

Manès Sperber is a novelist and essayist. This article was translated from the German for The New York Times by Joachim Neugroschel.

June 19, 1976

For political ends

Terrorism

From Robespierre to Arafat.
By Albert Parry.
Illustrated. 624 pp. New York:
The Vanguard Press. $17.50.

Guerrilla

A Historical and Critical Study.
By Walter Laqueur.
462 pp. Boston: Little, Brown & Co.
$17.50.

By CONOR CRUISE O'BRIEN

These books are part of a rapidly growing literature about the use of violence for political ends, or ostensibly for political ends. Both books range widely in time and space, and they overlap to a considerable extent. There may be a conceptual distinction between terrorism and guerrilla—though I confess it still eludes me after reading these two volumes—but in practice the two are so often found to be mixed up that differences between them become blurred.

This does not worry Albert Parry, who—as one might infer from his title—tends to see terrorism as the use of violence by people he doesn't like, an attitude with which I sympathize emotionally but must deprecate intellectually. Walter Laqueur's approach is more academic and—though this does not necessarily follow—his book is much the more valuable of the two. Yet he too fails to establish a clear and stable distinction between guerrilla and terrorism or to confine himself, in terms of his announced distinction, to his announced subject. He deprecates the term "urban guerrilla" and makes the valid point that it is used for propaganda purposes to avoid the pejorative connotations of the words, "terrorist" and "terrorism." Yet the grounds on which he would deny validity to the term "urban guerrilla" seem to me to lack solidity. "The essence of guerrilla warfare," says Mr. Laqueur in his preface, "lies in the fact that the guerrilla can hide in the countryside and this, quite self-evidently, is impossible to do in a city."

One has to agree that a gunman, however one chooses to denominate him, cannot "hide in the countryside" in the city. But he can and does hide in the city. Both in the city and in the country, gunmen can hide, emerge to kill and destroy, and go into hiding again. It is not at all self-evident that different names have to be applied to this pattern of activity, according as it is practiced in the city or in the country. By that criterion, applied to the Irish situation, the same I.R.A. gunman, when hiding in South Armagh, would be a guerrilla warrior but when hiding in Andersonstown, Belfast, would be a mere terrorist.

It is true that Mr. Laqueur also posits a distinction based on scale, which could rather more safely be maintained: "There have been guerrilla units of ten thousand men and women but an urban terrorist unit seldom, if ever, comprises more than a few people, and urban terrorist movements rarely consist of more than a few hundred members." Yet this distinction is also imperfect. Urban guerrilla/terrorist activities are carried out by small groups, but many *rural* guerrilla/terrorist activities have also been carried out by small groups, including one of the most successful of all in modern times, Castro's in the Sierra Maestra. If smallness makes the terrorist, these are rural terrorists.

The truth is that these are not purely analytical terms and cannot be made to work as such. They are heavily charged by the history of past human attitudes to violence, their use is conditioned by our own political judgments about particular uses of violence in the present, and by feelings affecting such judgments, and affected by them. By immemorial tradition war is legitimate violence. Guerrilla (little) war implies at least a degree of legitimacy; belligerent status may be round the corner. "Terror," "terrorism," "terrorist" — isolating the element of fear which all violence must inspire—necessarily evoke all our negative feelings about violence and place at a distance the calming concept of legitimacy.

Also, for English-speaking persons interested in discussing such topics, guerrilla has that halo of distance; romantic figures in foreign countries, engaged in some vaguely perceived opera of violence, evoke quite different feelings from the spectacle of your neighbors' legs, arms and heads being collected in plastic containers outside the bombed-out shell of your local supermarket. In this perspective "urban terrorism" is indeed very different from "guerrilla warfare." Country people, who have actually experienced the rural guerrilla, might not agree, but do not greatly influence published comment. The nearer the violence, the less likely it is to seem as legitimate. Compare the degrees of support for the I.R.A. among Irish-

---

Conor Cruise O'Brien is Minister for Posts and Telegraphs for the Republic of Ireland.

Americans and among Irish people actually living in Ireland.

The concept of legitimacy dictates the selection of examples in Mr. Parry's large and sprawling book, although the author nowhere clearly articulates such a concept. Why, for example, begin with Robespierre? Terror as an instrument of government is as old as government itself, and the terror of 1793 is by no means the bloodiest in recorded history. The reasons why that terror can be seen as *the* terror and why a writer like Mr. Parry finds it natural to begin there do not derive directly from a moral revulsion from political violence but from the political judgment that revolutionary violence is illegitimate, and from the tendency to restrict the application of the alarming word "terror" to violence seen as illegitimate. Similarly it is natural for Mr. Parry to exclude all acts committed in the course of war between sovereign states from the otherwise very wide scope of his survey of terrorism. An anarchist's bomb killing five or six people ranks as terrorism, but Hiroshima does not. The reason is not that Hiroshima was less terrible, or less intended to terrify, but that its terror is seen as legitimate and that legitimate terror is not called by that name.

I do not want to be taken as implying that the concept of legitimacy is irrelevant or that there is no such thing as legitimate use of force; only a thoroughgoing pacifist—who has necessarily also to be a thoroughgoing anarchist—could make such assertions. What I object to about Mr. Parry's approach is not the fact that he applies concepts of legitimacy and reflects them in his vocabulary, but that he shows no awareness that this is what he is doing or that there are difficult problems involved in the relations between authority and violence.

Both the books reviewed here often make fatiguing and depressing reading because of the great accumulation of violent case-histories they contain. In the case of "Guerrilla" the accumulation is drawn from an even larger span of time than in "Terrorism" because Mr. Laqueur begins his examples in classical times. But Mr. Laqueur, unlike Mr. Parry, does a great deal more than accumulate examples; he reasons about them and draws significant inferences from them. The concluding part of his book—Chapters 8 and 9, "Guerrilla Doctrine Today" and "A Summing Up"—is particularly important and deserves to be read by all who are seriously concerned with the problems of violence in modern society. He believes, rightly I think, that the strength and potential of guerrilla movements have been exaggerated mainly as a result of the successes and ostensible successes of these movements in the decolonization period when the people they were fighting often wanted to get out anyway. In this last part of the book he seems to lose sight—to his own advantage—of the distinction he sought to establish earlier between guerrilla and terrorism. In one of the most striking passages in the book he shows how the apparent helplessness of democracies in dealing with terrorism can be deceptive:

"Democratic regimes always seem highly vulnerable to terrorist attack. The constitutional restraints in these regimes make it difficult to combat terrorism and such failure exposes democratic governments to ridicule and contempt. If, on the other hand, they adopt stringent measures they are charged with oppression, and the violation of basic human rights. If terrorists are put on trial they will try to disrupt legal procedure and to make fair administration of justice impossible. Having been sentenced, terrorists and their sympathizers could then claim that they are victims of gross injustice. Up to this point, the media (always inclined to give wide publicity to acts of violence), are the terrorists' natural ally. But as terrorists' operations become more frequent, as insecurity spreads and as wide sections of the population are adversely affected, there is a growing demand for tougher action by the Government, even if this should involve occasional (or systematic) infringements of human rights. The swing in popular opinion is reflected in the media focusing no longer on the courage and unselfishness of the terrorists but on the psychopathological sources of terrorism and the criminal element—sometimes marginal, at others quite prominent, but always present in "urban guerrilla" operations. Unless the moral fiber of the regime is in a state of advanced decay, and the political will paralyzed, the urban terrorist will fail to make headway beyond the stage of provocation, in which, according to plan, public opinion should have been won over to their cause, but is in fact antagonized."

I think that in seeing the media as generally "reflecting," rather than shaping, public opinion Mr. Laqueur is right. In my opinion they tend to reflect it with a considerable time-lag, especially where political violence is concerned. But the whole question of the relation of the media to political violence on the one hand, and to democracy on the other, deserves to be the subject of a separate and detailed study. Mr. Laqueur might be the right person to undertake it. If he does, I can promise him a rich vein of material in Ireland, North and South. ■

January 23, 1977

The Liberators' Assault on Democracy

To the Editor:
During the past decade the ideology of terror has gained acceptance in many Western universities and in some segments of the press through the argument that its use is justified by the revolutionary epoch of liberation and because it is merely a temporary method. The argument is both unethical and spurious: In reality the terrorists' means and ends have long merged into a permanent totalitarian synthesis, consequently they can no longer be considered liberators.

The men of terror start out by rejecting traditional ethics, including its most emphatic command, respect for the lives of innocents. This self-inflicted demoralization provides them with a nihilistic license to attack civilians indiscriminately and—by the sheer magnitude of their cruelty—to pressure their target governments into making concessions. Their grim operations constitute, however, a steady descent into a treacherous underground—the void of deliberate violence —from which there is no return.

After victory this underground becomes the *permanent* foundation of their new regime, in which terror is being discreetly institutionalized through the establishment of a totali-

Perspectives on Terrorism

tarian police state. The masters of this system have absolute power over their masses, who are being deprived of civil rights and all basic freedoms. In the name of a perpetual revolution they must live in fear and by bread alone.

The victors in Cambodia and Mozambique have demonstrated the reality and the dimensions of this repressive pattern, which is, by definition, sanctioned at the U.N. General Assembly. Similarly, the Lebanese civil war has shown that the protagonists of this aggressive ideology can not live, even as guests, in the framework of democracy.

This global totalitarian trend presents an immediate danger to the emerging peoples in Asia and Africa, many of whom have not had a free day since their "liberation." It is, however, a threat in the long run to freedom everywhere, since its elitist partisans advocate it as a principle of universal validity. Strangely, the academic guardians of the West's liberal ideals have ignored this categorical claim, which is in fact a dogmatic assault on democracy. Their silence on this vital issue brings to mind the anemic era in the 1920's that prompted J. Benda to write his classic: "The Treason of the Intellectuals."   LASZLO T. KISS
New York, Feb. 14, 1977

February 20, 1977

Dangers to Liberty in Fighting Terrorism

By Irving Louis Horowitz

NEW BRUNSWICK, N.J.—A society free from the threat of terrorism is quite attainable. Fascist systems manage to reduce terrorism by a series of devices: mass organizations in which membership is compulsory; block-by-block spying networks; mandatory police-identification certificates, and clear delineations of "friends" and "enemies" of the regime.

With the increased sophistication of computerization techniques, such mechanisms for social and personal control loom ever larger. The question is not one of technique but of social policy: Does a citizenry wish to pay such a price for tranquillity?

The acceptance of some terrorism, like some protest violence, is a sign of a society's acceptance of the costs of liberty. The potential for terror is also a reminder that the state's force has its counterforce; and the hardware of the state is almost always greater, more pervasive, and more devastating than the disruptive possibilities that are available to terrorists.

If we evaluate terrorism in terms of the number of people that have been killed by design or by accident, there is clearly no comparison with the genocidal behavior of Stalin in Russia and Hitler in Germany.

The autocratic state has nearly unlimited power to terrorize entire communities, ethnic or racial groups, and, of course, religious networks. If terrorism is judged simply in terms of lives dispatched, the Nazi holocaust—the genocidal benchmark of our century—outstrips the desultory performances engaged in by contemporary terrorists.

If we consider terrorism in terms of its disruption of local political systems or social organizations, again there is scarcely any comparison between what terrorists achieve and the disruption caused by a major automobile accident on an urban superhighway or the large-scale temporary breakdown occasioned by a power failure in a big city. It is the symbolic effect of terrorism that represents its real impact.

When persons are assassinated or kidnapped because of their national origins or religious affiliations, this threatens the entire structure of intergroup toleration and support. Because terrorism involves death and destruction by design, it is clearly different from the random character of highway accidents or technological breakdowns.

The measurement of terrorism's success therefore is not only its ability to topple the social order but also its ability to loosen that order in symbolic terms, by weakening the legitimating capacities of elected officials and casting doubt on our concept of the rights of a society and the obligations of a state.

For example, the act of boarding an airplane involves an acceptance of commonplace procedures that a few short years ago would have been deemed a direct violation of civil liberties. Most people accept the frisking and new baggage procedures as the necessary cost of a safe flight. Nonetheless, one has a perfect right, even a duty, to raise questions about these new social costs of travel, certainly to inquire whether the new frisking procedures are permanent or transitory.

Risk is part of the nature of the democratic system—to permit modes of behavior that are uncontrolled and experimental. To insist that new mechanisms have to be created to prevent terror may be more risky than accepting the possibility of certain terrorist acts.

Under the banner of the anti-terrorist industry (airport-surveillance equipment, home-security systems, counter-terror research) enormous erosion of civil liberties could be made to seem all too rational and enlightened to the general public. The costliest aspect of terrorism may not be the destruction of physical property and loss of life—as terrorists intend—but the weakening of the social and political fabric, that complex series of norms and laws upon which democratic conflict-resolution ultimately rests.

Irving Louis Horowitz is professor of sociology and political science at Rutgers University. This was adapted from an article in the May issue of The Civil Liberties Review.

April 30, 1977

Terror and Tolerance

To the Editor:

A question for Irving Louis Horowitz ("Dangers to Liberty in Fighting Terrorism," Op-Ed April 30): Would his benevolence toward terrorism have been extended to the Nazi thugs and street gangs who plagued Weimar Germany in the 1920's and who were the forerunners of a regime which, in Horowitz's own words, gave us "the genocidal benchmark of our century?"

PAULA SUTTER FICHTNER
Associate Professor of History
Brooklyn College
Brooklyn, May 1, 1977

May 14, 1977

The Editorial Notebook

The Infection of Terrorism

Except for a fleeting encounter with Bernardine Dohrn, that bad Weather person, before she went underground, I have never knowingly been in the company of a terrorist, yet I feel intimately acquainted with several. The introductions were arranged, long before the current fashion for hijackings and hostages, by a few novelists who transmitted their fascination to the impressionable reader. For me, the prototype of the calling will always be The Professor, met in the pages of Joseph Conrad's "The Secret Agent" and never forgotten.

Conrad was not one to consort with terrorists, and the portraits he gives us are undoubtedly overwrought. But he struck some truths about an individual whose vocation it is to threaten murder and invite death. One of his revolutionaries, an old man who likes to call himself The Terrorist, characterizes his mission this way: "I have always dreamed of a band of men absolute in their resolve to discard all scruples in the choice of means, strong enough to give themselves frankly the name of destroyers, and free from the taint of that resigned pessimism which rots the world. No pity for anything on earth, including themselves, and death enlisted for good and all in the service of humanity—that's what I would have liked to see."

In Conrad's sardonic view, The Professor embodies such an ideal. A genius with explosives, he boasts that he walks with his right hand closed round an india-rubber ball in a trouser pocket. The squeezing of the ball would activate a detonator inside the glass flask full of dynamite close to his breast. Let the world beware of interfering with him.

In a memorable scene, he finds himself face to face with Chief Inspector Heat, the head of England's anti-terrorist squad. Their exasperation is mutual. Chief Heat, the bluff workaday policeman, cannot fathom what sort of game people like The Professor are playing. The Professor, rubber ball at the ready, dares Heat to arrest him, but when they part the terrorist feels defeated, unable to break through the obstinate English spirit of playing by the rules. "It is this country that is dangerous, with her idealistic conception of legalism. . . . Nothing would please me more than to see Inspector Heat and his likes take to shooting us down in broad daylight with the approval of the public. Half our battle would be won then; the disintegration of the old morality would have set in in its very temple."

•

Terrorists have changed since Conrad's time; they come now in different nationalities, flaunting different causes, but their main assaults are still against nations where liberal ideas of law prevail. The South Moluccans take no hostages in the South Moluccas; the Croatians invade no embassies in Croatia; if the Hanafi Muslims had played out their recent adventure in a Muslim land such as Iraq or Syria instead of Washington, D.C., they would certainly be much less comfortable today. Where terrorism might be justifiable because other methods of dissent are blocked, it rarely flourishes; there are no terrorists in Czechoslovakia or South Korea, unless one counts the rulers.

Conrad did not much care if the Czar were blown up; he was concerned about the effect of terrorism on the Britain he admired. In most of Europe today and emphatically in our country, the state is far more powerful than any illegitimate opposition; to wipe out that opposition illegitimately would be to surrender to the spirit of terrorism. "Madness and despair," cries The Professor. "Give me that lever and I'll move the world."

When the state itself becomes mad and despairing and subverts its own laws, then every exploit of its opponents is justified and criminals become martyrs. The list of countries where terrorism today holds power is long and perhaps growing. That is why the Dutch action in Assen, combining coolness, forbearance and controlled toughness, was so heartening.

"The Secret Agent" ends with The Professor, alone as usual, prowling the back streets of London. "He had no future. He disdained it. He was a force. His thoughts caressed the images of ruin and destruction. He moved on unsuspected and deadly, like a pest in the street full of men."

Though dangerous, The Professor has no future so long as England will not exchange its values for his, so long as the Dutch will not respond like lunatics to lunacy, so long as Americans, for all their perennial panic about extremists, resist using provocation as a pretext for persecution. So long as we keep our heads and our values, terrorism has no more future here than The Professor had in Conrad's London.

WALTER GOODMAN

June 28, 1977

The C.I.A., Cuba and Terrorism

By John Marks

WASHINGTON — Our Government should have no higher priority than stamping out terrorism. Civilization, as most Americans value it, breaks down as bombs explode in airports and trains full of children are seized. Yet, for the last 35 years, our Government has made regular use of terrorism as an instrument of foreign policy.

During World War II, there were no bleeding hearts arguing that we should not use any and all means against the Axis powers. And for the first two decades of Cold War that followed, blowing up buildings and sending forth assassins was standard American policy. Nevertheless, our leaders did not want to admit publicly that we did these things, so the American people were kept in the dark while our enemies knew exactly—because they were on the receiving end—to what level America would stoop.

These early covert struggles tended to be in faraway places, and their victims could be written off if not as Communists, at least as obscure foreigners. Around 1960, as CBS recently showed in a brilliant documentary, C.I.A. "unconventional warfare" came much closer to home—to Cuba. The agency trained thousands of Cuban exiles in poisoning crops, sabotaging factories, and even in killing. These Cubans, like most true believers, did not consider themselves to be terrorists —but rather, fighters for a just cause.

Sometimes at the C.I.A.'s order and sometimes for their own reasons, Cubans commandeered the Castro Government's planes and ships. Al-

Perspectives on Terrorism

ways the hijackers were greeted as heroes in Miami where C.I.A. propagandists encouraged the American press—which didn't need much encouragement—to praise these refugees from Castro's rule.

By the end of the 1960's, however, the hijacking flow had reversed, as politically and criminally inclined Americans forced planes to fly to Cuba. Suddenly, Americans had become the victims of terrorism, and for this and other reasons, our Government's role in promoting the same tactics against others rapidly declined.

At present, terrorism seems to have been eliminated from America's bag of dirty tricks (although the C.I.A. still maintains a "standby" capability). Yet, hundreds of the C.I.A.'s former anti-Castro warriors insist on continuing their fight, and they use Miami as the base for a worldwide campaign of bombing and killing. They are quite skilled at the covert arts because their C.I.A. case officers taught them well.

CBS reported that some of these same case officers, now retired, are advising the terrorists. An agency spokesman told me there is "no way the agency can keep tabs" on its ex-employees.

The spokesman also denied the C.I.A. was still plugged into the terrorist scene, but the fact remains that over the years the agency worked with and "penetrated" the various Cuban groups, and it retains large amounts of intelligence on them. The C.I.A., it is true, is specifically barred from any domestic law enforcement function, but this prohibition does not prevent it from providing information to domestic authorities. In fact, the C.I.A. has been extremely reluctant to give away its own secrets and to turn in some of its former agents and friends. The Cubans, for their part, have the C.I.A. over a barrel because of their extensive knowledge of agency operations which, if revealed, could be embarrassing or worse.

Last year, Dade County (Miami) policemen told a Congressional committee that the C.I.A. had not been cooperative in their probe of Cuban violence and that the C.I.A. had refused a specific request for the names of Cubans in the Miami area who had received explosives training. Recently, the C.I.A. spokesman said the agency still would not provide a "blanket list" of such people but would only give the police the names of "real suspects." The spokesman also said that C.I.A. personnel would report any criminal activity they came across.

In any case, the Cuban terrorists continue to operate with relative impunity from Miami, and their violent actions have seriously interfered with the current policy of better relations with Cuba.

Their admitted bombing last fall of a Cubana airliner, killing 73, caused Fidel Castro to suspend the U.S.-Cuban hijacking agreement, and their bombing last month of a Fort Lauderdale office caused an obviously frightened Mackey International Airlines to cancel its planned resumption of commercial air service to Cuba.

In the CBS program, a Cuban terrorist leader threatened violence against anyone trying to stop his group's bloody campaign. The Carter Administration had better accept that challenge right now and turn the full force of the Government against these Cubans.

An extraordinary effort is needed because their C.I.A.-provided technical proficiency and international contacts have made them, to a large extent, immune to normal law enforcement efforts. And as the first step in this special program, the Administration should make clear that the C.I.A. now must go all out *on our side* in the war against terrorism.

John Marks is an associate of the Center for National Security Studies.

June 28, 1977

Anarchists And Terrorists

By James Joll

LONDON—A little while ago the French Minister of Justice, Alain Peyrefitte, remarked, after the extradition of Klaus Croissant, the defense lawyer of some of the German terrorists: "We find ourselves facing a menace comparable to that of anarchism at the end of the 19th century. The Third Republic knew the answer to that menace. The Fifth knows it as well."

In fact, nobody knows the answer, and perhaps the wave of anarchist terrorism of 80 years ago that so alarmed the governments of Europe receded as much because of the passage of time and the anarchists' failure to achieve anything by their violence as because of any measures taken by the French Government.

Still, Mr. Peyrefitte's remark reminds us that the present use of terrorism by many different groups for many different purposes is not quite as new a phenomenon as some of those who are alarmed by it tend to imply.

Even if the aims are not always the same as those of the anarchists of the 1890's—though in some cases they are remarkably similar—the methods used have served as an example of how to attack the powerful structure of the modern state, and they have continued to attract desperate people who have realized that there is little chance of achieving their radical goals by more orthodox or more legitimate means.

"I shall not be killing an innocent man if I kill the first bourgeois to appear," a French terrorist said in 1893; and another, who threw a bomb into a crowded popular café, wounding 20 people and killing one, defended himself with the words: "I wanted to show the bourgeoisie that their pleas-

TERRORISM AND THE STATE TODAY

ures would no longer be complete, that their insolent triumphs would be disturbed, that their golden calf would tremble violently on its pedestal, until the final shock would cast it down in mud and blood."

Techniques have become more sophisticated since then; and the hijacking of an airliner, with every move watched on millions of television screens, is more effective as a means of attracting attention than the indiscriminate bombing of cafes and opera houses.

Moreover, there do seem to be more real international links between the terrorists today than between the anarchists of 80 years ago. While there is nothing new in committing armed robbery in order to replenish the funds of a revolutionary organization, there does seem to be something new in the feeling that the aims of total revolution toward which the Baader-Meinhof group seemed to be striving are somehow linked to the aspirations of the Palestinian liberation movement or even the Irish Republican Army.

The theory behind this is presumably an adaptation of a familiar Marxist idea that any movement that is likely to weaken the hold of the existing system is, in the short run, a potential ally, however much the ultimate picture of society after the revolution may differ.

What all these movements have in common—and this they share with their anarchist predecessors—is a belief that terrorism as a method can make the authorities lose their nerve and so take countermeasures that will be unacceptable to liberal opinion within the countries concerned, so that that opinion will eventually oblige the government to give way.

There are certainly examples in the history of European decolonization—

> 'The present use of terrorism . . . is not quite as new a phenomenon as some of those who are alarmed by it tend to imply'

in Palestine, Cyprus and Algeria, for example—where such methods have been successful.

But there is also an alternative view of the purpose of terrorism. This is based on a belief that the established political, social and economic system is a great deal more precarious than it seems, and that it only needs the example of one startling or shocking gesture to set off a conflagration.

In France in 1968 there were many students who believed that it only needed the detonator provided by the student movement to set off the explosion that would destroy bourgeois society. A crazy optimism with no basis in the real social or political system is as characteristic of terrorists both past and present as is the desperate desire to immolate themselves in the service of their cause.

For many of the anarchists of the last century, the destruction of existing society seemed more important than the building of a new one; and it is probably only in their personal psychological makeup that the explanation is to be found.

The great Russian anarchist Michael Bakunin, in his quarrel with Marx over 100 years ago, always maintained that the nature of society after a successful revolution would be determined by the structure of the revolutionary movement itself. A centralized authoritarian revolutionary movement would, he thought, inevitably produce a centralized authoritarian society after the revolution. And perhaps the same principle should be applied to the use of terrorism: A revolution based on terrorism will if successful lead to a government that relies on terrorism to maintain itself in power.

It is this that should make us see the illusion of the romantic appeal that terrorism still has for some people, who, while deploring terrorist actions, have too bad a conscience about the evils of contemporary society to condemn such acts when carried out by others.

And in the panic into which terrorism, especially in West Germany, has cast some people, it is perhaps also just as well to remember that there have always been people among the anarchists to condemn terrorism and to base their critique of contemporary society on the necessity for a moral reform, a reassessment of all values in the individual, rather than on wholesale destruction of the existing order, which would not distinguish the innocent from the guilty.

James Joll, author of "The Anarchists," is professor of international history at the University of London.

December 15, 1977

Suggested Reading

Alexander, Yonah, ed. *International Terrorism: National, Regional and Global Perspectives.* New York: AMS Press, 1976.

Allen, Richard. *Imperialism and Nationalism in the Fertile Crescent.* New York: Oxford University Press, 1974.

Amin, Samir. *Imperialism and Unequal Development.* New York: Monthly Review, 1977.

Amin, Samir. *Unequal Development.* New York: Monthly Review, 1976.

Arendt, Hannah. *On Violence.* New York: Harcourt, Brace and World, 1970.

Avineri, Shlomo, ed. *Israel and the Palestinians.* New York: St. Martin's, 1974.

Bell, J. Bowyer. *Terror Out of Zion: The Irgun, Lehi, Stern Gang and the Palestinian Underground, 1929-1949.* New York: St. Martin's, 1977.

Bernard, Stephane. *Franco-Moroccan Conflict, 1943-1956.* New Haven, Ct.: Yale University Press, 1968.

Cameron, James. *The Making of Israel.* New York: Taplinger, 1977.

Cesaire, Aime. *Discourse on Colonialism.* New York: Monthly Review, 1962 [1955].

Clutterbuck, Richard. *Guerrillas and Terrorists.* Salem, N.H.: Faber & Faber, 1977.

Dellinger, Dave. *Revolutionary Nonviolence.* Indianapolis, Ind.: Bobbs, Merrill, 1970.

Dobb, Maurice. *Studies in the Development of Capitalism.* London, England: International, 1963.

Dutt, Romesch Chunder. *The Economic History of India under Early British Rule.* London, England: K. Paul, Trench, Trubner & Co., 1906.

Edwards, A. *A Season in Hell* [Sepoy Rebellion]. New York: Taplinger, 1973.

Fein, Helen. *Imperial Crime and Punishment.* Honolulu, Hawaii: University Press of Hawaii, 1977.

Gough, Kathleen, and Hari P. Sharma, eds. *Imperialism and Revolution in South Asia.* New York: Monthly Review, 1973.

Green, Gil. *Terrorism—Is It Revolutionary?* New York: New Outlook, 1970.

Guha, Arun. *First Spark of Revolution: The Early Phase of India's Struggle for Independence, 1900-1920.* Port Washington, N.Y.: Kennikat, 1971.

Hay, Edward. *History of the Irish Insurrection.* Brooklyn, N.Y.: Revisionist Press, 1973.

Hentoff, Nat, ed. *The Essays of A.J. Muste.* New York: Simon & Schuster, 1970.

Hobsbawm, E.J. *The Age of Capital, 1848-1875.* London, England: Weidenfeld and Nicolson, 1975.

Hobson, J.A. *Imperialism.* Ann Arbor: University of Michigan, 1965 [1902].

Hutchins, F. *Illusion of Permanence: British Imperialism in India.* Princeton, N.J.: Princeton University Press, 1967.

El Kodsy, Ahmad, and Eli Lobel. *The Arab World and Israel.* New York: Monthly Review, 1976.

La Feber, Walter. *The New Empire.* Ithaca, N.Y.: Cornell University Press, 1963.

Lamb, Helen B. *Studies on India and Vietnam.* New York: Monthly Review, 1976.

Laquer, Walter. *Terrorism.* Boston, Mass.: Little, Brown, 1977.

Lewis, Gordon K. *Notes on the Puerto Rican Revolution.* New York: Monthly Review, 1974.

Magdoff, Harry. *The Age of Imperialism.* New York: Monthly Review, 1969.

Maldonado-Denis, Manuel. *Puerto Rico: A Socio-Historic Interpretation.* New York: Vintage, 1972.

Mansergh, Nicholas. *The Irish Question, 1840-1921.* Toronto, Ontario: University of Toronto Press, 1976.

Merleau-Pont, Maurice. *Humanism and Terror.* Boston, Mass.: Beacon, 1969 [1947].

O'Farrell, P.J. *England and Ireland Since 1800.* New York: Oxford University Press, 1975.

Parry, Albert. *Terrorism: Past, Present, Future.* New York: Vanguard, 1976.

Rabinowitch, Alexander. *The Bolsheviks Come to Power: The Revolution of 1917 in Petrograd.* New York: Norton, 1976.

Rhodes, Robert, ed. *Imperialism and Underdevelopment.* New York: Monthly Review, 1970.

Trotsky, Leon. *History of the Russian Revolution.* New York: Pathfinder Press, 1976.

Trotsky, Leon. *Terrorism and Communism.* Ann Arbor, Mich.: University of Michigan Press, 1961.

Wallerstein, Immanuel. *The Modern World-System.* New York: Academic Press, 1961.

Williams, William Appleman. *The Tragedy of American Diplomacy.* New York: Dell, 1962.

Index

Abbas, Ferhat, 94, 95, 100, 109, 114
Abdel-Fattah, Zaid, 197
Abdelkader, Sayah, 94
Abdullah, King, 165-66
Adwan, Kemal, 190
Aga Khan, 68
Agnew, Spiro, 283, 284, 286
Alami, Musa, 180
Albertz, Heinrich, 307-8
Albrecht, Susanne, 339, 340, 345
Alexander I, 12
Alexander II, 10-11, 15-16, 53
Alexander III, 19-20, 21
Alexandrovitch, Michael, 45
Algeria, 93-125; Algerian National Liberation Front, 99, 100, 101, 102-3, 113-14; Arab Nationalists, 94; arrests in, 96; assassination of Mayor, 101; ceasefire, 120; and French losses, 98-99, 112, 120-21; French vigilantes in, 103-4; guerrilla warfare, 98; independence vote, 125; martial law in, 100; mutiny ends, 115; Napoleon III and, 93; provisional government, 109; rebellion, 102-14; referendum, 110; reforms, 105; secret army, 121-22, 123, 124-25; terrorism in, 94, 116-19, 122-23, 124-25; terrorism in France, 108-9, 114; thoughts of J.P. Sartre on, 332, 333; Tunisia and, 106
Almirante, Giorgio, 352
Alpert, Jane, 299
Amery, L.S., 81
Amnesty International, 242, 343
Amri, Fakhri, 187
Amritsar affair, 65-66
anarchists, 336-38, 366-67
Anarchists, 3, 6-8
Anderson, John, 76, 85
Ansari, M.A., 77
anti-terrorism, 364
Arab League, 95-97, 99
Arab(s): assassination of Wasfi Tal, 182, 186; Black September, 184-85, 186-88; and British, 160; commandos, 182; and Deir Yasin, 163; at Entebbe, 202-3, 301; Fatah, al-, 172-74, 179, 181, 184-88, 190, 194, 290-10; hijackings, 176-79, 190-92, 202-3, 206-8; in Jerusalem, 199; vs. Jews, 128-212, 301; in Khartoum, 188; Menahem Begin on, 169-70; Olympic Games killings, 184, 186; OPEC meeting terrorism, 200-202; refugees, Palestinian, 171-72; in Rome, 190-91; Soviet Union aid to, 185; terrorism, 131, 134-36, 161-62, 165-66, 184-86, 188, 190-94, 199, 200-202, 208-10; treatment of, by Israelis, 205; *see also* Arafat, Yasir; individual countries; Middle East; Palestine
Arafat, Yasir: and Ali Salameh, 186-87; and Anwar el-Sadat, 197-98; and commando organization, 181; and independent Palestine, 194-95; and Jimmy Carter, 205; and Lebanon, 173-74; military defeat of, 203-4; and PLO, 172; portrait of, 179; and Soviet Union, 185, 194; and terrorism, 208; and United States, 204
Aragon, Louis, 320
Aron, Raymond, 102
Ashbel, Isaac, 148-49
Ashbel, Joseph, 147
assassinations: Aldo Moro, 354-56; Alexander II, 15-16, 53; Amédée Froger, 101; Count Folke Bernadotte, 167-68; E. Francis Riggs, 265; Governor-General Mayor of India, 57; Grand Duke Sergius, 30; Günter von Drenkman, 337; Hanns-Martin Schleyer, 343-44; in Ireland, 218; Jürgen Ponto, 339, 340; Kevin O'Higgins, 217-18; King Humbert, 5, 6; Lord Moyne, 140-41; M. de Plehve, 24; Michael Collins, 216-17; Michael O'Dwyer, 80-81; Mohandas Gandhi, 91-92; Russian officials, 22; Sadi Carnot, 4, 6; Siegfried Buback, 337, 340; statistics on, 307; T.E. Ewart-Biggs, 257-58; Wasfi Tal, 182; William Fox, 251; Yousef el-Sebai, 206-8
assassinations, attempted: Alexander II, 13; Charles de Gaulle, 116; Governor of Bengal, 78; Harry Truman, 267-68; John Taylor, 241; M. Pobiedonostseff, 19; P.A. Stolypin, 44; Russian royal family, 14; Viceroy of India, 62-63; William McKinley, 5, 6
Attlee, Clement, 84-85, 87-88
Auriol, Vincent, 107
Ayers, Bill, 276-80
Azad, Maulana Abul Kalam, 81-82
Azad, Mohamed Singh, 80

Baader, Andreas, 336-38, 342-43, 245, 247-50
Bachman, Simon, 3
Bachmann, Josef, 309
Bakunin, Michale, 367

371

Balfour Declaration, 129-30
Barcelo, Romero, 270
Barker, Evelyn, 148
Barr, Glen, 256
Barre, Siad, 342, 343
Bayley, John, 228-29
Beatles, the, 327
Beauvoir, Simone de, 330
Begin, Menahem: to Britain, 170-71; Irgun leadership, 157; and Israel, 166-67, 210-11; meeting with Anwar el-Sadat, 206; and terrorism, 169-70, 208
Beidas, Youssef, 180
Ben Bella, Mohammed, 99-101, 109, 125
Bender, Traugott, 343
Bendjelloul, Mohammed Salah, 97
Ben Gurion, David, 147, 153, 161, 164
Ben Khedda, Benyoussef, 125
Bentley, Alvin A., 266
Berlinguer, Enrico, 352, 354
Bernadotte, Folke (Count), 167-68
Besant, Annie, 64
Bevin, Ernest, 155
Beynon, William, 65
Black September, 302
"Bloody Sunday", 238-41
Blum, Leon, 94, 95
Bogdanovitch, Governor, 22
Bogroff, Dmitry, 44
Bokay, Yusuf Adan, 343
Bolling, Klaus, 342
Bolsheviks, 8, 51-53
Bose, Subhas, 77, 80, 84, 86
Boucher, Jean, 116
Boudin, Kathy, 281
Boudin, Leonard, 281
Bouin, Andre, 321
Bourges-Maunoury, Maurice, 96, 104
Bourguiba, Habib, 95, 172
Bouteflika, Abdelaziz, 358
Brady, Thomas, 104
Brandon, Henry, 345-46
Brandt, Willy, 307, 315, 347, 348
Bressi, Angelo, 5
Britain: bombings, 228, 241, 248-249; and Catholics, 242; Dublin and, 212, 240; grants independence to India, 88-90; and IRA, 246, 253; and Ireland, 214, 219; and Menahem Begin, 170-71; and Northern Ireland, 223-24, 226-29, 237-41, 243-44, 251-55, 257; and Palestine, 128-30, 134, 137, 143-44, 146-52, 154, 155, 163; recognition of Israel, 169; release of Jewish leaders, 153
Brown, George, 306
Brown, H. Rap, 281
Brown, Sam, 286, 291
Brzezinski, Zbigniew, 345
Buback, Siegfried, 337, 340
bubonic plague, Indian, 59
Bunche, Ralph J., 168
Bustani, Emile, 173
Byrnes, James F., 142-43

Callaghan, James, 170, 225, 257
Cameron, Lord, 226-27
Campos, Pedro Albizu, 265

Canning, Charles John Viscount, 57
Carnot, Sadi, 4
Carson, J.F., 261-62
Carter, Jimmy, 205, 270, 343
Casement, Roger, 212
Castro, Fidel, 330, 366
Castroism, 291
Catholic Church, 6, 113, 213-14, 247-48
Catholics: and British in Ulster, 228-29; critical of IRA, 253-54; vs. Protestants in Ulster, 222-61
Catroux, Georges, 120
Challe, Maurice, 115, 121
Chamberlain, Neville, 137, 219
Chavez, Cesar, 291
Chelmsford, Baron, 64
Chemali, Fouad, 185
Chevallier, Jacques, 104
Chichester-Clark, James D., 225, 226
Chichester-Clark, Robert, 224
China, 95, 335
Churchill, Winston, 87, 88, 141, 241
CIA, 365-66
Cinque, Field Marshal, 299-301
civil disobedience: in Algeria, 94; in India, 68, 69, 72, 75-76, 78, 81; of Jews in Palestine, 148
civil rights, 223-24, 265
Clark, Ramsey, 337
Cocteau, Jean, 320
Cohn-Bendit, Daniel, 315, 316, 318, 320, 321, 345
Cole, G.D.H., 293-94
Collazo, Oscar, 268
Collins, Michael, 216-17
Columbus, Christopher, 263
Communism, 329, 356
Communists: in Algeria, 99; bombing of Indian Legislative Assembly, 71; in French, 95, 316-17, 320-21, 324, 330-34, 335; in Germany, 345; and Indo-Chinese vs. French, 94-95; in Italy, 351-56; Jean-Paul Sartre on, 329-34; in Tunisia, 95
Conway, William, 238, 247, 250
Cooney, Patrick, 257
Cordero, Andres Figueroa, 266, 268, 270-71
Corrigan, Mairead, 259-60
Cosgrave, Liam, 251, 257, 258
Coty, René, 106-7
Cousins, Norman, 197-98
Cowan, Paul, 288-89
Craig, James, 215
Craig, William, 223, 227
Craigavon, Viscount, 218
Crépin, Jean, 111
Crimean War, 12
Cripps, Stafford, 85, 87, 88
Croatian hijacking, 359-61
Croissant, Klaus, 337
CS aerosol, 227, 228
Cuba, 261-63, 269, 325, 365-66
Cunningham, Alan G., 147-49, 153, 163
Curcio, Renato, 355-56
Cyprus, 152, 206-8
Czolgosz, Leon, 5

Dalton, Hugh, 142
Dane, Louis, 63, 80

Das, Jatindranath, 72
Dash, Samuel, 240
Davis, Clifford, 266
Davis, Leon, 291
Dayan, Moshe, 168, 183
Debré, Michel, 112, 123, 317
DeFreeze, Donald D., 300
Deir Yasin, 162-63
Delorme, Daniele, 112
Delouvrier, Paul, 121
democracy, 363-64
despotism, 2
Deva, Bima, 78
Devlin, Bernadette, 224-25, 227, 238-39
Dohrn, Bernadine, 279, 295, 297, 299
Doiselet, Daniel, 321
Doubassoff, Governor General, 35
Drenkmann, Günter von, 337
Drumm, Maire, 259
Duclos, Jacques, 95, 332
Dutschke, Rudi, 308-15
Duverger, Maurice, 102
Dyer, R.E.H., 65-66
Dylan, Bob, 317

Edward VII, 61
Egypt, 99, 165-66, 181, 206-8
Eisenhower, Dwight D., 141-42
Elbrick, Charles Burke, 301
Elizabeth, Empress, 6-7
England. *See* Britain
Ensslin, Gudrun, 338-40, 342-43, 345, 349-50
Entebbe raid, 202-3, 301
Eritrea, 95
d'Estaing, Valery Giscard, 317
Evarts, Benjamin, 131
Ewart-Biggs, T.E., 257-58
Exodus 1947, 160

Fallon, George H., 266
F.A.L.N. (Fuerzas Armadas de Liberacion Nacional Puertorriquena), 267-70
Farrell, Michael, 236
Farren, Neil, 238
Fatah, al-. *See* Arab(s), Fatah, al-
Faulkner, Brian, 234-36, 238-39, 243-44, 250-52, 256
Faure, Edgar, 98, 120
FBI, 268-69, 272, 298-99, 306
fedayeen, 181, 182
Feltrinelli, Giangiacomo, 351
Finland, 24-25
Fishman, J.L., 147, 153
Fitt, Gerald, 223, 250, 255
Flores, Irving, 266, 268
Fouchet, Christian, 319
Fox, William, 251
France: in Algeria, 93-125; and Arab Countries, 102; assassination attempt on Charles de Gaulle, 116; assassination of President, 4, 6; Citroen plant takeover, 321; Communists in, 95, 316-17, 320-21, 330-34, 335; Indo-China revolt, 94-95; intellectuals curbed in, 112; North African policy, 96, 97; Renault plant violence, 316, 331, 335; Sochaux incident, 322; student rebellion, 315-29, 330-34, 345; terrorism in, 108-9, 114, 366-67; and Tunisia, 96, and United Nations, 97
Frantz Fanon (Gendzier), 356-58
Fraser, Andrew, 61
Fraunces Tavern, 359
Freemasonry, 6
French North Africa, 95-97
Frey, Roger, 116
Frick, H.C., 3
Froger, Amedée, 101

Gandhi, Mohandas: advises suicide, 86; assassination of, 91-92; Bengal repression, 77; described, 66-67; end of civil disobedience, 75-76, 78; hails England, 87; Hindu accord, 78; and Hitlerism, 81; hunger strike, 78, 91; Indian Congress, 78-80; Indian home rule, 72, 74-75; Indian independence, 81, 89-90; jailed, 69, 73, 77; and Jawaharlal Nehru, 82; non-violent policy, 68-69; release from prison, 70; riots, 68; and Rowlatt Act, 66; Salt Act, 73; and 'untouchables', 87; vs. terrorism, 78, 81
Garlick, Judge, 76
Gaulle. Charles de: and Algeria, 106-8, 110, 112, 113-15, 121, 123; assassination attempt on, 116; and French forces, 93; Jean Paul Sartre on, 330; protest vs., 315-22
Gelber, David, 285-87
Gendzier, Irene L. *(Frantz Fanon)*, 356-58
Genet, Jean, 340
Genscher, Hans-Dietrich, 348
George V, 65
Gerassi, John, 330-34
Germany, 2, 132, 160, 347-48; *see also* West Germany
Giraud, Henri Honoré, 93
Godard, Jean Luc, 318
Godse, Nathuran Vinayak, 91-92
Goldman, Emma, 7, 8
Goodman, Walter, 365
Gopon, George, 28
Goulding, Cathal, 226, 237
Great Britain. *See* Britain
Greenhut, J.B., 22-23
Greiffenshagen, Martin, 346
Griffith, Arthur, 213, 216, 220
Groenewald, Kurt, 337
Gromyko, Andrei, 161, 186, 194
Gruenbaum, Isaac, 153
Gruenberg, Isaac, 147
Gruner, Dov Bela, 157
Grunewald, Armin, 339
Guerrilla (Walter Laqueur), 362-63
Gur, Mordechai, 210-11
Gurney, Henry, 153

Habash, George, 173, 178-79, 180, 181, 194, 212
Haddad, Wadi, 212
Haining, Robert H., 138
Hajj, Messali, 95
Hall, Camilla, 300-301

373

Halley, Malcolm, 69, 70
Hardinge, Lord, 62-63
Harkavi, Yehoshaphat, 186
Harris, Emily, 301
Harris, William, 301
Harrison, Earl G., 141-42
Hashad, Mohamed Nazih, 165
Hawary, el-, Ahmed, Mohamed, 165
Hawatmeh, Nayef, 180
Hayden, Tom, 287
Hays, Arthur Garfield, 265
Hearst, Patricia, 299-300
Heath, Edward, 238-39, 243-44, 249
Henderson, Arthur, 76
hijacking: Arab guerrillas, 176-79, 182, 190-92, 197, 202-3, 206-8, 305; Entebbe raid, 202-3; Lufthansa Airline in Somalia, 341-43, 350; TWA, 359-61; U.S.-Cuba agreement, 366
Ho Chi Minh, 94-95
Hoffman, Abbie, 287
Horkheimer, Max, 346
Horowitz, Irving Louis, 364
Hostos, E.M., 263
Hotson, Ernest, 76
Hourani, Cecil, 172
Howard, Vincent, 6
Howe, Irving, 289-96
Huggins, Erika, 332, 334
Humbert I, 5, 6
Hume, John, 238
Hungary, 330, 332
Hussein, King, 186, 194-95
Husseini, Jamal, 180
Hutchison, Barbara, 304

India, 56-92; Amritsar affair, 65-66; assassination attempt on British Viceroy, 62-63, 72; assassination attempt on Governor of Bengal, 78; assassination of Earl of Mayo, 57; assassination of Michael O'Dwyer, 80-81; assassination of Mohandas Gandhi, 91-92; Bengal disorder, 70, 76; bubonic plague, 59; cabinet created, 85-86; Communist bombing of Legislative Assembly, 71; disunity of, 82-83; dominion status of, 71; end of civil disobedience, 75-76, 78; English rule of, 56-92; equality law, 69; Europeans in, 56, 61; Hindu-Moslem conflict, 58, 66, 70, 80-81, 85, 86, 90-91; Hindus, 62, 67, 78; home rule, 64, 65, 72, 74-75, 77, 79; hunger strikes, 72, 78; independence in, 81, 85, 87-90; industrialization in, 66-67; government conflicts, 77; Moslems, 59-60, 86; mutiny of troops, 56; National Congress, 59, 61, 63, 78-81, 84; Pakistan nation, 84, 89-90; press censorship in, 74; reform in, 62; release of passive resistant prisoners, 81-82; riots in, 62, 64, 65-66, 67-68, 73, 83, 84, 91-92; Sikhs riots, 90-91; Simon Commission, 71, 74-75, 79; strikes in, 71; 'untouchables', 87; women's violence, 78; *see also* Gandhi, Mohandas
Indo-China, 94-95
International Red Cross, 343
international terrorism, 306
International War Crimes Tribunal, 330
Inverchapel, Lord, 154
IRA, 212-261, 359; assassination of T.E. Ewart-Biggs, 357-58; assassination of William Fox, 251; bombings in England, 241, 248-49, 253-55; Catholics critical of, 253-54; curbs vs, 253, 258; divided, 230-34; Dublin bombings, 251; and Eamon de Valera, 221, 222; internment law, 229, 235-36, 246; new campaign, 260-61; and peace marchers, 258-59; terrorism, 237, 246-47, 256-57; U.S. support of, 255-56
Iraq, 165-66, 171
Ireland, 212-61; accord with Britain, 219; assassination of Kevin O'Higgins, 217-18; assassination of Michael Collins, 216-217; assassination of T.E. Ewart-Biggs, 257-58; assassinations in, 218; Catholic Church in, 247-48; Dail Eireann, 215-16; history of rebellion, 214-15; Irish Home Rule, 214; republic born, 219; Sinn Fein Society, 212, 213, 215-16, 220, 221; terrorism, 250-51; *see also* Northern Ireland
Irwin, Lord, 72, 74, 76
Israel, 164-212; Arab hatred of, 187; Arab prisoners in, 205; Arab refugees in, 171-72; vs. Arabs, 171-212, 301; Entebbe raid, 202-3; Fatah, al-, raids, 194; Haganah, 166-68; Irgun Zvai Leumi, 157, 166-68; Jerusalem, 199; and Lebanon, 190, 193, 210-11; vs. Libya, 189; measures vs. Arab terrorists, 174-76; Olympic Games killings, 184, 186; proclamation of, 164; recognized by Britain, 169; reprisal for Olympic Games killings, 184; Stern gang in, 166, 167, 168; Tel Aviv terrorism, 165-66, 183, 209-10; terrorism in, 165-66, 183, 185-86, 189, 192-93, 199, 209-10, 305; terrorism outside Middle East, 185-86; and United Nations, 196, 358; and Yasir Arafat, 196; *see also* Palestine
Italy: assassination of Aldo Moro, 354-56; assassination of King, 5; Communists in, 351-56; politics in, 351-56; terrorism, 350-52
IWW, 8

Jabotinsky, A., 134
Jabotinsky, Vladimir, 131, 134, 136, 138-39
Jackson, George, 332, 333
Jackson, Stanley, 78
Japan, 31, 347
Jeanson, Francis, 112
Jenkins, Brian, 303-5
Jenkins, Roy, 253, 254
Jensen, Ben F., 266
Jews: admission to Palestine, 145-46; assassination of Folke Bernadotte, 167-68; assassination of Lord Moyne, 141; Civil War among, 136; displaced, 141-42; establishment of Israel, 164; leaders freed by British, 153; Kishineff Massacre, 22-23; Mohandas Gandhi advice, 87; and Nihilism, 15; and Palestine homeland, 128-212; and Pope Leo, 6; Russian, 37, 40; sent to Cyprus, 152; *see also* Israel; Palestine; Zionism
Jinnah, Mohammed Ali, 84, 87, 88, 89
Jiryis, Sabri Elias, 204
Johnson, Herschel V., 161
Jordan, 171, 181-82, 186-88, 302
Jouhaud, Edmond, 115
Joxe, Louis, 120, 121

Kaddoumi, Farouk, 200-201
Kanafani, Ghassan, 185

Kennedy, Edward, 240-41
Kennedy, Joseph, 137
Kennedy, Robert, 188, 356
Kent State, 288
Kerensky, Alexander, 49-53
Khaled, Leila, 178, 180
Khalef, Salah, 187
Khider, Mohammed, 99, 101
Kiep, Walter, 337
King, Martin Luther, 281, 309
Kishineff Massacre, 22-23
Kissinger, Henry, 195, 197-98, 301, 304-5
Kleindienst, Richard, 280
Kniaz Potemkine mutiny, 32-33
Koenig, Joseph-Pierre, 96
Kolakowski, Leszek, 345
Kollek, Teddy, 199
Korniloff, General, 50
Kreisky, Bruno, 200
Krim, Belkacem, 109
Krishna Menon, V.K., 97
Kristol, Irving, 282
Kunstler, William, 337
Kupperman, Robert, 306
Kuropatkin, General, 31
Kuznetsov, Vasily V., 194

Lacoste, Robert, 99, 100, 101, 102, 104, 120
Lagaillarde, Pierre, 111
Lamington, Lord, 80
Laqueur, Walter *(Guerrilla)*, 362-63
League of Nations, 128-30
Lebanon: freed from France, 94-95; and Israel, 165-66, 181, 190, 210-11; Palestinian commandos, 173-74; PLO defeat, 203-4; terrorism in, 192, 193
Lebron, Lolita, 266, 268
Leila, Abou, 196-97
Lenin, Nikolai, 47, 48, 52
Leonard, Roger, 96
Leonhardy, Terrance, 304
Libya, 187-88, 189
Lie, Trygve, 168
Lindbergh, Charles A., 264
Lloyd George, David, 214-16
Lluveras, Antonio Mattel, 264
Lod International Airport, 183
Lorenz, Peter, 336, 337
Lowenstein, Allard K., 291
Lundstrom, Aage, 167, 168
Luther, Angela, 337
Lynch, John, 229, 243, 247-48, 260

McBride, Sean, 361
McClure, Brooks, 306-7
McDade, James, 253
McDonald, James G., 166
MacDonald, Malcolm, 137
MacDonald, Ramsey, 74-75, 77, 137
Machtinger, Howard Norton, 299
McKinley, William, 5, 6, 263

McReynolds, David, 283-84
MacStiofain, Sean, 237
Madagascar, 95
Magill, Brendan, 253
Makhlouf, Eugene M., 180
Malatesta, Enrico, 6, 7
Malraux, Andre, 118
Manson, Charlie, 295
Mao Tse-tung, 320, 335
Maoism, 291, 318, 332-33, 335
March, Reginald, 254-55
Marcuse, Herbert, 318, 323-29, 345, 346
Mardam, Jamil, 166
Mari Bras, Juan, 268-69, 272
Martel, Robert, 111
Martinez, Noel Colon, 268
Martinez, Ruben, 268
Marty, Andre, 95
Massu, Jacques, 103-4, 106-7, 121 or Massu, Jean
Mastutchenko, 32-33
Maudling, Reginald, 241
Maximalists. *See* Bolsheviks
Mayo, Earl of, 57
Medani, el-, Ahmed Tewfik, 109
Meinhof, Ulrike, 335-38, 342-43, 347-50
Meins, Holger, 336-37
Meir, Golda, 175, 183, 192
Melouza massacre, 102-3
Mendes-France, Pierre, 120
Merk, Bruno, 184
Messali, Hadj, 102-3, 109, 114
Messmer, Pierre, 112
Metcalfe, H.A.F., 73
Middle East, 140-41, 175-76, 197-98; *see also* Arab League Arab(s); individual countries; Palestine
Miles, Nelson A., 264
Minutemen, 281
Miranda, Rafael C., 266
Mirbach, Andreas von, 338
Mitchell, John, 280, 286
Mitrione, Dan, 302
Mitterand, Francois, 96
Mohn, Paul, 168
Moller, Irmgard, 342, 350
Mollet, Guy, 99-100, 102, 120-21, 317
Montagu, Edwin S., 64, 66-67
Mooney, Thomas J., 47
Moore, George Curtis, 188, 302
Moro, Aldo, 354-56
Morocco, 97, 100
Morton, Geoffrey, 139
Mountbatten, Lord, 88, 89-90
Moyne, Lord, 140-41
Moynihan, Daniel P., 200
Mukden, 31
Munich, West Germany, 183, 186
Mury, Gilbert, 335
Musmar, Mohammed Rashad, 205

Nader, Ralph, 286, 291
Najjar, Mohammed Yussef, 190
Nanterre University, 317, 318, 319, 320

Napoleon III, 93
Nashashibi, Ragheb, 180
Nasser, Gamal Abdel, 99, 182
Nasser, Kemal, 180, 185
Nazi movement, 81, 132, 329, 345, 349
Nechayev, Serge, 16-17, 289
Nehru, Jawaharlal: arrest of, 77; British rule of India, 84; Indian home rule, 72; Indian independence, 87, 88, 89-90; Mohandas Gandhi's death and, 91-92; and Moslem League, 86; and National Congress, 79, 85-86; release from prison, 81-82; and Socialists, 79; succeeds Mohandas Gandhi, 82
Neubauer, Kurt, 308-9
New Left, 280, 281, 287-96, 323-29
Newman, Louis I., 139
New Popular Resistance, 335
Nicholas II: Black Hundred Massacre, 35; Duma dissolved, 39; and Jewish pogroms, 40; and Leo Tolstoy, 40-43; reforms of, 25-27, 31, 33-35; revolutions and, 27-28, 29, 45-47
Nihilism, 2, 10, 11-13, 15, 17, 22, 345
Nixon, Richard, 82-83, 286, 288-89, 298, 302, 335
Nobel Peace Prize, 259-60
Noel, Cleo A., 188, 302
Nogrette, Robert, 335
non-violence. *See* civil disobedience
North Africa, French, 95-97
Northern Ireland: assassination attempt on John Taylor, 241; Belfast, 225, 242; British in, 228-29, 237, 246, 251, 252; Catholics in, 226-27, 242; Catholic vs. Protestant conflict, 221-61; CS gas, 238; government of, 243-44, 250, 252; internment law, 229, 235-36, 246; march for peace, 258-59; Nobel Peace Prize, 259-60; riot-control gas, 227; riots, 238-40; terrorism in, 230-34, 237, 246-48, 256-57; terrorism in London, 253; Ulster Defense Association, 245; women tarred and feathered, 236

Obolensky, General, 22
O'Bradaigh, Ruairl, 261
O'Brien, Charles, 281
O'Brien Conor Cruise, 260, 262-63
Oceania, 95
O'Connell, David, 253
O'Dwyer, Michael, 66, 80-81
O' Higgins, Kevin, 217-18
Ohnesorg, Benno, 307-8, 321-13
Olympic Games (Munich), 184, 186, 301, 302
O'Neill, Terence, 222-25
OPEC (Organization of Petroleum Exporting Countries), 200-202
Orbeta, Enrique de, 265
Ormsby-Gore, William, 135
Ortiz, Joseph, 111
Ottoman Empire, 128-29
Oughton, Diana, 282-83
Overney, René-Pierre, 335

Padilla, Heberto, 330
Pahlevi, Mohammed Riza, 307
Paisley, Ian, 222, 227, 228, 255, 256
Pakistan, 84, 89-90

Palestine: Arab-Israeli conflict, 165-66, 171-212; and Arabs, 128-29; assassination of Count Folke Bernadotte, 167-68; background, 128-29; British and, 137, 155, 163, 205; and displaced Jews, 141-42; *Exodus 1947*, 160: Haganah, 146, 147-48, 153-54, 155, 159, 161, 162-63; independence arguments, 200-201; Irgun Zvai Leumi, 140, 144, 147-48, 149-51, 153-54, 155, 156, 157, 161, 162-63; Israel proclaimed, 164; Jewish capture of Deir Yasin, 162-63; Jewish Civil War; Jewish dissension, 156; Jewish immigration, 145-46, 152, 158-59; Jewish Revisionist Party, 134; Jewish rights to, 128-30; Jewish state boundaries, 133; Nazism and, 132; Palestinians, 179-80, 302, 359; Palmach terrorism, 146, 147; PLO, 171, 172, 180, 181, 194-96, 197, 198, 202, 203-5, 206, 208, 209-10, 358; Simpson Report, 130; Stern Gang, 139, 144, 147, 153, 162-63, 166; terrorism, 138, 139-41, 143-44, 146-52, 154, 155-56, 159, 161-62; at United Nations, 157; unrest in, 132; *see also* Israel; popular Front for the Liberation of Palestine
Palme, Olaf, 338
Pan-Slavists, 11
Parry, Albert *(Terrorism)*, 362-63
Pasha, Mahmoud Fahmy Nokrashy, 165
Patel, Sadar Vallabhai, 84, 86
Patterson, John, 304
Peres, Shimon, 183, 202
Peyrefitte, Alain, 318, 366
Pfimlin, Pierre, 107
Philippines, 261-62
Plehve, M. de, 24
PLO. *See* Palestine, PLO
Pobiedonostseff, M., 19, 24
Pompidou, Georges, 316-17
Ponce de Leon, Juan, 263
Ponto, Jürgen, 339, 340, 345, 347-48
Pope Leo XII, 6
Pope Paul VI, 351
Popular Front for the Liberation of Palestine, 178-79, 181, 183, 194, 212
Poujade, Robert, 317
Prasad, Rajendra, 89-90
President Warfield, 158-59
press, the, 24, 74
Protestants, 226-61
Puerto Rico, 359; annexation to United States, 261-63; assassination attempt on Harry Truman, 267-68; assassination of E. Francis Riggs, 265; and Charles Lindbergh, 264; and FBI, 268-69, 272; independence for, 270-71; riots, 265; shooting of U.S. Congressmen, 266, 268, 270-71; violence by revolutionists, 267-68; *see also* F.A.L.N.

Qaddafi, el-, Muammar, 187
Quester, George H., 199

Rabe, Robert, 307
Rabin, Yitzhak, 199
Radhakrishnan, S., 90
radical groups, 282-95, 298, 299, 307-15; *see also* Anarchists; F.A.L.N.; IRA; New Left; Palestine, PLO; SDS; Symbionese Liberation Army; United States, Weather-

men: West Germany, Baader-Meinhof gang
Rafael, Gideon, 189-90
Rand, Ayn, 287-88
Raspe, Jan-Carl, 340, 342-43, 345, 349-50
Rasputin, 45
Rauti, Giuseppe, 351
Reagan, Ronald, 292, 293
Rebmann, Kurt, 349-50
Red Army Faction, 336-37, 344
Red Brigades, 354-56
Rees, Marlyn, 252, 255, 257, 259
regicide, 2, 53
Reinders, Ralf, 337
Riggs, E. Francis, 265
Riley, William, 168
Roberts, Kenneth A., 266
Roche, James Anthony, 228
Roche, Jean, 318
Rockefeller, David, 345
Rohl, Klaus Rainer, 339
Rome, 190-91
Romeo, Rosario, 352-54
Roosevelt, Theodore, 7-8
Rovere, Richard H., 285
Rowlatt Act, 64, 66
Rudd, Mark, 299
Rumor, Mariano, 351
Russell, Charles A., 307
Russia: aid to Indian strikers, 71; Alexander Kerensky's dictatorship, 49; anti-Americanism, 47; assassination of Alexander II, 15-16, 53; assassination of Grand Duke Sergius, 30; assassination of M. de Plehve, 24; assassination attempt on M. Pobiendonostseff, 19; assassination of P.A. Stolypin, 44; autocracy, 18; Baku strike, 22; Black Hundred Massacre, 35; Black Sea Fleet, 32-33, 37; Bolshevik Revolution, 52-53; Constitutional Democrats, 35; demonstrations, 9, 12, 14, 19, 49; famine, 18; and Finland, 24-25; freedoms in, 21, 24, 25-26, 32, 47; fundamental law draft, 36; government, 31, 36-37, 39, 47, 49, 50-53; Jews in, 15, 24, 40; Kishineff Massacre, 22-23; Leo Tolstoy on, 40-43; military law in, 8, 10-11; Mukden disaster, 31; Nihilism in, 10, 11-13, 15-17; Nikolai Lenin and, 48; peasants, 23, 30-31, 48; People's Rights Part, 18; political parties, 22; reforms, 9, 14, 19-20, 21, 26-27, 53; revolution in, 27-28, 29, 30, 31, 39, 45-47, 52-53; St. Petersburg trial, 11; Siberian exile, 23, 24; socialism in, 2, 22, 38; Socialists' Revolutionary Party, 22; strike in, 18, 28-29, 33-35, 44; war weary, 47; women students in, 10; *see also* Soviet Union
Rustin, Bayard, 293

sabotage, 356
Sadat, el-, Anwar, 181, 195, 197-98, 206
Sagan, Françoise, 112
Salah, Abdullah, 182
Salameh, Ali Hassan, 186-87
Salan, Raoul, 106-8, 115, 121
Samuel, Herbert, 128-29
San Juan, Puerto Rico, 263
Santo, Cesare Giovanni, 4
Saragat, Giuseppe, 350-51
Sartawi, Isam, 172, 180

Sartre, Jean-Paul, 112, 321, 330-34, 357
Satyendra, Sinhha, 63
Saudi Arabia, 165-66
Sayigh, Youssef, 181
Schaap, William, 337
Scheel, Walter, 338, 347
Scheib, Israel, 168
Schlesinger, Jr., Arthur, 287
Schleyer, Hanns-Martin, 339-44, 347
Schmidt, Helmut, 339-40, 342, 343, 345, 347-48
Schryver, Harold, 267-68
Schuster, George, 71
SDS, 277-80, 282-83, 291-93
Seale, Bobby, 332, 334
Sebai, el-, Yousef, 206-8
serfs, Russian, 9, 14
Sergius, Grand Duke, 30
Serot, André Pierre, 167-68
Servan-Schreiber, Jean-Jacques, 102
Shah, of Iran, 312
Shankerlal, 69
Shennawy, el-, Mohamed Mamoun, 165
Shertok, Moshe, 147, 153, 167
Shipoff, M., 26
Shukairy, Ahmed, 148, 171, 172, 180
Signoret, Simone, 112
Simhon, Isaac, 147
Simkhon, Joseph, 148-49
Simon, John, 70, 71, 74, 79, 137
Singh, Kharah, 72
Singh, Sardar Balder, 87
Sinn Fein Society, 212, 213, 215-16, 220, 221
Sipianuine, 22
Sirhan, Sirhan, 188
Smythe, Tony, 240
Socialism, 2, 6, 38
Somalia, 341-42, 350
Sorbonne University, 318-19
Soustelle, Jacques, 97, 98, 104
Soviet Union: and Algerian revolution, 99; and Ho Chi Minh, 95; and Palestine, 160, 161; pensions to regicides, 53; and PLO, 194; weapons to Arabs, 185; *see also* Russia
Spain, 3-4, 262-64
Spencer, K.H., 149
Sperber, Manes, 361-62
Springer, Axel, 308, 309
Stammheim, Prison, 339, 343, 348, 349
Stern, Abraham, 139
Stern, Philip, 291
Stewart, Michael, 227
Stockholm, Sweden, 338
Stolypin, P.A., 37, 44
Straus, Oscar Solomon, 7-8
Strauss, Franz Josef, 343
Stubbs, Richard, 153
Sturmer, M., 45
Sviatopolk-Mirsky, Prince, 24-25, 26, 29
Symbionese Liberation Army, 299-300
Syria, 94-95, 165-66, 173-74, 203-4

Tal, Wasfi, 182, 186
Taylor, A.E., 149
Taylor, John, 241

Tekoah, Yosef, 195-96, 358
Tel Aviv Airport, 183
terrorism, 198, 364; *see also* individual countries
Terrorism (Parry), 362-63
Theosophical Society, 64
Thorez, Maurice, 95
Tolstoy, Leo, 17, 19-20, 40-43
Trans-Jordan, 165-66
Trepoff, Alexander, 45
Trilateral Commission, 345
Tripolitania, 95
Trotsky, Leon, 47, 50-52
Truman, Harry, 141-42, 145-46, 267-68
Tunisia: and Algeria, 103, 125; arrests in, 96; Communists in, 95; and France, 97, 106; liberation of, 100; Neo-Destour Party, 95

Uganda, 202-3
Ukhtomsky, Prince, 23, 24
Ulster. *See* Northern Ireland
United Arab Republic, 182
United Nations: assassination of Folke Bernadotte, 167-68; French walk-out, 97; Israel, 164, 166-67; Palestine question, 155, 157, 161; and PLO, 196-97; terrorism and, 358; and United States rule of Puerto Rico, 268-69; and Yasir Arafat, 195-96; on Zionism, 200
United States: annexations, 261-63; anti-terrorist training, 305-6; Army Mathematics Research Center, 296-97; assassination attempt on President, 5; bargaining with terrorists, 301-5; business and terrorism, 306-7; establishment, 284; and IRA, 255-56; and Palestine, 142-43, 154, 160, 161; and PLO, 204; and Puerto Rico, 264, 266-68, 270-71; radical groups, 282-95; riot-control gas, 227; vs. Russia, 47; and sabotage, 306; and Spain, 264; terrorism in, 281-82, 296-98, 305-6; war on Anarchists, 7-8; and Weathermen, 276-80; 291, 297-99, 345; and Zionism, 200
Urban George, 352-54
Uruguay, 302

Valera, Eamon de, 213, 216, 218, 219-22
Valera, Vivion de, 219, 251
Valpreda, Pietro, 351
Vanuxem, Paul, 116
Venezuela, 263
Victoria, Queen, 57
Vienna, 200-202
Vietnam, 95, 293, 308, 310, 330, 332, 333

Waldheim, Kurt, 200
Wallace-Dunlop, Arthur, 60-61
Warburg, Felix, 130
Warburton, G.C., 149
Wavell, Viscount, 85-86
Wazir, Khalil, 187
Weathermen. *See* United States, and Weathermen
Weiner, R.S.P., 228-29
Weiss, Peter, 337
Weizman, Ezer, 209-11
Weizmann, Chaim: Menahem Begin on, 157; and terrorism, 141, 147; and Zionism, 130, 131, 137, 139
Western society, 346
West Germany: anarchists in, 336-38; assassination of Günter von Drenkmann, 337; assassination of Hanns-Martin Schleyer, 343-44; assassination of Jürgen Ponto, 339, 340; assassination of Siegfried Buback, 337, 340; Baader-Meinhof gang, 335-39, 341-43, 344, 345-50; criminal laws changed, 337; democracy in, 347-48; guerrilla groups, 335-38; hijacking in Somalia, 341-42, 343; kidnapping of industrialists, 339-41; student demonstrations, 307-15; terrorism, 338, 340-41, 345, 366-67; *see also* Germany
West Indies, 262
Whitelaw, William, 243, 245, 256, 250
Widgery, Lord, 239, 240, 245
Wilkerson, Catherine Platt, 281, 283
Wilkins, Roy, 293
Williams, Betty, 259-60
Willingdon, Earl of, 76
Wilson, Harold, 223-24, 226, 243, 253, 255-57
Wise, Stephen S., 139

Yahya, al-, Abdel Razak, 181
Yellin, Nathan Friedman, 168
Yemen, 165-66
Yugoslavia, 360-61

Zaccagnini, Benigno, 355
Zetland, Marquess of, 80
Zionism: and David Ben Gurion, 101; death of Vladimir Jabotinsky, 138-39; and fascism, 131-32; Israel established, 164; and Jewish Civil War, 136; Menahem Begin on, 169-70; opposition to violence, 140, 153, 156, 159; and revisionism, 131-32; terrorism by, 143-44, 146-52; United Nations and, 200; and Winston Churchill, 141; World Zionist Organization, 131